Sears List of
Subject Headings

Sears List
of
Subject
Headings

17th Edition

Edited by

JOSEPH MILLER

New York • Dublin

The H. W. Wilson Company

2000

Printed in the United States of America

ISBN 0-8242-0989-3

Contents

Preface vii

Acknowledgments xiii

Principles of the Sears List xv

1. The Purpose of Subject Cataloging xv

2. Determining the Subject of the Work xvi

3. Specific and Direct Entry xvii

4. Types of Subject Headings xviii

    4. A. Topical Headings xviii

    4. B. Form Headings xix

    4. C. Geographic Headings xx

    4. D. Names xx

5. The Grammar of Subject Heading xx

    5. A. The Forms of Headings xxi

        5. A. i. Single Nouns xxi

        5. A. ii. Compound Headings xxi

        5. A. iii. Adjectives with Nouns xxi

        5. A. iv. Phrase Headings xxi

    5. B. Subdivisions xxii

        5. B. i. Topical Subdivisions xxii

        5. B. ii. Geographic Subdivisions xxii

        5. B. iii. Chronological Subdivisions xxiii

        5. B. iv. Form Subdivisions xxiv

        5. B. v. The Order of Subdivisions xxiv

        5. B. vi. Geographic Headings Subdivided by Topic . xxiv

        5. B. vii. Local Materials xxv

Principles of the Sears List—*Continued*

  6. Some Difficult Areas of Application xxv

      6. A. Biography xxv

         6. A. i. Collective Biographies xxv

         6. A. ii. Individual Biographies xxvi

      6. B. Nationalities xxvii

      6. C. Literature xxvii

         6. C. i. Works about Literature xxviii

         6. C. ii. Literary Works xxviii

         6. C. iii. Themes in Literature xxix

      6. D. Wars and Events xxx

      6. E. Nonbook Materials xxx

  7. Classification and Subject Headings xxx

  8. Maintaining a Catalog xxxi

      8. A. Adding New Headings xxxi

      8. B. Revising Subject Headings xxxii

      8. C. Making References xxxiii

         8. C. i. *See* References xxxiii

         8. C. ii. *See also* References xxxiv

         8. C. iii. General References xxxv

      8. D. Recording Headings and References xxxv

  9. Cataloging in the Twenty-first Century xxxvi

10. Bibliography xxxvii

Headings to be Added by the Cataloger xxxviii

"Key" Headings xxxix

Commonly Used Subdivisions xl

List of Canceled and Replacement Headings xli

Symbols Used xlvi

Sears List of Subject Headings 1

Preface

For nearly eight decades the Sears List of Subject Headings has served the needs of small and medium-sized libraries, suggesting headings appropriate for use in their catalogs and providing patterns and instructions for adding new headings as they are required. The successive editors of the List have faced the need to accommodate change while maintaining a sound continuity. The new and revised headings in each edition reflect developments in the literature and in the use of the English language, while the changes in the form of the headings and in the structure and display of the List reflect shifts in the prevailing philosophy of subject cataloging.

A major feature of this seventeenth edition of the Sears List is the revision of the headings for the native peoples of the Western Hemisphere. The headings **Indians, Indians of North America, Indians of Mexico**, etc., have been cancelled in favor of **Native Americans**, which may be subdivided geographically by continent, region, country, state, or city. Subdivisions formerly used under **Indians of North America** for classes of persons, such as *Women* or *Children*, and for things distinctly ethnic, such as *Medicine* or *Music*, have been cancelled in favor of phrase headings, such as **Native American women, Native American children, Native American medicine**, and **Native American music**. Subdivisions for things not of an ethnic nature, such as *Housing* or *Social conditions*, remain subdivisions under **Native Americans**. The heading **Native Americans** is now the pattern heading for all ethnic groups.

Also in this edition many new subdivisions have been added to those provided for in the List, among them *Biblical teaching, Interactive multimedia, Juvenile drama, Juvenile fiction, Juvenile poetry, Lists, Memorizing, Press coverage, Services for, Storage*, and *Tournaments*. For every subdivision provided for in Sears there is now an entry in the alphabetical List with instructions for the use of that particular subdivision. The List of Commonly Used Subdivisions formerly found in the front matter of Sears has been eliminated in favor of this more exhaustive treatment of subdivisions, each in its own place.

A further revision in this edition is the inclusion of many more notes reading (May subdiv. geog.). Such a note indicates that a heading may be subdivided geographically whenever the material warrants. Headings without this note either represent topics very unlikely to be given geographic treatment or cannot be subdivided geo-graphically because they are themselves used as subdivisions under geographic headings.

The Principles of the Sears List, which follows this Preface, has been extensively reorganized and rewritten, with renewed emphasis on the Principle of Specificity. This statement of principles is intended both as a statement of the theoretical foundations of the Sears List and as a concise introduction to subject cataloging in general.

A History of the Sears List

Minnie Earl Sears prepared the first edition of this work in response to demands for a list of subject headings that was better suited to the needs of the small library than the existing American Library Association and Library of Congress lists. Published in 1923, the *List of Subject Headings for Small Libraries* was based on the headings used by nine small libraries that were known to be well cataloged. Minnie Sears used only *See* and "refer from" references in the first edition. In the second edition (1926) she added *See also* references at the request of teachers of cataloging who were using the List as a textbook. To make the List more useful for that purpose, she wrote a chapter on "Practical Suggestions for the Beginner in Subject Heading Work" for the third edition (1933).

Isabel Stevenson Monro edited the fourth (1939) and fifth (1944) editions. A new feature of the fourth edition was the inclusion of Dewey Decimal Classification numbers as applied in the *Standard Catalog for Public Libraries*. The new subjects added to the List were based on those used in the Standard Catalog Series and on the catalog cards issued by the H.W. Wilson Company. Consequently, the original subtitle "Compiled from Lists used in Nine Representative Small Libraries" was dropped.

The sixth (1950), seventh (1954), and eighth (1959) editions were prepared by Bertha M. Frick. In recognition of the pioneering and fundamental contribution made by Minnie Sears the title was changed to *Sears List of Subject Headings* with the sixth edition. Since the List was being used by medium-sized libraries as well as small ones, the phrase "for Small Libraries" was deleted from the title. The symbols *x* and *xx* were substituted for the "Refer from (see ref.)" and "Refer from (see also ref.)" phrases to conform to the format adopted by the Library of Congress.

The ninth edition (1965), the first of four to be prepared by Barbara M. Westby, continued the policies of the earlier editions. With the eleventh edition, the "Practical Suggestions for the Beginner in Subject Heading Work" was retitled "Principles of the Sears List of Subject Headings" to emphasize "principles," and a section dealing with nonbook materials was added.

The thirteenth edition (1986), prepared by Carmen Rovira and Caroline Reyes, was the first to take advantage of computer validation capabilities. It also responded to the changing theory in subject analysis occasioned by the development of online public access catalogs. This effort was taken further in the fourteenth edition (1991) under the editorship of Martha T. Mooney, who reduced the number of compound terms, simplified many subdivisions, and advanced the work of uninverting inverted headings.

In accord with a suggestion of the Cataloging of Children's Materials Committee of the American Library Association, many of the headings from *Subject Headings for Children's Literature* (Library of Congress) were incorporated into the Sears List with the thirteenth edition. Since the Sears List is intended for both adult and juvenile collections, wherever the Library of Congress has two different headings for adult and juvenile approaches to a single subject, a choice of a single term was made for Sears. In cases where the Sears List uses the adult form, the cataloger of children's materials may prefer to use the juvenile form found in *Subject Headings for Children's Literature*.

In the fifteenth edition (1994), the first edited by Joseph Miller, the interval between publication of editions was shortened to provide a more timely updating of subject headings. In keeping with prevailing thinking in the field of library and information science, all remaining inverted headings were canceled in favor of the uninverted form. Likewise, the display of the List on the page was changed to conform to the NISO standards for thesauri approved in 1993. While Sears remains a list of subject headings and not a true thesaurus, it uses the labels BT, NT, RT, SA, and UF for broader terms, narrower terms, related terms, See Also, and Used for. A List of Canceled and Replacement Headings was added to facilitate the updating of catalogs, and the legend "[*Former heading*]" was introduced within the List to identify earlier forms of headings. Also in the fifteenth edition many headings were added to enhance access to individual works of fiction, poetry, drama, and other imaginative works, such as films and radio and television programs, based on the *Guidelines on Subject Access to*

Individual Works of Fiction, Drama, etc. prepared by a subcommittee of the Subject Analysis Committee of the ALA.

In the sixteenth edition (1997) the suggested classification numbers were revised to conform to the thirteenth edition of the Abridged Dewey Decimal Classification, further instructions were added for the application of subdivisions, and the headings in the field of religion were extensively revised to reduce their exclusively Christian application and make them more useful for cataloging materials on other religions.

The Scope of the Sears List

No list can possibly provide a heading for every idea, object, process, or relationship, especially not within the scope of a single volume. What Sears hopes to offer instead is a basic list that includes many of the headings most likely to be needed in small libraries together with patterns and examples that will guide the cataloger in creating additional headings as needed. New topics appear every day, and books on those topics require new subject headings. Headings for new topics can be developed from the Sears List in two ways, by establishing new terms as needed and by subdividing the headings already in the List. Instructions for creating new headings based on the pattern in Sears and sources for establishing the wording of new headings are given in the Principles of the Sears List. The various kinds of subdivisions and the rules for their application are also discussed in the Principles of the Sears List.

It is only by being flexible and expandable that Sears has been able over the years to fill the needs of various kinds of libraries. The degree or level of specificity required for a collection depends entirely on the material being collected. While a small library is unlikely to need very narrow topics of a technical or scientific nature, it is not at all unlikely that a small library might have a children's book on a single concept such as **Triangle** or a gardening book on **Irises**. Neither of these terms is in Sears, but the first would be added as a narrower term under **Shape** and the second as a narrower term under **Flowers**.

New Headings in this Edition

The new terms in the present edition represent developments in many different areas, especially computers, personal relations, politics, and popular culture. Among the new headings in the field of technology are **Cyberspace**, **Databases**, **Electronic discussion groups**, **Information retrieval**, **Internet addresses**, **Internet industry**, **Internet marketing**, **Internet searching**, **Internet shopping**, and **Technological literacy**. Among the new headings in other fields are **Achievement tests**, **Crisis intervention (Mental health services)**, **Feng-shui**, **Grandparents as parents**, **Land mines**, **Postcolonialism**, **Stalking**, and **Violence in mass media**.

Many of the headings new to this edition were suggested by librarians representing various sizes and types of libraries, by commercial vendors of bibliographic records, and by the catalogers and indexers at the H.W. Wilson Company who are responsible for the headings in the Standard Catalog Series, *Book Review Digest*, and such periodical indexes as *Readers' Guide to Periodical Literature*. In addition, *Library of Congress Subject Headings* was consulted.

Revised Headings in this Edition

Apart from the headings for Native Americans, this edition of Sears reflects many other examples of revision and updating of existing headings. Some terms have been changed to reflect current usage; for example, **Computer monitors** replaces **Video display terminals**,

Fax transmission replaces **Facsimile transmission**, **Moon rocks** replaces **Lunar petrology**, and **Commercial fishing** replaces **Fisheries**. In some cases two headings have been collapsed into one, such as **World history—19th century**, which replaces both **Nineteenth century** and **Modern history—1800-1899 (19th century)**. In other cases a single heading has been split into two, such as **Colonial architecture**, which is replaced by both **Architecture—United States—1600-1775, Colonial period** and **American colonial style in architecture**.

Many headings that formerly incorporated the word "modern" have been simplified and clarified. In previous editions of the List the terms **Modern history** and **Modern art** were subdivided by century for general histories of events and of art since the Middle Ages. In this edition **Modern history** is limited to the discipline of post-medieval history without period subdivisions. For general histories of the modern period the heading **World history** is now subdivided by century, as in **World history—19th century**. In this edition the art of the modern period is simply **Art**, subdivided by century as needed. For materials on the modernist movement in art the heading **Modernism in art** has been added, parallel to **Realism in art** and **Romanticism in art**.

The headings for government policy have been revised and regularized in this edition. In the past some policies were expressed by subdivisions under geographic headings and others were topics that could be subdivided geographically. Now all headings for policies are either phrase headings, such as **Economic policy** and **Environ-mental policy**, or topics subdivided by *Government policy*, such as **Homeless persons—Government policy** and **Genetic engineering—Government policy**, all subdivided geographically.

As in previous editions, certain headings of decreasing interest and some unnecessary examples have been deleted from the List, such as **Cicadas**, **Ground cushion phenomena**, and **Railroads—Electrification**. Such headings are not invalid and may be maintained in the catalog. Other headings that have been deleted are no longer valid and are now used as cross-references to other headings. These references appear in Sears in the alphabetical listings with the label "[*Former heading*]" and also in the List of Canceled and Replacement Headings.

Form of Headings

It was the policy of Minnie Sears to use the Library of Congress form of subject headings with some modification, chiefly the simplification of phrasing. The Sears List still reflects the usage of the Library of Congress unless there is some compelling reason to vary, but those instances of variation have become numerous over the years. A major difference between the two lists is that in Sears the direct form of entry has replaced the inverted form, on the theory that most library users search for multiple-word terms in the order in which they occur naturally in the language. In all cases cross-references have been made from the inverted form and from the Library of Congress form where it otherwise varies.

Scope Notes

As in previous editions, all the new and revised headings in this edition have been provided with scope notes where such notes are required. Scope notes are intended to clarify the specialized use of a term or to distinguish between terms that might be confused. If there is any question what a term means, the cataloger should simply consult a dictionary. There are times, however, when subject headings require a stricter limitation of a term than the common usage given in a dictionary would allow, as in the case of **Marketing**, a term in business and economics, not to be confused with **Grocery shopping**. Here a scope note is required. Some scope notes distinguish between topics and forms, such as the note at **Textbooks**, which indicates that that heading is applicable only to materials about textbooks, not to textbooks themselves. There are also scope notes in Sears that identify any headings in the area of literature that may be assigned to individual works of drama, fiction, poetry, etc.

Classification

The classification numbers in this edition of Sears are taken from the thirteenth edition of the *Abridged Dewey Decimal Classification.* The numbers are intended only to direct the cataloger to a place in the DDC schedules where material on that subject is often found. They are not intended as a substitute for consulting the schedules, notes, and manual of the DDC itself. The relationship between subject headings and classification is further discussed in the Principles of the Sears List.

Usually only one number is assigned to a subject heading. In some cases, however, when a subject can be treated in more than one discipline, the subject is then given more than one number in the List. The heading **Chemical industry**, for example, is given two numbers, **338.4** and **660**, which represent possible classification numbers for materials dealing with the chemical industry from the viewpoints of economics and technology respectively. Classification numbers are not assigned to a few very general subject headings, such as **Charters**, **Exhibitions**, **Hallmarks**, and **Identification**, which cannot be classified unless a specific application is identified. The alphabetic notation of B for individual biographies is occasionally provided in addition to Dewey classification numbers for such materials.

The Dewey numbers given in Sears are extended as far as is authorized by the *Abridged Dewey Decimal Classification*, which is seldom more than four places beyond the decimal point. When an item being classified has a particular form or geographic specificity, the number may be extended by adding form and geographic subdivisions from the Dewey tables. To demonstrate the building of these numbers, the Dewey number has been carried out when an example of a form or geographic subdivision is provided in the List; for example, **World War, 1939-1945—Pictorial works** is given the number **940.53022**, and **Antiques— United States** is given the number **745.10973**. A library preferring broad classification may elect to use the numbers found at the unsubdivided headings **World War, 1939-1945** and **Antiques**, that is, **940.53** and **745.1**. No library should feel the need to extend classification numbers beyond what is practical for the size of the library's collection. For libraries in which even relatively brief numbers are too long the cataloger should consult the discussion of close and broad classification in the introduction to the Dewey volume.

Style, Filing, Etc.

For spelling and definitions the editor has relied upon *Webster's Third New International Dictionary of the English Language, Unabridged* (1961) and the *Random House Webster's Unabridged Dictionary*, 2nd ed., revised and updated (1997). Capitalization and the forms of corporate and geographic names used as examples are based on the *Anglo-American Cataloguing Rules*, 2nd ed., 1998 revision. The filing of entries follows the *ALA Filing Rules* (1980).

Every term in the List that may be used as a subject heading is printed in boldface type whether it is a main term; a term in a USE reference; a broader, narrower, or related term; or an example in a scope note or general reference. If a term is not printed in boldface type, it is not used as a heading. Earlier forms of headings revised in this edition are found after the UF (Used for) label with the indication "[*Former heading*]" appended.

Acknowledgments

The editor wishes to acknowledge with gratitude the contributions to this edition of the individual catalogers, reference librarians, and vendors of cataloging services who have offered suggestions for headings to be added to the List. The Cataloging of Children's Materials Committee of the American Library Association has also been an important source of advice.

Thanks are extended to the editors and catalogers of the H.W. Wilson Company; to Patricia Kuhr, Editor, Subject Authority Files, for her assistance in formulating subject headings; and to Ann Case, Associate Director of Indexing Services.

The classification numbers given in this edition of Sears conform to the *Abridged Dewey Decimal Classification Edition 13*, published in 1997, by OCLC Forest Press. We extend special thanks to the editors of the *Dewey Decimal Classification* for providing information and advice on the application of Dewey numbers.

Every edition of the Sears List represents the work of many hands, especially those of the previous editors over the years. The contributions of the users of the List have also been invaluable. Every comment, suggestion, question, or request from a user represents an opportunity for improvement and is greatly valued.

J. Miller

Principles of the Sears List of Subject Headings

Certain principles and practices of subject cataloging should be understood before an attempt is made to assign subject headings to library materials. The discussion that follows makes reference to the *Sears List of Subject Headings*, henceforth referred to as the Sears List or the List, but the principles are applicable to other lists of subject headings as well.

1. THE PURPOSE OF SUBJECT CATALOGING

All library work is a matter of the storage and retrieval of information, and cataloging is that aspect of library work devoted to storage. The best cataloging is simply that which facilitates the most accurate and complete retrieval. The two basic branches of cataloging are descriptive cataloging and subject cataloging. Descriptive cataloging makes possible the retrieval of materials in a library by title, author, date, etc.—in short all the searchable elements of a cataloging record except the subjects. Only by conforming to the standards for descriptive cataloging can a librarian assure the user accurate retrieval on the descriptive elements, and those standards are codified in the *Anglo-American Cataloguing Rules*, which is now in its second revised edition (commonly known as *AACR2*).

Until the second half of the nineteenth century, descriptive cataloging was the only library cataloging that was found necessary. Libraries were much smaller than they are today, and scholarly librarians then were able, with the aid of printed bibliographies, to be familiar with everything available on a given subject and guide the users to it. With the rapid growth of knowledge in many fields in the course of the nineteenth century and the resulting increase in the volume of books and other library materials, it became desirable to do a preliminary subject analysis of such works and then to represent them in the catalog in such a way that they would be retrievable by subject.

Subject cataloging deals with what a book or other library item is about, and the purpose of subject cataloging is to list under one uniform word or phrase all the materials on a given topic that a library has in its collection. A subject heading is that uniform word or phrase used in the library catalog to express a topic. The use of authorized words or phrases only, with cross-references from unauthorized synonyms, is the essence of bibliographic control in subject cataloging. The purpose of a subject authority, such as the Sears List, is to provide a basic vocabulary of authorized terms together with suggestions for useful cross-references.

The two most common types of subject authorities are the thesaurus and the subject heading list. A true thesaurus, in the realm of information science, is a comprehensive controlled vocabulary of discrete unit terms, called descriptors, arranged is such a way as to display the hierarchical and associative relationships among terms. It is usually limited to a particular realm of knowledge, as in the case of the *Art and Architecture Thesaurus*. The American national standards for thesauri are spelled out in the NISO *Guidelines for the Construction, Format, and Management of Monolingual Thesauri*. A subject heading list, such as the Sears List or the *Library of Congress Subject Headings*, is simply an alphabetical list of terms that have been established over time as warranted by the materials being cataloged. A subject heading list also indicates relationships among terms but does not attempt to establish any comprehensive hierarchies. In addition to simple descriptors, a subject heading list can include pre-coordinated strings composed of subject terms with subdivisions.

The *Library of Congress Subject Headings*, which in print now comprises five large volumes, is primarily a list of headings that have been used in the Library. Likewise *Medical Subject Headings* is linked to the holdings of the National Library of Medicine. The Sears List is unique among subject heading lists in that it does not attempt to be a complete list of terms used in any single library but only a list of headings most likely to be needed in a typical small library and a skeleton or pattern for creating other headings as needed. By using the Sears List as a foundation, the cataloger in a small library can develop a local authority list that is consistent in form and comprehensive for that library. This has proven over the years to be a practical and economical solution to the cataloging needs of small libraries. In other ways, such as the use of uninverted headings only and of popular rather than technical vocabulary, the Sears List is specifically tailored to the needs of small libraries of any kind, including school libraries, small public libraries, church libraries, etc.

Because the Sears List is not a complete authority list, the cataloger using the Sears List must take an active part in developing a larger vocabulary of terms. As an aid in this process we offer the following discussion of the basic principles of subject analysis and the construction and control of subject headings.

2. DETERMINING THE SUBJECT OF THE WORK

The first and most important step in subject cataloging is to ascertain the true subject of the material being cataloged. This concept of "aboutness" should never be far from a subject cataloger's thoughts. It is a serious mistake to think of subject analysis as a matter of sorting through material and fitting it into the available categories, like sorting the mail, rather than focusing first on the material and determining what it is really about.

Many times the subject of a work is readily determined. **Hummingbirds** is obviously the subject of a book entitled *The Complete Book of Hummingbirds*. In others cases the subject is not so easy to discern, because it may be a complex one or the author may not express it in a manner clear to someone unfamiliar with the subject. The subject of a work cannot always be determined from the title alone, which is often uninformative or misleading, and undue dependence on it can result in error. A book entitled *Great Masters in Art* immediately suggests the subject **Artists**, but closer examination may reveal the book to be only about painters, not about artists in general. After reading the title page, the cataloger should examine the table of contents and skim the preface and introduction, and then, if the subject is still not clear, examine the text carefully and read parts of it, if necessary. In the case of nonbook materials, the cataloger should examine the container, the label, any accompanying guides, etc., and view or listen to the contents if possible. Only after this preliminary examination has been made is it possible to determine the subject of a work. If the meaning of a subject term is not clearly understood, reference sources should be consulted, not only an unabridged dictionary and general encyclopedia, but specialized reference books as well.

Only when the cataloger has determined the subject content of a work and identified it with explicit words can the Sears List be used to advantage. The List is consulted to determine one of three possibilities. If the word the cataloger chose to describe the subject content of the work is an established heading in the List, then that heading should be assigned to the work. If the word the cataloger chose is a synonym or alternate form of an established heading in the List, then the cataloger forgoes the word that first came to mind in favor of the term from the List. A third possibility is that there is no heading in the List for the subject of the work at hand, in which case the cataloger must formulate the appropriate heading, add it to the library's subject authority file with its attendant references, and then assign it to the work.

Many books are about more than one subject. In that case a second or third subject heading would be necessary. Theoretically there is no limit to the number of subject entries that could be made for one work, but in practice an excess of entries is a disservice to the user of the catalog. More than three subject headings should be assigned to a single item only after careful consideration. The need for more than three may be due to the cataloger's inability to identify precisely the single broader heading that would cover all the topics in the work. Similarly, a subject heading should not be assigned for a topic that comprises less than one third of a work. The commonest practice, known as the Rule of Three, may be stated as follows: As many as three specific subject headings in a given area may be assigned to a work, but if the work treats of more than three subjects, then a broader heading is used instead and the specific headings are omitted. A work about snakes and lizards, for example, would be assigned the headings **Snakes** and **Lizards**. If the work also included material on turtles, a third heading **Turtles** would be added. But if the work discussed alligators and crocodiles as well, the only subject heading assigned would be **Reptiles**.

Subject headings are used for materials that have definite, definable subjects. There are always a few works so indefinite in their subject content that it is better not to assign a heading at all. Such a work might be a collection of materials produced by several individuals on a variety of topics or one person's random thoughts and ideas. If a cataloger cannot determine a definite subject, the reader is unlikely to find the item under a makeshift or general heading. The headings **Human behavior** and **Happiness**, for example, would be misleading when assigned to a book titled *Appreciation*, which is a personal account of the sources of the author's pleasure in life. The book has no specific subject and so it should be assigned no subject headings.

3. SPECIFIC AND DIRECT ENTRY

The principle of specific and direct entry is fundamental in modern subject cataloging. According to that rule a work is entered in the catalog directly under the most specific subject heading that accurately represents its content. This term should be neither broader nor narrower but co-extensive in scope with the subject of the work cataloged. The principle was definitively formulated by Charles A. Cutter (1837-1903) in his *Rules for a Dictionary Catalog*. Cutter wrote: "Enter a work under its subject-heading, not under the heading of a class which includes that subject." His example is: "Put Lady Cust's book on 'The Cat' under Cat, not under Zoology or Mammals, or Domestic animals; and put Garnier's 'Le Fer' under Iron, not under Metals or Metallurgy." The reason this principle has become sacred to modern cataloging is simply that there is no other way to insure uniformity. In subject cataloging uniformity means simply that all materials on a single topic are assigned the same subject heading. If the headings **Cats, Zoology, Mammals**, and **Domestic animals** were all equally correct for a book on cats, as they would be without Cutter's rule, there would be no single heading for that topic and consequently no assurance of uniformity. One cataloger could assign the heading **Cats** to Lady Cust's book, another cataloger could assign the heading **Mammals** to another book on cats, and a third cataloguer could assign the heading **Domestic animals** or **Pets** to yet another book on cats. There would then be no simple way to retrieve all the materials on cats in the library's collection.

The principle of specific entry holds that a work is always entered under a specific term rather than under a broader heading that includes the specific concept. This principle is of particular importance to the cataloguer using the Sears List, since the heading of appropriate specificity must be added if it is not already there. If, for example, a work being catalogued is about penguins, it should be entered only under the most specific term that is not narrower than the scope of the book itself, that is, **Penguins**. It should not be assigned the heading **Birds** or **Water birds**. This is true even though the heading **Penguins** does not appear in the List. When a specific subject is not found in the List, the heading for the larger group or category to which it belongs should be consulted, in this case **Birds**. There the cataloger finds a general reference that reads: "SA [See also] types of birds, e.g. **Birds of prey; Canaries**; etc. {to be added as needed}." The cataloger must establish the heading **Penguins** as a narrower term under the heading **Birds** and then assign it to the book on penguins. In many cases the most specific entry will be a general subject. A book entitled

Birds of the World would have the subject heading **Birds**. Even though **Birds** is a very broad term, it is the narrowest term that comprehends the subject content of that work.

Having assigned a work the most specific subject heading that is applicable, the cataloger should not then make an additional entry under a broader heading. A work with the title *Birds of the Ocean* should not be entered under both **Birds** and **Water birds** but only under **Water birds**. To eliminate this duplication, the *See also* references in the public catalog direct the user from the broader subject headings to the more specific ones. At **Birds**, for example, the reference would read: "See also **Birds of Prey; Canaries; Pelicans; Penguins; Water birds**," etc.

The principle of direct entry holds that a subject heading should stand as a separate term rather than as a subdivision under a broader heading. If the reader wants information about owls, the direct approach is to consult the catalog under the heading **Owls**, not under the broader subject **Birds** subdivided by the narrower topic **Owls**. In other words, the cataloger has entered the book directly under **Owls**, not indirectly under "Birds—Owls," or under "Birds—Birds of prey—Owls." The latter two subject strings are both specific, but they are not direct.

4. TYPES OF SUBJECT HEADINGS

There are four types of subject headings: topical headings, form headings, geographic headings, and proper names.

4. A. TOPICAL HEADINGS

Topical subject headings are simply the words or phrases for common things or concepts that represent the content of various works. In choosing the word or phrase that makes the best subject heading several things should be considered. The first and most obvious is the literary warrant, or the language of the material being cataloged. The word most commonly used in the literature is most likely the word that best represents the item cataloged. If nine out of ten books on the subject use the phrase "Gun control," there is no reason to use any word or phrase other than **Gun control** as a subject heading, so long as that phrase meets certain other criteria.

A second consideration, and one of the criteria that a subject heading should meet, is that of common usage. In so far as possible a subject heading should represent the common usage of the English language. In American libraries this means current American spelling and terminology: **Labor** not Labour; **Elevators** not Lifts. (In British libraries these choices would be reversed.) Foreign terms such as **Romans à clef** are not used unless they have been fully incorporated into the English language. By the same token contemporary usage gradually should replace antiquated words or phrases. The heading **Blacks**, for example, replaced Negroes as common usage changed. In time the heading **African Americans** was added to the Sears List for greater specificity, as the use of that term stabilized. What is common usage depends, in part, upon who the users of a library are. In most small libraries the popular or common word for a thing is to be preferred to the scientific or technical word, when the two are truly synonymous. For example, **Desert animals** is preferable in most small libraries to Desert fauna. In such a case the scientific term should be a *See* reference to the established term.

In order to maintain uniformity in a library catalog two things are necessary. The first is abiding by Cutter's rule of specificity, and the second is choosing a single word or phrase from among its synonyms or near-synonyms in establishing a subject heading. If **Desert animals** and Desert fauna were both allowed as established headings, the material on one subject would end up in two places. Sometimes a single word or phrase must be chosen from among several choices that do not mean exactly the same thing but are too close to be easily distinguished. In the Sears List, for example, **Regional planning** is an established heading with *See* references from County planning, Metropolitan planning, and State planning. The term chosen as the established heading is the one that is most inclusive.

Another important consideration in establishing topical subject headings is that they should be clear and unambiguous. Sometimes the most common term for a topic is not suitable as a subject heading because it is ambiguous. Civil War, for example, must be rejected in favor of **United States—History—1861-1865, Civil War**, since not all civil wars are the American Civil War. The term **Civil war** could itself become a heading, if it were needed for general materials on rebellions or internal revolutions.

When a single word has several meanings, that word can be used as a subject heading only when it is somehow rendered unambiguous. The word Depression, for example, can mean either an economic or a mental state, but as subject headings one is formulated **Depressions** and the other **Depression (Psychology)**. Stress can mean either stress on materials or stress on the mind, and the two headings are **Strength of materials** and **Stress (Psychology)**. Notice that the ambiguous word is qualified even when the other meaning is expressed in other words. Furthermore, an ambiguous term such as Feedback should be qualified, **Feedback (Psychology)**, even when the other meaning, **Feedback (Electronics)**, does not yet exist in the catalog. Whenever identical words with different meanings are used in the catalog, both require a parenthetical qualifier, which is usually either a broader term or discipline of study, as in the case of **Seals (Animals)** and **Seals (Numismatics)**.

In choosing one term as a subject heading from among several possibilities the cataloger must also think of the spelling, number, and connotations of the various forms. When variant spellings are in use, one must be selected and uniformly applied, such as **Archeology** rather than Archaeology. A decision also must be made between the singular and plural form, which will be further discussed under Grammar of Subject Headings below. Sometimes variant forms of words can have different connotations, as with Arab, Arabian, and Arabic. It may seem inconsistent to use all three forms in subject headings, but, in fact, they are used consistently in the following ways: Arab relating to the people; Arabian referring to the geographical area and to horses; and Arabic for the language, script, or literature.

4. B. FORM HEADINGS

The second kind of heading that is found in a library catalog is the form heading, which describes not the subject content of a work but its form. In other words, a form heading tells us not what a work is about but what it is. Form in this context means intellectual form of the materials rather than the physical form of the item. The physical forms of such nonbook materials as videorecordings, computer files, etc., are considered general material designations (GMD), a part of the descriptive cataloging, rather than subject headings.

Some form headings describe the general arrangement of the material and the purpose of the work, such as **Almanacs**, **Directories**, **Gazetteers**, and **Encyclopedias and dictionaries**. These headings are customarily assigned to individual works as well as to materials about such forms. Theoretically, at least, any form can also be a topic, since it is possible for someone to write a book about almanacs or gazetteers.

Other form headings are the names of literary forms and genres. Headings for the major literary forms, **Fiction**, **Poetry**, **Drama**, and **Essays**, are usually used as topical subject headings. As form headings they are used for collections only rather than for individual literary works. Minor literary forms, also known as genres, such as **Science fiction**, **Epistolary poetry**, and **Children's plays**, are much more numerous and are often assigned to individual literary works. These headings will be discussed at greater length below under Literature. The distinction between form headings and topical headings in literature can sometimes be made by using the singular form for the topical heading and the plural for the form heading. **Short story**, for example, is topical, for materials about the short story as a literary form, while **Short stories** is a form. Likewise, **Essay** is topical, while **Essays** is a form. The peculiarities of language, however, do not always permit this distinction.

4. C. GEOGRAPHIC HEADINGS

Many works in a library's collection are about geographic areas, countries, cities, etc. The appropriate subject heading for such a work is the name of the place in question. Geographic headings are the established names of individual places, from places as large as **Africa** to places as small as **Walden Pond (Mass.)**. They signify not only physical places but also political jurisdictions. These headings differ from topical subject headings in that they refer to a unique entity rather than to an abstraction or category of things.

The Sears List does not attempt to provide geographic headings, which are numerous far beyond the scope of a single volume. The geographic headings that are found in Sears, such as **United States, Ohio**, and **Chicago (Ill.)**, are offered only as examples. The cataloger using the Sears List must establish geographic headings as needed with the aid of standard references sources. Some suggested sources are the most current editions of *The Columbia Gazetteer of the World*; *National Geographic Atlas of the World*; *Statesman's Year-book*; *Times Atlas of the World*; and *Merriam-Webster's Geographical Dictionary*. The geographic headings and geographic subdivisions found in Sears follow the form of abbreviation for qualifying states, provinces, etc., found in Appendix B (Abbreviations) of *AACR2*.

4. D. NAMES

Still other materials in a library's collection are about individual persons, families, corporate bodies, literary works, motion pictures, etc. The appropriate heading for such material is the unique name of the entity in question. The three major types of name headings are personal names, corporate names, and uniform titles. Individual or personal name headings are usually established in the inverted form, with dates if necessary, and with *See* references from alternate forms. The heading **Clinton, Bill**, for example, would require a *See* reference from "Clinton, William Jefferson," and if the library had material about any other person called Bill Clinton, the name heading for the president would need to take the form **Clinton, Bill, 1946-** . Corporate name headings are the commonly established names of corporate bodies, such as business firms, institutions, buildings, sports teams, performing groups, etc. Materials about a corporate body, such as **Rockefeller Center** or **Fort Lauderdale International Boat Show**, are entered directly under the corporate name heading as a subject. Uniform titles are the established names of periodicals, computer programs, motion pictures, radio and television programs, and certain literary works. Materials about a computer program, motion picture, etc., and materials about an anonymous literary work are entered directly under the uniform title, such as **Eudora (Computer file)** or **Beowulf**, as a subject. Materials about a literary work with a known author are entered under a name-title heading consisting of the author's name followed by the title, such as **Shakespeare, William, 1564-1616. Hamlet** for a book about Shakespeare's play.

Like geographic headings, name headings are numerous beyond the scope of the Sears List and must be established by the cataloger as needed. Suggested sources for personal and corporate names are *Who's Who*; *Who's Who in America*; *Merriam-Webster's Biographical Dictionary*; *The Dictionary of National Biography*; and the *Encyclopedia of Associations*. General encyclopedias and standard reference works limited to specific fields are also useful sources for names.

5. THE GRAMMAR OF SUBJECT HEADINGS

While many subject headings are simple terms like **Reptiles** or **Electricity**, other subjects can be very complex, in some cases involving several levels of subdivision. In order to construct subject headings consistently the cataloger should understand the grammar of subject headings.

5. A. THE FORMS OF HEADINGS

5. A. i. Single Nouns

A single noun is the ideal type of subject heading when the language supplies it. Such terms are not only the simplest in form but often the easiest to comprehend. A choice must be made between the singular and plural forms of a noun. The plural is the more common, but in practice both are used. Abstract ideas and the names of disciplines of study are usually stated in the singular, such as **Biology** or **Existentialism**. An action, such as **Editing** or **Child abuse**, is also expressed in the singular. Headings for concrete things are most commonly in the plural form, when those things can be counted, such as **Playgrounds** or **Children**. Concrete things that cannot be counted, such as **Steel** or **Milk**, obviously remain in the singular. In most cases common sense can be relied upon. In some instances both the singular and the plural of a word can be subject headings when they have two different meanings, such as **Theater** for the activity and **Theaters** for the buildings. In the case of **Arts** and **Art**, the one means the arts in general, while the other means the fine and decorative arts specifically.

5. A. ii. Compound Headings

Subject headings that consist of two nouns joined by "and" are of several types. Some headings link two things because together they form a single concept or topic, such as **Bow and arrow** or **Good and evil**; because they are so closely related they are rarely treated separately, such as **Forests and forestry** or **Publishers and publishing**; or because they are so closely synonymous they are seldom distinguished, such as **Cities and towns** or **Rugs and carpets**. Other headings that link two words with "and" stand for the relationship between the two things, such as **Church and state** or **Television and children**. Compound headings of this type should not be made without careful consideration. Often there is a better way to formulate the heading. A heading like "Medicine and religion," for example, is less accurate that the form established in Sears, which is **Medicine—Religious aspects**. (There is not likely to be material on the medical aspects of religion.) One question that arises in forming compound headings is word order. The only rule is that common usage takes precedence (no one says "Arrow and bow"), and, where there is no established common usage, alphabetic order is preferred. Whatever the order, a *See* reference should be made from either the second term or from the pair of terms reversed, as in Forestry, *See* **Forests and forestry**, or Children and television, *See* **Television and children**.

5. A. iii. Adjectives with Nouns

Often a specific concept is best expressed by a noun with an adjective, such as **Unemployment insurance** or **Buddhist art**. In the past the expression was frequently inverted (Insurance, Unemployment; Art, Buddhist). There were two possible reasons for inversion: 1) an assumption was made that the searcher would think first of the noun; or 2) the noun was placed first in order to keep all aspects of a broad subject together in an alphabetical listing, as in a card catalog. In recent years these arguments have been abandoned in favor of the direct order because users have become more and more accustomed to searching in the order of natural language. The only headings that have been retained in Sears in the inverted form are proper names, including the names of battles and massacres.

5. A. iv. Phrase Headings

Some concepts that involve two or more elements can be expressed only by more or less complex phrases. These are the least satisfactory headings, as they offer the greatest variation in wording, are often the longest, and may not be thought of readily by either the maker or the user of the catalog, but for many topics the English language seems to offer no more compact terminology. Examples are **Insects as carriers of disease** and **Violence in popular culture**.

5. B. SUBDIVISIONS

Specific entry in subject headings is achieved in two basic ways. The first, as noted above, is the creation of narrower terms as needed. The second is the use of subdivisions under an established term to designate aspects of that term, such as **Birds—Eggs** or **Food—Analysis**, or the form of the item itself, such as **Agriculture—Bibliography**. The scope of the Sears List can be expanded far beyond the actual headings printed through the use of subdivisions. Some subdivisions are applicable to only a few subjects. *Eggs*, for example, is applicable only under headings for oviparous animals. Other subdivisions, such as *Analysis*, are applicable under many subjects. Still other subdivisions, such as *Bibliography*, are applicable under nearly any heading. The Sears List does not attempt to list all possible subdivisions, but all those that are most likely to be used in a small library are included. For every subdivision included there is an instruction in the List for the use of that subdivision. Some subdivisions are also headings, such as **Bibliography**, and in such cases the instruction is given in a general reference as part of the entry for that heading. Other subdivisions, such as *Economic aspects*, are not themselves headings, and in such cases the instruction for the use of the subdivision is a free-standing general reference in the alphabetical List.

5. B. i. Topical Subdivisions

Topical subdivisions are those subdivisions that brings out the aspect of a subject or point of view presented in a particular work. A work may be a history of the subject, as in **Clothing and dress—History**; or it may deal with the philosophy of the subject, as in **Religion—Philosophy**; research in the field, as in **Oceanography—Research**; the laws about it, as in **Automobiles—Law and legislation**; or how to study and teach the subject, as in **Mathematics—Study and teaching**. The advantage of subdivisions over phrase headings for complex subjects is that uniformity can be more readily achieved with subdivisions. Once the subdivisions have been established, they can be appended to any applicable subject heading without guessing or straining the language for a suitable phrase. Subject strings with topical subdivisions can be read backwards: **Clothing and dress—History**, for example, means the history of clothing and dress, and **Oceanography—Research—Ethical aspects** means ethical aspects of research in the field of oceanography.

5. B. ii. Geographic Subdivisions

Another aspect of subjects that can be brought out in subdivisions is geographic specificity. The unit used as a subdivision may be the name of a country, state, city, or other geographic area. A topical heading with a geographic subdivision means simply that topic in a particular places. **Bridges—France**, for example, is the appropriate subject string for a work on bridges in France, and **Agriculture—Ohio** for a work on agriculture in Ohio.

Not every topical heading lends itself logically or practically to geographic subdivision. Some topics, such as **Internet addresses** or **Intuition**, are either non-physical or too abstract to have a geographic location. Other headings, such as **Pet therapy** or **Parenting**, are unlikely to be dealt with geographically, at least in works that would be found in a small library. Still other headings, such as **Exploration** or **Church history**, are not subdivided geographically because the same term is used instead as a subdivision under the geographic headings, as in **Arctic regions—Exploration** or **United States—Church history**.

Many subject headings in the Sears List are followed by the parenthetical phrase (May subdiv. geog.). In application this means that if the work in hand deals with that subject in general, only the heading itself is used; but if it deals with the subject in a particular place, the heading may be subdivided geographically. Some small libraries limit the use of geographic subdivision to countries other than the United States, since most of their material will be concerned with the United States. Furthermore, if a library prefers geographic subdivisions for subjects that are not so indicated in the List, the library should feel free to add them, provided, of course, that the heading is not itself used as a subdivision under geographic headings.

Some subjects, mostly in the fields of art and music, have general references that read: "SA [See also] art of particular countries or regions, e.g. **Greek art**." For these headings the geographic qualification is conveyed by a modifying adjective rather than by a subdivision. The Sears List historically has never distinguished between French art and Art in France (which is not necessarily French). Should a library have sufficient material to warrant such a distinction, **Art—France** could be established in addition to **French art**, which is suggested, and the art of particular countries could also be subdivided by other countries, as in **Italian art—Great Britain**. Such a decision should be based on the materials at hand and the purpose and needs of the library.

Geographic subdivisions can be either direct or indirect. The Sears List uses the direct form of subdivision, whereby topics are subdivided directly by cities, counties, metropolitan areas, etc., as in **Theater—Paris (France)** or **Hospitals—Chicago (Ill.)**. The indirect form of subdivision, used by the Library of Congress and certain other subject heading systems, interposes the name of the country or state (the larger geographic area) between the topical subject and the smaller area, as in "Theater—France—Paris" and "Hospitals—Illinois—Chicago."

5. B. iii. Chronological Subdivisions

In any catalog, large or small, there will be many works on American history. If these works are all entered under the general heading **United States—History**, the library user is required to look through many entries to find materials about any specific period of American history. Chronological subdivisions, which correspond to generally accepted periods of a country's history or to the spans of time most frequently treated in the literature, make such a search much simpler by bringing together all works on a single period of history, such as **United States—History—1945-1953**. If a chronological period has been given a name, this name is included in the heading following the dates, as in **United States—History—1600-1775, Colonial period**.

Historical periods vary from one country to another and usually correspond to major dynastic or governmental changes. The Sears List includes chronological subdivisions only for those countries about which a small library is likely to have much historical material, with the greatest number of period subdivisions under **United States**, **Canada**, **Great Britain**, **France**, **Germany**, and **Italy**, and a few subdivisions only under several other countries. Whenever there is only a small amount of material on the history of a country, it should simply be entered under the name of the country with the subdivision *History*, without a chronological subdivision. For most small libraries in North America the heading **Turkey—History** will suffice for all historical material about Turkey, even though Turkey has a very long history. If, however, a library should acquire a large amount of historical material about any such country or region, period subdivisions should be established beyond those spelled out in the Sears List. For these the cataloger may wish to consult *LC Period Subdivisions under Names of Places*.

The same chronological subdivisions that are used under a country's history may also be used under that country with the subdivision *Politics and government*. Other kinds of subjects, especially those relating to literature and the arts, may also be subdivided chronologically as appropriate, usually by century.

5. B. iv. Form Subdivisions

The most common item found in a library is an expository prose treatise on a subject. Many works, however, present their material in other forms, such as lists, tables, maps, pictures, etc. Form subdivisions specify the form an item takes. Like form headings they tell what an item is rather than what it is about. Some of the most common form subdivisions are *Bibliography*; *Catalogs*; *Dictionaries*; *Directories*; *Gazetteers*; *Handbooks, manuals, etc.*; *Indexes*; *Maps*; *Pictorial works*; *Portraits*; *Registers*; and *Statistics*.

Topical headings with form subdivisions, such as **Children's literature—Bibliography** or **Geology—Maps**, render such works retrievable by form and separate them from expository treatises. Apart from a few examples, these combinations of subject heading with form subdivision are not given in the Sears List but are to be added by the cataloger as needed. Form subdivisions are particularly valuable under headings for the large fields of knowledge that are represented by many entries in a library's catalog. In applying form subdivisions the cataloger should be guided by the character of an item itself, not by the title. Many works with titles beginning with Outline of, Handbook of, or Manual of, are in fact expository works. For example, H. G. Wells's *Outline of History* and H. J. Rose's *Handbook of Latin Literature* are lengthy, comprehensive treatises, and to use the form subdivisions that the titles suggest would be inaccurate. Other so-titled Outlines or Manuals or Handbooks may prove to be bibliographies, dictionaries, or statistics of the subject.

5. B. v. The Order of Subdivisions

At the Subject Subdivision Conference that took place at Airlie House, Virginia, in May 1991, organized by the Library of Congress, it was recommended that subdivisions follow the standard order of **[Topical]—[Geographic]—[Chronological]—[Form]**. Since that time the library community has endeavored to implement that recommendation. Only in a few subject areas, especially in the field of art, have exceptions been made. A cataloger using the Sears List can safely assume that subject strings made in the recommended order will provide the greatest uniformity. By following this standard the cataloger will know, for example, to prefer **Railroads—Rates—United States** to "Railroads—United States—Rates," and **Sports—United States—Statistics** to "Sports—Statistics—United States."

5. B. vi. Geographic Headings Subdivided by Topic

A longstanding exception to the practice of subdividing topics geographically, and one that remains apart from the Airlie House recommendation, is that of subdividing geographic headings by topics, when those topics pertain to the history, geography, or politics of a place. For works discussing the history of California, a census of Peru, the government of Italy, the boundaries of Bolivia, the population of Paris, or the climate of Alaska, the appropriate subject strings would be **California—History**; **Peru—Census**; **Italy—Politics and government**; **Bolivia—Boundaries**; **Paris (France)—Population**; and **Alaska—Climate**.

Many subdivisions, such as *Defenses* or *Race relations*, are used only under geographic headings; many subdivisions are never used under geographic headings; and others, such as *History* or *Biography*, are used under geographic headings exactly as they are under topical subjects. Specific instructions for the application of subdivisions are given at the general reference for the subdivision in the List. For example, at **Census** in the List the general reference reads: "SA [See also] names of countries, cities, etc., with the subdivision *Census* {to be added as needed}." Similar instructions appear under **Boundaries**; **Climate**; **Population**; etc. Some topics that are used as subdivisions under geographic headings are applicable to countries only. The subdivision *Foreign relations*, for example, can be used only under countries, since only countries have foreign relations. The instructions for applications are explicit. At *Foreign relations* in the List, for example, the general reference reads: "USE names of countries with the subdivision *Foreign relations*, e.g. **United States—Foreign relations** {to be added as needed}."

A list of suggested topical subdivisions that may be used under the name of any city is given in the List under **Chicago (Ill.)**; those that may be used under the name of any state are listed under **Ohio**; and those that may be used under the name of any country or region, except for *History* further subdivided chronologically, are given under **United States**. Since each country's history is unique, the period subdivisions for its history are also unique.

5. B. vii. Local Materials

If for any reason a library wishes to keep state, local, or community area materials together in the catalog, those materials may constitute an exception to the practice of geographic subdivision. All local materials are then entered under the name of the place with all topics as subdivisions. If, for example, a library in Honolulu chose this option, the headings **Public buildings—Honolulu (Hawaii)** and **Bridges—Honolulu (Hawaii)** would become **Honolulu (Hawaii)—Public buildings** and **Honolulu (Hawaii)—Bridges**. Materials with geographic specificity other than local materials would still be treated in the ordinary way, with most topics subdivided geographically.

6. SOME DIFFICULT AREAS OF APPLICATION

In many areas the application of subject headings and their appropriate subdivisions is a simple and straightforward matter. There are, however, areas in which either the complexity of the material or the vagaries of the English language create persistent problems. Even in these areas, by maintaining sound principles, following instructions carefully, and using common sense, it is possible to catalog library materials in such a way that users can find what they need. Some of these problem areas are dealt with here.

6. A. BIOGRAPHY

Discussions of biography as a form of writing are given the topical subject heading **Biography as a literary form**. Works that are themselves biographies are given either the form heading **Biography** or the form subdivision *Biography*. Such works are considered here in two groups, collective biographies and individual biographies.

6. A. i. Collective Biographies

Collective biographies are works containing biographies of more than three persons. Works consisting of biographies of three persons or fewer are treated as individual biographies and given headings for the names of the persons individually. Collective biographies not limited to any area or to any class of persons, such as *Lives of Famous Men and Women*, are simply assigned the heading **Biography**. Often collective biographies are devoted to persons of a single country or geographic area, such as *Who's Who in the Arab World*, or *Dictionary of American Biography*; or to ethnic groups, such as *Who's Who among Hispanic Americans*. For such works the appropriate subject heading is the name of the geographic area or ethnic group with the subdivision *Biography*, in this case **Arab countries—Biography**; **United States—Biography**; and **Hispanic Americans—Biography**. If there are many entries under any such heading, the biographical dictionaries, which list a large number of names in alphabetical order, may be separated from the works with longer articles intended for continuous reading by adding the form subdivision *Dictionaries*. The heading for such a work as *Dictionary of American Biography* or *Who's Who in America* would then be **United States—Biography—Dictionaries**.

Some collective biographies are devoted to lives of a particular class of persons, such as women, or persons of a particular occupation or profession, such as librarians. These are entered under the heading for the class of persons or occupational group with the subdivision *Biography*, such as **Women—Biography** or **Librarians—Biography**. Still other collective biographies are devoted to any or all persons connected with a particular industry, institution, or field of endeavor. For these works the appropriate heading is the heading for that industry, institution, or field with the subdivision *Biography*, such as **Computer industry—Biography**; **Catholic Church—Biography**; or **Baseball—Biography**. A subject is usually broader in scope than a single category of persons associated with that subject, and likewise **Baseball—Biography** is broader than **Baseball players—Biography** and would be more suitable for a collective biography that includes managers, owners of teams, and other persons associated with the sport.

6. A. ii. Individual Biographies

Usually the only subject heading needed for the life of an individual is the name of the person, established in the same way as an author entry. The rules for establishing names are in *AACR2*. If a work is an autobiography, the author's name is entered in the bibliographic record twice, once as the author and again as the subject. There are a few individual persons about whom much has been written other than biographical material, such as works about their writings or other activities. In such cases, subdivisions are added to the person's name to specify the various aspects treated, among them *Biography*. As examples of such persons, the Sears List includes **Jesus Christ** and **Shakespeare, William, 1564-1616**, with subdivisions appropriate to material written about them. The subdivisions listed under Shakespeare may also be used, if needed, under the name of any voluminous author. The subdivisions provided under **Presidents—United States** may also be used under the name of any president or other ruler, if applicable. The subdivisions needed will vary from one individual to another. Different topics will be applicable, for example, to the material on Martin Luther, Napoleon, and Sigmund Freud. It should be noted that this use of subdivisions represents the exceptional, not the usual, treatment. For most individual biographies the name alone is sufficient.

Occasionally a biography will include enough material about the field in which the person worked that a second subject heading is required in addition to the personal name. A life of Mary Baker Eddy, for example, may include an account of the development of Christian Science substantial enough to warrant the subject heading **Christian Science—History**. The additional subject headings should be used only when the work contains a significant amount of material about the field of endeavor in addition to the subject's personal life, not simply because the subject was prominent in that field.

It is not customary practice to categorize the subjects of individual biographies by race, sex, occupation, etc. with the subdivision *Biography*. Headings such as **African American musicians—Biography** or **Women politicians—Biography** are appropriate only to collective biographies. Some catalogers are tempted to assign such headings to individual biographies as well, but there are several compelling reasons for not doing so. The first and most obvious is that in the case of a collective biography it is the author or compiler of the work who classifies or categorizes the persons included, not the cataloger. For a book such as *Black Women Scientists in the United States*, the subject heading **African American women scientists** is applicable because the author has selected the subjects of the biographies expressly for being African Americans, women, and scientists. For a collective biography entitled *Just as I Am: Famous Men and Women with Disabilities*, the subject string **Handicapped—Biography** would be appropriate because the author has written about several handicapped persons with their handicapped condition as the common feature. It would be impertinent, however, for a cataloger to assign the subject string **Handicapped—Biography** to a biography of an individual person who happened to be handicapped, even if that condition were an important element of the person's story. In other words, three or more handicapped persons constitute the category Handicapped, but a single person can never constitute a category.

Another reason for not assigning categories of persons to individual biographies is that there is no way of controlling them. Consider the case of Maya Angelou, who is a woman, an African American, an author, a poet, a memoirist, a novelist, and a filmmaker, among other things. Given those seven categories alone, the number of subject headings that could be assigned to a biography of Maya Angelou would number in the dozens if not scores: **Women, American women, African Americans, African American women, Women authors**, etc. Unless the cataloger thought of every possible combination and made a heading for that category with the subdivision *Biography*, the catalog would be inconsistent and retrieval unreliable.

The real reason for not entering individual biographies under categories of persons is that it violates the principle of specific entry. The wisdom of Cutter's rule prevails. Any of dozens of categories would apply equally to a biography of Maya Angelou simply because none of them applies. The only heading that is neither broader nor narrower but is co-extensive in scope with the subject content of the work is the personal name heading **Angelou, Maya**. *See also* references can be made, if such references are deemed useful, from a category of persons to the names of individuals about whom the library has material. At the heading **African American women authors**, for example, one would then find any books that are really about African American women authors, followed by a reference: "See also **Angelou, Maya; McMillan, Terry; Morrison, Toni**," etc. Any inconsistencies in these *See also* references would limit retrieval but would not compromise the essential integrity of the catalog.

6. B. NATIONALITIES

An aspect of subject headings fraught with confusion is that of nationalities. Even though some headings are given national adjectives, the general rule is that the national aspects of subjects are expressed by geographic subdivisions under the topical subject headings. Headings for things that are always stationary are never given national adjectives but are instead subdivided geographically, such as **Architecture—France**. Things that are not stationary are also usually expressed as topical headings with a geographic subdivision, such as **Automobiles—Germany** or **Corporations—Japan**. When those things are replicated or transported to foreign countries, however, they are given national adjectives to express national style, ownership, or origin, and subdivided by the place where they are found, such as **German automobiles—United States** or **Japanese corporations—France**.

Headings for topics in literature and the arts are given national adjectives to express national character, such as **American literature**, **Spanish art**, etc. These headings may then be subdivided geographically by any place except for the country expressed in the national adjective. **American literature—Southern States** is therefore allowable, but not "Spanish art—Spain."

In the area of people, all headings for categories of persons are subdivided geographically in the Sears List with the exception of **Authors, Novelists, Dramatists**, and **Poets**, which are given national adjectives. All other categories of writers, such as **Biographers, Journalists**, etc., are subdivided geographically. A collective biography of American poets would be entered under **American poets—Biography**, but a collective biography of American composers or journalists would be given the heading **Composers—United States—Biography** or **Journalists—United States—Biography**. When a book deals with a category of persons from one country living or working in a foreign country, such as American composers in France, the book requires two subject strings rather than one, in this case **Composers—United States** and **Americans—France**.

6. C. LITERATURE

The field of literature presents special difficulties in cataloging because it includes two distinct types of material. The first consists of works about literature, and such works are assigned topical subject headings for whatever they are about. The second consists of literary works themselves, and those works are assigned form headings to describe what the item is rather than what it is about.

6. C. i. Works about Literature

The subject headings for works about the various literary forms are the headings for those forms, such as **Drama, Fiction,** and **Poetry.** A work about poetry is simply given the heading **Poetry.** Topical subdivisions are added to such headings as needed. A work about the history of poetry or about the criticism of poetry would be entered under **Poetry—History and criticism.** A work about the technique of writing plays would be entered under **Drama—Technique.** Form subdivisions may also be used under these headings to indicate the form the work takes, such as **Drama—Dictionaries** or **Poetry—Indexes.** In addition to the major forms of literature there are also lesser genres, which are subsets of the major literary forms, such as **Science fiction** or **Epic poetry.** These headings are also applicable to works about literature, with topical and form subdivisions added as needed.

Literary works are commonly studied and written about according to categories characterized by nationality, language, religions, etc. The primary consideration in discussing literature is nationality, as in **American literature, Mexican literature,** and **Brazilian literature.** These topics are never dealt with as subsets of **English literature, Spanish literature,** or **Portuguese literature** simply because they are written in the English, Spanish, and Portuguese languages. Nationality takes precedence over language. Only a few national literatures are included in the List, and others are to be added as needed. Works about the major literary forms of national literatures are entered under the direct phrase, such as **Italian poetry** or **Russian fiction,** and again specific aspects or forms are expressed by subdivisions, as in **Italian poetry—History and criticism** or **Russian fiction—Dictionaries.** The subdivisions that appear under **English literature** may be used under any national literature, and headings for the major literary forms for any national literature may be formulated by substituting its national name for the word English.

Apart from national literatures there are also literatures characterized by areas larger than countries, such as **Latin American literature** or **African literature;** by languages not limited to or identified with a single country, such as **Latin literature** or **Arabic literature;** or by religions, such as **Catholic literature** or **Buddhist literature.** All these kinds of literature are treated in the same way as national literatures. Where a national literature is written in two or more prominent languages, the language is identified in parentheses after the name of the literature for material specifically limited to literature in that language, such as **Canadian literature (French).** Materials about the literatures of minority groups within a country, written in the predominant language of that country's literature, are identified by subdivisions indicating the author group under the name of the literature, such as **American literature—African American authors.** Materials about the literatures of indigenous minority groups written in their own language are given the name of the language, such as **Navajo literature.**

6. C. ii. Literary Works

Items that are literary works themselves are of two types: collections of several authors, or anthologies, and works by a single author, or individual literary works. Literary anthologies are given a heading for the most specific literary form that includes every item in the anthology. Very general anthologies are given broad headings, such as **Literature—Collections; Poetry—Collections;** or **Drama—Collections.** Anthologies of national literatures and the forms of national literatures are given the headings for those literatures or forms with the subdivision *Collections,* such as **American literature—Collections** and **Italian poetry—Collections.** Headings for minor literary genres, such as **Science fiction** or **Pastoral poetry,** are usually assigned to anthologies without any subdivision.

Traditionally the literary works of individual authors receive no subject headings. Literary works are best known by author and title, and readers usually want a specific novel or play, or poetry by a specific poet—material that can be located in the catalog by the author and title entries. Headings describing the major literary forms (such as **Drama**, **Fiction**, and **Poetry**) and the headings for the major forms of a national literature (such as **Irish drama**, **Russian fiction**, and **Italian poetry**) are never assigned to an individual work or to a collection by a single author. It would be counterproductive, for example, to assign the heading **Fiction** to every novel in a library's collection, since the numbers of records with the same heading would be impracticably large. Furthermore, the form and national origin of a work are expressed in the classification.

In recent years, however, many libraries have felt the need for access by subject and genre to individual works of imaginative literature. In the Sears List the headings for minor literary forms and genres—such as **Ballads**, **Fables**, **Fairy tales**, **Horror fiction**, **Science fiction**, etc.—are identified in the scope notes as applicable to individual works as well as to collections and materials about the topic. If there is no scope note indicating that a literature heading can be applied to an individual work, it can be assumed that it is not intended to be so applied. This policy is in accordance with the *Guidelines on Subject Access to Individual Works of Fiction, Drama, etc.* prepared by the Subcommittee on Subject Access to Individual Works of Fiction, Drama, etc., of the ALA Subject Analysis Committee (ALA, 1990). It varies from the usage of the Library of Congress *Subject Cataloging Manual* in that it allows form and genre access to certain kinds of literary works that are often requested in libraries. Genre headings with national or linguistic adjectives, such as **Australian science fiction** or **Latin epic poetry**, are applicable to collections but are never assigned to individual works. If they were assigned to individual works, since all authors fall into the purview of one nationality or another, there would be nothing remaining under the heading **Science fiction** or **Epic poetry** but collections of international scope.

In some libraries subject access is provided to works of literature by using any applicable subject heading from the List with the subdivision *Fiction*, *Drama*, or *Poetry*. Hence a collection of stories all set in Los Angeles could be assigned the heading **Los Angeles (Calif.)—Fiction**; a collections of plays in which the main characters are all nurses could be assigned the heading **Nurses—Drama**; and a volume of poems by several authors all on the theme of baseball could be assigned the heading **Baseball—Poetry**. Personal and corporate names can always be added to the List in order to be used with the subdivisions *Fiction*, *Drama*, and *Poetry* to provide subject access to literary collections that deal with real persons or corporate entities.

Providing the same kind of access by setting, character, or theme to individual works of fiction, drama, or poetry is more problematic. For the collection of stories set in Los Angeles, the appropriate level of specificity can be determined by finding what is common to all the stories. The plays about nurses may be about a variety of nurses, one elderly, one Hispanic American, one male, etc., but their being nurses is what they have in common. The topic **Nurses**, then, is of equal specificity with the collection itself. In individual stories or plays, however, the characters and settings are unique. For a novel in which the main character is an Italian American woman who is anorexic and a Buddhist, drives a truck for a living, and runs for political office in California, the number of applicable subject headings would run to several dozen, from **Buddhists—California** to **Women political candidates**. These headings are all less specific than the unique character and the unique situation, and to assign any of them is to violate the principle of specificity and abandon uniformity in cataloging. To assign headings for those topics also violates the principle of "aboutness." The novel is not really about truck drivers or Buddhists or political candidates at all.

6. C. iii. Themes in Literature

Some libraries have a significant amount of material about topics, locales, or themes in imaginative literature. The appropriate headings for such material is simply "Topic in literature," according to the pattern found in the Sears List under **Literature—Themes**, such as **Dogs in literature**, **Ohio in literature**, etc. Headings of this type are for critical discussions only, not for literary works. Materials about the depiction of historical persons in drama, fiction, or poetry are entered under the person's name with the subdivision *In literature*, such as **Napoleon I, Emperor of the French, 1769-1821—In literature**. Materials about the depiction of a particular war in drama, fiction, or poetry are entered under the heading for the war with the subdivision *Literature and the war*, such as **World War, 1939-1945—Literature and the war**.

6. D. WARS AND EVENTS

Catalogers are often called upon to formulate headings as needed for wars and current events, when those wars or events generate books and other library materials. Wars fought between two or more nations are given a name, followed by a date or dates, as appropriate, such as **War of 1812**; **Israel-Arab War, 1967**; **World War, 1939-1945**; etc. Civil wars, insurrections, and invasions are entered under the history of the country involved (following the dates, as with other historical periods), such as **United States—History—1861-1865, Civil War**; **Cuba—History—1961, Invasion**; etc.

Events of short duration, including battles, are dealt with as isolated topics rather than as periods in a country's history. Events that have names are given a heading for the name, followed by the place, and then by the date, such as **Tiananmen Square Incident, Beijing (China), 1989**, and **World Trade Center Bombing, New York (N.Y.), 1993**. Battles are entered under the name of the battle, but in the inverted form, with the place of the battle qualified as needed, such as **Hastings (East Sussex, England), Battle of, 1066**, and **Gettysburg (Pa.), Battle of, 1863**. Recurring events, such as games, festivals, etc., are given the recurring name, followed by the date, with the place in parentheses, if the place changes, such as **Olympic Games, 1996 (Atlanta, Ga.)**. Unnamed events, such as individual riots or tornadoes, are entered under the kind of event subdivided by the place of the event, such as **Riots—Washington (D.C.)** or **Tornadoes—Moore (Okla.)**.

6. E. NONBOOK MATERIALS

The assignment of subject headings for electronic media and for audiovisual and special instructional materials should follow the same principles that are applied to books. The uniform application of the same headings to book and nonbook materials alike is especially important in an integrated catalog, which brings all materials on one subject together regardless of format. Because nonbook materials often concentrate on very small aspects of larger subjects, the cataloger may not find in the List the specific heading that should be used. In such instances the cataloger should be generous in adding new subjects as needed. There are many form and genre headings that apply equally to nonbook materials and to books about such materials, such as **Biographical films**; **Comedy television programs**; and **Science fiction comic books, strips, etc.**

Topical subject headings assigned to nonbook materials should not include form subdivisions to describe physical format, such as motion pictures, slides, sound recordings, etc. For libraries using integrated catalogs, *AACR2* provides the option of using general material designations (GMD), at the end of the title proper to alert users to the general class of material to which an item belongs. Additional information on this aspect of descriptive cataloging can be found in the most recent edition of *AACR2* and in the ALA's *Guidelines for Bibliographic Description of Interactive Multimedia*.

7. CLASSIFICATION AND SUBJECT HEADINGS

The cataloger should recognize a fundamental difference between classification and subject headings for the library catalog. In any system of classification that determines the arrangement of items on the shelves, a work can obviously have only one class number and stand in only one place, but in a catalog the same work can be entered, if necessary, under as many different points of entry as there are distinct subjects in the work (usually, however, not more than three). Classification is used to gather in one numerical place on the shelf works that give similar treatment to a subject. Subject headings gather in one alphabetical place in a catalog all treatments of a subject regardless of shelf location.

Another difference between classification and subject cataloging is that classification is frequently less precise than the subject entries for the catalog. Material on floriculture in general as well as on specific kinds of garden flowers are classed together in 635.9 in the Dewey Decimal Classification. A book on flower gardening, one on perennial gardening, and one on rose gardening will all three be classified in one number, while in the catalog each book will have its own specific subject heading: **Flower gardening**, **Perennials**, or **Roses**.

Library materials are classified by discipline, not by subject. A single subject may be dealt with in many disciplines. The Dewey classification numbers given with a heading in the Sears List are intended only to direct the cataloger to the disciplines where that subject is most likely to be treated. They are not meant to be absolute or cover all possibilities and should be used together with the Dewey Decimal Classification schedules. The cataloger must examine the work at hand and determine the discipline in which the author is writing. On the basis of that decision the cataloger classifies the work, not by the subject of the work alone.

8. MAINTAINING A CATALOG

The library catalog is a vital function at the very center of a library, and as such it is always growing and changing to reflect the growing collection and to meet the changing needs of the users. It is a challenge to the cataloger to add new records, revise existing records, and make all the appropriate references, and at the same time maintain the integrity of the catalog.

8. A. ADDING NEW HEADINGS

When a cataloger has determined what an item to be cataloged is about and formulated that concept into words, the next step is to find the subject heading that expresses that concept. The first thing to be determined is whether or not there is already an existing heading in the List for that concept. If, for example, there is a book on lawsuits, the cataloger may think of the terms Lawsuits, Suing, and Suits. Upon consulting the List it becomes clear that those words are not headings but references to the established heading **Litigation**. **Litigation** is slightly broader than Suing, but is more suitable as a subject heading because it includes the matter of defending oneself against lawsuits. In this case the cataloger enters the book into the catalog under the heading **Litigation**. A new heading is not necessary.

At other times the appropriate heading for a book is not a new heading but a new combination of an established heading and a subdivision. If, for example, there is a book on the use and abuse of alcohol on college campuses, the cataloger may first think of the term Drunkenness. In the Sears List Drunkenness is an unpreferred term and a reference to two established headings: **Alcoholism** and **Temperance**. The scope note at **Temperance** reads: "Use for materials on the virtue of temperance or on the temperance movement." The book is not about drunkenness in relation to either vice and virtue or the temperance movement, so that heading can be eliminated. Neither is the book really about alcoholism, but at the heading **Alcoholism**, there is a general reference that reads: "SA [See also] classes of persons with the subdivision *Alcohol use*, e.g. **Employees—Alcohol use**; **Youth—Alcohol use**; etc., {to be added as needed}." At this point the cataloger realizes that the appropriate Sears subject heading for the book at hand would be **College students—Alcohol use**. **College students** is already an established heading in the List, but it could be added if it were not.

The cataloger should always keep in mind that it is not only appropriate but essential that types of things and examples of things not found in the List be established as headings and added to the List locally as needed. If there is a book on gloves, for example, and there is no heading in the Sears List for Gloves, the cataloger thinks of the concept or category of thing that would include gloves. Clothing comes to mind. At the heading **Clothing and dress** in the List there is a general reference: "SA [See also] types of clothing articles and accessories {to be added as needed}." The cataloger then establishes the heading **Gloves** and enters the book into the catalog under **Gloves**. It would be inappropriate to enter the book under the heading **Clothing and dress** simply because **Clothing and dress** is in the List and **Gloves** is not. It would mean that a user looking in the catalog under Gloves would find nothing. The general references in the List should reinforce the point that the List does not aim at completeness and must be expanded. Even where there is no general reference, narrower terms for types of things and examples and instances of things must be added as needed.

At times it is nearly impossible to determine what broader concept or category a new subject might be included under. This should not deter the cataloger from establishing any heading that is needed. Take, for example, the case of a book on thumb sucking, a common phenomenon among small children. The nearest terms in the List might be **Child psychology**, **Child rearing**, or **Human behavior**, but they are none too near. Nowhere is there a general reference instructing the cataloger to add headings for common childhood phenomena, and still the only appropriate heading for the book would be **Thumb sucking**. Here the intrepid cataloger, thinking how useless the headings **Child psychology**, **Child rearing**, or **Human behavior** would be on such a book, adds the heading **Thumb sucking** to the List and enters the book into the catalog under that heading.

There are resources that a cataloger can turn to for help in establishing subject headings that are not in the List. Other available databases and catalogs in which books are listed by subject can always be consulted, such as the Standard Catalog Series; *American Book Publishing Record*; *Subject Guide to Books in Print*; and the *National Union Catalog: Books*. Periodical indexes, such as *Readers' Guide to Periodical Literature* or *Applied Science & Technology Index,* are especially helpful in establishing headings for current events and very new topics and trends. The index and the schedules of the *Dewey Decimal Classification* are a useful source of subject terminology as well as a way of seeing a topic in its relation to other topics. The Library of Congress issues lists of new subject headings in *Library of Congress Subject Headings Weekly Lists* on its World Wide Web site and includes new subject headings of current interest in its quarterly *Cataloging Service Bulletin*. Library of Congress cataloging information, including subject headings, emanating from its Cataloging in Publication (CIP) program, is available in various online databases and is also printed on the title page verso of many books.

8. B.   REVISING SUBJECT HEADINGS

Because the English language does not stand still, neither do subject headings. It would be impossible today for a catalog to maintain the headings Negroes or Dinosauria, since common usage has relegated these terms to history. The prevailing thinking about the form of subject headings also changes, and as a result whole groups of headings need to be revised. All the inverted headings in the Sears List, for example, were eventually revised to the uninverted form, such as **Health insurance** for "Insurance, Health." With each new edition of the Sears List a library should consult the List of Canceled and Replacement Headings in the front of the volume and revise its catalog accordingly. Any headings created locally based on the pattern set by a Sears heading, and strings consisting of a Sears heading and a subdivision, must also be revised if that heading is revised in Sears. If, for example, a library had added the headings "Insurance, Title" and "Insurance, Health—Law and legislation," those headings would need to be revised to **Title insurance** and **Health insurance—Law and legislation**.

How a library revises its catalog depends upon the kind of catalog. In a card catalog the subjects are physically erased and retyped, either on all the cards on which they appear or on the subject entry cards alone. If in a card catalog replacement of a term is desirable but the number of bibliographic records to be revised is prohibitive, a history note can be used instead. A history note is simply a card at both the old and the new form indicating the change. When, for example, the heading "Insurance, Health" is changed in Sears to **Health insurance**, the two cards would read as follows:

> **Insurance, Health**. For materials issued after [date] consult the following heading: **Health insurance**

and

> **Health insurance**. For materials issued before [date] consult the following heading: **Insurance, Health**.

In an online catalog the revision process depends upon the software employed in the catalog. If the software provides global update capability, the revision of many bibliographic records at once is simple. If they must be revised one by one, the process is still immensely easier than revising cards in a card catalog. There is also the option, provided the software allows for it, of displaying a history note in an online catalog in lieu of revising the bibliographic records.

8. C. MAKING REFERENCES

Once an item has been assigned a subject heading, either a heading found in the List or one added as needed, attention must be directed to insuring that the reader who is searching for this material will not fail to find it because of insufficient references to the proper heading. References direct the user from terms not used as headings to the term that is used, and from broader and related terms to the term chosen to represent a given subject. The Sears List uses the symbols found in most thesauri to point out the relationships among the terms found in the List and to assist the cataloger in establishing appropriate references in the public catalog based upon these relationships. There are three types of references: *See* references, *See also* references, and general references.

8. C. i. *See* References

In the public catalog *See* references direct the user from unpreferred or unestablished terms and phrases to the preferred or established terms that are used as subject headings. Under most headings in the Sears List, following the UF [Used for] label, is one or more suggested terms for *See* references in the public catalog. A cataloger may want to use some or all of them as references, and many catalogers add other *See* references they deem useful. In theory there is no limit to the number of *See* references to a particular term, but in practice there may well be, especially in a card catalog. The references will be more useful if the cataloger considers materials from the reader's point of view. The reader's profile depends on age, background, education, occupation, and geographical location, and takes into account the type of library, such as school, public, university, or special.

The following are some types of the unpreferred terms that might be used as *See* references in a catalog:

(1) Synonyms or terms so nearly synonymous that they would cover the same material. For example, **Instructional materials centers** requires a reference from School media centers.

(2) The second part of compound headings. For example, **Antique and vintage motorcycles** requires a reference from Vintage motorcycles.

(3) The inverted form of a heading, either an adjective-noun combination or a phrase heading, especially if the word brought forward is not also the broader term. For example, **Theory of knowledge** requires a reference from "Knowledge, Theory of," there being no heading Knowledge.

(4) Variant spellings. For example, **Archeology** requires a reference from Archaeology.

(5) The opposite of a term, when it is included in the meaning of a term without being specifically mentioned. For example, **School attendance** requires a reference from Absence from school and from Absenteeism (Schools), and **Equality** requires a reference from Inequality.

(6) The former forms of headings revised to reflect common usage, when the older term still has any currency. For example, Negroes remains as a reference to **Blacks** and to **African Americans**, but Dinosauria is no longer retained as a reference to **Dinosaurs**.

The first time a heading from the List is assigned to a work in the collection, the terms in the UF field in the List are entered, at the cataloger's discretion, as *See* references in the public catalog. When the same heading is subsequently assigned to other works, the references are already in place. When the cataloger adds a heading to the authority file as needed, all the appropriate *See* references are entered as well the first time the heading is used. For the heading **College students—Alcohol use**, in the example above, suitable *See* references might be Campus drinking, College drinking, and Drinking on campus.

8. C. ii. *See also* References

In the public catalog *See also* references direct the user from one established heading to another established heading. Under most headings in the Sears List, following the BT [Broader term] label, is a term that is broader in scope than the heading itself. As a rule, a term has only one broader term, unless it is an example or aspect of two or more things. The broader term serves two functions in the List. The first is to aid the cataloger in finding the best term to assign to a work. If the first term the cataloger thinks of to describe the contents of the work does not cover all aspects of work, the broader term may be the more appropriate heading for that work. The second function is to indicate where *See also* references should be made in the public catalog. A *See also* reference is made from a broader term to a narrower term, but not from a narrower term to a broader term. Take, for example, the broader term **Clothing and dress** on the heading **Gloves**. When the heading **Gloves** is assigned for the first time to a work in the collection, a reference is made at **Clothing and dress** "See also **Gloves**." If **Clothing and dress** has never been assigned to a work in the collection, it is entered in the catalog for the sake of the reference, and the reference "See also **Gloves**" is made. The point is that the user who is interested in works on clothing and dress in general may also be interested in works limited to gloves. The book on gloves need not be entered under both **Clothing and dress** and **Gloves**, but only under the appropriately specific heading, because the *See also* reference will direct the user from the broader to the narrower term. If the book on gloves were entered under both **Clothing and dress** and **Gloves**, the catalog would first list the book under the heading **Clothing and dress** and then direct the user to look as well under **Gloves** only to find the same book.

Under many headings in the Sears List, following the RT [Related term] label, one or more terms are listed that represent similar or associated subjects. These related terms are neither broader nor narrower than the main term but roughly equal in specificity. The term **Pardon**, for example, is related to **Amnesty**. The cataloger or the user may easily look first to one term only to realize that the other is the more precise term for the material being cataloged or being sought in the catalog. Related terms are reciprocal. When the term **Pardon** is assigned for the first time to a work in the collection, a reference is made in the catalog at **Amnesty** "See also **Pardon**." The reciprocal reference at **Pardon** "See also **Amnesty**" is also made, but only if **Amnesty** has also been assigned to a work in the collection. A reference is never made to a heading until there is a work entered under that heading in the collection, and if the only work entered under a heading is lost or discarded the references to that heading must be deleted. References to headings under which there is no material in the collection are called blind references and are to be avoided.

8. C. iii. General References

Under many headings in the Sears List, following the SA [See also] label, there is what is called a general reference, not to a specific heading but to a general group or category of things that may be established as headings as needed. In the example of **Clothing and dress** given above, the general reference is to "types of clothing articles and accessories, {to be added as needed}." This reference is addressed to the cataloger as a reminder not to be limited to the types of clothing and dress items given as examples in the List—**Hats, Hosiery, Shoes**, etc.—but to create a heading for any other clothing item, such as **Gloves**, when the need arises.

A second function of general references is to provide instruction in the application of subdivisions. Only a few subdivisions are universally applicable. All others apply only to certain types of headings. For every subdivision provided in the List, except those of unique application, there is a general reference spelling out the use of that subdivision. If the subdivision is also a heading, the general reference is given under the heading. **Folklore**, for example, is both a heading and a subdivision. Under the heading **Folklore** the general reference reads: "SA [See also] topics as themes in folklore with the subdivision *Folklore*, e.g. **Plants—Folklore**; names of ethnic or occupational groups with the subdivision *Folklore*, e.g. **Inuit—Folklore**; and names of individual legendary characters, e.g. **Bunyan, Paul (Legendary character)** {to be added as needed}." When the subdivision is not also a heading, there is a free-standing general reference in the alphabetical List with instructions on the use of that subdivision. For example, at *Industrial applications*, which is not a heading but only a subdivision, there is a general reference that reads: "USE types of scientific phenomena, chemicals, plants, and crops with the subdivision *Industrial applications*, e.g. **Ultrasonic waves—Industrial applications** {to be added as needed}."

Some libraries also display general references in the public catalog. Rather than make a specific *See also* reference from the broader term to every narrower term, they adapt the general reference in the List to address it to the user of the catalog. At **Flowers**, for example, rather than a specific *See also* reference to **Day lilies, Orchids, Peonies, Poppies, Roses, Tulips**, and **Violets**, there would be a general reference "See also types of flowers." The drawback of this procedure and the reason it is not recommended is that the user who wants to see all the books on specific flower types would have to think of every type of flower and look in dozens of places in the catalog. Many online catalogs are now able to provide the user with an expanded display of all the narrower terms under **Flowers** that have been used in the catalog.

8. D. RECORDING HEADINGS AND REFERENCES

The cataloger should keep a record of all the subject headings used in the catalog and all the references made to and from them. This local authority file may be kept on cards or on a computer. Some catalogers are tempted to forgo this process and merely consult the catalog whenever there is a question of previous practice. Without a local authority file, however, there can be no consistency in the cataloging. It is not possible to consult the catalog at the heading **Teachers—Ethics**, for example, and find what *See also* references were made to that term from any broader or related terms or what *See* references were made from unpreferred terms. Since **Teachers—Ethics** is not in the Sears List but was added as needed, consulting the List is not the answer. When a book appears on the ethics of psychologists, the cataloger will create **Psychologists—Ethics**, but without knowing what references were made to the heading **Teachers—Ethics**, there is no way the cataloger can create similar and consistent references for the new term. Likewise, if there is only one book entered under **Teachers—Ethics**, and if that book is lost or discarded, without a local authority file there would be no way of knowing what to delete in order to avoid blind references.

Many libraries today do little original cataloging but instead get their cataloging records from outside sources, either from computerized cooperative cataloging utilities or from vendors, often the same companies that sell them their books and other library materials. This procurement of cataloging from outside sources can save libraries a great deal of money, but it does not mean that there is no work for the cataloger in the library. Someone must order the cataloging, specifying to the vendor the particular needs of the library. If a library is devoted largely or entirely to children's materials, for example, a librarian will need to specify that the library does not want the subdivision *Juvenile literature* on every subject heading. A library using Sears subject headings will need to apprise the vendor of that fact. When the cataloging records arrive in the library, only a cataloger can check them to be sure they are what was ordered. And lastly, only a cataloger can made the appropriate references in the local catalog, tailored to that library's particular collection, which make the records useful to the users.

9. CATALOGING IN THE TWENTY-FIRST CENTURY

It is useful to view modern cataloging practice in an historical perspective. In the nineteenth century, as libraries grew and cataloging became more thorough, it was clear that some form of cooperation among libraries was desirable. For many years the distribution of printed library cards was the principal method of cooperative cataloging. Later computerized utilities replaced printed cards. From the beginning it was clear that without principles and standards guaranteeing uniformity, cooperative cataloging would be impossible. In the very first volume of the American Library Association's *Library Journal* (1876-77) there are several lengthy discussions of cooperative cataloging, including an article on the topic by Melvil Dewey. It was out of these discussions and the voluminous correspondence that ensued that the modern standards of cataloging developed, both the rules for descriptive cataloging and Cutter's *Rules for a Dictionary Catalog*. These rules are not arbitrary but are firmly grounded in logic. They have stood unchallenged for nearly a hundred years because they have served to facilitate accurate and comprehensive retrieval in the modern library.

The world of libraries in the twenty-first century is certain to be quite different from what it has been heretofore. More information will be available in machine-readable form, and ready access to the internet will no doubt change the way many users seek and find information. Traditional methods of storage and retrieval in libraries will likely be supplemented by new methods engendered by artificial intelligence. The challenge of catalogers in the future is to approach every new technology and theory knowledgeably and fearlessly, judge them against what we know are the soundest principles, and embrace the good and reject the spurious, always keeping in mind the ultimate goal of meeting, even anticipating, the changing needs of the library users.

10. BIBLIOGRAPHY

American Library Association. Filing Committee. *ALA Filing Rules*. Chicago: American Library Association, 1980.

Anglo-American Cataloguing Rules. 2nd ed., 1998 Revisions. Chicago: American Library Association, 1998.

Association for Library Collections and Technical Services. Subject Analysis Committee. *Guidelines on Subject Access to Individual Works of Fiction, Drama, etc*. Chicago: American Library Association, 1990.

Chan, Lois Mai. *Cataloging and Classification: an Introduction*. 2nd ed. New York: McGraw-Hill, 1994.

Chan, Lois Mai, Phyllis A. Richmond, and Elaine Svenonius, eds. *Theory of Subject Analysis: a Sourcebook*. Englewood, Colo.: Libraries Unlimited, 1985. [Contains excerpts from Charles A. Cutter's *Rules for a Dictionary Catalog*]

Dewey, Melvil. *Abridged Dewey Decimal Classification and Relative Index*. 13th ed. Edited by Joan S. Mitchell, et al. Albany, N.Y.: Forest Press, 1997.

Foskett, A. C. *The Subject Approach to Information*. 5th ed. London: Library Association Pub., 1996.

Haykin, David Judson. *Subject Headings: a Practical Guide*. Washington: U.S. Government Printing Office, 1951. Reprint. New York: Gordon Press, 1978.

Interactive Multimedia Guidelines Review Task Force. *Guidelines for Bibliographic Description of Interactive Multimedia*. Chicago: American Library Association, 1994.

Intner, Sheila S., and Jean Riddle Weihs. *Standard Cataloging for School and Public Libraries*. 2nd ed. Englewood, Colo.: Libraries Unlimited, 1996.

Lancaster, F. W. *Vocabulary Control for Information Retrieval*. 2nd ed. Arlington, Va.: Information Resources Press, 1986.

Library Literature & Information Science. New York: The H. W. Wilson Co., 1921-

Library of Congress. Cataloging Policy and Support Office. *Subject Cataloging Manual: Subject Headings*. 5th ed. Washington, D.C.: Library of Congress, 1996-

Library of Congress. Office for Subject Cataloging Policy. *LC Period Subdivisions under Names of Places*. 5th ed. Washington, D.C.: Library of Congress, 1994.

Lighthall, Lynne. *Sears List of Subject Headings: Canadian Companion*. 5th ed. New York: The H. W. Wilson Co., 1995.

Taylor, Arlene G. *The Organization of Information*. Englewood, Colo.: Libraries Unlimited, 1999.

Taylor, Arlene G. *Wynar's Introduction to Cataloging and Classification*. 9th ed. Englewood, Colo.: Libraries Unlimited, [in press 2000]

Zuiderveld, Sharon, ed. *Cataloging Correctly for Kids: An Introduction to the Tools*. 3rd ed. Chicago: American Library Association, 1998.

Headings to be Added by the Cataloger

Sears is not intended to be a complete list of subject headings but only a list of many of the most commonly used headings and a pattern for creating other headings as needed. Types of things and names of individual things must always be added when they are not already provided in the List. The general references in the List explicitly instruct the cataloger to create headings in areas where the need for such additions is most obvious (such as under **Flowers**, where the general reference reads "SA [See also] types of flowers, e.g. **Roses** {to be added as needed}"). Where there is no general reference the same instruction is implicit. A further discussion of adding headings can be found in the Principles of the Sears List. Some of the additional headings most likely to be needed are the following:

Topical Subjects
1. Types of common things—foods, tools, sports, musical instruments, etc.
2. Types of plants and animals—fruits, flowers, birds, fishes, etc.
3. Types of chemicals and minerals
4. Types of enterprises and industries
5. Types of diseases
6. Names of organs and regions of the body
7. Names of languages, language groups, and national literatures
8. Names of ethnic groups and nationalities
9. Names of wars, battles, treaties, etc.

Geographic Headings
1. Names of political jurisdictions—countries, states, cities, provinces, etc.
2. Groups of states, groups of countries, alliances, etc.
3. Names of geographic features—regions, mountain ranges, island groups, individual mountains, individual islands, rivers, river valleys, oceans, lakes, etc.

Names
1. Personal names—individual persons and families
2. Corporate names—associations, societies, government bodies, religious denominations, business firms, performing groups, colleges, libraries, hospitals, hotels, ships, etc.
3. Uniform titles—anonymous literary works, newspapers, periodicals, and sacred scriptures

The Key Headings on the following page can be used as a guide in applying subdivisions to any similar headings. Subdivisions not provided for in the **Sears List** may also be established and used as needed.

"Key" Headings

Certain headings in the Sears List have been chosen to serve as examples, at which the subdivisions particularly applicable to certain categories of headings are given. If a subdivision is provided under the "key" heading, it may also be used under any heading of that type.

Authors: **Shakespeare, William, 1564-1616** (to illustrate the subdivisions that may be used under any voluminous author, and in some cases other individual persons)

Ethnic groups: **Native Americans** (to illustrate the subdivisions that may be used under any ethnic group or native people)

Languages: **English language** (to illustrate the subdivisions that may be used under any language or group of languages)

Literature: **English literature** (to illustrate the subdivisions that may be used under any literature)

Places: **United States**
Ohio
Chicago (Ill.)
(to illustrate the subdivisions—except for historical periods—that may be used under any country, state, or city)

Public figures: **Presidents—United States** (to illustrate the subdivisions that may be used under the presidents, prime ministers, governors, and rulers of any country, state, etc., and in some cases under the names of individual presidents, prime ministers, etc.)

Wars: **World War, 1939-1945** (to illustrate the subdivisions that may be used under any war, and in some cases individual battles)

Commonly Used Subdivisions

To allow for a standardized formulation of many complex subjects, there are a large number of topical and form subdivisions that are widely applicable and may be used under a variety of subjects as needed. Altogether there are provisions and examples for more than twelve hundred subdivisions in the Sears List. The List of Commonly Used Subdivisions formerly found on this page has been replaced by an abundance of general references within the List itself. For each of the subdivisions provided for in Sears there is now a general reference in the alphabetical list with specific instructions as to what types of headings that subdivision can be used under.

SUBDIVISIONS OF BROAD APPLICATION

Some subdivisions are of very broad application and can be used under nearly any subject heading. The following are examples of two general references for such subdivisions—one for a topical subdivision, *Computer simulation*, which is also a heading, and one for a form subdivision, *Interactive multimedia*, which is only a subdivision:

Computer simulation
SA subjects with the subdivision *Computer simulation*, e.g. **Psychology—Computer simulation** [to be added as needed]

Interactive multimedia
USE subjects with the subdivision *Interactive multimedia*, e.g. **Geology—Interactive multimedia** [to be added as needed]

SUBDIVISIONS OF LIMITED APPLICATION

Some subdivisions are of limited application and can be used only under certain categories of subject heading. The following are examples of two general references for such subdivisions—one for a topical subdivision, *Satellites*, which is also a heading, and one for a form subdivision, *Facsimiles*, which is only a subdivision:

Satellites
SA names of planets with the subdivision *Satellites*, e.g. **Mars (Planet)—Satellites** [to be added as needed]

Facsimiles
SEE types of printed or written materials, documents, etc., with the subdivision *Facsimiles*, e.g. **Autographs—Facsimiles** [to be added as needed]

List of Canceled and Replacement Headings

CANCELED HEADINGS	REPLACEMENT HEADINGS
Accreditation (Education)	Schools—Accreditation
Aerospace industries	Aerospace industry
African American business people	African American businesspeople
African Americans in television	African Americans on television
Agricultural industries	Agricultural industry
American actors	Actors—United States
American architecture	Architecture—United States
American artists	Artists—United States
American arts	Arts—United States
American composers	Composers—United States
American decoration and ornament	Decoration and ornament—United States
American ethics	Ethics—United States
American folk dancing	Folk dancing—United States
American historians	Historians—United States
American illustrators	Illustrators—United States
American literature—American Indian authors	American literature—Native American authors
American musicians	Musicians—United States
American newspapers	Newspapers—United States
American painters	Painters—United States
American philosophers	Philosophers—United States
American sculptors	Sculptors—United States
Anglo-Saxon language	English language—Old English period
Anglo-Saxon literature	English literature—Old English period
Animal rights movements	Animal rights movement
Apple	Apples
Art forgeries	Art—Forgeries
Automobile engines	Automobiles—Motors
Black business people	Black businesspeople
Book industries	Book industry
Book industries—Exhibitions	Books—Exhibitions
Books—Classification	Library classification
Books—Reviews	Book reviews
Brothers and sisters	Siblings
Business people	Businesspeople
Buying	Purchasing
Carpets	Rugs and carpets
Cave drawings	Cave drawings and paintings
Ceramic industries	Ceramic industry
Charts	Charts, diagrams, etc.
Chicago (Ill.)—Social policy	Social policy—Chicago (Ill.)
Children and adults	Child-adult relationship
Children—Costume	Children's costumes
Children—Employment	Child labor
China—History—1989, Tiananman Square Incident	Tiananmen Square Incident, Beijing (China), 1989
Christian art and symbolism	Christian art
	Christian symbolism

CANCELED HEADINGS	REPLACEMENT HEADINGS
Christian unity	Christian union
	Church—Unity
	Ecumenical movement
	Interdenominational cooperation
Christmas plays	Christmas—Drama
Christmas poetry	Christmas—Poetry
City life	City and town life
Clay industries	Clay industry
Colonial architecture	American colonial style in architecture
	Architecture—United States—1600-1775, Colonial period
Computer aided design	Computer-aided design
Computer assisted instruction	Computer-assisted instruction
Congresses and conventions	Conferences
County libraries	Public libraries
	Regional libraries
Credit card crimes	Credit card fraud
Cross cultural studies	Cross-cultural studies
Customer service	Customer services
Cyclotron	Cyclotrons
Czechoslovakia—History—1989-1992	Czechoslovakia—History—1945-1992
D.D.T. (Insecticide)	DDT (Insecticide)
Defense industries	Defense industry
DNA fingerprints	DNA fingerprinting
Drapery	Draperies
Drilling and boring	Drilling and boring (Earth and rocks)
	Drilling and boring (Metal, wood, etc.)
Dual career family	Dual-career families
Education and state	Education—Government policy
Educational associations	Education—Societies
Eighteenth century	World history—18th century
Electric engineering	Electrical engineering
Electric industries	Electric products industry
Electronic date processing	Data processing
Electronic spreadsheets	Spreadsheet software
English language—Errors	English language—Errors of usage
English newspapers	Newspapers—Great Britain
Family violence	Domestic violence
Father and child	Father-child relationship
Fathers and daughters	Father-daughter relationship
Fathers and sons	Father-son relationship
Facsimile transmission	Fax transmission
Fifteenth century	World history—15th century
Fisheries	Commercial fishing
Fourteenth century	World history—14th century
France—History—1958-1969	France—History—1958-
France—History—1969-	France—History—1958-
French folk songs	Folk songs—France
Grandparent and child	Grandparent-grandchild relationship
Ground effect machines	Air-cushion vehicles
Home business	Home-based business
Human relations	Interpersonal relations
Indians	Native Americans
Indians of Central America	Native Americans—Central America
Indians of Central America—Guatemala	Native Americans—Guatemala
Indians of Mexico	Native Americans—Mexico

CANCELED HEADINGS	REPLACEMENT HEADINGS
Indians of North America	Native Americans
	Native Americans—North America
	Native Americans—United States
Indians of North America—Antiquities	Native Americans—Antiquities
Indians of North America—Architecture	Native American architecture
Indians of North America—Art	Native American art
Indians of North America—Canada	Native Americans—Canada
Indians of North America—Captivities	Native Americans—Captivities
Indians of North America—Children	Native American children
Indians of North America—Christian missions	Native Americans—Christian missions
Indians of North America—Claims	Native Americans—Claims
Indians of North America—Costume	Native American costume
Indians of North America—Dances	Native American dance
Indians of North America—Dwellings	Native Americans—Dwellings
Indians of North America—Economic conditions	Native Americans—Economic conditions
Indians of North America—Education	Native Americans—Education
Indians of North America—First contact with Europeans	Native Americans—First contact with Europeans
Indians of North America—Folklore	Native Americans—Folklore
Indians of North America—Games	Native American games
Indians of North America—Government relations	Native Americans—Government relations
Indians of North America—History	Native Americans—History
Indians of North America—History—Chronology	Native Americans—History—Chronology
Indians of North America—Industries	Native Americans—Industries
Indians of North America—Languages	Native American languages
Indians of North America—Literature	Native American literature
Indians of North America—Medicine	Native American medicine
Indians of North America—Music	Native American music
Indians of North America—Names	Native American names
Indians of North America—Origins	Native Americans—Origins
Indians of North America—Politics and government	Native Americans—Politics and government
Indians of North America—Psychology	Native Americans—Psychology
Indians of North America—Relations with early settlers	Native Americans—Relations with early settlers
Indians of North America—Religion	Native Americans—Religion
Indians of North America—Reservations	Native Americans—Reservations
Indians of North America—Rites and ceremonies	Native Americans—Rites and ceremonies
Indians of North America—Sign language	Native American sign language
Indians of North America—Silverwork	Native American silverwork
Indians of North America—Social conditions	Native Americans—Social conditions
Indians of North America—Social life and customs	Native Americans—Social life and customs
Indians of North America—Wars	Native Americans—Wars
Indians of North America—Women	Native American women
Indians of South America	Native Americans—South America
Indians of South America—Peru	Native Americans—Peru
Indians of the West Indies	Native Americans—West Indies
Industrial wastes	Industrial waste
Infants—Clothing	Infants' clothing
Lemon	Lemons
Libraries—Trustees	Library trustees

CANCELED HEADINGS	REPLACEMENT HEADINGS
Lime (Fruit)	Limes
Lime (Mineral)	Lime
Literature—Stories, plots, etc.	Stories, plots, etc.—Collections
Lord's Supper	Eucharist
Lunar petrology	Moon rocks
Man (Theology)	Human beings (Theology)
Mass	Mass (Liturgy)
Mathematics—Computer assisted instruction	Mathematics—Computer-assisted instruction
Minorities in television	Minorities on television
Men actors	Male actors
Middle Ages—History	Middle Ages
Military health	Military personnel—Health and hygiene
Models and model making	Models and modelmaking
Modern architecture	Modernism in architecture
Modern architecture—1600-1799 (17th and 18th centuries)	Architecture—17th and 18th centuries
Modern architecture—1800-1899 (19th century)	Architecture—19th century
Modern architecture—1900-1999 (20th century)	Architecture—20th century
Modern art—1800-1899 (19th century)	Art—19th century
Modern art—1900-1999 (20th century)	Art—20th century
Modern history—1800-1899 (19th century)	World history—19th century
Modern history—1900-1999 (20th century)	World history—20th century
Modern history—1945-	World history—1945-
Modern painting—1800-1899 (19th century)	Painting—19th century
Modern painting—1900-1999 (20th century)	Painting—20th century
Modern sculpture	Modernism in sculpture
Modern sculpture—1900-1999 (20th century)	Sculpture—20th century
Modernism (Art)	Modernism in art
Modernism (Arts)	Modernism (Aesthetics)
Moneymaking projects for children	Money-making projects for children
Moors	Muslims
Mother and child	Mother-child relationship
Mothers and daughters	Mother-daughter relationship
Mothers and sons	Mother-son relationship
Multimedia systems	Multimedia
Nineteenth century	World history—19th century
Noninstitutional churches	Non-institutional churches
Nonwage payments	Fringe benefits
Ohio—Economic policy	Economic policy—Ohio
Ohio—Social policy	Social policy—Ohio
Orange (Fruit)	Oranges
Organic chemistry—Synthesis	Organic compounds—Synthesis
Parent and child	Parent-child relationship
Parent-teacher relationships	Parent-teacher relationship
Pattern making	Patternmaking
Pecan	Pecans
Physics—Congresses	Physics—Conferences
Plots (Drama, fiction, etc.)	Stories, plots, etc.
Power plants	Electric power plants
Programming (Computers)	Computer programming
Programming languages (Computers)	Programming languages
Public relations—Libraries	Libraries—Public relations
Railroads—Consolidation	Railroads—Mergers
Religious art and symbolism	Religious art

CANCELED HEADINGS	REPLACEMENT HEADINGS
Renaissance architecture	Architecture—15th and 16th centuries
Renaissance art	Art—15th and 16th centuries
Renaissance decoration and ornament	Decoration and ornament—15th and 16th centuries
Rich people	Rich
Rugs	Rugs and carpets
Saving and thrift	Saving and investment
Science and state	Science—Government policy
Seventeenth century	World history—17th century
Single parent family	Single-parent families
Sixteenth century	World history—16th century
State aid to education	Government aid to education
State aid to libraries	Government aid to libraries
Stepfamily	Stepfamilies
Stealing	Theft
Stock exchange	Stock exchanges
Student life	College students
	Students
Talking books	Audiobooks
Teacher-student relationships	Teacher-student relationship
Thirteenth century	World history—13th century
Tiros (Meteorological satellite)	TIROS satellites
Transsexuality	Transsexualism
Twentieth century	World history—20th century
Twenty-first century	World history—21st century
Type and type founding	Type and type-founding
United States—Commercial policy	Commercial policy—United States
United States—Economic policy	Economic policy—United States
United States—History—1812-1815, War of 1812	War of 1812
United States—Military policy	Military policy—United States
United States—Social policy	Social policy—United States
Video display terminals	Computer monitors
Violence in television	Violence on television
Wages	Salaries, wages, etc.
World War, 1939-1945—Congresses	World War, 1939-1945—Conferences
World Wide Web servers	Web servers
Young adults' library services	Young adults' libraries

Symbols Used

UF = Used for

SA = See also

BT = Broader term

NT = Narrower term

RT = Related term

[Former heading] = Term that was once used as a heading and is no longer

(May subdiv. geog.) = Heading that may be subdivided by name of place

Sears List of Subject Headings

3-D photography
USE **Three dimensional photography**

4-H clubs   630.6
UF Four-H clubs
BT **Agriculture—Societies**
    Agriculture—Study and teaching
    Boys' clubs
    Girls' clubs

4th of July
USE **Fourth of July**

100 years' war
USE **Hundred Years' War, 1339-1453**

Abacus   513.028
BT **Calculators**

Abandoned children (May subdiv. geog.)   362.73
UF Exposed children
BT **Child welfare**
    Children
RT **Orphans**

Abandoned towns
USE **Extinct cities**
     Ghost towns

Abandonment of family
USE **Desertion and nonsupport**

Abbeys (May subdiv. geog.)   271; 726
SA names of individual abbeys [to be added as needed]
BT **Church architecture**
    Monasteries
NT **Westminster Abbey**
RT **Cathedrals**

Abbreviations   411
UF Contractions
    Symbols
BT **Writing**
NT **Acronyms**
    Code names
RT **Ciphers**
    Shorthand
    Signs and symbols

ABCs
USE **Alphabet**

Abduction
USE **Kidnapping**

Abilities
USE **Ability**

Ability   153.9
UF Abilities
    Aptitude
    Skill
    Skills
    Talent
    Talents
SA types of ability [to be added as needed]
NT **Creative ability**
    Executive ability
    Leadership
    Musical ability
RT **Success**

Ability grouping in education   371.2
UF Grouping by ability
BT **Education**
    Educational psychology
    Grading and marking (Education)
NT **Nongraded schools**

Ability—Testing   153.9; 371.26
UF Aptitude testing
BT **Educational tests and measurements**
    Intelligence tests
    Psychological tests

ABMs
USE **Antimissile missiles**

Abnormal children
USE **Exceptional children**
     Handicapped children

Abnormal growth
USE **Growth disorders**

Abnormal psychology   616.89
Use for systematic descriptions of mental disorders. Materials on clinical aspects of mental disorders, including therapy, are en-

1

Abnormal psychology—*Continued*
tered under **Psychiatry.** Popular materials and materials on regional or social aspects of mental disorders are entered under **Mental illness.**
- UF Mental diseases
     Pathological psychology
     Psychology, Pathological
     Psychopathology
     Psychopathy
- BT **Mind and body**
     Nervous system
- NT **Codependency**
     Compulsive behavior
     Depression (Psychology)
     Eating disorders
     Hallucinations and illusions
     Mental illness
     Mental retardation
     Multiple personality
     Neuroses
     Personality disorders
     Psychosomatic medicine
     Self-mutilation
- RT **Criminal psychology**
     Mental health
     Psychiatry
     Psychoanalysis

Abnormalities, Human
- USE **Birth defects**
     Growth disorders

Abolition of capital punishment
- USE **Capital punishment**

Abolition of slavery
- USE **Abolitionists**
     Slavery
     Slaves—Emancipation

Abolitionists (May subdiv. geog.)   **326; 920**
- UF Abolition of slavery
     Antislavery
- BT **Reformers**
- RT **Slavery**
     Slaves—Emancipation

Abominable snowman
- USE **Yeti**

Aborigines
- USE **Native peoples**

Aborigines, Australian
- USE **Australian aborigines**

Abortion (May subdiv. geog.)   **618.8**
- UF Induced abortion
     Termination of pregnancy

Abortion—Ethical aspects   179.7
- UF Abortion—Moral and religious aspects
- BT **Ethics**
- RT **Pro-choice movement**
     Pro-life movement

Abortion—Law and legislation (May subdiv. geog.)   **344; 363.46**
- BT **Law**
     Legislation

Abortion—Moral and religious aspects
- USE **Abortion—Ethical aspects**
     Abortion—Religious aspects

Abortion—Religious aspects   291.5
     May be further subdivided by religion or sect.
- UF Abortion—Moral and religious aspects
- RT **Pro-choice movement**
     Pro-life movement

Abortion—Religious aspects—Catholic Church   241

Abortion rights movement
- USE **Pro-choice movement**

Abrasives   553.6
- BT **Ceramics**

Absence from school
- USE **School attendance**

Absenteeism (Labor)   331.25; 658.3
- UF Employee absenteeism
     Labor absenteeism
- BT **Hours of labor**
     Personnel management
- RT **Employee morale**

Absenteeism (Schools)
- USE **School attendance**

Abstinence
- USE **Fasting**
     Temperance

Abstinence, Sexual
- USE **Sexual abstinence**

Abstract art (May subdiv. geog.)   **709.04; 759.06**
- UF Abstract painting
     Geometric art
     Nonobjective art
- BT **Art**

Abstract painting
- USE **Abstract art**

Abuse of animals
- USE **Animal welfare**

Abuse of children
    USE   **Child abuse**
Abuse of medications
    USE   **Medication abuse**
Abuse of medicines
    USE   **Medication abuse**
Abuse of persons
    USE   **Offenses against the person**
Abuse of the elderly
    USE   **Elderly abuse**
Abuse of wives
    USE   **Wife abuse**
Abuse, Verbal
    USE   **Invective**
Abused aged
    USE   **Elderly abuse**
Abused children
    USE   **Child abuse**
Abused wives
    USE   **Abused women**
          Wife abuse
Abused women   362.82
    UF   Abused wives
          Battered wives
          Battered women
    BT   **Victims of crimes**
          Women
    RT   **Wife abuse**
Academic achievement (May subdiv.
    geog.)   **370.1; 371.2**
    UF   Academic failure
          Achievement, Academic
          Educational achievement
          Scholastic achievement
          Student achievement
    BT   **Success**
    NT   **Achievement tests**
Academic advising
    USE   **Educational counseling**
Academic degrees   378.2
    UF   College degrees
          Degrees, Academic
          Doctors' degrees
          Honorary degrees
          University degrees
    BT   **Colleges and universities**
Academic dissertations
    USE   **Dissertations**
Academic failure
    USE   **Academic achievement**

Academic freedom (May subdiv. geog.)
    371.1; 378.1
    Use for materials on the freedom of teach-
    ers and students to teach, discuss, or investi-
    gate controversial subjects without penalty or
    restraint from officials, governments, or orga-
    nized groups.
    UF   Educational freedom
          Freedom, Academic
          Freedom of teaching
          Teaching, Freedom of
    BT   **Intellectual freedom**
          Toleration
Academic libraries (May subdiv. geog.)
    027.7
    UF   College and university libraries
          College libraries
          University libraries
    BT   **Libraries**
Accelerated reading
    USE   **Speed reading**
Accident insurance   368.38
    UF   Insurance, Accident
    BT   **Casualty insurance**
    NT   **Workers' compensation**
Accidents (May subdiv. geog.)   363.1
    UF   Emergencies
          Injuries
          Wrecks
    SA   types of accidents, e.g. **Railroad**
          accidents; subjects with the
          subdivision *Accidents,* e.g.
          Chemical industry—Acci-
          dents; Nuclear power
          plants—Accidents; etc.; and
          groups and classes of persons,
          animals, organs of the body,
          and plants and crops with the
          subdivision *Wounds and inju-*
          ries, e.g. **Horses—Wounds**
          and injuries; Foot—Wounds
          and injuries [to be added as
          needed]
    NT   **Aircraft accidents**
          Explosions
          Fires
          Home accidents
          Industrial accidents
          Poisons and poisoning
          Railroad accidents
          Shipwrecks
          Space vehicle accidents
          Traffic accidents

Accidents—*Continued*
    Wounds and injuries
  RT **Disasters**
    First aid
Accidents—Prevention   363.1; 658.3
  UF Prevention of accidents
    Safety measures
  SA subjects with the subdivision
    Safety devices or *Safety mea-*
    sures, e.g. **Railroads—Safety**
    devices; Radiation—Safety
    measures; etc. [to be added
    as needed]
  NT **Aeronautics—Safety measures**
    Radiation—Safety measures
    Railroads—Safety devices
    Safety education
    Safety regulations
    Water safety
  RT **Safety devices**
Acclimatization
  USE **Adaptation (Biology)**
    Environmental influence on
    humans
Accompaniment, Musical
  USE **Musical accompaniment**
Accountability
  USE **Liability (Law)**
Accountants   657.092; 920
  UF Bookkeepers
    Certified public accountants
  RT **Accounting**
Accounting (May subdiv. geog.)   657
  UF Financial accounting
  SA types of industries, professions,
    and organizations with the
    subdivision *Accounting* [to be
    added as needed]
  BT **Business**
    Business education
    Business mathematics
  NT **Corporations—Accounting**
    Cost accounting
  RT **Accountants**
    Auditing
    Bookkeeping
Accounting machines
  USE **Calculators**
Accounts, Collecting of
  USE **Collecting of accounts**

Accreditation
  USE types of hospitals and service
    institutions, types of educa-
    tional institutions, and names
    of individual institutions with
    the subdivision *Accreditation,*
    e.g. **Colleges and universi-**
    ties—Accreditation; and sub-
    jects with the subdivision
    Study and teaching, for ac-
    creditation of programs of
    study in those subjects, e.g.
    Mathematics—Study and
    teaching [to be added as
    needed]
Accreditation (Education)
  USE **Schools—Accreditation**
Acculturation (May subdiv. geog.)
    303.48
  UF Culture contact
  BT **Anthropology**
    Civilization
    Culture
    Ethnology
  NT **Ethnic relations**
    Multicultural education
    Race relations
    Socialization
  RT **East and West**
Achievement, Academic
  USE **Academic achievement**
Achievement tests (May subdiv. geog.)
    371.26
  UF Scholastic achievement tests
    School achievement tests
  BT **Academic achievement**
    Educational tests and measure-
    ments
Acid precipitation
  USE **Acid rain**
Acid rain   363.738; 628.5
  UF Acid precipitation
  BT **Rain**
    Water pollution
Acids   546; 661
  SA types of acids [to be added as
    needed]
  BT **Chemicals**
    Chemistry
  NT **Carbolic acid**

Acne   616.5
    UF   Blackheads (Acne)
          Pimples (Acne)
    BT   **Skin—Diseases**
ACOAs
    USE **Adult children of alcoholics**
Acoustics
    USE **Architectural acoustics**
          Hearing
          Music—Acoustics and physics
          Sound
Acquaintance rape
    USE **Date rape**
Acquired immune deficiency syndrome
    USE **AIDS (Disease)**
Acquisitions, Corporate
    USE **Corporate mergers and acquisitions**
Acquisitions (Libraries)
    USE **Libraries—Acquisitions**
Acrobats and acrobatics   791.3; 796.47
    SA   types of acrobatic activities, e.g.
          Tumbling [to be added as
          needed]
    BT   **Circus**
    NT   **Tumbling**
    RT   **Gymnastics**
Acronyms   411; 421, etc.
    UF   English language—Acronyms
          Initialisms
    BT   **Abbreviations**
          Code names
Acting   791.4; 792
    Use for materials on the art and technique of acting in any medium (stage, television, etc.) and on acting as a profession. Materials limited to the presentation of plays are entered under **Amateur theater** or **Theater—Production and direction.**
    UF   Dramatic art
          Stage
    BT   **Drama**
          Public speaking
    NT   **Mime**
          Pageants
          Pantomimes
    RT   **Actors**
          Amateur theater
          Drama in education
          Theater
Acting—Costume
    USE **Costume**

Actions and defenses
    USE **Litigation**
Activities curriculum
    USE **Creative activities**
Activity schools
    USE **Education—Experimental methods**
Actors (May subdiv. geog.)   **791.4; 792; 920**
    Use for materials on several persons of the acting profession, whether male or female. Materials on several female actors that emphasize their identity as women are entered under **Actresses.** Materials on several male actors that emphasize their identity as men are entered under **Male actors.**
    UF   Actors and actresses
          Motion picture actors and actresses
          Television actors
    SA   names of individual actors [to be added as needed]
    BT   **Entertainers**
    NT   **Actors—United States**
          Actresses
          African American actors
          Black actors
          Comedians
          Male actors
          Stunt performers
    RT   **Acting**
Actors and actresses
    USE **Actors**
Actors, Black
    USE **Black actors**
Actors—United States   791.4; 792; 920
    UF   American actors *[Former heading]*
          American actors and actresses
    BT   **Actors**
Actresses (May subdiv. geog.)   **791.4; 792; 920**
    Use for materials on several female actors that emphasize their identity as women. General materials on persons of the acting profession, whether male or female, are entered under **Actors.**
    UF   Female actors
          Women actors
    BT   **Actors**
Acupressure   615.8
    UF   Finger pressure therapy
          Myotherapy

Acupressure—*Continued*
    BT   **Alternative medicine**
         Massage
    RT   **Acupuncture**
Acupuncture   615.8
    BT   **Alternative medicine**
    RT   **Acupressure**
Adages
    USE   **Proverbs**
Adaptability (Psychology)
    USE   **Adjustment (Psychology)**
Adaptation (Biology)   578.4; 581.4; 591.4
    UF   Acclimatization
    BT   **Biology**
         Ecology
         Genetics
         Variation (Biology)
    NT   **Environmental influence on humans**
         Stress (Physiology)
Adaptation (Psychology)
    USE   **Adjustment (Psychology)**
Adaptations
    USE   **Film adaptations**
         Television adaptations
         and names of authors, titles of anonymous literary works, types of literature, and types of musical compositions with the subdivision *Adaptations,* for individual works, collections, or criticism and interpretation of literary, cinematic, video, or television adaptations, e.g., **Shakespeare, William, 1564-1616—Adaptations; Beowulf—Adaptations; Arthurian romances—Adaptations;** etc. [to be added as needed]
Addiction
    USE   types of addiction, e.g. **Alcoholism; Drug abuse; Exercise addiction;** etc. [to be added as needed]
Addiction to alcohol
    USE   **Alcoholism**
Addiction to drugs
    USE   **Drug abuse**
Addiction to exercise
    USE   **Exercise addiction**

Addiction to gambling
    USE   **Compulsive gambling**
Addiction to nicotine
    USE   **Tobacco habit**
Addiction to tobacco
    USE   **Tobacco habit**
Addiction to work
    USE   **Workaholism**
Addictive behavior
    USE   **Compulsive behavior**
Addicts
    USE   **Drug addicts**
Adding machines
    USE   **Calculators**
Additives, Food
    USE   **Food additives**
Addresses
    USE   **Lectures and lecturing**
         Speeches
Adhesives   620.1; 668; 691
    SA   types of adhesives [to be added as needed]
    BT   **Materials**
    NT   **Cement**
         Glue
         Mortar
Adjustment (Psychology)   155.2
    UF   Adaptability (Psychology)
         Adaptation (Psychology)
         Coping behavior
         Maladjustment (Psychology)
    BT   **Psychology**
Adjustment, Social
    USE   **Social adjustment**
Administration
    USE   **Civil service**
         Management
         Public administration
         and types of institutions in the sphere of health, education, and social services, and names of individual institutions with the subdivision *Administration,* e.g. **Libraries—Administration; Schools—Administration;** etc.; types of management, e.g. **Office management;** types of industries, types of industrial plants and processes, and names of individual corporate bodies, with

Administration—*Continued*
the subdivision *Management,*
e.g. **Information systems—
Management;** and names of
countries, cities, etc., with the
subdivision *Politics and gov-
ernment,* e.g. **United States—
Politics and government** [to
be added as needed]
Administration of criminal justice (May
subdiv. geog.) **353.4**
UF Criminal justice, Administration
of
BT **Administration of justice**
Criminal law
NT **Amnesty**
Corrections
Crime
Law enforcement
Pardon
Parole
Police
Prisons
Punishment
Administration of justice (May subdiv.
geog.) **347; 353.4**
UF Justice, Administration of
BT **Law**
NT **Administration of criminal jus-
tice**
Due process of law
Governmental investigations
Impeachments
RT **Courts**
Administrative ability
USE **Executive ability**
Administrative agencies (May subdiv.
geog.) **351**
Use for materials on governmental bodies,
such as boards, commissions, departments,
etc., responsible for implementing and admin-
istering legislation.
UF Administrative agencies—Law
and legislation
Executive agencies
Government agencies
Regulatory agencies
SA names of administrative agencies
[to be added as needed]
BT **Administrative law**
Public administration
NT **Executive departments**

Administrative agencies—Law and legisla-
tion
USE **Administrative agencies**
Administrative agencies—Reorganization
(May subdiv. geog.) **351**
UF Executive departments—Reorga-
nization
Executive reorganization
Government reorganization
Reorganization of administrative
agencies
**Administrative agencies—Reorganiza-
tion—Ohio 352.2**
UF Ohio—Executive departments—
Reorganization
**Administrative agencies—Reorganiza-
tion—United States 352.2**
UF United States—Executive depart-
ments—Reorganization
Administrative law (May subdiv. geog.)
342
BT **Law**
NT **Administrative agencies**
Civil service
Local government
Ombudsman
RT **Constitutional law**
Public administration
Administrators and executors
USE **Executors and administrators**
Admirals 359.0092; 920
BT **Military personnel**
Navies
Admissions applications
USE **College applications**
Admissions essays
USE **College applications**
Adolescence 155.5; 305.235
Use for materials on the process or the state
of growing to maturity. Materials on the time
of life between thirteen and twenty-five years,
and on people in this general age range, are
entered under **Youth.** Materials limited to teen
youth are entered under **Teenagers.** Materials
limited to people in the general age range of
eighteen through twenty-five years are entered
under **Young men** or **Young women.**
UF Teen age
Teenagers—Development
BT **Age**
RT **Youth**
Adolescence—Psychology
USE **Adolescent psychology**

Adolescent fathers
USE **Teenage fathers**
Adolescent mothers
USE **Teenage mothers**
Adolescent pregnancy
USE **Teenage pregnancy**
Adolescent prostitution
USE **Juvenile prostitution**
Adolescent psychiatry   616.89
UF   Teenagers—Psychiatry
BT   **Psychiatry**
Adolescent psychology   155.5
UF   Adolescence—Psychology
Teenagers—Psychology
BT   **Psychology**
Adolescents
USE   **Teenagers**
Adopted children   306.87; 362.82
BT   **Adoptees**
Children
RT   **Adoption**
Orphans
Adoptees   346.01; 362.73
Use for materials on anyone formally adopt-
ed as a dependent.
UF   Adult adoptees
NT   **Adopted children**
RT   **Adoption**
Birthparents
Adoption (May subdiv. geog.)   **346.01;
362.73**
UF   Child placing
Children—Adoption
Children—Placing out
BT   **Parent-child relationship**
NT   **Interracial adoption**
RT   **Adopted children**
Adoptees
Foster home care
Adoption—Corrupt practices   364.1
UF   Black market children
Sale of infants
Selling of infants
BT   **Criminal law**
Adult adoptees
USE   **Adoptees**
Adult child abuse victims   362.76
UF   Adult survivors of child abuse
Adults abused as children
Child abuse survivors
Grown-up abused children

BT   **Victims of crimes**
NT   **Adult child sexual abuse vic-
tims**
RT   **Child abuse**
**Adult child sexual abuse victims
362.76**
UF   Adult survivors of child sexual
abuse
Adults sexually abused as chil-
dren
BT   **Adult child abuse victims**
RT   **Child sexual abuse**
Adult children of alcoholics   362.292
UF   ACOAs
Alcoholic parents
BT   **Children of alcoholics**
RT   **Alcoholics**
Adult education (May subdiv. geog.)
374
UF   Education of adults
Lifelong education
BT   **Education**
Higher education
Secondary education
University extension
NT   **Agricultural extension work**
Prisoners—Education
RT   **Continuing education**
**Evening and continuation
schools**
Adult fiction
USE   **Erotic fiction**
Adult films
USE   **Erotic films**
Adult survivors of child abuse
USE   **Adult child abuse victims**
Adult survivors of child sexual abuse
USE   **Adult child sexual abuse vic-
tims**
Adulteration of food
USE   **Food adulteration and inspec-
tion**
Adultery   176; 306.73; 363.4
UF   Extramarital relationships
Marital infidelity
BT   **Sexual ethics**
Adults abused as children
USE   **Adult child abuse victims**
Adults and children
USE   **Child-adult relationship**

Adults sexually abused as children
  USE **Adult child sexual abuse victims**

Adventure and adventurers (May subdiv. geog.) **904; 904.092; 910.4; 920**
  NT **Escapes**
      Exploration
      Explorers
      Frontier and pioneer life
      Heroes and heroines
      Sea stories
      Seafaring life
      Shipwrecks
  RT **Voyages and travels**

Adventure and adventurers—Fiction
  USE **Adventure fiction**

Adventure fiction **808.83; 813, etc.**
  May be used for individual works, collections, or materials about adventure fiction.
  UF Adventure and adventurers—Fiction
      Adventure stories
      Suspense novels
      Swashbucklers
      Thrillers
  BT **Fiction**
  NT **Robinsonades**
      Romantic suspense novels
      Science fiction
      Sea stories
      Spy stories
      Western stories

Adventure films **791.43**
  May be used for individual works, collections, or materials about adventure films.
  UF Suspense films
      Swashbucklers
      Thrillers
  BT **Motion pictures**
  NT **Superhero films**
      Western films
  RT **Adventure television programs**

Adventure radio programs **791.44**
  May be used for individual works, collections, or materials about adventure radio programs.
  BT **Radio programs**
  NT **Superhero radio programs**

Adventure stories
  USE **Adventure fiction**

Adventure television programs **791.45**
  May be used for individual works, collections, or materials about adventure television programs.
  BT **Television programs**
  NT **Superhero television programs**
  RT **Adventure films**

Advertisement writing
  USE **Advertising copy**

Advertising (May subdiv. geog.) **659.1**
  May be subdivided by topic, e.g. **Advertising—Cosmetics;** to specify the thing advertised.
  BT **Business**
      Retail trade
  NT **Advertising and children**
      Advertising copy
      Advertising layout and typography
      Commercial art
      Commercial catalogs
      Coupons (Retail trade)
      Deceptive advertising
      Electric signs
      Fashion models
      Market surveys
      Newspaper advertising
      Packaging
      Posters
      Printing—Specimens
      Radio advertising
      Show windows
      Sign painting
      Signs and signboards
      Television advertising
  RT **Marketing**
      Propaganda
      Public relations
      Publicity
      Selling

Advertising and children **659.1**
  UF Children and advertising
  BT **Advertising**
      Children

Advertising art
  USE **Commercial art**

Advertising copy **659.13**
  UF Advertisement writing
      Copy writing
  BT **Advertising**
      Authorship

Advertising—Cosmetics **659.1**
  UF Cosmetics—Advertising

Advertising layout and typography
659.13
BT **Advertising**
Printing
Typography
Advertising, Newspaper
USE **Newspaper advertising**
Advertising—Newspapers 659.1
Use for materials on the advertising of newspapers. Materials on advertising in newspapers are entered under **Newspaper advertising.**
UF Newspapers—Advertising
Advisors
USE **Consultants**
Aerial bombs
USE **Bombs**
Aerial navigation
USE **Navigation (Aeronautics)**
Aerial operations
USE names of wars with the subdivision *Aerial operations,* e.g. **World War, 1939-1945—Aerial operations** [to be added as needed]
Aerial photography 778.3
BT **Photography**
NT **Remote sensing**
Aerial propellers 629.134
UF Airplanes—Propellers
Propellers, Aerial
BT **Airplanes**
Aerial reconnaissance 355.4; 358.4
UF Reconnaissance, Aerial
BT **Military aeronautics**
Remote sensing
Aerial rockets
USE **Rockets (Aeronautics)**
Aerial spraying and dusting
USE **Aeronautics in agriculture**
Aerobatics
USE **Stunt flying**
Aerobic dancing
USE **Aerobics**
Aerobic exercises
USE **Aerobics**
Aerobics 613.7
UF Aerobic dancing
Aerobic exercises
BT **Exercise**
RT **Dance**

Aerobiology
USE **Air—Microbiology**
Aerodromes
USE **Airports**
Aerodynamics 533; 629.132
UF Streamlining
BT **Air**
Dynamics
Pneumatics
NT **Supersonic aerodynamics**
RT **Aeronautics**
Aerodynamics, Supersonic
USE **Supersonic aerodynamics**
Aeronautical instruments 629.135
UF Airplanes—Instruments
Instruments, Aeronautical
SA types of instruments, e.g. **Gyroscope** [to be added as needed]
BT **Scientific apparatus and instruments**
NT **Airplanes—Electric equipment**
Gyroscope
Instrument flying
Aeronautical sports 797.5
SA types of aeronautical sports [to be added as needed]
BT **Aeronautics**
Sports
NT **Airplane racing**
Skydiving
Aeronautics (May subdiv. geog.) 629.13
Use for materials dealing collectively with various types of aircraft and for materials on the scientific or technical aspects of aircraft and their construction and operation. Materials on companies engaged in commercial aviation are entered under **Airlines.**
UF Air routes
Airways
Aviation
SA aeronautics in particular industries or fields of endeavor, e.g. **Aeronautics in agriculture** [to be added as needed]
BT **Engineering**
Locomotion
NT **Aeronautical sports**
Aeronautics and civilization
Aeronautics in agriculture
Air pilots
Airplanes
Airports

Aeronautics—*Continued*
        Airships
        Astronautics
        Balloons
        Gliders (Aeronautics)
        Gliding and soaring
        Helicopters
        High speed aeronautics
        Kites
        Lasers in aeronautics
        Meteorology in aeronautics
        Military aeronautics
        Navigation (Aeronautics)
        Parachutes
        Radio in aeronautics
        Rocketry
        Rockets (Aeronautics)
        Unidentified flying objects
  RT Aerodynamics
        Flight
Aeronautics—Accidents
  USE **Aircraft accidents**
Aeronautics and civilization   306
  UF Civilization and aeronautics
  BT **Aeronautics**
        Civilization
  NT **Astronautics and civilization**
Aeronautics, Commercial
  USE **Commercial aeronautics**
Aeronautics—Flights   387.7; 629.13
  UF Aeronautics—Voyages
        Flights around the world
        Transatlantic flights
  BT **Voyages and travels**
  NT **Space flight**
Aeronautics in agriculture   631.3
  UF Aerial spraying and dusting
        Airplanes in agriculture
        Crop dusting
        Crop spraying
  BT **Aeronautics**
        Agriculture
        Spraying and dusting
  RT **Agricultural pests**
Aeronautics—Medical aspects
  USE **Aviation medicine**
Aeronautics, Military
  USE **Military aeronautics**
Aeronautics—Navigation
  USE **Navigation (Aeronautics)**
Aeronautics—Piloting
  USE **Airplanes—Piloting**

Aeronautics—Safety measures   387.7;
     629.134
  BT Accidents—Prevention
  NT Air traffic control
Aeronautics—Study and teaching
     629.1307
  UF Flight training
  NT **Airplanes—Piloting**
Aeronautics—Voyages
  USE **Aeronautics—Flights**
Aeroplanes
  USE **Airplanes**
Aerosol sniffing
  USE **Solvent abuse**
Aerosols   541.3; 551.51; 660
  BT **Air pollution**
Aerospace industries
  USE **Aerospace industry**
Aerospace industry (May subdiv. geog.)
     338.4
  UF Aerospace industries *[Former
        heading]*
        Aircraft production
  BT **Industries**
  NT **Airplane industry**
Aerospace law
  USE **Space law**
Aerospace medicine
  USE **Aviation medicine**
        Space medicine
Aerothermodynamics   629.132; 629.4
  UF Thermoaerodynamics
  BT **Astronautics**
        High speed aeronautics
        Supersonic aerodynamics
        Thermodynamics
Aesthetics   111; 701; 801
  UF Beauty
        Esthetics
        Taste (Aesthetics)
  SA styles and movements in the
        arts, e.g. **Classicism; Post-
        modernism;** etc., and aesthet-
        ics of particular countries, e.g.
        Japanese aesthetics [to be
        added as needed]
  BT **Philosophy**
  NT **Art appreciation**
        Classicism
        Color
        Criticism

Aesthetics—*Continued*
        Japanese aesthetics
        Modernism (Aesthetics)
        Postmodernism
        Rhythm
        Romanticism
        Values
  RT **Arts**
Aesthetics, Japanese
  USE **Japanese aesthetics**
Affection
  USE **Friendship**
       Love
Affirmative action programs (May
    subdiv. geog.) **331.13; 658.3**
  UF Equal employment opportunity
      Equal opportunity in employ-
        ment
  BT **Discrimination in employment**
      Personnel management
Affliction
  USE **Joy and sorrow**
      Suffering
Affluent people
  USE **Rich**
Affordable housing
  USE **Housing**
Africa **960**
  NT **Central Africa**
      East Africa
      North Africa
      Northeast Africa
      Northwest Africa
      Pan-Africanism
      South Africa
      Southern Africa
      Sub-Saharan Africa
      West Africa
  RT **Africans**
Africa, Central
  USE **Central Africa**
Africa—Civilization **306.096; 960**
  UF African civilization
  BT **Civilization**
Africa, East
  USE **East Africa**
Africa, Eastern
  USE **East Africa**
Africa, French-speaking Equatorial
  USE **French-speaking Equatorial Af-**
       rica

Africa, French-speaking West
  USE **French-speaking West Africa**
Africa—History **960**
Africa—History—1960- **960.3**
Africa, North
  USE **North Africa**
Africa, Northeast
  USE **Northeast Africa**
Africa, Northwest
  USE **Northwest Africa**
Africa, Southern
  USE **Southern Africa**
Africa—Study and teaching **960.07**
  UF African studies
  BT **Area studies**
Africa, Sub-Saharan
  USE **Sub-Saharan Africa**
Africa, West
  USE **West Africa**
African American actors **791.4; 792;**
      920
  UF African American actors and ac-
      tresses
      Afro-American actors
  BT **Actors**
      Black actors
African American actors and actresses
  USE **African American actors**
African American art (May subdiv.
    geog.) **704**
    Use for materials on works of art by several
  African American artists. Materials on African
  Americans depicted in works of art are en-
  tered under **African Americans in art.**
  UF Afro-American art
  BT **Art**
      Black art
  NT **Harlem Renaissance**
  RT **African American artists**
African American artists **709.2; 920**
    Use for materials on several African Ameri-
  cans artists.
  UF Afro-American artists
  BT **Artists**
      Black artists
  RT **African American art**
African American athletes **796.092;**
      920
  UF Afro-American athletes
  BT **Athletes**
      Black athletes

African American authors   810.9; 920

Use for materials on several African American authors.

UF   Afro-American authors

SA   genres of American literature with the subdivision *African American authors,* e.g. **American poetry—African American authors;** etc. [to be added as needed]

BT   **American authors**
       Black authors

African American business people

USE   **African American businesspeople**

African American businesspeople   338.092; 658.0092; 920

UF   African American business people *[Former heading]*
       Afro-American businesspeople

BT   **Black businesspeople**
       Businesspeople

African American children   305.23

UF   Afro-American children

BT   **Black children**
       Children

African American elderly   305.26

BT   **Elderly**

African American folklore

USE   **African Americans—Folklore**

African American librarians   020.92; 920

UF   Afro-American librarians

BT   **Black librarians**
       Librarians

African American literature

USE   **American literature—African American authors**

African American men   305.38

UF   Afro-American men

BT   **Men**

African American music (May subdiv. geog.)   **780.089**

Use for materials on the music of African Americans. Materials on the music of Blacks not limited to the United States are entered under **Black music.**

UF   African American songs
       Afro-Americans—Music
       Songs, African American

BT   **Black music**
       Music

NT   **Blues music**
       Gospel music
       Harlem Renaissance
       Rap music

RT   **African American musicians**
       Spirituals (Songs)

African American musicians   780.92; 920

UF   Afro-American musicians

BT   **Black musicians**
       Musicians

RT   **African American music**

African American poetry

USE   **American poetry—African American authors**

African American songs

USE   **African American music**

African American suffrage

USE   **African Americans—Suffrage**

African American women   305.48

UF   Afro-American women

BT   **Black women**
       Women

African American youth   305.235

BT   **Youth**

African Americans (May subdiv. geog. by cities, states, or regions of the U.S.)   **305.896; 973**

Use for materials dealing collectively with Blacks in the United States. General materials and materials on Blacks in places other than the United States are entered under **Blacks.**

UF   Afro-Americans
       Black Americans
       Blacks—United States
       Negroes

SA   African Americans in various occupations and professions, e.g. **African American artists; African American librarians;** etc. [to be added as needed]

BT   **Blacks**

NT   **Libraries and African Americans**
       World War, 1939-1945—African Americans

African Americans and libraries

USE   **Libraries and African Americans**

African Americans—Biography   920

BT   **Blacks—Biography**

African Americans—Chicago (Ill.)
305.896; 977.3

African Americans—Civil rights (May
subdiv. geog.)   323.1; 342
   BT Blacks—Civil rights
        Civil rights
   NT African Americans—Suffrage

African Americans—Economic conditions
(May subdiv. geog.)   330.973
   BT Blacks—Economic conditions
        Economic conditions

African Americans—Education (May
subdiv. geog.)   370.89; 371.829
   BT Blacks—Education
        Education

African Americans—Employment (May
subdiv. geog.)   331.6
   BT Blacks—Employment
        Employment

African Americans—Folklore   398
   UF African American folklore
   BT Blacks—Folklore
        Folklore

African Americans—Housing (May
subdiv. geog.)   307.3; 363.5
   BT Blacks—Housing
        Housing

African Americans in art   704.9

Use for materials on African Americans depicted in works of art. Materials on the attainments of several African Americans in the area of art are entered under **African American artists.** Materials on works of art by several African American artists are entered under **African American art.**

   UF Afro-Americans in art
   BT **Art—Themes**

African Americans in literature   809

Use for materials on the theme of African Americans in works of literature. Materials on several African American authors are entered under **African American authors.** Materials on works of literature by several African American authors are entered under **American literature—African American authors** and the various forms of American literature with the subdivision *African American authors*, e.g. **American poetry—African American authors.**

   UF Afro-Americans in literature
   BT **Literature—Themes**

African Americans in motion pictures
791.43

Use for materials on the depiction of African Americans in motion pictures. Materials on several African American actors are entered under **African American actors.** Materials discussing all aspects of African Americans' involvement in motion pictures are entered under **African Americans in the motion picture industry.**

   BT **Blacks in motion pictures**
        Motion pictures

African Americans in television
   USE **African Americans on television**

African Americans in television broadcasting   791.45

Use for materials on all aspects of African Americans' involvement in the television industry. Materials on the portrayal of African Americans in television programs are entered under **African Americans on television.**

   UF African Americans in the television industry
        Afro-Americans in television broadcasting
   BT **Television broadcasting**

African Americans in the motion picture
industry   791.43092

Use for materials on all aspects of African Americans' involvement in motion pictures. Materials on the depiction of African Americans in motion pictures are entered under **African Americans in motion pictures.**

   BT **Blacks in the motion picture industry**
        Motion picture industry

African Americans in the television industry
   USE **African Americans in television broadcasting**

African Americans—Intellectual life
(May subdiv. geog.)   305.896
   BT **Blacks—Intellectual life**
        Intellectual life

African Americans—Ohio   305.896;
977.1

African Americans on television   791.45

Use for materials on the portrayal of African Americans in television programs. Materials on all aspects of African Americans' involvement in the television industry are entered under **African Americans in television broadcasting.**

   UF African Americans in television
        [Former heading]
        Afro-Americans on television
   BT **Television**

African Americans—Political activity
(May subdiv. geog.)   322.4; 324
   BT **Blacks—Political activity**
        Political participation

African Americans—Political activity—
Continued
  NT Black nationalism
      Black power
African Americans—Race identity
      305.896
  BT Blacks—Race identity
      Race awareness
  NT Black nationalism
African Americans—Religion   270.089;
      299
  BT Blacks—Religion
      Religion
` NT Black Muslims
African Americans—Segregation (May
      subdiv. geog.)   305.896
  BT Blacks—Segregation
      Segregation
African Americans—Social conditions
      (May subdiv. geog.)   305.896
  BT Blacks—Social conditions
      Social conditions
African Americans—Social life and cus-
      toms (May subdiv. geog.)
      305.896
  BT Blacks—Social life and cus-
      toms
      Manners and customs
African Americans—Southern States
      305.896; 975
  UF Southern States—African Ameri-
      cans
African Americans—Suffrage (May
      subdiv. geog.)   324.6
  UF African American suffrage
  BT African Americans—Civil
      rights
      Blacks—Suffrage
      Suffrage
African civilization
  USE Africa—Civilization
African literature (English)   820
  BT Literature
African peoples
  USE Africans
African relations
  USE Pan-Africanism
African songs   782.42096
  UF Songs, African
  BT Songs
African studies
  USE Africa—Study and teaching

Africans   305.896; 960
  UF African peoples
  SA names of African peoples, e.g.
      Yoruba (African people) [to
      be added as needed]
  NT Blacks—Africa
      Yoruba (African people)
  RT Africa
Afrikaaners
  USE Afrikaners
Afrikaners   305.83; 968
  UF Afrikaaners
      Boers
      South African Dutch
      South Africans, Afrikaans-
      speaking
Afro-American actors
  USE African American actors
Afro-American art
  USE African American art
Afro-American artists
  USE African American artists
Afro-American athletes
  USE African American athletes
Afro-American authors
  USE African American authors
Afro-American businesspeople
  USE African American businesspeo-
      ple
Afro-American children
  USE African American children
Afro-American librarians
  USE African American librarians
Afro-American men
  USE African American men
Afro-American musicians
  USE African American musicians
Afro-American women
  USE African American women
Afro-Americans
  USE African Americans
Afro-Americans and libraries
  USE Libraries and African Ameri-
      cans
Afro-Americans in art
  USE African Americans in art
Afro-Americans in literature
  USE African Americans in litera-
      ture

Afro-Americans in television broadcasting
    USE   **African Americans in television broadcasting**
Afro-Americans—Music
    USE   **African American music**
Afro-Americans on television
    USE   **African Americans on television**
After dinner speeches   808.5; 808.85
    BT   **Speeches**
    RT   **Toasts**
After school day care
    USE   **After school programs**
After school programs   362.71; 372.12
    UF   After school day care
    BT   **Student activities**
Afterlife
    USE   **Future life**
Afternoon teas   642
        Use for materials on the meal. Materials on
        the plant or on the beverage are entered under
        Tea.
    UF   Teas
    BT   **Cooking**
    RT   **Entertaining**
         Tea
Age   305.2
    UF   Age groups
    SA   types of animals, plants, and
         crops with the subdivision
         Age [to be added as needed]
    NT   **Adolescence**
         Age and employment
         Aging
         Children
         Drinking age
         Elderly
         Life expectancy
         Longevity
         Middle age
         Middle aged persons
         Old age
         Teenagers
         Youth
Age and employment   331.3
    UF   Employment and age
    BT   **Age**
         Employment
    NT   **Career changes**
         Child labor
         Teenagers—Employment
         Youth—Employment

Age discrimination   305.2
    BT   **Discrimination**
Age groups
    USE   **Age**
Age—Physiological effect
    USE   **Aging**
Aged
    USE   **Elderly**
Aged men
    USE   **Elderly men**
Aged parents
    USE   **Aging parents**
Aged women
    USE   **Elderly women**
Ageing
    USE   **Aging**
Agent Orange   363.17; 615.9
    BT   **Herbicides**
Ages—Pensions
    USE   **Old age pensions**
Aggregates
    USE   **Set theory**
Aggressive behavior
    USE   **Aggressiveness (Psychology)**
Aggressiveness (Psychology)   152.4; 155.2
    UF   Aggressive behavior
    BT   **Human behavior**
         Psychology
    NT   **Assertiveness (Psychology)**
         Bullies
         Violence
Aging   571.8; 612.6
    UF   Age—Physiological effect
         Ageing
         Senescence
    SA   types of animals, organs of the
         body, plants, and crops with
         the subdivision *Aging* [to be
         added as needed]
    BT   **Age**
         Elderly
         Gerontology
         Longevity
         Middle age
         Old age
    NT   **Male climacteric**
         Menopause

Aging parents (May subdiv. geog.)
    306.874
    UF   Aged parents
           Elderly parents
    BT   **Elderly**
           Parents
Aging persons
    USE **Elderly**
Agnosticism   **149; 211**
    BT   **Free thought**
           Religion
    RT   **Atheism**
           Belief and doubt
           Positivism
           Rationalism
           Skepticism
Agrarian question
    USE **Agriculture—Economic aspects**
          Agriculture—Government policy
          Land tenure
Agrarian reform
    USE **Land reform**
Agreements
    USE **Contracts**
          Covenants
Agribusiness
    USE **Agricultural industry**
Agricultural bacteriology   **630.2**
    UF   Bacteriology, Agricultural
           Diseases and pests
    SA   types of crops, plants, trees, etc.,
           with the subdivision *Diseases*
           and pests, e.g. **Fruit—Diseases and pests** [to be added
           as needed]
    BT   **Bacteriology**
    RT   **Soil microbiology**
Agricultural botany
    USE **Economic botany**
Agricultural chemicals   **631.8; 668**
    SA   types of agricultural chemicals
           and names of individual
           chemicals [to be added as
           needed]
    BT   **Agricultural chemistry**
           Chemicals
    NT   **Fertilizers**
           Herbicides
           Insecticides
           Pesticides

Agricultural chemistry   **630.2**
    BT   **Chemistry**
    NT   **Agricultural chemicals**
    RT   **Soils**
Agricultural clubs
    USE **Agriculture—Societies**
Agricultural cooperation
    USE **Cooperative agriculture**
Agricultural credit (May subdiv. geog.)
    332.7
    UF   Farm credit
           Farm loans
           Rural credit
    BT   **Agriculture—Economic aspects**
           Banks and banking
           Credit
Agricultural economics
    USE **Agriculture—Economic aspects**
Agricultural education
    USE **Agriculture—Study and teaching**
Agricultural engineering (May subdiv.
    geog.)   **630**
    UF   Agricultural mechanics
           Farm mechanics
    BT   **Engineering**
    NT   **Drainage**
           Electricity in agriculture
           Irrigation
    RT   **Agricultural machinery**
Agricultural experiment stations (May
    subdiv. geog.)   **630.7**
    UF   Experimental farms
    BT   **Agriculture—Government policy**
           Agriculture—Research
           Agriculture—Study and teaching
    RT   **Agricultural extension work**
Agricultural extension work (May subdiv.
    geog.)   **630.7**
    BT   **Adult education**
           Agriculture—Government policy
    NT   **County agricultural agents**
    RT   **Agricultural experiment stations**
           Agriculture—Study and teaching
           Community development

Agricultural industries
   USE **Agricultural industry**
Agricultural industry (May subdiv. geog.)
   338.1
   UF Agribusiness
         Agricultural industries *[Former heading]*
   BT **Agriculture—Economic aspects**
         Industries
   NT **Food industry**
Agricultural laborers (May subdiv. geog.)
   331.7
   UF Farm laborers
   BT **Labor**
   RT **Migrant labor**
         Peasantry
Agricultural machinery   **631.3**
   UF Agricultural tools
         Farm engines
         Farm equipment
         Farm implements
         Farm machinery
         Farm mechanics
         Implements, utensils, etc.
   SA types of farm machinery [to be added as needed]
   BT **Machinery**
         Tools
   NT **Electricity in agriculture**
         Harvesting machinery
         Plows
         Tractors
   RT **Agricultural engineering**
Agricultural mechanics
   USE **Agricultural engineering**
Agricultural pests   **632**
   UF Diseases and pests
         Garden pests
   SA types of crops, plants, trees, etc., with the subdivision *Diseases and pests,* e.g. **Fruit—Diseases and pests** [to be added as needed]
   BT **Economic zoology**
         Pests
   NT **Fruit—Diseases and pests**
         Fungi
         Pest control
         Plant diseases
         Spraying and dusting
         Weeds

   RT **Aeronautics in agriculture**
         Insect pests
Agricultural policy
   USE **Agriculture—Government policy**
Agricultural products
   USE **Farm produce**
Agricultural research
   USE **Agriculture—Research**
Agricultural societies
   USE **Agriculture—Societies**
Agricultural subsidies (May subdiv. geog.)   **338.9**
   UF Farm subsidies
   BT **Subsidies**
   RT **Agriculture—Government policy**
Agricultural tools
   USE **Agricultural machinery**
Agriculture (May subdiv. geog.)   **338.1; 630**
   UF Agronomy
         Farming
         Planting
   SA types of agriculture, e.g. **Truck farming;** types of agricultural products, e.g. **Corn;** and ethnic groups with the subdivision *Agriculture,* e.g. **Native Americans—Agriculture** [to be added as needed]
   BT **Life sciences**
   NT **Aeronautics in agriculture**
         Aquaculture
         Beekeeping
         Cooperative agriculture
         Crop rotation
         Cultivated plants
         Dairying
         Dry farming
         Economic botany
         Farmers
         Forests and forestry
         Fruit culture
         Gardening
         Horticulture
         Livestock industry
         Native Americans—Agriculture
         Organic farming
         Pastures
         Plant breeding

Agriculture—*Continued*
      Reclamation of land
      Soils
      Truck farming
  RT **Farms**
      Food supply
Agriculture and state
  USE **Agriculture—Government policy**
Agriculture—Bibliography   016.63
Agriculture, Cooperative
  USE **Cooperative agriculture**
Agriculture—Documentation   025
  BT **Documentation**
Agriculture—Economic aspects (May subdiv. geog.)   **338.1**
  UF Agrarian question
      Agricultural economics
  BT **Economics**
  NT **Agricultural credit**
      Agricultural industry
      Land tenure
  RT **Farm management**
      Farm produce—Marketing
Agriculture—Government policy (May subdiv. geog.)   **338.9**
  UF Agrarian question
      Agricultural policy
      Agriculture and state
      State and agriculture
  BT **Industrial policy**
  NT **Agricultural experiment stations**
      Agricultural extension work
  RT **Agricultural subsidies**
      Land reform
Agriculture—Research   **630.7**
  UF Agricultural research
  BT **Research**
  NT **Agricultural experiment stations**
Agriculture—Societies   **630.6**
  UF Agricultural clubs
      Agricultural societies
  SA names of agricultural societies
      [to be added as needed]
  BT **Associations**
      Country life
      Societies
  NT **4-H clubs**
      Grange

Agriculture—Statistics   **338.1; 630.2**
  UF Crop reports
  BT **Statistics**
Agriculture—Study and teaching   **630.7**
  UF Agricultural education
  BT **Vocational education**
  NT **4-H clubs**
      Agricultural experiment stations
      County agricultural agents
  RT **Agricultural extension work**
Agriculture—Tenant farming
  USE **Farm tenancy**
Agriculture—Tropics   **630.913**
  BT **Tropics**
Agriculture—United States   **630.973**
Agronomy
  USE **Agriculture**
AI (Artificial intelligence)
  USE **Artificial intelligence**
Aid to dependent children
  USE **Child welfare**
Aid to developing areas
  USE **Foreign aid**
      Technical assistance
AIDS (Disease) (May subdiv. geog.)   **616.97**
  UF Acquired immune deficiency syndrome
      HIV disease
  BT **Communicable diseases**
      Diseases
AIDS (Disease)—Prevention   **616.97**
    Use for materials on AIDS prevention in general not limited to safe sexual practices. Materials limited to safe sexual practices in the prevention of AIDS are entered under **Safe sex in AIDS prevention.**
  NT **Safe sex in AIDS prevention**
AIDS (Disease)—Treatment   **615.5**
  BT **Therapeutics**
Air   **533; 546**
    Use for materials dealing with air in general and with its chemical and physical properties. Materials on the body of air surrounding the earth are entered under **Atmosphere.**
  BT **Meteorology**
  NT **Aerodynamics**
      Atmosphere
      Ventilation
  RT **Atmosphere**
Air bases (May subdiv. geog.)   **358.4**
  UF Military air bases
      Naval air bases

Air bases—*Continued*
  BT **Airports**
      Military aeronautics
Air cargo
  USE **Commercial aeronautics**
Air carriers
  USE **Airlines**
Air charters
  USE **Airlines—Chartering**
Air conditioning   644; 697.9
  SA subjects with the subdivision *Air*
      conditioning [to be added as
      needed]
  NT **Automobiles—Air conditioning**
  RT **Refrigeration**
      Ventilation
Air crashes
  USE **Aircraft accidents**
Air-cushion vehicles   629.3
  UF Ground effect machines *[Former*
      heading]
      Hovercraft
  BT **Vehicles**
Air defenses (May subdiv. geog.)   363.3
    Use for materials on military defense
  against air attack. Materials on the protection
  of civilians from enemy attack are entered un-
  der **Civil defense.**
  UF Air raid defensive measures
  BT **Military aeronautics**
  NT **Radar defense networks**
Air freight
  USE **Commercial aeronautics**
Air lines
  USE **Airlines**
Air mail service   383
  BT **Commercial aeronautics**
      Postal service
Air—Microbiology   579
  UF Aerobiology
  BT **Microbiology**
Air, Moisture of
  USE **Humidity**
Air navigation
  USE **Navigation (Aeronautics)**
Air pilots   629.13092; 920
  UF Airplane pilots
      Aviators
      Pilots
      Test pilots

  BT **Aeronautics**
  NT **Astronauts**
      Women air pilots
Air piracy
  USE **Hijacking of airplanes**
Air pollution (May subdiv. geog.)
             363.739; 628.5
  UF Atmosphere—Pollution
      Pollution of air
  BT **Environmental health**
      Pollution
  NT **Aerosols**
Air pollution—Measurement   363.739;
             628.5
  BT **Measurement**
Air pollution—United States   363.739;
             628.5
Air power   358.4
  BT **Military aeronautics**
Air raid defensive measures
  USE **Air defenses**
Air raid shelters   363.3
  UF Blast shelters
      Bomb shelters
      Fallout shelters
      Nuclear bomb shelters
      Public shelters
      Shelters, Air raid
  BT **Civil defense**
Air rights law
  USE **Airspace law**
Air routes
  USE **Aeronautics**
Air-ships
  USE **Airships**
Air space law
  USE **Airspace law**
Air surfing
  USE **Gliding and soaring**
Air terminals
  USE **Airports**
Air traffic control   387.7
  UF Airports—Traffic control
  BT **Aeronautics—Safety measures**
Air transport
  USE **Commercial aeronautics**
Air warfare
  USE **Military aeronautics**
      Military airplanes

Aircraft
   USE   **Airplanes**
         Airships
         Balloons
         Gliders (Aeronautics)
         Helicopters
Aircraft accidents (May subdiv. geog.)
         363.12; 629.13
   UF   Aeronautics—Accidents
         Air crashes
         Airplane accidents
         Airplane crashes
         Airplanes—Accidents
         Aviation accidents
         Plane crashes
   BT   **Accidents**
   RT   **Survival after airplane acci-**
         dents, shipwrecks, etc.
Aircraft carriers   359.3; 623
   UF   Airplane carriers
   BT   **Military aeronautics**
         Warships
Aircraft industry
   USE   **Airplane industry**
Aircraft production
   USE   **Aerospace industry**
         Airplane industry
Airdromes
   USE   **Airports**
Airline hostesses
   USE   **Flight attendants**
Airline stewardesses
   USE   **Flight attendants**
Airline stewards
   USE   **Flight attendants**
Airlines (May subdiv. geog.)   **387.7**
      Use for materials on companies engaged in
   commercial aviation. Materials on various
   types of aircraft and on the scientific or tech-
   nical aspects of aircraft and their construction
   and operation are entered under **Aeronautics.**
   UF   Air carriers
         Air lines
   BT   **Commercial aeronautics**
   NT   **Flight attendants**
Airlines—Chartering   387.7
   UF   Air charters
         Airplanes—Chartering
         Charter flights
Airlines—Hijacking
   USE   **Hijacking of airplanes**
Airplane accidents
   USE   **Aircraft accidents**

Airplane carriers
   USE   **Aircraft carriers**
Airplane crashes
   USE   **Aircraft accidents**
Airplane engines   629.134
   UF   Airplane motors
         Airplanes—Engines
         Airplanes—Motors
   BT   **Engines**
   NT   **Jet propulsion**
Airplane hijacking
   USE   **Hijacking of airplanes**
Airplane industry (May subdiv. geog.)
         338.4; 387.7
   UF   Aircraft industry
         Aircraft production
   BT   **Aerospace industry**
Airplane motors
   USE   **Airplane engines**
Airplane pilots
   USE   **Air pilots**
Airplane racing   797.5
   UF   Airplanes—Racing
   BT   **Aeronautical sports**
         Racing
Airplane spotting
   USE   **Airplanes—Identification**
Airplanes   387.7; 629.133
   UF   Aeroplanes
         Aircraft
   SA   types of airplanes and specific
         makes of airplanes [to be
         added as needed]
   BT   **Aeronautics**
   NT   **Aerial propellers**
         Bombers
         Gliders (Aeronautics)
         Helicopters
         Jet planes
         Military airplanes
Airplanes—Accidents
   USE   **Aircraft accidents**
Airplanes—Chartering
   USE   **Airlines—Chartering**
Airplanes—Design and construction
         629.134
Airplanes—Electric equipment   629.135
   UF   Airplanes—Instruments
   BT   **Aeronautical instruments**
Airplanes—Engines
   USE   **Airplane engines**

Airplanes—Flight testing
    USE **Airplanes—Testing**
Airplanes—Hijacking
    USE **Hijacking of airplanes**
Airplanes—Identification 623.7;
    629.133
    UF Airplane spotting
          Airplanes—Recognition
    BT **Identification**
Airplanes in agriculture
    USE **Aeronautics in agriculture**
Airplanes—Inspection 387.7; 629.134
Airplanes—Instruments
    USE **Aeronautical instruments**
           Airplanes—Electric equipment
Airplanes—Maintenance and repair
    629.134
    UF Airplanes—Repair
Airplanes—Materials 629.134
    BT **Materials**
Airplanes, Military
    USE **Military airplanes**
Airplanes—Models 629.133
    UF Model airplanes
          Paper airplanes
    BT **Models and modelmaking**
Airplanes—Motors
    USE **Airplane engines**
Airplanes—Noise 629.132
    BT **Noise**
          Noise pollution
Airplanes—Operation
    USE **Airplanes—Piloting**
Airplanes—Piloting 629.132
    UF Aeronautics—Piloting
          Airplanes—Operation
          Flight training
    SA types and names of airplanes
          with the subdivision *Piloting*
          [to be added as needed]
    BT **Aeronautics—Study and teach-**
          ing
          Navigation (Aeronautics)
    NT **Helicopters—Piloting**
          Instrument flying
          Stunt flying
Airplanes—Propellers
    USE **Aerial propellers**
Airplanes—Racing
    USE **Airplane racing**

Airplanes—Recognition
    USE **Airplanes—Identification**
Airplanes—Repair
    USE **Airplanes—Maintenance and**
          repair
Airplanes, Rocket propelled
    USE **Rocket planes**
Airplanes—Testing 629.134
    UF Airplanes—Flight testing
          Test pilots
Airports (May subdiv. geog.) **387.7;**
    629.136
    UF Aerodromes
          Air terminals
          Airdromes
    SA names of individual airports [to
          be added as needed]
    BT **Aeronautics**
    NT **Air bases**
          Heliports
Airports—Traffic control
    USE **Air traffic control**
Airships 629.133
    Use for materials on self-propelled aircraft
that are lighter than air and steerable. Materi-
als on aircraft held aloft by hot air or light
gases that are nondirigible and propelled only
by the wind are entered under **Balloons.**
    UF Air-ships
          Aircraft
          Balloons, Dirigible
          Blimps
          Dirigible balloons
          Zeppelins
    BT **Aeronautics**
    RT **Balloons**
Airspace law 341.4
    UF Air rights law
          Air space law
    BT **Property**
Airways
    USE **Aeronautics**
Alaska Highway (Alaska and Canada)
    388.1; 979.8
    BT **Roads**
Alchemy 540.1
    Use for materials on medieval attempts to
change base metals into gold. Materials on the
transmutation of metals in nuclear physics are
entered under **Transmutation (Chemistry).**
    UF Hermetic art and philosophy
          Philosophers' stone
          Transmutation of metals

Alchemy—*Continued*
    BT   **Chemistry**
            Occultism
    RT   **Transmutation (Chemistry)**
Alcohol   **547; 661**
    UF   Alcohol use
            Intoxicants
    SA   classes of persons with the sub-
            division *Alcohol use,* e.g. **Em-**
            ployees—Alcohol use;
            Youth—Alcohol use; etc. [to
            be added as needed]
    BT   **Chemicals**
    NT   **Alcohol as fuel**
            Alcoholic beverages
            Denatured alcohol
    RT   **Alcoholism**
            Distillation
Alcohol and employees
    USE **Employees—Alcohol use**
Alcohol and teenagers
    USE **Teenagers—Alcohol use**
Alcohol and youth
    USE **Youth—Alcohol use**
Alcohol as fuel   **662**
    UF   Alcohol fuel
            Ethanol
            Ethyl alcohol fuel
    SA   types of alcohol fuels, e.g.
            Gasohol [to be added as
            needed]
    BT   **Alcohol**
            Fuel
    NT   **Gasohol**
Alcohol consumption
    USE **Drinking of alcoholic beverages**
Alcohol, Denatured
    USE **Denatured alcohol**
Alcohol fuel
    USE **Alcohol as fuel**
Alcohol in the workplace
    USE **Employees—Alcohol use**
Alcohol—Physiological effect   **615**
Alcohol use
    USE **Alcohol**
         Alcoholism
         Drinking of alcoholic beverages
         and classes of persons with the
         subdivision *Alcohol use,* e.g.
         Employees—Alcohol use;
         Youth—Alcohol use; etc. [to
         be added as needed]

Alcoholic beverage consumption
    USE **Drinking of alcoholic beverages**
Alcoholic beverages   **641.2**
    UF   Drinks
            Intoxicants
    BT   **Alcohol**
            Beverages
    NT   **Liquors**
            Wine and wine making
    RT   **Drinking of alcoholic beverages**
Alcoholic parents
    USE **Adult children of alcoholics**
         Children of alcoholics
Alcoholics   **362.292; 616.86**
    UF   Drunkards
    NT   **Recovering alcoholics**
    RT   **Adult children of alcoholics**
            Alcoholism
            Children of alcoholics
Alcoholism (May subdiv. geog.)
            362.292; 616.86
    UF   Addiction to alcohol
            Alcohol use
            Drinking problem
            Drunkenness
            Intemperance
            Intoxication
            Liquor problem
            Problem drinking
    SA   classes of persons with the sub-
            division *Alcohol use,* e.g. **Em-**
            ployees—Alcohol use;
            Youth—Alcohol use; etc. [to
            be added as needed]
    BT   **Social problems**
    RT   **Alcohol**
            Alcoholics
            Drinking of alcoholic beverages
            Temperance
            Twelve-step programs
Alfalfa   **583; 633.3**
    BT   **Forage plants**
Algae   **579.8**
    UF   Sea mosses
            Seaweeds
    BT   **Marine plants**
Algebra   **512**
    BT   **Mathematical analysis**
            Mathematics
    NT   **Graph theory**
            Group theory

Algebra—*Continued*
    Linear algebra
    Logarithms
    Number theory
    Probabilities
    Sequences (Mathematics)
Algebra, Boolean
  USE **Boolean algebra**
Algebras, Linear
  USE **Linear algebra**
Alienation (Social psychology)   302.5
  UF Estrangement (Social psychology)
      Rebels (Social psychology)
      Social alienation
  BT **Social psychology**
Aliens (May subdiv. geog.)   323.6
  UF Foreign population
      Foreigners
      Noncitizens
      Nonnationals
  SA national groups subdivided by the place of their residence, e.g. **Mexicans—United States** [to be added as needed]
  BT **Minorities**
  NT **Illegal aliens**
      Refugees
  RT **Citizenship**
      Immigrants
      Immigration and emigration
      Naturalization
Aliens from outer space
  USE **Extraterrestrial beings**
Aliens—United States   325.73
  UF United States—Foreign population
  NT **Mexicans—United States**
  RT **United States—Immigration and emigration**
All Fools' Day
  USE **April Fools' Day**
All Hallows' Eve
  USE **Halloween**
All terrain bicycles
  USE **Mountain bikes**
All terrain vehicles   629.22
  UF ATVs
  SA types of vehicles, e.g. **Snowmobiles** [to be added as needed]

  BT **Vehicles**
  NT **Mountain bikes**
      Snowmobiles
Allegories   808.88; 810.8, etc.
    May be used for individual works or for collections of allegories. Materials on allegory as a literary form or on allegory in the fine and decorative arts are entered under **Allegory.**
  BT **Fiction**
  RT **Fables**
      Parables
Allegory   704.9; 808
    Use for materials on allegory as a literary form as well as for allegory in the fine and decorative arts. Individual allegories and collections of allegories are entered under **Allegories.**
  BT **Arts**
      Fiction
  RT **Symbolism in literature**
Allergies
  USE **Allergy**
Allergies, Food
  USE **Food allergy**
Allergy   616.97
  UF Allergies
  SA types of allergies [to be added as needed]
  BT **Immunity**
  NT **Food allergy**
      Hay fever
Allergy, Food
  USE **Food allergy**
Alleys
  USE **Streets**
Allied health personnel   610.69
  UF Paramedical personnel
  SA types of allied health personnel [to be added as needed]
  NT **Emergency medical technicians**
      Medical technologists
      Nurse practitioners
Alligators   597.98
  BT **Reptiles**
  RT **Crocodiles**
Allocation of time
  USE **Time management**
Allowances, Children's
  USE **Children's allowances**
Alloys   669
  SA types of alloys [to be added as needed]

Alloys—*Continued*
- BT **Industrial chemistry**
  - **Metals**
- NT **Aluminum alloys**
  - **Brass**
  - **Pewter**
- RT **Metallurgy**

Allusions   031.02; 803
- SA names of individual persons with the subdivision *Allusions,* for materials on allusions to that person, e.g. **Shakespeare, William, 1564-1616—Allusions** [to be added as needed]
- RT **Terms and phrases**

Almanacs   030
- UF Annuals
- BT **Serial publications**
- NT **Nautical almanacs**
- RT **Calendars**
  - **Chronology**

Alphabet   411

Use for materials on the series of characters that form the elements of a written language and for materials to be used in teaching children the ABCs. Materials on the styles of alphabets used by artists, etc., are entered under **Alphabets.**
- UF ABCs
  - Alphabet books
  - Letters of the alphabet
- SA names of languages with the subdivision *Alphabet,* e.g. **English language—Alphabet** [to be added as needed]
- BT **Writing**
- NT **Alphabets**

Alphabet books
- USE **Alphabet**

Alphabetizing
- USE **Files and filing**

Alphabets   745.6

Use for materials on the styles of alphabets used by artists, etc. Materials on the series of characters that form the elements of a written language and for materials to be used in teaching children the ABCs are entered under **Alphabet.**
- UF Ornamental alphabets
- BT **Alphabet**
  - **Sign painting**
- NT **Monograms**
- RT **Illumination of books and manuscripts**
  - **Initials**

Lettering

Alpine animals
- USE **Mountain animals**

Alpine fauna
- USE **Mountain animals**

Alpine flora
- USE **Mountain plants**

Alpine plants
- USE **Mountain plants**

Alternate energy resources
- USE **Renewable energy resources**

Alternate work sites
- USE **Telecommuting**

Alternating current machinery
- USE **Electric machinery—Alternating current**

Alternating currents
- USE **Alternating electric currents**

Alternating electric currents   621.31
- UF Alternating currents
  - Electric currents, Alternating
- BT **Electric currents**

Alternative energy resources
- USE **Renewable energy resources**

Alternative histories   808.3; 813, etc.

May be used for individual works, collections, or materials about imaginative works featuring key changes in historical facts.
- BT **Fantasy fiction**

Alternative life styles
- USE **Alternative lifestyles**

Alternative lifestyle
- USE **Counter culture**

Alternative lifestyles (May subdiv. geog.)   306

Use for materials on ways of living regarded as unacceptable by conventional standards, especially those that reject consumerism, the work ethic, etc.
- UF Alternative life styles
- BT **Lifestyles**

Alternative medicine (May subdiv. geog.)   610; 613; 615.5
- UF Therapeutic systems
- SA types of alternative medicine [to be added as needed]
- BT **Medicine**
- NT **Acupressure**
  - **Acupuncture**
  - **Chiropractic**
  - **Health self-care**
  - **Holistic medicine**
  - **Homeopathy**

Alternative medicine—*Continued*
     Mental healing
     Naturopathy
     Reflexology
Alternative military service
    USE **National service**
Alternative press (May subdiv. geog.)
     070.4; 071, etc.
    Use for materials about publications issued clandestinely and contrary to government regulation and for materials about publications issued legally (and usually serially) and produced by radical, anti-establishment, or counter-culture groups.
    UF Underground literature
          Underground press
    BT **Press**
Alternative schools
    USE **Experimental schools**
Alternative universities
    USE **Free universities**
Alternative work schedules
    USE **Flexible hours of labor**
           Part-time employment
Altitude, Influence of
    USE **Environmental influence on humans**
Altruists
    USE **Philanthropists**
Aluminum   **669; 673**
    BT **Metals**
    NT **Aluminum foil**
Aluminum alloys   **669; 673**
    BT **Alloys**
Aluminum foil   **673**
    BT **Aluminum**
          Packaging
Aluminum—Recycling   **628.4; 673**
    BT **Recycling**
Alzheimer's disease   **616.8**
    BT **Brain—Diseases**
Amateur films   **778.5; 791.43**
    May be used for individual works, collections, or materials about amateur films.
    UF Amateur motion pictures
          Home movies
          Home video movies
          Personal films
    BT **Motion pictures**
    RT **Camcorders**
          Motion picture cameras
Amateur motion pictures
    USE **Amateur films**

Amateur radio stations   **384.54; 621.3841**
    UF Ham radio stations
    BT **Radio stations**
          Shortwave radio
Amateur theater (May subdiv. geog.)
     792
    UF Non-professional theater
          Play production
          Private theater
    BT **Amusements**
          Theater
    NT **Charades**
          Children's plays
          College and school drama
          One act plays
          Pantomimes
          Shadow pantomimes and plays
    RT **Acting**
          Drama in education
          Little theater movement
Ambassadors
    USE **Diplomats**
Amendments, Equal rights
    USE **Equal rights amendments**
America   **970**
    Use for general materials on the Western Hemisphere.
    SA names of individual countries of the Western Hemisphere [to be added as needed]
    NT **Latin America**
          North America
          South America
America—Antiquities   **970.01**
    BT **Antiquities**
America—Civilization   **970; 980**
    Use for general materials on the civilization of the Western Hemisphere in modern times. Materials on ancient civilizations in America are entered under **America—Antiquities;** under a region, country, city, etc., with the subdivision *Antiquities;* or under the name of an ancient people. Materials limited to the civilization of the United States are entered under **United States—Civilization.**
    UF American civilization
    BT **Civilization**
America—Discovery and exploration
    USE **America—Exploration**
America—Exploration   **970.01**
    UF America—Discovery and exploration

America—Exploration—*Continued*
BT Exploration
NT Northwest Passage
   United States—Exploration
America—History   970
UF American history
America—Politics and government   970
RT Pan-Americanism
American actors
USE Actors—United States
American actors and actresses
USE Actors—United States
American architecture
USE Architecture—United States
American art   709.73
UF Art, American
BT Art
NT American folk art
American artificial satellites   629.43;
   629.46
UF Artificial satellites, American
BT Artificial satellites
American artists
USE Artists—United States
American arts
USE Arts—United States
American authors   810.9; 920
UF Authors, American
BT Authors
NT African American authors
   American dramatists
   American novelists
   American poets
   Hispanic American authors
American ballads   811, etc.
BT American poetry
American Bicentennial
USE American Revolution Bicenten-
   nial, 1776-1976
American Bill of rights
USE United States. Constitution.
   1st-10th amendments
American bison
USE Bison
American characteristics
USE American national characteris-
   tics
American Civil War
USE United States—History—1861-
   1865, Civil War
American civilization
USE America—Civilization

American colonial style in architecture
   724
UF Colonial architecture *[Former
   heading]*
BT Architecture
American colonies
USE United States—History—1600-
   1775, Colonial period
American color prints   769.973
UF Color prints, American
BT Color prints
American composers
USE Composers—United States
American constitution
USE United States. Constitution
American cooking   641.5973
   Use for materials on cooking limited to
American national and regional styles.
UF Cookery, American
SA styles of regional American
   cooking, e.g. Southern cook-
   ing [to be added as needed]
BT Cooking
American decoration and ornament
USE Decoration and ornament—
   United States
American diaries   809; 920
   Use for collections of American diaries and
for materials about American diaries.
BT American literature
   Diaries
American diplomatic and consular ser-
   vice (May subdiv. geog.)   327.73;
   353.1
UF Diplomatic and consular service,
   American
   United States—Diplomatic and
   consular service
BT Diplomatic and consular ser-
   vice
American drama   812
   Use for general materials about American
drama, not for individual works.
BT American literature
   Drama
American drama—Collections   812.008
American drama—History and criticism
   812.009
American dramatists   812.009; 920
UF Dramatists, American
BT American authors
   Dramatists

American drawing   741.973
  UF   Drawing, American
  BT   **Drawing**
American economic assistance
  USE   **American foreign aid**
American engraving   760; 769
  UF   Engraving, American
  BT   **Engraving**
American espionage   327.1273; 355.3
  UF   Espionage, American
  BT   **Espionage**
American essays   814; 814.008
  BT   **American literature**
        Essays
American ethics
  USE   **Ethics—United States**
American exploring expeditions
  USE   **United States—Exploring expe-**
        ditions
American fables   813
  BT   **Fables**
American fiction   813
      May be used for collections or materials
      about American fiction, not for individual
      works.
  BT   **American literature**
        Fiction
American films
  USE   **Motion pictures—United States**
American flag
  USE   **Flags—United States**
American folk art   745.0973
  UF   Folk art, American
  BT   **American art**
        Folk art
American folk dancing
  USE   **Folk dancing—United States**
American folk music
  USE   **Folk music—United States**
American folk songs
  USE   **Folk songs—United States**
American foreign aid (May subdiv. geog.)
      338.91; 361.6
  UF   American economic assistance
        Economic assistance, American
  BT   **Foreign aid**
American furniture   684.100973;
      749.213
  UF   Furniture, American
  SA   styles of American furniture [to
        be added as needed]
  BT   **Furniture**

American government
  USE   **United States—Politics and**
        government
American graphic arts
  USE   **Graphic arts—United States**
American historians
  USE   **Historians—United States**
American history
  USE   **America—History**
        United States—History
American hostages (May subdiv. geog.
      except U.S.)   920
  BT   **Hostages**
American hostages—Iran   920
  NT   **Iran hostage crisis, 1979-1981**
American illustrators
  USE   **Illustrators—United States**
American Indian authors
  USE   **Native American authors**
American Indians
  USE   **Native Americans**
American letters   816; 816.008
  BT   **American literature**
        Letters
American literature (May subdiv. geog.
      by state or region)   810
      May be subdivided by the topical subdivi-
      sions and literary forms used under **English**
      literature; or geographically by states or re-
      gions of the United States for works by or
      about several authors from a state or region or
      writing about a state or region, e.g. **American**
      literature—Massachusetts; American litera-
      ture—Southern States; etc.
  SA   various forms of American liter-
        ature, e.g. **American poetry;**
        American satire; etc. [to be
        added as needed]
  BT   **Literature**
  NT   **American diaries**
        American drama
        American essays
        American fiction
        American letters
        American literature (Spanish)
        American poetry
        American prose literature
        American satire
        American speeches
        American wit and humor
        Beat generation

American literature—17th and 18th centuries 810

UF American literature—Colonial period

American literature—19th century 810

American literature—20th century 810

American literature—21st century 810

American literature—African American authors 810.8; 810.9

May be used for collections or materials about American literature by several African American authors, not for individual works. Use same pattern for literatures and literary forms written by other ethnic groups or classes of authors.

UF African American literature

American literature—Afro-American authors

American literature—Black authors

Black literature (American)

SA particular forms of American literature with the subdivision *African American authors;* e.g., **American poetry—African American authors** [to be added as needed]

NT **Harlem Renaissance**

American literature—Afro-American authors

USE **American literature—African American authors**

American literature—American Indian authors

USE **American literature—Native American authors**

American literature—Black authors

USE **American literature—African American authors**

American literature—Collections 810.8

Use for collections of both poetry and prose by several American authors. Collections consisting of prose only are entered under **American prose literature**; collections of poetry are entered under **American poetry—Collections.**

American literature—Colonial period

USE **American literature—17th and 18th centuries**

American literature—Hispanic American authors 810

Use for materials on American literature in English written by American authors of Spanish or Latin American origins. Materials on American literature written in Spanish are entered under **American literature (Spanish).**

UF American literature—Latin American authors

Hispanic American literature (English)

SA genres of American literature with the subdivision *Hispanic American authors;* and **American literature** and genres of American literature with subdivisions for specific groups of Hispanic American authors, e.g. **American literature—Mexican American authors** [to be added as needed]

NT **American literature—Mexican American authors**

American literature—Latin American authors

USE **American literature—Hispanic American authors**

American literature—Massachusetts 810

American literature—Mexican American authors 810

Use for materials on American literature written in English by American authors of Mexican origins.

UF Chicano literature (English)

Mexican American literature (English)

SA genres of American literature with the subdivision *Mexican American authors* [to be added as needed]

BT **American literature—Hispanic American authors**

American literature—Native American authors 810.8; 810.9

May be used for collections or materials about American literature written in English by several Native American authors, not for individual works. Collections or materials about literature written in Native American languages by several Native American authors are entered under **Native American literature.**

UF American literature—American Indian authors *[Former heading]*

American literature—Southern States 810

UF Southern literature

American literature (Spanish)   860

Use for materials on American literature written in Spanish. Materials on American literature in English written by American authors of Spanish or Latin American origins are entered under **American literature—Hispanic American authors.**

UF   Hispanic American literature
(Spanish)
Spanish American literature

SA   genres of American literature
with the qualifier (Spanish)
[to be added as needed]

BT   **American literature**

**American literature—Women authors
810.8; 810.9**

May be used for collections or for materials about several American women authors.

American Loyalists   973.3

UF   Loyalists, American
Tories, American

BT   **United States—History—1775-
1783, Revolution**

American military assistance (May
subdiv. geog.)   **355**

UF   Military assistance, American

BT   **Military assistance**

American motion pictures

USE   **Motion pictures—United States**

American music   780.973

UF   Music, American

BT   **Music**

American musicians

USE   **Musicians—United States**

**American national characteristics
306.0973; 973**

UF   American characteristics
National characteristics,
American
United States—National characteristics

BT   **National characteristics**

American national songs

USE   **National songs—United States**

American newspapers

USE   **Newspapers—United States**

American novelists   813.009; 920

UF   Novelists, American

BT   **American authors
Novelists**

American orations

USE   **American speeches**

American painters

USE   **Painters—United States**

American painting   759.13

UF   Painting, American

BT   **Painting**

American periodicals   051

BT   **Periodicals**

American personal names

USE   **Personal names—United States**

American philosophers

USE   **Philosophers—United States**

American philosophy   191

UF   Philosophy, American

BT   **Philosophy**

American poetry   811

Use for general materials about American poetry, not for individual works.

BT   **American literature
Poetry**

NT   **American ballads**

American poetry—African American authors   811, etc.

May be used for collections or materials about American poetry by several African American authors, not for individual works.

UF   African American poetry
American poetry—Afro-American
authors
American poetry—Black authors
Black poetry (American)

American poetry—Afro-American authors

USE   **American poetry—African
American authors**

American poetry—Black authors

USE   **American poetry—African
American authors**

American poetry—Collections   811.008

**American poetry—History and criticism
811.009**

American poets   811.009; 920

UF   Poets, American

BT   **American authors
Poets**

American politicians

USE   **Politicians—United States**

American politics

USE   **United States—Politics and
government**

American pottery   738.0973

UF   Pottery, American

BT   **Pottery**

American prints   769.973
  UF Prints, American
  BT **Prints**
American propaganda   303.3; 327.1
  UF Propaganda, American
  BT **Propaganda**
American prose literature   818
    Use for collections of prose writings by several American authors that may include a variety of literary forms, such as essays, fiction, orations, etc. May also be used for general materials about such prose writings.
  UF Prose literature, American
  BT **American literature**
American Revolution
  USE **United States—History—1775-1783, Revolution**
American Revolution Bicentennial, 1776-1976   973.3
  UF American Bicentennial
      Bicentennial celebrations—United States—1976
      United States—Bicentennial celebrations
      United States—History—1775-1783, Revolution—Centennial celebrations, etc.
  BT **United States—Centennial celebrations, etc.**
American Revolution Bicentennial, 1776-1976—Collectibles   973.3075
  BT **Collectors and collecting**
American satire   817; 817.008
  UF Satire, American
  BT **American literature**
      Satire
American schools
  USE **Schools—United States**
American sculptors
  USE **Sculptors—United States**
American sculpture   730.973
  BT **Sculpture**
American songs   782.420973
  BT **Songs**
  NT **Folk songs—United States**
      National songs—United States
      Spirituals (Songs)
American-Spanish War, 1898
  USE **Spanish-American War, 1898**
American speeches   815; 815.008
  UF American orations
      Speeches, addresses, etc., American

  BT **American literature**
      Speeches
American technical assistance (May subdiv. geog.)   338.91; 361.6
  UF Technical assistance, American
  BT **Technical assistance**
American teenagers
  USE **Teenagers—United States**
American tourists
  USE **American travelers**
American travelers   910.92; 920
  UF American tourists
  BT **Travelers**
American wit and humor   817; 817.008; 817.009
    Use for collections by several authors or for materials about American wit and humor. Individual works by American humorists are entered under **Wit and humor.**
  BT **American literature**
      Wit and humor
American youth
  USE **Youth—United States**
Americana   069; 973
    Use for materials about American objects of interest to collectors for their historical value, such as documents, relics, etc., including items of little intrinsic value. Materials about old American objects that have aesthetic as well as financial value, usually furniture or decorative arts, are entered under **Antiques—United States.**
  BT **Collectors and collecting**
      Popular culture—United States
      United States—Civilization
      United States—History
  RT **Antiques—United States**
Americanisms   427
    Use for materials on words and expressions peculiar to the United States.
  UF English language—Americanisms
  BT **English language—Dialects**
Americanization   305.813; 306.0973
  BT **Socialization**
  NT **United States—Immigration and emigration**
  RT **Immigration and emigration**
      Naturalization
Americans (May subdiv. geog. except U.S.)   305.813; 920; 973
    Use for materials on citizens of the United States.
  RT **United States**
Americans—Foreign countries   305.813; 920; 973

Americans—Greece   305.813

Amish   289.7
  BT   **Christian sects**
       Mennonites

Ammunition   623.4
  SA   types of ammunition, e.g.
       Bombs [to be added as need-
       ed]
  BT   **Explosives**
       Ordnance
       Projectiles
  NT   **Bombs**
  RT   **Firearms**
       Gunpowder

Amnesty   364.6
  BT   **Administration of criminal jus-
       tice**
       Executive power
  RT   **Forgiveness**
       Pardon

Amniocentesis   618.3
  BT   **Prenatal diagnosis**

Amphetamines   615
  UF   Pep pills
  SA   types of amphetamines, e.g.
       Methamphetamine [to be
       added as needed]
  BT   **Stimulants**
  NT   **Methamphetamine**

Amphibians (May subdiv. geog.)   567;
  597.8
  SA   types of amphibians [to be add-
       ed as needed]
  BT   **Animals**
  NT   **Frogs**
       Salamanders

Amphibious operations
  USE   names of wars with the subdivi-
        sion *Amphibious operations,*
        e.g. **World War, 1939-
        1945—Amphibious opera-
        tions** [to be added as needed]

Amplifiers (Electronics)   621.3815
  SA   types of amplifiers [to be added
       as needed]
  BT   **Electronics**
  NT   **Masers**
       Transistor amplifiers

Amplifiers, Transistor
  USE   **Transistor amplifiers**

Amusement parks (May subdiv. geog.)
  791.06
  UF   Theme parks
  SA   names of specific parks [to be
       added as needed]
  BT   **Parks**
  NT   **Walt Disney World (Fla.)**
  RT   **Carnivals**

Amusements (May subdiv. geog.)   790
  UF   Entertainments
       Pastimes
  SA   types of amusements, e.g. **Car-
       nivals** [to be added as need-
       ed]
  NT   **Amateur theater**
       Carnivals
       Charades
       Children's parties
       Christmas entertainments
       Church entertainments
       Circus
       Concerts
       Creative activities
       Dance
       Fireworks
       Fortune telling
       Hobbies
       Juggling
       Literary recreations
       Magic tricks
       Mathematical recreations
       Puzzles
       Riddles
       Scientific recreations
       Shadow pictures
       Skits
       Theater
       Toys
       Tricks
       Vaudeville
       Ventriloquism
  RT   **Entertaining**
       Games
       Indoor games
       Play
       Recreation
       Sports

Anabolic steroids
  USE   **Steroids**

Anaesthetics
  USE   **Anesthetics**

Analysis
    USE   types of chemicals and sub-
          stances with the subdivision
          Analysis, e.g. **Water—Analy-**
          sis; Milk—Analysis; etc., for
          materials on methods of ana-
          lyzing those items [to be add-
          ed as needed]

Analysis (Chemistry)
    USE   **Analytical chemistry**

Analysis (Mathematics)
    USE   **Calculus**
          Mathematical analysis

Analysis of food
    USE   **Food adulteration and inspec-**
          tion
          Food—Analysis

Analytic geometry   516.3
    UF   Geometry, Analytic
    BT   **Geometry**

Analytical chemistry   543
    UF   Analysis (Chemistry)
          Chemical analysis
          Chemistry, Analytic
          Qualitative analysis
          Quantitative analysis
    SA   types of substances with the
          subdivision *Analysis,* e.g. **Wa-**
          ter—Analysis [to be added as
          needed]
    BT   **Chemistry**
    NT   **Distillation**
          Food—Analysis
          Water—Analysis

Anarchism and anarchists   320.5; 335
    BT   **Freedom**
          Political crimes and offenses
          Political science
    RT   **Terrorism**

Anatomy   571.3; 611
    SA   names of organs and regions of
          the body and subjects with
          the subdivision *Anatomy,* e.g.
          Heart—Anatomy; Birds—
          Anatomy; etc. [to be added
          as needed]
    BT   **Biology**
          Medicine
    NT   **Animals—Anatomy**
          Artistic anatomy
          Birds—Anatomy

          Cardiovascular system
          Comparative anatomy
          Foot
          Glands
          Head
          Heart—Anatomy
          Human anatomy
          Immune system
          Musculoskeletal system
          Nervous system
          Plants—Anatomy
          Reproductive system
          Respiratory system
          Skin
          Stomach
          Throat
    RT   **Physiology**

Anatomy, Artistic
    USE   **Artistic anatomy**

Anatomy, Comparative
    USE   **Comparative anatomy**

Anatomy of animals
    USE   **Animals—Anatomy**

Anatomy of plants
    USE   **Plants—Anatomy**

Ancestor worship (May subdiv. geog.)
          291.2
    UF   Worship of the dead
    BT   **Religion**
    RT   **Shinto**

Ancestry
    USE   **Genealogy**
          Heredity

Ancient architecture (May subdiv. geog.)
          722
    UF   Architecture, Ancient
    BT   **Archeology**
          Architecture
    NT   **Byzantine architecture**
          Greek architecture
          Pyramids
          Roman architecture

Ancient art (May subdiv. geog.)   **709.01**
    UF   Art, Ancient
    BT   **Art**
    NT   **Byzantine art**
          Greek art
          Roman art

Ancient civilization   306.093; 930
- UF   Civilization, Ancient
- BT   **Ancient history**
          Civilization
- NT   **Classical civilization**

Ancient geography   913

Use for materials on the geography of the ancient world in general. Materials on the ancient geography of one country or region still existing in modern times are entered under the name of the place with the subdivision *Historical geography*. Materials on the geography of regions or countries of antiquity that no longer exist as such in modern times are entered under the name of the place with the subdivision *Geography*.

- UF   Classical geography
          Geography, Ancient
- SA   names of modern countries with the subdivision *Historical geography,* e.g. **Greece—Historical geography;** and names of places of antiquity with the subdivision *Geography,* e.g. **Gaul—Geography** [to be added as needed]
- BT   **Ancient history**
          Historical geography
- NT   **Gaul—Geography**
          Greece—Historical geography
          Rome—Geography

Ancient Greece
- USE   **Greece—History—0-323**

Ancient Greece—Description
- USE   **Greece—Description—0-323**

Ancient history   930

Use for materials on the history of the ancient world up to the fall of Rome not limited to a single country or region.

- UF   History, Ancient
- SA   names of ancient peoples, e.g. **Hittites;** and names of countries of antiquity, with the subdivision *History* [to be added as needed]
- BT   **World history**
- NT   **Ancient civilization**
          Ancient geography
          Bible
          Classical dictionaries
          Hittites
          Inscriptions
          Numismatics

Ancient philosophy   180
- UF   Greek philosophy
          Philosophy, Ancient
          Roman philosophy
- BT   **Philosophy**
- NT   **Stoics**

Androgyny   155.3; 305.3
- BT   **Sex differences (Psychology)**
          Sex role

Anecdotes   808.88; 818.008, etc.

May be used for collections of anecdotes and for materials about anecdotes.

- UF   Facetiae
          Stories
- SA   subjects with the subdivision *Anecdotes* [to be added as needed]
- NT   **Music—Anecdotes**
- RT   **Wit and humor**

Anesthetics   615; 617.9
- UF   Anaesthetics
- BT   **Materia medica**
- RT   **Pain**
          Surgery

Angels   235
- UF   Spirits
- BT   **Heaven**

Angina pectoris   616.1
- BT   **Heart diseases**

Anglican Church
- USE   **Church of England**

Angling
- USE   **Fishing**

Anglo-French intervention in Egypt, 1956
- USE   **Sinai Campaign, 1956**

Anglo-Saxon language
- USE   **English language—Old English period**

Anglo-Saxon literature
- USE   **English literature—Old English period**

Anglo-Saxons   305.82; 941.01
- BT   **Great Britain—History—0-1066**
          Teutonic peoples

Animal abuse
- USE   **Animal welfare**

Animal attacks   591.6
- UF   Attacks by animals
- BT   **Dangerous animals**

Animal babies   591.3

Use for materials on baby animals of several species. Baby animals of a particular spe-

Animal babies—*Continued*
cies are entered under the name of the species.
    UF   Animals—Infancy
          Baby animals
    BT   **Animals**
Animal behavior   591.5
    UF   Animals—Behavior
          Behavior
          Habits of animals
    SA   types of specific behavior, e.g.
          Animals—Migration; Hibernation; Sexual behavior in animals; etc.; and types of animals with the subdivision *Behavior,* e.g. **Birds—Behavior** [to be added as needed]
    BT   **Animals**
          Zoology
    NT   **Animal communication**
          Animal courtship
          Animal defenses
          Animal sounds
          Animals—Food
          Animals—Migration
          Birds—Behavior
          Hibernation
          Instinct
          Monkeys—Behavior
          Nest building
          Primates—Behavior
          Sexual behavior in animals
    RT   **Animal intelligence**
          Tracking and trailing
Animal camouflage
    USE **Camouflage (Biology)**
Animal communication   591.59
    UF   Animal language
          Animals—Language
          Communication among animals
    BT   **Animal behavior**
    RT   **Animal sounds**
Animal courtship   591.56
    UF   Animals—Courtship
          Courtship (Animal behavior)
          Courtship of animals
          Mate selection in animals
          Mating behavior
    BT   **Animal behavior**
          Sexual behavior in animals

Animal defenses   591.47
    UF   Defense mechanisms (Zoology)
          Self-defense in animals
          Self-protection in animals
    BT   **Animal behavior**
    NT   **Camouflage (Biology)**
Animal drawing
    USE **Animal painting and illustration**
Animal embryos, Frozen
    USE **Frozen embryos**
Animal experimentation   619
    UF   Experimentation on animals
          Laboratory animal experimentation
    BT   **Research**
    NT   **Vivisection**
    RT   **Animal welfare**
Animal exploitation
    USE **Animal welfare**
Animal-facilitated therapy
    USE **Pet therapy**
Animal flight   573.7
    UF   Animals—Flight
    SA   types of animals with the subdivision *Flight,* e.g. **Birds—Flight** [to be added as needed]
    BT   **Animal locomotion**
          Flight
    NT   **Birds—Flight**
Animal food
    USE **Animals—Food**
         Food of animal origin
Animal habitations
    USE **Animals—Habitations**
Animal homes
    USE **Animals—Habitations**
Animal housing   636.08
    Use for materials on houses or habitations provided by humans for either wild or domestic animals. Materials on the natural shelters and homes animals build for themselves, such as burrows, dens, lairs, etc., are entered under **Animals—Habitations.**
    UF   Animals—Housing
          Domestic animal dwellings
          Domestic animals—Housing
          Habitations of domestic animals
    SA   types of animals with the subdivision *Housing,* e.g. **Pets—Housing** [to be added as needed]

Animal housing—*Continued*
- BT **Animals**
- NT **Beehives**
  Birdhouses
  Pets—Housing
- RT **Animals—Habitations**

Animal husbandry
- USE **Livestock industry**

Animal industry
- USE **Livestock industry**

Animal instinct
- USE **Instinct**

Animal intelligence 591.5
- UF Animal psychology
  Intelligence of animals
- SA types of animals with the subdivision *Psychology* [to be added as needed]
- BT **Animals**
- NT **Dogs—Psychology**
  Psychology of learning
- RT **Animal behavior**
  Comparative psychology
  Instinct

Animal kingdom
- USE **Zoology**

Animal language
- USE **Animal communication**
  Animal sounds

Animal light
- USE **Bioluminescence**

Animal locomotion 573.7
- UF Animals—Movements
  Movements of animals
- BT **Animals**
  Locomotion
- NT **Animal flight**

Animal lore
- USE **Animals—Folklore**
  Animals in literature
  Mythical animals
  Natural history

Animal luminescence
- USE **Bioluminescence**

Animal magnetism
- USE **Hypnotism**

Animal migration
- USE **Animals—Migration**

Animal oils
- USE **Oils and fats**

Animal painting and illustration   704.9; 743.6; 758

Use for materials on the art of painting or drawing animals. Materials on the depiction of animals in works of art are entered under **Animals in art.** Popular materials consisting chiefly of photographs or illustrations of animals are entered under **Animals—Pictorial works.**
- UF Animal drawing
- BT **Painting**
- RT **Animals in art**
  Animals—Pictorial works
  Photography of animals

Animal parasites
- USE **Parasites**

Animal photography
- USE **Photography of animals**

Animal physiology
- USE **Zoology**

Animal pictures
- USE **Animals—Pictorial works**

Animal pounds
- USE **Animal shelters**

Animal products   338.1; 338.4
- UF Products, Animal
- SA types of animal products [to be added as needed]
- BT **Commercial products**
- NT **Dairy products**
  Hides and skins
  Ivory
  Leather
  Wool

Animal psychology
- USE **Animal intelligence**
  Comparative psychology

Animal reproduction   571.8
- UF Animals—Birth
  Animals—Reproduction
- BT **Animals**
  Reproduction

Animal rights (May subdiv. geog.)   **179**

Use for materials on the inherent rights attributed to animals. Materials on the protection and treatment of animals are entered under **Animal welfare.** Materials on the political movement to promote the idea of animal rights are entered under **Animal rights movement.**
- UF Animals' rights
  Rights of animals
- RT **Animal rights movement**
  Animal welfare

Animal rights movement (May subdiv. geog.) **179**
  UF Animal rights movements *[Former heading]*
      Animal welfare movement
      Antivivisection movement
  BT **Social movements**
  RT **Animal rights**
      Animal welfare
Animal rights movements
  USE **Animal rights movement**
Animal sexual behavior
  USE **Sexual behavior in animals**
Animal shelters **179; 636.08**
  UF Animal pounds
  BT **Animal welfare**
Animal signs
  USE **Animal tracks**
Animal sounds **573.9; 591.59**
  UF Animal language
      Animals—Sounds
  BT **Animal behavior**
  NT **Birdsongs**
  RT **Animal communication**
Animal stories
  USE **Animals—Fiction**
Animal tracks **590**
  UF Animal signs
      Tracks of animals
  BT **Tracking and trailing**
Animal training
  USE **Animals—Training**
Animal welfare **179**
  Use for materials on the protection and treatment of animals. Materials on the inherent rights attributed to animals are entered under **Animal rights.** Materials on the political movement to promote the idea of animal rights are entered under **Animal rights movement.**
  UF Abuse of animals
      Animal abuse
      Animal exploitation
      Animals—Mistreatment
      Animals—Protection
      Animals—Treatment
      Cruelty to animals
      Humane treatment of animals
      Laboratory animal welfare
      Prevention of cruelty to animals
      Protection of animals

  NT **Animal shelters**
  RT **Animal experimentation**
      Animal rights
      Animal rights movement
Animal welfare movement
  USE **Animal rights movement**
Animals (May subdiv. geog.) **590**
  Use for nonscientific materials. Materials on the science of animals are entered under **Zoology.** Subdivisions used under this heading may be used under the names of orders, classes, or individual species of animals.
  UF Beasts
      Fauna
      Wild animals
  SA names of orders and classes of the animal kingdom; kinds of animals characterized by their environments; and names of individual species [to be added as needed]
  NT **Amphibians**
      Animal babies
      Animal behavior
      Animal housing
      Animal intelligence
      Animal locomotion
      Animal reproduction
      Aquatic animals
      Birds
      Carnivorous animals
      Dangerous animals
      Desert animals
      Domestic animals
      Extinct animals
      Forest animals
      Furbearing animals
      Game and game birds
      Insects
      Invertebrates
      Jungle animals
      Mammals
      Mountain animals
      Pets
      Poisonous animals
      Predatory animals
      Prehistoric animals
      Rare animals
      Reptiles
      Spiders
      Stream animals
      Swamp animals
      Ticks

Animals—*Continued*
  Vertebrates
  Wildlife
  Working animals
  Worms
 RT **Zoology**
   Zoos
Animals—Anatomy 571.3
 UF Anatomy of animals
   Structural zoology
   Zoology—Anatomy
 BT **Anatomy**
   Zoology
 NT **Fur**
Animals and the handicapped 636.088
 UF Handicapped and animals
   Pets and the handicapped
 BT **Animals—Training**
 NT **Guide dogs**
   Hearing ear dogs
   Pet therapy
Animals as food
 USE **Food of animal origin**
Animals—Behavior
 USE **Animal behavior**
Animals—Birth
 USE **Animal reproduction**
Animals—Camouflage
 USE **Camouflage (Biology)**
Animals—Color 573.5; 591.47
 BT **Color**
Animals—Courtship
 USE **Animal courtship**
Animals—Diseases 571.9; 636.089
 UF Diseases of animals
   Domestic animals—Diseases
 SA types of animals with the subdi-
   vision *Diseases* [to be added
   as needed]
 BT **Diseases**
 NT **Horses—Diseases**
 RT **Veterinary medicine**
Animals, Edible
 USE **Food of animal origin**
Animals—Fiction 808.83; 813, etc.
 Use for collections of stories about animals.
 Materials about the portrayal of animals in lit-
 erature are entered under **Animals in litera-
 ture.**

 UF Animal stories
 SA types of animals with the subdi-
   vision *Fiction*, e.g. **Dogs—
   Fiction** [to be added as need-
   ed]
 RT **Animals in literature**
   Fables
Animals—Filmography 016.591
Animals—Flight
 USE **Animal flight**
Animals—Folklore 398.24
 UF Animal lore
 BT **Folklore**
 NT **Dragons**
   Monsters
 RT **Mythical animals**
Animals—Food 591.5
 Use for materials on the food and food hab-
 its of animals. Materials on human food of
 animal origin are entered under **Food of ani-
 mal origin.**
 UF Animal food
   Feeding behavior in animals
 SA types of animals and species of
   animals with the subdivision
   Food [to be added as needed]
 BT **Animal behavior**
   Food
 NT **Feeds**
   Food chains (Ecology)
Animals—Habitations 591.56
 Use for materials on the natural shelters and
 homes animals build for themselves, such as
 burrows, dens, lairs, etc. Materials on houses
 or habitations provided by humans for either
 wild or domestic animals are entered under
 Animal housing.
 UF Animal habitations
   Animal homes
   Habitations of wild animals
   Wild animal dwellings
 SA types of animals and individual
   species of animals with the
   subdivision *Habitations,* or
   Nests, e.g. **Beavers—Habita-
   tions; Birds—Nests;** etc. [to
   be added as needed]
 NT **Nest building**
 RT **Animal housing**
Animals—Hibernation
 USE **Hibernation**
Animals—Housing
 USE **Animal housing**

Animals in art   704.9

Use for materials on the depiction of animals in works of art. Materials on the art of painting or drawing animals are entered under **Animal painting and illustration.** Materials consisting chiefly of photographs or illustrations of animals are entered under **Animals—Pictorial works.**

BT   **Art—Themes**

RT   **Animal painting and illustration**

      Animals—Pictorial works

Animals in literature   809

Use for materials on the theme of animals in literature. Collections of poems or stories about animals are entered under **Animals—Poetry** or **Animals—Fiction.**

UF   Animal lore

SA   phrase headings for specific animals in literature, e.g. **Dogs in literature** [to be added as needed]

BT   **Literature—Themes**

RT   **Animals—Fiction**

      Animals—Poetry

Animals in motion pictures   791.43

BT   **Motion pictures**

Animals in police work   363.2; 636.088

BT   **Police**

      Working animals

Animals—Infancy

USE   **Animal babies**

Animals—Language

USE   **Animal communication**

Animals—Migration   591.56

UF   Animal migration

      Migration

SA   types of animals with the subdivision *Migration,* e.g. **Birds—Migration** [to be added as needed]

BT   **Animal behavior**

Animals—Mistreatment

USE   **Animal welfare**

Animals—Movements

USE   **Animal locomotion**

Animals, Mythical

USE   **Mythical animals**

Animals—Photography

USE   **Photography of animals**

Animals—Pictorial works   590.22

Use for popular materials consisting chiefly of photographs or illustrations of animals. Materials on the art of painting or drawing animals are entered under **Animal painting and illustration.** Materials on the depiction of animals in works of art are entered under **Animals in art.**

UF   Animal pictures

RT   **Animal painting and illustration**

      Animals in art

      Photography of animals

Animals—Poetry   808.81; 811, etc.; 811.008, etc.

Use for collections of poetry about animals. Materials on the theme of animals in literature are entered under **Animals in literature.**

RT   **Animals in literature**

Animals, Prehistoric

USE   **Prehistoric animals**

Animals—Protection

USE   **Animal welfare**

Animals—Reproduction

USE   **Animal reproduction**

Animals' rights

USE   **Animal rights**

Animals—Sexual behavior

USE   **Sexual behavior in animals**

Animals—Sounds

USE   **Animal sounds**

Animals—Temperature

USE   **Body temperature**

Animals—Training   636.088

UF   Animal training

      Training of animals

SA   types of animals with the subdivision *Training,* e.g. **Horses—Training** [to be added as needed]

NT   **Animals and the handicapped**

      Dogs—Training

Animals—Treatment

USE   **Animal welfare**

Animals—United States   591.973

UF   Zoology—United States

Animals, Useful and harmful

USE   **Economic zoology**

Animals—War use   355.4

UF   War use of animals

BT   **Working animals**

NT   **Dogs—War use**

Animated cartoons

USE   **Animated films**

Animated films   741.5; 791.43

May be used for individual works, collections, or materials about animated films.

Animated films—*Continued*
    UF   Animated cartoons
          Cartoons, Animated
          Motion picture cartoons
    BT   **Cartoons and caricatures**
          Motion pictures
    RT   **Animation (Cinematography)**

Animated television programs   791.45
    May be used for individual works, collections, or materials about animated television programs.
    UF   Cartoons, Television
          Television cartoons
    BT   **Television programs**

Animation (Cinematography)   741.5; 778.5
    BT   **Cinematography**
    RT   **Animated films**

Anniversaries
    USE **Birthdays**
          Holidays
          and ethnic groups, classes of persons, individuals, coporate bodies, places, religious denominations, or wars with the subdivision *Anniversaries,* for materials about anniversary celebrations, e.g. **Shakespeare, William, 1564-1616—Anniversaries** [to be added as needed]

Annual income guarantee
    USE **Guaranteed annual income**

Annuals
    USE **Almanacs**
          Calendars
          Periodicals
          School yearbooks
          and subjects and names of countries, cities, etc., individual persons, families, and corporate bodies with the subdivision *Periodicals,* e.g. **Engineering—Periodicals** [to be added as needed]

Annuals (Plants)   582.1; 635.9
    BT   **Cultivated plants**
          Flower gardening
          Flowers

Annuities   368.3
    BT   **Investments**
          Retirement income

    NT   **Pensions**
    RT   **Life insurance**

Annulment of marriage
    USE **Marriage—Annulment**

Anointing of the sick   265
    UF   Extreme unction
          Last rites (Sacraments)
          Last sacraments
    BT   **Sacraments**

Anonyms
    USE **Pseudonyms**

Anorexia nervosa   616.85
    BT   **Eating disorders**

Answers to questions
    USE **Questions and answers**

Antarctic expeditions
    USE **Antarctica—Exploration**

Antarctic regions
    USE **Antarctica**

Antarctica   998
    Use for materials on the continent of Antarctica and the regions adjacent to it.
    UF   Antarctic regions
    BT   **Earth**
          Polar regions
    RT   **South Pole**

Antarctica—Exploration   919.8
    UF   Antarctic expeditions
          Polar expeditions
    SA   names of expeditions, e.g. **Byrd Antarctic Expedition** [to be added as needed]
    BT   **Exploration**
          Scientific expeditions
    NT   **Byrd Antarctic Expedition**

Antenuptial contracts
    USE **Marriage contracts**

Anthologies   080; 808.8; 810.8, etc.
    Use for collections of general interest by several authors not limited to works of literature or focused on a single subject.
    UF   Collected papers (Anthologies)
          Collected works
          Collections (Anthologies)
          Collections of literature
          Literary collections
          Readings (Anthologies)
    SA   form headings for minor literary forms that represent collections of works of several authors, e.g. **Essays; American**

Anthologies—*Continued*

    essays; **Parodies; Short stories;** etc.; major literary forms and national literatures with the subdivision *Collections,* e.g. **Poetry—Collections; English literature—Collections;** etc.; and subjects with the subdivision *Literary collections,* for collections focused on a single subject by two or more authors involving two or more literary forms, e.g. **Cats—Literary collections** [to be added as needed]

  BT **Books**

Anthropogeography

  USE **Human geography**

Anthropology (May subdiv. geog.) **301; 599.9**

  UF Human race

  SA names of races and peoples, e.g. **Navajo Indians** [to be added as needed]

  BT **Social sciences**

  NT **Acculturation**
      Anthropometry
      Ethnopsychology
      Human geography
      Language and languages
      National characteristics
      Physical anthropology
      Social change

  RT **Civilization**
      Culture
      Ethnology
      Human beings

Anthropometry **599.9**

  UF Skeletal remains

  BT **Anthropology**
      Ethnology
      Human beings

  NT **Fingerprints**

Anti-abortion movement

  USE **Pro-life movement**

Anti-Americanism

  USE **United States—Foreign opinion**

Anti-apartheid movement **172; 320.5; 323.1**

  BT **Civil rights**
      Social movements
      South Africa—Race relations

  RT **Apartheid**

Anti-fascist movements

  USE **World War, 1939-1945—Underground movements**

Anti-Nazi movement

  USE **World War, 1939-1945—Underground movements**

Anti-poverty programs

  USE **Domestic economic assistance**

Anti-Reformation

  USE **Counter-Reformation**

Anti-utopias

  USE **Dystopias**

Anti-war films

  USE **War films**

Anti-war poetry

  USE **War poetry**

Anti-war stories

  USE **War stories**

Antiabortion movement

  USE **Pro-life movement**

Antiamericanism

  USE **United States—Foreign opinion**

Antiballistic missiles

  USE **Antimissile missiles**

Antibiotics **615**

  SA names of specific antibiotics [to be added as needed]

  BT **Drug therapy**

  NT **Penicillin**

Antibusing

  USE **Busing (School integration)**

Anticommunist movements (May subdiv. geog.) **322.4**

  BT **Communism**

Anticorrosive paint

  USE **Corrosion and anticorrosives**

Antimissile missiles **358.1; 623.4**

  UF ABMs
      Antiballistic missiles

  BT **Guided missiles**

Antinuclear movement (May subdiv. geog.) **303.48; 327.1; 363.17**

  UF Nuclear freeze movement

  BT **Arms control**
      Nuclear weapons
      Social movements

  RT **Nuclear power plants—Environmental aspects**

Antipoverty programs

  USE **Domestic economic assistance**

Antiquarian books
   USE **Rare books**
Antique and classic cars (May subdiv.
      geog.) **629.222**
   UF   Antique automobiles
        Antique cars
        Classic automobiles
        Classic cars
        Vintage automobiles
        Vintage cars
   BT   **Automobiles**
Antique and vintage motorcycles (May
      subdiv. geog.) **629.227**
   UF   Antique motorcycles
        Classic motorcycles
        Vintage motorcycles
   BT   **Motorcycles**
Antique automobiles
   USE **Antique and classic cars**
Antique cars
   USE **Antique and classic cars**
Antique motorcycles
   USE **Antique and vintage motorcycles**
Antiques (May subdiv. geog.) **745.1**
   Use for materials on old decorative or utilitarian objects that have aesthetic or historical importance and financial value. Materials on any objects of interest to collectors, including mass produced items of little intrinsic value, are entered under **Collectibles.**
   SA   subjects and names with the subdivision *Collectibles,* e.g. **American Revolution Bicentennial, 1776-1976—Collectibles;** and types of objects collected, excluding antiquities and natural objects, with the subdivision *Collectors and collecting,* e.g. **Boxes—Collectors and collecting** [to be added as needed]
   BT   **Antiquities**
        Collectors and collecting
        Decoration and ornament
        Decorative arts
   NT   **Art objects**
        Collectors and collecting
        Victoriana
Antiques—United States **745.10973**
   Use for materials about old American objects that have aesthetic as well as financial value, usually furniture or decorative arts. Ma-

terials about American objects of interest to collectors for their historical value, such as documents, relics, etc., including items of little intrinsic value, are entered under **Americana.**
   RT   **Americana**
Antiquities **930.1**
   Use for general materials on the relics or monuments of ancient times. Materials on the relics or monuments of an extinct city or town are entered under the name of the city or town.
   UF   Archeological specimens
        Ruins
   SA   names of extinct cities, e.g. **Delphi (Extinct city);** and names of groups of people extant in modern times and names of cities (except extinct cities), countries, regions, etc., with the subdivision *Antiquities,* e.g. **Native Americans—Antiquities; United States—Antiquities;** etc. [to be added as needed]
   NT   **America—Antiquities**
        Antiques
        Bible—Antiquities
        Chicago (Ill.)—Antiquities
        Christian antiquities
        Classical antiquities
        Egypt—Antiquities
        Jews—Antiquities
        Native Americans—Antiquities
        Ohio—Antiquities
        Prehistoric peoples
        United States—Antiquities
   RT   **Archeology**
Antiquities—Collection and preservation **069**
   UF   Preservation of antiquities
   BT   **Collectors and collecting**
Antiquity of man
   USE **Human origins**
Antisemitism (May subdiv. geog.) **305.892**
   BT   **Prejudices**
   NT   **Holocaust, 1933-1945**
        Jews—Persecutions
Antiseptics **614.4; 617.9**
   BT   **Therapeutics**
   RT   **Disinfection and disinfectants**
        Surgery

Antislavery
  USE **Abolitionists**
       Slavery
       Slaves—Emancipation
Antistalking laws
  USE **Stalking**
Antitrust law (May subdiv. geog.)
       343.07
  UF   Industrial trusts—Law and legis-
       lation
  BT   **Commercial law**
  RT   **Industrial trusts**
Antivivisection movement
  USE **Animal rights movement**
Antiwar movements
  USE **Peace movements**
Antonyms
  USE **Opposites**
       and names of languages with
       the subdivision *Synonyms and
       antonyms,* e.g. **English lan-
       guage—Synonyms and ant-
       onyms** [to be added as need-
       ed]
Ants   595.79
  BT   **Insects**
Anxieties
  USE **Anxiety**
Anxiety   152.4
  UF   Anxieties
       Anxiousness
  BT   **Emotions**
       Neuroses
       Stress (Psychology)
  NT   **Post-traumatic stress disorder**
       Separation anxiety in children
  RT   **Fear**
       Worry
Anxiousness
  USE **Anxiety**
Apartheid   320.5
    Use for materials on the economic, political,
  and social policies of the government of
  South Africa designed to segregate racial
  groups in South Africa and Namibia.
  UF   Separate development (Race re-
       lations)
  BT   **Segregation**
       South Africa—Race relations
  RT   **Anti-apartheid movement**

Apartment houses (May subdiv. geog.)
       647; 728
  BT   **Buildings**
       Domestic architecture
       Houses
       Housing
       Landlord and tenant
  NT   **Apartments**
       Condominiums
       Tenement houses
Apartments (May subdiv. geog.)   **643**
  UF   Flats
  BT   **Apartment houses**
Apiculture
  USE **Beekeeping**
Apocalyptic fantasies
  USE **Fantasy fiction**
       Fantasy films
       Fantasy television programs
       Robinsonades
       Science fiction
       War films
       War stories
Apollo project   629.45
  UF   Project Apollo
  BT   **Life support systems (Space
       environment)**
       **Orbital rendezvous (Space
       flight)**
       Space flight to the moon
Apologetic works
  USE **Apologetics**
       and religions and denominations
       with the subdivision *Apologet-
       ic works,* for materials de-
       fending those religions or de-
       nominations, e.g. **Christiani-
       ty—Apologetic works** for
       materials defending Christiani-
       ty; and religions, denomina-
       tions, religious orders, and sa-
       cred works with the subdivi-
       sion *Controversial literature,*
       for materials that argue
       against or express opposition
       to those groups or works, e.g.
       **Christianity—Controversial
       literature** for materials attack-
       ing Christianity [to be added
       as needed]

Apologetics   239; 291.2
   UF   Apologetic works
   SA   religions and denominations with
         the subdivision *Apologetic*
         works, for materials defending
         those religions or denomina-
         tions, e.g. **Christianity—**
         Apologetic works for materi-
         als defending Christianity; and
         religions, denominations, reli-
         gious orders, and sacred
         works with the subdivision
         Controversial literature, for
         materials that argue against or
         express opposition to those
         groups or works, e.g. **Chris-**
         tianity—Controversial litera-
         ture for materials attacking
         Christianity [to be added as
         needed]
   BT   **Theology**
   NT   **Christianity—Apologetic works**
         Natural theology

Apoplexy
   USE **Stroke**

Apostles   225.92
   UF   Disciples, Twelve
   BT   **Christian saints**
         Church history—30-600, Early
         church

Apostles' Creed   238
   BT   **Creeds**

Apostolic Church
   USE **Church history—30-600, Early**
         church

Apparatus, Chemical
   USE **Chemical apparatus**

Apparatus, Electric
   USE **Electric apparatus and appli-**
         ances

Apparatus, Electronic
   USE **Electronic apparatus and ap-**
         pliances

Apparatus, Scientific
   USE **Scientific apparatus and in-**
         struments

Apparitions   133.1
   UF   Phantoms
         Specters
         Spirits

   BT   **Parapsychology**
   NT   **Ghosts**
   RT   **Hallucinations and illusions**
         Spiritualism
         Visions

Appearance, Personal
   USE **Personal appearance**

Apperception   153.7
   BT   **Educational psychology**
         Psychology
   NT   **Attention**
         Consciousness
         Number concept
   RT   **Perception**
         Theory of knowledge

Apple
   USE **Apples**

Apple Macintosh (Computer)
   USE **Macintosh (Computer)**

Apples   641.3
   UF   Apple *[Former heading]*
   BT   **Fruit**

Appliances, Electric
   USE **Electric apparatus and appli-**
         ances
         Electric household appliances

Appliances, Electronic
   USE **Electronic apparatus and ap-**
         pliances

Applications for college
   USE **College applications**

Applications for positions   331.12;
           650.14
   UF   Employment applications
         Employment references
         Job applications
         Letters of recommendation
         Recommendations for positions
   BT   **Job hunting**
         Personnel management
   NT   **Interviewing**
         Résumés (Employment)

Applied arts
   USE **Decorative arts**

Applied mechanics   620.1
     Use for materials on the application of the
principles of mechanics to engineering structures other than machinery. Materials on the
application of the principles of mechanics to
the design, construction, and operation of machinery are entered under **Mechanical engineering.**

Applied mechanics—*Continued*
  UF Mechanics, Applied
  BT **Mechanics**
Applied psychology   158
  UF Industrial psychology
      Practical Psychology
      Psychology, Applied
  SA subjects with the subdivision
      Psychological aspects, e.g.
      Drugs—Psychological aspects
      [to be added as needed]
  BT **Psychology**
  NT **Behavior modification**
      Counseling
      Drugs—Psychological aspects
      Employee morale
      Human engineering
      Negotiation
      Pastoral psychology
      Psychological warfare
  RT **Educational psychology**
      Interviewing
      Social psychology
Applied science
  USE **Technology**
Appointment
  USE types of public officials and
       names of individual public of-
       ficials with the subdivision
       Appointment, e.g. **Presi-
       dents—United States—Ap-
       pointment** [to be added as
       needed]
Appointments and retirements
  USE names of armed forces with the
       subdivision *Appointments and
       retirements,* e.g. **United
       States. Army—Appointments
       and retirements** [to be added
       as needed]
Apportionment (Election law) (May
    subdiv. geog.)   **324; 328.3; 342**
  UF Legislative reapportionment
      Reapportionment (Election law)
  BT **Representative government and
      representation**
Appraisal
  USE **Tax assessment**
       Valuation
Appraisal of books
  USE **Book reviewing**
       Books and reading

Criticism
      **Literature—History and criti-
      cism**
Appreciation of art
  USE **Art appreciation**
Appreciation of music
  USE **Music appreciation**
Apprentices   331.5
  BT **Labor**
      Technical education
  RT **Employees—Training**
Apprenticeship novels
  USE **Bildungsromans**
Appropriations and expenditures
  USE names of countries and names
       of individual government de-
       partments, agencies, etc., with
       the subdivision *Appropriations
       and expenditures,* e.g. **United
       States—Appropriations and
       expenditures** [to be added as
       needed]
Approximate computation   372.7; 513.2
  UF Arithmetic—Estimation
      Computation, Approximate
      Estimation (Mathematics)
  BT **Numerical analysis**
April First
  USE **April Fools' Day**
April Fools' Day   394.262
  UF All Fools' Day
      April First
  BT **Holidays**
Aptitude
  USE **Ability**
Aptitude testing
  USE **Ability—Testing**
Aquaculture   639
  UF Aquiculture
      Freshwater aquaculture
      Mariculture
      Marine aquaculture
      Ocean farming
      Sea farming
  BT **Agriculture**
      Marine resources
  NT **Fish culture**
Aquarian Age movement
  USE **New Age movement**

Aquariums   597.073; 639.34
    SA   names of specific aquariums [to
          be added as needed]
    BT   **Freshwater biology**
         Natural history
    NT   **Marine aquariums**
    RT   **Fish culture**
         Fishes
Aquatic animals (May subdiv. geog.)
    591.76
    UF   Aquatic fauna
         Water animals
    BT   **Animals**
    NT   **Fishes**
         Freshwater animals
         Marine animals
         Shellfish
         Sponges
Aquatic birds
    USE **Water birds**
Aquatic fauna
    USE **Aquatic animals**
Aquatic plants
    USE **Freshwater plants**
         Marine plants
Aquatic sports
    USE **Water sports**
Aquatic sports—Safety measures
    USE **Water safety**
Aqueducts   628.1
    UF   Water conduits
    BT   **Civil engineering**
         Hydraulic structures
         Water supply
Aquiculture
    USE **Aquaculture**
Arab civilization   306.0917; 909
    UF   Civilization, Arab
    BT   **Civilization**
Arab countries   956
    Use for materials on several Arabic-
speaking countries. Materials on the region
consisting of northeastern Africa and Asia
west of Afghanistan are entered under **Middle
East.**
    BT   **Islamic countries**
         Middle East
Arab countries—Foreign relations—Israel
    956
    UF   Arab-Israel relations
         Arab-Israeli relations
         Israel-Arab relations
         Israeli-Arab relations

    NT   **Israel-Arab conflicts**
    RT   **Israel—Foreign relations—
         Arab countries**
         Jewish-Arab relations
Arab countries—Politics and government
    956
    BT   **Politics**
    NT   **Pan-Arabism**
Arab-Israel conflicts
    USE **Israel-Arab conflicts**
Arab-Israel relations
    USE **Arab countries—Foreign rela-
         tions—Israel**
         **Israel—Foreign relations—
         Arab countries**
Arab-Israel War, 1948-1949
    USE **Israel-Arab War, 1948-1949**
Arab-Israel War, 1956
    USE **Sinai Campaign, 1956**
Arab-Israel War, 1967
    USE **Israel-Arab War, 1967**
Arab-Israel War, 1973
    USE **Israel-Arab War, 1973**
Arab-Israeli conflict, 1987-
    USE **Intifada, 1987-**
Arab-Israeli conflicts
    USE **Israel-Arab conflicts**
Arab-Israeli relations
    USE **Arab countries—Foreign rela-
         tions—Israel**
         **Israel—Foreign relations—
         Arab countries**
Arab-Jewish relations
    USE **Jewish-Arab relations**
Arab refugees (May subdiv. geog.)   325
    UF   Refugees, Arab
    BT   **Refugees**
Arabia
    USE **Arabian Peninsula**
Arabian Peninsula   953
    UF   Arabia
    BT   **Peninsulas**
Arabs (May subdiv. geog.)   305.892; 909
    SA   names of specific Arab peoples
         [to be added as needed]
    NT   **Bedouins**
         Jewish-Arab relations
         Palestinian Arabs
Arabs—Palestine
    USE **Palestinian Arabs**

Arbitration and award 347

Use for materials on the settlement of civil disputes by arbitration instead of a court trial.

   UF   Awards (Law)

           Mediation

   BT   **Commercial law**

           Courts

   RT   **Litigation**

Arbitration, Industrial

   USE   **Industrial arbitration**

Arbitration, International

   USE   **International arbitration**

Arboriculture

   USE   **Forests and forestry**

            Fruit culture

            Trees

Arc light

   USE   **Electric lighting**

Arc welding

   USE   **Electric welding**

Archaeology

   USE   **Archeology**

Archeological specimens

   USE   **Antiquities**

Archeologists 920; 930.1092

   BT   **Historians**

Archeology (May subdiv. geog.) **930.1**

Use for materials on the discipline of archeology. General materials on the relics or monuments of ancient times are entered under **Antiquities.** Materials on the relics or monuments of an extinct city or town are entered under the name of the city or town.

   UF   Archaeology

            Prehistory

   SA   names of extinct cities, e.g. **Delphi (Extinct city)** [to be added as needed]; and names of groups of people and of cities (except extinct cities), countries, regions, etc., with the subdivision *Antiquities,* e.g. **Native Americans—Antiquities; United States—Antiquities;** etc. [to be added as needed]

   BT   **History**

   NT   **Ancient architecture**

           Bible—Antiquities

           Brasses

           Bronzes

           Burial

           Buried treasure

           Cliff dwellers and cliff dwellings

           Excavations (Archeology)

           Extinct cities

           Fossil hominids

           Gems

           Heraldry

           Historic sites

           Industrial archeology

           Inscriptions

           Mounds and mound builders

           Mummies

           Numismatics

           Obelisks

           Prehistoric peoples

           Pyramids

           Radiocarbon dating

           Rock drawings, paintings, and engravings

           Tombs

   RT   **Antiquities**

Archery 799.3

   BT   **Martial arts**

           Shooting

   RT   **Bow and arrow**

Architects 720.92; 920

   BT   **Artists**

Architectural acoustics 729; 690

   UF   Acoustics

   BT   **Sound**

   NT   **Soundproofing**

Architectural decoration and ornament 729

   UF   Architecture—Decoration and ornament

           Decoration and ornament, Architectural

   BT   **Architecture**

           Decoration and ornament

Architectural design 720

Use for materials on the process and methodology of designing buildings.

   BT   **Architecture**

           Design

Architectural designs

   USE   **Architecture—Designs and plans**

Architectural details

   USE   **Architecture—Details**

Architectural drawing 720.28

   BT   **Drawing**

Architectural engineering
    USE **Building**
          Structural analysis (Engineering)
          Structural engineering
Architectural features
    USE **Architecture—Details**
Architectural metalwork   721
    BT   **Metalwork**
Architectural perspective
    USE **Perspective**
Architecture (May subdiv. geog.)   **720**
    Use for materials on the design and style of structures. Materials on the process of construction are entered under **Building.** General materials on buildings are entered under **Buildings.**
    UF   Building design
          Construction
    SA   styles of architecture, e.g. **Byzantine architecture;** and types of buildings, e.g. **Farm buildings** [to be added as needed]
    BT   **Art**
    NT   **American colonial style in architecture**
          Ancient architecture
          Architectural decoration and ornament
          Architectural design
          Asian architecture
          Baroque architecture
          Byzantine architecture
          Church architecture
          Classicism in architecture
          Domestic architecture
          Greek architecture
          Industrial buildings—Design and construction
          Islamic architecture
          Landscape architecture
          Library architecture
          Lost architecture
          Medieval architecture
          Modernism in architecture
          Monuments
          Native American architecture
          Naval architecture
          Obelisks
          Roman architecture
          Romanesque architecture
          Spires
          Tombs
          Underground architecture
    RT   **Building**
          Buildings
Architecture—15th and 16th centuries (May subdiv. geog.)   **724**
    UF   Architecture, Renaissance
          Renaissance architecture *[Former heading]*
Architecture—17th and 18th centuries (May subdiv. geog.)   **724**
    UF   Architecture, Modern—17th-18th centuries
          Modern architecture—1600-1799 (17th and 18th centuries) *[Former heading]*
Architecture—19th century (May subdiv. geog.)   **724**
    UF   Architecture, Modern—19th century
          Modern architecture—1800-1899 (19th century) *[Former heading]*
Architecture—20th century (May subdiv. geog.)   **724**
    UF   Architecture, Modern—20th century
          Modern architecture—1900-1999 (20th century) *[Former heading]*
Architecture—21st century (May subdiv. geog.)   **724**
    UF   Architecture, Modern—21st century
          Modern architecture—2000-2099 (21st century)
Architecture, American
    USE **Architecture—United States**
Architecture, Ancient
    USE **Ancient architecture**
Architecture and the handicapped   720
    UF   Barrier free design
          Handicapped and architecture
    BT   **Handicapped**
Architecture—Awards   720.79
Architecture, Baroque
    USE **Baroque architecture**
Architecture, Byzantine
    USE **Byzantine architecture**

Architecture—Composition, proportion, etc.   720; 729
  UF Architecture—Proportion
       Proportion (Architecture)
  BT **Composition (Art)**
Architecture—Conservation and restoration   690; 720.28
  UF Architecture—Restoration
       Buildings, Restoration of
       Conservation of buildings
       Preservation of buildings
       Restoration of buildings
  RT **Buildings—Maintenance and repair**
Architecture—Decoration and ornament
  USE **Architectural decoration and ornament**
Architecture—Designs and plans   720.28; 729
  UF Architectural designs
       Architecture—Plans
       Designs, Architectural
  NT **Domestic architecture—Designs and plans**
Architecture—Details   721; 729
  UF Architectural details
       Architectural features
  SA types of architectural features, e.g. **Windows; Fireplaces;** etc. [to be added as needed]
  NT **Chimneys**
      Doors
      Fireplaces
      Floors
      Foundations
      Roofs
      Windows
      Woodwork
Architecture, Domestic
  USE **Domestic architecture**
Architecture, Gothic
  USE **Gothic architecture**
Architecture, Greek
  USE **Greek architecture**
Architecture, Islamic
  USE **Islamic architecture**
Architecture, Medieval
  USE **Medieval architecture**
Architecture, Modern
  USE **Modernism in architecture**

Architecture, Modern—17th-18th centuries
  USE **Architecture—17th and 18th centuries**
Architecture, Modern—19th century
  USE **Architecture—19th century**
Architecture, Modern—20th century
  USE **Architecture—20th century**
Architecture, Modern—21st century
  USE **Architecture—21st century**
Architecture—Plans
  USE **Architecture—Designs and plans**
Architecture—Proportion
  USE **Architecture—Composition, proportion, etc.**
Architecture, Renaissance
  USE **Architecture—15th and 16th centuries**
Architecture—Restoration
  USE **Architecture—Conservation and restoration**
Architecture, Roman
  USE **Roman architecture**
Architecture, Romanesque
  USE **Romanesque architecture**
Architecture, Rural
  USE **Farm buildings**
Architecture—United States   720.973
  UF American architecture *[Former heading]*
       Architecture, American
Architecture—United States—1600-1775, Colonial period   720.973
  UF Colonial architecture *[Former heading]*
Archives (May subdiv. geog.)   026; 027
  UF Documents
       Government records—Preservation
       Historical records—Preservation
       Preservation of historical records
       Public records—Preservation
       Records—Preservation
  SA subjects, ethnic groups, classes of persons, individuals, families, schools, and military services with the subdivision *Archives* [to be added as needed]
  BT **Bibliography**
      Documentation

Archives—*Continued*
     History—Sources
     Information services
  NT Manuscripts
     Presidents—United States—Archives
  RT Charters
     Libraries
Archives—United States   027.0973; 353.0071
  UF United States—Archives
Arctic expeditions
  USE **Arctic regions—Exploration**
Arctic regions   919.8; 998
  UF Far north
  BT **Earth**
     Polar regions
  NT **Northeast Passage**
     Northwest Passage
  RT **North Pole**
Arctic regions—Exploration   919.8
  UF Arctic expeditions
     Polar expeditions
  SA names of expeditions [to be added as needed]
  BT **Exploration**
     Scientific expeditions
Ardennes, Battle of the, 1944-1945 940.54
  UF Bastogne, Battle of
     Battle of the Bulge
     Bulge, Battle of the
  BT **World War, 1939-1945—Campaigns**
Area studies   940-999
  Use for general materials on area studies.
  UF Foreign area studies
  SA continents, countries, and geographic regions with the subdivision *Study and teaching* [to be added as needed]
  BT **Education**
  NT **Africa—Study and teaching**
Arena theater   725; 792
  UF Round stage
     Theater-in-the-round
  BT **Theater**
Argentine rummy
  USE **Canasta (Game)**
Argumentation
  USE **Debates and debating**
     Logic

Aristocracy (May subdiv. geog.)   305.5
  BT **Political science**
     Upper class
  RT **Nobility**
Arithmetic   513
  UF Computation (Mathematics)
  SA types of arithmetic operations [to be added as needed]
  BT **Mathematics**
     Set theory
  NT **Average**
     Calculators
     Cube root
     Fractions
     Mental arithmetic
     Metric system
     Multiplication
     Percentage
     Ratio and proportion
     Square root
     Subtraction
  RT **Numbers**
Arithmetic, Commercial
  USE **Business mathematics**
Arithmetic—Estimation
  USE **Approximate computation**
Arithmetic—Study and teaching   372.7; 513.07
  NT **Counting**
     Mathematical readiness
     Number games
Arithmetical readiness
  USE **Mathematical readiness**
Armada, 1588
  USE **Spanish Armada, 1588**
Armaments
  USE **Military readiness**
     Military weapons
Armaments industries
  USE **Defense industry**
Armed forces   343; 355
  UF Armed services
     Military forces
  SA specific branches of the armed forces under names of countries, e.g. **United States. Army;** and names of countries, regions, and international organizations with the subdivision *Armed forces,* e.g. **United States—Armed**

Armed forces—*Continued*
　　　　forces; United Nations—
　　　　Armed forces; etc. [to be
　　　　added as needed]
　BT　**Military art and science**
　NT　**Armies**
　　　　Military personnel
　　　　Navies
　　　　Ohio—Militia
　　　　Recruiting and enlistment
　　　　United Nations—Armed forces
　　　　United States—Armed forces
　　　　United States—Militia
　　　　Voluntary military service
　RT　**Military readiness**
　　　　War
Armed forces—Recruiting, enlistment, etc.
　USE　**Recruiting and enlistment**
Armed services
　USE　**Armed forces**
Armies　355.3
　UF　Army
　　　　Military power
　SA　names of countries with the sub-
　　　　head *Army,* e.g. **United**
　　　　States. Army [to be added as
　　　　needed]
　BT　**Armed forces**
　　　　Military personnel
　NT　**Draft**
　　　　Soldiers
　　　　United States. Army
　RT　**Military art and science**
Armies—Medical care　355.3
　SA　names of wars with the subdivi-
　　　　sion *Health aspects* or *Medi-*
　　　　cal care, e.g. **World War,**
　　　　1939-1945—Health aspects;
　　　　World War, 1939-1945—
　　　　Medical care; etc. [to be
　　　　added as needed]
　BT　**Medical care**
　　　　Military medicine
　RT　**Military personnel—Health**
　　　　and hygiene
Armistice Day
　USE　**Veterans Day**
Armistices
　USE　names of wars with the subdivi-
　　　　sion *Armistices,* e.g. **World**
　　　　War, 1939-1945—Armistices
　　　　[to be added as needed]

Armor　355.8; 623.4; 739.7
　　Use for materials on protective covering
worn as a defense against weapons.
　UF　Arms and armor
　　　　Suits of armor
　BT　**Art metalwork**
　　　　Costume
　　　　Military art and science
　RT　**Weapons**
Armored cars (Tanks)
　USE　**Military tanks**
Arms and armor
　USE　**Armor**
　　　　Weapons
Arms control (May subdiv. geog.)
　　　　327.1; 341.7
　UF　Disarmament
　　　　Limitation of armament
　　　　Non-proliferation of nuclear
　　　　　weapons
　　　　Nuclear non-proliferation
　　　　Nuclear test ban
　BT　**International relations**
　　　　International security
　　　　War
　NT　**Antinuclear movement**
　　　　Arms race
　RT　**International arbitration**
　　　　Military readiness
　　　　Peace
Arms proliferation
　USE　**Arms race**
Arms race (May subdiv. geog.)　**327.1;**
　　　　355
　　Use for materials on the competitive in-
crease in the military power of two or more
nations or blocs.
　UF　Arms proliferation
　　　　Proliferation of arms
　BT　**Arms control**
　　　　International security
　RT　**Arms transfers**
　　　　Military readiness
　　　　Military weapons
Arms sales
　USE　**Arms transfers**
　　　　Defense industry
　　　　Military assistance
　　　　Military weapons
Arms traffic
　USE　**Arms transfers**

Arms transfers (May subdiv. geog.)
    327.1; 382
    UF   Arms sales
           Arms traffic
           Foreign military sales
           Military sales
    BT   **International trade**
    RT   **Arms race**
           Defense industry
           Military assistance

Army
    USE **Armies**
          Military art and science
          and names of countries with the
            subhead *Army,* e.g. **United**
            States. Army [to be added as
            needed]

Army bases
    USE **Military bases**

Army desertion
    USE **Military desertion**

Army life
    USE **Soldiers**
          and names of armies with the
            subdivision *Military life,* e.g.
            United States. Army—Military life [to be added as
            needed]

Army posts
    USE **Military bases**

Army schools
    USE **Military education**

Army tests
    USE **United States. Army—Examinations**

Army vehicles
    USE **Military vehicles**

Aromatic plant products
    USE **Essences and essential oils**

Arrow
    USE **Bow and arrow**

Art 700
    Use for materials on the visual arts only (architecture, painting, etc.). Materials on the arts in general, including the visual arts, literature, and the performing arts, are entered under **Arts.**
    SA   types of art, e.g. **Commercial art;** art of particular religions, e.g. **Christian art;** movements in art, e.g. **Romanticism in art;** art and other

subjects, e.g. **Art and mythology;** subjects and themes in art, e.g. **Animals in art;** and art of particular countries, regions, or ethnic groups, e.g. **American art; Greek art; Native American art;** etc. [to be added as needed]
    BT   **Arts**
    NT   **Abstract art**
          African American art
          American art
          Ancient art
          Architecture
          Art and mythology
          Art and religion
          Art and society
          Art objects
          Artistic anatomy
          Artistic photography
          Artists' models
          Arts and crafts movement
          Asian art
          Baroque art
          Black art
          Botanical illustration
          Bronzes
          Buddhist art
          Byzantine art
          Christian art
          Collage
          Collectors and collecting
          Commercial art
          Composition (Art)
          Computer art
          Copy art
          Cubism
          Decoration and ornament
          Drawing
          Earthworks (Art)
          Engraving
          Erotic art
          Etching
          Expressionism (Art)
          Folk art
          Futurism (Art)
          Gems
          Graphic arts
          Greek art
          Illumination of books and manuscripts

Art—*Continued*
    Illustration of books
    Impressionism (Art)
    Interior design
    Islamic art
    Kinetic art
    Medieval art
    Modernism in art
    Municipal art
    Native American art
    Painting
    Performance art
    Pictures
    Portraits
    Postimpressionism (Art)
    Prehistoric art
    Realism in art
    Religious art
    Roman art
    Romanticism in art
    Sculpture
    Symbolism
    Video art
    World War, 1939-1945—Art
    and the war
  RT **Artists**
Art—15th and 16th centuries   709.02;
  709.03
  UF Art, Renaissance
    Renaissance art *[Former heading]*
Art—17th and 18th centuries   709.03
  UF Art, Modern—17th-18th centuries
Art—19th century   709.03
  UF Art, Modern—19th century
    Modern art—1800-1899 (19th
    century) *[Former heading]*
Art—20th century   709.04
  UF Art, Modern—20th century
    Modern art—1900-1999 (20th
    century) *[Former heading]*
  SA types of twentieth-century art,
    e.g. **Cubism** [to be added as
    needed]
Art—21st century   709.05
  UF Art, Modern—21st century
    Modern art—2000-2099 (21st
    century)
Art, American
  USE **American art**

Art—Analysis, interpretation, appreciation
  USE **Art appreciation**
    Art criticism
    Art—Study and teaching
Art, Ancient
  USE **Ancient art**
Art and mythology   704.9
  UF Mythology in art
  BT **Art**
    Mythology
  RT **Art and religion**
Art and religion   246; 291.1; 701
  UF Arts in the church
    Religion and art
  BT **Art**
    Religion
  RT **Art and mythology**
    Religious art
Art and society (May subdiv. geog.)
  701
  UF Art and sociology
    Society and art
    Sociology and art
  BT **Art**
  NT **Art patronage**
    Art—Political aspects
    Folk art
Art and sociology
  USE **Art and society**
Art and the war
  USE names of wars with the subdivision *Art and the war,* e.g.
    **World War, 1939-1945—Art
    and the war** [to be added as
    needed]
Art appreciation   701
  UF Appreciation of art
    Art—Analysis, interpretation, appreciation
  BT **Aesthetics**
    Art criticism
Art, Asian
  USE **Asian art**
Art, Baroque
  USE **Baroque art**
Art, Black
  USE **Black art**
Art, Buddhist
  USE **Buddhist art**
Art, Byzantine
  USE **Byzantine art**

Art collections (May subdiv. geog.)   708
    UF   Art—Collections
          Art—Private collections
          Collections of art, painting, etc.
          Private art collections
    SA   names of collectors or of the
          original owners of private art
          collections with the subdivi-
          sion *Art collections* [to be
          added as needed]
    RT   **Art museums**
          Collectors and collecting
Art—Collections
    USE **Art collections**
Art—Composition
    USE **Composition (Art)**
Art criticism   701; 709
    UF   Art—Analysis, interpretation, ap-
          preciation
    BT   **Criticism**
    NT   **Art appreciation**
Art education
    USE **Art—Study and teaching**
Art—Exhibitions   707.4
    BT   **Exhibitions**
Art—Federal aid
    USE **Federal aid to the arts**
Art—Forgeries   702.8; 751.5
    UF   Art forgeries *[Former heading]*
          Forgery of works of art
    BT   **Counterfeits and counterfeiting**
          Forgery
Art forgeries
    USE **Art—Forgeries**
Art galleries
    USE **Art museums**
Art, Gothic
    USE **Gothic art**
Art, Greek
    USE **Greek art**
Art—History   709
    BT   **History**
Art in advertising
    USE **Commercial art**
Art in motion
    USE **Kinetic art**
Art industries and trade
    USE **Decorative arts**
Art, Islamic
    USE **Islamic art**

Art, Kinetic
    USE **Kinetic art**
Art, Medieval
    USE **Medieval art**
Art metalwork   739; 745.56
    UF   Decorative metalwork
    SA   types of art metalwork [to be
          added as needed]
    BT   **Decorative arts**
          Metalwork
    NT   **Armor**
          Brasses
          Bronzes
          Goldwork
          Pewter
          Silverwork
Art, Modern—17th-18th centuries
    USE **Art—17th and 18th centuries**
Art, Modern—19th century
    USE **Art—19th century**
Art, Modern—20th century
    USE **Art—20th century**
Art, Modern—21st century
    USE **Art—21st century**
Art, Municipal
    USE **Municipal art**
Art museums (May subdiv. geog.)   708
    UF   Art galleries
          Collections of art, painting, etc.
          Picture galleries
    SA   names of individual art museums
          [to be added as needed]
    BT   **Museums**
    RT   **Art collections**
Art objects   700; 745
    Use for general materials about decorative
    articles of artistic merit such as snuff boxes,
    brasses, pottery, needlework, glassware, etc.
    Materials on old decorative objects having
    historical or financial value are entered under
    Antiques.
    UF   Objets d'art
    SA   types of art objects, e.g. **Furni-**
          ture; Pottery; etc. [to be
          added as needed]
    BT   **Antiques**
          Art
          Decoration and ornament
          Decorative arts
    NT   **Miniature objects**
Art, Oriental
    USE **Asian art**

Art patronage (May subdiv. geog.)   **700**

    Use for materials on patronage of the arts by individuals or corporations. Materials on government support of the arts are entered under **Arts—Government policy** or **Federal aid to the arts.**

    UF   Art patrons

           Business patronage of the arts

           Corporate patronage of the arts

           Corporations—Art patronage

           Funding for the arts

           Patronage of the arts

           Private funding of the arts

    BT   **Art and society**

    RT   **Arts—Government policy**

           Federal aid to the arts

Art patrons

    USE **Art patronage**

Art—Political aspects (May subdiv. geog.)   **701**

    BT   **Art and society**

Art, Prehistoric

    USE **Prehistoric art**

Art—Prices   **707.5**

    BT   **Prices**

Art—Private collections

    USE **Art collections**

Art, Renaissance

    USE **Art—15th and 16th centuries**

Art robberies

    USE **Art thefts**

Art, Roman

    USE **Roman art**

Art, Romanesque

    USE **Romanesque art**

Art schools

    USE **Art—Study and teaching**

Art—Study and teaching   **707**

    UF   Art—Analysis, interpretation, appreciation

           Art education

           Art schools

Art—Technique   **702.8**

Art thefts (May subdiv. geog.)   **364.16**

    UF   Art robberies

    BT   **Theft**

Art—Themes   **704.9**

    UF   Iconography

           Themes in art

    SA   topics in art, e.g. **Dogs in art;** and names of persons, families, and corporate bodies

with the subdivision *In art,* e.g. **Napoleon I, Emperor of the French, 1769-1821—In art** [to be added as needed]

    NT   **African Americans in art**

           Animals in art

           Blacks in art

           Children in art

           Dogs in art

           Flowers in art

           Napoleon I, Emperor of the French, 1769-1821—In art

           Nude in art

           Plants in art

           Women in art

Arthritis   **616.7**

    BT   **Diseases**

    NT   **Gout**

Arthritis—Physical therapy   **616.7**

Arthur, King—Romances

    USE **Arthurian romances**

Arthurian romances   **398.22; 808.8; 809**

    May be used for individual works, collections, or materials about Arthurian romances.

    UF   Arthur, King—Romances

           Knights of the Round Table

    BT   **Romances**

    RT   **Grail—Legends**

Arthurian romances—Adaptations   **808.8**

Articles of war

    USE **Military law**

Articulation (Education)   **371.2**

    Use for materials that discuss the integration of various elements of the school system, between levels, between schools, between subjects, or between the school's programs and outside activities, aimed at promoting a continuous advancement by the student.

    BT   **Education—Curricula**

           Schools—Administration

Artificial flies   **688.7; 799.1**

    UF   Fishing flies

           Flies, Artificial

    BT   **Fishing**

           Fly casting

Artificial flowers   **745.594**

    UF   Flowers, Artificial

    BT   **Decoration and ornament**

Artificial foods   **641.3; 664**

    UF   Synthetic foods

    BT   **Food**

           Synthetic products

Artificial fuels
USE **Synthetic fuels**
Artificial heart 617.4
BT **Artificial organs**
Heart
Artificial insemination 636.08
Use for general materials on artificial in-
semination and materials specifically on the
artificial insemination of livestock and other
animals. Materials limited to artificial insemi-
nation in humans are entered under **Human
artificial insemination.**
BT **Reproduction**
NT **Human artificial insemination**
Artificial insemination, Human
USE **Human artificial insemination**
Artificial intelligence 006.3
UF AI (Artificial intelligence)
Machine intelligence
BT **Computer science**
NT **Expert systems (Computer sci-
ence)**
Artificial limbs 617.5
UF Limbs, Artificial
Prosthesis
BT **Orthopedics**
Artificial organs 617.9
UF Organs, Artificial
Prosthesis
SA names of artificial organs, e.g.
Artificial heart [to be added
as needed]
BT **Surgery**
NT **Artificial heart**
Artificial reality
USE **Virtual reality**
Artificial respiration 617.1
UF Pulmonary resuscitation
Respiration, Artificial
Resuscitation, Pulmonary
BT **First aid**
Artificial satellites 629.43; 629.46
UF Orbiting vehicles
Satellites, Artificial
SA satellites of particular countries,
e.g. **American artificial satel-
lites;** types of satellites; and
names of specific satellites [to
be added as needed]
BT **Astronautics**
NT **American artificial satellites
Explorer (Artificial satellite)
Meteorological satellites**

Space stations
RT **Space vehicles**
Artificial satellites, American
USE **American artificial satellites**
**Artificial satellites—Control systems
629.46**
**Artificial satellites in telecommunication
384.5; 621.382**
UF Communication satellites
Communications relay satellites
Global satellite communications
systems
Satellite communication systems
SA names of specific satellites or
projects [to be added as need-
ed]
BT **Telecommunication**
NT **Telstar project**
Artificial satellites—Launching 629.43
UF Launching of satellites
BT **Rockets (Aeronautics)**
Artificial satellites—Law and legislation
USE **Space law**
Artificial satellites—Orbits 629.4
BT **Astrodynamics**
Artificial satellites—Tracking 629.43
UF Tracking of satellites
Artificial selection
USE **Breeding**
Artificial sweeteners
USE **Sugar substitutes**
Artificial weather control
USE **Weather control**
Artillery 355.8; 623.4
BT **Military art and science**
RT **Ordnance**
Artistic anatomy 704.9; 743.4
UF Anatomy, Artistic
Human anatomy in art
Human figure in art
BT **Anatomy
Art
Drawing
Nude in art**
NT **Figure drawing
Figure painting**
Artistic photography 770; 779
UF Photography—Aesthetics
Photography, Artistic
BT **Art
Photography**

Artists (May subdiv. geog.) **709.2; 920**
    SA   types of artists and names of in-
           dividual artists [to be added
           as needed]
    NT   **African American artists**
          Architects
          Black artists
          Child artists
          Engravers
          Etchers
          Illustrators
          Lithographers
          Painters
          Potters
          Sculptors
          Women artists
    RT   **Art**
          Arts
Artists, American
    USE **Artists—United States**
Artists, Black
    USE **Black artists**
Artists' materials   741.2; 751.2
    UF   Drawing materials
          Painters' materials
    SA   types of artists' materials [to be
           added as needed]
    BT   **Materials**
Artists' models   702.8
    UF   Models
          Models, Artists'
          Models (Persons)
    BT   **Art**
Artists—United States   709.2; 920
    UF   American artists *[Former head-
           ing]*
          Artists, American
Arts (May subdiv. geog.)   **700**
    Use for materials on the arts in general,
    including the visual arts, literature, and the
    performing arts. Materials on the visual arts
    only (architecture, painting, etc.) are entered
    under **Art.**
    BT   **Humanities**
    NT   **Allegory**
          Art
          Decorative arts
          Handicraft
          Performing arts
          Surrealism
          Visual literacy
    RT   **Aesthetics**
          Artists

Arts, American
    USE **Arts—United States**
Arts and crafts movement (May subdiv.
    geog.)   **745**
    Use for materials on the movement originat-
    ing in England in the nineteenth century that
    promoted a return to craftsmanship in the ap-
    plied and decorative arts.
    UF   Crafts (Arts)
    BT   **Art**
          Decoration and ornament
          Decorative arts
          Industrial arts
    RT   **Folk art**
          Handicraft
Arts and state
    USE **Arts—Government policy**
          Federal aid to the arts
Arts—Federal aid
    USE **Federal aid to the arts**
Arts—Government policy (May subdiv.
    geog.)   **353.7; 700**
    UF   Arts and state
          Funding for the arts
          State encouragement of the arts
    BT   **Social policy**
    RT   **Art patronage**
          Federal aid to the arts
Arts, Graphic
    USE **Graphic arts**
Arts in the church
    USE **Art and religion**
Arts—United States   700.973
    UF   American arts *[Former heading]*
          Arts, American
Asbestos   553.6; 620.1; 666; 691
    BT   **Minerals**
Asceticism   248.4; 291.4
    May be subdivided by religion or sect.
    BT   **Ethics**
          Religious life
    NT   **Fasting**
          Sexual abstinence
Asceticism—Catholic Church   248.4
Asia   950
    UF   East
          Orient
    SA   areas of Asia [to be added as
           needed]
    NT   **Central Asia**
          East Asia
          Middle East

Asia—*Continued*
      Southeast Asia
Asia, Central
    USE **Central Asia**
Asia—Civilization   306.095; 950
    UF   Asian civilization
          Civilization, Oriental
          Oriental civilization
    BT   **Civilization**
          East and West
Asia—Politics and government   950
    BT   **Politics**
Asia, Southeastern
    USE **Southeast Asia**
Asian architecture   720.95
    UF   Oriental architecture
    BT   **Architecture**
Asian art   709.5
    UF   Art, Asian
          Art, Oriental
          Oriental art
    BT   **Art**
Asian civilization
    USE **Asia—Civilization**
Asphyxiating gases
    USE **Poisonous gases**
Assassination   364.15
    SA   classes of persons and names of
          individuals with the subdivi-
          sion *Assassination* [to be add-
          ed as needed]
    BT   **Crime**
          Homicide
          Political crimes and offenses
    NT   **Presidents—United States—As-**
          sassination
Assault, Criminal
    USE **Offenses against the person**
Assault, Sexual
    USE **Rape**
Assembly programs, School
    USE **School assembly programs**
Assembly, Right of
    USE **Freedom of assembly**
Assertive behavior
    USE **Assertiveness (Psychology)**
Assertiveness (Psychology)   155.2; 158.2
    UF   Assertive behavior
    BT   **Aggressiveness (Psychology)**
          Psychology
    RT   **Self-confidence**

Assessment
    USE **Tax assessment**
Assessment, Tax
    USE **Tax assessment**
Assistance in emergencies
    USE **Helping behavior**
Assistance to developing areas
    USE **Foreign aid**
          Technical assistance
Assisted reproduction
    USE **Reproductive technology**
Association, Freedom of
    USE **Freedom of association**
Associations (May subdiv. geog.)   **060;**
          302.3; 366
    UF   Associations, institutions, etc.
          Networks (Associations, institu-
          tions, etc.)
          Organizations
          Voluntary associations
          Voluntary organizations
    SA   types of associations; subjects,
          classes of persons, ethnic
          groups, and names of individ-
          ual persons, families, and cor-
          porate bodies, with the subdi-
          vision *Societies;* and names of
          specific associations [to be
          added as needed]
    NT   **Agriculture—Societies**
          Charity organization
          Clubs
          Community life
          Cooperation
          Nonprofit organizations
          Religious institutions
          Societies
          Trade and professional associa-
          tions
Associations, institutions, etc.
    USE **Associations**
Associations, International
    USE **International agencies**
Asteroids   523.44
    UF   Minor planets
          Planetoids
    BT   **Astronomy**
          Solar system
    RT   **Planets**

Astrobiology
USE **Life on other planets**
Space biology
Astrochemistry
USE **Space chemistry**
Astrodynamics   521; 629.4
BT **Dynamics**
NT **Artificial satellites—Orbits**
Navigation (Astronautics)
RT **Astronautics**
Space flight
Astrogeology   559.9
SA names of planets with the subdi-
vision *Geology* [to be added
as needed]
BT **Geology**
NT **Lunar geology**
Mars (Planet)—Geology
Astrology   133.5
UF Hermetic art and philosophy
BT **Astronomy**
Divination
Occultism
NT **Horoscopes**
Zodiac
RT **Constellations**
Astronautical accidents
USE **Space vehicle accidents**
Astronautical communication systems
USE **Astronautics—Communication
systems**
Astronautical instruments   629.4
UF Instruments, Astronautical
Space vehicles—Instruments
BT **Navigation (Astronautics)**
Space optics
RT **Astronautics—Communication
systems**
Astronautics (May subdiv. geog.)   629.4
BT **Aeronautics**
NT **Aerothermodynamics**
Artificial satellites
Astronautics and civilization
Interplanetary voyages
Navigation (Astronautics)
Outer space
Rocketry
Space flight
Space flight to the moon
Space stations
Unidentified flying objects

RT **Astrodynamics**
Space sciences
Space vehicles
Astronautics—Accidents
USE **Space vehicle accidents**
Astronautics and civilization   306.4
UF Civilization and astronautics
Outer space and civilization
Space age
Space power
BT **Aeronautics and civilization**
Astronautics
Civilization
NT **Space colonies**
Space law
**Astronautics—Communication systems
629.47**
UF Astronautical communication sys-
tems
Space communication
BT **Interstellar communication**
Telecommunication
NT **Radio in astronautics**
RT **Astronautical instruments**
**Astronautics—International cooperation
629.4**
UF International space cooperation
BT **International cooperation**
Astronautics—Law and legislation
USE **Space law**
Astronautics—United States   629.40973
NT **Project Voyager**
Astronauts   629.450092; 920
UF Cosmonauts
BT **Air pilots**
Space flight
NT **Space vehicles—Piloting**
Astronauts—Clothing
USE **Space suits**
Astronauts—Nutrition   629.47
UF Space nutrition
BT **Nutrition**
Astronavigation
USE **Navigation (Astronautics)**
Astronomers   520.92; 920
BT **Scientists**
Astronomical instruments   522
UF Instruments, Astronomical
SA types of instruments, e.g. **Tele-
scopes** [to be added as need-
ed]

Astronomical instruments—*Continued*
BT   Scientific apparatus and instruments
       Space optics
NT   Astronomical photography
       Telescopes
Astronomical observatories   522
UF   Observatories, Astronomical
RT   Astronomy
Astronomical photography   522
UF   Astrophotography
BT   Astronomical instruments
       Photography
Astronomical physics
USE   Astrophysics
Astronomy   520
BT   Physical sciences
       Science
       Universe
NT   Asteroids
       Astrology
       Astrophysics
       Bible—Astronomy
       Black holes (Astronomy)
       Chronology
       Comets
       Galaxies
       Life on other planets
       Lunar eclipses
       Meteorites
       Meteors
       Moon
       Nautical astronomy
       Outer space
       Planetariums
       Planets
       Pulsars
       Quasars
       Radio astronomy
       Seasons
       Sky
       Solar eclipses
       Solar system
       Space environment
       Spectrum analysis
       Sun
       Zodiac
RT   Astronomical observatories
       Constellations
       Space sciences
       Stars

Astronomy—Atlases
USE   Stars—Atlases
Astronomy—Mathematics   520.1
BT   Mathematics
Astrophotography
USE   Astronomical photography
Astrophysics   523.01
UF   Astronomical physics
BT   Astronomy
       Physics
NT   Black holes (Astronomy)
       Spectrum analysis
Astros (Baseball team)
USE   Houston Astros (Baseball team)
Asylum   341.4
UF   Asylum, Right of
       Political asylum
       Right of asylum
       Sanctuary (Law)
BT   International law
NT   Political refugees
       Sanctuary movement
Asylum, Right of
USE   Asylum
Asylums
USE   Institutional care
At-home employment
USE   Home-based business
At risk students   371.93
    Use for materials on students considered prone to academic failure or other problems.
UF   Disadvantaged students
       High risk students
       Students with problems
       Underprivileged students
BT   Students
RT   Dropouts
       Socially handicapped children
Atheism   211
BT   Religion
       Secularism
       Theology
RT   Agnosticism
       Deism
       Rationalism
       Theism
Athletes (May subdiv. geog.)   796.092; 920
SA   types of athletes, e.g. Baseball players [to be added as needed]

Athletes—*Continued*
   NT   **African American athletes**
       Baseball players
       Black athletes
   RT   **Sports**
Athletes, Black
   USE **Black athletes**
Athletes—Drug use   362.29; 796
   UF   Drugs and sports
       Sports and drugs
   RT   **Steroids**
Athletic coaching
   USE **Coaching (Athletics)**
Athletic medicine
   USE **Sports medicine**
Athletics (May subdiv. geog.)   796
   SA   types of athletic activities [to be
        added as needed]
   NT   **Boxing**
       Coaching (Athletics)
       Gymnastics
       Martial arts
       Olymplc games
       Rowing
       Track athletics
       Weight lifting
       Wrestling
   RT   **Physical education**
       Sports
Atlantic Ocean   910.9163
   BT   **Ocean**
   NT   **Bermuda Triangle**
Atlantic States   974; 975
   UF   Eastern Seaboard
       Middle Atlantic States
       South Atlantic States
   BT   **United States**
Atlas (Missile)   623.4; 629.47
   BT   **Ballistic missiles**
       **Intercontinental ballistic mis-
        siles**
Atlases   912
   Use as a form heading for geographical at-
lases of world coverage. General materials
about maps and their history are entered under
Maps.
   UF   Geographical atlases
   SA   scientific and technical subjects
        with the subdivision *Atlases,*
        for materials consisting of
        comprehensive, often system-
        atically arranged, collections

of illustrative plates, charts,
etc., usually with explanatory
captions, e.g. **Human anatomy—Atlases;** and names of
countries, cities, etc., with the
subdivision *Maps,* e.g. **United
States—Maps** [to be added
as needed]
   BT   **Geography**
       Maps
   NT   **Bible—Geography**
       Historical atlases
       Human anatomy—Atlases
       Stars—Atlases
       United States—Maps
Atlases, Astronomical
   USE **Stars—Atlases**
Atmosphere   551.5
   Use for materials on the body of air sur-
rounding the earth. Materials on the chemical
and physical properties of air are entered un-
der **Air.**
   BT   **Air**
       Earth
   NT   **Clouds**
       Fog
       Sky
       Upper atmosphere
   RT   **Meteorology**
Atmosphere—Pollution
   USE **Air pollution**
Atmosphere, Upper
   USE **Upper atmosphere**
Atmospheric greenhouse effect
   USE **Greenhouse effect**
Atmospheric humidity
   USE **Humidity**
Atolls
   USE **Coral reefs and islands**
Atom smashing
   USE **Cyclotrons**
Atomic bomb   355.8; 623.4
   BT   **Bombs**
       Nuclear weapons
   NT   **Radioactive fallout**
   RT   **Hydrogen bomb**
Atomic bomb—Physiological effect
   616.9
   RT   **Radiation—Physiological effect**
Atomic bomb—Testing   623.4
Atomic bomb victims   940.54
   UF   Victims of atomic bombings

Atomic energy
USE **Nuclear energy**
Atomic industry
USE **Nuclear industry**
Atomic medicine
USE **Nuclear medicine**
Atomic nuclei
USE **Nuclear physics**
Atomic power
USE **Nuclear energy**
Atomic power plants
USE **Nuclear power plants**
Atomic-powered vehicles
USE **Nuclear propulsion**
Atomic submarines
USE **Nuclear submarines**
Atomic theory   539.7; 541.2
BT **Physical chemistry**
RT **Quantum theory**
Atomic warfare
USE **Nuclear warfare**
Atomic weapons
USE **Nuclear weapons**
Atoms   539.7; 541.2
BT **Physical chemistry**
NT **Cyclotrons**
Electrons
Isotopes
Neutrons
Protons
Transmutation (Chemistry)
Atonement—Christianity   232; 234
UF Jesus Christ—Atonement
Vicarious atonement
BT **Christianity**
Jesus Christ
Sacrifice
Salvation
Atonement, Day of
USE **Yom Kippur**
Atonement—Judaism   296.3
UF Atonement (Judaism)
BT **Judaism**
Atonement (Judaism)
USE **Atonement—Judaism**
Atrocities (May subdiv. geog.)   **909**
UF Military atrocities
SA names of wars with the subdivision *Atrocities,* e.g. **World War, 1939-1945—Atrocities;**

and names of specific atrocities [to be added as needed]
BT **Crime**
Cruelty
NT **Massacres**
Persecution
World War, 1939-1945—Atrocities
Attacks by animals
USE **Animal attacks**
Attempted suicide
USE **Suicide**
Attendance, School
USE **School attendance**
Attention   153.1; 153.7
UF Concentration
BT **Apperception**
Educational psychology
Memory
Psychology
Thought and thinking
NT **Listening**
Attitude (Psychology)   152.4
UF Attitudes
SA ethnic groups and classes of persons with the subdivision *Attitudes,* e.g. **Teenagers—Attitudes** [to be added as needed]
BT **Emotions**
Psychology
NT **Conformity**
Frustration
Job satisfaction
Prejudices
Racism
Sexism
Stereotype (Psychology)
Teenagers—Attitudes
RT **Public opinion**
Attitudes
USE **Attitude (Psychology)**
and ethnic groups and classes of persons with the subdivision *Attitudes,* e.g. **Teenagers—Attitudes** [to be added as needed]
Attorneys
USE **Lawyers**
ATVs
USE **All terrain vehicles**

Auction bridge
USE **Bridge (Game)**
Auctions   658.8
    UF   Sales, Auction
    BT   **Selling**
Audio amplifiers, Transistor
    USE   **Transistor amplifiers**
Audio cassettes
    USE   **Sound recordings**
Audiobooks   028
    Use for materials on sound recordings of books, including but not limited to materials recorded specifically for the blind.
    UF   Books on cassette
           Books on tape
           Cassette books
           Recorded books
           Talking books *[Former heading]*
    BT   **Sound recordings**
    RT   **Blind—Books and reading**
Audiodisc players
    USE   **Compact disc players**
Audiotapes
    USE   **Sound recordings**
Audiovisual aids
    USE   subjects with the subdivision *Audiovisual aids,* e.g. **Library education—Audiovisual aids;** and subjects with the subdivisions *Study and teaching—Audiovisual aids,* for the use of audiovisual aids in the teaching of those subjects, e.g. **Science—Study and teaching—Audiovisual aids** [to be added as needed]
Audiovisual education   371.33
    UF   Visual instruction
    SA   subjects with the subdivision *Audiovisual aids* [to be added as needed]
    BT   **Education**
    NT   **Audiovisual materials**
           Library education—Audiovisual aids
           Motion pictures in education
           Radio in education
           Television in education
Audiovisual materials   025.17; 371.33
    UF   Multimedia materials
           Nonbook materials
           Nonprint materials

    SA   subjects with the subdivision *Audiovisual aids;* and names of specific audiovisual materials [to be added as needed]
    BT   **Audiovisual education**
           Teaching—Aids and devices
    NT   **Filmstrips**
           Library education—Audiovisual aids
           Manipulatives
           Motion pictures
           Sound recordings
           Videodiscs
           Videotapes
Audiovisual materials centers
    USE   **Instructional materials centers**
Auditing (May subdiv. geog.)   **657**
    SA   topics and names of corporate bodies with the subdivision *Auding* [to be added as needed]
    BT   **Bookkeeping**
    RT   **Accounting**
Auricular confession
    USE   **Confession**
Aurora australis
    USE   **Auroras**
Aurora borealis
    USE   **Auroras**
Auroras   538
    UF   Aurora australis
           Aurora borealis
           Northern lights
           Polar lights
           Southern lights
    BT   **Geophysics**
           Meteorology
Australia   994
    May be subdivided like United States except for *History.*
    NT   **Australians**
Australian aborigines   305.89
    UF   Aborigines, Australian
    BT   **Australians**
           Native peoples
Australians   305.82; 994
    BT   **Australia**
    NT   **Australian aborigines**
Author and publisher
    USE   **Authors and publishers**

Authoring programs for computer-assisted
    instruction
    USE   **Computer-assisted instruction—**
            Authoring programs
Authoritarianism
    USE   **Fascism**
            Totalitarianism
Authors   809; 920
    UF   Writers
    SA   authors of particular countries,
            e.g. **American authors;** types
            of writers, e.g. **Poets;** names
            of national literatures with the
            subdivision for a particular
            kind of author, e.g. **American**
            literature—Women authors;
            American literature—African
            American authors; etc.; sub-
            jects and names of countries,
            cities, etc. with the subdivi-
            sion *Bio-bibliography;* and
            names of individual authors
            [to be added as needed]
    NT   **American authors**
            Black authors
            Child authors
            Dramatists
            English authors
            Historians
            Journalists
            Native American authors
            Novelists
            Poets
            Women authors
    RT   **Books**
            Literature—Bio-bibliography
Authors, American
    USE   **American authors**
Authors and publishers   070.5
    Use for materials on the relations between
    author and publisher.
    UF   Author and publisher
            Publishers and authors
    BT   **Authorship**
            Contracts
            Publishers and publishing
    RT   **Copyright**
Authors, Black
    USE   **Black authors**
Authors—Correspondence   816, etc.;
    808.86; 809.6
    BT   **Letters**

Authors, English
    USE   **English authors**
Authors—Homes and haunts
    USE   **Literary landmarks**
Authors—Interviews   809
    BT   **Interviews**
Authorship   808
    Use for general materials on being or be-
    coming an author. Materials concerning the
    composition of special types of literature are
    entered under more specific headings such as
    Fiction—Technique; Biography as a liter-
    ary form; Short story; etc.
    UF   Writing (Authorship)
    SA   individual writers, titles of liter-
            ary works, and sacred works
            with the subdivision *Author-*
            ship; e.g. **Shakespeare, Wil-**
            liam, 1564-1616—Authorship
            [to be added as needed]
    BT   **Literature**
    NT   **Advertising copy**
            Authors and publishers
            Biography as a literary form
            Creative writing
            Drama—Technique
            Editing
            Fiction—Technique
            Historiography
            Journalism
            Love stories—Technique
            Radio authorship
            Report writing
            Short story
            Technical writing
            Television authorship
            Versification
Authorship—Handbooks, manuals, etc.
    808
    RT   **Printing—Style manuals**
Autism   616.89; 618.92
    BT   **Child psychiatry**
Autobiographical fiction   808.83; 813,
    etc.
    May be used for individual works, collec-
    tions, or materials about autobiographical fic-
    tion.
    UF   Autobiographical novels
    BT   **Biographical fiction**
Autobiographical novels
    USE   **Autobiographical fiction**

Autobiographies   920

Use for collections of autobiographies. Materials about autobiography as a literary form are entered under **Autobiography.**

UF   Memoirs
     Personal narratives

SA   ethnic groups, classes of persons, and subjects with the subdivision *Biography* or *Correspondence,* e.g. **Women—Biography; Authors—Correspondence;** etc.; and names of diseases, events, and wars with the subdivision *Personal narratives* [to be added as needed]

BT   **Biography**

NT   **Holocaust, 1933-1945—Personal narratives**
     United States—History—1861-1865, Civil War—Personal narratives
     World War, 1939-1945—Personal narratives

RT   **Diaries**

Autobiography   809

Use for materials on autobiography as a literary form. Collections of autobiographies are entered under **Autobiographies.**

UF   Autobiography as a literary form
     Autobiography—History and criticism
     Autobiography—Technique
     Memoirs

BT   **Biography as a literary form**

Autobiography as a literary form
USE   **Autobiography**

Autobiography—History and criticism
USE   **Autobiography**

Autobiography—Technique
USE   **Autobiography**

Autographs   929.8

SA   classes of persons, ethnic groups, wars, and names of individual persons with the subdivision *Autographs,* or *Autographs—Facsimiles* [to be added as needed]

BT   **Biography**
     Writing

RT   **Manuscripts**

Autographs—Facsimiles   929.8

SA   classes of persons, ethnic groups, wars, and names of individual persons with the subdivisions *Autographs—Facsimiles* [to be added as needed]

Automata
USE   **Robots**

Automated cataloging   025.3

UF   Cataloging—Data processing

BT   **Cataloging**

Automatic bread machines
USE   **Bread machines**

Automatic control
USE   **Automation**
      Cybernetics
      Electric controllers
      Servomechanisms

Automatic data processing
USE   **Data processing**

Automatic drafting
USE   **Computer graphics**

Automatic drawing
USE   **Computer graphics**

Automatic machinery
USE   **Automation**

Automatic speech recognition   006.4

UF   Mechanical speech recognition
     Speech recognition, Automatic

BT   **Speech processing systems**
     Voice

Automation   629.8; 670.42

UF   Automatic control
     Automatic machinery
     Computer control

SA   subjects with the subdivision *Automation,* e.g. **Libraries—Automation** [to be added as needed]

BT   **Industrial equipment**
     Machinery in the workplace

NT   **Feedback control systems**
     Industrial robots
     Libraries—Automation
     Servomechanisms
     Systems engineering
     Telecommuting

Automatons
USE   **Robots**

Automobile accidents
USE **Traffic accidents**
Automobile design
USE **Automobiles—Design and construction**
Automobile driver education (May subdiv. geog.) **629.28**
UF Automobile drivers—Education
Car driver education
Driver education
BT **Education**
Automobile drivers 629.28
UF Automobile driving
Automobiles—Driving
Car drivers
Drivers, Automobile
Automobile drivers—Education
USE **Automobile driver education**
Automobile drivers' licenses
USE **Drivers' licenses**
Automobile driving
USE **Automobile drivers**
Automobile engines
USE **Automobiles—Motors**
Automobile guides
USE **Automobile travel—Guidebooks**
Automobile industry (May subdiv. geog.) **338.4; 388.3**
UF Automotive industry
Car industry
Motor vehicle industry
BT **Industries**
NT **Service stations**
Automobile industry—Production standards 658.5
BT **Production standards**
Automobile insurance 368
UF Car insurance
Insurance, Automobile
BT **Insurance**
Automobile motors
USE **Automobiles—Motors**
Automobile parts 629.28
UF Automobiles—Parts
Car parts
BT **Automobiles**
Automobile pools
USE **Car pools**

Automobile racing (May subdiv. geog.) **796.72**
UF Automobiles—Racing
Car racing
SA types of automobile racing and names of specific races [to be added as needed]
BT **Racing**
NT **Karts and karting**
Stock car racing
Automobile repairs
USE **Automobiles—Maintenance and repair**
Automobile styling
USE **Automobiles—Design and construction**
Automobile touring
USE **Automobile travel**
Automobile transmission
USE **Automobiles—Transmission devices**
Automobile travel (May subdiv. geog.) **796.7**
UF Automobile touring
Automobiles—Touring
Car travel
Motoring
BT **Travel**
Automobile travel—Guidebooks 912
UF Automobile guides
Automobiles—Road guides
Travel guides
BT **Maps**
RT **Road maps**
Automobiles (May subdiv. geog.) **388.3; 629.222**
UF Cars (Automobiles)
Motor cars
SA names of specific makes and models of automobiles, e.g. **Ford automobile** [to be added as needed]
BT **Highway transportation**
Vehicles
NT **Antique and classic cars**
Automobile parts
Buses
Compact cars
Diesel automobiles
Electric automobiles
Ford automobile

Automobiles—*Continued*
> Foreign automobiles
> Sports cars
> Trucks

Automobiles—Accidents
> USE **Traffic accidents**

Automobiles—Air conditioning   629.2
> BT **Air conditioning**

Automobiles—Brakes   629.2
> BT **Brakes**

Automobiles—Conservation and restoration   629.28
> UF Automobiles—Restoration
> Restoration of automobiles

Automobiles—Construction
> USE **Automobiles—Design and construction**

Automobiles—Design
> USE **Automobiles—Design and construction**

Automobiles—Design and construction   629.222
> UF Automobile design
> Automobile styling
> Automobiles—Construction
> Automobiles—Design
> Automotive engineering
> Car design
> BT **Industrial design**

Automobiles—Drivers' licenses
> USE **Drivers' licenses**

Automobiles—Driving
> USE **Automobile drivers**

Automobiles, Electric
> USE **Electric automobiles**

Automobiles—Electric equipment   629.25
> UF Electric equipment of automobiles

Automobiles—Engines
> USE **Automobiles—Motors**

Automobiles, Foreign
> USE **Foreign automobiles**

Automobiles—Fuel consumption   629.28
> BT **Energy consumption**
> **Fuel**

Automobiles—Gearing
> USE **Automobiles—Transmission devices**

Automobiles—Inspection (May subdiv. geog.)   **353.9**

Automobiles—Law and legislation (May subdiv. geog.)   **343.09**
> BT **Law**
> **Legislation**
> RT **Traffic regulations**

Automobiles—Maintenance and repair   629.28
> UF Automobile repairs
> Automobiles—Repairing
> Car maintenance
> Car repair

Automobiles—Models   629.22
> UF Model cars
> BT **Models and modelmaking**

Automobiles—Motors   629.25
> UF Automobile engines *[Former heading]*
> Automobile motors
> Automobiles—Engines
> Car engines
> SA types of automobiles and makes and models of automobiles with the subdivision *Motors* [to be added as needed]
> BT **Engines**

Automobiles—Painting   667
> UF Car painting
> BT **Industrial painting**

Automobiles—Parts
> USE **Automobile parts**

Automobiles—Pollution control devices   629.25
> UF Pollution control devices (Motor vehicles)
> BT **Pollution control industry**

Automobiles—Purchasing (May subdiv. geog.)   **381**

Automobiles—Racing
> USE **Automobile racing**

Automobiles—Repairing
> USE **Automobiles—Maintenance and repair**

Automobiles—Restoration
> USE **Automobiles—Conservation and restoration**

Automobiles—Road guides
> USE **Automobile travel—Guidebooks**

Automobiles—Touring
> USE **Automobile travel**

Automobiles—Trailers
> USE **Travel trailers and campers**

Automobiles—Transmission devices
629.2
   UF   Automobile transmission
         Automobiles—Gearing
         Car transmissions
         Transmissions, Automobile
   BT   **Gearing**
Automotive engineering
   USE **Automobiles—Design and construction**
Automotive industry
   USE **Automobile industry**
Autosuggestion
   USE **Hypnotism**
         Mental suggestion
Autumn   508; 525
   UF   Fall
   BT   **Seasons**
Avant-garde churches
   USE **Non-institutional churches**
Avant-garde films
   USE **Experimental films**
Avant-garde theater
   USE **Experimental theater**
Avenues
   USE **Streets**
Average   519.5
   BT   **Arithmetic**
         Probabilities
         Statistics
Aviation
   USE **Aeronautics**
Aviation accidents
   USE **Aircraft accidents**
Aviation medicine   616.9
   UF   Aeronautics—Medical aspects
         Aerospace medicine
   BT   **Medicine**
   NT   **Jet lag**
   RT   **Space medicine**
Aviators
   USE **Air pilots**
Avocations
   USE **Hobbies**
Awakening, Religious
   USE **Religious awakening**
Awards   001.4
   UF   Competitions
         Prizes (Rewards)
         Rewards (Prizes, etc.)

   SA   types of awards and prizes; subjects, corporate entities, persons, and military services with the subdivision *Awards,* e.g. **Architecture—Awards;** and names of specific awards and prizes, e.g. **Nobel Prizes** [to be added as needed]
   NT   **Literary prizes**
         Nobel Prizes
   RT   **Contests**
Awards (Law)
   USE **Arbitration and award**
Axiology
   USE **Values**
Aztecs   972.004
   BT   **Native Americans—Mexico**
B-52 bomber   623.7
   BT   **Bombers**
B and B accommodations
   USE **Bed and breakfast accommodations**
Babies
   USE **Infants**
Baby animals
   USE **Animal babies**
Baby care
   USE **Infants—Care**
Baby clothes
   USE **Infants' clothing**
Baby names
   USE **Personal names**
Baby sitters
   USE **Babysitters**
Baby sitting
   USE **Babysitting**
Babysitters   649
   UF   Baby sitters
         Sitters (Babysitters)
   RT   **Babysitting**
Babysitting   649
   UF   Baby sitting
   BT   **Child care**
         Infants—Care
   RT   **Babysitters**
Back packing
   USE **Backpacking**
Backpack cycling
   USE **Bicycle touring**

Backpacking   796.51
    UF Back packing
          Pack transportation
    BT **Camping**
          Hiking
Bacon-Shakespeare controversy
    USE **Shakespeare, William, 1564-1616—Authorship**
Bacon's Rebellion, 1676   973.2
    BT **United States—History—1600-1775, Colonial period**
Bacteria   579.3

    Use for general materials on bacteria. Materials on the science of studying bacteria are entered under **Bacteriology.**

    UF Disease germs
          Germs
          Microbes
    BT **Microorganisms**
          Parasites
    RT **Bacteriology**
Bacterial warfare
    USE **Biological warfare**
Bacteriology   579.3

    Use for materials on the science of studying bacteria. General materials on bacteria are entered under **Bacteria.**

    SA types of bacteriology, e.g. **Agricultural bacteriology;** types of microbiology, e.g. **Soil microbiology;** and subjects with the subdivision *Microbiology,* e.g. **Cheese—Microbiology** [to be added as needed]
    BT **Microbiology**
    NT **Agricultural bacteriology**
    RT **Bacteria**
Bacteriology, Agricultural
    USE **Agricultural bacteriology**
Badges of honor
    USE **Decorations of honor**
           Insignia
           Medals
Bahai Faith   297.9
    UF Bahaism
    BT **Religions**
Bahaism
    USE **Bahai Faith**
Baking   641.7
    SA types of baked products [to be added as needed]

    BT **Cooking**
    NT **Bread**
          Cake
          Pastry
    RT **Bread machines**
Balance of nature
    USE **Ecology**
Balance of payments (May subdiv. geog.) 382
    BT **International economic relations**
    RT **Balance of trade**
Balance of power   327.1
    UF Power politics
    BT **International relations**
Balance of trade (May subdiv. geog.) 382
    UF Trade, Balance of
          Trade deficits
          Trade surpluses
    BT **International trade**
    RT **Balance of payments**
Ball bearings
    USE **Bearings (Machinery)**
Ball games   796.3
    SA types of games, e.g. **Baseball;** and names of competitions [to be added as needed]
    BT **Games**
    NT **Baseball**
          Basketball
          Bowling
          Football
          Soccer
          Softball
          Table tennis
          Volleyball
Ballads   808.1; 808.81; 811, etc.

    May be used for individual works, collections, or materials about ballads. Materials on the folk tunes associated with these ballads and collections that include both words and music are entered under **Folk songs.**

    BT **Literature**
          Poetry
          Songs
    RT **Folk songs**
Ballet (May subdiv. geog.)   792.8

    Use for musical works composed for the ballet and for materials about the ballet. Individual ballet plots or collections of ballet plots are entered under **Ballet—Stories, plots, etc.**

Ballet—*Continued*
> UF Ballets
> BT **Dance**
> **Drama**
> **Performing arts**
> **Theater**
> RT **Pantomimes**

Ballet dancers **792.8092; 920**
> BT **Dancers**

Ballet plots
> USE **Ballet—Stories, plots, etc.**

Ballet—Stories, plots, etc. **792.8**
> UF Ballet plots

Ballets
> USE **Ballet**

Ballistic missiles **358.1; 623.4**
> Use for materials on high-altitude, high-speed missiles that are self-propelled and guided in the first stage of flight only and later have a natural and uncontrolled trajectory.
> UF Missiles, Ballistic
> SA types of ballistic missiles and names of specific missiles [to be added as needed]
> BT **Guided missiles**
> **Nuclear weapons**
> **Rockets (Aeronautics)**
> NT **Atlas (Missile)**
> **Intercontinental ballistic missiles**

Balloons **629.133**
> Use for materials on aircraft held aloft by hot air or light gases that are nondirigible and propelled only by the wind. Materials on self-propelled aircraft that are lighter than air and steerable are entered under **Airships.**
> UF Aircraft
> BT **Aeronautics**
> RT **Airships**

Balloons, Dirigible
> USE **Airships**

Ballot
> USE **Elections**

Ballparks
> USE **Stadiums**

Band music **784**
> BT **Instrumental music**
> **Military music**

Bandages **616.02**
> UF Bandages and bandaging
> BT **First aid**

Bandages and bandaging
> USE **Bandages**

Bandits
> USE **Thieves**

Bandmasters
> USE **Conductors (Music)**

Bands (Music) **784**
> SA types of bands and names of individual bands [to be added as needed]
> NT **Drum majoring**
> **Instrumentation and orchestration**
> RT **Conducting**
> **Orchestra**

Bank credit cards
> USE **Credit cards**

Bank debit cards
> USE **Debit cards**

Bank failures (May subdiv. geog.) **332.1**
> UF Failure of banks
> BT **Bankruptcy**
> **Banks and banking**
> **Business failures**

Banking
> USE **Banks and banking**

Bankruptcy (May subdiv. geog.) **332.7; 336.3; 346.07**
> UF Business mortality
> Failure in business
> Insolvency
> BT **Business failures**
> **Commercial law**
> **Debtor and creditor**
> **Finance**
> NT **Bank failures**

Banks and banking (May subdiv. geog.) **332.1**
> UF Banking
> Savings banks
> SA names of individual banks [to be added as needed]
> BT **Business**
> **Capital**
> **Commerce**
> **Finance**
> NT **Agricultural credit**
> **Bank failures**
> **Consumer credit**
> **Cooperative banks**
> **Debit cards**
> **Federal Reserve banks**
> **Foreign exchange**

Banks and banking—*Continued*
        Interest (Economics)
        Investments
        Negotiable instruments
        Savings and loan associations
  RT **Credit**
        Money
        Trust companies
Banks and banking, Cooperative
  USE **Cooperative banks**
Banks and banking—Credit cards
  USE **Credit cards**
Banks and banking—Data processing
    332.10285
  BT **Data processing**
Banks and banking—United States
    332.10973
Banned books
  USE **Books—Censorship**
Banners
  USE **Flags**
Banquets
  USE **Dining**
        Dinners
Baptism **234; 265**
  UF Christening
  BT **Sacraments**
Baptists **286**
  BT **Christian sects**
Bar
  USE **Lawyers**
Barbary States
  USE **North Africa**
Barbecue cookery
  USE **Barbecue cooking**
Barbecue cooking **641.7**
  UF Barbecue cookery
        Grill cooking
  BT **Outdoor cooking**
Barbering
  USE **Hair**
Bargaining
  USE **Negotiation**
Barns **631.2; 728**
  BT **Farm buildings**
Barometers **551.5; 681**
  BT **Meteorological instruments**
Baroque architecture (May subdiv. geog.)
    724
  UF Architecture, Baroque
  BT **Architecture**

Baroque art (May subdiv. geog.) **709.03**
  UF Art, Baroque
  BT **Art**
Barrier free design
  USE **Architecture and the handi-**
        capped
Barristers
  USE **Lawyers**
Barrooms
  USE **Bars**
Barrows
  USE **Mounds and mound builders**
Bars (May subdiv. geog.) **647.95**
    Use for materials on public drinking estab-
lishments.
  UF Barrooms
        Pubs
        Restaurants, bars, etc.
        Saloons
        Taverns
  BT **Liquor industry**
  RT **Restaurants**
Barter (May subdiv. geog.) **332**
  UF Exchange, Barter
  BT **Commerce**
        Economics
        Money
        Subsistence economy
        Underground economy
Basal readers **372.41; 418**
    Use for readers providing controlled vocab-
ulary in a series of books intended to be read
sequentially and for materials about such read-
ers.
  UF English language—Basal readers
  BT **Reading materials**
Baseball (May subdiv. geog.) **796.357**
  BT **Ball games**
        Sports
  NT **Baseball teams**
        Little League baseball
        Softball
  RT **Baseball players**
Baseball cards **769**
  BT **Sports cards**
Baseball clubs
  USE **Baseball teams**
Baseball—Fiction **808.83; 813, etc.**
    Use for collections of baseball stories.
  UF Baseball stories

Baseball players (May subdiv. geog.)
    796.357; 920
  BT **Athletes**
  RT **Baseball**
Baseball stories
  USE **Baseball—Fiction**
Baseball teams (May subdiv. geog.)
    796.35706
  UF Baseball clubs
  SA names of individual baseball
      teams [to be added as need-
      ed]
  BT **Baseball**
  NT **Houston Astros (Baseball
      team)**
Basements 721
  UF Cellars
  BT **Foundations
      Underground architecture**
Bases (Chemistry) 546; 661
  BT **Chemistry**
Bashfulness
  USE **Shyness**
Basic education (May subdiv. geog.)
    370.11
  UF Basic skills education
      Fundamental education
  BT **Education**
Basic life skills
  USE **Life skills**
Basic rights
  USE **Civil rights
      Human rights**
Basic skills education
  USE **Basic education**
Basket making 746.41
  BT **Weaving**
Basketball (May subdiv. geog.) **796.323**
  BT **Ball games
      Sports**
Bastogne, Battle of
  USE **Ardennes, Battle of the, 1944-
      1945**
Baths 613; 615.8
  BT **Cleanliness
      Hygiene
      Physical therapy**
  RT **Hydrotherapy**
Bathyscaphe 387.2; 623.8
  BT **Oceanography—Research
      Submersibles**

Batik 746.6
  BT **Dyes and dyeing**
Baton twirling 791.6
  RT **Drum majoring**
Bats 599.4
  BT **Mammals**
Battered elderly
  USE **Elderly abuse**
Battered wives
  USE **Abused women**
Battered women
  USE **Abused women**
Batteries, Electric
  USE **Electric batteries
      Storage batteries**
Batteries, Solar
  USE **Solar batteries**
Battering of wives
  USE **Wife abuse**
Battle of the Bulge
  USE **Ardennes, Battle of the, 1944-
      1945**
Battle ships
  USE **Warships**
Battle songs
  USE **War songs**
Battlefields (May subdiv. geog.) **904**
  UF Battlegrounds
  SA names of wars with the subdivi-
      sion *Battlefields,* e.g. **World
      War, 1939-1945—Battle-
      fields;** and names of individu-
      al battlefields [to be added as
      needed]
  BT **Battles**
Battlegrounds
  USE **Battlefields**
Battles (May subdiv. geog.) **355.4; 909;
    930-990**
  UF Fighting
      Sieges
  SA names of wars with the subdivi-
      sion *Campaigns,* e.g. **United
      States—History—1861-1865,
      Civil War—Campaigns;** and
      names of individual battles,
      e.g. **Ardennes, Battle of the,
      1944-1945** [to be added as
      needed]
  BT **Military art and science
      Military history**

Battles—*Continued*
  War
 NT **Battlefields**
   Naval battles
Battleships
 USE **Warships**
Bay of Pigs invasion
 USE **Cuba—History—1961, Invasion**
Bazaars
 USE **Fairs**
Beaches (May subdiv. geog.) **551.45**
 BT **Seashore**
Beadwork **746.5**
 BT **Crocheting**
   Embroidery
   Weaving
Bearings (Machinery) **621.8**
 UF Ball bearings
 BT **Machinery**
 RT **Lubrication and lubricants**
Beasts
 USE **Animals**
Beat generation **810.9**
 UF Beatniks
   Beats
 BT **American literature**
   Bohemianism
Beatniks
 USE **Beat generation**
Beats
 USE **Beat generation**
Beautification of landscape
 USE **Landscape protection**
Beauty
 USE **Aesthetics**
Beauty parlors
 USE **Beauty shops**
Beauty, Personal
 USE **Personal appearance**
   Personal grooming
Beauty salons
 USE **Beauty shops**
Beauty shops **646.7**
 UF Beauty parlors
   Beauty salons
 BT **Business enterprises**
 NT **Cosmetics**
Beavers **599.37**
 BT **Furbearing animals**
   Mammals
Beavers—Habitations **599.37**

Bed and breakfast accommodations (May subdiv. geog.) **647.94**
 UF B and B accommodations
 BT **Hotels and motels**
Bedouins (May subdiv. geog.) **305.892; 909**
 BT **Arabs**
Bedspreads **643; 746.9**
 UF Coverlets
 BT **Interior design**
Bedtime **306.4; 392.3**
 UF Getting ready for bed
 BT **Night**
   Sleep
 NT **Lullabies**
Bee culture
 USE **Beekeeping**
Bee hives
 USE **Beehives**
Bee houses
 USE **Beehives**
Beef **641.3; 664**
 BT **Meat**
Beef cattle **636.2**
 UF Steers
 SA names of breeds of beef cattle
   [to be added as needed]
 BT **Cattle**
 NT **Hereford cattle**
Beehives **638**
 UF Bee hives
   Bee houses
   Bees—Housing
 BT **Animal housing**
 RT **Beekeeping**
Beekeeping **638**
 UF Apiculture
   Bee culture
   Honeybee culture
 BT **Agriculture**
 RT **Beehives**
   Bees
Bees **595.79; 638**
 BT **Insects**
 RT **Beekeeping**
   Honey
Bees—Housing
 USE **Beehives**
Begging **362.5**
 UF Mendicancy
   Panhandling

Begging—*Continued*
　BT　**Poor**
　RT　**Tramps**
Beginning reading materials
　USE　**Easy reading materials**
Behavior
　USE　**Animal behavior**
　　　Human behavior
　　　and types of specific behavior,
　　　e.g. **Sexual behavior;** and
　　　types of animals with the
　　　subdivision *Behavior,* e.g.
　　　Birds—Behavior [to be add-
　　　ed as needed]
Behavior genetics　155.7
　UF　Psychogenetics
　BT　**Genetics**
　　　Psychology
Behavior, Helping
　USE　**Helping behavior**
Behavior modification　153.8
　BT　**Applied psychology**
　　　Human behavior
　　　Psychology of learning
　NT　**Brainwashing**
　　　Twelve-step programs
Behavior problems (Children)
　USE　**Emotionally disturbed children**
Behavioral psychology
　USE　**Psychophysiology**
Behaviorism　150.19
　Use for materials on empirical psychology
　dealing with the observable actions of organ-
　isms rather than with mental phenomena.
　UF　Behavioristic psychology
　　　Interbehaviorial psychology
　BT　**Human behavior**
　　　Psychology
　　　Psychophysiology
Behavioristic psychology
　USE　**Behaviorism**
Beijing Massacre, 1989
　USE　**Tiananmen Square Incident,**
　　　Beijing (China), 1989
Belief and doubt　121
　Use for materials on belief and doubt from
　the philosophical standpoint. Materials on reli-
　gious belief and doubt are entered under
　Faith.
　UF　Doubt
　BT　**Philosophy**
　　　Theory of knowledge

　NT　**Truth**
　RT　**Agnosticism**
　　　Faith
　　　Rationalism
　　　Skepticism
Bell System Telstar satellite
　USE　**Telstar project**
Belles lettres
　USE　**Literature**
Bells　786.8
　UF　Carillons
　　　Chimes
　　　Church bells
　BT　**Musical instruments**
Belts and belting　621.8
　UF　Chain belting
　BT　**Machinery**
　RT　**Power transmission**
Beneficial insects　591.6
　UF　Helpful insects
　　　Useful insects
　SA　types of beneficial insects, e.g.
　　　Silkworms [to be added as
　　　needed]
　BT　**Economic zoology**
　　　Insects
　NT　**Silkworms**
Benefits, Employee
　USE　**Fringe benefits**
Benefits, Fringe
　USE　**Fringe benefits**
Benevolent institutions
　USE　**Institutional care**
Beowulf—Adaptations　829
Bequests
　USE　**Gifts**
　　　Inheritance and succession
　　　Wills
Bereavement　155.9; 248.8
　Use for materials on the suffering of those
　who have lost a loved one. Materials on men-
　tal suffering or sorrow from other causes, es-
　pecially loss or remorse, are entered under
　Grief.
　UF　Mourning
　　　Sorrow
　　　Sympathy
　BT　**Emotions**
　RT　**Consolation**
　　　Grief
Bermuda Triangle　001.9
　UF　Devil's Triangle
　BT　**Atlantic Ocean**

Berries   634
    SA   types of berries, e.g. **Strawber-**
          ries [to be added as needed],
          in the plural form
    BT   **Fruit**
          Fruit culture
    NT   **Strawberries**

Best-book lists
    USE   **Best books**

Best books   011

Use for lists of recommended books and materials about recommended books. Materials on the principles of book selection for libraries are entered under **Book selection.**

    UF   Best-book lists
          Bibliography—Best books
          Book lists
          Books and reading—Best books
          Choice of books
          Evaluation of literature
          Literature—Evaluation
    BT   **Books**
    RT   **Book selection**

Best sellers (Books)   028; 070.5
    UF   Books—Best sellers
    BT   **Books and reading**

Betting
    USE   **Gambling**

Bevel gearing
    USE   **Gearing**

Beverage industry (May subdiv. geog.)
    338.4
    SA   types of beverage industries, e.g.
          Coffee industry [to be added
          as needed]
    BT   **Food industry**
    NT   **Coffee industry**
          Liquor industry
          Tea industry

Beverages   613; 641.2; 641.8; 663
    UF   Drinks
    SA   types of beverages and names of
          specific beverages [to be add-
          ed as needed]
    BT   **Diet**
          Food
    NT   **Alcoholic beverages**
          Cocoa
          Coffee
          Liquors
          Tea

Bias attacks
    USE   **Hate crimes**
Bias crimes
    USE   **Hate crimes**
Bias (Psychology)
    USE   **Prejudices**

Bible   220

The subdivisions provided under **Bible** may also be used with any part of the Bible, with single books of the Bible, and with groups of books, e.g. **Bible. O.T.—Biography; Bible. O.T. Pentateuch—Commentaries; Bible. O.T. Psalms—History; Bible. N.T. Gospels—Inspiration;** etc.

    UF   Holy Scriptures
          Scriptures, Holy
    BT   **Ancient history**
          Hebrew literature
          Jewish literature
          Sacred books
    NT   **Bible stories**

Bible and science   220.8
    UF   Bible—Science
          Science and the Bible
    BT   **Religion and science**
          Science
    RT   **Creationism**

Bible—Animals
    USE   **Bible—Natural history**

Bible—Antiquities   220.9
    UF   Biblical archeology
    BT   **Antiquities**
          Archeology
    NT   **Christian antiquities**

Bible as literature   809
    UF   Bible—Language, style, etc.
          Bible—Literary character
    NT   **Bible—Criticism**
          Bible—Parables
    RT   **Religious literature**

Bible—Astronomy   220.8
    BT   **Astronomy**

Bible—Biography   220.92
    UF   Biblical characters
    BT   **Biography**
    NT   **Women in the Bible**

Bible—Birds
    USE   **Bible—Natural history**
Bible—Botany
    USE   **Bible—Natural history**
Bible—Catechism, question books
    USE   **Bible—Catechisms**

Bible—Catechisms   220
    UF   Bible—Catechism, question
             books *[Former heading]*
           Bible—Question books
    BT   **Bible—Study and teaching**
           Catechisms

Bible—Chronology   220.9
    Use for materials on the dates of events related in the Bible and their correlation with the dates of general history.
    UF   Bible—History of biblical
             events—Chronology
           Chronology, Biblical
    BT   **Chronology**

Bible classes
    USE **Bible—Study and teaching**
          Religious summer schools
          Sunday schools

Bible—Commentaries   220.7
    UF   Bible—Interpretation
           Commentaries, Biblical

Bible—Concordances   220.3
    Use for works that list the words of the Bible and give the passages where each word occurs. Works that list topics or names found in the Bible and give the passages where those topics or names rather than exact words are found are entered under **Bible—Indexes.**

Bible—Cosmology
    USE **Biblical cosmology**

Bible—Criticism   220.6
    UF   Bible—Criticism, interpretation,
             etc.
           Bible—Exegesis
           Bible—Hermeneutics
           Bible—Interpretation
           Exegesis, Biblical
           Hermeneutics, Biblical
           Higher criticism
    BT   **Bible as literature**

Bible—Criticism, interpretation, etc.
    USE **Bible—Criticism**

Bible—Dictionaries   220.3
    BT   **Encyclopedias and dictionaries**

Bible—Drama
    USE **Bible plays**

Bible—Evidences, authority, etc.   220.1
    Use for materials that attempt to establish the truth of statements in the Bible or the authority of its precepts. Materials on the divine inspiration of the Bible are entered under **Bible—Inspiration.**
    UF   Evidences of the Bible
    BT   **Bible—Inspiration**

Bible—Exegesis
    USE **Bible—Criticism**

Bible fiction   808.83; 813, etc.
    May be used for individual works, collections, or materials about imaginative fiction in which characters and settings are taken from the Bible. Stories that are retold or adapted from the Bible while remaining faithful to the original are entered under **Bible stories.**
    UF   Bible—History of biblical
             events—Fiction
    SA   names of biblical characters with
             the subdivision *Fiction* [to be
             added as needed]
    BT   **Fiction**
    RT   **Bible stories**

Bible films   791.43
    May be used for individual works, collections, or materials about bible films.
    UF   Biblical films
    BT   **Motion pictures**
    RT   **Bible plays**

Bible—Flowers
    USE **Bible—Natural history**

Bible—Gardens
    USE **Bible—Natural history**

Bible—Geography   220.91
    UF   Bible—Maps
           Biblical geography
    BT   **Atlases**
          Geography

Bible—Hermeneutics
    USE **Bible—Criticism**

Bible—History   220.9
    Use for materials on the origin, authorship, and composition of the Bible as a book. Materials on historical events as described in the Bible are entered under **Bible—History of biblical events.**

Bible—History of biblical events   220.9
    Use for materials on historical events as described in the Bible. Materials on the origin, authorship, and composition of the Bible as a book are entered under **Bible—History.**
    UF   History, Biblical

Bible—History of biblical events—Chronology
    USE **Bible—Chronology**

Bible—History of biblical events—Fiction
    USE **Bible fiction**

Bible—Illustrations
    USE **Bible—Pictorial works**

Bible in literature   809
    Use for materials that discuss the Bible as a theme in literature.

Bible in literature—*Continued*
 BT Literature
 RT Religion in literature
Bible in the schools
 USE Religion in the public schools
Bible—Indexes 220.3
 Use for works that list topics or names found in the Bible and give the passages where those topics or names rather than exact words are found. Works that list the words of the Bible and give the passages where the exact word occurs are entered under Bible—Concordances.
Bible—Inspiration 220.1
 Use for materials on the divine inspiration of the Bible. Materials that attempt to establish the truth of statements in the Bible or the authority of its precepts are entered under Bible—Evidence, authority, etc.
 UF Inspiration, Biblical
 NT Bible—Evidences, authority, etc.
Bible—Interpretation
 USE Bible—Commentaries
  Bible—Criticism
Bible—Introductions
 USE Bible—Study and teaching
Bible—Language, style, etc.
 USE Bible as literature
Bible—Literary character
 USE Bible as literature
Bible—Maps
 USE Bible—Geography
Bible. N.T. 225
 Use same subdivisions as those given under Bible. They may also be used for groups of books, e.g. Bible. N.T. Gospels—Inspiration; and for single books, e.g. Bible. N.T. Matthew—Commentaries.
 UF New Testament
Bible—Natural history 220.8
 UF Bible—Animals
  Bible—Birds
  Bible—Botany
  Bible—Flowers
  Bible—Gardens
  Bible—Plants
  Bible—Zoology
  Botany of the Bible
  Nature in the bible
  Zoology of the Bible
 BT Natural history
Bible. O.T. 221
 Use same subdivisions as those given under Bible. They may also be used for groups of

books, e.g. Bible. O.T. Pentateuch—Commentaries; and for single books, e.g. Bible. O.T. Psalms—History.
 UF Old Testament
 NT Ten commandments
Bible—Parables 226.8
 BT Bible as literature
  Parables
 NT Jesus Christ—Parables
Bible—Pictorial works 220.022
 UF Bible—Illustrations
 RT Jesus Christ—Art
Bible—Plants
 USE Bible—Natural history
Bible plays 808.82; 812, etc.
 May be used for individual plays, collections, or materials about dramatizations of biblical events.
 UF Bible—Drama
  Biblical plays
  Plays, Bible
 SA names of biblical characters with the subdivision *Drama* [to be added as needed]
 BT Religious drama
 NT Mysteries and miracle plays
  Passion plays
 RT Bible films
Bible—Prophecies 220.1
 UF Prophecies (Bible)
 NT Jesus Christ—Prophecies
Bible—Psychology 220.8
 UF Biblical psychology
 BT Psychology
Bible—Question books
 USE Bible—Catechisms
Bible—Reading 220.5
 BT Books and reading
Bible—Science
 USE Bible and science
Bible stories 220.9
 May be used for individual works, collections, or materials about stories that are retold or adapted from the Bible while remaining faithful to the original. Imaginative fiction in which characters and settings are taken from the Bible is entered under Bible fiction.
 UF Stories
 BT Bible
 RT Bible fiction
Bible—Study
 USE Bible—Study and teaching

Bible—Study and teaching   220.07
   UF   Bible classes
        Bible—Introductions
        Bible—Study
   BT   **Christian education**
        Sunday schools
   NT   **Bible—Catechisms**
Bible—Use   220.6
   Use for materials that show how the Bible is used as a guide to living, to cultivation of a spiritual life, and to problems of doctrine.
Bible—Versions   220.4; 220.5
   Use for materials on the various versions and translations of the Bible.
Bible—Women
   USE   **Women in the Bible**
Bible—Zoology
   USE   **Bible—Natural history**
Biblical archeology
   USE   **Bible—Antiquities**
Biblical characters
   USE   **Bible—Biography**
Biblical cosmology   231.7; 291.2; 296.3
   UF   Bible—Cosmology
   BT   **Cosmology**
   RT   **Creation**
Biblical films
   USE   **Bible films**
Biblical geography
   USE   **Bible—Geography**
Biblical plays
   USE   **Bible plays**
Biblical psychology
   USE   **Bible—Psychology**
Biblical teaching
   USE   religious or secular topics with the subdivision *Biblical teaching,* e.g. **Salvation—Biblical teaching; Family—Biblical teaching;** etc. [to be added as needed]
Bibliographic control   025.3
   UF   Universal bibliographic control
   BT   **Documentation**
   NT   **Cataloging**
        Indexing
        Information systems
        MARC formats
Bibliographic data in machine readable form
   USE   **Machine readable bibliographic data**

Bibliographic instruction   025.5
   Use for materials on the instruction of readers in library use. Materials on the education of librarians are entered under **Library education.**
   UF   Library instruction
        Library orientation
        Library skills
        Library user orientation
   BT   **Library services**
Bibliography   010
   SA   subjects and names of persons and places with the subdivision *Bibliography,* e.g. **Agriculture—Bibliography; Shakespeare, William, 1564-1616—Bibliography; United States—Bibliography;** etc. [to be added as needed]
   BT   **Documentation**
   NT   **Archives**
        Editions
        Indexes
        Indexing
        Manuscripts
        Printing
        Reference books
        Serial publications
   RT   **Books**
        Cataloging
        Library science
Bibliography—Best books
   USE   **Best books**
Bibliography—Bilingual books
   USE   **Bilingual books**
Bibliography—Editions
   USE   **Editions**
Bibliography—First editions
   USE   **First editions**
Bibliography—Rare books
   USE   **Rare books**
Bibliography—Reprint editions
   USE   **Reprints (Publications)**
Bibliomania
   USE   **Book collecting**
Bibliophily
   USE   **Book collecting**
Bicentennial celebrations—United States—1976
   USE   **American Revolution Bicentennial, 1776-1976**

Biculturalism (May subdiv. geog.)
   306.44

   Use for materials on the presence of two distinct cultures within a single country or region. Materials on the coexistence of several distinct ethnic, religious, or cultural groups within one society are entered under **Pluralism (Social sciences)**. Materials on policies or programs that foster the preservation of various cultures or cultural identities within a unified society are entered under **Multiculturalism**

   BT   **Pluralism (Social sciences)**
   RT   **Multiculturalism**

Biculturalism—United States   306.44
Bicycle camping
   USE   **Bicycle touring**
Bicycle racing (May subdiv. geog.)
   796.6
   BT   **Cycling**
        Racing
   RT   **Bicycle touring**
        Bicycles
Bicycle touring (May subdiv. geog.)
   796.6
   UF   Backpack cycling
        Bicycle camping
        Touring, Bicycle
   BT   **Camping**
        Cycling
        Travel
   RT   **Bicycle racing**
        Bicycles
Bicycles   629.227
   UF   Bicycles and bicycling
        Bikes
   BT   **Vehicles**
   NT   **Minibikes**
        Motorcycles
        Mountain bikes
   RT   **Bicycle racing**
        Bicycle touring
        Cycling
Bicycles and bicycling
   USE   **Bicycles**
        Cycling
Bicycling
   USE   **Cycling**
Big bang cosmology
   USE   **Big bang theory**
Big bang theory   523.1
   UF   Big bang cosmology
   BT   **Cosmology**

Big books   372.41

   Use for books produced in an oversize format and intended for use in shared-reading learning experiences or for materials about such books.

   UF   Enlarged texts for shared reading
        Oversize books
        Oversized books for shared reading
        Shared reading books
   BT   **Children's literature**
        Reading materials
   RT   **Large print books**
Big foot
   USE   **Sasquatch**
Bigfoot
   USE   **Sasquatch**
Bigotry
   USE   **Prejudices**
        Toleration
Bigotry-motivated crimes
   USE   **Hate crimes**
Bikes
   USE   **Bicycles**
Biking
   USE   **Cycling**
Bildungsromans   808.3

   May be used for individual works, collections, or materials about fiction in which the theme is the development of a character from youth to adulthood.

   UF   Apprenticeship novels
        Coming of age stories
   BT   **Fiction**
Bilingual books   002; 011

   Use for materials about bilingual books. As a form heading for the bilingual materials themselves, use this heading subdivided by the languages, e.g. **Bilingual books—English-Spanish.**

   UF   Bibliography—Bilingual books
        Books—Bilingual editions
   BT   **Books**
        Editions
Bilingual books—English-Spanish

   Use as a form heading for bilingual materials in English and Spanish.

   UF   Bilingual books—Spanish-English
Bilingual books—Spanish-English
   USE   **Bilingual books—English-Spanish**

Bilingual education (May subdiv. geog.)
  370.117
  UF Education, Bilingual
  BT **Bilingualism**
      Multicultural education
Bilingualism (May subdiv. geog.)
  306.44; 400
  BT **Language and languages**
  NT **Bilingual education**
Bilingualism—United States 306.44;
  420
Bill collecting
  USE **Collecting of accounts**
Bill of rights (U.S.)
  USE **United States. Constitution.**
        1st-10th amendments
Billboards
  USE **Signs and signboards**
Bills and notes
  USE **Negotiable instruments**
Bills of credit
  USE **Credit**
        Negotiable instruments
Bills of fare
  USE **Menus**
Binary system (Mathematics) 513.5
  UF Pair system
  BT **Mathematics**
      Numbers
Binding of books
  USE **Bookbinding**
Binge eating behavior
  USE **Bulimia**
Binge-purge behavior
  USE **Bulimia**
Bio-bibliography
  USE subjects, groups and classes of
        persons, names of places, and
        names of individual persons
        with the subdivision *Bio-*
        bibliography, e.g. **English lit-**
        erature—Bio-bibliography;
        United States—Bio-
        bibliography; etc. [to be add-
        ed as needed]
Bioastronautics
  USE **Space medicine**
Biochemistry 572
  UF Biological chemistry
      Physiological chemistry

  BT **Biology**
      Chemistry
      Medicine
  NT **Clinical chemistry**
      Metabolism
      Molecular biology
      Nucleic acids
      Proteins
      Steroids
Bioconversion
  USE **Biomass energy**
Biodiversity
  USE **Biological diversity**
Bioethics 174
  UF Biological ethics
      Biology—Ethical aspects
      Biomedical ethics
      Life sciences ethics
  BT **Ethics**
  NT **Medical ethics**
      Transplantation of organs, tis-
      sues, etc.—Ethical aspects
Biofeedback training 152.1
  UF Visceral learning
  BT **Feedback (Psychology)**
      Mind and body
      Psychology of learning
      Psychotherapy
Biogeography (May subdiv. geog.)
  578.09
  Use for materials on the geographical distri-
  bution of animals and plants collectively or of
  animals only. Materials on the geographical
  distribution of plants are entered under
  Plants—Geographical distribution.
  UF Distribution of animals and
        plants
        Geographical distribution of ani-
        mals and plants
  SA types of plants and animals with
        the subdivision *Geographical*
        distribution, e.g. **Fishes—Geo-**
        graphical distribution [to be
        added as needed]
  BT **Ecology**
      Geography
  NT **Fishes—Geographical distribu-**
      tion
      Plants—Geographical distribu-
      tion
  RT **Natural history**
Biographical dictionaries
  USE **Biography—Dictionaries**

Biographical fiction   808.83; 813, etc.

May be used for individual works, collections, or materials about fictionalized accounts of the lives of real persons.

UF   Biographical novels

SA   names of real persons with the subdivision *Fiction,* e.g. **Napoleon I, Emperor of the French, 1769-1821—Fiction;** or *In literature,* e.g. **Napoleon I, Emperor of the French, 1769-1821—In literature;** [to be added as needed]

BT   **Fiction**

NT   **Autobiographical fiction**

RT   **Historical fiction**

Biographical films   791.43

May be used for individual works, collections, or materials about films depicting the lives of real persons.

BT   **Motion pictures**

Biographical novels

USE   **Biographical fiction**

Biographical radio programs   791.44

May be used for individual works, collections, or materials about radio programs recounting the lives of real persons.

BT   **Radio programs**

Biographical television programs 791.45

May be used for individual works, collections, or materials about television programs depicting the lives of real persons.

BT   **Television programs**

Biography   920

Use for collections of biographies not limited to one country or to one group or class of persons. Materials on the writing of biography are entered under **Biography as a literary form.**

UF   Life histories

Memoirs

Personal narratives

SA   subjects and names of places and corporate bodies with the subdivision *Biography;* ethnic groups and classes of persons with the subdivision *Biography* or *Correspondence;* and names of diseases, events, and wars with the subdivision *Personal narratives* [to be added as needed]

BT   **History**

NT   **Autobiographies**

Autographs

Bible—Biography

Blacks—Biography

Chicago (Ill.)—Biography

Christian biography

Epitaphs

Greece—Biography

Medicine—Biography

Men—Biography

Motion pictures—Biography

Musicians—Biography

Obituaries

Ohio—Biography

Portraits

Religious biography

Rome—Biography

United States. Army—Biography

United States—Biography

United States—History—1861-1865, Civil War—Biography

United States—History—1861-1865, Civil War—Personal narratives

United States. Navy—Biography

United States. Supreme Court—Biography

Women—Biography

World War, 1939-1945—Biography

World War, 1939-1945—Personal narratives

RT   **Genealogy**

Biography (as a literary form)

USE   **Biography as a literary form**

Biography as a literary form   809

Use for materials on the writing of biography.

UF   Biography (as a literary form)

Biography—History and criticism

Biography—Technique

BT   **Authorship**

Literature

NT   **Autobiography**

Biography—Dictionaries   920.02

Use for collections of biographies in dictionary form not limited to one group or class of persons.

Biography—Dictionaries—*Continued*
  UF   Biographical dictionaries
       Dictionaries, Biographical
  SA   subjects, groups or classes of
       persons, and names of places
       with the subdivisions *Biogra-
       phy—Dictionaries,* e.g. **Wom-
       en—Biography—Dictionaries;
       United States—Biography—
       Dictionaries;** etc. [to be add-
       ed as needed]
  BT   **Encyclopedias and dictionaries**
Biography—History and criticism
  USE **Biography as a literary form**
Biography—Technique
  USE **Biography as a literary form**
Biological anthropology
  USE **Physical anthropology**
Biological chemistry
  USE **Biochemistry**
Biological clocks
  USE **Biological rhythms**
Biological diversification
  USE **Biological diversity**
Biological diversity (May subdiv. geog.)
       333.95
  Use for materials on the variety and vari-
  ability among living organisms and the eco-
  logical complexes in which they occur,
  including ecosystem diversity, species diversi-
  ty, and genetic diversity.
  UF   Biodiversity
       Biological diversification
       Diversity, Biological
  BT   **Biology**
  RT   **Ecology**
Biological diversity conservation (May
       subdiv. geog.)   333.95
  UF   Conservation of biological diver-
       sity
       Maintenance of biological diver-
       sity
       Preservation of biological diver-
       sity
  BT   **Conservation of natural re-
       sources**
Biological ethics
  USE **Bioethics**
Biological form
  USE **Morphology**
Biological parents
  USE **Birthparents**

Biological physics
  USE **Biophysics**
Biological rhythms   571.7
  UF   Biological clocks
       Biology—Periodicity
       Biorhythms
  BT   **Cycles**
  NT   **Jet lag**
Biological structure
  USE **Morphology**
Biological warfare (May subdiv. geog.)
       358; 623.4
  UF   Bacterial warfare
       Germ warfare
  BT   **Military art and science
       Tactics**
Biologists (May subdiv. geog.)   **570.92;
       920**
  BT   **Naturalists
       Scientists**
Biology   570
  BT   **Life sciences
       Science**
  NT   **Adaptation (Biology)
       Anatomy
       Biochemistry
       Biological diversity
       Biomathematics
       Biophysics
       Botany
       Cells
       Cryobiology
       Death
       Ecology
       Embryology
       Fossils
       Freshwater biology
       Gaia hypothesis
       Genetics
       Heredity
       Life (Biology)
       Life cycles (Biology)
       Marine biology
       Microbiology
       Physiology
       Protoplasm
       Radiobiology
       Reproduction
       Sex (Biology)
       Space biology
       Symbiosis**

Biology—*Continued*
      Variation (Biology)
      Zoology
  RT **Evolution**
Biology—Ecology
  USE **Ecology**
Biology—Ethical aspects
  USE **Bioethics**
Biology, Molecular
  USE **Molecular biology**
Biology—Periodicity
  USE **Biological rhythms**
Biology—Social aspects
  USE **Sociobiology**
Bioluminescence   572
  UF Animal light
      Animal luminescence
      Light production in animals
  BT **Luminescence**
Biomass energy   333.95
   Use for materials on organic matter that can be converted to fuel and is therefore regarded as a potential energy source.
  UF Bioconversion
      Energy, Biomass
      Energy conversion, Microbial
      Microbial energy conversion
  SA types of matter as fuels, e.g.
      Waste products as fuel [to be added as needed]
  BT **Energy resources**
      Fuel
  RT **Waste products as fuel**
Biomathematics   570.1
  BT **Biology**
      Mathematics
Biomechanics
  USE **Human engineering**
      Human locomotion
Biomedical ethics
  USE **Bioethics**
Bionics   003
   Use for materials on the science of technological systems that function in the manner of living systems.
  BT **Biophysics**
      Cybernetics
      Systems engineering
Biophysics   571.4
  UF Biological physics
  BT **Biology**
      Physics

  NT **Bionics**
      Molecular biology
      Radiobiology
Biorhythms
  USE **Biological rhythms**
Biosciences
  USE **Life sciences**
Biotechnology   620.8; 660.6
   Use for materials on the application of living organisms or their biological systems or processes to the manufacture of products.
  BT **Chemical engineering**
      Microbiology
  NT **Reproductive technology**
  RT **Genetic engineering**
Bipolar depression
  USE **Manic-depressive illness**
Bipolar disorder
  USE **Manic-depressive illness**
Bird decoys (Hunting)
  USE **Decoys (Hunting)**
Bird eggs
  USE **Birds—Eggs**
Bird houses
  USE **Birdhouses**
Bird photography
  USE **Photography of birds**
Bird song
  USE **Birdsongs**
Bird watching   598.07
  BT **Natural history**
Birdbanding   598.07
  UF Birds—Banding
      Birds—Marking
  BT **Wildlife conservation**
Birdhouses   690
  UF Bird houses
  BT **Animal housing**
Birds (May subdiv. geog.)   **598**
  SA types of birds, e.g. **Birds of prey; Canaries;** etc. [to be added as needed]
  BT **Animals**
  NT **Birds of prey**
      Cage birds
      Canaries
      Ducks
      Eagles
      Game and game birds
      Geese
      Peacocks
      Pheasants

Birds—*Continued*
 Poultry
 Robins
 State birds
 Terns
 Turkeys
 Water birds
Birds—Anatomy   598
 BT Anatomy
Birds—Banding
 USE Birdbanding
Birds—Behavior   598.15
 UF Birds—Habits and behavior
 BT Animal behavior
Birds—Collection and preservation
  598.075
 BT Zoological specimens—Collection and preservation
Birds—Color   598.147
 BT Color
Birds—Eggs   598.14
 UF Bird eggs
  Birds' eggs
  Birds—Eggs and nests
 BT Eggs
Birds' eggs
 USE Birds—Eggs
Birds—Eggs and nests
 USE Birds—Eggs
  Birds—Nests
Birds—Flight   591.5; 598.15
 BT Animal flight
Birds—Habits and behavior
 USE Birds—Behavior
Birds—Marking
 USE Birdbanding
Birds—Migration   598.156
 UF Migration of birds
Birds—Nests   598.156
 UF Birds—Eggs and nests
  Birds' nests
Birds' nests
 USE Birds—Nests
Birds of prey   598.9
 SA names of specific birds of prey
  [to be added as needed]
 BT Birds
  Predatory animals
 NT Eagles
Birds—Photography
 USE Photography of birds

Birds—Protection   333.95; 639.9
 UF Protection of birds
 BT Wildlife conservation
 RT Game protection
Birds—Song
 USE Birdsongs
Birds—United States   598.0973
Birdsongs   598.159
 UF Bird song
  Birds—Song
 BT Animal sounds
Birth
 USE Childbirth
Birth attendants
 USE Midwives
Birth control (May subdiv. geog.)
  353.5; 363.9; 613.9
 UF Conception—Prevention
  Contraception
  Family planning
  Fertility control
  Planned parenthood
 BT Population
  Sexual hygiene
 NT Sterilization (Birth control)
 RT Birth rate
  Childlessness
  Family size
  Human fertility
  Infertility
Birth control—Ethical aspects   176
 UF Birth control—Moral and religious aspects
 BT Ethics
Birth control—Moral and religious aspects
 USE Birth control—Ethical aspects
  Birth control—Religious aspects
Birth control—Religious aspects   248.4;
  291.5
 UF Birth control—Moral and religious aspects
Birth customs
 USE Childbirth
Birth defects   616
 UF Abnormalities, Human
  Birth injuries
  Deformities
  Human abnormalities
  Infants—Birth defects
  Malformations, Congenital

Birth defects—*Continued*
   BT   **Medical genetics**
          Pathology
   RT   **Growth disorders**
Birth injuries
   USE   **Birth defects**
Birth, Multiple
   USE   **Multiple birth**
Birth order   **306.87**
   UF   Firstborn child
          Middle child
          Oldest child
          Sibling sequence
          Youngest child
   BT   **Children**
          Family
Birth rate (May subdiv. geog.)   **304.6**
   UF   Birthrate
   BT   **Vital statistics**
   NT   **Human fertility**
   RT   **Birth control**
          Population
Birth records
   USE   **Registers of births, etc.**
Birthday books
   USE   **Birthdays**
Birthdays   **394.2**
   UF   Anniversaries
          Birthday books
   BT   **Days**
Birthparents   **306.874**
   Use for materials on natural, i.e. biological, parents who relinquished their children for adoption.
   UF   Biological parents
          Natural parents
          Parents, Biological
   BT   **Parents**
   RT   **Adoptees**
Birthrate
   USE   **Birth rate**
Births, Registers of
   USE   **Registers of births, etc.**
Bison   **599.64; 636.2**
   UF   American bison
          Buffalo, American
   BT   **Mammals**
Black actors   **791.4; 792; 920**
   UF   Actors, Black
          Black actors and actresses
   BT   **Actors**
   NT   **African American actors**

Black actors and actresses
   USE   **Black actors**
Black Africa
   USE   **Sub-Saharan Africa**
Black Americans
   USE   **African Americans**
Black art (May subdiv. geog.)   **704.03**
   Use for materials on works of art by several Black artists. Materials on Blacks depicted in works of art are entered under **Blacks in art.**
   UF   Art, Black
          Blacks—Art
   BT   **Art**
   NT   **African American art**
   RT   **Black artists**
Black art (Magic)
   USE   **Magic**
          Witchcraft
Black artists (May subdiv. geog.)   **709.2; 920**
   Use for materials on several Black artists.
   UF   Artists, Black
   BT   **Artists**
   NT   **African American artists**
   RT   **Black art**
Black athletes (May subdiv. geog.)   **796.092; 920**
   UF   Athletes, Black
   BT   **Athletes**
   NT   **African American athletes**
Black authors   **809; 920**
   Use for collections and for materials on several Black authors not limited to a single national literature or literary form.
   UF   Authors, Black
   SA   names of national literatures other than American literature and forms of literature with the subdivision *Black authors,* e.g. **French literature—Black authors; French poetry—Black authors;** etc. [to be added as needed]
   BT   **Authors**
   NT   **African American authors**
Black business people
   USE   **Black businesspeople**
Black businesspeople (May subdiv. geog.)   **338.092; 658.0092; 920**
   UF   Black business people *[Former heading]*

Black businesspeople—*Continued*
- BT **Businesspeople**
- NT **African American businesspeople**

Black children (May subdiv. geog.)
305.23
- UF Blacks—Children
  Children, Black
- BT **Children**
- NT **African American children**

Black comedy (Literature)
- USE **Black humor (Literature)**

Black death
- USE **Plague**

Black folk songs
- USE **Black music**

Black folklore
- USE **Blacks—Folklore**

Black Hawk War, 1832   973.5
- BT **Native Americans—Wars**
  United States—History—1815-1861

Black holes (Astronomy)   523.8
- UF Frozen stars
- BT **Astronomy**
  Astrophysics
  Stars

Black humor (Literature)   808.7;
808.87; 813, etc.

May be used for individual works, collections, or materials about literary works characterized by a desperate, sardonic humor intended to induce laughter as the appropriate response to the apparent meaninglessness and absurdity of existence.
- UF Black comedy (Literature)
  Dark humor (Literature)
- BT **Fiction**
  Literature
  Wit and humor

Black lead
- USE **Graphite**

Black librarians   020.92; 920
- BT **Librarians**
- NT **African American librarians**

Black literature (American)
- USE **American literature—African American authors**

Black literature (French)
- USE **French literature—Black authors**

Black magic (Witchcraft)
- USE **Magic**
  Witchcraft

Black market (May subdiv. geog.)   381

Use for materials on illegal trade aimed at avoiding government regulations, such as fixed prices or rationing. Materials on goods and services that are produced and sold legally but not reported or taxed are entered under **Underground economy.**
- UF Grey market
- BT **Commerce**
- RT **Underground economy**

Black market children
- USE **Adoption—Corrupt practices**

Black music (May subdiv. geog.)
780.089

Use for general materials and for materials on the music of Blacks not in the United States. Materials on the music of African Americans are entered under **African American music.**
- UF Black folk songs
  Black songs
  Blacks—Music
  Blacks—Songs and music
- BT **Music**
- NT **African American music**
- RT **Black musicians**

Black musicians (May subdiv. geog.)
780.92; 920
- UF Musicians, Black
- BT **Musicians**
- NT **African American musicians**
- RT **Black music**

Black Muslims   297.8
- UF Nation of Islam
- BT **African Americans—Religion**
  Black nationalism
  Muslims—United States

Black nationalism   320.5
- UF Black separatism
  Nationalism, Black
  Separatism, Black
- BT **African Americans—Political activity**
  African Americans—Race identity
  Blacks—Political activity
  Blacks—Race identity
- NT **Black Muslims**
- RT **Black power**

Black poetry (American)
    USE **American poetry—African American authors**
Black poetry (French)
    USE **French poetry—Black authors**
Black power **322.4**
    BT **African Americans—Political activity**
          Blacks—Political activity
    RT **Black nationalism**
Black separatism
    USE **Black nationalism**
Black songs
    USE **Black music**
Black suffrage
    USE **Blacks—Suffrage**
Black women (May subdiv. geog.)
    305.48
    UF Women, Black
    BT **Women**
    NT **African American women**
Blackboard drawing
    USE **Chalk talks**
          Crayon drawing
Blackheads (Acne)
    USE **Acne**
Blackouts, Electric power
    USE **Electric power failures**
Blacks (May subdiv. geog. except U.S.)
    305.896

    Use for materials on the Black race in general or for materials on Blacks as an element in the population, especially in countries where they are a minority. Works on Black people in countries with a population predominantly Black are assigned headings appropriate for the country without the use of the heading **Blacks,** except when the works discuss Blacks as distinct from other groups in the country. Materials on Blacks in the United States are entered under **African Americans.**

    UF Negroes
    SA Blacks in various occupations and professions, e.g. **Black artists; Black librarians;** etc. [to be added as needed]
    NT **African Americans**
Blacks—Africa **305.896; 960**
    BT **Africans**
Blacks—Art
    USE **Black art**
Blacks—Biography **920**
    BT **Biography**
    NT **African Americans—Biography**

Blacks—Children
    USE **Black children**
Blacks—Civil rights (May subdiv. geog.)
    323.1; 342
    BT **Blacks—Political activity**
          Civil rights
    NT **African Americans—Civil rights**
Blacks—Economic conditions (May subdiv. geog.) **330.9**
    BT **Economic conditions**
    NT **African Americans—Economic conditions**
Blacks—Education (May subdiv. geog.)
    370.89; 371.829
    BT **Education**
    NT **African Americans—Education**
Blacks—Employment (May subdiv. geog.)
    331.6
    BT **Employment**
    NT **African Americans—Employment**
Blacks—Folklore **398**
    UF Black folklore
    BT **Folklore**
    NT **African Americans—Folklore**
Blacks—France **305.896; 944**
    UF France—Blacks
Blacks—Housing (May subdiv. geog.)
    307.3; 363.5
    BT **Housing**
    NT **African Americans—Housing**
Blacks in art **704.9**

    Use for materials on Blacks depicted in works of art. Materials on African Americans depicted in works of art are entered under **African Americans in art.** Materials on the attainments of several Blacks in the area of art are entered under **Black artists.** Materials on the attainments of several African Americans in the area of art are entered under **African American artists.** Materials on works of art by several Black artists are entered under **Black art.** Materials on works of art by several African American artists are entered under **African American art.**

    BT **Art—Themes**
Blacks in literature **809**

    Use for materials on the theme of Blacks in works of literature. Materials on the attainments of several Blacks in the area of literature are entered under **Black authors.** Materials on works of literature by several Black authors are entered under individual literatures and forms of literature with the subdivision *Black authors,* e.g. **French literature—Black**

Blacks in literature—*Continued*
   authors; French poetry—Black authors; etc.
   Materials on the theme of African Americans
   in works of literature are entered under
   African Americans in literature. Materials
   on the attainments of several African Americans in the area of literature are entered under
   African American authors. Materials on
   works of literature by several African
   American authors are entered under **American
   literature—African American authors** and
   the various forms of American literature with
   the subdivision *African American authors,* e.g.
   **American poetry—African American au-
   thors.**
   BT   **Literature—Themes**
Blacks in motion pictures   791.43
   Use for materials on the depiction of Blacks
   in motion pictures. Materials on several Black
   actors are entered under **Black actors.** Materials discussing all aspects of Blacks' involvement in motion pictures are entered under
   Blacks in the motion picture industry.
   BT   **Motion pictures**
   NT   **African Americans in motion
         pictures**
**Blacks in the motion picture industry
   791.43092**
   Use for materials on all aspects of Blacks'
   involvement in motion pictures. Materials on
   the depiction of Blacks in motion pictures are
   entered under **Blacks in motion pictures.**
   BT   **Motion picture industry**
   NT   **African Americans in the mo-
         tion picture industry**
Blacks—Intellectual life (May subdiv.
   geog.)   **305.896**
   BT   **Intellectual life**
   NT   **African Americans—Intellectu-
         al life**
Blacks—Music
   USE   **Black music**
Blacks—Political activity (May subdiv.
   geog.)   **322.4; 324**
   BT   **Political participation**
   NT   **African Americans—Political
         activity**
         Black nationalism
         Black power
         Blacks—Civil rights
Blacks—Race identity   305.896
   UF   Negritude
   BT   **Race awareness**
   NT   **African Americans—Race iden-
         tity**
         Black nationalism

Blacks—Religion   270.089; 299
   BT   **Religion**
   NT   **African Americans—Religion**
Blacks—Segregation (May subdiv. geog.)
   305.896
   BT   **Segregation**
   NT   **African Americans—Segrega-
         tion**
Blacks—Social conditions (May subdiv.
   geog.)   **305.896**
   BT   **Social conditions**
   NT   **African Americans—Social
         conditions**
Blacks—Social life and customs (May
   subdiv. geog.)   **305.896**
   BT   **Manners and customs**
   NT   **African Americans—Social life
         and customs**
Blacks—Songs and music
   USE   **Black music**
Blacks—Suffrage   324.6
   UF   Black suffrage
   BT   **Suffrage**
   NT   **African Americans—Suffrage**
Blacks—United States
   USE   **African Americans**
Blacksmithing   682
   BT   **Ironwork**
   NT   **Welding**
   RT   **Forging**
Blast furnaces   669
   BT   **Furnaces**
         Smelting
Blast shelters
   USE   **Air raid shelters**
Bleaching   667
   BT   **Cleaning**
         Industrial chemistry
         Textile industry
   RT   **Dyes and dyeing**
Blessed Virgin Mary
   USE   **Mary, Blessed Virgin, Saint**
Blimps
   USE   **Airships**
Blind   362.4
   BT   **Physically handicapped**
         Vision disorders

Blind—Books and reading   011.63;
      027.6; 028
   UF   Books for the blind
   BT   Books and reading
   NT   Large print books
   RT   Audiobooks
        Braille books
Blind—Education (May subdiv. geog.)
      371.91
   UF   Education of the blind
   BT   Education
Blind—Institutional care   362.4
   BT   Institutional care
Blizzards   551.55
   BT   Storms
   RT   Snow
Block printing
   USE   Color prints
         Linoleum block printing
         Textile printing
         Wood engraving
         Woodcuts
Block signal systems
   USE   Railroads—Signaling
Blockades
   USE   names of wars with the subdivi-
         sion *Blockades,* e.g. **World
         War, 1939-1945—Blockades**
         [to be added as needed]
Blood   573.1; 612.1
   BT   Physiology
   NT   Blood groups
        Blood pressure
Blood—Circulation   573.1; 612.1
   UF   Circulation of the blood
   RT   Blood pressure
        Cardiovascular system
Blood—Diseases   616.1
   UF   Diseases of the blood
   SA   types of blood diseases, e.g.
        Leukemia [to be added as
        needed]
   BT   Diseases
   NT   Leukemia
Blood groups   612.1
   UF   Rh factor
   BT   Blood
   RT   Blood—Transfusion

Blood pressure   612.1
   BT   Blood
   NT   Hypertension
   RT   Blood—Circulation
Blood—Transfusion   615
   RT   Blood groups
Blowing the whistle
   USE   Whistle blowing
Blowouts, Oil well
   USE   Oil wells—Blowouts
Blue collar workers
   USE   Labor
         Working class
Blue prints
   USE   Blueprints
Blueprints   604.2; 692
   UF   Blue prints
   BT   Mechanical drawing
Blues music   781.643; 782.421643
   UF   Blues songs
   BT   African American music
        Folk music—United States
        Popular music
   RT   Jazz music
Blues songs
   USE   Blues music
Board sailing
   USE   Windsurfing
Boarding houses
   USE   Hotels and motels
Boarding schools
   USE   Private schools
Boards of education
   USE   School boards
Boards of health
   USE   Health boards
Boards of trade
   USE   Chambers of commerce
Boards of trustees
   USE   Trusts and trustees
Boat building
   USE   Boatbuilding
Boat racing (May subdiv. geog.)   797.1
   UF   Regattas
   SA   types of boat racing and names
        of specific races [to be added
        as needed]
   BT   Boats and boating
        Racing

89

Boatbuilding   623.8
- UF   Boat building
  - Boats—Construction
- BT   **Naval architecture**
- NT   **Yachts and yachting**
- RT   **Boats and boating**
  - **Shipbuilding**

Boating
- USE   **Boats and boating**

Boats and boating   797.1
- UF   Boating
- BT   **Water sports**
- NT   **Boat racing**
  - **Canoes and canoeing**
  - **Catamarans**
  - **Houseboats**
  - **Hydrofoil boats**
  - **Iceboats**
  - **Marinas**
  - **Motorboats**
  - **Rowing**
  - **Steamboats**
  - **Tugboats**
  - **Yachts and yachting**
- RT   **Boatbuilding**
  - **Sailing**
  - **Ships**

Boats—Construction
- USE   **Boatbuilding**

Body
- USE   **Human body**

Body and mind
- USE   **Mind and body**

Body building
- USE   **Bodybuilding**

Body care
- USE   **Hygiene**

Body heat
- USE   **Body temperature**

Body image   128; 155.2

Use for materials on the visual, mental, or memory image of one's own body or another's body, and one's attitude towards that image.
- BT   **Human body**
  - **Mind and body**
  - **Personality**
  - **Self-perception**

Body language
- USE   **Nonverbal communication**

Body surfing
- USE   **Surfing**

Body temperature   571.7; 612
- UF   Animals—Temperature
  - Body heat
  - Temperature, Animal and human
  - Temperature, Body
- BT   **Diagnosis**
  - **Physiology**
- RT   **Fever**

Body weight   613
- BT   **Human body**
  - **Weight**
- NT   **Obesity**
  - **Weight loss**

Bodybuilding   646.7
- UF   Body building
  - Physique
- BT   **Exercise**
  - **Physical fitness**
- RT   **Weight lifting**

Boers
- USE   **Afrikaners**

Bogs (May subdiv. geog.)   **551.41**
- BT   **Wetlands**

Bohemianism (May subdiv. geog.)   **306**
- BT   **Counter culture**
  - **Manners and customs**
- NT   **Beat generation**
  - **Hippies**

Bolshevism
- USE   **Communism**

Bomb attacks
- USE   **Bombings**

Bomb shelters
- USE   **Air raid shelters**

Bombers   358.4; 623.7
- SA   types of bombers, e.g. **B-52 bomber** [to be added as needed]
- BT   **Airplanes**
  - **Military airplanes**
- NT   **B-52 bomber**

Bombings (May subdiv. geog.)   **364.1**

Use for materials on the use of explosive devices for the purposes of political terrorism or protest. Materials on bombs in general and on bombs launched from aircraft are entered under **Bombs.**
- UF   Bomb attacks
  - Terrorist bombings
- SA   names of individual bombings incidents [to be added as needed]

Bombings—*Continued*
  BT Offenses against public safety
      Political crimes and offenses
      Terrorism
Bombs 355.8; 623.4
  Use for materials on bombs in general and
  and on bombs launched from aircraft. Materi-
  als on the use of explosive devices for the
  purposes of political terrorism or protest are
  entered under **Bombings.**
  UF Aerial bombs
  SA types of bombs, e.g. **Atomic
      bomb** [to be added as need-
      ed]
  BT Ammunition
      Explosives
      Ordnance
      Projectiles
  NT Atomic bomb
      Guided missiles
      Hydrogen bomb
      Incendiary bombs
      Neutron bomb
Bonds 332.63
  BT Finance
      Investments
      Negotiable instruments
      Securities
      Stock exchanges
  NT Junk bonds
  RT Public debts
      Stocks
Bonds—Rating 332.63
Bones 573.7; 611; 612.7
  Use for comprehensive and systematic ma-
  terials on the anatomy of bones. Materials
  limited to the morphology or mechanics of the
  skeleton, human or animal, are entered under
  Skeleton.
  BT Musculoskeletal system
  NT Fractures
  RT Skeleton
Bonsai 635.9
  BT Dwarf trees
Book arts—Exhibitions
  USE Books—Exhibitions
Book awards
  USE Literary prizes
       and names of awards, e.g.
       **Caldecott Medal; Newbery
       Medal;** etc. [to be added as
       needed]
Book buying (Libraries)
  USE Libraries—Acquisitions

Book catalogs 017; 025.3
  Use for materials on library catalogs in
  book form. Retail book catalogs and book
  auction catalogs and materials about such cat-
  alogs are entered under **Booksellers' catalogs.**
  Publishers' book catalogs and materials about
  such catalogs are entered under **Publishers'
  catalogs.**
  UF Books—Catalogs
      Catalogs, Book
      Catalogs in book form
  BT Library catalogs
Book collecting 002.075
  UF Bibliomania
      Bibliophily
      Books—Collectors and collecting
  BT Book selection
      Collectors and collecting
  RT Bookplates
      Books
Book fairs
  USE Books—Exhibitions
Book illustration
  USE Illustration of books
Book industries
  USE Book industry
Book industries and trade
  USE Book industry
Book industries—Exhibitions
  USE Books—Exhibitions
Book industry (May subdiv. geog.) 686
  UF Book industries [*Former head-
      ing*]
      Book industries and trade
      Book trade
  BT Industries
  NT Bookbinding
      Booksellers and bookselling
      Printing
  RT Publishers and publishing
Book lending
  USE Library circulation
Book lists
  USE Best books
Book numbers, Publishers' standard
  USE Publishers' standard book
       numbers
Book plates
  USE Bookplates
Book prices
  USE Books—Prices

Book prizes
    USE   **Literary prizes**
         and names of prizes, e.g.
         Caldecott Medal; Newbery Medal; etc. [to be added as needed]
Book rarities
    USE   **Rare books**
Book reviewing   028.1; 808

    Use for materials on the technique of reviewing books. Collections of miscellaneous book reviews are entered under **Book reviews.**

    UF   Appraisal of books
         Books—Appraisal
         Evaluation of books
         Literature—Evaluation
         Reviewing (Books)
    SA   types of books with the subdivision *Reviews,* and topics, types of literature, ethnic groups, classes of persons, and names of places with the subdivision *Book reviews;* for collections of book reviews devoted to a particular type of book or subject, e.g. **Reference books—Reviews; Sociology—Book reviews; Children's literature—Book reviews;** etc. [to be added as needed]
    BT   **Books and reading**
         Criticism
    RT   **Book reviews**
Book reviews   028.1; 808.8

    Use for collections of book reviews. Materials on the technique of reviewing books are entered under **Book reviewing.**

    UF   Books—Reviews *[Former heading]*
    SA   types of books with the subdivision *Reviews,* and topics, types of literature, ethnic groups, classes of persons, and names of places with the subdivision *Book reviews;* for collections of book reviews devoted to a particular type of book or subject, e.g. **Reference books—Reviews; Sociology—Book reviews; Chil-**

dren's literature—Book reviews; etc. [to be added as needed]
    NT   **Book talks**
    RT   **Book reviewing**
Book sales
    USE   **Books—Prices**
Book selection   025.2

    Use for materials on the principles of book selection for libraries. Lists of recommended books and materials about recommended books are entered under **Best books.**

    UF   Books—Selection
         Choice of books
    BT   **Libraries—Acquisitions**
         Libraries—Collection development
    NT   **Book collecting**
    RT   **Best books**
Book talks   021.7; 028.1
    UF   Booktalking
         Booktalks
    BT   **Book reviews**
         Libraries—Public relations
         Public speaking
Book trade
    USE   **Book industry**
         Booksellers and bookselling
         Publishers and publishing
Book trade—Exhibitions
    USE   **Books—Exhibitions**
Book Week, National
    USE   **National Book Week**
Bookbinding (May subdiv. geog.)   **025.7; 095; 686.3**
    UF   Binding of books
    BT   **Book industry**
         Books
Bookkeepers
    USE   **Accountants**
Bookkeeping   657
    SA   types of industries, professions, and organizations with the subdivision *Accounting* [to be added as needed]
    BT   **Business**
         Business education
         Business mathematics
    NT   **Auditing**
         Corporations—Accounting
         Cost accounting
         Office equipment and supplies

Bookkeeping—*Continued*
RT Accounting
Bookmobiles 027.4
BT **Library extension**
Bookplates 025.7; 769.5
UF Book plates
Ex libris
BT **Prints**
RT **Book collecting**
Books 002
NT Anthologies
Best books
Bilingual books
Bookbinding
Books of hours
Braille books
Chapbooks
Early printed books
Illumination of books and
manuscripts
Illustration of books
Incunabula
Librettos
Manuscripts
Paperback books
Rare books
Reference books
Reprints (Publications)
Textbooks
RT Authors
Bibliography
Book collecting
Literature
Printing
Publishers and publishing
Books and reading (May subdiv. geog.)
028
Use for general materials on reading for in-
formation and culture, advice to readers, and
surveys of reading habits.
UF Appraisal of books
Books—Appraisal
Choice of books
Evaluation of literature
Literature—Evaluation
Reading interests
SA names of individuals and classes
of persons with the subdivi-
sion *Books and reading*, e.g.
Blind—Books and reading
[to be added as needed]

BT **Communication**
Education
Reading
NT **Best sellers (Books)**
Bible—Reading
Blind—Books and reading
Book reviewing
Children—Books and reading
National Book Week
Reference books
Teenagers—Books and reading
RT **Reading materials**
Books and reading—Best books
USE **Best books**
Books and reading for children
USE **Children—Books and reading**
Books and reading for teenagers
USE **Teenagers—Books and reading**
Books and reading for young adults
USE **Teenagers—Books and reading**
Books—Appraisal
USE **Book reviewing**
Books and reading
Criticism
**Literature—History and criti-
cism**
Books—Best sellers
USE **Best sellers (Books)**
Books—Bilingual editions
USE **Bilingual books**
Books—Catalogs
USE **Book catalogs**
Booksellers' catalogs
Publishers' catalogs
Books—Censorship 025.2; 323.44
UF Banned books
Index librorum prohibitorum
Prohibited books
BT **Censorship**
Books—Classification
USE **Library classification**
Books—Collectors and collecting
USE **Book collecting**
Books—Exhibitions (May subdiv. geog.)
070.5074; 686.074
UF Book arts—Exhibitions
Book fairs
Book industries—Exhibitions
[Former heading]
Book trade—Exhibitions
Library book fairs

Books—Exhibitions—*Continued*
           Publishers and publishing—Exhibitions
   BT   **Exhibitions**
Books—First editions
   USE   **First editions**
Books for children
   USE   **Children's literature**
Books for sight saving
   USE   **Large print books**
Books for teenagers
   USE   **Young adult literature**
Books for the blind
   USE   **Blind—Books and reading**
            Braille books
Books—Large print
   USE   **Large print books**
Books of hours (May subdiv. geog.)
       242; 745.6
   BT   **Books**
   RT   **Illumination of books and manuscripts**
Books of lists   **030**
   Use as a form heading for books consisting of miscellaneous lists of facts, names, etc.
   UF   Facts, Miscellaneous
         List books
         Lists
         Miscellanea
         Miscellaneous facts
   SA   topics with the subdivision *Lists,* e.g. **Sports—Lists** [to be added as needed]
Books on cassette
   USE   **Audiobooks**
Books on tape
   USE   **Audiobooks**
Books—Preservation
   USE   **Library resources—Conservation and restoration**
Books—Prices   **002.075**
   UF   Book prices
         Book sales
   BT   **Booksellers and bookselling**
         Prices
Books—Reviews
   USE   **Book reviews**
Books—Selection
   USE   **Book selection**

Booksellers and bookselling (May subdiv. geog.)   **070.5; 381; 658.8**
   UF   Book trade
   BT   **Book industry**
   NT   **Books—Prices**
         Booksellers' catalogs
   RT   **Publishers and publishing**
Booksellers' catalogs   **017**
   Use for retail book catalogs and book auction catalogs and materials about such catalogs. Materials on library catalogs in book form are entered under **Book catalogs.** Publishers' book catalogs and materials about such catalogs are entered under **Publishers' catalogs.**
   UF   Books—Catalogs
         Catalogs
         Catalogs, Booksellers'
   BT   **Booksellers and bookselling**
Booktalking
   USE   **Book talks**
Booktalks
   USE   **Book talks**
Boolean algebra   **511.3**
   UF   Algebra, Boolean
   BT   **Group theory**
         Set theory
         Symbolic logic
Boots
   USE   **Shoes**
Border life
   USE   **Frontier and pioneer life**
Borders (Geography)
   USE   **Boundaries**
Boring
   USE   **Drilling and boring (Earth and rocks)**
         Drilling and boring (Metal, wood, etc.)
Born again Christianity
   USE   **Regeneration (Christianity)**
Borrowing
   USE   **Loans**
Boss rule
   USE   **Political corruption**
Botanic gardens
   USE   **Botanical gardens**
Botanical chemistry   **572**
   UF   Plant chemistry
   BT   **Chemistry**
   NT   **Plants—Analysis**
Botanical classification
   USE   **Botany—Classification**

Botanical gardens (May subdiv. geog.)
580.73
   UF Botanic gardens
   SA names of individual botanical gardens [to be added as needed]
   BT **Gardens**
         Parks

Botanical illustration (May subdiv. geog.)
758
   UF Flower painting and illustration
         Fruit painting and illustration
   BT **Art**
         Illustration of books
   RT **Botany**
         Plants in art

Botanical specimens—Collection and preservation
   USE **Plants—Collection and preservation**

Botanists (May subdiv. geog.) **580.92;**
920
   BT **Naturalists**

Botany 580
   Use for materials on the science of plants. Nonscientific materials on plants are entered under **Plants.**
   UF Flora
         Vegetable kingdom
   BT **Biology**
         Science
   NT **Economic botany**
         Medical botany
         Photosynthesis
         Plant physiology
         Plants—Anatomy
   RT **Botanical illustration**
         Natural history
         Plants

Botany—Anatomy
   USE **Plants—Anatomy**

Botany—Classification 580.1
   UF Botanical classification
         Botany—Taxonomy
         Classification—Botany
         Classification—Plants
         Plant classification
         Plant taxonomy
         Plants—Classification
         Systematic botany
         Taxonomy (Botany)
   BT **Classification**

Botany—Ecology
   USE **Plant ecology**
Botany, Economic
   USE **Economic botany**
Botany, Medical
   USE **Medical botany**

Botany—Nomenclature 580.1
   Use for systematically derived lists of names or designations of plants and for materials about such names. Materials on the common or vernacular names of plants are entered under **Popular plant names.**
   UF Plants—Names
         Plants—Nomenclature
         Scientific names of plants
         Scientific plant names
   RT **Botany—Terminology**
         Popular plant names

Botany of the Bible
   USE **Bible—Natural history**
Botany—Pathology
   USE **Plant diseases**
Botany—Physiology
   USE **Plant physiology**
Botany—Structure
   USE **Plants—Anatomy**
Botany—Taxonomy
   USE **Botany—Classification**

Botany—Terminology 580.1
   Use for lists or discussions of words and expressions in the field of botany. Systematically derived lists of names or designations of plants and materials about such names are entered under **Botany—Nomenclature.** Materials on the common or vernacular names of plants are entered under **Popular plant names.**
   RT **Botany—Nomenclature**
         Popular plant names

Botany—United States
   USE **Plants—United States**
Boulder Dam (Ariz. and Nev.)
   USE **Hoover Dam (Ariz. and Nev.)**
Boulevards
   USE **Streets**

Boundaries 320.1; 341.4
   UF Borders (Geography)
         Frontiers
         Political boundaries
         Political geography
   SA names of wars with the subdivision *Territorial questions,* and countries, cities, etc., with the subdivision *Boundaries* [to be added as needed]

Boundaries—*Continued*
    BT   **Geography**
           International law
           International relations
    NT   **Chicago (Ill.)—Boundaries**
           Ohio—Boundaries
           United States—Boundaries
           World War, 1914-1918—Territorial questions
           World War, 1939-1945—Territorial questions
    RT   **Geopolitics**
Bourgeoisie
    USE **Middle class**
Bow and arrow   799.2028
    UF   Arrow
    BT   **Weapons**
    RT   **Archery**
Bowed instruments
    USE **Stringed instruments**
Bowling   794.6; 796.31
    UF   Tenpins
    BT   **Ball games**
Boxes   688.8; 745.593
    UF   Containers
           Crates
    BT   **Packaging**
Boxes—Collectors and collecting
    745.593
    BT   **Collectors and collecting**
Boxing   796.83
    UF   Fighting
           Prize fighting
           Pugilism
           Sparring
    BT   **Athletics**
           Self-defense
Boy Scouts (May subdiv. geog.)   369.43
    UF   Cub Scouts
    BT   **Boys' clubs**
           Scouts and scouting
Boycott
    USE **Boycotts**
Boycotts (May subdiv. geog.)   327.1;
    331.89; 338.6; 341.5
    UF   Boycott
           Consumer boycotts
    BT   **Commerce**
           Consumers
           Passive resistance
    RT   **Restraint of trade**

Boys   155.43; 305.23
    BT   **Children**
    RT   **Teenagers**
           Young men
Boys' clubs   369.42
    UF   Boys—Societies
    BT   **Clubs**
           Societies
    NT   **4-H clubs**
           Boy Scouts
Boys—Employment
    USE **Child labor**
Boys—Societies
    USE **Boys' clubs**
Boys' towns
    USE **Children—Institutional care**
Brahmanism   294.5
    BT   **Religions**
    RT   **Hinduism**
Braille books   011.63; 411
    UF   Books for the blind
    BT   **Books**
    RT   **Blind—Books and reading**
Brain   573.8; 611; 612.8
    BT   **Head**
           Nervous system
    NT   **Memory**
           Mind and body
           Phrenology
           Psychology
           Sleep
Brain damaged children   618.92
    BT   **Exceptional children**
           Handicapped children
Brain death   616.07
    UF   Irreversible coma
    BT   **Death**
Brain—Diseases   616.8
    BT   **Diseases**
    NT   **Alzheimer's disease**
           Cerebral palsy
           Stroke
Brain storming
    USE **Group problem solving**
Brainwashing   153.8
    Use for materials on the forcible indoctrination of an individual or group in order to alter basic political, social, religious, or moral beliefs.
    UF   Deprogramming
           Forced indoctrination
           Indoctrination, Forced

Brainwashing—*Continued*
    Mind control
    Thought control
    Will
  BT **Behavior modification**
    Mental suggestion
    Psychological warfare
    Psychology of learning

Brakes   **625.2; 629.2**
  SA types of vehicles with the subdi-
      vision *Brakes,* e.g. **Automo-**
      biles—Brakes [to be added
      as needed]
  NT **Automobiles—Brakes**

Branch stores
  USE **Chain stores**

Brand name products   **380.1; 658.8**
  UF Branded merchandise
  BT **Commercial products**
    Manufactures
  RT **Trademarks**

Branded merchandise
  USE **Brand name products**

Brass   **669; 673**
  BT **Alloys**
    Metals
  NT **Brasses**

Brass instruments   **788.9**
  BT **Wind instruments**

Brasses   **739.5**
  UF Monumental brasses
    Sepulchral brasses
  BT **Archeology**
    Art metalwork
    Brass
    Inscriptions
    Sculpture
    Tombs

Bravery
  USE **Courage**

Brazilian literature   **869**
  May use same subdivisions and names of
  literary forms as for **English literature.**
  BT **Latin American literature**
    Literature

Bread   **641.8; 664**
  BT **Baking**
    Cooking
    Food
  RT **Bread machines**

Bread machines   **641.7**
  UF Automatic bread machines
  BT **Kitchen utensils**
  RT **Baking**
    Bread

Break dancing   **793.3**
  BT **Dance**

Breakers
  USE **Ocean waves**

Breakfast cereals
  USE **Prepared cereals**

Breakfasts   **642**
  BT **Cooking**
    Menus
  NT **Prepared cereals**

Breakthroughs, Scientific
  USE **Discoveries in science**

Breast—Cancer
  USE **Breast cancer**

Breast cancer   **616.99**
  UF Breast—Cancer
  BT **Cancer**
    Women—Diseases

Breast feeding   **649**
  UF Nursing (Infant feeding)
  BT **Infants—Nutrition**

Breathing
  USE **Respiration**

Breeding (May subdiv. geog.)   **631.5;**
        636.08
  Use for materials on the controlled propaga-
  tion of plants and animals with the purpose of
  producing or maintaining desired characteris-
  tics.
  UF Artificial selection
    Selection, Artificial
  SA types of animals with the subdi-
      vision *Breeding* [to be added
      as needed]
  BT **Reproduction**
  NT **Dogs—Breeding**
    Heredity
    Horses—Breeding
    Livestock breeding
    Mendel's law
    Plant breeding
  RT **Genetics**

Breeding behavior
  USE **Sexual behavior in animals**

Bricklaying   693
   BT   Building
   RT   Bricks
         Masonry
Bricks   666; 691
   BT   Building materials
   RT   Bricklaying
Bridal customs
   USE   Marriage customs and rites
Bridge (Game)   795.41
   UF   Auction bridge
         Contract bridge
         Duplicate bridge
   BT   Card games
Bridges (May subdiv. geog.)   624; 725
     This heading may be subdivided by the
   names of rivers, lakes, canals, etc. as well as
   by countries, states, cities, etc.
   UF   Viaducts
   SA   types of bridges and names of
         individual bridges [to be add-
         ed as needed]
   BT   Civil engineering
         Transportation
   NT   Golden Gate Bridge (San
         Francisco, Calif.)
Bridges—Chicago (Ill.)   624
   UF   Chicago (Ill.)—Bridges
Bridges—Hudson River (N.Y. and N.J.)
   624
   UF   Hudson River (N.Y. and N.J.)—
         Bridges
Brigands
   USE   Thieves
Bright children
   USE   Gifted children
British Commonwealth countries
   USE   Commonwealth countries
British Commonwealth of Nations
   USE   Commonwealth countries
British Dominions
   USE   Commonwealth countries
British Empire
   USE   Great Britain—Colonies
Broadcast journalism (May subdiv. geog.)
   070.4
   UF   Radio journalism
         Television journalism
   BT   Broadcasting
         Journalism
         Press

   NT   Radio broadcasting of sports
         Television broadcasting of
          news
         Television broadcasting of
          sports
Broadcasting (May subdiv. geog.)
   384.54
   BT   Telecommunication
   NT   Broadcast journalism
         Equal time rule (Broadcasting)
         Fairness doctrine (Broadcast-
          ing)
         Minorities in broadcasting
         Radio broadcasting
         Television broadcasting
Bronze Age (May subdiv. geog.)   930.1
   BT   Civilization
Bronzes (May subdiv. geog.)   739.5
   BT   Archeology
         Art
         Art metalwork
         Decoration and ornament
         Metalwork
         Sculpture
Brothers   306.875
   BT   Men
         Siblings
Brothers and sisters
   USE   Siblings
Brownies (Girl Scouts)
   USE   Girl Scouts
Brownouts
   USE   Electric power failures
Brutality
   USE   Cruelty
Bubonic plague
   USE   Plague
Buccaneers
   USE   Pirates
Bucolic poetry
   USE   Pastoral poetry
Buddhism (May subdiv. geog.)   294.3
   BT   Religions
   NT   Zen Buddhism
Buddhism—Prayers   294.3
   UF   Buddhist prayers
   BT   Prayers
Buddhist art (May subdiv. geog.)   294.3;
   704.9
   UF   Art, Buddhist
   BT   Art

Buddhist prayers
USE **Buddhism—Prayers**
Budget (May subdiv. geog.) **352.4**
  Use for materials on government budgets or reports on governmental appropriations and expenditures. Materials on business budgets are entered under **Business budgets.** Materials on household budgets are entered under **Household budgets.** Materials on personal budgets are entered under **Personal finance.**
  UF Government budgets
  SA names of countries and names of individual government departments, agencies, etc., with the subdivision *Appropriations and expenditures,* e.g. **United States—Appropriations and expenditures** [to be added as needed]
  BT **Public finance**
Budget—United States 352.4
  UF Federal budget
    United States—Budget
  NT **United States—Appropriations and expenditures**
Budgets, Business
  USE **Business budgets**
Budgets, Household
  USE **Household budgets**
Budgets, Personal
  USE **Personal finance**
Buffalo, American
  USE **Bison**
Buffing
  USE **Grinding and polishing**
Bugging, Electronic
  USE **Eavesdropping**
Building 690
  Use for materials on the process of constructing buildings and other structures. Materials on the design and style of structures are entered under **Architecture.** General materials on buildings and materials on buildings in a particular place are entered under **Buildings.**
  UF Architectural engineering
    Construction
  SA types of buildings with the subdivision *Design and construction,* e.g. **Industrial buildings—Design and construction** [to be added as needed]
  BT **Structural engineering**
  NT **Bricklaying**
    Carpentry
    Concrete construction

  House construction
  Industrial buildings—Design and construction
  Masonry
  Plumbing
  Steel construction
  RT **Architecture**
    Building materials
Building and earthquakes
  USE **Buildings—Earthquake effects**
Building and loan associations
  USE **Savings and loan associations**
Building contracts
  USE **Construction contracts**
Building—Contracts and specifications
  USE **Construction contracts**
Building design
  USE **Architecture**
Building—Estimates 692
Building failures 690
  BT **Structural failures**
Building, Iron and steel
  USE **Steel construction**
Building materials 691
  UF Structural materials
  SA types of building materials, e.g. **Bricks** [to be added as needed]
  BT **Materials**
  NT **Bricks**
    Cement
    Concrete
    Glass
    Glass construction
    Reinforced concrete
    Stone
    Structural steel
    Stucco
    Terra cotta
    Tiles
    Wood
  RT **Building**
    Strength of materials
Building nests
  USE **Nest building**
Building repair
  USE **Buildings—Maintenance and repair**
Building—Repair and reconstruction
  USE **Buildings—Maintenance and repair**

Building security
USE **Burglary protection**
Buildings (May subdiv. geog.)   **690; 720**
   Use for general materials on buildings and, with geographic subdivisions, for materials on buildings in a particular place. Materials on the design and style of structures are entered under **Architecture.** Materials on the process of constructing buildings and other structures are entered under **Building.**
   UF   Edifices
         Structures
   SA   types of building features, e.g.
         Doors; Windows; etc.; types of buildings and construction, e.g. **Farm buildings;** types of institutions and names of individual institutions and corporate bodies with the subdivision *Buildings,* e.g. **Colleges and universities—Buildings;** and names of specific buildings [to be added as needed]
   NT   **Apartment houses**
         Castles
         Chimneys
         Church buildings
         Colleges and universities— Buildings
         Commercial buildings
         Doors
         Farm buildings
         Fireplaces
         Floors
         Foundations
         Historic buildings
         Houses
         Industrial buildings
         Office buildings
         Palaces
         Prefabricated buildings
         Public buildings
         Roofs
         Rooms
         School buildings
         Skyscrapers
         Synagogues
         Temples
         Theaters
         Walls
         Windows
   RT   **Architecture**

Buildings—Earthquake effects   693.8
   Use for materials on the design and construction of buildings to withstand earthquakes.
   UF   Building and earthquakes
         Earthquakes and building
   BT   **Earthquakes**
   NT   **Skyscrapers—Earthquake effects**
Buildings, Industrial
   USE   **Industrial buildings**
Buildings—Maintenance and repair   690
   UF   Building repair
         Building—Repair and reconstruction
         Buildings—Remodeling
   SA   types of buildings with the subdivision *Maintenance and repair,* e.g. **Houses—Maintenance and repair;** and types of buildings and parts of buildings with the subdivision *Remodeling,* e.g. **Houses—Remodeling; Kitchens—Remodeling;** etc. [to be added as needed]
   RT   **Architecture—Conservation and restoration**
Buildings, Office
   USE   **Office buildings**
Buildings, Prefabricated
   USE   **Prefabricated buildings**
Buildings—Remodeling
   USE   **Buildings—Maintenance and repair**
Buildings, Restoration of
   USE   **Architecture—Conservation and restoration**
Buildings, School
   USE   **School buildings**
Buildings—Security
   USE   **Burglary protection**
Built-in furniture   645; 684.1; 749
   BT   **Furniture**
Bulbs   584; 635.9
   BT   **Flower gardening**
         Plants
Bulge, Battle of the
   USE   **Ardennes, Battle of the, 1944- 1945**

Bulimia   616.85
  UF   Binge eating behavior
         Binge-purge behavior
         Gorge-purge syndrome
  BT   **Eating disorders**
Bulletin boards   371.33
  BT   **Teaching—Aids and devices**
  NT   **Computer bulletin boards**
Bullfights   791.8
  UF   Fighting
  BT   **Sports**
Bullies   155.4; 302.3; 646.7
  UF   Bullying
         Bullyism
  BT   **Aggressiveness (Psychology)**
Bullion
  USE **Precious metals**
Bullying
  USE **Bullies**
Bullyism
  USE **Bullies**
Bunnies
  USE **Rabbits**
Bunny rabbits
  USE **Rabbits**
Bunyan, Paul (Legendary character)
      398.22
  UF   Paul Bunyan
  BT   **Folklore—United States**
Bureaucracy (May subdiv. geog.)   302.3
  BT   **Political science**
         Public administration
  RT   **Civil service**
         Organizational sociology
Burglar alarms   621.389
  BT   **Burglary protection**
         Electric apparatus and appliances
Burglars
  USE **Thieves**
Burglary protection   621.389; 643
  UF   Building security
         Buildings—Security
         Protection against burglary
         Residential security
  SA   types of protective devices, e.g.
         Burglar alarms; and types of
         buildings with the subdivision
         Security measures, e.g. **Nuclear power plants—Security**

         measures [to be added as needed]
  BT   **Crime prevention**
  NT   **Burglar alarms**
         Locks and keys
Burial (May subdiv. geog.)   363.7; 393
  UF   Burial customs
         Burying grounds
         Graves
         Interment
  SA   names of individual persons and
         groups of notable persons
         with the subdivision *Death
         and burial,* e.g. **Presidents—
         United States—Death and
         burial** [to be added as needed]
  BT   **Archeology**
         Public health
  NT   **Catacombs**
         Cemeteries
         Cryonics
         Mounds and mound builders
         Mummies
         Tombs
  RT   **Cremation**
         Death
         Funeral rites and ceremonies
Burial customs
  USE **Burial**
Burial statistics
  USE **Mortality**
         Registers of births, etc.
         Vital statistics
Buried cities
  USE **Extinct cities**
Buried treasure   622; 910.4
  UF   Hidden treasure
         Sunken treasure
         Treasure trove
  BT   **Archeology**
         Underwater exploration
Burn out (Psychology)   158.7
  UF   Burnout syndrome
  BT   **Job satisfaction**
         Job stress
         Mental health
         Motivation (Psychology)
         Occupational health and safety
         Stress (Psychology)

Burnout syndrome
    USE **Burn out (Psychology)**
Burnt offering
    USE **Sacrifice**
Bursaries
    USE **Scholarships**
Burying grounds
    USE **Burial**
           Cemeteries
Buses   388.4; 629.222
    UF Motor buses
    BT **Automobiles**
          Highway transportation
          Local transit
Bush survival
    USE **Wilderness survival**
Business   650
    UF Trade
    BT **Commerce**
          Economics
    NT **Accounting**
          Advertising
          Banks and banking
          Bookkeeping
          Business budgets
          Business enterprises
          Business failures
          Businesspeople
          Competition
          Customer relations
          Department stores
          Economic conditions
          Entrepreneurship
          Home-based business
          Installment plan
          Mail-order business
          Management
          Marketing
          Markets
          Office management
          Profit
          Real estate business
          Selling
          Small business
          Trust companies
Business administration
    USE **Management**
Business and government
    USE **Economic policy**

Business and politics (May subdiv. geog.)
    322
    UF Business—Political activity
          Politics and business
    BT **Politics**
Business arithmetic
    USE **Business mathematics**
Business budgets   658.15
    UF Budgets, Business
    BT **Business**
Business colleges
    USE **Business schools**
Business correspondence
    USE **Business letters**
Business cycles (May subdiv. geog.)
    338.5
    UF Economic cycles
          Stabilization in industry
    SA types of business cycles, e.g.
          Depressions [to be added as
          needed]
    BT **Cycles**
          Economic conditions
    NT **Depressions**
          Economic forecasting
          Recessions
    RT **Financial crises**
Business—Databases   650
    BT **Databases**
Business depression, 1929-1939
    USE **Great Depression, 1929-1939**
Business depressions
    USE **Depressions**
Business education (May subdiv. geog.)
    650.07
    UF Business—Study and teaching
          Clerical work—Training
          Commercial education
          Office work—Training
    BT **Education**
    NT **Accounting**
          Bookkeeping
          Keyboarding (Electronics)
          Secretaries
          Shorthand
          Typewriting
Business English
    USE **English language—Business**
           English

Business enterprises (May subdiv. geog.)
  338.7

  Use for materials on business concerns as legal entities, regardless of the form of organization.

  UF Business organizations
      Businesses
      Companies
      Enterprises
      Firms
  SA types of businesses [to be added as needed]
  BT **Business**
  NT **Beauty shops**
      Corporations
      Government business enterprises
      Minority business enterprises
      Money-making projects for children
      Multinational corporations
      New business enterprises
Business entertaining **395.3; 658**
  BT **Entertaining**
      Public relations
Business ethics (May subdiv. geog.) **174**
  BT **Ethics**
      Professional ethics
  NT **Competition**
      Deceptive advertising
      Success
Business failures (May subdiv. geog.)
  338; 658
  UF Business mortality
      Failure in business
  BT **Business**
  NT **Bank failures**
      Bankruptcy
Business forecasting (May subdiv. geog.)
  338.5
  BT **Economic forecasting**
      Forecasting
Business—Government policy
  USE **Economic policy**
Business—Information resources **650**
  BT **Information resources**
Business—Information services (May subdiv. geog.) **658.4**
  BT **Information services**
Business—International aspects
  USE **Multinational corporations**

Business—Internet resources **650**
  BT **Internet resources**
Business—Internet resources—Directories
  650.025
Business Japanese
  USE **Japanese language—Business Japanese**
Business language
  USE names of languages with unique language subdivisions, e.g. **English language—Business English; Japanese language—Business Japanese;** etc. [to be added as needed]
Business law
  USE **Commercial law**
Business—Law and legislation
  USE **Commercial law**
Business letters **651.7**
  UF Business correspondence
      Commercial correspondence
      Correspondence
  BT **Letter writing**
Business libraries **026**

  Use for materials on libraries with a subject focus on business. Materials on libraries located within companies, firms, or private businesses, covering any subject area, are entered under **Corporate libraries.**

  UF Libraries, Business
  BT **Special libraries**
Business machines
  USE **Office equipment and supplies**
Business management
  USE **Management**
Business math
  USE **Business mathematics**
Business mathematics **650.01**
  UF Arithmetic, Commercial
      Business arithmetic
      Business math
      Commercial arithmetic
      Commercial mathematics
      Finance—Mathematics
  BT **Mathematics**
  NT **Accounting**
      Bookkeeping
      Interest (Economics)
Business mortality
  USE **Bankruptcy**
      Business failures
Business organizations
  USE **Business enterprises**

Business patronage of the arts
   USE   **Art patronage**
Business people
   USE   **Businesspeople**
Business—Political activity
   USE   **Business and politics**
Business recessions
   USE   **Recessions**
Business schools   650.071
   UF   Business colleges
   BT   **Schools**
Business secrets
   USE   **Trade secrets**
Business—Study and teaching
   USE   **Business education**
Businesses
   USE   **Business enterprises**
Businessmen (May subdiv. geog.)
      338.092; 658.0092; 920
   UF   Men in business
   BT   **Businesspeople**
Businesspeople (May subdiv. geog.)
      338.092; 658.0092; 920
   UF   Business people *[Former heading]*
   BT   **Business**
   NT   **African American businesspeople**
         Black businesspeople
         Businessmen
         Businesswomen
         Capitalists and financiers
         Entrepreneurs
         Merchants
         Self-employed
Businesswomen (May subdiv. geog.)
      338.092; 658.0092; 920
   UF   Women in business
   BT   **Businesspeople**
         Women
Busing (School integration)   379.2
   UF   Antibusing
         School busing
         Student busing
   BT   **School children—Transportation**
         School integration
Butter   637; 641.3
   BT   **Dairy products**
   NT   **Margarine**

Butterflies   595.78
   UF   Cocoons
         Lepidoptera
   BT   **Insects**
   NT   **Caterpillars**
   RT   **Moths**
Buttons   646; 687
   BT   **Clothing and dress**
Buy American policy
   USE   **Buy national policy—United States**
Buy national policy (May subdiv. geog.)
      352.5
      Use for materials on the requirement that a national government procure goods produced domestically.
   UF   Government policy
   BT   **Commercial policy**
         Government purchasing
Buy national policy—United States
      352.5
   UF   Buy American policy
Buyers' guides
   USE   **Consumer education**
         Shopping
Buying
   USE   **Purchasing**
Buyouts, Corporate
   USE   **Corporate mergers and acquisitions**
Buyouts, Leveraged
   USE   **Leveraged buyouts**
By-products
   USE   **Waste products**
Byrd Antarctic Expedition   919.8
   BT   **Antarctica—Exploration**
Byzantine architecture (May subdiv. geog.)   **723**
   UF   Architecture, Byzantine
   BT   **Ancient architecture**
         Architecture
         Medieval architecture
Byzantine art   709.02
   UF   Art, Byzantine
   BT   **Ancient art**
         Art
         Medieval art
Byzantine Empire   949.5
   UF   Eastern Empire
Cabala   135; 296.1
   UF   Cabbala
         Kabbala

Cabala—*Continued*
    BT   **Hebrew literature**
            Jewish literature
            Judaism
            Mysticism
            Occultism
    RT   **Symbolism of numbers**
Cabbala
    USE **Cabala**
Cabinet officers (May subdiv. geog.)
    352.24; 920
    UF   Ministers of state
    NT   **Prime ministers**
Cabinet work
    USE **Cabinetwork**
Cabinetwork   684.1
    Use for materials on the making and finishing of fine woodwork, such as furniture or interior details. Materials on the construction of a wooden building or the wooden portion of any building are entered under **Carpentry.**
    UF   Cabinet work
    BT   **Carpentry**
    NT   **Veneers and veneering**
    RT   **Furniture**
            Woodwork
Cabins
    USE **Log cabins and houses**
Cable railroads (May subdiv. geog.)
    385; 625.5
    UF   Funicular railroads
            Railroads, Cable
    BT   **Railroads**
    RT   **Street railroads**
Cable television (May subdiv. geog.)
    384.55
    BT   **Television broadcasting**
Cables   384.6; 621.319; 624.1
    BT   **Power transmission**
            Rope
Cables, Submarine
    USE **Submarine cables**
Cactus   583; 635.9
    BT   **Desert plants**
CAD
    USE **Computer-aided design**
CAD/CAM software
    USE **Computer-aided design software**
CAD software
    USE **Computer-aided design software**

Cafes
    USE **Coffeehouses**
            Restaurants
Cage birds   636.6
    SA   types of cage birds [to be added as needed]
    BT   **Birds**
    NT   **Canaries**
CAI
    USE **Computer-assisted instruction**
Cake   641.8; 664
    BT   **Baking**
            Confectionery
            Cooking
            Desserts
    RT   **Pastry**
Cake decorating   641.8
    BT   **Confectionery**
Calculating machines
    USE **Calculators**
Calculators   510.28; 651.8; 681
    Use for materials on present-day calculators or on calculators and mechanical computers made before 1945. Materials on modern electronic computers developed after 1945 are entered under **Computers.**
    UF   Accounting machines
            Adding machines
            Calculating machines
            Pocket calculators
    BT   **Arithmetic**
            Office equipment and supplies
    NT   **Abacus**
            Slide rule
    RT   **Computers**
Calculus   515
    UF   Analysis (Mathematics)
    BT   **Mathematical analysis**
            Mathematics
Caldecott Awards
    USE **Caldecott Medal**
Caldecott Medal   028.5
    UF   Caldecott Awards
            Caldecott Medal books
    BT   **Children's literature**
            Illustration of books
            Literary prizes
Caldecott Medal books
    USE **Caldecott Medal**

Calendars   529
　　UF　Annuals
　　SA　subjects, corporate bodies, and
　　　　names of countries, cities,
　　　　etc., with the subdivision *Cal-*
　　　　endars, for works that list re-
　　　　curring, coming, or past
　　　　events in those places or re-
　　　　lated to those topics or orga-
　　　　nizations [to be added as
　　　　needed]
　　BT　**Time**
　　NT　**Church year**
　　　　Days
　　　　Devotional calendars
　　　　Months
　　　　Week
　　RT　**Almanacs**
California—Gold discoveries   979.4
　　UF　California gold rush
California gold rush
　　USE　**California—Gold discoveries**
Calisthenics
　　USE　**Gymnastics**
　　　　Physical education
Calligraphy   745.6
　　BT　**Decorative arts**
　　　　Handwriting
　　　　Writing
Calvinism (May subdiv. geog.)   **284**
　　BT　**Reformation**
　　RT　**Congregationalism**
　　　　Puritans
Camcorders   621.388; 778.59
　　UF　Home video cameras
　　　　Video cameras, Home
　　BT　**Cameras**
　　　　Home video systems
　　　　Video recording
　　RT　**Amateur films**
Camels   599.63; 636.2
　　UF　Dromedaries
　　BT　**Desert animals**
　　　　Mammals
Cameras   681; 771.3
　　SA　types of cameras and names of
　　　　individual makes of cameras
　　　　[to be added as needed]
　　BT　**Photography**
　　　　Photography—Equipment and
　　　　　supplies

　　NT　**Camcorders**
　　　　Kodak camera
　　　　Motion picture cameras
Camouflage (Biology)   591.47
　　UF　Animal camouflage
　　　　Animals—Camouflage
　　BT　**Animal defenses**
Camouflage (Military science)   355.4;
　　　　623
　　BT　**Military art and science**
　　　　Naval art and science
Camp cooking
　　USE　**Outdoor cooking**
Camp Fire Girls   369.47
　　BT　**Girls' clubs**
Camp sites
　　USE　**Campgrounds**
Campaign funds (May subdiv. geog.)
　　　　324.7
　　UF　Elections—Finance
　　　　Political parties—Finance
　　BT　**Elections**
　　　　Politics
Campaign funds—United States   324.7
　　UF　Elections—United States—Fi-
　　　　nance
　　　　United States—Campaign funds
Campaign literature (May subdiv. geog.)
　　　　324.2
　　UF　Political campaign literature
　　BT　**Literature**
　　　　Politics
Campaigns
　　USE　names of wars with the subdivi-
　　　　sion *Campaigns,* e.g. **World**
　　　　War, 1939-1945—Cam-
　　　　paigns; which may be further
　　　　subdivided geographically [to
　　　　be added as needed]
Campaigns, Political
　　USE　**Politics**
Campaigns, Presidential—United States
　　USE　**Presidents—United States—**
　　　　Election
Campers and trailers
　　USE　**Travel trailers and campers**
Campgrounds (May subdiv. geog.)
　　　　796.54
　　UF　Camp sites
　　NT　**Trailer parks**
　　RT　**Camping**

Camping (May subdiv. geog.) **796.54**

    Use for materials on the technique of camping. Materials on camps with a definite program of activities are entered under **Camps.**

    BT   **Outdoor recreation**

    NT   **Backpacking**

          Bicycle touring

          Outdoor cooking

          Tents

          Travel trailers and campers

          Wilderness survival

    RT   **Campgrounds**

          Outdoor life

Camps (May subdiv. geog.) **796.54**

    Use for materials on camps with a definite program of activities. Materials on the technique of camping are entered under **Camping.**

    UF   Summer camps

    BT   **Recreation**

Camps (Military)

    USE **Military camps**

Campus disorders

    USE **College students—Political activity**

Canada   **971**

    May be subdivided like United States except for *History.*

    SA   names of individual provinces, territories, or regions [to be added as needed]

Canada—English-French relations
    305.811; 306.44

    UF   Canada—French-English relations

Canada—French-English relations

    USE **Canada—English-French relations**

Canada—History—0-1763 (New France)
    971.01

    UF   New France—History

Canada—History—1755-1763   971.01

Canada—History—1763-1791   971.02

Canada—History—1763-1867   971.02

Canada—History—1775-1783   971.02

Canada—History—1791-1841   971.03

Canada—History—19th century   971.03

Canada—History—1841-1867   971.04

Canada—History—1867-   971.05

Canada—History—1867-1914   971.05

Canada—History—20th century   971.06

Canada—History—1914-1945   971.06

Canada—History—1945-   971.06

Canada—History—21st century   971.06

Canadian Indians

    USE **Native Americans—Canada**

Canadian Invasion, 1775-1776   **973.3**

    BT   **United States—History—1775-1783, Revolution**

Canadian literature (May subdiv. geog.)
    810; C810

    Use for general materials not limited to literature in a particular language or form. May use same subdivision and names of literary forms as for **English literature;** e.g. **Canadian poetry;** etc.

    BT   **Literature**

    NT   **Canadian literature (English)**

          Canadian literature (French)

          Canadian poetry

Canadian literature (English) (May subdiv. geog.)   **810; C810**

    May use same subdivisions and names of literary forms as for **English literature;** e.g. **Canadian poetry (English);** etc.

    UF   English Canadian literature

    BT   **Canadian literature**

    NT   **Canadian poetry (English)**

Canadian literature (French) (May subdiv. geog.)   **840; C840**

    May use same subdivisions and names of literary forms as for **English literature;** e.g. **Canadian poetry (French);** etc.

    UF   French Canadian literature

          French literature—Canada

    BT   **Canadian literature**

    NT   **Canadian poetry (French)**

Canadian poetry (May subdiv. geog.)
    811; C811

    Use for general materials about Canadian poetry not limited to a particular language, not for individual works.

    BT   **Canadian literature**

    NT   **Canadian poetry (English)**

          Canadian poetry (French)

Canadian poetry (English) (May subdiv. geog.)   **811; C811**

    Use for general materials about Canadian poetry in English, not for individual works.

    UF   English Canadian poetry

    BT   **Canadian literature (English)**

          Canadian poetry

Canadian poetry (French) (May subdiv. geog.)   **841; C841**

    Use for general materials about Canadian poetry in French, not for individual works.

    UF   French Canadian poetry

    BT   **Canadian literature (French)**

          Canadian poetry

Canadians   305.811; 971
  NT   French Canadians
Canals (May subdiv. geog.)   386; 627
  SA   names of individual canals [to
        be added as needed]
  BT   Civil engineering
        Hydraulic structures
        Transportation
        Waterways
  NT   Panama Canal
  RT   Inland navigation
Canaries   598.8; 636.6
  BT   Birds
        Cage birds
Canasta (Game)   795.41
  UF   Argentine rummy
  BT   Card games
Cancer (May subdiv. geog.)   616.99
  UF   Carcinoma
        Malignant tumors
  SA   types of cancer [to be added as
        needed]
  BT   Diseases
        Tumors
  NT   Breast cancer
        Leukemia
        Lung cancer
Cancer—Chemotherapy   616.99
  UF   Chemotherapy
  BT   Drug therapy
Cancer—Diet therapy   616.99
  BT   Diet therapy
Cancer—Genetic aspects   616.99
  BT   Medical genetics
Cancer—Nursing   610.73
  BT   Nursing
Cancer patients
  USE   Cancer—Patients
Cancer—Patients   616.99
  UF   Cancer patients
  BT   Patients
Cancer—Surgery   616.99
  BT   Surgery
Candies
  USE   Candy
Candles   621.32; 745.593
  BT   Lighting
Candy   641.8
  UF   Candies
        Sweets
  BT   Confectionery

Caning of chairs
  USE   Chair caning
Cannabis
  USE   Marijuana
Canned goods
  USE   Canning and preserving
Cannibalism   291.3; 394
  BT   Ethnology
        Human behavior
Canning and preserving   641.4; 664
  UF   Canned goods
        Food, Canned
        Pickling
        Preserving
  SA   types of foods with the subdivi-
        sion *Preservation* [to be add-
        ed as needed]
  BT   Cooking
        Food—Preservation
        Industrial chemistry
  NT   Fruit—Preservation
        Vegetables—Preservation
Cannon
  USE   Ordnance
Canoes and canoeing   797.1
  BT   Boats and boating
        Water sports
Canon law
  USE   Ecclesiastical law
Canons, fugues, etc.
  USE   Fugue
Cantatas   782.2
    Use for musical scores and for materials on
  the cantata as a musical form.
  BT   Choral music
        Vocal music
Canvas embroidery
  USE   Needlepoint
Capital (May subdiv. geog.)   332
  BT   Economics
        Finance
  NT   Banks and banking
        Human capital
        Industrial trusts
        Interest (Economics)
        Investments
        Profit
        Saving and investment
  RT   Capitalism
        Wealth
Capital accumulation
  USE   Saving and investment

Capital and labor
  USE **Industrial relations**
Capital equipment
  USE **Industrial equipment**
Capital formation
  USE **Saving and investment**
Capital goods
  USE **Industrial equipment**
Capital punishment (May subdiv. geog.)
      179.7; 364.6
  UF   Abolition of capital punishment
       Death penalty
       Executions
       Hanging
  BT   **Criminal law**
       Punishment
Capital punishment—United States
      364.6
Capitalism (May subdiv. geog.)   **330.12**
  BT   **Economics**
       Labor
       Profit
  NT   **Entrepreneurship**
  RT   **Capital**
       Capitalists and financiers
       Free enterprise
Capitalists and financiers (May subdiv.
      geog.)   **332.092; 920**
  UF   Financiers
  BT   **Businesspeople**
  RT   **Capitalism**
Capitalization (Finance)
  USE **Corporations—Finance**
       Securities
       Valuation
Capitals (Cities)   307.76
    Use for materials on the capital cities of
    several countries or states.
  BT   **Cities and towns**
  NT   **Capitols**
Capitols   725
  BT   **Capitals (Cities)**
       Public buildings
Captivities
  USE ethnic groups with the subdivi-
       sion *Captivities,* e.g. **Native
       Americans—Captivities** [to
       be added as needed]
Car accidents
  USE **Traffic accidents**

Car design
  USE **Automobiles—Design and con-
       struction**
Car driver education
  USE **Automobile driver education**
Car drivers
  USE **Automobile drivers**
Car engines
  USE **Automobiles—Motors**
Car industry
  USE **Automobile industry**
Car insurance
  USE **Automobile insurance**
Car maintenance
  USE **Automobiles—Maintenance and
       repair**
Car painting
  USE **Automobiles—Painting**
Car parts
  USE **Automobile parts**
Car pools   388.4
  UF   Automobile pools
       Carpools
       Ride sharing
       Van pools
  BT   **Traffic engineering**
       Transportation
Car racing
  USE **Automobile racing**
Car repair
  USE **Automobiles—Maintenance and
       repair**
Car transmissions
  USE **Automobiles—Transmission de-
       vices**
Car travel
  USE **Automobile travel**
Car wheels
  USE **Wheels**
Car wrecks
  USE **Traffic accidents**
Carbines
  USE **Rifles**
Carbolic acid   547; 661
  BT   **Acids**
       Chemicals
Carbon   540; 660
  BT   **Chemical elements**
  NT   **Diamonds**
       Graphite

Carbon 14 dating
    USE **Radiocarbon dating**
Carbon dioxide greenhouse effect
    USE **Greenhouse effect**
Carburetors   621.43
    BT **Internal combustion engines**
Carcinoma
    USE **Cancer**
Card catalogs   025.3
    UF Catalogs, Card
    BT **Library catalogs**
Card games   795.4
    SA types of card games [to be add-
         ed as needed]
    BT **Games**
    NT **Bridge (Game)**
         Canasta (Game)
         Card tricks
         Solitaire (Game)
         Tarot
    RT **Playing cards**
Card tricks   795.4
    BT **Card games**
         Magic tricks
         Tricks
Cardiac diseases
    USE **Heart diseases**
Cardiac resuscitation   616.02; 616.1
    UF Heart resuscitation
         Resuscitation, Heart
    BT **First aid**
Cardinals   262
    BT **Catholic Church—Clergy**
Cardiovascular system   612.1
    UF Circulatory system
         Vascular system
    BT **Anatomy**
         Physiology
    NT **Heart**
    RT **Blood—Circulation**
Cards, Debit
    USE **Debit cards**
Cards, Greeting
    USE **Greeting cards**
Cards, Playing
    USE **Playing cards**
Cards, Sports
    USE **Sports cards**

Care
    USE parts of the body, classes of
            persons, and types of animals
            with the subdivision *Care,*
            e.g. **Foot—Care; Infants—**
            Care; Dogs—Care; etc.;
            classes of persons with the
            subdivisions *Medical care, In-*
            stitutional care, and *Home*
            care, e.g. **Elderly—Medical**
            care; Elderly—Institutional
            care; Elderly—Home care;
            etc.; ethnic groups and classes
            of persons with the subdivi-
            sion *Health and hygiene,* e.g.
            Infants—Health and hy-
            giene; and inanimate things
            with the subdivision *Mainte-*
            nance and repair, e.g. **Auto-**
            mobiles—Maintenance and
            repair [to be added as need-
            ed]
Care givers
    USE **Caregivers**
Care of children
    USE **Child care**
Care of the dying
    USE **Terminal care**
Career changes   650.14; 658.4
    UF Changing careers
         Mid-career changes
    SA fields of knowledge, professions,
         industries, and trades with the
         subdivision *Vocational guid-*
         ance [to be added as needed]
    BT **Age and employment**
         Vocational guidance
Career counseling
    USE **Vocational guidance**
Career development
    USE **Personnel management**
           Vocational guidance
Career education
    USE **Vocational education**
Career guidance
    USE **Vocational guidance**
Careers
    USE **Occupations**
           Professions
           Vocational guidance

Caregivers   362; 649.8

Use for materials on family and friends who on a voluntary basis provide personal home care for the elderly, ill, or handicapped.

UF   Care givers

Family caregivers

BT   **Volunteer work**

RT   **Home care services**

Caricatures and cartoons

USE   **Cartoons and caricatures**

Carillons

USE   **Bells**

Carnival (May subdiv. geog.)   394.25

Use for materials on festivals, merrymaking, and revelry before Lent. Materials on traveling amusement enterprises, consisting of sideshows, games of chance, etc., are entered under **Carnivals.**

UF   Mardi Gras

Pre-Lenten festivities

BT   **Festivals**

Carnivals (May subdiv. geog.)   394.25; 791

Use for materials on traveling amusement enterprises, consisting of sideshows, games of chance, merry-go-rounds, etc. Materials on festivals, merrymaking, and revelry before Lent are entered under **Carnival.**

BT   **Amusements**

Festivals

RT   **Amusement parks**

Circus

Fairs

Carnivora

USE   **Carnivorous animals**

Carnivores

USE   **Carnivorous animals**

Carnivorous animals   599.7

UF   Carnivora

Carnivores

Meat-eating animals

SA   types of carnivorous animals [to be added as needed]

BT   **Animals**

Carnivorous plants   583; 635.9

UF   Insect-eating plants

Insectivorous plants

BT   **Plants**

Carols   782.28

UF   Christmas carols

Easter carols

BT   **Church music**

Folk songs

Hymns

Songs

Vocal music

Carpentry   694

Use for materials on the construction of a wooden building or the wooden portion of any building. Materials on the making and finishing of fine woodwork, such as furniture or interior details, are entered under **Cabinetwork.**

BT   **Building**

NT   **Cabinetwork**

Turning

RT   **Woodwork**

Carpentry—Tools

USE   **Carpentry tools**

Carpentry tools   694

UF   Carpentry—Tools

SA   types of carpentry tools [to be added as needed]

BT   **Tools**

NT   **Saws**

Carpet cleaning

USE   **Rugs and carpets—Cleaning**

Carpetbag rule

USE   **Reconstruction (1865-1876)**

Carpets

USE   **Rugs and carpets**

Carpools

USE   **Car pools**

Carriages and carts   388.3; 688.6

UF   Carts

Stagecoaches

Wagons

BT   **Vehicles**

Cars (Automobiles)

USE   **Automobiles**

Cartels

USE   **Industrial trusts**

Cartography

USE   **Map drawing**

Maps

Cartoons and caricatures   741.5

Use for collections of pictorial humor and for materials about caricatures and cartoons.

UF   Caricatures and cartoons

SA   subjects, classes of persons, names of individuals, and names of wars with the subdivision *Cartoons and caricatures* [to be added as needed]

BT   **Pictures**

Portraits

Cartoons and caricatures—*Continued*
  NT Animated films
      Computers—Cartoons and caricatures
      World War, 1939-1945—Cartoons and caricatures
  RT Comic books, strips, etc.
Cartoons, Animated
  USE Animated films
Cartoons, Television
  USE Animated television programs
Carts
  USE Carriages and carts
Carts (Midget cars)
  USE Karts and karting
Carving (Arts)
  USE Carving (Decorative arts)
Carving (Decorative arts) (May subdiv. geog.) 731.4; 736
  UF Carving (Arts)
  SA types of carving, e.g. Wood carving [to be added as needed]
  BT Decorative arts
  NT Wood carving
  RT Sculpture
Carving (Meat, etc.) 642
  BT Dining
      Entertaining
      Meat
Carving, Wood
  USE Wood carving
Case studies
  USE subjects with the subdivision *Case studies,* e.g. Juvenile delinquency—Case studies [to be added as needed]
Case work, Social
  USE Social case work
Cassette books
  USE Audiobooks
Cassette recorders and recording
  USE Magnetic recorders and recording
Cassette tapes, Audio
  USE Sound recordings
Castaways
  USE Survival after airplane accidents, shipwrecks, etc.
Caste (May subdiv. geog.) 305.5
  BT Manners and customs
  NT Social classes

Casting
  USE Founding
       Plaster casts
Castles (May subdiv. geog.) 728.8
  UF Chateaux
  BT Buildings
  RT Medieval architecture
Casts, Plaster
  USE Plaster casts
Casualty insurance 368.5
  UF Insurance, Casualty
  BT Insurance
  NT Accident insurance
CAT scan
  USE Tomography
Catacombs 393; 726
  BT Burial
      Cemeteries
      Christian antiquities
      Tombs
  RT Church history—30-600, Early church
Cataloging 025.3
  UF Cataloguing
      Libraries—Cataloging
      Library cataloging
  SA cataloging of particular subjects, e.g., Cataloging of music [to be added as needed]
  BT Bibliographic control
      Documentation
      Library science
      Library technical processes
  NT Automated cataloging
      Cataloging of music
      International Standard Bibliographic Description
      Library classification
      Machine readable bibliographic data
      Subject headings
  RT Bibliography
      Indexing
      Library catalogs
Cataloging data in machine readable form
  USE Machine readable bibliographic data
Cataloging—Data processing
  USE Automated cataloging
Cataloging—Music
  USE Cataloging of music

Cataloging of music   025.3
    UF   Cataloging—Music
         Music—Cataloging
    BT   **Cataloging**
Catalogs
    USE **Booksellers' catalogs**
         Commercial catalogs
         Library catalogs
         Publishers' catalogs
         and subjects and names of museums with the subdivision *Catalogs,* e.g. **Motion pictures—Catalogs** [to be added as needed]
Catalogs, Book
    USE **Book catalogs**
Catalogs, Booksellers'
    USE **Booksellers' catalogs**
Catalogs, Card
    USE **Card catalogs**
Catalogs, Classified
    USE **Classified catalogs**
Catalogs, Film
    USE **Motion pictures—Catalogs**
Catalogs in book form
    USE **Book catalogs**
Catalogs, Library
    USE **Library catalogs**
Catalogs, Online
    USE **Online catalogs**
Catalogs, Publishers'
    USE **Publishers' catalogs**
Catalogs, Subject
    USE **Subject catalogs**
Cataloguing
    USE **Cataloging**
Catalysis   541.3
    BT   **Physical chemistry**
    RT   **Catalytic RNA**
Catalytic RNA   572.8
    UF   Ribozymes
    BT   **Enzymes**
         RNA
    RT   **Catalysis**
Catamarans   797.1
    BT   **Boats and boating**
Catastrophes
    USE **Disasters**

Catechisms   238; 291.2
    SA   names of religions and sects and titles of sacred works with the subdivision *Catechisms* [to be added as needed]
    BT   **Theology—Study and teaching**
    NT   **Bible—Catechisms**
    RT   **Creeds**
Categories of persons
    USE **Persons**
         and classes of persons, e.g. **Elderly; Handicapped; Explorers; Drug addicts;** etc. [to be added as needed]
Caterers and catering
    USE **Catering**
Catering   642
    UF   Caterers and catering
    BT   **Cooking**
         Food service
    RT   **Menus**
Caterpillars   595.78
    UF   Cocoons
    BT   **Butterflies**
         Moths
Cathedrals (May subdiv. geog.)   726.6
    SA   names of individual cathedrals [to be added as needed]
    BT   **Church buildings**
    RT   **Abbeys**
         Church architecture
         Gothic architecture
         Medieval architecture
Cathedrals—United States   726.60973
Cathode ray tubes   537.5; 621.3815
    UF   CRTs
    BT   **Vacuum tubes**
Catholic charismatic movement   282
    UF   Charismatic movement
         Charismatic renewal movement
    BT   **Catholic Church**
         Episcopal Church
    RT   **Pentecostalism**
         Spiritual gifts
Catholic Church (May subdiv. geog.)   282
    UF   Roman Catholic Church
    SA   religious subjects with the subdivision *Catholic Church,* e.g. **Asceticism—Catholic Church; Laity—Catholic**

Catholic Church—*Continued*

Church; etc., and other subjects with the subdivisions
*Religious aspects—Catholic
Church;* e.g. **Abortion—Religious aspects—Catholic
Church** [to be added as
needed]

BT   **Christian sects**

Christianity

NT   **Catholic charismatic movement**

Inquisition

Laity—Catholic Church

Papacy

RT   **Catholics**

Catholic Church—Charities   361.7

BT   **Charities**

Catholic Church—Clergy   253

BT   **Clergy**

Priests

NT   **Cardinals**

Ex-priests

Catholic Church—Converts

USE   **Converts to Catholicism**

Catholic Church—Creeds   238

Use for materials about the concise, formal,
authorized statements of Catholic doctrine and
for the texts of such statements.

UF   Catholic creeds

BT   **Creeds**

Catholic Church—Foreign relations (May
subdiv. geog.)   **282; 327.456**

Use for materials on diplomatic relations
between the Catholic Church and various governments or political bodies. When this heading is subdivided geographically, an additional
entry is provided with the Catholic Church
and the place in reversed positions. Materials
on the relations between the Catholic Church
and other churches or religions are entered
under **Catholic Church—Relations.**

UF   Catholic Church—Relations
(Diplomatic)

Vatican City—Foreign relations

BT   **International relations**

Catholic Church—Liturgy   264

Use for materials on the forms of prayers,
rituals, and ceremonies used in the official
public worship of the Catholic Church. Texts
of Catholic liturgies are entered under **Catholic Church—Liturgy—Texts.**

UF   Catholic liturgies

BT   **Liturgies**

Rites and ceremonies

Catholic Church—Liturgy—Texts   264

Catholic Church—Missions   266

BT   **Christian missions**

Catholic Church—Relations   282

Use for materials on relations between the
Catholic Church and other churches or religions. This heading may be further subdivided
by church or religion, in which case an additional entry is provided with the two churches
or religions in reversed positions. Materials on
diplomatic relations between the Catholic
Church and various governments or political
bodies are entered under **Catholic Church—
Foreign relations.**

Catholic Church—Relations (Diplomatic)

USE   **Catholic Church—Foreign relations**

Catholic Church—United States   282

Catholic colleges and universities (May
subdiv. geog.)   **378**

UF   Catholic universities and colleges

BT   **Colleges and universities**

Catholic converts

USE   **Converts to Catholicism**

Catholic creeds

USE   **Catholic Church—Creeds**

Catholic ex-nuns

USE   **Ex-nuns**

Catholic ex-priests

USE   **Ex-priests**

Catholic laity

USE   **Laity—Catholic Church**

Catholic literature   282; 808; 809

BT   **Christian literature**

Literature

Catholic liturgies

USE   **Catholic Church—Liturgy**

Catholic universities and colleges

USE   **Catholic colleges and universities**

Catholics (May subdiv. geog.)   **282.092;
305.6**

NT   **Converts to Catholicism**

RT   **Catholic Church**

Catholics—United States   282.092;
305.6

Cats (May subdiv. geog.)   599.75; 636.8

Use for materials on domestic cats. Materials on non-domesticated species of cats or domestic cats living in a wild state are entered
under **Wild cats.**

UF   Kittens

SA   names of specific breeds of cat
[to be added as needed]

BT   **Domestic animals**

Mammals

Cats—*Continued*
  RT **Wild cats**
Cats—Literary collections   808.8; 810.8,
    etc.
Cattle 599.64; 636.2
  UF Cows
  BT **Domestic animals**
       Mammals
  NT **Beef cattle**
       Dairy cattle
Cattle brands 636.2
Cattle—Vaccination 636.089
  BT **Vaccination**
Causes
  USE names of wars with the subdivi-
       sion *Causes,* e.g. **World**
       War, 1939-1945—Causes [to
       be added as needed]
Cautionary tales and verse
  USE **Fables**
       Parables
Cautionary tales and verses
  USE **Didactic fiction**
       Didactic poetry
Cave drawings
  USE **Cave drawings and paintings**
Cave drawings and paintings (May
    subdiv. geog.)   **743; 759.01**
  UF Cave drawings *[Former head-*
       ing]
       Cave paintings
  BT **Rock drawings, paintings, and**
       engravings
Cave dwellers 569.9; 930.1
  BT **Prehistoric peoples**
Cave paintings
  USE **Cave drawings and paintings**
Caves 551.44
  UF Grottoes
       Speleology
CB radio
  USE **Citizens band radio**
CD-I technology 006.7
  UF CDI technology
       Compact disc interactive technol-
       ogy
       Interactive CD technology
  BT **Compact discs**
       Optical storage devices
CD players
  USE **Compact disc players**

CD-ROM
  USE **CD-ROMs**
CD-ROMs 004.5
  UF CD-ROM
       CDROM
       CDROMs
       Compact disc read-only memory
  BT **Compact discs**
       Optical storage devices
CDI technology
  USE **CD-I technology**
CDROM
  USE **CD-ROMs**
CDROMs
  USE **CD-ROMs**
CDs (Compact discs)
  USE **Compact discs**
Celebrities (May subdiv. geog.)   **920**
  UF Famous people
       Public figures
  SA types of celebrities, e.g. **Actors;**
       Television personalities; and
       names of individual celebrities
       [to be added as needed]
  BT **Persons**
  NT **Television personalities**
Celery 635; 641.3
  BT **Vegetables**
Celibacy 248.4; 291.4
    Use for materials on the renunciation of
  marriage for religious reasons. Materials on
  the virtue that moderates and regulates the
  sexual appetite in human beings are entered
  under **Chastity.** Materials on abstinence from
  sexual activity are entered under **Sexual absti-**
  nence.
  UF Clerical celibacy
  BT **Clergy**
       Religious life
  RT **Chastity**
       Sexual abstinence
Cellars
  USE **Basements**
Cellists
  USE **Violoncellists**
Cello
  USE **Violoncellos**
Cello players
  USE **Violoncellists**
Cells 571.6
  UF Cytology
  BT **Biology**
       Physiology

Cells—*Continued*
        Reproduction
  NT DNA
  RT Embryology
        Protoplasm
Cells, Electric
  USE Electric batteries
Celtic legends   398.2
  BT Legends
Celtic mythology   299; 936
  UF Mythology, Celtic
  BT **Mythology**
Celts (May subdiv. geog.)   305.891;
      936.4
  UF Gaels
  BT **France—History—0-1328**
        Great Britain—History—0-1066
  NT **Druids and Druidism**
Cement   620.1; 666; 691
  UF Hydraulic cement
  BT **Adhesives**
        Building materials
        Ceramics
        Masonry
        Plaster and plastering
  RT **Concrete**
Cemeteries (May subdiv. geog.)   393;
      718
  UF Burying grounds
        Churchyards
        Graves
        Graveyards
  SA types of cemeteries and names
        of individual cemeteries [to
        be added as needed]
  BT **Burial**
        Public health
        Sanitation
  NT **Catacombs**
        Epitaphs
  RT **Tombs**
Censorship (May subdiv. geog.)   303.3;
      363.3
  Use for general materials on the limitation
of freedom of expression in various fields.
  SA subjects and names of wars with
        the subdivision *Censorship,*
        e.g. **Books—Censorship** [to
        be added as needed]
  BT **Intellectual freedom**
  NT **Books—Censorship**
        Freedom of speech

        Libraries—Censorship
        Motion pictures—Censorship
        Television—Censorship
        World War, 1939-1945—Censorship
  RT **Freedom of information**
        Freedom of the press
Census   304.6; 310; 352.7
  SA names of countries, cities, etc.,
        with the subdivision *Census*
        [to be added as needed]
  BT **Population**
        Statistics
        Vital statistics
  NT **Chicago (Ill.)—Census**
        Ohio—Census
        United States—Census
Centennial celebrations, etc.
  USE names of places, wars, and his-
        torical events with the subdi-
        vision *Centennial celebrations,*
        etc., e.g. **United States—History—1861-1865, Civil War—Centennial celebrations, etc.** [to be added as needed]
Centers for the performing arts   725;
      790.2
  SA names of individual centers [to
        be added as needed]
  BT **Performing arts**
  NT **Theaters**
Central Africa   967
  Use for materials dealing collectively with
the region of Africa that includes the Central
African Republic, Equatorial Guinea, Gabon,
Congo (Republic), and Congo (Democratic
Republic).
  UF Africa, Central
  BT **Africa**
  NT **French-speaking Equatorial Africa**
Central America   972.8
  BT **North America**
Central Asia   958
  UF Asia, Central
  BT **Asia**
Central Asia—History   958
Central Asia—History—1991-   958
Central Europe   943
  Use for materials on the area included in
the basins of the Danube, Elbe and Rhine riv-
ers.

Central Europe—*Continued*
    UF   Europe, Central
Central planning
    USE   **Economic policy**
Central States
    USE   **Middle West**
Centralization of schools
    USE   **Schools—Centralization**
Centralized processing (Libraries)
    USE   **Library technical processes**
Ceramic industries
    USE   **Ceramic industry**
Ceramic industry (May subdiv. geog.)
    338.4
    UF   Ceramic industries *[Former*
          heading]
    SA   types of ceramic industries, e.g.
          Glass manufacture [to be
          added as needed]
    BT   **Industries**
    NT   **Clay industry**
          Glass manufacture
    RT   **Ceramics**
Ceramic materials
    USE   **Ceramics**
Ceramic tiles
    USE   **Tiles**
Ceramics   **666**
     Use for materials on the technology of fired
earth products or on ceramic products intend-
ed for industrial use. Materials on ceramic
products intended for the table or decorative
use are entered under **Pottery** or **Porcelain.**
    UF   Ceramic materials
    BT   **Industrial chemistry**
          Materials
    NT   **Abrasives**
          Cement
          Clay
          Glass
          Glazes
          Pottery
          Tiles
    RT   **Ceramic industry**
Cereals
    USE   **Grain**
Cereals, Prepared
    USE   **Prepared cereals**
Cerebral palsy   **616.8**
    UF   Paralysis, Cerebral
    BT   **Brain—Diseases**
Cerebrovascular disease
    USE   **Stroke**

Ceremonies
    USE   **Etiquette**
          Manners and customs
          Rites and ceremonies
Certainty   **121**
    BT   **Logic**
          Theory of knowledge
    RT   **Truth**
Certified public accountants
    USE   **Accountants**
Chain belting
    USE   **Belts and belting**
Chain stores   **658.8**
    UF   Branch stores
    BT   **Retail trade**
          Stores
Chair caning   **684.1**
    UF   Caning of chairs
    BT   **Handicraft**
Chairs   **645; 684.1; 749**
    BT   **Furniture**
Chalk talks   **741.2**
    UF   Blackboard drawing
    BT   **Public speaking**
Challenger (Space shuttle)
    USE   **Challenger (Spacecraft)**
Challenger (Spacecraft)   **629.44**
    UF   Challenger (Space shuttle)
    BT   **Space shuttles**
Chamber music   **785**
    BT   **Instrumental music**
          Music
    NT   **Quintets**
Chambers of commerce (May subdiv.
    geog.)   **380.106; 381.06**
    UF   Boards of trade
          Trade, Boards of
    BT   **Commerce**
Change of life in men
    USE   **Male climacteric**
Change of life in women
    USE   **Menopause**
Change of sex
    USE   **Transsexualism**
Change, Organizational
    USE   **Organizational change**
Change, Social
    USE   **Social change**
Changing careers
    USE   **Career changes**

Chanties
USE **Sea songs**
Chants (Plain, Gregorian, etc.) 782.32
Use for books of chants and for materials about chants.
UF Gregorian chant
Plain chant
Plainsong
BT **Church music**
Chanukah
USE **Hanukkah**
Chaos (Science) 003
UF Chaotic behavior in systems
BT **Dynamics**
Science
System theory
Chaotic behavior in systems
USE **Chaos (Science)**
Chap-books
USE **Chapbooks**
Chapbooks 398
May be used for individual works, collections, or materials about chapbooks.
UF Chap-books
Jestbooks
BT **Books**
Folklore
Literature
Pamphlets
Periodicals
Wit and humor
RT **Comic books, strips, etc.**
Chaplains 253
SA corporate bodies and institutions with the subdivision *Chaplains,* e.g. **United States. Army—Chaplains** [to be added as needed]
BT **Clergy**
NT **United States. Army—Chaplains**
Character 155.2
BT **Personality**
NT **Human behavior**
RT **Temperament**
Character assassination
USE **Libel and slander**
Character education
USE **Moral education**
Characters
USE **Characters and characteristics in literature**

and names of authors with the subdivision *Characters;* e.g. **Shakespeare, William, 1564-1616—Characters** [to be added as needed]
Characters and characteristics in literature 809; 810.9, etc.
UF Characters
Fictional characters
Fictitious characters
Literary characters
SA names of authors with the subdivision *Characters;* e.g. **Shakespeare, William, 1564-1616—Characters;** racial and ethnic groups and classes of persons in literature, e.g. **African Americans in literature; Children in literature;** etc.; names of persons, families, and corporate bodies with the subdivision *In literature,* e.g. **Napoleon I, Emperor of the French, 1769-1821—In literature;** and individual literary characters established in the inverted form with the qualifier (Fictitious character), e.g. **Holmes, Sherlock (Fictitious character)** [to be added as needed]
BT **Literature**
RT **Literature—Themes**
Charades 793.2
BT **Amateur theater**
Amusements
Literary recreations
Riddles
Charcoal 662
BT **Fuel**
Charismata
USE **Spiritual gifts**
Charismatic movement
USE **Catholic charismatic movement**
Pentecostalism
Charismatic renewal movement
USE **Catholic charismatic movement**
Pentecostalism
Charitable institutions
USE **Charities**
Institutional care

Charitable institutions—*Continued*
  Orphanages
Charities (May subdiv. geog.) **361.7**
  Use for materials on privately supported welfare activities. Materials on tax supported welfare activities are entered under **Public welfare.** Materials on the methods employed in welfare work, public or private, are entered under **Social work.** General materials on the various policies, programs, services, and facilities to meet basic human needs, such as health, education, and welfare, are entered under **Human services.**
  UF Charitable institutions
      Endowed charities
      Homes (Institutions)
      Institutions, Charitable and philanthropic
      Poor relief
      Social welfare
      Welfare agencies
      Welfare work
  SA names of appropriate corporate bodies with the subdivision *Charities,* e.g. **Catholic Church—Charities;** and names of wars with the subdivision *Civilian relief,* e.g. **World War, 1939-1945—Civilian relief** [to be added as needed]
  BT **Human services**
      Social work
  NT **Catholic Church—Charities**
      Child welfare
      Disaster relief
      Food relief
      Institutional care
      Medical charities
      Orphanages
      Social settlements
      World War, 1939-1945—Civilian relief
  RT **Charity organization**
      Endowments
      Philanthropy
      Public welfare
      Volunteer work
Charities, Medical
  USE **Medical charities**
Charity **177**
  BT **Ethics**
      Virtue
  RT **Love—Religious aspects**

Charity organization **361**
  BT **Associations**
  RT **Charities**
      Philanthropy
Charlatans
  USE **Impostors and imposture**
Charms **133.4**
  UF Spells
      Talismans
  BT **Folklore**
      Superstition
Charter flights
  USE **Airlines—Chartering**
Charter schools (May subdiv. geog.) **371.01**
  Use for materials on legislatively authorized, independent, and innovative public schools that operate under the authority of a charter.
  BT **Schools**
Charters
  UF Documents
  BT **History—Sources**
  NT **Magna Carta**
  RT **Archives**
      Manuscripts
Chartography
  USE **Maps**
Charts
  USE **Charts, diagrams, etc.**
Charts, diagrams, etc. **912**
  UF Charts *[Former heading]*
  SA topics with the subdivision *Charts, diagrams, etc.,* for works consisting of charts or diagrams illustrating those topics, e.g. **Electric wiring—Charts, diagrams, etc.** [to be added as needed]
  RT **Maps**
Charts, Nautical
  USE **Nautical charts**
Chasidism
  USE **Hasidism**
Chastity **176**
  Use for materials on the virtue that moderates and regulates the sexual appetite in human beings. Materials on the renunciation of marriage for religious reasons are entered under **Celibacy.** Materials on abstinence from sexual activity are entered under **Sexual abstinence.**
  BT **Sexual ethics**
      Virtue

Chastity—*Continued*
    RT   **Celibacy**
           Sexual abstinence
Chat groups, Online
    USE **Online chat groups**
Chat rooms, Online
    USE **Online chat groups**
Chateaux
    USE **Castles**
Cheating in sports
    USE **Sports—Corrupt practices**
Checkers 794.2
    UF   Draughts
    BT   **Games**
Cheerleaders
    USE **Cheerleading**
Cheerleading 371.8; 791.6
    UF   Cheerleaders
           Cheers and cheerleading
    BT   **Student activities**
Cheers and cheerleading
    USE **Cheerleading**
Cheese 637; 641.3
    BT   **Dairy products**
Cheese—Bacteriology
    USE **Cheese—Microbiology**
Cheese—Microbiology 637
    UF   Cheese—Bacteriology
    BT   **Microbiology**
Chemical analysis
    USE **Analytical chemistry**
Chemical apparatus 542
    UF   Apparatus, Chemical
           Chemistry—Apparatus
    BT   **Scientific apparatus and instruments**
Chemical elements 546
    UF   Elements, Chemical
    SA   names of chemical elements [to be added as needed]
    BT   **Chemistry**
    NT   **Carbon**
           Gold
           Helium
           Hydrogen
           Iron
           Mercury
           Oxygen
           Radium
           Silver
           Sulphur
           Tin

           Uranium
           Zinc
    RT   **Periodic law**
Chemical engineering (May subdiv. geog.)
    660
    UF   Chemistry, Industrial
           Chemistry, Technical
    BT   **Engineering**
    NT   **Biotechnology**
           Fermentation
    RT   **Industrial chemistry**
           Metallurgy
Chemical equations 540
    UF   Equations, Chemical
    BT   **Chemical reactions**
Chemical geology
    USE **Geochemistry**
Chemical industries
    USE **Chemical industry**
Chemical industry (May subdiv. geog.)
    338.4; 660
    Use for materials about industries that produce chemicals or are based on chemical processes. General materials on chemicals, including their manufacture, are entered under **Chemicals.**
    UF   Chemical industries
           Chemistry, Industrial
           Chemistry, Technical
    SA   types of industries, e.g. **Plastics industry** [to be added as needed]
    BT   **Industries**
    NT   **Plastics industry**
    RT   **Chemicals**
           Industrial chemistry
Chemical industry—Accidents 363.11
    BT   **Industrial accidents**
Chemical industry—Employees 331.11
    UF   Chemical workers
    BT   **Employees**
**Chemical industry—Employees—Diseases
    616.9**
    UF   Chemical workers' diseases
    BT   **Occupational diseases**
**Chemical industry—Employees—Pensions
    331.25**
**Chemical industry—Employees—Salaries,
    wages, etc.** (May subdiv. geog.)
    331.2
    BT   **Salaries, wages, etc.**

Chemical industry—Law and legislation
(May subdiv. geog.) 343
 BT Law
 Legislation
Chemical industry—Waste disposal
363.72; 628.4
 BT Refuse and refuse disposal
Chemical landfills
 USE Hazardous waste sites
Chemical pollution
 USE Pollution
Chemical reactions 541.3
 UF Reactions, Chemical
 BT Chemistry
 NT Chemical equations
Chemical societies
 USE Chemistry—Societies
Chemical technology
 USE Industrial chemistry
Chemical warfare 358; 623.4
 UF Gas warfare
 Poisonous gases—War use
 SA names of wars with the subdivision Chemical warfare [to be added as needed]
 BT Military art and science
 War
 NT Incendiary weapons
 World War, 1914-1918—Chemical warfare
 World War, 1939-1945—Chemical warfare
Chemical workers
 USE Chemical industry—Employees
Chemical workers' diseases
 USE Chemical industry—Employees—Diseases
Chemicals 540; 661
 Use for general materials on chemicals, including their manufacture. Materials about industries that produce chemicals or are based on chemical processes are entered under **Chemical industry.**
 SA types of chemicals, e.g. **Acids; Agricultural chemicals;** etc.; and names of individual chemicals [to be added as needed]
 NT Acids
 Agricultural chemicals
 Alcohol
 Carbolic acid
 Deuterium oxide

 Nitrates
 Organic compounds
 Petrochemicals
 RT Chemical industry
 Industrial chemistry
Chemicals—Toxicology
 USE Toxicology
Chemistry 540
 BT Physical sciences
 Science
 NT Acids
 Agricultural chemistry
 Alchemy
 Analytical chemistry
 Bases (Chemistry)
 Biochemistry
 Botanical chemistry
 Chemical elements
 Chemical reactions
 Color
 Combustion
 Explosives
 Fermentation
 Fire
 Geochemistry
 Industrial chemistry
 Inorganic chemistry
 Microchemistry
 Organic chemistry
 Pharmaceutical chemistry
 Pharmacy
 Photographic chemistry
 Physical chemistry
 Space chemistry
 Spectrum analysis
Chemistry, Analytic
 USE Analytical chemistry
Chemistry—Apparatus
 USE Chemical apparatus
Chemistry, Diagnostic
 USE Clinical chemistry
Chemistry—Dictionaries 540.3
 BT Encyclopedias and dictionaries
Chemistry—Experiments 540; 542
Chemistry, Industrial
 USE Chemical engineering
 Chemical industry
Chemistry, Inorganic
 USE Inorganic chemistry
Chemistry—Laboratory manuals
540.78

Chemistry, Medical
    USE   **Clinical chemistry**
Chemistry of food
    USE   **Food—Analysis**
            Food—Composition
Chemistry, Organic
    USE   **Organic chemistry**
Chemistry, Physical and theoretical
    USE   **Physical chemistry**
Chemistry—Problems, exercises, etc.
    540.76
Chemistry—Societies   540.6
    UF   Chemical societies
    BT   **Societies**
Chemistry, Synthetic
    USE   **Organic compounds—Synthesis**
Chemistry, Technical
    USE   **Chemical engineering**
            Chemical industry
            Industrial chemistry
Chemistry, Textile
    USE   **Textile chemistry**
Chemists (May subdiv. geog.)   **540.92;**
    920
    BT   **Scientists**
Chemists' shops
    USE   **Drugstores**
Chemotherapy
    USE   **Cancer—Chemotherapy**
            Drug therapy
Chess   794.1
    BT   **Games**
Chicago (Ill.)   917.73; 977.3
    The subdivisions under **Chicago (Ill.)** may
    be used under the name of any city. The sub-
    divisions under **United States** may be further
    consulted as a guide for formulating other
    headings as needed.
Chicago (Ill.)—Antiquities   977.3
    BT   **Antiquities**
Chicago (Ill.)—Bibliography   015.773;
    016.9773
Chicago (Ill.)—Bio-bibliography   012
Chicago (Ill.)—Biography   920.0773
    BT   **Biography**
Chicago (Ill.)—Biography—Portraits
    920.0773
Chicago (Ill.)—Boundaries   977.3
    BT   **Boundaries**
Chicago (Ill.)—Bridges
    USE   **Bridges—Chicago (Ill.)**
Chicago (Ill.)—Census   317.73
    BT   **Census**

Chicago (Ill.)—City planning
    USE   **City planning—Chicago (Ill.)**
Chicago (Ill.)—Civil defense
    USE   **Civil defense—Chicago (Ill.)**
Chicago (Ill.)—Climate   551.69773
    BT   **Climate**
Chicago (Ill.)—Commerce   381
    BT   **Commerce**
Chicago (Ill.)—Description   917.73
Chicago (Ill.)—Description—Guidebooks
    USE   **Chicago (Ill.)—Guidebooks**
Chicago (Ill.)—Description—Views
    USE   **Chicago (Ill.)—Pictorial works**
Chicago (Ill.)—Directories   917.73
    Use for lists of names and addresses. Lists
    of names without addresses are entered under
    Chicago (Ill.)—Registers.
    BT   **Directories**
    NT   **Chicago (Ill.)—Telephone di-**
            rectories
    RT   **Chicago (Ill.)—Registers**
Chicago (Ill.)—Directories—Telephone
    USE   **Chicago (Ill.)—Telephone di-**
            rectories
Chicago (Ill.)—Economic conditions
    330.9773
    BT   **Economic conditions**
Chicago (Ill.)—Employees
    USE   **Chicago (Ill.)—Officials and**
            employees
Chicago (Ill.)—Government
    USE   **Chicago (Ill.)—Politics and**
            government
Chicago (Ill.)—Government employees
    USE   **Chicago (Ill.)—Officials and**
            employees
Chicago (Ill.)—Government publications
    USE   **Government publications—Chi-**
            cago (Ill.)
Chicago (Ill.)—Guidebooks   917.73
    UF   Chicago (Ill.)—Description—
            Guidebooks
Chicago (Ill.)—Historic buildings
    USE   **Historic buildings—Chicago**
            (Ill.)
Chicago (Ill.)—History   977.3
Chicago (Ill.)—History—Societies
    977.3006
    BT   **History—Societies**
Chicago (Ill.)—Industries
    USE   **Industries—Chicago (Ill.)**

Chicago (Ill.)—Intellectual life   977.3
   BT   Intellectual life
Chicago (Ill.)—Manufactures
   USE   Manufactures—Chicago (Ill.)
Chicago (Ill.)—Maps   912.773
   BT   Maps
Chicago (Ill.)—Moral conditions   977.3
   BT   Moral conditions
Chicago (Ill.)—Occupations
   USE   Occupations—Chicago (Ill.)
Chicago (Ill.)—Officials and employees
      352.1773
   UF   Chicago (Ill.)—Employees
         Chicago (Ill.)—Government em-
         ployees
Chicago (Ill.)—Pictorial works   917.73
   UF   Chicago (Ill.)—Description—
         Views
Chicago (Ill.)—Politics and government
      977.3
   UF   Chicago (Ill.)—Government
   BT   Municipal government
         Politics
Chicago (Ill.)—Popular culture
   USE   Popular culture—Chicago (Ill.)
Chicago (Ill.)—Population   304.609773
   BT   Population
Chicago (Ill.)—Public buildings
   USE   Public buildings—Chicago (Ill.)
Chicago (Ill.)—Public works
   USE   Public works—Chicago (Ill.)
Chicago (Ill.)—Race relations
      305.8009773
   BT   Race relations
Chicago (Ill.)—Registers   917.73
      Use for lists of names without addresses.
      Lists of names that include addresses are en-
      tered under Chicago (Ill.)—Directories.
   RT   Chicago (Ill.)—Directories
Chicago (Ill.)—Social conditions   977.3
   BT   Social conditions
Chicago (Ill.)—Social life and customs
      977.3
   BT   Manners and customs
Chicago (Ill.)—Social policy
   USE   Social policy—Chicago (Ill.)
Chicago (Ill.)—Statistics   317.73
   BT   Statistics
Chicago (Ill.)—Streets
   USE   Streets—Chicago (Ill.)
Chicago (Ill.)—Suburbs and environs
   USE   Chicago Suburban Area (Ill.)

Chicago (Ill.)—Telephone directories
      917.73
   UF   Chicago (Ill.)—Directories—
         Telephone
   BT   Chicago (Ill.)—Directories
Chicago (Ill.)—Urban renewal
   USE   Urban renewal—Chicago (Ill.)
Chicago Metropolitan Area (Ill.)   977.3
   RT   Chicago Suburban Area (Ill.)
Chicago Metropolitan Area (Ill.)—Poli-
      tics and government   977.3
   BT   Metropolitan government
Chicago Suburban Area (Ill.)   977.3
   UF   Chicago (Ill.)—Suburbs and en-
         virons
   RT   Chicago Metropolitan Area
         (Ill.)
Chicanas
   USE   Mexican American women
Chicano literature (English)
   USE   American literature—Mexican
         American authors
Chicanos
   USE   Mexican Americans
Chicken pox
   USE   Chickenpox
Chickenpox   616.9
   UF   Chicken pox
   BT   Diseases
         Viruses
Chief justices
   USE   Judges
Child abuse (May subdiv. geog.)
      362.76; 364.15
   UF   Abuse of children
         Abused children
         Child neglect
         Children—Abuse
         Cruelty to children
   BT   Child welfare
         Domestic violence
         Parent-child relationship
   NT   Child sexual abuse
   RT   Adult child abuse victims
Child abuse survivors
   USE   Adult child abuse victims
Child-adult relationship   305.23; 362.7;
      649
   UF   Adults and children
         Children and adults [Former
            heading]

123

Child-adult relationship—*Continued*
  BT **Children**
  NT **Child rearing**
      Children and strangers
      Conflict of generations
      Parent-child relationship
      Teacher-student relationship
Child and father
  USE **Father-child relationship**
Child and mother
  USE **Mother-child relationship**
Child and parent
  USE **Parent-child relationship**
Child artists   704; 709.2; 920
    Use for materials on children as artists and
  on works of art by children.
  UF Children as artists
  BT **Artists**
      Gifted children
  NT **Finger painting**
Child authors   809; 920
    Use for materials on children as authors and
  discussions of literary works written by chil-
  dren. Individual literary works and collections
  of literary works written by children are en-
  tered under the form heading **Children's
  writings.**
  UF Children as authors
  BT **Authors**
      Gifted children
  RT **Children's writings**
Child birth
  USE **Childbirth**
Child care (May subdiv. geog.)   649
  UF Care of children
      Children—Care
  NT **Babysitting**
      Child rearing
      Day care centers
      Infants—Care
Child care centers
  USE **Day care centers**
Child custody   306.89; 346.01; 362.7
  UF Children—Custody
      Custody of children
      Joint custody of children
      Parental custody
      Shared custody
  BT **Divorce mediation**
      Parent-child relationship
  NT **Parental kidnapping**
  RT **Visitation rights (Domestic re-
      lations)**

Child development   155.4; 305.231;
      612.6
  UF Child study
      Children—Development
  BT **Children**
  NT **Children—Growth**
  RT **Child psychology**
      Child rearing
Child labor (May subdiv. geog.)   331.3
  UF Boys—Employment
      Children—Employment *[Former
        heading]*
      Employment of children
      Girls—Employment
      Working children
  BT **Age and employment**
      Child welfare
      Labor
      Social problems
Child labor—United States   331.3
Child molesting
  USE **Child sexual abuse**
Child neglect
  USE **Child abuse**
Child placing
  USE **Adoption**
      Foster home care
Child prostitution
  USE **Juvenile prostitution**
Child psychiatry   616.89; 618.92
    Use for materials on the clinical and thera-
  peutic aspects of mental disorders in children.
  Materials on children suffering from mental or
  emotional illnesses are entered under **Emo-
  tionally distrubed children.**
  UF Children—Mental health
      Pediatric psychiatry
  BT **Psychiatry**
  NT **Autism**
      Mentally handicapped children
  RT **Child psychology**
      Emotionally disturbed children
Child psychology   155.4
  UF Child study
      Children—Psychology
  BT **Psychology**
  NT **Emotions in children**
      Imaginary playmates
      Intelligence tests
      Psychology of learning
      Separation anxiety in children
      Sibling rivalry

Child psychology—*Continued*
RT   **Child development**
      Child psychiatry
      Child rearing
      Educational psychology
Child raising
  USE   **Child rearing**
Child rearing   **392.1; 649**

Use for materials on the principles and techniques of rearing children. Materials on the psychological and social interaction between parents and their minor children are entered under **Parent-child relationship.** Materials on the skills, attributes, and attitudes needed for parenthood are entered under **Parenting.**

  UF   Child raising
      Children—Management
      Children—Training
      Discipline of children
      Training of children
  BT   **Child-adult relationship**
      Child care
      Parent-child relationship
  NT   **Children's allowances**
      Socialization
      Toilet training
  RT   **Child development**
      Child psychology
      Parenting
Child sex abuse
  USE   **Child sexual abuse**
Child sexual abuse (May subdiv. geog.)   **362.76; 364.15**
  UF   Child molesting
      Child sex abuse
      Children—Molesting
      Molesting of children
      Sexual abuse
      Sexually abused children
  BT   **Child abuse**
      Incest
      Sex crimes
  RT   **Adult child sexual abuse victims**
Child snatching by parents
  USE   **Parental kidnapping**
Child study
  USE   **Child development**
      Child psychology
Child support   **346.01**
  UF   Support of children
  BT   **Child welfare**
      Desertion and nonsupport

Divorce mediation
Child welfare (May subdiv. geog.)
  362.7

Use for materials on the aid, support, and protection of children, by the state or by private welfare organizations.

  UF   Aid to dependent children
      Children—Charities, protection, etc.
      Mothers' pensions
      Protection of children
  BT   **Charities**
      Public welfare
      Social work
  NT   **Abandoned children**
      Child abuse
      Child labor
      Child support
      Children—Institutional care
      Day care centers
      Foster home care
  RT   **Children's hospitals**
      Juvenile delinquency
      Orphanages
Childbirth (May subdiv. geog.)   **612.6; 618.2**
  UF   Birth
      Birth customs
      Child birth
      Labor (Childbirth)
      Obstetrics
  NT   **Midwives**
      Multiple birth
      Natural childbirth
  RT   **Pregnancy**
Childhood diseases
  USE   **Children—Diseases**
Childlessness   **306.85**
  BT   **Children**
      Family size
  RT   **Birth control**
      Human fertility
      Infertility
Children (May subdiv. geog.)   **305.23**

Use for materials on people from birth through age twelve. Materials limited to the first two years of a child's life are entered under **Infants.**

  UF   Preschool children
  SA   children of particular racial or ethnic groups, e.g. **African American children;** children

Children—*Continued*

and other subjects, e.g. **Children and war;** and names of wars with the subdivision *Children,* e.g. **World War, 1939-1945—Children** [to be added as needed]

BT   Age

Family

NT   **Abandoned children**

Adopted children

Advertising and children

African American children

Birth order

Black children

Boys

Child-adult relationship

Child development

Childlessness

Children and war

Children of alcoholics

Children of drug addicts

Children of immigrants

Computers and children

Exceptional children

Father-child relationship

Foster children

Girls

Handicapped children

Infants

Missing children

Mother-child relationship

Motion pictures and children

Native American children

Only child

Orphans

Parent-child relationship

Runaway children

School children

Television and children

Children, Abnormal

USE   **Handicapped children**

Children—Abuse

USE   **Child abuse**

Children—Adoption

USE   **Adoption**

Children and adults

USE   **Child-adult relationship**

Children and advertising

USE   **Advertising and children**

Children and motion pictures

USE   **Motion pictures and children**

Children and strangers   362.7

UF   Infants and strangers

Strangers and children

BT   **Child-adult relationship**

Children and television

USE   **Television and children**

Children and war (May subdiv. geog.)   **305.23**

UF   War and children

SA   names of particular wars with the subdivision *Children,* e.g. **World War, 1939-1945—Children** [to be added as needed]

BT   **Children**

War

NT   **World War, 1939-1945—Children**

Children as artists

USE   **Child artists**

Children as authors

USE   **Child authors**

Children as consumers

USE   **Young consumers**

Children, Black

USE   **Black children**

Children—Books and reading   011.62; 028.5

Use for materials on the reading interests of children and lists of books for children. Collections or materials about literature published for children are entered under **Children's literature.** Individual literary works and collections of literary works written by children are entered under **Children's writings.** Materials about works written by children and materials about children as authors are entered under **Child authors.**

UF   Books and reading for children

Children's reading

Reading interests of children

BT   **Books and reading**

Children—Care

USE   **Child care**

Children—Charities, protection, etc.

USE   **Child welfare**

Children—Civil rights   323.3; 342

BT   **Civil rights**

Children—Clothing

USE   **Children's clothing**

Children—Costume

USE   **Children's costumes**

Children, Crippled
  USE **Physically handicapped children**
Children—Custody
  USE **Child custody**
Children—Day care
  USE **Day care centers**
Children—Dental care 617.6
Children—Development
  USE **Child development**
Children—Diseases 618.92
  UF Childhood diseases
      Children's diseases
      Diseases of children
      Medicine, Pediatric
      Pediatrics
  SA types of diseases, e.g.
      Chickenpox [to be added as needed]
  BT **Diseases**
  RT **Children—Health and hygiene**
Children—Education
  USE **Elementary education**
       Preschool education
Children—Employment
  USE **Child labor**
Children—Food
  USE **Children—Nutrition**
Children, Gifted
  USE **Gifted children**
Children—Growth 155.4; 612.6
  BT **Child development**
Children—Health and hygiene (May subdiv. geog.) **613**
  UF Children—Hygiene
      Pediatrics
  BT **Health**
      Hygiene
  NT **Children—Nutrition**
      School hygiene
  RT **Children—Diseases**
      Children's hospitals
      Health education
Children—Hospitals
  USE **Children's hospitals**
Children—Hygiene
  USE **Children—Health and hygiene**
Children, Hyperactive
  USE **Hyperactive children**

Children in art 704.9
  Use for materials on children depicted in works of art. Materials on children as artists are entered under **Child artists.**
  BT **Art—Themes**
Children in literature 809
  Use for materials on the theme of children in works of literature. Individual literary works or collections of literary works written by children are entered under the form heading **Children's writings.** Materials about children as authors and about works written by children are entered under **Child authors.**
  BT **Literature—Themes**
Children—Institutional care (May subdiv. geog.) **362.73**
  UF Boys' towns
      Children's homes
  BT **Child welfare**
      Institutional care
  NT **Day care centers**
      Orphanages
      Reformatories
  RT **Foster home care**
Children—Language 155.4
  BT **Language and languages**
Children—Management
  USE **Child rearing**
Children—Medical examinations 616.07
  UF Medical inspection in schools
      School children—Medical examinations
Children—Mental health
  USE **Child psychiatry**
Children—Molesting
  USE **Child sexual abuse**
Children—Nutrition 613.2083; 641.1083; 649
  UF Children—Food
      Children's food
  BT **Children—Health and hygiene**
      Nutrition
  NT **School children—Food**
Children of alcoholics 362.292
  UF Alcoholic parents
      COAs
  BT **Children**
  NT **Adult children of alcoholics**
  RT **Alcoholics**
Children of divorced parents 306.874; 646.7
  BT **Divorce**
      Parent-child relationship
  RT **Part-time parenting**

Children of drug addicts 362.29
  UF Children of narcotic addicts
      Cocaine babies
      Crack babies
  BT **Children**
      Drug addicts
Children of immigrants 305.23
  UF First generation children
  BT **Children**
      Immigration and emigration
Children of narcotic addicts
  USE **Children of drug addicts**
Children of single fathers
  USE **Children of single parents**
Children of single mothers
  USE **Children of single parents**
Children of single parents 306.874
  UF Children of single fathers
      Children of single mothers
      Single parents' children
  BT **Single parents**
Children of working parents 306.874;
      362.7
  UF Working parents' children
  BT **Parent-child relationship**
  NT **Latchkey children**
Children—Placing out
  USE **Adoption**
      Foster home care
Children—Psychology
  USE **Child psychology**
Children, Retarded
  USE **Mentally handicapped children**
Children—Socialization
  USE **Socialization**
Children—Surgery 617
  UF Pediatric surgery
  BT **Surgery**
Children—Training
  USE **Child rearing**
Children—United States 305.230973
Children's allowances 332.024; 649
  UF Allowances, Children's
  BT **Child rearing**
      Money
      Personal finance
  RT **Money-making projects for
      children**
Children's books
  USE **Children's literature**

Children's clothing 391; 646.4
  Use for materials on children's clothing that
  is worn from day to day, including historical
  materials. Works on children's costumes for
  fancy dress of theatricals are entered under
  Children's costumes.
  UF Children—Clothing
  BT **Clothing and dress**
  NT **Infants' clothing**
  RT **Children's costumes**
Children's costumes 646.4; 792
  Use for materials on children's costumes for
  fancy dress or theatricals. Materials on chil-
  dren's clothing that is worn from day to day
  are entered under **Children's clothing.**
  UF Children—Costume *[Former
      heading]*
  BT **Costume**
  RT **Children's clothing**
Children's courts
  USE **Juvenile courts**
Children's day care centers
  USE **Day care centers**
Children's diseases
  USE **Children—Diseases**
Children's food
  USE **Children—Nutrition**
Children's homes
  USE **Children—Institutional care**
Children's hospitals 362.1
  UF Children—Hospitals
  BT **Hospitals**
  RT **Child welfare**
      Children—Health and hygiene
Children's libraries 027.62
  UF Libraries and children
      Library services to children
  BT **Libraries**
  RT **Libraries and schools**
Children's literature 808.8; 810.8, etc.
  Use for collections or materials about litera-
  ture published for children. Materials on the
  reading interests of children and lists of books
  for children are entered under **Children—
  Books and reading.** Individual literary works
  and collections of literary works written by
  children are entered under **Children's writings.** Materials about works written by children and materials about children as authors
  are entered under **Child authors.**
  UF Books for children
      Children's books
      Juvenile literature
  SA subjects and personal, corporate,
      and place names with the
      subdivision *Juvenile literature,*

Children's literature—*Continued*
for non-fiction materials e.g.
Computers—Juvenile literature; and with the subdivisions *Juvenile fiction; Juvenile poetry;* and *Juvenile drama;* for materials in those forms, e.g. **Christmas—Juvenile fiction; Christmas—Juvenile poetry; Christmas—Juvenile drama;** etc. [to be added as needed]

BT **Literature**
NT **Big books**
Caldecott Medal
Children's plays
Children's poetry
Children's stories
Easy reading materials
Fairy tales
Newbery Medal
Picture books for children
Plot-your-own stories
Reading materials
Storytelling

Children's literature—Book reviews
808.8; 810.8, etc.
Children's literature—History and criticism 809
Children's moneymaking projects
USE **Money-making projects for children**
Children's parties 395.3; 793.2
BT **Amusements**
Entertaining
Parties
Children's plays 808.82; 809.2; 812, etc.; 812.008, etc.; 812.009, etc.

May be used for individual works, collections, or materials about plays for children. Materials about plays for production in colleges and schools are entered under **College and school drama.** Individual works and collections of plays written by children are entered under **Children's writings.** Materials about plays written by children are entered under **Child authors.**

UF Plays for children
School plays
SA subjects and personal, corporate, and place names with the subdivision *Juvenile drama,* e.g. **Christmas—Juvenile drama** [to be added as needed]
BT **Amateur theater**
Children's literature
Drama
Theater
Children's poetry 808.81; 809.1; 811, etc.; 811.008, etc.; 811.009, etc.

Use for individual poems, collections, or materials about poetry written for children. Individual works and collections of poetry written by children are entered under **Children's writings.** Materials about poetry written by children are entered under **Child authors.**

UF Poetry for children
SA subjects and personal, corporate, and place names with the subdivision *Juvenile poetry;* e.g. **Christmas—Juvenile poetry** [to be added as needed]
BT **Children's literature**
Poetry
NT **Children's songs**
Lullabies
Nonsense verses
Nursery rhymes
Tongue twisters
Children's reading
USE **Children—Books and reading**
Reading
Children's songs 782.42

Use for collections of songs that contain both words and music, and for materials about songs for children. Collections of songs without the music are entered under **Children's poetry.**

UF Songs for children
BT **Children's poetry**
School songbooks
Songs
NT **Lullabies**
Nursery rhymes
Children's stories 808.83; 809.3; 813, etc.; 813.008, etc.; 813.009

Use for individual stories and collections of stories written for children. Individual works and collections of stories written by children are entered under **Children's writings.** Materials about stories written by children are entered under **Child authors.**

UF Fiction for children
Stories for children
SA subjects and personal, corporate, and place names with the subdivision *Juvenile fiction,*

Children's stories—*Continued*

> e.g. **Christmas—Juvenile fiction** [to be added as needed]

  BT **Children's literature**

        Fiction

Children's writings   808.8; 810.8, etc.

Use for individual literary works or collections of literary works written by children. Materials on children as authors and discussions of literary works written by children are entered under **Child authors.** Collections of works published for children are entered under **Children's literature.**

  UF School prose

        School verse

  RT **Child authors**

        College and school journalism

Chimes

  USE **Bells**

Chimneys   697; 721

  UF Smoke stacks

  BT **Architecture—Details**

        Buildings

  RT **Fireplaces**

China   951

Use as a heading or as a geographic subdivision for materials dealing with mainland China, regardless of time period, or with the People's Republic of China, or for comprehensive materials on China including Taiwan. Materials dealing with the island of Taiwan, regardless of time period, or with the post-1948 Republic of China are entered under **Taiwan.** May be subdivided like United States except for *History.*

  UF China (People's Republic of China)

        People's Republic of China

China—History   951

China—History—1912-1949   951.04

China—History—1949-   951.05

China—History—1949-1976   951.05

China—History—1976-   951.05

China—History—1989, Tiananmen Square Incident

  USE **Tiananmen Square Incident, Beijing (China), 1989**

China painting   738.1

  UF Porcelain painting

  BT **Decoration and ornament**

        Painting

        Porcelain

China (People's Republic of China)

  USE **China**

China (Porcelain)

  USE **Porcelain**

China (Republic)

  USE **Taiwan**

Chinaware

  USE **Porcelain**

Chinese Americans (May subdiv. geog.)   **305.895; 973**

Chinese satellite countries

  USE **Communist countries**

Chipmunks   599.36

  BT **Mammals**

        Squirrels

Chiropody

  USE **Podiatry**

Chiropractic   615.5

  BT **Alternative medicine**

        Massage

  RT **Naturopathy**

        Osteopathic medicine

Chivalry   394

  BT **Manners and customs**

  NT **Medieval tournaments**

  RT **Crusades**

        Feudalism

        Heraldry

        Knights and knighthood

        Medieval civilization

        Romances

Chivalry—Romances

  USE **Romances**

Chocolate   641.3

  BT **Food**

  RT **Cocoa**

        Desserts

Choice, Freedom of

  USE **Free will and determinism**

Choice of books

  USE **Best books**

        Book selection

        Books and reading

Choice of college

  USE **College choice**

Choice of profession, occupation, vocation, etc.

  USE **Vocational guidance**

Choice of school

  USE **School choice**

Choice (Psychology)   153.8

  BT **Psychology**

  RT **Decision making**

Choirs (Music)   782.5
  BT **Church music**
  RT **Choral conducting**
      Choral music
      Choral societies
      Singing
Cholesterol content of food
  USE **Food—Cholesterol content**
Choose-your-own story plots
  USE **Plot-your-own stories**
Choral conducting   782.5
  UF Conducting, Choral
  BT **Conducting**
  RT **Choirs (Music)**
      Choral music
      Conductors (Music)
Choral music   782.5
  UF Music, Choral
  BT **Church music**
      Vocal music
  NT **Cantatas**
  RT **Choirs (Music)**
      Choral conducting
      Choral societies
Choral societies   782.506
  UF Singing societies
  BT **Societies**
  RT **Choirs (Music)**
      Choral music
Choral speaking   808.5
  UF Speaking choirs
      Unison speaking
  BT **Drama**
      Recitations
Christ
  USE **Jesus Christ**
Christening
  USE **Baptism**
Christian antiquities (May subdiv. geog.)
    225.9; 270; 930.1
  UF Christian archeology
      Church antiquities
      Ecclesiastical antiquities
  BT **Antiquities**
      Bible—Antiquities
  NT **Catacombs**
  RT **Christian art**
Christian archeology
  USE **Christian antiquities**

Christian art (May subdiv. geog.)   246;
    704.9
  UF Christian art and symbolism
      [Former heading]
      Ecclesiastical art
  BT **Art**
      Religious art
  NT **Jesus Christ—Art**
      Mary, Blessed Virgin, Saint—
      Art
  RT **Christian antiquities**
      Christian symbolism
      Gothic art
Christian art and symbolism
  USE **Christian art**
      Christian symbolism
Christian biography   270.092; 920
  UF Christianity—Biography
      Christians—Biography
      Ecclesiastical biography
  BT **Biography**
      Religious biography
  NT **Fathers of the church**
Christian civilization   270; 909
  UF Civilization, Christian
  BT **Christianity**
      Civilization
Christian denominations
  USE **Christian sects**
Christian devotional calendars
  USE **Devotional calendars**
Christian doctrinal theology
  USE **Christianity—Doctrines**
Christian doctrine
  USE **Christianity—Doctrines**
Christian education (May subdiv. geog.)
    268
    Use for materials on the instruction of
Christian religion in schools and private life.
General materials on the instruction of reli-
gion in schools and private life are entered
under **Religious education.** Materials on the
relation of the church to education and materi-
als on the history of the part that the church
has taken in secular education are entered un-
der **Church and education.** Materials on
church supported and controlled elementary
and secondary schools are entered under
Church schools.
  UF Education, Christian
  BT **Religious education**
  NT **Bible—Study and teaching**
  RT **Church and education**

Christian ethics 241
  UF Christian moral theology
      Moral theology, Christian
  BT **Ethics**
  NT **Conscience**
  RT **Christian life**
Christian fasts and feasts
  USE **Christian holidays**
Christian fiction 808.83; 813, etc.
  Use for individual works, collections, or materials about fiction that promotes Christian teachings or exemplifies a Christian way of life.
  BT **Fiction**
      Religious fiction
Christian fundamentalism 230; 270.8
  Use for materials on the modern conservative movement in Protestantism emphasizing literal interpretation of the Bible, as opposed to religious liberalism, modernism, or evolutionism.
  UF Fundamentalism
      Modernist-fundamentalist controversy
  BT **Christianity—Doctrines**
      Religious fundamentalism
  RT **Modernism (Theology)**
Christian holidays 263; 394.266
  UF Christian fasts and feasts
      Christian holy days
      Fasts and feasts—Christianity
  SA names of Christian holidays, e.g.
      Christmas [to be added as needed]
  BT **Church year**
      Religious holidays
  NT **Christmas**
      Easter
      Good Friday
Christian holy days
  USE **Christian holidays**
Christian-Jewish relations
  USE **Christianity—Relations—Judaism**
      Judaism—Relations—Christianity
Christian life 248.4
  UF Religious life (Christian)
  BT **Religious life**
  RT **Christian ethics**
Christian life—Sermons 252
  BT **Sermons**

Christian literature Example under **Literature.** 230
  BT **Religious literature**
  NT **Catholic literature**
      Early Christian literature
      Papal encyclicals
      Sermons
Christian literature—30-600, Early
  USE **Early Christian literature**
Christian literature, Early
  USE **Early Christian literature**
Christian ministry 253
  BT **Ministry**
Christian missionaries 266.0092; 920
  UF Missionaries, Christian
  RT **Christian missions**
Christian missions (May subdiv. geog.) 266
  UF Foreign missions, Christian
      Home missions, Christian
      Missions, Christian
  SA names of Christian churches, denominations, religious orders, etc., with the subdivision *Missions,* e.g. **Catholic Church—Missions;** and names of peoples evangelized with the subdivision *Christian missions,* e.g. **Native Americans—Christian missions** [to be added as needed]
  BT **Christianity**
      Church history
      Church work
  NT **Catholic Church—Missions**
      Native Americans—Christian missions
      Salvation Army
  RT **Christian missionaries**
      Evangelistic work
Christian moral theology
  USE **Christian ethics**
Christian names
  USE **Personal names**
Christian philosophy 190; 230.01
  Use for materials on philosophy as practiced by Christian philosophers or on the nature, origins, or validity of Christian beliefs from a philosophical point of view.
  UF Christianity—Philosophy
  BT **Philosophy**

Christian saints   270.092; 920
   BT   Saints
   NT   Apostles
Christian Science   289.5
   UF   Church of Christ, Scientist
   BT   **Christian sects**
   RT   **Spiritual healing**
Christian sects (May subdiv. geog.)   280
   UF   Christian denominations
         Church denominations
         Denominations, Christian
   SA   names of Christian sects, e.g.
         Presbyterian Church [to be
         added as needed]
   BT   **Christianity**
         Church history
         Sects
   NT   **Amish**
         Baptists
         Catholic Church
         Christian Science
         Christian union
         Church of England
         Church of Jesus Christ of Latter-day Saints
         Community churches
         Congregationalism
         Eastern churches
         Ecumenical movement
         Episcopal Church
         Greek Orthodox Church
         Huguenots
         Interdenominational cooperation
         Mennonites
         Moravians
         Non-institutional churches
         Orthodox Eastern Church
         Pentecostal churches
         Presbyterian Church
         Protestant churches
         Puritans
         Russian Orthodox Church
         Salvation Army
         Shakers
         Society of Friends
         Unitarianism
Christian sociology (May subdiv. geog.)
    261
    Use for materials on social theory from a Christian point of view. Materials on religious sociology in general are entered under **Religion and sociology**. Materials on the practical treatment of social problems from the point of view of the church are entered under **Church and social problems**.
   UF   Sociology, Christian
   BT   **Religion and sociology**
         Sociology
   RT   **Christianity and economics**
         Church and social problems
Christian symbolism (May subdiv. geog.)
    246; 704.9
   UF   Christian art and symbolism
         [Former heading]
   BT   **Symbolism**
   RT   **Christian art**
Christian union (May subdiv. geog.)
    280
    Use for materials on prospective and actual mergers within and across denominational lines. Materials on unity as one of the marks of the church are entered under **Church—Unity**. Materials on a movement originating in the twentieth century aimed at promoting church cooperation and unity are entered under **Ecumenical movement**. Materials on religious activities planned and conducted cooperatively by two or more Christian sects are entered under **Interdenominational cooperation**.
   UF   Christian unity *[Former heading]*
         Christianity—Union between churches
         Ecumenism
   BT   **Christian sects**
         Church
   RT   **Ecumenical movement**
Christian unity
   USE   **Christian union**
         Church—Unity
         Ecumenical movement
         Interdenominational cooperation
Christian year
   USE   **Church year**
Christianity (May subdiv. geog.)   230
   SA   names of Christian churches and sects, e.g. **Catholic Church; Huguenots;** etc.; and Christianity and other subjects, e.g. **Christianity and economics** [to be added as needed]
   BT   **Religions**
   NT   **Atonement—Christianity**
         Catholic Church

Christianity—*Continued*

    Christian civilization
    Christian missions
    Christian sects
    Christianity and economics
    Councils and synods
    Counter-Reformation
    Eastern churches
    Pentecostalism
    Protestantism
    Reformation
RT **Christians**
    Church
    Jesus Christ

Christianity and economics   261.8
UF Economics and Christianity
BT **Christianity**
    Economics
RT **Christian sociology**
    Church and labor

Christianity and evolution
USE **Creationism**

Christianity and other religions   261.2
    Use for materials on the relations between Christianity and several other religions. Materials on the relations between Christianity and one other religion are entered under **Christianity** subdivided by *Relations* further subdivided by the other religion, and also under the other religion subdivided by *Relations—Christianity,* e.g. **Christianity—Relations—Judaism** and **Judaism—Relations—Christianity.** The same pattern is followed for sects and denominations.
UF Comparative religion
BT **Religions**
NT **Christianity—Relations—Judaism**
    Judaism—Relations—Christianity
    Paganism

Christianity and other religions—Judaism
USE **Christianity—Relations—Judaism**
    Judaism—Relations—Christianity

Christianity and politics   261.7; 322
UF Christianity—Political aspects
    Politics and Christianity
BT **Church and state**
    Religion and politics

Christianity—Apologetic works   239
    Use for materials defending Christianity. Materials attacking Christianity are entered under **Christianity—Controversial literature.**
BT **Apologetics**

Christianity—Biography
USE **Christian biography**

Christianity—Controversial literature 239
    Use for materials attacking Christianity. Materials defending Christianity are entered under **Christianity—Apologetic works.**

Christianity—Doctrines   230
UF Christian doctrinal theology
    Christian doctrine
BT **Doctrinal theology**
NT **Christian fundamentalism**
    Creationism
    God—Christianity
    Liberation theology
    Modernism (Theology)
    Regeneration (Christianity)
    Trinity

Christianity—History
USE **Church history**

Christianity—Origin
USE **Church history—30-600, Early church**

Christianity—Philosophy
USE **Christian philosophy**

Christianity—Political aspects
USE **Christianity and politics**

Christianity—Psychology   230.01; 253.5
BT **Psychology of religion**

Christianity—Relations—Judaism 261.2; 296.3
    Use for materials on the relations between Christianity and Judaism. When assigning this heading, provide an additional subject entry under **Judaism—Relations—Christianity.**
UF Christian-Jewish relations
    Christianity and other religions—Judaism
    Jewish-Christian relations
BT **Christianity and other religions**
    Judaism

Christianity—Union between churches
USE **Christian union**

Christians (May subdiv. geog.)   270.092
RT **Christianity**

Christians—Biography
USE **Christian biography**

Christians—Persecutions (May subdiv. geog.)   272
BT **Church history**
    Persecution

Christmas (May subdiv. geog.)   263;
    394.2663
    BT   Christian holidays
         Holidays
    NT   Christmas entertainments
         Santa Claus
    RT   Jesus Christ—Nativity
Christmas cards   741.6; 745.594
    BT   Greeting cards
Christmas carols
    USE   Carols
Christmas cooking (May subdiv. geog.)
    641.5
    BT   Cooking
Christmas decorations   394.2663;
    745.594
    UF   Christmas ornaments
    BT   Decoration and ornament
    NT   Christmas trees
Christmas—Drama   394.2663; 792;
    808.82; 812, etc.
    Use for collections of plays about Christ-
mas.
    UF   Christmas plays [Former head-
         ing]
Christmas entertainments   394.2663;
    791
    BT   Amusements
         Christmas
Christmas—Fiction   808.83; 813, etc.;
    813.008, etc.
    Use for collections of stories about Christ-
mas.
    UF   Christmas stories
Christmas—Juvenile drama   808.82;
    812, etc.; 812.008, etc.
    Use for collections of plays about Christmas
written for children.
Christmas—Juvenile fiction   808.83;
    813, etc.; 813.008; 8
    Use for collections of stories about Christ-
mas written for children.
Christmas—Juvenile poetry   808.81;
    811, etc.; 811.008, etc.
    Use for collections of poems about Christ-
mas written for children.
Christmas ornaments
    USE   Christmas decorations
Christmas plays
    USE   Christmas—Drama
Christmas poetry
    USE   Christmas—Poetry

Christmas—Poetry   808.81; 811, etc.;
    811.008, etc.
    Use for collections of poems about Christ-
mas.
    UF   Christmas poetry [Former head-
         ing]
Christmas stories
    USE   Christmas—Fiction
Christmas tree growing   635.9
    UF   Growing of Christmas trees
    BT   Forests and forestry
    RT   Christmas trees
         Tree planting
Christmas trees   394.2663; 745.594
    BT   Christmas decorations
         Trees
    RT   Christmas tree growing
Christmas—United States   394.2663
Christology
    USE   Jesus Christ
Chromosome mapping
    USE   Gene mapping
Chromosomes   572.8
    BT   Genetics
         Heredity
    NT   Genetic recombination
Chronicle history (Drama)
    USE   Historical drama
Chronicle plays
    USE   Historical drama
Chronology   529
    Use for materials on the science that deals
with measuring time by regular divisions and
that assigns proper dates to events.
    SA   individual persons, wars, sacred
         works, topics that are inher-
         ently historical, and topics not
         subdivided by History, such
         as art, music, literature, etc.,
         with the subdivision Chronol-
         ogy, e.g. Bible—Chronology;
         and ethnic groups, corporate
         bodies, military services, top-
         ics not inherently historical,
         and names of places with the
         subdivision History—Chronol-
         ogy, e.g. Native Americans—
         History—Chronology [to be
         added as needed]
    BT   Astronomy
         History
         Time

Chronology—*Continued*
- NT **Bible—Chronology**
  Day
  Historical chronology
  Months
  Night
  Week
- RT **Almanacs**

Chronology, Biblical
- USE **Bible—Chronology**

Chronology, Historical
- USE **Historical chronology**

Church   260

Use for materials on the concept and function of the Christian Church as a whole.
- SA   church and other subjects, e.g.
  Church and education [to be added as needed]
- BT **Theology**
- NT **Christian union**
  Church and education
  Church and social problems
  Church and state
  Church work
  Clergy
  Ecclesiastical law
  Ecumenical movement
  Laity
  Sacraments
- RT **Christianity**

Church and education   261

Use for materials on the relation of the church to education in general, and for materials on the history of the part that the church has taken in secular education. Materials on church supported and controlled elementary and secondary schools are entered under **Church schools.** Materials on the instruction of religion in schools and private life are entered under **Religious education,** and of Christian religion under **Christian education.**
- UF   Education and church
  Education and religion
  Fundamentalism and education
  Religion and education
- BT **Church**
  Education
- NT **Religion in the public schools**
- RT **Christian education**

Church and labor   261.8
- UF   Labor and the church
- BT **Labor**
- RT **Christianity and economics**

Church and race relations   261.8
- UF   Integrated churches
  Race relations and the church
- BT **Church work**

Church and social problems   261.8

Use for materials on the practical treatment of social problems from the point of view of the church. Materials on social theory from a Christian point of view are entered under **Christian sociology.** Materials on religious sociology in general are entered under **Religion and sociology.**
- UF   Religion and social problems
  Social problems and the church
- BT **Church**
  Social problems
- NT **Liberation theology**
  Sanctuary movement
- RT **Christian sociology**
  Church work

Church and state (May subdiv. geog.)
  261.7; 291.1; 322
- UF   Church—Government policy
  Religion and state
  Religion—Government policy
  Separation of church and state
- BT **Church**
  State, The
- NT **Christianity and politics**
  Religion in the public schools

Church and state—United States   322
- UF   United States—Church and state

Church antiquities
- USE **Christian antiquities**

Church architecture (May subdiv. geog.)
  726.5
- UF   Ecclesiastical architecture
- BT **Architecture**
- NT **Abbeys**
  Monasteries
  Mosques
  Spires
  Temples
- RT **Cathedrals**
  Church buildings
  Gothic architecture

Church attendance
- USE **Public worship**

Church bells
- USE **Bells**

Church buildings (May subdiv. geog.)
726.5

Use for general descriptive and historical materials on church buildings that cannot be entered under **Church architecture.**

UF   Churches
SA   names of individual churches, e.g. **Westminster Abbey** [to be added as needed]
BT   **Buildings**
NT   **Cathedrals**
      Westminster Abbey
RT   **Church architecture**

Church buildings—United States
726.50973

Church councils
USE   **Councils and synods**

Church denominations
USE   **Christian sects**
       Sects

Church entertainments   253.7
UF   Church sociables
      Socials
BT   **Amusements**
      Church work

Church fathers
USE   **Fathers of the church**

Church festivals
USE   **Religious holidays**

Church finance   254; 262.0068
BT   **Finance**
NT   **Tithes**

Church furniture   247
UF   Ecclesiastical furniture
BT   **Furniture**

Church—Government policy
USE   **Church and state**

Church history   270

Use for materials dealing with the development of Christianity and church organization.

UF   Christianity—History
      Ecclesiastical history
      Religious history
SA   names of countries, states, etc. with the subdivision *Church history,* e.g. **United States— Church history;** and names of individual denominations, sects, churches, etc. [to be added as needed]

BT   **History**
NT   **Christian missions**
      Christian sects
      Christians—Persecutions
      Councils and synods
      Martyrs
      Monasteries
      Ohio—Church history
      Papacy
      Popes
      Popes—Temporal power
      Protestant churches
      Protestantism
      Sects
      United States—Church history

Church history—30-600, Early church
270.1
UF   Apostolic Church
      Christianity—Origin
      Early church history
      Primitive Christianity
NT   **Apostles**
      Gnosticism
RT   **Catacombs**
      Early Christian literature

Church history—600-1500, Middle Ages
270.3
UF   Medieval church history
BT   **Middle Ages**
NT   **Crusades**

Church history—1500-, Modern period
270.6
UF   Modern church history
NT   **Counter-Reformation**
      Reformation

Church history—Ohio
USE   **Ohio—Church history**

Church history—United States
USE   **United States—Church history**

Church law
USE   **Ecclesiastical law**

Church libraries   027.6
UF   Parish libraries
BT   **Libraries**

Church music (May subdiv. geog.)
781.71

This heading may be subdivided by religion or denomination as needed.

UF   Religious music
      Sacred music

Church music—*Continued*

    SA   types of church music, e.g.
            Hymns [to be added as need-
            ed]

    BT   **Music**

    NT   **Carols**

          Chants (Plain, Gregorian, etc.)

          Choirs (Music)

          Choral music

          Gospel music

          Hymnals

          Hymns

          Oratorio

          Organ music

    RT   **Liturgies**

Church of Christ, Scientist

    USE   **Christian Science**

Church of England (May subdiv. geog.)
    283

    UF   Anglican Church

          England, Church of

    BT   **Christian sects**

Church of England—United States   **283**

Use for materials on the Episcopal Church in the United States prior to 1789. Materials on the Episcopal Church in the United States after 1789 are entered under **Episcopal Church.**

    RT   **Episcopal Church**

          Puritans

**Church of Jesus Christ of Latter-day
    Saints** (May subdiv. geog.)   **289.3**

    UF   Latter-day Saints

          Mormon Church

    BT   **Christian sects**

    RT   **Mormons**

Church schools (May subdiv. geog.)
    371.07

Use for materials on church supported and controlled elementary and secondary schools. Materials on the relation of the church to education and on the history of the part that the church has taken in secular education are entered under **Church and education.** Materials on the instruction of religion in schools and private life are entered under **Religious education,** and of Christian religion under **Christian education.**

    UF   Denominational schools

          Nonpublic schools

          Parochial schools

    BT   **Private schools**

          Schools

Church service books

    USE   **Liturgies**

Church settlements

    USE   **Social settlements**

Church sociables

    USE   **Church entertainments**

Church—Unity   **262**

Use for materials on unity as one of the marks of the church. Materials on prospective and actual mergers within and across denominational lines are entered under **Christian union.** Materials on a movement originating in the twentieth century aimed at promoting church cooperation and unity are entered under **Ecumenical movement.** Materials on religious activities planned and conducted cooperatively by two or more Christian sects are entered under **Interdenominational cooperation.**

    UF   Christian unity *[Former head-
          ing]*

Church work   **253; 291**

    SA   church work with particular
            groups of persons, e.g.
            Church work with the sick
            [to be added as needed]

    BT   **Church**

    NT   **Christian missions**

          Church and race relations

          Church entertainments

          Church work with the sick

          Church work with youth

          Evangelistic work

          **Interdenominational coopera-
          tion**

          Lay ministry

          Ministry

          Pastoral psychology

          Rural churches

          Sunday schools

    RT   **Church and social problems**

          Pastoral theology

Church work with the sick   **259;
    362.1023**

    BT   **Church work**

          Sick

Church work with youth   **259**

    BT   **Church work**

          Youth

Church year   **263**

Use for materials on the seasons of observance and Christian festivals with their cycles, as making up the Christian or church year. Works on the origins of Christian festivals and fasts are entered under **Christian holiday.**

    UF   Christian year

          Ecclesiastical year

          Liturgical year

Church year—*Continued*
 SA festival seasons and seasons of
  the church year, e.g. **Lent** [to
  be added as needed]
 BT **Calendars**
  Religious holidays
  Worship
 NT **Christian holidays**
  Holy Week
  Lent
Churches
 USE **Church buildings**
  Religious institutions
Churches, Community
 USE **Community churches**
Churches, Country
 USE **Rural churches**
Churches, Non-institutional
 USE **Non-institutional churches**
Churches, Rural
 USE **Rural churches**
Churches, Undenominational
 USE **Community churches**
Churchyards
 USE **Cemeteries**
Cigarettes 679
 BT **Smoking**
  Tobacco
Cigars 679
 BT **Smoking**
  Tobacco
Cinema
 USE **Motion pictures**
Cinematography 778.5
  Use for materials on the technical aspects
 of making motion pictures and their projection
 onto a screen. General materials on motion
 pictures, including motion pictures as an art
 form, are entered under **Motion pictures.**
 UF Motion picture photography
  Photography—Motion pictures
 BT **Photography**
 NT **Animation (Cinematography)**
  Motion picture cameras
Cinesiology
 USE **Kinesiology**
Cipher and telegraph codes 384.1
 UF Codes, Telegraph
  Morse code
  Telegraph codes
 BT **Ciphers**
  Telegraph

Ciphers 652
 UF Codes
  Contractions
 BT **Signs and symbols**
 NT **Cipher and telegraph codes**
 RT **Abbreviations**
  Cryptography
  Writing
Ciphers (Lettering)
 USE **Monograms**
Circuits, Electric
 USE **Electric circuits**
Circulation of library materials
 USE **Library circulation**
Circulation of the blood
 USE **Blood—Circulation**
Circulatory system
 USE **Cardiovascular system**
Circumnavigation
 USE **Voyages around the world**
Circus (May subdiv. geog.) **791.3**
 BT **Amusements**
 NT **Acrobats and acrobatics**
  Clowns
 RT **Carnivals**
CIS
 USE **Commonwealth of Independent
  States**
Cities and towns (May subdiv. geog.)
  307.76
  Use for general materials on cities and
 towns. For materials on large cities and their
 surrounding areas use **Metropolitan areas.**
 General materials on the government of cities
 are entered under **Municipal government.**
 General materials on local government other
 than that of cities are entered under **Local
 government.**
 UF Municipalities
  Towns
  Urban areas
 SA names of individual cities and
  towns [to be added as need-
  ed]
 BT **Sociology**
 NT **Capitals (Cities)**
  City and town life
  Extinct cities
  Inner cities
  Markets
  Municipal art
  Parks
  Streets

Cities and towns—*Continued*
    Urbanization
    Villages
  RT **Urban sociology**
Cities and towns—Civic improvement
    307.3; 354.3
  UF Civic improvement
    Municipal improvements
  NT **City planning**
    Community centers
Cities and towns—Finance
  USE **Municipal finance**
Cities and towns—Government
  USE **Municipal government**
Cities and towns—Growth   307.76
  UF Cities and towns, Movement to
    Urban development
  BT **Internal migration**
    Population
  NT **Metropolitan areas**
    Suburbs
  RT **Urbanization**
Cities and towns—Lighting
  USE **Streets—Lighting**
Cities and towns, Movement to
  USE **Cities and towns—Growth**
    Urbanization
Cities and towns—Planning
  USE **City planning**
Cities and towns—United States
    307.760973; 973
  UF United States—Cities and towns
Cities, Imaginary
  USE **Geographical myths**
Citizen participation
  USE **Political participation**
    and subjects designating govern-
    ment activity with the subdi-
    vision *Citizen participation,*
    e.g. **City planning—Citizen
    participation** [to be added as
    needed]
Citizens band radio   384.5; 621.3845
  UF CB radio
    Citizens radio service
  BT **Shortwave radio**
Citizen's defender
  USE **Ombudsman**
Citizens radio service
  USE **Citizens band radio**

Citizenship (May subdiv. geog.)   **172;
    323.6**
  UF Civics
    Franchise
    Nationality (Citizenship)
  BT **Constitutional law**
    Political ethics
    Political science
  NT **Patriotism**
    Suffrage
  RT **Aliens**
    Naturalization
Citrus
  USE **Citrus fruits**
Citrus fruit
  USE **Citrus fruits**
Citrus fruits   634
    Names of particular fruits may be used for
  either the fruit or the tree.
  UF Citrus
    Citrus fruit
  SA types of citrus fruits, e.g. **Lem-
    ons** [to be added as needed]
  BT **Fruit**
  NT **Lemons**
    Limes
    Oranges
City and town life (May subdiv. geog.)
    307.76
  UF City life *[Former heading]*
    Town life
    Urban life
  BT **Cities and towns**
    Urban sociology
City-federal relations
  USE **Federal-city relations**
City government
  USE **Municipal government**
City life
  USE **City and town life**
City manager
  USE **Municipal government by city
    manager**
City planning (May subdiv. geog.)
    307.1; 354.3; 711
    Use for materials on the architectural and
  engineering aspects of urban redevelopment.
  Materials on the economic, sociological, and
  political aspects are entered under **Urban re-
  newal.**
  UF Cities and towns—Planning
    Municipal planning
    Town planning

City planning—*Continued*
    Urban development
    Urban planning
  BT **Cities and towns—Civic improvement**
    Planning
  NT **Suburbs**
    Zoning
  RT **Community development**
    Housing
    Municipal art
    Public works
    Regional planning
    Urban renewal
City planning—Chicago (Ill.) 307.1;
  354.3; 711
  UF Chicago (Ill.)—City planning
City planning—Citizen participation
  (May subdiv. geog.) **307.1**
  BT **Political participation**
    Social action
City planning—United States 307.1;
  354.3; 711
City planning—Zone system
  USE **Zoning**
City schools
  USE **Urban schools**
City-state relations
  USE **State-local relations**
City traffic **388.4**
  UF Local traffic
    Street traffic
    Traffic, City
    Urban traffic
  BT **Streets**
    Traffic engineering
City transit
  USE **Local transit**
Civic art
  USE **Municipal art**
Civic improvement
  USE **Cities and towns—Civic improvement**
Civic involvement
  USE **Political participation**
    and subjects with the subdivision *Citizen participation,* e.g.
    City planning—United States—Citizen participation
    [to be added as needed]

Civics
  USE **Citizenship**
    Political science
Civil defense (May subdiv. geog.) **363.3**
    Use for materials on the protection of civilians from enemy attack. Materials on military defenses against air attack are entered under **Air defenses.**
  UF Civilian defense
  SA names of wars with the subdivision *Evacuation of civilians* [to be added as needed]
  BT **Military art and science**
  NT **Air raid shelters**
    Rescue work
    Survival skills
    World War, 1939-1945—Evacuation of civilians
Civil defense—Chicago (Ill.) **363.3**
  UF Chicago (Ill.)—Civil defense
Civil defense—United States **363.3**
  UF United States—Civil defense
Civil disobedience (May subdiv. geog.) **303.6; 322.4**
  BT **Resistance to government**
Civil disorders
  USE **Riots**
Civil engineering (May subdiv. geog.) **624**
  BT **Engineering**
  NT **Aqueducts**
    Bridges
    Canals
    Dams
    Drainage
    Dredging
    Excavation
    Extraterrestrial bases
    Harbors
    Highway engineering
    Hydraulic engineering
    Lunar bases
    Marine engineering
    Mechanical engineering
    Military engineering
    Mining engineering
    Public works
    Railroad engineering
    Reclamation of land
    Roads
    Streets
    Structural engineering

Civil engineering—*Continued*
    Structural steel
    Surveying
    Tunnels
    Walls
    Water supply engineering
Civil government
  USE **Political science**
Civil law suits
  USE **Litigation**
Civil liberty
  USE **Freedom**
Civil rights (May subdiv. geog.) **323;
    342**

    Use for materials on citizens' rights as established by law or protected by a constitution. Materials on the rights of persons regardless of their legal, socioeconomic, or cultural status and as recognized by the international community are entered under **Human rights.**

  UF Basic rights
      Constitutional rights
      Fundamental rights
  SA ethnic groups and classes of persons with the subdivision *Civil rights* [to be added as needed]
  BT **Constitutional law**
      Human rights
      Political science
  NT **African Americans—Civil rights**
      Anti-apartheid movement
      Blacks—Civil rights
      Children—Civil rights
      Due process of law
      Fair trial
      Freedom of assembly
      Freedom of association
      Freedom of information
      Freedom of movement
      Freedom of religion
      Freedom of speech
      Freedom of the press
      Right of privacy
      Women's rights
  RT **Civil rights demonstrations**
      Discrimination
      Freedom
Civil rights demonstrations (May subdiv. geog.) **322.4**
  UF Demonstrations for civil rights
      Freedom marches for civil rights

      Marches for civil rights
      Sit-ins for civil rights
  BT **Demonstrations**
  RT **Civil rights**
Civil rights (International law)
  USE **Human rights**
Civil servants
  USE **Civil service**
Civil service (May subdiv. geog.) **342;
    351; 352.6**

    Use for general materials on career government service and the laws governing it. Materials on civil service employees are entered under the name of the country, state, city, corporate body, or government agency with the subdivision *Officials and employees.*

  UF Administration
      Civil servants
      Employees and officials
      Government employees
      Government service
      Officials and employees
      Tenure of office
  SA names of countries, states, cities, etc., and corporate bodies with the subdivision *Officials and employees,* e.g. **United States—Officials and employees; Ohio—Officials and employees; Chicago (Ill.)—Officials and employees; United Nations—Officials and employees;** etc. [to be added as needed]
  BT **Administrative law**
      Political science
      Public administration
  NT **Municipal officials and employees**
  RT **Bureaucracy**
      Public officers
Civil service—Examinations **351.076**
  BT **Examinations**
Civil service—United States **351.73**
  UF United States—Civil service
  RT **United States—Officials and employees**
Civil War—England
  USE **Great Britain—History—1642-1660, Civil War and Commonwealth**

Civil War—United States
USE **United States—History—1861-**
1865, Civil War
Civilian defense
USE **Civil defense**
Civilian evacuation
USE **World War, 1939-1945—Evac-**
uation of civilians
Civilian relief
USE names of wars with the subdivi-
sion *Civilian relief,* e.g.
World War, 1939-1945—Ci-
vilian relief [to be added as
needed]
Civilization   306; 909

Use for materials on civilization in general
and on the development of social customs, art,
industry, religion, etc., of several countries or
peoples.

SA names of continents, regions,
countries, states, etc., with the
subdivision *Civilization,* e.g.
United States—Civilization;
and the civilizations of peo-
ples not confined to a single
place, e.g. **Arab civilization;**
Western civilization; etc. [to
be added as needed]
NT **Acculturation**
Aeronautics and civilization
Africa—Civilization
America—Civilization
Ancient civilization
Arab civilization
Asia—Civilization
Astronautics and civilization
Bronze Age
Christian civilization
Computers and civilization
Education
Iron Age
Jewish civilization
Learning and scholarship
Manners and customs
Medieval civilization
Modern civilization
Ohio—Civilization
Primitive societies
Progress
Religions
Renaissance
Science and civilization

Social sciences
Stone Age
Technology and civilization
United States—Civilization
War and civilization
Western civilization
RT **Anthropology**
Culture
Ethnology
History
Sociology
Civilization, Ancient
USE **Ancient civilization**
Civilization and aeronautics
USE **Aeronautics and civilization**
Civilization and astronautics
USE **Astronautics and civilization**
Civilization and computers
USE **Computers and civilization**
Civilization and science
USE **Science and civilization**
Civilization and technology
USE **Technology and civilization**
Civilization and war
USE **War and civilization**
Civilization, Arab
USE **Arab civilization**
Civilization, Christian
USE **Christian civilization**
Civilization, Classical
USE **Classical civilization**
Civilization, Greek
USE **Greece—Civilization**
Civilization, Medieval
USE **Medieval civilization**
Civilization, Modern
USE **Modern civilization**
Civilization, Oriental
USE **Asia—Civilization**
Civilization, Western
USE **Western civilization**
Claims
USE ethnic groups, places, and wars
with the subdivision *Claims,*
e.g. **Native Americans—**
Claims [to be added as need-
ed]
Clairvoyance   133.8
BT **Extrasensory perception**
Occultism
RT **Telepathy**

143

Clans (May subdiv. geog.)   306.85;
        941.1
    SA   names of clans or of families
            [to be added as needed]
    BT   **Family**
    NT   **Tartans**
    RT   **Kinship**
Clans—Scotland   941.1
    UF   Highland clans
            Scottish clans
Class conflict
    USE   **Social conflict**
Class consciousness   305.5
    BT   **Social classes**
            Social psychology
    RT   **Marxism**
Class distinction
    USE   **Social classes**
Class struggle
    USE   **Social conflict**
Classed catalogs
    USE   **Classified catalogs**
Classes (Mathematics)
    USE   **Set theory**
Classes of persons
    USE   **Persons**
            and classes of persons, e.g. **El-
            derly; Handicapped; Explor-
            ers; Drug addicts;** etc. [to be
            added as needed]
Classic automobiles
    USE   **Antique and classic cars**
Classic cars
    USE   **Antique and classic cars**
Classic motorcycles
    USE   **Antique and vintage motorcy-
            cles**
Classical antiquities   937; 938
    UF   Classical archeology
            Greek antiquities
            Roman antiquities
    SA   names of extinct cities of Greek
            and Roman antiquity e.g. **Del-
            phi (Extinct city);** and names
            of groups of people extant in
            modern times and names of
            cities (except extinct cities),
            countries, regions, etc., with
            the subdivision *Antiquities* [to
            be added as needed]

    BT   **Antiquities**
    NT   **Greece—Antiquities**
            Greek art
            Roman art
            Rome—Antiquities
            Rome (Italy)—Antiquities
Classical antiquities—Dictionaries
    USE   **Classical dictionaries**
Classical archeology
    USE   **Classical antiquities**
Classical art
    USE   **Greek art**
            Roman art
Classical biography
    USE   **Greece—Biography**
            Rome—Biography
Classical civilization (May subdiv. geog.)
        937
    Use for materials on both ancient Greek
    and Roman civilizations. Materials on the
    spread of Greek civilization throughout the
    ancient world following the conquests of Al-
    exander the Great are entered under **Helle-
    nism.**
    UF   Civilization, Classical
    BT   **Ancient civilization**
    NT   **Greece—Civilization**
            Rome—Civilization
    RT   **Classicism**
Classical dictionaries   937.003; 938.003
    UF   Classical antiquities—Dictionaries
            Dictionaries, Classical
    BT   **Ancient history**
            Encyclopedias and dictionaries
Classical education   370.11
    BT   **Education**
    RT   **Humanism**
            Humanities
Classical geography
    USE   **Ancient geography**
            Greece—Historical geography
            Rome—Geography
Classical languages
    USE   **Greek language**
            Latin language
Classical literature   870; 880
    BT   **Literature**
    RT   **Greek literature**
            Latin literature
Classical music
    USE   **Music**

Classical mythology   292.1
   UF   Greek mythology
          Mythology, Classical
          Roman mythology
   BT   **Mythology**
Classicism   709; 809
   BT   **Aesthetics**
          Literature
   NT   **Classicism in architecture**
   RT   **Classical civilization**
Classicism in architecture   723; 724
   BT   **Architecture**
          Classicism
Classification   001

   Use for materials on the organization of knowledge into a systematic arrangement of topics or categories. Materials on the classification of library materials are entered under **Library classification,** which may be subdivided by the type of literature or the subject of the materials classified.

   UF   Classification of knowledge
   SA   subjects with the subdivision
          Classification, e.g. **Botany—**
          Classification [to be added as
          needed]
   NT   **Botany—Classification**
          Library classification
Classification—Books
   USE **Library classification**
Classification—Botany
   USE **Botany—Classification**
Classification, Dewey Decimal
   USE **Dewey Decimal Classification**
Classification of knowledge
   USE **Classification**
Classification—Plants
   USE **Botany—Classification**
Classified catalogs   017; 025.3
   UF   Catalogs, Classified
          Classed catalogs
   BT   **Library catalogs**
   RT   **Library classification**
Classroom management   371.102
   BT   **School discipline**
          Teaching
Clay   553.6; 666; 738.1
   BT   **Ceramics**
          Soils
   NT   **Modeling**
Clay industries
   USE **Clay industry**

Clay industry (May subdiv. geog.)
          338.4; 666
   UF   Clay industries *[Former head-*
          ing]
   BT   **Ceramic industry**
   NT   **Pottery**
Clay modeling
   USE **Modeling**
Cleaning   648; 667
   SA   topics with the subdivision
          Cleaning, e.g. **Rugs and car-**
          pets—Cleaning [to be added
          as needed]
   BT   **Sanitation**
   NT   **Bleaching**
          Cleaning compounds
          Dry cleaning
          House cleaning
          Laundry
          Street cleaning
Cleaning compounds   648; 667
   BT   **Cleaning**
   NT   **Detergents**
          Soap
Cleanliness   391.6; 613; 646.7
   UF   Messiness
          Neatness
   BT   **Hygiene**
          Sanitation
   NT   **Baths**
Clearing of land
   USE **Reclamation of land**
Clergy (May subdiv. geog.)   **200.92;**
          270.092
   UF   Curates
          Ministers of the gospel
          Pastors
          Preachers
          Rectors
   SA   church denominations with the
          subdivision *Clergy,* e.g. **Cath-**
          olic Church—Clergy [to be
          added as needed]
   BT   **Church**
   NT   **Catholic Church—Clergy**
          Celibacy
          Chaplains
          Priests
          Rabbis
          Women clergy

Clergy—*Continued*
    RT   **Ministry**
         Ordination
         Pastoral theology
Clergy—Office
    USE **Ministry**
Clergy—Political activity   261.7; 291.1
    BT   **Political participation**
Clerical celibacy
    USE **Celibacy**
Clerical employees
    USE **Office workers**
Clerical personnel
    USE **Office workers**
Clerical psychology
    USE **Pastoral psychology**
Clerical work—Training
    USE **Business education**
Clerks
    USE **Office workers**
Clerks (Retail trade)
    USE **Sales personnel**
Cliff dwellers and cliff dwellings (May
    subdiv. geog.)   **979**
    BT   **Archeology**
         **Native Americans—Southwest-
         ern States**
Climacteric, Female
    USE **Menopause**
Climacteric, Male
    USE **Male climacteric**
Climate   **551.6**
    Use for materials on climate as it relates to
humans and to plant and animal life, including
the effects of changes of climate. Materials
limited to the climate of a particular region
are entered under the name of the place with
the subdivision *Climate*. Materials on the state
of the atmosphere at a given time and place
with respect to heat or cold, wetness or dryness, calm or storm, are entered under
Weather. Scientific materials on the atmosphere, especially weather factors, are entered
under **Meteorology.**
    UF   Climatology
    SA   names of countries, cities, etc.,
         with the subdivision *Climate*
         [to be added as needed]
    BT   **Earth sciences**
    NT   **Chicago (Ill.)—Climate**
         Forest influences
         Greenhouse effect
         Ohio—Climate
         Seasons
         United States—Climate

    RT   **Meteorology**
         Weather
Climate and forests
    USE **Forest influences**
Climatology
    USE **Climate**
Climbing plants   **582.1; 635.9**
    UF   Vines
    BT   **Gardening**
         Plants
Clinical chemistry   **616.07**
    Use for materials on the chemical diagnosis
of disease and health monitoring.
    UF   Chemistry, Diagnostic
         Chemistry, Medical
         Diagnostic chemistry
         Medical chemistry
    BT   **Biochemistry**
         Diagnosis
Clinical drug trials
    USE **Drugs—Testing**
Clinical genetics
    USE **Medical genetics**
Clinical trials of drugs
    USE **Drugs—Testing**
Clinics
    USE **Medical practice**
Clip art   **741.6**
    Use for materials on clipping art work from
published sources to use in creating docu-
ments, posters, newsletters, etc. Materials on
the use of photocopying machines to create
original works of art are entered under **Copy
art.**
    BT   **Graphic arts**
Clipper ships   **387.2; 623.8**
    BT   **Ships**
Clippings (Books, newspapers, etc.)
    025.17
    UF   Newspaper clippings
         Press clippings
    BT   **Newspapers**
Clocks and watches (May subdiv. geog.)
    681.1; 739.3
    UF   Horology
         Watches
    BT   **Time**
    NT   **Sundials**
Clog dancing   **793.3**
    UF   Clog-dancing
         Clogging (Dance)
    BT   **Dance**

Clog-dancing
USE **Clog dancing**
Clogging (Dance)
USE **Clog dancing**
Cloisters
USE **Convents**
Monasteries
Clones and cloning
USE **Cloning**
Cloning   571.8; 660.6
UF Clones and cloning
BT **Genetic engineering**
NT **Human cloning**
Molecular cloning
Cloning—Ethical aspects   174
BT **Ethics**
Closed caption television   384.55
BT **Deaf**
Television
Closed caption video recordings   384.55
UF Video recordings, Closed caption
Video recordings for the hearing
impaired
BT **Deaf**
Videodiscs
Videotapes
Closed-circuit television   384.55
UF Television, Closed-circuit
BT **Intercommunication systems**
Microwave communication systems
Television
Closed shop
USE **Open and closed shop**
Cloth
USE **Fabrics**
Clothes
USE **Clothing and dress**
Clothiers
USE **Clothing industry**
Clothing
USE types of clothing articles and accessories; costume of particular ethnic groups, e.g. **Native American costume;** and professions and classes of persons with the subdivision *Clothing,* e.g. **Handicapped—Clothing** [to be added as needed]

Clothing and dress (May subdiv. geog.)
391; 646.4
Use for materials on clothing and the art of dress from day to day in practical situations, including historical dress and the clothing of various professions or classes of persons. Materials on the characteristic costume of ethnic groups and on fancy dress and theatrical costumes are entered under **Costume.** Materials on the prevailing mode or style of dress are entered under **Fashion.**
UF Clothes
Dress
Garments
Style in dress
SA types of clothing articles and accessories; costume of particular ethnic groups, e.g. **Native American costume;** and professions and classes of persons with the subdivision *Clothing,* e.g. **Handicapped—Clothing** [to be added as needed]
BT **Manners and customs**
NT **Buttons**
Children's clothing
Dress accessories
Dressmaking
Fans
Fashion
Handicapped—Clothing
Hats
Hosiery
Infants' clothing
Jewelry
Leather garments
Men's clothing
Shoes
Tailoring
Umbrellas and parasols
Uniforms
Wigs
Women's clothing
RT **Clothing industry**
Costume
Personal appearance
Personal grooming
Clothing and dress—Dry cleaning
USE **Dry cleaning**
Clothing and dress—France   391
Use for materials on day to day dress in France.

Clothing and dress—France—History
391

Use for materials on day to day dress in France in the past.

Clothing and dress—History 391

Use for materials on day to day dress in the past.

Clothing and dress—Repairing 646.2
UF   Mending

Clothing industry (May subdiv. geog.)
338.4; 687
UF   Clothiers
      Clothing trade
      Fashion industry
      Garment industry
BT   **Industries**
NT   **Dressmaking**
      Fashion design
      Shoe industry
      Tailoring
RT   **Clothing and dress**

Clothing trade
USE   **Clothing industry**

Cloud seeding
USE   **Weather control**

Clouds 551.57
BT   **Atmosphere**
      Meteorology

Clowns 791.3; 791.3092; 920
BT   **Circus**
      Entertainers

Clubs (May subdiv. geog.) **367**
BT   **Associations**
NT   **Boys' clubs**
      Girls' clubs
      Men—Societies
      Scouts and scouting
      Women—Societies
RT   **Societies**

Co-dependence
USE   **Codependency**

Co-dependency
USE   **Codependency**

Co-ops
USE   **Cooperative societies**

Co-ops (Housing)
USE   **Cooperative housing**

Co-parenting
USE   **Part-time parenting**

Coaching
USE   **Coaching (Athletics)**
      Horsemanship

and types of sports with the subdivision *Coaching* [to be added as needed]

Coaching (Athletics) 796.07
UF   Athletic coaching
      Coaching
      Sports coaching
SA   types of sports with the subdivision *Coaching* [to be added as needed]
BT   **Athletics**
      Physical education
      Sports
NT   **Football—Coaching**

Coal (May subdiv. geog.) **553.2**
BT   **Fuel**
NT   **Coal gasification**
      Coal liquefaction
      Coal mines and mining

Coal gas
USE   **Gas**

Coal gasification 665.7
UF   Gasification of coal
BT   **Coal**

Coal liquefaction 622
UF   Liquefaction of coal
BT   **Coal**

Coal miners 622; 920
BT   **Miners**

Coal mines and mining (May subdiv. geog.) **622**
BT   **Coal**
      Mines and mineral resources
NT   **Mining engineering**

Coal oil
USE   **Petroleum**

Coal tar products 547; 661
BT   **Petroleum**
RT   **Gas**

COAs
USE   **Children of alcoholics**

Coast pilot guides
USE   **Pilot guides**

Coastal landforms
USE   **Coasts**

Coastal signals
USE   **Signals and signaling**

Coasts (May subdiv. geog.) **551.45**
UF   Coastal landforms
BT   **Landforms**
RT   **Seashore**

Coats of arms
USE **Heraldry**
Cocaine   362.29; 615
BT **Narcotics**
NT **Crack (Drug)**
Cocaine babies
USE **Children of drug addicts**
Cocoa   633.7; 641.3
BT **Beverages**
RT **Chocolate**
Cocoons
USE **Butterflies**
   Caterpillars
   Moths
   Silkworms
Code deciphering
USE **Cryptography**
Code enciphering
USE **Cryptography**
Code names   423
BT **Abbreviations**
   Names
NT **Acronyms**
Codependency   616.86
UF Co-dependence
   Co-dependency
   Codependent behavior
BT **Abnormal psychology**
Codependent behavior
USE **Codependency**
Codes
USE **Ciphers**
Codes, Penal
USE **Criminal law**
Codes, Telegraph
USE **Cipher and telegraph codes**
Coeducation (May subdiv. geog.)
   371.822
BT **Education**
RT **Girls—Education**
   Men—Education
   Women—Education
Coffee   633.7; 641.8
BT **Beverages**
RT **Coffee industry**
Coffee bars
USE **Coffeehouses**
Coffee houses
USE **Coffeehouses**

Coffee industry (May subdiv. geog.)
   338.1; 338.4
UF Coffee trade
BT **Beverage industry**
NT **Coffeehouses**
RT **Coffee**
Coffee shops
USE **Restaurants**
Coffee trade
USE **Coffee industry**
Coffeehouses (May subdiv. geog.)
   647.95
   Use for materials on public establishments devoted primarily to serving coffee. Materials on coffee shops and cafes as small inexpensive restaurants are entered under **Restaurants.**
UF Cafes
   Coffee bars
   Coffee houses
BT **Coffee industry**
   Restaurants
Cog wheels
USE **Gearing**
Cognition
USE **Theory of knowledge**
Cohabitation
USE **Unmarried couples**
Cohousing
USE **Cooperative housing**
Coiffure
USE **Hair**
Coin collecting
USE **Coins—Collectors and collecting**
Coinage (May subdiv. geog.)   **332.4**
   Use for materials on the processing and history of metal money. Lists of coins and general materials about coins are entered under **Coins.**
BT **Money**
NT **Counterfeits and counterfeiting**
RT **Gold**
   Mints
   Silver
Coinage of words
USE **New words**
Coins (May subdiv. geog.)   **737.4**
   Use for lists of coins and general materials about coins. Materials on coins from the point of view of art and archeology are entered under **Numismatics.** Materials on the processing of metal money are entered under **Coinage.**
UF Specie
BT **Money**

Coins—Collectors and collecting 737.4
    UF   Coin collecting
    RT   **Numismatics**
Cold 536; 551.5
    NT   **Cryobiology**
           Ice
    RT   **Low temperatures**
           Temperature
Cold (Disease) 616.2
    UF   Common cold
    BT   **Communicable diseases**
           Diseases
    NT   **Influenza**
Cold—Physiological effect 613
    BT   **Cryobiology**
Cold storage 641.4; 664
    BT   **Food—Preservation**
    NT   **Compressed air**
    RT   **Refrigeration**
Cold—Therapeutic use 615.8
    UF   Cryotherapy
    BT   **Therapeutics**
    NT   **Cryosurgery**
Cold war 909.82

    Use for materials on the rivalry between capitalist and communist nations following World War II.

    UF   Power politics
    BT   **World politics—1945-1991**
Collaborationists (May subdiv. geog.) 364.1
    UF   Collaborators (Traitors)
    SA   names of wars with the subdivision *Collaborationists,* e.g. **World War, 1939-1945—Collaborationists** [to be added as needed]
    BT   **Traitors**
    NT   **World War, 1939-1945—Collaborationists**
Collaborators (Traitors)
    USE **Collaborationists**
Collage 702.8; 751.4
    BT   **Art**
           Handicraft
Collapse of structures
    USE **Structural failures**
Collectables
    USE **Collectibles**
Collected papers (Anthologies)
    USE **Anthologies**

Collected works
    USE **Anthologies**
          Literature—Collections
          Storytelling—Collections
          and form headings for minor literary forms that represent collections of works of several authors, e.g. **Essays; American essays; Parodies; Short stories;** etc.; major literary forms and national literatures with the subdivision *Collections,* e.g. **Poetry—Collections; English literature—Collections;** etc.; and subjects with the subdivision *Literary collections,* for collections focused on a single subject by two or more authors involving two or more literary forms, e.g. **Cats—Literary collections** [to be added as needed]
Collectibles (May subdiv. geog.) 745.1

    Use for materials on any objects of interest to collectors, including mass produced items of little intrinsic value. Materials on old decorative or utilitarian objects that have aesthetic or historical importance and financial value are entered under **Antiques.**

    UF   Collectables
           Memorabilia
    SA   subjects and names with the subdivision *Collectibles,* e.g. **American Revolution Bicentennial, 1776-1976—Collectibles;** and types of objects collected, excluding antiquities and natural objects, with the subdivision *Collectors and collecting,* e.g. **Boxes—Collectors and collecting** [to be added as needed]
    BT   **Collectors and collecting**
    NT   **Victoriana**
Collecting
    USE **Collectors and collecting**
Collecting of accounts 658.8
    UF   Accounts, Collecting of
           Bill collecting
           Collection of accounts
    BT   **Commercial law**
           Credit
           Debt

Collecting of accounts—*Continued*
    Debtor and creditor
Collection and preservation
    USE   types of antiquities and types of
             natural objects, including ani-
             mal specimens and plant
             specimens, with the subdivi-
             sion *Collection and preserva-*
             tion, e.g. **Birds—Collection**
             and preservation; for materi-
             als on methods of collecting
             and preserving those objects
             [to be added as needed]
Collection development (Libraries)
    USE   **Libraries—Collection develop-**
             ment
Collection of accounts
    USE   **Collecting of accounts**
Collections
    USE   form headings for minor literary
             forms that represent collec-
             tions of works of several au-
             thors, e.g. **Essays; American**
             essays; Parodies; Short sto-
             ries; etc.; major literary forms
             and national literatures with
             the subdivision *Collections,*
             e.g. **Poetry—Collections; En-**
             glish literature—Collections;
             etc.; and subjects with the
             subdivision *Literary collec-*
             tions, for collections focused
             on a single subject by two or
             more authors involving two or
             more literary forms, e.g.
             Cats—Literary collections [to
             be added as needed]
Collections (Anthologies)
    USE   **Anthologies**
Collections of art, painting, etc.
    USE   **Art collections**
             Art museums
Collections of literature
    USE   **Anthologies**
             Literature—Collections
             Storytelling—Collections
             and form headings for minor
             literary forms that represent
             collections of works of sever-
             al authors, e.g. **Essays;**
             American essays; Parodies;

Short stories; etc.; major literary forms and national literatures with the subdivision
Collections, e.g. **Poetry—Collections; English literature—
Collections;** etc.; and subjects
with the subdivision *Literary
collections,* for collections focused on a single subject by
two or more authors involving
two or more literary forms,
e.g. **Cats—Literary collections** [to be added as needed]
Collections of natural specimens
    USE   **Plants—Collection and preser-**
             vation
             Zoological specimens—Collec-
             tion and preservation
             and types of natural specimens
             with the subdivision *Collec-*
             tion and preservation, e.g.
             Birds—Collection and pres-
             ervation [to be added as
             needed]
Collections of objects
    USE   **Collectors and collecting**
             and subjects and names with
             the subdivision *Collectibles,*
             e.g. **American Revolution Bi-**
             centennial, 1776-1976—Col-
             lectibles; and types of objects
             collected, excluding antiquities
             and natural objects, with the
             subdivision *Collectors and
             collecting,* e.g. **Boxes—Col-
             lectors and collecting** [to be
             added as needed]
Collective bargaining (May subdiv. geog.)
    331.89; 658.3
    May be subdivided by groups of profession-
al or nonprofessional workers, e.g. **Collective
bargaining—Librarians.**
    UF   Labor negotiations
    BT   **Industrial relations**
           Labor
           Labor disputes
           Negotiation
    RT   **Industrial arbitration**
           Labor contract
           Labor unions
           Participative management
           Strikes

Collective bargaining—Librarians
331.89
   UF   Librarians—Collective bargaining
         Libraries—Collective bargaining
Collective farms
   USE   **Collective settlements**
         Cooperative agriculture
Collective labor agreements
   USE   **Labor contract**
Collective security
   USE   **International security**
Collective settlements (May subdiv. geog.)
      307.77; 335
      Use for materials on traditional, formally
      organized communal ventures, usually based
      on ideological, political, or religious affilia-
      tion. Materials on arrangements in voluntary
      cooperative living, usually informal, are en-
      tered under **Communal living.**
   UF   Collective farms
         Communal settlements
         Communes
         Cooperative living
   SA   names of individual collective
         settlements [to be added as
         needed]
   BT   **Communism**
         Cooperation
         Socialism
   RT   **Communal living**
         Cooperative agriculture
         Counter culture
         Utopias
Collective settlements—Israel   307.77
   UF   Israel—Collective settlements
         Kibbutz
Collective settlements—United States
      307.77
Collectivism
   USE   **Communism**
         Socialism
Collectors and collecting (May subdiv.
      geog.)   **790.1**
   UF   Collecting
         Collections of objects
   SA   types of collecting, e.g. **Book
         collecting;** types of objects
         collected, excluding antiquities
         and natural objects, with the
         subdivision *Collectors and
         collecting,* e.g. **Postcards—
         Collectors and collecting;**

names of original owners of
private art collections with the
subdivision *Art collections;*
subjects and names with the
subdivision *Collectibles,* e.g.
**American Revolution Bicen-
tennial, 1776-1976—Collectibles;** and antiquities and
types of natural objects with
the subdivision *Collection and
preservation,* e.g. **Birds—Collection and preservation** [to
be added as needed]
   BT   **Antiques**
         Art
         Hobbies
   NT   **American Revolution Bicenten-
         nial, 1776-1976—Collectibles**
         Americana
         Antiques
         **Antiquities—Collection and
         preservation**
         Book collecting
         **Boxes—Collectors and collect-
         ing**
         Collectibles
         **Plants—Collection and preser-
         vation**
         Stamp collecting
         **Zoological specimens—Collec-
         tion and preservation**
   RT   **Art collections**
Collects
   USE   **Prayers**
College admissions essays
   USE   **College applications**
College and school drama   371.8; 792
      Use for materials about college and school
      drama. Individual works, collections, and ma-
      terials about plays for children are entered un-
      der **Children's plays.** Plays for children on a
      particular theme are entered under subjects
      and personal, corporate, and place names with
      the subdivision *Juvenile drama.*
   UF   College drama
         School plays
   BT   **Amateur theater**
         Drama
         Student activities
   RT   **Drama in education**
College and school journalism   371.8
   UF   College journalism
         College periodicals

College and school journalism—*Continued*
        School journalism
        School newspapers
  BT **Journalism**
        Student activities
  RT **Children's writings**
College and university libraries
  USE **Academic libraries**
College applications 378.1
  UF Admissions applications
        Admissions essays
        Applications for college
        College admissions essays
        Colleges and universities—Applications
  RT **Colleges and universities—Entrance requirements**
College athletics
  USE **College sports**
College choice 378
  UF Choice of college
        Colleges and universities—Selection
  BT **Colleges and universities**
        School choice
College costs 378.3
  UF Tuition
  BT **Colleges and universities—Finance**
  NT **Student aid**
        Student loan funds
College degrees
  USE **Academic degrees**
College drama
  USE **College and school drama**
College dropouts
  USE **Dropouts**
College entrance examinations
  USE **Colleges and universities—Entrance examinations**
College entrance requirements
  USE **Colleges and universities—Entrance requirements**
College fraternities
  USE **Fraternities and sororities**
College graduates (May subdiv. geog.)
        305.5; 378
  UF Graduates, College
        University graduates
  BT **Professions**
  RT **College students**

College journalism
  USE **College and school journalism**
College libraries
  USE **Academic libraries**
College life
  USE **College students**
College periodicals
  USE **College and school journalism**
College songs
  USE **Students' songs**
College sororities
  USE **Fraternities and sororities**
College sports (May subdiv. geog.)
        371.8; 796
  UF College athletics
        Intercollegiate athletics
        Varsity sports
  SA types of sports [to be added as needed]
  BT **Sports**
        Student activities
  RT **School sports**
College students (May subdiv. geog.)
        371.8; 378
  UF College life
        Colleges and universities—Students
        Student life *[Former heading]*
        Undergraduates
        University students
  BT **Students**
  RT **College graduates**
College students, Foreign
  USE **Foreign students**
College students—Political activity
        371.8; 378
  UF Campus disorders
  BT **Political participation**
College students—Sexual behavior
        371.8; 378
  BT **Sexual behavior**
College teachers
  USE **Colleges and universities—Faculty**
        Educators
        Teachers
College yearbooks
  USE **School yearbooks**

Colleges and universities (May subdiv. geog.) **378**
UF Universities
Universities and colleges
SA types of colleges and universities, e.g. **Catholic colleges and universities;** and names of individual colleges and universities [to be added as needed]
BT **Education**
Higher education
Professional education
Schools
NT **Academic degrees**
Catholic colleges and universities
College choice
Commencements
Dissertations
Fraternities and sororities
Free universities
Junior colleges
Law schools
Medical colleges
Teachers colleges
United States Military Academy
University extension
Colleges and universities—Accreditation **378; 379.1**
Colleges and universities—Applications
USE **College applications**
Colleges and universities—Buildings **727**
BT **Buildings**
Colleges and universities—Curricula **378.1**
UF Core curriculum
SA types of education and schools with the subdivision *Curricula,* e.g. **Library education—Curricula** [to be added as needed]
BT **Education—Curricula**
Colleges and universities—Employees (May subdiv. geog.) **378.1**
BT **Employees**

Colleges and universities—Employees—Salaries, wages, etc. (May subdiv. geog.) **331.2**
BT **Salaries, wages, etc.**
Colleges and universities—Endowments **378**
BT **Endowments**
Colleges and universities—Entrance examinations **378.1**
UF College entrance examinations
Entrance examinations for colleges
BT **Educational tests and measurements**
Examinations
NT **Graduate Record Examination**
Scholastic Aptitude Test
Colleges and universities—Entrance requirements **378.1**
UF College entrance requirements
Entrance requirements for colleges and universities
SA names of individual colleges and universities with the subdivision *Entrance requirements* [to be added as needed]
BT **Examinations**
RT **College applications**
Colleges and universities—Faculty **378.1**
UF College teachers
Faculty (Education)
BT **Teachers**
Colleges and universities—Faculty—Pensions **331.25**
Colleges and universities—Finance **378.1**
UF Tuition
BT **Finance**
NT **College costs**
RT **Federal aid to education**
Colleges and universities—Insignia **378.2**
BT **Insignia**
Colleges and universities—Selection
USE **College choice**
Colleges and universities—Students
USE **College students**
Colleges and universities—United States **378.73**

Collies   636.737
   BT   Dogs
Collisions, Railroad
   USE   Railroad accidents
Colloids   541.3
   BT   Physical chemistry
Colonial architecture
   USE   American colonial style in architecture
       Architecture—United States—1600-1775, Colonial period
Colonial history (U.S.)
   USE   United States—History—1600-1775, Colonial period
Colonialism
   USE   Colonies
       Imperialism
Colonies   321; 325

Use for materials on general colonial policy. Materials on the policy of settling immigrants or nationals abroad are entered under **Colonization.** Materials on migration from one country to another are entered under **Immigration and emigration.** Materials on the movement of population within a country for permanent settlement are entered under **Internal migration.**

   UF   Colonialism
       Dependencies
   SA   names of countries with the subdivision *Colonies,* or *Territories and possessions,* e.g.
       Great Britain—Colonies;
       United States—Territories and possessions; etc. [to be added as needed]
   BT   Imperialism
   NT   Great Britain—Colonies
       Land settlement
       Penal colonies
   RT   Colonization
Colonies, Space
   USE   Space colonies
Colonization   325

Use for materials on the policy of settling immigrants or nationals abroad. Materials on general colonial policy are entered under **Colonies.** Materials on migration from one country to another are entered under **Immigration and emigration.** Materials on the movement of population within a country for permanent settlement are entered under **Internal migration.**

   SA   names of countries with the subdivision *Immigration and emigration,* e.g. **United States—**

Immigration and emigration [to be added as needed]
   BT   **Imperialism**
       Land settlement
   NT   **Internal migration**
       Public lands
   RT   **Colonies**
       Immigration and emigration
Color   535.6; 701; 752
   UF   Colour
   SA   subjects with the subdivision *Color,* and names of specific colors [to be added as needed]
   BT   Aesthetics
       Chemistry
       Light
       Optics
       Painting
       Photometry
   NT   Animals—Color
       Birds—Color
       Dyes and dyeing
       Red
   RT   Pigments
Color blindness   617.7
   BT   Color sense
       Vision disorders
Color etchings
   USE   Color prints
Color photography   778.6
   UF   Color slides
       Photography, Color
   BT   Photography
Color printing   686.2

Use for materials on practical printing in color. Materials on hand-colored prints or on pictures printed in color are entered under **Color prints.**

   SA   types of color printing processes [to be added as needed]
   BT   Printing
   NT   Illustration of books
       Lithography
       Silk screen printing
   RT   Color prints
Color prints   769

Use for materials on hand-colored prints or on pictures printed in color. Materials on practical printing in color are entered under **Color printing.**

   UF   Block printing
       Color etchings

Color prints—*Continued*
    Painting—Color reproductions
  SA color prints of particular countries, e.g. **American color prints** [to be added as needed]
  BT **Prints**
  NT **American color prints**
       Japanese color prints
  RT **Color printing**
Color prints, American
  USE **American color prints**
Color prints, Japanese
  USE **Japanese color prints**
Color—Psychological aspects 152.14
  UF Psychology of color
  BT **Color sense**
       Psychology
Color sense 152.14
  BT **Psychophysiology**
       Senses and sensation
       Vision
  NT **Color blindness**
       Color—Psychological aspects
Color slides
  USE **Color photography**
       Slides (Photography)
Color television 621.388
  BT **Television**
Colorado River—Hoover Dam
  USE **Hoover Dam (Ariz. and Nev.)**
Coloring books 372.5
  UF Painting books
  BT **Picture books for children**
Colour
  USE **Color**
Columnists
  USE **Journalists**
Combustion 541.3; 621.402
  BT **Chemistry**
  NT **Fuel**
  RT **Fire**
       Heat
Comedians (May subdiv. geog.) 791; 792.2; 920
  BT **Actors**
       Entertainers
  NT **Fools and jesters**
Comedies 808.82; 812, etc.
  May be used for individual works or for collections. Materials about comedy as a literary form are entered under **Comedy.**

  UF Comic drama
       Comic plays
       Humorous plays
       Slapstick comedies
  BT **Drama**
       Wit and humor
  NT **Comedy films**
       Comedy television programs
       Farces
Comedy 792.2; 809.2
  Use for materials on comedy as a literary form. Individual works and collections of comedies are entered under **Comedies.**
  UF Comic drama
       Comic literature
  BT **Drama**
       Wit and humor
Comedy films 791.43
  May be used for individual works, collections, or materials about comedy films.
  UF Comic films
       Humorous films
       Slapstick comedies
  SA types of comedy films, e.g. **Three Stooges films** [to be added as needed]
  BT **Comedies**
       Motion pictures
  NT **Three Stooges films**
  RT **Comedy television programs**
Comedy radio programs 791.44
  May be used for individual works, collections, or materials about comedy radio programs.
  UF Radio comedies
       Radio comedy programs
  BT **Radio programs**
Comedy television programs 791.45
  May be used for individual works, collections, or materials about television comedies.
  UF Comic television programs
       Sitcoms
       Situation comedies
       Slapstick comedies
       Television comedies
       Television comedy programs
  BT **Comedies**
       Television programs
  RT **Comedy films**
Comets 523.6
  BT **Astronomy**
       Solar system
  NT **Halley's comet**

Comic books, strips, etc. (May subdiv. geog.) **741.5**

May be used for individual works, collections, or materials about printed comic strips, i.e. groups of cartoons in narrative sequence, and books and magazines consisting of comic strips, etc.

UF   Comic strips
       Funnies
       Humorous pictures

SA   ethnic groups, classes of persons, corporate bodies, individual persons, literary authors, or sacred works with the subdivision *Comic books, strips, etc.;* and names of comic books, comic strips, and comic strip characters [to be added as needed]

BT **Wit and humor**

NT **Mystery comic books, strips, etc.**
      Science fiction comic books, strips, etc.
      Superhero comic books, strips, etc.
      Western comic books, strips, etc.

RT **Cartoons and caricatures**
      Chapbooks

Comic drama
   USE **Comedies**
          Comedy

Comic epic literature
   USE **Mock-heroic literature**

Comic films
   USE **Comedy films**

Comic literature
   USE **Comedy**
          Parody
          Satire

Comic novels
   USE **Humorous fiction**

Comic opera
   USE **Opera**
          Operetta

Comic plays
   USE **Comedies**

Comic strips
   USE **Comic books, strips, etc.**

Comic television programs
   USE **Comedy television programs**

Comic verse
   USE **Humorous poetry**

Coming of age stories
   USE **Bildungsromans**

Commencements **394.2**

UF   Graduation

BT **Colleges and universities**
      High schools
      School assembly programs

Commentaries
   USE names of sacred works, including named parts of sacred works, with the subdivision *Commentaries,* e.g. **Bible—Commentaries** [to be added as needed]

Commentaries, Biblical
   USE **Bible—Commentaries**

Commerce **380.1**

Use for general materials on foreign and domestic commerce. Materials limited to commerce between states are entered under **Interstate commerce.**

UF   Distribution (Economics)
       Trade

SA   names of countries, cities, etc., with the subdivision *Commerce,* e.g. **United States—Commerce;** and names of articles of commerce, e.g. **Cotton** [to be added as needed]

BT **Economics**
      Finance

NT **Banks and banking**
      Barter
      Black market
      Boycotts
      Business
      Chambers of commerce
      Chicago (Ill.)—Commerce
      Commercial geography
      Commercial products
      Competition
      Contracts
      Cooperation
      Developing countries—Commerce
      Electronic commerce
      Exchange
      Industrial trusts
      International trade
      Interstate commerce

Commerce—*Continued*
    Marine insurance
    Markets
    Monopolies
    Multinational corporations
    Ohio—Commerce
    Prices
    Profit sharing
    Restraint of trade
    Retail trade
    Stocks
    Tourist trade
    Trade routes
    Trademarks
    United States—Commerce
  RT **Transportation**
Commerce—Law and legislation
  USE **Commercial law**
Commercial aeronautics (May subdiv. geog.) **387.7**
  UF Aeronautics, Commercial
      Air cargo
      Air freight
      Air transport
      Commercial aviation
  BT **Freight**
      Transportation
  NT **Air mail service**
      Airlines
Commercial arithmetic
  USE **Business mathematics**
Commercial art (May subdiv. geog.) **741.6**
  UF Advertising art
      Art in advertising
  BT **Advertising**
      Art
      Drawing
  NT **Fashion design**
      Posters
      Textile design
Commercial aviation
  USE **Commercial aeronautics**
Commercial buildings (May subdiv. geog.) **333.33; 725**
  UF Mercantile buildings
      Store buildings
  BT **Buildings**
  NT **Shopping centers and malls**
      Stores

Commercial catalogs **380.1029; 659.13**
  UF Catalogs
      Commercial products—Catalogs
      Mail order catalogs
      Trade catalogs
  SA types of merchandise, objects, products, etc., and names of individual companies with the subdivision *Catalogs* [to be added as needed]
  BT **Advertising**
Commercial correspondence
  USE **Business letters**
Commercial education
  USE **Business education**
Commercial employees
  USE **Office workers**
Commercial endeavors in space
  USE **Space industrialization**
Commercial fishing (May subdiv. geog.) **338.3; 639.2**
  Use for materials on the fishing industry. Materials on the cultivation of fish in captivity are entered under **Fish culture.** Materials on fishing as a sport are entered under **Fishing.**
  UF Fisheries *[Former heading]*
      Fishing, Commercial
      Fishing industry
      Sea fisheries
  BT **Industries**
  NT **Pearl fisheries**
      Whaling
Commercial fishing—United States **338.3; 639.2**
Commercial geography **330.9**
  UF Economic geography
      World economics
  BT **Commerce**
      Geography
  NT **Trade routes**
  RT **Economic conditions**
Commercial law (May subdiv. geog.) **346.07**
  UF Business law
      Business—Law and legislation
      Commerce—Law and legislation
      Mercantile law
  BT **Law**
  NT **Antitrust law**
      Arbitration and award
      Bankruptcy
      Collecting of accounts

Commercial law—*Continued*
- Contracts
- Corporation law
- Debtor and creditor
- Fraud
- Insider trading
- Landlord and tenant
- Licenses
- Negotiable instruments
- Restraint of trade
- Unfair competition
- RT Maritime law

Commercial mathematics
- USE **Business mathematics**

Commercial paper
- USE **Negotiable instruments**

Commercial photography 778
- BT **Photography**
- NT **Photojournalism**

Commercial policy (May subdiv. geog.)
380.1; 381.3; 382

Use for general materials on the various regulations by which governments seek to protect and increase the commerce of a country, such as subsidies, tariffs, free ports, etc.

- UF Government policy
  Government regulation of commerce
  Reciprocity
  Trade barriers
  World economics
- BT **Economic policy**
  International economic relations
- NT **Buy national policy**
  Commercial products
  Free trade
  Protectionism
  Tariff

Commercial policy—United States
380.1; 381.3; 382
- UF United States—Commercial policy *[Former heading]*

Commercial products (May subdiv. geog.)
338; 380.1
- UF Merchandise
  Products, Commercial
- SA types of products and names of specific products [to be added as needed]

- BT **Commerce**
- NT **Animal products**
  Brand name products
  Consumer goods
  Forest products
  Generic products
  Manufactures
  Marine resources
  Raw materials
  Substitute products

Commercial products—Catalogs
- USE **Commercial catalogs**

Commercial products recall
- USE **Product recall**

Commercial secrets
- USE **Trade secrets**

Commercials, Radio
- USE **Radio advertising**

Commercials, Television
- USE **Television advertising**

Commission government
- USE **Municipal government by commission**

Commission government with city manager
- USE **Municipal government by city manager**

Common cold
- USE **Cold (Disease)**

Common law marriage
- USE **Unmarried couples**

Common market
- USE **European Union**

Commonplaces
- USE **Terms and phrases**

Commonwealth countries 909

Use for materials dealing collectively with the member countries of the international organization that was founded in 1931 as the British Commonwealth of Nations, changed its name to the Commonwealth of Nations in 1950, and became known as the Commonwealth in 1969.

- UF British Commonwealth countries
  British Commonwealth of Nations
  British Dominions
  Commonwealth of Nations
  Dominions, British
- RT **Great Britain—Colonies**

Commonwealth of England
- USE **Great Britain—History—1642-1660, Civil War and Commonwealth**

Commonwealth of Independent States
947.086

Use for materials specifically on the federation of independent former Soviet republics that was established in December 1991 and does not include Georgia or the Baltic states. General materials on several or all of the countries that emerged from the dissolution of the Soviet Union in 1991 are entered under **Former Soviet republics.**

UF   CIS

RT   **Former Soviet republics**
      Russia (Federation)
      Soviet Union

Commonwealth of Nations

USE   **Commonwealth countries**

Commonwealth, The

USE   **Political science**
      Republics
      State, The

Communal living (May subdiv. geog.)
307.77

Use for materials on arrangements in voluntary cooperative living, usually informal. Materials on traditional, formally organized communal ventures, usually based on ideological, political, or religious affiliation are entered under **Collective settlements.**

UF   Communal settlements
      Communes
      Cooperative living
      Group living

BT   **Cooperation**

RT   **Collective settlements**
      Cooperative housing
      Counter culture

Communal settlements

USE   **Collective settlements**
      Communal living

Communes

USE   **Collective settlements**
      Communal living

Communicable diseases (May subdiv. geog.) **614.4; 616.9**

UF   Contagion and contagious diseases
      Contagious diseases
      Infection and infectious diseases
      Quarantine

SA   names of communicable diseases [to be added as needed]

BT   **Diseases**
      Public health

NT   **AIDS (Disease)**
      Cold (Disease)

      Fumigation
      Germ theory of disease
      Influenza
      Plague
      Rabies
      Sexually transmitted diseases

RT   **Epidemics**
      Immunity
      Insects as carriers of disease

Communicable diseases—Prevention
614.4

BT   **Preventive medicine**

Communication   302.2

Use for general materials on communication in its broadest sense, including the use of the spoken and written word, signs, symbols, or behavior.

UF   Mass communication

BT   **Sociology**

NT   **Books and reading**
      Conversation
      Cybernetics
      Deaf—Means of communication
      Information science
      Language and languages
      Language arts
      Mass media
      Nonverbal communication
      Popular culture
      Postal service
      Public speaking
      Signals and signaling
      Signs and symbols
      Telecommunication
      Writing

Communication among animals

USE   **Animal communication**

Communication arts

USE   **Language arts**

Communication satellites

USE   **Artificial satellites in telecommunication**

Communication systems

USE   subjects with the subdivision *Communication systems,* e.g. **Astronautics—Communication systems** [to be added as needed]

Communications relay satellites

USE   **Artificial satellites in telecommunication**

Communion
   USE   **Eucharist**
Communism (May subdiv. geog.)   **320.5;**
   321.9; 324.1; 335.43
   UF   Bolshevism
         Collectivism
   SA   communism and other subjects,
         e.g. **Communism and litera-**
         ture [to be added as needed]
   BT   **Political science**
         Totalitarianism
   NT   **Anticommunist movements**
         Collective settlements
         Communism and literature
         Communism and religion
         Dialectical materialism
   RT   **Marxism**
         Socialism
Communism and literature   **335.4; 809;**
   810.9, etc.
   UF   Literature and communism
   BT   **Communism**
         Literature
Communism and religion   **261.7; 335.4**
   UF   Communism—Religious aspects
         Religion and communism
   BT   **Communism**
         Religion
Communism—Religious aspects
   USE   **Communism and religion**
Communism—Soviet Union   **320.5;**
   335.430947; 947.084
   UF   Russian communism
         Soviet communism
         Soviet Union—Communism
Communism—United States   **320.5;**
   335.43; 973
Communist countries   **909**
   UF   Chinese satellite countries
         Iron curtain countries
         People's democracies
         Russian satellite countries
         Soviet bloc
Communities, Space
   USE   **Space colonies**
Community action
   USE   **Political participation**
Community and libraries
   USE   **Libraries and community**

Community and school (May subdiv.
   geog.)   **371.19**
   UF   School and community
   BT   **Community life**
   NT   **Parent-teacher associations**
Community based residences
   USE   **Group homes**
Community centers (May subdiv. geog.)
   374; 790.06
   UF   Neighborhood centers
         Play centers
         Recreation centers
         School buildings as recreation
           centers
         Schools as social centers
   BT   **Cities and towns—Civic im-**
         provement
         Community life
         Community organization
         Recreation
         Social settlements
   NT   **Youth hostels**
   RT   **Playgrounds**
Community chests
   USE   **Fund raising**
Community churches (May subdiv. geog.)
   254
     Use for materials on local churches that
   have no denominational affiliations.
   UF   Churches, Community
         Churches, Undenominational
         Nondenominational churches
         Undenominational churches
         Union churches
   BT   **Christian sects**
Community colleges
   USE   **Junior colleges**
Community councils
   USE   **Community organization**
Community development (May subdiv.
   geog.)   **307.1; 361.6**
   UF   Neighborhood development
   BT   **Domestic economic assistance**
         Social change
         Urban renewal
   RT   **Agricultural extension work**
         City planning
         Technical assistance
Community health services (May subdiv.
   geog.)   **362.1**
   BT   **Community services**
         Public health

Community history
  USE **Local history**
Community life (May subdiv. geog.)
    307
  BT **Associations**
  NT **Community and school**
      Community centers
      Community organization
      Neighborhood
      Scouts and scouting
Community organization (May subdiv.
    geog.) **307**
  UF Community councils
  BT **Community life**
      Social work
  NT **Community centers**
      Local government
  RT **Urban renewal**
Community services (May subdiv. geog.)
    361.7; 361.8
  SA types of services, e.g. **Commu-
      nity health services** [to be
      added as needed]
  BT **Social work**
  NT **Community health services**
Community surveys
  USE **Social surveys**
Community theater
  USE **Little theater movement**
Compact automobiles
  USE **Compact cars**
Compact cars **629.222**
  UF Compact automobiles
      Compacts (Automobiles)
      Economy cars
      Small cars
  SA names of specific makes and
      models of compact cars [to
      be added as needed]
  BT **Automobiles**
Compact disc interactive technology
  USE **CD-I technology**
Compact disc players **621.389**
  UF Audiodisc players
      CD players
      Digital audio disc players
  BT **Phonograph**
      **Sound—Recording and repro-
      ducing**
Compact disc read-only memory
  USE **CD-ROMs**

Compact discs **621.389; 780.26**
  Use for materials on small optical discs in
  general and on the compact disc format for
  sound recordings. Materials about sound
  recordings that emphasize the content of the
  recording rather than the format are entered
  under **Sound recordings.**
  UF CDs (Compact discs)
      Compact disks
      Digital compact discs
  BT **Optical storage devices**
      Sound recordings
  NT **CD-I technology**
      CD-ROMs
Compact disks
  USE **Compact discs**
Compacts (Automobiles)
  USE **Compact cars**
Companies
  USE **Business enterprises**
      Corporations
Companion-animal partnership
  USE **Pet therapy**
Company libraries
  USE **Corporate libraries**
Company symbols
  USE **Trademarks**
Comparative anatomy **571.3**
  UF Anatomy, Comparative
  BT **Anatomy**
      Zoology
  NT **Morphology**
Comparative government **320.3**
  UF Government, Comparative
  SA names of countries, cities, etc.,
      with the subdivision *Politics
      and government,* e.g. **United
      States—Politics and govern-
      ment** [to be added as needed]
  BT **Political science**
Comparative linguistics
  USE **Linguistics**
Comparative literature **809**
  UF Literature, Comparative
  BT **Literature**
Comparative morphology
  USE **Morphology**
Comparative philology
  USE **Linguistics**
Comparative physiology **571.1**
  UF Physiology, Comparative
  BT **Physiology**

Comparative psychology   156
    UF   Animal psychology
           Psychology, Comparative
    SA   types of animals with the subdivision *Psychology*, e.g. **Dogs—Psychology** [to be added as needed]
    BT   **Zoology**
    NT   **Dogs—Psychology**
           Sociobiology
    RT   **Animal intelligence**
           Instinct

Comparative religion
    USE **Christianity and other religions**
           Religions

Comparative studies
    USE religious topics and names of sacred works and individual Christian denominations with the subdivision *Comparative studies*, e.g. **Mysticism—Comparative studies** [to be added as needed]

Comparison
    USE names of languages with the subdivision *Comparison*, e.g. **English language—Comparison** [to be added as needed]

Comparison (English grammar)
    USE **English language—Comparison**

Comparison of cultures
    USE **Cross-cultural studies**

Compass   538; 623.8
    UF   Magnetic needle
           Mariner's compass
    BT   **Magnetism**
           Navigation

Compassion
    USE **Consolation**

Compensation
    USE **Pensions**
           Salaries, wages, etc.
           Workers' compensation

Compensatory spending
    USE **Deficit financing**

Competition (May subdiv. geog.)   338.6
    BT   **Business**
           Business ethics
           Commerce
    RT   **Industrial trusts**
           Monopolies

Competition, International
    USE **International competition**

Competition, Unfair
    USE **Unfair competition**

Competitions
    USE **Awards**
           Contests
           and subjects with the subdivision *Competitions*, e.g. **Literature—Competitions** [to be added as needed]

Composers (May subdiv. geog.)   780.92; 920
    UF   Songwriters
    BT   **Musicians**

Composers, American
    USE **Composers—United States**

Composers—United States   780.92; 920
    UF   American composers *[Former heading]*
           Composers, American

Composition
    USE types of natural substances of unfixed composition, including soils, plants and crops, animals, farm products, etc., with the subdivision *Composition*, for the results of analyses of those substances, e.g. **Food—Composition** [to be added as needed]

Composition and exercises
    USE names of languages with the subdivision *Composition and exercises*, e.g. **English language—Composition and exercises** [to be added as needed]

Composition (Art)   701
    UF   Art—Composition
    BT   **Art**
    NT   **Architecture—Composition, proportion, etc.**
    RT   **Painting**

Composition (Music)   781.3
    UF   Music—Composition
           Musical composition
           Song writing
           Songwriting
    BT   **Music**
           Music—Theory

Composition (Music)—*Continued*
   NT   **Counterpoint**
         Harmony
         Instrumentation and orchestration
         Musical accompaniment
         Musical form
         Popular music—Writing and publishing
Composition of natural substances
   USE   types of natural substances of unfixed composition, including soils, plants and crops, animals, farm products, etc., with the subdivision *Composition* for the results of analyses of those substances, e.g. **Food—Composition** [to be added as needed]
Composition (Printing)
   USE   **Typesetting**
Composition (Rhetoric)
   USE   **Rhetoric**
         and names of languages with the subdivision *Composition and exercises,* e.g. **English language—Composition and exercises** [to be added as needed]
Compost   **631.8**
   BT   **Fertilizers**
         Soils
   RT   **Organic gardening**
Comprehensive health care organizations
   USE   **Health maintenance organizations**
Compressed air   **621.5**
   UF   Pneumatic transmission
   BT   **Cold storage**
         Pneumatics
         Power (Mechanics)
Compulsion (Psychology)
   USE   **Compulsive behavior**
Compulsive behavior   **616.85**
   UF   Addictive behavior
         Compulsion (Psychology)
   SA   types of compulsive behavior [to be added as needed]
   BT   **Abnormal psychology**
         Human behavior
   NT   **Compulsive gambling**
         Exercise addiction

         Workaholism
   RT   **Twelve-step programs**
Compulsive exercising
   USE   **Exercise addiction**
Compulsive gambling   **616.85**
   UF   Addiction to gambling
   BT   **Compulsive behavior**
         Gambling
Compulsive working
   USE   **Workaholism**
Compulsory education   **379.2**
   UF   Compulsory school attendance
         Education, Compulsory
   BT   **Education—Government policy**
   NT   **Evening and continuation schools**
   RT   **School attendance**
Compulsory labor
   USE   **Forced labor**
Compulsory military service
   USE   **Draft**
Compulsory school attendance
   USE   **Compulsory education**
         School attendance
Computation, Approximate
   USE   **Approximate computation**
Computation (Mathematics)
   USE   **Arithmetic**
Computer-aided design   **620**
     Use for materials on the use of computer graphics to design tools, vehicles, buildings, etc.
   UF   CAD
         Computer aided design *[Former heading]*
         Computer-assisted design
         Electronic design
   BT   **Computer graphics**
         Design
   RT   **Computer-aided design software**
Computer aided design
   USE   **Computer-aided design**
Computer-aided design software   **006.6**
   UF   CAD/CAM software
         CAD software
   BT   **Computer software**
   RT   **Computer-aided design**
Computer art (May subdiv. geog.)   **700; 760**
     Use for materials on the use of computer graphics to create artistic designs, drawings, or other works of art.

Computer art—*Continued*
   BT   **Art**
        Computer graphics
Computer-assisted design
   USE   **Computer-aided design**
Computer-assisted instruction   371.33
    Use for materials on automated instruction in which a student interacts directly with a computer.
   UF   CAI
        Computer assisted instruction
        [Former heading]
        Computers—Educational use
        Education—Automation
        Education—Data processing
        Teaching—Data processing
   SA   subjects with the subdivision
        Computer-assisted instruction
        [to be added as needed]
   BT   **Programmed instruction**
   NT   **Mathematics—Computer-assisted instruction**
Computer assisted instruction
   USE   **Computer-assisted instruction**
Computer-assisted instruction—Authoring programs   005.3; 371.33
    Use for materials on computer programs that allow the user with comparatively little expertise to design customized computer programs for educational purposes.
   UF   Authoring programs for computer-assisted instruction
   BT   **Computer software**
Computer awareness
   USE   **Computer literacy**
Computer-based information systems
   USE   **Information systems**
        Management information systems
Computer-based multimedia information systems
   USE   **Multimedia**
Computer bulletin boards   004.693; 384.3
    Use for materials on services that allow users to post messages and retrieve messages from others who have some common interest. Materials on services that allow users to engage in conversations in real time are entered under **Online chat groups.** Materials on services, commonly called newsgroups or LISTSERV lists, that allow subscribers to post messages that are then distributed to other subscribers are entered under **Electronic discussion groups.**
   UF   Electronic bulletin boards
   BT   **Bulletin boards**
   RT   **Electronic discussion groups**
        Online chat groups
Computer control
   USE   **Automation**
Computer crimes (May subdiv. geog.)   **364.16**
   UF   Computer fraud
   BT   **Crime**
   NT   **Computer viruses**
   RT   **Computer security**
Computer drafting
   USE   **Computer graphics**
Computer drawing
   USE   **Computer graphics**
Computer fraud
   USE   **Computer crimes**
Computer games   794.8
   BT   **Computer software**
        Games
Computer graphics   006.6
    Use for materials on the production of drawings, pictures, or diagrams, as distinct from letters and numbers, on a computer screen or hard-copy output devices. Materials on the use of computer graphics to create artistic designs, drawings, or other works of art are entered under **Computer art.** Materials on the use of computer graphics to design tools, vehicles, buildings, etc., are entered under **Computer-aided design.**
   UF   Automatic drafting
        Automatic drawing
        Computer drafting
        Computer drawing
        Electronic drafting
        Electronic drawing
        Graphics, Computer
   BT   **Data processing**
   NT   **Computer-aided design**
        Computer art
Computer hardware
   USE   **Computers**
Computer industry (May subdiv. geog.)   **338.7**
   BT   **Industries**
   RT   **Computers**
Computer input-output equipment
   USE   **Computer peripherals**
Computer interfaces   004.6; 621.39
    Use for materials on equipment and techniques linking computers to peripheral devices or to other computers.

Computer interfaces—*Continued*
    UF   Interfaces, Computer
    BT   **Computer peripherals**
Computer keyboarding
    USE **Keyboarding (Electronics)**
Computer keyboards
    USE **Keyboards (Electronics)**
Computer languages
    USE **Programming languages**
Computer literacy   004
    Use for materials on the basic knowledge of computers a person needs in order to function in a computer-based society.
    UF   Computer awareness
    BT   **Computers and civilization**
          Literacy
Computer memory systems
    USE **Computer storage devices**
Computer modeling
    USE **Computer simulation**
Computer models
    USE **Computer simulation**
Computer monitors   004.7
    Use for materials on video display devices connected to a personal computer.
    UF   CRT display terminals
          Video display terminals *[Former heading]*
    BT   **Computer peripherals**
Computer music   786.7
    BT   **Music**
    RT   **Computer sound processing**
          Electronic music
Computer network resources
    USE **Internet resources**
Computer networks   004.6; 384.3
    Use for materials on systems consisting of two or more interconnected computers.
    UF   Information superhighway
          Networks, Computer
    SA   types of computer networks and names of specific computer networks [to be added as needed]
    BT   **Data transmission systems**
          Telecommunication
    NT   **Cyberspace**
          Internet
    RT   **Information networks**
Computer operating systems   005.4
    UF   Computers—Operating systems
          Operating systems (Computers)
    BT   **Computer software**

Computer peripherals   004.7; 621.39
    UF   Computer input-output equipment
          Input equipment (Computers)
          Output equipment (Computers)
    SA   types of computer peripherals [to be added as needed]
    BT   **Computers**
    NT   **Computer interfaces**
          Computer monitors
          Computer storage devices
          Computer terminals
          Keyboards (Electronics)
Computer program languages
    USE **Programming languages**
Computer programming   005.1
    UF   Computers—Programming
          Programming (Computers) *[Former heading]*
    SA   subjects with the subdivision *Computer programs,* e.g.
          Database management—Computer programs [to be added as needed]
    BT   **Computer science**
          Data processing
    RT   **Computer software**
          Programming languages
Computer programs
    USE **Computer software**
          and subjects with the subdivision *Computer programs,* e.g.
          Oceanography—Computer programs [to be added as needed]
Computer science   004
    Use for materials discussing collectively the disciplines that deal with the general theory and application of computers.
    BT   **Science**
    NT   **Artificial intelligence**
          Computer programming
          Database management
    RT   **Computers**
Computer science—Dictionaries   004.03
    UF   Computer terms
          Computers—Dictionaries
    BT   **Encyclopedias and dictionaries**
Computer security   005.8
    Use for materials on protecting computer hardware and software from accidental or malicious access, use, modification, disclosure, or destruction.

Computer security—*Continued*
UF Computers—Access control
     Computers—Security measures
BT **Computers**
RT **Computer crimes**
     Computer viruses
Computer sex 306.7
UF Cybersex
     On-line sex
     Online sex
BT **Sexual behavior**
Computer simulation 003
UF Computer modeling
     Computer models
     Simulation, computer
SA subjects with the subdivision
     Computer simulation, e.g.
     Psychology—Computer simu-
     lation [to be added as need-
     ed]
BT **Mathematical models**
NT **Psychology—Computer simula-**
     tion
     Virtual reality
Computer software 005.3
UF Computer programs
     Programs, Computer
     Software, Computer
SA types of computer software, e.g.
     Computer games; Spread-
     sheet software; etc.; subjects
     with the subdivision *Computer*
     programs, e.g. **Oceanogra-**
     phy—Computer programs;
     and names of individual com-
     puter programs [to be added
     as needed]
NT **Computer-aided design soft-**
     ware
     Computer-assisted instruction—
     Authoring programs
     Computer games
     Computer operating systems
     Computer viruses
     Database management—Com-
     puter programs
     Educational software
     Free computer software
     Image processing software
     Internet software
     Multimedia

Oceanography—Computer pro-
     grams
     Programming languages
     Shareware (Computer soft-
     ware)
     Spreadsheet software
     Utilities (Computer programs)
     Word processing software
RT **Computer programming**
     Computer software industry
     Computers
Computer software industry (May subdiv.
     geog.) **338.4**
BT **Industries**
RT **Computer software**
Computer sound processing 006.5
UF Sound processing, Computer
BT **Computers**
     Sound
RT **Computer music**
     Speech processing systems
Computer speech processing systems
USE **Speech processing systems**
Computer storage devices 004.5;
     621.39
UF Computer memory systems
     Computers—Memory systems
     Computers—Storage devices
     Memory devices (Computers)
     Storage devices, Computer
BT **Computer peripherals**
NT **Optical storage devices**
Computer terminals 004.7; 621.39
     Use for materials on video display devices
     connected to a mainframe computer.
UF Terminals, Computer
BT **Computer peripherals**
Computer terms
USE **Computer science—Dictionaries**
Computer utility programs
USE **Utilities (Computer programs)**
Computer viruses 005.8
UF Software viruses
     Viruses, Computer
BT **Computer crimes**
     Computer software
RT **Computer security**
Computerized tomography
USE **Tomography**
Computers 004; 621.39
     Use for materials on modern electronic
     computers developed after 1945. Materials on

167

Computers—*Continued*
present-day calculators and on calculating machines and mechanical computers made before 1945 are entered under **Calculators.**

- UF Computer hardware
- SA types of computers, e.g.
  Microcomputers; and names of specific computers, e.g. **IBM 7090 (Computer)** [to be added as needed]
- BT **Electronic apparatus and appliances**
- NT **Computer peripherals**
  Computer security
  Computer sound processing
  Computers and children
  Computers and civilization
  Data processing
  IBM 7090 (Computer)
  Information systems
  Macintosh (Computer)
  Microcomputers
  Microprocessors
  Portable computers
  Supercomputers
- RT **Calculators**
  Computer industry
  Computer science
  Computer software

Computers—Access control
- USE **Computer security**

Computers and children   004
- BT **Children**
  Computers

Computers and civilization   004; 303.48
- UF Civilization and computers
- BT **Civilization**
  Computers
  Technology and civilization
- NT **Computer literacy**

Computers—Cartoons and caricatures **621.39; 741.5**
- BT **Cartoons and caricatures**

Computers—Dictionaries
- USE **Computer science—Dictionaries**

Computers—Educational use
- USE **Computer-assisted instruction**

Computers—Juvenile literature   **004**

Computers—Memory systems
- USE **Computer storage devices**

Computers—Operating systems
- USE **Computer operating systems**

Computers—Programming
- USE **Computer programming**

Computers—Security measures
- USE **Computer security**

Computers—Storage devices
- USE **Computer storage devices**

Computers—Utility programs
- USE **Utilities (Computer programs)**

Con artists
- USE **Swindlers and swindling**

Con game
- USE **Swindlers and swindling**

Concentration
- USE **Attention**

Concentration camps (May subdiv. geog.) **365**
- UF Internment camps
- SA names of wars with the subdivision *Prisoners and prisons;* and names of individual camps [to be added as needed]
- BT **Military camps**
  Political crimes and offenses
- NT **World War, 1939-1945—Prisoners and prisons**
- RT **Prisoners of war**

Concept formation
- USE **Concept learning**

Concept learning   153.2; 370.15
  Use for materials on the process of discovering the distinguishing features of particular concepts and the ensuing ability to use the concepts appropriately.
- UF Concept formation
- BT **Concepts**
  Psychology of learning

Conception—Prevention
- USE **Birth control**

Concepts   153.2
- SA types of concepts and images, e.g. **Size; Shape;** etc. [to be added as needed]
- BT **Perception**
- NT **Concept learning**
  Opposites
  Shape
  Size

Concerto   784.18
  Use for musical scores and for materials on the concerto as a musical form.

Concerto—*Continued*
UF Concertos
BT **Musical form**
 Orchestral music
Concertos
 USE **Concerto**
Concerts 780.78
BT **Amusements**
 Music
RT **Music festivals**
Concordances 010

Use for works that list words with references to passages in a text where the exact word occurs. Works that list topics or names with references to books, articles, or passages where those topics or name are to be found are entered under **Indexes.**

SA names of individual authors, literary works, sacred works, literatures, and literary forms, with the subdivision *Concordances,* e.g. **Shakespeare, William, 1564-1616—Concordances; Bible—Concordances;** etc. [to be added as needed]
BT **Indexes**
Concrete 691; 693
BT **Building materials**
 Foundations
 Masonry
 Plaster and plastering
NT **Reinforced concrete**
RT **Cement**
 Concrete construction
Concrete building
 USE **Concrete construction**
Concrete construction 693
UF Concrete building
 Construction, Concrete
BT **Building**
RT **Concrete**
Concrete—Testing 620.1
BT **Strength of materials**
Condemnation of land
 USE **Eminent domain**
Condensers (Electricity) 621.31
UF Electric condensers
BT **Induction coils**
Condensers (Steam) 621.1
BT **Steam engines**
Condominium timesharing
 USE **Timesharing (Real estate)**

Condominiums (May subdiv. geog.)
 346.04; 643
BT **Apartment houses**
NT **Timesharing (Real estate)**
Conduct of life 170

Use for materials on standards of behavior and materials containing moral guidance and advice to the individual.

UF Morals
 Personal conduct
SA classes of persons with the subdivision *Conduct of life;* and names of vices and virtues [to be added as needed]
BT **Ethics**
 Human behavior
 Life skills
NT **Vice**
 Virtue
Conducting 781.45

Use for materials on orchestral conducting or a combination of orchestral and choral conducting. Materials limited to choral conducting are entered under **Choral conducting.**

BT **Music**
NT **Choral conducting**
RT **Bands (Music)**
 Conductors (Music)
 Orchestra
Conducting, Choral
 USE **Choral conducting**
Conductors, Electric
 USE **Electric conductors**
Conductors (Music) (May subdiv. geog.)
 784.2092; 920
UF Bandmasters
 Music conductors
BT **Musicians**
 Orchestra
RT **Choral conducting**
 Conducting
Confectionary
 USE **Confectionery**
Confectionery 641.8; 664
UF Confectionary
 Sweets
BT **Cooking**
NT **Cake**
 Cake decorating
 Candy
Confederacies
 USE **Federal government**

Confederate States of America   973.7
   BT   United States—History—1861-
        1865, Civil War
Confederation of American colonies
   USE   **United States—History—1783-
         1809**
Conference calls (Teleconferencing)
   USE   **Teleconferencing**
Conference papers
   USE   **Conference proceedings**
Conference proceedings (May subdiv.
        geog.)   **060**
   Use for materials about the papers and oth-
er documents stemming from a conference
and for collections of various conference pro-
ceedings. Materials about conferences apart
from the proceedings are entered under **Con-
ferences.**
   UF   Conference papers
   SA   topics and names of corporate
        bodies with the subdivision
        Conference proceedings [to be
        added as needed]
   BT   **Documentation**
   RT   **Conferences**
Conferences   **060**
   Use for materials about conferences, congresses, or conventions. Materials about the
papers and other documents stemming from a
conference and collections of various confer-
ence proceedings are entered under **Confer-
ence proceedings.**
   UF   Congresses
        Congresses and conventions
        [Former heading]
        Conventions
        International conferences
   SA   subjects and names of corporate
        bodies with the subdivision
        Conferences, e.g. **World
        War, 1939-1945—Confer-
        ences; Physics—Conferences;**
        names of specific conferences,
        congresses, or conventions;
        and subjects and names of
        corporate bodies with the sub-
        division *Conference proceed-
        ings* [to be added as needed]
   BT   **Intellectual cooperation
        International cooperation**
   NT   **Constitutional conventions
        Political conventions
        World War, 1939-1945—Con-
        ferences**

   RT   **Conference proceedings**
Conferences, Parent-teacher
   USE   **Parent-teacher conferences**
Confession   **265**
   UF   Auricular confession
        Forgiveness of sin
   RT   **Penance**
Confessions of faith
   USE   **Creeds**
Confidence game
   USE   **Swindlers and swindling**
Configuration (Psychology)
   USE   **Gestalt psychology**
Confirmation   **265**
   BT   **Sacraments**
Conflict of cultures
   USE   **Culture conflict**
Conflict of generations   306.874
   UF   Generation gap
   BT   **Child-adult relationship
        Interpersonal relations
        Parent-child relationship
        Social conflict**
Conflict of interests (May subdiv. geog.)
        172; 353.4
   BT   **Political ethics**
   NT   **Misconduct in office
        Political corruption**
Conflict, Social
   USE   **Social conflict**
Conformity   153.8; 302.5; 303.3
   UF   Nonconformity
        Social conformity
   BT   **Attitude (Psychology)
        Freedom**
   RT   **Dissent
        Individuality**
Confucianism (May subdiv. geog.)   181;
        299
   BT   **Religions**
Congenital diseases
   USE   **Medical genetics**
Conglomerate corporations (May subdiv.
        geog.)   338.8
   UF   Diversified corporations
   BT   **Corporations**
   RT   **Corporate mergers and acqui-
        sitions**

Congregationalism (May subdiv. geog.)
   285.8
   BT **Christian sects**
   NT **Unitarianism**
   RT **Calvinism**
        Puritans
Congregations
   USE **Religious institutions**
Congress (U.S.)
   USE **United States. Congress**
Congresses
   USE **Conferences**
       and subjects with the subdivision *Conferences,* e.g. **World War, 1939-1945—Conferences; Physics—Conferences;** and names of specific conferences, congresses, or conventions [to be added as needed]
Congresses and conventions
   USE **Conferences**
Congressional investigations
   USE **Governmental investigations**
Conjuring
   USE **Magic tricks**
Conscience **170; 241**
   BT **Christian ethics**
        Duty
        Ethics
   NT **Freedom of conscience**
Conscientious objectors (May subdiv. geog.) **343; 355.2**
   SA names of wars with the subdivision *Conscientious objectors* [to be added as needed]
   BT **Freedom of conscience**
        War—Religious aspects
   NT **World War, 1939-1945—Conscientious objectors**
   RT **Draft resisters**
        Pacifism
Consciousness **126; 153**
   BT **Apperception**
        Mind and body
        Perception
        Psychology
   NT **Gestalt psychology**
        Individuality
        Personality
        Self
        Theory of knowledge

   RT **Subconsciousness**
Consciousness expanding drugs
   USE **Hallucinogens**
Conscript labor
   USE **Forced labor**
Conscription, Military
   USE **Draft**
Conservation and restoration
   USE types of art objects, library materials, architecture, and land vehicles with the subdivision *Conservation and restoration,* e.g. **Automobiles—Conservation and restoration** [to be added as needed]
Conservation movement
   USE **Environmental movement**
Conservation of biological diversity
   USE **Biological diversity conservation**
Conservation of buildings
   USE **Architecture—Conservation and restoration**
Conservation of energy
   USE **Energy conservation**
        Force and energy
Conservation of forests
   USE **Forest conservation**
Conservation of natural resources (May subdiv. geog.) **333.7; 639.9**
   UF Preservation of natural resources
        Resource management
   SA types of conservation, e.g. **Soil conservation** [to be added as needed
   BT **Environmental protection**
        Natural resources
   NT **Biological diversity conservation**
        Energy conservation
        Forest conservation
        Nature conservation
        Plant conservation
        Soil conservation
        Water conservation
        Wildlife conservation
   RT **Environmental policy**
        National parks and reserves
        Wilderness areas
Conservation of nature
   USE **Nature conservation**

Conservation of photographs
    USE   **Photographs—Conservation and restoration**

Conservation of plants
    USE   **Plant conservation**

Conservation of power resources
    USE   **Energy conservation**

Conservation of the soil
    USE   **Soil conservation**

Conservation of water
    USE   **Water conservation**

Conservation of wildlife
    USE   **Wildlife conservation**

Conservation of works of art, books, etc.
    USE   subjects with the subdivision *Conservation and restoration,* e.g. **Library resources—Conservation and restoration; Painting—Conservation and restoration;** etc. [to be added as needed]

Conservatism (May subdiv. geog.)   320.5
    UF   Reaction (Political science)
         Right (Political science)
    BT   **Political science**
         Social sciences
    RT   **Right and left (Political science)**

Conservatories, Home
    USE   **Garden rooms**

Consolation   152.4; 155.9
    UF   Compassion
         Solace
         Sympathy
    BT   **Emotions**
         Human behavior
    RT   **Bereavement**
         Grief

Consolidation and merger of corporations
    USE   **Corporate mergers and acquisitions**

Consolidation of schools
    USE   **Schools—Centralization**

Consortia, Library
    USE   **Library cooperation**

Constellations   523.8
    SA   names of constellations [to be added as needed]
    BT   **Sky**
    RT   **Astrology**
         Astronomy

         Stars

Constitution (U.S.)
    USE   **United States. Constitution**

Constitutional amendments (May subdiv. geog.)   **342**
    Use for texts of constitutional amendments and materials about constitutional amendments and the amending process.
    SA   subjects dealt with in constitutional amendments with the subdivision *Law and legislation,* or *Legal status, laws, etc.* [to be added as needed]
    BT   **Constitutional law**
         Constitutions

Constitutional conventions (May subdiv. geog.)   **342**
    UF   Conventions, Constitutional
    BT   **Conferences**

Constitutional history (May subdiv. geog.)   **342**
    Use for materials on the history of constitutions. Texts of constitutions are entered under **Constitutions.**
    UF   Constitutional law—History
    BT   **History**
    NT   **Democracy**
         Monarchy
         Representative government and representation
         Republics
    RT   **Constitutions**

Constitutional history—Ohio   **342.771; 977.1**
    UF   Ohio—Constitutional history
    BT   **Ohio—History**

Constitutional history—United States   **342.73; 973**
    UF   United States—Constitutional history
    BT   **United States—History**

Constitutional law (May subdiv. geog.)   **342**
    Use for materials on constitutions or constitutional law. Texts of constitutions are entered under **Constitutions.**
    BT   **Law**
    NT   **Citizenship**
         Civil rights
         Constitutional amendments
         Democracy
         Eminent domain
         Executive power

Constitutional law—*Continued*
>> Federal government
>> Injunctions
>> Legislative bodies
>> Magna Carta
>> Monarchy
>> Proportional representation
>> Referendum
>> Representative government and representation
>> Republics
>> Separation of powers
>> Suffrage
>> War and emergency powers
> RT Administrative law
>> Constitutions

Constitutional law—History
> USE Constitutional history

Constitutional law—Ohio 342.771
> UF Ohio—Constitutional law

Constitutional law—United States 342.73
> UF United States—Constitutional law

Constitutional rights
> USE Civil rights

Constitutions (May subdiv. geog.) 342
> Use for texts of constitutions. Materials about constitutions are entered under either **Constitutional law** or **Constitutional history.**
> UF State constitutions
> BT Law
> NT Constitutional amendments
>> Equal rights amendments
> RT Constitutional history
>> Constitutional law

Constitutions—Ohio 342.771
> UF Ohio—Constitution

Constitutions—United States 342.73; 973
> Use for collections of texts of several state or federal constitutions. Materials about constitutions are entered under either **Constitutional history** or **Constitutional law.** Materials on the United States Constitution alone are entered under **United States—Constitution.**
> UF State constitutions
>> United States—Constitutions

Construction
> USE Architecture
>> Building
>> Engineering

Construction, Concrete
> USE Concrete construction

Construction contracts 692
> UF Building contracts
>> Building—Contracts and specifications
> BT Contracts

Construction, House
> USE House construction

Construction of roads
> USE Roads

Consular service
> USE Diplomatic and consular service

Consulates
> USE Diplomatic and consular service

Consuls
> USE Diplomats

Consultants 001
> UF Advisors
> SA types of consultants [to be added as needed]
> BT Counseling
> NT Educational consultants

Consultative management
> USE Participative management

Consumer behavior
> USE Consumers

Consumer boycotts
> USE Boycotts

Consumer credit 332.7
> BT Banks and banking
>> Credit
>> Personal finance
> NT Credit cards
>> Installment plan
>> Personal loans

Consumer demand
> USE Consumption (Economics)

Consumer education (May subdiv. geog.) 640.73
> Use for materials on the selection and efficient use of consumer goods and services and on methods of educating consumers. Materials on the decision-making processes, external factors, and individual characteristics of consumers that determine their purchasing behavior are entered under **Consumers.** Materials on the economic theory of consumption and on consumerism or consumer demand are entered under **Consumption (Economics).**
> UF Buyers' guides
>> Consumers' guides
>> Shoppers' guides

Consumer education—*Continued*
- BT **Education**
    Home economics
- RT **Consumers**
    Shopping

Consumer goods (May subdiv. geog.)
    338.4

Use for materials on products that are purchased for personal or household purposes.
- UF Consumer products
    Merchandise
- BT **Commercial products**
    Manufactures
- RT **Consumption (Economics)**

Consumer loans
- USE **Personal loans**

Consumer organizations
- USE **Cooperative societies**

Consumer price indexes   338.5
- UF Cost of living indexes
    Price indexes, Consumer
- BT **Cost and standard of living**
    Prices

Consumer products
- USE **Consumer goods**

Consumer protection (May subdiv. geog.)
    343.07; 381.3

Use for materials on governmental and private activities that guard consumers against dangers to their health, safety, or economic well-being.
- UF Consumerism
- BT **Industrial policy**
- NT **Drugs—Testing**
    Food adulteration and inspection
    Product recall
    Product safety

Consumer spending
- USE **Consumption (Economics)**

Consumerism
- USE **Consumer protection**
    Consumption (Economics)

Consumers (May subdiv. geog.)   **640.73;**
    658.8

Use for materials on the decision-making processes, external factors, and individual characteristics of consumers that determine their purchasing behavior. Materials on the selection and efficient use of consumer goods and services and on methods of educating consumers are entered under **Consumer education.** Materials on the economic theory of consumption and on consumerism or consumer demand are entered under **Consumption (Economics).**

- UF Consumer behavior
- NT **Boycotts**
    Young consumers
- RT **Consumer education**
    Consumption (Economics)
    Shopping

Consumers' cooperative societies
- USE **Cooperative societies**

Consumers' guides
- USE **Consumer education**

Consumers—Information services (May
    subdiv. geog.)   **658.8**
- BT **Information services**

Consumption (Economics) (May subdiv.
    geog.)   **339.4**

Use for materials on the economic theory of consumption and on consumerism or consumer demand. Materials on the decision-making processes, external factors, and individual characteristics of consumers that determine their purchasing behavior are entered under **Consumers.** Materials on the selection and efficient use of consumer goods and services and on methods of educating consumers are entered under **Consumer education.**

- UF Consumer demand
    Consumer spending
    Consumerism
- BT **Economics**
- NT **Prices**
- RT **Consumer goods**
    Consumers

Consumption of alcoholic beverages
- USE **Drinking of alcoholic beverages**

Consumption of energy
- USE **Energy consumption**

Contact lenses   617.7
- BT **Eyeglasses**
    Lenses

Contagion and contagious diseases
- USE **Communicable diseases**

Contagious diseases
- USE **Communicable diseases**

Container gardening   635.9
- BT **Gardening**
- RT **Flower gardening**
    House plants
    Indoor gardening
    Miniature gardens
    Window gardening

Containers
- USE **Boxes**

Contaminated food
- USE **Food contamination**

Contamination of environment
  USE **Pollution**
Contests   **001.4; 790.1**
  UF **Competitions**
  SA types of contests and names of
       specific contests, e.g. **Olym-
       pic games;** and subjects with
       the subdivision *Competitions*
       or *Tournaments,* e.g. **Litera-
       ture—Competitions; Ten-
       nis—Tournaments** [to be
       added as needed]
  NT **Literature—Competitions**
       Olympic games
       Sports tournaments
  RT **Awards**
Continental drift   551.1
  UF Drifting of continents
  BT **Continents**
       Geology
  RT **Plate tectonics**
Continental shelf   551.41
  BT **Geology**
  RT **Territorial waters**
Continents   551.41
  BT **Earth**
  NT **Continental drift**
Continuation schools
  USE **Evening and continuation
        schools**
Continuing care communities
  USE **Life care communities**
Continuing care retirement communities
  USE **Life care communities**
Continuing education (May subdiv. geog.)
       374
  UF Lifelong education
       Permanent education
       Recurrent education
  BT **Education**
  NT **Evening and continuation
        schools**
  RT **Adult education**
Contraband trade
  USE **Smuggling**
Contraception
  USE **Birth control**
Contract bridge
  USE **Bridge (Game)**

Contract labor (May subdiv. geog.)
       331.5
  UF Indentured servants
  BT **Labor**
  RT **Peonage**
Contractions
  USE **Abbreviations**
        Ciphers
Contracts   346.02
  UF Agreements
  SA types of contracts, e.g. **Con-
       struction contracts** [to be
       added as needed]
  BT **Commerce**
       Commercial law
  NT **Authors and publishers**
       Construction contracts
       Covenants
       Labor contract
       Liability (Law)
       Marriage contracts
       Negotiable instruments
       Trusts and trustees
Contrition
  USE **Penance**
Control
  USE types of control, e.g. **Flood con-
        trol; Weather control;** etc.,
        and animals, plants, or pro-
        cesses with the subdivision
        Control, e.g. **Mosquitoes—
        Control** [to be added as
        needed]
Control of guns
  USE **Gun control**
Controversial literature
  USE types of religions, denomina-
        tions, religious orders, and sa-
        cred works with the subdivi-
        sion *Controversial literature,*
        for materials that argue
        against or express opposition
        to those groups or works, e.g.
        **Christianity—Controversial
        literature** for materials attack-
        ing Christianity; and religions
        and denominations with the
        subdivision *Apologetic works,*
        for materials defending those
        religions or denominations,
        e.g. **Christianity—Apologetic**

Controversial literature—*Continued*
    works for materials defending Christianity [to be added as needed]
Conundrums
  USE **Riddles**
Convenience cooking
  USE **Quick and easy cooking**
Convenience foods   **641.3; 664**
    Use for materials on prepackaged foods that are easy to prepare for eating.
  UF Fast foods
  BT **Food**
  NT **Fast food restaurants**
Conventions
  USE **Conferences**
    and subjects with the subdivision *Conferences,* e.g. **World War, 1939-1945—Conferences; Physics—Conferences;** and names of specific conferences, congresses, or conventions [to be added as needed]
Conventions, Constitutional
  USE **Constitutional conventions**
Conventions, Political
  USE **Political conventions**
Convents (May subdiv. geog.)   **271; 726**
  UF Cloisters
      Nunneries
  BT **Monasteries**
  NT **Monasticism and religious orders for women**
Conversation   **808.56**
  UF Discussion
      Table talk
      Talking
  BT **Communication**
      Language and languages
  NT **Discussion groups**
      Interviews
      Online chat groups
Conversation and phrase books
  USE **Modern languages—Conversation and phrase books**
    and names of languages and groups of languages with the subdivision *Conversation and phrase books,* e.g. **English language—Conversation and phrase books** [to be added as needed]

Conversation in foreign languages
  USE **Modern languages—Conversation and phrase books**
Conversations and phrases
  USE **Modern languages—Conversation and phrase books**
Conversion   **248.2; 291.4**
  BT **Evangelistic work**
      Salvation
      Spiritual life
  NT **Converts**
  RT **Regeneration (Christianity)**
Conversion of saline water
  USE **Sea water conversion**
Conversion of waste products
  USE **Recycling**
Converts   **248.2; 291.4**
    Use for materials on converts from one religion or denomination to another.
  SA converts to a particular religion or denomination, e.g. **Converts to Catholicism** [to be added as needed]
  BT **Conversion**
  NT **Converts to Catholicism**
Converts to Catholicism   **282**
  UF Catholic Church—Converts
      Catholic converts
  BT **Catholics**
      Converts
Conveying machinery   **621.8**
  UF Conveyors
  BT **Machinery**
      Materials handling
  RT **Hoisting machinery**
Conveyors
  USE **Conveying machinery**
Convict labor (May subdiv. geog.)   **331.5; 365**
  UF Prison labor
  BT **Forced labor**
      Prisoners
Convicts
  USE **Criminals**
      Prisoners
Cook books
  USE **Cooking**
Cookbooks
  USE **Cooking**
Cookery
  USE **Cooking**

Cookery, American
    USE **American cooking**
Cookery for the sick
    USE **Cooking for the sick**
Cookery, French
    USE **French cooking**
Cooking (May subdiv. geog.) **641.5**

    Use a phrase heading, e.g. **French cooking;** **Southern cooking;** etc., for distinctive national or regional styles of cooking. For cooking as it is practiced in a particular city, state, province, etc., subdivide **Cooking** geographically.

    UF Cook books
          Cookbooks
          Cookery
          Food preparation
          Recipes
    SA types of cooking, e.g. **Microwave cooking;** cooking of particular countries or regions, e.g. **French cooking; American cooking; Southern cooking;** etc.; and, for materials on the cooking of specific foods or kinds of food, **Cooking** with a subdivision for the food, e.g. **Cooking—Vegetables; Cooking—Natural foods;** etc. [to be added as needed]
    BT **Home economics**
    NT **Afternoon teas**
          American cooking
          Baking
          Bread
          Breakfasts
          Cake
          Canning and preserving
          Catering
          Christmas cooking
          Confectionery
          Cooking for the sick
          Desserts
          Dinners
          Fish as food
          Flavoring essences
          French cooking
          Holiday cooking
          Luncheons
          Menus
          Microwave cooking
          Outdoor cooking

          Pastry
          Quantity cooking
          Quick and easy cooking
          Salads
          Sandwiches
          Sauces
          Soups
          Southern cooking
          Vegetarian cooking
    RT **Diet**
          Food
          Gastronomy
Cooking for institutions
    USE **Food service**
Cooking for large numbers
    USE **Quantity cooking**
Cooking for the sick **641.5**
    UF Cookery for the sick
          Food for invalids
          Invalid cooking
    SA types of diets, e.g. **Salt-free diet** [to be added as needed]
    BT **Cooking**
          Diet in disease
          Nursing
          Sick
    NT **Diet therapy**
          Salt-free diet
Cooking—Natural foods **641.5**
    UF Natural food cooking
    RT **Natural foods**
Cooking utensils
    USE **Kitchen utensils**
Cooking—Vegetables **641.6**
    BT **Vegetables**
    RT **Salads**
          Vegetarian cooking
Cooling appliances
    USE **Refrigeration**
Cooperation (May subdiv. geog.) **334**

    Use for general materials on the theory and history of cooperation and the cooperative movement. Materials dealing specifically with cooperative enterprises are entered under **Cooperative societies.**

    UF Cooperative distribution
          Distribution, Cooperative
    BT **Associations**
          Commerce
          Economics
    NT **Collective settlements**
          Communal living
          Cooperative agriculture

Cooperation—*Continued*
>   Cooperative banks
>   Cooperative housing
>   Cooperative societies
>   International cooperation
>   Savings and loan associations
> RT Profit sharing

Cooperation, Intellectual
> USE Intellectual cooperation

Cooperation, Interchurch
> USE Interdenominational cooperation

Cooperation, Interdenominational
> USE Interdenominational cooperation

Cooperative agriculture (May subdiv. geog.) 334
>   Use for materials on cooperation in the production and disposal of agricultural products.
> UF Agricultural cooperation
>   Agriculture, Cooperative
>   Collective farms
>   Farmers' cooperatives
> BT Agriculture
>   Cooperation
> RT Collective settlements

Cooperative banks (May subdiv. geog.) 334
> UF Banks and banking, Cooperative
>   People's banks
> BT Banks and banking
>   Cooperation
>   Cooperative societies
>   Personal loans
> NT Credit unions
> RT Savings and loan associations

Cooperative distribution
> USE Cooperation
>   Cooperative societies

Cooperative housing (May subdiv. geog.) 334
> UF Co-ops (Housing)
>   Cohousing
>   Housing, Cooperative
> BT Cooperation
>   Housing
> RT Communal living

Cooperative learning 371.3
>   Use for materials on the method of education that involves having students work together on projects in a structured manner.
> UF Group method in teaching
>   Group teaching

>   Group work in education
> BT Education
>   Teaching

Cooperative living
> USE Collective settlements
>   Communal living

Cooperative societies (May subdiv. geog.) 334; 658.8
>   Use for materials dealing specifically with cooperative enterprises. General materials on the theory and history of cooperation and the cooperative movement are entered under Cooperation.
> UF Co-ops
>   Consumer organizations
>   Consumers' cooperative societies
>   Cooperative distribution
>   Cooperative stores
>   Cooperatives
> SA types of cooperative societies, e.g. Credit unions [to be added as needed]
> BT Cooperation
>   Corporations
>   Societies
> NT Cooperative banks
>   Savings and loan associations

Cooperative stores
> USE Cooperative societies

Cooperatives
> USE Cooperative societies

Copiers
> USE Copying machines

Coping behavior
> USE Adjustment (Psychology)

Coping skills
> USE Life skills

Copper engraving
> USE Engraving

Copperwork 673; 739.5
> BT Metalwork

Copy art (May subdiv. geog.) 760
>   Use for materials on the use of photocopying machines to create original works of art. Materials on clipping art work from published sources to use in creating documents, posters, newsletters, etc., are entered under Clip art.
> UF Copying machine art
>   Reprographic art
>   Xerographic art
> BT Art
> RT Photocopying

Copy writing
> USE Advertising copy

Copying machine art
  USE **Copy art**
Copying machines   681
  UF Copiers
      Copying processes and machines
      Duplicating machines
      Photocopying machines
  BT **Office equipment and supplies**
  RT **Copying processes**
Copying processes   686
  UF Copying processes and machines
      Duplicating processes
      Reproduction processes
      Reprography
  SA names of specific processes [to
      be added as needed]
  BT **Documentation**
  NT **Photocopying**
  RT **Copying machines**
Copying processes and machines
  USE **Copying machines**
       Copying processes
Copyright (May subdiv. geog.)   **341.7;
  346.04; 352.7**
    May be subdivided by topic, e.g. **Copy-
  right—Sound recordings.**
  UF International copyright
      Literary property
  NT **Fair use (Copyright)**
  RT **Authors and publishers**
      Intellectual property
Copyright—Sound recordings (May
  subdiv. geog.)   **341.7; 346.04**
  UF Sound recordings—Copyright
Coral reefs and islands (May subdiv.
  geog.)   **551.42**
  UF Atolls
  BT **Geology**
      Islands
Corals   563; 593.6
  BT **Marine animals**
Cordials (Liquor)
  USE **Liquors**
Core curriculum
  USE **Colleges and universities—Cur-
       ricula**
       Education—Curricula
Corn (May subdiv. geog.)   **633.1; 633.2**
  UF Maize
  BT **Forage plants**
      Grain

Coronary heart diseases
  USE **Heart diseases**
Corporate acquisitions
  USE **Corporate mergers and acqui-
       sitions**
Corporate downsizing
  USE **Downsizing of organizations**
Corporate libraries   027.6
    Use for materials on libraries located within
  companies, firms, or private businesses, cover-
  ing any subject areas. Materials on libraries
  with a subject focus on business are entered
  under **Business libraries.**
  UF Company libraries
      Industrial libraries
      Libraries, Corporate
  BT **Special libraries**
Corporate mergers and acquisitions
    (May subdiv. geog.)   **338.8; 658.1**
  UF Acquisitions, Corporate
      Buyouts, Corporate
      Consolidation and merger of
        corporations
      Corporate acquisitions
      Corporate takeovers
      Industrial mergers
      Mergers
      Takeovers, Corporate
  SA types of institutions and types of
      industries and businesses with
      the subdivision *Mergers,* e.g.
      Railroads—Mergers [to be
      added as needed]
  NT **Leveraged buyouts**
      Railroads—Mergers
  RT **Conglomerate corporations**
      Industrial trusts
Corporate patronage of the arts
  USE **Art patronage**
Corporate symbols
  USE **Trademarks**
Corporate takeovers
  USE **Corporate mergers and acqui-
       sitions**
Corporate welfare
  USE **Subsidies**
Corporation law (May subdiv. geog.)
  346
  BT **Commercial law**
      Corporations
      Law

Corporation law—*Continued*
  NT **Public service commissions**
  RT **Industrial trusts**
      Monopolies
      Restraint of trade
Corporations (May subdiv. geog.)
      338.7; 658.1
  UF Companies
  BT **Business enterprises**
      Stocks
  NT **Conglomerate corporations**
      Cooperative societies
      Corporation law
      Multinational corporations
      Municipal ownership
      Public service commissions
      Trust companies
  RT **Industrial trusts**
Corporations—Accounting 657; 658.15
  BT **Accounting**
      Bookkeeping
Corporations—Art patronage
  USE **Art patronage**
Corporations—Finance 658.15
  UF Capitalization (Finance)
  BT **Finance**
Corporations, Multinational
  USE **Multinational corporations**
Corporations, Nonprofit
  USE **Nonprofit organizations**
Corpulence
  USE **Obesity**
Correctional institutions (May subdiv.
  geog.) **365**
  UF Penal institutions
  SA types of correctional institutions
      [to be added as needed]
  BT **Punishment**
  NT **Halfway houses**
      Penal colonies
      Prisons
      Reformatories
Correctional services
  USE **Corrections**
Corrections (May subdiv. geog.) **364.6**
  Use for materials on the rehabilitation and treatment of offenders through parole, penal custody, and probation programs, and on the administration of such programs.
  UF Correctional services
      Criminals—Rehabilitation programs

      Penology
      Reform of criminals
  BT **Administration of criminal justice**
  NT **Parole**
      Probation
      Punishment
Correspondence
  USE **Business letters**
      Letter writing
      Letters
      and ethnic groups, classes of persons, and names of individual persons and families with the subdivision *Correspondence,* e.g. **Authors—Correspondence** [to be added as needed]
Correspondence schools and courses
  (May subdiv. geog.) **374**
  UF Home education
      Home study courses
  BT **Distance education**
      Schools
      Technical education
      University extension
  RT **Self-instruction**
Corrosion and anticorrosives 620.1
  UF Anticorrosive paint
      Rust
      Rustless coatings
  BT **Industrial chemistry**
  RT **Paint**
Corrupt practices
  USE subjects with the subdivision *Corrupt practices,* e.g. **Adoption—Corrupt practices; Sports—Corrupt practices;** etc. [to be added as needed]
Corruption in politics
  USE **Political corruption**
Corruption in sports
  USE **Sports—Corrupt practices**
Corruption, Police
  USE **Police corruption**
Corsairs
  USE **Pirates**
Cosmetic surgery
  USE **Plastic surgery**

Cosmetics 646.7
 UF Makeup (Cosmetics)
 SA types of cosmetics [to be added
  as needed]
 BT Beauty shops
  Personal grooming
 NT Perfumes
  Theatrical makeup
 RT Toiletries
Cosmetics—Advertising
 USE Advertising—Cosmetics
Cosmic rays 539.7
 UF Millikan rays
 BT Nuclear physics
  Radiation
  Radioactivity
  Space environment
Cosmobiology
 USE Space biology
Cosmochemistry
 USE Space chemistry
Cosmogony
 USE Cosmology
  Universe
Cosmography
 USE Cosmology
  Universe
Cosmology 113; 523.1
 Use for general or theoretical materials on
 the science or philosophy of the universe. Ma-
 terials limited to the physical description of
 the universe are entered under Universe.
 UF Cosmogony
  Cosmography
 BT Universe
 NT Biblical cosmology
  Big bang theory
Cosmonauts
 USE Astronauts
Cost accounting 657
 BT Accounting
  Bookkeeping
Cost and standard of living (May subdiv.
 geog.) 339.4
 UF Cost of living
  Food, Cost of
  Household finances
  Standard of living
 BT Economics
  Home economics
  Quality of life
  Social conditions

 Wealth
 NT Consumer price indexes
  Household budgets
  Subsistence economy
 RT Prices
  Salaries, wages, etc.
Cost of living
 USE Cost and standard of living
Cost of living indexes
 USE Consumer price indexes
Cost of medical care
 USE Medical care—Costs
Costs
 USE subjects with the subdivision
  Costs, e.g. Medical care—
  Costs [to be added as need-
  ed]
Costume (May subdiv. geog.) 391; 792
 Use for materials on the characteristic cos-
 tume of ethnic or national groups and for ma-
 terials on fancy dress and theatrical costumes.
 For the traditional national costume of a par-
 ticular country subdivide geographically. Ma-
 terials on clothing and the art of dress from
 day to day in practical situations, including
 historical dress and the clothing of various
 professions or classes of persons, are entered
 under Clothing and dress. Materials on the
 prevailing mode or style of dress are entered
 under Fashion.
 UF Acting—Costume
  Fancy dress
  Style in dress
  Theatrical costume
 SA costume of particular ethnic
  groups, e.g. Native American
  costume; and professions and
  classes of persons with the
  subdivision Clothing, e.g.
  Handicapped—Clothing [to
  be added as needed]
 BT Decorative arts
  Ethnology
  Manners and customs
 NT Armor
  Children's costumes
  Fans
  Hats
  Jewelry
  Masks (Facial)
  Native American costume
  Theatrical makeup
  Uniforms
  Wigs
 RT Clothing and dress

Cot death
USE **Sudden infant death syndrome**
Cottage industry
USE **Home-based business**
Cotton   633.5; 677
BT **Economic botany**
Fabrics
Fibers
Yarn
Cotton manufacture   677
BT **Textile industry**
Councils and synods   262
UF Church councils
Ecumenical councils
Synods
SA names of specific councils and
synods, e.g. **Vatican Council
(2nd : 1962-1965)** [to be
added as needed]
BT **Christianity**
Church history
NT **Vatican Council (2nd : 1962-
1965)**
Counseling   361; 371.4
UF Guidance
SA types of counseling; and ethnic
groups and classes of persons
with the subdivision *Counsel-
ing of,* e.g. **Employees—
Counseling of** [to be added
as needed]
BT **Applied psychology**
Helping behavior
Personnel management
NT **Consultants**
Crisis centers
Drug abuse counseling
Educational counseling
Elderly—Counseling of
Employees—Counseling of
Family therapy
Health counseling
Hotlines (Telephone counseling)
Marriage counseling
Peer counseling
School counseling
Social group work
Vocational guidance
RT **Interviewing**
Social case work

Counseling of
USE classes of persons and ethnic
groups with the subdivision
Counseling of, e.g. **Elderly—
Counseling of** [to be added
as needed]
Counseling of the elderly
USE **Elderly—Counseling of**
Counseling with the aged
USE **Elderly—Counseling of**
Counter culture (May subdiv. geog.)
306
UF Alternative lifestyle
Counterculture
Nonconformity
Subculture
BT **Lifestyles**
Social conditions
NT **Bohemianism**
RT **Collective settlements**
Communal living
Radicalism
Counter-Reformation (May subdiv. geog.)
270.6
UF Anti-Reformation
BT **Christianity**
**Church history—1500-, Mod-
ern period**
RT **Reformation**
Counterculture
USE **Counter culture**
Counterespionage
USE **Intelligence service**
**Counterfeits and counterfeiting   332;
364.1**
BT **Coinage**
Crime
Forgery
Impostors and imposture
Money
Swindlers and swindling
NT **Art—Forgeries**
Literary forgeries
Counterintelligence
USE **Intelligence service**
Counterpoint   781.2
BT **Composition (Music)**
Music—Theory
NT **Fugue**
Counting   513.2
Use for materials on counting, including
counting books. Materials on numbers, num-

Counting—*Continued*
bering, and systems of numeration are entered under **Numbers.** Materials on the conceptualization of numbers are entered under **Number concept.**

- UF Counting books
- BT **Arithmetic—Study and teaching**
- NT **Number games**
- RT **Numbers**

Counting books
- USE **Counting**

Country and western music
- USE **Country music**

Country churches
- USE **Rural churches**

Country life (May subdiv. geog.)
  307.72; 630

Use for descriptive, popular, and literary materials on living in the country. Materials on social organization and conditions in rural communities are entered under **Rural sociology.**

- UF Rural life
- BT **Manners and customs**
- NT **Agriculture—Societies**
  Farm life
  Mountain life
  Plantation life
- RT **Outdoor life**
  Rural sociology

Country life—United States **307.72; 630**

Country music **781.642**
- UF Country and western music
  Hillbilly music
- BT **Folk music—United States**
  Popular music

Country schools
- USE **Rural schools**

County agricultural agents **630.7**
- BT **Agricultural extension work**
  Agriculture—Study and teaching

County government (May subdiv. geog.)
  320.8; 352.15
- UF County officers
- BT **Local government**

County libraries
- USE **Public libraries**
  Regional libraries

County officers
- USE **County government**

County planning
- USE **Regional planning**

Coupons (Retail trade) **659**
- BT **Advertising**

Coups d'état
- USE **Revolutions**

Courage **179**
- UF Bravery
  Heroism
- BT **Virtue**
- NT **Morale**
- RT **Heroes and heroines**

Courses of study
- USE **Education—Curricula**

Court fools
- USE **Fools and jesters**

Court life
- USE **Courts and courtiers**

Court martial
- USE **Courts martial and courts of inquiry**

Courtesy **177; 395**
- UF Manners
  Politeness
- BT **Etiquette**
  Virtue

Courtiers
- USE **Courts and courtiers**

Courting
- USE **Courtship**

Courtroom drama
- USE **Legal drama (Films)**
  Legal drama (Radio programs)
  Legal drama (Television programs)

Courts (May subdiv. geog.) **347**
- UF Judiciary
- BT **Law**
- NT **Arbitration and award**
  Courts martial and courts of inquiry
  Criminal procedure
  Jury
  Juvenile courts
  United States. Supreme Court
- RT **Administration of justice**
  Judges

Courts and courtiers **394; 929.7**
- UF Court life
  Courtiers

Courts and courtiers—*Continued*
 SA names of countries, cities, etc.,
   with the subdivision *Courts*
   and courtiers [to be added as
   needed]
 BT **Manners and customs**
 NT **Fools and jesters**
   Princes
   Princesses
 RT **Kings and rulers**
   Queens
Courts martial and courts of inquiry
 343
 UF Court martial
   Military courts
 BT **Courts**
   Trials
 RT **Military law**
Courts—United States 347.73
 UF Federal courts
   United States—Courts
Courtship (May subdiv. geog.) **306.73;**
 392.4
 UF Courting
 BT **Love**
 NT **Dating (Social customs)**
 RT **Marriage**
Courtship (Animal behavior)
 USE **Animal courtship**
Courtship of animals
 USE **Animal courtship**
Covenants 231.7; 291.2
 Use for materials on religious covenants.
 May be subdivided by religion as needed. Ma-
 terials on non-religious covenants are entered
 under **Contracts.**
 UF Agreements
 BT **Contracts**
   Theology
Covens
 USE **Witches**
Coverlets
 USE **Bedspreads**
   Quilts
Cowboys
 USE **Cowhands**
Cowgirls
 USE **Cowhands**
Cowhands (May subdiv. geog.) **636.2;**
 978
 UF Cowboys
   Cowgirls

   Gauchos
 BT **Frontier and pioneer life**
   Ranch life
 RT **Rodeos**
Cowhands—Songs 782.42
 UF Cowhands—Songs and music
 BT **Music**
   Songs
Cowhands—Songs and music
 USE **Cowhands—Songs**
Cows
 USE **Cattle**
Crabs 565; 595.3
 BT **Crustacea**
   Shellfish
Crack babies
 USE **Children of drug addicts**
Crack cocaine
 USE **Crack (Drug)**
Crack (Drug) 362.29; 615
 UF Crack cocaine
 BT **Cocaine**
Cradle songs
 USE **Lullabies**
Craft festivals
 USE **Craft shows**
Craft shows 745
 UF Craft festivals
 BT **Exhibitions**
   Festivals
   Handicraft
Crafts (Arts)
 USE **Arts and crafts movement**
   Handicraft
Cranes, derricks, etc. 621.8
 UF Derricks
 BT **Hoisting machinery**
Crank (Drug)
 USE **Ice (Drug)**
Cranks
 USE **Eccentrics and eccentricities**
Crashes (Finance)
 USE **Financial crises**
Crates
 USE **Boxes**
Crayon drawing 741.2
 UF Blackboard drawing
 BT **Drawing**
 RT **Pastel drawing**

Creation   213; 231.7
  BT   Natural theology
  RT   Biblical cosmology
      Creationism
      Evolution
      Universe
Creation (Literary, artistic, etc.)   153.3
  UF   Inspiration
  BT   Genius
      Imagination
      Intellect
      Inventions
  NT   Creative writing
      Planning
  RT   Creative ability
Creation—Study and teaching
  USE   Creationism
      Evolution—Study and teaching
Creationism   231.7
  Use for materials on the doctrine that the universe was created by God out of nothing in the initial seven days of time and that all biological species were created rather than evolving from pre-existing types through modifications in successive generations.
  UF   Christianity and evolution
      Creation—Study and teaching
      Evolution and Christianity
      Fundamentalism and education
      Fundamentalism and evolution
      Scientific creationism
  BT   Christianity—Doctrines
  RT   Bible and science
      Creation
      Evolution
      Evolution—Study and teaching
      Religion and science
Creative ability   153.3; 701; 801
  UF   Creativity
  BT   Ability
  NT   Creative thinking
  RT   Creation (Literary, artistic, etc.)
Creative activities   372.5
  Use for materials on activities for children that result in some form of personal expression such as painting, cooking, drama, etc.
  UF   Activities curriculum
  BT   Amusements
      Elementary education
      Kindergarten
  RT   Handicraft
Creative movement
  USE   Movement education

Creative thinking   153.4
  BT   Creative ability
Creative writing   808
  UF   Writing (Authorship)
  BT   Authorship
      Creation (Literary, artistic, etc.)
      Language arts
Creativity
  USE   Creative ability
Creature films
  USE   Horror films
Credibility
  USE   Truthfulness and falsehood
Credit (May subdiv. geog.)   332.7
  UF   Bills of credit
      Letters of credit
  BT   Finance
      Money
  NT   Agricultural credit
      Collecting of accounts
      Consumer credit
      Installment plan
      Negotiable instruments
  RT   Banks and banking
      Debtor and creditor
      Loans
Credit card crimes
  USE   Credit card fraud
Credit card fraud   364.16
  UF   Credit card crimes [Former heading]
  BT   Fraud
      Swindlers and swindling
Credit cards   332.7
  UF   Bank credit cards
      Banks and banking—Credit cards
  BT   Consumer credit
Credit unions (May subdiv. geog.)   334
  Use for materials on cooperative associations that make small loans to its members at low interest rates.
  BT   Cooperative banks
Creditor
  USE   Debtor and creditor
Creeds   238; 291.2
  Use for materials about the concise, formal, and authorized statements of doctrines and for the texts of those statements.

Creeds—*Continued*

UF   Confessions of faith

SA   names of religions and individual denominations with the
subdivision *Creeds,* e.g. **Catholic Church—Creeds** [to be
added as needed]

BT   **Doctrinal theology**

NT   **Apostles' Creed**

     Catholic Church—Creeds

     Nicene Creed

RT   **Catechisms**

Cremation   363.7; 393; 614

UF   Incineration

     Mortuary customs

BT   **Public health**

     Sanitation

RT   **Burial**

     Funeral rites and ceremonies

Creole folk songs   782.42162

UF   Folk songs, Creole

BT   **Folk songs**

Creoles (May subdiv. geog.)   **305.84;
972.9; 976**

BT   **Ethnic groups**

Crests

USE   **Heraldry**

Crew (Rowing)

USE   **Rowing**

Crewelwork   746.44

BT   **Embroidery**

Crib death

USE   **Sudden infant death syndrome**

Crime (May subdiv. geog.)   **364**

UF   Crimes

     Criminology

     Felony

SA   types of crimes, e.g. **Computer
crimes** [to be added as need-
ed]

BT   **Administration of criminal justice**

     Social problems

NT   **Assassination**

     Atrocities

     Computer crimes

     Counterfeits and counterfeiting

     Crime prevention

     Crimes against humanity

     Crimes without victims

     Criminals

     Drugs and crime

     Drunk driving

     Forgery

     Fraud

     Hate crimes

     Homicide

     Impostors and imposture

     Juvenile delinquency

     Lynching

     Offenses against property

     Offenses against public safety

     Offenses against the person

     Organized crime

     Racketeering

     Riots

     Sex crimes

     Smuggling

     Swindlers and swindling

     Theft

     Treason

     Victims of crimes

     Vigilance committees

     White collar crimes

RT   **Criminal law**

     Police

     Punishment

     Trials

     Vice

Crime and drugs

USE   **Drugs and crime**

Crime and narcotics

USE   **Drugs and crime**

Crime comics

USE   **Mystery comic books, strips,
etc.**

Crime films

USE   **Film noir**

     Gangster films

     Mystery films

Crime plays

USE   **Mystery and detective plays**

Crime prevention (May subdiv. geog.)
364.4

UF   Prevention of crime

BT   **Crime**

NT   **Burglary protection**

Crime prevention—Citizen participation
(May subdiv. geog.)   **364.4**

BT   **Political participation**

Crime programs

USE   **Mystery radio programs**

     Mystery television programs

Crime stories
    USE **Mystery fiction**
Crime syndicates
    USE **Organized crime**
           Racketeering
Crime—United States   364.973
Crime victims
    USE **Victims of crimes**
Crimean War, 1853-1856   947
    UF   Great Britain—History—1853-
          1856, Crimean War
          Russo-Turkish War, 1853-1856
Crimes
    USE **Crime**
Crimes against humanity (May subdiv.
    geog.)   **364.1**
    BT   **Crime**
    NT   **Forced labor**
          Genocide
          Slavery
          War crimes
Crimes against public safety
    USE **Offenses against public safety**
Crimes against the person
    USE **Offenses against the person**
Crimes, Military
    USE **Military offenses**
Crimes of hate
    USE **Hate crimes**
Crimes, Political
    USE **Political crimes and offenses**
Crimes without victims   364.1
    UF   Non-victim crimes
          Nonvictim crimes
          Victimless crimes
    BT   **Crime**
          Criminal law
Criminal assault
    USE **Offenses against the person**
Criminal investigation (May subdiv.
    geog.)   **363.25**
    BT   **Law enforcement**
    NT   **Criminals—Identification**
          Eavesdropping
          Fingerprints
          Lie detectors and detection
          Missing persons
          Wiretapping
    RT   **Detectives**
          Forensic sciences
          Police

Criminal justice, Administration of
    USE **Administration of criminal jus-**
          tice
Criminal law (May subdiv. geog.)   **345**
    UF   Codes, Penal
          Misdemeanors (Law)
          Penal codes
          Penal law
    SA   types of crimes, e.g. **Homicide**
          [to be added as needed]
    BT   **Law**
    NT   **Administration of criminal jus-**
          tice
          Adoption—Corrupt practices
          Capital punishment
          Crimes without victims
          Homicide
          Insanity defense
          Jury
          Kidnapping
          Military offenses
          Misconduct in office
          Obscenity (Law)
          Offenses against property
          Offenses against public safety
          Offenses against the person
          Political crimes and offenses
          Probation
          Prohibition
          Sports—Corrupt practices
          Trials
          Vigilance committees
    RT   **Crime**
          Criminal procedure
          Punishment
Criminal procedure (May subdiv. geog.)
    345
    BT   **Courts**
    NT   **Torture**
    RT   **Criminal law**
Criminal psychiatry
    USE **Criminal psychology**
Criminal psychology   364.3
    UF   Criminal psychiatry
    BT   **Psychology**
    RT   **Abnormal psychology**
Criminalistics
    USE **Forensic sciences**

Criminals (May subdiv. geog.) **364.3; 364.6**
  UF Convicts
        Delinquents
        Outlaws
  BT **Crime**
  NT **Gangs**
        Impostors and imposture
        Pirates
        Prisoners
        Swindlers and swindling
        Thieves
Criminals and drugs
  USE **Criminals—Drug use**
Criminals and narcotics
  USE **Criminals—Drug use**
Criminals—Drug use 362.29; 364.3
  UF Criminals and drugs
        Criminals and narcotics
        Drugs and criminals
        Narcotics and criminals
  RT **Drugs and crime**
Criminals—Identification 363.25
  BT **Criminal investigation**
        Identification
  NT **Fingerprints**
Criminals—Rehabilitation programs
  USE **Corrections**
Criminology
  USE **Crime**
Crippled children
  USE **Physically handicapped children**
Crippled people
  USE **Physically handicapped**
Crisis centers 361.3; 362
  UF Crisis intervention centers
  SA types of crisis centers, e.g. **Hotlines (Telephone counseling)** [to be added as needed]
  BT **Counseling**
        Social work
  RT **Hotlines (Telephone counseling)**
Crisis counseling
  USE **Hotlines (Telephone counseling)**
Crisis intervention centers
  USE **Crisis centers**

Crisis intervention (Mental health services) (May subdiv. geog.) **362.2; 616.89**
  UF Crisis intervention (Psychiatry)
        Emergency mental health services
  BT **Mental health services**
Crisis intervention (Psychiatry)
  USE **Crisis intervention (Mental health services)**
Crisis intervention telephone service
  USE **Hotlines (Telephone counseling)**
Crisis management 658.4
  BT **Management**
        Problem solving
Critical thinking 153.4; 160
  Use for materials on thinking that is based on sound logic and the careful evaluation of all pertinent evidence.
  BT **Decision making**
        Logic
        Problem solving
        Reasoning
        Thought and thinking
Criticism 801
  Use for materials on the history, principles, methods, etc., of criticism in general and of literary criticism in particular. Materials that are themselves histories or criticisms of literature are entered under **Literature—History and criticism.** Criticism of the work of an individual author, artist, composer, etc., is entered under that person's name as a subject; only in the case of voluminous authors is it necessary to add the subdivision *Criticism.* Criticism of a single work is entered under the name of the author, artist, or composer, followed by the title of the work.
  UF Appraisal of books
        Books—Appraisal
        Criticism and interpretation
        Criticism, interpretation, etc.
        Evaluation of literature
        Literary criticism
        Literature—Evaluation
  SA literature, film, and music subjects with the subdivision *History and criticism,* e.g. **English poetry—History and criticism;** and names of voluminous authors and of sacred works with the subdivision *Criticism,* e.g. **Shakespeare, William, 1564-1616—Criticism; Bible—Criticism;** etc. [to be added as needed]

Criticism—*Continued*
    BT   Aesthetics
            Literature
            Rhetoric
    NT   Art criticism
            Book reviewing
            Dramatic criticism
            Feminist criticism
    RT   Literary style
Criticism and interpretation
    USE   Criticism
            and literature, film, and music subjects with the subdivision *History and criticism,* e.g. **English poetry—History and criticism;** and names of voluminous authors and of sacred works with the subdivision *Criticism,* e.g. **Shakespeare, William, 1564-1616—Criticism; Bible—Criticism;** etc. [to be added as needed]
Criticism, Feminist
    USE   Feminist criticism
Criticism, interpretation, etc.
    USE   Criticism
            and literature, film, and music subjects with the subdivision *History and criticism,* e.g. **English poetry—History and criticism;** and names of voluminous authors and of sacred works with the subdivision *Criticism,* e.g. **Shakespeare, William, 1564-1616—Criticism; Bible—Criticism;** etc. [to be added as needed]
Cro-Magnons   569.9; 930.1
    UF   Cromagnons
    BT   Prehistoric peoples
Crocheting   746.43
    BT   Needlework
    NT   Beadwork
            Lace and lace making
Crockery
    USE   Pottery
Crocodiles (May subdiv. geog.)   597.98
    BT   Reptiles
    RT   Alligators
Cromagnons
    USE   Cro-Magnons

Crop dusting
    USE   Aeronautics in agriculture
Crop reports
    USE   Agriculture—Statistics
Crop rotation   631.5
    UF   Rotation of crops
    BT   Agriculture
Crop spraying
    USE   Aeronautics in agriculture
Crops
    USE   Farm produce
Cross cultural conflict
    USE   Culture conflict
Cross-cultural psychology
    USE   Ethnopsychology
Cross-cultural studies   306
    Use for materials on the systematic comparison of two or more cultural groups, either within the same country or in separate countries.
    UF   Comparison of cultures
            Cross cultural studies *[Former heading]*
            Intercultural studies
            Transcultural studies
    SA   topics with the subdivision *Cross-cultural studies,* e.g. **Marriage—Cross-cultural studies** [to be added as needed]
    BT   Culture
            Social sciences
Cross cultural studies
    USE   Cross-cultural studies
Cross-examination
    USE   Witnesses
Crossword puzzles   793.73
    BT   Puzzles
            Word games
Crowds   302.3
    UF   Mobs
    NT   Demonstrations
            Riot control
    RT   Riots
            Social psychology
Crown lands
    USE   Public lands
CRT display terminals
    USE   Computer monitors
CRTs
    USE   Cathode ray tubes

Crucifixion of Jesus Christ
    USE   **Jesus Christ—Crucifixion**
Crude oil
    USE   **Petroleum**
Cruelty   179
    UF   Brutality
    BT   **Ethics**
    NT   **Atrocities**
         Torture
Cruelty to animals
    USE   **Animal welfare**
Cruelty to children
    USE   **Child abuse**
Cruises
    USE   **Ocean travel**
Crusades   909.07
    BT   **Church history—600-1500,**
         Middle Ages
    RT   **Chivalry**
Crustacea   565; 595.3
    SA   names of specific crustaceans,
         e.g. **Lobsters** [to be added as
         needed]
    BT   **Shellfish**
    NT   **Crabs**
         Lobsters
Cryobiology   571.4
    UF   Freezing
         Low temperature biology
    BT   **Biology**
         Cold
         Low temperatures
    NT   **Cold—Physiological effect**
         Frozen embryos
Cryogenic interment
    USE   **Cryonics**
Cryogenic surgery
    USE   **Cryosurgery**
Cryogenics
    USE   **Low temperatures**
Cryonics   621.5
    UF   Cryogenic interment
         Freezing of human bodies
         Human cold storage
    BT   **Burial**
Cryosurgery   617
    UF   Cryogenic surgery
    BT   **Cold—Therapeutic use**
         Surgery
Cryotherapy
    USE   **Cold—Therapeutic use**

Cryptography   652
    UF   Code deciphering
         Code enciphering
         Secret writing
    BT   **Signs and symbols**
         Writing
    RT   **Ciphers**
Crystal gazing
    USE   **Divination**
Crystal meth (Drug)
    USE   **Ice (Drug)**
Crystallization
    USE   **Crystals**
Crystallography
    USE   **Crystals**
Crystals   548
    UF   Crystallization
         Crystallography
    SA   types of crystals, e.g. **Quartz** [to
         be added as needed]
    BT   **Physical chemistry**
         Solids
    NT   **Quartz**
    RT   **Minerals**
Cub Scouts
    USE   **Boy Scouts**
Cuba   972.91
    May be subdivided like United States ex-
    cept for *History.*
    BT   **Islands**
Cuba—History   972.91
Cuba—History—1958-1959, Revolution
         972.9106
Cuba—History—1959-   972.9106
Cuba—History—1961, Invasion
         972.9106
    UF   Bay of Pigs invasion
         Cuban invasion, 1961
         Invasion of Cuba, 1961
Cuban invasion, 1961
    USE   **Cuba—History—1961, Invasion**
Cube root   513.2
    BT   **Arithmetic**
Cubic measurement
    USE   **Volume (Cubic content)**
Cubism (May subdiv. geog.)   **709.04;**
         759.06
    BT   **Art**

Cultivated plants (May subdiv. geog.)
    581.6; 631.5
  UF Plants, Cultivated
  BT **Agriculture**
      Gardening
      Plants
  NT **Annuals (Plants)**
      House plants
      Ornamental plants
      Perennials

Cultivated plants—United States   **581.6; 631.5**

Cults (May subdiv. geog.)   **291.9; 306.6**

Use for materials on groups or movements whose beliefs or practices differ significantly from the traditional religions and are often focused upon a charismatic leader. Materials on the major world religions are entered under **Religions.** Materials on independent religious groups those teachings or practices fall within the normative bounds of the major world religions are entered under **Sects.**

  UF Religious cults
  BT **Religions**
  NT **New Age movement**
  RT **Sects**

Cultural anthropology
  USE **Ethnology**

Cultural change
  USE **Social change**

Cultural exchange programs
  USE **Exchange of persons programs**

Cultural heritage
  USE **Cultural property**

Cultural life
  USE **Intellectual life**

Cultural patrimony
  USE **Cultural property**

Cultural policy (May subdiv. geog.)   **306**

Use for materials on official government policy toward educational, artistic, intellectual, or other cultural activities and organizations in general.

  UF Government policy
      Intellectual life—Government policy
      State encouragement of science, literature, and art
  SA types of artistic or intellectual activities with the subdivision *Government policy* [to be added as needed]
  BT **Culture**
      Intellectual life
  NT **Cultural property—Protection**

Cultural policy—United States   **306**
  UF United States—Cultural policy

Cultural property (May subdiv. geog.)
    344

Use for materials on property that is considered essential to a nation's cultural heritage.

  UF Cultural heritage
      Cultural patrimony
      Heritage property
      National heritage
      National patrimony
      National treasure
  BT **Property**

Cultural property—Protection (May subdiv. geog.)   **344**

Use for materials on protecting cultural heritage property from theft, misappropriation, or exportation. Materials on identifying and preserving historically important towns, buildings, sites, etc., are entered under **Historic preservation.**

  UF Cultural property—Protection—Government policy
      Cultural resources management
  BT **Cultural policy**
  RT **Historic preservation**

Cultural property—Protection—Government policy
  USE **Cultural property—Protection**

Cultural relations   **306; 341.7**
  UF Intercultural relations
  BT **Intellectual cooperation**
      International cooperation
      International relations
  NT **Exchange of persons programs**
      Interfaith relations

Cultural resources management
  USE **Cultural property—Protection**

Culturally deprived
  USE **Socially handicapped**

Culturally deprived children
  USE **Socially handicapped children**

Culturally handicapped
  USE **Socially handicapped**

Culturally handicapped children
  USE **Socially handicapped children**

Culture   **306; 909**

Use for materials on the sum total of ways of living or thinking established by a group of human beings and transmitted from one generation to the next, including a concern for what is regarded as excellent in the arts, manners, scholarship, etc.

Culture—*Continued*
  SA   regions, countries, states, etc.,
       with the subdivisions *Intellec-
       tual life; Civilization;* or *So-
       cial life and customs,* e.g.
       **United States—Intellectual
       life; United States—Civiliza-
       tion; United States—Social
       life and customs;** etc. [to be
       added as needed]
  NT   **Acculturation**
       Cross-cultural studies
       Cultural policy
       Humanism
       Intellectual life
       Multiculturalism
       Pluralism (Social sciences)
       Popular culture
  RT   **Anthropology**
       Civilization
       Education
       Learning and scholarship
       Sociology
Culture conflict (May subdiv. geog.)
       155.8; 306; 155.8
  UF   Conflict of cultures
       Cross cultural conflict
       Culture shock
       Future shock
  BT   **Ethnic relations**
       Ethnopsychology
       Race relations
Culture contact
  USE **Acculturation**
Culture shock
  USE **Culture conflict**
Curates
  USE **Clergy**
Curiosities and wonders (May subdiv.
       geog.)   **030**
  UF   Enigmas
       Facts, Miscellaneous
       Miscellanea
       Miscellaneous facts
       Oddities
       Trivia
       Wonders
  SA   subjects with the subdivision
       Miscellanea, e.g. **Medicine—
       Miscellanea** [to be added as
       needed]

  NT   **Eccentrics and eccentricities**
       Medicine—Miscellanea
       Monsters
       World records
Currency
  USE **Money**
Currency devaluation
  USE **Monetary policy**
Current events   909.82
       Use for materials on the study and teaching
    of current events. Accounts or discussions of
    the events themselves are entered under the
    appropriate heading for historical period or
    history of a place. Periodicals and yearbooks
    devoted to current events are entered under
    History—Periodicals.
  BT   **Modern history—Study and
       teaching**
Currents, Electric
  USE **Electric currents**
Currents, Ocean
  USE **Ocean currents**
Curricula
  USE **Education—Curricula**
       and types of education and
       schools with the subdivision
       Curricula, e.g. **Library edu-
       cation—Curricula** [to be
       added as needed]
Curriculum development
  USE **Curriculum planning**
Curriculum materials centers
  USE **Instructional materials centers**
Curriculum planning (May subdiv. geog.)
       375
  UF   Curriculum development
  BT   **Education—Curricula**
       Planning
  NT   **Interdisciplinary approach in
       education**
Curtains
  USE **Draperies**
Custody kidnapping
  USE **Parental kidnapping**
Custody of children
  USE **Child custody**
Custom duties
  USE **Tariff**
Customer relations   658.8
  BT   **Business**
       Public relations
  NT   **Customer services**

Customer service
    USE **Customer services**
Customer services   658.8
    UF Customer service *[Former heading]*
        Service, Customer
        Service (in industry)
        Services, Customer
        Technical service
    BT **Customer relations**
Customs and practices
    USE religions, denominations, religious orders, and religious holidays with the subdivision *Customs and practices,* e.g. **Judaism—Customs and practices** [to be added as needed]
Customs, Social
    USE **Manners and customs**
Customs (Tariff)
    USE **Tariff**
Cybercommerce
    USE **Electronic commerce**
Cybernetics   003
    UF Automatic control
        Mechanical brains
    BT **Communication**
        Electronics
        System theory
    NT **Bionics**
        System analysis
        Systems engineering
Cybersex
    USE **Computer sex**
Cybershopping
    USE **Internet shopping**
Cyberspace   006
    Use for materials on the non-physical environment created by the Internet or other computer networks.
    BT **Computer networks**
        Space and time
Cycles   115
    UF Cyclic theory
        Natural cycles
        Periodicity
    NT **Biological rhythms**
        Business cycles
        Life cycles (Biology)
    RT **Rhythm**
        Time

Cyclic theory
    USE **Cycles**
Cycling   796.6
    UF Bicycles and bicycling
        Bicycling
        Biking
    BT **Exercise**
        Outdoor recreation
        Sports
    NT **Bicycle racing**
        Bicycle touring
        Motorcycling
    RT **Bicycles**
        Tricycles
Cyclones (May subdiv. geog.)   **551.55**
    Use for materials on large-scale storms that involve high winds rotating around a center of low atmospheric pressure. Materials on the cyclones of the West Indies are entered under **Hurricanes.** Materials on the cyclones of the China Seas and the Philippines are entered under **Typhoons.**
    BT **Meteorology**
        Storms
        Winds
    NT **Hurricanes**
        Typhoons
Cyclopedias
    USE **Encyclopedias and dictionaries**
Cyclotron
    USE **Cyclotrons**
Cyclotrons   539.7
    UF Atom smashing
        Cyclotron *[Former heading]*
        Magnetic resonance accelerator
    BT **Atoms**
        Nuclear physics
        Transmutation (Chemistry)
Cytology
    USE **Cells**
Czech Republic   943.71
    Use for materials on this part of the former country of Czechoslovakia since its becoming independent on January 1, 1993. May be subdivided like United States except for *History.*
    RT **Czechoslovakia**
Czechoslovakia   943.703
    Use for materials on the former country of Czechoslovakia through December 31, 1992. Materials on the two parts of the former country of Czechoslovakia, which became independent on January 1, 1993, are entered under **Czech Republic** and **Slovakia.**
    RT **Czech Republic**
        Slovakia

Czechoslovakia—History—1918-1968
943.703

Czechoslovakia—History—1945-1992
943.704
  UF Czechoslovakia—History—1989-
      1992 *[Former heading]*

Czechoslovakia—History—1968-1989
943.704

Czechoslovakia—History—1989-1992
  USE **Czechoslovakia—History—1945-1992**

D.D.T. (Insecticide)
  USE **DDT (Insecticide)**

D Day
  USE **Normandy (France), Attack on,
      1944**

Daily readings (Spiritual exercises)
  USE **Devotional calendars**

Dairies
  USE **Dairying**

Dairy cattle 636.2
  SA names of breeds of dairy cattle
      [to be added as needed]
  BT **Cattle**
      Dairying
  NT **Holstein-Friesian cattle**

Dairy farming
  USE **Dairying**

Dairy industry
  USE **Dairying**

Dairy products 637; 641.3
  UF Products, Dairy
  SA types of dairy products [to be
      added as needed]
  BT **Animal products**
  NT **Butter**
      Cheese
      Milk

Dairying (May subdiv. geog.) **636.2;
  637**

Use for materials on the production and
marketing of milk and milk products and for
general materials on dairy farming.
  UF Dairies
      Dairy farming
      Dairy industry
  BT **Agriculture**
      Livestock industry
  NT **Dairy cattle**
      Milk

Dams (May subdiv. geog.) **627**
  SA names of dams, e.g. **Hoover
      Dam (Ariz. and Nev.)** [to be
      added as needed]
  BT **Civil engineering**
      Hydraulic structures
      Water supply
  NT **Hoover Dam (Ariz. and Nev.)**

Dance (May subdiv. geog.) **792.8; 793.3**
Use for materials on recreational dancing as
well as performance dance.
  UF Dances
      Dancing
  SA types of dances and dancing [to
      be added as needed]
  BT **Amusements**
      Performing arts
  NT **Ballet**
      Break dancing
      Clog dancing
      Folk dancing
      Modern dance
      Tap dancing
  RT **Aerobics**
      Dance music

Dance music (May subdiv. geog.) **781.5;
  784.18**
  BT **Music**
  RT **Dance**

**Dance—United States 792.80973;
  793.30973**

Dancers (May subdiv. geog.) **792.8092;
  793.3092; 920**
  SA types of dancers, e.g. **Ballet
      dancers** [to be added as
      needed]
  BT **Entertainers**
  NT **Ballet dancers**

Dances
  USE **Dance**

Dancing
  USE **Dance**

Dangerous animals 591.6
  BT **Animals**
  NT **Animal attacks**
      Poisonous animals

Dangerous materials
  USE **Hazardous substances**

Dangerous occupations
  USE **Hazardous occupations**

Danish language 439.8
May be subdivided like **English language.**

Danish language—*Continued*
  BT Language and languages
      Norwegian language
      Scandinavian languages
Danish literature   839.81
      May use same subdivisions and names of
      literary forms as for **English literature.**
  BT Literature
      Scandinavian literature
Dark Ages
  USE Middle Ages
Dark humor (Literature)
  USE Black humor (Literature)
Dark night of the soul
  USE Mysticism
Darkroom technique in photography
  USE Photography—Processing
Darwinism
  USE Evolution
Data banks
  USE Databases
Data bases
  USE Databases
Data processing (May subdiv. geog.)
      004
  UF Automatic data processing
      Electronic data processing *[For-*
        mer heading]
  SA subjects with the subdivision
      Data processing, e.g. **Banks
      and banking—Data process-
      ing** [to be added as needed]
  BT Computers
      Information systems
  NT Banks and banking—Data pro-
      cessing
      Computer graphics
      Computer programming
      Database management
      Expert systems (Computer sci-
        ence)
      Optical data processing
  RT Computer science
Data processing—Keyboarding
  USE Keyboarding (Electronics)
Data retrieval
  USE Information retrieval
Data storage and retrieval systems
  USE Information systems

Data transmission systems   004.6;
      621.38; 621.39
  UF Transmission of data
  BT Telecommunication
  NT Computer networks
      Electronic mail systems
      Fax transmission
      Teletext systems
      Video telephone
      Videotex systems
Databanks
  USE Databases
Database management   005.74
  UF Systems, Database management
  BT Computer science
      Data processing
      Information systems
Database management—Computer pro-
      grams   005.74
  BT Computer software
Databases   025.04
      Use for materials on any type of organized
      body of information, including written, numer-
      ical, and visual information, not limited to a
      particular subject.
  UF Data banks
      Data bases
      Databanks
  SA subjects with the subdivision
      Databases, for materials about
      data files on a subject regard-
      less of the medium of distri-
      bution, e.g. **Business—
      Databases;** subjects with the
      subdivision *Information re-
      sources,* for general materials
      about information on a sub-
      ject, e.g. **Business—Informa-
      tion resources;** subjects with
      the subdivision *Internet re-
      sources,* for materials about
      information available on the
      Internet on a subject, e.g.
      Business—Internet resources;
      and headings for the providers
      or the users of information
      with the subdivision *Informa-
      tion services,* for materials
      about organizations that pro-
      vide information services, e.g.
      United Nations—Information

Databases—*Continued*
    services; Consumers—Information services; etc. [to be added as needed]
  BT **Information resources**
  NT **Business—Databases**
Date etiquette
  USE **Dating (Social customs)**
Date rape   362.883; 364.15
  UF Acquaintance rape
      Dating violence
  BT **Dating (Social customs)**
      Rape
Dates, Historical
  USE **Historical chronology**
Dating etiquette
  USE **Dating (Social customs)**
Dating, Radiocarbon
  USE **Radiocarbon dating**
Dating (Social customs) (May subdiv. geog.)   **306.73; 392.4; 646.7**
  UF Date etiquette
      Dating etiquette
  BT **Courtship**
      Etiquette
      Manners and customs
  NT **Date rape**
  RT **Man-woman relationship**
Dating violence
  USE **Date rape**
Daughters   306.874
  BT **Family**
      Women
  NT **Father-daughter relationship**
      Mother-daughter relationship
Daughters and fathers
  USE **Father-daughter relationship**
Daughters and mothers
  USE **Mother-daughter relationship**
Day   529
  BT **Chronology**
      Time
  RT **Night**
Day care centers (May subdiv. geog.)   **362.71**
  UF Child care centers
      Children—Day care
      Children's day care centers
      Day nurseries
      Nurseries, Day
  BT **Child care**
      Child welfare

Children—Institutional care
  RT **Nursery schools**
Day dreams
  USE **Fantasy**
Day nurseries
  USE **Day care centers**
Day of Atonement
  USE **Yom Kippur**
Days   394.2
  UF Days of the week
  SA types of days and names of particular days [to be added as needed]
  BT **Calendars**
  NT **Birthdays**
      Festivals
      Holidays
  RT **Week**
Days of the week
  USE **Days**
DDT (Insecticide)   668
  UF D.D.T. (Insecticide) *[Former heading]*
      Dichloro-diphenyl-trichloroethane
  BT **Insecticides**
Dead Sea scrolls   221.4; 229; 296.1
  UF Qumran texts
Deaf (May subdiv. geog.)   **362.4**
  BT **Hearing impaired**
      Physically handicapped
  NT **Closed caption television**
      Closed caption video recordings
Deaf—Education (May subdiv. geog.)   **371.91**
  UF Education of the deaf
  BT **Education**
Deaf—Institutional care   362.4
  BT **Institutional care**
Deaf—Means of communication   362.4; 419
    Use for general materials on communication in the broadest sense by people who are deaf. Materials on language systems based on hand gestures are entered under **Sign language.**
  UF Finger alphabet
      Lip reading
  BT **Communication**
  NT **Hearing ear dogs**
  RT **Nonverbal communication**
      Sign language

Deaf—Sign language
USE **Sign language**
Deafness   362.4; 617.8
BT **Ear**
NT **Hearing aids**
RT **Hearing**
Death (May subdiv. geog.)   128; 236;
306.9; 571.9
SA ethnic groups and classes of per-
sons with the subdivision
Death, e.g. **Infants—Death;**
and names of individual per-
sons and groups of notable
persons with the subdivision
Death and burial, e.g. **Presi-
dents—United States—Death
and burial** [to be added as
needed]
BT **Biology**
Eschatology
Life
NT **Brain death**
Future life
Infants—Death
Near-death experiences
Right to die
RT **Burial**
Mortality
Terminal care
Terminally ill
Death and burial
USE names of individual persons and
groups of notable persons
with the subdivision *Death
and burial,* e.g. **Presidents—
United States—Death and
burial** [to be added as need-
ed]
Death masks
USE **Masks (Sculpture)**
Death notices
USE **Obituaries**
Death penalty
USE **Capital punishment**
Death rate
USE **Mortality**
Vital statistics
Deaths, Registers of
USE **Registers of births, etc.**

Debates and debating   808.53
UF Argumentation
Discussion
Speaking
BT **Public speaking**
Rhetoric
NT **Parliamentary practice**
Radio addresses, debates, etc.
RT **Discussion groups**
Debit cards   332.1
UF Bank debit cards
Cards, Debit
BT **Banks and banking**
Debris in Space
USE **Space debris**
Debt (May subdiv. geog.)   332.7
Use for economic and statistical materials
on debt. Legal materials regarding debtor and
creditor are entered under **Debtor and credi-
tor.**
UF Indebtedness
BT **Finance**
NT **Collecting of accounts**
Public debts
RT **Debtor and creditor**
Debtor
USE **Debtor and creditor**
Debtor and creditor (May subdiv. geog.)
346.07
Use for legal materials regarding debtor and
creditor. Economic and statistical materials on
debt are entered under **Debt.**
UF Creditor
Debtor
BT **Commercial law**
NT **Bankruptcy**
Collecting of accounts
RT **Credit**
Debt
Debts, Public
USE **Public debts**
Decalogue
USE **Ten commandments**
Deceit
USE **Fraud**
Decentralization of schools
USE **Schools—Decentralization**
Deceptive advertising   343.07
UF False advertising
Fraudulent advertising
Misleading advertising
Misrepresentation in advertising
Truth in advertising

Deceptive advertising—*Continued*
   BT   Advertising
       Business ethics
Decimal system   513.5
   BT   Numbers
   RT   Metric system
Decision making (May subdiv. geog.)
      153.8; 302.3; 658.4
   NT   Critical thinking
       Group decision making
   RT   Choice (Psychology)
       Problem solving
Decks (Domestic architecture)
   USE **Patios**
Declamations
   USE **Monologues**
        Recitations
Declaration of independence (U.S.)
   USE **United States—Declaration of**
        independence
Decoration and ornament (May subdiv.
   geog.)   **745.4**

Use for general materials on the forms and styles of decoration in various fields of fine arts or applied art and on the history of various styles of ornament. In addition to geographic subdivision, this heading may be subdivided by date or by style of ornament, e.g. **Decoration and ornament—15th and 16th centuries; Decoration and ornament—Gothic style;** etc. Materials limited to the decoration of houses are entered under **Interior design.**

   UF   Decorative art
       Decorative design
       Decorative painting
       Ornament
       Painting, Decorative
   BT   Art
       Decorative arts
   NT   Antiques
       Architectural decoration and
         ornament
       Art objects
       Artificial flowers
       Arts and crafts movement
       Bronzes
       China painting
       Christmas decorations
       Decoupage
       Design
       Egg decoration
       Embroidery
       Enamel and enameling

       Flower arrangement
       Furniture
       Garden ornaments and furni-
         ture
       Gems
       Glass painting and staining
       Holiday decorations
       Illumination of books and
         manuscripts
       Illustration of books
       Interior design
       Ironwork
       Leather work
       Lettering
       Metalwork
       Monograms
       Mosaics
       Mural painting and decoration
       Needlework
       Picture frames and framing
       Pottery
       Sculpture
       Show windows
       Stencil work
       Stucco
       Table setting and decoration
       Tapestry
       Terra cotta
       Textile design
       Wood carving
   RT   Handicraft
       Painting
Decoration and ornament—15th and
   16th centuries (May subdiv. geog.)
   745.4
   UF   Decoration and ornament, Re-
        naissance
       Renaissance decoration and orna-
        ment *[Former heading]*
Decoration and ornament, American
   USE **Decoration and ornament—**
        United States
Decoration and ornament, Architectural
   USE **Architectural decoration and**
        ornament
Decoration and ornament, Gothic
   USE **Decoration and ornament—**
        Gothic style

Decoration and ornament—Gothic style
(May subdiv. geog.)   **745.4**

UF   Decoration and ornament, Gothic
Gothic decoration and ornament

Decoration and ornament, Renaissance

USE   **Decoration and ornament—
15th and 16th centuries**

**Decoration and ornament—United States
745.4**

UF   American decoration and orna-
ment *[Former heading]*
Decoration and ornament,
American

Decoration Day

USE   **Memorial Day**

Decorations, Holiday

USE   **Holiday decorations**

Decorations of honor (May subdiv. geog.)
355.1; 929.8

UF   Badges of honor
Emblems

SA   names of medals [to be added
as needed]

RT   **Heraldry
Insignia
Medals**

Decorative art

USE   **Decoration and ornament
Decorative arts**

Decorative arts (May subdiv. geog.)
745

Use for general materials on the various applied art forms having some utilitarian as well
as decorative purpose, including furniture, silverware, the decoration of buildings, etc.

UF   Applied arts
Art industries and trade
Decorative art
Minor arts

SA   types of decorative arts [to be
added as needed]

BT   **Arts**

NT   **Antiques
Art metalwork
Art objects
Arts and crafts movement
Calligraphy
Carving (Decorative arts)
Costume
Decoration and ornament
Decoupage
Enamel and enameling**

**Fabrics
Furniture
Glassware
Jewelry
Lacquer and lacquering
Leather work
Mosaics
Needlework
Porcelain
Pottery
Rugs and carpets
Silverware
Tapestry
Woodwork**

RT   **Folk art
Handicraft**

**Decorative arts—United States
745.0973**

Decorative design

USE   **Decoration and ornament**

Decorative metalwork

USE   **Art metalwork**

Decorative painting

USE   **Decoration and ornament**

Decoupage   745.54

BT   **Decoration and ornament
Decorative arts
Paper crafts**

Decoys (Hunting) (May subdiv. geog.)
745.593; 799.2

UF   Bird decoys (Hunting)

BT   **Hunting
Shooting**

Deduction (Logic)

USE   **Logic**

Deep diving (May subdiv. geog.)   **627**

Use for materials on underwater diving with
equipment. Materials on diving from a board
or platform are entered under **Diving.**

UF   Deep sea diving
Submarine diving
Underwater diving

BT   **Underwater exploration
Water sports**

NT   **Scuba diving
Skin diving**

RT   **Diving**

Deep sea diving

USE   **Deep diving**

Deep sea drilling (Petroleum)

USE   **Offshore oil well drilling**

Deep sea engineering
    USE **Ocean engineering**
Deep sea mining
    USE **Ocean mining**
Deep-sea Photography
    USE **Underwater photography**
Deer (May subdiv. geog.)   **599.65**
    UF Fawns
    BT **Game and game birds**
         Mammals
    NT **Reindeer**
Defamation
    USE **Libel and slander**
Defective speech
    USE **Speech disorders**
Defective vision
    USE **Vision disorders**
Defectors (May subdiv. geog.)   **325;
327.12**
    UF Political defectors
         Turncoats
    BT **Political refugees**
Defense industries
    USE **Defense industry**
Defense industry (May subdiv. geog.)
338.4

    Use for materials on the industries producing the implements of war. Materials on the implements of war themselves are entered under **Ordnance** or under **Military weapons.**

    UF Armaments industries
         Arms sales
         Defense industries *[Former
heading]*
         Military sales
         Military supplies industry
         Munitions
         Weapons industry
    BT **Industries**
    RT **Arms transfers**
         Military readiness
         Military weapons
         Ordnance
Defense (Law)
    USE **Litigation**
Defense mechanisms (Zoology)
    USE **Animal defenses**
Defense policy
    USE **Military policy**
Defense readiness
    USE **Military readiness**

Defenses
    USE types of defenses, e.g. **Air defenses;** and names of continents, regions, countries, and individual colonies with the subdivision *Defenses,* e.g. **United States—Defenses** [to be added as needed]
Defenses, Radar
    USE **Radar defense networks**
Deficit financing (May subdiv. geog.)
336.3
    UF Compensatory spending
         Deficit spending
    BT **Public finance**
    RT **Public debts**
Deficit spending
    USE **Deficit financing**
Defoliants
    USE **Herbicides**
Deformities
    USE **Birth defects**
Degrees, Academic
    USE **Academic degrees**
Degrees of latitude and longitude
    USE **Geodesy**
         Latitude
         Longitude
Dehydrated foods
    USE **Dried foods**
Dehydrated milk
    USE **Dried milk**
Deism (May subdiv. geog.)   **211**
    BT **Religion**
         Theology
    RT **Atheism**
         Free thought
         Positivism
         Rationalism
         Theism
Deities
    USE **Gods and goddesses**
Dejection
    USE **Depression (Psychology)**
Delayed memory
    USE **Recovered memory**
Delinquency, Juvenile
    USE **Juvenile delinquency**
Delinquents
    USE **Criminals**

Delivery of health care
    USE **Medical care**
Delivery of medical care
    USE **Medical care**
Delphi (Ancient city)
    USE **Delphi (Extinct city)**
Delphi (Extinct city)   938
    UF Delphi (Ancient city)
    BT **Extinct cities—Greece**
          Greece—Antiquities
Delusions
    USE **Hallucinations and illusions**
Demobilization
    USE names of armed forces with the
          subdivision *Demobilization,*
          e.g. **United States. Army—**
          Demobilization [to be added
          as needed]
Democracy (May subdiv. geog.)   **321.8**
    UF Popular government
          Self-government
    BT **Constitutional history**
          Constitutional law
          Political science
    NT **Freedom**
          Referendum
          Suffrage
    RT **Equality**
          Representative government and
          representation
          Republics
Democratic Party (U.S.)   324.2736
    BT **Political parties**
Demography
    USE **Population**
Demoniac possession   133.4
    BT **Demonology**
    RT **Devil**
          Exorcism
Demonology (May subdiv. geog.)   **133.4**
    UF Evil spirits
          Spirits
    BT **Occultism**
    NT **Demoniac possession**
    RT **Devil**
          Exorcism
Demonstrations (May subdiv. geog.)
    322.4; 361.2
    Use for materials on public gatherings,
marches, etc., organized for nonviolent protest
even though incidental disturbances or rioting
may occur.

    UF Marches (Demonstrations)
          Protest marches and rallies
          Protests, demonstrations, etc.
          Public demonstrations
          Rallies (Protest)
    SA names of specific wars or other
          objects of protest with the
          subdivision *Protest move-*
          ments, e.g. **World War,**
          1939-1945—Protest move-
          ments [to be added as need-
          ed]
    BT **Crowds**
          Public meetings
    NT **Civil rights demonstrations**
          Hunger strikes
    RT **Peace movements**
          Protest movements
          Riots
Demonstrations—Chicago (Ill.)
    322.409773
Demonstrations for civil rights
    USE **Civil rights demonstrations**
Demonstrations—United States
    322.40973; 361.2
Denationalization
    USE **Privatization**
Denatured alcohol   661
    UF Alcohol, Denatured
          Industrial alcohol
    BT **Alcohol**
Denominational schools
    USE **Church schools**
Denominations, Christian
    USE **Christian sects**
Denominations, Protestant
    USE **Protestant churches**
Denominations, Religious
    USE **Sects**
Dental care (May subdiv. geog.)   **617.6**
    Use for materials on the organization of
services and facilities for dental care. Materi-
als on the technical and medical aspects of
dental care are entered under **Dentistry.**
    SA ethnic groups, classes of per-
          sons, and military services
          with the subdivision *Dental*
          care, e.g. **Children—Dental**
          care [to be added as needed]
    BT **Medical care**
    RT **Dentistry**

Dentistry (May subdiv. geog.)   **617.6**
> Use for materials on the technical and medical aspects of dental care. Materials on the organization of services and facilities for dental care are entered under **Dental care.**

  SA ethnic groups, classes of persons, and military services with the subdivision *Dental care,* e.g. **Children—Dental care** [to be added as needed]
  BT **Medicine**
  RT **Dental care**
       Teeth

Deoxyribonucleic acid
  USE **DNA**

Department stores (May subdiv. geog.) **658.8**
  BT **Business**
       Retail trade
       Stores

Dependencies
  USE **Colonies**

Depression, Mental
  USE **Depression (Psychology)**

Depression (Psychology)   **616.85**
  UF Dejection
       Depression, Mental
       Depressive psychoses
       Melancholia
       Mental depression
       Mentally depressed
  BT **Abnormal psychology**
       Neuroses
  RT **Manic-depressive illness**

Depressions (May subdiv. geog.)   **338.5**
  UF Business depressions
       Economic depressions
  SA names of countries, states, cities, etc., with the subdivision *Economic conditions* [to be added as needed]
  BT **Business cycles**
  NT **Great Depression, 1929-1939**

Depressions—1929
  USE **Great Depression, 1929-1939**

Depressive psychoses
  USE **Depression (Psychology)**

Deprogramming
  USE **Brainwashing**

Derailments
  USE **Railroad accidents**

Dermatitis
  USE **Skin—Diseases**

Derricks
  USE **Cranes, derricks, etc.**

Desalination of water
  USE **Sea water conversion**

Desalting of water
  USE **Sea water conversion**

Descent
  USE **Genealogy**
       Heredity

Description
  USE names of cities (except extinct cities), countries, states, and regions with the subdivision *Description,* e.g. **Chicago (Ill.)—Description; United States—Description;** etc., for descriptive materials and accounts of travel, including the history of travel, in those places; names of places with the subdivision *Geography* for broad geographical materials about a specific place, e.g. **United States—Geography;** and names of extinct cities or towns, without further subdivision, for general descriptive materials on those places, e.g. **Delphi (Extinct city)** [to be added as needed]

Description and travel
  USE names of cities (except extinct cities), countries, states, etc., with the subdivision *Description,* e.g. **United States—Description;** and ethnic groups, classes of persons, and names of individuals with the subdivision *Travel,* e.g. **Handicapped—Travel** [to be added as needed]

Descriptive geometry   **516**
  UF Geometry, Descriptive
  BT **Geometrical drawing**
       Geometry
  NT **Perspective**

Desegregated schools
  USE **School integration**

Desegregation
USE **Segregation**
Desegregation in education
USE **School integration**
Desert animals (May subdiv. geog.)
     578.754
  UF Desert fauna
  SA types of desert animals, e.g.
       Camels [to be added as need-
       ed]
  BT **Animals**
       Deserts
  NT **Camels**
Desert fauna
USE **Desert animals**
Desert plants (May subdiv. geog.) **581.7**
  SA types of desert plants, e.g. **Cac-
       tus** [to be added as needed]
  BT **Deserts**
       Plant ecology
       Plants
  NT **Cactus**
Desertion
USE **Desertion and nonsupport**
       Military desertion
Desertion and nonsupport **306.88;
346.01**
  UF Abandonment of family
       Desertion
       Nonsupport
  BT **Divorce**
       Domestic relations
  NT **Child support**
       Runaway adults
Desertion, Military
USE **Military desertion**
Desertions
USE names of wars with the subdivi-
       sion *Desertions,* e.g. **World
       War, 1939-1945—Desertions**
       [to be added as needed]
Deserts **551.41**
  BT **Physical geography**
  NT **Desert animals**
       Desert plants
Design (May subdiv. geog.) **745.4**
  SA types of design, e.g. **Industrial
       design; Fashions design;** etc.;
       types of objects, structures,
       machines, equipment, etc., and
       types of educational tests and

examinations with the subdivision *Design and construction,*
e.g. **Automobiles—Design
and construction;** topical
headings with which the subdivision *Design and construction* would be inappropriate
with the subdivision *Design,*
e.g. **Quilts—Design; Pamphlets—Design;** etc.; and
types of architecture and landscape with the form subdivision *Designs and plans,* for
materials containing designs
and drawings, e.g. **Domestic
architecture—Designs and
plans** [to be added as needed]
  BT **Decoration and ornament**
  NT **Architectural design**
       Computer-aided design
       Fashion design
       Garden design
       Industrial design
       Interior design
       Machine design
       Pamphlets—Design
       Quilts—Design
       Textile design
       Web sites—Design
  RT **Patternmaking**
Design and construction
USE types of objects, structures, ma-
       chines, equipment, etc., and
       types of educational tests and
       examinations with the subdivi-
       sion *Design and construction,*
       e.g. **Airplanes—Design and
       construction** [to be added as
       needed]
Design, Industrial
USE **Industrial design**
Designed genetic change
USE **Genetic engineering**
Designer drugs **362.29; 615**
    Use for materials on illicit drugs manufac-
tured by altering the molecular structure of
existing drugs to mimic the effects of standard
narcotics, stimulants, or hallucinogens.
  UF Synthetic drugs of abuse
  SA types of designer drugs, e.g. **Ice
       (Drug)** [to be added as need-
       ed]

Designer drugs—*Continued*
  BT **Drugs**
  NT **Ice (Drug)**
Designs and plans
  USE types of architecture and landscape with the form subdivision *Designs and plans,* for materials containing designs and drawings, e.g. **Domestic architecture—Designs and plans** [to be added as needed]
Designs, Architectural
  USE **Architecture—Designs and plans**
Designs, Floral
  USE **Flower arrangement**
Desktop computers
  USE **Microcomputers**
Desktop publishing   070.5; 686.2
  Use for materials on the use of a personal computer with writing, graphics, and page layout software to produce printed material for publication. Materials on the process of publishing by which books and articles or any kind of data are made available as an electronic product are entered under **Electronic publishing.**
  RT **Electronic publishing**
     Word processing
Desserts   641.8
  SA types of desserts and names of specific desserts [to be added as needed]
  BT **Cooking**
  NT **Cake**
     Ice cream, ices, etc.
  RT **Chocolate**
Destiny
  USE **Fate and fatalism**
Destitution
  USE **Poverty**
Destruction and pillage
  USE names of wars with the subdivision *Destruction and pillage,* e.g. **World War, 1939-1945—Destruction and pillage** [to be added as needed]
Destruction of property
  USE **Vandalism**
Destructive insects
  USE **Insect pests**

Detective and mystery comic books, strips, etc.
  USE **Mystery comic books, strips, etc.**
Detective and mystery films
  USE **Mystery films**
Detective and mystery plays
  USE **Mystery and detective plays**
Detective and mystery radio programs
  USE **Mystery radio programs**
Detective and mystery stories
  USE **Mystery fiction**
Detective and mystery television programs
  USE **Mystery television programs**
Detective comics
  USE **Mystery comic books, strips, etc.**
Detective fiction
  USE **Mystery fiction**
Detective stories
  USE **Mystery fiction**
Detectives (May subdiv. geog.)   **363.25; 920**
  BT **Police**
  RT **Criminal investigation**
     Secret service
Detergent pollution of rivers, lakes, etc.
  USE **Water pollution**
Detergents   668
  UF Synthetic detergents
  BT **Cleaning compounds**
  RT **Soap**
Determinism and indeterminism
  USE **Free will and determinism**
Deuterium oxide   546
  UF Heavy water
  BT **Chemicals**
Devaluation of currency
  USE **Monetary policy**
Developing countries   330.9
  Use for comprehensive materials on countries that are not fully modernized or industrialized. This heading may be subdivided by the topical subdivisions used under countries, regions, etc., and may also be used as a geographic subdivision e.g. **Education—Developing countries.**
  UF Less developed countries
     Third World
     Underdeveloped areas
  BT **Economic conditions**
     Industrialization
  NT **New states**

Developing countries—Commerce
338.91; 382
  BT Commerce
Developing countries—Education
  USE Education—Developing countries
Development
  USE Embryology
      Evolution
      Growth disorders
      Modernization (Sociology)
Development, Economic
  USE Economic development
Deviation, Sexual
  USE Sexual deviation
Devices (Heraldry)
  USE Heraldry
      Insignia
Devil   235
  UF Satan
  RT Demoniac possession
      Demonology
Devil's Triangle
  USE Bermuda Triangle
Devotion
  USE Prayer
      Worship
Devotional calendars   242
  UF Christian devotional calendars
      Daily readings (Spiritual exercises)
      Devotional exercises (Daily readings)
  BT Calendars
      Devotional literature
Devotional exercises   242; 248.3

Use for general materials on acts of private prayer and private worship and for materials on religious practices other than the corporate worship of a congregation. Materials on the religious literature used as aids in devotional exercises are entered under **Devotional literature.**

  UF Devotional theology
      Devotions
      Family devotions
      Family prayers
  BT Worship
  NT Meditation
  RT Prayer
Devotional exercises (Daily readings)
  USE Devotional calendars

Devotional literature   242

Use for materials on the religious literature used as aids in devotional exercises. General materials on acts of private prayer and private worship and materials on religious practices other than the corporate worship of a congregation are entered under **Devotional exercises.**

  BT Religious literature
  NT Devotional calendars
      Meditations
      Prayers
Devotional theology
  USE Devotional exercises
      Prayer
Devotions
  USE Devotional exercises
Dewey Decimal Classification   025.4
  UF Classification, Dewey Decimal
  BT Library classification
Diagnosis   616.07
  UF Medical diagnosis
      Symptoms
  BT Medicine
  NT Body temperature
      Clinical chemistry
      Magnetic resonance imaging
      Pain
      Prenatal diagnosis
  RT Pathology
Diagnostic chemistry
  USE Clinical chemistry
Dialectical materialism   335.4
  UF Historical materialism
  BT Communism
      Socialism
  RT Marxism
Dialectics
  USE Logic
Dialects
  USE names of languages with the subdivision *Dialects,* e.g. **English language—Dialects** [to be added as needed]
Diamonds   553.8
  BT Carbon
      Precious stones
Diaries   809; 920

Use for collections of diaries from various countries and for materials about diaries in general.

Diaries—*Continued*
    UF   Journals (Diaries)
    SA   diaries of particular countries,
          e.g. **American diaries;** and
          classes of persons, ethnic
          groups, and names of individ-
          ual persons and families with
          the subdivision *Diaries* [to be
          added as needed]
    BT   **Literature**
    NT   **American diaries**
    RT   **Autobiographies**
Dichloro-diphenyl-trichloroethane
    USE **DDT (Insecticide)**
Dictators   321.9092; 920
    BT   **Heads of state**
          Totalitarianism
Dictionaries
    USE **Encyclopedias and dictionaries**
        and   subjects, names of lan-
        guages, and names of volumi-
        nous authors with the subdivi-
        sion *Dictionaries,* e.g. **English
        language—Dictionaries; Bi-
        ography—Dictionaries;
        Shakespeare, William, 1564-
        1616—Dictionaries** etc. [to be
        added as needed]
Dictionaries, Biographical
    USE **Biography—Dictionaries**
Dictionaries, Classical
    USE **Classical dictionaries**
Dictionaries, Machine readable
    USE **Machine readable dictionaries**
Dictionaries, Multilingual
    USE **Polyglot dictionaries**
Dictionaries, Picture
    USE **Picture dictionaries**
Dictionaries, Polyglot
    USE **Polyglot dictionaries**
Didactic drama   808.82; 812, etc.
    May be used for individual works, collec-
    tions, or materials about didactic drama.
    BT   **Drama**
Didactic fiction   808.83; 813, etc.
    May be used for individual works, collec-
    tions, or materials about didactic fiction.
    UF   Cautionary tales and verses
          Moral and philosophic stories
          Morality stories

    BT   **Fiction**
    RT   **Fables**
          Parables
Didactic poetry   808.81; 811, etc.
    May be used for individual works, collec-
    tions, or materials about didactic poetry.
    UF· Cautionary tales and verses
    BT   **Poetry**
    RT   **Fables**
          Parables
Dies (Metalworking)   621.9; 671.2
    BT   **Metalwork**
Diesel automobiles   629.222
    UF   Diesel cars
    BT   **Automobiles**
Diesel cars
    USE **Diesel automobiles**
Diesel engines   621.43
    BT   **Engines**
          Internal combustion engines
Diet (May subdiv. geog.)   613.2
    UF   Dietetics
    SA   types of diets, e.g. **Salt-free diet**
          [to be added as needed]
    BT   **Health**
          Hygiene
    NT   **Beverages**
          Dietetic foods
          Eating customs
          Fasting
          Gastronomy
          Menus
          Salt-free diet
          School children—Food
          Vegetarianism
    RT   **Cooking**
          Digestion
          Food
          Nutrition
          Weight loss
Diet in disease   613.2; 616.3
    SA   types of diets, e.g. **Salt-free diet**
          [to be added as needed]
    BT   **Therapeutics**
    NT   **Cooking for the sick**
          Diet therapy
          Salt-free diet
Diet—Therapeutic use
    USE **Diet therapy**
Diet therapy   615.8
    UF   Diet—Therapeutic use
          Invalid cooking

Diet therapy—*Continued*

  SA names of diseases with the subdivision *Diet therapy,* e.g. **Cancer—Diet therapy;** and types of food with the subdivision *Therapeutic use,* e.g. **Herbs—Therapeutic use** [to be added as needed]

  BT **Cooking for the sick**
  Diet in disease
  Therapeutics

  NT **Cancer—Diet therapy**

Dietary fiber
  USE **Food—Fiber content**

Dietetic foods   641.3; 664
  BT **Diet**
  Food

Dietetics
  USE **Diet**

Dieting
  USE **Weight loss**

Diets, Reducing
  USE **Weight loss**

Digestion   573.3; 612.3
  BT **Physiology**
  NT **Indigestion**
  RT **Diet**
  Nutrition
  Stomach

Digital audio disc players
  USE **Compact disc players**

Digital circuits
  USE **Digital electronics**

Digital compact discs
  USE **Compact discs**

Digital electronics   621.381
  UF Digital circuits
  BT **Electronics**

Dimension, Fourth
  USE **Fourth dimension**

Dining (May subdiv. geog.)   **641.01**

  Use for materials on dining customs and gastronomic travel. Materials on menus and recipes for dinners are entered under **Dinners.**

  UF Banquets
  Dinners and dining
  Eating

  BT **Food**
  NT **Carving (Meat, etc.)**
  RT **Dinners**
  Eating customs
  Entertaining

  Gastronomy
  Table etiquette

Dinners   642

  Use for materials on menus and recipes for dinners. Materials on dining customs and gastronomic travel are entered under **Dining.**

  UF Banquets
  Dinners and dining

  BT **Cooking**
  Menus

  RT **Dining**

Dinners and dining
  USE **Dining**
  Dinners

Dinosaur eggs
  USE **Dinosaurs—Eggs**

Dinosaurs (May subdiv. geog.)   **567.9**

  SA types of dinosaurs and names of specific dinosaurs [to be added as needed]

  BT **Fossil reptiles**
  Prehistoric animals

Dinosaurs—Eggs   567.9
  UF Dinosaur eggs
  BT **Eggs**

Dioptrics
  USE **Refraction**

Diphtheria   616.9
  BT **Diseases**

Diplomacy   327.2; 341.3

  SA names of countries with the subdivision *Foreign relations* [to be added as needed]

  BT **International relations**
  NT **Diplomats**
  Treaties
  United States—Foreign relations
  RT **Diplomatic and consular service**

Diplomatic and consular service (May subdiv. geog.)   **341.3**

  Use for materials on diplomatic and consular service in general or on the diplomatic and consular officials of various countries stationed abroad in various countries. Materials on the diplomatic and consular officials of various countries stationed in a specific country are entered under **Diplomatic and consular service** subdivided by the country where they are stationed. Materials on the diplomatic and consular officials of a specific country, regardless of where they are stationed, are entered under the appropriately modified heading, e.g. **American diplomatic and consular**

Diplomatic and consular service—*Continued*

service. Materials on the diplomatic and consular officials of a specific country stationed in a specific country are entered under the appropriately modified heading subdivided by the place where they are stationed.

    UF   Consular service

           Consulates

           Embassies

           Foreign service

           Legations

    SA   diplomatic and consular services of particular countries, e.g. **American diplomatic and consular service** [to be added as needed]

    BT   **International relations**

    NT   **American diplomatic and consular service**

    RT   **Diplomacy**

           Diplomats

Diplomatic and consular service, American

    USE **American diplomatic and consular service**

Diplomatic history

    USE names of wars with the subdivision *Diplomatic history,* e.g. **World War, 1939-1945—Diplomatic history** [to be added as needed]

Diplomats (May subdiv. geog.)

    327.2092; 920

    UF   Ambassadors

           Consuls

           Ministers (Diplomatic agents)

    BT   **Diplomacy**

           International relations

           Statesmen

    RT   **Diplomatic and consular service**

Direct current machinery

    USE **Electric machinery—Direct current**

Direct legislation

    USE **Referendum**

Direct primaries

    USE **Primaries**

Direct selling   **658.8**

    BT   **Marketing**

           Retail trade

           Selling

    NT   **Mail-order business**

           Peddlers and peddling

           Telemarketing

Direct taxation

    USE **Taxation**

Direction sense   **152.1; 912**

    UF   Orientation

           Sense of direction

    NT   **Left and right (Direction)**

    RT   **Hiking**

           Navigation

           Orienteering

Direction (Theater)

    USE **Theater—Production and direction**

Directories   **910.25**

Use for materials about directories and for bibliographies of directories.

    SA   subjects and names of countries, cities, etc., with the subdivision *Directories,* for lists of persons, organizations, objects, etc., together with addresses or other identifying data [to be added as needed]

    NT   **Chicago (Ill.)—Directories**

           Junior colleges—Directories

           Ohio—Directories

           Physicians—Directories

           United States—Directories

Directories—Telephone

    USE names of cities with the subdivision *Telephone directories,* e.g. **Chicago (Ill.)—Telephone directories** [to be added as needed]

Directors

    USE types of producers and directors in specific media, e.g. **Motion picture producers and directors; Theatrical producers and directors;** etc. [to be added as needed]

Directory, French, 1795-1799

    USE **France—History—1789-1799, Revolution**

Dirigible balloons

    USE **Airships**

Disability income insurance

    USE **Disability insurance**

Disability insurance   368.38
UF   Disability income insurance
     Insurance, Disability
BT   **Insurance**
Disability law
USE   **Handicapped—Legal status,**
     laws, etc.
Disabled
USE   **Handicapped**
Disadvantaged
USE   **Socially handicapped**
Disadvantaged children
USE   **Socially handicapped children**
Disadvantaged students
USE   **At risk students**
Disarmament
USE   **Arms control**
Disaster preparedness
USE   **Disaster relief**
Disaster relief (May subdiv. geog.)
     363.34
UF   Disaster preparedness
     Emergency preparedness
     Emergency relief
BT   **Charities**
     Public welfare
NT   **Food relief**
Disasters (May subdiv. geog.)   904
UF   Catastrophes
     Emergencies
SA   types of disasters [to be added
     as needed]
NT   **Fires**
     Natural disasters
     Railroad accidents
     Shipwrecks
RT   **Accidents**
Disciples, Twelve
USE   **Apostles**
Discipline
USE   **Punishment**
Discipline of children
USE   **Child rearing**
     School discipline
Discography
USE   **Sound recordings**
     and subjects and names of per-
     sons with the subdivision *Dis-*
     cography, e.g. **Music—Dis-**
     cography; Shakespeare, Wil-
     liam, 1564-1616—Discogra-

phy; etc., for lists or catalogs
     of sound recordings [to be
     added as needed]
Discount stores   381; 658.8
BT   **Retail trade**
     Stores
Discoverers
USE   **Explorers**
Discoveries and exploration
USE   **Exploration**
Discoveries in geography
USE   **Exploration**
Discoveries in science (May subdiv. geog.)
     500
UF   Breakthroughs, Scientific
     Discoveries, Scientific
     Scientific breakthroughs
     Scientific discoveries
BT   **Research**
     Science
Discoveries, Scientific
USE   **Discoveries in science**
Discrimination (May subdiv. geog.)
     177; 305
Use for general materials on discrimination
by race, religion, sex, age, social status, or
other factors, including reverse discrimination.
SA   phrase headings for discrimina-
     tion in particular realms of
     activity, e.g. **Discrimination**
     in employment; or discrimi-
     nation against particular ethnic
     groups or classes of persons,
     e.g. **Discrimination against**
     the handicapped; and ethnic
     groups and classes of persons
     with the subdivision *Civil*
     rights, or *Legal status, laws,*
     etc., e.g. **African Ameri-**
     cans—Civil rights; Handi-
     capped—Legal status, laws,
     etc. [to be added as needed]
BT   **Ethnic relations**
     Interpersonal relations
     Prejudices
     Race relations
     Social problems
     Social psychology
NT   **Age discrimination**
     Discrimination against the
     handicapped
     Discrimination in education

Discrimination—*Continued*
      Discrimination in employment
      Discrimination in housing
      Discrimination in public ac-
        commodations
      Hate crimes
      Race discrimination
      Sex discrimination
  RT **Civil rights**
      Minorities
      Segregation
      Toleration
Discrimination against disabled persons
  USE **Discrimination against the**
        handicapped
Discrimination against handicapped persons
  USE **Discrimination against the**
        handicapped
Discrimination against the disabled
  USE **Discrimination against the**
        handicapped
Discrimination against the handicapped
  305.9; 362.4
  UF Discrimination against disabled
      persons
      Discrimination against handi-
      capped persons
      Discrimination against the dis-
      abled
  BT **Discrimination**
      Handicapped
Discrimination in education (May subdiv.
  geog.) **379.2**
  BT **Discrimination**
  RT **Segregation in education**
Discrimination in employment (May
  subdiv. geog.) **331.13**
  UF Employment discrimination
      Equal employment opportunity
      Equal opportunity in employ-
      ment
      Fair employment practice
      Job discrimination
  SA ethnic groups and classes of per-
      sons with the subdivision *Em-*
      ployment, e.g. **African Amer-**
      icans—Employment [to be
      added as needed]
  BT **Discrimination**
  NT **Affirmative action programs**
      Equal pay for equal work

Discrimination in housing (May subdiv.
  geog.) **363.5**
  UF Fair housing
      Open housing
      Segregation in housing
  BT **Discrimination**
      Housing
Discrimination in public accommodations
  (May subdiv. geog.) **305**
  UF Public accommodations, Discrim-
      ination in
      Segregation in public accommo-
      dations
  BT **Discrimination**
Discussion
  USE **Conversation**
      Debates and debating
      Negotiation
Discussion groups **374**
  UF Forums (Discussions)
      Great books program
      Group discussion
      Panel discussions
  BT **Conversation**
  NT **Electronic discussion groups**
  RT **Debates and debating**
Disease germs
  USE **Bacteria**
      Germ theory of disease
Disease (Pathology)
  USE **Pathology**
Diseases (May subdiv. geog.) **614.4; 616**
  UF Illness
      Sickness
  SA types of diseases, e.g. **Commu-**
      nicable diseases; names of
      specific diseases, e.g. **Influen-**
      za; and types of animals,
      classes of persons, and parts
      of the body with the subdivi-
      sion *Diseases,* e.g. **Nervous**
      system—Diseases [to be add-
      ed as needed]
  NT **AIDS (Disease)**
      Animals—Diseases
      Arthritis
      Blood—Diseases
      Brain—Diseases
      Cancer
      Chickenpox
      Children—Diseases

Diseases—*Continued*
  Cold (Disease)
  Communicable diseases
  Diphtheria
  Elderly—Diseases
  Epidemics
  Heart diseases
  Hyperactivity
  Infants—Diseases
  Influenza
  Lungs—Diseases
  Lyme disease
  Malaria
  Men—Diseases
  Mental illness
  Nervous system—Diseases
  Occupational diseases
  Plant diseases
  Poliomyelitis
  Rheumatism
  Skin—Diseases
  Teeth—Diseases
  Typhoid fever
  Women—Diseases
 RT Health
  Medicine
  Pathology
  Sick
Diseases and pests
 USE Agricultural bacteriology
  Agricultural pests
  Fungi
  Household pests
  Insect pests
  Parasites
  Plant diseases
  and names of individual pests,
  e.g. **Locusts;** and types of
  crops, plants, trees, etc., with
  the subdivision *Diseases and
  pests,* e.g. **Fruit—Diseases
  and pests** [to be added as
  needed]
Diseases of animals
 USE Animals—Diseases
Diseases of children
 USE Children—Diseases
Diseases of plants
 USE Plant diseases
Diseases of the blood
 USE Blood—Diseases

Diseases of women
 USE Women—Diseases
Diseases—Prevention
 USE Preventive medicine
Diseases—Treatment
 USE Therapeutics
Diseases, Tropical
 USE Tropical medicine
Dishes
 USE Porcelain
  Pottery
  Tableware
Dishonesty
 USE Honesty
Disinfection and disinfectants   614.4
 UF Germicides
 BT Hygiene
  Pharmaceutical chemistry
  Public health
  Sanitation
 RT Antiseptics
  Fumigation
Disney World (Fla.)
 USE Walt Disney World (Fla.)
Disobedience
 USE Obedience
Displaced persons
 USE Political refugees
  Refugees
Disposal of medical waste
 USE Medical wastes
Disposal of refuse
 USE Refuse and refuse disposal
Dissent (May subdiv. geog.)   303.48;
   361.2
 UF Nonconformity
  Protest
 BT Freedom of conscience
  Freedom of religion
 RT Conformity
Dissertations   378.2; 808
  Use for materials about academic theses and
  dissertations.
 UF Academic dissertations
  Dissertations, Academic
  Doctoral theses
  Theses
 BT Colleges and universities
Dissertations, Academic
 USE Dissertations

Distance education (May subdiv. geog.)
    371.3

    Use for materials on the various forms of long-distance instruction, usually in the field of adult education, made possible by written, audiovisual, or electronic communication between a student and a teacher.

    UF   Distance learning

    BT   **Education**

    NT   **Correspondence schools and courses**

          University extension

Distance learning

    USE **Distance education**

Distillation   **641.2; 663**

    UF   Stills

    BT   **Analytical chemistry**

          Industrial chemistry

          Technology

    NT   **Essences and essential oils**

    RT   **Alcohol**

          Liquors

Distribution, Cooperative

    USE **Cooperation**

Distribution (Economics)

    USE **Commerce**

          Marketing

Distribution of animals and plants

    USE **Biogeography**

Distribution of wealth

    USE **Economics**

          Wealth

District libraries

    USE **Regional libraries**

District schools

    USE **Rural schools**

Districting (in city planning)

    USE **Zoning**

Diversified corporations

    USE **Conglomerate corporations**

Diversity, Biological

    USE **Biological diversity**

Diversity movement

    USE **Multiculturalism**

Dividends

    USE **Securities**

          Stocks

Divination (May subdiv. geog.)   **133.3**

    UF   Crystal gazing

          Necromancy

          Soothsaying

    BT   **Occultism**

    NT   **Astrology**

          Feng-shui

          Fortune telling

          Palmistry

    RT   **Oracles**

          Prophecies

Divine healing

    USE **Spiritual healing**

Diving   **797.2**

    Use for materials on diving from a board or platform. Materials on underwater diving with equipment are entered under **Deep diving.**

    BT   **Swimming**

          Water sports

    RT   **Deep diving**

Divinity of Jesus Christ

    USE **Jesus Christ—Divinity**

Division of powers

    USE **Separation of powers**

Divorce (May subdiv. geog.)   **173; 306.89; 346.01**

    UF   Separation (Law)

    BT   **Family**

    NT   **Children of divorced parents**

          Desertion and nonsupport

          Divorce mediation

    RT   **Domestic relations**

Divorce counseling

    USE **Divorce mediation**

Divorce mediation   **362.82**

    UF   Divorce counseling

          Mediation, Divorce

    BT   **Divorce**

    NT   **Child custody**

          Child support

    RT   **Marriage counseling**

DNA   **572.8**

    UF   Deoxyribonucleic acid

    BT   **Cells**

          Heredity

          Nucleic acids

    NT   **Recombinant DNA**

DNA cloning

    USE **Molecular cloning**

DNA fingerprinting   **614**

    UF   DNA fingerprints *[Former heading]*

          DNA identification

          DNA profiling

          Genetic fingerprinting

          Genetic fingerprints

DNA fingerprinting—*Continued*
    Genetic profiling
  BT **Identification**
      Medical jurisprudence
DNA fingerprints
  USE **DNA fingerprinting**
DNA identification
  USE **DNA fingerprinting**
DNA profiling
  USE **DNA fingerprinting**
Docks 386; 387.1; 627
  BT **Hydraulic structures**
      Marinas
  RT **Harbors**
Doctor films
  USE **Medical drama (Films)**
Doctor novels
  USE **Medical novels**
Doctor radio programs
  USE **Medical drama (Radio programs)**
Doctor television programs
  USE **Medical drama (Television programs)**
Doctoral theses
  USE **Dissertations**
Doctors
  USE **Physicians**
Doctors' degrees
  USE **Academic degrees**
Doctrinal theology (May subdiv. geog.)
    230; 291.2
  UF Dogmatic theology
      Dogmatics
      Systematic theology
      Theology, Doctrinal
  SA names of religions or individual denominations with the subdivision *Doctrines,* e.g. **Christianity—Doctrines; Judaism—Doctrines;** etc., and religious topics with the subdivision *History of doctrines,* e.g. **Salvation—History of doctrines** [to be added as needed]
  BT **Theology**
  NT **Christianity—Doctrines**
      Creeds
      Grace (Theology)
      Human beings (Theology)
      Judaism—Doctrines

      Salvation
      Salvation—History of doctrines
Doctrine of fairness (Broadcasting)
  USE **Fairness doctrine (Broadcasting)**
Doctrines
  USE names of religions or individual denominations with the subdivision *Doctrines,* e.g. **Christianity—Doctrines; Judaism—Doctrines;** etc. [to be added as needed]
Documentaries (Motion pictures)
  USE **Documentary films**
Documentary films (May subdiv. geog.)
    070.1
  UF Documentaries (Motion pictures)
      Nonfiction films
  BT **Motion pictures**
Documentation 025
  SA subjects with the subdivision *Documentation,* e.g. **Agriculture—Documentation** [to be added as needed]
  BT **Information science**
  NT **Agriculture—Documentation**
      Archives
      Bibliographic control
      Bibliography
      Cataloging
      Conference proceedings
      Copying processes
      Information retrieval
      Libraries
      Library science
  RT **Information services**
Documents
  USE **Archives**
      Charters
      Government publications
Dog
  USE **Dogs**
Dog breeding
  USE **Dogs—Breeding**
Dog care
  USE **Dogs—Care**
Dog guides
  USE **Guide dogs**
Dogmatic theology
  USE **Doctrinal theology**

Dogmatics
USE **Doctrinal theology**
Dogs (May subdiv. geog.)   **599.77; 636.7**
UF Dog
Puppies
SA types of dogs, e.g. **Guide dogs;**
and names of specific breeds
of dogs [to be added as need-
ed]
BT **Domestic animals**
Mammals
NT **Collies**
Guide dogs
Hearing ear dogs
Dogs—Breeding   636.7
UF Dog breeding
BT **Breeding**
Dogs—Care   636.7
UF Dog care
Dogs—Fiction   808.83; 813, etc.
Use for collections of stories about dogs.
Materials about dog stories are entered under
Dogs in literature.
Dogs for the blind
USE **Guide dogs**
Dogs for the deaf
USE **Hearing ear dogs**
Dogs in art   704.9
BT **Art—Themes**
Dogs in literature   809
Use for materials about the depiction of
dogs in literary works. Collections of dog sto-
ries are entered under **Dogs—Fiction.**
BT **Literature—Themes**
Dogs—Psychology   636.7
BT **Animal intelligence**
Comparative psychology
Psychology
Dogs—Training   636.7
BT **Animals—Training**
Dogs—War use   355.4
UF War use of dogs
BT **Animals—War use**
Doll
USE **Dolls**
Dollhouses   688.7
BT **Miniature objects**
Toys
Dolls (May subdiv. geog.)   **688.7**
UF Doll
BT **Toys**

Domesday book   942.02
UF Doomsday book
BT **Great Britain—History—1066-
1154, Norman period**
Domestic animal dwellings
USE **Animal housing**
Domestic animals (May subdiv. geog.)
636
Use for general materials on farm animals.
Materials limited to animals as pets are en-
tered under **Pets.** Materials on stock raising as
an industry are entered under **Livestock in-
dustry.**
UF Domestication
Farm animals
Livestock
SA types of domestic animals, e.g.
Cattle [to be added as need-
ed]
BT **Animals**
NT **Cats**
Cattle
Dogs
Pigs
Poultry
Reindeer
Sheep
Working animals
RT **Livestock industry**
Pets
Domestic animals—Diseases
USE **Animals—Diseases**
Domestic animals—Housing
USE **Animal housing**
Domestic appliances
USE **Electric household appliances**
**Household equipment and sup-
plies**
Domestic architecture (May subdiv.
geog.)   **728**
Use for materials on residential buildings
from the standpoint of style and design. Gen-
eral materials on buildings in which people
live are entered under **Houses.**
UF Architecture, Domestic
Dwellings
Residences
SA types of residential buildings,
e.g. **Apartment houses** [to be
added as needed]
BT **Architecture**
NT **Apartment houses**
House construction
Prefabricated houses

Domestic architecture—*Continued*
    Solar homes
  RT **Houses**
Domestic architecture—Designs and
    plans **728**
  UF Home designs
    House plans
  BT **Architecture—Designs and**
    plans
Domestic economic assistance (May
    subdiv. geog.) **338.9**
  UF Anti-poverty programs
    Antipoverty programs
    Economic assistance
    Economic assistance, Domestic
    Poor relief
  BT **Economic policy**
  NT **Community development**
    Government lending
    Public works
    Subsidies
    Transfer payments
  RT **Grants-in-aid**
    Poverty
    Unemployed
Domestic finance
  USE **Household budgets**
    Personal finance
Domestic relations (May subdiv. geog.)
    346.01
  UF Family relations
  BT **Interpersonal relations**
  NT **Desertion and nonsupport**
    Visitation rights (Domestic re-
    lations)
  RT **Divorce**
    Family
    Family life education
    Marriage
Domestic violence (May subdiv. geog.)
    362.82
  UF Family violence *[Former head-*
    ing]
    Household violence
  BT **Violence**
  NT **Child abuse**
    Elderly abuse
    Wife abuse
Domestic workers
  USE **Household employees**
Domestication
  USE **Domestic animals**

Dominion of the sea
  USE **Sea power**
Dominions, British
  USE **Commonwealth countries**
Donation of organs, tissues, etc. **362.1**
  UF Organ donation
    Tissue donation
  BT **Gifts**
  RT **Transplantation of organs, tis-**
    sues, etc.
Donations
  USE **Gifts**
Doomsday book
  USE **Domesday book**
Door to door selling
  USE **Peddlers and peddling**
Doors **721**
  BT **Architecture—Details**
    Buildings
Double consciousness
  USE **Multiple personality**
Doubt
  USE **Belief and doubt**
Down syndrome **616.85**
  UF Down's syndrome
  BT **Mental retardation**
Down's syndrome
  USE **Down syndrome**
Downsizing of organizations **658.1**
  UF Corporate downsizing
    Organizational downsizing
    Organizational retrenchment
    Retrenchment of organizations
  BT **Organizational change**
  RT **Employees—Dismissal**
Draft **355.2**
  UF Compulsory military service
    Conscription, Military
    Military conscription
    Military draft
    Military service, Compulsory
    Military training, Universal
    Selective service
    Universal military training
  BT **Armies**
    Military law
    Recruiting and enlistment
  RT **Draft resisters**
Draft dodgers
  USE **Draft resisters**

Draft evaders
USE **Draft resisters**
Draft resisters   355.2
UF   Draft dodgers
         Draft evaders
SA   names of wars with the subdivision *Draft resisters* [to be added as needed]
NT   **World War, 1939-1945—Draft resisters**
RT   **Conscientious objectors**
         Draft
         Military desertion
Drafting, Mechanical
USE   **Mechanical drawing**
Dragons   398.24
BT   **Animals—Folklore**
         Folklore
         Monsters
         Mythical animals
Drainage (May subdiv. geog.)   631.6
Use for materials on land drainage. Materials on house drainage are entered under **House drainage.**
UF   Land drainage
BT   **Agricultural engineering**
         Civil engineering
         Hydraulic engineering
         Municipal engineering
         Reclamation of land
         Sanitary engineering
RT   **Sewerage**
Drainage, House
USE   **House drainage**
Drama   808.2; 808.82
Use for general materials on drama, not for individual works. Materials on the history and criticism of drama as literature are entered under **Drama—History and criticism.** Materials on criticism of drama as presented on the stage are entered under **Dramatic criticism.** Materials on the presentation of plays are entered under **Acting; Amateur theater;** or **Theater—Production and direction.** Collections of plays are entered under **Drama—Collections; American drama—Collections; English drama—Collections;** etc.
UF   Stage
SA   subjects, historical events, names of countries, cities, etc., ethnic groups, classes of persons, and names of individual persons with the subdivision *Drama,* to express the theme or subject content of collections of plays, e.g. **Easter—Drama; United States—History—1861-1865, Civil War—Drama; Napoleon I, Emperor of the French, 1769-1821—Drama;** etc. [to be added as needed]
BT   **Literature**
NT   **Acting**
         American drama
         Ballet
         Children's plays
         Choral speaking
         College and school drama
         Comedies
         Comedy
         Didactic drama
         Drama in education
         Dramatists
         English drama
         Folk drama
         Historical drama
         Horror plays
         Masks (Plays)
         Melodrama
         Morality plays
         Motion picture plays
         Mystery and detective plays
         One act plays
         Opera
         Pantomimes
         Pastoral drama
         Puppets and puppet plays
         Radio plays
         Religious drama
         Science fiction plays
         Television plays
         Tragedies
         Tragedy
RT   **Dramatic criticism**
         Theater
Drama—Collections   808.82; 812.008, etc.
Use for collections of plays by several authors.
UF   Plays
Drama—History and criticism   809.2
Use for materials on criticism of drama as a literary form. Materials on criticism of drama as presented on the stage are entered under **Dramatic criticism.**

Drama—History and criticism—*Continued*
    NT   **English drama—History and criticism**
    RT   **Dramatic criticism**
Drama in education   372.66
    BT   **Drama**
    RT   **Acting**
          Amateur theater
          College and school drama
          School assembly programs
Drama—Technique   808.2
    UF   Play writing
          Playwriting
    BT   **Authorship**
    NT   **Motion picture plays—Technique**
          Radio plays—Technique
          Television plays—Technique
Dramatic art
    USE **Acting**
Dramatic criticism   792.9
    Use for materials on criticism of drama as presented on the stage. Materials on criticism of drama as a literary form are entered under **Drama—History and criticism; American drama—History and criticism;** etc.
    UF   Theater criticism
    BT   **Criticism**
    RT   **Drama**
          Drama—History and criticism
          Theater
Dramatic music
    USE **Musicals**
          Opera
          Operetta
Dramatic plots
    USE **Stories, plots, etc.**
Dramatic production
    USE names of dramatists with the subdivision *Dramatic production,* e.g. **Shakespeare, William, 1564-1616—Dramatic production** [to be added as needed]
Dramatists   809.2; 920
    Use for materials on the personal lives of several playwrights, not limited to a single national literature. Materials dealing with their literary work are entered under **Drama—History and criticism; English drama—History and criticism;** etc.

    UF   Playwrights
    SA   dramatists of particular countries, e.g. **American dramatists** [to be added as needed]
    BT   **Authors**
          Drama
    NT   **American dramatists**
Dramatists, American
    USE **American dramatists**
Draperies   645; 684
    UF   Curtains
          Drapery *[Former heading]*
    BT   **Interior design**
          Upholstery
Drapery
    USE **Draperies**
Draughts
    USE **Checkers**
Drawing   741; 743
    UF   Drawings
          Sketching
    SA   drawing of particular countries, e.g. **American drawing** [to be added as needed]
    BT   **Art**
          Graphic arts
    NT   **American drawing**
          Architectural drawing
          Artistic anatomy
          Commercial art
          Crayon drawing
          Figure drawing
          Geometrical drawing
          Graphic methods
          Landscape drawing
          Map drawing
          Mechanical drawing
          Pastel drawing
          Pen drawing
          Pencil drawing
          Shades and shadows
          Topographical drawing
    RT   **Illustration of books**
          Painting
          Perspective
Drawing, American
    USE **American drawing**
Drawing materials
    USE **Artists' materials**
Drawings
    USE **Drawing**

Dream interpretation
USE **Dreams**
Dreaming
USE **Dreams**
Dreams 154.6
UF Dream interpretation
Dreaming
BT **Visions**
NT **Fantasy**
RT **Sleep**
Subconsciousness
Dredging 627
BT **Civil engineering**
Hydraulic engineering
Dress
USE **Clothing and dress**
Dress accessories 391.4; 646
BT **Clothing and dress**
Dressage
USE **Horsemanship**
Dressing of ores
USE **Ore dressing**
Dressmaking 646.4; 687
UF Garment making
BT **Clothing and dress**
Clothing industry
RT **Needlework**
Sewing
Tailoring
Dressmaking—Patterns 646.4; 687
Dried flowers
USE **Flowers—Drying**
Dried foods 641.4; 664
UF Dehydrated foods
BT **Food**
NT **Dried milk**
Freeze-dried foods
RT **Food—Preservation**
Dried milk 637
UF Dehydrated milk
Powdered milk
BT **Dried foods**
Milk
Drifting of continents
USE **Continental drift**
Drill and minor tactics 355.5
UF Military drill
Minor tactics
BT **Tactics**
RT **Military art and science**

Drill (Nonmilitary)
USE **Marching drills**
Drilling and boring
USE **Drilling and boring (Earth and rocks)**
Drilling and boring (Metal, wood, etc.)
Drilling and boring (Earth and rocks) 622
Use for materials on the operation of cutting holes in earth or rock. Materials on workshop operations in metal, wood, etc., are entered under **Drilling and boring (Metal, wood, etc.)**.
UF Boring *[Former heading]*
Drilling and boring
Shaft sinking
Well boring
BT **Hydraulic engineering**
Mining engineering
Water supply engineering
NT **Oil well drilling**
RT **Tunnels**
Wells
Drilling and boring (Metal, wood, etc.) 621.9
Use for materials on workshop operations in metal, wood, etc. Materials on the operation of cutting holes in earth or rock are entered under **Drilling and boring (Earth and rocks)**.
UF Boring
Drilling and boring *[Former heading]*
BT **Machine shop practice**
RT **Machine tools**
Drilling, Oil well
USE **Oil well drilling**
Drilling platforms 627
UF Marine drilling platforms
Ocean drilling platforms
Oil drilling platforms
Platforms, Drilling
BT **Ocean engineering**
Offshore oil well drilling
Drills, Marching
USE **Marching drills**
Drinking age (May subdiv. geog.) 344; 363.4
UF Minimum drinking age
BT **Age**
Teenagers—Alcohol use
Youth—Alcohol use

Drinking and employees
  USE **Employees—Alcohol use**
Drinking and teenagers
  USE **Teenagers—Alcohol use**
Drinking and youth
  USE **Youth—Alcohol use**
Drinking in the workplace
  USE **Employees—Alcohol use**
Drinking of alcoholic beverages (May
    subdiv. geog.)   **178; 363.4; 394.1;
    613.81**

  Use for materials on drinking in its social
aspects and as a social problem.

  UF   Alcohol consumption
       Alcohol use
       Alcoholic beverage consumption
       Consumption of alcoholic bever-
         ages
       Drinking problem
       Liquor problem
       Social drinking
  SA   classes of persons and ethnic
         groups with the subdivision
         Alcohol use, e.g. **Employ-
         ees—Alcohol use; Youth—
         Alcohol use;** etc. [to be add-
         ed as needed]
  NT   **Drunk driving**
  RT   **Alcoholic beverages**
       Alcoholism
       Temperance
Drinking problem
  USE **Alcoholism**
       Drinking of alcoholic beverages
Drinking water (May subdiv. geog.)
    363.6; 628.1
  UF   Potable water
       Tap water
  BT   **Water**
       Water supply
Drinks
  USE **Alcoholic beverages**
       Beverages
       Liquors
Driver education
  USE **Automobile driver education**
Drivers, Automobile
  USE **Automobile drivers**
Drivers' licenses (May subdiv. geog.)
    353.9; 629.28
  UF   Automobile drivers' licenses
       Automobiles—Drivers' licenses

       Motor vehicles—Drivers' li-
         censes
  BT   **Safety regulations**
Driving under the influence of alcohol
  USE **Drunk driving**
Driving while intoxicated
  USE **Drunk driving**
Dromedaries
  USE **Camels**
Drop forging
  USE **Forging**
Dropouts (May subdiv. geog.)   **371.2**
  UF   College dropouts
       Elementary school dropouts
       High school dropouts
       School dropouts
       Student dropouts
       Teenage dropouts
  BT   **Students**
       Youth
  RT   **At risk students**
       Educational counseling
       School attendance
Droughts (May subdiv. geog.)   **551.57;
    632**
  BT   **Meteorology**
  NT   **Dust storms**
  RT   **Rain**
Drowning prevention
  USE **Water safety**
Drug abuse (May subdiv. geog.)   **362.29;
    613.8; 616.86**

  Use for general materials on the misuse or
abuse of drugs. Materials on the abuse of a
particular drug or kind of drugs are entered
under this heading and also under the drug or
kind of drugs, e.g. **Cocaine; Hallucinogens;**
etc.

  UF   Addiction to drugs
       Drug addiction
       Drug habit
       Drug misuse
       Drug use
       Drugs—Abuse
       Drugs—Misuse
       Narcotic abuse
       Narcotic addiction
       Narcotic habit
       Substance abuse
  SA   classes of persons with the sub-
         division *Drug use,* e.g. **Crim-
         inals—Drug use;** and types

Drug abuse—*Continued*

> of drug abuse, e.g. **Medica-tion abuse** [to be added as needed]

  BT **Social problems**
  NT **Medication abuse**
  RT **Drug addicts**
      Drugs
      Solvent abuse
      Twelve-step programs

Drug abuse counseling **362.29; 613.8**

  UF Drug addiction counseling
      Drug counseling
      Narcotic addiction counseling
  BT **Counseling**
  NT **Drug addicts—Rehabilitation**

Drug abuse education
  USE **Drug education**

Drug abuse—Physiological effect
  USE **Drugs—Physiological effect**

Drug abuse screening
  USE **Drug testing**

Drug abuse—Study and teaching
  USE **Drug education**

Drug abuse—Testing
  USE **Drug testing**

Drug abusing physicians
  USE **Physicians—Drug use**

Drug addicted physicians
  USE **Physicians—Drug use**

Drug addiction
  USE **Drug abuse**

Drug addiction counseling
  USE **Drug abuse counseling**

Drug addiction education
  USE **Drug education**

Drug addicts (May subdiv. geog.)
      362.29; 616.86

  UF Addicts
      Narcotic addicts
  SA classes of persons with the sub-division *Drug use,* e.g. **Crim-inals—Drug use** [to be added as needed]
  NT **Children of drug addicts**
      Recovering addicts
  RT **Drug abuse**

Drug addicts—Rehabilitation **362.29; 613.8; 616.86**

  BT **Drug abuse counseling**

Drug counseling
  USE **Drug abuse counseling**

Drug dealing
  USE **Drug traffic**

Drug education (May subdiv. geog.)
      362.29; 371.7; 613.8

  Use for materials on the study of drugs, including their source, abuse, chemical composition, and social, physical, and personal effects.

  UF Drug abuse education
      Drug abuse—Study and teaching
      Drug addiction education
  BT **Health education**

Drug habit
  USE **Drug abuse**

Drug misuse
  USE **Drug abuse**

Drug plants
  USE **Medical botany**

Drug pushers
  USE **Drug traffic**

Drug stores
  USE **Drugstores**

Drug testing **344; 658.3**

  Use for materials on testing to identify personal use or misuse of drugs. Materials on the testing of drugs for safety or effectiveness are entered under **Drugs—Testing.**

  UF Drug abuse screening
      Drug abuse—Testing
      Screening for drug abuse
      Testing for drug abuse
  SA classes of persons with the sub-division *Drug testing,* e.g. **Employees—Drug testing** [to be added as needed]
  NT **Employees—Drug testing**

Drug testing in the workplace
  USE **Employees—Drug testing**

Drug therapy **615.5**

  UF Chemotherapy
      Pharmacotherapy
  SA names of diseases other than cancer with the subdivision *Drug therapy,* e.g. **Mental ill-ness—Drug therapy** [to be added as needed]
  BT **Therapeutics**
  NT **Antibiotics**
      Cancer—Chemotherapy
      Mental illness—Drug therapy
  RT **Drugs**
      Pharmacology

Drug trade, Illicit
  USE **Drug traffic**
Drug traffic (May subdiv. geog.)
    363.45; 364.1
  UF Drug dealing
      Drug pushers
      Drug trade, Illicit
      Narcotic traffic
      Smuggling of drugs
      Trafficking in drugs
      Trafficking in narcotics
  BT **Drugs and crime**
Drug use
  USE **Drug abuse**
       Drugs
       and classes of persons with the
       subdivision *Drug use,* e.g.
       **Criminals—Drug use; Employees—Drug use;
       Teenagers—Drug use;
       Youth—Drug use;** etc. [to be
       added as needed]
Drugs 615
  UF Drug use
      Pharmaceuticals
  SA classes of persons with the sub-
      division *Drug use,* e.g. **Criminals—Drug use;** types of
      drugs, e.g. **Amphetamines;
      Hallucinogens; Narcotics;
      Stimulants;** etc.; and names
      of individual drugs, e.g.
      Crack (Drug); Marijuana;
      etc. [to be added as needed]
  BT **Pharmacy**
      Therapeutics
  NT **Designer drugs**
      Drugs and crime
      Generic drugs
      Hallucinogens
      Narcotics
      Nonprescription drugs
      Orphan drugs
      Psychotropic drugs
      Steroids
      Stimulants
      Sulfonamides
  RT **Drug abuse**
      Drug therapy
      Materia medica
      Pharmacology

Drugs—Abuse
  USE **Drug abuse**
Drugs—Adulteration and analysis
  USE **Pharmacology**
Drugs and crime (May subdiv. geog.)
    364.1
    Use for general materials on the relationship
    of drugs and crime. Materials on the illicit
    drug trade are entered under **Drug traffic.**
    Materials on the use of drugs by criminals are
    entered under **Criminals—Drug use.**
  UF Crime and drugs
      Crime and narcotics
      Narcotics and crime
  BT **Crime**
      Drugs
  NT **Drug traffic**
  RT **Criminals—Drug use**
Drugs and criminals
  USE **Criminals—Drug use**
Drugs and employees
  USE **Employees—Drug use**
Drugs and sports
  USE **Athletes—Drug use**
Drugs and teenagers
  USE **Teenagers—Drug use**
Drugs and youth
  USE **Youth—Drug use**
Drugs—Chemistry
  USE **Pharmaceutical chemistry**
Drugs—Generic substitution
  USE **Generic drugs**
Drugs in the workplace
  USE **Employees—Drug use**
Drugs—Misuse
  USE **Drug abuse**
Drugs, Nonprescription
  USE **Nonprescription drugs**
Drugs—Physiological effect   615; 616.86
    Use for materials limited to the effect of
    drugs on the functions of living organisms.
  UF Drug abuse—Physiological effect
  SA names of drugs with the subdi-
         vision *Physiological effect* [to
         be added as needed]
  BT **Pharmacology**
  NT **Opium—Physiological effect**
**Drugs—Psychological aspects   615;
    616.86**
  BT **Applied psychology**
Drugs—Testing   363.19
    Use for materials on the testing of drugs for
    safety or effectiveness. Materials on testing to

Drugs—Testing—*Continued*

identify the personal use or misuse or drugs are entered under **Drug testing.**

UF   Clinical drug trials

Clinical trials of drugs

BT   **Consumer protection**

Pharmacology

Drugstores   381

Use for materials on business establishments that sell drugs. Materials on the art or practice of preparing, preserving, and dispensing drugs are entered under **Pharmacy.**

UF   Chemists' shops

Drug stores

Pharmacies

BT   **Retail trade**

Stores

Druids and Druidism   299

BT   **Celts**

Religions

Drum

USE   **Drums**

Drum majoring   784.9; 791.6

BT   **Bands (Music)**

RT   **Baton twirling**

Drums   786.9

UF   Drum

BT   **Musical instruments**

Percussion instruments

Drunk driving   363.12; 364.1

UF   Driving under the influence of alcohol

Driving while intoxicated

BT   **Crime**

Drinking of alcoholic beverages

Drunkards

USE   **Alcoholics**

Drunkenness

USE   **Alcoholism**

Temperance

Dry cleaning   667

UF   Clothing and dress—Dry cleaning

BT   **Cleaning**

Dry farming (May subdiv. geog.)   **631.5**

UF   Farming, Dry

BT   **Agriculture**

Dry goods

USE   **Fabrics**

Drying   660

SA   materials, products, or objects dried with the subdivision *Drying,* e.g. **Flowers—Drying** [to be added as needed]

BT   **Industrial chemistry**

Dual-career couples

USE   **Dual-career families**

Dual-career families   306.85; 646.7

Use for materials on families in which both the husband and wife are pursuing careers.

UF   Dual-career couples

Dual career family *[Former heading]*

Dual-career marriage

Dual-income couples

Two-career couples

Two-career families

Two-career family

Two-income families

Working couples

BT   **Family**

RT   **Work and family**

Dual career family

USE   **Dual-career families**

Dual-career marriage

USE   **Dual-career families**

Dual-income couples

USE   **Dual-career families**

Ducks   598.4; 636.5

BT   **Birds**

Poultry

Ductless glands

USE   **Endocrine glands**

Due process of law (May subdiv. geog.)   **347**

Use for materials on the regular administration of the law, according to which citizens may not be denied their legal rights and all laws must conform to fundamental and accepted legal principles. Materials on legal hearings before an impartial and disinterested tribunal are entered under **Fair trial.**

UF   Procedural due process

Substantive due process

BT   **Administration of justice**

Civil rights

NT   **Fair trial**

Dueling (May subdiv. geog.)   **179.7; 394**

UF   Fighting

BT   **Manners and customs**

Martial arts

Dumps, Toxic

USE   **Hazardous waste sites**

Dunes
   USE   **Sand dunes**
Duplicate bridge
   USE   **Bridge (Game)**
Duplicating machines
   USE   **Copying machines**
Duplicating processes
   USE   **Copying processes**
Dust, Radioactive
   USE   **Radioactive fallout**
Dust storms   551.55
   BT   **Droughts**
        Erosion
        Storms
Dusting and spraying
   USE   **Spraying and dusting**
Duties
   USE   **Tariff**
        Taxation
Duty   170
   BT   **Ethics**
        Human behavior
   NT   **Conscience**
Dwarf trees   582.16; 635.9
   SA   types of dwarf trees, e.g. **Bonsai**
        [to be added as needed]
   BT   **Trees**
   NT   **Bonsai**
Dwarfism   616.4
   UF   Growth retardation
   BT   **Growth disorders**
Dwellings
   USE   **Domestic architecture**
        Houses
        Housing
        and ethnic groups and classes
        of persons with the subdivi-
        sion *Dwellings,* for materials
        on the residential buildings of
        a group from the standpoint
        of architecture, construction,
        or ethnology, e.g. **Native
        Americans—Dwellings;** and
        ethnic groups and classes of
        persons with the subdivision
        Housing, for materials on the
        social and economic aspects
        of providing housing for the
        group, e.g. **Physically handi-
        capped—Housing** [to be add-
        ed as needed]

Dyes and dyeing   646.6; 667; 746.6
   SA   types of dyes and types of dye-
        ing [to be added as needed]
   BT   **Color**
        Pigments
        Textile chemistry
        Textile industry
   NT   **Batik**
        Tie dyeing
   RT   **Bleaching**
Dying children
   USE   **Terminally ill children**
Dying patients
   USE   **Terminally ill**
Dynamics   531
   UF   Kinetics
   BT   **Mathematics**
        Mechanics
   NT   **Aerodynamics**
        Astrodynamics
        Chaos (Science)
        Hydrodynamics
        Kinematics
        Matter
        Motion
        Quantum theory
        Thermodynamics
   RT   **Force and energy**
        Physics
        Statics
Dynamite   662
   BT   **Explosives**
Dynamos
   USE   **Electric generators**
Dyslexia   371.91; 616.85
   BT   **Reading disability**
Dyspepsia
   USE   **Indigestion**
Dystopias   811, etc.; 813, etc.
     May be used for individual works, collec-
   tions, or materials about dystopias.
   UF   Anti-utopias
   BT   **Fantasy fiction**
        Science fiction
   RT   **Utopian fiction**
E-mail
   USE   **Electronic mail systems**
E-mail discussion groups
   USE   **Electronic discussion groups**
Eagles   598.9
   BT   **Birds**
        Birds of prey

Ear   611; 612.8
   BT   Head
   NT   Deafness
   RT   Hearing
Early Christian literature   270.1
   Use for individual works or collections of the writings of early Christian authors. Materials on the lives and thought of the leaders of the Christian church up to the time of Gregory the Great in the West and John of Damascus in the East are entered under **Fathers of the church.**
   UF   Christian literature—30-600, Early
        Christian literature, Early
   BT   **Christian literature**
        Literature
        Medieval literature
   RT   **Church history—30-600, Early church**
        Fathers of the church
        Latin literature
Early church history
   USE   **Church history—30-600, Early church**
Early printed books (May subdiv. geog.) **094**
   SA   subjects with the subdivision *Early works to 1800,* for materials on those subjects written before 1800, e.g. **Political science—Early works to 1800** [to be added as needed]
   BT   **Books**
Early printed books—15th century
   USE   **Incunabula**
Early works to 1800
   USE   subjects with the subdivision *Early works to 1800,* for materials on those subjects written before 1800, e.g. **Political science—Early works to 1800** [to be added as needed]
Earth   525; 550
   Use for general materials on the whole planet. Materials limited to the structure and composition of the earth and the physical changes it has undergone and is still undergoing are entered under **Geology.**
   UF   World
   BT   **Planets**
        Solar system
   NT   **Antarctica**
        Arctic regions

        Atmosphere
        Continents
        Earthquakes
        Gaia hypothesis
        Geodesy
        Geography
        Ice age
        Latitude
        Longitude
        Ocean
        Tropics
   RT   **Earth sciences**
        Geology
        Physical geography
Earth—Age   551.7
Earth—Chemical composition
   USE   **Geochemistry**
Earth—Crust   551.1
   BT   **Earth—Internal structure**
   NT   **Plate tectonics**
   RT   **Earth—Surface**
Earth, Effect of man on
   USE   **Human influence on nature**
Earth fills
   USE   **Landfills**
Earth—Internal structure   551.1
   NT   **Earth—Crust**
Earth sciences   550
   UF   Geoscience
   BT   **Physical sciences**
        Science
   NT   **Climate**
        Geochemistry
        Geography
        Geology
        Geophysics
        Meteorology
        Oceanography
        Water
   RT   **Earth**
Earth sheltered houses   690; 728
   UF   Underground houses
   BT   **House construction**
        Houses
        Underground architecture
Earth—Surface   551.1
   UF   Surface of the earth
   NT   **Landforms**
   RT   **Earth—Crust**
Earthenware
   USE   **Pottery**

Earthly paradise
USE **Paradise**
Earthquake effects
USE types of structures with the sub-
division *Earthquake effects,*
e.g. **Skyscrapers—Earth-
quake effects** [to be added as
needed]
Earthquake sea waves
USE **Tsunamis**
Earthquakes (May subdiv. geog.)
551.22
UF **Seismography**
Seismology
SA types of structures subject to
earthquake forces with the
subdivision *Earthquake effects,*
e.g. **Skyscrapers—Earth-
quake effects** [to be added as
needed]
BT **Earth**
Geology
Natural disasters
Physical geography
NT **Buildings—Earthquake effects**
**Skyscrapers—Earthquake ef-
fects**
Earthquakes and building
USE **Buildings—Earthquake effects**
Earthquakes—California   551.2209794
Earthquakes—United States   551.220973
Earthworks (Archeology)
USE **Excavations (Archeology)**
Earthworks (Art) (May subdiv. geog.)
709.04
UF Landscape sculpture
Site oriented art
BT **Art**
East
USE **Asia**
East Africa   967.6
Use for materials dealing collectively with
the eastern regions of Africa. The term usual-
ly includes the areas now occupied by Burun-
di, Kenya, Rwanda, Tanzania, Uganda, and
Somalia, and sometimes Malawi and Mozam-
bique as well.
UF Africa, East
Africa, Eastern
Eastern Africa
BT **Africa**

East and West   306; 909
Use for materials on both acculturation and
cultural conflict between Asian and Occidental
civilizations.
BT **International relations**
NT **Asia—Civilization**
Western civilization
RT **Acculturation**
East Asia   950
Use for materials that deal collectively with
the eastern regions of Asia including China,
Japan, Korea, and Taiwan.
UF East (Far East)
Far East
Orient
BT **Asia**
RT **Pacific rim**
East (Far East)
USE **East Asia**
East Germany
USE **Germany (East)**
East Goths
USE **Goths**
East Indians   305.891; 954
UF Indians (of India)
Easter (May subdiv. geog.)   **263;
394.2667**
BT **Christian holidays**
Holy Week
RT **Lent**
Easter carols
USE **Carols**
Easter—Drama   808.82; 812, etc.
Use for collections of plays about Easter.
BT **Religious drama**
Easter egg decoration
USE **Egg decoration**
Eastern Africa
USE **East Africa**
Eastern churches   281
BT **Christian sects**
Christianity
NT **Orthodox Eastern Church**
Eastern Empire
USE **Byzantine Empire**
Eastern Europe   947
UF Europe, Eastern
Eastern Europe—History   947
**Eastern Europe—History—1989-
947.085; 947.086**
Eastern Seaboard
USE **Atlantic States**

Easy and quick cooking
  USE **Quick and easy cooking**
Easy reading materials 372.41
  UF Beginning reading materials
      Preprimers
      Preschool reading materials
      Primers
  BT **Children's literature**
      Reading materials
Eating
  USE **Dining**
      Gastronomy
Eating customs (May subdiv. geog.)
      394.1
  UF Food customs
      Food habits
  BT **Diet**
      Human behavior
      Nutrition
  NT **Table etiquette**
  RT **Dining**
Eating disorders 616.85
  SA types of eating disorders [to be
      added as needed]
  BT **Abnormal psychology**
  NT **Anorexia nervosa**
      Bulimia
Eavesdropping 363.25
  UF Bugging, Electronic
      Electronic bugging
      Electronic eavesdropping
      Electronic listening devices
      Listening devices
  BT **Criminal investigation**
      Right of privacy
  RT **Wiretapping**
Eccentrics and eccentricities (May subdiv.
      geog.) **920**
  UF Cranks
  BT **Curiosities and wonders**
      Personality
  NT **Hermits**
Ecclesiastical antiquities
  USE **Christian antiquities**
Ecclesiastical architecture
  USE **Church architecture**
Ecclesiastical art
  USE **Christian art**
Ecclesiastical biography
  USE **Christian biography**

Ecclesiastical fasts and feasts
  USE **Religious holidays**
Ecclesiastical furniture
  USE **Church furniture**
Ecclesiastical history
  USE **Church history**
Ecclesiastical institutions
  USE **Religious institutions**
Ecclesiastical law 262.9
  UF Canon law
      Church law
  BT **Church**
      Law
  NT **Tithes**
Ecclesiastical rites and ceremonies
  USE **Rites and ceremonies**
Ecclesiastical year
  USE **Church year**
Eclipses, Lunar
  USE **Lunar eclipses**
Eclipses, Solar
  USE **Solar eclipses**
Eclogues
  USE **Pastoral poetry**
Eco-development
  USE **Economic development—Envi-**
      ronmental aspects
Ecodevelopment
  USE **Economic development—Envi-**
      ronmental aspects
Ecological movement
  USE **Environmental movement**
Ecology (May subdiv. geog.) **577**
  UF Balance of nature
      Biology—Ecology
      Ecosystems
  SA types of ecology, e.g. **Marine**
      ecology; and types of ani-
      mals, plants, and crops with
      the subdivision *Ecology* [to be
      added as needed]
  BT **Biology**
      Environment
  NT **Adaptation (Biology)**
      Biogeography
      Environmental protection
      Food chains (Ecology)
      Gaia hypothesis
      Marine ecology
      Plant ecology
      Symbiosis

Ecology—*Continued*
  RT **Biological diversity**
Ecology, Human
  USE **Human ecology**
Ecology, Social
  USE **Human ecology**
Economic aid
  USE **Foreign aid**
Economic aspects
  USE subjects with the subdivision
       Economic aspects, e.g. **Agri-
       culture—Economic aspects**
       [to be added as needed]
Economic assistance
  USE **Domestic economic assistance**
       Foreign aid
Economic assistance, American
  USE **American foreign aid**
Economic assistance, Domestic
  USE **Domestic economic assistance**
Economic biology
  USE **Economic botany**
       Economic zoology
Economic botany   581.6
  UF Agricultural botany
      Botany, Economic
      Economic biology
  BT **Agriculture**
      Botany
  NT **Cotton**
      Edible plants
      Forage plants
      Forest products
      Plant conservation
      Plant introduction
      Poisonous plants
      Weeds
Economic conditions   330.9
   Use for general materials on some or all of
the following: natural resources, business,
commerce, industry, labor, manufactures, fi-
nancial conditions. Materials on the history of
the economic development of several countries are entered under **Economic development.**
  UF Economic history
      National resources
      World economics
  SA racial and ethnic groups, classes
      of persons, and names of
      countries, cities, areas, etc.,
      with the subdivision *Economic*

conditions, e.g. **African
       Americans—Economic condi-
       tions; United States—Eco-
       nomic conditions;** etc. [to be
       added as needed]
  BT **Business**
      Economics
      Social conditions
      Wealth
  NT **African Americans—Economic
       conditions**
      Blacks—Economic conditions
      Business cycles
      **Chicago (Ill.)—Economic con-
       ditions**
      Developing countries
      Great Depression, 1929-1939
      Industrial revolution
      Jews—Economic conditions
      Labor supply
      **Native Americans—Economic
       conditions**
      Natural resources
      Ohio—Economic conditions
      Poverty
      Quality of life
      **United States—Economic con-
       ditions**
  RT **Commercial geography**
      Economic development
Economic cycles
  USE **Business cycles**
Economic depressions
  USE **Depressions**
Economic development   338.9
   Use for materials on the theory and policy
of economic development. Materials restricted
to a particular place are entered under the
name of the country, city, or area with the
subdivisions *Economic conditions; Economic
policy;* or *Industries.*
  UF Development, Economic
      Economic growth
  BT **Economic policy**
      Economics
  NT **Sustainable development**
  RT **Economic conditions**
**Economic development—Environmental
   aspects   333.7; 338.9**
   Use for general materials on the environmental impact of economic development. Materials on economic development that satisfies
the needs of the present generation without

227

Economic development—Environmental aspects—*Continued*
depleting natural resources for the future or having adverse environmental effects are entered under **Sustainable development.**
- UF Eco-development
  Ecodevelopment

Economic forecasting   338.5
- BT **Business cycles**
  Economics
  Forecasting
- NT **Business forecasting**
  Employment forecasting

Economic geography
- USE **Commercial geography**

Economic geology   553
- UF Geology, Economic
- SA types of geological products, e.g. **Asbestos; Gypsum;** etc. [to be added as needed]
- BT **Geology**
- NT **Mines and mineral resources**
  Petroleum geology
  Quarries and quarrying
  Soils
  Stone

Economic growth
- USE **Economic development**

Economic history
- USE **Economic conditions**

Economic mobilization
- USE **Industrial mobilization**

Economic planning
- USE **Economic policy**

Economic policy (May subdiv. geog.) **338.9**
Use for materials on the policy of government in economic affairs.
- UF Business and government
  Business—Government policy
  Central planning
  Economic planning
  Government and business
  Government policy
  National planning
  State planning
- SA subjects with the subdivision *Government policy,* e.g. **Agriculture—Government policy;** and types of activities, facilities, industries, services, and undertakings with the subdivision *Planning,* e.g. **Transportation—Planning** [to be added as needed]
- BT **Economics**
  Planning
- NT **Commercial policy**
  Domestic economic assistance
  Economic development
  Fiscal policy
  Foreign aid
  Free enterprise
  Government lending
  Government ownership
  Industrial mobilization
  Industrial policy
  Industrialization
  International economic relations
  Labor policy
  Land reform
  Monetary policy
  Municipal ownership
  Privatization
  Sanctions (International law)
  Subsidies
  Tariff
  Transfer payments
  Welfare state
- RT **National security**
  Social policy

Economic policy—Ohio   338.9771
- UF Ohio—Economic policy *[Former heading]*

Economic policy—United States 338.973
- UF United States—Economic policy *[Former heading]*

Economic recessions
- USE **Recessions**

Economic relations, Foreign
- USE **International economic relations**

Economic sanctions
- USE **Sanctions (International law)**

Economic sustainability
- USE **Sustainable development**

Economic zones (Maritime law)
- USE **Territorial waters**

Economic zoology   591.6
Use for general materials on animals injurious or beneficial to agriculture, and for mate-

Economic zoology—*Continued*
rials on the extermination of wild animals, venomous snakes, etc.

UF   Animals, Useful and harmful
Economic biology
Zoology, Economic

BT   **Zoology**

NT   **Agricultural pests**
Beneficial insects
Furbearing animals
Insect pests
Livestock industry
Pest control
Pests
Poisonous animals
Wildlife conservation
Working animals

Economics (May subdiv. geog.)   **330**

Use for materials on the science of economics. This heading may be subdivided geographically for materials on this branch of learning in a particular place. Materials on the economic conditions of a particular place are entered under the name of the place with the subdivision *Economic conditions.*

UF   Distribution of wealth
Political economy
Production

SA   subjects with the subdivision
Economic aspects, e.g. **Agriculture—Economic aspects;**
and countries, states, cities, regions, etc., with the subdivision *Economic conditions,* e.g.
United States—Economic conditions [to be added as needed]

BT   **Social sciences**

NT   **Agriculture—Economic aspects**
Barter
Business
Capital
Capitalism
Christianity and economics
Commerce
Consumption (Economics)
Cooperation
Cost and standard of living
Economic conditions
Economic development
Economic forecasting
Economic policy
Employment
Finance

Income
Individualism
Industrial trusts
Industries
Labor
Land use
Marxism
Medical economics
Money
Monopolies
Population
Prices
Profit
Property
Saving and investment
Socialism
Statistics
Underground economy
Waste (Economics)
Wealth

Economics and Christianity
USE   **Christianity and economics**

Economics—History   **330.09; 330.1**

Use for materials describing the development of economic theories. Materials on the economic conditions and development of countries are entered under **Economic conditions.**

Economics of war
USE   **War—Economic aspects**

Economy
USE   **Saving and investment**

Economy cars
USE   **Compact cars**

Economy, Underground
USE   **Underground economy**

Ecosystems
USE   **Ecology**

Ecumenical councils
USE   **Councils and synods**

Ecumenical movement (May subdiv. geog.)   **280**

Use for materials on a movement originating in the twentieth century aimed at promoting church cooperation and unity. Materials on unity as one of the marks of the church are entered under **Church—Unity.** Materials on prospective and actual mergers within and across denominational lines are entered under **Christian union.** Materials on religious activities planned and conducted cooperatively by two or more Christian sects are entered under **Interdenominational cooperation.**

UF   Christian unity *[Former heading]*
Ecumenism

Ecumenical movement—*Continued*
  BT   **Christian sects**
       Church
  RT   **Christian union**
Ecumenism
  USE **Christian union**
       Ecumenical movement
Eddas   839
    May be used for individual works, collections, or materials about eddas.
  BT   **Old Norse literature**
       Poetry
       Scandinavian literature
Eden
  USE **Paradise**
Edible plants   581.6
  UF   Food plants
       Plants, Edible
  BT   **Economic botany**
       Food
       Plants
Edifices
  USE **Buildings**
Editing   070.5; 808
    Use for materials on the editing of books and texts. Materials on the editing of newspapers and periodicals are entered under **Journalism—Editing.**
  SA   subjects and types of literature with the subdivision *Editing,* e.g. **Poetry—Editing;** etc. [to be added as needed]
  BT   **Authorship**
       Publishers and publishing
  NT   **Journalism—Editing**
       Poetry—Editing
Editions   016
  UF   Bibliography—Editions
  BT   **Bibliography**
  NT   **Bilingual books**
       First editions
       Paperback books
       Reprints (Publications)
Education (May subdiv. geog.)   **370**
    Subdivisions listed under this heading may be used under other education headings where applicable.
  UF   Instruction
       Pedagogy
       Study and teaching
  SA   types of education [to be added as needed], e.g. **Vocational education;** classes of persons and social and ethnic groups with the subdivision *Education,* e.g. **Deaf—Education; African Americans—Education;** etc.; and subjects with the subdivision *Study and teaching,* e.g. **Science—Study and teaching** [to be added as needed]
  BT   **Civilization**
  NT   **Ability grouping in education**
       Adult education
       African Americans—Education
       Area studies
       Audiovisual education
       Automobile driver education
       Basic education
       Blacks—Education
       Blind—Education
       Books and reading
       Business education
       Church and education
       Classical education
       Coeducation
       Colleges and universities
       Consumer education
       Continuing education
       Cooperative learning
       Deaf—Education
       Distance education
       Educational evaluation
       Educational games
       Educational technology
       Educational tests and measurements
       Educators
       Elementary education
       Evening and continuation schools
       Family life education
       Foreign study
       Girls—Education
       Health education
       Higher education
       Home and school
       Home schooling
       International education
       Labor—Education
       Library education
       Literacy
       Mainstreaming in education

Education—*Continued*
>   Men—Education
>   Mentally handicapped children—Education
>   Military education
>   Moral education
>   Multicultural education
>   Native Americans—Education
>   Nature study
>   Naval education
>   Outdoor education
>   Physical education
>   Preschool education
>   Professional education
>   Psychology of learning
>   Religious education
>   Scholarships
>   School choice
>   Secondary education
>   Self-instruction
>   Simulation games in education
>   Socialization
>   Special education
>   Study skills
>   Teaching
>   Technical education
>   Veterans—Education
>   Vocational education
>   Women—Education
>   World War, 1939-1945—Education and the war
> RT Culture
>   Learning and scholarship
>   Schools

Education—Aims and objectives   370.11
Education and church
> USE **Church and education**
Education and radio
> USE **Radio in education**
Education and religion
> USE **Church and education**
Education and state
> USE **Education—Government policy**
Education and television
> USE **Television in education**
Education and the war
> USE names of wars with the subdivision *Education and the war,* e.g. **World War, 1939-1945—Education and the war** [to be added as needed]

Education associations
> USE **Education—Societies**
Education—Automation
> USE **Computer-assisted instruction**
Education, Bilingual
> USE **Bilingual education**
Education, Christian
> USE **Christian education**
Education, Compulsory
> USE **Compulsory education**
Education—Computer programs
> USE **Educational software**
Education—Curricula   375
> UF Core curriculum
>   Courses of study
>   Curricula
>   Schools—Curricula
> SA types of education and schools with the subdivision *Curricula,* e.g. **Library education—Curricula** [to be added as needed]
> NT **Articulation (Education)**
>   **Colleges and universities—Curricula**
>   **Curriculum planning**
>   **Library education—Curricula**
Education—Data processing
> USE **Computer-assisted instruction**
Education—Developing countries   370.9172
> UF Developing countries—Education
Education, Elementary
> USE **Elementary education**
Education—Experimental methods   371.3
> UF Activity schools
>   Experimental methods in education
>   Progressive education
>   Teaching—Experimental methods
> SA types of experimental methods, e.g. **Nongraded schools; Open plan schools;** etc. [to be added as needed]
> NT **Experimental schools**
>   **Nongraded schools**
>   **Open plan schools**
>   **Whole language**
Education—Federal aid
> USE **Federal aid to education**

Education—Finance   371.2; 379.1
  UF   School finance
       School taxes
       Tuition
  BT   **Finance**
  NT   **Government aid to education**
  RT   **Federal aid to education**
Education for librarianship
  USE   **Library education**
Education—Government aid
  USE   **Government aid to education**
Education—Government policy (May
     subdiv. geog.)   **379**
  UF   Education and state *[Former
       heading]*
       Educational policy
  BT   **Social policy**
  NT   **Compulsory education**
       Federal aid to education
       Government aid to education
Education, Higher
  USE   **Higher education**
Education, Industrial
  USE   **Industrial arts education**
Education—Integration
  USE   **School integration**
       Segregation in education
Education of adults
  USE   **Adult education**
Education of children
  USE   **Elementary education**
Education of criminals
  USE   **Prisoners—Education**
Education of men
  USE   **Men—Education**
Education of prisoners
  USE   **Prisoners—Education**
Education of the blind
  USE   **Blind—Education**
Education of the deaf
  USE   **Deaf—Education**
Education of veterans
  USE   **Veterans—Education**
Education of women
  USE   **Women—Education**
Education of workers
  USE   **Labor—Education**
Education—Personnel service
  USE   **Educational counseling**
Education, Preschool
  USE   **Preschool education**

Education, Primary
  USE   **Elementary education**
Education, Secondary
  USE   **Secondary education**
Education—Segregation
  USE   **Segregation in education**
Education—Societies   **370.6**
  UF   Education associations
       Educational associations *[Former
       heading]*
  BT   **Societies**
  NT   **Parent-teacher associations**
Education—State aid
  USE   **Government aid to education**
Education—Statistics   **370**
  BT   **Statistics**
Education—Study and teaching   **370.7**
     Use for materials on the study of education
  as a discipline. Materials on the history and
  methods of training teachers, including the ed-
  ucational functions of teachers colleges, are
  entered under **Teachers—Training.** Materials
  on the art of teaching and methods of teach-
  ing are entered under **Teaching.**
  UF   Pedagogy
  NT   **Teachers colleges**
       Teachers—Training
Education, Theological
  USE   **Theology—Study and teaching**
Education—United States   **370.973**
Educational accreditation
  USE   **Schools—Accreditation**
Educational achievement
  USE   **Academic achievement**
Educational administration
  USE   **Schools—Administration**
Educational assessment
  USE   **Educational evaluation**
Educational associations
  USE   **Education—Societies**
Educational consultants (May subdiv.
     geog.)   **370.7**
  BT   **Consultants**
Educational counseling (May subdiv.
     geog.)   **371.4**
     Use for materials on the assistance given to
  students by schools, colleges, or universities
  in the selection of a program of studies suited
  to their abilities, interests, future plans, and
  general circumstances. Materials on the assistance given to students in understanding and
  coping with adjustment problems are entered
  under **School counseling.** Materials on the activities and programs designed to help people
  plan, choose, and succeed in their careers are
  entered under **Vocational guidance.**

Educational counseling—_Continued_
    UF   Academic advising
            Education—Personnel service
            Educational guidance
            Guidance counseling, Educational
            Personnel service in education
            Student guidance
            Students—Counseling
    BT   **Counseling**
    RT   **Dropouts**
            School counseling
            Vocational guidance
Educational evaluation (May subdiv.
    geog.)   **370.7; 379.1**
    UF   Educational assessment
            Educational program evaluation
            Evaluation research in education
            Instructional systems analysis
            Program evaluation in education
            Self-evaluation in education
    SA   topics in education with the sub-
            division _Evaluation,_ e.g. **Sci-
            ence—Study and teaching—
            Evaluation** [to be added as
            needed]
    BT   **Education**
Educational films
    USE   **Libraries and motion pictures**
            Motion pictures in education
Educational freedom
    USE   **Academic freedom**
Educational games   371.33
    UF   Instructional games
            Instructive games
    BT   **Education**
            Games
    NT   **Simulation games in education**
Educational gaming
    USE   **Simulation games in education**
Educational guidance
    USE   **Educational counseling**
Educational measurements
    USE   **Educational tests and measure-
            ments**
Educational media
    USE   **Teaching—Aids and devices**
Educational media centers
    USE   **Instructional materials centers**
Educational policy
    USE   **Education—Government policy**
Educational program evaluation
    USE   **Educational evaluation**

Educational psychology   370.15
    BT   **Psychology**
            Teaching
    NT   **Ability grouping in education**
            Apperception
            Attention
            Imagination
            Intelligence tests
            Listening
            Memory
            Psychology of learning
            Thought and thinking
    RT   **Applied psychology**
            Child psychology
Educational reports
    USE   **School reports**
Educational simulation games
    USE   **Simulation games in education**
Educational sociology (May subdiv. geog.)
    306.43
    UF   Social problems in education
    BT   **Sociology**
Educational software   005.3
    UF   Education—Computer programs
    BT   **Computer software**
Educational surveys (May subdiv. geog.)
    370
    UF   School surveys
    BT   **Surveys**
Educational technology (May subdiv.
    geog.)   **371.33**
    UF   Instructional technology
    BT   **Education**
    RT   **Teaching—Aids and devices**
Educational television
    USE   **Public television**
            Television in education
Educational tests and measurements
    (May subdiv. geog.)   **371.26**
    UF   Educational measurements
            Tests
    BT   **Education**
            Examinations
    NT   **Ability—Testing**
            Achievement tests
            **Colleges and universities—En-
            trance examinations**
            Examinations
            **Grading and marking (Educa-
            tion)**

Educational tests and measurements—
Continued
    RT   **Intelligence tests**
          Psychological tests
Educators (May subdiv. geog.)   **370.92;**
    920

    Use for materials on people engaged professionally in the field of education in general. Materials on educators engaged in classroom or other instruction are entered under **Teachers.**

    UF   College teachers
          Faculty (Education)
          Professors
    BT   **Education**
    NT   **Teachers**
EEC
    USE **European Union**
Efficiency, Industrial
    USE **Industrial efficiency**
Egg decoration   **745.59**
    UF   Easter egg decoration
    BT   **Decoration and ornament**
          Handicraft
Eggs   **636.5; 641**

    Use for materials on chicken eggs or on animal eggs in general.

    SA   types of animals other than
          chickens with the subdivision
          Eggs, e.g. **Dinosaurs—Eggs**
          [to be added as needed]
    BT   **Food**
    NT   **Birds—Eggs**
          Dinosaurs—Eggs
Egypt   **962**

    May be subdivided like United States except for *History.*

Egypt—Antiquities   **932**
    UF   Egyptology
    BT   **Antiquities**
Egypt—History   **932; 962**
    NT   **Sinai Campaign, 1956**
Egypt—History—1970-   **962.05**
Egyptology
    USE **Egypt—Antiquities**
Eight-hour day
    USE **Hours of labor**
Eighteenth century
    USE **World history—18th century**
Elder abuse
    USE **Elderly abuse**
Elder care
    USE **Elderly—Care**

Elderly (May subdiv. geog.)   **155.67;**
    305.26
    UF   Aged
          Aging persons
          Elderly persons
          Older persons
          Senior citizens
    SA   elderly of particular racial or
          ethnic groups [to be added as
          needed]
    BT   **Age**
          Gerontology
    NT   **African American elderly**
          Aging
          Aging parents
          Elderly men
          Elderly women
          Libraries and the elderly
          Social work with the elderly
    RT   **Old age**
          Retirees
Elderly abuse   **362.6**
    UF   Abuse of the elderly
          Abused aged
          Battered elderly
          Elder abuse
          Elderly—Mistreatment
          Elderly neglect
          Parent abuse
    BT   **Domestic violence**
Elderly and libraries
    USE **Libraries and the elderly**
Elderly—Care (May subdiv. geog.)
    362.6

    Use for general materials on the care of the dependent elderly.

    UF   Elder care
    NT   **Elderly—Home care**
          Elderly—Institutional care
          Elderly—Medical care
Elderly—Counseling of   **362.6**
    UF   Counseling of the elderly
          Counseling with the aged
    BT   **Counseling**
Elderly—Diseases   **618.97**
    UF   Geriatrics
    BT   **Diseases**
    RT   **Elderly—Health and hygiene**

Elderly—Health and hygiene (May subdiv. geog.) **618.97**
    UF   Geriatrics
    BT   **Health**
           Hygiene
    RT   **Elderly—Diseases**
Elderly—Home care (May subdiv. geog.) **362.6**
    BT   **Elderly—Care**
           Home care services
Elderly—Housing (May subdiv. geog.) **362.6**
    UF   Housing for the elderly
    BT   **Housing**
    NT   **Retirement communities**
Elderly—Institutional care (May subdiv. geog.) **362.6**
    UF   Homes for the elderly
           Old age homes
    BT   **Elderly—Care**
           Institutional care
Elderly—Life skills guides **362.6; 646.7**
    BT   **Life skills**
    RT   **Retirement**
Elderly—Medical care (May subdiv. geog.) **362.1; 618.97**
    UF   Medical care for the elderly
    BT   **Elderly—Care**
           Medical care
    NT   **Medicare**
Elderly men (May subdiv. geog.) **305.26**
    UF   Aged men
    BT   **Elderly**
Elderly—Mistreatment
    USE **Elderly abuse**
Elderly neglect
    USE **Elderly abuse**
Elderly parents
    USE **Aging parents**
Elderly persons
    USE **Elderly**
Elderly—Recreation **790.084**
    BT   **Recreation**
Elderly—Societies **367**
    BT   **Societies**
Elderly—United States **305.260973**
Elderly women (May subdiv. geog.) **305.26**
    UF   Aged women
    BT   **Elderly**

Elected officials
    USE **Public officers**
Election
    USE **Elections**
          and types of public officials and names of individual public officials with the subdivision *Election,* e.g. **Presidents—United States—Election** [to be added as needed]
Election (Theology)
    USE **Predestination**
Electioneering
    USE **Politics**
Elections (May subdiv. geog.) **324**
    UF   Ballot
           Election
           Franchise
           Polls
           Voting
    SA   types of public officials and names of individual public officials with the subdivision *Election,* e.g. **Presidents—United States—Election** [to be added as needed]
    BT   **Politics**
    NT   **Campaign funds**
           Presidents—United States—Election
           Primaries
           Referendum
           Suffrage
           Voter registration
    RT   **Proportional representation**
           Representative government and representation
Elections—Finance
    USE **Campaign funds**
Elections—United States **324.973**
    UF   United States—Elections
Elections—United States—Finance
    USE **Campaign funds—United States**
Electoral college
    USE **Presidents—United States—Election**
Electric apparatus and appliances **621.3028; 643**
    Use for materials on small electrical machines and appliances. Materials on large ma-

Electric apparatus and appliances—*Continued*
chines powered by electricity are entered under **Electric machinery.**

- UF   Apparatus, Electric
  - Appliances, Electric
  - Electric appliances
- SA   types of electric apparatus and appliances, e.g. **Burglar alarms** [to be added as needed]
- BT   **Scientific apparatus and instruments**
- NT   **Burglar alarms**
  - **Electric batteries**
  - **Electric generators**
  - **Electric household appliances**
  - **Electric lamps**
  - **Induction coils**
  - **Storage batteries**

Electric appliances
- USE   **Electric apparatus and appliances**
  - **Electric household appliances**

Electric automobiles   629.222
- UF   Automobiles, Electric
  - Electric cars
- BT   **Automobiles**

Electric batteries   621.31
- UF   Batteries, Electric
  - Cells, Electric
- BT   **Electric apparatus and appliances**
  - **Electrochemistry**
- NT   **Fuel cells**
  - **Solar batteries**
- RT   **Storage batteries**

Electric cars
- USE   **Electric automobiles**

Electric circuits   621.319
- UF   Circuits, Electric
- BT   **Electric lines**
  - **Electricity**
- NT   **Electronic circuits**

Electric companies
- USE   **Electric utilities**

Electric condensers
- USE   **Condensers (Electricity)**

Electric conductors   621.319
- UF   Conductors, Electric
- BT   **Electronics**
- NT   **Semiconductors**
  - **Superconductors**

Electric controllers   629.8
- UF   Automatic control
- BT   **Electric machinery**

Electric currents   537.6; 621.31
- UF   Currents, Electric
- BT   **Electricity**
- NT   **Alternating electric currents**
  - **Electric measurements**
  - **Electric transformers**

Electric currents, Alternating
- USE   **Alternating electric currents**

Electric distribution
- USE   **Electric lines**
  - **Electric power distribution**

Electric engineering
- USE   **Electrical engineering**

Electric equipment of automobiles
- USE   **Automobiles—Electric equipment**

Electric eye
- USE   **Photoelectric cells**

Electric generators   621.31
- UF   Dynamos
  - Generators, Electric
- BT   **Electric apparatus and appliances**
  - **Electric machinery**

Electric heating   621.402; 644; 697
- UF   Electricity in the home
- BT   **Heating**

Electric household appliances   643
- UF   Appliances, Electric
  - Domestic appliances
  - Electric appliances
  - Electricity in the home
  - Household appliances, Electric
  - Labor saving devices, Household
- SA   types of specific appliances [to be added as needed]
- BT   **Electric apparatus and appliances**
  - **Household equipment and supplies**

Electric industries
- USE   **Electric products industry**

Electric lamps   621.32; 645
    UF   Incandescent lamps
    BT   **Electric apparatus and appliances**
          Lamps
    RT   **Electric lighting**
Electric light
    USE **Electric lighting**
          Photometry
          Phototherapy
Electric light and power industry
    USE **Electric utilities**
Electric lighting   621.32
    UF   Arc light
          Electric light
          Electricity in the home
          Light, Electric
    BT   **Lighting**
    NT   **Fluorescent lighting**
    RT   **Electric lamps**
Electric lighting, Fluorescent
    USE **Fluorescent lighting**
Electric lines   621.319
    Use for materials on power transmission lines, their construction and properties.
    UF   Electric distribution
          Electric power transmission
          Electric transmission
          Electricity—Distribution
          Power transmission, Electric
          Transmission of power
    BT   **Electric power distribution**
    NT   **Electric circuits**
          Electric wiring
Electric machinery   621.31
    Use for materials on large machines powered by electricity. Materials on smaller machines and appliances are entered under **Electric apparatus and appliances.**
    BT   **Machinery**
    NT   **Electric controllers**
          Electric generators
          Electric motors
          Electric transformers
Electric machinery—Alternating current   621.319
    UF   Alternating current machinery
Electric machinery—Direct current   621.319
    UF   Direct current machinery

Electric measurements   621.37
    UF   Measurements, Electric
    BT   **Electric currents**
          Weights and measures
    NT   **Electric meters**
    RT   **Electric testing**
Electric meters   621.37
    UF   Meters, Electric
    BT   **Electric measurements**
Electric motors   621.46
    UF   Induction motors
          Motors
    BT   **Electric machinery**
    NT   **Electric transformers**
Electric power   621.31
    BT   **Electricity**
          Energy resources
          Power (Mechanics)
Electric power development
    USE **Electrification**
Electric power distribution   621.319
    UF   Electric distribution
          Electric power transmission
          Electric transmission
          Electricity—Distribution
          Power transmission, Electric
          Transmission of power
    BT   **Electrical engineering**
          Power transmission
    NT   **Electric lines**
          Electric utilities
          Electric wiring
Electric power failures   621.319
    UF   Blackouts, Electric power
          Brownouts
          Electric power interruptions
          Power blackouts
          Power failures
Electric power in mining
    USE **Electricity in mining**
Electric power industry
    USE **Electric utilities**
Electric power interruptions
    USE **Electric power failures**
Electric power plants (May subdiv. geog.)   621.31
    UF   Power plants *[Former heading]*
          Power stations
    SA   types of electric power plants, e.g. **Nuclear power plants** [to be added as needed]

Electric power plants—*Continued*
  NT **Hydroelectric power plants**
        Nuclear power plants
        Steam power plants
Electric power transmission
  USE **Electric lines**
         Electric power distribution
Electric products industry (May subdiv.
    geog.) **338.4**
    Use for materials on industries producing
products that contain electrical motors or oth-
erwise employ electricity.
  UF Electric industries *[Former head-*
        ing]
  BT **Industries**
Electric railroads (May subdiv. geog.)
    385; 621.33; 625.1
  UF Interurban railroads
  BT **Railroads**
  RT **Street railroads**
Electric signs 621.32; 659.13
  BT **Advertising**
        Signs and signboards
  NT **Neon tubes**
Electric smelting
  USE **Electrometallurgy**
Electric testing 621.37
  BT **Testing**
  RT **Electric measurements**
Electric toys 688.7
  BT **Toys**
Electric transformers 621.31
  UF Transformers, Electric
  BT **Electric currents**
        Electric machinery
        Electric motors
Electric transmission
  USE **Electric lines**
         Electric power distribution
Electric utilities (May subdiv. geog.)
    333.793
    Use for materials on businesses that sell
and distribute electricity to customers.
  UF Electric companies
        Electric light and power industry
        Electric power industry
  BT **Electric power distribution**
        Public utilities
  NT **Electrification**
Electric utilities—Government ownership
    (May subdiv. geog.) **333.793**

Electric waves 537; 621.381
  UF Hertzian waves
        Radio waves
  BT **Electricity**
        Waves
  NT **Electromagnetic waves**
        Microwaves
Electric welding 671.5
  UF Arc welding
        Resistance welding
        Spot welding
        Welding, Electric
  BT **Welding**
Electric wiring 621.319
  UF Wiring, Electric
  BT **Electric lines**
        Electric power distribution
Electric wiring—Charts, diagrams, etc.
    621.319
Electrical engineering (May subdiv. geog.)
    621.3
  UF Electric engineering *[Former*
        heading]
  BT **Engineering**
        Mechanical engineering
  NT **Electric power distribution**
        Electricity in mining
        Electrification
Electricity 537; 621.3
  SA electricity in various endeavors,
        e.g. **Electricity in agriculture**
        [to be added as needed]
  BT **Physics**
  NT **Electric circuits**
        Electric currents
        Electric power
        Electric waves
        Electricity in agriculture
        Electricity in mining
        Lightning
  RT **Magnetism**
Electricity—Distribution
  USE **Electric lines**
         Electric power distribution
Electricity in agriculture 333.79; 631.3
  UF Electricity on the farm
  BT **Agricultural engineering**
        Agricultural machinery
        Electricity
  RT **Rural electrification**

Electricity in medicine
  USE **Electrotherapeutics**
Electricity in mining **622**
  UF Electric power in mining
       Mining, Electric
  BT **Electrical engineering**
       Electricity
  RT **Mining engineering**
Electricity in the home
  USE **Electric heating**
       Electric household appliances
       Electric lighting
Electricity on the farm
  USE **Electricity in agriculture**
Electrification (May subdiv. geog.)
      621.319
  UF Electric power development
  BT **Electric utilities**
       Electrical engineering
  NT **Rural electrification**
Electrochemistry **541.3; 660**
  BT **Industrial chemistry**
       Physical chemistry
  NT **Electric batteries**
       Electrometallurgy
       Electroplating
       Electrotyping
       Fuel cells
Electromagnetic waves **539.2**
  UF Waves, Electromagnetic
  BT **Electric waves**
       Radiation
  NT **Gamma rays**
       Heat
       Infrared radiation
       Light
       Microwaves
       Ultraviolet rays
       X-rays
Electromagnetism **621.34**
  BT **Magnetism**
  NT **Masers**
Electromagnets **621.34**
  UF Magnet winding
  BT **Magnetism**
       Magnets
Electrometallurgy **669.028**
  UF Electric smelting
  BT **Electrochemistry**
       Metallurgy
       Smelting

  RT **Electroplating**
       Electrotyping
Electron microscope and microscopy
  USE **Electron microscopes**
Electron microscopes **502.8**
  UF Electron microscope and micros-
       copy
  BT **Microscopes**
Electron tubes
  USE **Vacuum tubes**
Electronic apparatus and appliances
      621.381
  UF Apparatus, Electronic
       Appliances, Electronic
  SA types of electronic apparatus and
       appliances, e.g. **Computers**
       [to be added as needed]
  BT **Electronics**
       Scientific apparatus and in-
       struments
  NT **Computers**
       Electronic toys
       Intercommunication systems
       Magnetic recorders and re-
       cording
       Vacuum tubes
Electronic art
  USE **Video art**
Electronic bugging
  USE **Eavesdropping**
Electronic bulletin boards
  USE **Computer bulletin boards**
Electronic circuits **621.319; 621.3815**
  BT **Electric circuits**
       Electronics
Electronic commerce (May subdiv. geog.)
      380.1; 658
    Use for materials on the exchange of goods
  and services and the transfer of funds through
  electronic communications.
  UF Cybercommerce
       Internet commerce
       Online commerce
  BT **Commerce**
  NT **Internet marketing**
       Internet shopping
Electronic data processing
  USE **Data processing**
Electronic design
  USE **Computer-aided design**

Electronic discussion groups   004.692

Use for materials on services, commonly called newsgroups or LISTSERV lists, that allow subscribers to post messages that are then distributed to other subscribers. Materials on services that allow users to engage in conversations in real time are entered under **Online chat groups.** Materials on services that allow users to post messages and retrieve messages from others who have some common interest are entered under **Computer bulletin boards.**

UF   E-mail discussion groups

Electronic newsgroups

Internet discussion groups

Internet newsgroups

LISTSERV lists

Newsgroups, Electronic

Online discussion groups

Online newsgroups

Usenet newsgroups

BT   **Discussion groups**

RT   **Computer bulletin boards**

Online chat groups

Electronic drafting

USE   **Computer graphics**

Electronic drawing

USE   **Computer graphics**

Electronic eavesdropping

USE   **Eavesdropping**

Electronic games

USE   **Video games**

Electronic listening devices

USE   **Eavesdropping**

Electronic mail systems   004.692; 384.3

Use for materials on the electronic transmission of letters, messages, etc., primarily through the use of computers.

UF   E-mail

Email

BT   **Data transmission systems**

Telecommunication

Electronic marketing

USE   **Telemarketing**

Electronic music   786.7

UF   Synthesizer music

BT   **Music**

RT   **Computer music**

Electronic musical instruments   786.7

UF   Musical instruments, Electronic

SA   types of instruments, e.g. **Synthesizer (Musical instrument)** [to be added as needed]

BT   **Musical instruments**

NT   **Synthesizers (Musical instruments)**

Electronic newsgroups

USE   **Electronic discussion groups**

Electronic publishing (May subdiv. geog.) **070.5; 686.2**

Use for materials on the process of publishing by which books and articles or any kind of data are made available as an electronic product. Materials on the use of a personal computer with writing, graphics, and page layout software to produce printed material for publication are entered under **Desktop publishing.**

UF   Online publishing

Web publishing

BT   **Information services**

Publishers and publishing

NT   **Teletext systems**

RT   **Desktop publishing**

Electronic speech processing systems

USE   **Speech processing systems**

Electronic spreadsheets

USE   **Spreadsheet software**

Electronic toys   688.7

BT   **Electronic apparatus and appliances**

Toys

NT   **Video games**

Electronics   537.5; 621.381

BT   **Engineering**

Physics

Technology

NT   **Amplifiers (Electronics)**

Cybernetics

Digital electronics

Electric conductors

Electronic apparatus and appliances

Electronic circuits

High-fidelity sound systems

Microelectronics

Semiconductors

Superconductors

Transistors

Electrons   539.7

BT   **Atoms**

Particles (Nuclear physics)

Electroplating   671.7

BT   **Electrochemistry**

Metalwork

RT   **Electrometallurgy**

Electrotherapeutics   615.8

UF   Electricity in medicine

Medical electricity

Electrotherapeutics—*Continued*
  BT Massage
      Physical therapy
      Therapeutics
  NT Radiotherapy
Electrotyping   686.2
  BT Electrochemistry
      Printing
  RT Electrometallurgy
Elegiac poetry   808.81; 811, etc.
    May be used for individual works, collec-
    tions, or materials about elegiac poetry.
  UF Elegies
      Lamentations
  BT Poetry
Elegies
  USE Elegiac poetry
Elementary education (May subdiv.
    geog.)   372
    Use for general materials on education of
    children below the secondary school level.
  UF Children—Education
      Education, Elementary
      Education of children
      Education, Primary
      Grammar schools
      Primary education
  BT Education
  NT Creative activities
      Exceptional children
      Kindergarten
      Montessori method of educa-
        tion
      Nursery schools
      Readiness for school
Elementary particles (Physics)
  USE Particles (Nuclear physics)
Elementary school dropouts
  USE Dropouts
Elementary school libraries   027.8
  BT School libraries
Elementary schools (May subdiv. geog.)
    373.236
  UF Grade schools
  BT Schools
  RT Middle schools
Elements, Chemical
  USE Chemical elements
Elephants (May subdiv. geog.)   599.67
  BT Mammals

Elevators   621.8
  UF Lifts
  BT Hoisting machinery
Elite (Social sciences) (May subdiv. geog.)
    305.5
  BT Leadership
      Power (Social sciences)
      Social classes
      Social groups
Elizabeth II, Queen of Great Britain,
    1926-   92; B
  BT Queens—Great Britain
Elocution
  USE Public speaking
Elves   398.21
  BT Folklore
Email
  USE Electronic mail systems
Emancipation
  USE Freedom
Emancipation of slaves
  USE Slaves—Emancipation
Emancipation of women
  USE Women's rights
Embarrassment
  USE Self-consciousness
Embassies
  USE Diplomatic and consular ser-
        vice
Emblems
  USE Decorations of honor
      Heraldry
      Insignia
      Mottoes
      National emblems
      Seals (Numismatics)
      Signs and symbols
Emblems, State
  USE State emblems
Embracing
  USE Hugging
Embroidery (May subdiv. geog.)   746.44
  SA types of embroidery [to be add-
        ed as needed]
  BT Decoration and ornament
      Needlework
      Sewing
  NT Beadwork
      Crewelwork
      Needlepoint
      Samplers

Embryology   571.8; 612.6
    UF   Development
    BT   **Biology**
           Zoology
    NT   **Fetus**
           Frozen embryos
           Genetics
    RT   **Cells**
           Protoplasm
           Reproduction

Embryos, Frozen
    USE **Frozen embryos**

Emergencies
    USE **Accidents**
           Disasters
           First aid

Emergency assistance
    USE **Helping behavior**

Emergency medical technicians   610.69;
        616.02
    UF   Emergency paramedics
           EMTs (Medicine)
           Paramedical personnel
           Paramedics, Emergency
    BT   **Allied health personnel**

Emergency medicine   616.02
    BT   **Medicine**

Emergency mental health services
    USE **Crisis intervention (Mental
           health services)**

Emergency paramedics
    USE **Emergency medical technicians**

Emergency powers
    USE **War and emergency powers**

Emergency preparedness
    USE **Disaster relief**

Emergency relief
    USE **Disaster relief**

Emergency survival
    USE **Survival skills**

Emigrants
    USE **Immigrants**

Emigration
    USE **Immigration and emigration**

Eminent domain   333.1; 343
    UF   Condemnation of land
           Expropriation
    BT   **Constitutional law**
           Land use
           Property

Emotional stress
    USE **Stress (Psychology)**

Emotionally disturbed children   155.4;
        362.2; 371.94; 618.92

Use for general materials on children suffering from mental or emotional illnesses. Materials on the clinical and therapeutic aspects of mental disorders in children are entered under **Child psychiatry.**

    UF   Behavior problems (Children)
           Maladjusted children
           Mentally ill children
           Neurotic children
           Problem children
           Psychotic children
    BT   **Exceptional children**
           Mentally ill
    RT   **Child psychiatry**
           Juvenile delinquency

Emotions   152.4
    UF   Feelings
           Passions
    SA   types of emotions [to be added
           as needed]
    BT   **Psychology**
           Psychophysiology
    NT   **Anxiety**
           Attitude (Psychology)
           Bereavement
           Consolation
           Emotions in children
           Fanaticism
           Fear
           Frustration
           Grief
           Happiness
           Hope
           Horror
           Joy and sorrow
           Laughter
           Loneliness
           Love
           Pain
           Pleasure
           Prejudices
           Self-confidence
           Shyness
           Worry

Emotions in children   155.4
    BT   **Child psychology**
           Emotions

Emperors (May subdiv. geog.)   **920; 929.7**
    UF   Rulers
           Sovereigns
    SA   names of emperors, e.g. **Nero, Emperor of Rome, 37-68** [to be added as needed]
    BT   **Kings and rulers**
Emperors—Rome   **920; 937**
    UF   Roman emperors
    SA   names of Roman emperors, e.g. **Nero, Emperor of Rome, 37-68** [to be added as needed]
    NT   **Nero, Emperor of Rome, 37-68**
Empiricism   **146**
    UF   Experience
    BT   **Philosophy**
           Rationalism
           Theory of knowledge
    RT   **Pragmatism**
Employee absenteeism
    USE **Absenteeism (Labor)**
Employee benefits
    USE **Fringe benefits**
Employee counseling
    USE **Employees—Counseling of**
Employee drinking
    USE **Employees—Alcohol use**
Employee drug testing
    USE **Employees—Drug testing**
Employee fringe benefits
    USE **Fringe benefits**
Employee health services
    USE **Occupational health services**
Employee morale   **158.7; 658.3**
    BT   **Applied psychology**
           Morale
           Personnel management
    NT   **Job satisfaction**
    RT   **Absenteeism (Labor)**
Employees   **331.11; 920**
    UF   Workers
    SA   types of employees, e.g. **Office workers;** types of industries, services, establishments, or institutions, with the subdivision *Employees;* e.g. **Chemical industry—Employees; Railroads—Employees;** etc.; and names of countries, states, cities, etc., and corporate bodies

with the subdivision *Officials and employees,* e.g. **United States—Officials and employees; Ohio—Officials and employees; Chicago (Ill.)—Officials and employees; United Nations—Officials and employees;** etc. [to be added as needed]
    BT   **Labor**
    NT   **Chemical industry—Employees**
           Colleges and universities—Employees
           Medical personnel
           Migrant labor
           Office workers
           Railroads—Employees
    RT   **Personnel management**
Employees—Accidents
    USE **Industrial accidents**
Employees—Alcohol use   **331.25; 658.3**
    UF   Alcohol and employees
           Alcohol in the workplace
           Drinking and employees
           Drinking in the workplace
           Employee drinking
           Employees and alcohol
Employees and alcohol
    USE **Employees—Alcohol use**
Employees and drugs
    USE **Employees—Drug use**
Employees and narcotics
    USE **Employees—Drug use**
Employees and officials
    USE **Civil service**
Employees—Counseling of   **658.3**
    UF   Employee counseling
           Industrial counseling
    BT   **Counseling**
Employees—Dismissal   **331.25; 658.3**
    BT   **Job security**
           Personnel management
    RT   **Downsizing of organizations**
Employees—Drug testing   **331.25; 344; 658.3**
    UF   Drug testing in the workplace
           Employee drug testing
    BT   **Drug testing**
Employees—Drug use   **331.25; 658.3**
    UF   Drugs and employees
           Drugs in the workplace

Employees—Drug use—*Continued*
    Employees and drugs
    Employees and narcotics
Employees—Pensions
    USE **Old age pensions**
Employees—Rating   331.25; 658.3
Employees' representation in management
    USE **Participative management**
Employees—Salaries, wages, etc.
    USE **Salaries, wages, etc.**
Employees—Training   331.25; 658.3
    Use for materials discussing on-the-job training. Materials on teaching people a skill during the educational process are entered under **Vocational education.** Materials on teaching people a skill after formal education are entered under **Occupational training.** Materials on retraining are entered under **Occupational retraining.**
    UF In-service training
          Inservice training
          Training of employees
    SA types of employees or personnel with the subdivision *Training,* e.g. **Teachers—Training;** or with the subdivision *In-service training,* e.g. **Librarians—In-service training** [to be added as needed]
    BT **Occupational training**
          Personnel management
          Vocational education
    NT **Occupational retraining**
    RT **Apprentices**
          Technical education
Employer-employee relations
    USE **Industrial relations**
Employers' liability
    USE **Workers' compensation**
Employment   331.1
    Use for materials on the economic theory of employment.
    SA racial and ethnic groups and classes of persons with the subdivision *Employment,* e.g. **African Americans—Employment; Veterans—Employment;** etc. [to be added as needed]
    BT **Economics**
          Labor
    NT **African Americans—Employment**
          Age and employment

          Blacks—Employment
          Labor supply
          Men—Employment
          Part-time employment
          Summer employment
          Teenagers—Employment
          Temporary employment
          Unemployment
          Veterans—Employment
          Women—Employment
          Youth—Employment
    RT **Occupations**
          Vocational guidance
Employment agencies (May subdiv. geog.)   331.12
    BT **Labor**
          Labor turnover
          Personnel management
          Recruiting of employees
          Unemployment
    NT **Job hunting**
    RT **Labor supply**
Employment and age
    USE **Age and employment**
Employment applications
    USE **Applications for positions**
Employment discrimination
    USE **Discrimination in employment**
Employment forecasting (May subdiv. geog.)   331.1
    UF Occupational forecasting
    BT **Economic forecasting**
    RT **Labor supply**
Employment guidance
    USE **Vocational guidance**
Employment management
    USE **Personnel management**
Employment of children
    USE **Child labor**
Employment references
    USE **Applications for positions**
Employment security
    USE **Job security**
Employment, Supplementary
    USE **Supplementary employment**
Employment, Temporary
    USE **Temporary employment**

Empresses (May subdiv. geog.)   920

    SA   names of empresses; and countries, cities, etc., with the subdivision *Kings and rulers* [to be added as needed]

    BT   **Monarchy**

    RT   **Queens**

EMTs (Medicine)

    USE   **Emergency medical technicians**

Enamel and enameling   738.4

    UF   Porcelain enamels

    BT   **Decoration and ornament**

            Decorative arts

Encounter groups

    USE   **Group relations training**

Encyclicals, Papal

    USE   **Papal encyclicals**

Encyclopedias

    USE   **Encyclopedias and dictionaries** and subjects, groups or classes of persons, and names of places with the subdivision *Encyclopedias,* e.g. **Philosophy—Encyclopedias; Jews—Encyclopedias;** etc., for materials that provide topical information usually in alphabetical order [to be added as needed]

Encyclopedias and dictionaries   030; 031, etc.; 403; 413, etc.

    Use for general materials about encyclopedias and dictionaries.

    UF   Cyclopedias

            Dictionaries

            Encyclopedias

            Glossaries

            Subject dictionaries

    SA   subjects and names of languages with the subdivision *Dictionaries,* for materials in alphabetical order that define terms or identify things, e.g. **Chemistry—Dictionaries; English language—Dictionaries;** etc.; subjects, groups or classes of persons, and names of places with the subdivision *Biography—Dictionaries,* for biographical dictionaries, e.g. **Women—Biography—Dic-**

tionaries; Ohio—Biography—Dictionaries; etc.; and subjects, groups or classes of persons, and names of places with the subdivision *Encyclopedias,* e.g. **Philosophy—Encyclopedias; Jews—Encyclopedias;** etc., for materials that provide topical information usually in alphabetical order [to be added as needed]

    BT   **Reference books**

    NT   **Bible—Dictionaries**

            Biography—Dictionaries

            Chemistry—Dictionaries

            Classical dictionaries

            Computer science—Dictionaries

            English language—Dictionaries

            English language—Dictionaries—French

            French language—Dictionaries—English

            Geography—Dictionaries

            History—Dictionaries

            Jews—Encyclopedias

            Literature—Dictionaries

            Machine readable dictionaries

            Philosophy—Encyclopedias

            Picture dictionaries

            Polyglot dictionaries

            Shakespeare, William, 1564-1616—Dictionaries

            Technology—Dictionaries

End of the earth

    USE   **End of the world**

End of the world   001.9; 236; 291.2; 523.1

    Use for materials on the end of the world from an eschatological point of view (including Judgment Day, signs, fulfillments of prophecies, etc.) or from a scientific point of view.

    UF   End of the earth

            End of the world (Astronomy)

    BT   **Eschatology**

End of the world (Astronomy)

    USE   **End of the world**

End-of-the-world fantasies

    USE   **Fantasy fiction**

            Fantasy films

            Fantasy television programs

            Robinsonades

            Science fiction

End-of-the-world fantasies—*Continued*
> **War films**
> **War stories**

Endangered species (May subdiv. geog.)
> **333.95; 578.68**
> UF   Threatened species
>   Vanishing species
> BT   **Environmental protection**
>   **Nature conservation**
> NT   **Plant conservation**
>   **Wildlife conservation**
> RT   **Rare animals**
>   **Rare plants**

Endocrine glands   616.4
> UF   Ductless glands
>   Glands, Ductless
> BT   **Endocrinology**
> RT   **Hormones**

Endocrinology   616.4
> BT   **Medicine**
> NT   **Endocrine glands**
>   **Hormones**

Endorphins   612.8; 615
Endowed charities
> USE   **Charities**
>   **Endowments**

Endowments (May subdiv. geog.)   **001.4;**
> **361.6; 361.7**
> UF   Endowed charities
>   Foundations (Endowments)
> SA   disciplines, types of corporate
>   bodies, and names of individ-
>   ual corporate bodies with the
>   subdivision *Endowments,* e.g.
>   **Colleges and universities—**
>   **Endowments** [to be added as
>   needed]
> BT   **Finance**
> NT   **Colleges and universities—En-**
>   **dowments**
>   **Scholarships**
> RT   **Charities**
>   **Philanthropy**

Endurance, Physical
> USE   **Physical fitness**

Energy
> USE   **Energy resources**
>   **Force and energy**

Energy and state
> USE   **Energy policy**

Energy, Biomass
> USE   **Biomass energy**

Energy conservation (May subdiv. geog.)
> **333.791**
> UF   Conservation of energy
>   Conservation of power resources
>   Power resources conservation
> SA   types of energy conservation,
>   e.g. **Recycling** [to be added
>   as needed]
> BT   **Conservation of natural re-**
>   **sources**
>   **Energy resources**
> NT   **Recycling**
> RT   **Energy consumption**
>   **Energy policy**

Energy consumption (May subdiv. geog.)
> **333.79**
> UF   Consumption of energy
> SA   subjects with the subdivision
>   *Fuel consumption,* e.g. **Auto-**
>   **mobiles—Fuel consumption**
>   [to be added as needed]
> BT   **Energy resources**
> NT   **Automobiles—Fuel consump-**
>   **tion**
> RT   **Energy conservation**

Energy consumption—Forecasting
> **333.79**
Energy conversion from waste
> USE   **Waste products as fuel**
Energy conversion, Microbial
> USE   **Biomass energy**

Energy development (May subdiv. geog.)
> **333.79**
> UF   Energy resources development
>   Power resources development
> BT   **Energy resources**
> NT   **Water resources development**

Energy policy (May subdiv. geog.)
> **333.79; 354.3**
> UF   Energy and state
>   Energy resources—Government
>   policy
>   Government policy
> BT   **Energy resources**
>   **Industrial policy**
> RT   **Energy conservation**

Energy resources (May subdiv. geog.)
> **333.79**
Use for materials on the available sources
of mechanical power in general. Materials on
the physics and engineering aspects of power
are entered under **Power (Mechanics).**

Energy resources—*Continued*
   UF   Energy
         Power resources
         Power supply
   BT   **Natural resources**
         Power (Mechanics)
   NT   **Biomass energy**
         Electric power
         Energy conservation
         Energy consumption
         Energy development
         Energy policy
         Fuel
         Ocean energy resources
         Renewable energy resources
         Solar energy
         Water power
         Wind power
Energy resources development
   USE **Energy development**
Energy resources—Government policy
   USE **Energy policy**
Energy technology
   USE **Power (Mechanics)**
Engineering (May subdiv. geog.)   **620**
   UF   Construction
   SA   types of engineering, e.g. **Chemical engineering** [to be added as needed]
   BT   **Industrial arts**
         Technology
   NT   **Aeronautics**
         Agricultural engineering
         Chemical engineering
         Civil engineering
         Electrical engineering
         Electronics
         Genetic engineering
         Highway engineering
         Human engineering
         Hydraulic engineering
         Marine engineering
         Mechanical drawing
         Military engineering
         Mining engineering
         Minorities in engineering
         Municipal engineering
         Nuclear engineering
         Ocean engineering
         Railroad engineering
         Reliability (Engineering)
         Sanitary engineering

         Steam engineering
         Structural engineering
         Systems engineering
         Traffic engineering
         Water supply engineering
   RT   **Engineers**
         Materials
Engineering and construction
   USE names of wars with the subdivision *Engineering and construction,* e.g. **World War, 1939-1945—Engineering and construction** [to be added as needed]
Engineering drawing
   USE **Mechanical drawing**
Engineering, Genetic
   USE **Genetic engineering**
Engineering instruments   **620.0028**
   UF   Instruments, Engineering
   BT   **Scientific apparatus and instruments**
Engineering materials
   USE **Materials**
Engineering—Periodicals   **620.005**
Engineering—Study and teaching
         620.007
   BT   **Technical education**
Engineers (May subdiv. geog.)
         620.0092; 920
   RT   **Engineering**
         Inventors
Engines   **621.4**
   UF   Motors
   SA   types of engines and motors, e.g. **Steam engines; Electric motors;** etc., and types of vehicles and makes and models of vehicles with the subdivision *Motors,* e.g. **Automobiles—Motors** [to be added as needed]
   BT   **Machinery**
   NT   **Airplane engines**
         Automobiles—Motors
         Diesel engines
         Fire engines
         Fuel
         Heat engines
         Internal combustion engines
         Marine engines

Engines—*Continued*
        Pumping machinery
        Solar engines
        Steam engines
        Turbines
England   942

    May be subdivided like United States except for *History,* and *Politics and government,* or any subdivisions relating to history or politics and government. Such materials are entered instead under **Great Britain.**

    BT   **Great Britain**
England, Church of
    USE **Church of England**
England—History
    USE **Great Britain—History**
English as a foreign language
    USE **English as a second language**
English as a second language   420.7; 428
    UF   English as a foreign language
          English for foreigners
          English language as a second language
          English language—Study and teaching, Foreign
          English language—Texts for foreigners
    BT   **English language—Study and teaching**
    NT   **English language—Conversation and phrase books**
English authors   820.9; 920
    UF   Authors, English
    BT   **Authors**
English authors—First editions
    USE **English literature—First editions**
English authors—Homes (May subdiv. geog.)   **820.9; 920**
    BT   **Literary landmarks**
English Canadian literature
    USE **Canadian literature (English)**
English Canadian poetry
    USE **Canadian poetry (English)**
English composition
    USE **English language—Composition and exercises**
English drama   822
    Use for general materials about English drama, not for individual works.
    BT   **Drama**
          English literature

    NT   **Morality plays**
          Mysteries and miracle plays
English drama—Collections   822.008
English drama—History and criticism 822.009
    BT   **Drama—History and criticism**
English essays   824; 824.008
    Use for collections of literary essays by several authors.
    BT   **English literature**
          Essays
English fiction   823
    May be used for collections or materials about English fiction, not for individual works.
    BT   **English literature**
          Fiction
English fiction—History and criticism 823.009
English for foreigners
    USE **English as a second language**
          English language—Conversation and phrase books
English grammar
    USE **English language—Grammar**
English history
    USE **Great Britain—History**
English language (May subdiv. geog.)   **420**
    Subdivisions used under this heading may be used under other languages unless otherwise specified.
    BT   **Language and languages**
English language—0-1100
    USE **English language—Old English period**
English language—Acronyms
    USE **Acronyms**
English language—Alphabet   421
English language—Americanisms
    USE **Americanisms**
English language—Antonyms
    USE **English language—Synonyms and antonyms**
English language as a second language
    USE **English as a second language**
English language—Basal readers
    USE **Basal readers**
English language—Business English 428; 808
    Business English is a unique subdivision for **English language.** Use same pattern with unique subdivisions for other languages, e.g. **Japanese language—Business Japanese;** etc.

English language—Business English—
Continued
  UF   Business English
English language—Comparison   425
  UF   Comparison (English grammar)
English language—Composition and ex-
    ercises   428; 808
  UF   English composition
  RT   **Rhetoric**
English language—Conversation and
    phrase books   428
  UF   English for foreigners
       English language—Conversations
         and phrases
  BT   **English as a second language**
English language—Conversations and
    phrases
  USE   **English language—Conversa-
         tion and phrase books**
English language—Dialects   427
  NT   **Americanisms**
English language—Dictionaries   423
    Use for English language dictionaries. Dic-
    tionaries from English to another language are
    entered under this heading further subdivided
    by the other language, e.g. **English lan-
    guage—Dictionaries—French.** French-
    English dictionaries are entered under **French
    language—Dictionaries—English.** Combined
    English-French and French-English diction-
    aries are entered under both headings.
  BT   **Encyclopedias and dictionaries**
  RT   **English language—Terms and
         phrases**
English language—Dictionaries—French
    443
    Use for English-French dictionaries. French-
    English dictionaries are entered under **French
    language—Dictionaries—English.** Combined
    English-French and French-English diction-
    aries are entered under both headings.
  UF   Foreign language dictionaries
  BT   **Encyclopedias and dictionaries**
  RT   **French language—Diction-
         aries—English**
English language—Errors
  USE   **English language—Errors of
         usage**
English language—Errors of usage   428
  UF   English language—Errors *[For-
         mer heading]*
English language—Etymology   422
  BT   **English language—History**
English language—Examinations   420.76
  BT   **Examinations**

English language—Examinations—Study
    guides   420.76
English language—Foreign words and
    phrases   422
    Use for materials on foreign words and
    phrases incorporated into the English lan-
    guage.
  UF   Foreign language phrases
English language—Grammar   425
  UF   English grammar
  SA   **English language** subdivided by
       topics in the study of gram-
       mar, e.g. **English language—
       Parts of speech; English lan-
       guage—Infinitive;** etc. [to be
       added as needed]
  BT   **Grammar**
  NT   **English language—Usage**
English language—History   420.9
  NT   **English language—Etymology**
English language—Homonyms   423
English language—Idioms   428
  RT   **English language—Provincial-
         isms**
English language—Infinitive   425
English language—Jargon   427
English language—Middle English period
    420
  UF   Middle English language
English language—Old English period
    429
  UF   Anglo-Saxon language *[Former
         heading]*
       English language—0-1100
       Old English language
English language—Orthography
  USE   **English language—Spelling**
English language—Parts of speech   425
English language—Phonetics
  USE   **English language—Pronuncia-
         tion**
English language—Phrases and terms
  USE   **English language—Terms and
         phrases**
English language—Programmed instruc-
    tion   420.7
  BT   **Programmed instruction**
English language—Pronunciation   421
  UF   English language—Phonetics
  BT   **Phonetics**
  NT   **Reading—Phonetic method**

English language—Provincialisms 427
   RT   English language—Idioms
English language—Punctuation
   USE   **Punctuation**
English language—Reading materials
   USE   **Reading materials**
English language—Rhetoric
   USE   **Rhetoric**
English language—Rhyme 808.1
   BT   **Rhyme**
English language—Slang 427
English language—Social aspects 420
English language—Spelling 421
   UF   English language—Orthography
   NT   **Spellers**
          Spelling reform
   RT   **Word skills**
English language—Spelling reform
   USE   **Spelling reform**
English language—Study and teaching
   420.7
   NT   **English as a second language**
English language—Study and teaching,
   Foreign
   USE   **English as a second language**
English language—Synonyms and ant-
   onyms 423
   UF   English language—Antonyms
   RT   **Opposites**
English language—Terms and phrases
   420

   Use for general lists of words and phrases
and for lists that are applicable to certain situations (collective nouns, curious expressions,
etc.) rather than to specific subjects. Lists of
words and phrases limited to specific subjects
are entered under the subject with the subdivision *Dictionaries,* e.g. **Chemistry—Dictionaries.**

   UF   English language—Phrases and
          terms
   RT   **English language—Dictionaries**
English language—Texts for foreigners
   USE   **English as a second language**
English language—Usage 428
   BT   **English language—Grammar**
English language—Versification
   USE   **Versification**
English language—Vocabulary
   USE   **Vocabulary**
English letters 826; 826.008
   BT   **English literature**
          Letters

English literature 820
   Subdivisions used under this heading may
be used under other literatures.
   BT   **Literature**
   NT   **English drama**
          English essays
          English fiction
          English letters
          English poetry
          English prose literature
          English satire
          English sermons
          English speeches
          English wit and humor
English literature—0-1100
   USE   **English literature—Old English
          period**
English literature—16th and 17th centu-
   ries 820
   UF   English literature—Early modern,
          1500-1700
          Renaissance English literature
English literature—18th century 820
English literature—19th century 820
   UF   Victorian literature
English literature—20th century 820
English literature—21st century 820
English literature—Bibliography 016.82
English literature—Bio-bibliography
   820.9
English literature—Collections 820.8
   Use for collections of English literature by
several authors in more than one genre. Col-
lections of prose are entered under **English
prose literature.** Collections of poetry are en-
tered under **English poetry—Collections.**
Collections of drama are entered under **En-
glish drama—Collections.**
English literature—Criticism
   USE   **English literature—History and
          criticism**
English literature—Dictionaries 820.3
   BT   **Literature—Dictionaries**
English literature—Early modern, 1500-
   1700
   USE   **English literature—16th and
          17th centuries**
English literature—Examinations
   820.76
   BT   **English literature—Study and
          teaching**
English literature—First editions 820
   UF   English authors—First editions

English literature—History and criticism
820.9
  UF English literature—Criticism
English literature—Indexes 016.82
English literature—Middle English peri-
  od 820
  UF Middle English literature
English literature—Old English period
  829
  UF Anglo-Saxon literature *[Former
      heading]*
      English literature—0-1100
      Old English literature
English literature—Outlines, syllabi, etc.
  820.2
  BT Literature—Outlines, syllabi,
      etc.
  RT English literature—Study and
      teaching
English literature—Study and teaching
  820.7
  NT English literature—Examina-
      tions
  RT English literature—Outlines,
      syllabi, etc.
English newspapers
  USE Newspapers—Great Britain
English orations
  USE English speeches
English periodicals 052
  BT Periodicals
English poetry 821
  Use for general materials about English po-
  etry, not for individual works.
  BT English literature
      Poetry
English poetry—Collections 821.008
English poetry—History and criticism
  821.009
English prose literature 828
  Use for collections of prose writings that
  may include several literary forms, such as es-
  says, fiction, orations, etc.
  UF Prose literature, English
  BT English literature
English public schools 373.2
  Use for materials on British endowed sec-
  ondary schools that are open to public admis-
  sion but are not financed or administered by
  any government body.
  UF Public schools, Endowed (Great
      Britain)
      Public schools, English

  BT Private schools
English satire 827; 827.008
  UF Satire, English
  BT English literature
      Satire
English sermons 252
  BT English literature
      Sermons
English speeches 825; 825.008
  UF English orations
      Speeches, addresses, etc., En-
      glish
  BT English literature
      Speeches
English wit and humor 827; 827.008;
  827.009
  Use for collections by several authors or for
  materials about English wit and humor. Indi-
  vidual works by English humorists are entered
  under Wit and humor.
  BT English literature
      Wit and humor
Engravers (May subdiv. geog.) 760.92;
  920
  BT Artists
  NT Etchers
Engraving 760; 765
  UF Copper engraving
      Engravings
      Line engraving
      Steel engraving
  SA engraving of particular countries,
      e.g. American engraving [to
      be added as needed]
  BT Art
      Graphic arts
      Illustration of books
      Pictures
  NT American engraving
      Gems
      Mezzotint engraving
      Photoengraving
      Wood engraving
  RT Etching
Engraving, American
  USE American engraving
Engravings
  USE Engraving
Enhanced radiation weapons
  USE Neutron weapons

251

Enigmas
> USE **Curiosities and wonders**
> **Riddles**

Enlarged texts for shared reading
> USE **Big books**

Enlarging (Photography)
> USE **Photography—Enlarging**

Enlightenment (May subdiv. geog.) **190; 909.7; 940.2**
> Use for materials on the philosophic movement of the 18th century marked by the questioning of traditional doctrines and values, naturalistic and individualistic tendencies, and an emphasis on the empirical method in science and the free use of reason.
>
> BT **Modern civilization**
> **Modern philosophy**
> **Rationalism**

Enlistment
> USE **Recruiting and enlistment**

Ensemble playing
> USE **Ensembles (Music)**

Ensembles (Mathematics)
> USE **Set theory**

Ensembles (Music) **782; 784**
> Use for materials on small instrumental or vocal groups and for the music written for such groups.
>
> UF Ensemble playing
> Instrumental ensembles
> Musical ensembles
> Vocal ensembles
> SA types of vocal or instrumental ensembles, e.g. **Jazz ensembles** [to be added as needed]
> BT **Music**
> **Musical form**
> **Musicians**
> NT **Jazz ensembles**
> RT **Orchestra**

Ensigns
> USE **Flags**

Enteric fever
> USE **Typhoid fever**

Enterprises
> USE **Business enterprises**

Entertainers (May subdiv. geog.) **791.092; 920**
> SA types of entertainers and names of individual entertainers [to be added as needed]
> NT **Actors**
> **Clowns**
> **Comedians**
> **Dancers**
> **Fools and jesters**

Entertaining (May subdiv. geog.) **395.3; 642**
> Use for materials on hospitality and the art of entertaining guests.
>
> UF Guests
> Hospitality
> BT **Etiquette**
> **Home economics**
> NT **Business entertaining**
> **Carving (Meat, etc.)**
> **Children's parties**
> **Games**
> **Parties**
> RT **Afternoon teas**
> **Amusements**
> **Dining**
> **Luncheons**

Entertainments
> USE **Amusements**

Entozoa
> USE **Parasites**

Entrance examinations
> USE types of educational institutions and names of individual institutions with the subdivision *Entrance examinations,* e.g. **Colleges and universities—Entrance examinations** [to be added as needed]

Entrance examinations for colleges
> USE **Colleges and universities—Entrance examinations**

Entrance requirements
> USE types of educational institutions and names of individual institutions with the subdivision *Entrance requirements,* e.g **Colleges and universities—Entrance requirements** [to be added as needed]

Entrance requirements for colleges and universities
> USE **Colleges and universities—Entrance requirements**

Entrepreneurs (May subdiv. geog.) **338; 920**
> BT **Businesspeople**
> **Self-employed**

Entrepreneurship (May subdiv. geog.)
    338; 658.4
  BT **Business**
      Capitalism
      Small business
Environment (May subdiv. geog.)
    304.2; 333.7; 363.7
    Use for materials on the habitat or sur-
roundings of a population or on all factors ex-
ternal to the individual.
  SA subjects with the subdivision *En-*
      vironmental aspects, e.g. **Nu-**
      clear power plants—Envi-
      ronmental aspects [to be
      added as needed]
  NT **Ecology**
      Environmental movement
      Environmental policy
      Environmental protection
      Nuclear power plants—Envi-
      ronmental aspects
      Pesticides—Environmental as-
      pects
      Work environment
Environment and pesticides
  USE **Pesticides—Environmental as-**
      pects
Environment and state
  USE **Environmental policy**
Environment—Government policy
  USE **Environmental policy**
Environment, Space
  USE **Space environment**
Environmental aspects
  USE subjects with the subdivision *En-*
      vironmental aspects, e.g. **Nu-**
      clear power plants—Envi-
      ronmental aspects; Economic
      development—Environmental
      aspects [to be added as need-
      ed]
Environmental health (May subdiv. geog.)
    616.9
  UF Health—Environmental aspects
  SA subjects with the subdivision *En-*
      vironmental aspects, e.g. **Nu-**
      clear power plants—Envi-
      ronmental aspects [to be
      added as needed]
  BT **Environmental influence on**
      humans
      Public health

  NT **Air pollution**
      Nuclear power plants—Envi-
      ronmental aspects
      Occupational health and safety
      Pollution
      Water pollution
Environmental health engineering
  USE **Sanitary engineering**
Environmental influence on humans
    (May subdiv. geog.)   **304.2; 599.9**
  UF Acclimatization
      Altitude, Influence of
      Man—Influence of environment
  BT **Adaptation (Biology)**
      Human ecology
      Human geography
  NT **Environmental health**
      Survival skills
      Weightlessness
Environmental lobby
  USE **Environmental movement**
Environmental movement (May subdiv.
    geog.) **322.4; 363.7**
  UF Conservation movement
      Ecological movement
      Environmental lobby
      Environmentalism
      Green movement
  BT **Environment**
      Social movements
Environmental policy (May subdiv. geog.)
    344; 354.3; 363.7
  UF Environment and state
      Environment—Government poli-
      cy
      Environmental quality—Govern-
      ment policy
      Government policy
      State and environment
  BT **Environment**
  RT **Conservation of natural re-**
      sources
Environmental policy—United States
    344; 354.30973; 363.7
  UF United States—Environmental
      policy
Environmental pollution
  USE **Pollution**

Environmental protection (May subdiv. geog.) **344; 363.7**
- UF Environmentalism
- Protection of environment
- BT **Ecology**
- **Environment**
- NT **Conservation of natural resources**
- **Endangered species**
- **Landscape protection**
- **Soil conservation**
- **Wildlife conservation**
- RT **Pollution**

Environmental protection—Standards (May subdiv. geog.) **354.3**

Environmental quality—Government policy
- USE **Environmental policy**

Environmental radioactivity
- USE **Radioactive pollution**

Environmentalism
- USE **Environmental movement**
- **Environmental protection**

Enzymes **547; 572**
- BT **Proteins**
- NT **Catalytic RNA**

Eolithic period
- USE **Stone Age**

Epic films **791.43**

May be used for individual works, collections, or materials about epic films.
- UF Film epics
- BT **Motion pictures**

Epic literature **800**

May be used for individual works, collections, or materials about epic literature.
- BT **Literature**
- NT **Epic poetry**
- RT **Mock-heroic literature**

Epic poetry **808.81; 811, etc.**

May be used for individual works, collections, or materials about epic poetry.
- BT **Epic literature**
- **Narrative poetry**
- RT **Romances**

Epidemics (May subdiv. geog.) **614.4**
- UF Pestilences
- SA names of contagious diseases, e.g. **AIDS (Disease)** [to be added as needed]
- BT **Diseases**
- **Public health**

- NT **Plague**
- RT **Communicable diseases**

Epigrams **808.88; 818, etc.**

May be used for collections of epigrams and for materials about epigrams.
- UF Sayings
- BT **Wit and humor**
- NT **Quotations**
- **Toasts**
- RT **Proverbs**

Epigraphy
- USE **Inscriptions**

Epilepsy **616.8**
- BT **Nervous system—Diseases**

Episcopal Church (May subdiv. geog.) **283**

Use for materials on the Episcopal Church in the United States after 1789. Materials on the Episcopal Church in the United States prior to 1789 are entered under **Church of England—United States.**
- UF Protestant Episcopal Church in the U.S.A.
- BT **Christian sects**
- NT **Catholic charismatic movement**
- RT **Church of England—United States**

Epistemology
- USE **Theory of knowledge**

Epistolary fiction **813, etc.**

May be used for individual works, collections, or materials about novels written in the form of a series of letters.
- UF Epistolary novels
- Novels in letters
- BT **Fiction**

Epistolary novels
- USE **Epistolary fiction**

Epistolary poetry **811, etc.**

May be used for individual works, collections, or materials about epistolary verse.
- UF Verse epistles
- BT **Poetry**

Epitaphs **929**
- UF Graves
- BT **Biography**
- **Cemeteries**
- **Inscriptions**
- **Tombs**

Epithets
- USE **Names**
- **Nicknames**

Epizoa
- USE **Parasites**

Equal employment opportunity
　　USE　**Affirmative action programs**
　　　　　Discrimination in employment
Equal opportunity in employment
　　USE　**Affirmative action programs**
　　　　　Discrimination in employment
Equal pay for equal work　331.2; 658.3
　　UF　Pay equity
　　BT　**Discrimination in employment**
　　　　　Salaries, wages, etc.
　　　　　Women—Employment
Equal rights amendments (May subdiv.
　　geog.)　305.42; 323.4; 342
　　UF　Amendments, Equal rights
　　　　　ERAs
　　BT　**Constitutions**
　　　　　Sex discrimination
Equal time rule (Broadcasting)　324
　　　Use for materials on the requirement that
　all qualified candidates for public office be
　granted equal broadcast time if one of one
　such candidates is permitted to broadcast. Ma-
　terials on the requirement that, if one side of
　a controversial issue of public importance is
　aired, the same opportunity must be given for
　the presentation of contrasting views are en-
　tered under **Fairness doctrine (Broadcast-
　ing.)**
　　UF　Rule of equal time (Broadcast-
　　　　　ing)
　　BT　**Broadcasting**
　　　　　Television and politics
　　RT　**Fairness doctrine (Broadcast-
　　　　　ing)**
Equality (May subdiv. geog.)　323.42
　　UF　Inequality
　　　　　Social equality
　　BT　**Political science**
　　　　　Sociology
　　NT　**Individualism**
　　RT　**Democracy**
　　　　　Freedom
Equations, Chemical
　　USE　**Chemical equations**
Equestrianism
　　USE　**Horsemanship**
Equipment and supplies
　　USE　subjects and names of wars with
　　　　　the subdivision *Equipment
　　　　　and supplies,* e.g. **Televi-
　　　　　sion—Equipment and sup-
　　　　　plies; World War, 1939-
　　　　　1945—Equipment and sup-
　　　　　plies** [to be added as needed]

ERAs
　　USE　**Equal rights amendments**
Ergonomics
　　USE　**Human engineering**
Erosion　551.3
　　SA　types of erosion, e.g. **Soil ero-
　　　　　sion** [to be added as needed]
　　BT　**Geology**
　　NT　**Dust storms**
　　　　　Soil erosion
　　RT　**Soil conservation**
Erotic art (May subdiv. geog.)　704.9
　　UF　Sex in art
　　BT　**Art**
　　　　　Erotica
Erotic fiction　808.83; 813, etc.
　　　May be used for individual works, collec-
　tions, or materials about erotic fiction.
　　UF　Adult fiction
　　　　　Erotic novels
　　　　　Erotic stories
　　BT　**Erotic literature**
　　　　　Fiction
Erotic films　791.43
　　　May be used for individual works, collec-
　tions, or materials about erotic films.
　　UF　Adult films
　　BT　**Motion pictures**
Erotic literature　808.8; 809
　　UF　Literature, Erotic
　　BT　**Erotica**
　　　　　Literature
　　NT　**Erotic fiction**
　　　　　Erotic poetry
Erotic novels
　　USE　**Erotic fiction**
Erotic poetry　811, etc.
　　　May be used for individual works, collec-
　tions, or materials about erotic poetry.
　　BT　**Erotic literature**
　　　　　Poetry
　　RT　**Love poetry**
Erotic stories
　　USE　**Erotic fiction**
Erotica　704.9; 809
　　SA　types of erotica, e.g. **Erotic art;
　　　　　Erotic literature;** etc. [to be
　　　　　added as needed]
　　NT　**Erotic art**
　　　　　Erotic literature
　　RT　**Obscenity (Law)**
　　　　　Pornography

Errors   001.9; 153.7; 165

Use for materials on errors of judgment, errors of observation, scientific errors, popular misconceptions, etc. Errors in language are entered under names of languages with the subdivision *Errors of usage,* e.g. **English language—Errors of usage.**

UF   Fallacies

Medical errors

Mistakes

Scientific errors

RT   **Superstition**

Errors of usage

USE   names of languages with the subdivision *Errors of usage,* e.g. **English language—Errors of usage** [to be added as needed]

Erudition

USE   **Learning and scholarship**

Eruptions

USE   **Geysers**

Escapes (May subdiv. geog.)   **365; 904**

UF   Hostage escapes

Prison escapes

BT   **Adventure and adventurers**

Prisons

Eschatology   236; 291.2

UF   Intermediate state

Last things (Theology)

BT   **Theology**

NT   **Death**

End of the world

Future life

Heaven

Hell

Immortality

Millennium

Purgatory

Second Advent

Eskimos

USE   **Inuit**

ESP

USE   **Extrasensory perception**

Esperanto   499

BT   **Universal language**

Espionage (May subdiv. geog.)   **327.12**

UF   Spying

SA   espionage practiced by particular countries, e.g. **American espionage** [to be added as needed]

BT   **Intelligence service**

Secret service

Subversive activities

NT   **American espionage**

Spies

Espionage, American

USE   **American espionage**

Espionage films

USE   **Spy films**

Espionage stories

USE   **Spy stories**

Espionage television programs

USE   **Spy television programs**

Esquimaux

USE   **Inuit**

Essay   808.4

Use for materials on the appreciation of the essay and on the technique of writing essays. Collections of essays are entered under **Essays; American essays;** etc.

BT   **Literature**

Essays   808.84

Use for collections of literary essays by authors of several nationalities. Collections of literary essays by American authors are entered under **American essays;** by English authors, under **English essays;** etc. Essays limited to a particular subject, by one or more authors, are entered under that subject. Materials on the appreciation of the essay and on the technique of writing essays are entered under **Essay.**

NT   **American essays**

English essays

Essences and essential oils   664; 668

UF   Aromatic plant products

Essential oils

Vegetable oils

Volatile oils

BT   **Distillation**

Oils and fats

NT   **Flavoring essences**

Perfumes

Essential oils

USE   **Essences and essential oils**

Estate planning (May subdiv. geog.)   **332.024; 343.05; 346.05**

BT   **Personal finance**

Planning

NT   **Inheritance and transfer tax**

Insurance

RT   **Investments**

Tax planning

Trusts and trustees

Estate tax
USE **Inheritance and transfer tax**

Esthetics
USE **Aesthetics**

Estimates
USE types of engineering, technical processes, industries, etc., with the subdivision *Estimates,* e.g. **Building—Estimates** [to be added as needed]

Estimation (Mathematics)
USE **Approximate computation**

Estrangement (Social psychology)
USE **Alienation (Social psychology)**

Etchers 769.92; 920
BT **Artists**
Engravers

Etching 767
UF Etchings
BT **Art**
Pictures
RT **Engraving**

Etchings
USE **Etching**

Eternal life
USE **Eternity**
Future life
Immortality

Eternal punishment
USE **Hell**

Eternity 115
Use for materials on the philosophical concept of eternity. Materials on the character and form of a future life are entered under **Future life.** Materials on the question of the endless existence of the soul are entered under **Immortality.**
UF Eternal life
RT **Future life**

Ethanol
USE **Alcohol as fuel**

Ethical aspects
USE subjects with the subdivision *Ethical aspects,* e.g. **Birth control—Ethical aspects** [to be added as needed]

Ethical education
USE **Moral education**

Ethics (May subdiv. geog.) **170**
UF Moral philosophy
Morality
Morals

SA types of ethics, e.g. **Business ethics;** ethics of particular religions, e.g. **Christian ethics;** names of individual persons, classes of persons, types of professions, and types of professional personnel with the subdivision *Ethics,* e.g. **Librarians—Ethics; Shakespeare, William, 1564-1616—Ethics;** etc., and subjects with the subdivision *Ethical aspects,* e.g. **Birth control—Ethical aspects** [to be added as needed]
BT **Philosophy**
NT **Abortion—Ethical aspects**
Asceticism
Bioethics
Birth control—Ethical aspects
Business ethics
Charity
Christian ethics
Cloning—Ethical aspects
Conduct of life
Conscience
Cruelty
Duty
Good and evil
Honesty
Human cloning—Ethical aspects
Jewish ethics
Justice
Legal ethics
Loyalty
Medical ethics
Moral education
Motion pictures—Ethical aspects
Natural law
Political ethics
Professional ethics
Secularism
Sexual ethics
Sin
Social ethics
Stoics
Utilitarianism
Values
Vice

Ethics—*Continued*
>> **Virtue**
>> **Work ethic**
>> **World War, 1939-1945—Ethical aspects**
> RT **Human behavior**
Ethics—United States 170.973
> UF American ethics *[Former heading]*
Ethiopian-Italian War, 1935-1936
> USE **Italo-Ethiopian War, 1935-1936**
Ethnic cleansing
> USE **Genocide**
Ethnic conflict
> USE **Ethnic relations**
Ethnic diversity
> USE **Pluralism (Social sciences)**
Ethnic groups (May subdiv. geog.)
> **305.8**
>> Use for materials on groups of people bound together by common ancestry and culture. Materials on indigenous minorities are entered under **Native peoples.** Materials on the subjective sense of belonging to a particular ethnic group are entered under **Ethnicity.** Materials on several ethnic groups in a particular region or country are entered under **Ethnology** subdivided geographically. Materials on individual ethnic groups are entered under the name of the group, e.g. **Mexican Americans.**
> UF People
> SA names of individual ethnic groups [to be added as needed]
> BT **Ethnology**
> NT **Creoles**
>> **Hispanic Americans**
>> **Mexican Americans**
> RT **Ethnic relations**
>> **Ethnicity**
Ethnic identity
> USE **Ethnicity**
>> and ethnic groups with the subdivision *Ethnic identity,* e.g. **Mexican Americans—Ethnic identity** [to be added as needed]
Ethnic psychology
> USE **Ethnopsychology**
Ethnic relations 305.8
> UF Ethnic conflict
>> Relations among ethnic groups

> SA names of regions, countries, cities, etc., with the subdivision *Ethnic relations;* e.g. **United States—Ethnic relations** [to be added as needed]
> BT **Acculturation**
>> **Ethnology**
>> **Sociology**
> NT **Culture conflict**
>> **Discrimination**
> RT **Ethnic groups**
>> **Minorities**
>> **Multiculturalism**
>> **Pluralism (Social sciences)**
>> **Race relations**
Ethnic relations—Political aspects
> **305.8**
Ethnic relations—Religious aspects
> **305.8**
Ethnicity (May subdiv. geog.) **305.8**
>> Use for materials on the subjective sense of belonging to a particular ethnic group. Materials on groups of people bound together by a common ancestry or culture are entered under **Ethnic groups.** Materials on several ethnic groups in a particular region or country are entered under **Ethnology.**
> UF Ethnic identity
> SA ethnic groups with the subdivision *Ethnic identity,* e.g. **Mexican Americans—Ethnic identity;** and racial groups with the subdivision *Race identity,* e.g. **African Americans—Race identity** [to be added as needed]
> BT **Identity (Psychology)**
> RT **Ethnic groups**
>> **Multiculturalism**
>> **Pluralism (Social sciences)**
Ethnobotany (May subdiv. geog.) **581.6**
> SA names of ethnic groups with the subdivision *Ethnobotany* [to be added as needed]
> BT **Ethnology**
>> **Plants—Folklore**
Ethnocide
> USE **Genocide**
Ethnography
> USE **Ethnology**

Ethnology (May subdiv. geog.) **305.8; 306; 599.97**

Use for materials on the disciplines of ethnology and cultural anthropology, and, with appropriate geographic subdivisions, for materials on the origin, distribution, and characteristics of the elements of the population of a particular region or country. General materials on groups of people who are bound together by common ties of ancestry and culture are entered under **Ethnic groups.** Materials on individual racial or ethnic groups are entered under the name of the group, e.g. **Australian aborigines.**

UF Cultural anthropology
     Ethnography
     Geographical distribution of people
     Races of people
     Social anthropology
SA names of countries with the subdivision *Social life and customs,* e.g. **United States—Social life and customs;** and names of individual ethnic groups [to be added as needed]
BT **Human beings**
NT **Acculturation**
     Anthropometry
     Cannibalism
     Costume
     Ethnic groups
     Ethnic relations
     Ethnobotany
     Ethnopsychology
     Folklore
     Human geography
     Kinship
     Language and languages
     Manners and customs
     Native peoples
     Physical anthropology
     Primitive societies
     Race
     Race relations
     Semitic peoples
     Totems and totemism
RT **Anthropology**
     Archeology
     Civilization

Ethnology—United States **305.813**

UF United States—Ethnology
     United States—Peoples

SA names of individual ethnic groups [to be added as needed]

Ethnopsychology (May subdiv. geog.) **155.8**

UF Cross-cultural psychology
     Ethnic psychology
     Folk psychology
     National psychology
     Race psychology
SA names of racial or ethnic groups with the subdivision *Psychology* [to be added as needed]
BT **Anthropology**
     Ethnology
     Psychology
     Sociology
NT **Culture conflict**
     Native Americans—Psychology
RT **National characteristics**
     Social psychology

Ethyl alcohol fuel
USE **Alcohol as fuel**

Etiquette (May subdiv. geog.) **395**

UF Ceremonies
     Manners
     Politeness
     Salutations
SA types of etiquette, e.g. **Table etiquette;** and names of countries with the subdivision *Social life and customs,* e.g. **United States—Social life and customs** [to be added as needed]
BT **Human behavior**
NT **Courtesy**
     Dating (Social customs)
     Entertaining
     Letter writing
     Table etiquette
RT **Manners and customs**

Etymology
USE **Language and languages—Etymology**
     and names of languages with the subdivision *Etymology,* e.g. **English language—Etymology** [to be added as needed]

Eucharist 234; 264

May be subdivided by Christian sect or de-nomination.

- UF Communion
  - Holy communion
  - Lord's Supper *[Former heading]*
- BT **Liturgies**
  - **Sacraments**
- RT **Mass (Liturgy)**

Eugenics (May subdiv. geog.) 363.9

- BT **Genetics**
  - **Population**
- RT **Heredity**

Europe 940

- UF Europe, Western
  - Western Europe

Europe, Central

- USE **Central Europe**

Europe, Eastern

- USE **Eastern Europe**

Europe—History 940

- NT **Holy Roman Empire**

Europe—History—0-476 936; 937

Europe—History—476-1492 940.1; 940.2

- NT **Hundred Years' War, 1339-1453**
- RT **Middle Ages**

Europe—History—1492-1789 940.2

- NT **Seven Years' War, 1756-1763**
  - **Thirty Years' War, 1618-1648**

Europe—History—18th century 940.2

Europe—History—1789-1815 940.2

- NT **Napoleonic Wars, 1800-1815**

Europe—History—1789-1900 940.2

- UF Europe—History—19th century

Europe—History—19th century

- USE **Europe—History—1789-1900**

Europe—History—1815-1848 940.2

Europe—History—1848-1871 940.2

Europe—History—1871-1918 940.2

- NT **World War, 1914-1918**

Europe—History—20th century 940.5

Europe—History—1918-1945 940.5

- NT **Russo-Finnish War, 1939-1940**
  - **World War, 1939-1945**

Europe—History—1945- 940.55

Europe—History—21st century 940.56

Europe—Politics and government 940

May be subdivided by period using the same subdivisions as are listed under **Europe—History.**

- NT **European federation**

Europe, Western

- USE **Europe**

European Common Market

- USE **European Union**

European Community

- USE **European Union**

European Economic Community

- USE **European Union**

European federation 321; 940

Use for general materials on the political or economic union of European countries. Materials on the corporate body formerly known as the European Economic Community and the European Community, which became known as the European Union upon ratification of the Treaty of European Union on October 29, 1993, are entered under **European Union.**

- UF Federation of Europe
- BT **Europe—Politics and government**
  - **Federal government**
  - **International organization**
- NT **European Union**

European Union 341.242; 382

Use for materials on the corporate body formerly known as the European Economic Community and the European Community, which became known as the European Union upon ratification of the Treaty on European Union on October 29, 1993. General materials on the political or economic union of European countries are entered under **European federation.**

- UF Common market
  - EEC
  - European Common Market
  - European Community
  - European Economic Community
- BT **European federation**

Euthanasia (May subdiv. geog.) 179.7

- UF Mercy killing
- BT **Homicide**
  - **Medical ethics**
- RT **Right to die**

Evacuation of civilians

- USE names of wars with the subdivision *Evacuation of civilians,* e.g. **World War, 1939-1945—Evacuation of civilians** [to be added as needed]

Evaluation

- USE types of evaluation, e.g. **Educational evaluation;** and names of corporate bodies and types

Evaluation—*Continued*
    of institutions, products, services, equipment, activities, projects, and programs with the subdivision *Evaluation,* e.g. **Public health—Evaluation; Science—Study and teaching—Evaluation;** etc. [to be added as needed]

Evaluation of books
  USE **Book reviewing**

Evaluation of literature
  USE **Best books**
      Books and reading
      Criticism
      Literature—History and criticism

Evaluation research in education
  USE **Educational evaluation**

Evangelism
  USE **Evangelistic work**

Evangelistic healing
  USE **Spiritual healing**

Evangelistic work (May subdiv. geog.)
    253; 269
  UF Evangelism
      Revival (Religion)
  BT **Church work**
  NT **Conversion**
      Revivals
  RT **Christian missions**

Evening and continuation schools **374**
  UF Continuation schools
      Evening schools
      Night schools
  BT **Compulsory education**
      Continuing education
      Education
      Public schools
      Schools
      Secondary education
      Technical education
  RT **Adult education**

Evening schools
  USE **Evening and continuation schools**

Evergreens **582.1; 635.9**
  BT **Landscape gardening**
      Shrubs
      Trees

Evidences of the Bible
  USE **Bible—Evidences, authority, etc.**

Evil
  USE **Good and evil**

Evil spirits
  USE **Demonology**

Evolution **576.8**
  UF Darwinism
      Development
      Mutation (Biology)
      Origin of species
  SA types of animals, plants, crops, chemicals, and organs of the body with the subdivision *Evolution* [to be added as needed]
  BT **Philosophy**
  NT **Life—Origin**
  RT **Biology**
      Creation
      Creationism
      Human origins
      Natural selection
      Religion and science
      Variation (Biology)

Evolution and Christianity
  USE **Creationism**

Evolution—Study and teaching **576.807**
  UF Creation—Study and teaching
  RT **Creationism**

Ex libris
  USE **Bookplates**

Ex-nuns **305.48**
  UF Catholic ex-nuns
      Former nuns
  BT **Nuns**

Ex-priests **305.33; 920**
  UF Catholic ex-priests
      Former priests
  BT **Catholic Church—Clergy**
      Priests

Ex-Soviet republics
  USE **Former Soviet republics**

Ex-Soviet states
  USE **Former Soviet republics**

Examinations (May subdiv. geog.)
    371.26
    Use for general materials on examinations. Materials discussing the requirements for examinations in particular branches of study, or

Examinations—*Continued*
compilations of questions and answers for such examinations, are entered under the subject with the subdivision *Examinations.*

UF   Tests

SA   branches of study with the subdivision *Examinations,* e.g. **English language—Examinations;** and names of individual examinations [to be added as needed]

BT   **Educational tests and measurements**

Questions and answers

Teaching

NT   **Civil service—Examinations**

Colleges and universities—Entrance examinations

Colleges and universities—Entrance requirements

Educational tests and measurements

English language—Examinations

Graduate Record Examination

Music—Examinations

Scholastic Aptitude Test

United States. Army—Examinations

Examinations—Design and construction 371.26

Examinations—Study guides 371.26

Use for materials that provide directions on how to prepare for and pass examinations, usually with practice questions and answers included.

UF   Preparation guides for examinations

Study guides for examinations

Test preparation guides

SA   subjects, educational levels, and names of educational institutions with the subdivisions *Examinations—Study guides,* e.g. **English language—Examinations—Study guides;** and named examinations with the subdivision *Study guides,* e.g. **Graduate Record Examination—Study guides** [to be added as needed]

BT   **Study skills**

Excavation 624.1

BT   **Civil engineering**

Tunnels

Excavations (Archeology) (May subdiv. geog.) **930.1**

UF   Earthworks (Archeology)

Ruins

BT   **Archeology**

RT   **Extinct cities**

Mounds and mound builders

Excavations (Archeology)—United States 973

Exceptional children 155.45

UF   Abnormal children

BT   **Children**

Elementary education

NT   **Brain damaged children**

Emotionally disturbed children

Gifted children

Handicapped children

Mainstreaming in education

Slow learning children

Wild children

Excess government property

USE   **Surplus government property**

Exchange 332.4; 332.64

BT   **Commerce**

NT   **Foreign exchange**

Money

Exchange, Barter

USE   **Barter**

Exchange of persons programs 327.1; 370.116

UF   Cultural exchange programs

Interchange of visitors

Specialists exchange programs

Visitors' exchange programs

SA   types of exchange programs for particular classes of persons, e.g. **Teacher exchange** [to be added as needed]

BT   **Cultural relations**

International cooperation

NT   **Teacher exchange**

Exchange of prisoners of war

USE   **Prisoners of war**

Exchange of teachers

USE   **Teacher exchange**

Exchange rates

USE   **Foreign exchange**

Executions
USE **Capital punishment**
Executive ability   658.4
  UF Administrative ability
  BT **Ability**
  NT **Leadership**
      Planning
Executive agencies
USE **Administrative agencies**
Executive departments (May subdiv.
    geog.) **351**
  Use for materials on major administrative
  divisions of the executive branch of govern-
  ment, usually headed by an officer of cabinet
  rank.
  UF Government departments
      Government ministries
      State ministries
  SA names of executive departments
      [to be added as needed]
  BT **Administrative agencies**
Executive departments—Ohio   352.2
  UF Ohio—Executive departments
  SA names of executive departments
      [to be added as needed]
Executive departments—Reorganization
USE **Administrative agencies—Reor-
      ganization**
**Executive departments—United States
    352.2**
  UF United States—Executive depart-
      ments
  SA names of executive departments
      [to be added as needed]
  NT **Presidents—United States—
      Staff**
Executive investigations
USE **Governmental investigations**
Executive power (May subdiv. geog.)
    351
  Use for materials on the powers of the ex-
  ecutive or administrative branch of govern-
  ment.
  UF Presidents—Powers
  BT **Constitutional law**
      Political science
  NT **Amnesty**
      Heads of state
      Monarchy
      Pardon
      Prime ministers
      Separation of powers
      War and emergency powers

  RT **Presidents**
**Executive power—United States
    352.230973**
  UF Presidents—United States—Pow-
      er
      United States—Executive power
Executive reorganization
USE **Administrative agencies—Reor-
      ganization**
Executors and administrators (May
    subdiv. geog.) **346.05**
  UF Administrators and executors
  BT **Inheritance and succession**
  RT **Trusts and trustees**
      Wills
Exegesis, Biblical
USE **Bible—Criticism**
Exercise (May subdiv. geog.) **613.7**
  SA types of exercises and physical
      activities [to be added as
      needed]
  BT **Health**
      Hygiene
  NT **Aerobics**
      Bodybuilding
      Cycling
      Gymnastics
      Hatha yoga
      Physical fitness
      Rowing
      Weight lifting
  RT **Physical education**
      Weight loss
Exercise addiction   616.85
  UF Addiction to exercise
      Compulsive exercising
  BT **Compulsive behavior**
Exercises, problems, etc.
USE subjects with the subdivision
      Problems, exercises, etc., for
      compilations of practice prob-
      lems or exercises for use in
      the study of a topic, e.g.
      **Chemistry—Problems, exer-
      cises, etc.** [to be added as
      needed]
Exhaustion
USE **Fatigue**
Exhibitions
  UF Exhibits
      Expositions

Exhibitions—*Continued*
International exhibitions
World's fairs
SA   types of exhibitions, e.g. **Flower shows;** subjects and names of individual persons with the subdivision *Exhibitions,* e.g. **Printing—Exhibitions;** and names of particular exhibitions, e.g. **Expo 92 (Seville, Spain)** [to be added as needed]
NT   **Art—Exhibitions**
Books—Exhibitions
Craft shows
Expo 92 (Seville, Spain)
Fashion shows
Flower shows
Printing—Exhibitions
Science—Exhibitions
Trade shows
RT   **Fairs**
Exhibits
USE   **Exhibitions**
Exiles
USE   **Refugees**
Existentialism   142
BT   **Metaphysics**
Modern philosophy
Phenomenology
Exorcism   133.4; 291.3
BT   **Supernatural**
RT   **Demoniac possession**
Demonology
Expansion (United States politics)
USE   **United States—Territorial expansion**
Expectancy of life
USE   **Life expectancy**
Expectation of life
USE   **Life expectancy**
Expeditions, Scientific
USE   **Scientific expeditions**
Experience
USE   **Empiricism**
Experimental farms
USE   **Agricultural experiment stations**
Experimental films (May subdiv. geog.)
791.43
May be used for individual works, collections, or materials about experimental films.

UF   Avant-garde films
Personal films
Underground films
BT   **Motion pictures**
Experimental methods in education
USE   **Education—Experimental methods**
Experimental schools (May subdiv. geog.)
371.04
Use for materials on schools in which new teaching methods, organizations of subject matter, educational theories, personnel practices, etc., are tested.
UF   Alternative schools
Free schools
Nonformal schools
Project schools
Schools, Nonformal
BT   **Education—Experimental methods**
Schools
RT   **Open plan schools**
Experimental theater (May subdiv. geog.)
792
UF   Avant-garde theater
BT   **Theater**
Experimental universities
USE   **Free universities**
Experimentation on animals
USE   **Animal experimentation**
Experimentation on humans, Medical
USE   **Human experimentation in medicine**
Experiments
USE   scientific subjects with the subdivision *Experiments,* e.g. **Chemistry—Experiments** [to be added as needed]
Experiments, Scientific
USE   **Science—Experiments**
Expert systems (Computer science)
006.3
UF   Knowledge-based systems (Computer science)
BT   **Artificial intelligence**
Data processing
Information systems
Exploration   910.9
Use for materials on voyages and explorations that have advanced geographic knowledge.
UF   Discoveries and exploration
Discoveries in geography

Exploration—*Continued*
Explorations
Maritime discoveries
SA   names of celestial bodies, continents, regions, countries,
states, etc., with the subdivision *Exploration* for materials
on the exploration of those
areas when they were unset-
tled or sparsely settled and
largely unknown to the world
at large, e.g. **America—Exploration;** or with the subdivision *Description* for materials on later and recent travels
is those areas, e.g. **United
States—Description;** and
names of countries, states,
etc., with the subdivision *Exploring expeditions* for materials on explorations sponsored
by those governments, e.g.
**United States—Exploring ex-
peditions** [to be added as
needed]
BT   **Adventure and adventurers**
Geography
History
NT   **America—Exploration**
Antarctica—Exploration
Arctic regions—Exploration
Northeast Passage
Outer space—Exploration
Underwater exploration
United States—Exploration
RT   **Explorers**
Scientific expeditions
Voyages and travels
Exploration of space
USE   **Outer space—Exploration**
Exploration—United States
USE   **United States—Exploration**
Explorations
USE   **Exploration**
Explorer (Artificial satellite)   629.46
BT   **Artificial satellites**
Explorers (May subdiv. geog.)   **910.92;
920**
UF   Discoverers
Navigators
Voyagers

SA   names of places explored with
the subdivision *Exploration,*
e.g. **America—Exploration;**
names of countries with the
subdivisions *Description* and
Exploring expeditions; and
names of individual explorers
[to be added as needed]
BT   **Adventure and adventurers**
Heroes and heroines
NT   **United States—Exploring expeditions**
RT   **Exploration**
Travelers
Voyages and travels
Exploring expeditions
USE   names of countries sponsoring
exploring expeditions with the
subdivision *Exploring expedi-
tions,* e.g. **United States—Ex-
ploring expeditions;** etc.; and
names of expeditions, e.g.
**Lewis and Clark Expedition
(1804-1806)** [to be added as
needed]
Explosions   904
BT   **Accidents**
Explosives   363.17; 363.3; 623.4; 662
SA   types of explosives and explo-
sive devices [to be added as
needed]
BT   **Chemistry**
NT   **Ammunition**
Bombs
Dynamite
Gunpowder
Land mines
Torpedoes
Expo 92 (Seville, Spain)   909.82
UF   Seville (Spain). World's Fair,
1992
World's Fair (1992 : Seville,
Spain)
BT   **Exhibitions**
Fairs
Exports (May subdiv. geog.)   **382**
BT   **International trade**
Exposed children
USE   **Abandoned children**
Expositions
USE   **Exhibitions**

265

Express highways (May subdiv. geog.)
      388.1; 625.7
    UF   Freeways
          Interstate highways
          Limited access highways
          Motorways
          Parkways
          Superhighways
          Toll roads
          Turnpikes (Modern)
    BT   **Roads**
          Traffic engineering

Express service   388
    BT   **Railroads**
          Transportation
    NT   **Pony express**

Expressionism (Art) (May subdiv. geog.)
      709.04; 759.06
    BT   **Art**

Expropriation
    USE **Eminent domain**

Expulsion
    USE **Penal colonies**

Extended care facilities
    USE **Long-term care facilities**

Extermination of pests
    USE **Pest control**

Extinct animals (May subdiv. geog.)
      560
    SA   types of extinct animals [to be
          added as needed]
    BT   **Animals**
    NT   **Mastodon**
    RT   **Fossils**
          Prehistoric animals
          Rare animals

Extinct cities (May subdiv. geog.)   **930**
    UF   Abandoned towns
          Buried cities
          Ruins
          Sunken cities
    SA   names of extinct cities and
          towns, e.g. **Delphi (Extinct
          city)** [to be added as needed]
    BT   **Archeology**
          Cities and towns
    NT   **Ghost towns**
    RT   **Excavations (Archeology)**

Extinct cities—Greece   938
    NT   **Delphi (Extinct city)**

Extinct plants
    USE **Fossil plants**

Extracurricular activities
    USE **Student activities**

Extragalactic nebulae
    USE **Galaxies**

Extramarital relationships
    USE **Adultery**

Extrasensory perception   133.8
    UF   ESP
    BT   **Parapsychology**
    NT   **Clairvoyance**
          Telepathy

Extraterrestrial bases   629.44
    Use for materials on bases established on
    natural extraterrestrial bodies for specific
    functions other than colonization. Materials on
    communities established in space or on natural
    extraterrestrial bodies are entered under **Space
    colonies.** Materials on manned installations
    orbiting in space for specific functions, such
    as servicing space ships, are entered under
    Space stations.
    BT   **Civil engineering**
    RT   **Space colonies**

Extraterrestrial beings   576.8
    UF   Aliens from outer space
          Interplanetary visitors
    BT   **Life on other planets**

Extraterrestrial communication
    USE **Interstellar communication**

Extraterrestrial environment
    USE **Space environment**

Extraterrestrial life
    USE **Life on other planets**

Extravehicular activity (Space flight)
      629.45
    UF   Space vehicles—Extravehicular
          activity
          Space walk
          Walking in space
    BT   **Space flight**

Extreme unction
    USE **Anointing of the sick**

Extremism (Political science)
    USE **Radicalism**

Eye   611; 612.8
    BT   **Face**
          Head
    RT   **Optometry**
          Vision

Eyeglasses   617.7; 681
    UF   Glasses
          Spectacles

Eyeglasses—*Continued*
    SA   types of eyeglasses, e.g. **Contact lenses** [to be added as needed]
    NT   **Contact lenses**
Fables   398.2; 808.8; 811, etc.; 813, etc.
    May be used for individual works, collections, or materials about short tales intended to teach moral lessons, often with animals or inanimate objects speaking and acting like human beings, and usually with the lesson stated briefly at the end.
    UF   Cautionary tales and verse
          Moral and philosophic stories
          Tales
    SA   fables of particular countries, e.g. **American fables** [to be added as needed]
    BT   **Fiction**
          Literature
    NT   **American fables**
    RT   **Allegories**
          Animals—Fiction
          Didactic fiction
          Didactic poetry
          Folklore
          Legends
          Parables
          Romances
Fabric design
    USE **Textile design**
Fabrics (May subdiv. geog.)   677
    UF   Cloth
          Dry goods
          Textiles
    SA   types of fabrics [to be added as needed]
    BT   **Decorative arts**
    NT   **Cotton**
          Linen
          Silk
          Synthetic fabrics
          Wool
    RT   **Weaving**
Face   611; 612
    BT   **Head**
    NT   **Eye**
          Nose
    RT   **Physiognomy**
Facetiae
    USE **Anecdotes**
          Wit and humor

Facsimile transmission
    USE **Fax transmission**
Facsimiles
    USE types of printed or written materials, documents, etc., with the subdivision *Facsimiles,* e.g. **Autographs—Facsimiles** [to be added as needed]
Factories (May subdiv. geog.)   338.6; 670; 725
    UF   Industrial plants
          Mill and factory buildings
          Plants, Industrial
    SA   types of factories [to be added as needed]
    BT   **Industrial buildings**
    RT   **Factory management**
          Mills
Factories—Management
    USE **Factory management**
Factory and trade waste
    USE **Industrial waste**
Factory management   658.5
    Use for materials on the technical aspects of manufacturing processes. Materials on general principles of management of industries are entered under **Management.**
    UF   Factories—Management
          Production engineering
          Shop management
    BT   **Management**
    NT   **Job analysis**
          Motion study
          Office management
          Participative management
          Supervisors
          Time study
    RT   **Factories**
          Personnel management
Factory waste
    USE **Industrial waste**
Factory workers
    USE **Labor**
          Working class
Facts, Miscellaneous
    USE **Books of lists**
          Curiosities and wonders
Faculty
    USE types of educational institutions and names of individual educational institutions with the

Faculty—*Continued*

> subdivision *Faculty*, e.g. **Colleges and universities—Faculty** [to be added as needed]

Faculty (Education)

 USE **Colleges and universities—Faculty**
 Educators
 Teachers

Faience

 USE **Pottery**

Failure in business

 USE **Bankruptcy**
 Business failures

Failure of banks

 USE **Bank failures**

Failure to thrive syndrome

 USE **Growth disorders**

Failures, Structural

 USE **Structural failures**

Fair employment practice

 USE **Discrimination in employment**

Fair housing

 USE **Discrimination in housing**

Fair trade

 USE **Unfair competition**

Fair trade (Tariff)

 USE **Free trade**

Fair trial (May subdiv. geog.)   345

> Use for materials on legal hearings before an impartial and disinterested tribunal. Materials on the regular administration of the law, according to which citizens may not be denied their legal rights and all laws must conform to fundamental and accepted legal principles, are entered under **Due Process of law.**

 UF Right to a fair trial
 BT **Civil rights**
 Due process of law
 NT **Freedom of the press and fair trial**

Fair trial and free press

 USE **Freedom of the press and fair trial**

Fair use (Copyright) (May subdiv. geog.)   341.7; 346.04

 BT **Copyright**

Fairies   398.21

 BT **Folklore**

Fairness doctrine (Broadcasting)   343.09

> Use for materials on the requirement that, if one side of a controversial issue of public importance is aired, the same opportunity must

be given for the presentation of contrasting views. Materials on the requirement that all qualified candidates for public office be granted equal broadcast time if any one such candidate is permitted to broadcast are entered under **Equal time rule (Broadcasting).**

 UF Doctrine of fairness (Broadcasting)
 BT **Broadcasting**
 Television and politics
 RT **Equal time rule (Broadcasting)**

Fairs (May subdiv. geog.)   381; 394; 607; 907.4

> Use for general materials on public showings that suggest a variety of kinds of display and entertainment, usually in an outdoor setting, sometimes for the promotion of sales and sometimes in competition for prizes of excellence.

 UF Bazaars
 World's fairs
 SA names of fairs, e.g. **Expo 92 (Seville, Spain)** [to be added as needed]
 NT **Expo 92 (Seville, Spain)**
 Trade shows
 RT **Carnivals**
 Exhibitions
 Markets

Fairy tales (May subdiv. geog.)   398.2; 808.83; 813, etc.; 813.008, etc.

> May be used for individual works, collections, or materials about short, simple narratives, often of folk origin and usually intended for children, involving fantastic forces and magical beings such as dragons, elves, fairies, goblins, witches, and wizards.

 UF Stories
 Tales
 BT **Children's literature**
 Fiction
 RT **Folklore**

Faith   121; 234; 291.1

> Use for materials on religious belief and doubt. Materials on belief and doubt from the philosophical standpoint are entered under **Belief and doubt.**

 UF Religious belief
 BT **Religion**
 Salvation
 Spiritual life
 Theology
 Virtue
 RT **Belief and doubt**

Faith cure

 USE **Spiritual healing**

Faith healing
   USE **Spiritual healing**
Faith—Psychology   200.1; 248; 253.5
   BT **Psychology of religion**
Faithfulness
   USE **Loyalty**
Falconry   799.2
   UF Hawking
   BT **Game and game birds**
          Hunting
Fall
   USE **Autumn**
Fallacies
   USE **Errors**
          Logic
Falling stars
   USE **Meteors**
Fallout, Radioactive
   USE **Radioactive fallout**
Fallout shelters
   USE **Air raid shelters**
False advertising
   USE **Deceptive advertising**
False memories
   USE **False memory syndrome**
False memory syndrome   616.85
   UF False memories
   BT **Memory**
   RT **Recovered memory**
Falsehood
   USE **Truthfulness and falsehood**
Family (May subdiv. geog.)   **306.85**

   Use for materials stressing the sociological concept and structure of the family. Materials stressing the everyday life, interaction, and relationships of family members are entered under **Family life.**

   SA types of family members, e.g.
          Children; Fathers; Mothers;
          etc., types of family relation-
          ships, e.g. **Mother-son rela-**
          tionship; and names of indi-
          vidual persons with the subdi-
          vision *Family* [to be added as
          needed]
   BT **Interpersonal relations**
          Sociology
   NT **Birth order**
          Children
          Clans
          Daughters
          Divorce
          Dual-career families

          Family life
          Family size
          Farm family
          Fathers
          Grandparent-grandchild rela-
          tionship
          Husbands
          Kinship
          Marriage
          Married people
          Mothers
          Parent-child relationship
          Parents
          Siblings
          Single-parent families
          Sons
          Stepfamilies
          Wives
          Work and family
   RT **Domestic relations**
          Family reunions
          Home
Family and work
   USE **Work and family**
Family—Biblical teaching   248.4; 261.8
Family budget
   USE **Household budgets**
Family caregivers
   USE **Caregivers**
Family counseling
   USE **Family therapy**
Family devotions
   USE **Devotional exercises**
          Family—Religious life
Family farms (May subdiv. geog.)
          338.1; 630
   BT **Farms**
   RT **Farm family**
          Farm life
Family finance
   USE **Personal finance**
Family group therapy
   USE **Family therapy**
Family histories
   USE **Genealogy**
Family life (May subdiv. geog.)   **306.85;**
          392.3; 646.7

   Use for materials stressing the everyday life, interaction, and relationships of family members. Materials on the sociological concept and structure of the family are entered under **Family.**

Family life—*Continued*
   UF   Family relations
         Home life
   BT   **Family**
Family life education (May subdiv. geog.)
       306.85; 362.82; 372.82
   BT   **Education**
   NT   **Home economics**
         Marriage counseling
         Sex education
   RT   **Domestic relations**
Family names
   USE **Personal names**
Family planning
   USE **Birth control**
Family prayers
   USE **Devotional exercises**
         Family—Religious life
Family psychotherapy
   USE **Family therapy**
Family relations
   USE **Domestic relations**
         Family life
Family—Religious life   **248.4; 249;**
       291.4
   UF   Family devotions
         Family prayers
         Family worship
   BT   **Religious life**
Family reunions   **394.2**
   UF   Reunions, Family
   RT   **Family**
Family size (May subdiv. geog.)   **304.6**
   BT   **Family**
   NT   **Childlessness**
         Only child
   RT   **Birth control**
Family social work
   USE **Social case work**
Family therapy   **616.89**
   UF   Family counseling
         Family group therapy
         Family psychotherapy
         Problem families—Counseling of
   BT   **Counseling**
         Psychotherapy
Family trees
   USE **Genealogy**
Family—United States   **306.850973**
Family violence
   USE **Domestic violence**

Family worship
   USE **Family—Religious life**
Famines (May subdiv. geog.)   **904**
   BT   **Food supply**
         Starvation
Famines—United States   **363.80973; 973**
Famous people
   USE **Celebrities**
Fanaticism   **152.4; 200.1; 303**
   UF   Intolerance
   BT   **Emotions**
Fancy dress
   USE **Costume**
Fans   **391.4**
   BT   **Clothing and dress**
         Costume
Fantastic fiction
   USE **Fantasy fiction**
Fantastic films
   USE **Fantasy films**
Fantastic poetry
   USE **Fantasy poetry**
Fantastic radio programs
   USE **Fantasy radio programs**
Fantastic television programs
   USE **Fantasy television programs**
Fantasy   **154.3**
     Use for materials on fantasy as an aspect of psychology. Literary fantasies are entered under **Fantasy fiction.**
   UF   Day dreams
   BT   **Dreams**
         Imagination
   RT   **Hallucinations and illusions**
Fantasy fiction   **808.83; 809.3; 813, etc.**
     May be used for individual works, collections, or materials about imaginative fiction with strange settings, grotesque or fanciful characters, and supernatural or impossible events or forces.
   UF   Apocalyptic fantasies
         End-of-the-world fantasies
         Fantastic fiction
   BT   **Fiction**
   NT   **Alternative histories**
         Dystopias
         Ghost stories
         Imaginary voyages
         Utopian fiction
   RT   **Horror fiction**
         Interplanetary voyages
         Occult fiction
         Science fiction

Fantasy films 791.43
> May be used for individual works, collections, or materials about fantasy films.

  UF   Apocalyptic fantasies
       End-of-the-world fantasies
       Fantastic films
  BT   **Motion pictures**
  RT   **Horror films**
       Science fiction films

Fantasy poetry 808.81; 811, etc.
> May be used for individual works, collections, or materials about fantasy poetry.

  UF   Fantastic poetry
  BT   **Poetry**

Fantasy radio programs 791.44
> May be used for individual works, collections, or materials about fantasy radio programs.

  UF   Fantastic radio programs
  BT   **Radio programs**

Fantasy television programs 791.45
> May be used for individual works, collections, or materials about fantasy television programs.

  UF   Apocalyptic fantasies
       End-of-the-world fantasies
       Fantastic television programs
  BT   **Television programs**
  RT   **Horror television programs**
       Science fiction television programs

Far East
  USE **East Asia**
Far north
  USE **Arctic regions**
Farces 808.82; 812, etc.
> May be used for individual works, collections, or materials about farces.

  BT   **Comedies**
Farm animals
  USE **Domestic animals**
Farm buildings (May subdiv. geog.)
    631.2; 728
  UF   Architecture, Rural
       Rural architecture
  SA   types of farm buildings [to be
       added as needed]
  BT   **Buildings**
  NT   **Barns**
Farm credit
  USE **Agricultural credit**
Farm crops
  USE **Farm produce**

Farm engines
  USE **Agricultural machinery**
Farm equipment
  USE **Agricultural machinery**
Farm family (May subdiv. geog.)
    306.85
  UF   Rural families
  BT   **Family**
  RT   **Family farms**
       Farm life
       Rural sociology
Farm implements
  USE **Agricultural machinery**
Farm laborers
  USE **Agricultural laborers**
Farm life (May subdiv. geog.) **306.3;
    630**
  UF   Rural life
  BT   **Country life**
       Farmers
  NT   **Ranch life**
  RT   **Family farms**
       Farm family
       Rural sociology
Farm life—United States 306.3; 630
Farm loans
  USE **Agricultural credit**
Farm machinery
  USE **Agricultural machinery**
Farm management 630
  BT   **Farms**
       Management
  RT   **Agriculture—Economic aspects**
Farm mechanics
  USE **Agricultural engineering**
       Agricultural machinery
Farm produce (May subdiv. geog.)
    338.1; 630; 631.5
  UF   Agricultural products
       Crops
       Farm crops
       Products, Agricultural
  SA   types of farm products [to be
       added as needed]
  BT   **Food**
       Raw materials
  NT   **Hay**
Farm produce—Marketing 338.1
  UF   Marketing of farm produce
  BT   **Marketing**
       Prices

Farm produce—Marketing—*Continued*
RT **Agriculture—Economic aspects**
Farm subsidies
USE **Agricultural subsidies**
Farm tenancy (May subdiv. geog.)
333.5

Use for materials on the economic and social aspects of farm tenancy. Materials on the legal aspects are entered under **Landlord and tenant.**

UF Agriculture—Tenant farming
Tenant farming
BT **Farms**
Land tenure
NT **Sharecropping**
RT **Landlord and tenant**
Farmers (May subdiv. geog.) **630.92; 920**
BT **Agriculture**
NT **Farm life**
Farmers' cooperatives
USE **Cooperative agriculture**
Farming
USE **Agriculture**
Farming, Dry
USE **Dry farming**
Farming, Organic
USE **Organic farming**
Farms 333.76; 630; 636
BT **Land use**
Real estate
NT **Family farms**
Farm management
Farm tenancy
Vineyards
RT **Agriculture**
Fascism (May subdiv. geog.) **320.53; 321.9; 335.6**

Use for materials on the political philosophy, movements, or regimes that advocate a centralized autocratic government, severe economic and social regimentation, and the exaltation of nation and race over the individual. Materials on fascism in Germany during the Nazi regime are entered under **National socialism.**

UF Authoritarianism
Neo-fascism
BT **Totalitarianism**
NT **National socialism**
Neo-Nazis
Fascism—United States 320.5; 973.9
Fashion (May subdiv. geog.) **391**

Use for materials on the prevailing mode or style of dress. Materials on the characteristic costume of ethnic or national groups and for materials on fancy dress and theatrical costumes are entered under **Costume.** Materials on clothing and the art of dress from day to day in practical situations, including historical dress and the clothing of various professions or classes of persons, are entered under **Clothing and dress.**

UF Style in dress
BT **Clothing and dress**
RT **Fashion design**
Fashion design (May subdiv. geog.)
746.9
BT **Clothing industry**
Commercial art
Design
RT **Fashion**
Fashion industry
USE **Clothing industry**
Fashion models 659.1; 746.9
UF Manikins (Fashion models)
Mannequins (Fashion models)
Models
Models (Persons)
Style manikins
BT **Advertising**
Fashion shows 391; 659.1
BT **Exhibitions**
Fashionable society
USE **Upper class**
Fast food restaurants (May subdiv. geog.)
647.95
BT **Convenience foods**
Restaurants
Fast foods
USE **Convenience foods**
Faster reading
USE **Speed reading**
Fasting 178; 248.4; 291.4; 296.7
UF Abstinence
BT **Asceticism**
Diet
NT **Hunger strikes**
RT **Hunger**
Religious holidays
Starvation
Fasts and feasts
USE **Religious holidays**
Fasts and feasts—Christianity
USE **Christian holidays**
Fasts and feasts—Judaism
USE **Jewish holidays**
Fatally ill children
USE **Terminally ill children**

Fatally ill patients
USE **Terminally ill**
Fate and fatalism   149
UF Destiny
Fortune
BT **Philosophy**
RT **Free will and determinism**
Predestination
Father and child
USE **Father-child relationship**
Father-child relationship   306.874
UF Child and father
Father and child *[Former heading]*
BT **Children**
Fathers
Parent-child relationship
NT **Father-daughter relationship**
Father-son relationship
Father-daughter relationship   306.874
UF Daughters and fathers
Fathers and daughters *[Former heading]*
BT **Daughters**
Father-child relationship
Fathers
Father-son relationship   306.874
UF Fathers and sons *[Former heading]*
Sons and fathers
BT **Father-child relationship**
Fathers
Sons
Fathers (May subdiv. geog.)   **306.8**
BT **Family**
Men
NT **Father-child relationship**
Father-daughter relationship
Father-son relationship
Teenage fathers
Unmarried fathers
Fathers and daughters
USE **Father-daughter relationship**
Fathers and sons
USE **Father-son relationship**
Fathers of the church   270.1; 920
Use for materials on the lives and thought of the leaders of the Christian church up to the time of Gregory the Great in the West and John of Damascus in the East. Individual works or collections of the writings of early Christian authors are entered under **Early Christian literature.**

UF Church fathers
Patristic philosophy
Patristics
BT **Christian biography**
RT **Early Christian literature**
Fatigue   152.1; 612; 613.7
UF Exhaustion
Weariness
BT **Physiology**
NT **Jet lag**
RT **Rest**
Fatness
USE **Obesity**
Fats
USE **Oils and fats**
Fauna
USE **Animals**
Zoology
Fawns
USE **Deer**
Fax machines
USE **Fax transmission**
Fax transmission   384.1; 621.382
Use for the machines, the processes, and the products of facsimile transmission.
UF Facsimile transmission *[Former heading]*
Fax machines
BT **Data transmission systems**
Telecommunication
Fear   152.4
BT **Emotions**
NT **Horror**
Phobias
RT **Anxiety**
Feast days
USE **Religious holidays**
Feast of Dedication
USE **Hanukkah**
Feast of Lights
USE **Hanukkah**
Fecundity
USE **Fertility**
Federal aid (May subdiv. geog.)   **336**
Use for materials on central government aid in federal systems. Materials on aid from governments at any level in non-federal systems and on aid from states, provinces, or local governments in federal systems are entered under **Government aid.**
SA federal aid to specific endeavors,
e.g. **Federal aid to the arts**
[to be added as needed]

Federal aid—*Continued*
  BT **Public finance**
  NT **Federal aid to education**
      Federal aid to libraries
      Federal aid to minority business enterprises
      Federal aid to the arts
  RT **Government aid**
Federal aid to education (May subdiv. geog.) **379.1**
  UF Education—Federal aid
  BT **Education—Government policy**
      Federal aid
  RT **Colleges and universities—Finance**
      Education—Finance
Federal aid to libraries (May subdiv. geog.) **021.8**
  UF Libraries—Federal aid
  BT **Federal aid**
      Libraries—Government policy
  RT **Library finance**
Federal aid to minority business enterprises (May subdiv. geog.) **338.6**
  UF Minority business enterprises—Federal aid
  BT **Federal aid**
      Subsidies
Federal aid to the arts (May subdiv. geog.) **353.7; 700**
  UF Art—Federal aid
      Arts and state
      Arts—Federal aid
      Funding for the arts
      State and the arts
      State encouragement of the arts
  BT **Federal aid**
  RT **Art patronage**
      Arts—Government policy
Federal budget
  USE **Budget—United States**
Federal-city relations **351.09**
  UF City-federal relations
      Federal-municipal relations
      Municipal-federal relations
      Urban-federal relations
  BT **Federal government**
      Municipal government
Federal courts
  USE **Courts—United States**
Federal debt
  USE **Public debts**

Federal government **321.02; 351**
  UF Confederacies
      Federalism
  BT **Constitutional law**
      Political science
      Republics
  NT **European federation**
      Federal-city relations
      Federal-state relations
  RT **State governments**
Federal-Indian relations
  USE **Native Americans—Government relations**
Federal libraries
  USE **Government libraries**
Federal-municipal relations
  USE **Federal-city relations**
Federal Republic of Germany
  USE **Germany**
      Germany (West)
Federal Reserve banks **332.1**
  BT **Banks and banking**
Federal revenue sharing
  USE **Revenue sharing**
Federal spending policy
  USE **United States—Appropriations and expenditures**
Federal-state relations **321.02**
  UF State-federal relations
  BT **Federal government**
      State governments
Federal-state tax relations
  USE **Intergovernmental tax relations**
Federalism
  USE **Federal government**
Federation of Europe
  USE **European federation**
Feedback control systems **629.8**
  BT **Automation**
  NT **Servomechanisms**
Feedback (Psychology) **153.1**
  BT **Psychology of learning**
  NT **Biofeedback training**
Feeding behavior in animals
  USE **Animals—Food**
Feeds **633.2; 633.3**
  UF Fodder
  SA types of feeds, e.g. **Oats** [to be added as needed]

274

Feeds—*Continued*
    BT   **Animals—Food**
    NT   **Forage plants**
            Oats
            Silage and silos
    RT   **Grasses**
            Hay
            Root crops
Feeling
    USE **Perception**
            Touch
Feelings
    USE **Emotions**
Fees
    USE **Salaries, wages, etc.**
Feet
    USE **Foot**
Felidae
    USE **Wild cats**
Fellowships
    USE **Scholarships**
Felony
    USE **Crime**
Female actors
    USE **Actresses**
Female climacteric
    USE **Menopause**
Female identity
    USE **Women—Identity**
Female-male relationship
    USE **Man-woman relationship**
Female role
    USE **Sex role**
Feminine identity
    USE **Women—Identity**
Feminine psychology
    USE **Women—Psychology**
Femininity (May subdiv. geog.)   **155.3**
    UF   Femininity (Psychology)
    BT   **Sex (Psychology)**
    RT   **Women**
Femininity of God   **212; 231**
    UF   God—Femininity .
    BT   **God**
Femininity (Psychology)
    USE **Femininity**
Feminism (May subdiv. geog.)   **305.42;**
       323.3
    Use for materials on the theory of the political and social equality of the sexes and women's perspectives on various subjects. Materials on activities aimed at obtaining equal rights and opportunities for women are entered under **Women's movement.**
    UF   Feminist theory
    SA   types of feminist endeavors, e.g. **Feminist criticism; Feminist theology;** etc. [to be added as needed]
    NT   **Women—History**
    RT   **Suffragists**
           Women's movement
           Women's rights
Feminist criticism   **801**
    UF   Criticism, Feminist
    BT   **Criticism**
Feminist theology   **230**
    Use for materials on the feminist critique of traditional theology and on alternative theology from a feminist perspective.
    BT   **Theology**
Feminist theory
    USE **Feminism**
Fencing   **796.86**
    UF   Fighting
    BT   **Physical education**
Feng-shui (May subdiv. geog.)   **133.3**
    BT   **Divination**
Feral animals
    USE **Wildlife**
Feral cats
    USE **Wild cats**
Feral children
    USE **Wild children**
Fermentation   **547; 660; 663**
    UF   Ferments
    BT   **Chemical engineering**
           Chemistry
           Microbiology
Ferments
    USE **Fermentation**
Ferns   **587; 635.9**
    BT   **Plants**
Fertility   **573.6; 591.1**
    Use for general materials on fertility in animals, including humans. Materials limited to fertility in humans are entered under **Human fertility.**
    UF   Fecundity
    BT   **Reproduction**
    NT   **Human fertility**
    RT   **Infertility**
Fertility control
    USE **Birth control**
Fertility, Human
    USE **Human fertility**

Fertilization in vitro   176; 618.1;
    636.089
UF   Fertilization in vitro, Human
        Fertilization, Test tube
        In vitro fertilization
        Laboratory fertilization
        Test tube babies
        Test tube fertilization
BT   **Genetic engineering**
        Reproduction
Fertilization in vitro, Human
USE   **Fertilization in vitro**
Fertilization of plants   575.6
UF   Plants—Fertilization
        Pollination
BT   **Plant physiology**
        Plants
Fertilization, Test tube
USE   **Fertilization in vitro**
Fertilizers   631.8; 668
UF   Fertilizers and manures
        Manures
BT   **Agricultural chemicals**
        Soils
NT   **Compost**
        Lime
        Nitrates
        Phosphates
        Potash
Fertilizers and manures
USE   **Fertilizers**
Festivals (May subdiv. geog.)   **394.26**
    Use for materials on occasions other than
holidays devoted to festive community obser-
vances or to programs of cultural events. Ma-
terials on days of general exemption from
work or days publicly dedicated to the com-
memoration of some person, event, or princi-
ple are entered under **Holidays.** Materials on
religious fasts and feasts are entered under
Religious holidays.
UF   Fiestas
SA   types of festivals and names of
        specific festivals, e.g. **Carni-
        val** [to be added as needed]
BT   **Days**
        Manners and customs
NT   **Carnival**
        Carnivals
        Craft shows
        Film festivals
        Music festivals
        Parades
        Powwows

RT   **Holidays**
        Pageants
        Religious holidays
Festivals—United States   394.260973
Fetal death
USE   **Miscarriage**
Fetus   571.8; 612.6
UF   Unborn child
BT   **Embryology**
        Reproduction
Feudalism (May subdiv. geog.)   321
UF   Fiefs
        Vassals
BT   **Land tenure**
        Medieval civilization
NT   **Peasantry**
RT   **Chivalry**
Fever   616
SA   types of fevers, e.g. **Malaria** [to
        be added as needed]
BT   **Pathology**
NT   **Malaria**
        Typhoid fever
RT   **Body temperature**
Fiber content of food
USE   **Food—Fiber content**
Fiber glass
USE   **Glass fibers**
Fiberglass
USE   **Glass fibers**
Fibers   677
UF   Textile fibers
NT   **Cotton**
        Flax
        Glass fibers
        Hemp
        Linen
        Paper
        Silk
        Wool
Fibers, Glass
USE   **Glass fibers**
Fiction   808.3
    Use for collections and materials about fic-
tion from several countries and for materials
on fiction as a literary form, not for individual
works.
UF   Novels
        Stories
SA   fiction of particular national lit-
        eratures, e.g. **American fic-
        tion;** genres of fiction, e.g.

Fiction—*Continued*
    Fantasy fiction; and subjects, names of places, and personal and corporate names with the subdivision *Fiction,* to express the theme or subject content of collections of fiction, e.g. **Slavery—United States—Fiction; United States—History—1861-1865, Civil War—Fiction; Ohio—Fiction; Napoleon I, Emperor of the French, 1769-1821—Fiction;** etc. [to be added as needed]
  BT **Literature**
  NT **Adventure fiction**
       Allegories
       Allegory
       American fiction
       Bible fiction
       Bildungsromans
       Biographical fiction
       Black humor (Literature)
       Children's stories
       Christian fiction
       Didactic fiction
       English fiction
       Epistolary fiction
       Erotic fiction
       Fables
       Fairy tales
       Fantasy fiction
       Folklore
       Historical fiction
       Horror fiction
       Humorous fiction
       Interplanetary voyages
       Jewish religious fiction
       Legal stories
       Legends
       Love stories
       Medical novels
       Movie novels
       Mystery fiction
       Occult fiction
       Pastoral fiction
       Picaresque literature
       Plot-your-own stories
       Radio and television novels
       Religious fiction
       Romances

       Romans à clef
       School stories
       Science fiction
       Sea stories
       Short stories
       Short story
       War stories
       Western stories
Fiction for children
  USE **Children's stories**
Fiction—History and criticism 809.3
Fiction—Technique 808.3
  BT **Authorship**
Fictional characters
  USE **Characters and characteristics in literature**
Fictional plots
  USE **Stories, plots, etc.**
Fictitious characters
  USE **Characters and characteristics in literature**
Fictitious names
  USE **Pseudonyms**
Fictitious places
  USE **Geographical myths**
Fiddle
  USE **Violins**
Fiduciaries
  USE **Trusts and trustees**
Fiefs
  USE **Feudalism**
       Land tenure
Field athletics
  USE **Track athletics**
Field hockey 796.35
  BT **Sports**
Field hospitals
  USE **Military hospitals**
       Military medicine
Field photography
  USE **Outdoor photography**
Field trips 069; 371.3
  UF School excursions
       School trips
  BT **Student activities**
Fiestas
  USE **Festivals**
Fifteenth century
  USE **World history—15th century**

Fifth column
  USE **Subversive activities**
       World War, 1939-1945—Col-
       laborationists
Fighting
  USE **Battles**
       Boxing
       Bullfights
       Dueling
       Fencing
       Gladiators
       Military art and science
       Naval art and science
       Self-defense
       Self-defense for women
       War
Figure drawing   743.4
  UF   Human figure in art
  BT   **Artistic anatomy**
       Drawing
  RT   **Figure painting**
Figure painting   757
  UF   Human figure in art
  BT   **Artistic anatomy**
       Painting
  RT   **Figure drawing**
       Portrait painting
Figure skating
  USE **Ice skating**
Files and filing   005.74; 025.3; 651.5
  UF   Alphabetizing
       Filing systems
  BT   **Office management**
  RT   **Indexing**
Filing systems
  USE **Files and filing**
Filling stations
  USE **Service stations**
Fills (Earthwork)
  USE **Landfills**
Film adaptations   791.43
    May be used for individual works, collec-
    tions, or materials about film adaptations of
    material from other media.
  UF   Adaptations
       Filmed books
       Films from books
       Literature—Film and video adap-
         tations
       Motion picture adaptations

  SA   names of authors, titles of anon-
       ymous literary works, types of
       literature, and types of musi-
       cal compositions with the
       subdivision *Adaptations,* for
       individual works, collections,
       or criticism and interpretation
       of literary, cinematic, video,
       or television adaptations, e.g.,
       Shakespeare, William, 1564-
       1616—Adaptations;
       Beowulf—Adaptations; Ar-
       thurian romances—Adapta-
       tions; etc. [to be added as
       needed]
  BT   **Motion pictures**
Film catalogs
  USE **Motion pictures—Catalogs**
Film direction
  USE **Motion pictures—Production**
       and direction
Film directors
  USE **Motion picture producers and**
       directors
Film epics
  USE **Epic films**
Film festivals   791.43
  UF   Motion picture festivals
       Movie festivals
  BT   **Festivals**
Film industry (Motion pictures)
  USE **Motion picture industry**
Film noir   791.43
  UF   Crime films
       Films noirs
  BT   **Motion pictures**
  RT   **Mystery films**
Film posters   741.6; 791.43
  UF   Motion picture posters
       Motion pictures—Posters
       Movie posters
       Playbills
  BT   **Posters**
Film producers
  USE **Motion picture producers and**
       directors
Film production
  USE **Motion pictures—Production**
       and direction
Film projectors
  USE **Projectors**

Film scripts
    USE **Motion picture plays**
Filmed books
    USE **Film adaptations**
Filmmaking
    USE **Motion pictures—Production
          and direction**
Filmography
    USE **Motion pictures—Catalogs**
          and types of motion pictures
          with the subdivision *Catalogs,*
          e.g. **Science fiction films—
          Catalogs;** and subjects, class-
          es of persons, corporate enti-
          ties, and names of individual
          persons with the subdivision
          Filmography, e.g. **Animals—
          Filmography; Shakespeare,
          William, 1564-1616—Filmog-
          raphy;** etc. [to be added as
          needed]
Films
    USE **Filmstrips
          Motion pictures**
Films from books
    USE **Film adaptations**
Films noirs
    USE **Film noir**
Filmstrips   371.33; 778.2
    UF   Films
          Strip films
    BT   **Audiovisual materials
          Photography**
    RT   **Slides (Photography)**
Finance (May subdiv. geog.)   **332**
      Use for general materials on the manage-
    ment of money and credit. Materials on the
    raising and expenditure of funds in the public
    sector are entered under **Public finance.**
    UF   Funding
          Funds
    SA   subjects, ethnic groups, names of
          wars, and names of corporate
          bodies with the subdivision
          Finance, e.g. **Education—Fi-
          nance** [to be added as need-
          ed]
    BT   **Economics**
    NT   **Bankruptcy
          Banks and banking
          Bonds
          Capital**

**Church finance
Colleges and universities—Fi-
    nance
Commerce
Corporations—Finance
Credit
Debt
Education—Finance
Endowments
Financial crises
Foreign exchange
Fund raising
Income
Inflation (Finance)
Insurance
Interest (Economics)
Investments
Library finance
Loans
Money
Personal finance
Prices
Public finance
Railroads—Finance
Securities
Speculation
Stock exchanges
United Nations—Finance
Wealth**
    RT   **Monetary policy**
Finance, Household
    USE **Household budgets**
Finance—Mathematics
    USE **Business mathematics**
Finance, Municipal
    USE **Municipal finance**
Finance, Personal
    USE **Personal finance**
Finance, Public
    USE **Public finance**
Finance—United States   **332.0973;
          336.73**
Financial accounting
    USE **Accounting**
Financial aid to students
    USE **Student aid**
Financial crashes
    USE **Financial crises**

Financial crises (May subdiv. geog.)
    338 5
  UF Crashes (Finance)
      Financial crashes
      Financial panics
      Panics (Finance)
      Stock exchange crashes
      Stock market panics
  BT **Finance**
  RT **Business cycles**
Financial panics
  USE **Financial crises**
Financial planning, Personal
  USE **Personal finance**
Financiers
  USE **Capitalists and financiers**
Finding things
  USE **Lost and found possessions**
Finger alphabet
  USE **Deaf—Means of communication**
Finger games
  USE **Finger play**
Finger marks
  USE **Fingerprints**
Finger painting   **751.4**
  UF Painting, Finger
  BT **Child artists**
      Painting
Finger play   **793.4**
  UF Finger games
  BT **Play**
Finger pressure therapy
  USE **Acupressure**
Finger prints
  USE **Fingerprints**
Fingerprints   **363.25**
  UF Finger marks
      Finger prints
  BT **Anthropometry**
      Criminal investigation
      Criminals—Identification
      Identification
Finishes and finishing   **667; 684.1; 698; 745.7**
  UF Finishing
      Finishing materials
  SA topics with the subdivision *Finishing,* e.g. **Metals—Finishing;** or with the subdivision *Painting,* e.g. **Automobiles—**

Painting [to be added as needed]
  BT **Materials**
  NT **Industrial painting**
      Lacquer and lacquering
      Metals—Finishing
      Paint
      Varnish and varnishing
      Wood finishing
Finishing
  USE **Finishes and finishing**
      and topics with the subdivision *Finishing,* e.g. **Metals—Finishing** [to be added as needed]
Finishing materials
  USE **Finishes and finishing**
Finno-Russian War, 1939-1940
  USE **Russo-Finnish War, 1939-1940**
Fire   **536; 541.3**
  BT **Chemistry**
  NT **Fires**
      Fuel
  RT **Combustion**
      Heat
Fire bombs
  USE **Incendiary bombs**
Fire departments (May subdiv. geog.)
    628.9
  UF Fire stations
  RT **Fire fighters**
Fire engines   **628.9**
  BT **Engines**
      Fire fighting
Fire fighters (May subdiv. geog.)
    363.37092; 920
  UF Firemen and firewomen
  RT **Fire departments**
Fire fighting (May subdiv. geog.)   **628.9**
  BT **Fire prevention**
      Fires
  NT **Fire engines**
Fire insurance   **368.1**
  UF Insurance, Fire
  BT **Insurance**
  NT **Fireproofing**

Fire prevention (May subdiv. geog.)
     363.37; 628.9
  UF Prevention of fire
  SA types of institutions, buildings,
       industries, and vehicles with
       the subdivision *Fires and fire*
       prevention, e.g. **Nuclear pow-**
       er plants—Fires and fire
       prevention [to be added as
       needed]
  BT **Fires**
  NT **Fire fighting**
       Fireproofing
       Nuclear power plants—Fires
       and fire prevention
Fire stations
  USE **Fire departments**
Firearms (May subdiv. geog.)   623.4;
     739.7
  UF Guns
       Small arms
  SA types of firearms [to be added
       as needed]
  BT **Weapons**
  NT **Gunpowder**
       Handguns
       Rifles
       Shotguns
  RT **Ammunition**
       Shooting
Firearms control
  USE **Gun control**
Firearms industry (May subdiv. geog.)
     338.4; 683.4
    Use for materials on the small arms indus-
    try. Materials on the production of military
    weapons are entered under **Defense industry.**
  UF Firearms industry and trade
       Firearms trade
       Gunsmithing
       Weapons industry
  BT **Industries**
Firearms industry and trade
  USE **Firearms industry**
Firearms—Law and legislation
  USE **Gun control**
Firearms trade
  USE **Firearms industry**
Firemen and firewomen
  USE **Fire fighters**

Fireplaces   697; 749
  BT **Architecture—Details**
       Buildings
       Heating
       Space heaters
  RT **Chimneys**
Fireproofing   628.9; 693.8
  BT **Fire insurance**
       Fire prevention
Fires (May subdiv. geog.)   363.37; 904
  SA types of institutions, buildings,
       industries, and vehicles with
       the subdivision *Fires and fire*
       prevention, e.g. **Nuclear pow-**
       er plants—Fires and fire
       prevention [to be added as
       needed]
  BT **Accidents**
       Disasters
       Fire
  NT **Fire fighting**
       Fire prevention
       Forest fires
       Nuclear power plants—Fires
       and fire prevention
Fires and fire prevention
  USE types of institutions, buildings,
       industries, and vehicles with
       the subdivision *Fires and fire*
       prevention, e.g. **Nuclear pow-**
       er plants—Fires and fire
       prevention [to be added as
       needed]
Fireworks   662
  BT **Amusements**
Firms
  USE **Business enterprises**
First aid   362.1; 616.02
  UF Emergencies
       Injuries
       Wounded, First aid to
  BT **Health self-care**
       Home accidents
       Medicine
       Nursing
       Rescue work
       Sick
  NT **Artificial respiration**
       Bandages
       Cardiac resuscitation

First aid—*Continued*
  RT Accidents
      Lifesaving
First editions 094
  UF Bibliography—First editions
      Books—First editions
  SA types of publications, types of
      literature, and names of au-
      thors and composers with the
      subdivision *First editions,* e.g.
      **English literature—First edi-
      tions** [to be added as needed]
  BT **Editions**
First generation children
  USE **Children of immigrants**
First ladies—United States
  USE **Presidents' spouses—United
       States**
First names
  USE **Personal names**
First nations
  USE **Native Americans—Canada**
First World War
  USE **World War, 1914-1918**
Firstborn child
  USE **Birth order**
Fiscal policy (May subdiv. geog.) **336.3**
  UF Government policy
  BT **Economic policy**
      Public finance
  RT **Monetary policy**
Fiscal policy—United States 336.73
  UF United States—Fiscal policy
Fish
  USE **Fish as food**
       Fishes
Fish as food 641.3
  UF Fish
  BT **Cooking**
      Fishes
      Food
  RT **Seafood**
Fish culture (May subdiv. geog.) **639.3**
  Use for materials on the cultivation of fish
  in captivity. Materials on fishing as an indus-
  try are entered under **Commercial fishing.**
  UF Fish farming
      Fish hatcheries
  BT **Aquaculture**
  RT **Aquariums**
Fish farming
  USE **Fish culture**

Fish hatcheries
  USE **Fish culture**
Fisheries
  USE **Commercial fishing**
Fishes (May subdiv. geog.) **597**
  UF Fish
      Ichthyology
  SA types of fishes, e.g. **Salmon** [to
      be added as needed]
  BT **Aquatic animals**
  NT **Fish as food**
      Goldfish
      Salmon
      Tropical fish
  RT **Aquariums**
**Fishes—Geographical distribution
597.09**
  BT **Biogeography**
Fishes—Photography
  USE **Photography of fishes**
Fishes—United States 597.0973
Fishing (May subdiv. geog.) **799.1**
  Use for materials on fishing as a sport. Ma-
  terials on fishing as an industry are entered
  under **Commercial fishing.**
  UF Angling
  SA types of fishing [to be added as
      needed]
  BT **Sports**
  NT **Artificial flies**
      Fly casting
      Spear fishing
      Trout fishing
Fishing, Commercial
  USE **Commercial fishing**
Fishing—Equipment and supplies 799.1
  UF Fishing tackle
Fishing flies
  USE **Artificial flies**
Fishing industry
  USE **Commercial fishing**
Fishing tackle
  USE **Fishing—Equipment and sup-
       plies**
Fishing—United States 799.10973
Fitness
  USE **Physical fitness**
Five-day work week
  USE **Hours of labor**
Fixing
  USE **Repairing**

Flags (May subdiv. geog.)   **929.9**
    UF   Banners
           Ensigns
    BT   **Heraldry**
    RT   **National emblems**
           Signals and signaling
Flags—United States   929.9
    UF   American flag
           United States—Flags
Flats
    USE **Apartments**
Flatware, Silver
    USE **Silverware**
Flavoring essences   664
    BT   **Cooking**
           Essences and essential oils
           Food
Flax   633.5; 677
    BT   **Fibers**
           Yarn
    RT   **Linen**
Flexible hours of labor   331.25
    UF   Alternative work schedules
           Flexible work hours
           Flextime
           Four-day week
           Hours of labor, Flexible
    BT   **Hours of labor**
Flexible work hours
    USE **Flexible hours of labor**
Flextime
    USE **Flexible hours of labor**
Flies   595.77
    UF   Fly
           House flies
    SA   types of flies [to be added as needed]
    BT   **Household pests**
           Insects
           Pests
    NT   **Fruit flies**
Flies, Artificial
    USE **Artificial flies**
Flight   629.13
    UF   Flying
    SA   types of animals with the subdivision *Flight,* e.g. **Birds—Flight** [to be added as needed]

BT   **Locomotion**
NT   **Animal flight**
RT   **Aeronautics**
Flight attendants   387.7
    UF   Airline hostesses
           Airline stewardesses
           Airline stewards
           Stewardesses, Airline
           Stewards, Airline
    BT   **Airlines**
Flight to the moon
    USE **Space flight to the moon**
Flight training
    USE **Aeronautics—Study and teaching**
              Airplanes—Piloting
Flights around the world
    USE **Aeronautics—Flights**
Flint implements
    USE **Stone implements**
Floating hospitals
    USE **Hospital ships**
Floats (Parades)
    USE **Parades**
Flood control (May subdiv. geog.)   627
    UF   Flood prevention
    BT   **Hydraulic engineering**
    RT   **Forest influences**
Flood prevention
    USE **Flood control**
Floods (May subdiv. geog.)   363.34; 551.48; 904
    May also be subdivided by names of rivers or river valleys, e.g. **Floods—Mississippi River.**
    BT   **Meteorology**
           Natural disasters
           Rain
           Water
    RT   **Rivers**
Floods and forests
    USE **Forest influences**
Floods—Mississippi River   363.34
Floors   690; 721
    BT   **Architecture—Details**
           Buildings
Flora
    USE **Botany**
           Plants
Floral decoration
    USE **Flower arrangement**

Floriculture
USE **Flower gardening**
Florists' designs
USE **Flower arrangement**
Flour   641.3; 664
RT **Grain**
Flour mills   664
UF Grist mills
Milling (Flour)
BT **Mills**
Flow charts
USE **Graphic methods**
System analysis
Flowcharting
USE **Graphic methods**
System analysis
Flower arrangement   745.92
Use for materials on the artistic arrangement of flowers, including decoration of houses, churches, etc., with flowers.
UF Designs, Floral
Floral decoration
Florists' designs
Flowers—Arrangement
BT **Decoration and ornament**
Flowers
Table setting and decoration
Flower drying
USE **Flowers—Drying**
Flower gardening (May subdiv. geog.)
635.9
Use for practical materials on the cultivation of flowering plants for either commercial or private purposes.
UF Floriculture
SA types of flowers, e.g. **Roses** [to be added as needed]
BT **Gardening**
Horticulture
NT **Annuals (Plants)**
Bulbs
Greenhouses
House plants
Ornamental plants
Perennials
RT **Container gardening**
Flowers
Window gardening
Flower painting and illustration
USE **Botanical illustration**
Flowers in art
Flower prints
USE **Flowers in art**

Flower shows   635.9074
UF Flowers—Exhibitions
BT **Exhibitions**
Flowers (May subdiv. geog.)   **575.6;**
582.13
Use for general materials on flowers. Materials limited to the cultivation of flowers are entered under **Flower gardening.**
SA types of flowers, e.g. **Roses** [to be added as needed]
BT **Plants**
NT **Annuals (Plants)**
Flower arrangement
Perennials
Roses
State flowers
Wild flowers
RT **Flower gardening**
Flowers—Arrangement
USE **Flower arrangement**
Flowers, Artificial
USE **Artificial flowers**
Flowers, Drying
USE **Flowers—Drying**
Flowers—Drying   745.92
UF Dried flowers
Flower drying
Flowers, Drying
BT **Plants—Collection and preservation**
Flowers—Exhibitions
USE **Flower shows**
Flowers in art   758
UF Flower painting and illustration
Flower prints
BT **Art—Themes**
Flowers—United States   582.130973
Flu
USE **Influenza**
Fluid mechanics   532; 620.1
Use for materials on the branch of mechanics dealing with the properties of liquids or gases, either at rest or in motion.
UF Hydromechanics
BT **Mechanics**
NT **Gases**
Hydraulic engineering
Hydraulics
Hydrodynamics
Hydrostatics
Liquids

Fluorescent lighting   621.32
  UF   Electric lighting, Fluorescent
  BT   **Electric lighting**
Fluoridation of water
  USE   **Water fluoridation**
Flute
  USE   **Flutes**
Flutes   788.3
  UF   Flute
  BT   **Wind instruments**
Fly
  USE   **Flies**
Fly casting   799.1
  UF   Fly fishing
  BT   **Fishing**
  NT   **Artificial flies**
Fly fishing
  USE   **Fly casting**
Flying
  USE   **Flight**
Flying saucers
  USE   **Unidentified flying objects**
FM radio
  USE   **Radio frequency modulation**
Foals
  USE   **Horses**
      Ponies
Fodder
  USE   **Feeds**
Fog   551.57
  BT   **Atmosphere**
      Meteorology
Fog signals
  USE   **Signals and signaling**
Foliage
  USE   **Leaves**
Folk art   745
  Use for materials on objects of fine or dec-
  orative art produced in a peasant, popular, or
  naive style, often in cultural isolation and by
  unschooled artists or artisans.
  UF   Peasant art
  SA   folk art of particular countries or
      ethnic groups, e.g. **American
      folk art** [to be added as
      needed]
  BT   **Art**
      Art and society
  NT   **American folk art**
  RT   **Arts and crafts movement**
      Decorative arts
      Handicraft

Folk art, American
  USE   **American folk art**
Folk beliefs
  USE   **Folklore**
      Superstition
Folk dances
  USE   **Folk dancing**
Folk dancing (May subdiv. geog.)   793.3
  UF   Folk dances
      National dances
  SA   dance of particular ethnic
      groups, e.g. **Native American
      dance** [to be added as need-
      ed]
  BT   **Dance**
  NT   **Native American dance**
      Square dancing
Folk dancing—United States   793.3
  UF   American folk dancing *[Former
      heading]*
Folk drama   808.82; 812, etc.; 812.008,
      etc.
  May be used for collections or materials
  about folk drama, not for individual works.
  UF   Folk plays
  BT   **Drama**
  NT   **Puppets and puppet plays**
Folk lore
  USE   **Folklore**
Folk medicine
  USE   **Traditional medicine**
Folk music (May subdiv. geog.)   781.62
  BT   **Music**
Folk music—United States   781.6200973
  UF   American folk music
  NT   **Blues music**
      Country music
Folk plays
  USE   **Folk drama**
Folk psychology
  USE   **Ethnopsychology**
Folk songs (May subdiv. geog.)
      782.42162
  Use for materials about folk songs and col-
  lections of folk songs that include both words
  and music. Materials about ballads and collec-
  tions of ballads without music are entered un-
  der **Ballads.**
  SA   folk songs of particular ethnic
      groups, e.g. **Creole folk
      songs** [to be added as need-
      ed]

Folk songs—*Continued*
  BT **Folklore**
      Songs
      Vocal music
  NT **Carols**
      Creole folk songs
  RT **Ballads**
      National songs
Folk songs, Creole
  USE **Creole folk songs**
Folk songs—France   782.4216200944
  UF Folk songs, French
      France—Folk songs
      French folk songs [*Former
          heading*]
Folk songs, French
  USE **Folk songs—France**
Folk songs—Ohio   782.42162009771
Folk songs—United States
          782.4216200973
  UF American folk songs
  BT **American songs**
  NT **Spirituals (Songs)**
Folk tales
  USE **Folklore**
       Legends
Folklore (May subdiv. geog.)   398
      Use for general materials on folklore. May
      also be used for individual works, collections,
      and materials about stories based on spoken
      rather than written traditions.
  UF Folk beliefs
      Folk lore
      Folk tales
      Tales
      Traditions
  SA topics as themes in folklore with
      the subdivision *Folklore,* e.g.
      Plants—Folklore; names of
      ethnic or occupational groups
      with the subdivision *Folklore,*
      e.g. **Inuit—Folklore;** types of
      folkloric creatures, e.g. **Elves;**
      and names of individual leg-
      endary characters, e.g. **Bun-
      yan, Paul (Legendary char-
      acter)** [to be added as need-
      ed]
  BT **Ethnology**
      Fiction
      Manners and customs

  NT **African Americans—Folklore**
      Animals—Folklore
      Blacks—Folklore
      Chapbooks
      Charms
      Dragons
      Elves
      Fairies
      Folk songs
      Ghosts
      Giants
      Gnomes
      Goblins
      Grail
      Inuit—Folklore
      Jews—Folklore
      Monsters
      Native Americans—Folklore
      Nursery rhymes
      Plants—Folklore
      Proverbs
      Roland (Legendary character)
      Sagas
      Superstition
      Tall tales
      Tongue twisters
      Vampires
      Weather—Folklore
      Wicca
      Witchcraft
  RT **Fables**
      Fairy tales
      Legends
      Mythology
      Storytelling
Folklore, Medical
  USE **Traditional medicine**
Folklore—United States   398.0973
  NT **Bunyan, Paul (Legendary char-
       acter)**
Folkways
  USE **Manners and customs**
Food   641; 641.3; 664
  SA types of foods, names of specif-
      ic foods, and subjects with
      the subdivision *Food* [to be
      added as needed]
  BT **Home economics**
  NT **Animals—Food**
      Artificial foods
      Beverages

Food—*Continued*
  Bread
  Chocolate
  Convenience foods
  Dietetic foods
  Dining
  Dried foods
  Edible plants
  Eggs
  Farm produce
  Fish as food
  Flavoring essences
  Food of animal origin
  Frozen foods
  Fruit
  Honey
  Meat
  Milk
  Natural foods
  Nuts
  Prepared cereals
  School children—Food
  Seafood
  Spices
  Sugar
  Vegetables
  Vitamins
  RT Cooking
      Diet
      Food industry
      Gastronomy
      Grocery trade
      Nutrition
Food additives   641.3; 664
  UF Additives, Food
  BT Food—Analysis
      Food—Preservation
Food adulteration and inspection (May
    subdiv. geog.)   363.19
  UF Adulteration of food
      Analysis of food
      Food inspection
      Inspection of food
      Pure food
  BT Consumer protection
      Public health
  NT Food contamination
      Meat inspection
      Milk supply
  RT Food—Law and legislation
Food allergies
  USE Food allergy

Food allergy   616.97
  UF Allergies, Food
      Allergy, Food
      Food allergies
  SA types of food allergies [to be
        added as needed]
  BT Allergy
Food—Analysis   664
    Use for materials on methods of analyzing
    foods. Materials presenting the results of the
    analysis of foods are entered under Food—
    Composition.
  UF Analysis of food
      Chemistry of food
      Food chemistry
  SA types of foods with the subdivi-
        sion *Analysis,* e.g. Milk—
        Analysis [to be added as
        needed]
  BT Analytical chemistry
      Industrial chemistry
  NT Food additives
  RT Food—Composition
Food assistance programs
  USE Food relief
Food buying
  USE Grocery shopping
Food, Canned
  USE Canning and preserving
Food chains (Ecology)   577
  BT Animals—Food
      Ecology
Food chemistry
  USE Food—Analysis
      Food—Composition
Food—Cholesterol content   613.2
  UF Cholesterol content of food
  BT Food—Composition
Food—Composition   641; 664
    Use for materials presenting the results of
    the analysis of foods. Materials on methods of
    analyzing foods are entered under Food—
    Analysis.
  UF Chemistry of food
      Food chemistry
  SA food and types of food with
        subdivisions to indicate the
        particular content being ana-
        lyzed, e.g. Food—Cholesterol
        content [to be added as need-
        ed]
  NT Food—Cholesterol content
      Food—Fiber content

Food—Composition—*Continued*
　　Food—Sodium content
　RT　Food—Analysis
Food contamination (May subdiv. geog.)
　　363.19
　UF　Contaminated food
　BT　Food adulteration and inspec-
　　　tion
Food contamination—Press coverage
　　(May subdiv. geog.)　070.4
Food control
　USE　Food supply
Food, Cost of
　USE　Cost and standard of living
Food coupons
　USE　Food stamps
Food customs
　USE　Eating customs
Food—Fiber content　613.2
　UF　Dietary fiber
　　　Fiber content of food
　　　Roughage
　BT　Food—Composition
Food for invalids
　USE　Cooking for the sick
Food for school children
　USE　School children—Food
Food, Freeze dried
　USE　Freeze-dried foods
Food habits
　USE　Eating customs
Food industry (May subdiv. geog.)
　　338.1
　　Use for materials on the processing and
　marketing of food.
　UF　Food preparation
　　　Food preparation industry
　　　Food processing
　　　Food processing industry
　　　Food trade
　SA　type of food industries, e.g.
　　　Beverage industry [to be
　　　added as needed]
　BT　Agricultural industry
　NT　Beverage industry
　　　Food service
　　　Grocery trade
　　　Meat industry
　RT　Food
Food inspection
　USE　Food adulteration and inspec-
　　　tion

Food—Labeling　363.19; 641
　UF　Food labels
Food labels
　USE　Food—Labeling
Food—Law and legislation (May subdiv.
　　geog.)　344
　UF　Food laws
　BT　Law
　　　Legislation
　RT　Food adulteration and inspec-
　　　tion
Food laws
　USE　Food—Law and legislation
Food of animal origin　641.3
　　Use for materials on human food of animal
　origin. Materials on the food and food habits
　of animals are entered under Animals—Food.
　UF　Animal food
　　　Animals as food
　　　Animals, Edible
　BT　Food
Food—Packaging　664
　UF　Groceries—Packaging
　BT　Packaging
Food plants
　USE　Edible plants
Food poisoning　615.9
　BT　Poisons and poisoning
Food preparation
　USE　Cooking
　　　Food industry
Food preparation industry
　USE　Food industry
Food—Preservation　641.4; 664
　UF　Preservation of food
　SA　types of foods with the subdivi-
　　　sion *Preservation* [to be add-
　　　ed as needed]
　NT　Canning and preserving
　　　Cold storage
　　　Food additives
　　　Fruit—Preservation
　RT　Dried foods
　　　Frozen foods
Food processing
　USE　Food industry
Food processing industry
　USE　Food industry
Food—Purchasing
　USE　Grocery shopping

Food relief (May subdiv. geog.)   **363.8**
  UF   Food assistance programs
  SA   types of food relief, e.g. **Meals on wheels programs;** and names of wars with the subdivision *Civilian relief* or *Food supply* [to be added as needed]
  BT   **Charities**
       Disaster relief
       Public welfare
       Unemployed
  NT   **Food stamps**
       Meals on wheels programs
       World War, 1939-1945—Civilian relief
       World War, 1939-1945—Food supply
Food service   **642; 647.95**
  Use for materials on the preparation, delivery, and serving of ready-to-eat foods in large quantities outside of the home. Materials solely on the preparation of food in large quantities are entered under **Quantity cooking.**
  UF   Cooking for institutions
       Mass feeding
       Volume feeding
  BT   **Food industry**
       Service industries
  NT   **Catering**
       Restaurants
       Waiters and waitresses
  RT   **Quantity cooking**
Food—Sodium content   **613.2**
  UF   Sodium content of food
  BT   **Food—Composition**
Food stamp program
  USE   **Food stamps**
Food stamps (May subdiv. geog.)   **363.8**
  UF   Food coupons
       Food stamp program
  BT   **Food relief**
Food supply (May subdiv. geog.)   **363.8**
  Use for economic materials on the availability of food in general and on the conservation of food in wartime.
  UF   Food control
  SA   names of wars with the subdivision *Food supply,* e.g. **World War, 1939-1945—Food supply** [to be added as needed]
  NT   **Famines**
  RT   **Agriculture**

Food trade
  USE   **Food industry**
Fools and jesters   **791.092; 920**
  UF   Court fools
       Jesters
  BT   **Comedians**
       Courts and courtiers
       Entertainers
Foot   **611; 612**
  UF   Feet
  BT   **Anatomy**
Foot—Care   **617.5**
  UF   Foot—Care and hygiene
  BT   **Podiatry**
Foot—Care and hygiene
  USE   **Foot—Care**
Foot injuries
  USE   **Foot—Wounds and injuries**
Foot—Wounds and injuries   **617.5**
  UF   Foot injuries
  RT   **Podiatry**
Football (May subdiv. geog.)   **796.332**
  BT   **Ball games**
       Sports
  NT   **Soccer**
Football—Coaching   **796.33207**
  BT   **Coaching (Athletics)**
Footwear
  USE   **Shoes**
Forage plants (May subdiv. geog.)   **633.2**
  SA   names of forage plants [to be added as needed]
  BT   **Economic botany**
       Feeds
       Plants
  NT   **Alfalfa**
       Corn
       Hay
       Silage and silos
       Soybean
  RT   **Grasses**
Force and energy   **531**
  UF   Conservation of energy
       Energy
  BT   **Power (Mechanics)**
  RT   **Dynamics**
       Mechanics
       Motion
       Quantum theory

Forced indoctrination
USE **Brainwashing**
Forced labor (May subdiv. geog.)
331.11
UF Compulsory labor
Conscript labor
BT **Crimes against humanity**
Labor
NT **Convict labor**
Peonage
RT **Slavery**
Forced removal of Indians
USE **Native Americans—Relocation**
Forced repatriation
USE names of wars with the subdivision *Forced repatriation,* e.g. **World War, 1939-1945—Forced repatriation** [to be added as needed]
Ford automobile   629.222
BT **Automobiles**
Forecasting   003
UF Forecasts
Futurology
Predictions
SA types of forecasting, e.g. **Weather forecasting;** and subjects and names of countries, cities, etc., with the subdivision *Forecasting,* e.g. **Energy consumption—Forecasting** [to be added as needed]
NT **Business forecasting**
Economic forecasting
Weather forecasting
Forecasts
USE **Forecasting**
Foreign affairs
USE **International relations**
Foreign aid (May subdiv. geog.)   **338.91**
Use for general materials on international economic aid given in the form of gifts, loans, relief grants, etc. Materials limited to foreign aid in the form of technical expertise are entered under **Technical assistance.**
UF Aid to developing areas
Assistance to developing areas
Economic aid
Economic assistance
Foreign aid program
Foreign assistance

SA foreign aid from particular countries, e.g. **American foreign aid** [to be added as needed]
BT **Economic policy**
International cooperation
International economic relations
NT **American foreign aid**
Technical assistance
World War, 1939-1945—Civilian relief
RT **Reconstruction (1914-1939)**
Reconstruction (1939-1951)
Foreign aid program
USE **Foreign aid**
Military assistance
Technical assistance
Foreign area studies
USE **Area studies**
Foreign assistance
USE **Foreign aid**
Foreign automobiles (May subdiv. geog.)
629.222
UF Automobiles, Foreign
Foreign cars
SA names of specific makes and models [to be added as needed]
BT **Automobiles**
Foreign cars
USE **Foreign automobiles**
Foreign commerce
USE **International trade**
Foreign countries
USE ethnic and national groups, individual languages and literatures, military services, and types of publications qualified by language or nationality with the subdivision *Foreign countries,* e.g. **Americans—Foreign countries** [to be added as needed]
Foreign economic relations
USE **International economic relations**
and names of countries with the subdivision *Foreign economic relations,* e.g. **United States—Foreign economic re-**

290

Foreign economic relations—*Continued*
      lations [to be added as need-
      ed]
Foreign economic relations—United States
  USE **United States—Foreign eco-
      nomic relations**
Foreign exchange (May subdiv. geog.)
      332.4
  UF Exchange rates
      International exchange
  BT **Banks and banking**
      Exchange
      Finance
      Money
Foreign influences
  USE subjects, ethnic groups, and liter-
      atures with the subdivision
      Foreign influences, e.g. **Unit-
      ed States—Civilization—For-
      eign influences** [to be added
      as needed]
Foreign investments (May subdiv. geog.)
      332.6
  UF International investment
      Investments, Foreign
  BT **Investments**
      Multinational corporations
Foreign language dictionaries
  USE **English language—Diction-
      aries—French**
      **French language—Diction-
      aries—English**
Foreign language laboratories
  USE **Language laboratories**
Foreign language phrases
  USE **English language—Foreign
      words and phrases**
      **Modern languages—Conversa-
      tion and phrase books**
Foreign military sales
  USE **Arms transfers**
Foreign missions, Christian
  USE **Christian missions**
Foreign opinion
  USE names of countries with the sub-
      division *Foreign opinion,*
      which may be further subdi-
      vided by the country holding
      the opinion, e.g. **United
      States—Foreign opinion;
      United States—Foreign opin-**

ion—**France;** etc. [to be add-
      ed as needed]
Foreign policy
  USE **International relations**
Foreign population
  USE **Aliens**
      Immigrants
      Immigration and emigration
      Minorities
      Population
      and names of countries with the
      subdivision *Population,* e.g.
      United States—Population;
      or with the subdivision *Immi-
      gration and emigration,* e.g.
      **United States—Immigration
      and emigration** [to be added
      as needed]
Foreign public opinion
  USE names of countries with the sub-
      division *Foreign opinion,*
      which may be further subdi-
      vided by the country holding
      the opinion, e.g. **United
      States—Foreign opinion;
      United States—Foreign opin-
      ion—France;** etc. [to be add-
      ed as needed]
Foreign relations
  USE **International relations**
      and names of countries with the
      subdivision *Foreign relations,*
      e.g. **United States—Foreign
      relations** [to be added as
      needed]
Foreign service
  USE **Diplomatic and consular ser-
      vice**
Foreign students (May subdiv. geog.)
      370.116
  UF College students, Foreign
      Students, Foreign
  BT **Students**
Foreign study (May subdiv. geog.)
      370.116
  UF Overseas study
      Study abroad
      Study, Foreign
      Study overseas
  BT **Education**

Foreign trade
    USE **International trade**
Foreign words and phrases
    USE names of languages with the subdivision *Foreign words and phrases,* e.g. **English language—Foreign words and phrases** [to be added as needed]
Foreigners
    USE **Aliens**
            Immigrants
Foremen
    USE **Supervisors**
Forensic medicine
    USE **Medical jurisprudence**
Forensic science
    USE **Forensic sciences**
Forensic sciences   363.25
    Use for materials on science as applied in courts of law or in criminal investigations.
    UF Criminalistics
          Forensic science
    BT **Science**
    NT **Medical jurisprudence**
    RT **Criminal investigation**
Foreordination
    USE **Predestination**
Forest animals (May subdiv. geog.)   578.73
    UF Forest fauna
    BT **Animals**
    NT **Jungle animals**
Forest conservation (May subdiv. geog.)   333.75
    UF Conservation of forests
          Forest preservation
          Preservation of forests
    BT **Conservation of natural resources**
    RT **Forest reserves**
          Forests and forestry
Forest fauna
    USE **Forest animals**
Forest fires   634.9
    BT **Fires**
Forest influences   577.3
    UF Climate and forests
          Floods and forests
          Forests and climate
          Forests and floods
          Forests and rainfall

Forests and water supply
          Rainfall and forests
    BT **Climate**
          Water supply
    RT **Flood control**
          Forests and forestry
          Plant ecology
          Rain
Forest plants (May subdiv. geog.)   581.7
    BT **Forests and forestry**
          Plant ecology
          Plants
Forest preservation
    USE **Forest conservation**
Forest products (May subdiv. geog.)   634.9; 674
    BT **Commercial products**
          Economic botany
          Raw materials
    NT **Gums and resins**
          Lumber and lumbering
          Rubber
          Wood
Forest reserves (May subdiv. geog.)   333.75; 719
    UF National forests
    BT **Public lands**
    NT **Wilderness areas**
    RT **Forest conservation**
          Forests and forestry
          National parks and reserves
Forestry
    USE **Forests and forestry**
Forests and climate
    USE **Forest influences**
Forests and floods
    USE **Forest influences**
Forests and forestry (May subdiv. geog.)   577.3; 578.73; 634.9
    UF Arboriculture
          Forestry
          Timber
          Woods
    BT **Agriculture**
          Natural resources
    NT **Christmas tree growing**
          Forest plants
          Jungles
          Logging
          Lumber and lumbering
          Pruning

Forests and forestry—*Continued*
　　Rain forests
　　Reforestation
　　Tree planting
　RT　Forest conservation
　　Forest influences
　　Forest reserves
　　Trees
　　Wood
Forests and forestry—United States
　　577.30973; 634.90973
Forests and rainfall
　USE　Forest influences
Forests and water supply
　USE　Forest influences
Forgeries
　USE　names of individual persons and
　　types of art objects, docu-
　　ments, etc., with the subdivi-
　　sion *Forgeries,* e.g. Art—
　　Forgeries [to be added as
　　needed]
Forgery　332; 364.16
　SA　names of individual persons and
　　types of art objects, docu-
　　ments, etc., with the subdivi-
　　sion *Forgeries,* e.g. Art—
　　Forgeries [to be added as
　　needed]
　BT　Crime
　　Fraud
　　Impostors and imposture
　NT　Art—Forgeries
　　Counterfeits and counterfeiting
　　Literary forgeries
Forgery of works of art
　USE　Art—Forgeries
Forging　671.3; 682
　UF　Drop forging
　BT　Metalwork
　NT　Welding
　RT　Blacksmithing
　　Ironwork
Forgiveness　179
　BT　Virtue
　RT　Amnesty
　　Pardon
Forgiveness of sin
　USE　Confession
　　Penance
Form in biology
　USE　Morphology

Formal gardens
　USE　Gardens
Former nuns
　USE　Ex-nuns
Former priests
　USE　Ex-priests
Former Soviet republics　947.086
　　Use for general materials on several or all
　of the countries that emerged from the disso-
　lution of the Soviet Union in 1991. Materials
　specifically on the federation of independent
　former Soviet republics that was established in
　1991 and does not include Georgia or the Bal-
　tic states are entered under Commonwealth
　of Independent States.
　UF　Ex-Soviet republics
　　Ex-Soviet states
　　Former Soviet states
　RT　Commonwealth of Independent
　　States
　　Soviet Union
Former Soviet states
　USE　Former Soviet republics
Formosa
　USE　Taiwan
Formula translation (Computer language)
　USE　FORTRAN (Computer lan-
　　guage)
Fortification (May subdiv. geog.)　623
　UF　Forts
　SA　names of countries with the sub-
　　division *Defenses* [to be add-
　　ed as needed]
　BT　Military art and science
　RT　Military engineering
FORTRAN (Computer language)
　　005.13
　UF　Formula translation (Computer
　　language)
　　FORTRAN (Computer program
　　language)
　BT　Programming languages
FORTRAN (Computer program language)
　USE　FORTRAN (Computer lan-
　　guage)
Forts
　USE　Fortification
Fortune
　USE　Fate and fatalism
　　Probabilities
　　Success

Fortune telling   133.3
   BT   Amusements
        Divination
   NT   Palmistry
        Tarot
Fortunes
   USE   Income
         Wealth
Forums (Discussions)
   USE   Discussion groups
Fossil botany
   USE   Fossil plants
Fossil hominids (May subdiv. geog.)
       569.9
   UF   Hominids, Fossil
       Human fossils
       Human paleontology
       Man, Prehistoric
       Prehistoric man
       Prehistory
   BT   Archeology
       Fossils
   RT   Human origins
Fossil mammals (May subdiv. geog.)
       569
   UF   Mammals, Fossil
   SA   types of extinct mammals [to be
       added as needed]
   BT   Fossils
       Mammals
   NT   Mastodon
Fossil plants (May subdiv. geog.)   561
   UF   Extinct plants
       Fossil botany
       Paleobotany
       Plants, Extinct
       Plants, Fossil
   BT   Fossils
       Plants
Fossil reptiles (May subdiv. geog.)
       567.9
   UF   Reptiles, Fossil
   SA   types of fossil reptiles, e.g. Di-
       nosaurs [to be added as
       needed]
   BT   Fossils
       Reptiles
   NT   Dinosaurs

Fossils (May subdiv. geog.)   560
   UF   Paleontology
   BT   Biology
       Natural history
       Science
       Stratigraphic geology
   NT   Fossil hominids
       Fossil mammals
       Fossil plants
       Fossil reptiles
       Prehistoric animals
   RT   Extinct animals
Foster children   306.874
   BT   Children
   RT   Foster home care
Foster grandparents   362.73
   BT   Grandparents
       Volunteer work
Foster home care   362.73
   UF   Child placing
       Children—Placing out
   BT   Child welfare
   RT   Adoption
       Children—Institutional care
       Foster children
       Group homes
Foundations   624.1; 721
   BT   Architecture—Details
       Buildings
       Structural engineering
   NT   Basements
       Concrete
   RT   Soil mechanics
Foundations (Endowments)
   USE   Endowments
Founding   671.2
   Use for materials on the melting and cast-
  ing of metals.
   UF   Casting
       Foundry practice
       Molding (Metal)
       Moulding (Metal)
   BT   Metalwork
   NT   Type and type-founding
   RT   Patternmaking
Foundlings
   USE   Orphans
Foundry practice
   USE   Founding
Four-day week
   USE   Flexible hours of labor

Four-H clubs
USE **4-H clubs**
Fourteenth century
USE **World history—14th century**
Fourth dimension   530.11
UF   Dimension, Fourth
Hyperspace
BT   **Mathematics**
NT   **Space and time**
Time travel
Fourth of July   394.2634
UF   4th of July
Independence Day (United
States)
July Fourth
BT   **Holidays**
United States—History—1775-
1783, Revolution
Fractal geometry
USE   **Fractals**
Fractals   514
Use for materials on shapes or mathematical
sets that have fractional, i.e. irregular, dimen-
sions as opposed to the regular dimensions of
Euclidean geometry.
UF   Fractal geometry
Sets, Fractal
Sets of fractional dimension
BT   **Geometry**
Mathematical models
Set theory
Topology
Fractions   513.2
BT   **Arithmetic**
Mathematics
Fractures   617.1
BT   **Bones**
Wounds and injuries
Framing of pictures
USE   **Picture frames and framing**
France   944
May be subdivided like United States ex-
cept for *History.*
France—Blacks
USE   **Blacks—France**
France—Folk songs
USE   **Folk songs—France**
France—History   944
France—History—0-1328   944
NT   **Celts**

France—History—1328-1589, House of
Valois   944
NT   **Hundred Years' War, 1339-**
1453
Saint Bartholomew's Day,
Massacre of, 1572
France—History—1589-1789, Bourbons
944
France—History—1789-1799, Revolution
944.04
UF   Directory, French, 1795-1799
French Revolution
Reign of Terror
Revolution, French
Terror, Reign of
BT   **Revolutions**
France—History—1799-1815   944.05
NT   **Napoleonic Wars, 1800-1815**
France—History—1815-1914   944.06-
944.08
France—History—20th century   944.081
France—History—1914-1940   944.081
France—History—1940-1945, German oc-
cupation   944.081
UF   German occupation of France,
1940-1945
France—History—1945-   944.082
France—History—1945-1958   944.082
France—History—1958-   944.083
UF   France—History—1958-1969
[Former heading]
France—History—1969- *[Former*
heading]
France—History—1958-1969
USE   **France—History—1958-**
France—History—1969-
USE   **France—History—1958-**
France—History—21st century   944.084
Franchise
USE   **Citizenship**
Elections
Suffrage
Franciscans   271
UF   Friars Minor
Gray Friars
Grey Friars
Mendicant orders
Minorites
Saint Francis, Order of
St. Francis, Order of

Franciscans—*Continued*
　　BT　**Monasticism and religious orders**
Fraternities and sororities　371.8
　　UF　College fraternities
　　　　College sororities
　　　　Greek letter societies
　　　　Sororities
　　BT　**Colleges and universities**
　　　　Students—Societies
　　RT　**Secret societies**
Fraud (May subdiv. geog.)　**364.16**
　　UF　Deceit
　　　　Ripoffs
　　BT　**Commercial law**
　　　　Crime
　　　　Offenses against property
　　　　White collar crimes
　　NT　**Credit card fraud**
　　　　Forgery
　　　　Securities fraud
　　RT　**Impostors and imposture**
　　　　Swindlers and swindling
Frauds, Literary
　　USE　**Literary forgeries**
Fraudulent advertising
　　USE　**Deceptive advertising**
Free agency
　　USE　**Free will and determinism**
Free coinage
　　USE　**Monetary policy**
Free computer software　005.3
　　UF　Free software
　　　　Freeware
　　　　Public domain software
　　BT　**Computer software**
　　　　Free material
Free diving
　　USE　**Scuba diving**
　　　　Skin diving
Free enterprise (May subdiv. geog.)
　　　　330.12
　　UF　Free markets
　　　　Laissez-faire
　　　　Private enterprise
　　BT　**Economic policy**
　　RT　**Capitalism**
Free fall
　　USE　**Weightlessness**
Free love　176; 306.7
　　BT　**Sexual ethics**

Free markets
　　USE　**Free enterprise**
Free material
　　UF　Freebies
　　　　Giveaways
　　BT　**Gifts**
　　NT　**Free computer software**
Free press
　　USE　**Freedom of the press**
Free press and fair trial
　　USE　**Freedom of the press and fair trial**
Free schools
　　USE　**Experimental schools**
Free software
　　USE　**Free computer software**
Free speech
　　USE　**Freedom of speech**
Free thought　211
　　BT　**Freedom of conscience**
　　NT　**Agnosticism**
　　　　Skepticism
　　RT　**Deism**
　　　　Rationalism
Free time (Leisure)
　　USE　**Leisure**
Free trade (May subdiv. geog.)　**382**
　　UF　Fair trade (Tariff)
　　　　Free trade and protection
　　BT　**Commercial policy**
　　　　International trade
　　RT　**Protectionism**
　　　　Tariff
Free trade and protection
　　USE　**Free trade**
　　　　Protectionism
Free universities (May subdiv. geog.)
　　　　378
　　UF　Alternative universities
　　　　Experimental universities
　　　　Open universities
　　BT　**Colleges and universities**
Free verse　808.1
　　　May be used for collections or materials about free verse, not for individual works.
　　UF　Vers libre
　　BT　**Poetry**
Free will and determinism　123
　　UF　Choice, Freedom of
　　　　Determinism and indeterminism
　　　　Free agency
　　　　Freedom of choice

Free will and determinism—*Continued*
      Freedom of the will
      Indeterminism
      Liberty of the will
      Will
  BT **Philosophy**
  RT **Fate and fatalism**
      Predestination
Freebies
  USE **Free material**
Freedom (May subdiv. geog.)   **323.4**
  UF Civil liberty
      Emancipation
      Liberty
      Personal freedom
  BT **Democracy**
      Political science
  NT **Anarchism and anarchists**
      Conformity
      Freedom of assembly
      Freedom of association
      Freedom of conscience
      Freedom of movement
      Freedom of religion
      Freedom of speech
      Freedom of the press
      Intellectual freedom
      Slaves—Emancipation
  RT **Civil rights**
      Equality
Freedom, Academic
  USE **Academic freedom**
Freedom marches for civil rights
  USE **Civil rights demonstrations**
Freedom of assembly (May subdiv. geog.)
    323.4
  UF Assembly, Right of
      Right of assembly
  BT **Civil rights**
      Freedom
  NT **Public meetings**
      Riots
  RT **Freedom of association**
      Freedom of speech
Freedom of association (May subdiv. geog.) **323.4**
  UF Association, Freedom of
      Right of association
  BT **Civil rights**
      Freedom
  RT **Freedom of assembly**

Freedom of choice
  USE **Free will and determinism**
Freedom of choice movement
  USE **Pro-choice movement**
Freedom of conscience (May subdiv. geog.) **323.44**
  UF Liberty of conscience
  BT **Conscience**
      Freedom
      Toleration
  NT **Conscientious objectors**
      Dissent
      Free thought
      Public opinion
  RT **Freedom of religion**
Freedom of information (May subdiv. geog.) **323.44**
  UF Information, Freedom of
      Right to know
  BT **Civil rights**
      Intellectual freedom
  NT **Press—Government policy**
  RT **Censorship**
      Freedom of speech
      Freedom of the press
Freedom of movement (May subdiv. geog.) **323.4**
  UF Movement, Freedom of
  BT **Civil rights**
      Freedom
Freedom of religion (May subdiv. geog.) **261.7; 291.1; 323.44**
  UF Freedom of worship
      Religious freedom
      Religious liberty
  BT **Civil rights**
      Freedom
      Toleration
  NT **Dissent**
  RT **Freedom of conscience**
      Persecution
Freedom of speech (May subdiv. geog.) **323.44**
  UF Free speech
      Liberty of speech
      Speech, Freedom of
  BT **Censorship**
      Civil rights
      Freedom
      Intellectual freedom

Freedom of speech—*Continued*
RT **Freedom of assembly**
Freedom of information
Libel and slander
Freedom of teaching
USE **Academic freedom**
Freedom of the press (May subdiv. geog.)
323.44
UF Free press
Liberty of the press
Press censorship
BT **Civil rights**
Freedom
Intellectual freedom
Press
NT **Freedom of the press and fair trial**
RT **Censorship**
Freedom of information
Libel and slander
Freedom of the press and fair trial
323.42; 323.44; 342
UF Fair trial and free press
Free press and fair trial
Prejudicial publicity
Trial by publicity
BT **Fair trial**
Freedom of the press
Press
Freedom of the will
USE **Free will and determinism**
Freedom of worship
USE **Freedom of religion**
Freelancers
USE **Self-employed**
Freemasons **366**
UF Masonic orders
Masons (Secret order)
BT **Secret societies**
Freeware
USE **Free computer software**
Freeways
USE **Express highways**
Freeze-dried foods **641.4; 664**
UF Food, Freeze dried
BT **Dried foods**
Freezing
USE **Cryobiology**
Frost
Ice
Refrigeration

Freezing of human bodies
USE **Cryonics**
Freight **388**
UF Freight and freightage
BT **Maritime law**
Materials handling
Railroads
Transportation
NT **Commercial aeronautics**
Trucking
RT **Railroads—Rates**
Freight and freightage
USE **Freight**
French and Indian War
USE **United States—History—1755-1763, French and Indian War**
French Canadian literature
USE **Canadian literature (French)**
French Canadian poetry
USE **Canadian poetry (French)**
French Canadians (May subdiv. geog.)
305.811; 971
BT **Canadians**
French cookery
USE **French cooking**
French cooking **641.5944**
UF Cookery, French
French cookery
BT **Cooking**
French Equatorial Africa
USE **French-speaking Equatorial Africa**
French folk songs
USE **Folk songs—France**
French language **440**
May be subdivided like **English language.**
BT **Language and languages**
Romance languages
French language—Conversation and phrase books **448**
UF French language—Conversations and phrases
French language—Conversations and phrases
USE **French language—Conversation and phrase books**
French language—Dictionaries—English
443
Use for French-English dictionaries. English-French dictionaries are entered under

298

French language—Dictionaries—English—*Continued*
    English language—Dictionaries—French.
    Combined French-English and English-French dictionaries are entered under both headings.
- UF   Foreign language dictionaries
- BT   **Encyclopedias and dictionaries**
- RT   **English language—Dictionaries—French**

French language—Reading materials
    448.6

French literature   840
    May use same subdivisions and names of literary forms as for **English literature.**
- BT   **Literature**
        Romance literature
- NT   **French poetry**

French literature—Black authors
    840.8; 840.9
    May be used for collections or materials about French literature by several Black authors, not for individual works.
- UF   Black literature (French)

French literature—Canada
- USE **Canadian literature (French)**

French poetry   841
- BT   **French literature**
        Poetry
- NT   **Troubadours**

French poetry—Black authors   841, etc.
    May be used for collections or materials about French poetry by several Black authors, not for individual works.
- UF   Black poetry (French)

French Revolution
- USE **France—History—1789-1799, Revolution**

French-speaking Equatorial Africa   967
    Use for materials dealing collectively with the region of Africa that includes Central African Republic, Chad, Congo (Republic), and Gabon. The former name for the region was French Equatorial Africa.
- UF   Africa, French-speaking Equatorial
        French Equatorial Africa
- BT   **Central Africa**

French-speaking West Africa   966
    Use for materials dealing collectively with the region of Africa that includes Benin, Burkina Faso, Guinea, Ivory Coast, Mali, Mauritania, Niger, Senegal, and Togo.
- UF   Africa, French-speaking West
        French West Africa
- BT   **West Africa**

French West Africa
- USE **French-speaking West Africa**

Frequency modulation, Radio
- USE **Radio frequency modulation**

Fresco painting
- USE **Mural painting and decoration**

Freshwater animals (May subdiv. geog.)
    591.76
- UF   Freshwater fauna
- SA   types of freshwater animals [to be added as needed]
- BT   **Aquatic animals**
- RT   **Freshwater biology**

Freshwater aquaculture
- USE **Aquaculture**

Freshwater biology   578.76
- BT   **Biology**
- NT   **Aquariums**
        Freshwater plants
- RT   **Freshwater animals**

Freshwater fauna
- USE **Freshwater animals**

Freshwater plants (May subdiv. geog.)
    581.7
- UF   Aquatic plants
        Water plants
- BT   **Freshwater biology**
        Plants
- RT   **Marine plants**

Friars Minor
- USE **Franciscans**

Friends
- USE **Friendship**

Friends and associates
- USE names of individuals with the subdivision *Friends and associates* [to be added as needed]

Friends, Society of
- USE **Society of Friends**

Friendship   177
- UF   Affection
        Friends
- BT   **Human behavior**
- RT   **Love**

Friesian cattle
- USE **Holstein-Friesian cattle**

Fringe benefits   331.25
- UF   Benefits, Employee
        Benefits, Fringe
        Employee benefits

Fringe benefits—*Continued*

        Employee fringe benefits

        Non-wage payments

        Nonwage payments *[Former heading]*

  BT **Salaries, wages, etc.**

Frogs (May subdiv. geog.)   **597.8**

  UF Tadpoles

  BT **Amphibians**

Frontier and pioneer life (May subdiv. geog.) **978**

  UF Border life

        Pioneer life

  BT **Adventure and adventurers**

  NT **Cowhands**

        Native Americans—Captivities

        Overland journeys to the Pacific

        Ranch life

Frontiers

  USE **Boundaries**

Frost   **551.57**

  UF Freezing

  BT **Meteorology**

        Water

  NT **Ice**

        Refrigeration

Frozen animal embryos

  USE **Frozen embryos**

Frozen embryos   **176; 571.8; 612.6**

  UF Animal embryos, Frozen

        Embryos, Frozen

        Frozen animal embryos

        Frozen human embryos

        Human embryos, Frozen

  BT **Cryobiology**

        Embryology

Frozen foods   **641.4; 664**

  BT **Food**

  NT **Ice cream, ices, etc.**

  RT **Food—Preservation**

Frozen human embryos

  USE **Frozen embryos**

Frozen stars

  USE **Black holes (Astronomy)**

Fruit (May subdiv. geog.)   **634; 641.3**

    Names of tree fruits may be used for either the fruit or the tree.

  SA types of fruits, e.g. **Berries; Apples; Citrus fruits;** etc. [to be added as needed]

  BT **Food**

        Plants

  NT **Apples**

        Berries

        Citrus fruits

        Fruit culture

        Grapes

Fruit—Canning

  USE **Fruit—Preservation**

Fruit culture (May subdiv. geog.)   **634**

    Names of tree fruits may be used for either the fruit or the tree.

  UF Arboriculture

        Orchards

  BT **Agriculture**

        Fruit

        Gardening

        Horticulture

        Trees

  NT **Berries**

        Nurseries (Horticulture)

        Plant propagation

        Pruning

Fruit—Diseases and pests   **634**

  BT **Agricultural pests**

        Insect pests

        Pests

        Plant diseases

  NT **Spraying and dusting**

Fruit flies (May subdiv. geog.)   **595.77**

  BT **Flies**

Fruit painting and illustration

  USE **Botanical illustration**

Fruit—Preservation   **641.4; 664**

  UF Fruit—Canning

  BT **Canning and preserving**

        Food—Preservation

Frustration   **152.4**

  UF Futility

  BT **Attitude (Psychology)**

        Emotions

Fuel (May subdiv. geog.)   **333.8; 662**

  SA types of fuel; and subjects with the subdivision *Fuel consumption* [to be added as needed]

  BT **Combustion**

        Energy resources

        Engines

        Fire

        Home economics

Fuel—*Continued*
  NT   Alcohol as fuel
       Automobiles—Fuel consumption
       Biomass energy
       Charcoal
       Coal
       Gas
       Gasoline
       Natural gas
       Petroleum as fuel
       Synthetic fuels
       Wood
  RT   Heating
Fuel cells   621.31
  BT   Electric batteries
       Electrochemistry
Fuel consumption
  USE subjects with the subdivision
       Fuel consumption, e.g. **Automobiles—Fuel consumption**
       [to be added as needed]
Fuel oil
  USE Petroleum as fuel
Fugue   784.18
       Use for musical scores and for materials on
       the fugue as a musical form.
  UF   Canons, fugues, etc.
       Fugues
       Prelude and fugue
       Preludes and fugues
  BT   Counterpoint
       Musical form
Fugues
  USE Fugue
Fulfillment, Self
  USE Self-realization
Fumigation   614.4; 648
  BT   Communicable diseases
       Insecticides
  RT   Disinfection and disinfectants
Functional competencies
  USE Life skills
Functional literacy   302.2; 374
  UF   Occupational literacy
  BT   Literacy
Fund raising (May subdiv. geog.)
       361.7068; 658.15
  UF   Community chests
       Money raising
  BT   Finance
  RT   Gifts

Fundamental education
  USE Basic education
Fundamental life skills
  USE Life skills
Fundamental rights
  USE Civil rights
       Human rights
Fundamentalism
  USE Christian fundamentalism
       Islamic fundamentalism
       Religious fundamentalism
Fundamentalism and education
  USE Church and education
       Creationism
       Religion in the public schools
Fundamentalism and evolution
  USE Creationism
Fundamentalist movements
  USE Religious fundamentalism
Funding
  USE Finance
Funding for the arts
  USE Art patronage
       Arts—Government policy
       Federal aid to the arts
Funds
  USE Finance
Funeral customs and rites
  USE Funeral rites and ceremonies
       and ethnic groups and native
       peoples with the subdivision
       Funeral customs and rites [to
       be added as needed]
Funeral directors
  USE Undertakers and undertaking
Funeral rites and ceremonies (May
       subdiv. geog.)   393
  UF   Funeral customs and rites
       Graves
       Mortuary customs
       Mourning customs
  SA   ethnic groups and native peoples
       with the subdivision *Funeral
       customs and rites* [to be added
       as needed]
  BT   Manners and customs
       Rites and ceremonies
  RT   Burial
       Cremation

Fungi 579.5
- UF Diseases and pests
  - Mycology
- BT **Agricultural pests**
  - **Pests**
  - **Plants**
- NT **Molds (Fungi)**
  - **Plant diseases**
  - **Yeast**
- RT **Mushrooms**

Fungicides 632; 668
- UF Germicides
- BT **Pesticides**
- RT **Spraying and dusting**

Funicular railroads
- USE **Cable railroads**

Funnies
- USE **Comic books, strips, etc.**

Fur 675; 685
- BT **Animals—Anatomy**
- RT **Hides and skins**

Fur-bearing animals
- USE **Furbearing animals**

Fur trade (May subdiv. geog.) 338.3
- BT **Trapping**

Furbearing animals (May subdiv. geog.)
599.7; 636.97
- UF Fur-bearing animals
- SA types of furbearing animals, e.g.
  - **Beavers** [to be added as needed]
- BT **Animals**
  - **Economic zoology**
- NT **Beavers**

Furnaces 697
- BT **Heating**
- NT **Blast furnaces**
  - **Smelting**

Furniture 645; 749
- SA furniture of particular countries, e.g. **American furniture;** types of furniture, and names of specific articles of furniture, e.g. **Tables; Chairs;** etc. [to be added as needed]
- BT **Decoration and ornament**
  - **Decorative arts**
  - **Interior design**
- NT **American furniture**
  - **Built-in furniture**
  - **Chairs**
  - **Church furniture**
  - **Furniture making**
  - **Garden ornaments and furniture**
  - **Libraries—Equipment and supplies**
  - **Mirrors**
  - **Schools—Equipment and supplies**
  - **Tables**
  - **Veneers and veneering**
- RT **Cabinetwork**
  - **Upholstery**

Furniture, American
- USE **American furniture**

Furniture building
- USE **Furniture making**

Furniture—Conservation and restoration
- USE **Furniture finishing**
  - **Furniture—Repairing**

Furniture finishing 684.1; 749
- UF Furniture—Conservation and restoration
  - Furniture—Refinishing
  - Furniture—Restoration
  - Refinishing furniture
  - Restoration of furniture
- BT **Furniture making**
  - **Handicraft**
  - **Wood finishing**
- RT **Furniture—Repairing**

Furniture making 684.1; 749
- UF Furniture building
- BT **Furniture**
  - **Woodwork**
- NT **Furniture finishing**
  - **Furniture—Repairing**

Furniture—Refinishing
- USE **Furniture finishing**

Furniture—Repairing 684.1; 749
- UF Furniture—Conservation and restoration
  - Furniture—Restoration
  - Restoration of furniture
- BT **Furniture making**
- RT **Furniture finishing**

Furniture—Restoration
- USE **Furniture finishing**
  - **Furniture—Repairing**

Futility
- USE **Frustration**

Future life   129; 236

    Use for materials on the character and form of a future existence. Materials on the question of the endless existence of the soul are entered under **Immortality.** Materials on the philosophical concept of eternity are entered under **Eternity.**

    UF   Afterlife
           Eternal life
           Intermediate state
           Life after death
           Life, Future
           Resurrection
           Retribution
    BT   **Death**
           Eschatology
    NT   **Heaven**
           Hell
           Paradise
           Soul
    RT   **Eternity**
           Immortality

Future shock
    USE **Culture conflict**

Futurism (Art) (May subdiv. geog.)   709.04; 759.06
    BT   **Art**

Futurology
    USE **Forecasting**

Fuzzy logic
    USE **Fuzzy systems**

Fuzzy systems   629.8
    UF   Fuzzy logic
           Systems, Fuzzy
    BT   **System analysis**

Gaels
    USE **Celts**

Gaia concept
    USE **Gaia hypothesis**

Gaia hypothesis   550.1; 570.1
    UF   Gaia concept
           Gaia principle
           Gaia theory
           Living earth theory
    BT   **Biology**
           Earth
           Ecology
           Life (Biology)

Gaia principle
    USE **Gaia hypothesis**

Gaia theory
    USE **Gaia hypothesis**

Galaxies   523.1
    UF   Extragalactic nebulae
           Nebulae, Extragalactic
    BT   **Astronomy**
           Stars

Gales
    USE **Winds**

Gambling (May subdiv. geog.)   175; 795
    UF   Betting
           Gaming
    SA   types of gambling, e.g. **Lotteries** [to be added as needed]
    BT   **Games**
    NT   **Compulsive gambling**
           Lotteries
    RT   **Horse racing**

Game and game birds (May subdiv. geog.)   636.6
    UF   Wild fowl
    SA   types of animals and birds, e.g. **Deer; Pheasants;** etc. [to be added as needed]
    BT   **Animals**
           Birds
           Wildlife
    NT   **Deer**
           Falconry
           Game protection
           Pheasants
    RT   **Hunting**
           Trapping

Game preserves
    USE **Game reserves**

Game protection (May subdiv. geog.)   333.95; 636.9
    UF   Game wardens
           Protection of game
    BT   **Game and game birds**
           Hunting
           Wildlife conservation
    RT   **Birds—Protection**

Game reserves (May subdiv. geog.)   333.95
    UF   Game preserves
    BT   **Hunting**
           Wildlife conservation

Game theory   519.3
    UF   Games, Theory of
           Theory of games
    BT   **Mathematical models**
           Mathematics

Game theory—*Continued*
    Probabilities
  NT **Simulation games in education**
Game wardens
  USE **Game protection**
Games (May subdiv. geog.) **790**
  UF Pastimes
  SA types of games and names of
        individual games [to be added
        as needed]
  BT **Entertaining**
    Physical education
    Recreation
  NT **Ball games**
    Card games
    Checkers
    Chess
    Computer games
    Educational games
    Gambling
    Indoor games
    Native American games
    Olympic games
    Singing games
    Video games
    Word games
  RT **Amusements**
    Play
    Sports
Games, Theory of
  USE **Game theory**
Gaming
  USE **Gambling**
Gaming, Educational
  USE **Simulation games in education**
Gamma rays **537.5; 539.7**
  BT **Electromagnetic waves**
    Radiation
    X-rays
Gangs (May subdiv. geog.) **302.3;**
    364.106
  UF Gangsters
    Street gangs
    Teenage gangs
  BT **Criminals**
    Juvenile delinquency
    Organized crime
Gangster films **791.43**
  May be used for individual works, collec-
tions, or materials about gangster films.

  UF Crime films
  BT **Motion pictures**
  RT **Mystery films**
Gangsters
  USE **Gangs**
Garage sales **381**
  UF Yard sales
  BT **Secondhand trade**
Garbage
  USE **Refuse and refuse disposal**
Garbage disposal
  USE **Refuse and refuse disposal**
Garden design (May subdiv. geog.) **712**
  UF Gardens—Design
  BT **Design**
    Gardening
  RT **Landscape gardening**
Garden farming
  USE **Truck farming**
Garden furniture
  USE **Garden ornaments and furni-
    ture**
Garden of Eden
  USE **Paradise**
Garden ornaments and furniture **717**
  UF Garden furniture
  BT **Decoration and ornament**
    Furniture
    Gardens
    Landscape architecture
  NT **Sundials**
Garden pests
  USE **Agricultural pests**
    Insect pests
    Plant diseases
Garden rooms **643**
  UF Conservatories, Home
    Home conservatories
  BT **Houses**
    Rooms
  RT **Greenhouses**
Gardening (May subdiv. geog.) **635**
  Use for materials on the practical aspects of
creating gardens and cultivating flowers,
fruits, vegetables, etc. Materials on the design
or rearrangement of extensive gardens or es-
tates are entered under **Landscape gardening.**
Materials on the scientific and economic aspects of the cultivation of plants are entered
under **Horticulture.** General materials about
gardens, the history of gardens, various types
of gardens, etc., are entered under **Gardens.**

Gardening—*Continued*
UF   Planting
BT   **Agriculture**
NT   **Climbing plants**
     Container gardening
     Cultivated plants
     Flower gardening
     Fruit culture
     Garden design
     Gardening in the shade
     Greenhouses
     Grounds maintenance
     Indoor gardening
     Landscape gardening
     Nurseries (Horticulture)
     Organic gardening
     Plant propagation
     Pruning
     Truck farming
     Vegetable gardening
     Weeds
     Window gardening
RT   **Gardens**
     Horticulture
     Plants

Gardening in the shade   635
UF   Gardens, Shade
     Shade gardens
     Shady gardens
BT   **Gardening**

Gardens (May subdiv. geog.)   635; 712
Use for general materials about gardens, the history of gardens, various types of gardens, etc. Materials on the design or rearrangement of extensive gardens or estates are entered under **Landscape gardening.** Materials on the practical aspects of creating gardens and cultivating flowers, fruits, vegetables, etc., are entered under **Gardening.**
UF   Formal gardens
SA   types of gardens, e.g. **Botanical gardens;** and names of individual gardens [to be added as needed]
NT   **Botanical gardens**
     Garden ornaments and furniture
     Miniature gardens
     Rock gardens
RT   **Gardening**
Gardens—Design
USE   **Garden design**
Gardens, Miniature
USE   **Miniature gardens**

Gardens, Shade
USE   **Gardening in the shade**
Garment industry
USE   **Clothing industry**
Garment making
USE   **Dressmaking**
     Tailoring
Garments
USE   **Clothing and dress**
Gas   665.7
UF   Coal gas
BT   **Fuel**
RT   **Coal tar products**
Gas and oil engines
USE   **Internal combustion engines**
Gas companies (May subdiv. geog.)   363.6
Use for materials on the sale and distribution of gas to consumers.
UF   Natural gas companies
     Natural gas utilities
BT   **Public utilities**
Gas engines
USE   **Internal combustion engines**
Gas stations
USE   **Service stations**
Gas turbines   621.43
BT   **Turbines**
Gas warfare
USE   **Chemical warfare**
Gases   530.4; 533
SA   types of gases, e.g. **Nitrogen** [to be added as needed]
BT   **Fluid mechanics**
     Hydrostatics
     Physics
NT   **Helium**
     Natural gas
     Nitrogen
     Oxygen
     Poisonous gases
RT   **Pneumatics**
Gases, Asphyxiating and poisonous
USE   **Poisonous gases**
Gasification of coal
USE   **Coal gasification**
Gasohol   662
BT   **Alcohol as fuel**
Gasoline   665.5
BT   **Fuel**
     Petroleum

Gasoline engines
USE **Internal combustion engines**
Gastronomy 641.01
UF Eating
BT **Diet**
RT **Cooking**
Dining
Food
Gauchos
USE **Cowhands**
Gaul—Geography 914.4
BT **Ancient geography**
Historical geography
Gay liberation movement (May subdiv.
geog.) **305.9**
BT **Homosexuality**
Gay lifestyle
USE **Homosexuality**
Gay marriage
USE **Same-sex marriage**
Gay men (May subdiv. geog.) **305.38;**
306.76
UF Gays, Male
Homosexuals, Male
BT **Men**
NT **Gays and lesbians in the mili-**
tary
RT **Gay men's writings**
Homosexuality
Gay men's writings 808.8; 810.8, etc.
Use for collections of gay men's writings
by more than one author and for materials
about such writings.
UF Writings of gay men
BT **Literature**
RT **Gay men**
Gay women
USE **Lesbians**
Gay women's writings
USE **Lesbians' writings**
Gays and lesbians in the military
355.008
UF Gays in the military
Lesbians and gays in the mili-
tary
Lesbians in the military
United States—Armed forces—
Gays
BT **Gay men**
Lesbians
Military personnel

Gays, Female
USE **Lesbians**
Gays in the military
USE **Gays and lesbians in the mili-**
tary
Gays, Male
USE **Gay men**
Gazetteers 910.3
SA names of countries, states, etc.,
with the subdivision *Gazet-*
teers, e.g. **United States—**
Gazetteers [to be added as
needed]
BT **Geography**
NT **Ohio—Gazetteers**
United States—Gazetteers
RT **Geographic names**
Gearing 621.8
UF Bevel gearing
Cog wheels
Gears
Spiral gearing
BT **Machinery**
Power transmission
Wheels
NT **Automobiles—Transmission de-**
vices
RT **Mechanical movements**
Gears
USE **Gearing**
Geese (May subdiv. geog.) **598.4; 636.5**
UF Goose
BT **Birds**
Poultry
Water birds
Gemini project 629.45
UF Project Gemini
BT **Orbital rendezvous (Space**
flight)
Space flight
Gems (May subdiv. geog.) **736**
Use for materials on cut and polished pre-
cious stones treated from the point of view of
art or antiquity. Materials on gem stones treat-
ed from a mineralogical or technological point
of view are entered under **Precious stones.**
Materials on gems in which the emphasis is
on the setting are entered under **Jewelry.**
UF Jewels
BT **Archeology**
Art
Decoration and ornament
Engraving

Gems—*Continued*
>> **Minerals**
> RT **Jewelry**
>> **Precious stones**

Gemstones
> USE **Precious stones**

Gender identity
> USE **Sex role**

Gene mapping   572.8
> UF Chromosome mapping
>> Genetic mapping
>> Genome mapping
> BT **Genetics**

Gene splicing
> USE **Genetic engineering**

Gene therapy   616

> Use for materials on therapeutic efforts involving the replacement or supplementation of genes in order to cure diseases caused by genetic defects.

> UF Therapy, Gene
> BT **Genetic engineering**
>> **Therapeutics**

Gene transfer
> USE **Genetic engineering**

Genealogy   929
> UF Ancestry
>> Descent
>> Family histories
>> Family trees
>> Pedigrees
> SA countries, cities, etc., corporate bodies, ethnic groups, and classes of persons with the subdivision *Genealogy;* names of individual persons with the subdivision *Family;* and names of families, e.g. **Lincoln family** [to be added as needed]
> BT **History**
> NT **Registers of births, etc.**
>> **Wills**
> RT **Biography**
>> **Heraldry**

Generals (May subdiv. geog.)   355.0092; 920
> BT **Military personnel**

Generation gap
> USE **Conflict of generations**

Generative organs
> USE **Reproductive system**

Generators, Electric
> USE **Electric generators**

Generic drugs   615
> UF Drugs—Generic substitution
> BT **Drugs**
>> **Generic products**

Generic products   658.8
> UF Products, Generic
> BT **Commercial products**
>> **Manufactures**
> NT **Generic drugs**

Genes
> USE **Heredity**

Genetic aspects
> USE types of diseases with the subdivision *Genetic aspects,* e.g. **Cancer—Genetic aspects** [to be added as needed]

Genetic code   572.8
> BT **Molecular biology**

Genetic counseling   616; 618
> BT **Medical genetics**
>> **Prenatal diagnosis**

Genetic engineering (May subdiv. geog.)   660.6
> UF Designed genetic change
>> Engineering, Genetic
>> Gene splicing
>> Gene transfer
>> Genetic intervention
>> Genetic surgery
>> Splicing of genes
>> Transgenics
> BT **Engineering**
>> **Genetic recombination**
> NT **Cloning**
>> **Fertilization in vitro**
>> **Gene therapy**
>> **Molecular cloning**
>> **Recombinant DNA**
> RT **Biotechnology**

Genetic engineering—Government policy (May subdiv. geog.)   353.7; 660.6

Genetic engineering—Social aspects   306.4

Genetic fingerprinting
> USE **DNA fingerprinting**

Genetic fingerprints
> USE **DNA fingerprinting**

Genetic intervention
> USE **Genetic engineering**

Genetic mapping
  USE **Gene mapping**
Genetic profiling
  USE **DNA fingerprinting**
Genetic recombination   572.8
  UF Recombination, Genetic
  BT **Chromosomes**
  NT **Genetic engineering**
       Genetic transformation
       Recombinant DNA
Genetic surgery
  USE **Genetic engineering**
Genetic transformation   576.5
  UF Transformation (Genetics)
  BT **Genetic recombination**
Genetics   576.5
  SA types of diseases with the subdi-
       vision *Genetic aspects,* e.g.
       Cancer—Genetic aspects [to
       be added as needed]
  BT **Biology**
       Embryology
       Life (Biology)
       Mendel's law
       Reproduction
  NT **Adaptation (Biology)**
       Behavior genetics
       Chromosomes
       Eugenics
       Gene mapping
       Medical genetics
       Natural selection
       Variation (Biology)
  RT **Breeding**
       Heredity
Genitalia
  USE **Reproductive system**
Genlus   153.9
  UF Talent
  BT **Psychology**
  NT **Creation (Literary, artistic,**
       etc.)
Genocide (May subdiv. geog.)   **179.7;**
       364.1
  UF Ethnic cleansing
       Ethnocide
  BT **Crimes against humanity**
Genome mapping
  USE **Gene mapping**

Geochemistry   551.9
  UF Chemical geology
       Earth—Chemical composition
       Geological chemistry
  BT **Chemistry**
       Earth sciences
       Petrology
  NT **Geothermal resources**
Geodesy   526
  UF Degrees of latitude and longi-
       tude
  BT **Earth**
       Measurement
  NT **Latitude**
       Longitude
  RT **Surveying**
Geographic names (May subdiv. geog.)
       910
  UF Names, Geographical
       Place names
  BT **Names**
  RT **Gazetteers**
Geographic names—United States
       917.3
  UF United States—Geographic
       names
Geographical atlases
  USE **Atlases**
Geographical distribution
  USE types of plants and animals with
       the subdivision *Geographical*
       distribution, e.g. **Fishes—Geo-**
       graphical distribution [to be
       added as needed]
Geographical distribution of animals and
       plants
  USE **Biogeography**
Geographical distribution of people
  USE **Ethnology**
       Human geography
Geographical distribution of plants
  USE **Plants—Geographical distribu-**
       tion
Geographical myths   398.23
  UF Cities, Imaginary
       Fictitious places
       Imaginary places
       Islands, Imaginary
       Places, Imaginary
  BT **Mythology**

Geography   910

Use for general materials, frequently school materials, that describe the surface of the earth and its interrelationship with various peoples, animals, natural products, and industries. Materials limited to a particular place are entered under the name of the place with the subdivision *Geography.* General descriptive materials and travel materials limited to a particular place are entered under the name of the place (except extinct cities) with the subdivision *Description.* Materials on the physical features of the earth's surface and its atmosphere are entered under **Physical geography.**

UF   Social studies
SA   names of countries, states, etc.,
        with the subdivisions *Descrip-*
        tion and *Geography;* and sa-
        cred works with the subdivi-
        sion *Geography,* e.g. **Bible—**
        Geography [to be added as
        needed]
BT   **Earth**
      Earth sciences
      World history
NT   **Atlases**
      Bible—Geography
      Biogeography
      Boundaries
      Commercial geography
      Exploration
      Gazetteers
      Greece—Geography
      Historical geography
      Human geography
      Maps
      Military geography
      Physical geography
      Regionalism
      Surveying
      United States—Description
      United States—Geography
      Voyages and travels

Geography, Ancient
USE   **Ancient geography**

Geography—Dictionaries   910.3

Use for dictionaries of geographic terms. Materials listing names and descriptions of places are entered under **Gazetteers.**

BT   **Encyclopedias and dictionaries**
Geography, Historical
USE   **Historical geography**
Geography, Political
USE   **Geopolitics**
Geological chemistry
USE   **Geochemistry**

Geological physics
USE   **Geophysics**
Geologists (May subdiv. geog.)   **551.092;**
    920
BT   **Scientists**
Geology (May subdiv. geog.)   **550**

Use for materials limited to the structure and composition of the earth and the physical changes it has undergone and is still undergoing. General materials on the whole planet are entered under **Earth.**

UF   Geoscience
SA   names of planets and types of
      ore with the subdivision *Geol-*
      ogy [to be added as needed]
BT   **Earth sciences**
      Science
NT   **Astrogeology**
      Continental drift
      Continental shelf
      Coral reefs and islands
      Earthquakes
      Economic geology
      Erosion
      Geysers
      Glaciers
      Landforms
      Minerals
      Ore deposits
      Physical geography
      Stratigraphic geology
      Submarine geology
      Volcanoes
RT   **Earth**
      Petrology
      Rocks
Geology, Dynamic
USE   **Geophysics**
Geology, Economic
USE   **Economic geology**
Geology—Interactive multimedia   551
Geology, Lunar
USE   **Lunar geology**
Geology—Maps   550.22
BT   **Maps**
Geology—Moon
USE   **Lunar geology**
Geology, Petroleum
USE   **Petroleum geology**
Geology, Stratigraphic
USE   **Stratigraphic geology**
Geology—United States   557.3

Geometric art
USE **Abstract art**
Geometric patterns
USE **Patterns (Mathematics)**
Geometrical drawing   516; 604.2
UF   Mathematical drawing
        Plans
BT   **Drawing**
        Geometry
NT   **Descriptive geometry**
        Graphic methods
        Perspective
RT   **Mechanical drawing**
Geometry   516
BT   **Mathematics**
NT   **Analytic geometry**
        Descriptive geometry
        Fractals
        Geometrical drawing
        Plane geometry
        Projective geometry
        Ratio and proportion
        Shape
        Solid Geometry
        Square
        Topology
        Trigonometry
        Volume (Cubic content)
Geometry, Analytic
USE   **Analytic geometry**
Geometry, Descriptive
USE   **Descriptive geometry**
Geometry, Plane
USE   **Plane geometry**
Geometry, Projective
USE   **Projective geometry**
Geometry, Solid
USE   **Solid Geometry**
Geophysics   550
UF   Geological physics
        Geology, Dynamic
        Physics, Terrestrial
        Terrestrial physics
BT   **Earth sciences**
        Physics
NT   **Auroras**
        Plate tectonics
Geopolitics   320.1; 327.101
UF   Geography, Political
        Political geography

BT   **International relations**
        Political science
RT   **Boundaries**
        Human geography
        World politics
Geoscience
USE   **Earth sciences**
        Geology
Geothermal resources (May subdiv.
    geog.)   **333.8**
UF   Natural steam energy
        Thermal waters
SA   types of geothermal resources,
        e.g. **Geysers** [to be added as
        needed]
BT   **Geochemistry**
        Ocean energy resources
        Renewable energy resources
NT   **Geysers**
Geriatrics
USE   **Elderly—Diseases**
        Elderly—Health and hygiene
Germ theory
USE   **Life—Origin**
Germ theory of disease   616
UF   Disease germs
        Germs
        Microbes
BT   **Communicable diseases**
Germ warfare
USE   **Biological warfare**
German Democratic Republic
USE   **Germany (East)**
German Federal Republic
USE   **Germany (West)**
German language   430
    May be subdivided like **English language.**
BT   **Language and languages**
German literature   830
    May use same subdivisions and names of
literary forms as for **English literature.**
BT   **Literature**
German occupation of France, 1940-1945
USE   **France—History—1940-1945,**
        German occupation
German occupation of Netherlands, 1940-
    1945
USE   **Netherlands—History—1940-**
        1945, German occupation
Germany   943
    Use for materials on Germany before or af-
ter the division of the country following

310

Germany—*Continued*

World War II and for materials on East and West Germany discussed collectively as occupied zones or countries. Materials limited to the eastern part of Germany from 1945 to 1990, the Russian occupation zone, or the German Democratic Republic, are entered under **Germany (East)**. Materials limited to the western part of Germany from 1945 to 1990, the American, British, and French occupation zones, or the German Federal Republic, are entered under **Germany (West)**. May be subdivided like United States except for *History*.

UF Federal Republic of Germany

NT **Germany (East)**

  Germany (West)

Germany (Democratic Republic)

USE **Germany (East)**

Germany (East) 943

Use for materials limited to the eastern part of Germany from 1945 to 1990, the Russian occupation zone, or the German Democratic Republic. Materials on Germany before or after the division of the country following World War II and materials on East and West Germany discussed collectively as occupied zones or countries are entered under **Germany**.

UF East Germany

  German Democratic Republic

  Germany (Democratic Republic)

BT **Germany**

Germany (Federal Republic)

USE **Germany (West)**

Germany—History 943

Germany—History—0-1517 943

Germany—History—1517-1740 943

NT **Thirty Years' War, 1618-1648**

Germany—History—1740-1815 943

Germany—History—1815-1866 943

Germany—History—1848-1849, Revolution 943

Germany—History—1866-1918 943.08

Germany—History—1918-1933 943.085

Germany—History—1933-1945 943.086

Germany—History—1945-1990 943.087

Germany—History—1990- 943.087

UF Germany—History—Unification, 1990

Germany—History—Unification, 1990

USE **Germany—History—1990-**

Germany (West) 943.087

Use for materials limited to the western part of Germany from 1945 to 1990, the American, British, and French occupation zones, or the German Federal Republic. Materials on Germany before or after the division of the country following World War II and

materials on East and West Germany discussed collectively as occupied zones or countries are entered under **Germany**.

UF Federal Republic of Germany

  German Federal Republic

  Germany (Federal Republic)

  West Germany

BT **Germany**

Germicides

USE **Disinfection and disinfectants**

  Fungicides

Germination 571.8

UF Seeds—Germination

BT **Plant physiology**

Germs

USE **Bacteria**

  Germ theory of disease

  Microorganisms

Gerontology 305.26; 362.6; 612.6

BT **Social sciences**

NT **Aging**

  Elderly

RT **Old age**

Gestalt psychology 150.19

UF Configuration (Psychology)

  Psychology, Structural

  Structural psychology

BT **Consciousness**

  Perception

  Psychology

  Senses and sensation

  Theory of knowledge

Getting ready for bed

USE **Bedtime**

Gettysburg (Pa.), Battle of, 1863 973.7

BT **United States—History—1861-1865, Civil War—Campaigns**

Geysers (May subdiv. geog.) 551.2

UF Eruptions

  Thermal waters

BT **Geology**

  Geothermal resources

  Physical geography

  Water

Ghettoes, Inner city

USE **Inner cities**

Ghost stories 808.83; 813, etc.

May be used for individual works, collections, or materials about ghost stories.

UF Ghosts—Fiction

  Terror tales

BT **Fantasy fiction**

  Horror fiction

Ghost stories—*Continued*
    Occult fiction
    RT **Gothic novels**
        Mystery fiction
Ghost towns (May subdiv. geog.)
        307.76
    UF Abandoned towns
        Towns, abandoned
    BT **Extinct cities**
Ghosts (May subdiv. geog.)   **133.1**
    UF Haunted houses
        Phantoms
        Poltergeists
        Specters
        Spirits
    BT **Apparitions**
        Folklore
    RT **Parapsychology**
Ghosts—Fiction
    USE **Ghost stories**
Giantism   616.4
    Use for materials on excessive growth in humans. Materials on beings with a human form but with superhuman size or strength in folklore or imaginative literature are entered under **Giants.**
    UF Gigantism
    BT **Growth disorders**
Giants   398.21
    Use for materials on beings with a human form but with superhuman size or strength in folklore or imaginative literature. Materials on excessive growth in humans are entered under **Giantism.**
    BT **Folklore**
        Monsters
Gift of tongues
    USE **Glossolalia**
Gift wrapping   745.54
    UF Wrapping of gifts
    BT **Packaging**
        Paper crafts
Gifted children   155.45
    UF Bright children
        Children, Gifted
        Precocious children
    BT **Exceptional children**
    NT **Child artists**
        Child authors
Gifts   306.4; 361.7
    UF Bequests
        Donations
        Presents

    BT **Manners and customs**
    NT **Donation of organs, tissues, etc.**
        Free material
    RT **Fund raising**
Gifts of grace
    USE **Spiritual gifts**
Gifts of the Holy Spirit
    USE **Spiritual gifts**
Gifts, Spiritual
    USE **Spiritual gifts**
Gigantism
    USE **Giantism**
Gipsies
    USE **Gypsies**
Girl Scouts (May subdiv. geog.)
        369.463
    UF Brownies (Girl Scouts)
    BT **Girls' clubs**
        Scouts and scouting
Girls (May subdiv. geog.)   **155.43; 305.23**
    BT **Children**
    RT **Teenagers**
        Young women
Girls' clubs (May subdiv. geog.)   **369.46**
    UF Girls—Societies and clubs
    BT **Clubs**
        Societies
    NT **4-H clubs**
        Camp Fire Girls
        Girl Scouts
Girls—Education (May subdiv. geog.)
        371.822
    BT **Education**
    RT **Coeducation**
Girls—Employment
    USE **Child labor**
        Women—Employment
Girls—Societies and clubs
    USE **Girls' clubs**
GIs
    USE **Soldiers—United States**
Giveaways
    USE **Free material**
Glacial epoch
    USE **Ice age**
Glaciers (May subdiv. geog.)   **551.3**
    BT **Geology**
        Ice
        Physical geography

Gladiators   796.8092; 920
  UF   Fighting
Gladness
  USE   **Happiness**
Glands   571.7; 573.4; 611; 612.4
  BT   **Anatomy**
       Physiology
Glands, Ductless
  USE   **Endocrine glands**
Glass   666
  BT   **Building materials**
       Ceramics
  NT   **Glass fibers**
Glass construction   693
  BT   **Building materials**
Glass fibers   666
  UF   Fiber glass
       Fiberglass
       Fibers, Glass
       Glass, Spun
       Spun glass
  BT   **Fibers**
       Glass
Glass industry
  USE   **Glass manufacture**
Glass manufacture (May subdiv. geog.)
       666
  UF   Glass industry
  BT   **Ceramic industry**
Glass painting and staining (May subdiv.
       geog.)   **748.5**
  UF   Glass, Stained
       Painted glass
       Stained glass
       Windows, Stained glass
  BT   **Decoration and ornament**
       Painting
Glass, Spun
  USE   **Glass fibers**
Glass, Stained
  USE   **Glass painting and staining**
Glasses
  USE   **Eyeglasses**
Glassware (May subdiv. geog.)   642;
       748.2
  BT   **Decorative arts**
       Tableware
  RT   **Vases**
Glassware—Trademarks   748.2
  BT   **Trademarks**

Glazes   666; 738.1
  BT   **Ceramics**
       Pottery
Gliders (Aeronautics)   629.133
  UF   Aircraft
       Sailplanes (Aeronautics)
  BT   **Aeronautics**
       Airplanes
Gliding and soaring   797.5
  UF   Air surfing
       Hang gliding
       Soaring flight
  BT   **Aeronautics**
Global satellite communications systems
  USE   **Artificial satellites in telecom-**
         munication
Global warming
  USE   **Greenhouse effect**
Globes   912
  BT   **Maps**
Glossaries
  USE   **Encyclopedias and dictionaries**
Glossolalia   234
  UF   Gift of tongues
       Speaking in tongues
       Speaking with tongues
  BT   **Spiritual gifts**
  RT   **Pentecostalism**
Glow-in-the-dark books
  UF   Luminescent books
       Luminous books
  BT   **Picture books for children**
       Toy and movable books
Glue   668
  BT   **Adhesives**
Glue sniffing
  USE   **Solvent abuse**
Gnomes   398.21
  BT   **Folklore**
Gnosticism   273; 299
  BT   **Church history—30-600, Early**
       church
       Philosophy
       Religions
Go-karts
  USE   **Karts and karting**
Goblins   398.21
  BT   **Folklore**
God   211; 212; 231
       May subdivide by religion as needed, e.g.
       God—Christianity.

313

God—*Continued*
- NT Femininity of God
  - Providence and government of God
  - Revelation
- RT Metaphysics
  - Religion
  - Theism
  - Theology

God—Christianity 231
- BT **Christianity—Doctrines**
- NT **Holy Spirit**
  - **Jesus Christ**
  - **Trinity**

God—Femininity
- USE **Femininity of God**

God—Providence and government
- USE **Providence and government of God**

God—Sovereignty
- USE **Providence and government of God**

Goddess movement
- USE **Goddess religion**

Goddess religion (May subdiv. geog.) 291.2
- UF Goddess movement
  - Mother Goddess religion
- BT **Paganism**
- RT **Gods and goddesses**
  - **Wicca**
  - **Women—Religious life**

Goddesses
- USE **Gods and goddesses**

Gods
- USE **Gods and goddesses**

Gods and goddesses 291.2
- UF Deities
  - Goddesses
  - Gods
- SA names of gods and goddesses, e.g. **Zeus (Greek deity); Vesta (Roman deity);** etc. [to be added as needed]
- NT **Vesta (Roman deity)**
  - **Zeus (Greek deity)**
- RT **Goddess religion**
  - **Mythology**
  - **Religions**

Gold (May subdiv. geog.) **332.4; 553.4; 669**
- BT **Chemical elements**
  - **Precious metals**
- NT **Goldwork**
- RT **Coinage**
  - **Gold mines and mining**
  - **Money**

Gold articles
- USE **Goldwork**

Gold discoveries
- USE names of places with the subdivision *Gold discoveries,* e.g. **California—Gold discoveries** [to be added as needed]

Gold fish
- USE **Goldfish**

Gold mines and mining (May subdiv. geog.) **622**
- UF Gold rush
  - Gold rushes
- SA names of places with the subdivision *Gold discoveries,* e.g. **California—Gold discoveries** [to be added as needed]
- BT **Mines and mineral resources**
- NT **Prospecting**
- RT **Gold**

Gold plate
- USE **Plate**

Gold rush
- USE **Gold mines and mining**

Gold rushes
- USE **Gold mines and mining**

Gold work
- USE **Goldwork**

Golden Gate Bridge (San Francisco, Calif.) 624; 979.4
- BT **Bridges**

Goldfish 597.5
- UF Gold fish
- BT **Fishes**

Goldsmithing
- USE **Goldwork**

Goldwork (May subdiv. geog.) **739.2**
- UF Gold articles
  - Gold work
  - Goldsmithing
- BT **Art metalwork**
  - **Gold**
  - **Metalwork**

Goldwork—*Continued*
  NT **Plate**
Golf courses 796.352
  BT **Grounds maintenance**
Good and evil 170; 214; 241
  UF Evil
      Wickedness
  BT **Ethics**
      Philosophy
      Theology
  NT **Sin**
Good Friday 263
  BT **Christian holidays**
      Holy Week
      Lent
  RT **Jesus Christ—Crucifixion**
Good grooming
  USE **Personal grooming**
Goose
  USE **Geese**
Gorge-purge syndrome
  USE **Bulimia**
Gospel music 781.71; 782.25
  UF Music, Gospel
      Revivals—Music
  BT **African American music**
      Church music
      Popular music
  RT **Spirituals (Songs)**
Gossip 070.4; 177; 302.2
  BT **Journalism**
      Libel and slander
Gothic architecture (May subdiv. geog.)
    723
  UF Architecture, Gothic
  BT **Medieval architecture**
  RT **Cathedrals**
      Church architecture
      Gothic art
Gothic art (May subdiv. geog.) 709.02
  UF Art, Gothic
  BT **Medieval art**
  RT **Christian art**
      Gothic architecture
Gothic decoration and ornament
  USE **Decoration and ornament—**
        Gothic style
Gothic fiction
  USE **Gothic novels**
Gothic novels 813, etc.
  May be used for individual works, collections, or materials about novels that have a

medieval setting and usually include castles and ghosts.
  UF Gothic fiction
  BT **Historical fiction**
      Horror fiction
      Occult fiction
  RT **Ghost stories**
      Love stories
      Romantic suspense novels
Goths 305.83
  UF East Goths
      Ostrogoths
  BT **Teutonic peoples**
Gout 616.3
  BT **Arthritis**
      Rheumatism
Government
  USE **Political science**
      and names of countries, cities, etc., with the subdivision *Politics and government,* e.g. **United States—Politics and government** [to be added as needed]
Government agencies
  USE **Administrative agencies**
Government aid (May subdiv. geog.)
    336
  Use for materials on aid from governments at any level in non-federal systems and on aid from state, provincial, or local governments in federal systems. Materials on central government aid in federal systems are entered under **Federal aid.**
  SA government aid to specific endeavors, e.g. **Government aid to libraries** [to be added as needed]
  BT **Public finance**
  NT **Government aid to education**
      Government aid to libraries
  RT **Federal aid**
Government aid to education (May subdiv. geog.) 379.1
  UF Education—Government aid
      Education—State aid
      State aid to education *[Former heading]*
  BT **Education—Finance**
      Education—Government policy
      Government aid

Government aid to libraries (May subdiv. geog.) **021.8**
    UF   Libraries—Government aid
            Libraries—State aid
            State aid to libraries *[Former heading]*
    BT   **Government aid**
            Libraries—Government policy
            Library finance
Government and business
    USE **Economic policy**
Government and the press
    USE **Press—Government policy**
Government budgets
    USE **Budget**
Government buildings
    USE **Public buildings**
Government business enterprises (May subdiv. geog.) **338.7**
    UF   Government companies
            Nationalized companies
            Public enterprises
    SA   types of industries with the subdivision *Government ownership,* e.g. **Electric utilities—Government ownership;** which may be further subdivided geographically [to be added as needed]
    BT   **Business enterprises**
Government by commission
    USE **Municipal government by commission**
Government companies
    USE **Government business enterprises**
Government, Comparative
    USE **Comparative government**
Government debts
    USE **Public debts**
Government departments
    USE **Executive departments**
Government documents
    USE **Government publications**
Government employees
    USE **Civil service**
Government health insurance
    USE **National health insurance**
Government housing
    USE **Public housing**

Government investigations
    USE **Governmental investigations**
Government lending (May subdiv. geog.) **332.7; 354.8**
    BT   **Domestic economic assistance**
            Economic policy
            Loans
            Public finance
Government libraries (May subdiv. geog.) **027.5**
    Use for materials on special libraries maintained by government funds.
    UF   Federal libraries
            Libraries, Governmental
    BT   **Special libraries**
    NT   **National libraries**
            State libraries
Government, Local
    USE **Local government**
Government, Military
    USE **Military government**
Government ministries
    USE **Executive departments**
Government, Municipal
    USE **Municipal government**
Government officials
    USE **Public officers**
Government ownership (May subdiv. geog.) **333.1; 338.9**
    UF   Nationalization
            Public ownership
            Socialization of industry
            State ownership
    SA   types of industries with the subdivision *Government ownership,* e.g. **Electric utilities—Government ownership;** which may be further subdivided geographically [to be added as needed]
    BT   **Economic policy**
            Industrial policy
            Socialism
    NT   **Municipal ownership**
            Railroads—Government policy
    RT   **Privatization**
Government ownership of railroads
    USE **Railroads—Government policy**
Government policy
    USE **Buy national policy**
            Commercial policy
            Cultural policy

Government policy—*Continued*
    Economic policy
    Energy policy
    Environmental policy
    Fiscal policy
    Industrial policy
    Labor policy
    Military policy
    Monetary policy
    Social policy
    Wage-price policy
    and subjects, ethnic groups, and classes of persons with the subdivision *Government policy,* e.g. **Genetic engineering—Government policy; Homeless persons—Government policy;** etc., which may be further subdivided geographically [to be added as needed]

Government procurement
    USE **Government purchasing**
Government property, Surplus
    USE **Surplus government property**
Government publications (May subdiv. geog.) **011; 015; 025.17**
    UF Documents
        Government documents
        Official publications
        Public documents
    BT **Library resources**
Government publications—Chicago (Ill.)
    015.773
    UF Chicago (Ill.)—Government publications
Government publications—Ohio
    015.771
    UF Ohio—Government publications
Government publications—United States
    015.73; 025.17
    UF United States—Government publications
Government purchasing (May subdiv. geog.) **352.5**
    UF Government procurement
        Procurement, Government
        Public procurement
        Public purchasing
    BT **Purchasing**
    NT **Buy national policy**

Government records—Preservation
    USE **Archives**
Government regulation of commerce
    USE **Commercial policy**
          Industrial laws and legislation
          Interstate commerce
Government regulation of industry
    USE **Industrial policy**
Government regulation of railroads
    USE **Railroads—Government policy**
Government relations
    USE ethnic groups with the subdivision *Government relations,* e.g. **Native Americans—Government relations** [to be added as needed]
Government reorganization
    USE **Administrative agencies—Reorganization**
Government, Resistance to
    USE **Resistance to government**
Government service
    USE **Civil service**
Government spending policy
    USE **United States—Appropriations and expenditures**
Government subsidies
    USE **Subsidies**
Government surveys
    USE **Surveys**
Government transfer payments
    USE **Transfer payments**
Governmental investigations (May subdiv. geog.) **328.3; 353.4**
    Use for materials on investigations initiated by the legislative, executive, or judicial branches of the government, usually of some particular problem of public interest.
    UF Congressional investigations
        Executive investigations
        Government investigations
        Judicial investigations
        Legislative investigations
    BT **Administration of justice**
Governmental investigations—United States **328.3; 353.4**
    UF United States—Governmental investigations
Governments in exile
    USE names of wars with the subdivision *Governments in exile,* e.g. **World War, 1939-**

Governments in exile—*Continued*

       1945—Governments in exile

       [to be added as needed]

Governors (May subdiv. geog.) **352.23; 920**

  BT **State governments**

Grace (Theology) 234; 291.2

  BT **Doctrinal theology**

      Salvation

  NT **Sacraments**

      Spiritual gifts

Grade repetition

  USE **Promotion (School)**

Grade retention

  USE **Promotion (School)**

Grade schools

  USE **Elementary schools**

Grading and marking (Education) 371.27

  UF Grading and marking (Students)

      Marking and grading (Education)

      Students—Grading and marking

  BT **Educational tests and measurements**

  NT **Ability grouping in education**

      Promotion (School)

  RT **School reports**

Grading and marking (Students)

  USE **Grading and marking (Education)**

Graduate Record Examination 378.1

  UF GRE

  BT **Colleges and universities—Entrance examinations**

      Examinations

Graduate Record Examination—Study guides 378.1

Graduates, College

  USE **College graduates**

Graduation

  USE **Commencements**

Graffiti (May subdiv. geog.) **080; 808.88**

  BT **Inscriptions**

      Vandalism

Graft in politics

  USE **Political corruption**

Grafting 631.5

  BT **Plant propagation**

Grail 398

  UF Holy Grail

  BT **Folklore**

Grail—Legends 398; 809

  RT **Arthurian romances**

Grain 633.1

  UF Cereals

  SA types of cereal plants, e.g. **Corn; Wheat;** etc. [to be added as needed]

  NT **Corn**

      Wheat

  RT **Flour**

Grain—Storage (May subdiv. geog.) **633.1**

Grammar 415

  SA names of languages with the subdivision *Grammar* [to be added as needed]

  BT **Language and languages**

      Linguistics

  NT **English language—Grammar**

Grammar schools

  USE **Elementary education**

Gramophone

  USE **Phonograph**

Grandparent and child

  USE **Grandparent-grandchild relationship**

Grandparent-grandchild relationship 306.874

    Use for materials on the interaction between grandparents and their grandchildren. Materials restricted to the legal right of grandparents to visit their grandchildren are entered under **Visitation rights (Domestic relations).** Materials on the skills, etc., needed for being an effective grandparent are entered under **Grandparenting.**

  UF Grandparent and child *[Former heading]*

  BT **Family**

      Grandparents

Grandparenting 306.874

    Use for materials on the skills, etc., needed for being an effective grandparent. Materials on the interaction between grandparents and their grandchildren are entered under **Grandparent-grandchild relationship.**

  BT **Grandparents**

      Parenting

Grandparents 306.874

  BT **Parents**

  NT **Foster grandparents**

      Grandparent-grandchild relationship

      Grandparenting

      Grandparents as parents

Grandparents as parents   306.874
- UF   Parenting by grandparents
- BT   **Grandparents**
      Parenting

Grange   334
- BT   **Agriculture—Societies**

Granite   552; 553.5
- BT   **Rocks**
      Stone

Grants
- USE   **Grants-in-aid**
       Subsidies

Grants-in-aid (May subdiv. geog.)
   336.1; 352.73

   Use for materials on grants of money made
   from a central government to a local government.

- UF   Grants
- SA   federal aid to particular endeav-
      ors, e.g. **Federal aid to edu-**
      cation [to be added as need-
      ed]
- BT   **Public finance**
- RT   **Domestic economic assistance**

Grapes   634.8; 641.3
- UF   Viticulture
- BT   **Fruit**
- RT   **Vineyards**
      Wine and wine making

Graph theory   511
- UF   Graphs, Theory of
      Theory of graphs
- BT   **Algebra**
      Mathematical analysis
      Topology

Graphic arts (May subdiv. geog.)   760
- UF   Arts, Graphic
- SA   types of graphic arts [to be add-
      ed as needed]
- BT   **Art**
- NT   **Clip art**
      Drawing
      Engraving
      Painting
      Photography
      Printing
      Prints
      Typography

Graphic arts—United States   760.0973
- UF   American graphic arts

Graphic methods   001.4; 511
- UF   Flow charts
      Flowcharting
      Graphs
- BT   **Drawing**
      Geometrical drawing
      Mechanical drawing
- NT   **Statistics—Graphic methods**

Graphics, Computer
- USE   **Computer graphics**

Graphite   553.2
- UF   Black lead
- BT   **Carbon**

Graphology   137; 155.2

   Use for materials on handwriting as an expression of the writer's character. General materials on the history and art of writing are entered under **Writing.** Materials on writing
   with a pen or pencil and practical or prescriptive guides to penmanship are entered under
   Handwriting.

- BT   **Handwriting**
      Writing

Graphs
- USE   **Graphic methods**

Graphs, Theory of
- USE   **Graph theory**

Grass (Drug)
- USE   **Marijuana**

Grasses (May subdiv. geog.)   584; 633.2
- BT   **Plants**
- RT   **Feeds**
      Forage plants
      Hay
      Lawns

Grasslands (May subdiv. geog.)   577.4;
   578.74
- BT   **Land use**
- NT   **Prairies**

Graves
- USE   **Burial**
       Cemeteries
       Epitaphs
       Funeral rites and ceremonies
       Mounds and mound builders
       Tombs

Graveyards
- USE   **Cemeteries**

Gravitation   521; 531
- UF   Gravity
- BT   **Physics**
- RT   **Relativity (Physics)**

Gravity
    USE   **Gravitation**
Gravity free state
    USE   **Weightlessness**
Gray Friars
    USE   **Franciscans**
GRE
    USE   **Graduate Record Examination**
Grease
    USE   **Lubrication and lubricants**
           Oils and fats
Great books program
    USE   **Discussion groups**
Great Britain   941

> Use for materials on the United Kingdom of Great Britain and Northern Ireland, which comprises England, Scotland, Wales, and Northern Ireland, as well as for materials on the island of Great Britain. May be subdivided like United States except for *History*. Materials limited to one of the constituent parts of the United Kingdom, apart from materials relating to history or politics and government, are entered under that part, e.g. **England.**

    NT   **England**
Great Britain—Colonies   325
    UF   British Empire
    BT   **Colonies**
    RT   **Commonwealth countries**
Great Britain—History   941
    UF   England—History
          English history
Great Britain—History—0-1066   941.01
    NT   **Anglo-Saxons**
          Celts
Great Britain—History—1066-1154, Norman period   941.02
    NT   **Domesday book**
          Hastings (East Sussex, England), Battle of, 1066
          Normans
Great Britain—History—1066-1485, Medieval period   941.03
    NT   **Hundred Years' War, 1339-1453**
Great Britain—History—1154-1399, Plantagenets   941.03
    NT   **Magna Carta**
Great Britain—History—1399-1485, Lancaster and York   941.04
Great Britain—History—1455-1485, Wars of the Roses   941.04
    UF   Wars of the Roses, 1455-1485

Great Britain—History—1485-1603, Tudors   941.05
    NT   **Spanish Armada, 1588**
Great Britain—History—1603-1714, Stuarts   941.06
Great Britain—History—1642-1660, Civil War and Commonwealth   941.06
    UF   Civil War—England
          Commonwealth of England
Great Britain—History—1714-1837   941.07
    NT   **War of 1812**
Great Britain—History—19th century   941.081
    RT   **Industrial revolution**
Great Britain—History—1853-1856, Crimean War
    USE   **Crimean War, 1853-1856**
Great Britain—History—20th century   941.082
Great Britain—History—1945-1952   941.085
Great Britain—History—1952-   941.085
Great Britain—History—21st century   941.086
Great Britain—Kings and rulers   920; 941.092
    UF   Great Britain—Kings, queens, rulers, etc.
    BT   **Kings and rulers**
Great Britain—Kings, queens, rulers, etc.
    USE   **Great Britain—Kings and rulers**
Great Britain—Prime ministers
    USE   **Prime ministers—Great Britain**
Great Britain—Queens
    USE   **Queens—Great Britain**
Great Depression, 1929-1939 (May subdiv. geog.)   **338.5; 909.82**
    UF   Business depression, 1929-1939
          Depressions—1929
    BT   **Depressions**
          Economic conditions
Greece   938; 949.5

> May be subdivided like United States except for *History*.

Greece, Ancient
    USE   **Greece—History—0-323**
Greece—Antiquities   938
    BT   **Classical antiquities**
    NT   **Delphi (Extinct city)**

Greece—Biography   920.038; 920.0495
   UF   Classical biography
   BT   **Biography**
Greece—Civilization   938
   Use for materials on the civilization of Greece, ancient and modern. Materials on the spread of Greek civilization throughout the ancient world following the conquests of Alexander the Great are entered under **Hellenism.** Materials on both ancient Greek and Roman civilizations are entered under **Classical civilization.**
   UF   Civilization, Greek
         Greek civilization
   BT   **Classical civilization**
   NT   **Hellenism**
Greece—Description   914.95
   Use for descriptive materials on modern Greece, including materials for travelers. Descriptive materials on ancient Greece, including accounts by travelers in ancient times, are entered under **Greece—Description—0-323.**
   UF   Greece—Description and travel
Greece—Description—0-323   913.8
   Use for descriptive materials on ancient Greece including accounts by travelers of ancient times.
   UF   Ancient Greece—Description
Greece—Description and travel
   USE   **Greece—Description**
Greece—Geography   914.95
   Use for materials on the geography of modern Greece. Materials on the geography of ancient Greece are entered under **Greece—Historical geography.**
   BT   **Geography**
   NT   **Greece—Historical geography**
Greece—Historical geography   911; 913.8
   UF   Classical geography
   BT   **Ancient geography**
         Greece—Geography
         Historical geography
Greece—History   938; 949.5
Greece—History—0-323   938
   UF   Ancient Greece
         Greece, Ancient
Greece—History—323-1453   949.5
   UF   Medieval Greece
Greece—History—1453-   949.5
   UF   Greece, Modern
Greece—History—20th century   949.507
Greece—History—1967-1974   949.507
Greece—History—1974-   949.507
Greece, Modern
   USE   **Greece—History—1453-**

Greek antiquities
   USE   **Classical antiquities**
Greek architecture (May subdiv. geog.)   722
   UF   Architecture, Greek
   BT   **Ancient architecture**
         Architecture
Greek art   709.38; 709.495
   UF   Art, Greek
         Classical art
   BT   **Ancient art**
         Art
         Classical antiquities
Greek Church
   USE   **Greek Orthodox Church**
Greek civilization
   USE   **Greece—Civilization**
Greek language   480
   Use for classical Greek. Modern Greek is entered under **Modern Greek language.** May be subdivided like **English language.**
   UF   Classical languages
   BT   **Language and languages**
   RT   **Modern Greek language**
Greek language, Modern
   USE   **Modern Greek language**
Greek letter societies
   USE   **Fraternities and sororities**
Greek literature   880
   May use same subdivisions and names of literary forms as for **English literature.**
   BT   **Literature**
   RT   **Classical literature**
Greek literature, Modern
   USE   **Modern Greek literature**
Greek mythology
   USE   **Classical mythology**
Greek Orthodox Church (May subdiv. geog.)   281.9
   UF   Greek Church
   BT   **Christian sects**
         Orthodox Eastern Church
Greek philosophy
   USE   **Ancient philosophy**
Greek sculpture   730.938; 730.9495
   UF   Sculpture, Greek
   BT   **Sculpture**
Green movement
   USE   **Environmental movement**

Greenhouse effect (May subdiv. geog.)
  363.738; 551.5; 551.6
  UF   Atmospheric greenhouse effect
       Carbon dioxide greenhouse effect
       Global warming
       Greenhouse effect, Atmospheric
  BT   **Climate**
       Solar radiation
Greenhouse effect, Atmospheric
  USE **Greenhouse effect**
Greenhouses   631.5
  UF   Hothouses
  BT   **Flower gardening**
       Gardening
       Horticulture
  RT   **Garden rooms**
Greeting cards   741.6; 745.594
  UF   Cards, Greeting
  SA   types of greeting cards [to be
       added as needed]
  NT   **Christmas cards**
Gregorian chant
  USE **Chants (Plain, Gregorian, etc.)**
Grey Friars
  USE **Franciscans**
Grey market
  USE **Black market**
Grief   152.4; 155.9
  Use for materials on mental suffering or
  sorrow from causes such as loss or remorse
  other than the loss of a loved one. Materials
  on the suffering of those who have lost a
  loved one are entered under **Bereavement.**
  UF   Sorrow
  BT   **Emotions**
  RT   **Bereavement**
       Consolation
       Joy and sorrow
Grievance procedures (Public administration)
  USE **Ombudsman**
Grill cooking
  USE **Barbecue cooking**
Grinding and polishing   621.9
  UF   Buffing
       Polishing
  BT   **Machine shop practice**
  RT   **Machine tools**
Grist mills
  USE **Flour mills**
Groceries—Packaging
  USE **Food—Packaging**

Groceries—Purchasing
  USE **Grocery shopping**
Grocery shopping   641.3
  Use for materials on food buying. Materials
  on the principles and methods involved in the
  transfer of merchandise from producer to consumer
  are entered under **Marketing.**
  UF   Food buying
       Food—Purchasing
       Groceries—Purchasing
       Marketing (Home economics)
       Supermarket shopping
  BT   **Home economics**
       Shopping
Grocery trade (May subdiv. geog.)
  338.4
  BT   **Food industry**
  NT   **Supermarkets**
  RT   **Food**
Grooming
  USE types of animals with the subdivision
       Grooming [to be added
       as needed]
Grooming, Personal
  USE **Personal grooming**
Grottoes
  USE **Caves**
Ground effect machines
  USE **Air-cushion vehicles**
Grounds maintenance   712
  Use for materials on maintenance of public,
  industrial, and institutional grounds and large
  estates.
  BT   **Gardening**
  NT   **Golf courses**
       Roadside improvement
Group decision making   302.3; 658.4
  BT   **Decision making**
Group discussion
  USE **Discussion groups**
Group dynamics
  USE **Social groups**
Group homes   362; 363.5
  Use for materials on planned housing for
  groups of unrelated people needing supervision.
  UF   Community based residences
       Group residences
       Residential treatment centers
  BT   **Institutional care**
       Social work
  NT   **Halfway houses**
  RT   **Foster home care**

Group hospitalization
USE **Hospitalization insurance**
Group insurance   368.3
Use for materials on group life insurance. Materials on group insurance in other fields are entered under the specific kind of insurance, e.g. **Health insurance.**
UF   Insurance, Group
BT   **Life insurance**
Group living
USE   **Communal living**
Group medical practice
USE   **Medical practice**
Group medical practice, Prepaid
USE   **Health maintenance organizations**
Group medical service
USE   **Health insurance**
Group method in teaching
USE   **Cooperative learning**
Group problem solving   153.4
UF   Brain storming
Team problem solving
Think tanks
BT   **Problem solving**
Group relations training   302
UF   Encounter groups
Sensitivity training
T groups
BT   **Interpersonal relations**
Group residences
USE   **Group homes**
Group social work
USE   **Social group work**
Group teaching
USE   **Cooperative learning**
Group theory   512
UF   Groups, Theory of
BT   **Algebra**
Mathematics
Number theory
NT   **Boolean algebra**
Group travel
USE   **Travel**
Group values
USE   **Social values**
Group work in education
USE   **Cooperative learning**
Group work, Social
USE   **Social group work**
Grouping by ability
USE   **Ability grouping in education**

Groups of persons
USE   **Persons**
Groups, Social
USE   **Social groups**
Groups, Theory of
USE   **Group theory**
Growing of Christmas trees
USE   **Christmas tree growing**
Grown-up abused children
USE   **Adult child abuse victims**
Growth   155; 571.8; 612.6
SA   subjects with the subdivision *Growth,* e.g. **Children—Growth; Cities and towns—Growth; Plants—Growth;** etc. [to be added as needed]
BT   **Physiology**
Growth disorders   616.4
UF   Abnormal growth
Abnormalities, Human
Development
Failure to thrive syndrome
Human abnormalities
BT   **Metabolism**
NT   **Dwarfism**
Giantism
RT   **Birth defects**
Growth retardation
USE   **Dwarfism**
Guaranteed annual income (May subdiv. geog.)   **362.5**
Use for materials on compensation provided by a government to anyone whose annual income falls below a specified level.
UF   Annual income guarantee
Guaranteed income
BT   **Income**
Guaranteed income
USE   **Guaranteed annual income**
Guerillas
USE   **Guerrillas**
Guerrilla warfare (May subdiv. geog.)   **355.02; 355.4**
Use for materials on the military aspects of irregular warfare. General and historical materials are entered under **Guerrillas.**
UF   Unconventional warfare
BT   **Insurgency**
Military art and science
Tactics
War

Guerrillas (May subdiv. geog.)   356

    Use for general and historical materials. Materials on the military aspects of irregular warfare are entered under **Guerrilla warfare.**

    UF   Guerillas

           Partisans

    SA   names of wars with the subdivision *Underground movements,* e.g. **World War, 1939-1945—Underground movements** [to be added as needed]

    BT   **National liberation movements**

Guests

    USE **Entertaining**

Guidance

    USE **Counseling**

Guidance counseling, Educational

    USE **Educational counseling**

Guidance counseling, School

    USE **School counseling**

Guidance, Vocational

    USE **Vocational guidance**

Guide dogs   636.7

    UF   Dog guides

           Dogs for the blind

           Seeing eye dogs

    BT   **Animals and the handicapped**

           Dogs

           Working animals

Guidebooks

    USE names of cities (except ancient cities), countries, states, etc., with the subdivision *Guidebooks,* e.g. **Chicago (Ill.)—Guidebooks; United States—Guidebooks;** etc. [to be added as needed]

Guided missiles   358.1; 623.4

    UF   Missiles, Guided

    SA   types of missiles and names of specific missiles [to be added as needed]

    BT   **Bombs**

           Projectiles

           Rocketry

           Rockets (Aeronautics)

    NT   **Antimissile missiles**

           Ballistic missiles

           Nike rocket

Guitar

    USE **Guitars**

Guitar music   787.87

    BT   **Instrumental music**

Guitars   787.87

    UF   Guitar

    BT   **Stringed instruments**

Gulf States (U.S.)   976

    BT   **United States**

Gulf War, 1991

    USE **Persian Gulf War, 1991**

Gums and resins   547; 668

    UF   Resins

           Rosin

    BT   **Forest products**

           Industrial chemistry

           Plastics

Gun control (May subdiv. geog.)   323.4; 344; 363.3

    Use for materials about existing laws governing the purchase and use of firearms and for materials about the political controversy over limiting legal access to firearms and stopping the traffic in illegal firearms.

    UF   Control of guns

           Firearms control

           Firearms—Law and legislation

           Guns—Control

           Handgun control

           Right to bear arms

    BT   **Law**

           Legislation

Gunpowder   623.4

    UF   Powder, Smokeless

           Smokeless powder

    BT   **Explosives**

           Firearms

    RT   **Ammunition**

Guns

    USE **Firearms**

          Ordnance

          Rifles

          Shotguns

Guns—Control

    USE **Gun control**

Gunsmithing

    USE **Firearms industry**

Gymnastics   613.7; 796.44

    UF   Calisthenics

    BT   **Athletics**

           Exercise

           Sports

    RT   **Acrobats and acrobatics**

           Physical education

Gynecology
USE **Women—Diseases**
Women—Health and hygiene
Gypsies 305.891
UF Gipsies
Romanies
Gypsum 553.6
BT **Minerals**
Gyroscope 629.135; 681
BT **Aeronautical instruments**
Habit 152.3
BT **Human behavior**
Psychology
NT **Tobacco habit**
RT **Instinct**
Habitations
USE types of animals with the subdivision *Habitations,* for materials on the natural shelters and homes animals build for themselves, such as burrows, dens, lairs, etc., e.g. **Beavers—Habitations** [to be added as needed]
Habitations, Human
USE **Housing**
Habitations of domestic animals
USE **Animal housing**
Habitations of wild animals
USE **Animals—Habitations**
Habits of animals
USE **Animal behavior**
Hades
USE **Hell**
Haiku 808.1; 808.81; 811, etc.
May be used for collections of haiku by one or several authors or for materials about haiku.
BT **Poetry**
Hair 612.7; 646.7
Use for general materials on hair as well for as materials on hairdressing and haircutting.
UF Barbering
Coiffure
Haircutting
Hairdressing
Hairstyles
Hairstyling
BT **Head**
Personal grooming
NT **Wigs**

Haircutting
USE **Hair**
Hairdressing
USE **Hair**
Hairstyles
USE **Hair**
Hairstyling
USE **Hair**
Halftone process
USE **Photoengraving**
Halfway houses (May subdiv. geog.)
362; 365
Use for materials on centers for formerly institutionalized individuals, such as mental patients or drug addicts, that are designed to facilitate their readjustment to private life.
BT **Correctional institutions**
Group homes
Halley's comet 523.6
BT **Comets**
Hallmarks
UF Marks
Marks on plate
SA types of things with identifying marks, other than plate, with the subdivision *Marks,* e.g. **Pottery—Marks** [to be added as needed]
BT **Plate**
Halloween 394.2646
UF All Hallows' Eve
BT **Holidays**
Hallucinations and illusions 616.85;
616.89
UF Delusions
Illusions
BT **Abnormal psychology**
Parapsychology
Subconsciousness
Visions
NT **Optical illusions**
RT **Apparitions**
Fantasy
Magic
Magic tricks
Personality disorders
Hallucinogenic drugs
USE **Hallucinogens**
Hallucinogenic plants
USE **Hallucinogens**

Hallucinogens   615
   UF Consciousness expanding drugs
         Hallucinogenic drugs
         Hallucinogenic plants
   SA types of hallucinogens [to be
         added as needed]
   BT **Drugs**
         Psychotropic drugs
         Stimulants
Ham radio stations
   USE **Amateur radio stations**
Hand shadows
   USE **Shadow pictures**
Hand weaving
   USE **Weaving**
Handbooks, manuals, etc.
   USE subjects, classes of persons, and
         names of places, corporate
         bodies, individual literary au-
         thors, and sacred works with
         the subdivision *Handbooks,*
         manuals, etc., e.g. **Photogra-**
         phy—Handbooks, manuals,
         etc.; United States. Army—
         Handbooks, manuals, etc. [to
         be added as needed]
Handedness
   USE **Left- and right-handedness**
Handgun control
   USE **Gun control**
Handguns (May subdiv. geog.)   **683.4**
   UF Pistols
         Revolvers
   BT **Firearms**
Handheld computers
   USE **Portable computers**
Handicapped (May subdiv. geog.)
   305.9; 362.4
   UF Disabled
   NT **Architecture and the handi-**
         capped
         Discrimination against the
         handicapped
         Handicapped children
         Mentally handicapped
         Physically handicapped
         Sick
         Socially handicapped
         Sports for the handicapped
         Vocational guidance for the
         handicapped

Handicapped and animals
   USE **Animals and the handicapped**
Handicapped and architecture
   USE **Architecture and the handi-**
         capped
Handicapped children (May subdiv.
   geog.)   **362.7**
   UF Abnormal children
         Children, Abnormal
   BT **Children**
         Exceptional children
         Handicapped
   NT **Brain damaged children**
         Hyperactive children
         Mainstreaming in education
         Mentally handicapped children
         Physically handicapped chil-
         dren
         Socially handicapped children
Handicapped—Clothing   646.4
   BT **Clothing and dress**
Handicapped—Legal status, laws, etc.
   (May subdiv. geog.)   **346.01**
   UF Disability law
   BT **Law**
Handicapped—Nazi persecution (May
   subdiv. geog.)   **940.53**
   UF Nazi persecution of the handi-
         capped
   BT **Persecution**
         World War, 1939-1945—Atroc-
         ities
Handicapped—Salaries, wages, etc. (May
   subdiv. geog.)   **331.2**
   BT **Salaries, wages, etc.**
Handicapped—Services for (May subdiv.
   geog.)   **362.4**
   UF Services for the handicapped
   BT **Human services**
         Social work
Handicapped—Travel   910.2
   BT **Travel**
Handicraft (May subdiv. geog.)   **745.5;**
   746

   Use for materials on creative work done by
   hand, sometimes with the aid of simple tools
   or machines.

   UF Crafts (Arts)
   SA types of handicrafts [to be added
         as needed]

Handicraft—*Continued*
  BT   Arts
  NT   Chair caning
       Collage
       Craft shows
       Egg decoration
       Furniture finishing
       Hooked rugs
       Industrial arts
       Leather work
       Models and modelmaking
       Nature craft
       Paper crafts
       Picture frames and framing
       Quilting
       Weaving
  RT   Arts and crafts movement
       Creative activities
       Decoration and ornament
       Decorative arts
       Folk art
       Hobbies
       Occupational therapy
Handling of materials
  USE   Materials handling
Handwriting   652
    Use for materials on writing with a pen or
  pencil and for practical or prescriptive guides
  to penmanship. General materials on the his-
  tory and art of writing are entered under
  Writing. Materials on handwriting as an ex-
  pression of the writer's character are entered
  under **Graphology.**
  UF   Legibility of handwriting
       Penmanship
       Writing—Study and teaching
  BT   Writing
  NT   Calligraphy
       Graphology
       Writing of numerals
Hang gliding
  USE   Gliding and soaring
Hanging
  USE   Capital punishment
Hanukkah (May subdiv. geog.)   296.4;
           394.267
  UF   Chanukah
       Feast of Dedication
       Feast of Lights
  BT   Jewish holidays
Happening (Art)
  USE   Performance art

Happiness   158
  UF   Gladness
  BT   Emotions
  NT   Mental health
  RT   Joy and sorrow
       Pleasure
Harassment, Sexual
  USE   Sexual harassment
Harbors (May subdiv. geog.)   386;
           387.1; 627
  UF   Ports
  BT   Civil engineering
       Hydraulic structures
       Merchant marine
       Navigation
       Shipping
       Transportation
  NT   Marinas
  RT   Docks
Hard-of-hearing
  USE   Hearing impaired
Hares
  USE   Rabbits
Harlem Renaissance   810.9; 974.7
  UF   New Negro Movement
  BT   African American art
       African American music
       American literature—African
           American authors
Harmful insects
  USE   Insect pests
Harmony   781.2
  BT   Composition (Music)
       Music
       Music—Theory
Harry S. Truman Library   026
  BT   Presidents—United States—Ar-
           chives
Harvesting machinery   631.3
  UF   Reapers
  BT   Agricultural machinery
Hashish
  USE   Marijuana
Hasidism (May subdiv. geog.)   296.8
  UF   Chasidism
       Hassidism
  BT   Judaism
Hassidism
  USE   Hasidism

Hastings (East Sussex, England), Battle
 of, 1066   941.02
  BT   Great Britain—History—1066-
       1154, Norman period
Hate crimes (May subdiv. geog.)   364
  UF   Bias attacks
       Bias crimes
       Bigotry-motivated crimes
       Crimes of hate
       Prejudice-motivated crimes
  BT   Crime
       Discrimination
       Violence
Hatha yoga   613.7
  UF   Yoga exercises
       Yoga, Hatha
  BT   Exercise
       Yoga
Hats (May subdiv. geog.)   391.4; 646.5;
       687
  UF   Millinery
  BT   Clothing and dress
       Costume
Haunted houses
  USE Ghosts
Hawking
  USE Falconry
Hay   633.2
  SA   types of hay crops, e.g. Alfalfa
       [to be added as needed]
  BT   Farm produce
       Forage plants
  RT   Feeds
       Grasses
Hay fever   616.2
  BT   Allergy
Hazardous materials
  USE Hazardous substances
Hazardous occupations   331.7
  UF   Dangerous occupations
  BT   Occupations
  RT   Industrial accidents
       Occupational diseases
       Occupational health and safety
Hazardous substances   363.17; 604.7
  UF   Dangerous materials
       Hazardous materials
       Inflammable substances
       Toxic substances

  BT   Materials
  NT   Hazardous wastes
       Poisons and poisoning
Hazardous substances—Transportation
       363.17; 604.7
  BT   Transportation
Hazardous waste disposal
  USE Hazardous wastes
Hazardous waste sites (May subdiv.
  geog.)   363.72; 628.4
  UF   Chemical landfills
       Dumps, Toxic
       Toxic dumps
  BT   Landfills
  NT   Love Canal Chemical Waste
       Landfill (Niagara Falls,
       N.Y.)
Hazardous wastes   363.72
  UF   Hazardous waste disposal
       Toxic wastes
       Wastes, Hazardous
  BT   Hazardous substances
       Industrial waste
       Refuse and refuse disposal
  RT   Medical wastes
       Pollution
HDTV (Television)
  USE High definition television
Head   611; 612
  BT   Anatomy
  NT   Brain
       Ear
       Eye
       Face
       Hair
       Nose
       Phrenology
       Teeth
Heads of state (May subdiv. geog.)
       352.23; 920
  UF   Rulers
       State, Heads of
  SA   names of individual heads of
       state [to be added as needed]
  BT   Executive power
       Statesmen
  NT   Dictators
       Kings and rulers
       Presidents
Healing, Mental
  USE Mental healing

Healing, Spiritual
USE **Spiritual healing**
Health   613

Use for materials on physical, mental, and social well-being. Materials on personal body care are entered under **Hygiene.**

UF Personal health
SA parts of the body with the subdivision *Care,* e.g. **Foot—Care;** classes of persons and ethnic groups with the subdivision *Health and hygiene,* e.g. **Women—Health and hygiene;** and subjects and names of wars with the subdivision *Health aspects,* e.g. **World War, 1939-1945—Health aspects** [to be added as needed]
BT **Medicine**
Physiology
Preventive medicine
NT **Children—Health and hygiene**
Diet
Elderly—Health and hygiene
Exercise
Health education
Health self-care
Infants—Health and hygiene
Mental health
Nutrition
Physical fitness
Public health
Rest
Sleep
Women—Health and hygiene
RT **Diseases**
Holistic medicine
Hygiene
Health and hygiene
USE classes of persons and ethnic groups with the subdivision *Health and hygiene,* e.g. **Women—Health and hygiene;** and parts of the body with the subdivision *Care,* e.g. **Foot—Care; Skin—Care;** etc. [to be added as needed]

Health aspects
USE subjects, industries, and wars with the subdivision *Health aspects,* e.g. **World War, 1939-1945—Health aspects** [to be added as needed]
Health boards   614.06
UF Boards of health
Public health boards
BT **Public health**
Health care
USE **Medical care**
Health care delivery
USE **Medical care**
Health care personnel
USE **Medical personnel**
Health care reform (May subdiv. geog.) **362.1**
UF Health reform
Health system reform
Medical care reform
Reform of health care delivery
Reform of medical care delivery
RT **Health insurance**
Medical care
Health care, Self
USE **Health self-care**
Health clubs
USE **Physical fitness centers**
Health counseling   362.1; 613
BT **Counseling**
Health education
Health education (May subdiv. geog.) **372.3; 613.07**
UF Health—Study and teaching
Hygiene—Study and teaching
BT **Education**
Health
NT **Drug education**
Health counseling
School hygiene
RT **Children—Health and hygiene**
School nurses
Health—Environmental aspects
USE **Environmental health**
Health examinations
USE **Periodic health examinations**
Health foods
USE **Natural foods**
Health, Industrial
USE **Occupational health and safety**

Health insurance (May subdiv. geog.)
   368.38
   UF   Group medical service
          Health plans, Prepaid
          Insurance, Health
          Medical care, Prepaid
          Medical insurance
          Prepaid health plans
          Prepaid medical care
   BT   **Insurance**
   NT   **Health maintenance organiza-
          tions**
          Hospitalization insurance
          National health insurance
          Workers' compensation
   RT   **Health care reform**
Health maintenance organizations (May
   subdiv. geog.)   **368.38; 610.6**
   UF   Comprehensive health care orga-
          nizations
          Group medical practice, Prepaid
          HMOs
          Prepaid group medical practice
   BT   **Health insurance**
          Medical practice
Health personnel
   USE   **Medical personnel**
Health plans, Prepaid
   USE   **Health insurance**
Health professions
   USE   **Medical personnel**
Health program evaluation
   USE   **Public health—Evaluation**
Health reform
   USE   **Health care reform**
Health resorts (May subdiv. geog.)   **613**
   UF   Health resorts, spas, etc.
          Health spas
          Sanatoriums
          Spas
          Watering places
   BT   **Resorts**
   RT   **Hydrotherapy**
Health resorts, spas, etc.
   USE   **Health resorts**
Health sciences personnel
   USE   **Medical personnel**
Health self-care   **613; 616**
   UF   Health care, Self
          Medical self-care
          Self-care, Health

          Self-care, Medical
          Self-examination, Medical
          Self health care
          Self-help medical care
          Self-medication
   BT   **Alternative medicine**
          Health
          Medical care
   NT   **First aid**
          Physical fitness
   RT   **Holistic medicine**
          Popular medicine
Health services personnel
   USE   **Medical personnel**
Health spas
   USE   **Health resorts**
          Physical fitness centers
Health—Study and teaching
   USE   **Health education**
Health system reform
   USE   **Health care reform**
Healths, Drinking of
   USE   **Toasts**
Hearing   **152.1; 612.8**
   UF   Acoustics
   BT   **Senses and sensation**
          Sound
   RT   **Deafness**
          Ear
          Listening
Hearing aids   **617.8**
   BT   **Deafness**
Hearing ear dogs   **636.7**
   UF   Dogs for the deaf
   BT   **Animals and the handicapped**
          **Deaf—Means of communica-
          tion**
          Dogs
Hearing impaired   **362.4; 617.8**
   UF   Hard-of-hearing
          Partial hearing
          Partially hearing
   BT   **Physically handicapped**
   NT   **Deaf**
Heart   **573.1; 611; 612.1**
   BT   **Cardiovascular system**
   NT   **Artificial heart**
Heart—Anatomy   **573.1; 611**
   BT   **Anatomy**

Heart attack   616.1
   UF   Heart—Infarction
          Myocardial infarction
   BT   **Heart diseases**
Heart disease
   USE **Heart diseases**
Heart—Diseases
   USE **Heart diseases**
Heart diseases   616.1
   UF   Cardiac diseases
          Coronary heart diseases
          Heart disease
          Heart—Diseases
   BT   **Diseases**
   NT   **Angina pectoris**
          Heart attack
Heart diseases—Prevention   616.1
   BT   **Preventive medicine**
Heart—Infarction
   USE **Heart attack**
Heart—Physiology   612.1
   BT   **Physiology**
Heart resuscitation
   USE **Cardiac resuscitation**
Heart—Surgery   617.4
   UF   Open heart surgery
   BT   **Surgery**
Heart—Surgery—Nursing   610.73; 617.4
   BT   **Nursing**
Heart—Transplantation   617.4
   BT   **Transplantation of organs, tissues, etc.**
Heat   536
   BT   **Electromagnetic waves**
   NT   **Steam**
          Thermometers
   RT   **Combustion**
          Fire
          Temperature
          Thermodynamics
Heat—Conduction   536
Heat engines   621.4
   UF   Hot air engines
   BT   **Engines**
          Thermodynamics
Heat insulating materials
   USE **Insulation (Heat)**
Heat pumps   621.4
   BT   **Pumping machinery**
          Thermodynamics

Heat—Transmission   536
Heathenism
   USE **Paganism**
Heating   644; 697
   SA   subjects with the subdivision
          Heating and ventilation, e.g.
          Houses—Heating and ventilation [to be added as needed]
   BT   **Home economics**
   NT   **Electric heating**
          Fireplaces
          Furnaces
          Hot air heating
          Hot water heating
          Houses—Heating and ventilation
          Insulation (Heat)
          Oil burners
          Radiant heating
          Solar heating
          Space heaters
          Steam heating
          Stoves
   RT   **Fuel**
          Ventilation
Heating and ventilation
   USE types of buildings with the subdivision *Heating and ventilation,* e.g. **Houses—Heating and ventilation** [to be added as needed]
Heaven   236; 291.2
   BT   **Eschatology**
          Future life
   NT   **Angels**
   RT   **Paradise**
Heavy water
   USE **Deuterium oxide**
Hebrew language   492.4
   May be subdivided like **English language.**
   UF   Jewish language
          Jews—Language
   BT   **Language and languages**
Hebrew literature   892.4
   May use same subdivisions and names of literary forms as for **English literature.**
   UF   Jews—Literature
   BT   **Literature**
   NT   **Bible**
          Cabala
          Talmud

Hebrew literature—*Continued*
  RT   Jewish literature
Hebrews
  USE   Jews
Heirs
  USE   Inheritance and succession
Helicopters   387.7; 629.133
  UF   Aircraft
  BT   Aeronautics
       Airplanes
Helicopters—Piloting   629.132
  BT   Airplanes—Piloting
Heliports   387.7
  BT   Airports
Helium   546
  BT   Chemical elements
       Gases
Hell   236; 291.2
  UF   Eternal punishment
       Hades
       Retribution
  BT   Eschatology
       Future life
Hellenism   938
    Use for materials on the spread of Greek
    civilization throughout the ancient world fol-
    lowing the conquests of Alexander the Great.
    Materials limited to the civilization of Greece,
    ancient and modern, are entered under
    Greece—Civilization. Materials on both an-
    cient Greek and Roman civilizations are en-
    tered under **Classical civilization.**
  BT   Greece—Civilization
Helpful insects
  USE   Beneficial insects
Helpfulness
  USE   Helping behavior
Helping behavior   158
  UF   Assistance in emergencies
       Behavior, Helping
       Emergency assistance
       Helpfulness
  BT   Human behavior
       Interpersonal relations
  NT   Counseling
Hemp   633.5; 677
  BT   Fibers
  RT   Rope
Heraldry (May subdiv. geog.)   929.6
  UF   Coats of arms
       Crests
       Devices (Heraldry)
       Emblems
       Pedigrees

  BT   Archeology
       Signs and symbols
       Symbolism
  NT   Flags
       Insignia
       Mottoes
       Seals (Numismatics)
  RT   Chivalry
       Decorations of honor
       Genealogy
       Knights and knighthood
       National emblems
       Nobility
Herb remedies
  USE   Herbs—Therapeutic use
Herbal medicine
  USE   Herbs—Therapeutic use
       Medical botany
Herbals
  USE   Herbs
       Materia medica
Herbaria
  USE   Plants—Collection and preser-
         vation
Herbicides   632; 668
  UF   Defoliants
       Weed killers
  SA   types of herbicides, e.g. **Agent
       Orange** [to be added as need-
       ed]
  BT   Agricultural chemicals
       Pesticides
  NT   Agent Orange
  RT   Plants
       Spraying and dusting
Herbs   581.6; 635
  UF   Herbals
  BT   Plants
Herbs—Therapeutic use   615
  UF   Herb remedies
       Herbal medicine
       Medicinal herbs
  BT   Therapeutics
Hereditary diseases
  USE   Medical genetics
Hereditary succession
  USE   Inheritance and succession
Heredity   576.5
  UF   Ancestry
       Descent
       Genes

Heredity—*Continued*
    Inheritance (Biology)
  BT **Biology**
      Breeding
  NT **Chromosomes**
      DNA
      Variation (Biology)
  RT **Eugenics**
      Genetics
      Mendel's law
      Natural selection
Heredity of diseases
  USE **Medical genetics**
Hereford cattle 636.2
  BT **Beef cattle**
Heritage property
  USE **Cultural property**
Hermeneutics, Biblical
  USE **Bible—Criticism**
Hermetic art and philosophy
  USE **Alchemy**
      Astrology
      Occultism
Hermits (May subdiv. geog.) 920
  UF Recluses
  BT **Eccentrics and eccentricities**
  RT **Monasticism and religious orders**
Heroes and heroines 920
  UF Heroines
      Heroism
  BT **Adventure and adventurers**
  NT **Explorers**
      Martyrs
  RT **Courage**
      Mythology
Heroin 362.29; 615
  BT **Morphine**
      Narcotics
Heroines
  USE **Heroes and heroines**
Heroism
  USE **Courage**
      Heroes and heroines
Hertzian waves
  USE **Electric waves**
Hi-fi systems
  USE **High-fidelity sound systems**
Hibernation 591.56
  UF Animals—Hibernation
  BT **Animal behavior**

Hidden economy
  USE **Underground economy**
Hidden treasure
  USE **Buried treasure**
Hides and skins 636.088; 675
  UF Pelts
      Skins
  BT **Animal products**
  RT **Fur**
      Leather
      Tanning
Hieroglyphics 411
  BT **Inscriptions**
      Writing
  NT **Rosetta stone inscription**
  RT **Picture writing**
High blood pressure
  USE **Hypertension**
High definition television 621.388
  UF HDTV (Television)
  BT **Television**
High-fidelity sound systems 621.389
  UF Hi-fi systems
  BT **Electronics**
      Sound—Recording and reproducing
  NT **Stereophonic sound systems**
  RT **Phonograph**
High-frequency radio
  USE **Shortwave radio**
High income people
  USE **Rich**
High rise buildings
  USE **Skyscrapers**
High risk students
  USE **At risk students**
High school dropouts
  USE **Dropouts**
High school education
  USE **Secondary education**
High school libraries (May subdiv. geog.)
      027.8
  UF Junior high school libraries
      Secondary school libraries
  BT **School libraries**
High school life
  USE **High school students**
High school students (May subdiv. geog.)
      373
  UF High school life
      High schools—Students

High school students—*Continued*
  BT **Students**
High school yearbooks
  USE **School yearbooks**
High schools (May subdiv. geog.) **373**
  UF Secondary schools
  BT **Public schools**
      Schools
  NT **Commencements**
      Junior high schools
  RT **Secondary education**
High schools, Rural
  USE **Rural schools**
High schools—Students
  USE **High school students**
High society
  USE **Upper class**
High speed aerodynamics
  USE **Supersonic aerodynamics**
High speed aeronautics **629.132**
  BT **Aeronautics**
  NT **Aerothermodynamics**
      Rocket planes
      Rockets (Aeronautics)
      Supersonic aerodynamics
High tech
  USE **Technology**
High technology
  USE **Technology**
High treason
  USE **Treason**
High-yield junk bonds
  USE **Junk bonds**
Higher criticism
  USE **Bible—Criticism**
Higher education (May subdiv. geog.)
      378
  Use for general materials on education
  above the secondary level.
  UF Education, Higher
  BT **Education**
  NT **Adult education**
      Colleges and universities
      Junior colleges
      Professional education
      Technical education
      University extension
Highland clans
  USE **Clans—Scotland**
Highland costume
  USE **Tartans**

Highway accidents
  USE **Traffic accidents**
Highway beautification
  USE **Roadside improvement**
Highway construction
  USE **Roads**
Highway engineering (May subdiv. geog.)
      625.7
  UF Road engineering
  BT **Civil engineering**
      Engineering
  NT **Traffic engineering**
  RT **Roads**
Highway transportation (May subdiv.
  geog.) **388.3**
  UF Transportation, Highway
  BT **Transportation**
  NT **Automobiles**
      Buses
      Trucks
Highwaymen
  USE **Thieves**
Highways
  USE **Roads**
Hijacking of aircraft
  USE **Hijacking of airplanes**
Hijacking of airplanes (May subdiv.
  geog.) **364.15**
  Use same form for the hijacking of other
  modes of transportation.
  UF Air piracy
      Airlines—Hijacking
      Airplane hijacking
      Airplanes—Hijacking
      Hijacking of aircraft
  BT **Offenses against public safety**
Hiking (May subdiv. geog.) **796.51**
  SA types of hiking, e.g.
      Backpacking [to be added as
      needed]
  BT **Outdoor life**
  NT **Backpacking**
      Orienteering
  RT **Direction sense**
      Walking
Hillbilly music
  USE **Country music**
Hindu philosophy **181**
  UF Philosophy, Hindu
  BT **Philosophy**
  NT **Yoga**

Hinduism (May subdiv. geog.) **294.5**
  BT **Religions**
  NT **Vedas**
       Yoga
  RT **Brahmanism**
       Hindus

Hindus (May subdiv. geog.) **294.5092**
  RT **Hinduism**

Hippies (May subdiv. geog.) **306**
  BT **Bohemianism**

Hippies—United States **306**

Hispanic American authors **810.9; 920**
  SA genres of American literature
      with the subdivision *Hispanic*
      American authors [to be add-
      ed as needed]
  BT **American authors**
  NT **Mexican American authors**

Hispanic American literature (English)
  USE **American literature—Hispanic**
       American authors

Hispanic American literature (Spanish)
  USE **American literature (Spanish)**

Hispanic Americans **305.868; 973**
  Use for materials on United States citizens
  of Latin American descent. Materials on citi-
  zens of Latin American countries are entered
  under **Latin Americans.**
  UF Latinos (U.S.)
  SA names of groups of United
      States citizens from specific
      countries, e.g. **Mexican**
      Americans [to be added as
      needed]
  BT **Ethnic groups**
  NT **Mexican Americans**

Historians (May subdiv. geog.) **907;**
920
  UF Historiographers
  BT **Authors**
  NT **Archeologists**
  RT **Historiography**
      History

Historians, American
  USE **Historians—United States**

Historians—United States **907; 920**
  UF American historians *[Former*
      heading]
      Historians, American

Historic buildings (May subdiv. geog.)
363.6; 720.9
  Use for materials on buildings that are associated with notable persons or events in history. Materials on buildings that are merely
  old are entered under **Buildings;** or under various types of buildings, e.g. **Castles; Church**
  buildings; Theaters; etc.
  UF Historic houses
  BT **Buildings**
      Historic sites
      Monuments
  NT **Literary landmarks**

Historic buildings—Chicago (Ill.) **977.3**
  UF Chicago (Ill.)—Historic buildings

Historic buildings—Ohio **977.1**
  UF Ohio—Historic buildings

Historic buildings—United States **973**
  UF United States—Historic buildings

Historic houses
  USE **Historic buildings**

Historic preservation (May subdiv. geog.)
363.6
  Use for materials on identifying and preserving historically important towns, buildings, sites, etc. Materials on protecting cultural heritage property from theft, misappropriation, or exportation are entered under **Cultur-**
  al property—Protection.
  UF Preservationism (Historic preser-
      vation)
  SA types of objects, architecture,
      etc., with the subdivision
      Conservation and restoration,
      e.g. **Theaters—Conservation**
      and restoration [to be added
      as needed]
  NT **Theaters—Conservation and**
      restoration
  RT **Cultural property—Protection**

Historic sites (May subdiv. geog.) **363.6**
  UF Historical sites
  BT **Archeology**
      History
  NT **Historic buildings**
  RT **National monuments**

Historical atlases **911**
  UF Historical geography—Maps
      History—Atlases
      Maps, Historical
  BT **Atlases**
  RT **Historical geography**

Historical chronology **902**
  Use for materials in which historical events
  are arranged by date.

Historical chronology—*Continued*
- UF   Chronology, Historical
  Dates, Historical
  History—Chronology
- SA   ethnic groups, corporate bodies, military services, topics not inherently historical, and names of places with the subdivision *History—Chronology,* e.g. **Native Americans—History—Chronology; United States—History—Chronology;** and names of individual persons, wars, sacred works, topics that are inherently historical, and topics not subdivided by *History,* such as art, music, literture, etc., with the subdivision *Chronology,* e.g. **Bible—Chronology** [to be added as needed]
- BT   **Chronology**
  History

Historical dictionaries
- USE   **History—Dictionaries**

Historical drama   808.82; 812, etc.
  May be used for individual works, collections, or materials about historical drama.
- UF   Chronicle history (Drama)
  Chronicle plays
  History plays
- SA   historical topics, events, or personages with the subdivision *Drama,* e.g. **United States—History—1861-1865, Civil War—Drama; Napoleon I, Emperor of the French, 1769-1821—Drama** [to be added as needed]
- BT   **Drama**
- NT   **United States—History—1861-1865, Civil War—Drama**
  United States—History—Drama
  War films
  Western films

Historical fiction   808.83; 813, etc
  May be used for individual works, collections, or materials about fiction set during a time significantly prior to the time in which it was written.
- UF   Historical novels
  Historical romances

- SA   historical topics, events, or personages with the subdivision *Fiction,* e.g. **Slavery—United States—Fiction; United States—History—1861-1865, Civil War—Fiction; Napoleon I, Emperor of the French, 1769-1821—Fiction;** etc. [to be added as needed]
- BT   **Fiction**
- NT   **Gothic novels**
  Regency novels
  War stories
  Western stories
- RT   **Biographical fiction**
  History

Historical geography   911
  Use for materials that discuss the extent of territory held by the states or nations at a given period of history. Materials limited to one country or region still existing in modern times are entered under the name of the place with the subdivision *Historical geography*. Materials on the geography of regions or countries of antiquity that no longer exist as such in modern times are entered under the name of the place with the subdivision *Geography*.
- UF   Geography, Historical
- SA   names of modern countries or regions with the subdivision *Historical geography,* e.g. **Greece—Historical geography; United States—Historical geography;** etc.; and names of places of antiquity with the subdivision *Geography,* e.g. **Gaul—Geography** [to be added as needed]
- BT   **Geography**
  History
- NT   **Ancient geography**
  Gaul—Geography
  Greece—Historical geography
  Rome—Geography
  United States—Historical geography
- RT   **Historical atlases**

Historical geography—Maps
- USE   **Historical atlases**

Historical geology
- USE   **Stratigraphic geology**

Historical materialism
- USE   **Dialectical materialism**

Historical novels
    USE **Historical fiction**
Historical poetry   808.81; 811, etc.
    May be used for individual works, collections, or materials about historical poetry.
    UF   Poetry, Historical
    BT   **Narrative poetry**
    NT   **United States—History—Poetry**
           World War, 1939-1945—Poetry
Historical records—Preservation
    USE **Archives**
Historical romances
    USE **Historical fiction**
Historical sites
    USE **Historic sites**
Historical societies
    USE **History—Societies**
Historiographers
    USE **Historians**
Historiography   907
    Use for materials limited to the study and criticism of sources of history, methods of historical research, and the writing of history. General materials on history as a science, including the principles of history, the influence of various factors on history, and the relation of the science of history to other subjects, are entered under **History**. Materials on the interpretation and meaning of history and on the course of events and their resulting consequences are entered under **History—Philosophy**.
    UF   History—Criticism
          History—Historiography
    SA   subjects, wars, historical events, and names of countries, cities, etc., with the subdivision *Historiography* [to be added as needed]
    BT   **Authorship**
          History
    NT   **History—Sources**
          Local history
          Philosophy—Historiography
          United States—Historiography
          United States—History—1861-1865, Civil War—Historiography
    RT   **Historians**
History   900
    Use for general materials on history as a science, including the principles of history, the influence of various factors on history, and the relation of the science of history to other subjects. Materials on the interpretation and meaning of history and on the course of

events and their resulting consequences are entered under **History—Philosophy**. Materials limited to the study and criticism of sources of history, methods of historical research, and the writing of history are entered under **Historiography**. Materials on past events themselves are entered under **World history**; or under the names of regions, countries, cities, etc., with the subdivision *History*.
    UF   Social studies
    SA   countries, states, etc., with the subdivisions *Antiquities; Foreign relations; History;* or *Politics and government;* and subjects with the subdivision *History,* or, for literature, film, and music headings, *History and criticism,* e.g. **Art—History; English literature—History and criticism** [to be added as needed]
    BT   **Humanities**
          Social sciences
    NT   **Archeology**
          Art—History
          Biography
          Chronology
          Church history
          Constitutional history
          Exploration
          Genealogy
          Historic sites
          Historical chronology
          Historical geography
          Historiography
          Local history
          Massacres
          Military history
          Naval history
          Numismatics
          Oral history
          Seals (Numismatics)
          Women—History
          World history
    RT   **Civilization**
          Historians
          Historical fiction
History, Ancient
    USE **Ancient history**
History and criticism
    USE types of literature, music, and other arts with the subdivision *History and criticism,* e.g.

History and criticism—*Continued*
>> **English literature—History and criticism** [to be added as needed]

History—Atlases
>> USE **Historical atlases**

History, Biblical
>> USE **Bible—History of biblical events**

History—Chronology
>> USE **Historical chronology**

History—Criticism
>> USE **Historiography**

History—Dictionaries   903
>> UF   Historical dictionaries
>> BT   **Encyclopedias and dictionaries**
>> NT   **United States—History—Dictionaries**

History—Historiography
>> USE   **Historiography**

History, Military
>> USE   **Military history**

History, Modern
>> USE   **Modern history**

History, Modern—16th century
>> USE   **World history—16th century**

History, Modern—17th century
>> USE   **World history—17th century**

History, Modern—18th century
>> USE   **World history—18th century**

History, Modern—19th century
>> USE   **World history—19th century**

History, Modern—20th century
>> USE   **World history—20th century**

History, Modern—1945-
>> USE   **World history—1945-**

History, Modern—21st century
>> USE   **World history—21st century**

History of doctrines
>> USE   religious topics with the subdivision *History of doctrines,* e.g. **Salvation—History of doctrines** [to be added as needed]

History—Periodicals   905

History—Philosophy   901
>> Use for materials on the interpretation and meaning of history and on the course of events and their resulting consequences. General materials on history as a science, including the principles of history, the influences of various factors on history, and the relation of the science of history to other subjects, are entered under **History.** Materials limited to the study and criticism of the sources of history, methods of historical research, and the writing of history are entered under **Historiography.**
>> UF   Philosophy of history
>> BT   **Philosophy**

History plays
>> USE   **Historical drama**

History—Societies   906
>> UF   Historical societies
>> BT   **Societies**
>> NT   **Chicago (Ill.)—History—Societies**
>> **Ohio—History—Societies**
>> **United States—History—Societies**

History—Sources   900
>> Use for collections of documents, records, and other source materials upon which narrative history is based and for materials about such sources.
>> SA   historical subjects, periods of history, individual literary and sacred works, and names of wars with the subdivision *Sources,* e.g. **World War, 1939-1945—Sources;** and subjects, ethnic groups, classes of persons, coporate bodies, and names of countries, states, etc., with the subdivision *History—Sources;* e.g. **United States—History—Sources** [to be added as needed]
>> BT   **Historiography**
>> NT   **Archives**
>> **Charters**

Hittites   939
>> BT   **Ancient history**

HIV disease
>> USE   **AIDS (Disease)**

HMOs
>> USE   **Health maintenance organizations**

Hoaxes
>> USE   **Impostors and imposture**

Hobbies   790.1
>> UF   Avocations
>> SA   types of hobbies [to be added as needed]

Hobbies—*Continued*
  BT **Amusements**
      Leisure
      Recreation
  NT **Collectors and collecting**
  RT **Handicraft**
Hoboes
  USE **Tramps**
Hockey (May subdiv. geog.)   **796.962**
  UF Ice hockey
  BT **Winter sports**
Hogs
  USE **Pigs**
Hoisting machinery **621.8**
  UF Lifts
  SA types of hoisting machinery [to
      be added as needed]
  BT **Machinery**
  NT **Cranes, derricks, etc.**
      Elevators
  RT **Conveying machinery**
Holiday cooking (May subdiv. geog.)
    641.5
  SA cooking for particular holidays,
      e.g. **Christmas cooking** [to
      be added as needed]
  BT **Cooking**
Holiday decorations **394.26; 745.5**
  UF Decorations, Holiday
  BT **Decoration and ornament**
Holidays (May subdiv. geog.) **394.26**
  Use for materials on days of general ex-
emption from work or days publicly dedicated
to the commemoration of some person, event,
or principle. Materials on occasions other than
holidays devoted to festive community obser-
vances or to programs of cultural events are
entered under **Festivals.**
  UF Anniversaries
      Legal holidays
      National holidays
  SA names of holidays [to be added
      as needed]
  BT **Days**
      Manners and customs
  NT **April Fools' Day**
      Christmas
      Fourth of July
      Halloween
      Lincoln's Birthday
      Martin Luther King Day
      Memorial Day
      Religious holidays

      Thanksgiving Day
      Valentine's Day
      Veterans Day
  RT **Festivals**
      Vacations
Holidays, Jewish
  USE **Jewish holidays**
Holistic health
  USE **Holistic medicine**
Holistic medicine (May subdiv. geog.)
    610; 615.5
  UF Holistic health
      Wholistic medicine
  BT **Alternative medicine**
      Medicine
  RT **Health**
      Health self-care
      Mind and body
Holland
  USE **Netherlands**
Holmes, Sherlock (Fictitious character)
    823
  UF Sherlock Holmes (Fictitious
      character)
Holocaust, 1933-1945 **940.53**
  UF Holocaust, Jewish (1939-1945)
      Jewish Holocaust (1933-1945)
  SA names of concentration camps
      [to be added as needed]
  BT **Antisemitism**
      Jews—Persecutions
  NT **Holocaust survivors**
      Righteous Gentiles in the
      Holocaust
  RT **World War, 1939-1945—Jews**
Holocaust, 1933-1945—Personal narra-
    tives **920**
  BT **Autobiographies**
Holocaust, Jewish (1939-1945)
  USE **Holocaust, 1933-1945**
Holocaust survivors (May subdiv. geog.)
    940.53
  Use for materials on Jews who survived
persecution or imprisonment under the Nazis.
Accounts by Holocaust survivors are entered
under **Holocaust, 1933-1945—Personal nar-
ratives.**
  BT **Holocaust, 1933-1945**
Holography **774**
  UF Laser photography
      Lensless photography
  BT **Laser recording**
      Photography

Holography—*Continued*
  RT **Three dimensional photography**
Holstein-Friesian cattle **636.2**
  UF Friesian cattle
  BT **Dairy cattle**
Holy communion
  USE **Eucharist**
Holy days
  USE **Religious holidays**
Holy Ghost
  USE **Holy Spirit**
Holy Grail
  USE **Grail**
Holy Office
  USE **Inquisition**
Holy Roman Empire **943**
  BT **Europe—History**
Holy Scriptures
  USE **Bible**
Holy See
  USE **Papacy**
      Popes
Holy Spirit **231**
  UF Holy Ghost
  BT **God—Christianity**
      Trinity
  RT **Spiritual gifts**
Holy Week **263**
  BT **Church year**
      Lent
  NT **Easter**
      Good Friday
Home **306.8; 640**
  RT **Family**
      Home economics
Home accidents **363.13**
  BT **Accidents**
  NT **First aid**
Home and school **371.19**
  UF School and home
  BT **Education**
  RT **Parent-teacher associations**
      Parent-teacher relationship
Home-based business (May subdiv. geog.)
      338.6; 658
  UF At-home employment
      Cottage industry
      Home business *[Former heading]*
      Home labor
      Work at home

      Working at home
  BT **Business**
      Self-employed
      Small business
Home-based education
  USE **Home schooling**
Home business
  USE **Home-based business**
Home buying
  USE **Houses—Buying and selling**
Home care
  USE **Home care services**
      and classes of persons with the subdivision *Home care*, e.g. **Elderly—Home care** [to be added as needed]
Home care services (May subdiv. geog.)
      362.1
  UF Home care
      Home health care
      Home medical care
      Respite care
  SA classes of persons with the subdivision *Home care*, e.g. **Elderly—Home care** [to be added as needed]
  BT **Medical care**
  NT **Elderly—Home care**
      Home nursing
Home computers
  USE **Microcomputers**
Home conservatories
  USE **Garden rooms**
Home construction
  USE **House construction**
Home decoration
  USE **Interior design**
Home delivered meals programs
  USE **Meals on wheels programs**
Home designs
  USE **Domestic architecture—Designs and plans**
Home economics (May subdiv. geog.)
      640
  UF Homemaking
      Household management
      Housekeeping
  BT **Family life education**
  NT **Consumer education**
      Cooking
      Cost and standard of living

Home economics—*Continued*
       Entertaining
       Food
       Fuel
       Grocery shopping
       Heating
       House cleaning
       Household employees
       Household equipment and supplies
       Household pests
       Interior design
       Laundry
       Mobile home living
       Moving
       Sewing
       Shopping
       Storage in the home
       Ventilation
  RT Home
       Homemakers
Home economics—Accounting
  USE Household budgets
Home education
  USE Correspondence schools and courses
       Home schooling
       Self-instruction
Home health care
  USE Home care services
Home instruction
  USE Home schooling
Home labor
  USE Home-based business
Home life
  USE Family life
Home loans
  USE Mortgages
Home medical care
  USE Home care services
Home missions, Christian
  USE Christian missions
Home movies
  USE Amateur films
Home nursing   649.8
  BT Home care services
       Nursing
  RT Sick
Home purchase
  USE Houses—Buying and selling
Home remodeling
  USE Houses—Remodeling

Home repairing
  USE Houses—Maintenance and repair
Home repairs
  USE Houses—Maintenance and repair
Home schooling (May subdiv. geog.)
       371.04
    Use for materials on the provision of compulsory education in the home as an alternative to traditional public or private schooling. General materials on the instruction of children in the home are entered under **Child rearing.**
  UF Home-based education
       Home education
       Home instruction
       Home teaching by parents
       Homeschooling
  BT **Education**
Home sharing
  USE Shared housing
Home storage
  USE Storage in the home
Home study courses
  USE Correspondence schools and courses
       Self-instruction
Home teaching by parents
  USE Home schooling
Home video cameras
  USE Camcorders
Home video movies
  USE Amateur films
Home video systems   384.55; 621.388;
       778.59
  BT Television
  NT Camcorders
       Videotapes
  RT Video recording
Homeless
  USE Homeless persons
       Homelessness
Homeless people
  USE Homeless persons
Homeless persons (May subdiv. geog.)
       305.5; 362.5
  UF Homeless
       Homeless people
       Street people
  BT Poor
  NT Refugees
       Runaway children

Homeless persons—*Continued*
      Runaway teenagers
      Tramps
  RT Homelessness
Homeless persons—Government policy
    (May subdiv. geog.) 362.5
  BT Social policy
Homelessness (May subdiv. geog.)
    305.5; 362.5
  UF Homeless
  BT Housing
      Poverty
      Social problems
  RT Homeless persons
Homemakers 306.85; 640
  UF Househusbands
      Housewives
  RT Home economics
Homemaking
  USE Home economics
Homeopathy 615.5
  BT Alternative medicine
      Pharmacy
Homes
  USE Houses
      and ethnic groups, classes of
      persons, and names of corpo-
      rate bodies, families, and indi-
      vidual persons with the subdi-
      vision *Homes,* e.g. **English
      authors—Homes;** which may
      be further subdivided geo-
      graphically [to be added as
      needed]
Homes for the elderly
  USE Elderly—Institutional care
Homes (Institutions)
  USE Charities
      Institutional care
      Orphanages
Homeschooling
  USE Home schooling
Homework 371.3028
  BT Study skills
Homicide (May subdiv. geog.) 364.15
  UF Manslaughter
      Murder
  BT Crime
      Criminal law
      Offenses against the person
  NT Assassination
      Euthanasia

      Poisons and poisoning
      Trials (Homicide)
  RT Suicide
Homicide trials
  USE Trials (Homicide)
Hominids
  USE Human origins
Hominids, Fossil
  USE Fossil hominids
Homo sapiens
  USE Human beings
Homonyms
  USE names of languages with the
      subdivision *Homonyms,* e.g.
      **English language—Hom-
      onyms** [to be added as need-
      ed]
Homosexual marriage
  USE Same-sex marriage
Homosexuality (May subdiv. geog.)
    306.76
  UF Gay lifestyle
  BT Sexual behavior
  NT Gay liberation movement
      Lesbianism
  RT Gay men
      Lesbians
Homosexuals, Female
  USE Lesbians
Homosexuals, Male
  USE Gay men
Honesty 179
  UF Dishonesty
  BT Ethics
      Human behavior
  RT Truthfulness and falsehood
Honey 638; 641.3
  BT Food
  RT Bees
Honeybee culture
  USE Beekeeping
Honorary degrees
  USE Academic degrees
Hooked rugs 746.7
  BT Handicraft
      Rugs and carpets
Hoover Dam (Ariz. and Nev.) 627
  UF Boulder Dam (Ariz. and Nev.)
      Colorado River—Hoover Dam
  BT Dams

Hope   152.4; 179; 234
    BT   Emotions
         Spiritual life
         Virtue
Hormones   571.7; 573.4; 612.4
    BT   Endocrinology
    RT   Endocrine glands
         Steroids
Hornbooks   028.5; 096; 372.41
    BT   Reading materials
Horology
    USE   Clocks and watches
          Sundials
          Time
Horoscopes   133.5
    BT   Astrology
Horror   152.4
    BT   Emotions
         Fear
Horror—Fiction
    USE   Horror fiction
Horror fiction   808.83; 809.3; 813, etc.
    May be used for individual works, collec-
    tions, or materials about horror fiction.
    UF   Horror—Fiction
         Horror novels
         Horror stories
         Horror tales
         Terror tales
    BT   Fiction
    NT   Ghost stories
         Gothic novels
    RT   Fantasy fiction
         Occult fiction
Horror films   791.43
    May be used for individual works, collec-
    tions, or materials about horror films.
    UF   Creature films
         Horror movies
         Monster films
    SA   types of horror films, e.g. **Vam-
         pire films** [to be added as
         needed]
    BT   Motion pictures
    NT   Vampire films
    RT   Fantasy films
Horror movies
    USE   Horror films
Horror novels
    USE   Horror fiction

Horror plays   808.82; 812, etc.
    May be used for individual works, collec-
    tions, or materials about horror plays.
    BT   Drama
Horror radio programs   791.44
    May be used for individual works, collec-
    tions, or materials about horror radio pro-
    grams.
    BT   Radio programs
Horror stories
    USE   Horror fiction
Horror tales
    USE   Horror fiction
Horror television programs   791.45
    May be used for individual works, collec-
    tions, or materials about horror television pro-
    grams.
    BT   Television programs
    RT   Fantasy television programs
Horse breeding
    USE   Horses—Breeding
Horse racing   798.4
    BT   Racing
    RT   Gambling
         Horsemanship
Horse riding
    USE   Horsemanship
Horseback riding
    USE   Horsemanship
Horsebreaking
    USE   Horses—Training
Horsemanship (May subdiv. geog.)
             798.2
    UF   Coaching
         Dressage
         Equestrianism
         Horse riding
         Horseback riding
         Riding
    BT   Locomotion
    NT   Horses—Training
    RT   Horse racing
         Rodeos
Horses (May subdiv. geog.)   599.665;
             636.1
    UF   Foals
    BT   Mammals
    NT   Ponies
Horses—Breeding   636.1
    UF   Horse breeding
    BT   Breeding
Horses—Diseases   636.089
    BT   Animals—Diseases

Horses—Training 636.1
    UF   Horsebreaking
    BT   **Horsemanship**
Horses—Wounds and injuries 636.1
Horticulture (May subdiv. geog.) **635**
    Use for materials on the scientific and economic aspects of the cultivation of flowers, fruits, vegetables, etc. Materials on the practical aspects of creating gardens and cultivating plants are entered under **Gardening.** General materials about gardens, the history of gardens, various types of gardens, etc., are entered under **Gardens.**
    BT   **Agriculture**
          Plants
    NT   **Flower gardening**
          Fruit culture
          Greenhouses
          Hydroponics
          Landscape gardening
          Organic gardening
          Plant breeding
          Truck farming
          Vegetable gardening
    RT   **Gardening**
Hosiery 391.4; 687
    UF   Stockings
    BT   **Clothing and dress**
          Textile industry
Hospices (May subdiv. geog.) **362.1**
    BT   **Hospitals**
          Social medicine
          Terminal care
Hospital libraries (May subdiv. geog.) **027.6**
    UF   Libraries, Hospital
    BT   **Libraries**
Hospital personnel administration
    USE **Hospitals—Personnel management**
Hospital ships 362.1; 623.8
    UF   Floating hospitals
    BT   **Hospitals**
          Ships
Hospital wastes
    USE **Medical wastes**
Hospitality
    USE **Entertaining**
Hospitalization insurance 368.38
    UF   Group hospitalization
          Insurance, Hospitalization
    BT   **Health insurance**

Hospitals (May subdiv. geog.) **362.1**
    UF   Infirmaries
          Sanatoriums
    SA   types of hospitals and names of individual hospitals [to be added as needed]
    BT   **Institutional care**
          Public health
    NT   **Children's hospitals**
          Hospices
          Hospital ships
          Life support systems (Medical environment)
          Long-term care facilities
          Military hospitals
          Nursing homes
          Psychiatric hospitals
    RT   **Medical centers**
          Medical charities
Hospitals—Personnel management (May subdiv. geog.) **362.1**
    UF   Hospital personnel administration
    BT   **Personnel management**
Hospitals—Sanitation 614.4
    BT   **Sanitation**
Hospitals—United States 362.1
Hostage escapes
    USE **Escapes**
Hostage negotiation 363.3
    BT   **Hostages**
          Negotiation
Hostages (May subdiv. geog.) **920**
    SA   hostages from a particular country, e.g. **American hostages** [to be added as needed]
    BT   **Terrorism**
    NT   **American hostages**
          Hostage negotiation
Hot air engines
    USE **Heat engines**
Hot air heating 697
    UF   Warm air heating
    BT   **Heating**
Hot water heating 697
    BT   **Heating**
Hotels and motels (May subdiv. geog.) **647.94; 728**
    Use for materials on public accommodations, including inns and guest houses.
    UF   Boarding houses
          Inns
          Motels

Hotels and motels—*Continued*
    Rooming houses
    Tourist accommodations
  BT **Service industries**
  NT **Bed and breakfast accommodations**
      Youth hostels
Hotels and motels—United States
    647.9473; 728
Hothouses
  USE **Greenhouses**
Hotlines (Telephone counseling)   **361;**
    362.2
  UF Crisis counseling
    Crisis intervention telephone service
    Switchboard hotlines
    Telephone counseling
  BT **Counseling**
      Information services
      Social work
  RT **Crisis centers**
Hours of labor   331.25
  UF Eight-hour day
    Five-day work week
    Overtime
    Working day
    Working hours
  BT **Labor**
  NT **Absenteeism (Labor)**
      Flexible hours of labor
      Part-time employment
Hours of labor, Flexible
  USE **Flexible hours of labor**
House boats
  USE **Houseboats**
House buying
  USE **Houses—Buying and selling**
House cleaning   648
  BT **Cleaning**
      Home economics
      Household sanitation
House construction (May subdiv. geog.)
    690
  UF Construction, House
    Home construction
  SA types of house construction and
      special kinds of houses [to be
      added as needed]
  BT **Building**
      Domestic architecture

  NT **Earth sheltered houses**
      House painting
      Houses—Remodeling
      Log cabins and houses
      Prefabricated houses
  RT **Houses**
House decoration
  USE **Interior design**
House drainage   690
    Use for materials on house drainage. Materials on land drainage are entered under **Drainage.**
  UF Drainage, House
  BT **Household sanitation**
  NT **Sewerage**
  RT **Plumbing**
House flies
  USE **Flies**
House furnishing
  USE **Interior design**
House of Representatives (U.S.)
  USE **United States. Congress. House**
House painting   698
  BT **House construction**
  RT **Industrial painting**
House plans
  USE **Domestic architecture—Designs and plans**
House plants   635.9
  BT **Cultivated plants**
      Flower gardening
      Plants
      Window gardening
  RT **Container gardening**
      Indoor gardening
House purchase
  USE **Houses—Buying and selling**
House repairing
  USE **Houses—Maintenance and repair**
House repairs
  USE **Houses—Maintenance and repair**
House sanitation
  USE **Household sanitation**
House selling
  USE **Houses—Buying and selling**
House sharing
  USE **Shared housing**
House trailers
  USE **Mobile homes**
      Travel trailers and campers

Houseboats 728.7
    UF   House boats
    BT   **Boats and boating**
Household appliances
    USE **Household equipment and supplies**
Household appliances, Electric
    USE **Electric household appliances**
Household budgets 640
    UF   Budgets, Household
         Domestic finance
         Family budget
         Finance, Household
         Home economics—Accounting
         Household finances
    BT   **Cost and standard of living**
         Personal finance
Household employees 640
    UF   Domestic workers
         Housemaids
         Servants
    BT   **Home economics**
         Labor
**Household equipment and supplies
    643; 683**
    UF   Domestic appliances
         Household appliances
         Implements, utensils, etc.
         Labor saving devices, Household
    BT   **Home economics**
    NT   **Electric household appliances**
         Kitchen utensils
Household finances
    USE **Cost and standard of living**
         Household budgets
Household management
    USE **Home economics**
Household moving
    USE **Moving**
Household pests 648
    UF   Diseases and pests
         Vermin
    SA   types of pests, e.g. **Flies** [to be
         added as needed]
    BT   **Home economics**
         Household sanitation
         Pests
    NT   **Flies**
    RT   **Insect pests**

Household repairs
    USE **Houses—Maintenance and repair**
Household sanitation 648
    UF   House sanitation
         Sanitation, Household
    BT   **Sanitation**
    NT   **House cleaning**
         House drainage
         Household pests
         Laundry
         Ventilation
    RT   **Plumbing**
Household utensils
    USE **Kitchen utensils**
Household violence
    USE **Domestic violence**
Househusbands
    USE **Homemakers**
Housekeeping
    USE **Home economics**
Housemaids
    USE **Household employees**
Houses (May subdiv. geog.) **643; 728**
    Use for general materials on buildings in which people live. Materials on residential buildings from the standpoint of style and design are entered under **Domestic architecture.**
    UF   Dwellings
         Homes
         Residences
    SA   types of houses, e.g. **Earth sheltered houses;** types of architectural features, e.g. **Windows; Fireplaces;** etc.; and rooms and parts of the house, e.g. **Kitchens** [to be added as needed]
    BT   **Buildings**
    NT   **Apartment houses**
         Earth sheltered houses
         Garden rooms
         Housing
         Kitchens
         Log cabins and houses
         Prefabricated houses
         Rooms
         Solar homes
    RT   **Domestic architecture**
         House construction

Houses—Buying and selling   333.33
  UF   Home buying
        Home purchase
        House buying
        House purchase
        House selling
  BT   **Real estate business**
  NT   **Urban homesteading**
Houses—Heating and ventilation   644;
      697
  BT   **Heating**
Houses—Maintenance and repair   643
  UF   Home repairing
        Home repairs
        House repairing
        House repairs
        Household repairs
Houses—Remodeling   643
  UF   Home remodeling
        Remodeling (Architecture)
        Remodeling of houses
  SA   types of houses and parts of
        houses with the subdivision
        Remodeling, e.g. **Kitchens—**
        Remodeling [to be added as
        needed]
  BT   **House construction**
Housewives
  USE   **Homemakers**
Housing (May subdiv. geog.)   307.3;
      363.5
    Use for materials on the social and econom-
  ic aspects of housing. Materials on the social
  and economic aspects of housing as it pertains
  to specific ethnic groups or classes of persons
  are entered under that group or class of persons with the subdivision *Housing*. Materials
  on the residential buildings of ethnic groups
  or classes of persons from the standpoint of
  architecture, construction, or ethnology are entered under the name of the ethnic group or
  class of persons with the subdivision *Dwell-*
  ings.
  UF   Affordable housing
        Dwellings
        Habitations, Human
        Housing needs
        Urban housing
  SA   ethnic groups, classes of per-
        sons, and domestic animals
        with the subdivision *Housing;*
        e.g. **Native Americans—**
        Housing; Physically handi-
        capped—Housing; etc. [to be
        added as needed]

  BT   **Houses**
        Landlord and tenant
  NT   **African Americans—Housing**
        Apartment houses
        Blacks—Housing
        Cooperative housing
        Discrimination in housing
        Elderly—Housing
        Homelessness
        Labor—Housing
        Mobile homes
        Native Americans—Housing
        Physically handicapped—Hous-
          ing
        Public housing
        Shared housing
        Timesharing (Real estate)
        Urban homesteading
  RT   **City planning**
Housing, Cooperative
  USE   **Cooperative housing**
Housing for the elderly
  USE   **Elderly—Housing**
Housing for the physically handicapped
  USE   **Physically handicapped—Hous-**
          ing
Housing needs
  USE   **Housing**
Housing projects, Government
  USE   **Public housing**
Houston Astros (Baseball team)
      796.357
  UF   Astros (Baseball team)
        Houston (Tex.). Baseball Club
          (National League)
  BT   **Baseball teams**
Houston (Tex.). Baseball Club (National
    League)
  USE   **Houston Astros (Baseball**
          team)
Hovercraft
  USE   **Air-cushion vehicles**
How to start a business
  USE   **New business enterprises**
How-to-stop-smoking programs
  USE   **Smoking cessation programs**
How to study
  USE   **Study skills**

HTML (Document markup language)
   005.7
   UF   HyperText Markup Language
          (Document markup language)
   BT   **Programming languages**
Hudson River (N.Y. and N.J.)—Bridges
   USE **Bridges—Hudson River (N.Y.
        and N.J.)**
Hugging   158; 302.2; 395
   UF   Embracing
        Hugs
   BT   **Manners and customs
        Nonverbal communication
        Touch**
Hugs
   USE **Hugging**
Huguenots (May subdiv. geog.)   284
   BT   **Christian sects
        Reformation**
   NT   **Saint Bartholomew's Day,
        Massacre of, 1572**
Hull House
   USE **Hull House (Chicago, Ill.)**
Hull House (Chicago, Ill.)   361.4
   UF   Hull House
   BT   **Social settlements**
Human abnormalities
   USE **Birth defects
        Growth disorders**
Human anatomy   611
   SA   parts of the body, e.g. **Foot;** and
        names of organs and regions
        of the body with the subdivi-
        sion *Anatomy,* e.g. **Heart—
        Anatomy** [to be added as
        needed]
   BT   **Anatomy**
   RT   **Human body**
Human anatomy—Atlases   611
   BT   **Atlases**
Human anatomy in art
   USE **Artistic anatomy
        Nude in art**
**Human artificial insemination   346.01;
   618.1**
   UF   Artificial insemination, Human
   BT   **Artificial insemination
        Reproduction**
Human assets
   USE **Human capital**

Human behavior   150; 302
   UF   Behavior
        Morals
        Social behavior
   BT   **Character
        Psychology
        Social sciences**
   NT   **Aggressiveness (Psychology)
        Behavior modification
        Behaviorism
        Cannibalism
        Compulsive behavior
        Conduct of life
        Consolation
        Duty
        Eating customs
        Etiquette
        Friendship
        Habit
        Helping behavior
        Honesty
        Lifestyles
        Love
        Patience
        Patriotism
        Sexual behavior
        Social adjustment
        Sportsmanship
        Suicide—Psychological aspects
        Truthfulness and falsehood
        Vice
        Virtue**
   RT   **Ethics
        Interpersonal relations
        Life skills**
Human beings (May subdiv. geog.)
   128; 599.9
   Use for materials on the human species
   from the point of view of biology or anthro-
   pology. Materials on human beings as individ-
   uals are entered under **Persons.**
   UF   Homo sapiens
        Human race
        Man
   BT   **Primates**
   NT   **Anthropometry
        Ethnology
        Human body
        Persons
        Prehistoric peoples**
   RT   **Anthropology**

Human beings (Theology)   218; 233;
291.2
  UF   Man (Theology) *[Former head-ing]*
  BT   **Doctrinal theology**
  NT   **Soul**
Human body   612
Use for materials on the human body not limited to anatomy or physiology.
  UF   Body
  SA   parts of the body, e.g. **Foot** [to be added as needed]
  BT   **Human beings**
       Self
  NT   **Body image**
       Body weight
  RT   **Human anatomy**
       Mind and body
       Physiology
Human capital (May subdiv. geog.)
658.3
Use for materials on investments of capital in training and educating employees to improve their productivity. Materials on the strength of a country in terms of available personnel, both military and industrial, are entered under **Manpower.**
  UF   Human assets
       Human resources
  BT   **Capital**
  RT   **Labor supply**
Human cloning   571.8; 660.6
  BT   **Cloning**
Human cloning—Ethical aspects   174
  BT   **Ethics**
Human cold storage
  USE   **Cryonics**
Human ecology (May subdiv. geog.)
304.2
  UF   Ecology, Human
       Ecology, Social
       Social ecology
  BT   **Sociology**
  NT   **Environmental influence on**
       humans
       Human geography
       Human influence on nature
       Population
       Social psychology
       Survival skills
Human embryos, Frozen
  USE   **Frozen embryos**

Human engineering (May subdiv. geog.)
620.8
Use for materials on engineering design as related to human anatomical, physiological, and psychological capabilities and limitations.
  UF   Biomechanics
       Ergonomics
  BT   **Applied psychology**
       Engineering
       Industrial design
       Psychophysiology
  NT   **Life support systems (Space**
       environment)
       Life support systems (Submarine environment)
  RT   **Machine design**
Human experimentation in medicine
(May subdiv. geog.)   610.7
  UF   Experimentation on humans, Medical
       Medical experimentation on humans
  BT   **Medical ethics**
       Medicine—Research
Human fertility (May subdiv. geog.)
304.6; 612.6; 616.6
  UF   Fertility, Human
  BT   **Birth rate**
       Fertility
       Population
  RT   **Birth control**
       Childlessness
Human figure in art
  USE   **Artistic anatomy**
        Figure drawing
        Figure painting
        Nude in art
Human fossils
  USE   **Fossil hominids**
Human geography (May subdiv. geog.)
304.2
  UF   Anthropogeography
       Geographical distribution of people
       Social geography
  BT   **Anthropology**
       Ethnology
       Geography
       Human ecology
       Immigration and emigration
  NT   **Environmental influence on**
       humans

Human geography—*Continued*
  RT **Geopolitics**
Human influence on nature (May subdiv. geog.) **304.2; 363.7**
  UF Earth, Effect of man on
       Man—Influence on nature
       Nature—Effect of human beings on
  BT **Human ecology**
  NT **Pollution**
Human locomotion **152.3; 612.7**
  UF Biomechanics
       Human mechanics
       Human movement
  BT **Locomotion**
       Physiology
  NT **Kinesiology**
  RT **Musculoskeletal system**
Human mechanics
  USE **Human locomotion**
Human movement
  USE **Human locomotion**
Human origins **599.9**
  UF Antiquity of man
       Hominids
       Man—Antiquity
       Man—Origin
       Origin of man
  BT **Physical anthropology**
  RT **Evolution**
       Fossil hominids
       Prehistoric peoples
Human paleontology
  USE **Fossil hominids**
Human physiology
  USE **Physiology**
Human race
  USE **Anthropology**
       Human beings
Human records
  USE **World records**
Human relations
  USE **Interpersonal relations**
Human resource management
  USE **Personnel management**
Human resources
  USE **Human capital**
       Manpower
Human rights (May subdiv. geog.) **323; 341.4**
  Use for materials on the rights of persons regardless of their legal, socioeconomic, or cultural status, as recognized by the international community. Materials on citizens' rights as established by law or protected by a constitution are entered under **Civil rights.**
  UF Basic rights
       Civil rights (International law)
       Fundamental rights
       Rights, Human
       Rights of man
  NT **Civil rights**
Human services (May subdiv. geog.) **361**
  Use for general materials on the various policies, programs, services, and facilities to meet basic human needs, such as health, education, and welfare. Materials on the methods employed in social work, public or private, are entered under **Social work.** Materials on privately supported welfare activities are entered under **Charities.** Materials on tax-supported welfare activities are entered under **Public welfare.**
  SA ethnic groups and classes of persons with the subdivision *Services for,* e.g. **Handicapped—Services for** [to be added as needed]
  NT **Charities**
       Handicapped—Services for
       Public health
       Public welfare
       Social work
Human survival skills
  USE **Survival skills**
Human values
  USE **Values**
Humane treatment of animals
  USE **Animal welfare**
Humanism (May subdiv. geog.) **001.2; 880**
  Use for materials on culture founded on the study of the classics, or more narrowly on Greek and Roman scholarship. Materials on any intellectual or philosophical movement or set of beliefs that promotes human values as separate and distinct from religious doctrines are entered under **Secularism.**
  BT **Culture**
       Literature
       Philosophy
  NT **Humanities**
  RT **Classical education**
       Learning and scholarship
       Renaissance
       Secularism
Humanism, Secular
  USE **Secularism**

Humanitarians
USE **Philanthropists**
Humanities (May subdiv. geog.)   **001.3**
  BT   **Humanism**
        Learning and scholarship
  NT   **Arts**
        History
        Literature
        Music
        Philosophy
        Science and the humanities
  RT   **Classical education**
Humanities and science
USE **Science and the humanities**
Humans in space
USE **Space flight**
Humidity   **551.57**
  UF Air, Moisture of
       Atmospheric humidity
       Relative humidity
  BT   **Meteorology**
        Weather
Humor
  USE **Wit and humor**
       and subjects with the subdivi-
       sion *Humor,* e.g. **World War,**
       1939-1945—Humor [to be
       added as needed]
Humorists (May subdiv. geog.)   **809.7;**
  920
  BT   **Wit and humor**
Humorous fiction   **808.83; 813, etc.**
  May be used for individual works, collec-
  tions, or materials about humorous fiction.
  UF Comic novels
       Humorous stories
  BT   **Fiction**
        Wit and humor
  RT   **Mock-heroic literature**
Humorous films
USE **Comedy films**
Humorous pictures
USE **Comic books, strips, etc.**
Humorous plays
USE **Comedies**
Humorous poetry   **808.81; 811, etc.;**
  811.008, etc.
  May be used for individual works, collec-
  tions, or materials about humorous poetry.
  UF Comic verse
       Humorous verse
       Light verse

  BT   **Poetry**
        Wit and humor
  NT   **Limericks**
        Nonsense verses
Humorous stories
USE **Humorous fiction**
Humorous verse
  USE **Humorous poetry**
Hundred Years' War, 1339-1453   **944**
  UF 100 years' war
  BT   **Europe—History—476-1492**
        France—History—1328-1589,
          House of Valois
        Great Britain—History—1066-
          1485, Medieval period
Hungary—History   **943.9**
Hungary—History—1956, Revolution
  943.905
  BT   **Revolutions**
Hunger (May subdiv. geog.)   **363.8**
  RT   **Fasting**
        Starvation
Hunger strikes (May subdiv. geog.)
  303.6
  BT   **Demonstrations**
        Fasting
        Nonviolence
        Passive resistance
        Resistance to government
Hunting (May subdiv. geog.)   **799.2**
  SA types of hunting, e.g. **Whaling;**
       and ethnic groups with the
       subdivision *Hunting,* e.g. **Na-**
       tive Americans—Hunting [to
       be added as needed]
  NT   **Decoys (Hunting)**
        Falconry
        Game protection
        Game reserves
        Native Americans—Hunting
        Tracking and trailing
        Whaling
  RT   **Game and game birds**
        Shooting
        Trapping
Hunting—United States   **799.2973**
Hurricanes (May subdiv. geog.)   **551.55**
  Use for cyclonic storms originating in the
  region of the West Indies.
  SA names of specific hurricanes [to
       be added as needed]

Hurricanes—*Continued*
    BT   Cyclones
           Storms
           Winds
    RT   Typhoons
Husbands   306.872
    UF   Married men
           Spouses
    BT   Family
           Marriage
           Married people
           Men
Husbands, Runaway
    USE **Runaway adults**
Hybridization
    USE **Plant breeding**
Hydraulic cement
    USE **Cement**
Hydraulic engineering (May subdiv.
      geog.)   **627**
    BT   Civil engineering
           Engineering
           Fluid mechanics
           Water power
    NT   Drainage
           Dredging
           Drilling and boring (Earth and
              rocks)
           Flood control
           Hydraulic structures
           Hydrodynamics
           Hydrostatics
           Irrigation
           Pumping machinery
           Reclamation of land
           Wells
    RT   Hydraulics
           Rivers
           Water
           Water supply engineering
Hydraulic machinery   621.2
    BT   Machinery
           Water power
    NT   Turbines
Hydraulic structures   627
    SA   types of hydraulic structures [to
           be added as needed]
    BT   Hydraulic engineering
           Structural engineering
    NT   Aqueducts
           Canals
           Dams

           Docks
           Harbors
           Pipelines
           Reservoirs
Hydraulics   621.2; 627
    Use for materials on technical applications
of the theory of hydrodynamics.
    UF   Water flow
    BT   Fluid mechanics
           Liquids
           Mechanics
           Physics
    NT   Hydrodynamics
           Hydrostatics
           Water
           Water power
    RT   Hydraulic engineering
Hydrodynamics   532
    Use for materials on the theory of the mo-
tion and action of fluids. Materials on the experimental investigation and technical application of this theory are entered under **Hydraulics.**
    BT   Dynamics
           Fluid mechanics
           Hydraulic engineering
           Hydraulics
           Liquids
           Mechanics
    NT   Hydrostatics
           Viscosity
           Waves
Hydroelectric power
    USE **Water power**
Hydroelectric power plants (May subdiv.
      geog.)   **621.31**
    UF   Power plants, Hydroelectric
    BT   Electric power plants
           Water power
Hydrofoil boats   623.8
    BT   Boats and boating
Hydrogen   546
    BT   Chemical elements
Hydrogen bomb   623.4
    BT   Bombs
           Nuclear weapons
    NT   Radioactive fallout
    RT   Atomic bomb
Hydrogen nucleus
    USE **Protons**
Hydrology
    USE **Water**

Hydromechanics
USE **Fluid mechanics**
Hydropathy
USE **Hydrotherapy**
Hydrophobia
USE **Rabies**
Hydroponics   631.5; 635
UF Plants—Soilless culture
Soilless agriculture
Water farming
BT **Horticulture**
Hydrostatics   532
BT **Fluid mechanics**
Hydraulic engineering
Hydraulics
Hydrodynamics
Liquids
Mechanics
Physics
Statics
NT **Gases**
Hydrotherapy   615.8
UF Hydropathy
Water cure
BT **Physical therapy**
Therapeutics
Water
RT **Baths**
Health resorts
Hygiene   613
UF Body care
Personal cleanliness
Personal hygiene
SA parts of the body with the sub-
division *Care,* e.g. **Foot—
Care;** and classes of persons
and ethnic groups with the
subdivision *Health and hy-
giene,* e.g. **Women—Health
and hygiene** [to be added as
needed]
BT **Medicine**
Preventive medicine
NT **Baths**
Children—Health and hygiene
Cleanliness
Diet
Disinfection and disinfectants
Elderly—Health and hygiene
Exercise
Infants—Health and hygiene

**Military personnel—Health
and hygiene**
Personal grooming
Rest
School hygiene
Sexual hygiene
Sleep
Ventilation
Women—Health and hygiene
RT **Health**
Sanitation
Hygiene, Military
USE **Military personnel—Health
and hygiene**
Hygiene, Sexual
USE **Sexual hygiene**
Hygiene, Social
USE **Public health**
Hygiene—Study and teaching
USE **Health education**
Hymn books
USE **Hymnals**
Hymnals   782.27
Use for collections of sacred songs that
contain both words and music. Materials
about hymns are entered under **Hymns.**
UF Hymn books
Hymnbooks
BT **Church music**
Hymns
Songbooks
Hymnbooks
USE **Hymnals**
Hymnology
USE **Hymns**
Hymns   264; 782.27
Use for materials about hymns. Collections
of hymns that contain both words and music
are entered under **Hymnals.**
UF Hymnology
BT **Church music**
Liturgies
Songs
Vocal music
NT **Carols**
Hymnals
Spirituals (Songs)
RT **Religious poetry**
Hyperactive children   155.4; 618.92
UF Children, Hyperactive
Hyperkinetic children
BT **Handicapped children**
RT **Hyperactivity**

Hyperactivity   616.85; 616.92
    UF   Hyperkinesia
    BT   **Diseases**
    RT   **Hyperactive children**
Hyperkinesia
    USE   **Hyperactivity**
Hyperkinetic children
    USE   **Hyperactive children**
Hyperspace
    USE   **Fourth dimension**
Hypertension   616.1
    UF   High blood pressure
    BT   **Blood pressure**
Hypertext   005.75
    Use for materials on document retrieval networks having text files and dynamic indexes for links among documents.
    UF   Hypertext systems
    BT   **Multimedia**
HyperText Markup Language (Document markup language)
    USE   **HTML (Document markup language)**
Hypertext systems
    USE   **Hypertext**
Hypnosis
    USE   **Hypnotism**
Hypnotism   154.7
    UF   Animal magnetism
          Autosuggestion
          Hypnosis
          Mesmerism
    BT   **Mental healing**
          Psychophysiology
    RT   **Mental suggestion**
          Mind and body
          Psychoanalysis
          Subconsciousness
          Suggestive therapeutics
IBM 7090 (Computer)   621.39
    BT   **Computers**
ICBM
    USE   **Intercontinental ballistic missiles**
Ice (May subdiv. geog.)   551.3
    UF   Freezing
    BT   **Cold**
          Frost
          Physical geography
          Water
    NT   **Glaciers**
          Icebergs

Ice age   551.7
    UF   Glacial epoch
    BT   **Earth**
Ice boats
    USE   **Iceboats**
Ice cream, ices, etc.   637; 641.8
    UF   Ices
    BT   **Desserts**
          Frozen foods
Ice (Drug)   362.29; 615
    UF   Crank (Drug)
          Crystal meth (Drug)
    BT   **Designer drugs**
          Methamphetamine
Ice hockey
    USE   **Hockey**
Ice skating   796.91
    UF   Figure skating
          Skating
    BT   **Winter sports**
Ice sports
    USE   **Winter sports**
Icebergs   551.3
    BT   **Ice**
          Ocean
          Physical geography
Iceboats   623.8
    UF   Ice boats
    BT   **Boats and boating**
Icelandic language   439
    BT   **Language and languages**
          Scandinavian languages
Icelandic language—0-1500
    USE   **Old Norse language**
Icelandic literature   839
    UF   Icelandic literature, Modern
    BT   **Literature**
          Scandinavian literature
    RT   **Old Norse literature**
Icelandic literature, Modern
    USE   **Icelandic literature**
Ices
    USE   **Ice cream, ices, etc.**
Ichthyology
    USE   **Fishes**
Icongraphy
    USE   **Art—Themes**
Ideal states
    USE   **Utopian fiction**
          Utopias

Idealism   141
  BT   Philosophy
  RT   Materialism
       Realism
       Transcendentalism
Identification
  SA   subjects with the subdivision
       Identification [to be added as
       needed]
  NT   Airplanes—Identification
       Criminals—Identification
       DNA fingerprinting
       Fingerprints
Identity
  USE Identity (Psychology)
       Individuality
       Personality
       and classes of persons with the
       subdivision *Identity*, e.g.
       Women—Identity; ethnic
       groups with the subdivision
       Ethnic identity, e.g. Mexican
       Americans—Ethnic identity;
       and racial groups with the
       subdivision *Race identity*, e.g.
       African Americans—Race
       identity [to be added as
       needed]
Identity (Psychology)   126
  UF   Identity
  SA   classes of persons with the sub-
       division *Identity*, e.g. Wom-
       en—Identity; ethnic groups
       with the subdivision *Ethnic
       identity*, e.g. Mexican Ameri-
       cans—Ethnic identity; and
       racial groups with the subdi-
       vision *Race identity*, e.g.
       African Americans—Race
       identity [to be added as
       needed]
  BT   Personality
       Psychology
       Self
  NT   Ethnicity
       Women—Identity
Ideology (May subdiv. geog.)   140
  BT   Philosophy
       Political science
       Psychology
       Theory of knowledge

       Thought and thinking
  NT   Political correctness
Idioms
  USE names of languages with the
       subdivision *Idioms*, e.g. En-
       glish language—Idioms [to
       be added as needed]
Idyllic poetry
  USE Pastoral poetry
Illegal aliens (May subdiv. geog.)   323.6;
       325; 342
  UF   Undocumented aliens
  BT   Aliens
       Immigration and emigration
       Underground economy
  RT   Sanctuary movement
Illegitimacy (May subdiv. geog.)
       306.874; 346.01
  UF   Illegitimate children
       Legitimacy (Law)
  RT   Unmarried fathers
       Unmarried mothers
Illegitimate children
  USE Illegitimacy
Illiteracy
  USE Literacy
Illness
  USE Diseases
Illuminated manuscripts
  USE Illumination of books and
       manuscripts
Illumination
  USE Lighting
Illumination of books and manuscripts
       (May subdiv. geog.)   096; 745.6
  UF   Illuminated manuscripts
       Manuscripts, Illuminated
       Miniatures (Illumination of
       books and manuscripts)
       Ornamental alphabets
  BT   Art
       Books
       Decoration and ornament
       Illustration of books
       Manuscripts
       Medieval art
  RT   Alphabets
       Books of hours
       Initials

Illusions
USE **Hallucinations and illusions**
Optical illusions
Illustration of books (May subdiv. geog.)
741.6
UF Book illustration
SA types of illustration, e.g. **Botanical illustration** [to be added as needed]
BT **Art**
Books
Color printing
Decoration and ornament
NT **Botanical illustration**
Caldecott Medal
Engraving
Illumination of books and manuscripts
Photomechanical processes
RT **Drawing**
Picture books for children
Illustrations
USE subjects, names, and uniform titles with the subdivision *Pictorial works,* e.g. **Animals—Pictorial works; United States—History—1861-1865, Civil War—Pictorial works;** etc. [to be added as needed]
Illustrators (May subdiv. geog.)
741.6092; 920
BT **Artists**
Illustrators, American
USE **Illustrators—United States**
Illustrators—United States   741.6092; 920
UF American illustrators *[Former heading]*
Illustrators, American
Image processing software   006.6
BT **Computer software**
Imaginary animals
USE **Mythical animals**
Imaginary companions
USE **Imaginary playmates**
Imaginary creatures
USE **Mythical animals**
Imaginary friends
USE **Imaginary playmates**
Imaginary places
USE **Geographical myths**

Imaginary playmates   155.4
UF Imaginary companions
Imaginary friends
Make-believe playmates
BT **Child psychology**
Imagination
Play
Imaginary voyages   808.83; 813, etc.
May be used for individual works, collections, or materials about imaginary voyages.
UF Space flight (Fiction)
Voyages to the moon
BT **Fantasy fiction**
Science fiction
NT **Robinsonades**
RT **Interplanetary voyages**
Imagination   153.3
BT **Educational psychology**
Intellect
Psychology
NT **Creation (Literary, artistic, etc.)**
Fantasy
Imaginary playmates
Imaging, Magnetic resonance
USE **Magnetic resonance imaging**
Imitations
USE types of literature and names of prominent authors with the subdivision *Parodies, imitations, etc.,* e.g. **Shakespeare, William, 1564-1616—Parodies, imitations, etc.** [to be added as needed]
Immigrants (May subdiv. geog.)   **304.8**
Use for materials on foreign-born persons who enter a country intending to become permanent residents or citizens. This heading may be locally subdivided by the names of places where immigrants have settled.
UF Emigrants
Foreign population
Foreigners
SA names of immigrant ethnic groups, e.g. **Mexican Americans;** and, for immigrants who are not citizens, the names of national groups with the appropriate subdivision for the country of their residence, e.g. **Mexicans—United States** [to be added as needed]

Immigrants—*Continued*
BT **Minorities**
RT **Aliens**
Immigration and emigration
Immigrants—United States   325.73
UF   United States—Foreign population
NT   **Mexican Americans**
RT   **United States—Immigration and emigration**
Immigration and emigration   304.8; 325
Use for materials on migration from one country to another. Materials on the movement of population within a country for permanent settlement are entered under **Internal migration.**
UF   Emigration
Foreign population
Migration
SA   names of countries with the subdivision *Immigration and emigration,* e.g. **United States—Immigration and emigration;** and names of immigrant minorities and national groups, e.g. **Mexican Americans; Mexicans—United States;** etc. [to be added as needed]
BT   **Population**
NT   **Children of immigrants**
Human geography
Illegal aliens
Naturalization
Refugees
United States—Immigration and emigration
RT   **Aliens**
Americanization
Colonization
Immigrants
Internal migration
Immortality   129
Use for materials on the question of the endless existence of the soul. Materials on the character and form of a future existence are entered under **Future life.** Materials on the philosophical concept of eternity are entered under **Eternity.**
UF   Eternal life
Life after death
BT   **Eschatology**
Soul
Theology
RT   **Future life**

Immune system   616.07
UF   Immunological system
BT   **Anatomy**
Physiology
RT   **Immunity**
Immunity   571.9; 616.07
NT   **Allergy**
Immunization
RT   **Immune system**
Immunization (May subdiv. geog.)   614.4
Use for materials on any process, active or passive, that leads to increased immunity. Materials on active immunization with a vaccine are entered under **Vaccination.**
BT   **Immunity**
Public health
NT   **Vaccination**
Immunological system
USE   **Immune system**
Impaired vision
USE   **Vision disorders**
Impeachment
USE   types of public officials and names of individual public officials with the subdivision *Impeachment,* e.g. **Presidents—United States—Impeachment** [to be added as needed]
Impeachments (May subdiv. geog.)   342
SA   types of public officials and names of individual officials with the subdivision **Impeachment** [to be added as needed]
BT   **Administration of justice**
NT   **Recall (Political science)**
Imperialism   325
UF   Colonialism
SA   names of countries with the subdivision *Foreign relations* or *Colonies* [to be added as needed]
BT   **Political science**
NT   **Colonies**
Colonization
Implements, utensils, etc.
USE   **Agricultural machinery**
Household equipment and supplies
Stone implements

Implements, utensils, etc.—*Continued*
    Tools
Imports (May subdiv. geog.)   **382**
    BT **International trade**
Impostors and imposture (May subdiv.
      geog.)   **364.1**
    UF Charlatans
          Hoaxes
          Pretenders
    BT **Crime**
          Criminals
    NT **Counterfeits and counterfeiting**
          Forgery
          Quacks and quackery
    RT **Fraud**
          Swindlers and swindling
Impressionism (Art) (May subdiv. geog.)
      709.03; 759.05
    UF Neo-impressionism (Art)
    BT **Art**
Imprisonment
    USE **Prisons**
In art
    USE names of persons, families, and
          corporate bodies with the sub-
          division *In art,* for materials
          about the depiction of those
          persons or bodies in works of
          art, e.g. **Napoleon I, Emper-**
          or of the French, 1769-
          1821—In art; and phrase
          headings denoting particular
          themes in art for materials
          about those themes, e.g. **Dogs**
          in art [to be added as need-
          ed]
In-line skating   **796.2**
    UF Rollerblading
    BT **Roller skating**
In literature
    USE names of persons, families, and
          corporate bodies with the sub-
          division *In literature,* for ma-
          terials about the depiction of
          those persons or bodies in lit-
          erary works, e.g. **Napoleon I,**
          Emperor of the French,
          1769-1821—In literature; and
          phrase headings denoting par-
          ticular themes in literature for
          materials about those themes,

          e.g. **Dogs in literature** [to be
          added as needed]
In-service training
    USE **Employees—Training**
          and types of employees or per-
          sonnel with the subdivision
          In-service training, e.g. **Li-**
          brarians—In-service training
          [to be added as needed]
In vitro fertilization
    USE **Fertilization in vitro**
Inaudible sound
    USE **Ultrasonics**
Inaugural addresses
    USE types of public officials and
          names of individual public of-
          ficials with the subdivision
          Inaugural addresses, e.g.
          Presidents—United States—
          Inaugural addresses [to be
          added as needed]
Inauguration
    USE types of public officials and
          names of individual public of-
          ficials with the subdivision
          Inauguration, e.g. **Presi-**
          dents—United States—Inau-
          guration [to be added as
          needed]
Incandescent lamps
    USE **Electric lamps**
Incas   **985**
    BT **Native Americans—South**
          America
Incendiary bombs   **623.4**
    UF Fire bombs
    BT **Bombs**
          Incendiary weapons
Incendiary weapons   **623.4**
    BT **Chemical warfare**
    NT **Incendiary bombs**
Incentive (Psychology)
    USE **Motivation (Psychology)**
Incest   **306.877; 616.85**
    BT **Sex crimes**
    NT **Child sexual abuse**
Incineration
    USE **Cremation**
          Refuse and refuse disposal

Income (May subdiv. geog.) **331.2; 339.3**
UF Fortunes
BT **Economics**
    Finance
    Property
    Wealth
NT **Guaranteed annual income**
    Retirement income
    Salaries, wages, etc.
RT **Profit**
Income tax (May subdiv. geog.) **336.24**
UF Personal income tax
BT **Internal revenue**
    Taxation
NT **Tax credits**
Incunabula (May subdiv. geog.) **093**
Use for materials on books printed before the year 1501.
UF Early printed books—15th century
SA subjects with the subdivision *Early works to 1800,* for materials on those subjects written before 1800, e.g. **Political science—Early works to 1800** [to be added as needed]
BT **Books**
Indebtedness
USE **Debt**
Indentured servants
USE **Contract labor**
Independence Day (United States)
USE **Fourth of July**
Independent schools
USE **Private schools**
Independent study **371.39**
Use for materials on individual study that may be directed or assisted by instructional staff through periodic consultations.
BT **Study skills**
    Tutors and tutoring
Indeterminism
USE **Free will and determinism**
Index librorum prohibitorum
USE **Books—Censorship**
Indexes **016**
Use for works that list topics or names with references to books, articles, or passages where those topics or names are to be found. Works that list words with references to passages in a text where the exact word occurs are entered under **Concordances.**

SA subjects with the subdivision *Indexes,* e.g. **Newspapers—Indexes; Short stories—Indexes; English literature—Indexes;** etc. [to be added as needed]
BT **Bibliography**
NT **Concordances**
    Subject headings
Indexing **025.3**
BT **Bibliographic control**
    Bibliography
RT **Cataloging**
    Files and filing
Indian languages (North American)
USE **Native American languages**
Indian literature (East Indian)
USE **Indic literature**
Indian missions
USE **Native Americans—Christian missions**
Indian removal
USE **Native Americans—Relocation**
Indian reservations
USE **Native Americans—Reservations**
    and names of native peoples, tribes, etc., with the subdivision *Reservations* [to be added as needed]
Indians
USE **Native Americans**
Indians of Canada
USE **Native Americans—Canada**
Indians of Central America
USE **Native Americans—Central America**
Indians of Central America—Guatemala
USE **Native Americans—Guatemala**
Indians (of India)
USE **East Indians**
Indians of Mexico
USE **Native Americans—Mexico**
Indians of North America
USE **Native Americans**
    Native Americans—North America
    Native Americans—United States
Indians of North America—Agriculture
USE **Native Americans—Agriculture**

Indians of North America—Antiquities
    USE **Native Americans—Antiquities**
Indians of North America—Architecture
    USE **Native American architecture**
Indians of North America—Art
    USE **Native American art**
Indians of North America—Canada
    USE **Native Americans—Canada**
Indians of North America—Captivities
    USE **Native Americans—Captivities**
Indians of North America—Children
    USE **Native American children**
Indians of North America—Christian missions
    USE **Native Americans—Christian missions**
Indians of North America—Claims
    USE **Native Americans—Claims**
Indians of North America—Costume
    USE **Native American costume**
Indians of North America—Dances
    USE **Native American dance**
Indians of North America—Dwellings
    USE **Native Americans—Dwellings**
Indians of North America—Economic conditions
    USE **Native Americans—Economic conditions**
Indians of North America—Education
    USE **Native Americans—Education**
Indians of North Amcrica—First contact with Europeans
    USE **Native Americans—First contact with Europeans**
Indians of North America—Folklore
    USE **Native Americans—Folklore**
Indians of North America—Games
    USE **Native American games**
Indians of North America—Government relations
    USE **Native Americans—Government relations**
Indians of North America—History
    USE **Native Americans—History**
Indians of North America—History—Chronology
    USE **Native Americans—History—Chronology**
Indians of North America—Industries
    USE **Native Americans—Industries**

Indians of North America—Languages
    USE **Native American languages**
Indians of North America—Literature
    USE **Native American literature**
Indians of North America—Medicine
    USE **Native American medicine**
Indians of North America—Music
    USE **Native American music**
Indians of North America—Names
    USE **Native American names**
Indians of North America—Origin
    USE **Native Americans—Origin**
Indians of North America—Politics and government
    USE **Native Americans—Politics and government**
Indians of North America—Psychology
    USE **Native Americans—Psychology**
Indians of North America—Relations with early settlers
    USE **Native Americans—Relations with early settlers**
Indians of North America—Religion
    USE **Native Americans—Religion**
Indians of North America—Reservations
    USE **Native Americans—Reservations**
Indians of North America—Rites and ceremonies
    USE **Native Americans—Rites and ceremonies**
Indians of North America—Schools
    USE **Native Americans—Education**
Indians of North America—Sign language
    USE **Native American sign language**
Indians of North America—Silverwork
    USE **Native American silverwork**
Indians of North America—Social conditions
    USE **Native Americans—Social conditions**
Indians of North America—Social life and customs
    USE **Native Americans—Social life and customs**
Indians of North America—Wars
    USE **Native Americans—Wars**
Indians of North America—Women
    USE **Native American women**

Indians of South America
USE **Native Americans—South America**
Indians of South America—Peru
USE **Native Americans—Peru**
Indians of the West Indies
USE **Native Americans—West Indies**
Indic literature   891.4
UF Indian literature (East Indian)
BT **Literature**
Indigenous peoples
USE **Native peoples**
Indigestion   616.3
UF Dyspepsia
BT **Digestion**
Individual retirement accounts   332.024
UF IRAs (Pensions)
BT **Pensions**
Retirement income
Individualism (May subdiv. geog.)   **141; 302.5; 330.1**
BT **Economics**
Equality
Political science
Sociology
RT **Persons**
Individuality   155.2
UF Identity
BT **Consciousness**
Psychology
NT **Self**
RT **Conformity**
Personality
Individualized instruction   371.39
Use for materials on the adaptation of instruction to meet individual needs within a group. General materials on one-on-one instruction are entered under **Tutors and tutoring.**
BT **Tutors and tutoring**
RT **Open plan schools**
Indochina   959
Use for the area comprising Laos, Cambodia, and Vietnam.
BT **Southeast Asia**
Indoctrination, Forced
USE **Brainwashing**
Indoor games   793
BT **Games**
RT **Amusements**

Indoor gardening   635.9
BT **Gardening**
NT **Terrariums**
Window gardening
RT **Container gardening**
House plants
Miniature gardens
Induced abortion
USE **Abortion**
Induction coils   537.6; 621.319
BT **Electric apparatus and appliances**
NT **Condensers (Electricity)**
Induction (Logic)
USE **Logic**
Induction motors
USE **Electric motors**
Industrial accidents (May subdiv. geog.)   **363.11; 658.3**
UF Employees—Accidents
Industrial disasters
Industrial injuries
Labor—Accidents
Occupational accidents
Occupational injuries
SA industries with the subdivision *Accidents,* e.g. **Chemical industry—Accidents** [to be added as needed]
BT **Accidents**
NT **Chemical industry—Accidents**
RT **Hazardous occupations**
Industrial alcohol
USE **Denatured alcohol**
Industrial antiquities
USE **Industrial archeology**
Industrial applications
USE types of scientific phenomena, chemicals, plants, and crops with the subdivision *Industrial applications,* e.g. **Ultrasonic waves—Industrial applications** [to be added as needed]
Industrial arbitration (May subdiv. geog.)   **331.89**
UF Arbitration, Industrial
Industrial conciliation
Labor arbitration
Labor courts
Labor negotiations
Mediation, Industrial

Industrial arbitration—*Continued*

       Trade agreements (Labor)

  BT   **Industrial relations**

       Labor

       Labor disputes

       Labor unions

       Negotiation

  RT   **Collective bargaining**

       Strikes

Industrial archaeology

  USE **Industrial archeology**

Industrial archeology (May subdiv. geog.)
     609

    Use for materials on the study of the physical remains of industries from the eighteenth and nineteenth centuries, including buildings, machinery, and tools.

  UF   Industrial antiquities

       Industrial archaeology

  BT   **Archeology**

       Industries—History

Industrial arts   **600**

  UF   Mechanic arts

       Trades

  SA   types of industries, arts, and trades; and names of countries, cities, etc., with the subdivision *Industries* [to be added as needed]

  BT   **Handicraft**

  NT   **Arts and crafts movement**

       Engineering

       Industrial arts education

       Printing

  RT   **Technology**

Industrial arts education (May subdiv. geog.)   **607**

  UF   Education, Industrial

       Industrial education

       Industrial schools

       Manual training

  BT   **Industrial arts**

       Vocational education

  RT   **Technical education**

Industrial arts shops

  USE **School shops**

Industrial buildings (May subdiv. geog.)
     725

  UF   Buildings, Industrial

  BT   **Buildings**

  NT   **Factories**

Industrial buildings—Design and construction   **690**

  BT   **Architecture**

       Building

Industrial chemistry   **660**

  UF   Chemical technology

       Chemistry, Technical

       Technical chemistry

  SA   types of industries and products, e.g. **Clay industry; Dyes and dyeing;** etc. [to be added as needed]

  BT   **Chemistry**

       Technology

  NT   **Alloys**

       Bleaching

       Canning and preserving

       Ceramics

       Corrosion and anticorrosives

       Distillation

       Drying

       Electrochemistry

       Food—Analysis

       Gums and resins

       Synthetic products

       Tanning

       Textile chemistry

       Waste products

  RT   **Chemical engineering**

       Chemical industry

       Chemicals

       Metallurgy

Industrial conciliation

  USE **Industrial arbitration**

Industrial councils

  USE **Participative management**

Industrial counseling

  USE **Employees—Counseling of**

Industrial design (May subdiv. geog.)
     745.2

  UF   Design, Industrial

  BT   **Design**

  NT   **Automobiles—Design and construction**

       Human engineering

       Systems engineering

Industrial disasters

  USE **Industrial accidents**

Industrial diseases

  USE **Occupational diseases**

Industrial disputes
USE **Labor disputes**
Industrial drawing
USE **Mechanical drawing**
Industrial education
USE **Industrial arts education**
Technical education
Industrial efficiency (May subdiv. geog.)
658

Use for materials on the various means of increasing efficiency and output in business and industries, including time and motion studies and materials on the application of psychological principles to industrial production.

UF Efficiency, Industrial
BT **Management**
NT **Job analysis**
Labor productivity
Motion study
Office management
Time study
Industrial equipment   621.8
UF Capital equipment
Capital goods
Industries—Equipment and supplies
Machinery in industry
SA types of industries with the subdivision *Equipment and supplies* [to be added as needed]
BT **Machinery**
NT **Automation**
Industrial robots
Industrial exhibitions
USE **Trade shows**
Industrial health
USE **Occupational health and safety**
Industrial injuries
USE **Industrial accidents**
Industrial laws and legislation (May subdiv. geog.)   **343**
UF Government regulation of commerce
Industries—Law and legislation
SA types of industries with the subdivision *Law and legislation,* e.g. **Chemical industry—Law and legislation** [to be added as needed]
BT **Law**
Legislation

Industrial libraries
USE **Corporate libraries**
Industrial management
USE **Management**
Industrial materials
USE **Materials**
Industrial mergers
USE **Corporate mergers and acquisitions**
Industrial mobilization (May subdiv. geog.)   **355.2**

Use for materials on industrial and labor policies and programs for defense mobilization.

UF Economic mobilization
Industry and war
Mobilization, Industrial
National defenses
BT **Economic policy**
Military art and science
War—Economic aspects
RT **Military readiness**
Industrial organization
USE **Management**
Industrial painting   698
SA topics with the subdivision *Painting;* e.g. **Automobiles—Painting** [to be added as needed]
BT **Finishes and finishing**
NT **Automobiles—Painting**
Lettering
Sign painting
RT **House painting**
Industrial plants
USE **Factories**
Industrial policy (May subdiv. geog.)   **338.9; 354**
UF Government policy
Government regulation of industry
Industries—Government policy
Industries—Organization, control, etc.
Industry and state
State regulation of industry
BT **Economic policy**
NT **Agriculture—Government policy**
Consumer protection
Energy policy
Government ownership

Industrial policy—*Continued*
>Privatization
>Public service commissions
>Railroads—Government policy

Industrial policy—United States
>338.973; 354
>UF Industries—Government policy—
>United States
>United States—Industrial policy

Industrial psychology
>USE Applied psychology

Industrial relations (May subdiv. geog.)
>331

Use for general materials on employer-employee relations. Materials on problems of personnel and relations from the employer's point of view are entered under **Personnel management.**

>UF Capital and labor
>Employer-employee relations
>Labor and capital
>Labor-management relations
>Labor relations
>BT Labor
>Management
>NT Collective bargaining
>Industrial arbitration
>Labor contract
>Labor disputes
>Labor unions
>Participative management
>Personnel management
>Strikes

Industrial revolution (May subdiv. geog.)
>330.9; 909.81

Use for materials on the historical shift from home-based industries to large-scale factory production. Materials on the development of organized productions as industries, especially factory-based industries, are entered under **Industrialization.**

>SA names of countries with the subdivision *Economic conditions* [to be added as needed]
>BT Economic conditions
>Industries—History
>RT Great Britain—History—19th century
>Industrialization
>Technology and civilization

Industrial robots 629.8
>UF Robots, Industrial
>Working robots

>BT Automation
>Industrial equipment
>Robots

Industrial safety
>USE Occupational health and safety

Industrial schools
>USE Industrial arts education
>Technical education

Industrial secrets
>USE Trade secrets

Industrial trusts 338.8; 658

Use for materials on combinations in restraint of trade in which stock ownership is transferred to trustees, who in turn issue trust certificates and dividends and who attempt to achieve monopolistic control over output, prices, or markets.

>UF Cartels
>Trusts, Industrial
>BT Capital
>Commerce
>Economics
>RT Antitrust law
>Competition
>Corporate mergers and acquisitions
>Corporation law
>Corporations
>Monopolies
>Restraint of trade

Industrial trusts—Law and legislation
>USE Antitrust law

Industrial uses of space
>USE Space industrialization

Industrial waste 363.72; 628.4
>UF Factory and trade waste
>Factory waste
>Industrial wastes *[Former heading]*
>Trade waste
>BT Refuse and refuse disposal
>Waste products
>NT Hazardous wastes
>RT Pollution
>Water pollution

Industrial wastes
>USE Industrial waste

Industrial welfare (May subdiv. geog.)
>658.3
>UF Welfare work in industry
>BT Labor
>Management
>Social work

Industrial welfare—*Continued*
  NT **Social settlements**
Industrial workers
  USE **Labor**
       Working class
Industrialization (May subdiv. geog.)
    338
    Use for materials on the development of or-
ganized productions as industries, especially
factory-based industries. Materials on the his-
torical shift from home-based industries to
large-scale factory production are entered un-
der **Industrial revolution.**
  BT **Economic policy**
       Industries
  NT **Developing countries**
       Space industrialization
  RT **Industrial revolution**
       Modernization (Sociology)
Industries (May subdiv. geog.) **338**
    Apart from **Manufacturing industries** and
Service industries, all headings for types of
industries are formulated in the singular.
  UF Industry
       Production
  SA types of industries, e.g. **Steel in-
dustry;** and ethnic groups
with the subdivision *Indus-
tries,* e.g. **Native Ameri-
cans—Industries** [to be add-
ed as needed]
  BT **Economics**
  NT **Aerospace industry**
       Agricultural industry
       Automobile industry
       Book industry
       Ceramic industry
       Chemical industry
       Clothing industry
       Commercial fishing
       Computer industry
       Computer software industry
       Defense industry
       Electric products industry
       Firearms industry
       Industrialization
       Internet industry
       Iron industry
       Leather industry
       Management
       Manufactures
       Manufacturing industries
       Motion picture industry
       Native Americans—Industries

       Nuclear industry
       Paper industry
       Petroleum industry
       Pollution control industry
       Radio supplies industry
       Service industries
       Steel industry
       Textile industry
Industries—Chicago (Ill.) **338.09773**
  UF Chicago (Ill.)—Industries
Industries—Equipment and supplies
  USE **Industrial equipment**
Industries—Government policy
  USE **Industrial policy**
Industries—Government policy—United
    States
  USE **Industrial policy—United
       States**
Industries—History (May subdiv. geog.)
    338.09
  NT **Industrial archeology**
       Industrial revolution
Industries—Law and legislation
  USE **Industrial laws and legislation**
Industries—Ohio **338.09771**
  UF Ohio—Industries
Industries—Organization, control, etc.
  USE **Industrial policy**
Industries—United States **338.0973**
  UF United States—Industries
Industry
  USE **Industries**
Industry and state
  USE **Industrial policy**
Industry and war
  USE **Industrial mobilization**
       War—Economic aspects
Inequality
  USE **Equality**
Infallibility of the Pope
  USE **Popes—Infallibility**
Infant care
  USE **Infants—Care**
Infant mortality
  USE **Infants—Mortality**
Infant sudden death
  USE **Sudden infant death syndrome**
Infantile paralysis
  USE **Poliomyelitis**

Infants (May subdiv. geog.)   155.42;
  305.232; 362.7; 618.92
  Use for materials about children in the ear-
  liest period of life, usually the first two years
  only.
  UF   Babies
  BT   **Children**
Infants and strangers
  USE   **Children and strangers**
Infants—Birth defects
  USE   **Birth defects**
Infants—Care   649
  UF   Baby care
       Infant care
  BT   **Child care**
  NT   **Babysitting**
Infants—Clothing
  USE   **Infants' clothing**
Infants' clothing   646.4
  UF   Baby clothes
       Infants—Clothing *[Former head-
         ing]*
  BT   **Children's clothing**
       Clothing and dress
Infants—Death   306.9; 618.92
  Use for general materials on the death of
  infants. Materials on infant death rates and
  causes are entered under **Infants—Mortality.**
  BT   **Death**
  NT   **Sudden infant death syndrome**
Infants—Diseases   618.92
  UF   Pediatrics
  BT   **Diseases**
  RT   **Infants—Health and hygiene**
Infants—Education
  USE   **Preschool education**
Infants—Health and hygiene   613;
  618.92
  UF   Infants—Hygiene
       Pediatrics
  BT   **Health**
       Hygiene
  RT   **Infants—Diseases**
Infants—Hygiene
  USE   **Infants—Health and hygiene**
Infants—Mortality (May subdiv. geog.)
  304.6
  Use for materials on infant death rates and
  causes. General materials on the death of in-
  fants are entered under **Infants—Death.**
  UF   Infant mortality
  BT   **Mortality**

Infants—Nutrition   613.2; 649
  BT   **Nutrition**
  NT   **Breast feeding**
Infection and infectious diseases
  USE   **Communicable diseases**
Infectious wastes
  USE   **Medical wastes**
Infertility   616.6
  Use for materials on infertility in humans
  and in animals.
  UF   Sterility in animals
       Sterility in humans
  BT   **Reproduction**
  RT   **Birth control**
       Childlessness
       Fertility
       Human fertility
Infinitive
  USE   names of languages with the
        subdivision *Infinitive,* e.g. **En-
        glish language—Infinitive** [to
        be added as needed]
Infirmaries
  USE   **Hospitals**
Inflammable substances
  USE   **Hazardous substances**
Inflation (Finance) (May subdiv. geog.)
  332.4
  BT   **Finance**
  NT   **Wage-price policy**
  RT   **Monetary policy**
       Paper money
Influence
  USE   subjects, corporate bodies, indi-
        vidual persons, literary au-
        thors, religions, denomina-
        tions, sacred works, and wars
        with the subdivision *Influence,*
        e.g. **World War, 1939-
        1945—Influence; Shake-
        speare, William, 1564-1616—
        Influence** [to be added as
        needed]
Influenza   616.2
  UF   Flu
  BT   **Cold (Disease)**
       Communicable diseases
       Diseases
Informal sector (Economics)
  USE   **Underground economy**
Information centers
  USE   **Information services**

Information clearinghouses
　USE **Information services**
Information, Freedom of
　USE **Freedom of information**
Information networks　004.6
　Use for materials on the interconnection through telecommunications of a geographically dispersed group of libraries or information centers for the purpose of sharing their total information resources.
　UF　Information superhighway
　　　Networks, Information
　SA　types of information networks and names of specific networks [to be added as needed]
　BT　**Information systems**
　NT　**Internet**
　　　Library information networks
　RT　**Computer networks**
Information resources (May subdiv. geog.)　**025.04**
　Use for materials on sources of information in general, not limited to a specific topic or format. Materials on organizations that provide information services are entered under **Information services.**
　UF　Information sources
　SA　subjects with the subdivision *Information resources,* for general materials about information on a subject, e.g. **Business—Information resources;** subjects with the subdivision *Internet resources,* for materials about information available on the Internet on a subject, e.g. **Business—Internet resources;** subjects with the subdivision *Databases,* for materials about data files on a subject regardless of the medium of distribution, e.g. **Business—Databases;** and headings for the providers or the users of information with the subdivision *Information services,* for materials about organizations that provide information services, e.g. **United Nations—Information services; Consumers—Information services;** etc. [to be added as needed]

　BT　**Information science**
　NT　**Business—Information resources**
　　　Databases
　　　Information services
　　　Internet resources
Information retrieval　025.5
　UF　Data retrieval
　　　Information storage and retrieval
　　　Retrieval of information
　BT　**Documentation**
　　　Information science
　NT　**Internet searching**
　RT　**Information systems**
Information science (May subdiv. geog.)　**020**
　BT　**Communication**
　NT　**Documentation**
　　　Information resources
　　　Information retrieval
　　　Information systems
　　　Library science
Information services (May subdiv. geog.)　**025.5**
　Use for materials on organizations that provide information services. Materials on sources of information, not limited to a specific topic or format, are entered under **Information resources.**
　UF　Information centers
　　　Information clearinghouses
　SA　headings for the providers or the users of information with the subdivision *Information services,* for materials about organizatons that provide information services, e.g. **United Nations—Information services; Consumers—Information services;** etc.; subjects with the subdivision *Information resources,* for general materials about information on a subject, e.g. **Business—Information resources;** subjects with the subdivision *Internet resources,* for materials about information available on the Internet on a subject, e.g. **Business—Internet resources;** and subjects with the subdivision *Databases,* for materials

Information services—*Continued*
about data files on a subject
regardless of the medium of
distribution, e.g. **Business—
Databases** [to be added as
needed]
- BT **Information resources**
- NT **Archives**
  Business—Information services
  Consumers—Information services
  Electronic publishing
  Hotlines (Telephone counseling)
  **Machine readable bibliographic
  data**
  Reference services (Libraries)
  **United Nations—Information
  services**
- RT **Documentation**
  Information systems
  Libraries
  Research

Information society (May subdiv. geog.)
303.48
Use for materials on a society whose primary activity is the production and communication of information by means of computer networks and other advanced technology.
- BT **Sociology**

Information sources
- USE **Information resources**

Information storage and retrieval
- USE **Information retrieval**

Information storage and retrieval systems
- USE **Information systems**

Information superhighway
- USE **Computer networks**
  Information networks
  Internet

Information systems **025.04**
- UF Computer-based information systems
  Data storage and retrieval systems
  Information storage and retrieval systems
- BT **Bibliographic control**
  Computers
  Information science
- NT **Data processing**
  Database management

Expert systems (Computer science)
Information networks
**Machine readable bibliographic
data**
Management information systems
Multimedia
Teletext systems
Videotex systems
- RT **Information retrieval**
  Information services
  Libraries—Automation

Information systems—Management
025.04
Use for materials on the management of information systems.
- BT **Management**

Information technology (May subdiv.
geog.) **004; 303.48**
Use for materials on the acquisition, processing, storage, and dissemination of any type of information by microelectronics, computers, and telecommunication.
- BT **Technology**
- RT **Knowledge management**

Infrared radiation **535.01; 621.36**
- BT **Electromagnetic waves**
  Radiation

Inhalant abuse
- USE **Solvent abuse**

Inhalation abuse of solvents
- USE **Solvent abuse**

Inheritance and succession (May subdiv.
geog.) **346.05**
- UF Bequests
  Heirs
  Hereditary succession
  Intestacy
  Legacies
- BT **Wealth**
- NT **Executors and administrators**
  Inheritance and transfer tax
- RT **Trusts and trustees**
  Wills

Inheritance and transfer tax (May
subdiv. geog.) **343.05**
- UF Estate tax
  Taxation of legacies
  Transfer tax
- BT **Estate planning**
  Inheritance and succession
  Internal revenue

Inheritance and transfer tax—*Continued*
  Taxation
Inheritance (Biology)
  USE **Heredity**
Initialisms
  USE **Acronyms**
Initials 745.6
  NT **Printing—Specimens**
  RT **Alphabets**
    **Illumination of books and
      manuscripts**
    Lettering
    Monograms
    Type and type-founding
Initiative and referendum
  USE **Referendum**
Injunctions (May subdiv. geog.) 331.89
  BT **Constitutional law**
    Labor unions
  RT **Strikes**
Injuries
  USE **Accidents**
    First aid
    Wounds and injuries
Injurious insects
  USE **Insect pests**
Ink drawing
  USE **Pen drawing**
Inland navigation (May subdiv. gcog.)
  386
    May be subdivided by the names of rivers,
    lakes, canals, etc., as well as by countries,
    states, cities, etc.
  BT **Navigation**
    Shipping
    Transportation
  RT **Canals**
    Lakes
    Rivers
    Waterways
Inner cities (May subdiv. geog.) 307.76
    Use for materials on the densely populated,
    economically depressed, central areas of large
    cities.
  UF Ghettoes, Inner city
    Inner city ghettoes
    Inner city problems
  BT **Cities and towns**
Inner city ghettoes
  USE **Inner cities**
Inner city problems
  USE **Inner cities**

Inner city schools
  USE **Urban schools**
Inns
  USE **Hotels and motels**
Innuit
  USE **Inuit**
Inoculation
  USE **Vaccination**
Inorganic chemistry 546
  UF Chemistry, Inorganic
  BT **Chemistry**
  NT **Metals**
Input equipment (Computers)
  USE **Computer peripherals**
Inquisition (May subdiv. geog.) 272
  UF Holy Office
  BT **Catholic Church**
Insane
  USE **Mentally ill**
Insanity defense (May subdiv. geog.)
  345
  UF Insanity—Jurisprudence
    Insanity plea
    Mental illness—Jurisprudence
  BT **Criminal law**
Insanity—Jurisprudence
  USE **Insanity defense**
Insanity plea
  USE **Insanity defense**
Inscriptions (May subdiv. geog.) 411
  UF Epigraphy
  BT **Ancient history**
    Archeology
  NT **Brasses**
    Epitaphs
    Graffiti
    Hieroglyphics
    Seals (Numismatics)
Insect-eating plants
  USE **Carnivorous plants**
Insect pests (May subdiv. geog.) 632
  UF Destructive insects
    Diseases and pests
    Garden pests
    Harmful insects
    Injurious insects
  SA types of insect pests, e.g. **Lo-
      custs;** etc.; and types of
      crops, plants, trees, etc., with
      the subdivision *Diseases and
      pests,* e.g. **Fruit—Diseases**

Insect pests—*Continued*
      and pests [to be added as needed]
  BT **Economic zoology**
      Insects
      Pests
  NT **Fruit—Diseases and pests**
      Insects as carriers of disease
      Locusts
  RT **Agricultural pests**
      Household pests
      Parasites

Insecticides   632; 668
  SA types of insecticides [to be added as needed]
  BT **Agricultural chemicals**
      Pesticides
  NT **DDT (Insecticide)**
      Fumigation
  RT **Spraying and dusting**

Insecticides—Toxicology   615.9
  BT **Poisons and poisoning**

Insectivorous plants
  USE **Carnivorous plants**

Insects (May subdiv. geog.)   **595.7**
  SA types of insects [to be added as needed]
  BT **Animals**
  NT **Ants**
      Bees
      Beneficial insects
      Butterflies
      Flies
      Insect pests
      Locusts
      Mosquitoes
      Moths
      Silkworms
      Wasps

Insects as carriers of disease   614.4
  BT **Insect pests**
  RT **Communicable diseases**

Inservice training
  USE **Employees—Training**

Insider trading   346.07; 364.16
  UF Securities trading, Insider
      Stocks—Insider trading
  BT **Commercial law**
      Securities
      Stock exchanges

Insignia   929.9
  UF Badges of honor
      Devices (Heraldry)
      Emblems
  SA armies, navies, and other appropriate subjects with the subdivision *Insignia* or *Medals, badges, decorations, etc.* [to be added as needed]
  BT **Heraldry**
  NT **Colleges and universities—Insignia**
      United States. Army—Insignia
      United States. Army—Medals, badges, decorations, etc.
      United States. Navy—Insignia
      United States. Navy—Medals, badges, decorations, etc.
  RT **Decorations of honor**
      Medals
      National emblems

Insolvency
  USE **Bankruptcy**

Insomnia   616.8
  UF Sleeplessness
      Wakefulness
  RT **Sleep**

Inspection
  USE topics with the subdivision *Inspection,* e.g. **Automobiles—Inspection** [to be added as needed]

Inspection of food
  USE **Food adulteration and inspection**

Inspection of meat
  USE **Meat inspection**

Inspection of schools
  USE **School supervision**
      Schools—Administration

Inspiration
  USE **Creation (Literary, artistic, etc.)**

Inspiration, Biblical
  USE **Bible—Inspiration**

Installment plan   658.8
  UF Instalment plan
  BT **Business**
      Consumer credit
      Credit
      Purchasing

Instalment plan
  USE **Installment plan**
Instinct 152.3; 156
  UF Animal instinct
  BT **Animal behavior**
      Psychology
  RT **Animal intelligence**
      Comparative psychology
      Habit
Institutional care 361
  UF Asylums
      Benevolent institutions
      Charitable institutions
      Homes (Institutions)
  SA classes of persons with the sub-
      division *Institutional care* [to
      be added as needed]
  BT **Charities**
      Medical charities
      Public welfare
  NT **Blind—Institutional care**
      Children—Institutional care
      Deaf—Institutional care
      Elderly—Institutional care
      Group homes
      Hospitals
      Mentally ill—Institutional care
      Nursing homes
Institutions, Charitable and philanthropic
  USE **Charities**
Institutions, Ecclesiastical
  USE **Religious institutions**
Institutions, Religious
  USE **Religious institutions**
Instruction
  USE **Education**
      Teaching
Instructional games
  USE **Educational games**
Instructional materials
  USE **Teaching—Aids and devices**
Instructional materials centers (May
    subdiv. geog.) **027.7**
  UF Audiovisual materials centers
      Curriculum materials centers
      Educational media centers
      Learning resource centers
      Media centers (Education)
      Multimedia centers
      School media centers

  BT **Libraries**
  NT **School libraries**
Instructional supervision
  USE **School supervision**
Instructional systems analysis
  USE **Educational evaluation**
Instructional technology
  USE **Educational technology**
Instructive games
  USE **Educational games**
Instrument flying 629.132
  BT **Aeronautical instruments**
      Airplanes—Piloting
Instrumental ensembles
  USE **Ensembles (Music)**
Instrumental music 784
  SA types of instrumental music [to
      be added as needed]
  BT **Music**
  NT **Band music**
      Chamber music
      Guitar music
      Orchestral music
      Organ music
      Piano music
  RT **Musical instruments**
Instrumentalists (May subdiv. geog.)
      784
  SA types of instrumentalists, e.g. **Vi-**
      olinists [to be added as need-
      ed]
  BT **Musicians**
  NT **Organists**
      Pianists
      Violinists
      Violoncellists
Instrumentation and orchestration
      781.3; 784.13
  UF Orchestration
  BT **Bands (Music)**
      Composition (Music)
      Music
      Orchestra
  RT **Musical instruments**
Instruments, Aeronautical
  USE **Aeronautical instruments**
Instruments, Astronautical
  USE **Astronautical instruments**
Instruments, Astronomical
  USE **Astronomical instruments**

Instruments, Engineering
    USE **Engineering instruments**
Instruments, Measuring
    USE **Measuring instruments**
Instruments, Meteorological
    USE **Meteorological instruments**
Instruments, Musical
    USE **Musical instruments**
Instruments, Negotiable
    USE **Negotiable instruments**
Instruments, Optical
    USE **Optical instruments**
Instruments, Scientific
    USE **Scientific apparatus and instruments**
Insulation (Heat)   **691; 693.8**
    UF Heat insulating materials
        Thermal insulation
    BT **Heating**
Insulation (Sound)
    USE **Soundproofing**
Insults
    USE **Invective**
Insurance (May subdiv. geog.)   **368**
    SA types of insurance, e.g. **Automobile insurance** [to be added as needed]
    BT **Estate planning**
        Finance
        Personal finance
    NT **Automobile insurance**
        Casualty insurance
        Disability insurance
        Fire insurance
        Health insurance
        Life insurance
        Malpractice insurance
        Marine insurance
        Unemployment insurance
Insurance, Accident
    USE **Accident insurance**
Insurance, Automobile
    USE **Automobile insurance**
Insurance, Casualty
    USE **Casualty insurance**
Insurance, Disability
    USE **Disability insurance**
Insurance, Fire
    USE **Fire insurance**
Insurance, Group
    USE **Group insurance**

Insurance, Health
    USE **Health insurance**
Insurance, Hospitalization
    USE **Hospitalization insurance**
Insurance, Life
    USE **Life insurance**
Insurance, Malpractice
    USE **Malpractice insurance**
Insurance, Marine
    USE **Marine insurance**
Insurance, Professional liability
    USE **Malpractice insurance**
Insurance, Social
    USE **Social security**
Insurance, Unemployment
    USE **Unemployment insurance**
Insurance, Workers' compensation
    USE **Workers' compensation**
Insurgency (May subdiv. geog.)   **322.4; 355.02**
    UF Rebellions
    BT **Revolutions**
    NT **Guerrilla warfare**
        Subversive activities
        Terrorism
    RT **Internal security**
        Resistance to government
Integrated churches
    USE **Church and race relations**
Integrated curriculum
    USE **Interdisciplinary approach in education**
Integrated language arts (Holistic)
    USE **Whole language**
Integrated schools
    USE **School integration**
Integration in education
    USE **School integration**
        Segregation in education
Integration, Racial
    USE **Race relations**
Intellect   **153.4**
    UF Intelligence
        Mind
        Understanding
    BT **Psychology**
    NT **Creation (Literary, artistic, etc.)**
        Imagination
        Logic
        Memory

Intellect—*Continued*

      Perception

      Reason

      Senses and sensation

RT   **Reasoning**

      Theory of knowledge

      Thought and thinking

Intellectual cooperation   327.1; 370.116

UF   Cooperation, Intellectual

BT   **International cooperation**

NT   **Conferences**

      Cultural relations

RT   **International education**

Intellectual freedom   323.44

BT   **Freedom**

NT   **Academic freedom**

      Censorship

      Freedom of information

      Freedom of speech

      Freedom of the press

Intellectual life   001.1

Use for general materials on learning and scholarship, literature, the arts, etc. Materials on literature, art, music, motion pictures, etc. produced for a mass audience are entered under **Popular culture.**

UF   Cultural life

SA   classes of persons, ethnic groups, and names of countries, cities, etc., with the subdivision *Intellectual life* [to be added as needed]

BT   **Culture**

NT   **African Americans—Intellectual life**

      Blacks—Intellectual life

      Chicago (Ill.)—Intellectual life

      Cultural policy

      Learning and scholarship

      Ohio—Intellectual life

      Popular culture

      United States—Intellectual life

Intellectual life—Government policy

USE   **Cultural policy**

Intellectual property (May subdiv. geog.) 346.04

UF   Literary property

      Proprietary rights

      Rights, Proprietary

BT   **Property**

RT   **Copyright**

      Patents

Intellectuals (May subdiv. geog.)   **305.5**

UF   Intelligentsia

SA   ethnic groups, classes of persons, and names of countries, cities, etc., with the subdivision *Intellectual life,* e.g. **African Americans—Intellectual life; United States—Intellectual life;** etc. [to be added as needed]

BT   **Persons**

      Social classes

Intelligence

USE   **Intellect**

Intelligence agents

USE   **Spies**

Intelligence of animals

USE   **Animal intelligence**

Intelligence service (May subdiv. geog.) **327.12; 355.3**

Use for materials on a government agency that is engaged in obtaining information, usually about an enemy but sometimes about an ally or a neutral country, and also in blocking the attempts by foreign agents to obtain information about one's own national secrets.

UF   Counterespionage

      Counterintelligence

BT   **Public administration**

      Research

NT   **Espionage**

RT   **Secret service**

Intelligence service—United States 327.1273; 355.3

UF   United States—Intelligence service

Intelligence testing

USE   **Intelligence tests**

Intelligence tests   153.9

UF   Intelligence testing

      IQ tests

      Mental tests

BT   **Child psychology**

      Educational psychology

NT   **Ability—Testing**

RT   **Educational tests and measurements**

Intelligentsia

USE   **Intellectuals**

Intemperance

USE   **Alcoholism**

      Temperance

Inter-American relations
  USE **Pan-Americanism**
Interactive CD technology
  USE **CD-I technology**
Interactive media
  USE **Multimedia**
Interactive multimedia
  USE **Multimedia**
       and subjects with the subdivi-
       sion *Interactive multimedia,*
       e.g. **Geology—Interactive
       multimedia** [to be added as
       needed]
Interactive videotex
  USE **Videotex systems**
Interbehaviorial psychology
  USE **Behaviorism**
Interchange of visitors
  USE **Exchange of persons programs**
Interchurch cooperation
  USE **Interdenominational coopera-
       tion**
Intercollegiate athletics
  USE **College sports**
**Intercommunication systems   621.38;
  651.7**
  UF Interoffice communication sys-
      tems
  BT **Electronic apparatus and ap-
      pliances
      Telecommunication**
  NT **Closed-circuit television
      Microwave communication sys-
      tems**
Intercontinental ballistic missiles   623.4
  UF ICBM
  SA names of specific ICBM mis-
      siles, e.g. **Atlas (Missile)** [to
      be added as needed]
  BT **Ballistic missiles**
  NT **Atlas (Missile)**
Intercultural education
  USE **Multicultural education**
Intercultural relations
  USE **Cultural relations**
Intercultural studies
  USE **Cross-cultural studies**
Interdenominational cooperation (May
  subdiv. geog.)   **280**
  Use for materials on religious activities
  planned and conducted cooperatively by two
or more Christian sects. Materials on unity as
one of the marks of the church are entered
under **Church—Unity.** Materials on prospec-
tive and actual mergers within and across denominational lines are entered under **Christian union.** Materials on a movement originating in the twentieth century aimed at promoting church cooperation and unity are entered under **Ecumenical movement.**
  UF Christian unity *[Former head-
      ing]*
      Cooperation, Interchurch
      Cooperation, Interdenominational
      Interchurch cooperation
  BT **Christian sects
      Church work**
Interdisciplinarity in education
  USE **Interdisciplinary approach in
       education**
**Interdisciplinary approach in education
  375**
  UF Integrated curriculum
      Interdisciplinarity in education
      Interdisciplinary studies
  BT **Curriculum planning**
Interdisciplinary studies
  USE **Interdisciplinary approach in
       education**
Interest centers approach to teaching
  USE **Open plan schools**
Interest (Economics)   332.8
  BT **Banks and banking
      Business mathematics
      Capital
      Finance
      Loans**
Interest groups
  USE **Lobbying
       Political action committees**
Interfaces, Computer
  USE **Computer interfaces**
**Interfaith marriage   261.8; 291.1;
  306.84**
  UF Mixed marriage
  BT **Intermarriage**
Interfaith relations   261.2; 291.1
  BT **Cultural relations**
Intergovernmental tax relations (May
  subdiv. geog.)   **336.2**
  UF Federal-state tax relations
      State-local tax relations
      Tax relations, Intergovernmental
      Tax sharing

Intergovernmental tax relations—*Continued*

    BT   **Taxation**

    NT   **Revenue sharing**

Interior decoration

    USE **Interior design**

Interior design (May subdiv. geog.)
    729; 747

    Use for materials on the art and techniques of planning and supervising the design and execution of architectural interiors and their furnishings.

    UF   Home decoration

          House decoration

          House furnishing

          Interior decoration

    BT   **Art**

          Decoration and ornament

          Design

          Home economics

    NT   **Bedspreads**

          Draperies

          Furniture

          Lighting

          Mural painting and decoration

          Paperhanging

          Quilts

          Rugs and carpets

          Tapestry

          Upholstery

          Wallpaper

    RT   **Rooms**

Interlibrary loans (May subdiv. geog.)
    025.6

    BT   **Library circulation**

          Library cooperation

Interlocking signals

    USE **Railroads—Signaling**

Intermarriage (May subdiv. geog.)
    306.84

    Use for materials that discuss collectively marriage between persons of different religions, religious denominations, races, or ethnic groups.

    UF   Mixed marriage

    BT   **Marriage**

    NT   **Interfaith marriage**

          Interracial marriage

Intermediate schools

    USE **Middle schools**

Intermediate state

    USE **Eschatology**

          Future life

Interment

    USE **Burial**

Internal combustion engines   **621.43**

    UF   Gas and oil engines

          Gas engines

          Gasoline engines

          Oil engines

          Petroleum engines

    BT   **Engines**

    NT   **Carburetors**

          Diesel engines

Internal migration   **304.8**

    Use for materials on the movement of population within a country for permanent settlement. Materials on casual or seasonal workers who move from place to place in search of employment are entered under **Migrant labor.** Materials on migration from one country to another are entered under **Immigration and emigration.**

    UF   Migration, Internal

          Rural-urban migration

          Urban-rural migration

    BT   **Colonization**

          Population

    NT   **Cities and towns—Growth**

    RT   **Immigration and emigration**

          Land settlement

          Migrant labor

Internal revenue   **336.2**

    BT   **Taxation**

    NT   **Income tax**

          Inheritance and transfer tax

Internal revenue law (May subdiv. geog.)
    343.04

    BT   **Law**

Internal security (May subdiv. geog.)
    353.3; 363.2

    UF   Loyalty oaths

          Security, Internal

    RT   **Insurgency**

          Subversive activities

Internal security—United States   **353.3; 363.2**

    UF   United States—Internal security

International agencies (May subdiv. geog.)   **060**

    UF   Associations, International

          International associations

          International organizations

    SA   names of individual agencies [to be added as needed]

    BT   **International cooperation**

International arbitration   341.5
  UF Arbitration, International
        International mediation
        Mediation, International
  BT **International cooperation**
        International law
        International relations
        International security
        Treaties
  NT **League of Nations**
        United Nations
  RT **Arms control**
        Peace
International associations
  USE **International agencies**
International business enterprises
  USE **Multinational corporations**
International competition   337; 382; 658
  UF Competition, International
        World economics
  BT **International relations**
        International trade
  RT **War—Economic aspects**
International conferences
  USE **Conferences**
International cooperation   327.1; 341.7
  Use for general materials on international cooperative activities, with or without the participation of governments.
  SA subjects with the subdivision *International cooperation,* e.g. **Astronautics—International cooperation** [to be added as needed]
  BT **Cooperation**
        International law
        International relations
  NT **Astronautics—International cooperation**
        Conferences
        Cultural relations
        Exchange of persons programs
        Foreign aid
        Intellectual cooperation
        International agencies
        International arbitration
        International police
        League of Nations
        Space sciences—International cooperation
        United Nations

  RT **International education**
        International organization
        Reconstruction (1914-1939)
        Reconstruction (1939-1951)
        Technology transfer
International copyright
  USE **Copyright**
International economic relations   382
  UF Economic relations, Foreign
        Foreign economic relations
  BT **Economic policy**
        International relations
  NT **Balance of payments**
        Commercial policy
        Foreign aid
        International trade
        Multinational corporations
        Sanctions (International law)
        Technical assistance
        United States—Foreign economic relations
International education (May subdiv. geog.)   **370.116**
  Use for materials on education for international understanding, world citizenship, etc.
  BT **Education**
  NT **Teacher exchange**
  RT **Intellectual cooperation**
        International cooperation
        Multicultural education
International exchange
  USE **Foreign exchange**
International exhibitions
  USE **Exhibitions**
International investment
  USE **Foreign investments**
International language
  USE **Universal language**
International law (May subdiv. geog.)   **341**
  UF Law of nations
  BT **Law**
  NT **Asylum**
        Boundaries
        International arbitration
        International cooperation
        Intervention (International law)
        Mandates
        Marine salvage
        Maritime law
        Military law
        Naturalization

International law—*Continued*
      Neutrality
      Pirates
      Political refugees
      Privateering
      Sanctions (International law)
      Slave trade
      Space law
      Treaties
      War crimes
  RT International organization
      International relations
      Natural law
      War

International mediation
  USE **International arbitration**

International organization   341.2
    Use for materials on plans leading towards political organization of nations.
  UF World government
      World organization
  SA names of specific organizations,
      e.g. **United Nations** [to be
      added as needed]
  BT **International relations**
      International security
  NT **European federation**
      International police
      League of Nations
      Mandates
      North Atlantic Treaty Organization
      United Nations
  RT **International cooperation**
      International law
      World politics

International organizations
  USE **International agencies**

International police   341.7
  UF Interpol
      Police, International
  BT **International cooperation**
      International organization
      International relations
      International security

International politics
  USE **World politics**

International relations   327; 341.3
    Use for materials on the theory of international relations. Historical accounts are entered under **World politics; Europe—Politics and government;** etc. Materials on the for-
eign relations of an individual country are entered under the name of the country with the subdivison *Foreign relations.* Materials limited to diplomatic relations between two countries are entered under the name of each country with the subdivision *Foreign relations* further subdivided by the name of the other country, e.g. **United States—Foreign relations—Iran** and also **Iran—Foreign relations—United States.**
  UF Foreign affairs
      Foreign policy
      Foreign relations
      Peaceful coexistence
      World order
  SA names of countries with the subdivision *Foreign relations,*
      e.g. **United States—Foreign relations** [to be added as needed]
  NT **Arms control**
      Balance of power
      Boundaries
      Catholic Church—Foreign relations
      Cultural relations
      Diplomacy
      Diplomatic and consular service
      Diplomats
      East and West
      Geopolitics
      International arbitration
      International competition
      International cooperation
      International economic relations
      International organization
      International police
      International security
      Mandates
      Monroe Doctrine
      Nationalism
      Neutrality
      Peace
      Political refugees
      Treaties
      United States—Foreign relations
  RT **International law**
      National security
      Technology transfer
      World politics

International security 327.1; 341.7
- UF   Collective security
-       Security, International
- BT   **International relations**
- NT   **Arms control**
-       **Arms race**
-       **International arbitration**
-       **International organization**
-       **International police**
-       **Neutrality**
- RT   **Peace**

International space cooperation
- USE   **Astronautics—International co-operation**

International Standard Bibliographic Description 025.3
- UF   ISBD
- BT   **Cataloging**

International Standard Book Numbers 070.5
- UF   ISBN
- BT   **Publishers' standard book numbers**

International Standard Serial Numbers 070.5
- UF   ISSN
- RT   **Serial publications**

International trade (May subdiv. geog.) 382

Use for general materials about trade among nations. Materials on foreign trade of specific countries, cities, etc., are entered under the name of the place with the subdivision *Commerce*. Materials limited to trade between two countries are entered under the name of each country with the subdivision *Commerce* further subdivided by the name of the other country, i.e. **United States—Commerce—Japan** and also **Japan—Commerce—United States.**
- UF   Foreign commerce
-       Foreign trade
-       Trade, International
- BT   **Commerce**
-       **International economic relations**
- NT   **Arms transfers**
-       **Balance of trade**
-       **Exports**
-       **Free trade**
-       **Imports**
-       **International competition**

Internet 004.67
- UF   Information superhighway
-       Internet (Computer network)
- BT   **Computer networks**
-       **Information networks**
- NT   **Internet addresses**
-       **Internet resources**
-       **World Wide Web**

Internet access providers
- USE   **Internet service providers**

Internet addresses 004.67
- BT   **Internet**

Internet addresses—Directories 025.04
- SA   topics, names of places, categories of persons, ethnic groups, etc., with the subdivisions *Internet resources—Directories,* e.g. **Business—Internet resources—Directories** [to be added as needed]

Internet chat groups
- USE   **Online chat groups**

Internet commerce
- USE   **Electronic commerce**

Internet companies
- USE   **Internet industry**

Internet (Computer network)
- USE   **Internet**

Internet—Computer programs
- USE   **Internet software**

Internet discussion groups
- USE   **Electronic discussion groups**

Internet—Home shopping services
- USE   **Internet marketing**
-       **Internet shopping**

Internet industry (May subdiv. geog.) 004.67; 338.7
- UF   Internet companies
- BT   **Industries**
- NT   **Internet service providers**

Internet marketing (May subdiv. geog.) 658.8
- UF   Internet—Home shopping services
-       Online marketing
-       Online selling
- BT   **Electronic commerce**
-       **Marketing**
- RT   **Internet shopping**

Internet newsgroups
- USE   **Electronic discussion groups**

Internet resources   004.67
  UF   Computer network resources
  SA   subjects with the subdivision
        Internet resources, for materi-
        als about information avail-
        able on the Internet on a sub-
        ject, e.g. **Business—Internet
        resources;** subjects with the
        subdivision *Information re-
        sources,* for general materials
        about information on a sub-
        ject, e.g. **Business—Informa-
        tion resources;** subjects with
        the subdivision *Databases,* for
        materials about data files on a
        subject regardless of the me-
        dium of distribution, e.g.
        Business—Databases; and
        headings for the providers or
        the users of information with
        the subdivision *Information
        services,* for materials about
        organizations that provide in-
        formation services, e.g. **Unit-
        ed Nations—Information ser-
        vices; Consumers—Informa-
        tion services;** etc. [to be add-
        ed as needed]
  BT   **Information resources**
        Internet
  NT   **Business—Internet resources**
        Web sites
Internet searching   004.67; 025.5
  UF   Searching the Internet
  BT   **Information retrieval**
Internet service providers (May subdiv.
        geog.)   004.67
  UF   Internet access providers
  BT   **Internet industry**
Internet shopping (May subdiv. geog.)
        381; 640
  UF   Cybershopping
        Internet—Home shopping ser-
           vices
        Online shopping
        Shopping—Computer network re-
           sources
        Shopping—Internet resources
  BT   **Electronic commerce**
        Shopping
  RT   **Internet marketing**

Internet software   005.7
  UF   Internet—Computer programs
  BT   **Computer software**
Internment camps
  USE   **Concentration camps**
Interoffice communication systems
  USE   **Intercommunication systems**
Interpersonal relations (May subdiv.
        geog.)   **158; 302**
     Use for materials on group behavior, social
  relations between persons, and problems aris-
  ing from organizational and interpersonal rela-
  tions.
  UF   Human relations *[Former head-
           ing]*
  SA   relations between particular
        groups of persons or individu-
        als, e.g. **Jewish-Arab rela-
        tions; Parent-child relation-
        ship;** etc. [to be added as
        needed]
  BT   **Social psychology**
  NT   **Conflict of generations**
        Discrimination
        Domestic relations
        Family
        Group relations training
        Helping behavior
        Life skills
        Man-woman relationship
        Personal space
        Prejudices
        Social adjustment
        Teacher-student relationship
        Toleration
  RT   **Human behavior**
Interplanetary communication
  USE   **Interstellar communication**
Interplanetary visitors
  USE   **Extraterrestrial beings**
Interplanetary voyages   808.83; 813,
        etc.; 919.904
     Use for general materials about travel to
  other planets and for individual works, collec-
  tions, or materials about imaginary accounts
  of such travels. Materials on the physics and
  technical details of flight beyond the earth's
  atmosphere are entered under **Space flight.**
  UF   Interstellar travel
        Space travel
  BT   **Astronautics**
        Fiction

Interplanetary voyages—*Continued*
  NT **Outer space—Exploration**
  RT **Fantasy fiction**
      Imaginary voyages
      Rockets (Aeronautics)
      Science fiction
      Space flight
Interplanetary warfare
  USE **Space warfare**
Interpol
  USE **International police**
Interpreting and translating
  USE **Translating and interpreting**
Interpretive dance
  USE **Modern dance**
Interracial adoption (May subdiv. geog.)
      362.73
  BT **Adoption**
      Race relations
Interracial marriage (May subdiv. geog.)
      306.84
  UF Marriage, Interracial
      Racial intermarriage
  BT **Intermarriage**
Interracial relations
  USE **Race relations**
Interscholastic sports
  USE **School sports**
Interstate commerce 381
    Use for materials limited to commerce be-
  tween states. General materials on foreign and
  domestic commerce are entered under **Com-
  merce.**
  UF Government regulation of com-
      merce
  BT **Commerce**
Interstate highways
  USE **Express highways**
Interstellar communication 621.382
  UF Extraterrestrial communication
      Interplanetary communication
      Outer space—Communication
      Space communication
      Space telecommunication
  BT **Life on other planets**
      Telecommunication
  NT **Astronautics—Communication**
        systems
      Radio astronomy
Interstellar travel
  USE **Interplanetary voyages**

Interstellar warfare
  USE **Space warfare**
Interurban railroads
  USE **Electric railroads**
      Street railroads
Intervention (International law) 341.5
  UF Military intervention
  BT **International law**
      War
  NT **Monroe Doctrine**
  RT **Neutrality**
Interviewing 158
  BT **Applications for positions**
      Social psychology
  NT **Talk shows**
  RT **Applied psychology**
      Counseling
      Interviews
Interviewing (Journalism)
  USE **Reporters and reporting**
Interviews 920
    Use for materials about interviews and for
  collections of diverse interviews.
  SA subjects, ethnic groups, classes
        of persons, and names of cor-
        porate bodies and individual
        persons with the subdivision
        Interviews, e.g. **Authors—In-
        terviews** [to be added as
        needed]
  BT **Conversation**
  NT **Authors—Interviews**
  RT **Interviewing**
Interviews, Parent-teacher
  USE **Parent-teacher conferences**
Intestacy
  USE **Inheritance and succession**
Intifada, 1987- 956.9405
  UF Arab-Israeli conflict, 1987-
      Israeli-Arab conflict, 1987-
      Palestinian-Israeli conflict, 1987-
      Palestinian uprising, 1987-
  BT **Israel-Arab conflicts**
Intolerance
  USE **Fanaticism**
      Toleration
Intoxicants
  USE **Alcohol**
      Alcoholic beverages
      Liquors

Intoxication
USE **Alcoholism**
Temperance
Intuition 153.4
BT **Philosophy**
Psychology
Rationalism
Theory of knowledge
RT **Perception**
Inuit (May subdiv. geog.) **970.004**
Use for materials on the native peoples of the arctic regions of Alaska, Canada, and Greenland. If local usage dictates, libraries may establish **Eskimos** as a broader term than **Inuit;** and the names of other groups of Arctic peoples may be added as needed.
UF Eskimos
Esquimaux
Innuit
BT **Native peoples**
Inuit—Folklore 398
BT **Folklore**
Invalid cooking
USE **Cooking for the sick**
Diet therapy
Invalids
USE **Physically handicapped**
Sick
Invasion of Cuba, 1961
USE **Cuba—History—1961, Invasion**
Invasion of privacy
USE **Right of privacy**
Invective 808.88
UF Abuse, Verbal
Insults
Verbal abuse
BT **Satire**
Inventions (May subdiv. geog.) **608**
BT **Technology**
NT **Creation (Literary, artistic, etc.)**
Technology transfer
RT **Inventors**
Patents
Inventors (May subdiv. geog.) **609.2; 920**
RT **Engineers**
Inventions
Inventory control 658.7
UF Stock control
BT **Management**
Retail trade

Invertebrates 592
BT **Animals**
Investment and saving
USE **Saving and investment**
Investment companies
USE **Mutual funds**
Investment in real estate
USE **Real estate investment**
Investment trusts
USE **Mutual funds**
Investments (May subdiv. geog.) **332.6**
BT **Banks and banking**
Capital
Finance
NT **Annuities**
Bonds
Foreign investments
Mutual funds
Real estate investment
Savings and loan associations
Securities
RT **Estate planning**
Loans
Saving and investment
Speculation
Stock exchanges
Stocks
Investments, Foreign
USE **Foreign investments**
Invincible Armada
USE **Spanish Armada, 1588**
IQ tests
USE **Intelligence tests**
Iran 935; 955
May be subdivided like United States except for *History.*
UF Persia
Iran-Contra Affair, 1985-1990 973.927
UF Iran-Contra Arms Scandal, 1985-1990
BT **United States—History—1974-1989**
United States—History—1989-
Iran-Contra Arms Scandal, 1985-1990
USE **Iran-Contra Affair, 1985-1990**
Iran—Foreign relations—United States 327.55073
NT **Iran hostage crisis, 1979-1981**
Iran—History—1941-1979 955.05
Iran—History—1979- 955.05

Iran hostage crisis, 1979-1981
    327.55073; 327.73055; 955
  BT   American hostages—Iran
       Iran—Foreign relations—Unit-
       ed States
       United States—Foreign rela-
       tions—Iran
IRAs (Pensions)
  USE Individual retirement accounts
Iron   669; 672
  BT   Chemical elements
       Metals
  NT   Iron ores
       Ironwork
       Steel
Iron Age (May subdiv. geog.)   930.1
  BT   Civilization
Iron and steel building
  USE Steel construction
Iron curtain countries
  USE Communist countries
Iron industry (May subdiv. geog.)   338.2
  UF   Iron industry and trade
  BT   Industries
  RT   Steel industry
Iron industry and trade
  USE Iron industry
Iron ores   553.3
  BT   Iron
       Ores
Ironing
  USE Laundry
Ironwork (May subdiv. geog.)   672;
    682; 739.4
  UF   Wrought iron work
  BT   Decoration and ornament
       Iron
       Metalwork
  NT   Blacksmithing
       Welding
  RT   Forging
Irreversible coma
  USE Brain death
Irrigation (May subdiv. geog.)   333.91;
    627; 631.5
  BT   Agricultural engineering
       Hydraulic engineering
       Water resources development
       Water supply
  RT   Reclamation of land

Irrigation—United States   333.91; 627;
    631.5
ISBD
  USE International Standard Biblio-
       graphic Description
ISBN
  USE International Standard Book
       Numbers
Islam (May subdiv. geog.)   297
    Use for materials on the religion. Materials
  on the believers in this religion are entered
  under **Muslims.**
  BT   Religions
  NT   Islam—Relations—Judaism
       Islamic fundamentalism
       Judaism—Relations—Islam
       Koran
       Mysticism—Islam
  RT   Islamic law
       Muslims
Islam—Relations—Judaism   297
    Use for materials on the relations between
  Islam and Judaism. When assigning this head-
  ing, provide an additional subject entry under
  Judaism—Relations—Islam. Materials on the
  conflicts between the Arab countries and Isra-
  el are entered under **Israel-Arab conflicts.**
  Materials that discuss collectively the relations
  between Arabs and Jews, including religious,
  ethnic, and ideological relations, are entered
  under **Jewish-Arab relations.**
  UF   Islamic-Jewish relations
       Jewish-Islamic relations
  BT   Islam
       Judaism
  RT   Jewish-Arab relations
Islam—Sermons
  USE Islamic sermons
Islamic architecture (May subdiv. geog.)
    720.917
  UF   Architecture, Islamic
       Moorish architecture
       Muslim architecture
  BT   Architecture
  NT   Mosques
Islamic art (May subdiv. geog.)   709.1
  UF   Art, Islamic
       Mohammedan art
       Muslim art
       Saracenic art
  BT   Art
Islamic countries   956
  UF   Muslim countries
  NT   Arab countries

Islamic fundamentalism (May subdiv. geog.) **297.09**
  UF Fundamentalism
  BT **Islam**
      Religious fundamentalism
Islamic-Jewish relations
  USE **Islam—Relations—Judaism**
      Judaism—Relations—Islam
Islamic law (May subdiv. geog.) **340.5**
  UF Muslim law
  BT **Law**
  RT **Islam**
Islamic literature **297**
  UF Muslim literature
  BT **Religious literature**
  NT **Islamic sermons**
Islamic mysticism
  USE **Mysticism—Islam**
Islamic sermons **297**
  UF Islam—Sermons
      Muslim sermons
  SA individual Islamic sects with the subdivision *Sermons* [to be added as needed]
  BT **Islamic literature**
      Sermons
Islands (May subdiv. geog.) **551.42**
  SA names of islands and groups of islands [to be added as needed]
  NT **Coral reefs and islands**
      Cuba
      Islands of the Pacific
Islands, Imaginary
  USE **Geographical myths**
Islands of the Pacific **990**
  Use for comprehensive materials on all the islands of the Pacific Ocean. Materials restricted to comprehensive treatment of the island groups of Melanesia, Micronesia, and Polynesia are entered under **Oceania.**
  UF Pacific Islands
      Pacific Ocean Islands
  BT **Islands**
  NT **Oceania**
  RT **Pacific rim**
Isotopes **539.7; 541.3**
  BT **Atoms**
  NT **Radioisotopes**
Israel **956.94**
  May be subdivided like United States except for *History.*
  BT **Middle East**

Israel-Arab conflicts **965.04; 956.05**
  Use for materials on the conflicts between the Arab countries and Israel. Materials that discuss collectively the relations between Arabs and Jews, including religious, ethnic, and ideological relations, are entered under **Jewish-Arab relations.** Materials on relations between the religions of Judaism and Islam are entered under **Judaism—Relations—Islam** and under **Islam—Relations—Judaism.**
  UF Arab-Israel conflicts
      Arab-Israeli conflicts
      Israeli-Arab conflicts
  BT **Arab countries—Foreign relations—Israel**
      Israel—Foreign relations—Arab countries
  NT **Intifada, 1987-**
      Israel-Arab War, 1948-1949
      Israel-Arab War, 1967
      Israel-Arab War, 1973
      Lebanon—History—1982-1984, Israeli intervention
      Sinai Campaign, 1956
  RT **Jewish-Arab relations**
Israel-Arab relations
  USE **Arab countries—Foreign relations—Israel**
      Israel—Foreign relations—Arab countries
Israel-Arab War, 1948-1949 **956.04**
  UF Arab-Israel War, 1948-1949
  BT **Israel-Arab conflicts**
Israel-Arab War, 1956
  USE **Sinai Campaign, 1956**
Israel-Arab War, 1967 **956.04**
  UF Arab-Israel War, 1967
      Six Day War, 1967
  BT **Israel-Arab conflicts**
Israel-Arab War, 1973 **956.04**
  UF Arab-Israel War, 1973
      Yom Kippur War, 1973
  BT **Israel-Arab conflicts**
Israel—Collective settlements
  USE **Collective settlements—Israel**
Israel—Foreign relations—Arab countries **956**
  UF Arab-Israel relations
      Arab-Israeli relations
      Israel-Arab relations
      Israeli-Arab relations
  NT **Israel-Arab conflicts**
  RT **Arab countries—Foreign relations—Israel**

Israel—Foreign relations—Arab countries—*Continued*
>   **Jewish-Arab relations**

Israeli-Arab conflict, 1987-
>   USE   **Intifada, 1987-**

Israeli-Arab conflicts
>   USE   **Israel-Arab conflicts**

Israeli-Arab relations
>   USE   **Arab countries—Foreign relations—Israel**
>   **Israel—Foreign relations—Arab countries**

Israeli intervention in Lebanon, 1982-1984
>   USE   **Lebanon—History—1982-1984, Israeli intervention**

Israelis (May subdiv. geog.)   **305.892; 920; 956.94**
>   BT   **Jews**

Israelites
>   USE   **Jews**

ISSN
>   USE   **International Standard Serial Numbers**

Italo-Ethiopian War, 1935-1936   963
>   UF   Ethiopian-Italian War, 1935-1936

Italy   945
>   May be subdivided like United States except for *History.*

Italy—History   945

Italy—History—0-1559   945

Italy—History—1559-1789   945

Italy—History—1789-1815   945

Italy—History—1815-1914   945; 945.09

Italy—History—1914-1945   945.091

Italy—History—1945-1976   945.092

Italy—History—1976-   945.092

Ivory   679
>   BT   **Animal products**

Jails
>   USE   **Prisons**

Japan   952
>   May be subdivided like United States except for *History.*

Japan—Commerce—United States   382

Japan—History   952

Japan—History—0-1868   952

Japan—History—1868-1945   952.03

Japan—History—1945-1952, Allied occupation   952.04

Japan—History—1952-   952.04

Japanese aesthetics   111; 701; 801
>   UF   Aesthetics, Japanese
>   BT   **Aesthetics**

Japanese color prints   769.952
>   UF   Color prints, Japanese
>   BT   **Color prints**

Japanese language   495.6
>   May be subdivided like **English language.**
>   BT   **Language and languages**

Japanese language—Business Japanese   495.6
>   *Business Japanese* is a unique subdivision for **Japanese language.**
>   UF   Business Japanese

Japanese paper folding
>   USE   **Origami**

Jargon
>   USE   subjects and names of languages with the subdivision *Jargon,* e.g. **English language—Jargon** [to be added as needed]

Jazz ensembles   784.4
>   BT   **Ensembles (Music)**

Jazz music (May subdiv. geog.)   **781.65; 782.42165**
>   BT   **Music**
>   RT   **Blues music**

Jestbooks
>   USE   **Chapbooks**

Jesters
>   USE   **Fools and jesters**

Jesus Christ   232
>   UF   Christ
>   Christology
>   BT   **God—Christianity**
>   NT   **Atonement—Christianity**
>   **Second Advent**
>   RT   **Christianity**

Jesus Christ—Art   704.9
>   UF   Jesus Christ—Iconography
>   Jesus Christ in art
>   BT   **Christian art**
>   RT   **Bible—Pictorial works**

Jesus Christ—Atonement
>   USE   **Atonement—Christianity**

Jesus Christ—Birth
>   USE   **Jesus Christ—Nativity**

Jesus Christ—Crucifixion   232.96
>   UF   Crucifixion of Jesus Christ
>   RT   **Good Friday**

Jesus Christ—Divinity   232
  UF   Divinity of Jesus Christ
  RT   **Trinity**
Jesus Christ—Drama   808.82; 812, etc.
  Use for collections of plays about Jesus
  Christ.
  BT   **Religious drama**
  NT   **Passion plays**
Jesus Christ—Historicity   232.9
Jesus Christ—Iconography
  USE   **Jesus Christ—Art**
Jesus Christ in art
  USE   **Jesus Christ—Art**
Jesus Christ—Last Supper
  USE   **Last Supper**
Jesus Christ—Messiahship   232
Jesus Christ—Nativity   232.92
  UF   Jesus Christ—Birth
       Nativity of Jesus Christ
  RT   **Christmas**
Jesus Christ—Parables   226.8; 232.9
  BT   **Bible—Parables**
       Parables
Jesus Christ—Prayers   232.9
  NT   **Lord's prayer**
Jesus Christ—Prophecies   232
  BT   **Bible—Prophecies**
Jesus Christ—Resurrection   232.9
  UF   Resurrection of Jesus Christ
Jesus Christ—Second Advent
  USE   **Second Advent**
Jesus Christ—Sermon on the mount
  USE   **Sermon on the mount**
Jesus Christ—Teachings   232.9
  UF   Teachings of Jesus Christ
Jet airplanes
  USE   **Jet planes**
Jet lag   616.9
  BT   **Aviation medicine**
       Biological rhythms
       Fatigue
Jet planes   629.133
  UF   Jet airplanes
       Jets (Airplanes)
  BT   **Airplanes**
  NT   **Supersonic transport planes**
Jet propulsion   621.43
  BT   **Airplane engines**
  RT   **Rockets (Aeronautics)**
Jets (Airplanes)
  USE   **Jet planes**

Jewelry (May subdiv. geog.)   **391.7;
       739.27**
  Use for general materials on jewelry and
  for materials on gems in which the emphasis
  is on the setting. Materials on cut and pol-
  ished precious stones treated from the point of
  view of art or antiquity are entered under
  Gems. Materials on gem stones treated from
  the mineralogical or technological point of
  view are entered under **Precious stones.**
  UF   Jewels
  SA   styles of jewelry and types of
       jewelry items [to be added as
       needed]
  BT   **Clothing and dress**
       Costume
       Decorative arts
  RT   **Gems**
Jewels
  USE   **Gems**
       Jewelry
       Precious stones
Jewish-Arab relations   956
  Use for materials that discuss collectively
  the relations between Arabs and Jews, includ-
  ing religious, ethnic, and ideological relations.
  Materials on the conflicts between the Arab
  countries and Israel are entered under **Israel-
  Arab conflicts.** Materials on relations be-
  tween the religions of Judaism and Islam are
  entered under **Judaism—Relations—Islam;**
  and **Islam—Relations—Judaism.**
  UF   Arab-Jewish relations
  BT   **Arabs**
       Judaism
  RT   **Arab countries—Foreign rela-
       tions—Israel**
       Islam—Relations—Judaism
       Israel-Arab conflicts
       **Israel—Foreign relations—
       Arab countries**
       Judaism—Relations—Islam
       Palestinian Arabs
Jewish-Christian relations
  USE   **Christianity—Relations—Juda-
       ism**
       **Judaism—Relations—Christian-
       ity**
Jewish civilization   909
  UF   Jews—Civilization
  BT   **Civilization**
Jewish customs
  USE   **Jews—Social life and customs**
       **Judaism—Customs and prac-
       tices**

Jewish doctrines
USE **Judaism—Doctrines**
Jewish ethics 296.3
BT **Ethics**
Jewish folklore
USE **Jews—Folklore**
Jewish holidays 296.4; 394.267
UF Fasts and feasts—Judaism
Holidays, Jewish
Jews—Festivals
SA names of individual holidays,
e.g. **Hanukkah** [to be added
as needed]
BT **Judaism**
Religious holidays
NT **Hanukkah**
Passover
Yom Kippur
Jewish Holocaust (1933-1945)
USE **Holocaust, 1933-1945**
Jewish-Islamic relations
USE **Islam—Relations—Judaism**
Judaism—Relations—Islam
Jewish language
USE **Hebrew language**
Yiddish language
Jewish legends 296.1; 398.2
May be used for individual works, collec-
tions, or materials about Jewish legends.
UF Jews—Legends
Legends, Jewish
BT **Legends**
Jewish life
USE **Jews—Social life and customs**
**Judaism—Customs and prac-
tices**
Jewish literature 296; 808.8
UF Jews—Literature
BT **Literature**
Religious literature
NT **Bible**
Cabala
Jewish religious fiction
Talmud
Yiddish literature
RT **Hebrew literature**
Jewish liturgies
USE **Judaism—Liturgy**
Jewish religion
USE **Judaism**

**Jewish religious fiction 808.83; 813,
etc.**
Use for individual works, collections, or
materials about fiction that promotes Jewish
teachings or exemplifies a Jewish religious
way of life.
BT **Fiction**
Jewish literature
Religious fiction
Jewish theology
USE **Judaism—Doctrines**
Jews (May subdiv. geog.) **296.092;
305.892; 909**
UF Hebrews
Israelites
NT **Israelis**
World War, 1939-1945—Jews
RT **Judaism**
Jews—Antiquities 933
BT **Antiquities**
Jews—Civilization
USE **Jewish civilization**
Jews—Customs
USE **Jews—Social life and customs**
**Judaism—Customs and prac-
tices**
**Jews—Economic conditions 305.892;
330.9**
BT **Economic conditions**
Jews—Encyclopedias 909
BT **Encyclopedias and dictionaries**
Jews—Festivals
USE **Jewish holidays**
Jews—Folklore 398
UF Jewish folklore
BT **Folklore**
Jews—Language
USE **Hebrew language**
Yiddish language
Jews—Legends
USE **Jewish legends**
Jews—Literature
USE **Hebrew literature**
Jewish literature
Jews—Persecutions (May subdiv. geog.)
909; 933
BT **Antisemitism**
Persecution
NT **Holocaust, 1933-1945**
**World War, 1939-1945—
Jews—Rescue**

Jews—Political activity   909; 956.94
    BT   Political participation
Jews—Religion
    USE   Judaism
Jews—Restoration   956.94
    Use for materials on the belief that the
    Jews, in fulfillment of Biblical prophecy,
    would some day return to Palestine.
    RT   Zionism
Jews—Rites and ceremonies
    USE   Judaism—Customs and prac-
            tices
Jews—Ritual
    USE   Judaism—Customs and prac-
            tices
          Judaism—Liturgy
Jews—Social conditions   305.892; 909
    BT   Social conditions
Jews—Social life and customs   305.892
    Use for materials on Jewish social customs.
    General materials on Jewish religious prac-
    tices are entered under Judaism—Customs
    and practices. Materials on the forms of pub-
    lic worship in Judaism are entered under Ju-
    daism—Liturgy.
    UF   Jewish customs
          Jewish life
          Jews—Customs
    BT   Manners and customs
Job analysis   658.3
    UF   Personnel classification
    BT   Factory management
          Industrial efficiency
          Management
          Occupations
          Personnel management
          Salaries, wages, etc.
    NT   Motion study
          Time study
Job applications
    USE   Applications for positions
Job discrimination
    USE   Discrimination in employment
Job hunting   650.14
    UF   Job searching
    SA   fields of knowledge, professions,
          industries, and trades with the
          subdivision Vocational guid-
          ance [to be added as needed]
    BT   Employment agencies
          Vocational guidance
    NT   Applications for positions
          Résumés (Employment)

Job performance standards
    USE   Performance standards
Job placement guidance
    USE   Vocational guidance
Job résumés
    USE   Résumés (Employment)
Job retraining
    USE   Occupational retraining
Job satisfaction   650.1; 658.3
    UF   Work satisfaction
    BT   Attitude (Psychology)
          Employee morale
          Personnel management
          Work
    NT   Burn out (Psychology)
Job searching
    USE   Job hunting
Job security   331.25; 650.1; 658.3
    UF   Employment security
    BT   Personnel management
    NT   Employees—Dismissal
Job sharing   331.2; 658.3
    UF   Sharing of jobs
    BT   Part-time employment
Job stress   158.7; 658.3
    UF   Occupational stress
          Organizational stress
          Work stress
    BT   Stress (Physiology)
          Stress (Psychology)
    NT   Burn out (Psychology)
Job training
    USE   Occupational training
Jobless people
    USE   Unemployed
Joblessness
    USE   Unemployment
Jobs
    USE   Occupations
          Professions
Jogging   613.7
    BT   Running
Joint custody of children
    USE   Child custody
          Part-time parenting
Joke books
    USE   Jokes
Jokes   808.7; 808.88; 818, etc.
    May be used for collections of jokes and
    for materials about jokes.

Jokes—*Continued*
- UF Joke books
- BT **Wit and humor**
- NT **Practical jokes**

Journalism (May subdiv. geog.)   **070.4**

Use for materials on writing for the periodical press or on journalism as an occupation. Materials limited to the history, organization, and management of newspapers are entered under **Newspapers.**
- SA types of journalism, e.g. **Scientific journalism;** and topics with the subdivision *Press coverage,* e.g. **Food contamination—Press coverage** [to be added as needed]
- BT **Authorship**
  Literature
- NT **Broadcast journalism**
  College and school journalism
  Gossip
  Libel and slander
  Photojournalism
  Press
  Reporters and reporting
  Scientific journalism
- RT **Journalists**
  Newspapers
  Periodicals

Journalism—Editing   **070.4**
- UF Magazine editing
  News editing
  Newspapers—Editing
  Periodicals—Editing
- BT **Editing**

Journalism—Objectivity   **070.4**
- UF Slanted journalism
- BT **Professional ethics**

Journalism, Scientific
- USE **Scientific journalism**

Journalistic photography
- USE **Photojournalism**

Journalists (May subdiv. geog.)   **070.92; 920**
- UF Columnists
- SA names of wars with the subdivision *Journalists,* e.g. **World War, 1939-1945—Journalists** [to be added as needed]
- BT **Authors**
- NT **World War, 1939-1945—Journalists**
- RT **Journalism**

Journals
- USE **Periodicals**

Journals (Diaries)
- USE **Diaries**

Journeys
- USE **Travel**
  Voyages and travels

Joy and sorrow   **152.4**
- UF Affliction
  Sorrow
- BT **Emotions**
- NT **Pleasure**
- RT **Grief**
  Happiness
  Suffering

Judaism (May subdiv. geog.)   **296**
- UF Jewish religion
  Jews—Religion
- SA names of Jewish sects, e.g. **Hasidism** [to be added as needed]
- BT **Religions**
- NT **Atonement—Judaism**
  Cabala
  Christianity—Relations—Judaism
  Hasidism
  Islam—Relations—Judaism
  Jewish-Arab relations
  Jewish holidays
  Judaism—Relations—Christianity
  Judaism—Relations—Islam
  Rabbis
  Sabbath
  Talmud
- RT **Jews**
  Synagogues

Judaism—Customs and practices   **296.4**

Use for materials on Jewish religious practices in general. Materials on the forms of public worship in Judaism are entered under **Judaism—Liturgy.** Materials on Jewish social customs are entered under **Jews—Social life and customs.**
- UF Jewish customs
  Jewish life
  Jews—Customs
  Jews—Rites and ceremonies
  Jews—Ritual
- BT **Rites and ceremonies**
- RT **Judaism—Liturgy**

Judaism—Doctrines 296.3
   UF   Jewish doctrines
         Jewish theology
   BT   **Doctrinal theology**
Judaism—Liturgy 296.4
   Use for materials on the forms of public worship in Judaism. Materials on Jewish religious practices in general are entered under **Judaism—Customs and practices**. Materials on Jewish social customs are entered under **Jews—Social life and customs.**
   UF   Jewish liturgies
         Jews—Ritual
   BT   **Liturgies**
   RT   **Judaism—Customs and practices**
Judaism—Relations—Christianity 261.2; 296.3
   Use for materials on the relations between Judaism and Christianity. When assigning this heading, provide an additional subject entry under **Christianity—Relations—Judaism.**
   UF   Christian-Jewish relations
         Christianity and other religions—Judaism
         Jewish-Christian relations
   BT   **Christianity and other religions**
         Judaism
Judaism—Relations—Islam 296.3
   Use for materials on the relations between Judaism and Islam. When assigning this heading, provide an additional subject entry under **Islam—Relations—Judaism.** Materials on the conflicts between the Arab countries and Israel are entered under **Israel-Arab conflicts.** Materials that discuss collectively the relations between Arabs and Jews, including religious, ethnic, and ideological relations, are entered under **Jewish-Arab relations.**
   UF   Islamic-Jewish relations
         Jewish-Islamic relations
   BT   **Islam**
         Judaism
   RT   **Jewish-Arab relations**
Judges (May subdiv. geog.) **347; 920**
   UF   Chief justices
   BT   **Lawyers**
   NT   **Women judges**
   RT   **Courts**
Judicial investigations
   USE   **Governmental investigations**
Judiciary
   USE   **Courts**
Judo 796.815
   BT   **Physical education**
         Self-defense

         Wrestling
   NT   **Karate**
Juggling 793.8
   UF   Legerdemain
         Sleight of hand
   BT   **Amusements**
         Tricks
July Fourth
   USE   **Fourth of July**
Jungle animals (May subdiv. geog.) **578.734**
   UF   Jungle fauna
   BT   **Animals**
         Forest animals
Jungle fauna
   USE   **Jungle animals**
Jungles (May subdiv. geog.) **634.9**
   Use for materials on impenetrable thickets of second-growth vegetation replacing tropical rain forests that have been disturbed or degraded. Materials on forests of broad-leaved, mainly evergreen trees found in moist climates in the tropics, subtropics, and some parts of the temperate zones, are entered under **Rain forests.**
   UF   Tropical jungles
   BT   **Forests and forestry**
   RT   **Rain forests**
Junior colleges (May subdiv. geog.) **378.1**
   UF   Community colleges
         Two-year colleges
   BT   **Colleges and universities**
         Higher education
Junior colleges—Directories 378.1
   BT   **Directories**
Junior high school libraries
   USE   **High school libraries**
Junior high schools (May subdiv. geog.) **373.236**
   UF   Secondary schools
   BT   **High schools**
         Public schools
         Schools
   RT   **Middle schools**
         Secondary education
Junk
   USE   **Waste products**
Junk bonds 332.63
   UF   High-yield junk bonds
   BT   **Bonds**
Junk in space
   USE   **Space debris**

Jurisprudence
USE **Law**
Jurisprudence, Medical
USE **Medical jurisprudence**
Jurists
USE **Lawyers**
Jury   345; 347
UF   Trial by jury
BT   **Courts**
      Criminal law
Justice   340
BT   **Ethics**
      Law
      Virtue
Justice, Administration of
USE   **Administration of justice**
Juvenile courts (May subdiv. geog.)   **345**
UF   Children's courts
BT   **Courts**
RT   **Juvenile delinquency**
      Probation
Juvenile delinquency (May subdiv. geog.)
      364.3
UF   Delinquency, Juvenile
      Juvenile delinquents
BT   **Crime**
      Social problems
NT   **Gangs**
      Juvenile prostitution
      School violence
RT   **Child welfare**
      Emotionally disturbed children
      Juvenile courts
      Reformatories
      Teenagers—Drug use
      Youth—Drug use
Juvenile delinquency—Case studies
      364.3
Juvenile delinquents
USE   **Juvenile delinquency**
Juvenile drama
USE   subjects and names with the
       subdivision *Juvenile drama,*
       e.g. **Christmas—Juvenile**
       drama [to be added as need-
       ed]
Juvenile fiction
USE   subjects and names with the
       subdivision *Juvenile fiction,*
       e.g. **Christmas—Juvenile fic-**
       tion [to be added as needed]

Juvenile literature
USE   **Children's literature**
       and subjects and names with
       the subdivision *Juvenile liter-*
       ature, e.g. **Computers—Juve-**
       nile literature [to be added
       as needed]
Juvenile poetry
USE   subjects and names with the
       subdivision *Juvenile poetry,*
       e.g. **Christmas—Juvenile po-**
       etry [to be added as needed]
Juvenile prostitution (May subdiv. geog.)
       176; 306.74; 362.7; 363.4;
       364.1
UF   Adolescent prostitution
      Child prostitution
      Teenage prostitution
BT   **Juvenile delinquency**
      Prostitution
Kabbala
USE   **Cabala**
Karate   796.815
BT   **Judo**
      Self-defense
Kart racing
USE   **Karts and karting**
Karting
USE   **Karts and karting**
Karts and karting   796.7
UF   Carts (Midget cars)
      Go-karts
      Kart racing
      Karting
      Karts (Midget cars)
      Midget cars
BT   **Automobile racing**
Karts (Midget cars)
USE   **Karts and karting**
Keyboarding (Electronics)   004.7; 652.5
UF   Computer keyboarding
      Data processing—Keyboarding
      Word processor keyboarding
BT   **Business education**
      Office practice
RT   **Typewriting**
Keyboards (Electronics)   004.7
UF   Computer keyboards
BT   **Computer peripherals**
      Office equipment and supplies

Keyboards (Musical instruments) 786
    BT   Organs (Musical instruments)
         Pianos
Keys
    USE Locks and keys
Kibbutz
    USE Collective settlements—Israel
Kidnapping (May subdiv. geog.) 364.15
    UF   Abduction
    BT   Criminal law
         Offenses against the person
Kidnapping, Parental
    USE Parental kidnapping
Kindergarten (May subdiv. geog.)
         372.21
    BT   Elementary education
         Schools
    NT   Creative activities
         Montessori method of educa-
         tion
    RT   Nursery schools
         Preschool education
Kinematics 531
    BT   Dynamics
    NT   Mechanical movements
    RT   Mechanics
         Motion
Kinesiology 613.7
    UF   Cinesiology
    BT   Human locomotion
         Physical fitness
Kinetic art (May subdiv. geog.) 709.04
    UF   Art in motion
         Art, Kinetic
    BT   Art
    NT   Kinetic sculpture
Kinetic sculpture 731; 735
    UF   Sculpture in motion
    BT   Kinetic art
         Sculpture
    NT   Mobiles (Sculpture)
Kinetics
    USE Dynamics
         Motion
King Philip's War, 1675-1676 973.2
    UF   United States—History—1675-
         1676, King Philip's War
    BT   Native Americans—Wars
         United States—History—1600-
         1775, Colonial period

King William's War, 1689-1697
    USE United States—History—1689-
         1697, King William's War
Kings and rulers 920; 929.7
    Use for materials on monarchs and other
heads of state not democratically elected.
    UF   Kings, queens, rulers, etc.
         Monarchs
         Royal houses
         Royalty
         Rulers
         Sovereigns
    SA   names of places with the subdi-
         vision *Kings and rulers,* e.g.
         Great Britain—Kings and
         rulers; and names of individ-
         ual monarchs or rulers [to be
         added as needed]
    BT   Heads of state
    NT   Emperors
         Great Britain—Kings and rul-
         ers
    RT   Courts and courtiers
         Monarchy
         Queens
Kings, queens, rulers, etc.
    USE Kings and rulers
Kinship (May subdiv. geog.) 306.83
    SA   ethnic groups with the subdivi-
         sion *Kinship* [to be added as
         needed]
    BT   Ethnology
         Family
    RT   Clans
Kitchen gardens
    USE Vegetable gardening
Kitchen remodeling
    USE Kitchens—Remodeling
Kitchen renovation
    USE Kitchens—Remodeling
Kitchen utensils 643; 683
    UF   Cooking utensils
         Household utensils
         Kitchenware
         Utensils, Kitchen
    SA   types of kitchen utensils, e.g.
         Bread machines [to be added
         as needed]
    BT   Household equipment and sup-
         plies
    NT   Bread machines

Kitchens 643
  BT Houses
      Rooms
Kitchens—Remodeling 643
  UF Kitchen remodeling
      Kitchen renovation
      Remodeling of kitchens
Kitchenware
  USE Kitchen utensils
Kites 629.133; 796.1
  BT Aeronautics
Kittens
  USE Cats
Knighthood
  USE Knights and knighthood
Knights and knighthood (May subdiv.
      geog.) 394; 940.1
  UF Knighthood
  BT Middle Ages
      Nobility
  RT Chivalry
      Heraldry
Knights of the Round Table
  USE Arthurian romances
Knitting 677; 746.43
  BT Needlework
Knots and splices 623.88
  UF Splicing
  BT Navigation
      Rope
Knowledge
  USE names of individual persons with
       the subdivision *Knowledge,*
       e.g. **Shakespeare, William,
       1564-1616—Knowledge;**
       which may be further subdi-
       vided by the subject known,
       e.g. **Shakespeare, William,
       1564-1616—Knowledge—Ani-
       mals** [to be added as needed]
Knowledge-based systems (Computer sci-
      ence)
  USE **Expert systems (Computer sci-
       ence)**
Knowledge management (May subdiv.
      geog.) 658.4
  UF Management of knowledge as-
       sets
  BT Management
  RT Information technology

Knowledge, Theory of
  USE Theory of knowledge
Kodak camera 771.3
  BT Cameras
Koran 297.1
  UF Qur'an
  BT Islam
      Sacred books
Korea 951.9
      Use for comprehensive materials on all of
  Korea and for materials on Korea before it
  was divided in 1948 into two separate repub-
  lics.
  NT Korea (North)
      Korea (South)
Korea (Democratic People's Republic)
  USE Korea (North)
Korea (North) 951.93
      Use for materials on the Democratic Peo-
  ple's Republic of Korea, established in 1948.
  May be subdivided like United States except
  for *History.*
  UF Korea (Democratic People's Re-
       public)
      North Korea
  BT Korea
Korea (Republic)
  USE Korea (South)
Korea (South) 951.95
      Use for materials on the Republic of Korea,
  established in 1948. May be subdivided like
  United States except for *History.*
  UF Korea (Republic)
      South Korea
  BT Korea
Korean War, 1950-1953 951.904
Ku Klux Klan 322.4
  UF Ku-Klux Klan (1866-1869)
      Ku Klux Klan (1915-)
  BT Secret societies
  RT Reconstruction (1865-1876)
Ku-Klux Klan (1866-1869)
  USE Ku Klux Klan
Ku Klux Klan (1915-)
  USE Ku Klux Klan
Labeling
  USE subjects with the subdivision *La-
       beling,* e.g. **Food—Labeling**
       [to be added as needed]
Labor (May subdiv. geog.) 331
      Use for materials on the collective human
  activities involved in the production and dis-
  tribution of goods and services in an econo-
  my, especially activities performed by workers

Labor—*Continued*

for wages as distinguished from those performed by entrepreneurs for profits. Also use for general materials on workers. Materials on laborers as a social class are entered under **Working class.** Materials on the physical or mental exertion of individuals to produce or accomplish something are entered under **Work.**

UF Blue collar workers

      Factory workers

      Industrial workers

      Labor and laboring classes

      Laborers

      Manual workers

      Workers

SA types of laborers, e.g. **Agricultural laborers; Miners;** etc. [to be added as needed]

BT **Economics**

      Social conditions

      Sociology

NT **Agricultural laborers**

      Apprentices

      Capitalism

      Child labor

      Church and labor

      Collective bargaining

      Contract labor

      Employees

      Employment

      Employment agencies

      Forced labor

      Hours of labor

      Household employees

      Industrial arbitration

      Industrial relations

      Industrial welfare

      Labor supply

      Labor unions

      Libraries and labor

      Migrant labor

      Miners

      Open and closed shop

      Part-time employment

      Peasantry

      Proletariat

      Skilled labor

      Supplementary employment

      Unskilled labor

RT **Labor movement**

      Work

      Working class

Labor absenteeism

    USE **Absenteeism (Labor)**

Labor—Accidents

    USE **Industrial accidents**

Labor and capital

    USE **Industrial relations**

Labor and laboring classes

    USE **Labor**

            Labor movement

            Working class

Labor and libraries

    USE **Libraries and labor**

Labor and state

    USE **Labor policy**

Labor and the church

    USE **Church and labor**

Labor arbitration

    USE **Industrial arbitration**

Labor (Childbirth)

    USE **Childbirth**

Labor contract (May subdiv. geog.)

        331.1; 331.89

Use for materials on agreements between employer and employee in which the latter agrees to perform work in return for compensation from the former.

    UF Collective labor agreements

         Trade agreements (Labor)

    BT **Contracts**

         Industrial relations

    NT **Open and closed shop**

    RT **Collective bargaining**

Labor courts

    USE **Industrial arbitration**

Labor disputes (May subdiv. geog.)

        331.89

    UF Industrial disputes

    BT **Industrial relations**

    NT **Collective bargaining**

         Industrial arbitration

         Strikes

Labor—Education (May subdiv. geog.)

        331.25

    UF Education of workers

    BT **Education**

Labor force

    USE **Labor supply**

Labor—Government policy

    USE **Labor policy**

Labor—Housing (May subdiv. geog.)

        363.5

    BT **Housing**

Labor—Insurance
USE **Unemployment insurance**
Labor-management relations
USE **Industrial relations**
Labor market
USE **Labor supply**
Labor movement (May subdiv. geog.)
331.8
Use for materials on the efforts of organizations and individuals to improve conditions for labor.
UF Labor and laboring classes
BT **Social movements**
RT **Labor**
Labor unions
Labor negotiations
USE **Collective bargaining**
Industrial arbitration
Labor organizations
USE **Labor unions**
Labor output
USE **Labor productivity**
Labor participation in management
USE **Participative management**
Labor policy (May subdiv. geog.) **331**
UF Government policy
Labor and state
Labor—Government policy
Manpower policy
BT **Economic policy**
Labor productivity (May subdiv. geog.)
331.11
UF Labor output
Productivity of labor
SA types of industries, occupations, and processes with the subdivision *Labor productivity,* e.g. **Steel industry—Labor productivity** [to be added as needed]
BT **Industrial efficiency**
NT **Production standards**
Steel industry—Labor productivity
Labor relations
USE **Industrial relations**
Labor saving devices, Household
USE **Electric household appliances**
Household equipment and supplies

Labor supply (May subdiv. geog.)
331.11
UF Labor force
Labor market
BT **Economic conditions**
Employment
Labor
NT **Occupational retraining**
Unemployed
Unemployment
RT **Employment agencies**
Employment forecasting
Human capital
Manpower
Labor turnover 331.12
BT **Personnel management**
NT **Employment agencies**
Labor unions (May subdiv. geog.)
331.88
UF Labor organizations
Organized labor
Trade-unions
Unions, Labor
SA types of unions and names of individual labor unions [to be added as needed]
BT **Industrial relations**
Labor
Societies
NT **Industrial arbitration**
Injunctions
Librarians' unions
Open and closed shop
United Steelworkers of America
RT **Collective bargaining**
Labor movement
Strikes
Labor unions—United States
331.880973
Labor—United States 331.0973
Laboratory animal experimentation
USE **Animal experimentation**
Laboratory animal welfare
USE **Animal welfare**
Laboratory fertilization
USE **Fertilization in vitro**
Laboratory manuals
USE scientific and technical subjects with the subdivision *Laboratory manuals,* e.g. **Chemis-**

Laboratory manuals—*Continued*
>   try—**Laboratory manuals** [to
>   be added as needed]

Laborers
    USE   **Labor**
>   **Working class**
>   and types of laborers, e.g. **Ag-
>   ricultural laborers; Miners;**
>   etc. [to be added as needed]

Laboring class
    USE   **Working class**

Laboring classes
    USE   **Working class**

Lace and lace making (May subdiv.
>   geog.)   **677; 746.2**
    BT   **Crocheting**
>   **Needlework**
>   **Weaving**

Lacquer and lacquering (May subdiv.
>   geog.)   **667; 745.7**
    BT   **Decorative arts**
>   **Finishes and finishing**

Laissez-faire
    USE   **Free enterprise**

Laity   262
>   May be subdivided by religion or sect.
    UF   Laymen
    BT   **Church**
    RT   **Lay ministry**

Laity—Catholic Church   262
    UF   Catholic laity
    BT   **Catholic Church**

Lakes (May subdiv. geog.)   **551.48**
    SA   names of lakes [to be added as
>   needed]
    BT   **Physical geography**
>   **Water**
>   **Waterways**
    RT   **Inland navigation**

Lakes—United States   551.48

Lamaze method of childbirth
    USE   **Natural childbirth**

Lambs
    USE   **Sheep**

Lamentations
    USE   **Elegiac poetry**

Lamps   621.32; 749
    BT   **Lighting**
    NT   **Electric lamps**

Land
    USE   **Land use**
>   **Landforms**

Land drainage
    USE   **Drainage**

Land forms
    USE   **Landforms**

Land mines (May subdiv. geog.)   **355.8;
>   623.4**
    BT   **Explosives**
>   **Ordnance**

Land question
    USE   **Land tenure**

Land, Reclamation of
    USE   **Reclamation of land**

Land reform (May subdiv. geog.)   **333.3**
    UF   Agrarian reform
>   Reform, Agrarian
    BT   **Economic policy**
>   **Land use**
>   **Social policy**
    NT   **Land tenure**
    RT   **Agriculture—Government poli-
>   cy**

Land settlement (May subdiv. geog.)
>   **304.8; 325**
    UF   Resettlement
>   Settlement of land
    BT   **Colonies**
>   **Land use**
    NT   **Colonization**
    RT   **Internal migration**

**Land settlement—United States   304.8;
>   325.73**
    UF   United States—Land settlement
>   Westward movement

Land surveying
    USE   **Surveying**

Land surveys
    USE   **Surveying**

Land tenure (May subdiv. geog.)   **333.3**
>   Use for general and historical materials on
>   systems of holding land. Materials on the le-
>   gal relationships between landlord and tenant
>   are entered under **Landlord and tenant.**
    UF   Agrarian question
>   Fiefs
>   Land question
>   Tenure of land
    BT   **Agriculture—Economic aspects**
>   **Land reform**
>   **Land use**
    NT   **Farm tenancy**
>   **Feudalism**
>   **Landlord and tenant**

Land tenure—*Continued*
  RT **Peasantry**
       Real estate
Land use (May subdiv. geog.) **333.73**
    Use for general materials that cover such topics as types of land; the utilization, distribution, and development of land; and the economic factors affecting the value of land. Materials dealing only with ownership of land are entered under **Real estate.**
  UF Land
  BT **Economics**
  NT **Eminent domain**
       Farms
       Grasslands
       Land reform
       Land settlement
       Land tenure
       Landfills
       Pastures
       Public lands
       Real estate
       Reclamation of land
       Regional planning
Landfills (May subdiv. geog.) **363.72; 628.3; 628.4**
    Use for materials on places for waste disposal in which waste is buried in layers of earth in low ground.
  UF Earth fills
       Fills (Earthwork)
       Sanitary landfills
  SA names of landfills [to be added as needed]
  BT **Land use**
  NT **Hazardous waste sites**
       Love Canal Chemical Waste Landfill (Niagara Falls, N.Y.)
Landforms (May subdiv. geog.) **551.41**
  UF Land
       Land forms
  SA types of landforms, e.g. **Mountains; Coasts;** etc. [to be added as needed]
  BT **Earth—Surface**
       Geology
  NT **Coasts**
       Mountains
       Seashore
       Wetlands

Landlord and tenant (May subdiv. geog.) **333.5; 346.04**
    Use for materials on the legal relationships between landlord and tenant. General and historical materials on systems of holding land are entered under **Land tenure.**
  UF Tenant and landlord
  BT **Commercial law**
       Land tenure
       Real estate
  NT **Apartment houses**
       Housing
  RT **Farm tenancy**
Landmarks, Literary
  USE **Literary landmarks**
Landmarks, Preservation of
  USE **National monuments**
        Natural monuments
Landscape architecture (May subdiv. geog.) **712**
    Use for materials on modifying or arranging the features of a landscape, urban area, etc., for aesthetic or pragmatic purposes.
  UF Landscape design
  BT **Architecture**
  NT **Garden ornaments and furniture**
       Parks
       Patios
       Roadside improvement
  RT **Landscape gardening**
       Landscape protection
Landscape design
  USE **Landscape architecture**
Landscape drawing **743**
  BT **Drawing**
  RT **Landscape painting**
Landscape gardening (May subdiv. geog.) **712**
    Use for materials on the design or rearrangement of extensive gardens or estates.
  UF Planting
  BT **Gardening**
       Horticulture
  NT **Evergreens**
       Lawns
       Ornamental plants
  RT **Garden design**
       Landscape architecture
       Shrubs
       Trees

Landscape painting 758
  BT **Painting**
  RT **Landscape drawing**
Landscape protection (May subdiv. geog.)
      333.73
  UF Beautification of landscape
      Natural beauty conservation
      Preservation of natural scenery
      Protection of natural scenery
      Scenery
  BT **Environmental protection**
      Nature conservation
  NT **Natural monuments**
  RT **Landscape architecture**
      Regional planning
Landscape sculpture
  USE **Earthworks (Art)**
Language
  USE **Language and languages**
      and disciplines, classes of persons, types of newspapers, and names of individual persons, corporate bodies, and literary works entered under title with the subdivision *Language,* e.g. **Technology—Language; Children—Language;** etc. [to be added as needed]

Language and languages 400
  Use for general materials on the history, philosophy, origin, etc., of language. Materials on the scientific study of speech and comparative studies of language are entered under **Linguistics.**
  UF Language
      Languages
      Philology
  SA names of languages or groups of languages, e.g. **English language; Scandinavian languages; Native American languages;** etc.; disciplines, classes of persons, types of newspapers, and names of individual persons, corporate bodies, and literary works entered under title with the subdivison *Language,* e.g. **Technology—Language; Children—Language;** etc.; and names countries, cities, etc., with the subdivison *Languages,* for materials on the several languages spoken in a place, e.g. **United States—Languages;** etc. [to be added as needed]
  BT **Anthropology**
      Communication
      Ethnology
  NT **Bilingualism**
      Children—Language
      Conversation
      Danish language
      English language
      French language
      German language
      Grammar
      Greek language
      Hebrew language
      Icelandic language
      Japanese language
      Latin language
      Linguistics
      Modern Greek language
      Modern languages
      Native American languages
      Norwegian language
      Old Norse language
      Phonetics
      Programming languages
      Rhetoric
      Romance languages
      Russian language
      Scandinavian languages
      Semantics
      Sign language
      Sociolinguistics
      Spanish language
      Swedish language
      Translating and interpreting
      Universal language
      Verbal learning
      Vocabulary
      Voice
      Writing
      Yiddish language
  RT **Speech**

Language and languages—Business language
  USE   names of languages with unique language subdivisions, e.g. **English language—Business English; Japanese language—Business Japanese;** etc. [to be added as needed]
Language and languages—Comparative philology
  USE   **Linguistics**
Language and languages—Etymology 412
  UF   Etymology
        Word histories
  SA   names of languages with the subdivision *Etymology,* e.g. **English language—Etymology** [to be added as needed]
Language and languages—Political aspects   400
  Use for general materials on the political aspects of languages.
  SA   names of countries, cities, etc., with the subdivision *Languages,* e.g. **United States—Languages;** or with the two subdivisions *Languages—Political aspects;* and names of individual languages and groups of languages with the subdivision *Political aspects* [to be added as needed]
Language and society
  USE   **Sociolinguistics**
Language arts   372.6; 400
  Use for materials on language and literature considered comprehensively as a school subject at the elementary level.
  UF   Communication arts
  BT   **Communication**
  NT   **Creative writing**
        Literature
        Reading
        Speech
        Whole language
        Writing
Language arts (Holistic)
  USE   **Whole language**
Language arts—Patterning   372.6
  UF   Patterns (Language arts)
        Reading—Patterning
        Writing—Patterning
Language experience approach in education
  USE   **Whole language**
Language games
  USE   **Literary recreations**
Language, International
  USE   **Universal language**
Language laboratories   407
  UF   Foreign language laboratories
  RT   **Modern languages—Study and teaching**
Language, Universal
  USE   **Universal language**
Languages
  USE   **Language and languages**
        and countries, cities, etc., with the subdivision *Languages,* for materials on the several languages spoken in a place, e.g. **United States—Languages;** etc. [to be added as needed]
Languages, Modern
  USE   **Modern languages**
Languages—Vocabulary
  USE   **Vocabulary**
Lantern slides
  USE   **Slides (Photography)**
Laptop computers
  USE   **Portable computers**
Larceny
  USE   **Theft**
Large and small
  USE   **Size**
Large print books   028
  UF   Books for sight saving
        Books—Large print
        Large type books
        Sight saving books
  BT   **Blind—Books and reading**
  RT   **Big books**
Large type books
  USE   **Large print books**
Laser-beam recording
  USE   **Laser recording**
Laser photography
  USE   **Holography**
Laser recording   621.36; 621.38
  UF   Laser-beam recording
        Recording, Laser

Laser recording—*Continued*
- BT **Optical data processing**
- NT **Holography**
- RT **Lasers**
  Optical storage devices

Lasers 621.36
- SA lasers in particular subjects or fields of endeavor, e.g. **Lasers in aeronautics** [to be added as needed]
- BT **Light**
- NT **Lasers in aeronautics**
- RT **Laser recording**

Lasers in aeronautics 629.13
- BT **Aeronautics**
  Lasers

Last rites (Sacraments)
- USE **Anointing of the sick**

Last sacraments
- USE **Anointing of the sick**

Last Supper 232.9

Use for materials on the final meal of Jesus with his apostles, where the sacrament of the Eurcharist was instituted.
- UF Jesus Christ—Last Supper

Last things (Theology)
- USE **Eschatology**

Latchkey children 306.874; 362.7; 640
- BT **Children of working parents**

Lateness
- USE **Punctuality**

Lathe work
- USE **Lathes**
  Turning

Lathes 621.9
- UF Lathe work
- BT **Woodworking machinery**
- RT **Turning**

Latin America 980

Use for materials that discuss collectively several or all of the countries of the Western Hemisphere south of the United States in which Spanish, Portuguese, or French is the principal language.
- UF Spanish America
- SA names of individual Latin American countries [to be added as needed]
- BT **America**
- NT **Pan-Americanism**

Latin America—Politics and government 980
- BT **Politics**

Latin American literature 860

Use for materials on the French, Portuguese, or Spanish literature of several Latin American countries. May use same subdivisions and names of literary forms as for **English literature.**
- UF South American literature
  Spanish American literature
- SA names of individual Latin American literatures [to be added as needed]
- BT **Literature**
- NT **Brazilian literature**
  Mexican literature

Latin Americans (May subdiv. geog.) **920; 980**

Use for materials on citizens of Latin American countries. Materials on United States citizens of Latin American descent are entered under **Hispanic Americans.**

Latin language 470

May be subdivided like **English language.**
- UF Classical languages
- BT **Language and languages**
- RT **Romance languages**

Latin literature 870

May use same subdivisions and names of literary forms as for **English literature.**
- UF Roman literature
- BT **Literature**
- RT **Classical literature**
  Early Christian literature

Latinos (U.S.)
- USE **Hispanic Americans**

Latitude 526; 527
- UF Degrees of latitude and longitude
- BT **Earth**
  Geodesy
  Nautical astronomy

Latter-day Saints
- USE **Church of Jesus Christ of Latter-day Saints**

Laughter 152.4
- BT **Emotions**

Launching of satellites
- USE **Artificial satellites—Launching**

Laundry 648
- UF Ironing
  Washing
- BT **Cleaning**
  Home economics
  Household sanitation

Law (May subdiv. geog.) 340
  UF Jurisprudence
        Laws
        Statutes
  SA names of particular legal sys-
        tems, e.g. **Islamic law;** spe-
        cial branches of law, e.g.
        Criminal law; subjects with
        the subdivision *Law and leg-*
        islation, e.g. **Automobiles—**
        Law and legislation; and eth-
        nic groups and classes of per-
        sons with the subdivision *Le-*
        gal status, laws, etc., e.g.
        Handicapped—Legal status,
        laws, etc. [to be added as
        needed]
  BT **Political science**
  NT **Abortion—Law and legislation**
        Administration of justice
        Administrative law
        Automobiles—Law and legisla-
        tion
        Chemical industry—Law and
        legislation
        Commercial law
        Constitutional law
        Constitutions
        Corporation law
        Courts
        Criminal law
        Ecclesiastical law
        Food—Law and legislation
        Gun control
        Handicapped—Legal status,
        laws, etc.
        Industrial laws and legislation
        Internal revenue law
        International law
        Islamic law
        Justice
        Law reform
        Lawyers
        Libraries—Law and legislation
        Litigation
        Maritime law
        Medicine—Law and legislation
        Military law
        Natural law
        Safety regulations
        Space law

        Water rights
  RT **Legislation**
Law and legislation
  USE subjects with the subdivision
        Law and legislation, e.g. **Au-**
        tomobiles—Law and legisla-
        tion [to be added as needed]
Law enforcement (May subdiv. geog.)
        363.2
  BT **Administration of criminal jus-**
        tice
  NT **Criminal investigation**
        Police
Law—Fiction
  USE **Legal stories**
Law of nations
  USE **International law**
Law of nature
  USE **Natural law**
Law of the sea
  USE **Maritime law**
Law reform (May subdiv. geog.) 340
  UF Legal reform
  BT **Law**
Law schools (May subdiv. geog.)
        340.071
  BT **Colleges and universities**
Law suits
  USE **Litigation**
Law—United States 349.73
  UF United States—Law
Law—Vocational guidance 340.023
  BT **Professions**
        Vocational guidance
Lawn tennis
  USE **Tennis**
Lawns 635.9; 712
  BT **Landscape gardening**
  RT **Grasses**
Laws
  USE **Law**
        Legislation
Lawsuits
  USE **Litigation**
Lawyers (May subdiv. geog.) 340.092;
        920
  UF Attorneys
        Bar
        Barristers
        Jurists
        Legal profession

Lawyers—*Continued*
    Solicitors
  BT **Law**
  NT **Judges**
       Legal ethics
  RT **Legal ethics**
Lawyers—Fiction
  USE **Legal stories**
Lawyers—Salaries, wages, etc. (May
    subdiv. geog.) **331.2**
  BT **Salaries, wages, etc.**
Lay ministry **253**
  UF Volunteers in church work
  BT **Church work**
  RT **Laity**
Laymen
  USE **Laity**
Lead poisoning **615.9**
  UF Lead—Toxicology
  BT **Occupational diseases**
       Poisons and poisoning
Lead—Toxicology
  USE **Lead poisoning**
Leadership **158; 303.3**
  BT **Ability**
       Executive ability
       Social groups
       Success
  NT **Elite (Social sciences)**
League of Nations **341.22**
  BT **International arbitration**
       International cooperation
       International organization
       World War, 1914-1918—Peace
League of Nations—Mandatory system
  USE **Mandates**
Learned institutions and societies
  USE **Learning and scholarship**
Learned societies
  USE **Societies**
Learning and scholarship (May subdiv.
    geog.) **001.2**
  UF Erudition
       Learned institutions and societies
       Scholarship
  BT **Civilization**
       Intellectual life
  NT **Humanities**
       Professional education
  RT **Culture**
       Education
       Humanism

      Research
Learning center approach to teaching
  USE **Open plan schools**
Learning disabilities **153.1; 371.9;**
      616.85
  SA types of learning disabilities [to
       be added as needed]
  BT **Psychology of learning**
       Slow learning children
  NT **Reading disability**
Learning, Psychology of
  USE **Psychology of learning**
Learning resource centers
  USE **Instructional materials centers**
Learning, Verbal
  USE **Verbal learning**
Lease and rental services **333.5**
  UF Lease services
       Rental services
  BT **Service industries**
Lease services
  USE **Lease and rental services**
Leather **675**
  BT **Animal products**
  RT **Hides and skins**
       Leather industry
       Tanning
Leather clothing
  USE **Leather garments**
Leather garments **391; 685**
  UF Leather clothing
  BT **Clothing and dress**
       Leather work
Leather industry (May subdiv. geog.)
      338.4
  UF Leather industry and trade
  BT **Industries**
  NT **Shoe industry**
  RT **Leather**
Leather industry and trade
  USE **Leather industry**
Leather work **745.53**
  BT **Decoration and ornament**
       Decorative arts
       Handicraft
  NT **Leather garments**
Leaves **575.5; 581.4**
  UF Foliage
  BT **Plants**
Lebanon **956.92**
    May be subdivided like United States ex-
    cept for *History.*

Lebanon—History   956.92

Lebanon—History—1975-1976, Civil War   956.9204

Lebanon—History—1982-1984, Israeli intervention   956.05

    UF   Israeli intervention in Lebanon, 1982-1984

    BT   **Israel-Arab conflicts**

Lectures and lecturing   808.5

    Use for general materials on lectures and the art of delivering speeches on academic subjects. Collections of speeches on several subjects and materials about non-academic speeches are entered under **Speeches.** Collections of lectures on a single subject are entered under that subject.

    UF   Addresses

           Speaking

    BT   **Public speaking**

           Rhetoric

           Teaching

    NT   **Radio addresses, debates, etc.**

    RT   **Speeches**

Left and right

    USE **Left and right (Direction)**

          Right and left (Political science)

Left and right (Direction)   152.1

    Use for children's materials on left and right as indications of location or direction. Materials on political views or attitudes are entered under **Right and left (Political science).** Materials on the physical characteristics of favoring one hand or the other are entered under **Left- and right-handedness.**

    UF   Left and right

           Right and left

    BT   **Direction sense**

Left- and right-handedness   152.3

    UF   Handedness

           Right- and left-handedness

    BT   **Psychophysiology**

Left (Political science)

    USE **Liberalism**

          Right and left (Political science)

Legacies

    USE **Inheritance and succession**

          Wills

Legal aid (May subdiv. geog.)   **362.5**

    Use for materials on legal services to the poor, usually provided under the sponsorship of local bar associations or governmental units.

    UF   Legal assistance to the poor

           Legal representation of the poor

           Legal services for the poor

    BT   **Public welfare**

Legal assistance to the poor

    USE **Legal aid**

Legal drama (Films)   791.43

    May be used for individual works, collections, or materials about motion pictures dealing with trials or litigations.

    UF   Courtroom drama

    BT   **Motion pictures**

Legal drama (Radio programs)   791.44

    May be used for individual works, collections, or materials about radio programs dealing with trials or litigations.

    UF   Courtroom drama

    BT   **Radio programs**

Legal drama (Television programs)   791.45

    May be used for individual works, collections, or materials about television programs dealing with trials or litigations.

    UF   Courtroom drama

    BT   **Television programs**

Legal ethics (May subdiv. geog.)   **174; 340**

    BT   **Ethics**

           Lawyers

           Professional ethics

Legal fiction (Literature)

    USE **Legal stories**

Legal holidays

    USE **Holidays**

Legal medicine

    USE **Medical jurisprudence**

Legal novels

    USE **Legal stories**

Legal profession

    USE **Lawyers**

Legal reform

    USE **Law reform**

Legal representation of the poor

    USE **Legal aid**

Legal responsibility

    USE **Liability (Law)**

Legal services for the poor

    USE **Legal aid**

Legal status, laws, etc.

    USE ethnic groups and classes of persons with the subdivision *Legal status, laws, etc.,* e.g. **Handicapped—Legal status, laws, etc.** [to be added as needed]

Legal stories   808.83; 813, etc.
May be used for individual works, collections, or materials about fiction dealing with trials or litigations.
UF   Law—Fiction
Lawyers—Fiction
Legal fiction (Literature)
Legal novels
Trials—Fiction
BT   **Fiction**

Legal tender
USE   **Money**

Legations
USE   **Diplomatic and consular service**

Legendary characters
USE   names of individual legendary characters, e.g. **Bunyan, Paul (Legendary character)** [to be added as needed]

Legends (May subdiv. geog.)   398.2
May be used for individual works, collections, or materials about tales coming down from the past, especially those relating to actual events or persons. Collections of tales written between the eleventh and fourteenth centuries and dealing with the age of chivalry or the supernatural are entered under **Romances.**
UF   Folk tales
Stories
Tales
Traditions
SA   relgious topics and names of individual persons or sacred works with the subdivision *Legends;* e.g. **Grail—Legends;** legends of particular ethnic or religious groups, e.g. **Jewish legends;** and names of individual legendary characters, e.g. **Bunyan, Paul (Legendary character)** [to be added as needed]
BT   **Fiction**
Literature
NT   **Celtic legends**
Jewish legends
Mythology
Norse legends
Tall tales
RT   **Fables**
Folklore
Romances

Legends, Jewish
USE   **Jewish legends**
Legends—United States   398.20973; 973
Legerdemain
USE   **Juggling**
Magic tricks
Legibility of handwriting
USE   **Handwriting**
Legislation (May subdiv. geog.)   328
Use for materials on the theory of lawmaking and descriptions of the preparation and enactment of laws.
UF   Laws
SA   subjects with the subdivision *Law and legislation* [to be added as needed]
BT   **Political science**
NT   **Abortion—Law and legislation**
Automobiles—Law and legislation
Chemical industry—Law and legislation
Food—Law and legislation
Gun control
Industrial laws and legislation
Legislative bodies
Libraries—Law and legislation
Medicine—Law and legislation
Parliamentary practice
RT   **Law**

Legislation, Direct
USE   **Referendum**
Legislative bodies (May subdiv. geog.)   328.3
Use for materials on various law making bodies considered collectively.
UF   Legislatures
Parliaments
SA   names of individual legislative bodies, e.g. **United States. Congress** [to be added as needed]
BT   **Constitutional law**
Legislation
Representative government and representation
NT   **Parliamentary practice**
Term limits (Public office)
United States. Congress
War and emergency powers

Legislative investigations
USE   **Governmental investigations**

Legislative reapportionment
  USE **Apportionment (Election law)**
Legislatures
  USE **Legislative bodies**
Legitimacy (Law)
  USE **Illegitimacy**
Leisure (May subdiv. geog.) **790.01**
  UF Free time (Leisure)
       Leisure time
  NT **Hobbies**
       Retirement
  RT **Recreation**
Leisure time
  USE **Leisure**
Lemon
  USE **Lemons**
Lemons **634; 641.3**
  UF Lemon *[Former heading]*
  BT **Citrus fruits**
Lending
  USE **Loans**
Lending of library materials
  USE **Library circulation**
Lenses **535**
  SA types of lenses, e.g. **Contact lenses** [to be added as needed]
  BT **Optical instruments**
  NT **Contact lenses**
Lensless photography
  USE **Holography**
Lent **263**
  BT **Church year**
  NT **Good Friday**
       Holy Week
       Lenten sermons
  RT **Easter**
Lent—Meditations **242**
  BT **Meditations**
Lenten sermons **252**
    Use for collections of sermons on any subject preached during the season of Lent.
  BT **Lent**
       Sermons
Lepidoptera
  USE **Butterflies**
       Moths
Lesbian marriage
  USE **Same-sex marriage**
Lesbianism (May subdiv. geog.) **306.76**
  BT **Homosexuality**
  RT **Lesbians**

Lesbians (May subdiv. geog.) **305.48; 306.76**
  UF Gay women
       Gays, Female
       Homosexuals, Female
  BT **Women**
  NT **Gays and lesbians in the military**
  RT **Homosexuality**
       Lesbianism
       Lesbians' writings
Lesbians and gays in the military
  USE **Gays and lesbians in the military**
Lesbians in the military
  USE **Gays and lesbians in the military**
Lesbians' writings **808.8; 810.8, etc.**
    Use for collections of lesbians' writings by more than one author and for materials about such writings.
  UF Gay women's writings
       Writings of lesbians
  BT **Literature**
  RT **Lesbians**
Less developed countries
  USE **Developing countries**
Letter-sound association
  USE **Reading—Phonetic method**
Letter writing **383; 808.6**
    Use for materials on composition, forms, and etiquette of correspondence. Materials limited to business correspondence are entered under **Business letters.** Collections of literary letters are entered under **Letters.**
  UF Correspondence
  BT **Etiquette**
       Literary style
       Rhetoric
  NT **Business letters**
Lettering **745.6**
  UF Ornamental alphabets
  BT **Decoration and ornament**
       Industrial painting
       Mechanical drawing
  NT **Monograms**
  RT **Alphabets**
       Initials
       Sign painting
Letters **808.86**
    Use for collections of literary letters. Materials on the composition, forms, and etiquette of correspondence are entered under **Letter**

Letters—*Continued*

writing. Materials limited to business correspondence are entered under **Business letters.**

  UF   Correspondence

  SA   ethnic groups, classes of per-
         sons, and names of individual
         persons and families with the
         subdivision *Correspondence,*
         e.g. **Authors—Correspon-
         dence** [to be added as need-
         ed]

  NT   **American letters**

       Authors—Correspondence

       English letters

Letters of credit

  USE **Credit**

       Negotiable instruments

Letters of marque

  USE **Privateering**

Letters of recommendation

  USE **Applications for positions**

Letters of the alphabet

  USE **Alphabet**

Leukemia 616.99

  BT   **Blood—Diseases**

       Cancer

Levant

  USE **Middle East**

Leveraged buyouts 338.8; 658.1

  UF   Buyouts, Leveraged

       Management buyouts

  BT   **Corporate mergers and acqui-
       sitions**

**Lewis and Clark Expedition (1804-1806)
  973.4**

  BT   **United States—Exploring expe-
       ditions**

       **United States—History—1783-
       1809**

Liability (Law) (May subdiv. geog.)
  346.02

  UF   Accountability

       Legal responsibility

       Responsibility, Legal

  BT   **Contracts**

  NT   **Malpractice**

Liability, Professional

  USE **Malpractice**

Libel and slander (May subdiv. geog.)
  346.03

  UF   Character assassination

       Defamation

       Slander (Law)

  BT   **Journalism**

  NT   **Gossip**

  RT   **Freedom of speech**

       Freedom of the press

Liberalism (May subdiv. geog.) **148;
  320.5**

  UF   Left (Political science)

  BT   **Political science**

       Social sciences

  RT   **Right and left (Political sci-
       ence)**

Liberation movements, National

  USE **National liberation movements**

Liberation theology 261.8

  UF   Theology of liberation

  BT   **Christianity—Doctrines**

       Church and social problems

       Theology

Liberty

  USE **Freedom**

Liberty of conscience

  USE **Freedom of conscience**

Liberty of speech

  USE **Freedom of speech**

Liberty of the press

  USE **Freedom of the press**

Liberty of the will

  USE **Free will and determinism**

Librarians (May subdiv. geog.) **020.92;
  920**

  NT   **African American librarians**

       Black librarians

       Library technicians

  RT   **Libraries**

Librarians—Collective bargaining

  USE **Collective bargaining—Librari-
      ans**

Librarians—Education

  USE **Library education**

Librarians—Ethics 174

  UF   Librarians—Professional ethics

  BT   **Professional ethics**

Librarians—In-service training 023

  BT   **Library education**

Librarians—Professional ethics

  USE **Librarians—Ethics**

Librarians—Rating 023

Librarians—Recruiting 023

  BT   **Recruiting of employees**

Librarians—Training
   USE **Library education**
Librarians' unions   **331.88**
   UF Library unions
   BT **Labor unions**
Librarianship
   USE **Library science**
Libraries (May subdiv. geog.)   **027**
   SA types of libraries, e.g. **Academic libraries;** names of individual libraries, e.g. **Library of Congress;** libraries and particular groups of people, e.g. **Libraries and African Americans;** and libraries and other subjects, e.g. **Libraries and motion pictures** [to be added as needed]
   BT **Documentation**
   NT **Academic libraries**
         Children's libraries
         Church libraries
         Hospital libraries
         Instructional materials centers
         Libraries and community
         Libraries and motion pictures
         Libraries and pictures
         Libraries and schools
         Library architecture
         Library catalogs
         Library cooperation
         Library of Congress
         Library resources
         Library services
         Library technical processes
         Public libraries
         School libraries
         Special libraries
         Young adults' libraries
   RT **Archives**
         Information services
         Librarians
Libraries—Acquisitions   **025.2**
   UF Acquisitions (Libraries)
         Book buying (Libraries)
         Libraries—Order department
         Library acquisitions
   BT **Libraries—Collection development**
         Library technical processes
   NT **Book selection**

Libraries—Administration   **025.1**
   UF Library administration
         Library policies
   NT **Library finance**
         Library trustees
Libraries and African Americans   **027.6**
   UF African Americans and libraries
         Afro-Americans and libraries
         Library services to African Americans
   BT **African Americans**
         Library services
Libraries and children
   USE **Children's libraries**
Libraries and community   **021.2**
   UF Community and libraries
   BT **Libraries**
   NT **Libraries—Public relations**
Libraries and labor   **027.6**
   UF Labor and libraries
         Library services to labor
   BT **Labor**
         Library services
Libraries and motion pictures   **021**
   UF Educational films
         Motion pictures and libraries
   BT **Libraries**
         Motion pictures
         Motion pictures in education
Libraries and pictures   **021**
   BT **Libraries**
         Pictures
Libraries and readers
   USE **Library services**
Libraries and schools   **021**
   UF Schools and libraries
   BT **Libraries**
         Schools
   NT **Libraries and students**
   RT **Children's libraries**
         School libraries
Libraries and state
   USE **Libraries—Government policy**
Libraries and students   **027.62**
   UF Students and libraries
   BT **Libraries and schools**
         Library services
         School libraries
Libraries and the elderly   **027.6**
   UF Elderly and libraries
         Library services to the elderly

Libraries and the elderly—*Continued*
  BT **Elderly**
      Library services
Libraries—Automation 025.04
  UF Library automation
  SA names of projects, formats, and
        systems, e.g. **MARC formats**
        [to be added as needed]
  BT **Automation**
  NT **Machine readable bibliographic**
        data
  RT **Information systems**
      Online catalogs
Libraries—Boards of trustees
  USE **Library trustees**
Libraries, Business
  USE **Business libraries**
Libraries—Cataloging
  USE **Cataloging**
Libraries—Catalogs
  USE **Library catalogs**
Libraries—Censorship 025.2
  BT **Censorship**
Libraries—Centralization 021.6
  UF Library systems
Libraries—Circulation, loans
  USE **Library circulation**
Libraries—Collection development
  025.2
  UF Collection development (Librar-
        ies)
  BT **Library technical processes**
  NT **Book selection**
      Libraries—Acquisitions
Libraries—Collective bargaining
  USE **Collective bargaining—Librari-**
        ans
Libraries—Cooperation
  USE **Library cooperation**
Libraries, Corporate
  USE **Corporate libraries**
Libraries—Equipment and supplies
  022
  UF Library equipment and supplies
      Library supplies
  BT **Furniture**
Libraries—Federal aid
  USE **Federal aid to libraries**
Libraries—Finance
  USE **Library finance**
Libraries—Government aid
  USE **Government aid to libraries**

Libraries—Government policy (May
  subdiv. geog.) **021.8**
  UF Libraries and state
  BT **Social policy**
  NT **Federal aid to libraries**
      Government aid to libraries
Libraries, Governmental
  USE **Government libraries**
Libraries, Hospital
  USE **Hospital libraries**
Libraries—Law and legislation (May
  subdiv. geog.) **344**
  UF Library laws
      Library legislation
  BT **Law**
      Legislation
Libraries—Lighting 022
  BT **Lighting**
Libraries, Music
  USE **Music libraries**
Libraries, National
  USE **National libraries**
Libraries—Order department
  USE **Libraries—Acquisitions**
Libraries, Presidential
  USE **Presidents—United States—Ar-**
        chives
Libraries—Public relations (May subdiv.
  geog.) **021.7**
  UF Public relations—Libraries *[For-*
        mer heading]
  BT **Libraries and community**
  NT **Book talks**
Libraries, Regional
  USE **Regional libraries**
Libraries—Special collections 026
    May be subdivided by subject or form, e.g.
    Libraries—Special collections—Science fic-
    tion; Libraries—Special collections—Video-
    tapes; etc.
  UF Special collections in libraries
Libraries—State aid
  USE **Government aid to libraries**
Libraries—Statistics 020
  BT **Statistics**
Libraries—Technical services
  USE **Library technical processes**
Libraries—Trustees
  USE **Library trustees**
Libraries—United States 027.073
Library acquisitions
  USE **Libraries—Acquisitions**

Library administration
　USE　**Libraries—Administration**
Library architecture (May subdiv. geog.)
　　727
　　Use for materials on the design of library
　buildings.
　BT　**Architecture**
　　　Libraries
Library assistants
　USE　**Library technicians**
Library automation
　USE　**Libraries—Automation**
Library boards
　USE　**Library trustees**
Library book fairs
　USE　**Books—Exhibitions**
Library cataloging
　USE　**Cataloging**
Library catalogs　017; 025.3
　UF　Catalogs
　　　Catalogs, Library
　　　Libraries—Catalogs
　SA　types of library catalogs, e.g.
　　　　Online catalogs [to be added
　　　　　as needed]
　BT　**Libraries**
　NT　**Book catalogs**
　　　Card catalogs
　　　Classified catalogs
　　　Online catalogs
　　　Subject catalogs
　RT　**Cataloging**
Library circulation　025.6
　UF　Book lending
　　　Circulation of library materials
　　　Lending of library materials
　　　Libraries—Circulation, loans
　BT　**Library services**
　NT　**Interlibrary loans**
Library classification　025.4
　　May be further subdivided by a type of lit-
　erature or by the subject of the materials clas-
　sified.
　UF　Books—Classification *[Former
　　　　heading]*
　　　Classification—Books
　BT　**Cataloging**
　　　Classification
　　　Library technical processes
　NT　**Dewey Decimal Classification**
　RT　**Classified catalogs**

Library clerks
　USE　**Library technicians**
Library consortia
　USE　**Library cooperation**
Library cooperation (May subdiv. geog.)
　　021.6
　UF　Consortia, Library
　　　Libraries—Cooperation
　　　Library consortia
　BT　**Libraries**
　NT　**Interlibrary loans**
　　　Library information networks
Library education (May subdiv. geog.)
　　020.71
　　Use for materials on the education of librar-
　ians. Materials on the instruction of readers in
　library use are entered under **Bibliographic
　instruction.**
　UF　Education for librarianship
　　　Librarians—Education
　　　Librarians—Training
　　　Library science—Study and
　　　　teaching
　BT　**Education**
　　　Professional education
　NT　**Librarians—In-service training**
　　　Library schools
Library education—Audiovisual aids
　　020.71
　BT　**Audiovisual education**
　　　Audiovisual materials
Library education—Curricula　020.71
　BT　**Education—Curricula**
Library equipment and supplies
　USE　**Libraries—Equipment and
　　　　supplies**
Library extension　021.6
　BT　**Library services**
　NT　**Bookmobiles**
Library finance (May subdiv. gcog.)
　　025.1
　UF　Libraries—Finance
　BT　**Finance**
　　　Libraries—Administration
　NT　**Government aid to libraries**
　RT　**Federal aid to libraries**
Library information networks (May
　　subdiv. geog.)　**021.6**
　　Use for materials on networks that facilitate
　the sharing of information resources among
　several libraries.
　UF　Library networks
　　　Library systems

Library information networks—*Continued*
    BT   **Information networks**
         Library cooperation
Library instruction
    USE   **Bibliographic instruction**
Library laws
    USE   **Libraries—Law and legislation**
Library legislation
    USE   **Libraries—Law and legislation**
Library materials
    USE   **Library resources**
Library networks
    USE   **Library information networks**
Library of Congress   027.573
    UF   United States. Library of Con-
         gress
    BT   **Libraries**
Library orientation
    USE   **Bibliographic instruction**
Library policies
    USE   **Libraries—Administration**
Library processing
    USE   **Library technical processes**
Library reference services
    USE   **Reference services (Libraries)**
Library resources (May subdiv. geog.)
    025
    Use for materials on the resources and col-
    lections available in libraries for research not
    limited to a single subject or discipline.
    UF   Library materials
    SA   subjects, ethnic groups, classes
         of persons, corporate bodies,
         individual persons, literary au-
         thors, and names of countries,
         cities, etc., with the subdivi-
         sion *Library resources,* e.g.
         **United States—History—Li-
         brary resources** [to be added
         as needed]
    BT   **Libraries**
    NT   **Government publications**
**Library resources—Conservation and
    restoration   025.8**
    UF   Books—Preservation
         Library resources—Preservation
         Preservation of library resources
Library resources—Preservation
    USE   **Library resources—Conserva-
         tion and restoration**

Library schools (May subdiv. geog.)
    020.71
    BT   **Library education**
Library science (May subdiv. geog.)
    020
    Use for general materials on the knowledge
    and skill necessary for the organization and
    administration of libraries. Materials on ser-
    vices offered by libraries to patrons are en-
    tered under **Library services.**
    UF   Librarianship
    BT   **Documentation**
         Information science
    NT   **Cataloging**
         Library surveys
         Library technical processes
    RT   **Bibliography**
         Library services
Library science—Study and teaching
    USE   **Library education**
Library services (May subdiv. geog.)
    025.5
    Use for materials on services offered by li-
    braries to patrons. General materials on the
    knowledge and skill necessary for the organi-
    zation and administration of libraries are en-
    tered under **Library science.**
    UF   Libraries and readers
         Library services to readers
         Reader services (Libraries)
         Readers and libraries
    SA   libraries and specific types of
         users or specific activities for
         which services are provided,
         e.g. **Libraries and the elder-
         ly** [to be added as needed]
    BT   **Libraries**
    NT   **Bibliographic instruction**
         **Libraries and African Ameri-
         cans**
         Libraries and labor
         Libraries and students
         Libraries and the elderly
         Library circulation
         Library extension
         Reference services (Libraries)
    RT   **Library science**
Library services to African Americans
    USE   **Libraries and African Ameri-
         cans**
Library services to children
    USE   **Children's libraries**
Library services to labor
    USE   **Libraries and labor**

Library services to readers
 USE **Library services**
Library services to teenagers
 USE **Young adults' libraries**
Library services to the elderly
 USE **Libraries and the elderly**
Library services to young adults
 USE **Young adults' libraries**
Library skills
 USE **Bibliographic instruction**
Library supplies
 USE **Libraries—Equipment and supplies**
Library surveys   020
 BT **Library science**
  Surveys
Library systems
 USE **Libraries—Centralization**
  Library information networks
Library technical processes   025
 Use for materials on the activities and processes concerned with the acquisition, organization, and preparation of library materials for use.
 UF Centralized processing (Libraries)
  Libraries—Technical services
  Library processing
  Processing (Libraries)
  Technical services (Libraries)
 BT **Libraries**
  Library science
 NT **Cataloging**
  Libraries—Acquisitions
  Libraries—Collection development
  Library classification
Library technicians (May subdiv. geog.) **020.92**
 UF Library assistants
  Library clerks
  Paraprofessional librarians
 BT **Librarians**
  Paraprofessionals
Library trustees   021.8
 UF Libraries—Boards of trustees
  Libraries—Trustees *[Former heading]*
  Library boards
 BT **Libraries—Administration**
  Trusts and trustees
Library unions
 USE **Librarians' unions**

Library user orientation
 USE **Bibliographic instruction**
Librettos   780; 780.26
 Use for collections of miscellaneous librettos and for materials on the history and criticism of librettos and on writing librettos. Individual librettos and collections of librettos of a specific type are entered under the specific type of libretto.
 SA types of librettos, e.g. **Opera librettos** [to be added as needed]
 BT **Books**
 NT **Opera librettos**
Licenses (May subdiv. geog.)   **352.8**
 Use for general works on legal permissions to engage in business or perform other work or activities.
 SA occupational groups, types of industries, and types of vehicles with the subdivision *Licenses,* e.g. **Physicians—Licenses;** which may be further subdivided geographically [to be added as needed]
 BT **Commercial law**
  Public administration
Lie detectors and detection   363.2
 UF Polygraph
 BT **Criminal investigation**
  Medical jurisprudence
  Truthfulness and falsehood
Life   128
 Use for materials on philosophical or religious considerations of life. Materials on life from a scientific point of view are entered under **Life (Biology).**
 NT **Death**
  Life expectancy
 RT **Life (Biology)**
Life after death
 USE **Future life**
  Immortality
Life (Biology)   570.1
 Use for materials on life from a scientific point of view. Materials on philosophical or religious considerations of life are entered under **Life.**
 BT **Biology**
 NT **Gaia hypothesis**
  Genetics
  Life cycles (Biology)
  Middle age
  Protoplasm
  Reproduction

410

Life (Biology)—*Continued*
  RT **Life**
Life care communities (May subdiv.
    geog.) **362.1; 363.5**
    Use for materials on retirement communi-
    ties that guarantee services and medical care
    for the rest of a person's life.
  UF Continuing care communities
        Continuing care retirement com-
          munities
  BT **Retirement communities**
Life cycles
  USE **Life cycles (Biology)**
        and types of plants or animals
          with the subdivision *Life cy-*
          cles [to be added as needed]
Life cycles (Biology) **571.8**
  UF Life cycles
  SA types of plants or animals with
        the subdivision *Life cycles* [to
        be added as needed]
  BT **Biology**
      Cycles
      Life (Biology)
Life expectancy (May subdiv. geog.)
    304.6
  UF Expectancy of life
        Expectation of life
  BT **Age**
      Life
      Vital statistics
  NT **Longevity**
Life, Future
  USE **Future life**
Life histories
  USE **Biography**
Life insurance (May subdiv. geog.)
    368.32
  UF Insurance, Life
  BT **Insurance**
  NT **Group insurance**
  RT **Annuities**
Life on other planets **576.8**
    Use for materials on the possibility of in-
    digenous life in outer space. Materials on the
    biology of humans or other earth creatures
    while in outer space are entered under **Space
    biology.**
  UF Astrobiology
        Extraterrestrial life
  BT **Astronomy**
      Planets
      Universe

  NT **Extraterrestrial beings**
      Interstellar communication
Life—Origin **113**
  UF Germ theory
        Origin of life
  BT **Evolution**
Life quality
  USE **Quality of life**
Life saving
  USE **Lifesaving**
Life sciences (May subdiv. geog.) **570**
  UF Biosciences
  BT **Science**
  NT **Agriculture**
      Biology
      Medicine
Life sciences ethics
  USE **Bioethics**
Life skills (May subdiv. geog.) **158; 640**
    Use for materials on skills needed by an in-
    dividual to exist in modern society, including
    skills related to education, employment, fi-
    nance, etc.
  UF Basic life skills
        Coping skills
        Functional competencies
        Fundamental life skills
        Life skills guides
        Living skills
        Personal life skills
  SA groups and classes of persons
        with the subdivision *Life*
        skills guides, e.g. **Elderly—
        Life skills guides** [to be add-
        ed as needed]
  BT **Interpersonal relations**
      Success
  NT **Conduct of life**
      Elderly—Life skills guides
      Self-improvement
      Study skills
      Survival skills
  RT **Human behavior**
Life skills guides
  USE **Life skills**
        and groups and classes of per-
        sons with the subdivision *Life*
        skills guides, e.g. **Elderly—
        Life skills guides** [to be add-
        ed as needed]
Life span prolongation
  USE **Longevity**

Life styles
   USE **Lifestyles**
Life support systems (Medical environ-
      ment) 362.1
   BT **Hospitals**
       Terminal care
Life support systems (Space environ-
      ment) 629.47
   BT **Human engineering**
       Space medicine
   NT **Apollo project**
       Lunar bases
       Space suits
Life support systems (Submarine envi-
      ronment) 627
   BT **Human engineering**
Lifelong education
   USE **Adult education**
       Continuing education
Lifesaving 363.1
   UF Life saving
   BT **Rescue work**
   RT **First aid**
Lifestyles (May subdiv. geog.) **306**
   UF Life styles
   SA types of lifestyles [to be added
       as needed]
   BT **Human behavior**
       Manners and customs
   NT **Alternative lifestyles**
       Counter culture
       Unmarried couples
Lifts
   USE **Elevators**
       Hoisting machinery
Light 535
   BT **Electromagnetic waves**
       Physics
   NT **Color**
       Lasers
       Lighting
       Luminescence
       Refraction
   RT **Optics**
       Photometry
       Radiation
       Spectrum analysis
Light and shade
   USE **Shades and shadows**
Light, Electric
   USE **Electric lighting**

Light production in animals
   USE **Bioluminescence**
Light ships
   USE **Lightships**
Light—Therapeutic use
   USE **Phototherapy**
Light verse
   USE **Humorous poetry**
Lighthouses (May subdiv. geog.) **387.1;**
      623.89; 627
   BT **Navigation**
   NT **Lightships**
Lighting (May subdiv. geog.) **621.32**
   UF Illumination
   SA types of lighting and types of
      buildings, structures, rooms,
      installations, etc., with the
      subdivision *Lighting,* e.g. **Li-**
      braries—Lighting [to be add-
      ed as needed]
   BT **Interior design**
       Light
   NT **Candles**
       Electric lighting
       Lamps
       Libraries—Lighting
       Photography—Lighting
       Stage lighting
       Streets—Lighting
Lightning 551.56
   BT **Electricity**
       Meteorology
       Thunderstorms
Lightships 623.89; 627
   UF Light ships
   BT **Lighthouses**
       Ships
Limbs, Artificial
   USE **Artificial limbs**
Lime 631.8; 666
   UF Lime (Mineral) *[Former head-*
      ing]
   BT **Fertilizers**
       Minerals
Lime (Fruit)
   USE **Limes**
Lime (Mineral)
   USE **Lime**

Limericks   808.81; 811, etc.; 811.008, etc.

   May be used for collections of limericks by one or several authors or for materials about limericks.

   UF   Rhymes

   BT   **Humorous poetry**

   RT   **Nonsense verses**

Limes   634

   UF   Lime (Fruit) *[Former heading]*

   BT   **Citrus fruits**

Limitation of armament

   USE   **Arms control**

Limited access highways

   USE   **Express highways**

Lincoln, Abraham, 1809-1865   92; B

   BT   **Presidents—United States**

Lincoln Day

   USE   **Lincoln's Birthday**

Lincoln family   920; 929

Lincoln's Birthday   394.261

   UF   Lincoln Day

   BT   **Holidays**

Line engraving

   USE   **Engraving**

Linear algebra   512

   UF   Algebras, Linear

   BT   **Algebra**

          Mathematical analysis

   RT   **Topology**

Linear system theory

   USE   **System analysis**

Linen   677

   BT   **Fabrics**

          Fibers

   RT   **Flax**

Linguistic science

   USE   **Linguistics**

Linguistics (May subdiv. geog.)   **410**

   Use for materials on the scientific study of speech and for comparative studies of languages. General materials on the history, philosophy, origin, etc., of languages are entered under **Language and languages.**

   UF   Comparative linguistics

          Comparative philology

          Language and languages—Comparative philology

          Linguistic science

          Philology

          Philology, Comparative

   BT   **Language and languages**

   NT   **Grammar**

          Semantics

          Sociolinguistics

          Universal language

Linoleum block printing   761

   UF   Block printing

   BT   **Printing**

          Prints

Linotype   686.2

   BT   **Printing**

          Type and type-founding

          Typesetting

Lip reading

   USE   **Deaf—Means of communication**

Liquefaction of coal

   USE   **Coal liquefaction**

Liqueurs

   USE   **Liquors**

Liquid fuel

   USE   **Petroleum as fuel**

Liquids   532

   BT   **Fluid mechanics**

          Physics

   NT   **Hydraulics**

          Hydrodynamics

          Hydrostatics

Liquor industry (May subdiv. geog.)   **338.4**

   BT   **Beverage industry**

   NT   **Bars**

   RT   **Liquors**

Liquor problem

   USE   **Alcoholism**

          Drinking of alcoholic beverages

Liquors   663; 641.2

   UF   Cordials (Liquor)

          Drinks

          Intoxicants

          Liqueurs

          Liquors and liqueurs

   SA   types of liquors and liqueurs [to be added as needed]

   BT   **Alcoholic beverages**

          Beverages

   RT   **Distillation**

          Liquor industry

Liquors and liqueurs

   USE   **Liquors**

List books
USE **Books of lists**
Listening 153.6; 153.7
BT **Attention**
Educational psychology
RT **Hearing**
Listening devices
USE **Eavesdropping**
Lists
USE **Books of lists**
and topics with the subdivision
Lists, e.g. **Sports—Lists** [to
be added as needed]
LISTSERV lists
USE **Electronic discussion groups**
Literacy (May subdiv. geog.) 302.2;
379.2
UF Illiteracy
BT **Education**
NT **Computer literacy**
Functional literacy
Media literacy
Technological literacy
Visual literacy
Literacy, Visual
USE **Visual literacy**
Literary awards
USE **Literary prizes**
Literary characters
USE **Characters and characteristics**
in literature
Literary collections
USE **Anthologies**
Literature—Collections
and form headings for minor
literary forms that represent
collections of works of several
authors, e.g. **Essays;**
American essays; Parodies;
Short stories; etc.; major literary
forms and national literatures
with the subdivision
Collections, e.g. **Poetry—Collections;**
English literature—
Collections; etc.; and subjects
with the subdivision *Literary*
collections, for collections focused
on a single subject by
two or more authors involving
two or more literary forms,

e.g. **Cats—Literary collections** [to be added as needed]
Literary criticism
USE **Criticism**
Literature—History and criticism
Literary forgeries 098
UF Frauds, Literary
BT **Counterfeits and counterfeiting**
Forgery
Literary landmarks (May subdiv. geog.)
809; 810.9, etc.
UF Authors—Homes and haunts
Landmarks, Literary
BT **Historic buildings**
Literature—History and criticism
NT **English authors—Homes**
Literary landmarks—United States
810.9
Literary prizes (May subdiv. geog.)
807.9
UF Book awards
Book prizes
Literary awards
Literature—Prizes
SA names of awards, e.g. **Caldecott**
Medal [to be added as needed]
BT **Awards**
NT **Caldecott Medal**
Literature—Competitions
Newbery Medal
Literary property
USE **Copyright**
Intellectual property
Literary recreations 793.73
UF Language games
Recreations, Literary
BT **Amusements**
NT **Charades**
Plot-your-own stories
Rebuses
Riddles
Word games
Literary style 808; 809
UF Style, Literary
BT **Literature**
NT **Letter writing**
RT **Criticism**
Rhetoric

Literary themes
USE **Literature—Themes**

Literature 800

Literatures are described by countries or geographic regions. In countries or regions with more than one major language the literature may be further qualified by the language in parentheses, e.g. **Canadian literature (French)**. There is no distinction made in subject headings between literary works in their original languages and in translations.

UF Belles lettres
Modern literature

SA literatures of countries or of regions larger than a single country, e.g. **English literature; French literature; Scandinavian literature;** etc.; national or regional literatures qualified if needed by the language in which the literature was originally written or subdivided by a sub-set of authors within the literature, e.g. **African literature (English); American literature— African American authors;** etc.; literatures of particular religions, e.g. **Christian literature;** literatures of languages not identified with a particular country, e.g. **Latin literature;** and subjects, themes, and stylistic features in literature, e.g. **Bible in literature; Children in literature; Characters and characteristics in literature; Symbolism in literature;** etc. [to be added as needed]

BT **Humanities**
Language arts

NT **African literature (English)**
American literature
Authorship
Ballads
Bible in literature
Biography as a literary form
Black humor (Literature)
Brazilian literature
Campaign literature
Canadian literature
Catholic literature
Chapbooks

Characters and characteristics in literature
Children's literature
Classical literature
Classicism
Communism and literature
Comparative literature
Criticism
Danish literature
Diaries
Drama
Early Christian literature
English literature
Epic literature
Erotic literature
Essay
Fables
Fiction
French literature
Gay men's writings
German literature
Greek literature
Hebrew literature
Humanism
Icelandic literature
Indic literature
Jewish literature
Journalism
Latin American literature
Latin literature
Legends
Lesbians' writings
Literary style
Medieval literature
Mexican literature
Mock-heroic literature
Modern Greek literature
Modernism in literature
Multicultural literature
Music and literature
Native American literature
Norwegian literature
Old Norse literature
Parody
Picaresque literature
Poetry
Portuguese literature
Realism in literature
Religion in literature
Religious literature
Romance literature

Literature—*Continued*
> **Romances**
> **Russian literature**
> **Sagas**
> **Satire**
> **Scandinavian literature**
> **Short story**
> **Soviet literature**
> **Spanish literature**
> **Speeches**
> **Stories, plots, etc.**
> **Swedish literature**
> **Symbolism in literature**
> **West Indian literature (French)**
> **Wit and humor**
> **World War, 1939-1945—Literature and the war**
> **Young adult literature**
> RT **Books**

Literature and communism
> USE **Communism and literature**

Literature and music
> USE **Music and literature**

Literature and the war
> USE names of wars with the subdivision *Literature and the war,* e.g. **World War, 1939-1945—Literature and the war** [to be added as needed]

Literature—Bio-bibliography 809
> RT **Authors**

Literature—Collections 808.8
> Use for collections of literary works by several authors not limited to a single literature or literary form or focused on a single subject.
> UF Collected works
> Collections of literature
> Literary collections
> Literature—Selections
> SA form headings for minor literary forms that represent collections of works of several authors, e.g. **Essays; American essays; Parodies; Short stories;** etc.; major literary forms and national literatures with the subdivision *Collections,* e.g. **Poetry—Collections; English literature—Collections;** etc.; and subjects with the subdivision *Literary collections,* for collections focused on a single subject by two or more authors involving two or more literary forms, e.g. **Cats—Literary collections** [to be added as needed]

Literature, Comparative
> USE **Comparative literature**

Literature—Competitions 807.9
> BT **Contests**
> **Literary prizes**

Literature—Criticism
> USE **Literature—History and criticism**

Literature—Dictionaries 803
> BT **Encyclopedias and dictionaries**
> NT **English literature—Dictionaries**

Literature, Erotic
> USE **Erotic literature**

Literature—Evaluation
> USE **Best books**
> **Book reviewing**
> **Books and reading**
> **Criticism**
> **Literature—History and criticism**

Literature—Film and video adaptations
> USE **Film adaptations**
> **Television adaptations**

Literature—History and criticism 809
> Use for materials that are themselves histories or criticisms of literature in general. Materials on the history, principles, methods, etc., of literary criticism are entered under **Criticism.**
> UF Appraisal of books
> Books—Appraisal
> Evaluation of literature
> Literary criticism
> Literature—Criticism
> Literature—Evaluation
> NT **Literary landmarks**

Literature—Indexes 016.8

Literature, Medieval
> USE **Medieval literature**

Literature—Outlines, syllabi, etc. 802
> NT **English literature—Outlines, syllabi, etc.**

Literature—Prizes
> USE **Literary prizes**

Literature—Selections
> USE **Literature—Collections**

Literature—Stories, plots, etc.
    USE **Stories, plots, etc.—Collections**
Literature—Themes   809
    UF   Literary themes
         Themes in literature
    SA   subjects, racial and ethnic
         groups, and classes of persons
         in literature, e.g. **Dogs in literature; Women in literature;** etc., and names of persons, families, and corporate bodies with the subdivision *In art,* e.g. **Napoleon I, Emperor of the French, 1769-1821—In literature** [to be added as needed]
    NT **African Americans in literature**
        Animals in literature
        Blacks in literature
        Children in literature
        Dogs in literature
        Napoleon I, Emperor of the French, 1769-1821—In literature
        Nature in literature
        Travel in literature
        Women in literature
    RT **Characters and characteristics in literature**
Literatures of the Soviet Union
    USE **Soviet literature**
Lithographers (May subdiv. geog.) **763.092; 920**
    BT **Artists**
Lithography (May subdiv. geog.)   **686.2; 763; 764**
    UF   Lithoprinting
    BT **Color printing**
        Printing
        Prints
    NT **Offset printing**
Lithoprinting
    USE **Lithography**
        Offset printing
Litigation (May subdiv. geog.)   **347**
    UF   Actions and defenses
        Civil law suits
        Defense (Law)
        Law suits
        Lawsuits

        Personal actions (Law)
        Suing (Law)
        Suits (Law)
    BT **Law**
    NT **Witnesses**
    RT **Arbitration and award**
Littering
    USE **Refuse and refuse disposal**
Little League baseball   796.357
    BT **Baseball**
Little theater movement   792
    UF   Community theater
    BT **Theater**
    RT **Amateur theater**
Liturgical year
    USE **Church year**
Liturgics
    USE **Liturgies**
Liturgies   264; 291.3
    Use for general materials on the forms of prayers, rituals, and ceremonies used in public worship, including the theological and historical study of liturgies, and for texts of liturgies from more than one religion.
    UF   Church service books
        Liturgics
        Liturgy
        Ritual
        Service books (Liturgy)
    SA   names of individual religions and denominations with the subdivision *Liturgy* or *Liturgy—Texts;* e.g. **Catholic Church—Liturgy; Catholic Church—Liturgy—Texts** etc. [to be added as needed]
    BT **Religion**
        Rites and ceremonies
    NT **Catholic Church—Liturgy**
        Eucharist
        Hymns
        Judaism—Liturgy
        Mass (Liturgy)
    RT **Church music**
Liturgy
    USE **Liturgies**
        and names of individual religions and denominations with the subdivision *Liturgy* e.g. **Judaism—Liturgy; Catholic Church—Liturgy;** etc. [to be added as needed]

Live poliovirus vaccine
USE **Poliomyelitis vaccine**
Livestock
USE **Domestic animals**
Livestock industry
Livestock breeding (May subdiv. geog.)
636.08
UF Livestock—Breeding
BT **Breeding**
Livestock industry
Livestock—Breeding
USE **Livestock breeding**
Livestock industry (May subdiv. geog.)
636
Use for materials on stock raising as an industry. General materials on farm and other domestic animals are entered under **Domestic animals.**
UF Animal husbandry
Animal industry
Livestock
Stock raising
BT **Agriculture**
Economic zoology
NT **Dairying**
Livestock breeding
Livestock judging
RT **Domestic animals**
Livestock judging 636
UF Stock judging
BT **Livestock industry**
Living earth theory
USE **Gaia hypothesis**
Living skills
USE **Life skills**
Living together
USE **Unmarried couples**
Living wills 344
BT **Wills**
RT **Right to die**
Terminal care
Livres à clef
USE **Romans à clef**
Lizards (May subdiv. geog.) 597.95
BT **Reptiles**
Loan associations
USE **Savings and loan associations**
Loan funds, Student
USE **Student loan funds**
Loans (May subdiv. geog.) 332.7
UF Borrowing
Lending

BT **Finance**
NT **Government lending**
Interest (Economics)
Mortgages
Personal loans
Public debts
Savings and loan associations
Student aid
RT **Credit**
Investments
Loans, Personal
USE **Personal loans**
Lobbying (May subdiv. geog.) 328.3
Use for materials on groups that promote their own interests with public officials. Materials on special interest groups that support sympathetic candidates for public office through campaign contributions are entered under **Political action committees.**
UF Interest groups
Lobbying and lobbyists
Lobbyists
Pressure groups
SA names of specific lobbying and pressure groups [to be added as needed]
BT **Politics**
Propaganda
RT **Political action committees**
Lobbying and lobbyists
USE **Lobbying**
Lobbyists
USE **Lobbying**
Lobsters (May subdiv. geog.) 595.3
BT **Crustacea**
Shellfish
Local government (May subdiv. geog.)
320.8; 352.14
Use for materials on the government of districts, counties, townships, etc. Materials limited to county government only are entered under **County government.** Materials limited to the government of cities and towns are entered under **Municipal government.**
UF Government, Local
Town meeting
Township government
BT **Administrative law**
Community organization
Political science
NT **County government**
Metropolitan government
Municipal government
Public administration

Local government—*Continued*
　　State-local relations
Local history 907
　　Use for materials on the writing and compiling of local histories. Collective histories of several localities are entered under the country, state, etc., with the subdivision *Local history*. Individual local histories are entered under the city, county, or other locality with the subdivision *History*.
　UF　Community history
　　　　Regional history
　SA　names of countries, states, etc., with the subdivision *Local history,* e.g. **United States—Local history; Ohio—Local history;** etc.; and names of cities, counties, or other localities with the subdivision *History,* e.g. **Chicago (Ill.)—History** [to be added as needed]
　BT　**Historiography**
　　　　History
　NT　**Ohio—Local history**
　　　　United States—Local history
Local-state relations
　USE　**State-local relations**
Local traffic
　USE　**City traffic**
Local transit (May subdiv. geog.) 388.4
　　Use for materials on the various modes of local public transportation.
　UF　City transit
　　　　Mass transit
　　　　Municipal transit
　　　　Public transit
　　　　Rapid transit
　　　　Transit systems
　　　　Urban transportation
　BT　**Traffic engineering**
　　　　Transportation
　NT　**Buses**
　　　　Street railroads
　　　　Subways
Localism
　USE　**Regionalism**
Localisms
　USE　names of languages with the subdivision *Provincialisms,* e.g. **English language—Provincialisms** [to be added as needed]
Lockouts
　USE　**Strikes**

Locks and keys 683
　UF　Keys
　BT　**Burglary protection**
Locomotion 152.3; 388
　NT　**Aeronautics**
　　　　Animal locomotion
　　　　Flight
　　　　Horsemanship
　　　　Human locomotion
　　　　Navigation
　　　　Transportation
　　　　Walking
Locomotives (May subdiv. geog.) 625.26
　BT　**Railroads**
　NT　**Steam locomotives**
Locomotives—Models 625.1
　UF　Model trains
　BT　**Models and modelmaking**
Locusts 595.7; 632
　BT　**Insect pests**
　　　　Insects
Log cabins and houses (May subdiv. geog.) 728
　UF　Cabins
　BT　**House construction**
　　　　Houses
Logarithms 513.2
　BT　**Algebra**
　　　　Mathematics—Tables
　　　　Trigonometry—Tables
　NT　**Slide rule**
Logging (May subdiv. geog.) 634.9
　　Use for materials on the felling of trees and the transportation of logs to sawmills. Materials on lumber and the preparation of lumber are entered under **Lumber and lumbering.**
　UF　Timber—Harvesting
　BT　**Forests and forestry**
Logic 160
　UF　Argumentation
　　　　Deduction (Logic)
　　　　Dialectics
　　　　Fallacies
　　　　Induction (Logic)
　BT　**Intellect**
　　　　Philosophy
　　　　Science—Methodology
　NT　**Certainty**
　　　　Critical thinking
　　　　Probabilities
　　　　Symbolic logic
　　　　Theory of knowledge

Logic—*Continued*
  RT **Reasoning**
      Thought and thinking
Logic, Symbolic and mathematical
  USE **Symbolic logic**
Lone Ranger films   791.43
    May be used for individual works, collections, or materials about Lone Ranger films.
  BT **Western films**
Loneliness   155.9; 158
  UF Social isolation
      Solitude
  BT **Emotions**
Long distance running
  USE **Marathon running**
Long distance swimming
  USE **Marathon swimming**
Long distance telephone service (May subdiv. geog.)   **384.6**
  UF Telephone—Long distance
  BT **Telephone**
Long life
  USE **Longevity**
Long-term care facilities (May subdiv. geog.)   **362.1**
  UF Extended care facilities
  BT **Hospitals**
      Medical care
  NT **Nursing homes**
Longevity (May subdiv. geog.)   **612.6; 613**
  UF Life span prolongation
      Long life
  BT **Age**
      Life expectancy
  NT **Aging**
  RT **Middle age**
      Old age
Longitude   526; 527
  UF Degrees of latitude and longitude
  BT **Earth**
      Geodesy
      Nautical astronomy
Looking glasses
  USE **Mirrors**
Looms   677; 746.1
  BT **Weaving**
Loran   621.384
  BT **Navigation**
Lord's Day
  USE **Sabbath**

Lord's prayer   226.9; 242
  BT **Jesus Christ—Prayers**
Lord's Supper
  USE **Eucharist**
Losing things
  USE **Lost and found possessions**
Lost and found possessions   330.1
  UF Finding things
      Losing things
      Lost possessions
      Lost things
  BT **Property**
Lost architectural heritage
  USE **Lost architecture**
Lost architecture (May subdiv. geog.)   **720**
    Use for materials on buildings and structures that have been destroyed or demolished.
  UF Lost architectural heritage
      Lost buildings
  BT **Architecture**
Lost buildings
  USE **Lost architecture**
Lost children
  USE **Missing children**
Lost possessions
  USE **Lost and found possessions**
Lost things
  USE **Lost and found possessions**
Lotteries (May subdiv. geog.)   **336.1**
  BT **Gambling**
Louisiana Purchase   973.4; 976.3
  BT **United States—History—1783-1809**
Love   152.4; 177; 306.7
  UF Affection
  BT **Emotions**
      Human behavior
  NT **Courtship**
  RT **Friendship**
Love Canal Chemical Waste Landfill (Niagara Falls, N.Y.)   363.72
  BT **Hazardous waste sites**
      Landfills
Love poetry   808.81; 811, etc.
    May be used for individual works, collections, or materials about love poetry.
  BT **Poetry**
  RT **Erotic poetry**
Love—Religious aspects   231 ; 291.2
  UF Love (Theology)
  RT **Charity**

Love stories   808.83; 813, etc.

May be used for individual works, collections, or materials about love stories.

UF   Romance novels

Romances (Love stories)

Romantic fiction

Romantic stories

BT   **Fiction**

RT   **Erotic fiction**

Gothic novels

Romantic suspense novels

Love stories—Technique   808.3

BT   **Authorship**

Love (Theology)

USE   **Love—Religious aspects**

Low income housing

USE   **Public housing**

Low sodium diet

USE   **Salt-free diet**

Low temperature biology

USE   **Cryobiology**

Low temperatures   536; 621.5

UF   Cryogenics

BT   **Temperature**

NT   **Cryobiology**

RT   **Cold**

Refrigeration

Loyalists, American

USE   **American Loyalists**

Loyalty   172

UF   Faithfulness

BT   **Ethics**

Virtue

NT   **Patriotism**

Loyalty oaths

USE   **Internal security**

Lubrication and lubricants   621.8

UF   Grease

BT   **Machinery**

RT   **Bearings (Machinery)**

Oils and fats

Lullabies   782.42

UF   Cradle songs

BT   **Bedtime**

Children's poetry

Children's songs

Songs

Lumber and lumbering (May subdiv. geog.)   **634.9; 674**

Use for general materials on lumber and the preparation of lumber. Materials on the felling of trees and the transportation of logs to sawmills are entered under **Logging.**

UF   Timber

Woods

BT   **Forest products**

Forests and forestry

Trees

Wood

Luminescence   535

BT   **Light**

Radiation

NT   **Bioluminescence**

Phosphorescence

Luminescent books

USE   **Glow-in-the-dark books**

Luminous books

USE   **Glow-in-the-dark books**

Lunar bases   629.45

UF   Moon bases

BT   **Civil engineering**

Life support systems (Space environment)

Lunar eclipses   523.3

UF   Eclipses, Lunar

Moon—Eclipses

BT   **Astronomy**

Lunar expeditions

USE   **Space flight to the moon**

Lunar exploration

USE   **Moon—Exploration**

Lunar geology   559.9

UF   Geology, Lunar

Geology—Moon

Moon—Geology

BT   **Astrogeology**

NT   **Lunar soil**

Moon rocks

Lunar petrology

USE   **Moon rocks**

Lunar probes   629.43

UF   Moon probes

SA   names of specific lunar probe projects [to be added as needed]

BT   **Space probes**

NT   **Project Ranger**

Lunar rocks

USE   **Moon rocks**

Lunar soil   523.3; 552.0999; 631.4

UF   Moon soil

Soils, Lunar

BT   **Lunar geology**

RT   **Moon—Surface**

Lunar surface
  USE **Moon—Surface**
Lunar surface radio communication
  USE **Radio in astronautics**
Luncheons   642
  BT **Cooking**
       Menus
  RT **Entertaining**
Lunchrooms
  USE **Restaurants**
Lung cancer   616.99
  UF Lungs—Cancer
  BT **Cancer**
       Lungs—Diseases
Lungs   611; 612.2
  BT **Respiratory system**
Lungs—Cancer
  USE **Lung cancer**
Lungs—Diseases   616.2
  SA types of lung diseases [to be
       added as needed]
  BT **Diseases**
  NT **Lung cancer**
       Pneumonia
       Tuberculosis
Lying
  USE **Truthfulness and falsehood**
Lyme disease   616.9
  BT **Diseases**
Lymphatic system   573.1; 612.4; 616.4
  BT **Physiology**
Lynching (May subdiv. geog.)   **364.1**
  BT **Crime**
  RT **Vigilance committees**
Lyricists (May subdiv. geog.)   **782.0092;**
       920
  UF Songwriters
  BT **Poets**
Lyrics
  USE **Popular music—Texts**
Machine design   621.8
  UF Machinery—Construction
       Machinery—Design and con-
       struction
  SA types of machines, equipment,
       etc., with the subdivision *De-
       sign and construction,* e.g.
       **Airplanes—Design and con-
       struction** [to be added as
       needed]

  BT **Design**
       Machinery
  NT **Machinery—Models**
Machine intelligence
  USE **Artificial intelligence**
Machine language
  USE **Programming languages**
**Machine readable bibliographic data
       025.3**
  UF Bibliographic data in machine
       readable form
       Cataloging data in machine read-
       able form
  SA names of projects, formats, and
       systems, e.g. **MARC formats**
       [to be added as needed]
  BT **Cataloging**
       Information services
       Information systems
       Libraries—Automation
  NT **MARC formats**
Machine readable catalog system
  USE **MARC formats**
Machine readable dictionaries   423, etc.
  UF Dictionaries, Machine readable
  BT **Encyclopedias and dictionaries**
Machine shop practice   670.42
  UF Shop practice
  NT **Drilling and boring (Metal,
       wood, etc.)**
       Grinding and polishing
  RT **Machine shops**
Machine shops   670.42
  RT **Machine shop practice**
Machine tools   621.9
  SA types of machine tools [to be
       added as needed]
  BT **Machinery**
       Tools
  NT **Planing machines**
  RT **Drilling and boring (Metal,
       wood, etc.)**
       Grinding and polishing
Machinery   621.8
  UF Machines
  BT **Manufactures**
       Mechanical engineering
       Power (Mechanics)
       Technology
       Tools

Machinery—*Continued*

NT Agricultural machinery
Bearings (Machinery)
Belts and belting
Conveying machinery
Electric machinery
Engines
Gearing
Hoisting machinery
Hydraulic machinery
Industrial equipment
Lubrication and lubricants
Machine design
Machine tools
Mechanical drawing
Metalworking machinery
Robots
Simple machines
Woodworking machinery

RT Mechanics
Mills
Power transmission

Machinery—Construction
USE Machine design

Machinery—Design and construction
USE Machine design

Machinery—Drawing
USE Mechanical drawing

Machinery in industry
USE Industrial equipment
Machinery in the workplace

Machinery in the workplace 338

Use for materials on the social and economic aspects of mechanization in the area of work.

UF Machinery in industry
Technology in the workplace

BT Work environment

NT Automation

Machinery—Models 621.8

UF Mechanical models
Models, Mechanical

BT Machine design
Models and modelmaking

Machines
USE Machinery

Machines, Simple
USE Simple machines

Macintosh (Computer) 004.165

UF Apple Macintosh (Computer)

BT Computers

Made-for-TV movies
USE Television movies

Madonna
USE Mary, Blessed Virgin, Saint

Magazine editing
USE Journalism—Editing

Magazines
USE Periodicals

Maghreb
USE North Africa

Magic (May subdiv. geog.) 133.4

Use for materials on charms, spells, etc., believed to have supernatural power. Materials on types of entertainment involving illusionistic tricks are entered under **Magic tricks.**

UF Black art (Magic)
Black magic (Witchcraft)
Necromancy
Sorcery
Spells

BT Occultism

RT Hallucinations and illusions
Magic tricks
Witchcraft

Magic lanterns
USE Projectors

Magic tricks 793.8

UF Conjuring
Legerdemain
Prestidigitation
Sleight of hand

BT Amusements
Tricks

NT Card tricks

RT Hallucinations and illusions
Magic

Magna Carta 342; 942.03

BT Charters
Constitutional law
Great Britain—History—1154-1399, Plantagenets

Magnet schools (May subdiv. geog.)
373.24

Use for materials on schools offering special courses not available in the regular school curriculum and designed to attract students without reference to the usual attendance zone rules, often as an aid to voluntary school desegregation.

BT Public schools
School integration
Schools

Magnet winding
USE **Electromagnets**
Magnetic needle
USE **Compass**
Magnetic recorders and recording
621.382

Use for general materials on audio, computer, and video recording on a magnetizable medium.

UF Cassette recorders and recording
Tape recorders
BT **Electronic apparatus and appliances**
Magnetic resonance accelerator
USE **Cyclotrons**
Magnetic resonance imaging 616.07
UF Imaging, Magnetic resonance
MRI (Magnetic resonance imaging)
Nuclear magnetic resonance imaging
BT **Diagnosis**
Magnetism 538
BT **Physics**
NT **Compass**
Electromagnetism
Electromagnets
Magnets
RT **Electricity**
Magnets 538; 621.34
BT **Magnetism**
NT **Electromagnets**
Mail-order business (May subdiv. geog.)
658.8; 659.13
UF Mail order catalogs
BT **Business**
Direct selling
Selling
Mail order catalogs
USE **Commercial catalogs**
Mail-order business
Mail service
USE **Postal service**
Mainstreaming in education (May subdiv. geog.) **371.9**
BT **Education**
Exceptional children
Handicapped children
RT **Special education**

Maintenance and repair
USE **Repairing**
and types of things that require maintenance with the subdivision *Maintenance and repair,* e.g. **Automobiles—Maintenance and repair; Buildings—Maintenance and repair;** etc.; and types of things that require no maintenance with the subdivision *Repairing,* e.g. **Radio—Repairing** [to be added as needed]
Maintenance of biological diversity
USE **Biological diversity conservation**
Maize
USE **Corn**
Make-believe playmates
USE **Imaginary playmates**
Makeup (Cosmetics)
USE **Cosmetics**
Makeup, Theatrical
USE **Theatrical makeup**
Making-choices stories
USE **Plot-your-own stories**
Maladjusted children
USE **Emotionally disturbed children**
Maladjustment (Psychology)
USE **Adjustment (Psychology)**
Malaria (May subdiv. geog.) **616.9**
BT **Diseases**
Fever
Male actors (May subdiv. geog.) **791.4; 792; 920**

Use for materials on several male actors that emphasize their identity as men. General materials on persons of the acting profession, whether male or female, are entered under **Actors.**

UF Men actors *[Former heading]*
BT **Actors**
Male change of life
USE **Male climacteric**
Male climacteric 612.6
UF Change of life in men
Climacteric, Male
Male change of life
Male menopause
Menopause, Male
BT **Aging**
Male-female relationship
USE **Man-woman relationship**

Male menopause
USE **Male climacteric**
Male role
USE **Sex role**
Malfeasance in office
USE **Misconduct in office**
Malformations, Congenital
USE **Birth defects**
Malignant tumors
USE **Cancer**
Malls, Shopping
USE **Shopping centers and malls**
Malnutrition (May subdiv. geog.)   **362.1;**
      616.3
    BT **Nutrition**
    RT **Starvation**
Malpractice (May subdiv. geog.)   **346.03**
    UF Liability, Professional
          Professional liability
          Professions—Tort liability
          Tort liability of professions
    SA types of professional personnel
          with the subdivision *Malprac-*
          tice [to be added as needed]
    BT **Liability (Law)**
    NT **Medical personnel—Malprac-**
          tice
          Physicians—Malpractice
Malpractice insurance (May subdiv.
    geog.)   **368.5**
    UF Insurance, Malpractice
          Insurance, Professional liability
          Professional liability insurance
    BT **Insurance**
Mammals (May subdiv. geog.)   **599**
    SA types of mammals, e.g. **Marine**
          mammals; Primates; Bats;
          etc. [to be added as needed]
    BT **Animals**
    NT **Bats**
          Beavers
          Bison
          Camels
          Cats
          Cattle
          Chipmunks
          Deer
          Dogs
          Elephants
          Fossil mammals
          Horses

          Marine mammals
          Mice
          Pigs
          Primates
          Rabbits
          Reindeer
          Seals (Animals)
          Sheep
          Squirrels
          Whales
          Wild cats
Mammals, Fossil
    USE **Fossil mammals**
Man
    USE **Human beings**
Man—Antiquity
    USE **Human origins**
Man in space
    USE **Space flight**
Man—Influence of environment
    USE **Environmental influence on**
          humans
Man—Influence on nature
    USE· **Human influence on nature**
Man—Origin
    USE **Human origins**
Man power
    USE **Manpower**
Man, Prehistoric
    USE **Fossil hominids**
          Prehistoric peoples
Man, Primitive
    USE **Primitive societies**
Man (Theology)
    USE **Human beings (Theology)**
Man-woman relationship (May subdiv.
    geog.)   **306.7**
    UF Female-male relationship
          Male-female relationship
          Men—Relations with women
          Men-women relationship
          Relationships, Man-woman
          Woman-man relationship
          Women-men relationship
          Women—Relations with men
    BT **Interpersonal relations**
    RT **Dating (Social customs)**
Management (May subdiv. geog.)   **658**
    Use for materials on the theory of manage-
   ment and on the application of management
   principles to business and industry.

Management—*Continued*
UF Administration
Business administration
Business management
Industrial management
Industrial organization
Management science
Organization and management
Scientific management
SA types of management, e.g. **Office management;** types of businesses and industries, types of industrial plants and processes, and names of individual corporate bodies, with the subdivision *Management,* e.g. **Information systems— Management;** and types of institutions in the spheres of health, education, and social services, and names of individual institutions with the subdivision *Administration,* e.g. **Libraries—Administration; Schools—Administration;** etc. [to be added as needed]
BT **Business**
Industries
NT **Crisis management**
Factory management
Farm management
Industrial efficiency
Industrial relations
Industrial welfare
Information systems—Management
Inventory control
Job analysis
Knowledge management
Marketing
Materials handling
Natural resources—Management
Occupational health and safety
Office management
Organizational change
Personnel management
Planning
Production standards
Purchasing
Sales management

Time management
RT **Operations research**
Management buyouts
USE **Leveraged buyouts**
Management—Employee participation
USE **Participative management**
Management information systems (May subdiv. geog.) **658.4**
UF Computer-based information systems
BT **Information systems**
Management of knowledge assets
USE **Knowledge management**
Management science
USE **Management**
Managers
USE **Supervisors**
Mandates (May subdiv. geog.) **321**
UF League of Nations—Mandatory system
BT **International law**
International organization
International relations
Mania
USE **Manic-depressive illness**
Manic depression
USE **Manic-depressive illness**
Manic-depressive illness 616.89
UF Bipolar depression
Bipolar disorder
Mania
Manic depression
Manic-depressive psychoses
Manic-depressive psychosis
Melancholia
BT **Mental illness**
RT **Depression (Psychology)**
Manic-depressive psychoses
USE **Manic-depressive illness**
Manic-depressive psychosis
USE **Manic-depressive illness**
Manifest destiny (United States)
USE **United States—Territorial expansion**
Manikins (Fashion models)
USE **Fashion models**
Manipulative materials
USE **Manipulatives**
Manipulatives 371.33
Use for works on educational materials designed to be handled or touched by students in learning mathematical concepts.

Manipulatives—*Continued*
  UF Manipulative materials
       Manipulatives (Education)
  BT **Audiovisual materials**
       Mathematics—Study and
         teaching
       Teaching—Aids and devices
Manipulatives (Education)
  USE **Manipulatives**
Manned space flight
  USE **Space flight**
Manned undersea research stations
  USE **Undersea research stations**
Mannequins (Fashion models)
  USE **Fashion models**
Manners
  USE **Courtesy**
       Etiquette
Manners and customs   **390**
  UF Ceremonies
       Customs, Social
       Folkways
       Social customs
       Social life and customs
       Traditions
  SA ethnic groups and names of
       countries, cities, etc., with the
       subdivision *Social life and*
       customs [to be added as need-
       ed]
  BT **Civilization**
       Ethnology
  NT **African Americans—Social life**
       and customs
       Blacks—Social life and cus-
         toms
       Bohemianism
       Caste
       Chicago (Ill.)—Social life and
         customs
       Chivalry
       Clothing and dress
       Costume
       Country life
       Courts and courtiers
       Dating (Social customs)
       Dueling
       Festivals
       Folklore
       Funeral rites and ceremonies
       Gifts
       Holidays

       Hugging
       Jews—Social life and customs
       Lifestyles
       Marriage customs and rites
       Native Americans—Social life
       and customs
       Ohio—Social life and customs
       Seafaring life
       Tattooing
       Travel
       United States—Social life and
       customs
  RT **Etiquette**
       Rites and ceremonies
Manpower (May subdiv. geog.)   **331.11**
    Use for materials on the strength of a coun-
    try in terms of available personnel, both mili-
    tary and industrial. Materials on personnel in
    specific fields are entered under kinds of
    workers, e.g. **Agricultural laborers; Nurses;**
    etc. Materials on investments of capital in
    training and educating employees to improve
    their productivity are entered under **Human**
    capital.
  UF Human resources
       Man power
  SA names of wars with the subdivi-
       sion *Manpower;* e.g. **World**
       War, 1939-1945—Manpower
       [to be added as needed]
  RT **Labor supply**
       Military readiness
Manpower policy
  USE **Labor policy**
Manslaughter
  USE **Homicide**
Manual training
  USE **Industrial arts education**
Manual workers
  USE **Labor**
       Working class
Manufactures (May subdiv. geog.)
       338.4; 670
  SA types of industries and names of
       manufactured articles [to be
       added as needed]
  BT **Commercial products**
       Industries
  NT **Brand name products**
       Consumer goods
       Generic products
       Machinery
       Mills
       Papermaking

Manufactures—*Continued*
    Patents
    Prices
    Trademarks
    Waste products
    RT Manufacturing industries
Manufactures—Chicago (Ill.)   338.4
    UF Chicago (Ill.)—Manufactures
Manufactures—Defects
    USE Product recall
Manufactures—Ohio   338.4
    UF Ohio—Manufactures
Manufactures recall
    USE Product recall
Manufactures—United States   338.4
    UF United States—Manufactures
Manufacturing in space
    USE Space industrialization
Manufacturing industries (May subdiv.
    geog.)   338.4
    BT Industries
    RT Manufactures
Manures
    USE Fertilizers
Manuscripts (May subdiv. geog.)   091
    SA subjects, literatures, groups of
        authors, individual literary au-
        thors, literary works entered
        under title, and sacred works
        with the subdivision *Manu-
        scripts* [to be added as need-
        ed]
    BT Archives
        Bibliography
        Books
    NT Illumination of books and
        manuscripts
    RT Autographs
        Charters
Manuscripts, Illuminated
    USE Illumination of books and
        manuscripts
Map drawing   526.022
    UF Cartography
        Plans
    BT Drawing
    RT Topographical drawing
Maple sugar   641.3; 664
    BT Sugar
Maps   912
    Use for general materials about maps and
    their history. Materials on the methods of map

making and the mapping of areas are entered
under **Map drawing.** Geographical atlases of
world coverage are entered under **Atlases.**
    UF Cartography
        Chartography
        Plans
    SA types of maps, e.g. **Road maps;**
        subjects with the subdivision
        Maps, e.g. **Geology—Maps;**
        and names of countries, cities,
        etc., and names of wars with
        the subdivision *Maps* [to be
        added as needed]
    BT Geography
    NT Atlases
        Automobile travel—Guidebooks
        Chicago (Ill.)—Maps
        Geology—Maps
        Globes
        Moon—Maps
        Nautical charts
        Ohio—Maps
        Road maps
        United States—Maps
        World War, 1939-1945—Maps
    RT Charts, diagrams, etc.
Maps, Historical
    USE Historical atlases
Maps, Military
    USE Military geography
Marathon running   796.42
    UF Long distance running
    BT Running
Marathon swimming   797.2
    UF Long distance swimming
    BT Swimming
Marble   552; 553.5
    BT Rocks
        Stone
MARC formats   025.3
    UF Machine readable catalog system
        MARC system
    BT Bibliographic control
        Machine readable bibliographic
        data
MARC system
    USE MARC formats
Marches (Demonstrations)
    USE Demonstrations
Marches (Exercises)
    USE Marching drills

Marches for civil rights
    USE   **Civil rights demonstrations**
Marches (Music)   783.18
    BT   **Military music**
Marching
    USE   **Marching drills**
Marching drills   613.7
    UF   Drill (Nonmilitary)
          Drills, Marching
          Marches (Exercises)
          Marching
    BT   **Physical education**
Mardi Gras
    USE   **Carnival**
Margarine   641.3; 664
    UF   Oleomargarine
    BT   **Butter**
Mariculture
    USE   **Aquaculture**
Marihuana
    USE   **Marijuana**
Marijuana   362.29; 613.8; 615; 633.7
    UF   Cannabis
          Grass (Drug)
          Hashish
          Marihuana
          Pot (Drug)
    BT   **Narcotics**
Marinas (May subdiv. geog.)   **387.1**
    UF   Yacht basins
    BT   **Boats and boating**
          Harbors
          Yachts and yachting
    NT   **Docks**
Marine animals (May subdiv. geog.)
    591.77
    UF   Marine fauna
          Sea animals
    BT   **Aquatic animals**
    NT   **Corals**
          Marine mammals
    RT   **Marine biology**
Marine aquaculture
    USE   **Aquaculture**
Marine aquariums   597.073; 639.34
    UF   Salt water aquariums
          Sea water aquariums
    SA   names of specific marine aquari-
          ums [to be added as needed]
    BT   **Aquariums**
    NT   **Marineland (Fla.)**

Marine architecture
    USE   **Naval architecture**
Marine biology   578.77
    UF   Ocean life
          Sea life
    BT   **Biology**
          Oceanography
    NT   **Marine ecology**
          Marine plants
          Marine resources
    RT   **Marine animals**
Marine disasters
    USE   **Shipwrecks**
Marine drilling platforms
    USE   **Drilling platforms**
Marine ecology   578.77
    BT   **Ecology**
          Marine biology
Marine engineering (May subdiv. geog.)
    623.8
        Use for materials on engineering as applied
        to ships and their machinery.
    UF   Naval engineering
    BT   **Civil engineering**
          Engineering
          Mechanical engineering
          Naval architecture
          Naval art and science
          Steam navigation
Marine engines   623.8
    BT   **Engines**
          Shipbuilding
          Steam engines
Marine fauna
    USE   **Marine animals**
Marine flora
    USE   **Marine plants**
Marine geology
    USE   **Submarine geology**
Marine insurance   368.2
    UF   Insurance, Marine
    BT   **Commerce**
          Insurance
          Maritime law
          Merchant marine
          Shipping
Marine law
    USE   **Maritime law**
Marine mammals (May subdiv. geog.)
    599.5
    SA   types of marine mammals [to be
          added as needed]

Marine mammals—*Continued*
   BT   **Mammals**
         Marine animals
   NT   **Seals (Animals)**
         Whales
Marine mineral resources (May subdiv.
     geog.)   **333.8; 553**
   UF   Mineral resources, Marine
         Ocean mineral resources
   BT   **Marine resources**
         Mines and mineral resources
         Ocean bottom
         Ocean engineering
   NT   **Ocean mining**
   RT   **Ocean energy resources**
Marine painting   **758**
   UF   Sea in art
         Seascapes
         Ships in art
   BT   **Painting**
Marine plants (May subdiv. geog.)   **579**
   UF   Aquatic plants
         Marine flora
         Water plants
   BT   **Marine biology**
         Plants
   NT   **Algae**
   RT   **Freshwater plants**
Marine pollution (May subdiv. geog.)
     363.739
   UF   Ocean pollution
         Offshore water pollution
         Sea pollution
   BT   **Oceanography**
         Water pollution
   RT   **Oil pollution of water**
Marine resources (May subdiv. geog.)
     333.91; 591.77
   UF   Ocean—Economic aspects
         Ocean resources
         Resources, Marine
         Sea resources
   BT   **Commercial products**
         Marine biology
         Natural resources
         Oceanography
   NT   **Aquaculture**
         Marine mineral resources
         Ocean energy resources
         Ocean engineering
         Seafood

Marine salvage   **387.5; 627**
   UF   Ship salvage
   BT   **International law**
         Maritime law
         Salvage
   RT   **Shipwrecks**
Marine transportation
   USE   **Shipping**
Marineland (Fla.)   **597.073; 639.34**
   BT   **Marine aquariums**
Mariners
   USE   **Sailors**
Mariner's compass
   USE   **Compass**
Marionettes
   USE   **Puppets and puppet plays**
Marital counseling
   USE   **Marriage counseling**
Marital infidelity
   USE   **Adultery**
Maritime discoveries
   USE   **Exploration**
Maritime law (May subdiv. geog.)
     341.7; 343.09
   UF   Law of the sea
         Marine law
         Merchant marine—Law and leg-
           islation
         Naval law
         Navigation—Law and legislation
         Sea laws
   BT   **International law**
         Law
         Shipping
   NT   **Freight**
         Marine insurance
         Marine salvage
         Merchant marine
         Pirates
         Ships—Safety regulations
   RT   **Commercial law**
         Territorial waters
Market gardening
   USE   **Truck farming**
Market surveys (May subdiv. geog.)
     658.8
   BT   **Advertising**
         Surveys
   RT   **Public opinion polls**

Marketing (May subdiv. geog.)   **380.1; 658.8**

Use for materials on the principles and methods involved in the transfer of merchandise from producer to consumer. Materials on food buying are entered under **Grocery shopping.**

UF   Distribution (Economics)
     Merchandising

SA   subjects with the subdivision
     Marketing, e.g. **Farm pro-**
     duce—Marketing [to be add-
     ed as needed]

BT   **Business**
     Management

NT   **Direct selling**
     Farm produce—Marketing
     Internet marketing
     Sales management
     Telemarketing

RT   **Advertising**
     Selling

Marketing (Home economics)

USE   **Grocery shopping**
      Shopping

Marketing of farm produce

USE   **Farm produce—Marketing**

Markets (May subdiv. geog.)   **381; 658.8**

Use for materials on places where many buyers and sellers are brought into contract with one another in order to exhange goods and services.

BT   **Business**
     Cities and towns
     Commerce

NT   **Stock exchanges**

RT   **Fairs**

Marking and grading (Education)

USE   **Grading and marking (Educa-**
      tion)

Marks

USE   **Hallmarks**
      and types of things with identi-
      fying marks, other than plate,
      with the subdivision *Marks,*
      e.g. **Pottery—Marks** [to be
      added as needed]

Marks on plate

USE   **Hallmarks**

Marriage (May subdiv. geog.)   **306.81; 346.01**

UF   Married life
     Matrimony

BT   **Family**
     Sacraments

NT   **Husbands**
     Intermarriage
     Marriage contracts
     Marriage counseling
     Marriage customs and rites
     Married people
     Remarriage
     Same-sex marriage
     Weddings
     Wives

RT   **Courtship**
     Domestic relations

Marriage—Annulment   **262.9; 346.01**

UF   Annulment of marriage

Marriage contracts (May subdiv. geog.)   **306.81; 346.01**

UF   Antenuptial contracts
     Premarital contracts
     Prenuptial agreements
     Prenuptial contracts

BT   **Contracts**
     Marriage

Marriage counseling   **362.82**

UF   Marital counseling
     Premarital counseling

BT   **Counseling**
     Family life education
     Marriage

RT   **Divorce mediation**

Marriage—Cross-cultural studies   **306.81**

Marriage customs and rites (May subdiv. geog.)   **392.5**

UF   Bridal customs

BT   **Manners and customs**
     Marriage
     Rites and ceremonies
     Weddings

Marriage, Interracial

USE   **Interracial marriage**

Marriage registers

USE   **Registers of births, etc.**

Marriage statistics

USE   **Vital statistics**

Married life

USE   **Marriage**

Married men

USE   **Husbands**

Married people (May subdiv. geog.)
  306.872
  UF Married persons
  BT **Family**
      Marriage
  NT **Husbands**
      Wives
Married persons
  USE **Married people**
Married women
  USE **Wives**
Mars (Planet) 523.43
  BT **Planets**
  NT **Mars probes**
Mars (Planet)—Exploration 629.43
  BT **Planets—Exploration**
Mars (Planet)—Geology 559.9
  BT **Astrogeology**
Mars (Planet)—Pictorial works 523.43;
  778.3
  BT **Space photography**
Mars (Planet)—Satellites 523.9
  UF Satellites—Mars
  BT **Satellites**
Mars probes 629.43
  UF Martian probes
  BT **Mars (Planet)**
      Space probes
Marshall Plan
  USE **Reconstruction (1939-1951)**
Marshes (May subdiv. geog.) 551.41
  BT **Wetlands**
Martial arts (May subdiv. geog.) 796.8
  BT **Athletics**
  NT **Archery**
      Dueling
  RT **Self-defense**
      Self-defense for women
Martian probes
  USE **Mars probes**
Martin Luther King Day 394.261
  BT **Holidays**
Martyrs 200.92; 272.092
  BT **Church history**
      Heroes and heroines
  RT **Persecution**
      Saints
Marxian theory
  USE **Marxism**

Marxism (May subdiv. geog.) 335.4
  Use for materials on the system of econom-
  ic and political thought developed by Karl
  Marx, Friedrich Engels, or their followers.
  UF Marxian theory
      Marxist theory
  BT **Economics**
      Philosophy
      Political science
      Sociology
  RT **Class consciousness**
      Communism
      Dialectical materialism
      Socialism
Marxist theory
  USE **Marxism**
Mary, Blessed Virgin, Saint 232.91
  UF Blessed Virgin Mary
      Madonna
      Virgin Mary
  BT **Saints**
Mary, Blessed Virgin, Saint—Art 704.9
  BT **Christian art**
Mary, Blessed Virgin, Saint—Prayers
  242
  BT **Prayers**
Masculine psychology
  USE **Men—Psychology**
Masculinity (May subdiv. geog.) 155.3
  UF Masculinity (Psychology)
  BT **Sex (Psychology)**
  RT **Men**
Masculinity (Psychology)
  USE **Masculinity**
Masers 621.381
  BT **Amplifiers (Electronics)**
      Electromagnetism
      Microwaves
Masks (Facial) 391.4
  BT **Costume**
Masks (Plays) 808.82; 812, etc.
  May be used for individual works, collec-
  tions, or materials about masks.
  UF Masques (Plays)
  BT **Drama**
      Pageants
      Theater
Masks (Sculpture) (May subdiv. geog.)
  731
  UF Death masks
  BT **Sculpture**

Masonic orders
USE **Freemasons**
Masonry (May subdiv. geog.) 693
BT **Building**
Stone
NT **Cement**
Concrete
Plaster and plastering
Stonecutting
RT **Bricklaying**
Masons (Secret order)
USE **Freemasons**
Masques (Plays)
USE **Masks (Plays)**
Mass
USE **Mass (Liturgy)**
Mass communication
USE **Communication**
Mass media
Telecommunication
Mass culture
USE **Popular culture**
Mass feeding
USE **Food service**
Mass (Liturgy) 264
UF Mass *[Former heading]*
BT **Liturgies**
RT **Eucharist**
Mass media (May subdiv. geog.) 302.23
UF Mass communication
Media
SA topics with the subdivision *Press coverage*, e.g. **Food contamination—Press coverage** [to be added as needed]
BT **Communication**
NT **Motion pictures**
Newspapers
Periodicals
Radio broadcasting
Sex in mass media
Television broadcasting
Violence in mass media
RT **Popular culture**
Mass media literacy
USE **Media literacy**
Mass political behavior
USE **Political participation**
Political psychology
Mass psychology
USE **Social psychology**

Mass spectra
USE **Mass spectrometry**
Mass spectrometry 543; 547
UF Mass spectra
Mass spectrum analysis
BT **Spectrum analysis**
Mass spectrum analysis
USE **Mass spectrometry**
Mass transit
USE **Local transit**
Massacres (May subdiv. geog.) **179.7; 904**
SA names of individual massacres, e.g. **Saint Bartholomew's Day, Massacre of, 1572** [to be added as needed]
BT **Atrocities**
History
Persecution
NT **Saint Bartholomew's Day, Massacre of, 1572**
Massage 615.8; 646.7
BT **Physical therapy**
NT **Acupressure**
Chiropractic
Electrotherapeutics
RT **Osteopathic medicine**
Mastodon 569
BT **Extinct animals**
Fossil mammals
Mate selection in animals
USE **Animal courtship**
Materia medica (May subdiv. geog.) **615**
UF Herbals
Pharmacopoeias
SA types of drugs [to be added as needed]
BT **Medicine**
Therapeutics
NT **Anesthetics**
Narcotics
RT **Drugs**
Pharmacology
Pharmacy
Materialism (May subdiv. geog.) 146
BT **Philosophy**
Positivism
RT **Idealism**
Realism

Materials   620.1

Use for comprehensive works on the basic processed materials used in engineering and industry. Works on unprocessed minerals and unprocessed animal and vegetable products are entered under **Raw materials.**

UF   Engineering materials
      Industrial materials
      Strategic materials

SA   types of materials, e.g. **Building materials; Hazardous substances;** etc.; and scientific and technical disciplines and types of equipment and construction with the subdivision *Materials* [to be added as needed]

NT   **Adhesives**
      Airplanes—Materials
      Artists' materials
      Building materials
      Ceramics
      Finishes and finishing
      Hazardous substances

RT   **Engineering**

Materials handling   388; 658.7

UF   Handling of materials
      Mechanical handling

BT   **Management**

NT   **Conveying machinery**
      Freight

RT   **Trucks**

Maternity
USE   **Mothers**

Mathematical analysis   515

UF   Analysis (Mathematics)

BT   **Mathematics**

NT   **Algebra**
      Calculus
      Graph theory
      Linear algebra
      Numerical analysis

Mathematical drawing
USE   **Geometrical drawing**
      Mechanical drawing

Mathematical logic
USE   **Symbolic logic**

Mathematical models   511

UF   Models
      Models, Mathematical

SA   subjects with the subdivision *Mathematical models,* e.g. **Pollution—Mathematical models** [to be added as needed]

BT   **Mathematics**

NT   **Computer simulation**
      Fractals
      Game theory
      Pollution—Mathematical models
      System analysis

Mathematical notation   510

Use for materials on the system of graphic symbols used in mathematics as well as for materials on the process or method of setting these down.

UF   Mathematical symbols
      Mathematics—Notation
      Mathematics—Symbols
      Notation, Mathematical
      Symbols, Mathematical

RT   **Mathematics**

Mathematical readiness   372.7

UF   Arithmetical readiness
      Mathematics readiness
      Number readiness
      Readiness for mathematics

BT   **Arithmetic—Study and teaching**
      Mathematics—Study and teaching

Mathematical recreations   793.7

UF   Recreations, Mathematical

BT   **Amusements**
      Puzzles
      Scientific recreations

NT   **Number games**

Mathematical sequences
USE   **Sequences (Mathematics)**

Mathematical sets
USE   **Set theory**

Mathematical symbols
USE   **Mathematical notation**

Mathematicians (May subdiv. geog.)   510.92; 920

BT   **Scientists**

RT   **Mathematics**

Mathematics (May subdiv. geog.)   510

SA   subjects with the subdivision *Mathematics,* e.g. **Astronomy—Mathematics** [to be added as needed]

Mathematics—*Continued*
   BT   Science
   NT   Algebra
         Arithmetic
         Astronomy—Mathematics
         Binary system (Mathematics)
         Biomathematics
         Business mathematics
         Calculus
         Dynamics
         Fourth dimension
         Fractions
         Game theory
         Geometry
         Group theory
         Mathematical analysis
         Mathematical models
         Measurement
         Metric system
         Number theory
         Patterns (Mathematics)
         Probabilities
         Sequences (Mathematics)
         Set theory
         Symbolic logic
         Trigonometry
   RT   Mathematical notation
         Mathematicians
Mathematics—Computer-assisted instruc-
   tion   372.7; 510.78
   BT   Computer-assisted instruction
Mathematics—Notation
   USE   Mathematical notation
Mathematics readiness
   USE   Mathematical readiness
Mathematics—Study and teaching
   372.7; 510.7
   NT   Manipulatives
         Mathematical readiness
Mathematics—Symbols
   USE   Mathematical notation
Mathematics—Tables   510
   UF   Ready reckoners
   NT   Logarithms
         Trigonometry—Tables
Mating behavior
   USE   Animal courtship
         Sexual behavior in animals
Matrimony
   USE   Marriage

Matter   117; 530
   BT   Dynamics
         Physics
Mausoleums
   USE   Tombs
Maxims
   USE   Proverbs
Mayas   972.004
   BT   Native Americans—Central
           America
         Native Americans—Mexico
Meal planning
   USE   Menus
         Nutrition
Meals
   USE   types of meals, e.g. **Breakfasts;**
         Dinners; etc. [to be added as
         needed]
Meals for school children
   USE   School children—Food
Meals on wheels programs   362
      Use for materials on programs that deliver
   meals to the homebound.
   UF   Home delivered meals programs
   BT   Food relief
Measurement   389; 530.8
   UF   Metrology
   SA   subjects with the subdivision
         Measurement, e.g. **Air pollu-**
         tion—Measurement [to be
         added as needed]
   BT   Mathematics
   NT   Air pollution—Measurement
         Geodesy
         Measuring instruments
         Photometry
         Surveying
         Volume (Cubic content)
   RT   Weights and measures
Measurements, Electric
   USE   Electric measurements
Measures
   USE   Weights and measures
Measuring instruments   389; 681
   UF   Instruments, Measuring
   BT   Measurement
         Weights and measures
Meat   641.3; 664
   SA   types of meat [to be added as
         needed]

Meat—*Continued*
  BT **Food**
  NT **Beef**
      Carving (Meat, etc.)
Meat-eating animals
  USE **Carnivorous animals**
Meat industry (May subdiv. geog.)
    338.1
  UF Meat industry and trade
      Meat packing industry
      Packing industry
      Stockyards
  BT **Food industry**
  NT **Meat inspection**
Meat industry and trade
  USE **Meat industry**
Meat inspection (May subdiv. geog.)
    363.19
  UF Inspection of meat
  BT **Food adulteration and inspection**
      tion
      Meat industry
      Public health
Meat packing industry
  USE **Meat industry**
Mechanic arts
  USE **Industrial arts**
Mechanical brains
  USE **Cybernetics**
Mechanical drawing **604.2**
  UF Drafting, Mechanical
      Engineering drawing
      Industrial drawing
      Machinery—Drawing
      Mathematical drawing
      Plans
      Structural drafting
  BT **Drawing**
      Engineering
      Machinery
      Patternmaking
  NT **Blueprints**
      Graphic methods
      Lettering
  RT **Geometrical drawing**
Mechanical engineering (May subdiv.
    geog.) **621**
    Use for materials on the application of the
    principles of mechanics to the design, con-
    struction, and operation of machnery. Materi-
    als on the application of the principles of me-
    chanics to engineering structures other than

machinery are entered under **Applied me-
chanics.**
  BT **Civil engineering**
  NT **Electrical engineering**
      Machinery
      Marine engineering
      Mechanical movements
      Power (Mechanics)
      Power transmission
  RT **Steam engineering**
Mechanical handling
  USE **Materials handling**
Mechanical models
  USE **Machinery—Models**
Mechanical movements **531**
  UF Mechanisms (Machinery)
  BT **Kinematics**
      Mechanical engineering
      Mechanics
      Motion
  NT **Robots**
      Simple machines
  RT **Gearing**
Mechanical musical instruments **786.6**
  UF Musical instruments, Mechanical
  SA types of instruments, e.g. **Music
      boxes** [to be added as need-
      ed]
  BT **Musical instruments**
  NT **Music boxes**
Mechanical properties testing
  USE **Testing**
Mechanical speech recognition
  USE **Automatic speech recognition**
Mechanics **530; 531**
  BT **Physics**
  NT **Applied mechanics**
      Dynamics
      Fluid mechanics
      Hydraulics
      Hydrodynamics
      Hydrostatics
      Mechanical movements
      Power (Mechanics)
      Simple machines
      Soil mechanics
      Statics
      Strains and stresses
      Strength of materials
      Vibration
      Viscosity
      Wave mechanics

Mechanics—*Continued*
RT   Force and energy
      Kinematics
      Machinery
      Motion
Mechanics, Applied
USE   Applied mechanics
Mechanics (Persons)   920
Mechanisms (Machinery)
USE   Mechanical movements
Medallions
USE   Medals
Medals (May subdiv. geog.)   355.1; 737
UF   Badges of honor
      Medallions
SA   names of military services and
      other appropriate subjects with
      the subdivision *Medals,
      badges, decorations, etc.* [to
      be added as needed]
NT   United States. Army—Medals,
      badges, decorations, etc.
      United States. Navy—Medals,
      badges, decorations, etc.
RT   Decorations of honor
      Insignia
      Numismatics
Medals, badges, decorations, etc.
USE   types of armed forces with the
      subdivision *Medals, badges,
      decorations, etc.,* e.g. United
      States. Army—Medals,
      badges, decorations, etc. [to
      be added as needed]
Media
USE   Mass media
Media centers (Education)
USE   Instructional materials centers
Media coverage
USE   topics with the subdivision *Press
      coverage,* e.g. Food contami-
      nation—Press coverage [to
      be added as needed]
Media literacy (May subdiv. geog.)
      302.23
Use for materials on a person's knowledge
of and ability to use, interpret, and evaluate
the mass media.
UF   Mass media literacy
BT   Literacy
Mediation
USE   Arbitration and award

Mediation, Divorce
USE   Divorce mediation
Mediation, Industrial
USE   Industrial arbitration
Mediation, International
USE   International arbitration
Medicaid (May subdiv. geog.)   368.4
UF   Medical care for the poor
BT   National health insurance
      Poor—Medical care
      State medicine
RT   Medicare
Medical appointments and schedules
USE   Medical practice
Medical botany   581.6
UF   Botany, Medical
      Drug plants
      Herbal medicine
      Medicinal herbs
      Medicinal plants
      Plants, Medicinal
BT   Botany
      Medicine
      Pharmacy
Medical care (May subdiv. geog.)   362.1
Use for materials on the organization of
services and facilities for medical care. Mate-
rials on the technical and scientific aspects of
medical care are entered under Medicine.
UF   Delivery of health care
      Delivery of medical care
      Health care
      Health care delivery
      Medical services
      Personal health services
SA   ethnic groups, classes of per-
      sons, and names of wars with
      the subdivision *Medical care,*
      e.g. Native Americans—Med-
      ical care; Elderly—Medical
      care; etc. [to be added as
      needed]
BT   Public health
NT   Armies—Medical care
      Dental care
      Elderly—Medical care
      Health self-care
      Home care services
      Long-term care facilities
      Medical charities
      Mental health services

Medical care—*Continued*

> Native Americans—Medical
> care
> Occupational health services
> Poor—Medical care
> Sports medicine
> Terminal care
> United States—History—1861-
> 1865, Civil War—Medical
> care
> World War, 1939-1945—Medi-
> cal care
>
> RT **Health care reform**
> **Medicine**

Medical care—Costs   362.1

> UF Cost of medical care
> Medical service, Cost of
> Medicine—Cost of medical care
> BT **Medical economics**

Medical care—Ethical aspects

> USE **Medical ethics**

Medical care for the elderly

> USE **Elderly—Medical care**
> **Medicare**

Medical care for the poor

> USE **Medicaid**
> **Poor—Medical care**

Medical care, Prepaid

> USE **Health insurance**

Medical care reform

> USE **Health care reform**

Medical care—Social aspects

> USE **Social medicine**

Medical centers (May subdiv. geog.)
610.71

> RT **Hospitals**

Medical charities (May subdiv. geog.)
362.1

> UF Charities, Medical
> BT **Charities**
> **Medical care**
> **Public health**
> NT **Institutional care**
> RT **Hospitals**

Medical chemistry

> USE **Clinical chemistry**

Medical colleges (May subdiv. geog.)
610.71

> UF Medical schools
> BT **Colleges and universities**
> RT **Medicine—Study and teaching**

Medical consultation

> USE **Medical practice**

Medical diagnosis

> USE **Diagnosis**

Medical drama (Films)   791.43

> May be used for individual works, collec-
> tions, or materials about medical films.
> UF Doctor films
> BT **Motion pictures**

Medical drama (Radio programs)
791.44

> May be used for individual works, collec-
> tions, or materials about medical radio pro-
> grams.
> UF Doctor radio programs
> BT **Radio programs**

Medical drama (Television programs)
791.45

> May be used for individual works, collec-
> tions, or materials about medical television
> programs.
> UF Doctor television programs
> BT **Television programs**

Medical economics   338.4

> Use for comprehensive materials on the
> economic aspects of medical service from the
> point of view of both the practitioner and the
> public.
> SA types of medical services with
> the subdivision *Costs* [to be
> added as needed]
> BT **Economics**
> NT **Medical care—Costs**

Medical education

> USE **Medicine—Study and teaching**

Medical electricity

> USE **Electrotherapeutics**

Medical errors

> USE **Errors**
> **Medical personnel—Malprac-**
> **tice**
> **Physicians—Malpractice**

Medical ethics (May subdiv. geog.)   174

> UF Medical care—Ethical aspects
> Medicine—Ethical aspects
> SA types of medical practices and
> procedures with the subdivi-
> sion *Ethical aspects*, e.g.
> **Transplantation of organs,**
> **tissues, etc.—Ethical aspects**
> [to be added as needed]
> BT **Bioethics**
> **Ethics**
> **Professional ethics**

Medical ethics—*Continued*
NT   **Euthanasia**
Human experimentation in medicine
Right to die
RT   **Social medicine**
Medical examinations
USE   **Periodic health examinations**
and subjects, classes of persons, ethnic groups, and military services with the subdivision *Medical examinations,* e.g. **Children—Medical examinations** [to be added as needed]
Medical experimentation on humans
USE   **Human experimentation in medicine**
Medical fiction
USE   **Medical novels**
Medical folklore
USE   **Traditional medicine**
Medical genetics (May subdiv. geog.) **616**
UF   Clinical genetics
Congenital diseases
Hereditary diseases
Heredity of diseases
SA   names of diseases with the subdivision *Genetic aspects* [to be added as needed]
BT   **Genetics**
Pathology
NT   **Birth defects**
Cancer—Genetic aspects
Genetic counseling
Medical inspection in schools
USE   **Children—Medical examinations**
Medical insurance
USE   **Health insurance**
Medical insurance, National
USE   **National health insurance**
Medical jurisprudence (May subdiv. geog.) **614**
Use for materials on the application of medical knowledge to questions of law. Materials on the law as it affects medicine and the medical profession are entered under **Medicine—Law and legislation.**
UF   Forensic medicine
Jurisprudence, Medical
Legal medicine

BT   **Forensic sciences**
NT   **DNA fingerprinting**
Lie detectors and detection
Poisons and poisoning
Suicide
RT   **Medicine—Law and legislation**
Medical laws and legislation
USE   **Medicine—Law and legislation**
Medical malpractice
USE   **Medical personnel—Malpractice**
Medical missions (May subdiv. geog.) **362.1**
UF   Missions, Medical
BT   **Medicine**
Medical novels **813, etc.**
May be used for individual works, collections, or materials about novels with a medical setting.
UF   Doctor novels
Medical fiction
Medicine—Fiction
BT   **Fiction**
Medical offices
USE   **Medical practice**
Medical partnership
USE   **Medical practice**
Medical personnel (May subdiv. geog.) **610.69**
UF   Health care personnel
Health personnel
Health professions
Health sciences personnel
Health services personnel
Medical profession
BT   **Employees**
NT   **Nurses**
Physicians
RT   **Medicine**
Medical personnel—Malpractice (May subdiv. geog.) **346.03**
UF   Medical errors
Medical malpractice
SA   classes of persons in the medical field with the subdivision *Malpractice;* e.g. **Physicians—Malpractice** [to be added as needed]
BT   **Malpractice**
Medicine—Law and legislation

Medical photography   621.36; 778.3
   BT   **Photography**
       **Photography—Scientific appli-
         cations**
Medical practice (May subdiv. geog.)
    610.6

Use for materials on the organization and management of medicine as a profession. Scientific materials on the practice of medicine are entered under **Medicine.**

   UF   Clinics
       Group medical practice
       Medical appointments and sched-
         ules
       Medical consultation
       Medical offices
       Medical partnership
       Medical profession
       Medicine—Practice
   SA   types of medicine with the sub-
        division *Practice,* e.g. **Nucle-
        ar medicine—Practice** [to be
        added as needed]
   BT   **Medicine**
   NT   **Health maintenance organiza-
        tions**
       Nuclear medicine—Practice
Medical profession
   USE   **Medical personnel**
        Medical practice
        Medicine
Medical research
   USE   **Medicine—Research**
Medical schools
   USE   **Medical colleges**
Medical sciences
   USE   **Medicine**
Medical self-care
   USE   **Health self-care**
Medical service, Cost of
   USE   **Medical care—Costs**
Medical services
   USE   **Medical care**
Medical sociology
   USE   **Social medicine**
Medical technologists (May subdiv. geog.)
    610.69
   BT   **Allied health personnel**
Medical technology (May subdiv. geog.)
    610.28
   BT   **Medicine**

Medical transplantation
   USE   **Transplantation of organs, tis-
        sues, etc.**
Medical waste disposal
   USE   **Medical wastes**
Medical wastes   363.72
   UF   Disposal of medical waste
       Hospital wastes
       Infectious wastes
       Medical waste disposal
       Wastes, Medical
   BT   **Refuse and refuse disposal**
   RT   **Hazardous wastes**
Medicare (May subdiv. geog.)   **368.4**
   UF   Medical care for the elderly
   BT   **Elderly—Medical care**
       National health insurance
       State medicine
   RT   **Medicaid**
Medication abuse   362.29; 613.8; 616.86

Use for materials on the abuse or misuse of therapeutic or medicinal drugs, either prescription or non-prescription.

   UF   Abuse of medications
       Abuse of medicines
       Pharmaceutical abuse
       Prescription drug abuse
   BT   **Drug abuse**
Medicinal chemistry
   USE   **Pharmaceutical chemistry**
Medicinal herbs
   USE   **Herbs—Therapeutic use**
       Medical botany
Medicinal plants
   USE   **Medical botany**
Medicine (May subdiv. geog.)   **610**

Use for materials on the technical and scientific aspects of medical care. Materials on the organization of services and facilities for medical care are entered under **Medical Care.** Materials on the organization and management of medicine as a profession are entered under **Medical practice.**

   UF   Medical profession
       Medical sciences
   SA   types of medicine, e.g. **Sports
        medicine;** and names of dis-
        eases and groups of diseases,
        e.g. **AIDS (Disease); Fever;
        Nervous system—Diseases;**
        etc., and traditional medicine
        of particular ethnic groups,
        e.g.**Native American medi-
        cine** [to be added as needed]

Medicine—*Continued*
- BT **Life sciences**
  Therapeutics
- NT **Alternative medicine**
  Anatomy
  Aviation medicine
  Biochemistry
  Dentistry
  Diagnosis
  Emergency medicine
  Endocrinology
  First aid
  Health
  Holistic medicine
  Hygiene
  Materia medica
  Medical botany
  Medical missions
  Medical practice
  Medical technology
  Military medicine
  Mind and body
  Native American medicine
  Nuclear medicine
  Nursing
  Orthopedics
  Osteopathic medicine
  Pathology
  Periodic health examinations
  Pharmacology
  Pharmacy
  Physiology
  Podiatry
  Popular medicine
  Preventive medicine
  Psychiatry
  Psychosomatic medicine
  Quacks and quackery
  Social medicine
  Space medicine
  Sports medicine
  State medicine
  Submarine medicine
  Surgery
  Therapeutics
  Toxicology
  Traditional medicine
  Tropical medicine
  Veterinary medicine
- RT **Diseases**
  Medical care
  Medical personnel

Physicians
Medicine and religion
  USE **Medicine—Religious aspects**
Medicine—Biography   610.92; 920
- BT **Biography**
Medicine—Cost of medical care
  USE **Medical care—Costs**
Medicine—Ethical aspects
  USE **Medical ethics**
Medicine—Fiction
  USE **Medical novels**
Medicine—Law and legislation (May
    subdiv. geog.)   **344**
> Use for materials on the law as it affects medicine and the medical profession. Materials on the application of medical knowledge to questions of law are entered under **Medical jurisprudence.**
- UF Medical laws and legislation
- BT **Law**
  Legislation
- NT **Medical personnel—Malpractice**
  Physicians—Licenses
  Physicians—Malpractice
  Right to die
- RT **Medical jurisprudence**
Medicine, Military
  USE **Military medicine**
Medicine—Miscellanea   610.2
- BT **Curiosities and wonders**
Medicine, Pediatric
  USE **Children—Diseases**
Medicine—Physiological effect
  USE **Pharmacology**
Medicine, Popular
  USE **Popular medicine**
Medicine—Practice
  USE **Medical practice**
Medicine, Preventive
  USE **Preventive medicine**
Medicine, Psychosomatic
  USE **Psychosomatic medicine**
**Medicine—Religious aspects   261.5;
    291.1; 615.8**
- UF Medicine and religion
  Religion and medicine
- NT **Spiritual healing**
Medicine—Research   610.7
- UF Medical research
- BT **Research**
- NT **Human experimentation in medicine**

441

Medicine—Social aspects
  USE **Social medicine**
Medicine, State
  USE **State medicine**
Medicine—Study and teaching   **610.7**
  UF Medical education
  RT **Medical colleges**
Medicine—United States   **610.973**
Medieval architecture (May subdiv.
    geog.)   **723**
  UF Architecture, Medieval
  BT **Architecture**
     Medieval civilization
  NT **Byzantine architecture**
     Gothic architecture
     Romanesque architecture
  RT **Castles**
     Cathedrals
Medieval art (May subdiv. geog.)
    709.02
  UF Art, Medieval
  BT **Art**
     Medieval civilization
  NT **Byzantine art**
     Gothic art
     Illumination of books and
      manuscripts
     Romanesque art
Medieval church history
  USE **Church history—600-1500,**
     Middle Ages
Medieval civilization   **909.07**
  Use for materials on cultural and intellectu-
  al developments in the Middle Ages not limit-
  ed to a single country or region.
  UF Civilization, Medieval
  BT **Civilization**
  NT **Feudalism**
     Medieval architecture
     Medieval art
     Medieval literature
     Medieval philosophy
     Medieval tournaments
  RT **Chivalry**
     Middle Ages
Medieval Greece
  USE **Greece—History—323-1453**
Medieval literature   **809**
  May use same subdivisions as for **Litera-
  ture.**

  UF Literature, Medieval
  BT **Literature**
     Medieval civilization
  NT **Early Christian literature**
     Old Norse literature
Medieval philosophy   **189**
  UF Philosophy, Medieval
  BT **Medieval civilization**
     Philosophy
Medieval tournaments (May subdiv.
    geog.)   **394**
  Use for materials on medieval contests in
  which mounted and armored contestants
  fought for a prize with blunted weapons and
  in accordance with certain rules, and for mate-
  rials on modern re-enactments of such events.
  UF Tournaments
  BT **Chivalry**
     Medieval civilization
     Pageants
Meditation   **158; 248.3; 291.4; 296.7**
  Use for materials on spiritual contemplation
  or mental prayer. Collections of personal re-
  flections or thoughts for use in meditation are
  entered under **Meditations.**
  BT **Devotional exercises**
     Spiritual life
  NT **Transcendental meditation**
  RT **Meditations**
Meditations   **242; 291.4**
  Use for collections of personal reflections
  or thoughts for use in meditation. Materials on
  spiritual contemplation or mental prayer are
  entered under **Meditation.**
  SA religious topics, names of indi-
     vidual persons, and titles of
     sacred works with the subdi-
     vision *Meditations,* e.g.
     Lent—Meditations [to be
     added as needed]
  BT **Devotional literature**
     Prayers
  NT **Lent—Meditations**
  RT **Meditation**
Meetings, Public
  USE **Public meetings**
Melancholia
  USE **Depression (Psychology)**
     Manic-depressive illness
Melodrama   **808.82; 812, etc.**
  May be used for individual works, collec-
  tions, or materials about melodrama.
  BT **Drama**

Memoirs
  USE **Autobiographies**
       Autobiography
       Biography
Memorabilia
  USE **Collectibles**
Memorial Day   394.262
  UF   Decoration Day
  BT   **Holidays**
Memorizing
  USE subjects, types of literature, and
       titles of sacred works with
       the subdivision *Memorizing,*
       e.g. **Poetry—Memorizing** [to
       be added as needed]
Memory   153.1
  SA   subjects, types of literature, and
       titles of sacred works with
       the subdivision *Memorizing,*
       e.g. **Poetry—Memorizing** [to
       be added as needed]
  BT   **Brain**
       Educational psychology
       Intellect
       Psychology
       Psychophysiology
       Thought and thinking
  NT   **Attention**
       False memory syndrome
       Psychology of learning
       Recovered memory
  RT   **Mnemonics**
Memory devices (Computers)
  USE **Computer storage devices**
Men (May subdiv. geog.)   **305.31**
  SA   men of particular racial or eth-
       nic groups, e.g. **African
       American men;** and men in
       various occupations and pro-
       fessions, e.g. **Male actors** [to
       be added as needed]
  NT   **African American men**
       Brothers
       Fathers
       Gay men
       Husbands
       Single men
       Sons
       Widowers
       Young men
  RT   **Masculinity**

Men actors
  USE **Male actors**
Men—Biography   920
  BT   **Biography**
Men—Clothing
  USE **Men's clothing**
Men—Diseases   616.0081
  BT   **Diseases**
Men—Education (May subdiv. geog.)
       370.81
  UF   Education of men
  BT   **Education**
  RT   **Coeducation**
Men—Employment   331.11
  BT   **Employment**
Men in business
  USE **Businessmen**
Men—Psychology   155.3
  UF   Masculine psychology
  BT   **Psychology**
Men—Relations with women
  USE **Man-woman relationship**
Men—Social conditions   305.32
  BT   **Social conditions**
  NT   **Men's movement**
Men—Societies   367
  UF   Men's clubs
       Men's organizations
  BT   **Clubs**
       Societies
Men-women relationship
  USE **Man-woman relationship**
Mendel's law   576.5
  BT   **Breeding**
       Variation (Biology)
  NT   **Genetics**
  RT   **Heredity**
Mendicancy
  USE **Begging**
Mendicant orders
  USE **Franciscans**
Mending
  USE **Clothing and dress—Repairing**
       Repairing
Mennonites (May subdiv. geog.)   **289.7**
  BT   **Christian sects**
  NT   **Amish**
Menopause   612.6; 618.1
  UF   Change of life in women
       Climacteric, Female
       Female climacteric

Menopause—*Continued*

   BT   **Aging**

Menopause, Male

   USE   **Male climacteric**

Men's clothing   646; 687

   UF   Men—Clothing

   BT   **Clothing and dress**

Men's clubs

   USE   **Men—Societies**

Men's liberation movement

   USE   **Men's movement**

Men's movement   305.32

   UF   Men's liberation movement

   BT   **Men—Social conditions**

Men's organizations

   USE   **Men—Societies**

Menstruation   612.6

   BT   **Reproduction**

   NT   **Premenstrual syndrome**

Mental arithmetic   513

   UF   Mental calculation

   BT   **Arithmetic**

Mental calculation

   USE   **Mental arithmetic**

Mental deficiency

   USE   **Mental retardation**

Mental depression

   USE   **Depression (Psychology)**

Mental diseases

   USE   **Abnormal psychology**

          Mental illness

Mental healing   615.8

Use for materials on psychic or psychological means to treat illness. Materials on the use of faith, prayer, or religious means to treat illness are entered under **Spiritual healing.**

   UF   Healing, Mental

          Mind cure

          Psychic healing

   BT   **Alternative medicine**

   NT   **Hypnotism**

   RT   **Mental suggestion**

          Mind and body

          Psychotherapy

          Spiritual healing

          Subconsciousness

          Suggestive therapeutics

Mental health (May subdiv. geog.)

       362.2

   UF   Mental hygiene

   SA   ethnic groups, classes of persons, and names of individual persons with the subdivision *Mental health,* e.g. **Women—Mental health** [to be added as needed]

   BT   **Happiness**

          Health

   NT   **Burn out (Psychology)**

          Occupational therapy

          Stress (Psychology)

          Women—Mental health

   RT   **Abnormal psychology**

          Mental illness

          Mind and body

          Psychiatry

          Psychology

Mental health care

   USE   **Mental health services**

Mental health services (May subdiv. geog.)   **362.2; 616.89**

   UF   Mental health care

          Psychiatric care

          Psychiatric services

   SA   ethnic groups, classes of persons, and names of individual educational institutions with the subdivision *Mental health services* [to be added as needed]

   BT   **Medical care**

   NT   **Crisis intervention (Mental health services)**

Mental hospitals

   USE   **Psychiatric hospitals**

Mental hygiene

   USE   **Mental health**

Mental illness (May subdiv. geog.)   **362.2; 616.89**

Use for popular materials and materials on regional or social aspects of mental disorders. Materials on clinical aspects of mental disorders, including therapy, are entered under **Psychiatry.** Systematic descriptions of mental disorders are entered under **Abnormal psychology.**

   UF   Mental diseases

          Psychoses

Mental illness—*Continued*
- SA   names of specific illnesses, e.g.
  Manic-depressive illness [to
  be added as needed]
- BT   **Abnormal psychology**
  Diseases
- NT   **Manic-depressive illness**
  Multiple personality
  Neurasthenia
- RT   **Mental health**
  Mentally ill
  Personality disorders
  Psychiatry

Mental illness—Drug therapy   616.89
- BT   **Drug therapy**

Mental illness—Jurisprudence
- USE   **Insanity defense**

Mental illness—Physiological aspects
   616.89
- BT   **Physiology**

Mental institutions
- USE   **Mentally ill—Institutional care**

Mental patients
- USE   **Mentally ill**

Mental retardation (May subdiv. geog.)
   362.3; 616.85
- UF   Mental deficiency
- BT   **Abnormal psychology**
- NT   **Down syndrome**
- RT   **Mentally handicapped**

Mental stereotype
- USE   **Stereotype (Psychology)**

Mental stress
- USE   **Stress (Psychology)**

Mental suggestion   131; 154.7; 615.8
- UF   Autosuggestion
  Suggestion, Mental
- BT   **Mind and body**
  Parapsychology
  Subconsciousness
- NT   **Brainwashing**
- RT   **Hypnotism**
  Mental healing
  Suggestive therapeutics

Mental telepathy
- USE   **Telepathy**

Mental tests
- USE   **Intelligence tests**
  Psychological tests

Mentally depressed
- USE   **Depression (Psychology)**

Mentally deranged
- USE   **Mentally ill**

Mentally handicapped (May subdiv.
   geog.)   305.9; 362.2; 362.3
- UF   Mentally retarded
- BT   **Handicapped**
- NT   **Mentally handicapped children**
- RT   **Mental retardation**

Mentally handicapped children (May
   subdiv. geog.)   155.45; 362.2;
   362.3
- UF   Children, Retarded
  Mentally retarded children
  Retarded children
- BT   **Child psychiatry**
  Handicapped children
  Mentally handicapped
- RT   **Slow learning children**

Mentally handicapped children—Educa-
   tion (May subdiv. geog.)   371.92
- BT   **Education**
  Special education

Mentally ill (May subdiv. geog.)   362.2;
   616.89
- UF   Insane
  Mental patients
  Mentally deranged
  Psychotics
- BT   **Sick**
- NT   **Emotionally disturbed children**
- RT   **Mental illness**

Mentally ill children
- USE   **Emotionally disturbed children**

Mentally ill—Institutional care   362.2
- UF   Mental institutions
- BT   **Institutional care**
- RT   **Psychiatric hospitals**

Mentally retarded
- USE   **Mentally handicapped**

Mentally retarded children
- USE   **Mentally handicapped children**

Menus   642
- UF   Bills of fare
  Meal planning
- BT   **Cooking**
  Diet
- NT   **Breakfasts**
  Dinners
  Luncheons
- RT   **Catering**

Mercantile buildings
USE **Commercial buildings**
Mercantile law
USE **Commercial law**
Mercenary soldiers (May subdiv. geog.)
355.3
UF Mercenary troops
Soldiers of fortune
BT **Military personnel**
Soldiers
Mercenary troops
USE **Mercenary soldiers**
Merchandise
USE **Commercial products**
Consumer goods
Merchandising
USE **Marketing**
Retail trade
Merchant marine (May subdiv. geog.)
387.5
BT **Maritime law**
Sailors
Ships
Transportation
NT **Harbors**
Marine insurance
RT **Shipping**
Merchant marine—Law and legislation
USE **Maritime law**
Merchant marine—Safety regulations
USE **Ships—Safety regulations**
Merchant marine—United States
387.50973
Merchants (May subdiv. geog.)
380.1092; 920
BT **Businesspeople**
Mercury **546; 669**
UF Quicksilver
BT **Chemical elements**
Metals
Mercy killing
USE **Euthanasia**
Mergers
USE **Corporate mergers and acqui-**
sitions
and types of institutions and
types of industries and busi-
nesses with the subdivision
Mergers, e.g. **Railroads—**
Mergers [to be added as
needed]

Mermaids and mermen **398.21**
BT **Mythical animals**
Mesmerism
USE **Hypnotism**
Messages
USE types of public officials and
names of individual public of-
ficials with the subdivision
Messages, e.g. **Presidents—**
United States—Messages [to
be added as needed]
Messages to Congress
USE **Presidents—United States—**
Messages
Messiness
USE **Cleanliness**
Metabolism **572**
BT **Biochemistry**
NT **Growth disorders**
Metal finishing
USE **Metals—Finishing**
Metal work
USE **Metalwork**
Metallography **669**
Use for materials on the science of metal
structures and alloys, especially the study of
such structures with the microscope. Materials
on the process of extracting metals from their
ores, refining them, and preparing them for
use, are entered under **Metallurgy.**
UF Metallurgical analysis
Microscopic analysis
BT **Metals**
Metallurgical analysis
USE **Metallography**
Metallurgy (May subdiv. geog.) **669**
Use for materials on the process of extract-
ing metals from their ores, refining them, and
preparing them for use. Materials on the sci-
ence of metal structures and alloys, especially
the study of such structures with the micro-
scope, are entered under **Metallography.**
NT **Electrometallurgy**
RT **Alloys**
Chemical engineering
Industrial chemistry
Metals
Ores
Smelting
Metals **669**
SA types of metals [to be added as
needed]
BT **Inorganic chemistry**
Ores

Metals—*Continued*
NT   **Alloys**
    Aluminum
    Brass
    Iron
    Mercury
    Metallography
    Pewter
    Precious metals
    Soldering
    Tin
    Zinc
RT   **Metallurgy**
    Metalwork

Metals—Finishing   671.7
UF   Metal finishing
BT   **Finishes and finishing**
    Metalwork

Metalwork (May subdiv. geog.)   **671;
739**
UF   Metal work
BT   **Decoration and ornament**
NT   **Architectural metalwork**
    Art metalwork
    Bronzes
    Copperwork
    Dies (Metalworking)
    Electroplating
    Forging
    Founding
    Goldwork
    Ironwork
    Metals—Finishing
    Plate metalwork
    Sheet metalwork
    Silverwork
    Soldering
    Steel
    Tinwork
    Welding
RT   **Metals**
    Metalworking machinery

Metalworking machinery   621.9
BT   **Machinery**
RT   **Metalwork**

Metaphysics   110
BT   **Philosophy**
NT   **Existentialism**
    Space and time
    Theory of knowledge
RT   **God**

Meteorites   523.5
BT   **Astronomy**
    Meteors

Meteorological instruments   551.5028
UF   Instruments, Meteorological
SA   types of meteorological instruments [to be added as needed]
BT   **Scientific apparatus and instruments**
NT   **Barometers**
    Thermometers

Meteorological observatories   551.5028
UF   Meteorology—Observatories
    Observatories, Meteorological
    Weather stations
RT   **Meteorology**

Meteorological satellites   551.63
UF   Weather satellites
SA   names of satellites, e.g. **TIROS satellites** [to be added as needed]
BT   **Artificial satellites**
NT   **TIROS satellites**

Meteorology (May subdiv. geog.)   **551.5**
    Use for scientific materials on the atmosphere, especially weather factors. Materials on climate as it relates to humans and to plant and animal life, including the effects of changes of climate, are entered under **Climate.** Materials on the state of the atmosphere at a given time and place with respect to heat or cold, wetness or dryness, calm or storm, are entered under **Weather.**
BT   **Earth sciences**
NT   **Air**
    Auroras
    Clouds
    Cyclones
    Droughts
    Floods
    Fog
    Frost
    Humidity
    Lightning
    Meteorology in aeronautics
    Precipitation (Meteorology)
    Rainbow
    Seasons
    Solar radiation
    Storms
    Sunspots
    Thunderstorms
    Tornadoes

Meteorology—*Continued*
>> Weather control
>> Weather—Folklore
>> Weather forecasting
>> Winds
> RT Atmosphere
>> Climate
>> Meteorological observatories
>> Weather

Meteorology in aeronautics   629.132
> BT **Aeronautics**
>> **Meteorology**

Meteorology—Observatories
> USE **Meteorological observatories**

Meteorology—Tables   551.5

Meteors   523.5
> UF Falling stars
>> Shooting stars
> BT **Astronomy**
>> **Solar system**
> NT **Meteorites**

Meter
> USE **Musical meter and rhythm**
>> **Versification**

Meters, Electric
> USE **Electric meters**

Meth (Drug)
> USE **Methamphetamine**

Methamphetamine   362.29; 615
> UF Meth (Drug)
>> Speed (Drug)
> BT **Amphetamines**
> NT **Ice (Drug)**

Methodology
> USE subjects with the subdivision
>> *Methodology,* e.g. **Science—**
>> **Methodology** [to be added as
>> needed]

Metric system   389; 530.8
> BT **Arithmetic**
>> **Mathematics**
> RT **Decimal system**
>> **Weights and measures**

Metrical romances
> USE **Romances**

Metrology
> USE **Measurement**
>> **Weights and measures**

Metropolitan areas (May subdiv. geog.)
>>   307.76
> UF Urban areas
> SA names of metropolitan areas, e.g.
>> **Chicago Metropolitan Area**
>> **(Ill.)** [to be added as needed]
> BT **Cities and towns—Growth**
> NT **Suburbs**
>> **Urban renewal**

Metropolitan finance   336
> Use for general materials on the public finance of metropolitan areas. Materials on the finance of a particular metropolitan area are entered under **Public finance** with a geographic subdivision.
> BT **Municipal finance**
>> **Public finance**

Metropolitan government   320.8; 352.16
> SA names of metropolitan areas
>> with the subdivision *Politics*
>> *and government* [to be added
>> as needed]
> BT **Local government**
> NT **Chicago Metropolitan Area**
>> **(Ill.)—Politics and govern-**
>> **ment**
> RT **Municipal government**

Metropolitan planning
> USE **Regional planning**

Mexican American authors   810.9; 920
> SA genres of American literature
>> with the subdivision *Mexican*
>> *American authors* [to be added as needed]
> BT **Hispanic American authors**

Mexican American literature (English)
> USE **American literature—Mexican**
>> **American authors**

Mexican American women (May subdiv. geog.)   **305.868**
> UF Chicanas
> BT **Mexican Americans**
>> **Women**

Mexican Americans (May subdiv. geog.)
>>   **305.868; 973**
> Use for materials on American citizens of Mexican descent. Materials on noncitizens from Mexico are entered under **Mexicans—United States.** Use these same patterns for other ethnic groups in the U.S. and other countries.
> UF Chicanos
> BT **Ethnic groups**
>> **Hispanic Americans**

Mexican Americans—*Continued*
      Immigrants—United States
      Minorities
  NT Mexican American women
  RT Mexicans—United States
Mexican Americans—Ethnic identity
     305.868
Mexican literature   860; M860
  May use same subdivisions and names of literary forms as for **English literature.**
  BT **Latin American literature**
      Literature
Mexican War, 1846-1848   973.6
  UF United States—History—1845-
      1848, War with Mexico
  BT **United States—History—1815-
      1861**
Mexicans (May subdiv. geog.)   305.868;
     920; 972
Mexicans—United States   305.868
  Use for materials on noncitizens from Mexico. Materials on American citizens of Mexican descent are entered under **Mexican Americans.** Use these same patterns for other ethnic groups in the U.S. and other countries.
  BT **Aliens—United States**
      Minorities
  RT **Mexican Americans**
Mexico—Presidents
  USE **Presidents—Mexico**
Mezzotint engraving   766
  BT **Engraving**
MIAs
  USE **Missing in action**
Mice   599.35; 636.088
  UF Mouse
  BT **Mammals**
Microbes
  USE **Bacteria**
      Germ theory of disease
      Microorganisms
      Viruses
Microbial energy conversion
  USE **Biomass energy**
Microbiology   579
  SA subjects with the subdivision *Microbiology* [to be added as needed]
  BT **Biology**
  NT **Air—Microbiology**
      Bacteriology
      Biotechnology
      Cheese—Microbiology

      Fermentation
      Soil microbiology
  RT **Microorganisms**
Microchemistry   540
  BT **Chemistry**
Microcomputers   004.16; 621.39
  Use for materials on small, usually desktop-sized computers that have a self-contained central processing unit.
  UF Desktop computers
      Home computers
      PC computers
      PCs
      Personal computers
  SA types of personal computers, e.g.
      Macintosh (Computer) [to be added as needed]
  BT **Computers**
Microelectronics   621.381
  UF Microminiature electronic equipment
      Microminiaturization (Electronics)
  BT **Electronics**
      Semiconductors
Microfilming
  USE **Microphotography**
Microfilms   302.23; 686.4
  BT **Microforms**
Microforms   302.23; 686.4
  UF Micropublications
  SA types of microforms [to be added as needed]
  NT **Microfilms**
  RT **Microphotography**
Microminiature electronic equipment
  USE **Microelectronics**
Microminiaturization (Electronics)
  USE **Microelectronics**
Microorganisms   579
  UF Germs
      Microbes
      Microscopic organisms
  NT **Bacteria**
      Protozoa
      Viruses
  RT **Microbiology**
Microphotography   686.4
  Use for materials on the photographing of objects of any size to produce minute images. Materials on the photographing of minute objects through a microscope are entered under **Photomicrography.**

Microphotography—*Continued*
   UF   Microfilming
   BT   **Photography**
   RT   **Microforms**
Microprocessors   004.16
     Use for materials on the silicon chip that contains the central processing units of a microcomputer or other electronic device.
   BT   **Computers**
Micropublications
   USE   **Microforms**
Microscope and microscopy
   USE   **Microscopes**
Microscopes   502.8
   UF   Microscope and microscopy
       Microscopic analysis
   BT   **Optical instruments**
   NT   **Electron microscopes**
   RT   **Photomicrography**
Microscopic analysis
   USE   **Metallography**
        Microscopes
Microscopic organisms
   USE   **Microorganisms**
Microwave communication systems 621.381
   BT   **Intercommunication systems**
       Shortwave radio
       Telecommunication
   NT   **Closed-circuit television**
Microwave cookery
   USE   **Microwave cooking**
Microwave cooking   641.5
   UF   Microwave cookery
   BT   **Cooking**
Microwaves   537.5
   BT   **Electric waves**
       Electromagnetic waves
       Shortwave radio
   NT   **Masers**
Mid-career changes
   USE   **Career changes**
Middle age   305.24
   BT   **Age**
       Life (Biology)
   NT   **Aging**
   RT   **Longevity**
       Middle aged persons
Middle aged men (May subdiv. geog.)
   305.244
   BT   **Middle aged persons**

Middle aged persons (May subdiv. geog.)
   305.24
   BT   **Age**
   NT   **Middle aged men**
       Middle aged women
   RT   **Middle age**
Middle aged women (May subdiv. geog.)
   305.244
   BT   **Middle aged persons**
Middle Ages   909.07
     Use for materials on the history of the medieval world not limited to a single country or region.
   UF   Dark Ages
       Middle Ages—History *[Former heading]*
   BT   **World history**
   NT   **Church history—600-1500, Middle Ages**
       Knights and knighthood
       World history—12th century
       World history—13th century
       World history—14th century
       World history—15th century
   RT   **Europe—History—476-1492**
       Medieval civilization
Middle Ages—History
   USE   **Middle Ages**
Middle Atlantic States
   USE   **Atlantic States**
Middle child
   USE   **Birth order**
Middle class (May subdiv. geog.)   **305.5**
   UF   Bourgeoisie
   BT   **Social classes**
Middle East   956
     Use for materials on the region consisting of northeastern Africa and Asia west of Afghanistan. Materials on several Arabic-speaking countries are entered under **Arab countries.**
   UF   Levant
       Near East
       Orient
   BT   **Asia**
   NT   **Arab countries**
       Israel
Middle East—Strategic aspects   956
   BT   **Military geography**
       Strategy
Middle East War, 1991
   USE   **Persian Gulf War, 1991**

Middle English language
USE **English language—Middle English period**
Middle English literature
USE **English literature—Middle English period**
Middle schools (May subdiv. geog.)
373.236
UF Intermediate schools
BT **Schools**
RT **Elementary schools**
Junior high schools
Middle West 977
UF Central States
Midwest
North Central States
BT **Mississippi River Valley**
United States
RT **Old Northwest**
Midget cars
USE **Karts and karting**
Midwest
USE **Middle West**
Midwifery
USE **Midwives**
Midwives (May subdiv. geog.) **618.2**
UF Birth attendants
Midwifery
Nurse midwives
BT **Childbirth**
Natural childbirth
Nurses
Migrant labor (May subdiv. geog.)
331.5; 362.85
Use for materials on casual or seasonal workers who move from place to place in search of employment. Materials on the movement of population within a country for permanent settlement are entered under **Internal migration.**
UF Migratory workers
BT **Employees**
Labor
RT **Agricultural laborers**
Internal migration
Migration
USE **Animals—Migration**
Immigration and emigration
and types of animals with the subdivision *Migration*, e.g.
Birds—Migration [to be added as needed]

Migration, Internal
USE **Internal migration**
Migration of birds
USE **Birds—Migration**
Migratory workers
USE **Migrant labor**
Military aeronautics (May subdiv. geog.)
358.4
UF Aeronautics, Military
Air warfare
Naval aeronautics
SA names of wars with the subdivision *Aerial operations*, e.g.
World War, 1939-1945—Aerial operations [to be added as needed]
BT **Aeronautics**
Military art and science
War
NT **Aerial reconnaissance**
Air bases
Air defenses
Air power
Aircraft carriers
Military airplanes
Parachute troops
World War, 1939-1945—Aerial operations
Military aid
USE **Military assistance**
Military air bases
USE **Air bases**
Military airplanes (May subdiv. geog.)
623.7
UF Air warfare
Airplanes, Military
Naval airplanes
SA types of military airplanes [to be added as needed]
BT **Airplanes**
Military aeronautics
NT **Bombers**
Military art and science (May subdiv. geog.) **355**
UF Army
Fighting
Military power
Military science
NT **Armed forces**
Armor
Artillery

Military art and science—*Continued*
> **Battles**
> **Biological warfare**
> **Camouflage (Military science)**
> **Chemical warfare**
> **Civil defense**
> **Fortification**
> **Guerrilla warfare**
> **Industrial mobilization**
> **Military aeronautics**
> **Military camps**
> **Military transportation**
> **Ordnance**
> **Psychological warfare**
> **Signals and signaling**
> **Strategy**
> **Tactics**
> **Veterans**
> RT **Armies**
> **Drill and minor tactics**
> **Military personnel**
> **Naval art and science**
> **War**
> **Weapons**

Military art and science—Study and teaching
  USE **Military education**

Military assistance   355
  UF Arms sales
    Foreign aid program
    Military aid
    Military sales
    Mutual defense assistance program
  SA military assistance from particular countries, e.g. **American military assistance** [to be added as needed]
  BT **Military policy**
  NT **American military assistance**
  RT **Arms transfers**

Military assistance, American
  USE **American military assistance**

Military atrocities
  USE **Atrocities**
    War crimes

Military bases (May subdiv. geog.) **355.7**
  UF Army bases
    Army posts
    Military facilities
    Military installations

Military posts

Military biography
  USE names of armies and navies with the subdivision *Biography,* e.g. **United States. Army—Biography; United States. Navy—Biography;** etc. [to be added as needed]

Military camps   355.7
  UF Camps (Military)
  BT **Military art and science**
  NT **Concentration camps**

Military conscription
  USE **Draft**

Military courts
  USE **Courts martial and courts of inquiry**

Military crimes
  USE **Military offenses**

Military desertion (May subdiv. geog.) **343; 355.1**
  UF Army desertion
    Desertion
    Desertion, Military
  SA names of wars with the subdivision *Desertions* [to be added as needed]
  BT **Military offenses**
  NT **World War, 1939-1945—Desertions**
  RT **Draft resisters**

Military desertion—United States   343
  UF United States. Army—Desertions

Military draft
  USE **Draft**

Military drill
  USE **Drill and minor tactics**

Military education (May subdiv. geog.) **355.007; 355.5**
  UF Army schools
    Military art and science—Study and teaching
    Military schools
    Military training
    Schools, Military
  SA names of military schools, e.g. **United States Military Academy** [to be added as needed]
  BT **Education**
  NT **Military training camps**

Military engineering (May subdiv. geog.)
623
SA   names of wars with the subdivision *Engineering and construction* [to be added as needed]
BT   Civil engineering
      Engineering
NT   World War, 1939-1945—Engineering and construction
RT   Fortification
Military facilities
USE   Military bases
Military forces
USE   Armed forces
Military geography   355.4
UF   Maps, Military
      Military maps
SA   areas of the world with the subdivision *Strategic aspects* [to be added as needed]
BT   Geography
NT   Middle East—Strategic aspects
Military government   341.6; 355.4
      Use for general materials on governments under military regimes, not limited to a single country.
UF   Government, Military
SA   names of countries with the subdivision *Politics and government,* or *History,* with appropriate dates as needed, for materials on governments of particular countries under military rule; and names of countries occupied by foreign military governments with the appropriate subdivision under *History,* e.g., **Netherlands—History—1940-1945, German occupation; Japan—History—1945-1952, Allied Occupation;** etc. [to be added as needed]
BT   Public administration
RT   Military occupation
Military health
USE   Military personnel—Health and hygiene
Military history   355.009
UF   History, Military
      Wars

SA   names of countries with the sub-head *Army* or the subdivision *Military history,* e.g. **United States. Army; United States—Military history;** and names of wars, battles, sieges, etc. [to be added as needed]
BT   History
NT   Battles
      Military policy
      United States. Army
      United States—Military history
RT   Naval history
Military hospitals (May subdiv. geog.)
355.7
UF   Field hospitals
      Veterans—Hospitals
SA   names of wars with the subdivision *Medical care,* e.g. **World War, 1939-1945—Medical care** [to be added as needed]
BT   Hospitals
      Military medicine
RT   Veterans
Military installations
USE   Military bases
Military intervention
USE   Intervention (International law)
Military law (May subdiv. geog.)   343
UF   Articles of war
      War, Articles of
BT   International law
      Law
NT   Draft
      Military offenses
      Veterans—Legal status, laws, etc.
RT   Courts martial and courts of inquiry
      War
Military life
USE   Military personnel
      and names of countries with the subdivision *Armed forces* or the subheads *Army* or *Navy;* etc., with the subdivision *Military life,* e.g. **United States—Armed forces—Military life; United States. Army—Military life;** etc. [to be added as needed]

Military maps
USE **Military geography**
Military medicine   616.9
UF   Field hospitals
Medicine, Military
SA   names of wars with the subdivision *Medical care,* e.g. **World War, 1939-1945—Medical care** [to be added as needed]
BT   **Medicine**
NT   **Armies—Medical care**
Military hospitals
RT   **Military personnel—Health and hygiene**
Military music   781.5
SA   names of wars with the subdivision *Songs* [to be added as needed]
BT   **Music**
NT   **Band music**
Marches (Music)
World War, 1939-1945—Songs
Military occupation   341.6; 355.4
UF   Occupation, Military
Occupied territory
SA   names of occupied countries with the appropriate subdivision under *History,* e.g., **Netherlands—History—1940-1945, German occupation; Japan—History—1945-1952, Allied occupation;** etc. [to be added as needed]
BT   **War**
NT   **World War, 1939-1945—Occupied territories**
RT   **Military government**
Military offenses (May subdiv. geog.)
343; 355.1
UF   Crimes, Military
Military crimes
Naval offenses
Offenses, Military
SA   types of military offenses, e.g. **Military desertion** [to be added as needed]
BT   **Criminal law**
Military law
NT   **Military desertion**

Military offenses—United States   343; 355.1
UF   United States. Army—Crimes and misdemeanors
United States—Military offenses
Military pensions (May subdiv. geog.)
331.25
UF   Naval pensions
Pensions, Naval
War pensions
BT   **Pensions**
RT   **Veterans**
Military personnel (May subdiv. geog.)
355.3
UF   Military life
Servicemen
Servicewomen
SA   names of countries with the subdivision *Armed forces* or the subheads *Army* or *Navy,* etc., with the subdivision *Military life* or *Officers,* e.g. **United States—Armed forces—Military life; United States. Army—Officers;** etc. [to be added as needed]
BT   **Armed forces**
War
NT   **Admirals**
Armies
Gays and lesbians in the military
Generals
Mercenary soldiers
Navies
Recruiting and enlistment
Sailors
Soldiers
United States—Armed forces—Military life
United States. Army—Military life
United States. Army—Officers
United States. Navy—Officers
RT   **Military art and science**
Veterans
Military personnel—Health and hygiene
613.6
UF   Hygiene, Military
Military health *[Former heading]*

Military personnel—Health and hygiene—
Continued
>Soldiers—Hygiene
>SA names of wars with the subdivision *Health aspects* or *Medical care,* e.g. **World War, 1939-1945—Health aspects; World War, 1939-1945—Medical care;** etc. [to be added as needed]
>BT **Hygiene**
>RT **Armies—Medical care**
>   **Military medicine**

Military personnel missing in action
>USE **Missing in action**

Military personnel—United States
355.30973
>UF United States—Military personnel

Military policy (May subdiv. geog.) **355**
>UF Defense policy
>   Government policy
>BT **Military history**
>NT **Military assistance**
>   **Military readiness**
>RT **National security**

Military policy—United States **355**
>UF United States—Military policy
>   *[Former heading]*
>NT **Strategic Defense Initiative**

Military posts
>USE **Military bases**

Military power
>USE **Armies**
>   **Military art and science**
>   **Navies**
>   **Sea power**

Military preparedness
>USE **Military readiness**

Military readiness **355**
>Use for materials on military strength, including military personnel, munitions, natural resources, and industrial war potential. Materials on the implements of war are entered under **Ordnance** or **Military weapons.** Materials on the industries producing them are entered under **Defense industry.**
>>UF Armaments
>>   Defense readiness
>>   Military preparedness
>>   National defenses

>SA names of countries with the subdivision *Defenses,* e.g. **United States—Defenses** [to be added as needed]
>BT **Military policy**
>NT **United States—Defenses**
>RT **Armed forces**
>   **Arms control**
>   **Arms race**
>   **Defense industry**
>   **Industrial mobilization**
>   **Manpower**

Military sales
>USE **Arms transfers**
>   **Defense industry**
>   **Military assistance**

Military schools
>USE **Military education**

Military science
>USE **Military art and science**

Military service, Compulsory
>USE **Draft**

Military service, Voluntary
>USE **Voluntary military service**

Military signaling
>USE **Signals and signaling**

Military strategy
>USE **Strategy**

Military supplies industry
>USE **Defense industry**

Military tactics
>USE **Tactics**

Military tanks **358; 623.7**
>UF Armored cars (Tanks)
>   Tanks (Military science)
>BT **Military vehicles**

Military training
>USE **Military education**

Military training camps (May subdiv. geog.) **355.7**
>UF Students' military training camps
>   Training camps, Military
>BT **Military education**

Military training, Universal
>USE **Draft**

Military transportation **358**
>UF Transportation, Military
>SA names of wars with the subdivision *Transportation,* e.g. **World War, 1939-1945—**

Military transportation—*Continued*
　　　　Transportation [to be added
　　　　as needed]
　BT　**Military art and science**
　　　　Transportation
　NT　**Military vehicles**
Military uniforms　355.1
　UF　Naval uniforms
　　　　Uniforms, Military
　　　　Uniforms, Naval
　SA　names of military services with
　　　　the subdivision *Uniforms,* e.g.
　　　　United States. Army—Uni-
　　　　forms [to be added as need-
　　　　ed]
　BT　**Uniforms**
Military vehicles　355.8
　UF　Army vehicles
　　　　Vehicles, Military
　BT　**Military transportation**
　　　　Vehicles
　NT　**Military tanks**
Military weapons (May subdiv. geog.)
　　　　355.8; 623.4
　UF　Armaments
　　　　Arms sales
　　　　Munitions
　SA　names of wars with the subdivi-
　　　　sion *Equipment and supplies*
　　　　[to be added as needed]
　BT　**Ordnance**
　　　　Weapons
　NT　**Nuclear weapons**
　　　　Space weapons
　　　　World War, 1939-1945—
　　　　Equipment and supplies
　RT　**Arms race**
　　　　Defense industry
Militia
　USE　names of countries and states
　　　　with the subdivision *Militia,*
　　　　e.g. **United States—Militia**
　　　　[to be added as needed]
Militia movements (May subdiv. geog.)
　　　　303.48
　　Use for materials on anti-government
　paramilitary social movements.
　UF　Militias
　　　　Paramilitary militia movements
　BT　**Radicalism**
　　　　Social movements

Militias
　USE　**Militia movements**
Milk　637; 641.3
　BT　**Dairy products**
　　　　Dairying
　　　　Food
　NT　**Dried milk**
Milk—Analysis　637; 641.3
Milk supply　338.1
　BT　**Food adulteration and inspec-**
　　　　tion
　　　　Public health
Mill and factory buildings
　USE　**Factories**
Millenarianism
　USE　**Millennium**
Millennialism
　USE　**Millennium**
Millennium　236
　UF　Millenarianism
　　　　Millennialism
　BT　**Eschatology**
　RT　**Second Advent**
Millikan rays
　USE　**Cosmic rays**
Millinery
　USE　**Hats**
Milling (Flour)
　USE　**Flour mills**
Millionaires (May subdiv. geog.)　**920**
　BT　**Rich**
Mills (May subdiv. geog.)　**670.42**
　UF　Mills and millwork
　SA　types of mills [to be added as
　　　　needed]
　BT　**Manufactures**
　　　　Technology
　NT　**Flour mills**
　RT　**Factories**
　　　　Machinery
Mills and millwork
　USE　**Mills**
Mime　792.3
　BT　**Acting**
　RT　**Pantomimes**
Mind
　USE　**Intellect**
　　　　Psychology

Mind and body   128; 150
UF   Body and mind
BT   **Brain**
     Medicine
     Parapsychology
     Philosophy
NT   **Abnormal psychology**
     Biofeedback training
     Body image
     Consciousness
     Mental suggestion
     Psychosomatic medicine
     Sleep
     Temperament
RT   **Holistic medicine**
     Human body
     Hypnotism
     Mental healing
     Mental health
     Phrenology
     Psychoanalysis
     Psychophysiology
     Spiritual healing
     Subconsciousness

Mind control
USE   **Brainwashing**
Mind cure
USE   **Mental healing**
Mind reading
USE   **Telepathy**

Mine surveying   622.028
BT   **Mining engineering**
     Prospecting
     Surveying

Mineral lands
USE   **Mines and mineral resources**
Mineral resources
USE   **Mines and mineral resources**
Mineral resources, Marine
USE   **Marine mineral resources**
Mineralogy
USE   **Minerals**
     Natural history

Minerals (May subdiv. geog.)   **549**
Use for materials on the chemical and geological aspects of natural compounds extracted from the earth. Materials on mines and mining and the potential economic value of minerals are entered under **Mines and mineral resources.**

UF   Mineralogy
SA   names of minerals, e.g. **Quartz**
     [to be added as needed]

BT   **Geology**
NT   **Asbestos**
     Gems
     Gypsum
     Lime
     Ores
     Precious stones
     Quartz
RT   **Crystals**
     Mines and mineral resources
     Natural history
     Petrology

Miners (May subdiv. geog.)   **622.092; 920**
SA   types of miners [to be added as needed]
BT   **Labor**
NT   **Coal miners**

Miners—Diseases   616.9
UF   Miners' diseases
BT   **Occupational diseases**

Miners' diseases
USE   **Miners—Diseases**

Mines and mineral resources (May subdiv. geog.)   **333.8; 338.2**
Use for materials on mines and mining and the potential economic value of minerals. Materials on the chemical or geological aspects of natural compounds extracted from the earth are entered under **Minerals.**

UF   Mineral lands
     Mineral resources
     Mining
SA   types of mines and mining, e.g.
     Coal mines and mining [to be added as needed]
BT   **Economic geology**
     Natural resources
     Raw materials
NT   **Coal mines and mining**
     Gold mines and mining
     Marine mineral resources
     Mining engineering
     Precious metals
     Prospecting
     Silver mines and mining
RT   **Minerals**

Mines and mineral resources—United States   333.8; 338.2

Miniature gardens   635.9
UF   Gardens, Miniature
     Tray gardens

Miniature gardens—*Continued*
   BT   Gardens
          Miniature objects
   RT   Container gardening
          Indoor gardening
          Terrariums
Miniature objects   688; 745.592
   UF   Miniatures
          Tiny objects
   SA   types of objects with the subdi-
          vision *Models* [to be added as
          needed]
   BT   Art objects
   NT   Dollhouses
          Miniature gardens
          Miniature painting
          Models and modelmaking
   RT   Toys
Miniature painting   751.7; 757
   UF   Miniatures (Portraits)
          Portrait miniatures
   BT   Miniature objects
          Painting
   RT   Portrait painting
Miniatures
   USE   Miniature objects
Miniatures (Illumination of books and
   manuscripts)
   USE   Illumination of books and
           manuscripts
Miniatures (Portraits)
   USE   Miniature painting
Minibikes   629.227
   BT   Bicycles
          Motorcycles
Minimum drinking age
   USE   Drinking age
Minimum wage (May subdiv. geog.)
   331.2
   BT   Salaries, wages, etc.
Mining
   USE   Mines and mineral resources
           Mining engineering
Mining, Electric
   USE   Electricity in mining
Mining engineering (May subdiv. geog.)
   622
   UF   Mining
   BT   Civil engineering
          Coal mines and mining
          Engineering
          Mines and mineral resources

   NT   Drilling and boring (Earth and
           rocks)
          Mine surveying
          Ocean mining
   RT   Electricity in mining
Mining, Ocean
   USE   Ocean mining
Ministers (Diplomatic agents)
   USE   Diplomats
Ministers of state
   USE   Cabinet officers
Ministers of the gospel
   USE   Clergy
Ministry   253; 291.6
   UF   Clergy—Office
   SA   ministries of particular religions,
          e.g. Christian ministry [to be
          added as needed]
   BT   Church work
          Pastoral theology
   NT   Christian ministry
   RT   Clergy
Minor arts
   USE   Decorative arts
Minor planets
   USE   Asteroids
Minor tactics
   USE   Drill and minor tactics
Minorites
   USE   Franciscans
Minorities (May subdiv. geog.)   305.8;
   323.1
   UF   Foreign population
          Minority groups
   SA   names of particular ethnic and
          racial minorities and of na-
          tional groups in a foreign
          country, e.g. African Ameri-
          cans; Mexican Americans;
          Mexicans—United States;
          etc.; names of places with the
          subdivision *Race relations,*
          e.g. United States—Race re-
          lations; names of places with
          the subdivision *Ethnic rela-*
          tions, e.g. United States—
          Ethnic relations; and head-
          ings for minorities in various
          industries and fields of en-
          deavor, e.g., Minorities in

Minorities—*Continued*
        broadcasting [to be added as needed]
  NT **Aliens**
        Immigrants
        Mexican Americans
        Mexicans—United States
        Minorities in broadcasting
        Minorities in television broadcasting
        Minorities on television
        Minority business enterprises
  RT **Discrimination**
        Ethnic relations
        Race relations
        Segregation

Minorities in broadcasting   384.5; 791.4
  Use for materials on minority involvement in the broadcasting industry.
  UF Minority groups in broadcasting
  SA names of particular minority groups in broadcasting or in particular broadcast media, e.g. **African Americans in television broadcasting** [to be added as needed]
  BT **Broadcasting**
        Minorities
  NT **Minorities in television broadcasting**

Minorities in engineering   620
  UF Minority groups in engineering
  BT **Engineering**

Minorities in television
  USE **Minorities on television**

Minorities in television broadcasting   791.45
  Use for materials on all aspects of minority involvement in television. Materials on the portrayal of minorities in television programs are entered under **Minorities on television.**
  UF Minorities in the television industry
  SA names of particular minority groups in television broadcasting, e.g. **African Americans in television broadcasting** [to be added as needed]
  BT **Minorities**
        Minorities in broadcasting
        Television broadcasting

Minorities in the television industry
  USE **Minorities in television broadcasting**

Minorities on television   791.45
  Use for materials on the portrayal of minorities in television programs. Materials on all aspects of minority involvement in television are entered under **Minorities in television broadcasting.**
  UF Minorities in television *[Former heading]*
  SA names of particular minority groups in television, e.g. **African Americans on television** [to be added as needed]
  BT **Minorities**
        Television

Minority business enterprises   338.6
  UF Minority businesses
        Minority-owned business enterprises
  BT **Business enterprises**
        Minorities

Minority business enterprises—Federal aid
  USE **Federal aid to minority business enterprises**

Minority businesses
  USE **Minority business enterprises**

Minority groups
  USE **Minorities**

Minority groups in broadcasting
  USE **Minorities in broadcasting**

Minority groups in engineering
  USE **Minorities in engineering**

Minority-owned business enterprises
  USE **Minority business enterprises**

Minstrels   791.092; 920
  BT **Poets**
  NT **Troubadours**

Mints   332.4
  BT **Money**
  RT **Coinage**

Miracle plays
  USE **Mysteries and miracle plays**

Miracles   212; 231.7; 291.2
  Use for materials on miracles in any or all religious traditions.
  RT **Spiritual healing**
        Supernatural

Mirrors   748.8
  UF Looking glasses
  BT **Furniture**

Miscarriage   618.3
   UF   Fetal death
   BT   **Pregnancy**
Miscellanea
   USE   **Books of lists**
          Curiosities and wonders
          and subjects with the subdivision *Miscellanea,* e.g. **Medicine—Miscellanea** [to be added as needed]
Miscellaneous facts
   USE   **Books of lists**
          Curiosities and wonders
Misconduct in office (May subdiv. geog.)
   353.4
   UF   Malfeasance in office
          Official misconduct
   SA   names of specific incidents and offenses [to be added as needed]
   BT   **Conflict of interests**
          Criminal law
   NT   **Police corruption**
   RT   **Political corruption**
Misdemeanors (Law)
   USE   **Criminal law**
Misleading advertising
   USE   **Deceptive advertising**
Misrepresentation in advertising
   USE   **Deceptive advertising**
Missiles, Ballistic
   USE   **Ballistic missiles**
Missiles, Guided
   USE   **Guided missiles**
Missing children (May subdiv. geog.)
   362.82; 363.2
   UF   Lost children
   BT   **Children**
          Missing persons
   NT   **Runaway children**
Missing in action   341.6
   UF   MIAs
          Military personnel missing in action
   SA   names of wars with the subdivision *Missing in action* [to be added as needed]
   BT   **Prisoners of war**
          Soldiers
   NT   **World War, 1939-1945—Missing in action**

Missing persons (May subdiv. geog.)
   363.2
   BT   **Criminal investigation**
   NT   **Missing children**
          Runaway adults
          Runaway teenagers
Missionaries, Christian
   USE   **Christian missionaries**
Missions
   USE   names of Christian churches, denominations, religious orders, etc., with the subdivision *Missions,* e.g. **Catholic Church—Missions;** and names of peoples evangelized with the subdivision *Christian missions,* e.g. **Native Americans—Christian missions** [to be added as needed]
Missions, Christian
   USE   **Christian missions**
Missions, Medical
   USE   **Medical missions**
Mississippi River Valley   977
   UF   Mississippi Valley
   BT   **United States**
   NT   **Middle West**
Mississippi River Valley—History   977
   UF   New France—History
Mississippi Valley
   USE   **Mississippi River Valley**
Mistakes
   USE   **Errors**
Mixed marriage
   USE   **Interfaith marriage**
          Intermarriage
Mnemonics   153.1
   SA   subjects, types of literature, and titles of sacred works with the subdivision *Memorizing,* e.g. **Poetry—Memorizing** [to be added as needed]
   NT   **Poetry—Memorizing**
   RT   **Memory**
Mobile home living   643; 728.7
   BT   **Home economics**
          Mobile homes
   NT   **Trailer parks**
          Van life
Mobile home parks
   USE   **Trailer parks**

Mobile homes   643; 728.7

Use for materials on stationary transportable structures designed for year-round living. Materials on structures mounted upon a truck or towed by a truck or automobile for the purpose of temporary dwelling or cargo hauling are entered under **Travel trailers and campers.**

UF   House trailers

Trailers

BT   **Housing**

NT   **Mobile home living**

RT   **Travel trailers and campers**

Mobiles (Sculpture)   731

BT   **Kinetic sculpture**

Sculpture

Mobilization, Industrial

USE   **Industrial mobilization**

Mobs

USE   **Crowds**

Riots

Mock epic literature

USE   **Mock-heroic literature**

Mock-heroic literature   800

May be used for individual works, collections, or materials about mock-heroic literature.

UF   Comic epic literature

Mock epic literature

BT   **Literature**

Wit and humor

RT   **Epic literature**

Humorous fiction

Model airplanes

USE   **Airplanes—Models**

Model cars

USE   **Automobiles—Models**

Model making

USE   **Models and modelmaking**

Model ships

USE   **Ships—Models**

Model trains

USE   **Locomotives—Models**

Railroads—Models

Modeling   731.4; 738.1

UF   Clay modeling

BT   **Clay**

Sculpture

NT   **Soap sculpture**

RT   **Sculpture—Technique**

Modelmaking

USE   **Models and modelmaking**

Models

USE   **Artists' models**

Fashion models

Mathematical models

Models and modelmaking

and types of objects with the subdivision *Models*, e.g. **Airplanes—Models** [to be added as needed]

Models and model making

USE   **Models and modelmaking**

Models and modelmaking   688

UF   Model making

Modelmaking

Models

Models and model making *[Former heading]*

SA   types of objects with the subdivision *Models*, e.g. **Airplanes—Models** [to be added as needed]

BT   **Handicraft**

Miniature objects

NT   **Airplanes—Models**

Automobiles—Models

Locomotives—Models

Machinery—Models

Motorboats—Models

Patternmaking

Railroads—Models

Ships—Models

Models, Artists'

USE   **Artists' models**

Models, Mathematical

USE   **Mathematical models**

Models, Mechanical

USE   **Machinery—Models**

Models (Persons)

USE   **Artists' models**

Fashion models

Modern architecture

USE   **Modernism in architecture**

Modern architecture—1600-1799 (17th and 18th centuries)

USE   **Architecture—17th and 18th centuries**

Modern architecture—1800-1899 (19th century)

USE   **Architecture—19th century**

Modern architecture—1900-1999 (20th
century)

    USE   **Architecture—20th century**

Modern architecture—2000-2099 (21st
century)

    USE   **Architecture—21st century**

Modern art

    USE   **Modernism in art**

Modern art—1800-1899 (19th century)

    USE   **Art—19th century**

Modern art—1900-1999 (20th century)

    USE   **Art—20th century**

Modern art—2000-2099 (21st century)

    USE   **Art—21st century**

Modern church history

    USE   **Church history—1500-, Modern period**

Modern civilization   306.09; 909

    Use for materials on cultural and intellectual developments since 1453 not limited to a single country or region.

    UF   Civilization, Modern

    BT   **Civilization**

    NT   **Enlightenment**

Modern civilization—1950-   306.09; 909.82

    Use for materials on cultural and intellectual developments since 1950 not limited to a single country or region.

Modern dance   792.8

    UF   Interpretive dance

    BT   **Dance**

Modern Greek language   489

    May be subdivided like **English language.**

    UF   Greek language, Modern

           Romaic language

    BT   **Language and languages**

    RT   **Greek language**

Modern Greek literature   889

    May use same subdivisions and names of literary forms as for **English literature.**

    UF   Greek literature, Modern

           Neo-Greek literature

           Romaic literature

    BT   **Literature**

Modern history   909.08

    Use for materials covering the period after 1453.

    UF   History, Modern

    BT   **World history**

Modern history—1800-1899 (19th century)

    USE   **World history—19th century**

Modern history—1900-1999 (20th century)

    USE   **World history—20th century**

Modern history—1945-

    USE   **World history—1945-**

**Modern history—Study and teaching
907**

    NT   **Current events**

Modern languages   410

    Use for materials dealing collectively with living literary languages. May be subdivided like **English language.**

    UF   Languages, Modern

    BT   **Language and languages**

**Modern languages—Conversation and
phrase books   418**

    Use for instructional materials or for books of convenient conversations and phrases for travelers.

    UF   Conversation and phrase books

           Conversation in foreign languages

           Conversations and phrases

           Foreign language phrases

    SA   names of languages with the subdivision *Conversation and phrase books,* e.g. **French language—Conversation and phrase books** [to be added as needed]

**Modern languages—Study and teaching
418**

    RT   **Language laboratories**

Modern literature

    USE   **Literature**

           Modernism in literature

Modern painting—1800-1899 (19th
century)

    USE   **Painting—19th century**

Modern painting—1900-1999 (20th
century)

    USE   **Painting—20th century**

Modern painting—2000-2099 (21st century)

    USE   **Painting—21st century**

Modern philosophy   190

    Use for materials on developments in Western philosophy since the Middle Ages.

    UF   Philosophy, Modern

    BT   **Philosophy**

    NT   **Enlightenment**

           Existentialism

           Phenomenology

Modern sculpture

    USE   **Modernism in sculpture**

Modern sculpture—1900-1999 (20th
century)
    USE   **Sculpture—20th century**
Modernism
    USE   **Modernism (Aesthetics)**
            Modernism (Theology)
Modernism (Aesthetics)   700.1
    Use for materials on the philosophy and
practice of the arts since the nineteenth
century characterized by a self-conscious
break with the past and a search for new
forms of expression.
    UF   Modernism
           Modernism (Arts) *[Former head-
              ing]*
    BT   **Aesthetics**
    NT   **Modernism in architecture**
           Modernism in art
           Modernism in literature
           Modernism in sculpture
    RT   **Postmodernism**
Modernism (Art)
    USE   **Modernism in art**
Modernism (Arts)
    USE   **Modernism (Aesthetics)**
Modernism in architecture   724
    Use for materials on the theory and practice
of modernism in the architecture.
    UF   Architecture, Modern
           Modern architecture *[Former
              heading]*
    BT   **Architecture**
           Modernism (Aesthetics)
Modernism in art   709.04
    Use for materials on the theory and practice
of modernism in the visual arts.
    UF   Modern art *[Former heading]*
           Modernism (Art)
    BT   **Art**
           Modernism (Aesthetics)
Modernism in literature   801
    UF   Modern literature
           Modernism (Literature)
    BT   **Literature**
           Modernism (Aesthetics)
Modernism in sculpture   735
    UF   Modern sculpture *[Former head-
              ing]*
           Modernism (Sculpture)
           Sculpture, Modern
    BT   **Modernism (Aesthetics)**
           Sculpture

Modernism (Literature)
    USE   **Modernism in literature**
Modernism (Sculpture)
    USE   **Modernism in sculpture**
Modernism (Theology)   230; 273
    Use for materials on the movement in the
Christian churches that applies modern critical
methods to biblical study and the history of
dogma, and emphasizes the spiritual and ethi-
cal side of religion over historic dogmas and
creeds.
    UF   Modernism
           Modernist-fundamentalist contro-
              versy
    BT   **Christianity—Doctrines**
    RT   **Christian fundamentalism**
Modernist-fundamentalist controversy
    USE   **Christian fundamentalism**
           Modernism (Theology)
Modernization
    USE   **Modernization (Sociology)**
Modernization (Sociology) (May subdiv.
    geog.)   **303.44**
    Use for materials on the process by which
traditional societies achieve the political, cul-
tural, economic, and social characteristics of
modernity.
    UF   Development
           Modernization
    BT   **Social change**
    RT   **Industrialization**
Mohammedan art
    USE   **Islamic art**
Mold (Fungi)
    USE   **Molds (Fungi)**
Molding (Metal)
    USE   **Founding**
Molds (Botany)
    USE   **Molds (Fungi)**
Molds (Fungi)   579.5
    UF   Mold (Fungi)
           Molds (Botany)
    BT   **Fungi**
Molecular biochemistry
    USE   **Molecular biology**
Molecular biology   591.6
    UF   Biology, Molecular
           Molecular biochemistry
           Molecular biophysics
    BT   **Biochemistry**
           Biophysics
    NT   **Genetic code**
Molecular biophysics
    USE   **Molecular biology**

Molecular cloning   572.8
    UF   DNA cloning
    BT   **Cloning**
           Genetic engineering
Molecules   539; 541.2
    BT   **Physical chemistry**
Molesting of children
    USE **Child sexual abuse**
Mollusks   594
    Use for materials on mollusks and for systematic and comprehensive materials on shells. Popular materials on shells and shell collecting are entered under **Shells.**
    BT   **Shellfish**
    RT   **Shells**
Monarchs
    USE **Kings and rulers**
Monarchy (May subdiv. geog.)   321; 321.8
    UF   Royal houses
           Royalty
           Sovereigns
    BT   **Constitutional history**
           Constitutional law
           Executive power
           Political science
    NT   **Empresses**
           Queens
    RT   **Kings and rulers**
Monasteries (May subdiv. geog.)   255; 271; 726
    UF   Cloisters
    BT   **Church architecture**
           Church history
    NT   **Abbeys**
           Convents
    RT   **Monasticism and religious orders**
Monastic orders
    USE **Monasticism and religious orders**
Monasticism
    USE **Monasticism and religious orders**
Monasticism and religious orders (May subdiv. geog.)   255; 271
    Use for materials on the institution of monasticism and for general materials on religious orders not limited to orders for a single sex. This heading may be subdivided by religion or denomination as needed.
    UF   Monastic orders
           Monasticism
           Orders, Monastic

           Religious orders
    SA   names of monastic and religious orders, e.g. **Franciscans** [to be added as needed]
    NT   **Franciscans**
           Monasticism and religious orders for men
           Monasticism and religious orders for women
    RT   **Hermits**
           Religious life
Monasticism and religious orders for men   255; 271
    This heading may be subdivided by religion or denomination as needed.
    UF   Religious orders for men
    BT   **Monasticism and religious orders**
    RT   **Monks**
Monasticism and religious orders for women   255; 271
    This heading may be subdivided by religion or denomination as needed.
    UF   Religious orders for women
           Sisterhoods
    BT   **Convents**
           Monasticism and religious orders
    RT   **Nuns**
Monetary policy (May subdiv. geog.)   332.4
    UF   Currency devaluation
           Devaluation of currency
           Free coinage
           Government policy
    BT   **Economic policy**
    RT   **Finance**
           Fiscal policy
           Inflation (Finance)
           Money
Monetary policy—United States   332.4
    UF   United States—Monetary policy
Money (May subdiv. geog.)   332.4
    Use for materials on currency as a medium of exchange or measure of value and for general materials on various types of money.
    UF   Currency
           Legal tender
           Standard of value
    BT   **Economics**
           Exchange
           Finance

Money—*Continued*
  NT Barter
      Children's allowances
      Coinage
      Coins
      Counterfeits and counterfeiting
      Credit
      Foreign exchange
      Mints
      Paper money
  RT Banks and banking
      Gold
      Monetary policy
      Silver
      Wealth
Money-making projects for children
  332.024; 650.1
  UF Children's moneymaking projects
      Moneymaking projects for children *[Former heading]*
  BT Business enterprises
  RT Children's allowances
Money raising
  USE Fund raising
Moneymaking projects for children
  USE Money-making projects for children
Monkeys (May subdiv. geog.) 599.8
  BT Primates
Monkeys—Behavior 599.8
  UF Monkeys—Habits and behavior
  BT Animal behavior
Monkeys—Habits and behavior
  USE Monkeys—Behavior
Monks 255; 271
  RT Monasticism and religious orders for men
Monograms 745.6
  UF Ciphers (Lettering)
  BT Alphabets
      Decoration and ornament
      Lettering
  RT Initials
Monologues 808.85; 815, etc.
    May be used for individual works, collections, or materials about monologues. Monologues with incidental musical background and musical works in which spoken language is an integral part are entered under **Monologues with music.**
  UF Declamations
      Narrations

  BT Recitations
  RT Monologues with music
Monologues with music 808.85; 815, etc.; 782.2
    Use for musical scores and for materials about monologues with incidental musical background and musical works in which spoken language is an integral part. Individual monologues without music, collections, and materials about monologues without music are entered under **Monologues.**
  UF Musical declamation
      Narration with music
      Recitations with music
  BT Recitations
  RT Monologues
Monopolies (May subdiv. geog.) 338.8
  BT Commerce
      Economics
  RT Competition
      Corporation law
      Industrial trusts
      Restraint of trade
Monorail railroads 385; 625.1
  UF Railroads, Single rail
      Single rail railroads
  BT Railroads
Monroe Doctrine 327.73
  BT International relations
      Intervention (International law)
      United States—Foreign relations
Monster films
  USE Horror films
Monsters 001.9; 398.2
    Use for materials on legendary animals combining features of human and animal form or having the forms of various animals in combination. Materials on human abnormalities are entered under either **Birth defects** or **Growth disorders.**
  BT Animals—Folklore
      Curiosities and wonders
      Folklore
      Mythology
  NT Dragons
      Giants
      Sasquatch
      Yeti
Montessori method of education 371.39
  BT Elementary education
      Kindergarten
      Teaching

Months   529
  SA   names of the months [to be add-
       ed as needed]
  BT   **Calendars**
       Chronology
Monumental brasses
  USE   **Brasses**
Monuments (May subdiv. geog.)   **725**
  UF   Statues
  SA   ethnic groups, classes of per-
       sons, individual persons, fami-
       lies, and wars with the subdi-
       vision *Monuments,* e.g. **World
       War, 1939-1945—Monu-
       ments** [to be added as need-
       ed]
  BT   **Architecture**
       Sculpture
  NT   **Historic buildings**
       National monuments
       Natural monuments
       Obelisks
       Pyramids
       Tombs
       **World War, 1939-1945—Monu-
       ments**
Moon   523.3
  BT   **Astronomy**
       Solar system
Moon bases
  USE   **Lunar bases**
Moon—Eclipses
  USE   **Lunar eclipses**
Moon—Exploration   629.45
  UF   Lunar exploration
  BT   **Space flight to the moon**
Moon—Geology
  USE   **Lunar geology**
Moon (in religion, folklore, etc.)
  USE   **Moon worship**
Moon—Maps   523.3022
  BT   **Maps**
Moon—Photographs
  USE   **Moon—Pictorial works**
Moon—Pictorial works   523.3; 778.3
  UF   Moon—Photographs
  BT   **Space photography**
Moon probes
  USE   **Lunar probes**

Moon rocks   552.0999
  UF   Lunar petrology *[Former head-
       ing]*
       Lunar rocks
  BT   **Lunar geology**
       Petrology
Moon soil
  USE   **Lunar soil**
Moon—Surface   523.3
  UF   Lunar surface
  RT   **Lunar soil**
Moon, Voyages to
  USE   **Space flight to the moon**
Moon worship   291.2
  UF   Moon (in religion, folklore, etc.)
  BT   **Religion**
Moonlighting
  USE   **Supplementary employment**
Moons
  USE   **Satellites**
Moorish architecture
  USE   **Islamic architecture**
Moors
  USE   **Muslims**
Moral and philosophic stories
  USE   **Didactic fiction**
       Fables
       Parables
Moral conditions   301; 306; 900
  UF   Morals
  SA   names of countries, cities, etc.,
       with the subdivision *Moral
       conditions* [to be added as
       needed]
  BT   **Social conditions**
  NT   **Chicago (Ill.)—Moral condi-
       tions**
       Ohio—Moral conditions
       **United States—Moral condi-
       tions**
Moral education (May subdiv. geog.)
  370.11
  UF   Character education
       Ethical education
  BT   **Education**
       Ethics
  RT   **Religious education**
Moral philosophy
  USE   **Ethics**
Moral theology, Christian
  USE   **Christian ethics**

Morale   152.4
> SA   types of morale, e.g. **Employee morale** [to be added as needed]
> BT   **Courage**
> NT   **Employee morale**
> **Psychological warfare**

Moralities
> USE   **Morality plays**

Morality
> USE   **Ethics**

Morality plays   792.1; 808.82; 812, etc.
> May be used for individual works, collections, or materials about plays in which the chief characters are personifications of abstract qualities.
> UF   Moralities
> BT   **Drama**
> **English drama**
> **Religious drama**
> **Theater**
> RT   **Mysteries and miracle plays**

Morality stories
> USE   **Didactic fiction**

Morality tales
> USE   **Parables**

Morals
> USE   **Conduct of life**
> **Ethics**
> **Human behavior**
> **Moral conditions**

Moravians (May subdiv. geog.)   **284**
> UF   United Brethren
> BT   **Christian sects**

Mormon Church
> USE   **Church of Jesus Christ of Latter-day Saints**

Mormons (May subdiv. geog.)   **289.3092**
> RT   **Church of Jesus Christ of Latter-day Saints**

Morphine   362.29; 615
> BT   **Narcotics**
> NT   **Heroin**
> RT   **Opium**

Morphology   571.3
> UF   Biological form
> Biological structure
> Comparative morphology
> Form in biology
> Structure in biology

> SA   animals, languages, plants, and crops with the subdivision *Morphology* [to be added as needed]
> BT   **Comparative anatomy**

Morse code
> USE   **Cipher and telegraph codes**

Mortality (May subdiv. geog.)   **304.6**
> UF   Burial statistics
> Death rate
> Mortuary statistics
> SA   ethnic groups, classes of persons, diseases, and animals with the subdivision *Mortality,* for works on the number of deaths during a given time among a particular groups or due to a particular cause, e.g. **Infants—Mortality; Tuberculosis—Mortality;** etc. [to be added as needed]
> BT   **Population**
> **Vital statistics**
> NT   **Infants—Mortality**
> RT   **Death**

Mortar   666; 691
> BT   **Adhesives**
> **Plaster and plastering**

Mortgage loans
> USE   **Mortgages**

Mortgages (May subdiv. geog.)   **332.63; 332.7**
> UF   Home loans
> Mortgage loans
> BT   **Loans**
> **Securities**

Morticians
> USE   **Undertakers and undertaking**

Mortuary customs
> USE   **Cremation**
> **Funeral rites and ceremonies**

Mortuary statistics
> USE   **Mortality**
> **Vital statistics**

Mosaics   729; 738.5; 748.5
> BT   **Decoration and ornament**
> **Decorative arts**
> RT   **Mural painting and decoration**

Moslems
> USE   **Muslims**

Mosques (May subdiv. geog.)   726
   BT   Church architecture
      Islamic architecture
      Temples
Mosquitoes   595.77
   BT   Insects
Mosquitoes—Control   363.7
   BT   Pest control
Mosses (May subdiv. geog.)   588
   BT   Plants
Motels
   USE   Hotels and motels
Mother and child
   USE   Mother-child relationship
Mother-child relationship   306.874
   UF   Child and mother
      Mother and child *[Former heading]*
   BT   Children
      Mothers
      Parent-child relationship
   NT   Mother-daughter relationship
      Mother-son relationship
Mother-daughter relationship   305.4; 306.874
   UF   Daughters and mothers
      Mothers and daughters *[Former heading]*
   BT   Daughters
      Mother-child relationship
      Mothers
Mother Goddess religion
   USE   Goddess religion
Mother-son relationship   306.874
   UF   Mothers and sons *[Former heading]*
      Sons and mothers
   BT   Mother-child relationship
      Mothers
      Sons
Mothers (May subdiv. geog.)   306.874
   UF   Maternity
   BT   Family
      Women
   NT   Mother-child relationship
      Mother-daughter relationship
      Mother-son relationship
      Surrogate mothers
      Teenage mothers
      Unmarried mothers

Mothers and daughters
   USE   Mother-daughter relationship
Mothers and sons
   USE   Mother-son relationship
Mothers' pensions
   USE   Child welfare
Moths (May subdiv. geog.)   595.78
   UF   Cocoons
      Lepidoptera
   BT   Insects
   NT   Caterpillars
      Silkworms
   RT   Butterflies
Motion   531
   UF   Kinetics
   BT   Dynamics
   NT   Mechanical movements
      Speed
   RT   Force and energy
      Kinematics
      Mechanics
Motion picture actors and actresses
   USE   Actors
Motion picture adaptations
   USE   Film adaptations
Motion picture cameras   778.5
   UF   Movie cameras
   BT   Cameras
      Cinematography
   RT   Amateur films
Motion picture cartoons
   USE   Animated films
Motion picture direction
   USE   Motion pictures—Production and direction
Motion picture directors
   USE   Motion picture producers and directors
Motion picture festivals
   USE   Film festivals
Motion picture industry (May subdiv. geog.)   384; 791.43
   UF   Film industry (Motion pictures)
   BT   Industries
   NT   African Americans in the motion picture industry
      Blacks in the motion picture industry
      Motion picture producers and directors

Motion picture industry—*Continued*
> Motion pictures—Production
> and direction
> Women in the motion picture
> industry
RT Motion pictures
Motion picture musicals
USE **Musical films**
Motion picture photography
USE **Cinematography**
Motion picture plays   808.82; 812, etc.
May be used for individual works, collections, or materials about motion picture plays.
UF Film scripts
Motion picture scripts
Movie scripts
Screenplays
BT **Drama**
Motion picture plays—Technique   808.2
UF Motion pictures—Play writing
Play writing
Playwriting
BT **Drama—Technique**
Motion picture posters
USE **Film posters**
Motion picture producers
USE **Motion picture producers and
directors**
Motion picture producers and directors
(May subdiv. geog.)   791.43; 920
UF Film directors
Film producers
Motion picture directors
Motion picture producers
BT **Motion picture industry**
RT **Motion pictures—Production
and direction**
Motion picture production
USE **Motion pictures—Production
and direction**
Motion picture projectors
USE **Projectors**
Motion picture scripts
USE **Motion picture plays**
Motion picture serials   791.43
May be used for individual works, collections, or materials about motion picture serials.
BT **Motion pictures**
Motion pictures (May subdiv. geog.)
384; 791.43
Use for general materials on motion pictures, including motion pictures as an art

form. Materials on the technical aspects of making motion pictures and their projection onto a screen are entered under **Cinematography.** For materials on motion pictures produced by the motion picture industry of an individual country or on the motion pictures shown in a country, subdivide geographically, e.g. **Motion pictures—United States.**
UF Cinema
Films
Movies
SA types of motion pictures, e.g.
**Documentary films; Horror
films;** motion pictures and
particular groups of persons,
e.g., **Motion pictures and
children;** motion pictures as
used in various industries or
fields of endeavor, e.g. **Motion pictures in education;**
subjects and groups of persons portrayed in motion pictures, e.g. **Animals in motion
pictures; Women in motion
pictures;** groups of persons in
the motion picture industry,
e.g. **Women in the motion
picture industry;** and names
of individual motion pictures
[to be added as needed]
BT **Audiovisual materials**
Mass media
Performing arts
NT **Adventure films**
**African Americans in motion
pictures**
Amateur films
Animals in motion pictures
Animated films
Bible films
Biographical films
Blacks in motion pictures
Comedy films
Documentary films
Epic films
Erotic films
Experimental films
Fantasy films
Film adaptations
Film noir
Gangster films
Horror films
Legal drama (Films)
Libraries and motion pictures

Motion pictures—*Continued*
>> Medical drama (Films)
>> Motion picture serials
>> Motion pictures and children
>> Motion pictures in education
>> Musical films
>> Mystery films
>> Science fiction films
>> Sherlock Holmes films
>> Short films
>> Silent films
>> Sports drama (Films)
>> Spy films
>> Star Wars films
>> Television movies
>> Three Stooges films
>> Vampire films
>> War films
>> Western films
>> Women in motion pictures
>> World War, 1939-1945—Motion pictures and the war
> RT   Motion picture industry

Motion pictures, American
> USE   **Motion pictures—United States**

Motion pictures and children   **305.23; 649; 791.43**
> Use for materials on the effect of motion pictures on children and youth.
> UF   Children and motion pictures
> BT   **Children**
>> **Motion pictures**

Motion pictures and libraries
> USE   **Libraries and motion pictures**

Motion pictures and the war
> USE   names of wars with the subdivision *Motion pictures and the war,* e.g. **World War, 1939-1945—Motion pictures and the war** [to be added as needed]

Motion pictures—Biography   **791.43092; 920**
> BT   **Biography**

Motion pictures—Catalogs   **016.79143**
> UF   Catalogs, Film
>> Film catalogs
>> Filmography
> SA   types of motion pictures with the subdivision *Catalogs,* e.g. **Science fiction films—Cata-**

logs; and subjects, classes of persons, corporate entities, and names of individual persons with the subdivision *Filmography,* e.g. **Animals—Filmography; Shakespeare, William, 1564-1616—Filmography;** etc. [to be added as needed]

Motion pictures—Censorship (May subdiv. geog.)   **791.43**
> BT   **Censorship**

Motion pictures—Ethical aspects   **791.43**
> UF   Motion pictures—Moral and religious aspects
> BT   **Ethics**

Motion pictures in education   **371.33**
> UF   Educational films
> BT   **Audiovisual education**
>> **Motion pictures**
>> **Teaching—Aids and devices**
> NT   **Libraries and motion pictures**

Motion pictures—Moral and religious aspects
> USE   **Motion pictures—Ethical aspects**
>> **Motion pictures—Religious aspects**

Motion pictures—Play writing
> USE   **Motion picture plays—Technique**

Motion pictures—Posters
> USE   **Film posters**

Motion pictures—Production and direction   **384; 791.43**
> UF   Film direction
>> Film production
>> Filmmaking
>> Motion picture direction
>> Motion picture production
> BT   **Motion picture industry**
> RT   **Motion picture producers and directors**

Motion pictures—Religious aspects   **248.4; 291.4; 791.43**
> UF   Motion pictures—Moral and religious aspects

Motion pictures—Reviews   **791.43**

Motion pictures—Television adaptations
> USE   **Television adaptations**

Motion pictures—United States
    791.430973

Use for materials on motion pictures produced by the motion picture industry of the United States or on motion pictures shown in the United States.

    UF   American films
          American motion pictures
          Motion pictures, American
Motion study   658.5
    BT   **Factory management**
          Industrial efficiency
          Job analysis
          Personnel management
          Production standards
    RT   **Time study**
Motivation (Psychology)   153.8
    UF   Incentive (Psychology)
    BT   **Psychology**
    NT   **Burn out (Psychology)**
          Wishes
Motor boats
    USE   **Motorboats**
Motor buses
    USE   **Buses**
Motor cars
    USE   **Automobiles**
Motor coordination
    USE   **Movement education**
Motor cycles
    USE   **Motorcycles**
Motor trucks
    USE   **Trucks**
Motor vehicle industry
    USE   **Automobile industry**
Motor vehicles—Drivers' licenses
    USE   **Drivers' licenses**
Motorboats   623.8
    UF   Motor boats
          Power boats
    BT   **Boats and boating**
Motorboats—Models   623.8
    BT   **Models and modelmaking**
Motorcycles (May subdiv. geog.)
    629.227
    UF   Motor cycles
    SA   specific makes and models of
          motorcycles [to be added as
          needed]
    BT   **Bicycles**
    NT   **Antique and vintage motorcycles**

    Minibikes
    RT   **Motorcycling**
Motorcycling (May subdiv. geog.)   **796.7**
    BT   **Cycling**
    RT   **Motorcycles**
Motoring
    USE   **Automobile travel**
Motors
    USE   **Electric motors**
          Engines
          and types of engines and motors, e.g. **Steam engines;**
          Electric motors; etc., and
          types of vehicles and makes
          and models of vehicles with
          the subdivision *Motors,* e.g.
          Automobiles—Motors [to be
          added as needed]
Motorways
    USE   **Express highways**
Mottoes   808.88; 818.008, etc.; 929.8
          May be used for collections of mottoes and
    for materials about mottoes.
    UF   Emblems
    BT   **Heraldry**
    RT   **National emblems**
Moulding (Metal)
    USE   **Founding**
Mound-builders
    USE   **Mounds and mound builders**
Mounds and mound builders (May
    subdiv. geog.)   **930.1; 970.004**
    UF   Barrows
          Graves
          Mound-builders
    BT   **Archeology**
          Burial
          Tombs
    RT   **Excavations (Archeology)**
Mount Rainier (Wash.)   979.7
    BT   **Mountains**
Mountain animals (May subdiv. geog.)
    591.75
    UF   Alpine animals
          Alpine fauna
          Mountain fauna
    BT   **Animals**
Mountain bicycles
    USE   **Mountain bikes**
Mountain bikes   629.227
    UF   All terrain bicycles
          Mountain bicycles

Mountain bikes—*Continued*
    BT   **All terrain vehicles**
           Bicycles
Mountain climbing
    USE **Mountaineering**
Mountain fauna
    USE **Mountain animals**
Mountain flora
    USE **Mountain plants**
Mountain life (May subdiv. geog.)
    307.72
    BT   **Country life**
Mountain plants (May subdiv. geog.)
    581.7; 635.9
    UF   Alpine flora
           Alpine plants
           Mountain flora
    BT   **Plant ecology**
           Plants
Mountaineering 796.52
    UF   Mountain climbing
           Rock climbing
    BT   **Outdoor life**
Mountains (May subdiv. geog.)   **551.43**
    SA   names of mountain ranges and
           of individual mountains [to be
           added as needed]
    BT   **Landforms**
           Physical geography
    NT   **Mount Rainier (Wash.)**
           Rocky Mountains
           Volcanoes
Mourning
    USE **Bereavement**
Mourning customs
    USE **Funeral rites and ceremonies**
Mouse
    USE **Mice**
Movable books
    USE **Toy and movable books**
Movement education 152.3; 153.7;
    372.86
    UF   Creative movement
           Motor coordination
    BT   **Physical education**
Movement, Freedom of
    USE **Freedom of movement**
Movements of animals
    USE **Animal locomotion**
Movie cameras
    USE **Motion picture cameras**

Movie festivals
    USE **Film festivals**
Movie novelizations
    USE **Movie novels**
Movie novels 813, etc.
    May be used for individual works, collections, or materials about novels based on movies.
    UF   Movie novelizations
           Movie tie-ins
    BT   **Fiction**
    RT   **Radio and television novels**
Movie posters
    USE **Film posters**
Movie scripts
    USE **Motion picture plays**
Movie tie-ins
    USE **Movie novels**
Movies
    USE **Motion pictures**
Moving 648
    Use for materials on changing the location of possessions, household, office, etc.
    UF   Household moving
           Moving, household
    BT   **Home economics**
Moving, household
    USE **Moving**
MRI (Magnetic resonance imaging)
    USE **Magnetic resonance imaging**
Multi-age grouping
    USE **Nongraded schools**
Multicultural education (May subdiv.
    geog.) **370.117**
    Use for materials on the attempt to eradicate racial and religious prejudices through the study of various races, creeds, and immigrant cultures.
    UF   Intercultural education
    BT   **Acculturation**
           Education
           Multiculturalism
    NT   **Bilingual education**
    RT   **International education**
           Multicultural literature
Multicultural literature 808.8
    Use for collections that bring together literatures of various cultures for the purpose of illustrating racial, religious, or ethnic diversity.
    BT   **Literature**
           Multiculturalism
    RT   **Multicultural education**

Multiculturalism (May subdiv. geog.)
305.8; 306.44

Use for materials on policies or programs that foster the preservation of various cultures or cultural identities within a unified society. Materials on the coexistence of several distinct ethnic, religious, or cultural groups within one society are entered under **Pluralism (Social sciences).** Materials on the presence of two distinct cultures within a single country or region are entered under **Biculturalism.**

UF Diversity movement
BT **Culture**
    Social policy
NT **Multicultural education**
    Multicultural literature
RT **Biculturalism**
    Ethnic relations
    Ethnicity
    Pluralism (Social sciences)
    Race relations

Multilingual dictionaries
USE **Polyglot dictionaries**

Multilingual glossaries, phrase books, etc.
USE **Polyglot dictionaries**

Multimedia   006.7

Use for materials on computer systems, software, or data items that allow users to manipulate diverse integrated media, such as text, graphics, sound, etc.

UF Computer-based multimedia information systems
    Interactive media
    Interactive multimedia
    Multimedia computing
    Multimedia information systems
    Multimedia knowledge systems
    Multimedia systems *[Former heading]*
SA subjects with the subdivision *Interactive multimedia,* e.g. **Geology—Interactive multimedia** [to be added as needed]
BT **Computer software**
    Information systems
NT **Hypertext**

Multimedia centers
USE **Instructional materials centers**

Multimedia computing
USE **Multimedia**

Multimedia information systems
USE **Multimedia**

Multimedia knowledge systems
USE **Multimedia**

Multimedia materials
USE **Audiovisual materials**

Multimedia systems
USE **Multimedia**

Multinational corporations (May subdiv. geog.)   **338.8; 658**

UF Business—International aspects
    Corporations, Multinational
    International business enterprises
BT **Business enterprises**
    Commerce
    Corporations
    International economic relations
NT **Foreign investments**

Multiple birth   618.2

UF Birth, Multiple
SA types of multiple births, e.g. **Twins** [to be added as needed]
BT **Childbirth**
NT **Twins**

Multiple personalities
USE **Multiple personality**

Multiple personality   616.85

UF Double consciousness
    Multiple personalities
    Personality, Multiple
    Split personality
BT **Abnormal psychology**
    Mental illness
    Personality disorders
    Psychology

Multiple plot stories
USE **Plot-your-own stories**

Multiplication   513.2

BT **Arithmetic**

Mummies (May subdiv. geog.)   **393**

BT **Archeology**
    Burial

Municipal administration
USE **Municipal government**

Municipal art (May subdiv. geog.)   **711**

UF Art, Municipal
    Civic art
    Municipal improvements
BT **Art**
    Cities and towns
RT **City planning**

Municipal civil service
  USE **Municipal officials and em-**
       ployees
Municipal employees
  USE **Municipal officials and em-**
       ployees
Municipal engineering (May subdiv.
    geog.) **628**
  BT **Engineering**
      Public works
  NT **Drainage**
      Refuse and refuse disposal
      Sewerage
      Street cleaning
  RT **Sanitary engineering**
Municipal-federal relations
  USE **Federal-city relations**
Municipal finance (May subdiv. geog.)
    336
      Use for general materials on city finance
    and, when subdivided by country, state, or re-
    gion, for general considerations of municipal
    finance in those places. Materials on the fi-
    nance of individual cities, towns, or metropol-
    itan areas are entered under the name of the
    city, town, or area with the subdivision *Public
    finance.*
  UF Cities and towns—Finance
      Finance, Municipal
  SA names of cities with the subdivi-
      sion *Public finance* [to be
      added as needed]
  BT **Municipal government**
      Public finance
  NT **Metropolitan finance**
Municipal government (May subdiv.
    geog.) **320.8; 352.16**
      Use for materials on the government of cit-
    ies in general and, when subdivided by coun-
    try, state, or region, for general consideration
    of municipal government in those places. Ma-
    terials on the government of individual cities,
    towns, or metropolitan areas are entered under
    the name of the city, town, or area with the
    subdivision *Politics and government.*
  UF Cities and towns—Government
      City government
      Government, Municipal
      Municipal administration
      Municipalities
  SA names of cities, towns, and met-
      ropolitan areas with the subdi-
      vision *Politics and govern-
      ment* [to be added as needed]
  BT **Local government**
      Political science

  NT **Chicago (Ill.)—Politics and**
      government
      Federal-city relations
      Municipal finance
      Municipal government by city
      manager
      Municipal government by com-
      mission
      Public administration
      State-local relations
  RT **Metropolitan government**
      Municipal officials and em-
      ployees
Municipal government by city manager
    320.8; 352.16
  UF City manager
      Commission government with
      city manager
  BT **Municipal government**
Municipal government by commission
    320.8; 352.16
  UF Commission government
      Government by commission
  BT **Municipal government**
Municipal government—United States
    320.8; 352.160973
  UF United States—Municipal gov-
      ernment
Municipal improvements
  USE **Cities and towns—Civic im-**
       provement
       Municipal art
Municipal officers
  USE **Municipal officials and em-**
       ployees
Municipal officials and employees
    352.16
  UF Municipal civil service
      Municipal employees
      Municipal officers
      Town officers
  SA names of cities with the subdivi-
      sion *Officials and employees,*
      e.g. **Chicago (Ill.)—Officials**
      and employees [to be added
      as needed]
  BT **Civil service**
  RT **Municipal government**

Municipal ownership   338.9; 352.5
UF Public ownership
BT Corporations
Economic policy
Government ownership
Municipal planning
USE City planning
Municipal transit
USE Local transit
Municipalities
USE Cities and towns
Municipal government
Munitions
USE Defense industry
Military weapons
Mural painting and decoration (May
subdiv. geog.)   729; 751.7
UF Fresco painting
Wall decoration
Wall painting
BT Decoration and ornament
Interior design
Painting
RT Mosaics
Murder
USE Homicide
Murder mysteries
USE Mystery and detective plays
Mystery fiction
Mystery films
Mystery radio programs
Mystery television programs
Murder trials
USE Trials (Homicide)
Muscles   611; 612.7
BT Musculoskeletal system
Muscular system
USE Musculoskeletal system
Musculoskeletal system   611; 612.7
UF Muscular system
BT Anatomy
Physiology
NT Bones
Muscles
Skeleton
RT Human locomotion
Museums (May subdiv. geog.)   069; 708
SA appropriate subjects and names
of wars and of corporate bod-
ies with the subdivision *Mu-
seums*, e.g. **World War,**

1939-1945—Museums; and
names of individual galleries
and museums [to be added as
needed]
NT Art museums
Museums and schools
World War, 1939-1945—Muse-
ums
Museums and schools   069
UF Schools and museums
BT Museums
Schools
Museums—Ohio   708.171
Museums—United States   708.13
Mushrooms   579.6; 635
UF Toadstools
BT Plants
RT Fungi
Music   780
UF Classical music
SA music of particular countries or
ethnic groups, e.g. **American
music; Native American mu-
sic;** etc.; types of music, e.g.
Vocal music; and subjects,
classes of persons, and names
of individual persons, corpo-
rate bodies, places, or wars,
with the subdivision *Songs* for
collections of songs or materi-
als about songs pertaining to
the topic or entity named, e.g.
**Cowhands—Songs; Surfing—
Songs; United States Mili-
tary Academy—Songs** [to be
added as needed]
BT Humanities
NT African American music
American music
Black music
Chamber music
Church music
Composition (Music)
Computer music
Concerts
Conducting
Cowhands—Songs
Dance music
Electronic music
Ensembles (Music)
Folk music

Music—*Continued*
> Harmony
> Instrumental music
> Instrumentation and orchestration
> Jazz music
> Military music
> Music and literature
> Musical notation
> Musicians
> Native American music
> Orchestral music
> Organ music
> Piano music
> Popular music
> Radio and music
> Rock music
> Singing
> Violin music
> Vocal music

Music—Acoustics and physics   781.2
> UF   Acoustics
> BT   **Music—Theory**
> Physics
> RT   Sound

Music, American
> USE   **American music**

Music—Analysis, appreciation
> USE   **Music appreciation**
> **Music—History and criticism**

Music and literature   780
> UF   Literature and music
> Music and poetry
> Poetry and music
> BT   **Literature**
> Music

Music and poetry
> USE   **Music and literature**

Music and radio
> USE   **Radio and music**

Music—Anecdotes   780
> UF   Music—Anecdotes, facetiae, satire, etc.
> BT   **Anecdotes**

Music—Anecdotes, facetiae, satire, etc.
> USE   **Music—Anecdotes**
> **Music—Humor**

Music appreciation   781.1
> UF   Appreciation of music
> Music—Analysis, appreciation
> Musical appreciation

> BT   **Music—Study and teaching**
> RT   **Music—History and criticism**

Music box
> USE   **Music boxes**

Music boxes   786.6
> UF   Music box
> BT   **Mechanical musical instruments**

Music—Cataloging
> USE   **Cataloging of music**

Music, Choral
> USE   **Choral music**

Music—Composition
> USE   **Composition (Music)**

Music conductors
> USE   **Conductors (Music)**

Music—Criticism
> USE   **Music—History and criticism**

Music—Discography   016.78

Music education
> USE   **Music—Study and teaching**

Music—Examinations   780.76
> UF   Music—Examinations, questions, etc.
> BT   **Examinations**

Music—Examinations, questions, etc.
> USE   **Music—Examinations**

Music festivals (May subdiv. geog.)   780.79
> BT   **Festivals**
> RT   **Concerts**

Music, Gospel
> USE   **Gospel music**

Music—History and criticism   780.9
> UF   Music—Analysis, appreciation
> Music—Criticism
> Musical criticism
> RT   **Music appreciation**

Music—Humor   780
> UF   Music—Anecdotes, facetiae, satire, etc.
> BT   **Wit and humor**

Music—Instruction and study
> USE   **Music—Study and teaching**

Music libraries (May subdiv. geog.)   026
> UF   Libraries, Music
> BT   **Special libraries**

Music—Notation
> USE   **Musical notation**

Music—Psychological aspects   781
  UF   Psychology of music
  BT   **Psychology**
Music—Publishing (May subdiv. geog.)
       070.5
  BT   **Publishers and publishing**
Music—Study and teaching   780.7
  UF   Music education
       Music—Instruction and study
       Musical education
       Musical instruction
       School music
  NT   **Music appreciation**
Music—Theory   781
  NT   **Composition (Music)**
       Counterpoint
       Harmony
       Music—Acoustics and physics
       Musical form
       Musical meter and rhythm
Music videos   **384.55; 778.59**
       May be used for individual works, collec-
       tions, or materials about music videos.
  UF   Videos, Music
  BT   **Television programs**
       Videodiscs
       Videotapes
Musical ability   780.7
  UF   Musical talent
  BT   **Ability**
Musical accompaniment   781.47
  UF   Accompaniment, Musical
  BT   **Composition (Music)**
Musical appreciation
  USE   **Music appreciation**
Musical comedies
  USE   **Musicals**
Musical composition
  USE   **Composition (Music)**
Musical criticism
  USE   **Music—History and criticism**
Musical declamation
  USE   **Monologues with music**
Musical education
  USE   **Music—Study and teaching**
Musical ensembles
  USE   **Ensembles (Music)**
Musical films   791.43
       May be used for individual works, collec-
       tions, or materials about musical films.
  UF   Motion picture musicals
       Musicals (Motion pictures)

  BT   **Motion pictures**
  RT   **Musicals**
Musical form   784.18
  SA   names of musical forms ex-
       pressed in the singular, to be
       used both for musical scores
       and for materials about the
       musical form, e.g. **Concerto**
       [to be added as needed]
  BT   **Composition (Music)**
       Music—Theory
  NT   **Concerto**
       Ensembles (Music)
       Fugue
       Opera
       Operetta
       Oratorio
       Sonata
       Suite (Music)
       Symphony
Musical instruction
  USE   **Music—Study and teaching**
Musical instruments (May subdiv. geog.)
       784.19
  UF   Instruments, Musical
  SA   types of instruments, e.g. **Per-
       cussion instruments** [to be
       added as needed]
  NT   **Bells**
       Drums
       Electronic musical instruments
       **Mechanical musical instru-
       ments**
       Organs (Musical instruments)
       Percussion instruments
       Stringed instruments
       Wind instruments
  RT   **Instrumental music**
       **Instrumentation and orchestra-
       tion**
       Orchestra
       Tuning
Musical instruments, Electronic
  USE   **Electronic musical instruments**
Musical instruments, Mechanical
  USE   **Mechanical musical instru-
       ments**
Musical meter and rhythm   781.2
  UF   Meter
  BT   **Music—Theory**
       Rhythm

Musical notation   780.1
    UF   Music—Notation
    BT   **Music**
Musical revues, comedies, etc.
    USE **Musicals**
Musical talent
    USE **Musical ability**
Musicals (May subdiv. geog.)   **782.1; 792.6**

    Use for scores and for materials about musical comedies and revues.

    UF   Dramatic music
         Musical comedies
         Musical revues, comedies, etc.
    BT   **Theater**
    RT   **Musical films**
         Operetta
Musicals (Motion pictures)
    USE **Musical films**
Musicians (May subdiv. geog.)   **780.92; 920**
    SA   types of musicians and names of individual musicians [to be added as needed]
    BT   **Music**
    NT   **African American musicians**
         Black musicians
         Composers
         Conductors (Music)
         Ensembles (Music)
         Instrumentalists
         Singers
Musicians—Biography   780.92; 920
    BT   **Biography**
Musicians, Black
    USE **Black musicians**
Musicians—Portraits   780.92
Musicians—United States   780.92; 920
    UF   American musicians *[Former heading]*
Muslim architecture
    USE **Islamic architecture**
Muslim art
    USE **Islamic art**
Muslim countries
    USE **Islamic countries**
Muslim law
    USE **Islamic law**
Muslim literature
    USE **Islamic literature**
Muslim sermons
    USE **Islamic sermons**

Muslims (May subdiv. geog.)   **297.092**
    UF   Moors *[Former heading]*
         Moslems
    RT   **Islam**
Muslims—United States   297.092
    NT   **Black Muslims**
Mutation (Biology)
    USE **Evolution**
         Variation (Biology)
Mutual defense assistance program
    USE **Military assistance**
Mutual funds (May subdiv. geog.)   **332.63**
    UF   Investment companies
         Investment trusts
    BT   **Investments**
Mutualism (Biology)
    USE **Symbiosis**
Mycology
    USE **Fungi**
Myocardial infarction
    USE **Heart attack**
Myotherapy
    USE **Acupressure**
Mysteries
    USE **Mysteries and miracle plays**
         Mystery and detective plays
         Mystery fiction
         Mystery films
         Mystery radio programs
         Mystery television programs
Mysteries and miracle plays   792.1; 808.82; 822, etc.

    May be used for individual plays, collections, or materials about medieval plays depicting the life of Jesus or legends of the saints.

    UF   Miracle plays
         Mysteries
         Mystery plays
    BT   **Bible plays**
         English drama
         Pageants
         Religious drama
         Theater
    NT   **Passion plays**
    RT   **Morality plays**
Mystery and detective comics
    USE **Mystery comic books, strips, etc.**
Mystery and detective films
    USE **Mystery films**

Mystery and detective plays   808.82; 812, etc.

May be used for individual works, collections, or materials about mystery and detective dramas.

UF   Crime plays
      Detective and mystery plays
      Murder mysteries
      Mysteries
      Mystery plays
      Private eye stories
      Whodunits
BT   **Drama**

Mystery and detective radio programs
USE   **Mystery radio programs**

Mystery and detective stories
USE   **Mystery fiction**

Mystery and detective television programs
USE   **Mystery television programs**

Mystery comic books, strips, etc.   741.5

May be used for individual works, collections, or materials about mystery and detective comics.

UF   Crime comics
      Detective and mystery comic books, strips, etc.
      Detective comics
      Mystery and detective comics
BT   **Comic books, strips, etc.**

Mystery fiction   808.83; 813, etc.

May be used for individual works, collections, or materials about mystery fiction.

UF   Crime stories
      Detective and mystery stories
      Detective fiction
      Detective stories
      Murder mysteries
      Mysteries
      Mystery and detective stories
      Mystery stories
      Private eye stories
      Suspense novels
      Whodunits
BT   **Fiction**
RT   **Ghost stories**
      Horror fiction
      Romantic suspense novels
      Spy stories

Mystery films   791.43

May be used for individual works, collections, or materials about mystery and detective films.

UF   Crime films
      Detective and mystery films

Murder mysteries
      Mysteries
      Mystery and detective films
      Private eye stories
      Suspense films
      Whodunits
SA   particular kinds of detective and mystery films, e.g. **Sherlock Holmes films** [to be added as needed]
BT   **Motion pictures**
NT   **Sherlock Holmes films**
RT   **Film noir**
      Gangster films
      Spy films

Mystery plays
USE   **Mysteries and miracle plays**
       Mystery and detective plays

Mystery radio programs   791.44

May be used for individual works, collections, or materials about mystery and detective radio programs.

UF   Crime programs
      Detective and mystery radio programs
      Murder mysteries
      Mysteries
      Mystery and detective radio programs
      Private eye stories
      Suspense programs
      Whodunits
BT   **Radio programs**

Mystery stories
USE   **Mystery fiction**

Mystery television programs   791.45

May be used for individual works, collections, or materials about mystery and detective television programs.

UF   Crime programs
      Detective and mystery television programs
      Murder mysteries
      Mysteries
      Mystery and detective television programs
      Private eye stories
      Suspense programs
      Whodunits
BT   **Television programs**
RT   **Spy television programs**

Mystical theology
USE   **Mysticism**

Mysticism (May subdiv. geog.)   **248.2; 291.4**

May be subdivided by religion or sect, e.g. **Mysticism—Islam.**

UF   Dark night of the soul

Mystical theology

BT   **Spiritual life**

NT   **Cabala**

Theosophy

Mysticism—Comparative studies   **248.2; 291.4**

Mysticism—Islam (May subdiv. geog.)   **297.4**

UF   Islamic mysticism

BT   **Islam**

NT   **Sufism**

Mythical animals   **398.24**

UF   Animal lore

Animals, Mythical

Imaginary animals

Imaginary creatures

SA   types of mythical animals [to be added as needed]

BT   **Mythology**

NT   **Dragons**

Mermaids and mermen

Sasquatch

Yeti

RT   **Animals—Folklore**

Mythology   **291.1; 398.2**

UF   Myths

SA   mythology of particular national or ethnic groups or of particular geographic areas, e.g. **Celtic mythology** [to be added as needed]

BT   **Legends**

Religion

Religions

NT   **Art and mythology**

Celtic mythology

Classical mythology

Geographical myths

Monsters

Mythical animals

Symbolism

Totems and totemism

RT   **Folklore**

Gods and goddesses

Heroes and heroines

Mythology, Celtic

USE   **Celtic mythology**

Mythology, Classical

USE   **Classical mythology**

Mythology in art

USE   **Art and mythology**

Myths

USE   **Mythology**

Name

USE   names of countries, cities, etc., individual persons, dieties, corporate bodies, ethnic groups, wars, etc., with the subdivision *Name,* for materials on the name's origin, history, validity, etc. [to be added as needed]

Names   **929.4**

UF   Epithets

Proper names

SA   types of names, e.g. **Geographic names;** types of objects, domestic animals, events, organization, and institutions with the subdivision *Names,* for materials on the naming of those items, e.g. **Pets—Names;** and names of countries, cities, etc., individual persons, dieties, corporate bodies, ethnic groups, wars, etc., with the subdivision *Name,* for materials on the name's origin, history, validity, etc. [to be added as needed]

NT   **Code names**

Geographic names

Native American names

Personal names

Pseudonyms

Terms and phrases

Names, Geographical

USE   **Geographic names**

Names, Personal

USE   **Personal names**

Names—Pronunciation   **421**

Napoleon I, Emperor of the French, 1769-1821—Drama   **808.82; 812, etc.**

Use for collections of plays about Napoleon. Materials on Napoleon as a character in drama are entered under **Napoleon I, Emperor of the French, 1769-1821—In literature.**

Napoleon I, Emperor of the French, 1769-1821—Fiction 813, etc.

Use for collections of fiction about Napoleon. Materials on Napoleon as a character in fiction are entered under **Napoleon I, Emperor of the French, 1769-1821—In literature.**

Napoleon I, Emperor of the French, 1769-1821—In art 704.9

Use for materials about the depiction of Napoleon in works of art.

UF   Napoleon in art

BT   **Art—Themes**

Napoleon I, Emperor of the French, 1769-1821—In literature 809

Use for materials about Napoleon as a character or as he is portrayed in works of fiction, drama, or poetry. Collections in which Napoleon is a character are entered under **Napoleon I, Emperor of the French, 1769-1821—Fiction; Napoleon I, Emperor of the French, 1769-1821—Drama;** or **Napoleon I, Emperor of the French, 1769-1821—Poetry;** as appropriate.

UF   Napoleon in fiction, drama, poetry, etc.

BT   **Literature—Themes**

Napoleon I, Emperor of the French, 1769-1821—Poetry 808.81; 811, etc.

Use for collections of poetry about Napoleon. Materials on Napoleon as portrayed in poetry are entered under **Napoleon I, Emperor of the French, 1769-1821—In literature.**

Napoleon in art

USE   **Napoleon I, Emperor of the French, 1769-1821—In art**

Napoleon in fiction, drama, poetry, etc.

USE   **Napoleon I, Emperor of the French, 1769-1821—In literature**

Napoleonic Wars, 1800-1815 940.2

BT   **Europe—History—1789-1815**
      France—History—1799-1815

Narcotic abuse

USE   **Drug abuse**

Narcotic addiction

USE   **Drug abuse**

Narcotic addiction counseling

USE   **Drug abuse counseling**

Narcotic addicts

USE   **Drug addicts**

Narcotic habit

USE   **Drug abuse**

Narcotic traffic

USE   **Drug traffic**

Narcotics   178; 394.1; 615

Use for materials limited to those drugs that induce sleep or lethargy or deaden pain.

UF   Opiates
      Soporifics

SA   types of narcotics [to be added as needed]

BT   **Drugs**
      Materia medica
      Psychotropic drugs

NT   **Cocaine**
      Heroin
      Marijuana
      Morphine
      Opium

Narcotics and crime

USE   **Drugs and crime**

Narcotics and criminals

USE   **Criminals—Drug use**

Narcotics and teenagers

USE   **Teenagers—Drug use**

Narcotics and youth

USE   **Youth—Drug use**

Narration with music

USE   **Monologues with music**

Narrations

USE   **Monologues**
       Recitations

Narrative poetry   808.81; 811, etc.

May be used for individual works, collections, or materials about narrative poetry. Rhyming stories for very young children are entered under the form heading **Stories in rhyme.**

BT   **Poetry**

NT   **Epic poetry**
      Historical poetry
      Stories in rhyme

Nation of Islam

USE   **Black Muslims**

National anthems

USE   **National songs**

National Book Week   021.7

UF   Book Week, National

BT   **Books and reading**

National characteristics   305.8

UF   National images
      National psychology

SA   national characteristics of particular countries, e.g. **American national characteristics** [to be added as needed]

National characteristics—*Continued*
 BT   Anthropology
      Nationalism
      Social psychology
 NT   American national characteristics
 RT   Ethnopsychology
National characteristics, American
 USE American national characteristics
National community service
 USE National service
National consciousness
 USE Nationalism
National dances
 USE Folk dancing
National debts
 USE Public debts
National defenses
 USE Industrial mobilization
      Military readiness
National emblems (May subdiv. geog.)
      929.9
 UF   Emblems
      National symbols
 SA   types of national emblems and
      national symbols, e.g. Flags
      [to be added as needed]
 BT   Signs and symbols
 RT   Flags
      Heraldry
      Insignia
      Mottoes
      Seals (Numismatics)
      State emblems
National forests
 USE Forest reserves
National Guard (U.S.)
 USE United States. National Guard
National health insurance (May subdiv.
      geog.)   368.4
 UF   Government health insurance
      Medical insurance, National
      National health service
      Socialized medicine
 BT   Health insurance
 NT   Medicaid
      Medicare
 RT   State medicine
National health service
 USE National health insurance
      State medicine

National heritage
 USE Cultural property
National holidays
 USE Holidays
National hymns
 USE National songs
National images
 USE National characteristics
National interest
 USE Public interest
National landmarks
 USE National monuments
National liberation movements (May
      subdiv. geog.)   320.5
   Use for materials on minority or other
 groups in armed rebellion against a colonial
 government or against a national government
 charged with corruption or foreign domina-
 tion, usually in the period since World War II.
 UF   Liberation movements, National
 SA   names of individual liberation
      movements [to be added as
      needed]
 BT   Nationalism
      Revolutions
 NT   Guerrillas
National libraries (May subdiv. geog.)
      027.5
   Use for materials on libraries maintained by
 government funds that serve a country as a
 whole, particularly in collecting and preserv-
 ing that country's publications.
 UF   Libraries, National
 SA   names of individual national li-
      braries [to be added as need-
      ed]
 BT   Government libraries
National monuments (May subdiv. geog.)
      917.3
   Use for materials on monuments, such as
 historic sites or geographic areas, that are
 owned and maintained in the public interest
 by a country's government.
 UF   Landmarks, Preservation of
      National landmarks
 SA   names of individual national
      monuments [to be added as
      needed]
 BT   Monuments
      National parks and reserves
 RT   Historic sites
      Natural monuments

National parks and reserves (May subdiv. geog.)   **338.78; 363.6; 719**
  SA   names of individual national parks [to be added as needed]
  BT   **Parks**
        Public lands
  NT   **National monuments**
  RT   **Conservation of natural resources**
        Forest reserves
        Natural monuments
        Wilderness areas
National parks and reserves—United States   719; 917.3
  UF   United States—National parks and reserves
  NT   **Yosemite National Park (Calif.)**
National patrimony
  USE   **Cultural property**
National planning
  USE   **Economic policy**
        Social policy
National psychology
  USE   **Ethnopsychology**
        National characteristics
National resources
  USE   **Economic conditions**
        Natural resources
        United States—Economic conditions
National security (May subdiv. geog.)   **355**
  RT   **Economic policy**
        International relations
        Military policy
National security—United States   355
  UF   United States—National security
National service   361.2
  UF   Alternative military service
        National community service
  BT   **Public welfare**
  RT   **Volunteer work**
National socialism   320.5; 335.6
  Use for materials limited to fascism in Germany during the Nazi regime.
  UF   Nazism
  BT   **Fascism**
        World War, 1939-1945—Causes
  RT   **Neo-Nazis**
        Socialism

National songs (May subdiv. geog.)   **782.42**
  UF   National anthems
        National hymns
        Patriotic songs
  BT   **Songs**
  NT   **War songs**
  RT   **Folk songs**
        Patriotic poetry
National songs—United States   782.42
  UF   American national songs
        United States—National songs
  BT   **American songs**
National symbols
  USE   **National emblems**
National treasure
  USE   **Cultural property**
Nationalism (May subdiv. geog.)   **320.5**
  UF   National consciousness
  BT   **International relations**
        Political science
  NT   **National characteristics**
        National liberation movements
  RT   **Patriotism**
        Regionalism
Nationalism, Black
  USE   **Black nationalism**
Nationalism—United States   320.5
Nationalist China
  USE   **Taiwan**
Nationality (Citizenship)
  USE   **Citizenship**
Nationalization
  USE   **Government ownership**
Nationalization of railroads
  USE   **Railroads—Government policy**
Nationalized companies
  USE   **Government business enterprises**
Native American architecture (May subdiv. geog.)   **720.97; 970.004**
  UF   Indians of North America—Architecture [Former heading]
  BT   **Architecture**
  RT   **Native Americans—Dwellings**
Native American art (May subdiv. geog.)   **704; 709.01**
  UF   Indians of North America—Art [Former heading]
  BT   **Art**

Native American authors   810.9; 920
  UF   American Indian authors
  BT   **Authors**
Native American children (May subdiv.
    geog.)   **305.23; 970.004**
  UF   Indians of North America—Children *[Former heading]*
  BT   **Children**
Native American costume (May subdiv.
    geog.)   **970.004**
  UF   Indians of North America—Costume *[Former heading]*
  BT   **Costume**
Native American dance (May subdiv.
    geog.)   **793.3; 970.004**
  UF   Indians of North America—Dances *[Former heading]*
  BT   **Folk dancing**
Native American games (May subdiv.
    geog.)   **790.1; 970.004**
  UF   Indians of North America—Games *[Former heading]*
  BT   **Games**
       Native Americans—Social life and customs
Native American languages (May subdiv.
    geog.)   **497**
  Use for materials on the several languages of Native Americans.
  UF   Indian languages (North American)
       Indians of North America—Languages *[Former heading]*
  SA   names of individual languages, e.g. **Navajo language** [to be added as needed]
  BT   **Language and languages**
  NT   **Navajo language**
Native American legends
  USE   **Native Americans—Folklore**
Native American literature (May subdiv.
    geog.)   **897**
  Use for collections or materials about literature written in Native American languages by several Native American authors. Collections or materials about literature written in English by several Native American authors are entered under **American literature—Native American authors.**
  UF   Indians of North America—Literature *[Former heading]*
  BT   **Literature**

Native American medicine (May subdiv.
    geog.)   **615.8**
  UF   Indians of North America—Medicine *[Former heading]*
  BT   **Medicine**
Native American music (May subdiv.
    geog.)   **780.89**
  Use for musical transcriptions or for materials about the music of the Native Americans.
  UF   Indians of North America—Music *[Former heading]*
  BT   **Music**
Native American mythology
  USE   **Native Americans—Folklore**
       Native Americans—Religion
Native American names (May subdiv.
    geog.)   **929.4**
  UF   Indians of North America—Names *[Former heading]*
  BT   **Names**
Native American sign language   419
  UF   Indians of North America—Sign language *[Former heading]*
  BT   **Sign language**
Native American silverwork   739.2
  UF   Indians of North America—Silverwork *[Former heading]*
  BT   **Silverwork**
Native American women (May subdiv.
    geog.)   **305.4; 970.004**
  UF   Indians of North America—Women *[Former heading]*
  BT   **Women**
Native Americans (May subdiv. geog.)
    970.004
  Use for general materials on the native peoples of the Western Hemisphere. Libraries that prefer not to subdivide by *United States* may also use this heading for materials limited to the native peoples of the United States. Phrase headings derived from this term may be similarly established for other ethnic groups and for specific Native American peoples and linguistic families. Topical subdivisions provided under this heading may also be used under other ethnic groups and under specific Native American peoples and linguistic families.
  UF   American Indians
       Indians *[Former heading]*
       Indians of North America *[Former heading]*
       Native peoples—America
       Pre-Columbian Americans

Native Americans—*Continued*
SA names of particular Native
American peoples and linguis-
tic families, e.g. **Aztecs; Nav-
ajo Indians** etc. [to be added
as needed]
BT **Native peoples**
Native Americans—Agriculture (May
subdiv. geog.) **338.1; 630**
UF Indians of North America—Agri-
culture
BT **Agriculture**
Native Americans—Amusements
USE **Native Americans—Social life
and customs**
Native Americans—Antiquities (May
subdiv. geog.) **970.004**
UF Indians of North America—An-
tiquities [*Former heading*]
BT **Antiquities**
Native Americans—Canada 971.004
UF Canadian Indians
First nations
Indians of Canada
Indians of North America—Can-
ada [*Former heading*]
Native Americans—Captivities (May
subdiv. geog.) **970.004**
UF Indians of North America—Cap-
tivities [*Former heading*]
BT **Frontier and pioneer life**
**Native Americans—Central America
972.8004**
UF Indians of Central America
[*Former heading*]
NT **Mayas**
Native Americans—Christian missions
(May subdiv. geog.) **266**
UF Indian missions
Indians of North America—
Christian missions [*Former
heading*]
BT **Christian missions**
Native Americans—Chronology
USE **Native Americans—History—
Chronology**
Native Americans—Claims (May subdiv.
geog.) **323.1; 970.004**
UF Indians of North America—
Claims [*Former heading*]
Native Americans—Land claims

Native Americans—Customs
USE **Native Americans—Social life
and customs**
Native Americans—Dwellings (May
subdiv. geog.) **728; 970.004**
UF Indians of North America—
Dwellings [*Former heading*]
NT **Tepees**
RT **Native American architecture**
Native Americans—Economic conditions
(May subdiv. geog.) **970.004**
UF Indians of North America—Eco-
nomic conditions [*Former
heading*]
BT **Economic conditions**
Native Americans—Education (May
subdiv. geog.) **371.829; 970.004**
UF Indians of North America—Edu-
cation [*Former heading*]
Indians of North America—
Schools
BT **Education**
**Native Americans—First contact with
Europeans** (May subdiv. geog.)
970.004
UF Indians of North America—First
contact with Europeans [*For-
mer heading*]
BT **Native Americans—History**
RT **Native Americans—Relations
with early settlers**
Native Americans—Folklore (May subdiv.
geog.) **398**
Use for collections of Native American leg-
ends, myths, tales, etc., and for materials
about the folklore and mythology of Native
Americans.
UF Indians of North America—Folk-
lore [*Former heading*]
Native American legends
Native American mythology
BT **Folklore**
Native Americans—Forced Removal
USE **Native Americans—Relocation**
Native Americans—Government policy
USE **Native Americans—Govern-
ment relations**
Native Americans—Government relations
(May subdiv. geog.) **323.1;
970.004**
Use for materials on the Indian policy of
the United States government and on relations

Native Americans—Government relations—*Continued*
between North American governments and the Native Americans.

UF Federal-Indian relations
  Indians of North America—Government relations *[Former heading]*
  Native Americans—Government policy

RT **Native Americans—Relations with early settlers**

Native Americans—Guatemala 972.81004

UF Indians of Central America—Guatemala *[Former heading]*

Native Americans—History 970.004

UF Indians of North America—History *[Former heading]*

NT **Native Americans—First contact with Europeans**
  Native Americans—Relations with early settlers
  Native Americans—Wars

Native Americans—History—Chronology 970.004

Use for materials that list events and dates in the history of the Native Americans in the order of their occurrence.

UF Indians of North America—History—Chronology *[Former heading]*
  Native Americans—Chronology

Native Americans—Housing (May subdiv. geog.) **307.3; 363.5**

BT **Housing**

Native Americans—Hunting (May subdiv. geog.) **970.004**

BT **Hunting**

Native Americans—Industries (May subdiv. geog.) **338.4; 680; 970.004**

UF Indians of North America—Industries *[Former heading]*

BT **Industries**

Native Americans—Land claims

USE **Native Americans—Claims**

Native Americans—Medical care (May subdiv. geog.) **362.1**

BT **Medical care**

Native Americans—Mexico 972.004

UF Indians of Mexico *[Former heading]*

NT **Aztecs**
  Mayas

Native Americans—North America 970.004

UF Indians of North America *[Former heading]*

SA names of particular Native American peoples and linguistic families, e.g. **Navajo Indians** [to be added as needed]

Native Americans—Origin 970.004

UF Indians of North America—Origin *[Former heading]*

Native Americans—Peru 985

UF Indians of South America—Peru *[Former heading]*

Native Americans—Politics and government (May subdiv. geog.) **970.004**

UF Indians of North America—Politics and government *[Former heading]*
  Native Americans—Tribal government

BT **Politics**

Native Americans—Psychology 155.8

UF Indians of North America—Psychology *[Former heading]*

BT **Ethnopsychology**

Native Americans—Relations with early settlers (May subdiv. geog.) **970.004**

UF Indians of North America—Relations with early settlers *[Former heading]*

BT **Native Americans—History**

RT **Native Americans—First contact with Europeans**
  Native Americans—Government relations

Native Americans—Religion (May subdiv. geog.) **270.089; 299**

UF Indians of North America—Religion *[Former heading]*
  Native American mythology

BT **Religion**

Native Americans—Relocation (May subdiv. geog.) **970.004**

UF Forced removal of Indians
  Indian removal

Native Americans—Relocation—*Continued*
    Native Americans—Forced Removal
    Native Americans—Removal
    Removal of Indians
Native Americans—Removal
    USE **Native Americans—Relocation**
Native Americans—Reservations (May subdiv. geog.)   **333.1; 970.004**
    UF Indian reservations
        Indians of North America—Reservations *[Former heading]*
    SA names of native peoples, tribes, etc., with the subdivision *Reservations* [to be added as needed]
Native Americans—Rites and ceremonies
    970.004
    UF Indians of North America—Rites and ceremonies *[Former heading]*
    BT **Rites and ceremonies**
    NT **Powwows**
Native Americans—Social conditions (May subdiv. geog.)   **970.004**
    UF Indians of North America—Social conditions *[Former heading]*
    BT **Social conditions**
Native Americans—Social life and customs (May subdiv. geog.)
    970.004
    UF Indians of North America—Social life and customs *[Former heading]*
        Native Americans—Amusements
        Native Americans—Customs
    BT **Manners and customs**
    NT **Native American games**
        Powwows
Native Americans—South America   **980**
    UF Indians of South America *[Former heading]*
    NT **Incas**
Native Americans—Southwestern States
    979
    NT **Cliff dwellers and cliff dwellings**
        Navajo Indians
Native Americans—Tribal government
    USE **Native Americans—Politics and government**

Native Americans—United States
    970.004
    UF Indians of North America *[Former heading]*
Native Americans—Wars (May subdiv. geog.)   **970.004**
    UF Indians of North America—Wars *[Former heading]*
    BT **Native Americans—History**
    NT **Black Hawk War, 1832**
        King Philip's War, 1675-1676
        Pontiac's Conspiracy, 1763-1765
        United States—History—1689-1697, King William's War
        United States—History—1755-1763, French and Indian War
Native Americans—West Indies
    972.9004
    UF Indians of the West Indies *[Former heading]*
Native peoples (May subdiv. geog.)
    305.8
    Use for materials on indigenous groups within a colonial area or modern state where the group does not control the government. General materials on people bound together by common ancestry and culture are entered under **Ethnic groups.** Materials on the various ethnic groups or native peoples in a particular region or country are entered under **Ethnology** subdivided geographically.
    UF Aborigines
        Indigenous peoples
        Natives
        People
    SA names of individual native peoples e.g. **Yoruba (African people)** [to be added as needed]
    BT **Ethnology**
    NT **Australian aborigines**
        Inuit
        Native Americans
        Yoruba (African people)
Native peoples—America
    USE **Native Americans**
Natives
    USE **Native peoples**
Nativity of Jesus Christ
    USE **Jesus Christ—Nativity**

NATO
  USE   North Atlantic Treaty Organi-
        zation
Natural beauty conservation
  USE   Landscape protection
Natural childbirth   618.4
  UF   Lamaze method of childbirth
  BT   Childbirth
  NT   Midwives
Natural cycles
  USE   Cycles
Natural disasters (May subdiv. geog.)
        904
  SA   types of natural disasters [to be
        added as needed]
  BT   Disasters
  NT   Earthquakes
        Floods
        Storms
        Tsunamis
Natural disasters—United States   973
Natural food cooking
  USE   Cooking—Natural foods
Natural foods   641.3
  UF   Health foods
        Organically grown foods
  BT   Food
  RT   Cooking—Natural foods
Natural gardening
  USE   Organic gardening
Natural gas (May subdiv. geog.)   553.2;
        665.7
  BT   Fuel
        Gases
Natural gas companies
  USE   Gas companies
Natural gas utilities
  USE   Gas companies
Natural history (May subdiv. geog.)
        508
    Use for materials on the unsystematic study
  of zoology, botany, mineralogy, etc., the col-
  lecting of specimens, and, with a geographic
  subdivision, the description of nature in a par-
  ticular place. Materials on the study of ani-
  mals and plants as an elementary school sub-
  ject are entered under Nature study. General
  and theoretical materials on the natural world
  are entered under Nature.
  UF   Animal lore
        Mineralogy
  BT   Science
  NT   Aquariums
        Bible—Natural history

        Bird watching
        Fossils
        Nature photography
  RT   Biogeography
        Botany
        Minerals
        Nature
        Zoology
Natural history—United States   508.73
  UF   Nature study—United States
Natural law   340
  UF   Law of nature
        Natural rights
  BT   Ethics
        Law
  RT   International law
Natural monuments (May subdiv. geog.)
        719
    Use for general materials on natural objects
  of historic or scientific interest such as caves,
  cliffs, and natural bridges.
  UF   Landmarks, Preservation of
        Preservation of natural scenery
        Protection of natural scenery
        Scenery
  SA   names of individual natural
        monuments [to be added as
        needed]
  BT   Landscape protection
        Monuments
        Nature conservation
  RT   National monuments
        National parks and reserves
Natural monuments—United States
        719; 917.3
Natural parents
  USE   Birthparents
Natural pesticides   668
  BT   Pesticides
Natural religion
  USE   Natural theology
Natural resources (May subdiv. geog.)
        333.7
  UF   National resources
  SA   types of natural resources [to be
        added as needed]
  BT   Economic conditions
  NT   Conservation of natural re-
        sources
        Energy resources
        Forests and forestry
        Marine resources

Natural resources—*Continued*
        Mines and mineral resources
        Water resources development
        Water supply
  RT **Public lands**
Natural resources—Management   333.7
  BT **Management**
Natural resources—United States   333.7
Natural rights
  USE **Natural law**
Natural satellites
  USE **Satellites**
Natural selection   576.8
  UF Survival of the fittest
  BT **Genetics**
        Variation (Biology)
  RT **Evolution**
        Heredity
Natural steam energy
  USE **Geothermal resources**
Natural theology   210
    Use for materials on the knowledge of God's existence obtained by observing the visible processes of nature.
  UF Natural religion
  BT **Apologetics**
        Theology
  NT **Creation**
  RT **Religion and science**
Natural therapy
  USE **Naturopathy**
Naturalism in art
  USE **Realism in art**
Naturalism in literature
  USE **Realism in literature**
Naturalists (May subdiv. geog.)
        508.092; 920
  SA types of naturalists, e.g. **Botanists** [to be added as needed]
  BT **Scientists**
  NT **Biologists**
        Botanists
Naturalization   323.6
  BT **Immigration and emigration**
        International law
        Suffrage
  RT **Aliens**
        Americanization
        Citizenship
Nature   508
    Use for general and theoretical materials on the natural world. Materials on the study of

animals and plants as an elementary school subject are entered under **Nature study.** Materials on the unsystematic study of zoology, botany, mineralogy, etc., the collecting of specimens, and the description of nature in a particular place are entered under **Natural history.**
  RT **Natural history**
        Nature study
Nature conservation (May subdiv. geog.)
        333.7
  UF Conservation of nature
        Nature protection
        Preservation of natural scenery
        Protection of natural scenery
  BT **Conservation of natural resources**
  NT **Endangered species**
        Landscape protection
        Natural monuments
        Plant conservation
        Wildlife conservation
Nature craft   745.5
    Use for materials on crafts using objects found in nature, such as leaves, shells, etc.
  UF Naturecraft
  BT **Handicraft**
Nature—Effect of human beings on
  USE **Human influence on nature**
Nature in literature   809
  BT **Literature—Themes**
Nature in the bible
  USE **Bible—Natural history**
Nature photography   778.9
  UF Photography of nature
  SA photography of particular subjects in nature, e.g. **Photography of birds** [to be added as needed]
  BT **Natural history**
        Photography
  NT **Photography of animals**
        Photography of birds
        Photography of fishes
        Photography of plants
  RT **Outdoor photography**
Nature poetry   809.1; 811, etc.
    May be used for individual works or collections of poetry about nature.
  UF Nature—Poetry
  BT **Poetry**
Nature—Poetry
  USE **Nature poetry**

Nature protection
USE **Nature conservation**
Nature study   372.3; 508.07
Use for materials on the study of animals and plants as an elementary school subject. Materials on the unsystematic study of zoology, botany, mineralogy, etc., the collecting of specimens, and the description of nature in a particular place are entered under **Natural history**. General and theoretical materials on the natural world are entered under **Nature**.
BT **Education**
   Science—Study and teaching
RT **Nature**
   Outdoor education
   Outdoor life
Nature study—United States
USE **Natural history—United States**
Naturecraft
USE **Nature craft**
Naturopathy   615.5
UF Natural therapy
BT **Alternative medicine**
   Therapeutics
RT **Chiropractic**
Nautical almanacs   528
BT **Almanacs**
   Navigation
Nautical astronomy   527
BT **Astronomy**
NT **Latitude**
   Longitude
RT **Navigation**
   Time
Nautical charts   623.89
UF Charts, Nautical
   Navigation charts
   Navigation maps
   Pilot charts
BT **Maps**
   Navigation
Navaho Indians
USE **Navajo Indians**
Navaho language
USE **Navajo language**
Navajo Indians   970.004
UF Navaho Indians
BT **Native Americans—Southwestern States**
Navajo language   497
UF Navaho language
BT **Native American languages**

Naval administration
USE **Naval art and science**
   and names of countries with the subhead *Navy,* e.g. **United States. Navy** [to be added as needed]
Naval aeronautics
USE **Military aeronautics**
Naval air bases
USE **Air bases**
Naval airplanes
USE **Military airplanes**
Naval architecture   623.8
UF Marine architecture
BT **Architecture**
NT **Boatbuilding**
   Marine engineering
   Shipbuilding
   Steamboats
   Warships
Naval art and science (May subdiv. geog.)   **359**
UF Fighting
   Naval administration
   Naval science
   Naval warfare
   Navy
SA names of wars with the subdivision *Naval operations,* e.g. **World War, 1939-1945—Naval operations** [to be added as nccdcd]
NT **Camouflage (Military science)**
   Marine engineering
   Navy yards and naval stations
   Privateering
   Sailors
   Sea power
   Signals and signaling
   Strategy
   Submarine warfare
   Torpedoes
   Warships
RT **Military art and science**
   Navies
   Navigation
   War
Naval art and science—Study and teaching
USE **Naval education**
Naval bases
USE **Navy yards and naval stations**

Naval battles   359.4; 904
  UF   Naval warfare
  SA   names of countries with the sub-
         division *Naval history;* names
         of wars with the subdivision
         Naval operations, e.g. **World
         War, 1939-1945—Naval op-
         erations;** and names of spe-
         cific naval battles [to be add-
         ed as needed]
  BT   **Battles**
  RT   **Naval history**
Naval biography
  USE   names of navies with the subdi-
         vision *Biography,* e.g. **United
         States. Navy—Biography** [to
         be added as needed]
Naval education (May subdiv. geog.)
         359.007
  UF   Naval art and science—Study
         and teaching
         Naval schools
  BT   **Education**
Naval engineering
  USE   **Marine engineering**
Naval history   **359.009**
  UF   Wars
  SA   names of countries with the sub-
         head *Navy* or the subdivision
         Naval history [to be added as
         needed]
  BT   **History**
  NT   **Pirates**
         Privateering
         United States—Naval history
  RT   **Military history**
         Naval battles
         Sea power
Naval law
  USE   **Maritime law**
Naval offenses
  USE   **Military offenses**
Naval operations
  USE   names of wars with the subdivi-
         sion *Naval operations,* e.g.
         **World War, 1939-1945—Na-
         val operations** [to be added
         as needed]
Naval pensions
  USE   **Military pensions**

Naval personnel
  USE   **Sailors**
Naval power
  USE   **Sea power**
Naval schools
  USE   **Naval education**
Naval science
  USE   **Naval art and science**
Naval shipyards
  USE   **Navy yards and naval stations**
Naval signaling
  USE   **Signals and signaling**
Naval strategy
  USE   **Strategy**
Naval uniforms
  USE   **Military uniforms**
Naval warfare
  USE   **Naval art and science**
         Naval battles
         Submarine warfare
Navies   359.3
  UF   Military power
         Navy
         Sea life
  SA   names of countries with the sub-
         head *Navy,* e.g. **United
         States. Navy** [to be added as
         needed]
  BT   **Armed forces**
         Military personnel
  NT   **Admirals**
         Sailors
         United States. Navy
  RT   **Naval art and science**
         Sea power
         Warships
Navigation (May subdiv. geog.)   **623.89;
         629.04**
  UF   Pilots and pilotage
         Seamanship
  BT   **Locomotion**
  NT   **Compass**
         Harbors
         Inland navigation
         Knots and splices
         Lighthouses
         Loran
         Nautical almanacs
         Nautical charts
         Ocean currents
         Orienteering

Navigation—*Continued*
>> Pilot guides
>> Radar
>> Shipwrecks
>> Signals and signaling
>> Steam navigation
>> Winds
> RT Direction sense
>> Nautical astronomy
>> Naval art and science
>> Sailing
>> Ship pilots

Navigation (Aeronautics)   629.132
> UF Aerial navigation
>> Aeronautics—Navigation
>> Air navigation
> BT Aeronautics
> NT Airplanes—Piloting
>> Radio in aeronautics

Navigation (Astronautics)   629.45
> UF Astronavigation
>> Space navigation
> BT Astrodynamics
>> Astronautics
> NT Astronautical instruments
>> Radio in astronautics
>> Space vehicles—Piloting
> RT Space flight

Navigation charts
> USE Nautical charts

Navigation—Law and legislation
> USE Maritime law

Navigation maps
> USE Nautical charts

Navigators
> USE Explorers
>> Sailors

Navy
> USE Naval art and science
>> Navies
>> Sea power
>> and names of countries with the subhead *Navy*, e.g. **United States. Navy** [to be added as needed]

Navy Sealab project
> USE Sealab project

Navy yards and naval stations (May subdiv. geog.)   **359.7**
> UF Naval bases
>> Naval shipyards
> BT Naval art and science

Nazi persecution
> USE religious groups and classes of persons with the subdivision *Nazi persecution,* e.g. **Handicapped—Nazi persecution** [to be added as needed]

Nazi persecution of the handicapped
> USE **Handicapped—Nazi persecution**

Nazism
> USE **National socialism**

Near-death experiences   133.9; 155.9
> Use for materials on the paranormal experiences of those who have survived near death or apparent death.
> BT Death
> RT Parapsychology

Near East
> USE Middle East

Neatness
> USE Cleanliness

Nebulae, Extragalactic
> USE Galaxies

Necrologies
> USE Obituaries

Necromancy
> USE Divination
>> Magic

Needlepoint   746.44
> UF Canvas embroidery
> BT Embroidery
>> Needlework

Needlework   746.4
> SA types of needlework [to be added as needed]
> BT Decoration and ornament
>> Decorative arts
> NT Crocheting
>> Embroidery
>> Knitting
>> Lace and lace making
>> Needlepoint
>> Samplers
>> Tapestry
> RT Dressmaking
>> Sewing

Negotiable instruments (May subdiv. geog.)   **332.7**
> UF Bills and notes
>> Bills of credit
>> Commercial paper
>> Instruments, Negotiable
>> Letters of credit

Negotiable instruments—*Continued*
  BT Banks and banking
      Commercial law
      Contracts
      Credit
  NT Bonds
Negotiation 158; 302.3
  UF Bargaining
      Discussion
  BT Applied psychology
  NT Collective bargaining
      Hostage negotiation
      Industrial arbitration
Negritude
  USE Blacks—Race identity
Negroes
  USE African Americans
       Blacks
Neighborhood (May subdiv. geog.)
      307.3
  UF Neighborhoods
  BT Community life
      Social groups
Neighborhood centers
  USE Community centers
       Social settlements
Neighborhood development
  USE Community development
Neighborhoods
  USE Neighborhood
Neo-fascism
  USE Fascism
       Neo-Nazis
Neo-Greek literature
  USE Modern Greek literature
Neo-impressionism (Art)
  USE Impressionism (Art)
Neo-Latin languages
  USE Romance languages
Neo-Nazis (May subdiv. geog.) 320.5
      Use for materials on political groups whose
      social beliefs or political agendas are reminis-
      cent of those of Hitler's Nazis.
  UF Neo-fascism
      Neo-nazism
  BT Fascism
  RT National socialism
Neo-nazism
  USE Neo-Nazis
Neolithic period
  USE Stone Age

Neon tubes 621.32
  BT Electric signs
Nero, Emperor of Rome, 37-68 92; B
  BT Emperors—Rome
Nerves 611; 612.8
  BT Nervous system
Nerves—Diseases
  USE Nervous system—Diseases
Nervous breakdown
  USE Neurasthenia
Nervous exhaustion
  USE Neurasthenia
Nervous prostration
  USE Neurasthenia
Nervous system 611; 612.8
  UF Neurology
  BT Anatomy
      Physiology
  NT Abnormal psychology
      Brain
      Nerves
      Psychophysiology
Nervous system—Diseases 616.8
  UF Nerves—Diseases
      Neuropathology
  BT Diseases
  NT Epilepsy
Nest building 591.56
  UF Building nests
      Nesting (Animal behavior)
      Nesting behavior
  SA types of animals and individual
      species on animals with the
      subdivision *Nests*, e.g.
      Birds—Nests [to be added as
      needed]
  BT Animal behavior
      Animals—Habitations
Nesting (Animal behavior)
  USE Nest building
Nesting behavior
  USE Nest building
Nests
  USE types of animals and individual
       species of animals with the
       subdivision *Nests*, e.g.
       Birds—Nests [to be added as
       needed]
Netherlands 949.2
      May be subdivided like United States ex-
      cept for *History*.
  UF Holland

493

Netherlands—History 949.2

Netherlands—History—1940-1945, German occupation 949.207

UF   German occupation of Netherlands, 1940-1945

Network theory

USE **System analysis**

Networks (Associations, institutions, etc.)

USE **Associations**

Networks, Computer

USE **Computer networks**

Networks, Information

USE **Information networks**

Neurasthenia 616.85

UF   Nervous breakdown

Nervous exhaustion

Nervous prostration

BT   **Mental illness**

Neurology

USE **Nervous system**

Neuropathology

USE **Nervous system—Diseases**

Neuroses 616.85

BT   **Abnormal psychology**

NT   **Anxiety**

Depression (Psychology)

Phobias

Post-traumatic stress disorder

Psychosomatic medicine

Neurotic children

USE **Emotionally disturbed children**

Neutrality (May subdiv. geog.) 327.1; 341.6

UF   Nonalignment

BT   **International law**

International relations

International security

RT   **Intervention (International law)**

Neutrality—United States 327.73

UF   United States—Neutrality

RT   **United States—Foreign relations**

Neutron bomb 623.4

UF   Neutron bombs

BT   **Bombs**

Neutron weapons

Neutron bombs

USE **Neutron bomb**

Neutron weapons 623.4

UF   Enhanced radiation weapons

BT   **Nuclear weapons**

NT   **Neutron bomb**

Neutrons 539.7

BT   **Atoms**

Particles (Nuclear physics)

New Age movement (May subdiv. geog.) 131; 133; 299

Use for materials on any of various post-1970 cults and organizations that incorporate Eastern or Native American religions, occult beliefs and practices, mysticism, or meditation techniques in an attempt to enhance consciousness and develop human potential.

UF   Aquarian Age movement

BT   **Cults**

Occultism

Social movements

New birth (Theology)

USE **Regeneration (Christianity)**

New business enterprises (May subdiv. geog.) 338.7

UF   How to start a business

Starting a business

BT   **Business enterprises**

New countries

USE **New states**

New England 974

BT   **United States**

New France—History

USE **Canada—History—0-1763 (New France)**

Mississippi River Valley—History

New nations

USE **New states**

New Negro Movement

USE **Harlem Renaissance**

New states 321

UF   New countries

New nations

States, New

BT   **Developing countries**

New Testament

USE **Bible. N.T.**

New words 417; 427, etc.

UF   Coinage of words

Words, New

BT   **Vocabulary**

New York (N.Y.)—Streets

USE **Streets—New York (N.Y.)**

Newbery Award
    USE **Newbery Medal**
Newbery Medal **028.5**
    UF Newbery Award
          Newbery Prize books
    BT **Children's literature**
          Literary prizes
Newbery Prize books
    USE **Newbery Medal**
News agencies (May subdiv. geog.)
    070.4
    UF News services
          Wire services
    BT **Press**
News editing
    USE **Journalism—Editing**
News photography
    USE **Photojournalism**
News services
    USE **News agencies**
Newsgroups, Electronic
    USE **Electronic discussion groups**
Newspaper advertising **659.13**
    Use for materials on advertising in newspapers. Materials on the advertising of newspapers are entered under **Advertising—Newspapers.**
    UF Advertising, Newspaper
    BT **Advertising**
          Newspapers
Newspaper clippings
    USE **Clippings (Books, newspapers, etc.)**
Newspaper work
    USE **Reporters and reporting**
Newspapers (May subdiv. geog.) **070**
    Use for materials limited to the history, organization, and management of newspapers. Materials on writing for the periodical press, on the editing of such writing, and on journalism as an occupation, are entered under **Journalism.**
    SA names of individual newspapers [to be added as needed]
    BT **Mass media**
          Serial publications
    NT **Clippings (Books, newspapers, etc.)**
          Newspaper advertising
          Reporters and reporting
    RT **Journalism**
          Periodicals
          Press

Newspapers—Advertising
    USE **Advertising—Newspapers**
Newspapers—Editing
    USE **Journalism—Editing**
Newspapers—Great Britain **072**
    UF English newspapers *[Former heading]*
Newspapers—Indexes **070.1**
Newspapers—United States **071**
    UF American newspapers *[Former heading]*
Nicene Creed **238**
    BT **Creeds**
Nicknames **929.4**
    UF Epithets
          Sobriquets
    BT **Personal names**
Nicotine habit
    USE **Tobacco habit**
Night **529**
    BT **Chronology**
          Time
    NT **Bedtime**
    RT **Day**
Night schools
    USE **Evening and continuation schools**
Nike rocket **623.4**
    BT **Guided missiles**
Nineteenth century
    USE **World history—19th century**
Nitrates **553.6**
    BT **Chemicals**
          Fertilizers
Nitrogen **546; 665**
    BT **Gases**
Nobel Prizes **001.4; 807.9**
    BT **Awards**
Nobility (May subdiv. geog.) **305.5; 929.7**
    UF Peerage
    BT **Upper class**
    NT **Knights and knighthood**
    RT **Aristocracy**
          Heraldry
Noise **363.74**
    SA subjects with the subdivision *Noise* [to be added as needed]
    BT **Public health**
          Sound
    NT **Airplanes—Noise**

Noise pollution (May subdiv. geog.)
    363.74
    SA   subjects with the subdivision
          Noise [to be added as needed]
    BT   **Pollution**
    NT   **Airplanes—Noise**
Nomadic peoples
    USE **Nomads**
Nomads (May subdiv. geog.)   **304.2;**
    306.08
    UF   Nomadic peoples
          Pastoral peoples
    BT   **Primitive societies**
Nomenclature
    USE types of scientific and technical
          disciplines and types of sub-
          stances, plants, and animals
          with the subdivision *Nomen-*
          clature, for systematically de-
          rived lists of names or desig-
          nations that have been formal-
          ly adopted or sanctioned, and
          for discussions of the princi-
          ples involved in the creation
          and application of such
          names, e.g. **Botany—Nomen-**
          clature; scientific and techni-
          cal disciplines and types of
          animals, plants, and crops
          with the subdivision *Nomen-*
          clature (Popular), for lists or
          materials about popular, non-
          technical names or designa-
          tions of substances, species,
          etc., e.g. **Trees—Nomencla-**
          ture (Popular); and subjects,
          classes of persons, sacred
          works, and religious sects
          with the subdivision *Terminol-*
          ogy, for lists or discussions of
          words and expressions found
          in those works or used in
          those fields, e.g. **Botany—**
          Terminology [to be added as
          needed]
Nomenclature (Popular)
    USE types of scientific and technical
          disciplines and types of ani-
          mals, plants, and crops with
          the subdivision *Nomenclature*
          (Popular), for lists of popular

or non-technical names or
designations of substances,
species, etc., e.g. **Trees—No-**
menclature (Popular); and
scientific and technical disciplines and types of sub-
stances, plants, and animals
with the subdivision *Nomen-*
clature, for systematically derived lists of names or designations that have been formally adopted or sanctioned, and
for discussions of the principles involved in the creation
and application of such
names, e.g. **Botany—Nomen-**
clature [to be added as need-
ed]
Nomination
    USE types of public officials and
          names of individual public of-
          ficials with the subdivision
          Nomination, e.g. **Presidents—**
          United States—Nomination
          [to be added as needed]
Nomination of presidents
    USE **Presidents—United States—**
          Nomination
Non-institutional churches   **289.9**
    UF   Avant-garde churches
          Churches, Non-institutional
          Noninstitutional churches *[For-*
          mer heading]
    BT   **Christian sects**
Non-professional theater
    USE **Amateur theater**
Non-proliferation of nuclear weapons
    USE **Arms control**
Non-promotion (School)
    USE **Promotion (School)**
Non-victim crimes
    USE **Crimes without victims**
Non-wage payments
    USE **Fringe benefits**
Nonalignment
    USE **Neutrality**
Nonbook materials
    USE **Audiovisual materials**
Noncitizens
    USE **Aliens**

Nonconformity
USE **Conformity**
Counter culture
Dissent
Nondenominational churches
USE **Community churches**
Nonfiction films
USE **Documentary films**
Nonformal schools
USE **Experimental schools**
Nonfossil fuels
USE **Synthetic fuels**
Nongraded schools (May subdiv. geog.)
371.2
UF Multi-age grouping
Ungraded schools
BT **Ability grouping in education**
Education—Experimental
methods
Schools
Noninstitutional churches
USE **Non-institutional churches**
Nonlinguistic communication
USE **Nonverbal communication**
Nonnationals
USE **Aliens**
Nonnutritive sweeteners
USE **Sugar substitutes**
Nonobjective art
USE **Abstract art**
Nonprescription drugs **615**
UF Drugs, Nonprescription
Over-the-counter drugs
Patent medicines
BT **Drugs**
Nonprint materials
USE **Audiovisual materials**
Nonprofit corporations
USE **Nonprofit organizations**
Nonprofit organizations (May subdiv.
geog.) **346; 658**
UF Corporations, Nonprofit
Nonprofit corporations
Nonprofit sector
Nonprofits
Not-for-profit organizations
Organizations, Nonprofit
BT **Associations**
Nonprofit sector
USE **Nonprofit organizations**

Nonprofitable drugs
USE **Orphan drugs**
Nonprofits
USE **Nonprofit organizations**
Nonpublic schools
USE **Church schools**
Private schools
Nonsense verses **808.81; 811, etc.;**
811.008, etc.
May be used for individual works, collec-
tions, or materials about nonsense verse.
UF Rhymes
BT **Children's poetry**
Humorous poetry
Wit and humor
NT **Tongue twisters**
RT **Limericks**
Nonsupport
USE **Desertion and nonsupport**
Nonverbal communication **153.6; 302.2**
UF Body language
Nonlinguistic communication
BT **Communication**
NT **Hugging**
Personal space
RT **Deaf—Means of communica-**
tion
Nonvictim crimes
USE **Crimes without victims**
Nonviolence (May subdiv. geog.) **179;**
303.6
NT **Hunger strikes**
RT **Pacifism**
Passive resistance
Nonviolent noncooperation
USE **Passive resistance**
Nonwage payments
USE **Fringe benefits**
Nonword stories
USE **Stories without words**
Nordic peoples
USE **Teutonic peoples**
Normal schools
USE **Teachers colleges**
Normandy (France), Attack on, 1944
940.54
UF D Day
BT **World War, 1939-1945—Cam-**
paigns
Normans (May subdiv. geog.) **941.02**
BT **Great Britain—History—1066-**
1154, Norman period

497

Normans—*Continued*

    RT   **Vikings**

Norse languages

    USE   **Old Norse language**

           Scandinavian languages

Norse legends   398.2

    BT   **Legends**

Norse literature

    USE   **Old Norse literature**

           Scandinavian literature

Norsemen

    USE   **Vikings**

North Africa   961

    Use for materials dealing collectively with the region of Africa that includes Morocco, Algeria, Tunisia, and Libya.

    UF   Africa, North

           Barbary States

           Maghreb

    BT   **Africa**

North America   970

    BT   **America**

    NT   **Central America**

           Northwest Coast of North America

           Pacific Northwest

North Atlantic Treaty Organization 341.7

    UF   NATO

    BT   **International organization**

North Central States

    USE   **Middle West**

North Korea

    USE   **Korea (North)**

North Pole   910.9163; 998

    BT   **Polar regions**

    RT   **Arctic regions**

Northeast Africa   960

    Use for materials dealing collectively with the region of Africa that includes Sudan, Ethiopia, Eritrea, Somalia, and Djibouti.

    UF   Africa, Northeast

    BT   **Africa**

Northeast Passage   998

    BT   **Arctic regions**

           Exploration

           Voyages and travels

Northern lights

    USE   **Auroras**

Northmen

    USE   **Vikings**

Northwest Africa   964

    Use for materials dealing collectively with the region of Africa that includes Morocco, Western Sahara, Mauritania, Algeria, Mali, Tunisia, Libya, Niger, and Chad.

    UF   Africa, Northwest

    BT   **Africa**

Northwest Coast of North America 979.5

    UF   Northwest, Pacific coast

           Pacific Northwest coast

    BT   **North America**

Northwest, Old

    USE   **Old Northwest**

Northwest, Pacific

    USE   **Pacific Northwest**

Northwest, Pacific coast

    USE   **Northwest Coast of North America**

Northwest Passage   971.9

    BT   **America—Exploration**

           Arctic regions

Northwest Territory

    USE   **Old Northwest**

Norwegian language   439.8

    May be subdivided like **English language.**

    BT   **Language and languages**

           Scandinavian languages

    NT   **Danish language**

Norwegian language—0-1350

    USE   **Old Norse language**

Norwegian literature   839.82

    May use same subdivisions and names of literary forms as for **English literature.**

    BT   **Literature**

           Scandinavian literature

Nose   611; 612.2

    BT   **Face**

           Head

    RT   **Smell**

Not-for-profit organizations

    USE   **Nonprofit organizations**

Notation, Mathematical

    USE   **Mathematical notation**

Novelists   809.3; 920

    SA   novelists of particular countries, e.g. **American novelists;** and names of individual novelists [to be added as needed]

    BT   **Authors**

    NT   **American novelists**

Novelists, American

    USE   **American novelists**

Novels
    USE   **Fiction**
Novels in letters
    USE   **Epistolary fiction**
Nuclear bomb shelters
    USE   **Air raid shelters**
Nuclear energy (May subdiv. geog.)
        333.792; 539.7
    UF   Atomic energy
          Atomic power
          Nuclear power
    BT   **Nuclear physics**
    NT   **Nuclear engineering**
          Nuclear propulsion
          Nuclear reactors
    RT   **Nuclear industry**
          Nuclear power plants
Nuclear engineering (May subdiv. geog.)
        621.48
    BT   **Engineering**
          Nuclear energy
          Nuclear physics
    NT   **Nuclear reactors**
          Radioactive waste disposal
          Radioisotopes
Nuclear freeze movement
    USE   **Antinuclear movement**
Nuclear industry (May subdiv. geog.)
        333.792
    UF   Atomic industry
    BT   **Industries**
    RT   **Nuclear energy**
Nuclear magnetic resonance imaging
    USE   **Magnetic resonance imaging**
Nuclear medicine   616.07
    UF   Atomic medicine
    BT   **Medicine**
    RT   **Radiation—Physiological effect**
Nuclear medicine—Practice   616.07
    BT   **Medical practice**
Nuclear non-proliferation
    USE   **Arms control**
Nuclear particles
    USE   **Particles (Nuclear physics)**
Nuclear physics   539.7
    UF   Atomic nuclei
    BT   **Physics**
    NT   **Cosmic rays**
          Cyclotrons
          Nuclear energy
          Nuclear engineering

          Nuclear reactors
          Particles (Nuclear physics)
          Radiobiology
          Transmutation (Chemistry)
    RT   **Physical chemistry**
          Radioactivity
Nuclear pollution
    USE   **Radioactive pollution**
Nuclear power
    USE   **Nuclear energy**
Nuclear power plants (May subdiv. geog.)
        621.48
    UF   Atomic power plants
          Power plants, Nuclear
    BT   **Electric power plants**
    RT   **Nuclear energy**
Nuclear power plants—Accidents
        363.17
Nuclear power plants—Environmental
    aspects   333.792; 621.48
    BT   **Environment**
          Environmental health
    NT   **Radioactive waste disposal**
    RT   **Antinuclear movement**
Nuclear power plants—Fires and fire
    prevention   363.37; 628.9
    BT   **Fire prevention**
          Fires
Nuclear power plants—Security mea-
    sures   621.48
Nuclear propulsion   621.48
    UF   Atomic-powered vehicles
    SA   specific applications of nuclear
          propulsion, e.g. **Nuclear sub-**
          marines [to be added as
          needed]
    BT   **Nuclear energy**
    NT   **Nuclear submarines**
    RT   **Nuclear reactors**
Nuclear reactors   621.48
    UF   Reactors (Nuclear physics)
    BT   **Nuclear energy**
          Nuclear engineering
          Nuclear physics
    RT   **Nuclear propulsion**
Nuclear submarines (May subdiv. geog.)
        623.8
    UF   Atomic submarines
    BT   **Nuclear propulsion**
          Submarines

Nuclear test ban
   USE **Arms control**
Nuclear warfare 355.02
   UF Atomic warfare
   BT **War**
   RT **Nuclear weapons**
Nuclear waste disposal
   USE **Radioactive waste disposal**
Nuclear weapons (May subdiv. geog.)
   355.8; 623.4
   UF Atomic weapons
        Weapons, Atomic
        Weapons, Nuclear
   SA types of nuclear weapons, e.g.
        Atomic bomb [to be added
        as needed]
   BT **Military weapons**
   NT **Antinuclear movement**
        Atomic bomb
        Ballistic missiles
        Hydrogen bomb
        Neutron weapons
   RT **Nuclear warfare**
Nucleic acids 547; 572.8
   UF Polynucleotides
   BT **Biochemistry**
   NT **DNA**
        RNA
Nucleons
   USE **Particles (Nuclear physics)**
Nude in art 704.9; 743.4
   UF Human anatomy in art
        Human figure in art
   BT **Art—Themes**
   NT **Artistic anatomy**
Number concept 119; 155.4; 372.7
   Use for materials on the apperception and
   conceptualization of numbers. Materials on
   numbers, numbering, and systems of numera-
   tion are entered under **Numbers.** Materials on
   counting, including counting books, are en-
   tered under **Counting.**
   BT **Apperception**
        Psychology
   RT **Numbers**
Number games 793.7
   BT **Arithmetic—Study and teach-
        ing**
        Counting
        Mathematical recreations
Number patterns
   USE **Patterns (Mathematics)**

Number readiness
   USE **Mathematical readiness**
Number symbolism
   USE **Numerology**
        Symbolism of numbers
Number systems
   USE **Numbers**
Number theory 512
   Use for materials on that branch of mathe-
   matics that involves the study of integers and
   their relation to one another.
   UF Theory of numbers
   BT **Algebra**
        Mathematics
        Set theory
   NT **Group theory**
   RT **Numbers**
Numbers 119; 513
   Use for materials on numbers, numbering,
   and systems of numeration. Materials on the
   conceptualization of numbers are entered un-
   der **Number concept.** Materials on counting,
   including counting books, are entered under
   Counting. Materials on the graphic represen-
   tation of numbers are entered under **Numer-
   als.**
   UF Number systems
        Numeration
   SA names of individual numbers,
        e.g. **Three (The number);**
        and systems of numeration,
        e.g. **Decimal system** [to be
        added as needed]
   NT **Binary system (Mathematics)**
        Decimal system
        Three (The number)
   RT **Arithmetic**
        Counting
        Number concept
        Number theory
        Numerals
        Symbolism of numbers
Numeral formation
   USE **Writing of numerals**
Numeral writing
   USE **Writing of numerals**
Numerals 513
   Use for materials on the graphic representa-
   tion of numbers.
   SA types of numerals, e.g. **Roman
        numerals** [to be added as
        needed]
   NT **Roman numerals**
        Writing of numerals

Numerals—*Continued*
  RT **Numbers**
Numerals, Writing of
  USE **Writing of numerals**
Numeration
  USE **Numbers**
Numerical analysis 515
  BT **Mathematical analysis**
  NT **Approximate computation**
Numerical sequences
  USE **Sequences (Mathematics)**
Numerology 133.3
  Use for materials on the occult significance
  of numbers. General materials on the symbol-
  ism of numbers, as in philosophy, religion, or
  literature, are entered under **Symbolism of
  numbers.**
  UF Number symbolism
      Sacred numbers
      Symbolic numbers
  BT **Occultism**
      Symbolism of numbers
Numismatics (May subdiv. geog.) **737**
  Use for materials on coins, paper money,
  medals, and tokens considered as works of
  art, as historical specimens, or as aids to the
  study of history, archeology, etc.
  BT **Ancient history**
      Archeology
      History
  NT **Seals (Numismatics)**
  RT **Coins—Collectors and collect-
      ing**
      Medals
Nunneries
  USE **Convents**
Nuns (May subdiv. geog.) **255; 271**
  UF Sisters (Religious)
  BT **Women**
  NT **Ex-nuns**
  RT **Monasticism and religious or-
      ders for women**
Nurse clinicians
  USE **Nurse practitioners**
Nurse midwives
  USE **Midwives**
Nurse practitioners (May subdiv. geog.)
      610.73092; 920
  UF Nurse clinicians
  BT **Allied health personnel**
      Nurses
Nurseries, Day
  USE **Day care centers**

Nurseries (Horticulture) (May subdiv.
      geog.) **631.5; 635**
  BT **Fruit culture**
      Gardening
  NT **Plant propagation**
Nursery rhymes 398.8
  May be used for collections of nursery
  rhymes or for materials about nursery rhymes.
  UF Poetry for children
      Rhymes
  BT **Children's poetry**
      Children's songs
      Folklore
Nursery schools 372.21
  BT **Elementary education**
      Schools
  RT **Day care centers**
      Kindergarten
      Preschool education
Nurses (May subdiv. geog.) **610.73092;
      920**
  SA types of nurses [to be added as
      needed]
  BT **Medical personnel**
  NT **Midwives**
      Nurse practitioners
      Practical nurses
      School nurses
  RT **Nursing**
Nursing (May subdiv. geog.) **610.73;
      649.8**
  SA types of nursing, e.g. **Home
      nursing;** and diseases and
      medical procedures with the
      subdivision *Nursing* [to be
      added as needed]
  BT **Medicine**
      Therapeutics
  NT **Cancer—Nursing**
      Cooking for the sick
      First aid
      Heart—Surgery—Nursing
      Home nursing
      Practical nursing
  RT **Nurses**
      Sick
Nursing homes (May subdiv. geog.)
      362.1
  BT **Hospitals**
      Institutional care
      Long-term care facilities

Nursing (Infant feeding)
    USE **Breast feeding**
Nutrition (May subdiv. geog.)   **613.2**
    UF   Meal planning
    SA   animals, plants and crops, ethnic
           groups, and classes of persons
           with the subdivision *Nutrition,*
           e.g. **Children—Nutrition;**
           names of diseases with the
           subdivision *Diet therapy,* e.g.
           Cancer—Diet therapy; and
           types of foods with the subdi-
           vision *Therapeutic use;* e.g.
           Herbs—Therapeutic use [to
           be added as needed]
    BT   **Health**
         Physiology
         Therapeutics
    NT   **Astronauts—Nutrition**
         Children—Nutrition
         Eating customs
         Infants—Nutrition
         Malnutrition
         Plants—Nutrition
         Vitamins
    RT   **Diet**
         Digestion
         Food
Nuts   **581.4; 634**
    Names of specific kinds of nuts may be
    used for materials on the nut or the tree.
    SA   types of nuts, e.g. **Pecans** [to be
           added as needed]
    BT   **Food**
         Seeds
    NT   **Pecans**
Nylon   **677**
    BT   **Synthetic fabrics**
Oak   **583**
    UF   Oaks
    BT   **Trees**
         Wood
Oaks
    USE **Oak**
Oats   **633.1**
    BT   **Feeds**
Obedience   **179**
    UF   Disobedience
    BT   **Virtue**
Obelisks (May subdiv. geog.)   **721**
    BT   **Archeology**
         Architecture

         Monuments
         Pyramids
Obesity   **613.2; 616.3**
    UF   Corpulence
         Fatness
         Overweight
    BT   **Body weight**
Obituaries (May subdiv. geog.)   **920**
    UF   Death notices
         Necrologies
    SA   ethnic groups and classes of per-
           sons with the subdivision
           Obituaries [to be added as
           needed]
    BT   **Biography**
Objets d'art
    USE **Art objects**
Obscene materials
    USE **Obscenity (Law)**
           Pornography
Obscenity (Law) (May subdiv. geog.)
    345
    UF   Obscene materials
    BT   **Criminal law**
    RT   **Erotica**
         Pornography
Observatories, Astronomical
    USE **Astronomical observatories**
Observatories, Meteorological
    USE **Meteorological observatories**
Obstetrics
    USE **Childbirth**
Occidental civilization
    USE **Western civilization**
Occult fiction   **808.83; 813, etc.**
    May be used for individual works, collec-
    tions, or materials about fiction dealing with
    supernatural powers.
    BT   **Fiction**
    NT   **Ghost stories**
         Gothic novels
    RT   **Fantasy fiction**
Occult sciences
    USE **Occultism**
Occultism (May subdiv. geog.)   **133**
    UF   Hermetic art and philosophy
         Occult sciences
         Sorcery
    BT   **Religions**
         Supernatural
    NT   **Alchemy**
         Astrology

Occultism—*Continued*
    Cabala
    Clairvoyance
    Demonology
    Divination
    Magic
    New Age movement
    Numerology
    Oracles
    Palmistry
    Prophecies
    Spiritualism
    Witchcraft
  RT Parapsychology
Occupation, Military
  USE **Military occupation**
Occupational accidents
  USE **Industrial accidents**
Occupational crimes
  USE **White collar crimes**
Occupational diseases (May subdiv. geog.)
    616.9
  UF Industrial diseases
      Occupations—Diseases
  SA occupational groups with the
      subdivision *Diseases,* e.g.
      Miners—Diseases; types of
      industries with the subdivi-
      sions *Employees—Diseases;*
      e.g. **Chemical industry—Em-
      ployees—Diseases;** and names
      of occupational diseases [to
      be added as needed]
  BT **Diseases**
  NT **Chemical industry—Employ-
      ees—Diseases**
    Lead poisoning
    Miners—Diseases
  RT **Hazardous occupations**
    Occupational health and safety
Occupational forecasting
  USE **Employment forecasting**
Occupational guidance
  USE **Vocational guidance**
Occupational health and safety (May
    subdiv. geog.) **363.11; 658.3**
  UF Health, Industrial
      Industrial health
      Industrial safety
      Safety, Industrial
  BT **Environmental health**
    Management

    Public health
  NT **Burn out (Psychology)**
  RT **Hazardous occupations**
    Occupational diseases
    Occupational health services
Occupational health services (May
    subdiv. geog.) **362.1; 613.6;
    658.3**
  Use for materials on health services for em-
  ployees, usually provided at the place of
  work.
  UF Employee health services
  BT **Medical care**
  RT **Occupational health and safety**
Occupational injuries
  USE **Industrial accidents**
Occupational literacy
  USE **Functional literacy**
Occupational retraining (May subdiv.
    geog.) **331.25**
  UF Job retraining
      Retraining, Occupational
  BT **Employees—Training**
    Labor supply
    Occupational training
    Technical education
    Unemployed
    Vocational education
Occupational stress
  USE **Job stress**
Occupational therapy **615.8**
  BT **Mental health**
    Physical therapy
    **Physically handicapped—Reha-
    bilitation**
    Therapeutics
  RT **Handicraft**
Occupational training (May subdiv.
    geog.) **331.25; 374**
  Use for materials on teaching people a skill
  after formal education. Materials on teaching
  a skill during the educational process are en-
  tered under **Vocational education.** Materials
  discussing on-the-job training are entered under **Employees—Training.** Materials on
  retraining are entered under **Occupational
  retraining.**
  UF Job training
      Training, Occupational
      Training, Vocational
      Vocational training
  BT **Technical education**
    Vocational education

Occupational training—*Continued*
NT   **Employees—Training**
      Occupational retraining
Occupations (May subdiv. geog.)   **331.7**
   Use for descriptions and lists of occupations.
UF   Careers
      Jobs
      Trades
      Vocations
SA   fields of knowledge, professions, industries, and trades with the subdivision *Vocational guidance,* and ethnic groups and classes of persons with the subdivision *Employment,* e.g. **Women—Employment** [to be added as needed]
NT   **Hazardous occupations**
      Job analysis
      Paraprofessionals
      Professions
RT   **Employment**
      Vocational guidance
      Work
Occupations—Chicago (Ill.)   **331.7**
UF   Chicago (Ill.)—Occupations
Occupations—Diseases
USE   **Occupational diseases**
Occupations—Ohio   **331.7**
UF   Ohio—Occupations
Occupations—United States   **331.7**
UF   United States—Occupations
Occupied territories
USE   names of wars with the subdivision *Occupied territories,* e.g. **World War, 1939-1945—Occupied territories** [to be added as needed]
Occupied territory
USE   **Military occupation**
Ocean   **551.46**
UF   Oceans
      Sea
SA   names of oceans and seas [to be added as needed]
BT   **Earth**
      Physical geography
      Water
NT   **Atlantic Ocean**
      Icebergs
      Ocean bottom

      Ocean currents
      Ocean waves
      Tides
RT   **Oceanography**
      Seashore
Ocean bottom   **551.46**
UF   Ocean floor
      Sea bed
BT   **Ocean**
      Submarine geology
NT   **Marine mineral resources**
Ocean cables
USE   **Submarine cables**
Ocean currents   **551.47**
UF   Currents, Ocean
BT   **Navigation**
      Ocean
Ocean drilling platforms
USE   **Drilling platforms**
Ocean—Economic aspects
USE   **Marine resources**
      Shipping
Ocean energy resources   **333.91**
BT   **Energy resources**
      Marine resources
      Ocean engineering
NT   **Geothermal resources**
RT   **Marine mineral resources**
Ocean engineering (May subdiv. geog.)   **627**
   Use for materials on engineering beneath the surface of the ocean.
UF   Deep sea engineering
      Submarine engineering
      Undersea engineering
BT   **Engineering**
      Marine resources
      Oceanography
NT   **Drilling platforms**
      Marine mineral resources
      Ocean energy resources
      Ocean mining
      Offshore oil well drilling
Ocean farming
USE   **Aquaculture**
Ocean floor
USE   **Ocean bottom**
Ocean life
USE   **Marine biology**
Ocean mineral resources
USE   **Marine mineral resources**

Ocean mining (May subdiv. geog.)   **622**
  UF Deep sea mining
        Mining, Ocean
  BT **Marine mineral resources**
        Mining engineering
        Ocean engineering
Ocean pollution
  USE **Marine pollution**
Ocean resources
  USE **Marine resources**
Ocean routes
  USE **Trade routes**
Ocean transportation
  USE **Shipping**
Ocean travel   **910.4**
  UF Cruises
        Sea travel
  BT **Transportation**
        Travel
        Voyages and travels
  NT **Steamboats**
        Yachts and yachting
Ocean waves   **551.47**
  UF Breakers
        Sea waves
        Surf
        Swell
  BT **Ocean**
        Waves
  NT **Tsunamis**
Oceania   **995**
  Use for comprehensive materials on the lands and area of the central and southern Pacific Ocean, including Micronesia, Melanesia, and Polynesia. Comprehensive works on all the islands of the Pacific Ocean are entered under **Islands of the Pacific.**
  UF South Pacific region
        South Sea Islands
        South Seas
        Southwest Pacific region
  BT **Islands of the Pacific**
Oceanographic research
  USE **Oceanography—Research**
Oceanography (May subdiv. geog.)
      551.46
  UF Oceanology
  BT **Earth sciences**
  NT **Marine biology**
        Marine pollution
        Marine resources
        Ocean engineering
        Submarine geology

      Underwater exploration
  RT **Ocean**
Oceanography—Atlantic Ocean   **551.46**
Oceanography—Computer programs
      551.46
  BT **Computer software**
Oceanography—Research   **551.46**
  UF Oceanographic research
  BT **Research**
  NT **Bathyscaphe**
        Undersea research stations
Oceanology
  USE **Oceanography**
Oceans
  USE **Ocean**
Oddities
  USE **Curiosities and wonders**
Offenses against property (May subdiv. geog.)   **364.16**
  UF Property, Crimes against
        Property, Offenses against
  SA types of offenses, e.g. **Vandalism** [to be added as needed]
  BT **Crime**
        Criminal law
  NT **Fraud**
        Theft
        Vandalism
Offenses against public safety (May subdiv. geog.)   **364.1**
  UF Crimes against public safety
        Public safety, Crimes against
  SA types of offenses, e.g. **Hijacking of airplanes** [to be added as needed]
  BT **Crime**
        Criminal law
  NT **Bombings**
        Hijacking of airplanes
        Riots
        Sabotage
Offenses against the person (May subdiv. geog.)   **364.15**
  UF Abuse of persons
        Assault, Criminal
        Crimes against the person
        Criminal assault
  SA types of offenses, e.g. **Kidnapping** [to be added as needed]
  BT **Crime**
        Criminal law

Offenses against the person—*Continued*
- NT **Homicide**
  - **Kidnapping**
  - **Rape**
  - **Stalking**

Offenses, Military
- USE **Military offenses**

Office buildings (May subdiv. geog.)
725
- UF Buildings, Office
- BT **Buildings**

Office employees
- USE **Office workers**

Office equipment and supplies 651
- UF Business machines
  - Office machines
  - Office supplies
- SA types of office equipment and supplies [to be added as needed]
- BT **Bookkeeping**
  - **Office management**
- NT **Calculators**
  - **Copying machines**
  - **Keyboards (Electronics)**
  - **Typewriters**

Office machines
- USE **Office equipment and supplies**

Office management 651.3
- UF Office procedures
- BT **Business**
  - **Factory management**
  - **Industrial efficiency**
  - **Management**
- NT **Files and filing**
  - **Office equipment and supplies**
  - **Office practice**
  - **Secretaries**
  - **Word processing**
- RT **Personnel management**

Office practice 651.3
- UF Secretarial practice
- BT **Office management**
- NT **Keyboarding (Electronics)**
  - **Shorthand**
  - **Typewriting**
  - **Word processing**
- RT **Office workers**

Office procedures
- USE **Office management**

Office romance
- USE **Sex in the workplace**

Office supplies
- USE **Office equipment and supplies**

Office work—Training
- USE **Business education**

Office workers (May subdiv. geog.)
331.7; 651.3
- UF Clerical employees
  - Clerical personnel
  - Clerks
  - Commercial employees
  - Office employees
- BT **Employees**
- RT **Office practice**

Office workers—Salaries, wages, etc.
(May subdiv. geog.) **331.2**
- BT **Salaries, wages, etc.**

Officers
- USE names of armed forces with the subdivision *Officers,* e.g. **United States. Army—Officers** [to be added as needed]

Official misconduct
- USE **Misconduct in office**

Official publications
- USE **Government publications**

Officials and employees
- USE **Civil service**
  - **Public officers**
  - and names of countries, states, cities, etc., and corporate bodies with the subdivision *Officials and employees,* e.g. **United States—Officials and employees; Ohio—Officials and employees; Chicago (Ill.)—Officials and employees; United Nations—Officials and employees;** etc. [to be added as needed]

Offset printing 686.2
- UF Lithoprinting
- BT **Lithography**
  - **Printing**

Offshore oil industry (May subdiv. geog.)
338.2
- UF Oil industry, Offshore
- BT **Petroleum industry**
- NT **Offshore oil well drilling**

506

Offshore oil well drilling (May subdiv.
  geog.)   **622**
  UF   Deep sea drilling (Petroleum)
       Oil well drilling, Offshore
       Oil well drilling, Submarine
       Submarine oil well drilling
       Underwater drilling (Petroleum)
  BT   **Ocean engineering**
       Offshore oil industry
       Oil well drilling
  NT   **Drilling platforms**
Offshore water pollution
  USE   **Marine pollution**
Ohio   977.1
  The subdivisions under **Ohio** may be used
  under the name of any state of the United
  States or province of Canada. The subdivi-
  sions under **United States** may be further
  consulted as a guide for formulating other
  headings as needed.
Ohio—Antiquities   977.1
  BT   **Antiquities**
Ohio—Bibliography   015.771; 016.9771
Ohio—Bio-bibliography   012
Ohio—Biography   920.0771
  BT   **Biography**
Ohio—Biography—Dictionaries
       920.0771
Ohio—Biography—Portraits   920.0771
Ohio—Boundaries   977.1
  BT   **Boundaries**
Ohio—Census   317.71
  BT   **Census**
Ohio—Church history   277.71
  UF   Church history—Ohio
       Ohio—Religious history
  BT   **Church history**
  RT   **Ohio—Religion**
Ohio—Civilization   977.1
  BT   **Civilization**
Ohio—Climate   551.69771
  BT   **Climate**
Ohio—Commerce   381
  BT   **Commerce**
Ohio—Constitution
  USE   **Constitutions—Ohio**
Ohio—Constitutional history
  USE   **Constitutional history—Ohio**
Ohio—Constitutional law
  USE   **Constitutional law—Ohio**
Ohio—Description   917.71
  UF   Ohio—Description and travel
       Ohio—Travel

Ohio—Description and travel
  USE   **Ohio—Description**
Ohio—Description—Guidebooks
  USE   **Ohio—Guidebooks**
Ohio—Description—Views
  USE   **Ohio—Pictorial works**
Ohio—Directories   917.710025
  Use for lists of names and addresses. Lists
  of names without addresses are entered under
  Ohio—Registers.
  BT   **Directories**
  RT   **Ohio—Registers**
Ohio—Economic conditions   330.9771
  BT   **Economic conditions**
Ohio—Economic policy
  USE   **Economic policy—Ohio**
Ohio—Employees
  USE   **Ohio—Officials and employees**
Ohio—Executive departments
  USE   **Executive departments—Ohio**
Ohio—Executive departments—Reorganiza-
       tion
  USE   **Administrative agencies—Reor-
       ganization—Ohio**
Ohio—Fiction   808.83; 813, etc.
  Use for collections of stories about Ohio.
Ohio—Gazetteers   917.71
  BT   **Gazetteers**
Ohio—Government employees
  USE   **Ohio—Officials and employees**
Ohio—Government publications
  USE   **Government publications—
       Ohio**
Ohio—Guidebooks   917.7104
  UF   Ohio—Description—Guidebooks
Ohio—Historic buildings
  USE   **Historic buildings—Ohio**
Ohio—History   977.1
  NT   **Constitutional history—Ohio**
Ohio—History—Societies   977.106
  BT   **History—Societies**
Ohio—History—Sources   977.1
Ohio—Industries
  USE   **Industries—Ohio**
Ohio—Intellectual life   977.1
  BT   **Intellectual life**
Ohio—Local history   977.1
  BT   **Local history**
Ohio—Manufactures
  USE   **Manufactures—Ohio**
Ohio—Maps   912.771
  BT   **Maps**

Ohio—Militia 355.3
   BT   Armed forces
Ohio—Moral conditions 977.1
   BT   Moral conditions
Ohio—Occupations
   USE   Occupations—Ohio
Ohio—Officials and employees 351.771
   UF   Ohio—Employees
        Ohio—Government employees
Ohio—Officials and employees—Salaries,
   wages, etc. 331.2
   BT   Salaries, wages, etc.
Ohio—Pictorial works 917.710022
   UF   Ohio—Description—Views
Ohio—Politics and government 977.1
Ohio—Population 304.609771
   BT   Population
Ohio—Public buildings
   USE   Public buildings—Ohio
Ohio—Public lands
   USE   Public lands—Ohio
Ohio—Public works
   USE   Public works—Ohio
Ohio—Race relations 305.8009771
   BT   Race relations
Ohio—Registers 917.710025
   Use for lists of names without addresses.
   Lists of names that include addresses are en-
   tered under Ohio—Directories.
   RT   Ohio—Directories
Ohio—Religion 277.71
   BT   Religion
   RT   Ohio—Church history
Ohio—Religious history
   USE   Ohio—Church history
Ohio—Rural conditions 307.7209771
   BT   Rural sociology
Ohio—Social conditions 977.1
   BT   Social conditions
Ohio—Social life and customs 977.1
   BT   Manners and customs
Ohio—Social policy
   USE   Social policy—Ohio
Ohio—Statistics 317.71
   BT   Statistics
Ohio—Travel
   USE   Ohio—Description
Oil
   USE   Oils and fats
        Petroleum

Oil burners 697
   BT   Heating
        Petroleum as fuel
Oil drilling platforms
   USE   Drilling platforms
Oil engines
   USE   Internal combustion engines
Oil fuel
   USE   Petroleum as fuel
Oil industry
   USE   Petroleum industry
Oil industry, Offshore
   USE   Offshore oil industry
Oil painting
   USE   Painting
Oil pollution of rivers, harbors, etc.
   USE   Oil pollution of water
Oil pollution of water (May subdiv.
   geog.) 363.739; 628.1
   UF   Oil pollution of rivers, harbors,
        etc.
        Petroleum pollution of water
        Water—Oil pollution
   BT   Water pollution
   NT   Oil spills
   RT   Marine pollution
Oil spills (May subdiv. geog.) 363.738
   BT   Oil pollution of water
Oil well drilling (May subdiv. geog.)
   622
   UF   Drilling, Oil well
        Petroleum—Well boring
        Well drilling, Oil
   BT   Drilling and boring (Earth and
        rocks)
        Petroleum industry
   NT   Offshore oil well drilling
        Oil wells—Blowouts
   RT   Oil wells
Oil well drilling, Offshore
   USE   Offshore oil well drilling
Oil well drilling, Submarine
   USE   Offshore oil well drilling
Oil wells (May subdiv. geog.) 622
   BT   Petroleum industry
   RT   Oil well drilling
Oil wells—Blowouts 622
   UF   Blowouts, Oil well
   BT   Oil well drilling

Oils and fats   665
   UF Animal oils
         Fats
         Grease
         Oil
         Vegetable oils
   NT **Essences and essential oils**
         Petroleum
   RT **Lubrication and lubricants**
Old age (May subdiv. geog.)   **305.26**
   BT **Age**
   NT **Aging**
         Retirement
   RT **Elderly**
         Gerontology
         Longevity
Old age homes
   USE **Elderly—Institutional care**
Old age pensions (May subdiv. geog.)
       331.25; 368.3
   UF Ages—Pensions
         Employees—Pensions
   BT **Pensions**
         Retirement income
Old English language
   USE **English language—Old English period**
Old English literature
   USE **English literature—Old English period**
Old Icelandic language
   USE **Old Norse language**
Old Norse language   439
   UF Icelandic language—0-1500
         Norse languages
         Norwegian language—0-1350
         Old Icelandic language
         Old Norwegian language
   BT **Language and languages**
         Scandinavian languages
Old Norse literature   839
   UF Norse literature
   BT **Literature**
         Medieval literature
   NT **Eddas**
         Sagas
   RT **Icelandic literature**
         Scandinavian literature
Old Northwest   977
   Use for materials on the region between the Ohio and Mississippi rivers and the Great Lakes.

   UF Northwest, Old
         Northwest Territory
   BT **United States**
   RT **Middle West**
Old Norwegian language
   USE **Old Norse language**
Old Southwest   976
   Use for materials on that section of the United States that comprised the southwestern part before the cessions of land from Mexico following the Mexican War. It included Louisiana, Texas, Arkansas, Tennessee, Kentucky and Missouri.
   UF Southwest, Old
   BT **United States**
Old Testament
   USE **Bible. O.T.**
Older persons
   USE **Elderly**
Oldest child
   USE **Birth order**
Oleomargarine
   USE **Margarine**
Olympic games   796.48; 796.98
   UF Olympics
   SA topical headings for Olympic events of a particular year, e.g. **Olympic games, 1996 (Atlanta, Ga.)** [to be added as needed]
   BT **Athletics**
         Contests
         Games
         Sports
   NT **Olympic games, 1996 (Atlanta, Ga.)**
         Special Olympics
Olympic games, 1996 (Atlanta, Ga.)   796.48
   BT **Olympic games**
Olympics
   USE **Olympic games**
Ombudsman (May subdiv. geog.)   328.3; 342; 352.8
   UF Citizen's defender
         Grievance procedures (Public administration)
   BT **Administrative law**
         Public interest
On-line sex
   USE **Computer sex**

One act plays   808.82; 812, etc.

    May be used for individual works, collections, or materials about one-act plays.

    UF   Plays

            Short plays

    BT   **Amateur theater**

            Drama

One parent family

    USE   **Single-parent families**

Online catalogs   025.3

    UF   Catalogs, Online

            Online public access catalogs

            OPACs (Online public access catalogs)

    BT   **Library catalogs**

    RT   **Libraries—Automation**

Online chat groups   004.69

    Use for materials on services that allow users to engage in conversations in real time. Materials on services, commonly called newsgroups or LISTSERV lists, that allow subscribers to post messages that are then distributed to other subscribers are entered under **Electronic discussion groups.** Materials on services that allow users to post messages and retrieve messages from others who have some common interest are entered under **Computer bulletin boards.**

    UF   Chat groups, Online

            Chat rooms, Online

            Internet chat groups

            Online chat rooms

    BT   **Conversation**

    RT   **Computer bulletin boards**

            Electronic discussion groups

Online chat rooms

    USE   **Online chat groups**

Online commerce

    USE   **Electronic commerce**

Online discussion groups

    USE   **Electronic discussion groups**

Online marketing

    USE   **Internet marketing**

Online newsgroups

    USE   **Electronic discussion groups**

Online public access catalogs

    USE   **Online catalogs**

Online publishing

    USE   **Electronic publishing**

Online reference services

    USE   **Reference services (Libraries)**

Online selling

    USE   **Internet marketing**

Online sex

    USE   **Computer sex**

Online shopping

    USE   **Internet shopping**

Only child   155.44; 306.874

    UF   Single child

    BT   **Children**

            Family size

OPACs (Online public access catalogs)

    USE   **Online catalogs**

Opaque projectors

    USE   **Projectors**

Open and closed shop (May subdiv. geog.)   331.88

    UF   Closed shop

            Right to work

            Union shop

    BT   **Labor**

            Labor contract

            Labor unions

Open classroom approach to teaching

    USE   **Open plan schools**

Open education

    USE   **Open plan schools**

Open heart surgery

    USE   **Heart—Surgery**

Open housing

    USE   **Discrimination in housing**

Open plan schools (May subdiv. geog.)   371.2

    Use for materials on schools without interior walls.

    UF   Interest centers approach to teaching

            Learning center approach to teaching

            Open classroom approach to teaching

            Open education

    BT   **Education—Experimental methods**

    RT   **Experimental schools**

            Individualized instruction

Open universities

    USE   **Free universities**

Opera (May subdiv. geog.)   782.1; 792.5

    Use for musical scores and for materials about the opera.

    UF   Comic opera

            Dramatic music

            Operas

    BT   **Drama**

            Musical form

            Performing arts

Opera—*Continued*
    Vocal music
  NT **Operetta**
Opera librettos   782.1026
    Use for individual opera librettos and for collections of opera librettos.
  UF Operas—Librettos
  BT **Librettos**
  RT **Opera—Stories, plots, etc.**
Opera plots
  USE **Opera—Stories, plots, etc.**
Opera—Stories, plots, etc.   782.1026
  UF Opera plots
  RT **Opera librettos**
Operas
  USE **Opera**
Operas—Librettos
  USE **Opera librettos**
Operating systems (Computers)
  USE **Computer operating systems**
Operation Desert Storm
  USE **Persian Gulf War, 1991**
Operational analysis
  USE **Operations research**
Operational research
  USE **Operations research**
Operations research   658.5
  UF Operational analysis
       Operational research
  BT **Research**
       System theory
  RT **Management**
       Systems engineering
Operations, Surgical
  USE **Surgery**
Operetta (May subdiv. geog.)   **782.1; 792.5**
    Use for musical scores and for materials on the operetta as a musical form.
  UF Comic opera
       Dramatic music
       Operettas
  BT **Musical form**
       Opera
       Vocal music
  RT **Musicals**
Operettas
  USE **Operetta**
Opiates
  USE **Narcotics**
Opinion polls
  USE **Public opinion polls**

Opinion, Public
  USE **Public opinion**
Opium   615
  BT **Narcotics**
  RT **Morphine**
Opium—Physiological effect   615
  BT **Drugs—Physiological effect**
Opposites   153.2
  UF Antonyms
       Polarity
  BT **Concepts**
  RT **English language—Synonyms and antonyms**
Optical data processing   006.4; 621.36; 621.39
  BT **Data processing**
  NT **Laser recording**
Optical discs
  USE **Optical storage devices**
Optical illusions   152.14
  UF Illusions
  BT **Hallucinations and illusions**
       Psychophysiology
       Vision
Optical instruments   681
  UF Instruments, Optical
  BT **Scientific apparatus and instruments**
  NT **Lenses**
       Microscopes
       Telescopes
  RT **Optics**
       Space optics
Optical storage devices   004.5; 621.39
    Use for materials on data storage devices in which audio, video, or other data are optically encoded.
  UF Optical discs
  BT **Computer storage devices**
  NT **CD-I technology**
       CD-ROMs
       Compact discs
       Videodiscs
  RT **Laser recording**
Optics   535; 621.36
  BT **Physics**
  NT **Color**
       Perspective
       Radiation
       Refraction
       Space optics
       Spectrum analysis

Optics—*Continued*
  Vision
  RT **Light**
    Optical instruments
    Photometry
Optometry 617.7
  RT **Eye**
Oracles 133.3
  BT **Occultism**
  RT **Divination**
    Prophecies
Oral history 907
  Use for materials on recording oral recollections of places, events, etc., from persons drawing on their own life experiences. Oral histories that focus on a particular topic or place are entered under that topic or place.
  BT **History**
Oral interpretation
  USE **Recitations**
Orange (Fruit)
  USE **Oranges**
Oranges 634 ; 641.3
  UF Orange (Fruit) *[Former heading]*
  BT **Citrus fruits**
Orations
  USE **Speeches**
Oratorio 782.23
  Use for musical scores and for materials on the oratorio as a musical form.
  UF Oratorios
  BT **Church music**
    Musical form
    Vocal music
Oratorios
  USE **Oratorio**
Oratory
  USE **Public speaking**
Orbital laboratories
  USE **Space stations**
Orbital rendezvous (Space flight)
  629.45
  UF Rendezvous in space
    Space orbital rendezvous
  SA names of projects, e.g. **Apollo project; Gemini project;** etc.; and names of specific space ships [to be added as needed]
  BT **Space flight**
    Space stations
    Space vehicles
  NT **Apollo project**
    Gemini project

Orbiting vehicles
  USE **Artificial satellites**
    Space stations
Orchards
  USE **Fruit culture**
Orchestra 784.2
  SA types of orchestras [to be added as needed]
  NT **Conductors (Music)**
    Instrumentation and orchestration
    Orchestral music
  RT **Bands (Music)**
    Conducting
    Ensembles (Music)
    Musical instruments
Orchestral music 784.2
  SA types of orchestral music, e.g. **Symphony** [to be added as needed]
  BT **Instrumental music**
    Music
    Orchestra
  NT **Concerto**
    String orchestra music
    Suite (Music)
    Symphonic poems
    Symphony
Orchestration
  USE **Instrumentation and orchestration**
Orders, Monastic
  USE **Monasticism and religious orders**
Ordination 262; 265
  BT **Rites and ceremonies**
    Sacraments
  NT **Ordination of women**
  RT **Clergy**
Ordination of women 262
  UF Women—Ordination
  BT **Ordination**
  RT **Women clergy**
Ordnance 355.8; 623.4
  Use for materials on military supplies including weapons, ammunition, and vehicles, and the task of procuring, testing, storing, and issuing such supplies.
  UF Cannon
    Guns

Ordnance—*Continued*
- SA types of military ordnance, e.g. **Bombs;** names of armies with the subdivision *Ordnance,* e.g. **United States. Army—Ordnance;** and names of wars with the subdivision *Equipment and supplies,* e.g. **World War, 1939-1945—Equipment and supplies** [to be added as needed]
- BT **Military art and science**
- NT **Ammunition**
  Bombs
  Land mines
  Military weapons
  United States. Army—Ordnance
- RT **Artillery**
  Defense industry
  Projectiles

Ore deposits (May subdiv. geog.)   **553**
- SA types of ores, e.g. **Iron ores** [to be added as needed]
- BT **Geology**
- RT **Ores**

Ore dressing   622
- UF Dressing of ores
- BT **Smelting**

Oregon country
- USE **Pacific Northwest**

Oregon Trail   978
- BT **Overland journeys to the Pacific**
  United States

Ores   553
- SA types of ores, e.g. **Iron ores** [to be added as needed]
- BT **Minerals**
- NT **Iron ores**
  Metals
- RT **Metallurgy**
  Ore deposits

Organ
- USE **Organs (Musical instruments)**

Organ donation
- USE **Donation of organs, tissues, etc.**

Organ music   786.5
- BT **Church music**
  Instrumental music
  Music

Organ preservation (Anatomy)
- USE **Preservation of organs, tissues, etc.**

Organ transplants
- USE **Transplantation of organs, tissues, etc.**

Organic agriculture
- USE **Organic farming**

Organic chemicals
- USE **Organic compounds**

Organic chemistry   547
- UF Chemistry, Organic
- BT **Chemistry**
- NT **Organic compounds**

Organic chemistry—Synthesis
- USE **Organic compounds—Synthesis**

Organic compounds   547
- UF Organic chemicals
- SA types of organic compounds and individual organic substances [to be added as needed]
- BT **Chemicals**
  Organic chemistry

Organic compounds—Synthesis   547
- UF Chemistry, Synthetic
  Organic chemistry—Synthesis
  [Former heading]
  Synthetic chemistry
- NT **Polymers**
- RT **Synthetic products**

Organic farming (May subdiv. geog.)
  631.5
- UF Farming, Organic
  Organic agriculture
  Organiculture
- BT **Agriculture**

Organic gardening (May subdiv. geog.)
  635
- UF Natural gardening
  Organiculture
- BT **Gardening**
  Horticulture
- RT **Compost**

Organic waste as fuel
- USE **Waste products as fuel**

Organically grown foods
- USE **Natural foods**

Organiculture
- USE **Organic farming**
  Organic gardening

Organists (May subdiv. geog.)
786.5092; 920
BT   Instrumentalists
Organization and management
USE   Management
Organization development
USE   Organizational change
Organization (Sociology)
USE   Organizational sociology
Organization theory
USE   Organizational sociology
Organizational change (May subdiv.
geog.)   338.7; 658.4
UF   Change, Organizational
Organization development
Organizational development
Organizational innovation
BT   Management
NT   Downsizing of organizations
Organizational development
USE   Organizational change
Organizational downsizing
USE   Downsizing of organizations
Organizational innovation
USE   Organizational change
Organizational retrenchment
USE   Downsizing of organizations
Organizational sociology   302.3
UF   Organization (Sociology)
Organization theory
Sociology of organizations
BT   Sociology
RT   Bureaucracy
Organizational stress
USE   Job stress
Organizations
USE   Associations
Organizations, Nonprofit
USE   Nonprofit organizations
Organized crime (May subdiv. geog.)
364.106
UF   Crime syndicates
SA   types of organized crime, e.g.
Racketeering [to be added as
needed]
BT   Crime
NT   Gangs
Racketeering
Organized labor
USE   Labor unions

Organs (Anatomy)—Preservation
USE   Preservation of organs, tissues,
etc.
Organs, Artificial
USE   Artificial organs
Organs (Musical instruments) (May
subdiv. geog.)   786.5
UF   Organ
Pipe organs
BT   Musical instruments
NT   Keyboards (Musical instru-
ments)
Organs—Transplantation
USE   Transplantation of organs, tis-
sues, etc.
Orient
USE   Asia
East Asia
Middle East
Oriental architecture
USE   Asian architecture
Oriental art
USE   Asian art
Oriental civilization
USE   Asia—Civilization
Oriental rugs (May subdiv. geog.)   746.7
SA   types of Oriental rugs [to be
added as needed]
BT   Rugs and carpets
Orientation
USE   Direction sense
Orienteering   796.58
Use for materials on the cross-country sport
in which competitors using maps and com-
passes proceed on foot to checkpoints through
unknown terrain.
BT   Hiking
Navigation
Racing
Running
Sports
RT   Direction sense
Origami   736
UF   Japanese paper folding
Paper folding
BT   Paper crafts
Origin
USE   subjects, ethnic groups, classes
of persons, animals, plants,
crops, and religions with the
subdivision Origin, e.g.

Origin—*Continued*
        Life—Origin; Native Americans—Origin; etc. [to be added as needed]
Origin of life
  USE **Life—Origin**
Origin of man
  USE **Human origins**
Origin of species
  USE **Evolution**
Orlando (Legendary character)
  USE **Roland (Legendary character)**
Ornament
  USE **Decoration and ornament**
Ornamental alphabets
  USE **Alphabets**
       Illumination of books and manuscripts
       Lettering
Ornamental plants (May subdiv. geog.) **635.9; 715**
  UF Plants, Ornamental
  BT **Cultivated plants**
       Flower gardening
       Landscape gardening
  RT **Shrubs**
Orphan drugs 615
  Use for materials on drugs that appear to be useful for the treatment of rare disorders but owing to their limited commercial value have difficulty in finding funding for research and marketing.
  UF Nonprofitable drugs
  BT **Drugs**
Orphanages (May subdiv. geog.) **362.73**
  UF Charitable institutions
       Homes (Institutions)
  BT **Charities**
       Children—Institutional care
  RT **Child welfare**
Orphans (May subdiv. geog.) **362.73**
  UF Foundlings
  BT **Children**
  RT **Abandoned children**
       Adopted children
Orthodox Eastern Church (May subdiv. geog.) **281.9**
  BT **Christian sects**
       Eastern churches
  NT **Greek Orthodox Church**
       Russian Orthodox Church

Orthography
  USE **Spelling reform**
      and names of languages with the subdivision *Spelling,* e.g. **English language—Spelling** [to be added as needed]
Orthopedic surgery
  USE **Orthopedics**
Orthopedics 616.7; 617.4
  UF Orthopedic surgery
  BT **Medicine**
       Surgery
  NT **Artificial limbs**
  RT **Physically handicapped**
Osteopathic medicine 610; 615.5
  Use for materials on the therapeutic system based on the theory that disease is caused by loss of a structural integrity that can be restored by manipulation of the bones and muscles.
  UF Osteopathy
  BT **Medicine**
  RT **Chiropractic**
       Massage
Osteopathy
  USE **Osteopathic medicine**
Ostrogoths
  USE **Goths**
Out-of-doors education
  USE **Outdoor education**
Out-of-work people
  USE **Unemployed**
Outdoor cooking 641.5
  UF Camp cooking
  BT **Camping**
       Cooking
  NT **Barbecue cooking**
Outdoor education 371.3
  UF Out-of-doors education
  BT **Education**
  RT **Nature study**
       Outdoor life
Outdoor life (May subdiv. geog.) **796.5**
  UF Rural life
  SA types of outdoor life, education, or activities [to be added as needed]
  NT **Hiking**
       Mountaineering
       Wilderness survival
  RT **Camping**
       Country life
       Nature study

Outdoor life—*Continued*
      Outdoor education
      Sports
Outdoor photography   778.7
  UF Field photography
  BT **Photography**
  RT **Nature photography**
Outdoor recreation (May subdiv. geog.)
  796
  SA types of outdoor recreation, e.g.
      Camping [to be added as
      needed]
  BT **Recreation**
  NT **Camping**
      Cycling
      Parks
      Recreational vehicles
      Roller skating
Outdoor survival
  USE **Wilderness survival**
Outer space   523.1
  UF Space, Outer
  BT **Astronautics**
      Astronomy
      Space sciences
  NT **Space environment**
      Space warfare
Outer space and civilization
  USE **Astronautics and civilization**
Outer space—Colonies
  USE **Space colonies**
Outer space—Communication
  USE **Interstellar communication**
Outer space—Exploration   629.4
  UF Exploration of space
      Space exploration (Astronautics)
      Space research
  BT **Exploration**
      Interplanetary voyages
      Space flight
  NT **Planets—Exploration**
      Space probes
Outlaws
  USE **Criminals**
      Thieves
Outlines, syllabi, etc.
  USE subjects with the subdivision
      Outlines, syllabi, etc., e.g.
      English literature—Outlines,
      syllabi, etc. [to be added as
      needed]

Output equipment (Computers)
  USE **Computer peripherals**
Output standards
  USE **Production standards**
Over-the-counter drugs
  USE **Nonprescription drugs**
Overland journeys to the Pacific   978
    Use for materials on the pioneers' crossing
    of the American continent toward the Pacific
    by foot, horseback, wagon, etc.
  UF Transcontinental journeys
      (American continent)
  BT **Frontier and pioneer life**
      Voyages and travels
  NT **Oregon Trail**
  RT **West (U.S.)—Exploration**
Overseas study
  USE **Foreign study**
Oversize books
  USE **Big books**
Oversized books for shared reading
  USE **Big books**
Overtime
  USE **Hours of labor**
Overweight
  USE **Obesity**
Ownership
  USE **Property**
Oxyacetylene welding
  USE **Welding**
Oxygen   546; 547; 665.8
  BT **Chemical elements**
      Gases
  NT **Ozone**
Ozone   665.8
  BT **Oxygen**
Ozone layer   363.738; 551.51
  UF Ozonosphere
      Stratospheric ozone
  BT **Stratosphere**
Ozonosphere
  USE **Ozone layer**
Pacific Islands
  USE **Islands of the Pacific**
Pacific Northwest   979.5
    Use for materials on the old Oregon coun-
    try, comprising the present states of Oregon,
    Washington, and Idaho, parts of Montana and
    Wyoming, and the province of British Colum-
    bia.
  UF Northwest, Pacific
      Oregon country

Pacific Northwest—*Continued*
　BT　North America
　　　United States
　　　West (U.S.)
Pacific Northwest coast
　USE　Northwest Coast of North
　　　America
Pacific Ocean Islands
　USE　Islands of the Pacific
Pacific rim　330.99; 990
　　Use for materials on the periphery of the
　　Pacific Ocean, especially as a region of inter-
　　dependent economies.
　RT　East Asia
　　　Islands of the Pacific
Pacific States　979
　BT　West (U.S.)
Pacifism　174; 303.6
　　Use for materials on the renunciation of of-
　　fensive or defensive military actions on moral
　　grounds. Materials on social movements
　　adovcating peace are entered under **Peace
　　movements.**
　BT　**War—Religious aspects**
　NT　**Peace movements**
　RT　**Conscientious objectors**
　　　Nonviolence
　　　Peace
　　　Peace movements
Pack transportation
　USE　**Backpacking**
Packaging　658.5
　SA　types of packaging and packag-
　　　ing materials, and subjects
　　　with the subdivision *Packag-
　　　ing*, e.g. **Food—Packaging**
　　　[to be added as needed]
　BT　**Advertising**
　　　Retail trade
　NT　**Aluminum foil**
　　　Boxes
　　　Food—Packaging
　　　Gift wrapping
Packing industry
　USE　**Meat industry**
PACs (Political action committees)
　USE　**Political action committees**
Paganism (May subdiv. geog.)　**291; 292**
　UF　Heathenism
　BT　**Christianity and other religions**
　　　Religions
　NT　**Goddess religion**
　　　Wicca

Pageants (May subdiv. geog.)　**394;
　　791.6**
　BT　Acting
　NT　Masks (Plays)
　　　Medieval tournaments
　　　Mysteries and miracle plays
　　　Parades
　RT　Festivals
Pain　152.1; 612.8
　BT　**Diagnosis**
　　　Emotions
　　　Psychophysiology
　　　Senses and sensation
　RT　**Anesthetics**
　　　Pleasure
　　　Suffering
Paint　645; 667
　BT　**Finishes and finishing**
　RT　**Corrosion and anticorrosives**
　　　Pigments
Paint sniffing
　USE　**Solvent abuse**
Painted glass
　USE　**Glass painting and staining**
Painters (May subdiv. geog.)　**759; 920**
　BT　Artists
Painters' materials
　USE　**Artists' materials**
Painters—United States　759.13; 920
　UF　American painters *[Former
　　　heading]*
Painting　750
　UF　Oil painting
　　　Paintings
　SA　painting of particular countries,
　　　e.g. **American painting;**
　　　types of painting, e.g. **Land-
　　　scape painting;** and topics
　　　with the subdivision *Painting;*
　　　e.g. **Automobiles—Painting**
　　　[to be added as needed]
　BT　Art
　　　Graphic arts
　NT　**American painting**
　　　**Animal painting and illustra-
　　　tion**
　　　China painting
　　　Color
　　　Figure painting
　　　Finger painting
　　　Glass painting and staining

Painting—*Continued*
  Landscape painting
  Marine painting
  Miniature painting
  Mural painting and decoration
  Perspective
  Portrait painting
  Scene painting
  Stencil work
  Textile painting
  Watercolor painting
  RT Composition (Art)
      Decoration and ornament
      Drawing
      Pictures
Painting—15th and 16th centuries
    709.02; 709.03
  UF Painting, Renaissance
      Renaissance painting
Painting—17th and 18th centuries
    759.04
  UF Painting, Modern—17th-18th
      centuries
Painting—19th century 759.05
  UF Modern painting—1800-1899
      (19th century) [*Former head-
      ing*]
      Painting, Modern—19th century
Painting—20th century 759.06
  UF Modern painting—1900-1999
      (20th century) [*Former head-
      ing*]
      Painting, Modern—20th century
  SA types of twentieth-century paint-
      ing, e.g. **Cubism** [to be added
      as needed]
Painting—21st century 759.07
  UF Modern painting—2000-2099
      (21st century)
      Painting, Modern—21st century
Painting, American
  USE American painting
Painting books
  USE Coloring books
Painting—Color reproductions
  USE Color prints
Painting—Conservation and restoration
    751.6
Painting, Decorative
  USE Decoration and ornament
Painting, Finger
  USE Finger painting

Painting, Modern—17th-18th centuries
  USE Painting—17th and 18th centu-
       ries
Painting, Modern—19th century
  USE Painting—19th century
Painting, Modern—20th century
  USE Painting—20th century
Painting, Modern—21st century
  USE Painting—21st century
Painting, Renaissance
  USE Painting—15th and 16th centu-
       ries
Painting, Romanesque
  USE Romanesque painting
Painting—Technique 751.4
Paintings
  USE Painting
Pair system
  USE Binary system (Mathematics)
Palaces (May subdiv. geog.) 728.8
  BT Buildings
Paleobotany
  USE Fossil plants
Paleolithic period
  USE Stone Age
Paleontology
  USE Fossils
Palestinian Arabs (May subdiv. geog.)
       305.892; 956.94
  UF Arabs—Palestine
      Palestinians
  BT Arabs
  RT Jewish-Arab relations
Palestinian-Israeli conflict, 1987-
  USE Intifada, 1987-
Palestinian uprising, 1987-
  USE Intifada, 1987-
Palestinians
  USE Palestinian Arabs
Palmistry 133.6
  BT Divination
      Fortune telling
      Occultism
Pamphlets 025.17
  UF Street literature
  BT Press
  NT Chapbooks
Pamphlets—Design 686.2
  BT Design
Pan-Africanism 320.5; 327
      Use for materials on the advocacy of either
      political alliance or close economic, cultural,

Pan-Africanism—*Continued*
and military cooperation among the countries
of Africa.
  UF African relations
  BT **Africa**
Pan-Americanism 320.5; 327
  Use for materials on the advocacy of either
  political alliance or close economic, cultural,
  and military cooperation among the countries
  of North and South America.
  UF Inter-American relations
  BT **Latin America**
  RT **America—Politics and govern-
      ment**
Pan-Arabism 320.5
  Use for materials on the advocacy of either
  political alliance or close economic, cultural,
  and military cooperation among the Arab
  countries.
  UF Panarabism
  BT **Arab countries—Politics and
      government**
Panama Canal 972.87
  BT **Canals**
Panarabism
  USE **Pan-Arabism**
Panel discussions
  USE **Discussion groups**
Panel heating
  USE **Radiant heating**
Panhandling
  USE **Begging**
Panics (Finance)
  USE **Financial crises**
Pantomimes 792.3
  BT **Acting
      Amateur theater
      Drama
      Theater**
  NT **Shadow pantomimes and plays**
  RT **Ballet
      Mime**
Papacy 262
  UF Holy See
  BT **Catholic Church
      Church history**
  RT **Popes**
Papal encyclicals 262.9
  UF Encyclicals, Papal
  BT **Christian literature**
Papal visits (May subdiv. geog.) **262**
  UF Popes—Travel
      Popes—Voyages and travels
  BT **Voyages and travels**

Paper 676
  BT **Fibers**
  NT **Papermaking**
  RT **Paper industry**
Paper airplanes
  USE **Airplanes—Models**
Paper bound books
  USE **Paperback books**
Paper crafts 745.54
  UF Paper folding
      Paper sculpture
      Paper work
      Papier-mâché
  SA types of paper crafts [to be add-
      ed as needed]
  BT **Handicraft**
  NT **Decoupage
      Gift wrapping
      Origami**
  RT **Papermaking**
Paper folding
  USE **Origami
      Paper crafts**
Paper hanging
  USE **Paperhanging**
Paper industry (May subdiv. geog.)
        338.4
  Use for materials on the business of making
  and selling paper. Materials on the technology
  and craft of making paper are entered under
  Papermaking.
  UF Papermaking industry
  BT **Industries**
  RT **Paper**
Paper making
  USE **Papermaking**
Paper manufacture
  USE **Papermaking**
Paper money (May subdiv. geog.) **332.4**
  BT **Money**
  RT **Inflation (Finance)**
Paper sculpture
  USE **Paper crafts**
Paper work
  USE **Paper crafts**
Paperback books 070.5
  UF Paper bound books
  BT **Books
      Editions**

Paperhanging 698
UF Paper hanging
BT **Interior design**
RT **Wallpaper**
Papermaking (May subdiv. geog.) 676
Use for materials on the technology and craft of making paper. Materials on the business of making and selling paper are entered under **Paper industry.**
UF Paper making
Paper manufacture
BT **Manufactures**
Paper
RT **Paper crafts**
Papermaking industry
USE **Paper industry**
Papier-mâché
USE **Paper crafts**
Parables 808
May be used for individual works, collections, or materials about parables.
UF Cautionary tales and verse
Moral and philosophic stories
Morality tales
NT **Bible—Parables**
Jesus Christ—Parables
RT **Allegories**
Didactic fiction
Didactic poetry
Fables
Parachute troops 356
UF Paratroops
SA names of armies with the subdivision *Parachute troops*, e.g. **United States. Army—Parachute troops** [to be added as needed]
BT **Military aeronautics**
Parachutes
NT **United States. Army—Parachute troops**
Parachutes 629.134
BT **Aeronautics**
NT **Parachute troops**
Parade floats
USE **Parades**
Parades (May subdiv. geog.) 791.6
UF Floats (Parades)
Parade floats
Pomp
Processions
BT **Festivals**
Pageants

Paradise 236; 291.2
Use for materials on the earthly paradise or on a blessed intermediate state in the afterlife.
UF Earthly paradise
Eden
Garden of Eden
BT **Future life**
RT **Heaven**
Utopias
Parallel economy
USE **Underground economy**
Paralysis, Cerebral
USE **Cerebral palsy**
Paramedical personnel
USE **Allied health personnel**
Emergency medical technicians
Paramedics, Emergency
USE **Emergency medical technicians**
Paramilitary militia movements
USE **Militia movements**
Paranormal phenomena
USE **Parapsychology**
Paraprofessional librarians
USE **Library technicians**
Paraprofessionals 331.7
UF Paraprofessions and paraprofessionals
SA types of paraprofessional personnel, e.g. **Library technicians;** and fields of knowledge, professions, industries, and trades with the subdivision *Vocational guidance* [to be added as needed]
BT **Occupations**
Professions
NT **Library technicians**
Paraprofessions and paraprofessionals
USE **Paraprofessionals**
Parapsychology (May subdiv. geog.) 133
Use for materials on investigations of phenomena that appear to be contrary to physical laws and beyond the normal sense perceptions.
UF Paranormal phenomena
Psi (Parapsychology)
Psychic phenomena
Psychical research
BT **Psychology**
Research
Supernatural

Parapsychology—*Continued*
 NT **Apparitions**
  Extrasensory perception
  Hallucinations and illusions
  Mental suggestion
  Mind and body
  Psychokinesis
  Subconsciousness
  Visions
 RT **Ghosts**
  Occultism
  Spiritualism
Parasites   577.8; 578.6
 UF Animal parasites
  Diseases and pests
  Entozoa
  Epizoa
 SA types of animals and parts of
   the body with the subdivision
   Parasites [to be added as
   needed]
 BT **Pests**
 NT **Bacteria**
 RT **Insect pests**
  Symbiosis
Parasols
 USE **Umbrellas and parasols**
Paratroops
 USE **Parachute troops**
Parcel post
 USE **Postal service**
Pardon   364.6
 BT **Administration of criminal jus-
   tice**
  Executive power
 RT **Amnesty**
  Forgiveness
Parent abuse
 USE **Elderly abuse**
Parent and child
 USE **Parent-child relationship**
Parent-child relationship   306.874
  Use for materials on the psychological and
  social interaction between parents and their
  minor children. Materials on the skills, attri-
  butes, and attitudes needed for parenthood are
  entered under **Parenting.** Materials on the
  principles and techniques of rearing children
  are entered under **Child rearing.** Materials restricted to the legal right of parents to visit
  their children in situations of separation, divorce, etc., are entered under **Visitation
  rights (Domestic relations).**

 UF Child and parent
  Parent and child *[Former head-
   ing]*
 BT **Child-adult relationship**
  Children
  Family
  Parents
 NT **Adoption**
  Child abuse
  Child custody
  Child rearing
  Children of divorced parents
  Children of working parents
  Conflict of generations
  Father-child relationship
  Mother-child relationship
  Parenting
Parent-teacher associations (May subdiv.
 geog.)   **371.19**
 UF Parents' and teachers' associa-
   tions
  PTAs
 BT **Community and school**
  Education—Societies
  Parent-teacher relationship
  Societies
 RT **Home and school**
Parent-teacher conferences   371.103
 UF Conferences, Parent-teacher
  Interviews, Parent-teacher
  Teacher-parent conferences
 BT **Parent-teacher relationship**
Parent-teacher relationship   371.19
 UF Parent-teacher relationships *[For-
   mer heading]*
  Parents and teachers
  Teacher-parent relationship
  Teachers and parents
 NT **Parent-teacher associations**
  Parent-teacher conferences
 RT **Home and school**
Parent-teacher relationships
 USE **Parent-teacher relationship**
Parental behavior
 USE **Parenting**
Parental custody
 USE **Child custody**
Parental kidnapping (May subdiv. geog.)
   362.82
 UF Child snatching by parents
  Custody kidnapping

Parental kidnapping—*Continued*
    Kidnapping, Parental
  BT **Child custody**
Parenting (May subdiv. geog.) **306.874; 649**

    Use for materials on the skills, attributes, and attitudes needed for parenthood. Materials on the psychological and social interaction between parents and their minor children are entered under **Parent-child relationship.** Materials on the principles and techniques of rearing children are entered under **Child rearing.**

  UF Parental behavior
  BT **Parent-child relationship**
  NT **Grandparenting**
      Grandparents as parents
      Part-time parenting
  RT **Child rearing**
Parenting by grandparents
  USE **Grandparents as parents**
Parenting, Part-time
  USE **Part-time parenting**
Parents (May subdiv. geog.) **306.874**
  BT **Family**
  NT **Aging parents**
      Birthparents
      Grandparents
      Parent-child relationship
      Single parents
      Teenage parents
Parents and teachers
  USE **Parent-teacher relationship**
Parents' and teachers' associations
  USE **Parent-teacher associations**
Parents, Biological
  USE **Birthparents**
Parents' choice of school
  USE **School choice**
Parents, Unmarried
  USE **Unmarried fathers**
      Unmarried mothers
Parish libraries
  USE **Church libraries**
Parish registers
  USE **Registers of births, etc.**
Parks (May subdiv. geog.) **363.6; 712**
  BT **Cities and towns**
      Landscape architecture
      Outdoor recreation
  NT **Amusement parks**
      Botanical gardens
      National parks and reserves
      Zoos

  RT **Playgrounds**
Parks—United States **363.6; 712; 917.3**
Parkways
  USE **Express highways**
Parliamentary government
  USE **Representative government and representation**
Parliamentary practice **060.4**
  UF Rules of order
  BT **Debates and debating**
      Legislation
      Legislative bodies
      Public meetings
Parliaments
  USE **Legislative bodies**
Parochial schools
  USE **Church schools**
Parodies **808.87; 817, etc.**

    Use for collections of parodies. Materials on the literary form of parody, that is, satirical or humorous imitation of a serious piece of literature, are entered under **Parody.**

  UF Travesties
  SA types of literature, individual literary works entered under title, and names of prominent authors with the subdivision *Parodies, imitations, etc.,* e.g. **Shakespeare, William, 1564-1616—Parodies, imitations, etc.** [to be added as needed]
Parodies, imitations, etc.
  USE types of literature, individual literary works entered under title, and names of prominent authors with the subdivision *Parodies, imitations, etc.,* e.g. **Shakespeare, William, 1564-1616—Parodies, imitations, etc.** [to be added as needed]
Parody **808.7**

    Use for materials about the literary form of parody, that is, satirical or humorous imitation of a serious piece of literature. Collections of parodies are entered under **Parodies.**

  UF Comic literature
  BT **Literature**
      Satire
      Wit and humor
Parole (May subdiv. geog.) **364.6**
  BT **Administration of criminal justice**
      Corrections

Parole—*Continued*
        Punishment
        Social case work
  RT **Probation**
Part-time employment   331.25
  UF Alternative work schedules
  BT **Employment**
        Hours of labor
        Labor
  NT **Job sharing**
        Supplementary employment
Part-time parenting   306.874; 649
    Use for materials on parenting skills for separated, divorced, or surrogate parents who live apart from their children and spend less than full time with them.
  UF Co-parenting
        Joint custody of children
        Parenting, Part-time
        Shared parenting
  BT **Parenting**
  RT **Children of divorced parents**
Partial hearing
  USE **Hearing impaired**
Partially hearing
  USE **Hearing impaired**
Participative management   331.89; 658.3
  UF Consultative management
        Employees' representation in management
        Industrial councils
        Labor participation in management
        Management—Employee participation
        Workers' participation in management
        Workshop councils
  BT **Factory management**
        Industrial relations
        Personnel management
  RT **Collective bargaining**
Particles (Nuclear physics)   539.7
  UF Elementary particles (Physics)
        Nuclear particles
        Nucleons
  SA names of particles [to be added as needed]
  BT **Nuclear physics**
  NT **Electrons**
        Neutrons
        Protons
        Quarks
Parties   793.2
  SA types of parties [to be added as needed]
  BT **Entertaining**
  NT **Children's parties**
        Showers (Parties)
Parties, Political
  USE **Political parties**
Partisans
  USE **Guerrillas**
Partita
  USE **Suite (Music)**
Parts of speech
  USE names of languages with the subdivision *Parts of speech,* e.g. **English language—Parts of speech** [to be added as needed]
Passion plays   792.1; 808.82; 822, etc.
    May be used for individual plays, collections, or materials about medieval plays depicting the Passion of Christ.
  BT **Bible plays**
        Jesus Christ—Drama
        Mysteries and miracle plays
        Religious drama
        Theater
Passions
  USE **Emotions**
Passive resistance (May subdiv. geog.)   303.6; 322.4
  UF Nonviolent noncooperation
  BT **Resistance to government**
  NT **Boycotts**
        Hunger strikes
  RT **Nonviolence**
Passover (May subdiv. geog.)   296.4; 394.267
  UF Pesach
  BT **Jewish holidays**
Pastel drawing   741.2
  BT **Drawing**
  RT **Crayon drawing**
Pastimes
  USE **Amusements**
        Games
        Recreation
Pastoral drama   808.82; 812, etc.
    May be used for individual works, collections, or materials about pastoral drama.

Pastoral drama—*Continued*
  UF   Rural comedies
  BT   **Drama**
Pastoral fiction   808.83; 813, etc.
    May be used for individual works, collections, or materials about novels or short stories with a rural setting and a tone of romantic nostalgia.
  UF   Pastoral romances
          Rural comedies
  BT   **Fiction**
Pastoral peoples
  USE   **Nomads**
Pastoral poetry   808.81; 811, etc.
    May be used for individual works, collections, or materials about pastoral poetry.
  UF   Bucolic poetry
          Eclogues
          Idyllic poetry
          Rural poetry
  BT   **Poetry**
Pastoral psychiatry
  USE   **Pastoral psychology**
Pastoral psychology   253.5; 291.6
    Use for materials on the application of psychology and psychiatry by the clergy to the spiritual problems of individuals.
  UF   Clerical psychology
          Pastoral psychiatry
          Psychology, Pastoral
          Psychology, Religious
          Religious psychology
  BT   **Applied psychology**
          Church work
          Psychology of religion
  RT   **Pastoral theology**
Pastoral romances
  USE   **Pastoral fiction**
Pastoral theology (May subdiv. geog.)
          253; 291.6
    May be subdivided by sect or denomination.
  UF   Pastoral work
  BT   **Theology**
  NT   **Ministry**
          Preaching
  RT   **Church work**
          Clergy
          Pastoral psychology
Pastoral work
  USE   **Pastoral theology**
Pastors
  USE   **Clergy**
          Priests

Pastry   641.8
  BT   **Baking**
          Cooking
  RT   **Cake**
Pastures (May subdiv. geog.)   **333.74**
  BT   **Agriculture**
          Land use
Patchwork quilts
  USE   **Quilts**
Patent medicines
  USE   **Nonprescription drugs**
Patents (May subdiv. geog.)   **608**
  BT   **Manufactures**
  RT   **Intellectual property**
          Inventions
          Trademarks
Pathological psychology
  USE   **Abnormal psychology**
Pathology   616.07
  UF   Disease (Pathology)
  BT   **Medicine**
  NT   **Birth defects**
          Fever
          Medical genetics
          Therapeutics
  RT   **Diseases**
          Preventive medicine
Patience   179
  BT   **Human behavior**
          Virtue
Patience (Game)
  USE   **Solitaire (Game)**
Patients   362.1
  SA   diseases with the subdivision
          Patients, e.g. **Cancer—Patients;** and organs or regions of the body with the subdivisions *Surgery—Patients,* or *Transplantation—Patients* [to be added as needed]
  NT   **Cancer—Patients**
  RT   **Sick**
Patios   643
  UF   Decks (Domestic architecture)
  BT   **Landscape architecture**
Patriotic poetry   808.81; 811, etc.;
          811.008, etc.
    May be used for individual works, collections, or materials about patriotic poetry.
  BT   **Poetry**
  RT   **National songs**

Patriotic songs
    USE **National songs**
Patriotism (May subdiv. geog.)   **172**
    BT   **Citizenship**
          Human behavior
          Loyalty
    RT   **Nationalism**
Patristic philosophy
    USE **Fathers of the church**
Patristics
    USE **Fathers of the church**
Patronage of the arts
    USE **Art patronage**
Pattern making
    USE **Patternmaking**
Patternmaking   **671.2**
    UF   Pattern making *[Former heading]*
    BT   **Models and modelmaking**
    NT   **Mechanical drawing**
    RT   **Design**
          Founding
Patterns
    USE types of handicrafts and manufactures with the subdivision *Patterns,* e.g. **Dressmaking—Patterns** [to be added as needed]
Patterns (Language arts)
    USE **Language arts—Patterning**
Patterns (Mathematics)   **372.7**
    UF   Geometric patterns
          Number patterns
    BT   **Mathematics**
Paul Bunyan
    USE **Bunyan, Paul (Legendary character)**
Pauperism
    USE **Poverty**
Pavements (May subdiv. geog.)   **625.8**
    RT   **Roads**
          Streets
Pay equity
    USE **Equal pay for equal work**
Pay-per-view television
    USE **Subscription television**
Pay television
    USE **Subscription television**
Payroll taxes
    USE **Unemployment insurance**

PC computers
    USE **Microcomputers**
PCs
    USE **Microcomputers**
Peace   **172; 327.1; 341.7**
    SA   names of wars with the subdivision *Peace* e.g. **World War, 1939-1945—Peace** [to be added as needed]
    BT   **International relations**
    NT   **World War, 1914-1918—Peace**
    RT   **Arms control**
          International arbitration
          International security
          Pacifism
          Peace movements
          War
Peace keeping forces
    USE **United Nations—Armed forces**
Peace movements (May subdiv. geog.)   **327.1**

Use for materials on social movements advocating peace. Materials on the renunciation of offensive or defensive military actions on moral grounds are entered under **Pacifism.**

    UF   Antiwar movements
          War protest movements
    SA   names of wars with the subdivision *Protest movements,* e.g. **World War, 1939-1945—Protest movements** [to be added as needed]
    BT   **Social movements**
    RT   **Demonstrations**
          Peace
Peaceful coexistence
    USE **International relations**
Peacocks   **598.6**
    UF   Peafowl
          Peahens
    BT   **Birds**
Peafowl
    USE **Peacocks**
Peahens
    USE **Peacocks**
Pearl fisheries   **338.3; 639**
    UF   Pearlfisheries
    BT   **Commercial fishing**
Pearl Harbor (Oahu, Hawaii), Attack on, 1941   **940.54**
    BT   **World War, 1939-1945—Campaigns**

Pearlfisheries
USE **Pearl fisheries**
Peasant art
USE **Folk art**
Peasantry (May subdiv. geog.)   **305.5;**
307.72
 BT **Feudalism**
Labor
 RT **Agricultural laborers**
Land tenure
Rural sociology
Pecan
USE **Pecans**
Pecans   583; 634
 UF Pecan *[Former heading]*
 BT **Nuts**
Pedagogy
USE **Education**
Education—Study and teaching
Teaching
Peddlers and peddling (May subdiv.
geog.)   **658.8**
 UF Door to door selling
 BT **Direct selling**
Sales personnel
Pediatric psychiatry
USE **Child psychiatry**
Pediatric surgery
USE **Children—Surgery**
Pediatrics
USE **Children—Diseases**
Children—Health and hygiene
Infants—Diseases
Infants—Health and hygiene
Pedigrees
USE **Genealogy**
Heraldry
Peer counseling   158; 361.3
 UF Peer counseling in rehabilitation
Peer counseling of students
Peer group counseling
Rehabilitation peer counseling
Student to student counseling
 BT **Counseling**
Peer counseling in rehabilitation
USE **Peer counseling**
Peer counseling of students
USE **Peer counseling**
Peer group counseling
USE **Peer counseling**

Peer group influence
USE **Peer pressure**
Peer pressure   303.3; 364.2
 UF Peer group influence
 BT **Socialization**
Peerage
USE **Nobility**
Pelts
USE **Hides and skins**
Pen drawing   741.2
 UF Ink drawing
 BT **Drawing**
Pen names
USE **Pseudonyms**
Penal codes
USE **Criminal law**
Penal colonies (May subdiv. geog.)   **365**
 UF Expulsion
Transportation of criminals
 BT **Colonies**
Correctional institutions
Penal institutions
USE **Correctional institutions**
Prisons
Reformatories
Penal law
USE **Criminal law**
Penal reform
USE **Prison reform**
Penance (May subdiv. geog.)   **265**
 UF Contrition
Forgiveness of sin
Reconciliation, Sacrament of
Sacrament of Reconciliation
 BT **Sacraments**
 RT **Confession**
Pencil drawing   741.2
 BT **Drawing**
Penicillin   615
 BT **Antibiotics**
Peninsulas (May subdiv. geog.)   **551.41**
 SA names of peninsulas [to be add-
ed as needed]
 NT **Arabian Peninsula**
Penitentiaries
USE **Prisons**
Penmanship
USE **Handwriting**
Pennsylvania Dutch   974.8
 UF Pennsylvania Germans

Pennsylvania Germans
USE **Pennsylvania Dutch**
Penology
USE **Corrections**
Punishment
Pensions (May subdiv. geog.) **331.25;**
353.5; 658.3
UF Compensation
SA ethnic groups, classes of persons, and employees in particular industries with the subdivision *Pensions,* e.g. **Teachers—Pensions; Chemical industry—Employees—Pensions;** etc. [to be added as needed]
BT **Annuities**
Retirement income
NT **Individual retirement accounts**
Military pensions
Old age pensions
Social security
Pensions, Naval
USE **Military pensions**
Pentecostal churches (May subdiv. geog.)
289.9
Use for general materials on Christian denominations of the Pentecostal type. Materials on Christian movements that stress the personal experience of the Holy Spirit in daily life, with emphasis on personal holiness and spiritual gifts, especially the gift of tongues, are entered under **Pentecostalism.**
BT **Christian sects**
Protestantism
RT **Pentecostalism**
Pentecostal movement
USE **Pentecostalism**
Pentecostalism (May subdiv. geog.)
270.8
Use for materials on Christian movements that stress the personal experience of the Holy Spirit in daily life, with emphasis on personal holiness and spiritual gifts, especially the gift of tongues. General materials on Christian denominations of the Pentecostal type are entered under **Pentecostal churches.**
UF Charismatic movement
Charismatic renewal movement
Pentecostal movement
BT **Christianity**
RT **Catholic charismatic movement**
Glossolalia
Pentecostal churches
Spiritual gifts

Peonage (May subdiv. geog.) **306.3;**
331.5
UF Servitude
BT **Forced labor**
RT **Contract labor**
Slavery
People
USE **Ethnic groups**
Native peoples
Persons
and racial and ethnic groups and native peoples, e.g. **African Americans; Mexican Americans; Yoruba (African people);** etc., and classes of persons, e.g. **Elderly; Handicapped; Explorers; Drug addicts;** etc. [to be added as needed]
People in space
USE **Space flight**
People's banks
USE **Cooperative banks**
People's democracies
USE **Communist countries**
People's Republic of China
USE **China**
Pep pills
USE **Amphetamines**
Percentage **513.2**
BT **Arithmetic**
Perception **152.1; 153.7**
UF Feeling
SA types of concepts and images, e.g. **Size; Shape;** etc. [to be added as needed]
BT **Intellect**
Psychology
Senses and sensation
Theory of knowledge
Thought and thinking
NT **Concepts**
Consciousness
Gestalt psychology
Shape
Size
RT **Apperception**
Intuition

Percussion instruments   786.8
    SA   types of percussion instruments,
           e.g. **Drums** [to be added as
           needed]
    BT   **Musical instruments**
    NT   **Drums**
          Pianos
Perennials   635.9
    BT   **Cultivated plants**
          Flower gardening
          Flowers
Perfectionism (Personality trait)   155.2
    UF   Self-expectations, Perfectionist
    BT   **Personality**
Performance art (May subdiv. geog.)
    700

Use for materials on live performances by artists, drawing on literature, theater, music, film, etc., and combining elements of the various arts in untraditional ways.

    UF   Happening (Art)
    BT   **Art**
          Performing arts
Performance standards   658.5
    UF   Job performance standards
          Rating
          Work performance standards
    SA   subjects and classes of persons
           with the subdivision *Rating,*
           e.g. **Bonds—Rating; Employ-
           ees—Rating;** etc. [to be add-
           ed as needed]
Performing arts (May subdiv. geog.)
    790.2
    UF   Show business
    SA   specific art forms performed on
           stage or screen [to be added
           as needed]
    BT   **Arts**
    NT   **Ballet**
          **Centers for the performing
           arts**
          Dance
          Motion pictures
          Opera
          Performance art
          Theater
Perfumes   391.6; 668
    BT   **Cosmetics**
          Essences and essential oils

Periodic health examinations   616.07
    UF   Health examinations
          Medical examinations
          Physical examinations (Medicine)
    SA   subjects, classes of persons, eth-
           nic groups, and military ser-
           vices with the subdivision
           Medical examinations, e.g.
           **Children—Medical examina-
           tions** [to be added as needed]
    BT   **Medicine**
Periodic law   541.2
    BT   **Physical chemistry**
    RT   **Chemical elements**
Periodicals   050
    UF   Annuals
          Journals
          Magazines
          Yearbooks
    SA   periodicals of particular coun-
           tries, e.g. **American periodi-
           cals;** subjects with the subdi-
           vision *Periodicals,* e.g. **Engi-
           neering—Periodicals;** and
           names of individual periodi-
           cals [to be added as needed]
    BT   **Mass media**
          Serial publications
    NT   **American periodicals**
          Chapbooks
          English periodicals
    RT   **Journalism**
          Newspapers
          Press
Periodicals—Editing
    USE **Journalism—Editing**
Periodicals—Indexes   050
Periodicity
    USE **Cycles**
Permanent education
    USE **Continuing education**
Persecution (May subdiv. geog.)   **291;
    909**
    UF   Persecutions
          Religious persecution
    SA   religious groups with the subdi-
           vision *Persecutions,* e.g.
           **Christians—Persecutions;
           Jews—Persecutions;** etc.; and
           religious groups and classes
           of persons with the subdivi-

Persecution—*Continued*

      sion *Nazi persecution,* e.g.
      Handicapped—Nazi persecu-tion [to be added as needed]
- BT **Atrocities**
- NT **Christians—Persecutions**
      Handicapped—Nazi persecution
      Jews—Persecutions
      Massacres
- RT **Freedom of religion**
      Martyrs

Persecutions
- USE **Persecution**
      and religious groups with the subdivision *Persecutions,* e.g. **Christians—Persecutions; Jews—Persecutions;** etc.; and religious groups and classes of persons with the subdivision *Nazi persecution,* e.g. **Handicapped—Nazi persecu-tion** [to be added as needed]

Persia
- USE **Iran**

Persian Gulf War, 1991   956.7044
- UF Gulf War, 1991
      Middle East War, 1991
      Operation Desert Storm
- BT **United States—History—1989-**

Personal actions (Law)
- USE **Litigation**

Personal appearance   391.6
- UF Appearance, Personal
      Beauty, Personal
      Physical appearance
      Self image
- NT **Personal grooming**
      Tattooing
- RT **Clothing and dress**

Personal cleanliness
- USE **Hygiene**

Personal computers
- USE **Microcomputers**

Personal conduct
- USE **Conduct of life**

Personal development
- USE **Personality**
      Self-improvement
      Success

Personal films
- USE **Amateur films**
      Experimental films

Personal finance (May subdiv. geog.)
      332.024
- UF Budgets, Personal
      Domestic finance
      Family finance
      Finance, Personal
      Financial planning, Personal
- SA ethnic groups, classes of persons, and names of individual persons with the subdivision *Personal finance,* e.g. **Retir-ees—Personal finance** [to be added as needed]
- BT **Finance**
- NT **Children's allowances**
      Consumer credit
      Estate planning
      Household budgets
      Insurance
      Saving and investment
      Tax planning

Personal freedom
- USE **Freedom**

Personal grooming   391.6; 646.7
- UF Beauty, Personal
      Good grooming
      Grooming, Personal
- BT **Hygiene**
      Personal appearance
- NT **Cosmetics**
      Hair
      Toiletries
- RT **Clothing and dress**

Personal growth
- USE **Self-improvement**

Personal health
- USE **Health**

Personal health services
- USE **Medical care**

Personal hygiene
- USE **Hygiene**

Personal income tax
- USE **Income tax**

Personal life skills
- USE **Life skills**

Personal loans   332.7
    Use for materials on loans to individuals for personal rather than business uses.
- UF Consumer loans
      Loans, Personal
      Small loans

Personal loans—*Continued*
  BT **Consumer credit**
      Loans
  NT **Cooperative banks**
      Savings and loan associations
Personal names (May subdiv. geog.)
    929.4
  UF Baby names
      Christian names
      Family names
      First names
      Names, Personal
      Surnames
  SA personal names of particular na-
      tional or ethnic origins re-
      gardless of the place where
      they are found, e.g. **Scottish**
      personal names [to be added
      as needed]
  BT **Names**
  NT **Nicknames**
      Pseudonyms
      Scottish personal names
Personal names—United States
    929.40973
  UF American personal names
Personal narratives
  USE **Autobiographies**
      Biography
      and subjects with the subdivi-
      sion *Biography* or *Correspon-*
      dence; and names of diseases,
      events, and wars with the
      subdivision *Personal narra-*
      tives, e.g. **World War, 1939-**
      1945—Personal narratives
      [to be added as needed]
Personal space   **153.6; 302.2**
    Use for materials on the sense of physical
  space required for psychological comfort.
  UF Space, Personal
  BT **Interpersonal relations**
      Nonverbal communication
      Space and time
Personal time management
  USE **Time management**
Personality   **155.2**
  UF Identity
      Personal development
  BT **Consciousness**
      Psychology

  NT **Body image**
      Character
      Eccentrics and eccentricities
      Identity (Psychology)
      Perfectionism (Personality
        trait)
      Self
  RT **Individuality**
      Persons
Personality disorders   **616.85**
  BT **Abnormal psychology**
  NT **Multiple personality**
  RT **Hallucinations and illusions**
      Mental illness
Personality, Multiple
  USE **Multiple personality**
Personnel administration
  USE **Personnel management**
Personnel classification
  USE **Job analysis**
Personnel management (May subdiv.
    geog.)   **658.3**
  UF Career development
      Employment management
      Human resource management
      Personnel administration
      Supervision of employees
  SA names of corporate bodies and
      military services and types of
      industries, services, and orga-
      nizations with the subdivision
      Personnel management, e.g.
      Hospitals—Personnel man-
      agement [to be added as
      needed]
  BT **Industrial relations**
      Management
  NT **Absenteeism (Labor)**
      Affirmative action programs
      Applications for positions
      Counseling
      Employee morale
      Employees—Dismissal
      Employees—Training
      Employment agencies
      Hospitals—Personnel manage-
      ment
      Job analysis
      Job satisfaction
      Job security
      Labor turnover

Personnel management—*Continued*
    Motion study
    Participative management
    Recruiting of employees
    Supervisors
    Time study
  RT **Employees**
    Factory management
    Office management
Personnel service in education
  USE **Educational counseling**
Persons 128

    Use for materials on human beings as individuals. Materials on the human species from the point of view of biology or anthropology are entered under **Human beings.**

  UF Categories of persons
    Classes of persons
    Groups of persons
    People
  SA classes of persons, e.g. **Elderly;**
    Handicapped; Explorers;
    Drug addicts; etc. [to be
    added as needed]
  BT **Human beings**
  NT **Celebrities**
    Intellectuals
  RT **Individualism**
    Personality
Perspective 701
  UF Architectural perspective
  BT **Descriptive geometry**
    Geometrical drawing
    Optics
    Painting
  RT **Drawing**
Persuasion (Rhetoric)
  USE **Public speaking**
    Rhetoric
Perversion, Sexual
  USE **Sexual deviation**
Pesach
  USE **Passover**
Pest control 363.7; 628.9; 632
  UF Extermination of pests
    Pest extermination
    Pests—Biological control
    Pests—Control
    Pests—Extermination

  SA types of pests with the subdivision *Control*, e.g. **Mosquitoes—Control** [to be added as needed]
  BT **Agricultural pests**
    Economic zoology
    Pests
  NT **Mosquitoes—Control**
    Pesticides
Pest extermination
  USE **Pest control**
Pesticide pollution
  USE **Pesticides—Environmental aspects**
Pesticides (May subdiv. geog.) 632; 668
  BT **Agricultural chemicals**
    Pest control
    Poisons and poisoning
  NT **Fungicides**
    Herbicides
    Insecticides
    Natural pesticides
Pesticides and wildlife 590
  UF Wildlife and pesticides
  BT **Pesticides—Environmental aspects**
    Wildlife conservation
Pesticides—Environmental aspects 363.7; 632
  UF Environment and pesticides
    Pesticide pollution
  BT **Environment**
    Pollution
  NT **Pesticides and wildlife**
Pestilences
  USE **Epidemics**
Pests 591.6; 632
    Use for materials on detrimental or annoying animals or organisms.
  UF Vermin
  SA types of pests, e.g. **Agricultural pests; Flies;** etc.; and names of crops, trees, etc., with the subdivision *Diseases and pests,* e.g. **Fruit—Diseases and pests** [to be added as needed]
  BT **Economic zoology**
  NT **Agricultural pests**
    Flies
    Fruit—Diseases and pests
    Fungi

Pests—*Continued*
> > Household pests
> > Insect pests
> > Parasites
> > Pest control

Pests—Biological control
> USE Pest control

Pests—Control
> USE Pest control

Pests—Extermination
> USE Pest control

Pet-facilitated psychotherapy
> USE Pet therapy

Pet therapy   615.8
> UF Animal-facilitated therapy
> > Companion-animal partnership
> > Pet-facilitated psychotherapy
> BT Animals and the handicapped
> > Therapeutics

Petrochemicals   661
> UF Petroleum chemicals
> BT Chemicals

Petroglyphs
> USE Rock drawings, paintings, and
> > engravings

Petroleum (May subdiv. geog.)   553.2;
> 665.5
> UF Coal oil
> > Crude oil
> > Oil
> BT Oils and fats
> NT Coal tar products
> > Gasoline
> RT Petroleum geology
> > Petroleum industry

Petroleum as fuel   338.4; 665.5
> UF Fuel oil
> > Liquid fuel
> > Oil fuel
> BT Fuel
> NT Oil burners

Petroleum chemicals
> USE Petrochemicals

Petroleum engines
> USE Internal combustion engines

Petroleum geology (May subdiv. geog.)
> 553.2
> UF Geology, Petroleum
> BT Economic geology
> > Prospecting
> RT Petroleum

Petroleum industry (May subdiv. geog.)
> 338.2
> UF Oil industry
> > Petroleum industry and trade
> BT Industries
> NT Offshore oil industry
> > Oil well drilling
> > Oil wells
> > Service stations
> RT Petroleum

Petroleum industry and trade
> USE Petroleum industry

Petroleum pipelines (May subdiv. geog.)
> 338.2; 665.5
> BT Pipelines

Petroleum pollution of water
> USE Oil pollution of water

Petroleum—United States   553.2; 665.5

Petroleum—Well boring
> USE Oil well drilling

Petrology (May subdiv. geog.)   552
> SA types of rocks, e.g. Granite [to
> > be added as needed]
> BT Science
> NT Geochemistry
> > Moon rocks
> RT Geology
> > Minerals
> > Rocks
> > Stone

Pets (May subdiv. geog.)   636.088
> SA types of common pets, e.g.
> > Dogs; and types of animals
> > not ordinarily kept as pet, e.g.
> > Snakes as pets [to be added
> > as needed]
> BT Animals
> NT Snakes as pets
> RT Domestic animals

Pets and the handicapped
> USE Animals and the handicapped

Pets—Housing   690
> BT Animal housing

Pets—Names   636.088

Petting zoos   590.73
> BT Zoos

Pewter   673; 739.5
> BT Alloys
> > Art metalwork
> > Metals

Phantoms
USE **Apparitions**
Ghosts
Pharmaceutical abuse
USE **Medication abuse**
Pharmaceutical chemistry 615
UF Drugs—Chemistry
Medicinal chemistry
BT **Chemistry**
NT **Disinfection and disinfectants**
RT **Pharmacy**
Therapeutics
Pharmaceuticals
USE **Drugs**
Pharmacies
USE **Drugstores**
Pharmacodynamics
USE **Pharmacology**
Pharmacology 615
Use for materials on the action and proper-
ties of drugs in general. Materials limited to
the effect of drugs on the functions of living
organisms are entered under **Drugs—Physio-
logical effect.** Materials on the art or practice
of preparing, preserving, and dispensing drugs
are entered under **Pharmacy.**
UF Drugs—Adulteration and analysis
Medicine—Physiological effect
Pharmacodynamics
BT **Medicine**
NT **Drugs—Physiological effect**
Drugs—Testing
Toxicology
RT **Drug therapy**
Drugs
Materia medica
Pharmacy
Pharmacopoeias
USE **Materia medica**
Pharmacotherapy
USE **Drug therapy**
Pharmacy 615
Use for materials on the art or practice of
preparing, preserving, and dispensing drugs.
Materials on the action and properties of
drugs are entered under **Pharmacology.** Mate-
rials on business establishments that sell drugs
are entered under **Drugstores.**
BT **Chemistry**
Medicine
NT **Drugs**
Homeopathy
Medical botany
RT **Materia medica**
Pharmaceutical chemistry

Pharmacology
Pheasants 598.6; 636.5
BT **Birds**
Game and game birds
Phenomenology 142
BT **Modern philosophy**
NT **Existentialism**
Philanthropists (May subdiv. geog.)
361.7092; 920
UF Altruists
Humanitarians
RT **Philanthropy**
Philanthropy (May subdiv. geog.) 177;
361.7
RT **Charities**
Charity organization
Endowments
Philanthropists
Philately
USE **Stamp collecting**
Philology
USE **Language and languages**
Linguistics
Philology, Comparative
USE **Linguistics**
Philosophers (May subdiv. geog.) 180;
190; 920
RT **Philosophy**
Philosophers, American
USE **Philosophers—United States**
Philosophers' stone
USE **Alchemy**
Philosophers—United States 191; 920
UF American philosophers *[Former
heading]*
Philosophers, American
Philosophy 100
SA movements in philosophy, e.g.
Positivism; philosophy of par-
ticular countries, e.g.
American philosophy; philos-
ophy associated with particu-
lar religions, e.g. **Christian
philosophy;** and subjects with
the subdivision *Philosophy,*
e.g. **History—Philosophy** [to
be added as needed]
BT **Humanities**
NT **Aesthetics**
American philosophy
Ancient philosophy

Philosophy—*Continued*
    Belief and doubt
    Christian philosophy
    Empiricism
    Ethics
    Evolution
    Fate and fatalism
    Free will and determinism
    Gnosticism
    Good and evil
    Hindu philosophy
    History—Philosophy
    Humanism
    Idealism
    Ideology
    Intuition
    Logic
    Marxism
    Materialism
    Medieval philosophy
    Metaphysics
    Mind and body
    Modern philosophy
    Philosophy and religion
    Positivism
    Pragmatism
    Psychology
    Rationalism
    Realism
    Reality
    Skepticism
    Soul
    Theism
    Theory of knowledge
    Transcendentalism
    Truth
  RT **Philosophers**
Philosophy, American
  USE **American philosophy**
Philosophy, Ancient
  USE **Ancient philosophy**
Philosophy and religion   210
    Use for materials on the reciprocal relationship and influence between philosophy and religion. Materials on the nature, origin, or validity of religion from a philosophical point of view are entered under **Religion—Philosophy.**
  UF Religion and philosophy
  BT **Philosophy**
      Religion
  RT **Religion—Philosophy**
Philosophy—Encyclopedias   103
  BT **Encyclopedias and dictionaries**

Philosophy, Hindu
  USE **Hindu philosophy**
Philosophy—Historiography   109
  BT **Historiography**
Philosophy, Medieval
  USE **Medieval philosophy**
Philosophy, Modern
  USE **Modern philosophy**
Philosophy of history
  USE **History—Philosophy**
Philosophy of religion
  USE **Religion—Philosophy**
Phobias   616.85
  BT **Fear**
      Neuroses
Phonetic spelling
  USE **Spelling reform**
Phonetics   414
  UF Phonics
      Phonology
  SA names of languages with the subdivision *Pronunciation* [to be added as needed]
  BT **Language and languages**
      Sound
  NT **English language—Pronunciation**
  RT **Reading—Phonetic method**
      Speech
      Voice
Phonics
  USE **Phonetics**
      Reading—Phonetic method
Phonograph   621.389
  UF Gramophone
  BT **Sound—Recording and reproducing**
  NT **Compact disc players**
      Sound—Recording and reproducing
  RT **High-fidelity sound systems**
Phonograph records
  USE **Sound recordings**
Phonology
  USE **Phonetics**
      and names of languages with the subdivision *Pronunciation,* e.g. **English language—Pronunciation** [to be added as needed]

Phosphates   546; 553.6; 631.8
   BT   Fertilizers
Phosphorescence   535
   BT   Luminescence
          Radioactivity
Photo journalism
   USE Photojournalism
Photocopying   686.4
   UF   Photocopying processes
         Photoduplication
         Photographic reproduction
         Xerography
   BT   Copying processes
   RT   Copy art
Photocopying machines
   USE Copying machines
Photocopying processes
   USE Photocopying
Photoduplication
   USE Photocopying
Photoelectric cells   537.5; 621.3815
   UF   Electric eye
Photoengraving   686.2
   UF   Halftone process
   BT   Engraving
   RT   Photomechanical processes
Photographic chemistry   771
   Use for materials on the chemical processes
   employed in photography.
   BT   Chemistry
   NT   Photography—Processing
   RT   Photography
Photographic film
   USE Photography—Film
Photographic reproduction
   USE Photocopying
Photographic slides
   USE Slides (Photography)
Photographic supplies
   USE Photography—Equipment and
           supplies
Photographs   770
   Use for materials that discuss photographs
   as objects, including their classification, cata-
   loging, copying, coloring, mounting, etc.
   UF   Photos
         Snapshots
   SA   subjects, classes of persons,
         names of wars, and names of
         cities, states, countries, and
         named entities, such as indi-

vidual parks, structures, etc.,
with the subdivision *Pictorial
works,* e.g. **Animals—Pictori-
al works; United States—
History—1861-1865, Civil
War—Pictorial works;** etc.;
and names of persons or
groups of persons with the
subdivision *Pictorial works,* or
Portraits [to be added as
needed]
   BT   Pictures
   RT   Photography
Photographs—Conservation and restora-
   tion   771
   UF   Conservation of photographs
         Preservation of photographs
         Restoration of photographs
Photographs from space
   USE Space photography
Photography (May subdiv. geog.)   770
   SA   kinds of photography, e.g. **Por-
         trait photography;** photogra-
         phy of particular subjects, e.g.
         Photography of birds; and
         subjects, classes of persons,
         names of wars, and names of
         cities, states, countries, and
         named entities, such as indi-
         vidual parks, structures, etc.,
         with the subdivision *Pictorial
         works* [to be added as need-
         ed]
   BT   Graphic arts
   NT   Aerial photography
         Artistic photography
         Astronomical photography
         Cameras
         Cinematography
         Color photography
         Commercial photography
         Filmstrips
         Holography
         Medical photography
         Microphotography
         Nature photography
         Outdoor photography
         Photojournalism
         Photomechanical processes
         Photomicrography
         Portrait photography

Photography—*Continued*

> Slides (Photography)
> Space photography
> Telephotography
> Three dimensional photogra-
> phy
> Underwater photography
> RT Photographic chemistry
> Photographs

Photography—Aesthetics
 USE **Artistic photography**
Photography, Artistic
 USE **Artistic photography**
Photography, Color
 USE **Color photography**
Photography—Darkroom technique
 USE **Photography—Processing**
Photography—Developing and developers
 771
 BT **Photography—Processing**
Photography—Enlarging   771
 UF Enlarging (Photography)
Photography—Equipment and supplies
 771
 UF Photographic supplies
 NT **Cameras**
Photography—Film   771
 UF Photographic film
Photography—Handbooks, manuals, etc.
 770.2
Photography in astronautics
 USE **Space photography**
Photography—Lighting   771; 778.7
 BT **Lighting**
Photography—Motion pictures
 USE **Cinematography**
Photography of animals   778.9
 Use for materials on the technique of pho-
 tographing animals. Materials consisting of
 photographs and pictures of animals are en-
 tered under **Animals—Pictorial works.**
 UF Animal photography
  Animals—Photography
 BT **Nature photography**
 RT **Animal painting and illustra-**
  tion
  Animals—Pictorial works
Photography of birds   778.9
 UF Bird photography
  Birds—Photography
 BT **Nature photography**

Photography of fishes   778.9
 UF Fishes—Photography
 BT **Nature photography**
Photography of nature
 USE **Nature photography**
Photography of plants   778.9
 UF Plants—Photography
 BT **Nature photography**
Photography—Printing processes   771
 BT **Photography—Processing**
Photography—Processing   771
 UF Darkroom technique in photogra-
  phy
  Photography—Darkroom tech-
  nique
 SA types of photographic processing
  techniques, e.g. **Photogra-**
  phy—Developing and devel-
  opers; Photography—Print-
  ing processes; etc. [to be
  added as needed]
 BT **Photographic chemistry**
 NT **Photography—Developing and**
  developers
  Photography—Printing process-
  es
Photography—Retouching   771
 UF Retouching (Photography)
Photography—Scientific applications
 778.3
 SA specific applications, e.g. **Medi-**
  cal photography [to be added
  as needed]
 NT **Medical photography**
  Space photography
Photography, Stereoscopic
 USE **Three dimensional photogra-**
  phy
Photojournalism (May subdiv. geog.)
 070.4; 779
 UF Journalistic photography
  News photography
  Photo journalism
 BT **Commercial photography**
  Journalism
  Photography
Photomechanical processes   686.2
 SA types of photomechanical pro-
  cesses, e.g. **Photoengraving**
  [to be added as needed]

Photomechanical processes—*Continued*
    BT   **Illustration of books**
            Photography
    RT   **Photoengraving**
Photometry 535
    UF   Electric light
    BT   **Measurement**
    NT   **Color**
    RT   **Light**
            Optics
Photomicrography 778.3
    Use for materials on the photographing of minute objects through a miscroscope. Materials on the photographing of objects of any size to produce minute images are entered under **Microphotography.**
    BT   **Photography**
    RT   **Microscopes**
Photos
    USE   **Photographs**
Photosynthesis 572
    BT   **Botany**
Phototherapy 615.8
    UF   Electric light
            Light—Therapeutic use
    BT   **Physical therapy**
            Therapeutics
    RT   **Radiotherapy**
            Ultraviolet rays
Photovoltaic power generation 621.31
    UF   Solar cells
    BT   **Solar energy**
    NT   **Solar batteries**
Phrenology (May subdiv. geog.) **139**
    BT   **Brain**
            Head
            Psychology
    RT   **Mind and body**
            Physiognomy
Physical anthropology (May subdiv. geog.) **599.9**
    UF   Biological anthropology
    BT   **Anthropology**
            Ethnology
    NT   **Human origins**
Physical appearance
    USE   **Personal appearance**
Physical chemistry 541
    UF   Chemistry, Physical and theoretical
            Theoretical chemistry
    BT   **Chemistry**
            Physics

    NT   **Atomic theory**
            Atoms
            Catalysis
            Colloids
            Crystals
            Electrochemistry
            Molecules
            Periodic law
            Polymers
            Radiochemistry
            Solids
            Thermodynamics
    RT   **Nuclear physics**
            Quantum theory
Physical culture
    USE   **Physical education**
Physical education (May subdiv. geog.) **613.7; 796.07**
    UF   Calisthenics
            Physical culture
            Physical education and training
            Physical training
    SA   types of sports activities with the subdivision *Training,* e.g. **Soccer—Training;** and names of sports and types of physical exercise [to be added as needed]
    BT   **Education**
    NT   **Coaching (Athletics)**
            Fencing
            Games
            Judo
            Marching drills
            Movement education
            Physical fitness
            Posture
            Soccer—Training
    RT   **Athletics**
            Exercise
            Gymnastics
            Sports
Physical education and training
    USE   **Physical education**
Physical education—Medical aspects
    USE   **Sports medicine**
Physical examinations (Medicine)
    USE   **Periodic health examinations**

Physical fitness (May subdiv. geog.)
    613.7
  UF Endurance, Physical
      Fitness
      Physical stamina
      Stamina, Physical
  BT **Exercise**
      Health
      Health self-care
      Physical education
  NT **Bodybuilding**
      Kinesiology
      Physical fitness centers
Physical fitness centers (May subdiv.
    geog.) **613.7**
  UF Health clubs
      Health spas
      Recreation centers
      Spas
  BT **Physical fitness**
Physical geography (May subdiv. geog.)
    910
    Use for materials on the physical features
of the earth's surface and its atmosphere.
General materials, frequently school materials,
describing the surface of the earth and its in-
terrelationship with various peoples, animals,
natural products, and industries are entered
under **Geography.**
  BT **Geography**
      Geology
  NT **Deserts**
      Earthquakes
      Geysers
      Glaciers
      Ice
      Icebergs
      Lakes
      Mountains
      Ocean
      Rivers
      Volcanoes
      Winds
  RT **Earth**
Physical geography—United States
    917.3
Physical sciences   **500.2**
  BT **Science**
  NT **Astronomy**
      Chemistry
      Earth sciences
      Physics

Physical stamina
  USE **Physical fitness**
Physical therapy   **615.8**
  UF Physiotherapy
  SA types of physical therapy, e.g.
      Hydrotherapy; and types of
      disabilities, injuries, or dis-
      eases with the subdivision
      Physical therapy, e.g. **Arthri-**
      tis—Physicial therapy [to be
      added as needed]
  BT **Therapeutics**
  NT **Baths**
      Electrotherapeutics
      Hydrotherapy
      Massage
      Occupational therapy
      Phototherapy
      Radiotherapy
Physical training
  USE **Physical education**
Physically handicapped (May subdiv.
    geog.) **362.4**
  UF Crippled people
      Invalids
  SA types of physically handicapped
      persons, e.g. **Blind; Deaf;** etc.
      [to be added as needed]
  BT **Handicapped**
  NT **Blind**
      Deaf
      Hearing impaired
      Physically handicapped chil-
      dren
  RT **Orthopedics**
Physically handicapped children (May
    subdiv. geog.) **155.45; 362.4**
  UF Children, Crippled
      Crippled children
  BT **Handicapped children**
      Physically handicapped
Physically handicapped—Housing (May
    subdiv. geog.) **362.4**
  UF Housing for the physically hand-
      icapped
  BT **Housing**
Physically handicapped—Rehabilitation
    362.4
  NT **Occupational therapy**

Physicians (May subdiv. geog.) 610.69;
  920
  UF Doctors
  SA types of medical specialists [to
        be added as needed]
  BT Medical personnel
  NT Radiologists
      Surgeons
      Women physicians
  RT Medicine
Physicians—Directories 610.69
  BT Directories
Physicians—Drug use 362.29; 610.69
  UF Drug abusing physicians
      Drug addicted physicians
Physicians—Licenses (May subdiv. geog.)
  344
  BT Medicine—Law and legislation
Physicians—Malpractice (May subdiv.
  geog.) 346.03
  UF Medical errors
  BT Malpractice
      Medicine—Law and legislation
Physicists (May subdiv. geog.) 530.092;
  920
  BT Scientists
Physics 530
  BT Physical sciences
      Science
  NT Astrophysics
      Biophysics
      Electricity
      Electronics
      Gases
      Geophysics
      Gravitation
      Hydraulics
      Hydrostatics
      Light
      Liquids
      Magnetism
      Matter
      Mechanics
      Music—Acoustics and physics
      Nuclear physics
      Optics
      Physical chemistry
      Pneumatics
      Quantum theory
      Radiation
      Radioactivity

Relativity (Physics)
      Solids
      Sound
      Statics
      Thermodynamics
      Weight
      Weights and measures
  RT Dynamics
Physics—Conferences 530
  UF Physics—Congresses [Former
        heading]
Physics—Congresses
  USE Physics—Conferences
Physics, Terrestrial
  USE Geophysics
Physiognomy 138
  BT Psychology
  RT Face
      Phrenology
Physiological aspects
  USE types of activities and mental
        conditions with the subdivi-
        sion Physiological aspects,
        e.g. Mental illness—Physio-
        logical aspects [to be added
        as needed]
Physiological chemistry
  USE Biochemistry
Physiological effect
  USE types of drugs, chemicals, or en-
        vironmental phenomena or
        conditions with the subdivi-
        sion Physiological effect, e.g.
        Alcohol—Physiological effect;
        Radiation—Physiological ef-
        fect; etc. [to be added as
        needed]
Physiological psychology
  USE Psychophysiology
Physiological stress
  USE Stress (Physiology)
Physiology 571; 612
  Use for general materials on physiology and
  for materials on human physiology. Materials
  on the physiology of other animals or of
  plants are entered under the appropriate head-
  ing with the subdivision Physiology.
  UF Human physiology
  SA names of organs and regions of
        the body, types of plants and
        animals, and classes of per-
        sons with the subdivision

Physiology—*Continued*

Physiology, e.g. **Heart—Physiology; Reptiles—Physiology;** etc.; activities and mental conditions with the subdivision *Physiological aspects,* e.g. **Mental illness—Physiological aspects;** and drugs, chemicals, and environmental phenomena or conditions with the subdivision *Physiological effect,* e.g. **Alcohol—Physiological effect; Radiation—Physiological effect;** etc. [to be added as needed]

- BT   **Biology**
- **Medicine**
- **Science**
- NT   **Blood**
- **Body temperature**
- **Cardiovascular system**
- **Cells**
- **Comparative physiology**
- **Digestion**
- **Fatigue**
- **Glands**
- **Growth**
- **Health**
- **Heart—Physiology**
- **Human locomotion**
- **Immune system**
- **Lymphatic system**
- **Mental illness—Physiological aspects**
- **Musculoskeletal system**
- **Nervous system**
- **Nutrition**
- **Psychophysiology**
- **Reproduction**
- **Reproductive system**
- **Reptiles—Physiology**
- **Respiration**
- **Respiratory system**
- **Senses and sensation**
- **Skin**
- **Stress (Physiology)**
- RT   **Anatomy**
- **Human body**

Physiology, Comparative
   USE   **Comparative physiology**

Physiology of plants
   USE   **Plant physiology**

Physiotherapy
   USE   **Physical therapy**

Physique
   USE   **Bodybuilding**

Phytogeography
   USE   **Plants—Geographical distribution**

Pianists (May subdiv. geog.)   **786.2092; 920**
   BT   **Instrumentalists**

Piano
   USE   **Pianos**

Piano music   **786.2**
   BT   **Instrumental music**
       Music

Pianos   **786.2**
   UF   Piano
   BT   **Percussion instruments**
   NT   **Keyboards (Musical instruments)**

Pianos—Tuning   **786.2**
   BT   **Tuning**

Picaresque literature   **800**

May be used for individual works, collections, or materials about episodic accounts of the adventures of an engagingly roguish hero.

   UF   Picaresque novels
       Rogues and vagabonds—Fiction
   BT   **Fiction**
       Literature

Picaresque novels
   USE   **Picaresque literature**

Picketing
   USE   **Strikes**

Pickling
   USE   **Canning and preserving**

Pickup campers
   USE   **Travel trailers and campers**

Pictographs
   USE   **Picture writing**

Pictorial works
   USE   **Pictures**
       and subjects, classes of persons, names of wars, and names of cities, states, countries, and named entities, such as individual parks, structures, etc., with the subdivision *Pictorial works,* e.g. **Animals—Pictorial works; United States—History—1861-1865, Civil**

Pictorial works—*Continued*

War—Pictorial works; Chicago (Ill.)—Pictorial works; Yosemite National Park (Calif.)—Pictorial works; etc.; and names of persons or groups of persons with the subdivisions *Cartoons and caricatures; Pictorial works;* or *Portraits* [to be added as needed]

Picture books
   USE **Pictures**

Picture books for children
   BT **Children's literature**
   NT **Coloring books**
        Glow-in-the-dark books
        Stories without words
        Toy and movable books
   RT **Illustration of books**

Picture books for children, Wordless
   USE **Stories without words**

Picture dictionaries   413; 423, etc.
   UF Dictionaries, Picture
        Word books
   BT **Encyclopedias and dictionaries**

Picture frames and framing   684; 749
   UF Framing of pictures
   BT **Decoration and ornament**
        Handicraft

Picture galleries
   USE **Art museums**

Picture postcards
   USE **Postcards**

Picture telephone
   USE **Video telephone**

Picture writing   411
   Use for materials on the recording of events or the expression of messages by pictures representing actions or facts.
   UF Pictographs
   BT **Writing**
   RT **Hieroglyphics**

Pictures   025.17; 760
   Use for general materials on the study and use of pictures and for miscellaneous collections of pictures.
   UF Pictorial works
        Picture books
   SA subjects, classes of persons, names of wars, and names of cities, states, countries, and named entities, such as individual parks, structures, etc., with the subdivision *Pictorial works,* e.g. Animals—Pictorial works; United States—History—1861-1865, Civil War—Pictorial works; Chicago (Ill.)—Pictorial works; Yosemite National Park (Calif.)—Pictorial works; etc.; and names of persons or groups of persons with the subdivisions *Cartoons and caricatures; Pictorial works;* or *Portraits* [to be added as needed]
   BT **Art**
   NT **Cartoons and caricatures**
        Engraving
        Etching
        Libraries and pictures
        Photographs
        Portraits
        Views
   RT **Painting**

Pigments   547; 667; 751.2
   NT **Dyes and dyeing**
   RT **Color**
        Paint

Pigs   599.63; 636.4
   UF Hogs
        Swine
   BT **Domestic animals**
        Mammals

Pilgrims and pilgrimages (May subdiv. geog.)   **263; 291.3**
   BT **Voyages and travels**
   RT **Shrines**

Pilgrims (New England colonists)   974.4
   BT **Puritans**
        United States—History—1600-1775, Colonial period

Pilot charts
   USE **Nautical charts**

Pilot guides   623.89
   UF Coast pilot guides
   BT **Navigation**

Piloting
    USE   types of aircraft with the subdivision *Piloting*, e.g. **Airplanes—Piloting** [to be added as needed]

Piloting (Astronautics)
    USE   **Space vehicles—Piloting**

Pilots
    USE   **Air pilots**
           Ship pilots

Pilots and pilotage
    USE   **Navigation**
           Ship pilots

Pimples (Acne)
    USE   **Acne**

Ping-pong
    USE   **Table tennis**

Pioneer life
    USE   **Frontier and pioneer life**

Pipe fitting   696
    RT   **Plumbing**

Pipe lines
    USE   **Pipelines**

Pipe organs
    USE   **Organs (Musical instruments)**

Pipelines (May subdiv. geog.)   **388.5; 621.8**
    UF   Pipe lines
    SA   types of pipelines [to be added as needed]
    BT   **Hydraulic structures**
           Transportation
    NT   **Petroleum pipelines**

Pipes, Tobacco
    USE   **Tobacco pipes**

Piracy
    USE   **Pirates**

Pirates (May subdiv. geog.)   **364.16; 910.4**
    UF   Buccaneers
           Corsairs
           Piracy
    BT   **Criminals**
           International law
           Maritime law
           Naval history
    NT   **Privateering**

Pistols
    USE   **Handguns**

Place names
    USE   **Geographic names**

Places, Imaginary
    USE   **Geographical myths**

Places of retirement
    USE   **Retirement communities**

Places of work
    USE   **Work environment**

Plague (May subdiv. geog.)   **616.9**
    UF   Black death
           Bubonic plague
    BT   **Communicable diseases**
           Epidemics

Plain chant
    USE   **Chants (Plain, Gregorian, etc.)**

Plainsong
    USE   **Chants (Plain, Gregorian, etc.)**

Plane crashes
    USE   **Aircraft accidents**

Plane geometry   516.22
    UF   Geometry, Plane
    BT   **Geometry**

Plane trigonometry
    USE   **Trigonometry**

Planetariums   520.74
    BT   **Astronomy**

Planetary satellites
    USE   **Satellites**

Planetoids
    USE   **Asteroids**

Planets   523.4
    SA   names of planets, e.g. **Saturn (Planet)** [to be added as needed]
    BT   **Astronomy**
           Solar system
    NT   **Earth**
           Life on other planets
           Mars (Planet)
           Saturn (Planet)
    RT   **Asteroids**

Planets—Exploration   523.4
    SA   names of planets with the subdivision *Exploration* [to be added as needed]
    BT   **Outer space—Exploration**
    NT   **Mars (Planet)—Exploration**

Planets—Satellites
    USE   **Satellites**

Planing machines   621.9
    BT   **Machine tools**

Planned parenthood
    USE   **Birth control**

Planning (May subdiv. geog.)   **338.9; 658.4**

SA   types of planning, e.g. **Curriculum planning;** and types of activities, facilities, industries, services, and undertakings with the subdivision *Planning,* e.g. **Transportation—Planning** [to be added as needed]

BT   **Creation (Literary, artistic, etc.)**
Executive ability
Management

NT   **City planning**
Curriculum planning
Economic policy
Estate planning
Regional planning
Social policy
Tax planning
Transportation—Planning

Plans
USE   **Geometrical drawing**
Map drawing
Maps
Mechanical drawing

Plant anatomy
USE   **Plants—Anatomy**

Plant breeding   631.5

Use for materials on attempts to produce new or improved varieties of plants through controlled reproduction. Materials on the continuance or multiplication of plants by successive production are entered under **Plant propagation.**

UF   Hybridization
BT   **Agriculture**
Breeding
Horticulture
RT   **Plant propagation**

Plant chemistry
USE   **Botanical chemistry**
Plants—Analysis

Plant classification
USE   **Botany—Classification**

Plant conservation (May subdiv. geog.)   **333.95; 639.9**

UF   Conservation of plants
Plants—Conservation
Protection of plants
Wild flowers—Conservation

BT   **Conservation of natural resources**

Economic botany
Endangered species
Nature conservation
NT   **Scarecrows**
RT   **Rare plants**

Plant diseases (May subdiv. geog.)   **571.9; 632**

UF   Botany—Pathology
Diseases and pests
Diseases of plants
Garden pests
Plant pathology
Plants—Diseases

SA   types of crops, plants, trees, etc., with the subdivision *Diseases and pests* [to be added as needed]

BT   **Agricultural pests**
Diseases
Fungi

NT   **Fruit—Diseases and pests**

Plant distribution
USE   **Plants—Geographical distribution**

Plant ecology (May subdiv. geog.)   **581.7**

UF   Botany—Ecology
Plants—Ecology

SA   types of plants and crops with the subdivision *Ecology* [to be added as needed]

BT   **Ecology**
NT   **Desert plants**
Forest plants
Mountain plants
RT   **Forest influences**
Symbiosis

Plant introduction (May subdiv. geog.)   **581.6; 631.5**

BT   **Economic botany**

Plant lore
USE   **Plants—Folklore**

Plant nutrition
USE   **Plants—Nutrition**

Plant pathology
USE   **Plant diseases**

Plant physiology   571.2

UF   Botany—Physiology
Physiology of plants

BT   **Botany**
NT   **Fertilization of plants**
Germination

Plant physiology—*Continued*
>> **Plants—Growth**
>> **Plants—Nutrition**

Plant propagation   631.5
> Use for materials on the continuance or multiplication of plants by successive production. Materials on attempts to produce new or improved varieties of plants through controlled reproduction are entered under **Plant breeding.**
>> UF   Plants—Propagation
>> Propagation of plants
>> BT   **Fruit culture**
>> **Gardening**
>> **Nurseries (Horticulture)**
>> NT   **Grafting**
>> **Seeds**
>> RT   **Plant breeding**

Plant taxonomy
> USE   **Botany—Classification**

Plantation life (May subdiv. geog.)
**   307.72**
>> BT   **Country life**

Planting
> USE   **Agriculture**
> **Gardening**
> **Landscape gardening**
> **Tree planting**

Plants (May subdiv. geog.)   **580**
> Use for nonscientific materials. Materials on the science of plants are entered under **Botany.** Subdivisions used under this heading may be used under the names of orders, classes, or individual species of plants.
>> UF   Flora
>> Vegetable kingdom
>> SA   types of plants characterized by their physical characteristics, environment, or use, e.g. **Climbing plants; Desert plants; Forage plants;** etc.; and names of botanical categories of plants, c.g. **Ferns** [to be added as needed]
>> NT   **Bulbs**
>> **Carnivorous plants**
>> **Climbing plants**
>> **Cultivated plants**
>> **Desert plants**
>> **Edible plants**
>> **Ferns**
>> **Fertilization of plants**
>> **Flowers**
>> **Forage plants**

>> **Forest plants**
>> **Fossil plants**
>> **Freshwater plants**
>> **Fruit**
>> **Fungi**
>> **Grasses**
>> **Herbs**
>> **Horticulture**
>> **House plants**
>> **Leaves**
>> **Marine plants**
>> **Mosses**
>> **Mountain plants**
>> **Mushrooms**
>> **Poisonous plants**
>> **Popular plant names**
>> **Rare plants**
>> **Seeds**
>> **Shrubs**
>> **Tobacco**
>> **Trees**
>> **Vegetables**
>> **Weeds**
>> RT   **Botany**
>> **Gardening**
>> **Herbicides**

Plants—Analysis   572
>> UF   Plant chemistry
>> Plants—Chemical analysis
>> BT   **Botanical chemistry**

Plants—Anatomy   571.3
>> UF   Anatomy of plants
>> Botany—Anatomy
>> Botany—Structure
>> Plant anatomy
>> BT   **Anatomy**
>> **Botany**

Plants—Chemical analysis
> USE   **Plants—Analysis**

Plants—Classification
> USE   **Botany—Classification**

Plants—Collection and preservation
**   580.75**
>> UF   Botanical specimens—Collection and preservation
>> Collections of natural specimens
>> Herbaria
>> Preservation of botanical specimens
>> Specimens, Preservation of

Plants—Collection and preservation—
Continued
   BT   **Collectors and collecting**
   NT   **Flowers—Drying**
Plants—Conservation
   USE **Plant conservation**
Plants, Cultivated
   USE **Cultivated plants**
Plants—Diseases
   USE **Plant diseases**
Plants—Ecology
   USE **Plant ecology**
Plants, Edible
   USE **Edible plants**
Plants, Extinct
   USE **Fossil plants**
Plants—Fertilization
   USE **Fertilization of plants**
Plants—Folklore   398.24
   UF   Plant lore
   BT   **Folklore**
   NT   **Ethnobotany**
Plants, Fossil
   USE **Fossil plants**
**Plants—Geographical distribution
   581.9**
   UF   Geographical distribution of
         plants
         Phytogeography
         Plant distribution
   SA   types of plants with the subdivi-
         sion *Geographical distribution*
         [to be added as needed]
   BT   **Biogeography**
Plants—Growth   571.8
   BT   **Plant physiology**
Plants in art   704.9
   SA   types of plants in art, e.g. **Flow-
         ers in art** [to be added as
         needed]
   BT   **Art—Themes**
   RT   **Botanical illustration**
Plants, Industrial
   USE **Factories**
Plants, Medicinal
   USE **Medical botany**
Plants—Names
   USE **Botany—Nomenclature
         Popular plant names**
Plants—Nomenclature
   USE **Botany—Nomenclature
         Popular plant names**

Plants—Nutrition   575.7; 631.5
   UF   Plant nutrition
   BT   **Nutrition
         Plant physiology**
Plants, Ornamental
   USE **Ornamental plants**
Plants—Photography
   USE **Photography of plants**
Plants—Propagation
   USE **Plant propagation**
Plants—Soilless culture
   USE **Hydroponics**
Plants—United States   581.973
   UF   Botany—United States
Plaster and plastering   693
   UF   Plastering
   BT   **Masonry**
   NT   **Cement
         Concrete
         Mortar
         Stucco**
Plaster casts   731.4
   UF   Casting
         Casts, Plaster
   BT   **Sculpture**
Plastering
   USE **Plaster and plastering**
Plastic industries
   USE **Plastics industry**
Plastic materials
   USE **Plastics**
Plastic surgery   617.9
   UF   Cosmetic surgery
         Reconstructive surgery
         Surgery, Plastic
   BT   **Surgery**
Plastics   668.4
   UF   Plastic materials
   SA   names of specific plastics [to be
         added as needed]
   BT   **Polymers
         Synthetic products**
   NT   **Gums and resins
         Synthetic rubber**
   RT   **Plastics industry**
Plastics industry (May subdiv. geog.)
         338.4; 668.4
   UF   Plastic industries
   BT   **Chemical industry**
   RT   **Plastics**

Plate 739.2
>UF Gold plate
>>Silver plate
>BT **Goldwork**
>>**Silverwork**
>NT **Hallmarks**
>>**Sheffield plate**

Plate metalwork 671.8
>BT **Metalwork**
>>**Sheet metalwork**

Plate tectonics 551.1
>BT **Earth—Crust**
>>**Geophysics**
>RT **Continental drift**
>>**Submarine geology**

Platforms, Drilling
>USE **Drilling platforms**

Play 790
>BT **Recreation**
>NT **Finger play**
>>**Imaginary playmates**
>>**Sports**
>RT **Amusements**
>>**Games**

Play centers
>USE **Community centers**
>>**Playgrounds**

Play direction (Theater)
>USE **Theater—Production and direction**

Play production
>USE **Amateur theater**
>>**Theater—Production and direction**

Play writing
>USE **Drama—Technique**
>>**Motion picture plays—Technique**
>>**Radio plays—Technique**
>>**Television plays—Technique**

Playbills
>USE **Film posters**

Playgrounds (May subdiv. geog.) 796.06
>UF Play centers
>>Public playgrounds
>>School playgrounds
>BT **Recreation**
>>**Sports facilities**
>RT **Community centers**
>>**Parks**

Playhouses
>USE **Theaters**

Playing cards 795.4
>UF Cards, Playing
>NT **Tarot**
>RT **Card games**

Plays
>USE **Drama—Collections**
>>**One act plays**

Plays, Bible
>USE **Bible plays**

Plays for children
>USE **Children's plays**

Playwrights
>USE **Dramatists**

Playwriting
>USE **Drama—Technique**
>>**Motion picture plays—Technique**
>>**Radio plays—Technique**
>>**Television plays—Technique**

Pleasure 152.4
>BT **Emotions**
>>**Joy and sorrow**
>>**Senses and sensation**
>RT **Happiness**
>>**Pain**

Plot-your-own stories 808.3; 813, etc.
>UF Choose-your-own story plots
>>Making-choices stories
>>Multiple plot stories
>>Which-way stories
>BT **Children's literature**
>>**Fiction**
>>**Literary recreations**

Plots (Drama, fiction, etc.)
>USE **Stories, plots, etc.**

Plows 631.3
>BT **Agricultural machinery**

Plumbing 696
>BT **Building**
>NT **Sewerage**
>RT **House drainage**
>>**Household sanitation**
>>**Pipe fitting**

Pluralism (Social sciences) (May subdiv. geog.) 305.8
Use for materials on the coexistence of several distinct ethnic, religious, or cultural groups within one society. Materials on the presence of two distinct cultures within a single country or region are entered under

Pluralism (Social sciences)—*Continued*
Biculturalism. Materials on policies or programs that foster the preservation of various cultures or cultural identities within a unified society are entered under **Multiculturalism.**

    UF   Ethnic diversity
    BT   **Culture**
    NT   **Biculturalism**
    RT   **Ethnic relations**
          Ethnicity
          Multiculturalism
          Race relations

Plywood   674
    BT   **Wood**

PMS (Gynecology)
    USE **Premenstrual syndrome**

Pneumatic transmission
    USE **Compressed air**

Pneumatics   533; 621.5
    BT   **Physics**
    NT   **Aerodynamics**
          Compressed air
          Sound
    RT   **Gases**

Pneumonia   616.2
    BT   **Lungs—Diseases**

Pocket calculators
    USE **Calculators**

Podiatry   617.5
    UF   Chiropody
    BT   **Medicine**
    NT   **Foot—Care**
    RT   **Foot—Wounds and injuries**

Poetics   808.1
Use for materials on the art and technique of poetry. General materials on the appreciation, philosophy, etc., of poetry are entered under **Poetry.**

    UF   Poetry—Technique
    BT   **Poetry**
    NT   **Rhyme**
          Rhythm
          Versification

Poetry   809.1
Use for general materials on poetry, not for individual works. Materials on the history and criticism of poetry from more than one literature are entered under **Poetry—History and criticism.** Materials on the art and technique of poetry are entered under **Poetics.** Collections of poetry are entered under **Poetry—Collections; English poetry—Collections;** etc.

    UF   Poetry—Philosophy
    SA   types of poetry, e.g. **Haiku;** and subjects, historical events, names of places, ethnic groups, classes of persons, and names of individual persons with the subdivision *Poetry,* to express the theme or subject content of collections of poetry, e.g. **Animals—Poetry; World War, 1939-1945—Poetry; Napoleon I, Emperor of the French, 1769-1821—Poetry;** etc. [to be added as needed]
    BT   **Literature**
    NT   **American poetry**
          Ballads
          Children's poetry
          Didactic poetry
          Eddas
          Elegiac poetry
          English poetry
          Epistolary poetry
          Erotic poetry
          Fantasy poetry
          Free verse
          French poetry
          Haiku
          Humorous poetry
          Love poetry
          Narrative poetry
          Nature poetry
          Pastoral poetry
          Patriotic poetry
          Poetics
          Religious poetry
          Science fiction poetry
          Sea poetry
          Songs
          War poetry

Poetry and music
    USE **Music and literature**

Poetry—Collections   808.81; 811.08, etc.
    UF   Poetry—Selections
          Rhymes

Poetry—Editing   070.5
    BT   **Editing**

Poetry for children
    USE **Children's poetry**
          Nursery rhymes

Poetry, Historical
    USE **Historical poetry**
Poetry—History and criticism   809.1
Poetry—Memorizing   153.1
    BT **Mnemonics**
Poetry—Philosophy
    USE **Poetry**
Poetry—Selections
    USE **Poetry—Collections**
Poetry—Technique
    USE **Poetics**
Poets   809.1; 920
    Use for materials on the lives of several po-
    ets, not limited to a single national literature.
    SA   poets of particular countries, e.g.
            American poets [to be added
            as needed]
    BT   **Authors**
    NT   **American poets**
            Lyricists
            Minstrels
            Troubadours
Poets, American
    USE   **American poets**
Poison ivy   583
    BT   **Poisonous plants**
Poisonous animals (May subdiv. geog.)
            591.6
    SA   types of poisonous animals, e.g.
            Rattlesnakes [to be added as
            needed]
    BT   **Animals**
            Dangerous animals
            Economic zoology
            Poisons and poisoning
    NT   **Rattlesnakes**
Poisonous gases   363.17
    UF   Asphyxiating gases
            Gases, Asphyxiating and poison-
            ous
    BT   **Gases**
            Poisons and poisoning
    NT   **Radon**
Poisonous gases—War use
    USE   **Chemical warfare**
Poisonous plants (May subdiv. geog.)
            581.6
    UF   Toxic plants
    SA   types of poisonous plants, e.g.
            Poison ivy [to be added as
            needed]

    BT   **Economic botany**
            Plants
            Poisons and poisoning
    NT   **Poison ivy**
Poisonous substances
    USE   **Poisons and poisoning**
Poisons and poisoning   363.17; 615.9
    Use for materials on poisonous substances
    and their use. Materials on the science that
    treats of poisons and their antidotes are en-
    tered under **Toxicology.**
    UF   Poisonous substances
            Toxic substances
    SA   types of poisons or poisoning,
            e.g. **Lead poisoning;** and
            types of poisonous substances
            with the subdivision *Toxicolo-
            gy,* for materials on the influ-
            ence of particular substances
            on humans and animals, e.g.
            Insecticides—Toxicology [to
            be added as needed]
    BT   **Accidents**
            Hazardous substances
            Homicide
            Medical jurisprudence
    NT   **Food poisoning**
            Insecticides—Toxicology
            Lead poisoning
            Pesticides
            Poisonous animals
            Poisonous gases
            Poisonous plants
    RT   **Toxicology**
Polar expeditions
    USE   **Antarctica—Exploration**
            Arctic regions—Exploration
            Scientific expeditions
Polar lights
    USE   **Auroras**
Polar regions   998
    Use for materials on both the Antarctic and
    Arctic regions.
    NT   **Antarctica**
            Arctic regions
            North Pole
            South Pole
Polarity
    USE   **Opposites**
Police (May subdiv. geog.)   **363.2**
    UF   Police officers
            Policemen

Police—*Continued*
- BT **Administration of criminal justice**
  Law enforcement
- NT **Animals in police work**
  Detectives
  Police brutality
  Police corruption
  Policewomen
  Secret service
  State police
- RT **Crime**
  Criminal investigation

Police brutality (May subdiv. geog.) **363.2**
- UF Police—Complaints against
  Police cruelty
  Police repression
  Police violence
- BT **Police**

Police—Complaints against
- USE **Police brutality**
  Police corruption

Police—Corrupt practices
- USE **Police corruption**

Police corruption (May subdiv. geog.) **363.2**
- UF Corruption, Police
  Police—Complaints against
  Police—Corrupt practices
- BT **Misconduct in office**
  Police

Police cruelty
- USE **Police brutality**

Police, International
- USE **International police**

Police officers
- USE **Police**

Police repression
- USE **Police brutality**

Police, State
- USE **State police**

Police—United States **363.20973**
- UF United States—Police

Police violence
- USE **Police brutality**

Policemen
- USE **Police**

Policewomen (May subdiv. geog.) **363.2**
- UF Women police officers
- BT **Police**
  Women

Polio
- USE **Poliomyelitis**

Poliomyelitis **616.8**
- UF Infantile paralysis
  Polio
- BT **Diseases**

Poliomyelitis vaccine **614.4; 615**
- UF Live poliovirus vaccine
  Sabin vaccine
  Salk vaccine
- BT **Vaccination**

Polishing
- USE **Grinding and polishing**

Politeness
- USE **Courtesy**
  Etiquette

Political action committees (May subdiv. geog.) **322.4; 324**
  Use for materials on special interest groups that support sympathetic candidates for public office through campaign contributions. Materials on groups that promote their own interests with public officials are entered under **Lobbying.**
- UF Interest groups
  PACs (Political action committees)
  Pressure groups
- BT **Political participation**
- RT **Lobbying**

Political activity
- USE **Political participation**
  and classes of persons, types of industries, military services, and religious denominations, and names of corporate bodies and families with the subdivision *Political activity,* e.g. **Women—Political activity** [to be added as needed]

Political aspects
- USE subjects with the subdivision *Political aspects,* e.g. **Ethnic relations—Political aspects** [to be added as needed]

Political asylum
- USE **Asylum**

Political behavior
- USE **Political participation**
  Political psychology

Political boundaries
- USE **Boundaries**

Political campaign literature
  USE **Campaign literature**
Political campaigns
  USE **Politics**
Political conventions **324.5**
  UF Conventions, Political
  BT **Conferences**
  NT **Primaries**
  RT **Political parties**
Political correctness **306**
  BT **Ideology**
Political corruption (May subdiv. geog.)
    324; 353.4
  UF Boss rule
      Corruption in politics
      Graft in politics
      Political scandals
      Politics—Corrupt practices
      Spoils system
  BT **Conflict of interests**
      Political crimes and offenses
      Political ethics
      Politics
  NT **Whistle blowing**
  RT **Misconduct in office**
Political crimes and offenses (May
  subdiv. geog.) **364.1**
  UF Crimes, Political
      Sedition
  BT **Criminal law**
      Political ethics
      Subversive activities
  NT **Anarchism and anarchists**
      Assassination
      Bombings
      Concentration camps
      Political corruption
      Political prisoners
      Terrorism
      Treason
Political defectors
  USE **Defectors**
Political economy
  USE **Economics**
Political ethics (May subdiv. geog.) **172**
  BT **Ethics**
      Political science
      Politics
      Social ethics
  NT **Citizenship**
      Conflict of interests

      Political corruption
      Political crimes and offenses
      Resistance to government
Political extremism
  USE **Radicalism**
Political geography
  USE **Boundaries**
      Geopolitics
Political participation (May subdiv. geog.)
    323
  UF Citizen participation
      Civic involvement
      Community action
      Mass political behavior
      Political activity
      Political behavior
  SA subjects designating government
      activity with the subdivision
      Citizen participation, e.g.
      Crime prevention—Citizen
      participation; and corporate
      bodies, families, classes of
      persons, industries, military
      services, and religious denom-
      inations with the subdivision
      Political activity, e.g. **Wom-**
      en—Political activity [to be
      added as needed]
  BT **Politics**
  NT **African Americans—Political**
      activity
      Blacks—Political activity
      City planning—Citizen partici-
      pation
      Clergy—Political activity
      College students—Political ac-
      tivity
      Crime prevention—Citizen par-
      ticipation
      Jews—Political activity
      Political action committees
      Students—Political activity
      Women—Political activity
  RT **Social action**
Political parties (May subdiv. geog.)
    324.2
  UF Parties, Political
  SA names of parties [to be added as
      needed]
  BT **Political science**
      Politics

Political parties—*Continued*
  NT **Democratic Party (U.S.)**
      Politics
      Republican Party (U.S.)
      Right and left (Political science)
      Third parties (United States politics)
  RT **Political conventions**
Political parties—Finance
  USE **Campaign funds**
Political prisoners (May subdiv. geog.)
    365
  UF Prisoners of conscience
  BT **Political crimes and offenses**
      Prisoners
Political psychology   **302**
  UF Mass political behavior
      Political behavior
      Politics—Psychological aspects
  BT **Political science**
      Psychology
      Social psychology
  NT **Propaganda**
      Public opinion
Political refugees (May subdiv. geog.)
    325
  UF Displaced persons
      Refugees, Political
  SA refugees of particular countries, geographic regions, or ethnic groups, e.g. **Vietnamese refugees; Arab refugees;** etc., and names of wars with the subdivision *Refugees,* e.g. **World War, 1939-1945—Refugees** [to be added as needed]
  BT **Asylum**
      International law
      International relations
      Refugees
  NT **Defectors**
      World War, 1939-1945—Refugees
Political scandals
  USE **Political corruption**
Political science (May subdiv. geog.)
    320
    Use for materials on the science of politics. Materials on the various aspects of practical politics, such as electioneering, political machines, etc., are entered under **Politics.** Materials on the political processes of particular regions, countries, cities, etc., are entered under the place with the subdivision *Politics and government.*
  UF Civics
      Civil government
      Commonwealth, The
      Government
      Political theory
  SA movements in political philosophy, e.g. **Marxism;** topics with the subdivision *Political aspects,* e.g. **Ethnic relations—Political aspects;** and names of continents, areas, countries, cities, etc., and native peoples with the subdivision *Politics and government,* e.g. **United States—Politics and government; Native Americans—Politics and government** [to be added as needed]
  BT **Social sciences**
  NT **Anarchism and anarchists**
      Aristocracy
      Bureaucracy
      Citizenship
      Civil rights
      Civil service
      Communism
      Comparative government
      Conservatism
      Democracy
      Equality
      Executive power
      Federal government
      Freedom
      Geopolitics
      Ideology
      Imperialism
      Individualism
      Law
      Legislation
      Liberalism
      Local government
      Marxism
      Monarchy
      Municipal government
      Nationalism
      Political ethics

Political science—*Continued*
  Political parties
  Political psychology
  Postcolonialism
  Power (Social sciences)
  Progressivism (United States politics)
  Public administration
  Public opinion
  Radicalism
  Representative government and representation
  Republics
  Resistance to government
  Revolutions
  Right and left (Political science)
  Separation of powers
  Social contract
  Socialism
  State governments
  State rights
  Suffrage
  Taxation
  Totalitarianism
  United States—Politics and government
  Utopias
  World politics
 RT Politics
  State, The
Political science—Early works to 1800
  (May subdiv. geog.)   320
Political science—Religious aspects
 USE Religion and politics
Political theory
 USE Political science
Political violence
 USE Sabotage
  Terrorism
Politicians (May subdiv. geog.)
  324.2092; 920
 BT Statesmen
 NT Women politicians
Politicians—United States   324.2092; 920
 UF American politicians
  United States—Politicians
Politics   324.7
  Use for materials on the various aspects of practical politics, such as electioneering, polit-

ical machines, etc. Materials on the science of politics are entered under **Political science.**
 UF Campaigns, Political
  Electioneering
  Political campaigns
  Politics, Practical
  Practical politics
 SA subjects with the subdivision *Political aspects,* e.g. **Ethnic relations—Political aspects;** names of continents, areas, countries, cities, etc., and native peoples, with the subdivision *Politics and government;* and ethnic groups and classes of persons with the subdivision *Political activity,* e.g. **College students—Political activity** [to be added as needed]
 BT Political parties
 NT Arab countries—Politics and government
  Asia—Politics and government
  Business and politics
  Campaign funds
  Campaign literature
  Chicago (Ill.)—Politics and government
  Elections
  Latin America—Politics and government
  Lobbying
  Native Americans—Politics and government
  Political corruption
  Political ethics
  Political participation
  Political parties
  Primaries
  Regionalism
  Religion and politics
  Television and politics
  United States—Politics and government
 RT Political science
Politics and business
 USE Business and politics
Politics and Christianity
 USE Christianity and politics

552

Politics and government
    USE   names of continents, areas, countries, cities, etc., and native peoples with the subdivision *Politics and government,* e.g. **United States—Politics and government; Arab countries—Politics and government; Native Americans—Politics and government;** etc. [to be added as needed]

Politics and religion
    USE   **Religion and politics**

Politics and students
    USE   **Students—Political activity**

Politics and television
    USE   **Television and politics**

Politics—Corrupt practices
    USE   **Political corruption**

Politics, Practical
    USE   **Politics**

Politics—Psychological aspects
    USE   **Political psychology**

Politics—Religious aspects
    USE   **Religion and politics**

Pollination
    USE   **Fertilization of plants**

Polls
    USE   **Elections**
            Public opinion polls

Pollution (May subdiv. geog.) **304.2; 363.73**
    UF   Chemical pollution
            Contamination of environment
            Environmental pollution
    SA   types of pollution, e.g. **Air pollution** [to be added as needed]
    BT   **Environmental health**
            Human influence on nature
            Public health
            Sanitary engineering
            Sanitation
    NT   **Air pollution**
            Noise pollution
            Pesticides—Environmental aspects
            Radioactive pollution
            Space debris
            Water pollution

    RT   **Environmental protection**
            Hazardous wastes
            Industrial waste
            Pollution control industry
            Refuse and refuse disposal

Pollution control
    USE   **Pollution control industry**

Pollution control devices (Motor vehicles)
    USE   **Automobiles—Pollution control devices**

Pollution control industry (May subdiv. geog.) **338.4; 363.73**
    UF   Pollution control
            Pollution—Prevention
    BT   **Industries**
    NT   **Automobiles—Pollution control devices**
            Recycling
            Refuse and refuse disposal
    RT   **Pollution**

Pollution—Mathematical models 304.2; 363.73
    BT   **Mathematical models**

Pollution of air
    USE   **Air pollution**

Pollution of water
    USE   **Water pollution**

Pollution—Prevention
    USE   **Pollution control industry**

Pollution, Radioactive
    USE   **Radioactive pollution**

Poltergeists
    USE   **Ghosts**

Polyglot dictionaries 413
    UF   Dictionaries, Multilingual
            Dictionaries, Polyglot
            Multilingual dictionaries
            Multilingual glossaries, phrase books, etc.
            Polyglot glossaries, phrase books, etc.
    BT   **Encyclopedias and dictionaries**

Polyglot glossaries, phrase books, etc.
    USE   **Polyglot dictionaries**

Polygraph
    USE   **Lie detectors and detection**

Polymerization
    USE   **Polymers**

Polymers   541.3; 547; 668.9
  UF   Polymerization
  SA   types of polymers, e.g. **Plastics**
         [to be added as needed]
  BT   **Organic compounds—Synthesis**
         Physical chemistry
  NT   **Plastics**
Polynucleotides
  USE   **Nucleic acids**
Pomp
  USE   **Parades**
Ponds (May subdiv. geog.)   551.48
  BT   **Water**
Ponies   636.1
  UF   Foals
  BT   **Horses**
Pontiac's Conspiracy, 1763-1765   973.2
  BT   **Native Americans—Wars**
         United States—History—1600-
         1775, Colonial period
Pony express   383
  BT   **Express service**
         Postal service
Pools
  USE   **Swimming pools**
Poor (May subdiv. geog.)   305.5; 362.5
  UF   Poor people
         Poor persons
  BT   **Poverty**
         Public welfare
  NT   **Begging**
         Homeless persons
         Tramps
         Unemployed
Poor—Medical care   362.1
  UF   Medical care for the poor
  BT   **Medical care**
  NT   **Medicaid**
Poor people
  USE   **Poor**
Poor persons
  USE   **Poor**
Poor relief
  USE   **Charities**
         Domestic economic assistance
         Public welfare
Pop culture
  USE   **Popular culture**
Pop-up books
  USE   **Toy and movable books**

Popes   262; 920
  UF   Holy See
  BT   **Church history**
  RT   **Papacy**
Popes—Infallibility   262
  UF   Infallibility of the Pope
Popes—Temporal power   262
  UF   Temporal power of the Pope
  BT   **Church history**
Popes—Travel
  USE   **Papal visits**
Popes—Voyages and travels
  USE   **Papal visits**
Popular arts
  USE   **Popular culture**
Popular culture (May subdiv. geog.)
         306.4
    Use for materials on literature, art, music,
  motion pictures, etc., produced for a mass au-
  dience. General materials on learning and
  scholarship, literature, the arts, etc., are en-
  tered under **Intellectual life.**
  UF   Mass culture
         Pop culture
         Popular arts
  BT   **Communication**
         Culture
         Intellectual life
         Recreation
  NT   **Sex in popular culture**
         Violence in popular culture
  RT   **Mass media**
Popular culture—Chicago (Ill.)   977.3
  UF   Chicago (Ill.)—Popular culture
Popular culture—United States   973
  UF   United States—Popular culture
  NT   **Americana**
Popular government
  USE   **Democracy**
Popular medicine   616.02
    Use for medical books written for the lay-
  man.
  UF   Medicine, Popular
  BT   **Medicine**
  NT   **Traditional medicine**
  RT   **Health self-care**
Popular music (May subdiv. geog.)
         781.64; 782.42164
  UF   Popular songs
  SA   types of popular music [to be
         added as needed]
  BT   **Music**
         Songs

Popular music—*Continued*
NT   Blues music
     Country music
     Gospel music
     Rap music
     Rock music
Popular music—Texts   782.42164
UF   Lyrics
     Popular song lyrics
     Song lyrics
Popular music—Writing and publishing
     070.5; 781.3
UF   Song writing
     Songwriting
BT   **Composition (Music)**
Popular plant names   580.1
    Use for materials on the common or vernacular names of plants. Systematically derived lists of names or designations of plants and materials about such names are entered under **Botany—Nomenclature.**
UF   Plants—Names
     Plants—Nomenclature
SA   types of plants with the subdivision *Nomenclature (Popular),* e.g. **Trees—Nomenclature (Popular)** [to be added as needed]
BT   **Plants**
NT   **Trees—Nomenclature (Popular)**
RT   **Botany—Nomenclature**
Popular song lyrics
USE   **Popular music—Texts**
Popular songs
USE   **Popular music**
Popularity   158
BT   **Social psychology**
Population   304.6; 363.9
UF   Demography
     Foreign population
SA   ethnic groups and names of countries, cities, etc., with the subdivision *Population* [to be added as needed]
BT   **Economics**
     Human ecology
     Sociology
     Vital statistics
NT   **Birth control**
     Census
     Chicago (Ill.)—Population
     Cities and towns—Growth
     Eugenics

     Human fertility
     Immigration and emigration
     Internal migration
     Mortality
     Ohio—Population
     United States—Population
RT   **Birth rate**
Porcelain (May subdiv. geog.)   738.2
    Use for materials on chinaware and porcelain for the table or decorative use. Materials on the technology of fired earthen products or on clay products intended for industrial use are entered under **Ceramics.**
UF   China (Porcelain)
     Chinaware
     Dishes
SA   types of porcelain [to be added as needed]
BT   **Decorative arts**
     Pottery
     Tableware
NT   **China painting**
Porcelain enamels
USE   **Enamel and enameling**
Porcelain painting
USE   **China painting**
Pornography (May subdiv. geog.)   176; 363.4; 364.1
UF   Obscene materials
RT   **Erotica**
     Obscenity (Law)
Portable computers   004.16
UF   Handheld computers
     Laptop computers
BT   **Computers**
Portrait miniatures
USE   **Miniature painting**
Portrait painting   757
UF   Portraiture
BT   **Painting**
     Portraits
RT   **Figure painting**
     Miniature painting
Portrait photography (May subdiv. geog.)   778.9; 779
UF   Portraiture
BT   **Photography**
     Portraits
Portraits (May subdiv. geog.)   704.9; 757
SA   headings for collective and individual biography, classes of persons, and names of indi-

Portraits—*Continued*
viduals with the subdivision
Portraits, e.g. **United
States—Biography—Por-
traits; Musicians—Portraits;
Shakespeare, William, 1564-
1616—Portraits;** etc. [to be
added as needed]
  BT **Art**
      Biography
      Pictures
  NT **Cartoons and caricatures**
      Portrait painting
      Portrait photography
Portraiture
  USE **Portrait painting**
       Portrait photography
Ports
  USE **Harbors**
Portuguese literature 869
  BT **Literature**
      Romance literature
Position analysis
  USE **Topology**
Positivism 146
  BT **Philosophy**
      Rationalism
  NT **Materialism**
      Pragmatism
  RT **Agnosticism**
      Deism
      Realism
Post cards
  USE **Postcards**
Post-colonialism
  USE **Postcolonialism**
Post-impressionism
  USE **Postimpressionism (Art)**
Post-modernism
  USE **Postmodernism**
Post office
  USE **Postal service**
Post-traumatic stress disorder 616.85
  UF Posttraumatic stress disorder
      Traumatic stress syndrome
  BT **Anxiety**
      Neuroses
      Stress (Psychology)
Postage stamp collecting
  USE **Stamp collecting**

Postage stamps (May subdiv. geog.)
    383; 769.56
  UF Stamps, Postage
  BT **Postal service**
  RT **Stamp collecting**
Postage stamps—Collectors and collecting
  USE **Stamp collecting**
Postal cards
  USE **Postcards**
Postal delivery code
  USE **Zip code**
Postal service (May subdiv. geog.)
    354.75; 383
  UF Mail service
      Parcel post
      Post office
  BT **Communication**
      Transportation
  NT **Air mail service**
      Pony express
      Postage stamps
      Zip code
**Postal service—United States 354.75;
383**
  UF United States—Mail
      United States—Postal service
Postcards 383; 741.6
  UF Picture postcards
      Post cards
      Postal cards
**Postcards—Collectors and collecting
790.1**
Postcolonial theory
  USE **Postcolonialism**
Postcolonialism (May subdiv. geog.) **325**
  UF Post-colonialism
      Postcolonial theory
  BT **Political science**
Posters (May subdiv. geog.) **741.6**
  SA types of posters, e.g. **Film post-
ers;** and subjects, ethnic
groups, classes of persons, in-
dividual persons, corporate
bodies, and names of wars
with the subdivision *Posters*
[to be added as needed]
  BT **Advertising**
      Commercial art
  NT **Film posters**
  RT **Signs and signboards**

Postimpressionism (Art) (May subdiv. geog.) **709.03**
    UF   Post-impressionism
    BT   **Art**
Postmodernism (May subdiv. geog.)
    190; 700.1
    UF   Post-modernism
    BT   **Aesthetics**
    RT   **Modernism (Aesthetics)**
Posttraumatic stress disorder
    USE **Post-traumatic stress disorder**
Posture   **613.7**
    BT   **Physical education**
Pot (Drug)
    USE **Marijuana**
Potable water
    USE **Drinking water**
Potash   **631.8; 668**
    BT   **Fertilizers**
Potatoes   **635; 641.3**
    BT   **Vegetables**
Potters (May subdiv. geog.)   **738.092;**
    920
    BT   **Artists**
Potters' marks
    USE **Pottery—Marks**
Pottery   **666; 738**
    Use for materials on pottery for the table or for decorative use. Materials on the technology of fired earthen products or on clay products intended for industrial use are entered under **Ceramics.**
    UF   Crockery
           Dishes
           Earthenware
           Faience
           Stoneware
    SA   types of pottery and pottery of particular countries, e.g.
           American pottery [to be added as needed]
    BT   **Ceramics**
           Clay industry
           Decoration and ornament
           Decorative arts
           Tableware
    NT   **American pottery**
           Glazes
           Porcelain
           Terra cotta
    RT   **Vases**
Pottery, American
    USE **American pottery**

Pottery—Marks   **738**
    UF   Potters' marks
Poultry   **598.6; 636.5**
    SA   types of domesticated birds, e.g.
           Ducks [to be added as needed]
    BT   **Birds**
           Domestic animals
    NT   **Ducks**
           Geese
           Turkeys
Poverty   **305.5; 362.5**
    UF   Destitution
           Pauperism
    SA   names of countries with the subdivisions *Economic conditions* and *Social conditions* [to be added as needed]
    BT   **Economic conditions**
           Social problems
    NT   **Homelessness**
           Poor
    RT   **Domestic economic assistance**
           Public welfare
           Subsistence economy
Powder, Smokeless
    USE **Gunpowder**
Powdered milk
    USE **Dried milk**
Power blackouts
    USE **Electric power failures**
Power boats
    USE **Motorboats**
Power failures
    USE **Electric power failures**
Power (Mechanics)   **531; 621**
    Use for materials on the physics and engineering aspects of power. Materials on the available sources of mechanical power in general are entered under **Energy resources.**
    UF   Energy technology
    BT   **Mechanical engineering**
           Mechanics
    NT   **Compressed air**
           Electric power
           Energy resources
           Force and energy
           Machinery
           Power transmission
           Steam
           Water power
           Wind power

Power plants
USE **Electric power plants**
Power plants, Hydroelectric
USE **Hydroelectric power plants**
Power plants, Nuclear
USE **Nuclear power plants**
Power politics
USE **Balance of power**
Cold war
Power resources
USE **Energy resources**
Power resources conservation
USE **Energy conservation**
Power resources development
USE **Energy development**
Power (Social sciences) (May subdiv.
geog.) **303.3**
BT **Political science**
NT **Elite (Social sciences)**
Power stations
USE **Electric power plants**
Power supply
USE **Energy resources**
Power tools 621.9
BT **Tools**
Power transmission 621.8
UF Transmission of power
BT **Mechanical engineering**
Power (Mechanics)
NT **Cables**
Electric power distribution
Gearing
RT **Belts and belting**
Machinery
Power transmission, Electric
USE **Electric lines**
Electric power distribution
Powers, Separation of
USE **Separation of powers**
POWs
USE **Prisoners of war**
Powwows 394.2; 970.004
BT **Festivals**
**Native Americans—Rites and
ceremonies**
**Native Americans—Social life
and customs**
Practical jokes 818, etc.
UF Pranks
BT **Jokes**
Wit and humor

Practical nurses (May subdiv. geog.)
610.73; 920
BT **Nurses**
Practical nursing 610.73; 649.8
BT **Nursing**
Practical politics
USE **Politics**
Practical Psychology
USE **Applied psychology**
Practice
USE types of professions with the
subdivision *Practice*, e.g. **Nu-
clear medicine—Practice** [to
be added as needed]
Practice teaching
USE **Student teaching**
Pragmatism 144
BT **Philosophy**
Positivism
Realism
Theory of knowledge
RT **Empiricism**
Reality
Truth
Utilitarianism
Prairies (May subdiv. geog.) **577.4;
578.74**
BT **Grasslands**
Pranks
USE **Practical jokes**
Prayer 248.3; 291.4
May be subdivided by religion or sect. Use
for materials about prayer. Collections of
prayers are entered under **Prayers.**
UF Devotion
Devotional theology
BT **Worship**
RT **Devotional exercises**
Prayers
Prayer-books
USE **Prayers**
Prayer-books and devotions
USE **Prayers**
Prayer in the public schools (May
subdiv. geog.) **379.2**
Use for materials on the inclusion of
prayers or a period for silent prayer or medi-
tation in the daily schedule of public schools.
Materials on the teaching of religion in the
public schools or on the religious freedom of
students and school employees are entered un-
der **Religion in the public schools.**
UF Prayers in the public schools
School prayer

Prayer in the public schools—*Continued*
  BT **Religion in the public schools**
Prayers 242; 264; 291.4
  Use for collections of prayers. Materials about prayer are entered under **Prayer.**
  UF Collects
      Prayer-books
      Prayer-books and devotions
  SA names of religions, denominations, religious orders, classes of persons for whose use the prayers are intended, and names of saints and deities to whom the prayers are directed with the subdivision *Prayers,* e.g. **Buddhism—Prayers; Sick—Prayers; Mary, Blessed Virgin, Saint— Prayers;** etc. [to be added as needed]
  BT **Devotional literature**
  NT **Buddhism—Prayers**
      Mary, Blessed Virgin, Saint— Prayers
      Meditations
      Sick—Prayers
  RT **Prayer**
Prayers in the public schools
  USE **Prayer in the public schools**
Pre-Columbian Americans
  USE **Native Americans**
Pre-Lenten festivities
  USE **Carnival**
Preachers
  USE **Clergy**
Preaching (May subdiv. geog.) **251; 291.6**
  Use for materials on the art of writing and delivering sermons. Collections of sermons not limited to a single topic, occasion, or Christian denomination are entered under **Sermons.**
  UF Speaking
  BT **Pastoral theology**
      Public speaking
      Rhetoric
  RT **Sermons**
Precious metals (May subdiv. geog.) **553.4; 669**
  UF Bullion
  BT **Metals**
      Mines and mineral resources

  NT **Gold**
      Silver
Precious stones (May subdiv. geog.) **553.8**
  Use for mineralogical or technological materials on gem stones. Materials on cut and polished precious stones treated from the point of view of art or antiquity are entered under **Gems.** Materials on gems in which the emphasis is on the setting are entered under **Jewelry.**
  UF Gemstones
      Jewels
  SA names of precious stones [to be added as needed]
  BT **Minerals**
  NT **Diamonds**
  RT **Gems**
Precipitation forecasting
  USE **Weather forecasting**
Precipitation (Meteorology) (May subdiv. geog.) **551.57**
  BT **Meteorology**
      Water
      Weather
  NT **Rain**
      Snow
Precocious children
  USE **Gifted children**
Predators
  USE **Predatory animals**
Predatory animals 591.5
  UF Predators
  SA types of predatory animals [to be added as needed]
  BT **Animals**
  NT **Birds of prey**
Predestination 234; 291.2
  UF Election (Theology)
      Foreordination
  BT **Theology**
  RT **Fate and fatalism**
      Free will and determinism
Predictions
  USE **Forecasting**
      Prophecies
Prefabricated buildings 693
  UF Buildings, Prefabricated
  BT **Buildings**
  NT **Prefabricated houses**
Prefabricated houses 693; 728
  BT **Domestic architecture**
      House construction

Prefabricated houses—*Continued*
    Houses
    Prefabricated buildings
Pregnancy 599; 612.6; 618.2
  BT **Reproduction**
  NT **Miscarriage**
      Prenatal care
      Teenage pregnancy
  RT **Childbirth**
Prehistoric animals 560
  UF Animals, Prehistoric
  BT **Animals**
      Fossils
  NT **Dinosaurs**
  RT **Extinct animals**
Prehistoric art (May subdiv. geog.)
    709.01
  UF Art, Prehistoric
  BT **Art**
  NT **Rock drawings, paintings, and**
      engravings
Prehistoric man
  USE **Fossil hominids**
      Prehistoric peoples
Prehistoric peoples (May subdiv. geog.)
    930.1
  UF Man, Prehistoric
      Prehistoric man
      Prehistory
  SA names of prehistoric peoples,
      e.g. **Cro-Magnons;** etc.; and
      names of countries, cities,
      etc., with the subdivision *An-*
      tiquities, e.g. **United States—**
      Antiquities [to be added as
      needed]
  BT **Antiquities**
      Archeology
      Human beings
  NT **Cave dwellers**
      Cro-Magnons
  RT **Human origins**
Prehistory
  USE **Archeology**
      Fossil hominids
      Prehistoric peoples
Prejudice
  USE **Prejudices**
Prejudice-motivated crimes
  USE **Hate crimes**

Prejudices (May subdiv. geog.)   **152.4;**
    177; 303.3
  UF Bias (Psychology)
      Bigotry
      Prejudice
  SA types of prejudice [to be added
      as needed]
  BT **Attitude (Psychology)**
      Emotions
      Interpersonal relations
  NT **Antisemitism**
      Discrimination
      Racism
      Sexism
Prejudicial publicity
  USE **Freedom of the press and fair**
      trial
Prelude and fugue
  USE **Fugue**
Preludes and fugues
  USE **Fugue**
Premarital contracts
  USE **Marriage contracts**
Premarital counseling
  USE **Marriage counseling**
Premenstrual syndrome 618.1
  UF PMS (Gynecology)
      Premenstrual tension
  BT **Menstruation**
Premenstrual tension
  USE **Premenstrual syndrome**
Premiers
  USE **Prime ministers**
Prenatal care (May subdiv. geog.)   **618.2**
  BT **Pregnancy**
Prenatal diagnosis 618.3
  BT **Diagnosis**
  NT **Amniocentesis**
      Genetic counseling
Prenuptial agreements
  USE **Marriage contracts**
Prenuptial contracts
  USE **Marriage contracts**
Prepaid group medical practice
  USE **Health maintenance organiza-**
      tions
Prepaid health plans
  USE **Health insurance**
Prepaid medical care
  USE **Health insurance**

Preparation guides for examinations
USE **Examinations—Study guides**
Prepared cereals   641.3; 664
UF   Breakfast cereals
Cereals, Prepared
BT   **Breakfasts**
Food
Preprimers
USE   **Easy reading materials**
Presbyterian Church (May subdiv. geog.)
285
BT   **Christian sects**
Presbyterian Church—Sermons   252
BT   **Sermons**
Preschool children
USE   **Children**
Preschool education (May subdiv. geog.)
372.21
UF   Children—Education
Education, Preschool
Infants—Education
BT   **Education**
NT   **Readiness for school**
RT   **Kindergarten**
Nursery schools
Preschool reading materials
USE   **Easy reading materials**
Prescription drug abuse
USE   **Medication abuse**
Presents
USE   **Gifts**
Preservation
USE   types of foods and other things
preserved with the subdivision
Preservation, e.g. **Fruit—**
Preservation; Wood—Preser-
vation; etc.; antiquities and
types of natural objects,
including animal specimens
and plant specimens, with the
subdivision *Collection and*
preservation, e.g. **Birds—Col-**
lection and preservation; and
types of art objects, library
materials, architecture, and
land vehicles with the subdivision *Conservation and res-*
toration, e.g. **Automobiles—**
Conservation and restoration
[to be added as needed]

Preservation of antiquities
USE   **Antiquities—Collection and**
preservation
Preservation of biological diversity
USE   **Biological diversity conserva-**
tion
Preservation of botanical specimens
USE   **Plants—Collection and preser-**
vation
Preservation of buildings
USE   **Architecture—Conservation**
and restoration
Preservation of food
USE   **Food—Preservation**
Preservation of forests
USE   **Forest conservation**
Preservation of historical records
USE   **Archives**
Preservation of library resources
USE   **Library resources—Conserva-**
tion and restoration
Preservation of natural resources
USE   **Conservation of natural re-**
sources
Preservation of natural scenery
USE   **Landscape protection**
Natural monuments
Nature conservation
Preservation of organs, tissues, etc.
617.9
UF   Organ preservation (Anatomy)
Organs (Anatomy)—Preservation
RT   **Transplantation of organs, tis-**
sues, etc.
Preservation of photographs
USE   **Photographs—Conservation**
and restoration
Preservation of specimens
USE   **Taxidermy**
Preservation of wildlife
USE   **Wildlife conservation**
Preservation of wood
USE   **Wood—Preservation**
Preservation of works of art
USE   subjects with the subdivision
Conservation and restoration,
e.g. **Painting—Conservation**
and restoration [to be added
as needed]

Preservation of zoological specimens
USE **Zoological specimens—Collection and preservation**
Preservationism (Historic preservation)
USE **Historic preservation**
Preserving
USE **Canning and preserving**
Presidential aides
USE **Presidents—United States—Staff**
Presidential campaigns—United States
USE **Presidents—United States—Election**
Presidential libraries
USE **Presidents—United States—Archives**
Presidents (May subdiv. geog.) **352.23; 920**
SA names of presidents [to be added as needed]
BT **Heads of state**
NT **Vice-presidents**
RT **Executive power**
Presidents—Mexico 920; 972
UF Mexico—Presidents
Presidents—Powers
USE **Executive power**
Presidents' spouses—United States 920
UF First ladies—United States
Presidents—United States—Spouses
Presidents' wives—United States
Wives of presidents—United States
Presidents—United States 352.230973; 920
When applicable, the subdivisions under this heading may be used under names of presidents, prime ministers, and other rulers.
UF United States—Presidents
SA names of presidents [to be added as needed]
NT **Lincoln, Abraham, 1809-1865**
Presidents—United States—Appointment 352.23
Presidents—United States—Archives 026
UF Libraries, Presidential
Presidential libraries
Presidents—United States—Libraries

SA names of individual libraries [to be added as needed]
BT **Archives**
NT **Harry S. Truman Library**
Presidents—United States—Assassination 364.15; 973
BT **Assassination**
Presidents—United States—Burial
USE **Presidents—United States—Death and burial**
Presidents—United States—Children 920
Presidents—United States—Death and burial 393; 973
UF Presidents—United States—Burial
Presidents—United States—Funeral and memorial services
Presidents—United States—Memorial services
Presidents—United States—Election 324.973
May further subdivide by date.
UF Campaigns, Presidential—United States
Electoral college
Presidential campaigns—United States
BT **Elections**
Presidents—United States—Family 920
Presidents—United States—Fathers 920
Presidents—United States—Funeral and memorial services
USE **Presidents—United States—Death and burial**
Presidents—United States—Health 352.23; 920
UF Presidents—United States—Illness
Presidents—United States—Homes 728
Presidents—United States—Illness
USE **Presidents—United States—Health**
Presidents—United States—Impeachment 342
Presidents—United States—Inability
USE **Presidents—United States—Succession**
Presidents—United States—Inaugural addresses 352.23
BT **Speeches**

Presidents—United States—Inauguration
352.23

Presidents—United States—Libraries
USE   Presidents—United States—Archives

Presidents—United States—Medals
352.23

Presidents—United States—Memorial ser-
vices
USE   Presidents—United States—
Death and burial

Presidents—United States—Messages
352.23
UF   Messages to Congress
Presidents—United States—State
of the Union message
State of the Union messages

Presidents—United States—Mothers
920

Presidents—United States—Nomination
324.50973
UF   Nomination of presidents

Presidents—United States—Portraits
973

Presidents—United States—Power
USE   Executive power—United
States

Presidents—United States—Press relations   070.4; 352.230973

Presidents—United States—Protection
352.23

Presidents—United States—Quotations
818
BT   Quotations

Presidents—United States—Relations
with Congress   328.73; 352.23

Presidents—United States—Religion
920

Presidents—United States—Resignation
352.23

Presidents—United States—Sports   920

Presidents—United States—Spouses
USE   Presidents' spouses—United
States

Presidents—United States—Staff   352.23
UF   Presidential aides
BT   Executive departments—United
States

Presidents—United States—State of the
Union message
USE   Presidents—United States—
Messages

Presidents—United States—Succession
342; 352.23
UF   Presidents—United States—Inability

Presidents—United States—Tombs
917.3

Presidents—United States—Travel
352.23
UF   Presidents—United States—Voyages and travels

Presidents—United States—Voyages and
travels
USE   Presidents—United States—
Travel

Presidents' wives—United States
USE   Presidents' spouses—United
States

Press (May subdiv. geog.)   070
SA   topics with the subdivision Press
coverage, e.g. Food contami-
nation—Press coverage [to
be added as needed]
BT   Journalism
Propaganda
Publicity
NT   Alternative press
Broadcast journalism
Freedom of the press
Freedom of the press and fair
trial
News agencies
Pamphlets
RT   Newspapers
Periodicals
Public opinion

Press and government
USE   Press—Government policy

Press censorship
USE   Freedom of the press

Press clippings
USE   Clippings (Books, newspapers,
etc.)

Press coverage
USE   topics with the subdivision Press
coverage, e.g. Food contamination—Press coverage [to
be added as needed]

Press—Government policy (May subdiv. geog.) **323.44**
   UF   Government and the press
         Press and government
   BT   **Freedom of information**
Press relations
   USE   types of public officials and names of individual public officials with the subdivision *Press relations,* e.g. **Presidents—United States—Press relations** [to be added as needed]
Press working of metal
   USE   **Sheet metalwork**
Pressure groups
   USE   **Lobbying**
         Political action committees
Prestidigitation
   USE   **Magic tricks**
Pretenders
   USE   **Impostors and imposture**
Prevention
   USE   types of diseases, medical conditions, and situations to be avoided with the subdivision *Prevention,* e.g. **AIDS (Disease)—Prevention; Accidents—Prevention;** etc. [to be added as needed]
Prevention of accidents
   USE   **Accidents—Prevention**
Prevention of crime
   USE   **Crime prevention**
Prevention of cruelty to animals
   USE   **Animal welfare**
Prevention of disease
   USE   **Preventive medicine**
Prevention of fire
   USE   **Fire prevention**
Prevention of smoke
   USE   **Smoke prevention**
Preventive medicine   **613**
   UF   Diseases—Prevention
         Medicine, Preventive
         Prevention of disease
   SA   names of diseases with the subdivision *Prevention,* e.g. **AIDS (Disease)—Prevention** [to be added as needed]

   BT   **Medicine**
   NT   **Communicable diseases—Prevention**
         Health
         Heart diseases—Prevention
         Hygiene
         Vaccination
   RT   **Pathology**
Price controls
   USE   **Wage-price policy**
Price indexes, Consumer
   USE   **Consumer price indexes**
Price-wage policy
   USE   **Wage-price policy**
Prices (May subdiv. geog.)   **338.5**
   SA   subjects with the subdivision *Prices,* e.g. **Art—Prices** [to be added as needed]
   BT   **Commerce**
         Consumption (Economics)
         Economics
         Finance
         Manufactures
   NT   **Art—Prices**
         Books—Prices
         Consumer price indexes
         Farm produce—Marketing
         Wage-price policy
   RT   **Cost and standard of living**
         Salaries, wages, etc.
Priests (May subdiv. geog.)   **200.92; 270.092**
   UF   Pastors
   SA   names of church denominations with the subdivision *Clergy,* e.g. **Catholic Church—Clergy** [to be added as needed]
   BT   **Clergy**
   NT   **Catholic Church—Clergy**
         Ex-priests
Primaries (May subdiv. geog.)   **324.5**
   UF   Direct primaries
   BT   **Elections**
         Political conventions
         Politics
Primary education
   USE   **Elementary education**
Primates (May subdiv. geog.)   **599.8**
   SA   types of primates, e.g. **Monkeys** [to be added as needed]

Primates—*Continued*
    BT   **Mammals**
    NT   **Human beings**
           Monkeys
Primates—Behavior   599.8
    UF   Primates—Habits and behavior
    BT   **Animal behavior**
Primates—Habits and behavior
    USE **Primates—Behavior**
Prime ministers (May subdiv. geog.)
          352.23; 920

    May use same subdivisions, following geographic subdivision, as for **Presidents—United States.**

    UF   Premiers
    BT   **Cabinet officers**
           Executive power
Prime ministers—Great Britain
          352.230941; 920
    UF   Great Britain—Prime ministers
Primers
    USE **Easy reading materials**
Primitive Christianity
    USE **Church history—30-600, Early church**
Primitive man
    USE **Primitive societies**
Primitive societies (May subdiv. geog.)
          306; 305.8

    Use for materials on nonliterate, nonindustrialized peoples.

    UF   Man, Primitive
           Primitive man
           Primitive society
           Society, Primitive
    BT   **Civilization**
           Ethnology
    NT   **Nomads**
Primitive society
    USE **Primitive societies**
Princes (May subdiv. geog.)   920
    UF   Princes and princesses
           Royalty
    BT   **Courts and courtiers**
Princes and princesses
    USE **Princes**
          Princesses
Princesses (May subdiv. geog.)   920
    UF   Princes and princesses
           Royalty
    BT   **Courts and courtiers**

Printing (May subdiv. geog.)   **686.2**
    SA   types of printing processes [to be added as needed]
    BT   **Bibliography**
           Book industry
           Graphic arts
           Industrial arts
           Publishers and publishing
    NT   **Advertising layout and typography**
           Color printing
           Electrotyping
           Linoleum block printing
           Linotype
           Lithography
           Offset printing
           Proofreading
           Textile printing
           Type and type-founding
           Typesetting
           Typography
    RT   **Books**
           Prints
Printing—Exhibitions   **686.2074**
    BT   **Exhibitions**
Printing—Specimens   **686.2**
    UF   Type specimens
    BT   **Advertising**
           Initials
    RT   **Type and type-founding**
Printing—Style manuals   **686.02**
    UF   Style manuals
    RT   **Authorship—Handbooks, manuals, etc.**
Prints   769
    SA   prints of particular countries, e.g. **American prints** [to be added as needed]
    BT   **Graphic arts**
    NT   **American prints**
           Bookplates
           Color prints
           Linoleum block printing
           Lithography
           Woodcuts
    RT   **Printing**
Prints, American
    USE **American prints**
Prison escapes
    USE **Escapes**

Prison labor
  USE **Convict labor**
Prison reform   365
  UF   Penal reform
  BT   **Social problems**
Prison schools
  USE **Prisoners—Education**
Prisoners (May subdiv. geog.)   365
  UF   Convicts
       Prisoners and prisons
  BT   **Criminals**
  NT   **Convict labor**
       Political prisoners
  RT   **Prisoners of war**
       Prisons
Prisoners and prisons
  USE **Prisoners**
       Prisoners of war
       Prisons
       and names of wars with the
       subdivision *Prisoners and
       prisons,* e.g. **World War,
       1939-1945—Prisoners and
       prisons** [to be added as need-
       ed]
Prisoners—Education (May subdiv. geog.)
  365
  UF   Education of criminals
       Education of prisoners
       Prison schools
  BT   **Adult education**
       Prisons
Prisoners of conscience
  USE **Political prisoners**
Prisoners of war (May subdiv. geog.)
  341.6; 355.7
  UF   Exchange of prisoners of war
       POWs
       Prisoners and prisons
  SA   names of wars with the subdivi-
       sion *Prisoners and prisons,*
       e.g. **World War, 1939-
       1945—Prisoners and prisons**
       [to be added as needed]
  BT   **War**
  NT   **Missing in action**
       **United States—History—1861-
       1865, Civil War—Prisoners
       and prisons**
       **World War, 1939-1945—Pris-
       oners and prisons**

  RT   **Concentration camps**
       Prisoners
       Prisons
Prisons (May subdiv. geog.)   365
  UF   Imprisonment
       Jails
       Penal institutions
       Penitentiaries
       Prisoners and prisons
  SA   types of prisons, names of indi-
       vidual prisons, and names of
       wars with the subdivision
       Prisoners and prisons, e.g.
       **World War, 1939-1945—
       Prisoners and prisons** [to be
       added as needed]
  BT   **Administration of criminal jus-
       tice**
       Correctional institutions
       Punishment
  NT   **Escapes**
       Prisoners—Education
       Probation
       Reformatories
       **United States—History—1861-
       1865, Civil War—Prisoners
       and prisons**
       **World War, 1939-1945—Pris-
       oners and prisons**
  RT   **Prisoners**
       Prisoners of war
Prisons—United States   365
  UF   United States—Prisons
Privacy, Right of
  USE **Right of privacy**
Private art collections
  USE **Art collections**
Private enterprise
  USE **Free enterprise**
Private eye stories
  USE **Mystery and detective plays**
       Mystery fiction
       Mystery films
       Mystery radio programs
       Mystery television programs
Private funding of the arts
  USE **Art patronage**
Private schools (May subdiv. geog.)
  371.02; 373.2
  UF   Boarding schools
       Independent schools

Private schools—*Continued*
  Nonpublic schools
  BT   **Schools**
  NT   **Church schools**
       English public schools
Private theater
  USE   **Amateur theater**
Privateering (May subdiv. geog.)   **341**
  UF   Letters of marque
  BT   **International law**
       Naval art and science
       Naval history
       Pirates
Privatization (May subdiv. geog.)   **338.9**
   Use for materials on the transfer of public assets and service functions to the private sector.
  UF   Denationalization
  BT   **Economic policy**
       Industrial policy
  RT   **Government ownership**
Prize fighting
  USE   **Boxing**
Prizes (Rewards)
  USE   **Awards**
Pro-abortion movement
  USE   **Pro-choice movement**
Pro-choice movement   **179.7; 363.46**
  UF   Abortion rights movement
       Freedom of choice movement
       Pro-abortion movement
       Right to choose movement
  BT   **Social movements**
  RT   **Abortion—Ethical aspects**
       Abortion—Religious aspects
       Women's rights
Pro-life movement   **179.7; 363.46**
  UF   Anti-abortion movement
       Antiabortion movement
       Right-to-life movement (Anti-
          abortion movement)
  BT   **Social movements**
  RT   **Abortion—Ethical aspects**
       Abortion—Religious aspects
       Women's rights
Probabilities   **519.2**
  UF   Fortune
       Statistical inference
  BT   **Algebra**
       Logic
       Mathematics
       Statistics

  NT   **Average**
       Game theory
       Reliability (Engineering)
       Sampling (Statistics)
Probation (May subdiv. geog.)   **364.6**
  UF   Reform of criminals
       Suspended sentence
  BT   **Corrections**
       Criminal law
       Prisons
       Punishment
       Reformatories
       Social case work
  RT   **Juvenile courts**
       Parole
Problem children
  USE   **Emotionally disturbed children**
Problem drinking
  USE   **Alcoholism**
Problem families—Counseling of
  USE   **Family therapy**
Problem solving   **153.4; 510.76**
  BT   **Psychology**
  NT   **Crisis management**
       Critical thinking
       Group problem solving
  RT   **Decision making**
Problems, exercises, etc.
  USE   subjects with the subdivision
        Problems, exercises, etc., for
        compilations of practice prob-
        lems or exercises for use in
        the study of a topic, e.g.
        **Chemistry—Problems, exer-
        cises, etc.** [to be added as
        needed]
Procedural due process
  USE   **Due process of law**
Processing (Libraries)
  USE   **Library technical processes**
Processions
  USE   **Parades**
Procurement, Government
  USE   **Government purchasing**
Producers
  USE   types of producers and directors
        in specific media, e.g. **Motion
        picture producers and direc-
        tors; Theatrical producers
        and directors;** etc. [to be
        added as needed]

Product recall 658.5
  UF Commercial products recall
       Manufactures—Defects
       Manufactures recall
       Recall of products
  BT **Consumer protection**
Product safety 363.19; 658.5
  UF Unsafe products
  BT **Consumer protection**
Production
  USE **Economics**
       Industries
Production engineering
  USE **Factory management**
Production standards 658.5
  Use for materials on the unit time value for
  the accomplishment of a work task as deter-
  mined by work measurement techniques.
  UF Output standards
       Standards of output
       Time production standards
       Work standards
  SA types of industries and processes
       with the subdivision *Produc-
       tion standards,* e.g. **Automo-
       bile industry—Production
       standards** [to be added as
       needed]
  BT **Labor productivity**
       Management
  NT **Automobile industry—Produc-
       tion standards**
       Motion study
       Time study
Productivity of labor
  USE **Labor productivity**
Products, Agricultural
  USE **Farm produce**
Products, Animal
  USE **Animal products**
Products, Commercial
  USE **Commercial products**
Products, Dairy
  USE **Dairy products**
Products, Generic
  USE **Generic products**
Professional associations
  USE **Trade and professional associa-
       tions**

Professional education (May subdiv.
  geog.) 378
  SA types of professions with the
       subdivision *Study and teach-
       ing,* e.g. **Medicine—Study
       and teaching** [to be added as
       needed]
  BT **Education**
       Higher education
       Learning and scholarship
  NT **Colleges and universities**
       Library education
  RT **Technical education**
       Vocational education
Professional ethics (May subdiv. geog.)
  174
  SA types of professional ethics, e.g.
       Medical ethics; professions
       and types of professional per-
       sonnel with the subdivision
       Ethics, e.g. **Librarians—Eth-
       ics;** and subjects with the
       subdivision *Ethical aspects* [to
       be added as needed]
  BT **Ethics**
  NT **Business ethics**
       Journalism—Objectivity
       Legal ethics
       Librarians—Ethics
       Medical ethics
Professional liability
  USE **Malpractice**
Professional liability insurance
  USE **Malpractice insurance**
Professional sports (May subdiv. geog.)
  796
  SA types of sports [to be added as
       needed]
  BT **Sports**
Professions (May subdiv. geog.) 331.7
  UF Careers
       Jobs
       Vocations
  SA types of professions with the
       subdivision *Vocational guid-
       ance,* e.g. **Law—Vocational
       guidance** [to be added as
       needed]
  BT **Occupations**
       Self-employed

Professions—*Continued*
NT   College graduates
      Law—Vocational guidance
      Paraprofessionals
RT   Vocational guidance
Professions—Tort liability
USE   Malpractice
Professors
USE   Educators
      Teachers
Profit   338.5; 658.15
BT   Business
      Capital
      Economics
      Wealth
NT   Capitalism
RT   Income
Profit sharing (May subdiv. geog.)
    658.3; 331.2
BT   Commerce
      Salaries, wages, etc.
RT   Cooperation
Program evaluation in education
USE   Educational evaluation
Programmed instruction   371.39
UF   Programmed textbooks
SA   subjects with the subdivision
      Programmed instruction [to
      be added as needed]
BT   Teaching—Aids and devices
NT   Computer-assisted instruction
      English language—Pro-
      grammed instruction
      Teaching machines
Programmed textbooks
USE   Programmed instruction
Programming (Computers)
USE   Computer programming
Programming languages   005.13
UF   Computer languages
      Computer program languages
      Machine language
      Programming languages (Com-
      puters) *[Former heading]*
      Programming languages (Elec-
      tronic computers)
SA   names of specific languages, e.g.
      FORTRAN (Computer lan-
      guage) [to be added as need-
      ed]
BT   Computer software
      Language and languages

NT   FORTRAN (Computer lan-
      guage)
      HTML (Document markup
      language)
RT   Computer programming
Programming languages (Computers)
USE   Programming languages
Programming languages (Electronic com-
    puters)
USE   Programming languages
Programs, Computer
USE   Computer software
Programs, Radio
USE   Radio programs
Programs, Television
USE   Television programs
Programs, Twelve-step
USE   Twelve-step programs
Progress   303.44
BT   Civilization
NT   Science and civilization
Progressive education
USE   Education—Experimental
      methods
Progressivism (United States politics)
    320.973
BT   Political science
Prohibited books
USE   Books—Censorship
Prohibition (May subdiv. geog.)   344
    Use for materials on the legal prohibition of
  liquor traffic and liquor manufacture.
BT   Criminal law
RT   Temperance
Project Apollo
USE   Apollo project
Project Gemini
USE   Gemini project
Project method in teaching   371.3
BT   Teaching
Project Ranger   629.43
UF   Ranger project
BT   Lunar probes
Project schools
USE   Experimental schools
Project Sealab
USE   Sealab project
Project Telstar
USE   Telstar project
Project Voyager   629.43
UF   Voyager project
BT   Astronautics—United States

Projectiles   623.4
UF   Shells (Projectiles)
NT   **Ammunition**
Bombs
Guided missiles
Rockets (Aeronautics)
RT   **Ordnance**
Projective geometry   516
UF   Geometry, Projective
BT   **Geometry**
Projectors   778.2
UF   Film projectors
Magic lanterns
Motion picture projectors
Opaque projectors
Slide projectors
Stereopticon
Proletariat   305.5
BT   **Labor**
Socialism
Working class
Proliferation of arms
USE   **Arms race**
Promotion in school
USE   **Promotion (School)**
Promotion (School)   371.2
UF   Grade repetition
Grade retention
Non-promotion (School)
Promotion in school
Retention, Grade
School grade retention
School promotion
Student promotion
BT   **Grading and marking (Education)**
Promptness
USE   **Punctuality**
Pronunciation
USE   names of languages with the
subdivision *Pronunciation*, e.g.
English language—Pronunciation [to be added as needed]
Proofreading   070.5; 686.2
BT   **Printing**
Propaganda   303.3; 327.1
SA   propaganda of particular countries, e.g. **American propaganda;** and names of wars with the subdivision *Propaganda*, e.g. **World War,**

1939-1945—Propaganda [to be added as needed]
BT   **Political psychology**
Public opinion
NT   **American propaganda**
Lobbying
Press
Psychological warfare
World War, 1939-1945—Propaganda
RT   **Advertising**
Publicity
Propaganda, American
USE   **American propaganda**
Propagation of plants
USE   **Plant propagation**
Propellers, Aerial
USE   **Aerial propellers**
Proper names
USE   **Names**
Property (May subdiv. geog.)   330.1
UF   Ownership
BT   **Economics**
NT   **Airspace law**
Cultural property
Eminent domain
Income
Intellectual property
Lost and found possessions
Real estate
Surplus government property
RT   **Wealth**
Property, Crimes against
USE   **Offenses against property**
Property, Offenses against
USE   **Offenses against property**
Property tax—Assessment
USE   **Tax assessment**
Prophecies   133.3; 291.2
UF   Predictions
Prophecies (Occult sciences)
Prophecies (Occultism)
Prophecy
SA   subjects, titles of sacred works,
and names of persons with
the subdivision *Prophecies*,
e.g. **Bible—Prophecies** [to be
added as needed]
BT   **Occultism**
Supernatural

Prophecies—*Continued*
  RT **Divination**
      Oracles
Prophecies (Bible)
  USE **Bible—Prophecies**
Prophecies (Occult sciences)
  USE **Prophecies**
Prophecies (Occultism)
  USE **Prophecies**
Prophecy
  USE **Prophecies**
Prophets (May subdiv. geog.)   **200.92**
  BT **Religious biography**
Proportion (Architecture)
  USE **Architecture—Composition,**
       proportion, etc.
Proportional representation (May subdiv.
     geog.)   **328.3**
  UF Representation, Proportional
  BT **Constitutional law**
      Representative government and
      representation
  RT **Elections**
Proprietary rights
  USE **Intellectual property**
Prose literature, American
  USE **American prose literature**
Prose literature, English
  USE **English prose literature**
Prosody
  USE **Versification**
Prospecting (May subdiv. geog.)   **622**
  BT **Gold mines and mining**
      Mines and mineral resources
      Silver mines and mining
  NT **Mine surveying**
      Petroleum geology
Prosthesis
  USE **Artificial limbs**
       Artificial organs
Prostitution (May subdiv. geog.)   **176;**
     306.74; 363.4; 364.1
  BT **Sexual ethics**
      Social problems
      Women—Social conditions
  NT **Juvenile prostitution**
Protection
  USE subjects with the subdivision
       Protection, e.g. **Birds—Pro-**
       tection [to be added as need-
       ed]

Protection against burglary
  USE **Burglary protection**
Protection of animals
  USE **Animal welfare**
Protection of birds
  USE **Birds—Protection**
Protection of children
  USE **Child welfare**
Protection of environment
  USE **Environmental protection**
Protection of game
  USE **Game protection**
Protection of natural scenery
  USE **Landscape protection**
       Natural monuments
       Nature conservation
Protection of plants
  USE **Plant conservation**
Protection of wildlife
  USE **Wildlife conservation**
Protectionism (May subdiv. geog.)   **382**
  UF Free trade and protection
  BT **Commercial policy**
  RT **Free trade**
      Tariff
Proteins   **547; 572**
  BT **Biochemistry**
  NT **Enzymes**
Protest
  USE **Dissent**
Protest marches and rallies
  USE **Demonstrations**
Protest movements (May subdiv. geog.)
     303.48
  SA names of wars and other objects
      of protest with the subdivision
      Protest movements, e.g.
      World War, 1939-1945—
      Protest movements [to be
      added as needed]
  BT **Social movements**
  NT **World War, 1939-1945—Pro-**
      test movements
  RT **Demonstrations**
Protestant churches (May subdiv. geog.)
     280
      Use for materials on Protestant denomina-
      tions treated collectively. Works on Protestant
      church buildings are entered under **Church**
      buildings.
  UF Denominations, Protestant
      Protestant denominations

Protestant churches—*Continued*
  SA   names of Protestant churches,
       e.g. **Presbyterian Church** [to
       be added as needed]
  BT   **Christian sects**
       Church history
       Protestantism
Protestant denominations
  USE   **Protestant churches**
Protestant Episcopal Church in the U.S.A.
  USE   **Episcopal Church**
Protestant Reformation
  USE   **Reformation**
Protestant work ethic
  USE   **Work ethic**
Protestantism (May subdiv. geog.)   **280**
  BT   **Christianity**
       Church history
  NT   **Pentecostal churches**
       Protestant churches
  RT   **Reformation**
Protests, demonstrations, etc.
  USE   **Demonstrations**
Protons   539.7
  UF   Hydrogen nucleus
  BT   **Atoms**
       Particles (Nuclear physics)
Protoplasm   571.6
  BT   **Biology**
       Life (Biology)
  RT   **Cells**
       Embryology
Protozoa   579.4
  BT   **Microorganisms**
Proverbs   398.9
  UF   Adages
       Maxims
       Sayings
  BT   **Folklore**
       Quotations
  RT   **Epigrams**
Providence and government of God
       214; 231; 291.2
  UF   God—Providence and govern-
       ment
       God—Sovereignty
  BT   **God**
Provincialism
  USE   **Regionalism**

Provincialisms
  USE   names of languages with the
       subdivision *Provincialisms,*
       e.g. **English language—Pro-**
       vincialisms [to be added as
       needed]
Pruning   631.5
  BT   **Forests and forestry**
       Fruit culture
       Gardening
       Trees
Pseudonyms   929.4
  UF   Anonyms
       Fictitious names
       Pen names
  BT   **Names**
       Personal names
Psi (Parapsychology)
  USE   **Parapsychology**
Psychiatric care
  USE   **Mental health services**
Psychiatric hospitals (May subdiv. geog.)
       362.2
  UF   Mental hospitals
  BT   **Hospitals**
  RT   **Mentally ill—Institutional care**
Psychiatric services
  USE   **Mental health services**
Psychiatrists (May subdiv. geog.)   **920;**
       926
  UF   Psychopathologists
  BT   **Psychologists**
Psychiatry (May subdiv. geog.)   **616.89**
       Use for materials on clinical aspects of
       mental disorders, including therapy. Popular
       materials and materials on regional or social
       aspects of mental disorders are entered under
       Mental illness. Systematic descriptions of
       mental disorders are entered under **Abnormal**
       psychology.
  BT   **Medicine**
  NT   **Adolescent psychiatry**
       Child psychiatry
       Psychotherapy
  RT   **Abnormal psychology**
       Mental health
       Mental illness
Psychic healing
  USE   **Mental healing**
Psychic phenomena
  USE   **Parapsychology**
Psychical research
  USE   **Parapsychology**

Psychoactive drugs
USE **Psychotropic drugs**
Psychoanalysis (May subdiv. geog.)
150.19; 616.89
BT **Psychology**
NT **Psychosomatic medicine**
RT **Abnormal psychology**
Hypnotism
Mind and body
Subconsciousness
Psychogenetics
USE **Behavior genetics**
Psychokinesis   133.8
UF Telekinesis
BT **Parapsychology**
Spiritualism
Psychological aspects
USE subjects with the subdivision
Psychological aspects, e.g.
Drugs—Psychological aspects; World War, 1939-1945—Psychological aspects;
etc. [to be added as needed]
Psychological stress
USE **Stress (Psychology)**
Psychological tests   150.28
UF Mental tests
BT **Psychology**
NT **Ability—Testing**
RT **Educational tests and measurements**
Psychological warfare   355.3
Use for materials on methods used to undermine the morale of the civilian population and the military forces of an enemy country.
UF War of nerves
SA names of wars with the subdivision *Psychological aspects* [to be added as needed]
BT **Applied psychology**
Military art and science
Morale
Propaganda
War
NT **Brainwashing**
World War, 1939-1945—Psychological aspects
Psychologists (May subdiv. geog.)
150.92; 920
NT **Psychiatrists**
School psychologists
RT **Psychology**

Psychology (May subdiv. geog.)   **150**
UF Mind
SA religions, theological topics, titles of individual sacred works, types of animals, classes of persons, ethnic groups, and names of individual persons, including individual literary authors, with the subdivision *Psychology,* e.g. **Christianity—Psychology; Women—Psychology; Native Americans—Psychology;** etc.; and subjects with the subdivision *Psychological aspects* for materials on the relationship of particular situations, conditions, activities, environments, or objects to the mental condition or personality of the individual, e.g. **Color—Psychological aspects** [to be added as needed]
BT **Brain**
Philosophy
Soul
NT **Adjustment (Psychology)**
Adolescent psychology
Aggressiveness (Psychology)
Apperception
Applied psychology
Assertiveness (Psychology)
Attention
Attitude (Psychology)
Behavior genetics
Behaviorism
Bible—Psychology
Child psychology
Choice (Psychology)
Color—Psychological aspects
Consciousness
Criminal psychology
Dogs—Psychology
Educational psychology
Emotions
Ethnopsychology
Genius
Gestalt psychology
Habit
Human behavior
Identity (Psychology)

Psychology—*Continued*
        Ideology
        Imagination
        Individuality
        Instinct
        Intellect
        Intuition
        Memory
        Men—Psychology
        Motivation (Psychology)
        Multiple personality
        Music—Psychological aspects
        Number concept
        Parapsychology
        Perception
        Personality
        Phrenology
        Physiognomy
        Political psychology
        Problem solving
        Psychoanalysis
        Psychological tests
        Psychology of religion
        Psychophysiology
        Reasoning
        Self-acceptance
        Self-consciousness
        Self-control
        Self-esteem
        Self-perception
        Self-realization
        Senses and sensation
        Sex (Psychology)
        Social psychology
        Stress (Psychology)
        Subconsciousness
        Temperament
        Thought and thinking
        Values
        Women—Psychology
  RT Mental health
        Psychologists
Psychology and religion
  USE **Psychology of religion**
Psychology, Applied
  USE **Applied psychology**
Psychology, Comparative
  USE **Comparative psychology**
Psychology—Computer simulation   150
  BT **Computer simulation**
Psychology of color
  USE **Color—Psychological aspects**

Psychology of learning   153.1
  UF Learning, Psychology of
  BT **Animal intelligence**
        Child psychology
        Education
        Educational psychology
        Memory
  NT **Behavior modification**
        Biofeedback training
        Brainwashing
        Concept learning
        Feedback (Psychology)
        Learning disabilities
        Reading comprehension
        Verbal learning
Psychology of music
  USE **Music—Psychological aspects**
Psychology of religion   200.1
  UF Psychology and religion
        Psychology, Religious
        Religion and psychology
        Religion—Psychological aspects
        Religious psychology
  SA religious topics, titles of individ-
        ual sacred works, and names
        of religions with the subdivi-
        sion *Psychology* [to be added
        as needed]
  BT **Psychology**
        Religion
  NT **Christianity—Psychology**
        Faith—Psychology
        Pastoral psychology
Psychology, Pastoral
  USE **Pastoral psychology**
Psychology, Pathological
  USE **Abnormal psychology**
Psychology, Religious
  USE **Pastoral psychology**
        Psychology of religion
Psychology, Structural
  USE **Gestalt psychology**
Psychopathologists
  USE **Psychiatrists**
Psychopathology
  USE **Abnormal psychology**
Psychopathy
  USE **Abnormal psychology**
Psychopharmaceuticals
  USE **Psychotropic drugs**

Psychophysics

USE **Psychophysiology**

Psychophysiology 152

Use for materials on the relationship between psychological and physiological processes.

UF   Behavioral psychology
      Physiological psychology
      Psychophysics

BT   **Nervous system**
      Physiology
      Psychology

NT   **Behaviorism**
      Color sense
      Emotions
      Human engineering
      Hypnotism
      Left- and right-handedness
      Memory
      Optical illusions
      Pain
      Senses and sensation
      Sleep
      Temperament

RT   **Mind and body**

Psychoses

USE **Mental illness**

Psychosomatic medicine 616.08

UF   Medicine, Psychosomatic

BT   **Abnormal psychology**
      Medicine
      Mind and body
      Neuroses
      Psychoanalysis

Psychotherapy (May subdiv. geog.)
      616.89

UF   Therapy, Psychological

BT   **Psychiatry**
      Therapeutics

NT   **Biofeedback training**
      Family therapy
      Sex therapy
      Transactional analysis

RT   **Mental healing**
      Suggestive therapeutics

Psychotic children

USE **Emotionally disturbed children**

Psychotics

USE **Mentally ill**

Psychotropic drugs 615

Use for general materials on the group of drugs that act on the central nervous system

to affect behavior, mental activity, or perception, including the antipsychotic drugs, antidepressants, hallucinogenic agents, and tranquilizers.

UF   Psychoactive drugs
      Psychopharmaceuticals

SA   types of drugs and names of individual drugs [to be added as needed]

BT   **Drugs**

NT   **Hallucinogens**
      Narcotics
      Stimulants

PTAs

USE **Parent-teacher associations**

Public accommodations, Discrimination in

USE **Discrimination in public accommodations**

Public administration 351

Use for general materials on the conduct of public business not limited to a specific place.

UF   Administration

SA   names of countries, states, cities, etc., with the subdivision *Politics and government,* e.g. **United States—Politics and government** [to be added as needed

BT   **Local government**
      Municipal government
      Political science

NT   **Administrative agencies**
      Bureaucracy
      Civil service
      Intelligence service
      Licenses
      Military government
      United States—Politics and government

RT   **Administrative law**
      Public officers

Public assistance

USE **Public welfare**

Public buildings (May subdiv. geog.)
      352.5; 725

Use for materials on buildings owned by the public and maintained at public expense, such as government office buildings, public libraries, public schools, etc. Materials on buildings that are privately owned and maintained and are open to the public for business or entertainment are entered under **Buildings** or under the specific type of building.

Public buildings—*Continued*
 UF Government buildings
 SA names of individual public
  buildings [to be added as
  needed]
 BT **Buildings**
  Public works
 NT **Capitols**
Public buildings, American
 USE **Public buildings—United States**
Public buildings—Chicago (Ill.)
 725.09773
 UF Chicago (Ill.)—Public buildings
Public buildings—Ohio 725.09771
 UF Ohio—Public buildings
Public buildings—United States 352.5;
 725.0973
  Use for materials on U.S. federal govern-
  ment buildings located in or outside of the
  United States, including materials on U.S em-
  bassy or consulate buildings abroad.
 UF Public buildings, American
  United States—Government
   buildings
  United States—Public buildings
Public debts (May subdiv. geog.) **336.3**
  Use for materials on government debts.
 UF Debts, Public
  Federal debt
  Government debts
  National debts
 SA names of wars with the subdivi-
  sion *Finance*, e.g. **World**
  War, 1939-1945—Finance [to
  be added as needed]
 BT **Debt**
  Loans
  Public finance
 RT **Bonds**
  Deficit financing
Public debts—United States 336.3
 UF United States—Public debts
Public demonstrations
 USE **Demonstrations**
Public documents
 USE **Government publications**
Public domain
 USE **Public lands**
Public domain software
 USE **Free computer software**
Public enterprises
 USE **Government business enter-**
  prises

Public figures
 USE **Celebrities**
Public finance (May subdiv. geog.) **336**
  Use for materials on the raising and expen-
  diture of funds in the public sector.
 UF Finance, Public
 BT **Finance**
 NT **Budget**
  Deficit financing
  Federal aid
  Fiscal policy
  Government aid
  Government lending
  Grants-in-aid
  Metropolitan finance
  Municipal finance
  Public debts
  Tariff
  Taxation
Public health (May subdiv. geog.)
 362.1; 614
 UF Hygiene, Social
  Public hygiene
  Social hygiene
 BT **Health**
  Human services
  Social problems
  State medicine
 NT **Burial**
  Cemeteries
  Communicable diseases
  Community health services
  Cremation
  Disinfection and disinfectants
  Environmental health
  Epidemics
  Food adulteration and inspec-
   tion
  Health boards
  Hospitals
  Immunization
  Meat inspection
  Medical care
  Medical charities
  Milk supply
  Noise
  Occupational health and safety
  Pollution
  Refuse and refuse disposal
  School hygiene
  Sewage disposal
  Social medicine

Public health—*Continued*
  Street cleaning
  Vaccination
  Water pollution
 RT **Sanitation**
Public health boards
 USE **Health boards**
Public health—Evaluation 362.1
 UF Health program evaluation
Public health—United States
  362.10973; 614
 UF United States—Public health
Public housing (May subdiv. geog.)
  363.5
 UF Government housing
  Housing projects, Government
  Low income housing
 BT **Housing**
Public hygiene
 USE **Public health**
Public interest (May subdiv. geog.)
  172; 320.01; 344
 UF National interest
 BT **State, The**
 NT **Ombudsman**
  Whistle blowing
Public lands (May subdiv. geog.) 333.1
 UF Crown lands
  Public domain
 BT **Colonization**
  Land use
 NT **Forest reserves**
  National parks and reserves
 RT **Natural resources**
Public lands—Ohio 333.109771
 UF Ohio—Public lands
Public lands—United States 333.10973
 UF United States—Public lands
Public libraries (May subdiv. geog.)
  027.4
 UF County libraries *[Former heading]*
 BT **Libraries**
 NT **Regional libraries**
Public meetings 302.3
 UF Meetings, Public
 BT **Freedom of assembly**
 NT **Demonstrations**
  Parliamentary practice

Public officers 320
 Use for general materials on elected government officials not limited to a particular jurisdiction.
 UF Elected officials
  Government officials
  Officials and employees
  Public officials
 SA names of countries, states, cities, etc., with the subdivision *Officials and employees* [to be added as needed]
 NT **Term limits (Public office)**
 RT **Civil service**
  Public administration
Public officials
 USE **Public officers**
Public opinion (May subdiv. geog.)
  303.3
 UF Opinion, Public
 SA subjects with the subdivision *Public opinion,* e.g. **World War, 1939-1945—Public opinion;** and names of countries with the subdivision *Foreign opinion* for materials dealing with foreign public opinion about the country, e.g. **United States—Foreign opinion** [to be added as needed]
 BT **Freedom of conscience**
  Political psychology
  Political science
  Social psychology
 NT **Propaganda**
  Public opinion polls
  Publicity
  United States—Foreign opinion
  World War, 1939-1945—Public opinion
 RT **Attitude (Psychology)**
  Press
  Public relations
Public opinion polls 303.3
 Use for general materials and for materials on the technique of polling public opinion. Materials on polls on a specific topic are entered under the appropriate heading for the topic with the subdivision *Public opinion.* Materials on polls taken in a specific place are entered **Public opinion** subdivided geographically. Materials on polls limited to a specific class of persons are entered under the appro-

Public opinion polls—*Continued*
priate heading for the class of persons with
the subdivision *Attitudes.*

    UF   Opinion polls
           Polls
           Straw votes
    BT   **Public opinion**
    RT   **Market surveys**

Public ownership
    USE **Government ownership**
           Municipal ownership

Public playgrounds
    USE **Playgrounds**

Public procurement
    USE **Government purchasing**

Public purchasing
    USE **Government purchasing**

Public records—Preservation
    USE **Archives**

Public relations (May subdiv. geog.)
    659.2

    SA   topics with the subdivision *Pub-*
         lic relations, e.g. **Libraries—**
         Public relations [to be added
         as needed]
    NT   **Business entertaining**
           Customer relations
    RT   **Advertising**
           Public opinion
           Publicity

Public relations—Libraries
    USE **Libraries—Public relations**

Public safety, Crimes against
    USE **Offenses against public safety**

Public schools (May subdiv. geog.)
    371.01

Use for materials on preschool, elementary,
and secondary schools supported by state and
local government. Materials on British endowed secondary schools that are open to
public admission but are not financed or administered by any government body are entered under **English public schools.**

    BT   **Schools**
    NT   **Evening and continuation**
           schools
           High schools
           Junior high schools
           Magnet schools
           Religion in the public schools
           Rural schools
           Summer schools

Public schools and religion
    USE **Religion in the public schools**

Public schools, Endowed (Great Britain)
    USE **English public schools**

Public schools, English
    USE **English public schools**

Public schools—United States
    371.010973

    UF   United States—Public schools

Public service commissions (May subdiv.
    geog.) **354.72**

Use for materials on bodies appointed to
regulate or control public utilities.

    UF   Public utility commissions
    BT   **Corporation law**
           Corporations
           Industrial policy

Public service corporations
    USE **Public utilities**

Public shelters
    USE **Air raid shelters**

Public speaking **808.5**

Use for materials on the art of delivering
speeches. Collections of speeches on several
subjects and materials about speeches that
have already been delivered are entered under
Speeches. Materials limited to scholarly lectures are entered under **Lectures and lecturing.**

    UF   Elocution
           Oratory
           Persuasion (Rhetoric)
           Speaking
    BT   **Communication**
    NT   **Acting**
           Book talks
           Chalk talks
           Debates and debating
           Lectures and lecturing
           Preaching
           Voice culture
    RT   **Speeches**
           Voice

Public television (May subdiv. geog.)
    384.55

    UF   Educational television
    BT   **Television broadcasting**

Public transit
    USE **Local transit**

Public utilities (May subdiv. geog.)
    343.09; 354.72; 363.6

    UF   Public service corporations
           Utilities, Public
    NT   **Electric utilities**
           Gas companies
           Telegraph

Public utilities—*Continued*
    Telephone
    Water supply
Public utility commissions
    USE **Public service commissions**
Public welfare (May subdiv. geog.)
    361.6

Use for materials on tax-supported welfare activities. Materials on privately supported welfare activities are entered under **Charities.** Materials on the methods employed in welfare work, public or private, are entered under **Social work.** General materials on the various policies, programs, services, and facilities to meet basic human needs, such as health, education, and welfare, are entered under **Human services.**

    UF Poor relief
          Public assistance
          Relief, Public
          Social welfare
          Welfare, Public
          Welfare reform
    BT **Human services**
          Social work
    NT **Child welfare**
          Disaster relief
          Food relief
          Institutional care
          Legal aid
          National service
          Poor
          Social medicine
          Volunteer work
          Welfare state
    RT **Charities**
          Poverty
Public works (May subdiv. geog.)
    352.7; 363
    BT **Civil engineering**
          Domestic economic assistance
    NT **Municipal engineering**
          Public buildings
    RT **City planning**
Public works—Chicago (Ill.)   **363.09773**
    UF Chicago (Ill.)—Public works
Public works—Ohio   **352.7; 363.09771**
    UF Ohio—Public works
Public works—United States   **352.7; 363.0973**
    UF United States—Public works
Public worship   **264; 291.3**

May be subdivided by religion or sect.

    UF Church attendance
    BT **Worship**
Publicity   **659**
    BT **Public opinion**
    NT **Press**
    RT **Advertising**
          Propaganda
          Public relations
Publishers and authors
    USE **Authors and publishers**
Publishers and publishing (May subdiv. geog.)   **070.5**
    UF Book trade
          Publishing
    SA types of literature, types of published materials, and names of individual corporate bodies and religious denominations with the subdivision *Publishing,* e.g. **Music—Publishing** [to be added as needed]
    NT **Authors and publishers**
          Editing
          Electronic publishing
          Music—Publishing
          Printing
          Publishers' catalogs
          Publishers' standard book numbers
          Serial publications
    RT **Book industry**
          Books
          Booksellers and bookselling
Publishers and publishing—Exhibitions
    USE **Books—Exhibitions**
Publishers' catalogs   **015**

Use for catalogs produced by publishers and for materials about such catalogs. Retail book catalogs and book auction catalogs and materials about such catalogs are entered under **Booksellers' catalogs.**

    UF Books—Catalogs
          Catalogs
          Catalogs, Publishers'
    BT **Publishers and publishing**
Publishers' standard book numbers
    070.5
    UF Book numbers, Publishers' standard
          Standard book numbers
    BT **Publishers and publishing**
    NT **International Standard Book Numbers**

Publishing
    USE **Publishers and publishing**
        and types of literature, types of
        published materials, and
        names of individual corporate
        bodies and religious denomi-
        nations with the subdivision
        Publishing, e.g. **Music—Pub-
        lishing** [to be added as need-
        ed]

Pubs
    USE **Bars**

Pugilism
    USE **Boxing**

Pulmonary resuscitation
    USE **Artificial respiration**

Pulsars 523.8
    UF Pulsating radio sources
    BT **Astronomy**

Pulsating radio sources
    USE **Pulsars**

Pumping machinery 621.6
    UF Pumps
    SA types of pumping machinery,
        e.g. **Heat pumps** [to be add-
        ed as needed]
    BT **Engines**
        Hydraulic engineering
    NT **Heat pumps**

Pumps
    USE **Pumping machinery**

Punctuality 640
    UF Lateness
        Promptness
        Tardiness
    BT **Time**
        Virtue

Punctuation 411; 421, etc.
    UF English language—Punctuation
    BT **Rhetoric**

Punishment (May subdiv. geog.) **364.6**
    UF Discipline
        Penology
    BT **Administration of criminal jus-
        tice**
        Corrections
    NT **Capital punishment**
        Correctional institutions
        Parole
        Prisons
        Probation

        Reformatories
        Torture
    RT **Crime**
        Criminal law

Punishment in schools
    USE **School discipline**

Puns 808.88; 818, etc.
    May be used for collections of puns or for
  materials about puns.
    UF Puns and punning
    BT **Wit and humor**

Puns and punning
    USE **Puns**

Puppets and puppet plays 791.5
    UF Marionettes
    SA types of puppets or puppet plays
        [to be added as needed]
    BT **Drama**
        Folk drama
        Theater
    NT **Shadow pantomimes and plays**

Puppies
    USE **Dogs**

Purchasing (May subdiv. geog.) **658.7**
    Use for general materials on buying and
  materials on buying by commercial enterprises. Materials on consumer buying are entered under **Shopping.**
    UF Buying *[Former heading]*
    SA types of products and services
        with the subdivision *Purchas-
        ing,* e.g. **Automobiles—Pur-
        chasing** [to be added as need-
        ed]
    BT **Management**
    NT **Government purchasing**
        Installment plan
        Shopping

Pure food
    USE **Food adulteration and inspec-
        tion**

Purgatory 236; 291.2
    BT **Eschatology**

Purification of water
    USE **Water purification**

Puritans (May subdiv. geog.) **285**
    BT **Christian sects**
    NT **Pilgrims (New England colo-
        nists)**
    RT **Calvinism**
        **Church of England—United
        States**
        Congregationalism

Puzzles   793.73
   BT   Amusements
   NT   Crossword puzzles
        Mathematical recreations
        Rebuses
   RT   Riddles
Pyramids (May subdiv. geog.)   722; 909
   BT   Ancient architecture
        Archeology
        Monuments
   NT   Obelisks
Quacks and quackery   615.8
   BT   Impostors and imposture
        Medicine
        Swindlers and swindling
Quakers
   USE   Society of Friends
Qualitative analysis
   USE   Analytical chemistry
Quality control   519.8; 658.5
   SA   industries, processes, and materi-
        als with the subdivision *Qual-
        ity control* [to be added as
        needed]
   BT   Reliability (Engineering)
        Sampling (Statistics)
   NT   Steel industry—Quality control
Quality of life (May subdiv. geog.)
        303.3
   Use for materials on the objective standards
   and subjective attitudes by which individuals
   and groups assess their life situations.
   UF   Life quality
   BT   Economic conditions
        Social conditions
   NT   Cost and standard of living
Quantitative analysis
   USE   Analytical chemistry
Quantity cookery
   USE   Quantity cooking
Quantity cooking   641.5
   Use for materials limited to the preparation
   and cooking of food in large quantities. Mate-
   rials on the preparation, delivery, and serving
   of ready-to-eat foods in large quantities out-
   side of the home are entered under **Food ser-
   vice.**
   UF   Cooking for large numbers
        Quantity cookery
   BT   Cooking
   RT   Food service
Quantum mechanics
   USE   Quantum theory

Quantum theory   530.12
   UF   Quantum mechanics
   BT   Dynamics
        Physics
   NT   Wave mechanics
   RT   Atomic theory
        Force and energy
        Physical chemistry
        Radiation
        Relativity (Physics)
        Thermodynamics
Quarantine
   USE   Communicable diseases
Quarks   539.7
   BT   Particles (Nuclear physics)
Quarries and quarrying (May subdiv.
        geog.)   622
   UF   Stone quarries
   BT   Economic geology
   RT   Stone
Quartz   549
   UF   Rock crystal
   BT   Crystals
        Minerals
Quasars   523.1
   UF   Quasi-stellar radio sources
   BT   Astronomy
        Radio astronomy
Quasi-stellar radio sources
   USE   Quasars
Québec (Province)   971.4
Québec (Province)—History   971.4
Québec (Province)—History—Autonomy
   and independence movements
        971.4
   UF   Québec (Province)—Separatist
        movement
        Separatist movement in Québec
        (Province)
Québec (Province)—Separatist movement
   USE   Québec (Province)—History—
        Autonomy and independence
        movements
Queens (May subdiv. geog.)   920; 929.7
   Use for materials on women monarchs as
   well as on wives or consorts of monarchs.
   UF   Royalty
        Rulers
        Sovereigns
   SA   names of queens, e.g. **Elizabeth
        II, Queen of Great Britain,
        1926- ;** ethnic groups with

Queens—*Continued*

  the subdivision *Queens,* and countries, cities, etc., with the subdivision *Kings and rulers* [to be added as needed]
  BT **Monarchy**
  RT **Courts and courtiers**
      Empresses
      Kings and rulers

Queens—Great Britain   920; 941
  UF Great Britain—Queens
  SA names of British queens, e.g.
      Elizabeth II, Queen of Great Britain, 1926- [to be added as needed]
  NT **Elizabeth II, Queen of Great Britain, 1926-**

Queries
  USE **Questions and answers**

Questions and answers   793.73
  Use for collections of informal quizzes on various subjects. Informal quizzes on a particular subject are entered under the subject with the subdivision *Miscellanea.* Materials on formal examinations are entered under **Examinations.** Examination questions on a particular subject are entered under the subject with the subdivision *Examinations,* e.g. **Music—Examinations.** Compilations of practice problems or exercises for use in the study of a topic are entered under the topic with the subdivision *Problems, exercises, etc.,* e.g. **Chemistry—Problems, exercises, etc.**
  UF Answers to questions
      Queries
      Quizzes
      Trivia
  SA subjects with the subdivision *Miscellanea,* e.g. **Medicine—Miscellanea** [to be added as needed]
  NT **Examinations**

Quick and easy cookery
  USE **Quick and easy cooking**

Quick and easy cooking   641.5
  Use for materials containing recipes or cooking techniques emphasizing economy of preparation time and the use of readily available ingredients.
  UF Convenience cooking
      Easy and quick cooking
      Quick and easy cookery
      Quick-meal cooking
      Time saving cooking
  BT **Cooking**

Quick-meal cooking
  USE **Quick and easy cooking**
Quicksilver
  USE **Mercury**
Quilt designing
  USE **Quilts—Design**

Quilting   746.46
  BT **Handicraft**
  RT **Quilts**

Quilts (May subdiv. geog.)   746.46
  UF Coverlets
      Patchwork quilts
  BT **Interior design**
  RT **Quilting**

Quilts—Design   746.46
  UF Quilt designing
  BT **Design**

Quintets   785
  BT **Chamber music**

Quislings
  USE **World War, 1939-1945—Collaborationists**

Quit-smoking programs
  USE **Smoking cessation programs**
Quizzes
  USE **Questions and answers**
Qumran texts
  USE **Dead Sea scrolls**

Quotations   080; 808.88
  UF Sayings
  SA subjects, classes of persons, ethnic groups, and names of individuals with the subdivision *Quotations* [to be added as needed]
  BT **Epigrams**
  NT **Presidents—United States—Quotations**
      Proverbs

Qur'an
  USE **Koran**

Rabbis (May subdiv. geog.)   296.6; 920
  BT **Clergy**
      Judaism

Rabbits   599.32; 636
  UF Bunnies
      Bunny rabbits
      Hares
  BT **Mammals**

Rabies 616.9; 636.089
   UF   Hydrophobia
   BT   **Communicable diseases**
Race 599.97
   BT   **Ethnology**
Race awareness (May subdiv. geog.)
   305.8
   UF   Race identity
        Racial identity
   SA   names of racial groups with the
        subdivision *Race identity* [to
        be added as needed]
   BT   **Race relations**
   NT   **African Americans—Race identity**
        Blacks—Race identity
        Racism
Race discrimination (May subdiv. geog.)
   305.8
   Use for materials on the restriction or denial of rights, privileges, or choice because of race. Materials on prejudicial attitudes about particular groups because of their race are entered under **Racism.**
   UF   Racial discrimination
   SA   types of discrimination, e.g. **Discrimination in education** [to
        be added as needed]
   BT   **Discrimination**
        Race relations
        Racism
        Social problems
Race identity
   USE **Race awareness**
        and names of racial groups
        with the subdivision *Race
        identity,* e.g. **Blacks—Race identity; African Americans—Race identity;** etc. [to
        be added as needed]
Race prejudice
   USE **Racism**
Race problems
   USE **Race relations**
Race psychology
   USE **Ethnopsychology**
Race relations 305.8
   UF   Integration, Racial
        Interracial relations
        Race problems
        Racial integration

   SA   names of countries, cities, etc.,
        with the subdivision *Race relations,* e.g. **United States—Race relations** [to be added
        as needed]
   BT   **Acculturation**
        Ethnology
        Sociology
   NT   **Chicago (Ill.)—Race relations**
        Culture conflict
        Discrimination
        Interracial adoption
        Ohio—Race relations
        Race awareness
        Race discrimination
        Racism
        School integration
        Segregation
        South Africa—Race relations
        United States—Race relations
        White supremacy movements
   RT   **Ethnic relations**
        Minorities
        Multiculturalism
        Pluralism (Social sciences)
Race relations and the church
   USE **Church and race relations**
Races of people
   USE **Ethnology**
Racial balance in schools
   USE **School integration**
        Segregation in education
Racial bias
   USE **Racism**
Racial discrimination
   USE **Race discrimination**
Racial identity
   USE **Race awareness**
Racial integration
   USE **Race relations**
Racial intermarriage
   USE **Interracial marriage**
Racing 796
   SA   types of racing [to be added as
        needed]
   BT   **Sports**
   NT   **Airplane racing**
        Automobile racing
        Bicycle racing
        Boat racing
        Horse racing

Racing—*Continued*
      Orienteering
      Soap box derbies
  RT **Running**
Racism (May subdiv. geog.)   **305.8;**
      320.5
    Use for materials on prejudicial attitudes about particular groups because of their race. Materials on the restriction or denial of rights, privileges, or choice because of race are entered under **Race discrimination.**
  UF Race prejudice
      Racial bias
  BT **Attitude (Psychology)**
      Prejudices
      Race awareness
      Race relations
  NT **Race discrimination**
      White supremacy movements
Racketeering (May subdiv. geog.)
      364.106
  UF Crime syndicates
  BT **Crime**
      Organized crime
Radar 621.3848
  BT **Navigation**
      Radio
      Remote sensing
Radar defense networks 623
  UF Defenses, Radar
  BT **Air defenses**
Radiant heating 697
  UF Panel heating
  BT **Heating**
Radiation 539.2
  BT **Optics**
      Physics
      Waves
  NT **Cosmic rays**
      Electromagnetic waves
      Gamma rays
      Infrared radiation
      Luminescence
      Radioactivity
      Radium
      Sound
      Spectrum analysis
      Ultraviolet rays
      X-rays
  RT **Light**
      Quantum theory
Radiation biology
  USE **Radiobiology**

Radiation—Physiological effect 612
  RT **Atomic bomb—Physiological**
      effect
      Nuclear medicine
Radiation—Safety measures 363.1; 612
  BT **Accidents—Prevention**
Radiation, Solar
  USE **Solar radiation**
Radiation therapy
  USE **Radiotherapy**
Radicalism (May subdiv. geog.) **320.5**
    Use for materials on extremist social and political movements of either the right or the left.
  UF Extremism (Political science)
      Political extremism
      Radicals and radicalism
  BT **Political science**
      Revolutions
      Right and left (Political science)
  NT **Militia movements**
  RT **Counter culture**
Radicals and radicalism
  USE **Radicalism**
Radio 621.384
  UF Wireless
  SA radio and other subjects, e.g.
      Radio and music; and radio in various industries or fields of endeavor, e.g. **Radio in aeronautics** [to be added as needed]
  BT **Telecommunication**
  NT **Radar**
      Radio and music
      Radio frequency modulation
      Radio in aeronautics
      Radio in astronautics
      Radio in education
      Shortwave radio
Radio addresses, debates, etc. 384.54;
      808.5; 808.85
  UF Radio lectures
  BT **Debates and debating**
      Lectures and lecturing
      Radio broadcasting
      Radio scripts
Radio advertising 659.14
  UF Commercials, Radio
      Radio commercials

Radio advertising—*Continued*
    BT   **Advertising**
          Radio broadcasting
Radio and music   780; 781.5
    UF   Music and radio
    BT   **Music**
          Radio
Radio and television novels   813, etc.
    May be used for individual works, collections, or materials about novels based on radio or television programs.
    UF   Radio novels
          Television novels
    BT   **Fiction**
    RT   **Movie novels**
Radio astronomy   522
    SA   names of celestial radio sources, e.g. **Quasars** [to be added as needed]
    BT   **Astronomy**
          Interstellar communication
    NT   **Quasars**
Radio authorship   808
    UF   Radio script writing
          Radio writing
    BT   **Authorship**
          Radio broadcasting
    NT   **Radio plays—Technique**
    RT   **Radio scripts**
Radio broadcasting (May subdiv. geog.)
    384.54
    UF   Radio industry
    SA   radio broadcasting of particular kinds of programs, e.g. **Radio broadcasting of sports** [to be added as needed]
    BT   **Broadcasting**
          Mass media
    NT   **Radio addresses, debates, etc.**
          Radio advertising
          Radio authorship
          Radio broadcasting of sports
          Radio programs
          Radio stations
Radio broadcasting of sports   070.4
    UF   Sports broadcasting
          Sports in radio
    BT   **Broadcast journalism**
          Radio broadcasting
Radio chemistry
    USE   **Radiochemistry**

Radio comedies
    USE   **Comedy radio programs**
Radio comedy programs
    USE   **Comedy radio programs**
Radio commercials
    USE   **Radio advertising**
Radio drama
    USE   **Radio plays**
Radio—Equipment and supplies
    621.384028
    NT   **Radio—Receivers and reception**
    RT   **Radio supplies industry**
Radio equipment industry
    USE   **Radio supplies industry**
Radio frequency modulation   621.384
    UF   FM radio
          Frequency modulation, Radio
    BT   **Radio**
    NT   **Shortwave radio**
Radio in aeronautics   629.135
    BT   **Aeronautics**
          Navigation (Aeronautics)
          Radio
Radio in astronautics   629.4
    UF   Lunar surface radio communication
    BT   **Astronautics—Communication systems**
          Navigation (Astronautics)
          Radio
Radio in education   371.33
    UF   Education and radio
    BT   **Audiovisual education**
          Radio
          Teaching—Aids and devices
Radio industry
    USE   **Radio broadcasting**
          Radio supplies industry
Radio journalism
    USE   **Broadcast journalism**
Radio lectures
    USE   **Radio addresses, debates, etc.**
Radio novels
    USE   **Radio and television novels**
Radio operators   621.3841
Radio plays   808.82; 812, etc.
    May be used for individual works, collections, or materials about radio plays.
    UF   Radio drama
          Scenarios

Radio plays—*Continued*
BT **Drama**
Radio programs
NT **Soap operas**
RT **Radio scripts**
Radio plays—Technique   808.2
UF Play writing
Playwriting
BT **Drama—Technique**
Radio authorship
RT **Television plays—Technique**
Radio programs   384.54
May be used for individual works, collections, or materials about radio programs.
UF Programs, Radio
SA types of programs and names of specific programs [to be added as needed]
BT **Radio broadcasting**
NT **Adventure radio programs**
Biographical radio programs
Comedy radio programs
Fantasy radio programs
Horror radio programs
Legal drama (Radio programs)
Medical drama (Radio programs)
Mystery radio programs
Radio plays
Radio serials
Science fiction radio programs
Sports drama (Radio programs)
Spy radio programs
Talk shows
Variety shows (Radio programs)
War radio programs
Westerns (Radio programs)
RT **Radio scripts**
Radio—Receivers and reception   621.384
UF Radio reception
Radios
BT **Radio—Equipment and supplies**
Radio reception
USE **Radio—Receivers and reception**
Radio—Repairing   621.384
UF Radio repairs
Radio servicing

Radio repairs
USE **Radio—Repairing**
Radio script writing
USE **Radio authorship**
Radio scripts   791.44; 808.8; 818, etc.
May be used for individual works, collections, or materials about radio scripts.
NT **Radio addresses, debates, etc.**
RT **Radio authorship**
Radio plays
Radio programs
Radio serials   791.44
May be used for individual works, collections, or materials about radio serials.
BT **Radio programs**
RT **Soap operas**
Radio servicing
USE **Radio—Repairing**
Radio stations (May subdiv. geog.)   384.54
SA names of specific radio stations [to be added as needed]
BT **Radio broadcasting**
NT **Amateur radio stations**
Radio supplies industry (May subdiv. geog.)   338.4
UF Radio equipment industry
Radio industry
BT **Industries**
RT **Radio—Equipment and supplies**
Radio waves
USE **Electric waves**
Radio writing
USE **Radio authorship**
Radioactive fallout (May subdiv. geog.)   539.7
UF Dust, Radioactive
Fallout, Radioactive
BT **Atomic bomb**
Hydrogen bomb
Radioactive pollution
Radioactive isotopes
USE **Radioisotopes**
Radioactive pollution (May subdiv. geog.)   363.17; 363.73; 621.48
UF Environmental radioactivity
Nuclear pollution
Pollution, Radioactive
BT **Pollution**
Radioactivity

Radioactive pollution—*Continued*
   NT   **Radioactive fallout**
   RT   **Radioactive waste disposal**
Radioactive substances
   USE **Radioactivity**
Radioactive waste disposal (May subdiv.
    geog.)   **363.72; 621.48**
   UF   Nuclear waste disposal
   BT   **Nuclear engineering**
         Nuclear power plants—Envi-
           ronmental aspects
         Radioactivity
         Refuse and refuse disposal
   RT   **Radioactive pollution**
Radioactivity   **539.7**
   UF   Radioactive substances
   BT   **Physics**
         Radiation
   NT   **Cosmic rays**
         Phosphorescence
         Radioactive pollution
         Radioactive waste disposal
         Radiobiology
         Radiochemistry
         Radiotherapy
         Transmutation (Chemistry)
   RT   **Nuclear physics**
         Radium
         Radon
         Uranium
Radiobiology   **571.4**
   UF   Radiation biology
   BT   **Biology**
         Biophysics
         Nuclear physics
         Radioactivity
Radiocarbon dating   **539.7**
   UF   Carbon 14 dating
         Dating, Radiocarbon
   BT   **Archeology**
Radiochemistry   **541.3**
   UF   Radio chemistry
   BT   **Physical chemistry**
         Radioactivity
Radiography
   USE **X-rays**
Radioisotopes   **621.48**
   UF   Radioactive isotopes
   BT   **Isotopes**
         Nuclear engineering

Radiologists (May subdiv. geog.)   **920**
   BT   **Physicians**
   RT   **Radiotherapy**
Radios
   USE **Radio—Receivers and recep-**
           tion
Radiotherapy   **615.8**
   UF   Radiation therapy
   BT   **Electrotherapeutics**
         Physical therapy
         Radioactivity
         Therapeutics
   RT   **Phototherapy**
         Radiologists
         Radium
         Ultraviolet rays
         X-rays
Radium   **546; 661; 669**
   BT   **Chemical elements**
         Radiation
   RT   **Radioactivity**
         Radiotherapy
Radium emanation
   USE **Radon**
Radon   **363.738; 546**
   UF   Radium emanation
   BT   **Poisonous gases**
   RT   **Radioactivity**
Railroad accidents (May subdiv. geog.)
    363.12
   UF   Collisions, Railroad
         Derailments
         Railroads—Accidents
         Train wrecks
   BT   **Accidents**
         Disasters
Railroad construction
   USE **Railroad engineering**
Railroad engineering (May subdiv. geog.)
    625.1
   UF   Railroad construction
   BT   **Civil engineering**
         Engineering
         Railroads
Railroad fares
   USE **Railroads—Rates**
Railroad mergers
   USE **Railroads—Mergers**
Railroad rates
   USE **Railroads—Rates**

Railroad workers
USE **Railroads—Employees**
Railroads (May subdiv. geog.) **385;
625.1**
UF Railways
Trains
SA names of individual railroads [to
be added as needed]
BT **Transportation**
NT **Cable railroads
Electric railroads
Express service
Freight
Locomotives
Monorail railroads
Railroad engineering
Street railroads
Subways**
Railroads—Accidents
USE **Railroad accidents**
Railroads and state
USE **Railroads—Government policy**
Railroads, Cable
USE **Cable railroads**
Railroads—Consolidation
USE **Railroads—Mergers**
Railroads—Employees (May subdiv.
geog.) **331.7**
UF Railroad workers
BT **Employees**
Railroads—Fares
USE **Railroads—Rates**
Railroads—Finance 385
BT **Finance**
NT **Railroads—Rates**
Railroads—Government ownership
USE **Railroads—Government policy**
Railroads—Government policy (May
subdiv. geog.) **354.6; 385**
UF Government ownership of rail-
roads
Government regulation of rail-
roads
Nationalization of railroads
Railroads and state
Railroads—Government owner-
ship
Railroads, Nationalization of
State and railroads
State ownership of railroads

BT **Government ownership
Industrial policy**
NT **Railroads—Rates**
Railroads—Mergers (May subdiv. geog.)
338.8
UF Railroad mergers
Railroads—Consolidation *[For-
mer heading]*
BT **Corporate mergers and acqui-
sitions**
Railroads—Models 625.1
UF Model trains
BT **Models and modelmaking**
Railroads, Nationalization of
USE **Railroads—Government policy**
Railroads—Rates (May subdiv. geog.)
385
UF Railroad fares
Railroad rates
Railroads—Fares
BT **Railroads—Finance
Railroads—Government policy**
RT **Freight**
Railroads—Safety appliances
USE **Railroads—Safety devices**
Railroads—Safety devices 625.10028
UF Railroads—Safety appliances
BT **Accidents—Prevention
Safety devices**
NT **Railroads—Signaling**
Railroads—Signaling 625.1
UF Block signal systems
Interlocking signals
BT **Railroads—Safety devices
Signals and signaling**
Railroads, Single rail
USE **Monorail railroads**
Railroads—Statistics 385
BT **Statistics**
Railways
USE **Railroads**
Rain (May subdiv. geog.) **551.57**
UF Rain and rainfall
Rainfall
BT **Precipitation (Meteorology)**
NT **Acid rain
Floods**
RT **Droughts
Forest influences
Storms**

Rain and rainfall
USE **Rain**
Rain forests (May subdiv. geog.)
577.34; 634.9

Use for materials on forests of broad-leaved, mainly evergreen trees found in moist climates in the tropics, subtropics, and some parts of the temperate zones. Materials on impenetrable thickets of second-growth vegetation replacing tropical rain forests that have been disturbed or degraded are entered under **Jungles.**

UF   Rainforests
  Tropical rain forests
BT   **Forests and forestry**
RT   **Jungles**
Rain making
USE   **Weather control**
Rainbow   551.56
BT   **Meteorology**
RT   **Refraction**
Rainfall
USE   **Rain**
Rainfall and forests
USE   **Forest influences**
Rainforests
USE   **Rain forests**
Rallies (Protest)
USE   **Demonstrations**
Ranch life (May subdiv. geog.)   **307.72;
636**
BT   **Farm life**
  Frontier and pioneer life
NT   **Cowhands**
Random sampling
USE   **Sampling (Statistics)**
Ranger project
USE   **Project Ranger**
Rank
USE   **Social classes**
Rap music   782.421649
UF   Rap songs
  Rapping (Music)
BT   **African American music**
  Popular music
Rap songs
USE   **Rap music**
Rape (May subdiv. geog.)   **362.883;
364.15**
UF   Assault, Sexual
  Sexual assault
BT   **Offenses against the person**
  Sex crimes

NT   **Date rape**
Rapid reading
USE   **Speed reading**
Rapid transit
USE   **Local transit**
Rapping (Music)
USE   **Rap music**
Rare animals (May subdiv. geog.)
591.68
SA   names of specific animals, e.g.
  Bison [to be added as needed]
BT   **Animals**
RT   **Endangered species**
  Extinct animals
  Wildlife conservation
Rare books (May subdiv. geog.)   **090**
UF   Antiquarian books
  Bibliography—Rare books
  Book rarities
BT   **Books**
Rare plants (May subdiv. geog.)   **581.68**
BT   **Plants**
RT   **Endangered species**
  Plant conservation
Rates
USE   types of services, utilities, transportation systems, etc., with the subdivision *Rates,* e.g. **Railroads—Rates** [to be added as needed]
Rating
USE   **Performance standards**
  and subjects and classes of persons with the subdivision *Rating,* e.g. **Bonds—Rating; Employees—Rating;** etc. [to be added as needed]
Ratio and proportion   513.2
BT   **Arithmetic**
  Geometry
Rationalism   149; 211
BT   **Philosophy**
  Religion
  Secularism
  Theory of knowledge
NT   **Empiricism**
  Enlightenment
  Intuition
  Positivism
  Reason

Rationalism—*Continued*

      Skepticism

RT   **Agnosticism**

      Atheism

      Belief and doubt

      Deism

      Free thought

      Realism

Rattlesnakes   597.96

BT   **Poisonous animals**

      Snakes

Raw materials (May subdiv. geog.)
    333.7

Use for works on unprocessed minerals and unprocessed animal and vegetable products. Comprehensive works on the basic processed materials used in engineering and industry are entered under **Materials.**

BT   **Commercial products**

NT   **Farm produce**

      Forest products

      Mines and mineral resources

Rayon   677

BT   **Synthetic fabrics**

Rays, Ultra-violet

  USE   **Ultraviolet rays**

Re-enlistment

  USE   **Recruiting and enlistment**

Reaction (Political science)

  USE   **Conservatism**

Reactions, Chemical

  USE   **Chemical reactions**

Reactors (Nuclear physics)

  USE   **Nuclear reactors**

Reader services (Libraries)

  USE   **Library services**

Readers

  USE   **Reading materials**

Readers and libraries

  USE   **Library services**

Readers' theater   792

Use for materials on the dramatic reading of plays before an audience.

BT   **Theater**

Readiness for mathematics

  USE   **Mathematical readiness**

Readiness for reading

  USE   **Reading readiness**

Readiness for school   372.21

UF   School readiness

BT   **Elementary education**

      Preschool education

Reading   372.4; 418

Use for materials on methods of teaching reading and for general materials on the art of reading. Materials on teaching slow readers are entered under **Reading—Remedial teaching.** Materials on the cultural or informational aspects of reading and general discussions of books are entered under **Books and reading.**

UF   Children's reading

      Reading—Study and teaching

BT   **Language arts**

NT   **Books and reading**

      Reading comprehension

      Reading disability

      Reading—Phonetic method

      Reading readiness

      Speed reading

      Word skills

Reading clinics

  USE   **Reading—Remedial teaching**

Reading comprehension   372.48

BT   **Psychology of learning**

      Reading

      Verbal learning

Reading disability   371.91

SA   types of reading disabilities, e.g.
      Dyslexia [to be added as needed]

BT   **Learning disabilities**

      Reading

NT   **Dyslexia**

Reading interests

  USE   **Books and reading**

Reading interests of children

  USE   **Children—Books and reading**

Reading interests of teenagers

  USE   **Teenagers—Books and reading**

Reading interests of young adults

  USE   **Teenagers—Books and reading**

Reading materials   372.41; 418

Use for materials in English intended to be used in teaching reading or language skills. Such materials in other languages are entered under the language with the subdivision *Reading materials.*

UF   English language—Reading materials

      Readers

SA   names of languages other than English with the subdivision *Reading materials,* e.g. **French language—Reading materials** [to be added as needed]

Reading materials—*Continued*
  BT   Children's literature
  NT   Basal readers
       Big books
       Easy reading materials
       Hornbooks
       Recitations
  RT   Books and reading
Reading—Patterning
  USE   Language arts—Patterning
Reading—Phonetic method   372.46
  UF   Letter-sound association
       Phonics
  BT   English language—Pronuncia-
       tion
       Reading
  RT   Phonetics
Reading readiness   372.41
  UF   Readiness for reading
  BT   Reading
Reading—Remedial teaching   372.43
  UF   Reading clinics
       Remedial reading
Reading—Study and teaching
  USE   Reading
Readings and recitations
  USE   Recitations
Readings (Anthologies)
  USE   Anthologies
Ready reckoners
  USE   Mathematics—Tables
Real estate (May subdiv. geog.)   333.3
    Use for materials on land and buildings
    considered as property. Materials on the buy-
    ing and selling of real property are entered
    under **Real estate business.** General materials
    on land apart from the aspect of ownership
    are entered under **Land use.**
  UF   Real property
       Realty
  BT   Land use
       Property
  NT   Farms
       Landlord and tenant
       Real estate business
       Real estate investment
  RT   Land tenure
Real estate business (May subdiv. geog.)
       333.33; 346.04
    Use for materials limited to the buying and
    selling of real property. General materials on
    land and buildings considered as property are
    entered under **Real estate.**

  BT   Business
       Real estate
  NT   Houses—Buying and selling
Real estate investment (May subdiv.
    geog.)   332.63
  UF   Investment in real estate
       Real property investment
  BT   Investments
       Real estate
       Speculation
Real estate investment—Taxation
    343.05
  BT   Taxation
Real estate timesharing
  USE   Timesharing (Real estate)
Real property
  USE   Real estate
Real property investment
  USE   Real estate investment
Real property tax—Assessment
  USE   Tax assessment
Realism   149
  BT   Philosophy
  NT   Pragmatism
  RT   Idealism
       Materialism
       Positivism
       Rationalism
Realism in art   709.03
  UF   Naturalism in art
  BT   Art
Realism in literature   809
  UF   Naturalism in literature
  BT   Literature
Reality   111
  BT   Philosophy
       Truth
  RT   Pragmatism
       Theory of knowledge
Realty
  USE   Real estate
Reapers
  USE   Harvesting machinery
Reapportionment (Election law)
  USE   Apportionment (Election law)
Reason   128; 160
  BT   Intellect
       Rationalism
  NT   Reasoning

591

Reasoning   153.4; 160
    BT   Psychology
         Reason
         Thought and thinking
    NT   Critical thinking
    RT   Intellect
         Logic
Rebellions
    USE Insurgency
         Revolutions
Rebels (Social psychology)
    USE Alienation (Social psychology)
Rebirth
    USE Reincarnation
Rebuses   793.73
    BT   Literary recreations
         Puzzles
         Riddles
Recall of products
    USE Product recall
Recall (Political science) (May subdiv.
    geog.)   324.6
    BT   Impeachments
         Representative government and
         representation
Recessions (May subdiv. geog.)   338.5
    UF   Business recessions
         Economic recessions
    SA   names of countries, states, cities,
         etc., with the subdivision *Eco-*
         nomic conditions [to be added
         as needed]
    BT   Business cycles
Recipes
    USE Cooking
Reciprocity
    USE Commercial policy
Recitations   808.85
    Use for collections of material written or
selected for oral presentation and for materials
about recitation.
    UF   Declamations
         Narrations
         Oral interpretation
         Readings and recitations
    BT   Reading materials
         School assembly programs
    NT   Choral speaking
         Monologues
         Monologues with music
Recitations with music
    USE Monologues with music

Reclamation of land (May subdiv. geog.)
    627; 631.6
    Use for general materials on reclamation,
including drainage and irrigation.
    UF   Clearing of land
         Land, Reclamation of
    BT   Agriculture
         Civil engineering
         Hydraulic engineering
         Land use
    NT   Drainage
    RT   Irrigation
Recluses
    USE Hermits
Recombinant DNA   572.8
    BT   DNA
         Genetic engineering
         Genetic recombination
Recombination, Genetic
    USE Genetic recombination
Recommendations for positions
    USE Applications for positions
Reconciliation, Sacrament of
    USE Penance
Reconnaissance, Aerial
    USE Aerial reconnaissance
Reconstruction (1865-1876)   973.8
    UF   Carpetbag rule
         United States—History—1861-
         1865, Civil War—Reconstruc-
         tion
    BT   United States—History—1865-
         1898
    RT   Ku Klux Klan
Reconstruction (1914-1939)   940.3
    UF   World War, 1914-1918—Recon-
         struction
    RT   Foreign aid
         International cooperation
         World War, 1914-1918—Eco-
         nomic aspects
Reconstruction (1939-1951) (May subdiv.
    geog. except U.S.)   940.53
    UF   Marshall Plan
         World War, 1939-1945—Recon-
         struction
    NT   World War, 1939-1945—Civil-
         ian relief
         World War, 1939-1945—Repa-
         rations
    RT   Foreign aid
         International cooperation

Reconstruction (1939-1951)—*Continued*
    World War, 1939-1945—Eco-
        nomic aspects
Reconstructive surgery
    USE **Plastic surgery**
Recorded books
    USE **Audiobooks**
Recording, Laser
    USE **Laser recording**
Recordings, Sound
    USE **Sound recordings**
Records of achievement
    USE **World records**
Records of births, etc.
    USE **Registers of births, etc.**
        Vital statistics
Records, Phonograph
    USE **Sound recordings**
Records—Preservation
    USE **Archives**
Records, Sports
    USE **Sports records**
Records, World
    USE **World records**
Recovered memories
    USE **Recovered memory**
Recovered memory   616.85
    UF Delayed memory
        Recovered memories
        Repressed memory
    BT **Memory**
    RT **False memory syndrome**
Recovering addicts   362.29; 616.86
    BT **Drug addicts**
    RT **Recovering alcoholics**
Recovering alcoholics   362.292; 616.86
    BT **Alcoholics**
    RT **Recovering addicts**
Recovery of space vehicles
    USE **Space vehicles—Recovery**
Recreation (May subdiv. geog.)   **790**
    UF Pastimes
        Relaxation
    SA classes of persons with the sub-
        division *Recreation,* e.g. **El-**
        derly—Recreation [to be
        added as needed]
    NT **Camps**
        Community centers
        Elderly—Recreation
        Games
        Hobbies

        Outdoor recreation
        Play
        Playgrounds
        Popular culture
        Resorts
        Sports
        Vacations
    RT **Amusements**
        Leisure
        Sports facilities
Recreation centers
    USE **Community centers**
        Physical fitness centers
Recreational vehicles   629.226
    UF RVs
    SA types of recreational vehicles,
        e.g. **Travel trailers and**
        campers [to be added as
        needed]
    BT **Outdoor recreation**
        Vehicles
    NT **Travel trailers and campers**
Recreations, Literary
    USE **Literary recreations**
Recreations, Mathematical
    USE **Mathematical recreations**
Recreations, Scientific
    USE **Scientific recreations**
Recruiting
    USE **Recruiting and enlistment**
        Recruiting of employees
        and types of employees and
        professions with the subdivi-
        sion *Recruiting,* e.g. **Librari-**
        ans—Recruiting; and names
        of armed forces and of armies
        and navies with the subdivi-
        sion *Recruiting, enlistment,*
        etc. [to be added as needed]
Recruiting and enlistment   355.2
    UF Armed forces—Recruiting, enlist-
        ment, etc.
        Enlistment
        Re-enlistment
        Recruiting
        Recruiting, enlistment, etc.
    SA names of armed forces and of
        armies and navies with the
        subdivision *Recruiting, enlist-*
        ment, etc., e.g. **United**
        States—Armed Forces—Re-

Recruiting and enlistment—*Continued*
cruiting, enlistment, etc.;
United States. Army—Re-
cruiting, enlistment, etc.; etc.
[to be added as needed]
BT Armed forces
Military personnel
NT Draft
United States—Armed
Forces—Recruiting, enlist-
ment, etc.
United States. Army—Recruit-
ing, enlistment, etc.
United States. Navy—Recruit-
ing, enlistment, etc.
Voluntary military service
Recruiting, enlistment, etc.
USE Recruiting and enlistment
and names of armed forces and
of armies and navies with the
subdivision *Recruiting, enlist-
ment, etc.,* e.g. United
States—Armed Forces—Re-
cruiting, enlistment, etc.;
United States. Army—Re-
cruiting, enlistment, etc.; etc.
[to be added as needed]
Recruiting of employees 658.3
UF Recruiting
SA types of employees and profes-
sions with the subdivision *Re-
cruiting,* e.g. Librarians—Re-
cruiting [to be added as
needed]
BT Personnel management
NT Employment agencies
Librarians—Recruiting
Rectors
USE Clergy
Recurrent education
USE Continuing education
Recycling (May subdiv. geog.) 628.4
UF Conversion of waste products
Recycling (Waste, etc.)
SA subjects with the subdivision
Recycling, e.g. Aluminum—
Recycling [to be added as
needed]
BT Energy conservation
Pollution control industry
Salvage

NT Aluminum—Recycling
RT Refuse and refuse disposal
Waste products
Recycling (Waste, etc.)
USE Recycling
Red 535.6; 752
BT Color
Redemption
USE Salvation
Reducing
USE Weight loss
Reference books (May subdiv. geog.)
028.7
Use for materials about reference books.
Reference books themselves are entered under
Encyclopedias and dictionaries; or under the
appropriate subjects with the subdivisions *Dic-
tionaries; Bibliography;* etc., as needed.
BT Bibliography
Books
Books and reading
NT Encyclopedias and dictionaries
Reference books—Reviews 028.1
Reference services (Libraries) (May
subdiv. geog.) 025.5
Use for materials on activities designed to
make information available to library users,
including direct personal assistance.
UF Library reference services
Online reference services
Reference work (Libraries)
BT Information services
Library services
Reference work (Libraries)
USE Reference services (Libraries)
Referendum (May subdiv. geog.) 328.2
UF Direct legislation
Initiative and referendum
Legislation, Direct
BT Constitutional law
Democracy
Elections
Refinishing furniture
USE Furniture finishing
Reflexology 615.8
BT Alternative medicine
Reforestation (May subdiv. geog.)
333.75; 634.9
BT Forests and forestry
RT Tree planting
Reform, Agrarian
USE Land reform

Reform of criminals
   USE   **Corrections**
          Probation
          Reformatories
Reform of health care delivery
   USE   **Health care reform**
Reform of medical care delivery
   USE   **Health care reform**
Reform schools
   USE   **Reformatories**
Reform, Social
   USE   **Social problems**
Reformation (May subdiv. geog.)   **270.6**
   UF   Protestant Reformation
   SA   names of religious sects, e.g.
          Huguenots [to be added as
          needed]
   BT   **Christianity**
          Church history—1500-, Modern period
   NT   **Calvinism**
          Huguenots
   RT   **Counter-Reformation**
          Protestantism
Reformatories (May subdiv. geog.)   **365**
   UF   Penal institutions
          Reform of criminals
          Reform schools
   BT   **Children—Institutional care**
          Correctional institutions
          Prisons
          Punishment
   NT   **Probation**
   RT   **Juvenile delinquency**
Reformers (May subdiv. geog.)   **920**
    Use for materials about political, social, or
religious reformers.
   NT   **Abolitionists**
          Suffragists
Refraction   **535**
   UF   Dioptrics
   BT   **Light**
          Optics
   RT   **Rainbow**
Refrigeration   **621.5**
   UF   Cooling appliances
          Freezing
          Refrigeration and refrigerating
            machinery
          Refrigerators

   BT   **Frost**
   RT   **Air conditioning**
          Cold storage
          Low temperatures
Refrigeration and refrigerating machinery
   USE   **Refrigeration**
Refrigerators
   USE   **Refrigeration**
Refugees (May subdiv. geog.)   **325; 341.4; 362.87**
   UF   Displaced persons
          Exiles
   SA   refugees of particular countries,
          geographic regions, or ethnic
          groups, e.g. **Vietnamese refugees; Arab refugees;** etc.,
          and names of wars with the
          subdivision *Refugees,* e.g.
          World War, 1939-1945—Refugees [to be added as
          needed]
   BT   **Aliens**
          Homeless persons
          Immigration and emigration
   NT   **Arab refugees**
          Political refugees
          Vietnamese refugees
   RT   **Sanctuary movement**
Refugees, Arab
   USE   **Arab refugees**
Refugees, Political
   USE   **Political refugees**
Refuse and refuse disposal (May subdiv. geog.)   **363.72; 628.4**
   UF   Disposal of refuse
          Garbage
          Garbage disposal
          Incineration
          Littering
          Solid waste disposal
          Waste disposal
   SA   types of refuse, e.g. **Industrial waste;** types of waste disposal, e.g. **Radioactive waste disposal; Sewage disposal;** etc.; and types of industries, plants, and facilities with the subdivision *Waste disposal,* e.g. **Chemical industry—Waste disposal** [to be added as needed]

Refuse and refuse disposal—*Continued*
- BT **Municipal engineering**
  Pollution control industry
  Public health
  Sanitary engineering
  Sanitation
- NT **Chemical industry—Waste disposal**
  Hazardous wastes
  Industrial waste
  Medical wastes
  Radioactive waste disposal
  Sewage disposal
- RT **Pollution**
  Recycling
  Salvage
  Street cleaning
  Waste products

Regattas
- USE **Boat racing**

Regency novels   813, etc.

    May be used for individual works, collections, or materials about historical novels set during or around the period when the future George IV of England acted as Regent for George III (1811-1820).
- BT **Historical fiction**

Regeneration (Christianity)   234; 248.2
- UF Born again Christianity
  New birth (Theology)
  Regeneration (Theology)
- BT **Christianity—Doctrines**
  Salvation
- RT **Conversion**

Regeneration (Theology)
- USE **Regeneration (Christianity)**

Regimental histories
- USE names of wars with the subdivision *Regimental histories,* e.g.
  World War, 1939-1945—Regimental histories [to be added as needed]

Regional history
- USE **Local history**

Regional libraries (May subdiv. geog.)
  027.4

    Use for materials on public libraries serving several communities, counties, or other regions.
- UF County libraries *[Former heading]*
  District libraries
  Libraries, Regional

- BT **Public libraries**

Regional planning (May subdiv. geog.)
  307.1; 711
- UF County planning
  Metropolitan planning
  State planning
- BT **Land use**
  Planning
- RT **City planning**
  Landscape protection

Regionalism (May subdiv. geog.)   **320.4; 330.9**

    Use for materials on the political or economic power or interests of geographic areas within nations or beyond national boundaries.
- UF Localism
  Provincialism
  Sectionalism
- BT **Geography**
  Politics
- RT **Nationalism**

Regionalism—United States   917.3; 973
- UF Sectionalism (United States)

Registers
- USE **Registers of births, etc.**
  and subjects, ethnic groups, classes of persons, names of countries, cities, etc., and names of families and of corporate bodies, such as colleges and universities, with the subdivision *Registers,* for lists of persons or organizations without addresses or other identifying data, e.g.
  United States—Registers; United States Military Academy—Registers; etc. [to be added as needed]

Registers of births, etc. (May subdiv. geog.)   **929**
- UF Birth records
  Births, Registers of
  Burial statistics
  Deaths, Registers of
  Marriage registers
  Parish registers
  Records of births, etc.
  Registers
  Vital records

Registers of births, etc.—*Continued*
   BT   **Genealogy**
   NT   **Wills**
   RT   **Vital statistics**
Registration of voters
   USE   **Voter registration**
Regulatory agencies
   USE   **Administrative agencies**
Rehabilitation
   USE   classes of persons with the subdivision *Rehabilitation,* e.g. **Drug addicts—Rehabilitation; Physically handicapped—Rehabilitation;** etc. [to be added as needed]
Rehabilitation peer counseling
   USE   **Peer counseling**
Reign of Terror
   USE   **France—History—1789-1799, Revolution**
Reincarnation   129
   UF   Rebirth
   BT   **Theosophy**
   RT   **Soul**
Reindeer (May subdiv. geog.)   **599.65; 636.2**
   BT   **Deer**
         Domestic animals
         Mammals
Reinforced concrete   691
   BT   **Building materials**
         Concrete
Relations among ethnic groups
   USE   **Ethnic relations**
Relations with Congress
   USE   names of presidents with the subdivision *Relations with Congress* [to be added as needed]
Relationships, Man-woman
   USE   **Man-woman relationship**
Relative humidity
   USE   **Humidity**
Relativity (Physics)   530.11
   BT   **Physics**
   RT   **Gravitation**
         Quantum theory
         Space and time
Relaxation
   USE   **Recreation**
         Rest

Reliability (Engineering)   620
   UF   Reliability of equipment
         Systems reliability
   BT   **Engineering**
         Probabilities
         Systems engineering
   NT   **Quality control**
         Structural failures
         Testing
Reliability of equipment
   USE   **Reliability (Engineering)**
Relief, Public
   USE   **Public welfare**
Religion   200
   SA   names of peoples, ethnic groups, countries, states, etc., and individual persons with the subdivision *Religion,* e.g. **Native Americans—Religion; African Americans—Religion; United States—Religion; Shakespeare, William, 1564-1616—Religion;** etc.; religious subjects subdivided by religion or sect, e.g. **Laity—Catholic Church;** and other subjects with the subdivision *Religious aspects,* e.g. **Ethnic relations—Religious aspects; Love—Religious aspects;** etc., which may be further subdivided by religion or sect [to be added as needed]
   NT   **African Americans—Religion**
         Agnosticism
         Ancestor worship
         Art and religion
         Atheism
         Blacks—Religion
         Communism and religion
         Deism
         Faith
         Liturgies
         Moon worship
         Mythology
         Native Americans—Religion
         Ohio—Religion
         Philosophy and religion
         Psychology of religion
         Rationalism
         Religion and politics

Religion—*Continued*
      Religion and science
      Religion and sociology
      Religion in literature
      Religious awakening
      Religious education
      Religious fundamentalism
      Religious institutions
      Religious life
      Sun worship
      Supernatural
      Theism
      United States—Religion
      Visions
      War—Religious aspects
      Worship
  RT God
      Religions
      Theology
Religion and art
  USE Art and religion
Religion and communism
  USE Communism and religion
Religion and education
  USE Church and education
Religion and literature
  USE Religion in literature
      Religious literature
Religion and medicine
  USE Medicine—Religious aspects
Religion and philosophy
  USE Philosophy and religion
Religion and politics (May subdiv. geog.)
      261.7; 291.1; 322
  UF Political science—Religious aspects
      Politics and religion
      Politics—Religious aspects
      Religion—Political aspects
      Religions—Political aspects
  BT Politics
      Religion
  NT Christianity and politics
Religion and psychology
  USE Psychology of religion
Religion and science (May subdiv. geog.)
      215
  UF Science and religion
      Science—Religious aspects
  BT Religion
      Science

  NT Bible and science
  RT Creationism
      Evolution
      Natural theology
Religion and social problems
  USE Church and social problems
Religion and society
  USE Religion and sociology
Religion and sociology (May subdiv.
      geog.) **306.6**
    Use for materials on religious sociology in general. Materials on the sociology of Christian denominations and on social theory from a Christian point of view are entered under **Christian sociology.** Materials on the practical treatment of social problems from the point of view of the church are entered under **Church and social problems.**
  UF Religion and society
      Religion—Social aspects
      Religious sociology
      Society and religion
      Society—Religious aspects
      Sociology and religion
      Sociology of religion
  SA sociology associated with particular religions, e.g. **Christian sociology** [to be added as needed]
  BT **Religion**
      Sociology
  NT **Christian sociology**
Religion and state
  USE Church and state
Religion and war
  USE War—Religious aspects
Religion—Government policy
  USE Church and state
Religion in literature 809
  UF Religion and literature
  BT **Literature**
      Religion
  RT **Bible in literature**
Religion in the public schools (May
      subdiv. geog.) **379.2**
    Use for materials on the teaching of religion in the public schools or on the religious freedom of students and school employees. Materials on the inclusion of prayers or a period for silent prayer or meditation in the daily schedule of public schools are entered under **Prayer in the public schools.**
  UF Bible in the schools
      Fundamentalism and education
      Public schools and religion

Religion in the public schools—*Continued*
- BT   **Church and education**
-      **Church and state**
-      **Public schools**
-      **Religious education**
- NT   **Prayer in the public schools**

Religion—Philosophy   210

Use for materials on the nature, origin, or validity of religion from a philosophical point of view. Materials on the reciprocal relationship and influence between philosophy and religion are entered under **Philosophy and religion.**
- UF   Philosophy of religion
- RT   **Philosophy and religion**

Religion—Political aspects
- USE   **Religion and politics**

Religion—Psychological aspects
- USE   **Psychology of religion**

Religion—Social aspects
- USE   **Religion and sociology**

Religion—Study and teaching
- USE   **Theology—Study and teaching**

Religions   291

Use for materials on the major world religions. Materials on independent religious groups whose teachings or practices fall within the normative bounds of the major world religions are entered under **Sects.** Materials on groups or movements whose beliefs or practices differ significantly from the traditional religions, often focused upon a charismatic leader, are entered under **Cults.**
- UF   Comparative religion
- SA   names of religions and of sects within the major world religions [to be added as needed]
- BT   **Civilization**
- NT   **Bahai Faith**
-      **Brahmanism**
-      **Buddhism**
-      **Christianity**
-      **Christianity and other religions**
-      **Confucianism**
-      **Cults**
-      **Druids and Druidism**
-      **Gnosticism**
-      **Hinduism**
-      **Islam**
-      **Judaism**
-      **Mythology**
-      **Occultism**
-      **Paganism**
-      **Sects**
-      **Shinto**

-      **Taoism**
-      **Theosophy**
-      **Voodooism**
- RT   **Gods and goddesses**
-      **Religion**

Religions—Biography
- USE   **Religious biography**

Religions—Political aspects
- USE   **Religion and politics**

Religious and ecclesiastical institutions
- USE   **Religious institutions**

Religious art (May subdiv. geog.)   **291.3; 704.9**
- UF   Religious art and symbolism *[Former heading]*
-      Religious painting
-      Religious sculpture
-      Sacred art
- BT   **Art**
- NT   **Christian art**
- RT   **Art and religion**

Religious art and symbolism
- USE   **Religious art**

Religious aspects
- USE   subjects with the subdivision *Religious aspects,* e.g. **Ethnic relations—Religious aspects; Love—Religious aspects;** etc., which may be further subdivided by the names of religions or sects [to be added as needed]

Religious awakening (May subdiv. geog.)   **269; 291.4**

Use for materials on a renewal of interest in religion.
- UF   Awakening, Religious
-      Revival (Religion)
- BT   **Religion**

Religious belief
- USE   **Faith**

Religious biography   200.92; 920
- UF   Religions—Biography
- SA   biography of particular religions, e.g. **Christian biography** [to be added as needed]
- BT   **Biography**
- NT   **Christian biography**
-      **Prophets**
-      **Saints**

Religious ceremonies
- USE   **Rites and ceremonies**

Religious cults
USE **Cults**
Religious denominations
USE **Sects**
Religious drama   792.1; 808.82; 812, etc.

May be used for collections or materials about religious drama, not for individual works.
BT **Drama**
   Religious literature
NT **Bible plays**
   Easter—Drama
   Jesus Christ—Drama
   Morality plays
   Mysteries and miracle plays
   Passion plays
Religious education (May subdiv. geog.)
   291.7

Use for materials on the instruction of religion in schools and private life. Materials limited to the instruction of Christian religion in schools and private life are entered under **Christian education.** Materials on the relation of the church to education and on the history of the part that the church has taken in secular education are entered under **Church and education.** Materials on church supported and controlled elementary and secondary schools are entered under **Church schools.**
UF Theological education
BT **Education**
   Religion
NT **Christian education**
   Religion in the public schools
   Sunday schools
RT **Moral education**
   Theology—Study and teaching
Religious festivals
USE **Religious holidays**
Religious fiction   808.83; 813, etc.

Use for individual works, collections, or materials about fiction that promotes religious teachings or exemplifies a religious way of life.
SA fiction associated with particular religions, e.g. **Christian fiction** [to be added as needed]
BT **Fiction**
NT **Christian fiction**
   Jewish religious fiction
Religious freedom
USE **Freedom of religion**

Religious fundamentalism (May subdiv. geog.)   **291**

Use for religious groups opposed to modernity and secularism and seeking a revival of orthodox or conservative beliefs and practices.
UF Fundamentalism
   Fundamentalist movements
SA fundamentalism of various religions, e.g. **Islamic fundamentalism** [to be added as needed]
BT **Religion**
NT **Christian fundamentalism**
   Islamic fundamentalism
Religious history
USE **Church history**
Religious holidays (May subdiv. geog.)
   263; 394.265

Use for materials on religious holidays in general. Materials on secular holidays are entered under **Holidays.** Materials on secular festivals other than holidays are entered under **Festivals.**
UF Church festivals
   Ecclesiastical fasts and feasts
   Fasts and feasts
   Feast days
   Holy days
   Religious festivals
SA holidays of particular religions, e.g. **Jewish holidays;** and names of specific religious holidays and observances, e.g. **Christmas; Lent;** etc. [to be added as needed]
BT **Holidays**
   Rites and ceremonies
NT **Christian holidays**
   Church year
   Jewish holidays
   Thanksgiving Day
RT **Fasting**
   Festivals
Religious institutions (May subdiv. geog.)
   260; 291.6
UF Churches
   Congregations
   Ecclesiastical institutions
   Institutions, Ecclesiastical
   Institutions, Religious
   Religious and ecclesiastical institutions
   Religious organizations

Religious institutions—*Continued*
    BT **Associations**
        Religion
Religious liberty
    USE **Freedom of religion**
Religious life   248.4; 291.4
    Use for materials that describe or promote personal or community religious and devotional life.
    SA groups and classes of persons with the subdivision *Religious life* [to be added as needed]
    BT **Religion**
    NT **Asceticism**
        Celibacy
        Christian life
        Family—Religious life
        Spiritual life
        Teenagers—Religious life
        Women—Religious life
        Youth—Religious life
    RT **Monasticism and religious orders**
Religious life (Christian)
    USE **Christian life**
Religious literature   800
    UF Religion and literature
    SA literatures of particular religions or denominations, e.g. **Catholic literature** [to be added as needed]
    BT **Literature**
    NT **Christian literature**
        Devotional literature
        Islamic literature
        Jewish literature
        Religious drama
        Religious poetry
        Sacred books
    RT **Bible as literature**
Religious music
    USE **Church music**
Religious orders
    USE **Monasticism and religious orders**
Religious orders for men
    USE **Monasticism and religious orders for men**
Religious orders for women
    USE **Monasticism and religious orders for women**

Religious organizations
    USE **Religious institutions**
Religious painting
    USE **Religious art**
Religious persecution
    USE **Persecution**
**Religious poetry   808.81; 811, etc.;
        811.008, etc.**
    May be used for collections or materials about religious poetry, not for individual works.
    BT **Poetry**
        Religious literature
    RT **Hymns**
Religious psychology
    USE **Pastoral psychology**
        Psychology of religion
Religious sculpture
    USE **Religious art**
Religious sociology
    USE **Religion and sociology**
Religious summer schools (May subdiv. geog.)   **268; 291.7**
    UF Bible classes
        Vacation church schools
        Vacation schools, Religious
    BT **Schools**
        Summer schools
Relocation
    USE ethnic groups and classes of persons with the subdivision *Relocation,* e.g. **Native Americans—Relocation;** which may be further subdivided geographically [to be added as needed]
Remarriage (May subdiv. geog.)   **306.84**
    BT **Marriage**
Remedial reading
    USE **Reading—Remedial teaching**
Remedial teaching
    USE school subjects with the subdivision *Remedial teaching,* e.g. **Reading—Remedial teaching** [to be added as needed]
Remodeling
    USE types of buildings and parts of buildings with the subdivision *Remodeling,* e.g. **Houses—Remodeling; Kitchens—Remodeling;** etc. [to be added as needed]

Remodeling (Architecture)
 USE **Houses—Remodeling**
Remodeling of houses
 USE **Houses—Remodeling**
Remodeling of kitchens
 USE **Kitchens—Remodeling**
Remote sensing (May subdiv. geog.)
 621.36
 UF Sensing, Remote
  Terrain sensing, Remote
 BT **Aerial photography**
 NT **Aerial reconnaissance**
  Radar
 RT **Space optics**
Removal of Indians
 USE **Native Americans—Relocation**
Renaissance (May subdiv. geog.) **940.2**
 Use for materials on cultural and intellectu-
 al developments in the fifteenth and sixteenth
 centuries not limited to a single country or re-
 gion.
 BT **Civilization**
 RT **Humanism**
Renaissance architecture
 USE **Architecture—15th and 16th
  centuries**
Renaissance art
 USE **Art—15th and 16th centuries**
Renaissance decoration and ornament
 USE **Decoration and ornament—
  15th and 16th centuries**
Renaissance English literature
 USE **English literature—16th and
  17th centuries**
Renaissance painting
 USE **Painting—15th and 16th centu-
  ries**
Rendezvous in space
 USE **Orbital rendezvous (Space
  flight)**
Renewable energy resources (May subdiv.
 geog.) **333.79**
 UF Alternate energy resources
  Alternative energy resources
 SA types of renewable resources [to
  be added as needed]
 BT **Energy resources**
 NT **Geothermal resources**
  Solar energy
  Water power
  Wind power

Rental services
 USE **Lease and rental services**
Reorganization of administrative agencies
 USE **Administrative agencies—Reor-
  ganization**
Repairing 620
 UF Fixing
  Maintenance and repair
  Mending
  Repairs
 SA types of things that require
  maintenance with the subdivi-
  sion *Maintenance and repair,*
  e.g. **Automobiles—Mainte-
  nance and repair; Build-
  ings—Maintenance and re-
  pair;** etc.; and types of things
  that require no maintenance
  with the subdivision *Repair-
  ing,* e.g. **Radio—Repairing**
  [to be added as needed]
Repairs
 USE **Repairing**
Reparations
 USE names of wars with the subdivi-
  sion *Reparations,* e.g. **World
  War, 1939-1945—Repara-
  tions** [to be added as needed]
Report writing 808
 UF Reports—Preparation
  Research paper writing
  Term paper writing
 BT **Authorship**
 NT **School reports**
Reporters and reporting (May subdiv.
 geog.) **070.4**
 UF Interviewing (Journalism)
  Newspaper work
 BT **Journalism**
  Newspapers
Reports—Preparation
 USE **Report writing**
Reports, Teachers'
 USE **School reports**
Representation
 USE **Representative government and
  representation**
Representation, Proportional
 USE **Proportional representation**

Representative government and represen-
tation (May subdiv. geog.)   321.8
   UF   Parliamentary government
         Representation
         Self-government
   BT   **Constitutional history**
         Constitutional law
         Political science
   NT   **Apportionment (Election law)**
         Legislative bodies
         Proportional representation
         Recall (Political science)
   RT   **Democracy**
         Elections
         Republics
         Suffrage
Representatives, House of (U.S.)
   USE **United States. Congress. House**
Repressed memory
   USE **Recovered memory**
Reprint editions
   USE **Reprints (Publications)**
Reprints (Publications)   016
   UF   Bibliography—Reprint editions
         Reprint editions
   BT   **Books**
         Editions
Reproduction   573.6; 612.6
   BT   **Biology**
         Life (Biology)
         Physiology
   NT   **Animal reproduction**
         Artificial insemination
         Breeding
         Cells
         Fertility
         Fertilization in vitro
         Fetus
         Genetics
         Human artificial insemination
         Infertility
         Menstruation
         Pregnancy
   RT   **Embryology**
         Reproductive system
         Sex (Biology)
Reproduction processes
   USE **Copying processes**
Reproduction—Technological innovations
   USE **Reproductive technology**

Reproductive behavior
   USE **Sexual behavior in animals**
Reproductive organs
   USE **Reproductive system**
Reproductive system   573.6; 611; 612.6
   UF   Generative organs
         Genitalia
         Reproductive organs
         Sex organs
   BT   **Anatomy**
         Physiology
         Sex (Biology)
   RT   **Reproduction**
Reproductive technology (May subdiv.
geog.)   612.6
   UF   Assisted reproduction
         Reproduction—Technological in-
           novations
   BT   **Biotechnology**
Reprographic art
   USE **Copy art**
Reprography
   USE **Copying processes**
Reptiles (May subdiv. geog.)   597.9
   SA   types of reptiles [to be added as
         needed]
   BT   **Animals**
   NT   **Alligators**
         Crocodiles
         Fossil reptiles
         Lizards
         Snakes
         Turtles
Reptiles, Fossil
   USE **Fossil reptiles**
Reptiles—Physiology   597.9
   BT   **Physiology**
Republic of China, 1949-
   USE **Taiwan**
Republic of South Africa
   USE **South Africa**
Republican Party (U.S.)   324.2734
   BT   **Political parties**
Republics   321.8
   UF   Commonwealth, The
   BT   **Constitutional history**
         Constitutional law
         Political science

Republics—*Continued*
  NT Federal government
  RT Democracy
      Representative government and
        representation
Rescue of Jews, 1939-1945
  USE World War, 1939-1945—
        Jews—Rescue
Rescue operations, Space
  USE Space rescue operations
Rescue work (May subdiv. geog.) 363.3
  UF Search and rescue operations
  BT Civil defense
  NT First aid
      Lifesaving
      Space rescue operations
  RT Survival after airplane acci-
        dents, shipwrecks, etc.
Research (May subdiv. geog.) 001.4
  UF Research and development
  SA subjects with the subdivision *Re-
        search* [to be added as need-
        ed]
  NT Agriculture—Research
      Animal experimentation
      Discoveries in science
      Intelligence service
      Medicine—Research
      Oceanography—Research
      Operations research
      Parapsychology
      Surveys
  RT Information services
      Learning and scholarship
Research and development
  USE Research
Research paper writing
  USE Report writing
Reservations
  USE names of native peoples, tribes,
        etc., with the subdivision *Res-
        ervations,* e.g. Native Ameri-
        cans—Reservations [to be
        added as needed]
Reservoirs (May subdiv. geog.) 627;
        628.1
  BT Hydraulic structures
Resettlement
  USE Land settlement
Residences
  USE Domestic architecture
      Houses

Residential security
  USE Burglary protection
Residential treatment centers
  USE Group homes
Resignation
  USE classes of persons and names of
        individual persons with the
        subdivision *Resignation,* e.g.
        Presidents—United States—
        Resignation [to be added as
        needed]
Resins
  USE Gums and resins
Resistance of materials
  USE Strength of materials
Resistance to government (May subdiv.
        geog.) 322.4
  UF Government, Resistance to
  BT Political ethics
      Political science
  NT Civil disobedience
      Hunger strikes
      Passive resistance
  RT Insurgency
      Revolutions
Resistance welding
  USE Electric welding
Resorts (May subdiv. geog.) 790
  BT Recreation
  NT Health resorts
      Summer resorts
      Winter resorts
Resource management
  USE Conservation of natural re-
        sources
Resources, Marine
  USE Marine resources
Respiration 573.2; 612.2
  UF Breathing
  BT Physiology
  RT Respiratory system
Respiration, Artificial
  USE Artificial respiration
Respiratory organs
  USE Respiratory system
Respiratory system 573.2; 611; 612.2
  UF Respiratory organs
  BT Anatomy
      Physiology
  NT Lungs
  RT Respiration

Respite care
USE **Home care services**
Responsibility, Legal
USE **Liability (Law)**
Rest 613.7
UF Relaxation
BT **Health**
Hygiene
NT **Sleep**
RT **Fatigue**
Restaurants (May subdiv. geog.) 647.95
UF Cafes
Coffee shops
Lunchrooms
Restaurants, bars, etc.
SA types of restaurants [to be added
as needed]
BT **Food service**
NT **Coffeehouses**
Fast food restaurants
Tearooms
RT **Bars**
Restaurants, bars, etc.
USE **Bars**
Restaurants
Restoration of automobiles
USE **Automobiles—Conservation**
and restoration
Restoration of buildings
USE **Architecture—Conservation**
and restoration
Restoration of furniture
USE **Furniture finishing**
Furniture—Repairing
Restoration of photographs
USE **Photographs—Conservation**
and restoration
Restoration of works of art
USE subjects with the subdivision
Conservation and restoration,
e.g. **Painting—Conservation**
and restoration [to be added
as needed]
Restraint of trade (May subdiv. geog.)
338.6
UF Restrictive trade practices
Trade, Restraint of
BT **Commerce**
Commercial law
RT **Boycotts**
Corporation law

Industrial trusts
Monopolies
Unfair competition
Restrictive trade practices
USE **Restraint of trade**
Résumés (Employment) 650.14; 808
UF Job résumés
BT **Applications for positions**
Job hunting
Resurrection
USE **Future life**
Resurrection of Jesus Christ
USE **Jesus Christ—Resurrection**
Resuscitation, Heart
USE **Cardiac resuscitation**
Resuscitation, Pulmonary
USE **Artificial respiration**
Retail stores
USE **Stores**
Retail trade (May subdiv. geog.) **381;**
658.8
UF Merchandising
BT **Commerce**
NT **Advertising**
Chain stores
Department stores
Direct selling
Discount stores
Drugstores
Inventory control
Packaging
Sales personnel
Selling
Shopping centers and malls
Stores
Supermarkets
Retarded children
USE **Mentally handicapped children**
Retention, Grade
USE **Promotion (School)**
Retired people
USE **Retirees**
Retired persons
USE **Retirees**
Retirees (May subdiv. geog.) **155.67;**
305.9
UF Retired people
Retired persons
RT **Elderly**
Retirement
Retirees—Personal finance 332.024

Retirement (May subdiv. geog.) **305.26;**
306.3
  BT **Leisure**
    Old age
  NT **Retirement income**
  RT **Elderly—Life skills guides**
    Retirees
Retirement communities (May subdiv.
  geog.) **307.7; 363.5**
  UF Places of retirement
  BT **Elderly—Housing**
  NT **Life care communities**
Retirement income (May subdiv. geog.)
  331.25; 353.5
  BT **Income**
    Retirement
  NT **Annuities**
    Individual retirement accounts
    Old age pensions
    Pensions
Retouching (Photography)
  USE **Photography—Retouching**
Retraining, Occupational
  USE **Occupational retraining**
Retrenchment of organizations
  USE **Downsizing of organizations**
Retribution
  USE **Future life**
    Hell
Retrieval of information
  USE **Information retrieval**
Reunions, Family
  USE **Family reunions**
Revelation **231.7; 291.2**
  BT **God**
    Supernatural
    Theology
Revenue
  USE **Tariff**
    Taxation
Revenue sharing (May subdiv. geog.)
  336.1
    Use for materials on the practice of return-
    ing a percentage of federal tax money to state
    and local governments for locally directed and
    controlled public service programs.
  UF Federal revenue sharing
    Tax sharing
  BT **Intergovernmental tax relations**
Reviewing (Books)
  USE **Book reviewing**

Reviews
  USE topics and types of books with
    the subdivision *Reviews,* e.g.
    Motion picture—Reviews;
    Reference books—Reviews;
    etc.; and topics, types of liter-
    ature, ethnic groups, classes
    of persons, and names of
    places with the subdivision
    Book reviews; e.g. **Sociolo-**
    gy—Book reviews; Chil-
    dren's literature—Book re-
    views; etc., for collections of
    reviews [to be added as need-
    ed]
Revival (Religion)
  USE **Evangelistic work**
    Religious awakening
    Revivals
Revivals (May subdiv. geog.) **269; 291.4**
  UF Revival (Religion)
  BT **Evangelistic work**
Revivals—Music
  USE **Gospel music**
Revolution, American
  USE **United States—History—1775-**
    1783, Revolution
Revolution, French
  USE **France—History—1789-1799,**
    Revolution
Revolutions (May subdiv. geog.) **303.6**
  UF Coups d'état
    Rebellions
    Sedition
  SA names of countries with the ap-
    propriate subdivision under
    History, e.g. **France—His-**
    tory—1789-1799, Revolution
    [to be added as needed]
  BT **Political science**
  NT **France—History—1789-1799,**
    Revolution
    Hungary—History—1956, Rev-
    olution
    Insurgency
    National liberation movements
    Radicalism
    Slave revolts
    Soviet Union—History—1917-
    1921, Revolution

Revolutions—*Continued*
United States—History—1775-
1783, Revolution
RT Resistance to government
Revolvers
USE Handguns
Rewards (Prizes, etc.)
USE Awards
Rh factor
USE Blood groups
Rhetoric 808
UF Composition (Rhetoric)
English language—Rhetoric
Persuasion (Rhetoric)
Speaking
SA names of languages with the
subdivision *Composition and
exercises,* e.g. **English lan-
guage—Composition and ex-
ercises** [to be added as need-
ed]
BT Language and languages
NT Criticism
Debates and debating
Lectures and lecturing
Letter writing
Preaching
Punctuation
Satire
RT English language—Composition
and exercises
Literary style
Rheumatism 616.7
BT Diseases
NT Gout
Rhyme 808.1
SA names of languages with the
subdivision *Rhyme* [to be add-
ed as needed]
BT Poetics
Versification
NT English language—Rhyme
Stories in rhyme
Rhymes
USE Limericks
Nonsense verses
Nursery rhymes
Poetry—Collections
Rhythm 808.1
BT Aesthetics
Poetics

NT Musical meter and rhythm
Versification
RT Cycles
Ribonucleic acid
USE RNA
Ribose nucleic acid
USE RNA
Ribozymes
USE Catalytic RNA
Rich (May subdiv. geog.) 305.5; 920
UF Affluent people
High income people
Rich people
Rich persons
Wealthy people
BT Social classes
NT Millionaires
Rich people
USE Rich
Rich persons
USE Rich
Riches
USE Wealth
Riddles 398.6; 793.735; 808.88; 818,
etc.
Use for collections of riddles considered as
folklore, as games, or as literary exercises, by
one or several authors, and for materials about
riddles.
UF Conundrums
Enigmas
BT Amusements
Literary recreations
NT Charades
Rebuses
RT Puzzles
Ride sharing
USE Car pools
Riding
USE Horsemanship
Rifles 683.4
UF Carbines
Guns
BT Firearms
Right and left
USE Left and right (Direction)
Right and left (Political sci-
ence)
Right- and left-handedness
USE Left- and right-handedness

Right and left (Political science)   320.5

Use for general materials on political views or attitudes, i.e. conservative, traditional, liberal, radical, etc. Materials on the physical characteristics of favoring one hand or the other are entered under **Left- and right-handedness**. Materials on left and right as indications of location or direction are entered under **Left and right (Direction)**.

- UF   Left and right
- Left (Political science)
- Right and left
- Right (Political science)
- BT   **Political parties**
- **Political science**
- NT   **Radicalism**
- RT   **Conservatism**
- **Liberalism**

Right of assembly
- USE   **Freedom of assembly**

Right of association
- USE   **Freedom of association**

Right of asylum
- USE   **Asylum**

Right of privacy (May subdiv. geog.) **323.44**
- UF   Invasion of privacy
- Privacy, Right of
- BT   **Civil rights**
- NT   **Eavesdropping**
- **Trade secrets**
- **Wiretapping**

Right (Political science)
- USE   **Conservatism**
- **Right and left (Political science)**

Right to a fair trial
- USE   **Fair trial**

Right to bear arms
- USE   **Gun control**

Right to choose movement
- USE   **Pro-choice movement**

Right to die (May subdiv. geog.)   **179.7**
- BT   **Death**
- **Medical ethics**
- **Medicine—Law and legislation**
- RT   **Euthanasia**
- **Living wills**
- **Suicide**

Right to know
- USE   **Freedom of information**

Right-to-life movement (Anti-abortion movement)
- USE   **Pro-life movement**

Right to work
- USE   **Open and closed shop**

Righteous Gentiles in the Holocaust (May subdiv. geog.)   **940.53**
- BT   **Holocaust, 1933-1945**
- **World War, 1939-1945—Jews—Rescue**

Rights, Human
- USE   **Human rights**

Rights of animals
- USE   **Animal rights**

Rights of man
- USE   **Human rights**

Rights of women
- USE   **Women's rights**

Rights, Proprietary
- USE   **Intellectual property**

Riot control (May subdiv. geog.)   **303.6**
- UF   Riots—Control
- BT   **Crowds**
- **Riots**

Riots (May subdiv. geog.)   **303.6**
- UF   Civil disorders
- Mobs
- SA   names of institutions with the subdivision *Riots;* and names of specific riots [to be added as needed]
- BT   **Crime**
- **Freedom of assembly**
- **Offenses against public safety**
- NT   **Riot control**
- RT   **Crowds**
- **Demonstrations**

Riots—Control
- USE   **Riot control**

Ripoffs
- USE   **Fraud**

Rites and ceremonies (May subdiv. geog.) **390**
- UF   Ceremonies
- Ecclesiastical rites and ceremonies
- Religious ceremonies
- Ritual
- Traditions

Rites and ceremonies—*Continued*

    SA   classes of persons and ethnic groups with the subdivision *Rites and ceremonies,* e.g. **Native Americans—Rites and ceremonies;** and names of individual religions and denominations with the subdivision *Liturgy* or *Customs and practices,* e.g. **Catholic Church—Liturgy; Judaism—Customs and practices;** etc. [to be added as needed]

    NT   **Catholic Church—Liturgy**
           Funeral rites and ceremonies
           Judaism—Customs and practices
           Liturgies
           Marriage customs and rites
           Native Americans—Rites and ceremonies
           Ordination
           Religious holidays
           Sacraments
           Secret societies
    RT   **Manners and customs**

Ritual
    USE   **Liturgies**
           Rites and ceremonies

River animals
    USE   **Stream animals**

River pollution
    USE   **Water pollution**

Rivers (May subdiv. geog.)   **551.48**

    SA   names of rivers [to be added as needed]
    BT   **Physical geography**
           Water
           Waterways
    NT   **Stream animals**
           Water power
    RT   **Floods**
           Hydraulic engineering
           Inland navigation

RNA   **572.8**
    UF   Ribonucleic acid
           Ribose nucleic acid
    BT   **Nucleic acids**
    NT   **Catalytic RNA**

Road construction
    USE   **Roads**

Road engineering
    USE   **Highway engineering**

Road maps   **912**
    UF   Roads—Maps
    SA   names of countries, areas, states, cities, etc., with the subdivision *Maps* [to be added as needed]
    BT   **Maps**
    RT   **Automobile travel—Guidebooks**

Road signs
    USE   **Signs and signboards**

Roads (May subdiv. geog.)   **388.1; 625.7**
    UF   Construction of roads
           Highway construction
           Highways
           Road construction
           Thoroughfares
    BT   **Civil engineering**
           Transportation
    NT   **Alaska Highway (Alaska and Canada)**
           Express highways
           Roadside improvement
           Street cleaning
    RT   **Highway engineering**
           Pavements
           Soil mechanics
           Streets

Roads—Maps
    USE   **Road maps**

Roadside improvement (May subdiv. geog.)   **713**
    UF   Highway beautification
    BT   **Grounds maintenance**
           Landscape architecture
           Roads

Robbers
    USE   **Thieves**

Robins   **598.8**
    BT   **Birds**

Robinsonades   **808.83; 813, etc.**
    May be used for individual works, collections, or materials about fictional works describing a character's survival without the aid of civilization, as on a desert island.
    UF   Apocalyptic fantasies
           End-of-the-world fantasies
    BT   **Adventure fiction**
           Imaginary voyages

Robotics
    USE   **Robots**

Robots 629.8

Use for general materials on robots and robotics. Materials limited to robots in industry are entered under **Industrial robots.**

UF   Automata

      Automatons

      Robotics

BT   **Machinery**

      Mechanical movements

NT   **Industrial robots**

Robots, Industrial

USE   **Industrial robots**

Rock and roll music

USE   **Rock music**

Rock climbing

USE   **Mountaineering**

Rock crystal

USE   **Quartz**

Rock drawings

USE   **Rock drawings, paintings, and engravings**

Rock drawings, paintings, and engravings (May subdiv. geog.)   **759.01**

UF   Petroglyphs

      Rock drawings

      Rock engravings

      Rock paintings

BT   **Archeology**

      Prehistoric art

NT   **Cave drawings and paintings**

Rock engravings

USE   **Rock drawings, paintings, and engravings**

Rock gardens (May subdiv. geog.)   **635.9**

BT   **Gardens**

Rock music (May subdiv. geog.)   **781.66; 782.42166**

UF   Rock and roll music

BT   **Music**

      Popular music

Rock paintings

USE   **Rock drawings, paintings, and engravings**

Rock tombs

USE   **Tombs**

Rocket airplanes

USE   **Rocket planes**

Rocket flight

USE   **Space flight**

Rocket planes   **629.133**

UF   Airplanes, Rocket propelled

      Rocket airplanes

SA   names of rocket planes, e.g. **X-15 (Rocket aircraft)** [to be added as needed]

BT   **High speed aeronautics**

      Space vehicles

NT   **X-15 (Rocket aircraft)**

Rocketry   **621.43**

BT   **Aeronautics**

      Astronautics

NT   **Guided missiles**

      Rockets (Aeronautics)

      Space vehicles

Rockets (Aeronautics)   **629.133**

UF   Aerial rockets

SA   types of rockets and missiles and names of specific rockets and missiles [to be added as needed]

BT   **Aeronautics**

      High speed aeronautics

      Projectiles

      Rocketry

NT   **Artificial satellites—Launching**

      Ballistic missiles

      Guided missiles

RT   **Interplanetary voyages**

      Jet propulsion

Rocks (May subdiv. geog.)   **552**

Use for general materials on naturally occurring solid minerals. Materials on stone as a building material are entered under **Stone.**

SA   varieties of rock, e.g. **Granite** [to be added as needed]

NT   **Granite**

      Marble

RT   **Geology**

      Petrology

      Stone

Rocky Mountains   **978**

BT   **Mountains**

Rodeos (May subdiv. geog.)   **791.8**

BT   **Sports**

RT   **Cowhands**

      Horsemanship

Roentgen rays

USE   **X-rays**

Rogues and vagabonds—Fiction

USE   **Picaresque literature**

Roland (Legendary character)   398.22
UF   Orlando (Legendary character)
BT   **Folklore**
Roland (Legendary character)—Romances   821, etc.
Role conflict   302.5
Use for materials on the conflict within one person who is being called upon to fulfill two or more competing roles.
BT   **Social conflict**
Social role
Role playing   302
BT   **Social role**
Role, Social
USE   **Social role**
Roller skating   796.2
UF   Skating
BT   **Outdoor recreation**
NT   **In-line skating**
Rollerblading
USE   **In-line skating**
Romaic language
USE   **Modern Greek language**
Romaic literature
USE   **Modern Greek literature**
Roman antiquities
USE   **Classical antiquities**
Rome—Antiquities
Rome (Italy)—Antiquities
Roman architecture (May subdiv. geog.)   722
UF   Architecture, Roman
BT   **Ancient architecture**
Architecture
Roman art (May subdiv. geog.)   709.37
UF   Art, Roman
Classical art
BT   **Ancient art**
Art
Classical antiquities
Roman Catholic Church
USE   **Catholic Church**
Roman civilization
USE   **Rome—Civilization**
Roman emperors
USE   **Emperors—Rome**
Roman Empire
USE   **Rome**
Roman literature
USE   **Latin literature**
Roman mythology
USE   **Classical mythology**

Roman numerals   513
BT   **Numerals**
Roman philosophy
USE   **Ancient philosophy**
Romance languages   440
UF   Neo-Latin languages
SA   names of languages belonging to the Romance group, e.g. **French language** [to be added as needed]
BT   **Language and languages**
NT   **French language**
Spanish language
RT   **Latin language**
Romance literature   840
SA   names of literatures belonging to the Romance group, e.g. **French literature** [to be added as needed]
BT   **Literature**
NT   **French literature**
Portuguese literature
Spanish literature
Romance novels
USE   **Love stories**
Romances   808.8; 821, etc.; 823, etc.
May be used for individual works, collections, or materials about medieval tales dealing with the age of chivalry or the supernatural. They may be either in verse or in prose and may or may not have a basis in fact. Contemporary romance novels are entered under **Love stories** or **Romantic suspense novels.**
UF   Chivalry—Romances
Metrical romances
Stories
SA   names of historic persons and legendary characters with the subdivision *Romances,* e.g. **Roland (Legendary character)—Romances** [to be added as needed]
BT   **Fiction**
Literature
NT   **Arthurian romances**
RT   **Chivalry**
Epic poetry
Fables
Legends
Romances (Love stories)
USE   **Love stories**

Romanesque architecture (May subdiv. geog.) **723**

UF Architecture, Romanesque

BT **Architecture**

Medieval architecture

Romanesque art (May subdiv. geog.) **709.02**

UF Art, Romanesque

BT **Medieval art**

NT **Romanesque painting**

Romanesque painting (May subdiv. geog.) **759.02**

UF Painting, Romanesque

BT **Romanesque art**

Romanies

USE **Gypsies**

Romans à clef 808.83; 813, etc.

May be used for individual works, collections, or materials about novels in which fictional characters and events can be readily identified with real persons and events.

UF Livres à clef

BT **Fiction**

Romantic fiction

USE **Love stories**

Romantic stories

USE **Love stories**

Romantic suspense novels 813, etc.

May be used for individual works, collections, or materials about modern romantic suspense novels. Medieval tales are entered under **Romances.**

UF Suspense novels

BT **Adventure fiction**

RT **Gothic novels**

Love stories

Mystery fiction

Spy stories

Romanticism (May subdiv. geog.) **141; 709.03; 809**

BT **Aesthetics**

Romanticism in art 709.03

BT **Art**

Rome 937

Use for materials about the city of Rome in antiquity or about the Roman Empire. Materials on the modern city of Rome are entered under **Rome (Italy).** Materials on the ruins and remains of ancient Rome, the city and its environs, are entered under **Rome (Italy)—Antiquities.** Materials on Roman antiquities in several countries are entered under **Rome—Antiquities.** Materials on Roman antiquities limited to one modern country, city, etc., are entered under the place with the subdivision *Antiquities.*

UF Roman Empire

Rome—Antiquities 937

Use for materials on Roman antiquities in several countries. Materials on Roman antiquities limited to one modern country, city, etc., are entered under the place with the subdivision *Antiquities.* Materials on the ruins and remains of ancient Rome, the city and its environs, are entered under **Rome (Italy)—Antiquities.**

UF Roman antiquities

BT **Classical antiquities**

Rome—Biography 920.037

UF Classical biography

BT **Biography**

Rome—Civilization 937

Use for materials on the civilization of ancient Rome. Materials on both ancient Greek and Roman civilizations are entered under **Classical civilization.**

UF Roman civilization

BT **Classical civilization**

Rome—Description 913.7; 937

Use for descriptive materials on the Roman Empire including accounts by travelers of ancient times.

Rome—Geography 913.7

Use for geographic materials on ancient Rome.

UF Classical geography

BT **Ancient geography**

Historical geography

Rome—History 937

Rome (Italy) 945

Use for materials on the modern city of Rome. Materials about the city of Rome in antiquity or about the Roman Empire are entered under **Rome.**

Rome (Italy)—Antiquities 937

Use for materials on the ruins and remains of ancient Rome, the city and its environs. Materials on Roman antiquities in several countries are entered under **Rome—Antiquities.** Materials on Roman antiquities limited to one modern country, city, etc., are entered under the place with the subdivision *Antiquities.*

UF Roman antiquities

BT **Classical antiquities**

Rome (Italy)—Description 914.5

Rome (Italy)—History 945

Roofs 690; 695; 721

BT **Architecture—Details**

Buildings

Rooming houses

USE **Hotels and motels**

Roommates 643

RT **Shared housing**

Rooms   643; 645
    SA   types of rooms [to be added as
         needed]
    BT   Buildings
         Houses
    NT   Garden rooms
         Kitchens
    RT   Interior design
Root crops   633; 635
    BT   Vegetables
    RT   Feeds
Rope   623.88; 677
    NT   Cables
         Knots and splices
    RT   Hemp
Roses (May subdiv. geog.)   583; 635.9
    BT   Flowers
Rosetta stone inscription   493
    BT   Hieroglyphics
Rosin
    USE Gums and resins
Rotation of crops
    USE Crop rotation
Roughage
    USE Food—Fiber content
Round stage
    USE Arena theater
Routes of trade
    USE Trade routes
Rowing   797.1
    UF   Crew (Rowing)
         Sculling
    BT   Athletics
         Boats and boating
         Exercise
         Sports
         Water sports
Royal houses
    USE Kings and rulers
         Monarchy
Royalty
    USE Kings and rulers
         Monarchy
         Princes
         Princesses
         Queens
Rubber   678
    BT   Forest products
Rubber, Artificial
    USE Synthetic rubber

Rubber, Synthetic
    USE Synthetic rubber
Rubber tires
    USE Tires
Rug cleaning
    USE Rugs and carpets—Cleaning
Rugs
    USE Rugs and carpets
Rugs and carpets (May subdiv. geog.)
         645; 677; 746.7
    UF   Carpets [Former heading]
         Rugs [Former heading]
    BT   Decorative arts
         Interior design
    NT   Hooked rugs
         Oriental rugs
Rugs and carpets—Cleaning   677
    UF   Carpet cleaning
         Rug cleaning
Ruins
    USE Antiquities
         Excavations (Archeology)
         Extinct cities
Rule of equal time (Broadcasting)
    USE Equal time rule (Broadcasting)
Rulers
    USE Emperors
         Heads of state
         Kings and rulers
         Queens
Rules of order
    USE Parliamentary practice
Runaway adults   173; 306.88
    UF   Husbands, Runaway
         Runaway husbands
         Runaway wives
         Wives, Runaway
    BT   Desertion and nonsupport
         Missing persons
Runaway children   362.74
    BT   Children
         Homeless persons
         Missing children
Runaway husbands
    USE Runaway adults
Runaway teenagers   362.74
    BT   Homeless persons
         Missing persons
         Teenagers
Runaway wives
    USE Runaway adults

Running 796.42
  BT **Track athletics**
  NT **Jogging**
     Marathon running
     Orienteering
  RT **Racing**
Rural architecture
  USE **Farm buildings**
Rural churches (May subdiv. geog.)
  254
  UF Churches, Country
     Churches, Rural
     Country churches
  BT **Church work**
Rural comedies
  USE **Pastoral drama**
     Pastoral fiction
Rural conditions
  USE names of countries, states, etc.,
     with the subdivision *Rural
     conditions,* e.g. **United
     States—Rural conditions;
     Ohio—Rural conditions;** etc.
     [to be added as needed]
Rural credit
  USE **Agricultural credit**
Rural electrification (May subdiv. geog.)
  621.319
  BT **Electrification**
  RT **Electricity in agriculture**
Rural families
  USE **Farm family**
Rural high schools
  USE **Rural schools**
Rural life
  USE **Country life**
     Farm life
     Outdoor life
Rural poetry
  USE **Pastoral poetry**
Rural schools (May subdiv. geog.)   **371**
  UF Country schools
     District schools
     High schools, Rural
     Rural high schools
  BT **Public schools**
     Schools
Rural sociology 307.72
  Use for materials on the discipline of rural sociology and the theory of social organization in rural areas. Materials on the rural con-

ditions of particular regions, countries, cities, etc., are entered under the place with the subdivision *Rural conditions.* Descriptive, popular, and literary materials on living in the country are entered under **Country life.**
  UF Sociology, Rural
  SA names of countries, states, etc.,
     with the subdivision *Rural
     conditions* [to be added as
     needed]
  BT **Sociology**
  NT **Ohio—Rural conditions**
     **United States—Rural condi-
     tions**
     Urbanization
  RT **Country life**
     Farm family
     Farm life
     Peasantry
Rural-urban migration
  USE **Internal migration**
Russia 947
  Use for materials on Russia (including the Russian Empire) prior to 1917. Materials on the Union of Soviet Socialist Republics from its inception in 1917 until its dissolution in December 1991 are entered under **Soviet Union.** Materials on the independent republic of Russia since its establishment in December 1991 are entered under **Russia (Federation).**
  UF Russian Empire
  NT **Russians**
  RT **Russia (Federation)**
     Soviet Union
Russia (Federation) 947.086
  Use for materials on the independent republic, established in December 1991. Materials on Russia and the Russian Empire before 1917 are entered under **Russia.** Materials on the Union of Soviet Socialist Republics between 1917 and 1991 are entered under **Soviet Union.**
  NT **Russians**
  RT **Commonwealth of Independent
     States**
     Russia
     Soviet Union
Russia (Federation)—History—1991-
  947.086
Russia—History 947
  Use for materials on the history of Russia and the Russian empire before 1917.
Russia—History—1905, Revolution
  947.08
Russian Church
  USE **Russian Orthodox Church**

Russian communism
USE **Communism—Soviet Union**
Russian Empire
USE **Russia**
Russian language   491.7
May be subdivided like **English language.**
BT **Language and languages**
Russian literature   891.7
Use for materials on literature in the Russian language. Materials on several of the literatures of the Soviet Union are entered under **Soviet literature.** May use same subdivisions and names of literary forms as for **English literature.**
BT **Literature**
RT **Soviet literature**
Russian Orthodox Church (May subdiv. geog.)   **281.9**
UF **Russian Church**
BT **Christian sects**
Orthodox Eastern Church
Russian revolution
USE **Soviet Union—History—1917- 1921, Revolution**
Russian satellite countries
USE **Communist countries**
Russians (May subdiv. geog.)   **920; 947**
Use for materials on the dominant Slavic-speaking ethnic group of Russia. Materials on the citizens of the Soviet Union between 1917 and 1991, not limited to a single national or linguistic group, are entered under **Soviets (People).**
BT **Russia**
Russia (Federation)
Soviet Union
Russo-Finnish War, 1939-1940 948.9703
UF Finno-Russian War, 1939-1940
Soviet Union—History—1939-1940, War with Finland
BT **Europe—History—1918-1945**
Russo-Turkish War, 1853-1856
USE **Crimean War, 1853-1856**
Rust
USE **Corrosion and anticorrosives**
Rustless coatings
USE **Corrosion and anticorrosives**
RVs
USE **Recreational vehicles**
Sabbath   263; 296.4
UF Lord's Day
BT **Judaism**

Sabin vaccine
USE **Poliomyelitis vaccine**
Sabotage (May subdiv. geog.)   **331.89; 364.16**
UF Political violence
BT **Offenses against public safety**
Strikes
Subversive activities
Terrorism
Sacrament of Reconciliation
USE **Penance**
Sacraments   234; 265
BT **Church**
Grace (Theology)
Rites and ceremonies
NT **Anointing of the sick**
Baptism
Confirmation
Eucharist
Marriage
Ordination
Penance
Sacred art
USE **Religious art**
Sacred books   291.8
SA names of sacred books [to be added as needed]
BT **Religious literature**
NT **Bible**
Koran
Vedas
Sacred music
USE **Church music**
Sacred numbers
USE **Numerology**
Symbolism of numbers
Sacrifice   291.3
UF Burnt offering
BT **Worship**
NT **Atonement—Christianity**
Safe sex
USE **Safe sex in AIDS prevention**
Sexually transmitted diseases— Prevention
Safe sex in AIDS prevention   613.9; 616.97
Use for materials limited to safe sexual practices in the prevention of AIDS. Materials on AIDS prevention in general not limited to safe sexual practices are entered under **AIDS (Disease)—Prevention.**

Safe sex in AIDS prevention—*Continued*
  UF   Safe sex
  BT   AIDS (Disease)—Prevention
       Sexual hygiene
Safety appliances
  USE **Safety devices**
Safety devices   363.19; 620.8
  UF   Safety appliances
       Safety equipment
  SA   subjects with the subdivision
       Safety devices, e.g. **Rail-
       roads—Safety devices** [to be
       added as needed]
  NT   **Railroads—Safety devices**
  RT   **Accidents—Prevention**
Safety education (May subdiv. geog.)
       363.1; 371.7
  BT   **Accidents—Prevention**
Safety equipment
  USE **Safety devices**
Safety, Industrial
  USE **Occupational health and safety**
Safety measures
  USE **Accidents—Prevention**
       and subjects with the subdivi-
       sion *Safety measures,* e.g.
       **Aeronautics—Safety mea-
       sures** [to be added as needed]
Safety regulations (May subdiv. geog.)
       343; 363.1
  Use for collections or materials about rules
  regarding safety that have the force of law.
  SA   subjects with the subdivision
       Law and legislation or *Safety
       regulations,* e.g. **Food—Law
       and legislation; Ships—Safe-
       ty regulations;** etc. [to be
       added as needed]
  BT   **Accidents—Prevention**
       Law
  NT   **Drivers' licenses**
       Ships—Safety regulations
       Traffic regulations
Sagas   398.22; 839
  BT   **Folklore**
       Literature
       Old Norse literature
       Scandinavian literature
Sailboarding
  USE **Windsurfing**

Sailing (May subdiv. geog.)   **623.88;
       797.1**
  BT   **Ships**
       Water sports
  NT   **Windsurfing**
  RT   **Boats and boating**
       Navigation
       Yachts and yachting
Sailors (May subdiv. geog.)   **387.5092;
       623.88092; 920**
  UF   Mariners
       Naval personnel
       Navigators
       Sailors' life
       Sea life
       Seamen
  SA   names of navies, e.g. **United
       States. Navy** [to be added as
       needed]
  BT   **Military personnel**
       Naval art and science
       Navies
  NT   **Merchant marine**
       Ship pilots
  RT   **Seafaring life**
Sailors—Fiction
  USE **Sea stories**
Sailors' handbooks
  USE **United States. Navy—Hand-
       books, manuals, etc.**
Sailors' life
  USE **Sailors**
       Seafaring life
Sailors' song
  USE **Sea songs**
Sailplanes (Aeronautics)
  USE **Gliders (Aeronautics)**
**Saint Bartholomew's Day, Massacre of,
       1572   944**
  UF   St. Bartholomew's Day, Massa-
       cre of, 1572
  BT   **France—History—1328-1589,
       House of Valois**
       Huguenots
       Massacres
Saint Francis, Order of
  USE **Franciscans**
Saint Valentine's Day
  USE **Valentine's Day**

Saints (May subdiv. geog.)   **200.92; 920**
  SA saints of particular religions, e.g.
      Christian saints; and names
      of individual saints [to be
      added as needed]
  BT **Religious biography**
  NT **Christian saints**
      Mary, Blessed Virgin, Saint
  RT **Martyrs**
Salads   641.8
  BT **Cooking**
  RT **Cooking—Vegetables**
Salamanders   597.6
  BT **Amphibians**
Salaries
  USE **Salaries, wages, etc.**
Salaries, wages, etc. (May subdiv. geog.)
    331.2; 658.3

Use for materials on all forms of compensation for work performed or services rendered,
including salaries, wages, fees, commissions,
fringe benefits, and pensions.

  UF Compensation
      Employees—Salaries, wages, etc.
      Fees
      Salaries
      Wages *[Former heading]*
  SA types of professional personnel,
      types of workers, and classes
      of persons with the subdivi-
      sion *Salaries, wages, etc.,* e.g.
      Lawyers—Salaries, wages,
      etc.; Office workers—Sala-
      ries, wages, etc.; Handi-
      capped—Salaries, wages,
      etc.; industries and types of
      institutions with the subdivi-
      sions *Employees—Salaries,*
      wages, etc., e.g. **Chemical in-**
      dustry—Employees—Sala-
      ries, wages, etc.; Colleges
      and universities—Employ-
      ees—Salaries, wages, etc.;
      and countries, states, cities,
      etc., with the subdivisions *Of-*
      ficials and employees—Sala-
      ries, wages, etc., e.g. **Ohio—**
      Officials and employees—
      Salaries, wages, etc. [to be
      added as needed]

  BT **Income**
  NT **Chemical industry—Employ-**
      ees—Salaries, wages, etc.
      Colleges and universities—Em-
      ployees—Salaries, wages, etc.
      Equal pay for equal work
      Fringe benefits
      Handicapped—Salaries, wages,
      etc.
      Job analysis
      Lawyers—Salaries, wages, etc.
      Minimum wage
      Office workers—Salaries, wag-
      es, etc.
      Ohio—Officials and employ-
      ees—Salaries, wages, etc.
      Profit sharing
      Wage-price policy
  RT **Cost and standard of living**
      Prices
Sale of infants
  USE **Adoption—Corrupt practices**
Sales agents
  USE **Sales personnel**
Sales, Auction
  USE **Auctions**
Sales management   658.8
  BT **Management**
      Marketing
      Selling
Sales personnel (May subdiv. geog.)
    381.092; 658.85
  UF Clerks (Retail trade)
      Sales agents
      Salesmen
      Saleswomen
      Traveling sales personnel
  BT **Retail trade**
  NT **Peddlers and peddling**
Sales tax (May subdiv. geog.)   **336.2**
  BT **Taxation**
Salesmanship
  USE **Selling**
Salesmen
  USE **Sales personnel**
Saleswomen
  USE **Sales personnel**
Saline water
  USE **Sea water**
Saline water conversion
  USE **Sea water conversion**

Salk vaccine
USE Poliomyelitis vaccine
Salmon 597.5
BT Fishes
Saloons
USE Bars
Salt free diet
USE Salt-free diet
Salt-free diet 613.2
UF Low sodium diet
Salt free diet
BT Cooking for the sick
Diet
Diet in disease
Salt water
USE Sea water
Salt water aquariums
USE Marine aquariums
Salutations
USE Etiquette
Salvage (May subdiv. geog.) 627; 628.4
Use for materials on the recovery of equip-
ment, parts, cargo, merchandise, structures, or
waste, not limited to ships or shipwrecks.
UF Salvage (Waste, etc.)
Utilization of waste
Waste reclamation
NT Marine salvage
Recycling
Waste products as fuel
RT Refuse and refuse disposal
Salvage (Waste, etc.)
USE Salvage
Salvation 234; 291.2
UF Redemption
BT Doctrinal theology
NT Atonement—Christianity
Conversion
Faith
Grace (Theology)
Regeneration (Christianity)
Sanctification
Salvation Army 287.9
BT Christian missions
Christian sects
Salvation—Biblical teaching 234
Salvation history
USE Salvation—History of doctrines
Salvation—History of doctrines 234;
291.2
UF Salvation history
BT Doctrinal theology

Same-sex marriage (May subdiv. geog.)
306.81; 346.01
UF Gay marriage
Homosexual marriage
Lesbian marriage
BT Marriage
Samplers 746.3
BT Embroidery
Needlework
Sampling (Statistics) 519.5
UF Random sampling
BT Probabilities
Statistics
NT Quality control
Sanatoriums
USE Health resorts
Hospitals
Sanctification 234; 291.2
BT Salvation
Sanctions (International law) 341.5
UF Economic sanctions
BT Economic policy
International economic rela-
tions
International law
Sanctuary (Law)
USE Asylum
Sanctuary movement (May subdiv. geog.)
261.8
Use for materials on any network of reli-
gious congregations or churches that shelter
refugees or illegal aliens.
BT Asylum
Church and social problems
Social movements
RT Illegal aliens
Refugees
Sand dunes (May subdiv. geog.) 551.3
UF Dunes
BT Seashore
Sandwiches 641.8
BT Cooking
Sanitary affairs
USE Sanitary engineering
Sanitation
Sanitary engineering (May subdiv. geog.)
628
UF Environmental health engineering
Sanitary affairs
BT Engineering
NT Drainage
Pollution

Sanitary engineering—*Continued*
　　　　Refuse and refuse disposal
　　　　Sewerage
　　　　Soil microbiology
　　　　Street cleaning
　　RT　**Municipal engineering**
　　　　Sanitation
Sanitary landfills
　　USE　**Landfills**
Sanitation (May subdiv. geog.)　**363.72;**
　　　648
　　UF　Sanitary affairs
　　SA　subjects, types of industries, and
　　　　names of individual corporate
　　　　bodies with the subdivision
　　　　Sanitation, e.g. **Hospitals—**
　　　　Sanitation [to be added as
　　　　needed]
　　NT　**Cemeteries**
　　　　Cleaning
　　　　Cleanliness
　　　　Cremation
　　　　Disinfection and disinfectants
　　　　Hospitals—Sanitation
　　　　Household sanitation
　　　　Pollution
　　　　Refuse and refuse disposal
　　　　School hygiene
　　　　Smoke prevention
　　　　Ventilation
　　　　Water purification
　　RT　**Hygiene**
　　　　Public health
　　　　Sanitary engineering
Sanitation, Household
　　USE　**Household sanitation**
Santa Claus　**394.2663**
　　BT　**Christmas**
Saracenic art
　　USE　**Islamic art**
Sasquatch　**001.9**
　　UF　Big foot
　　　　Bigfoot
　　BT　**Monsters**
　　　　Mythical animals
SAT
　　USE　**Scholastic Aptitude Test**
Satan
　　USE　**Devil**
Satellite communication systems
　　USE　**Artificial satellites in telecom-**
　　　　munication

Satellites　**523.9**
　　UF　Moons
　　　　Natural satellites
　　　　Planetary satellites
　　　　Planets—Satellites
　　SA　names of planets with the subdi-
　　　　vision *Satellites,* e.g. **Mars**
　　　　(Planet)—Satellites [to be
　　　　added as needed]
　　BT　**Solar system**
　　NT　**Mars (Planet)—Satellites**
Satellites, Artificial
　　USE　**Artificial satellites**
Satellites—Mars
　　USE　**Mars (Planet)—Satellites**
Satire　**808.7; 808.87**
　　UF　Comic literature
　　SA　satire of particular countries, e.g.
　　　　American satire [to be added
　　　　as needed]
　　BT　**Literature**
　　　　Rhetoric
　　　　Wit and humor
　　NT　**American satire**
　　　　English satire
　　　　Invective
　　　　Parody
Satire, American
　　USE　**American satire**
Satire, English
　　USE　**English satire**
Saturn (Planet)　**523.46**
　　BT　**Planets**
Saucers, Flying
　　USE　**Unidentified flying objects**
Sauces　**641.8**
　　BT　**Cooking**
Saving and investment (May subdiv.
　　geog.)　**332.024**
　　UF　Capital accumulation
　　　　Capital formation
　　　　Economy
　　　　Investment and saving
　　　　Saving and thrift *[Former head-*
　　　　ing]
　　　　Thrift
　　BT　**Capital**
　　　　Economics
　　　　Personal finance
　　　　Wealth

Saving and investment—*Continued*
    NT   **Savings and loan associations**
    RT   **Investments**
Saving and thrift
    USE **Saving and investment**
Savings and loan associations (May
       subdiv. geog.)   **332.3**
    UF   Building and loan associations
          Loan associations
    BT   **Banks and banking**
          Cooperation
          Cooperative societies
          Investments
          Loans
          Personal loans
          Saving and investment
    RT   **Cooperative banks**
Savings banks
    USE **Banks and banking**
Saws   **621.9**
    BT   **Carpentry tools**
          Tools
Sayings
    USE **Epigrams**
          Proverbs
          Quotations
Scandinavian languages   **439**
    UF   Norse languages
    BT   **Language and languages**
    NT   **Danish language**
          Icelandic language
          Norwegian language
          Old Norse language
          Swedish language
Scandinavian literature   **839**
    UF   Norse literature
    BT   **Literature**
    NT   **Danish literature**
          Eddas
          Icelandic literature
          Norwegian literature
          Sagas
          Swedish literature
    RT   **Old Norse literature**
Scandinavians (May subdiv. geog.)   **920;**
    948
    Use for materials on the people of Scandi-
navia since the tenth century. Materials on
earlier Scandinavians are entered under **Vikings.**
    NT   **Vikings**

Scarecrows   **632**
    BT   **Plant conservation**
Scenarios
    USE **Radio plays**
          Stories, plots, etc.
          Television plays
Scene painting   **751.7**
    BT   **Painting**
          **Theaters—Stage setting and
            scenery**
Scenery
    USE **Landscape protection**
          Natural monuments
          Views
          Wilderness areas
Scenery (Stage)
    USE **Theaters—Stage setting and
            scenery**
Scepticism
    USE **Skepticism**
Scholarship
    USE **Learning and scholarship**
Scholarship funds
    USE **Scholarships**
Scholarships (May subdiv. geog.)   **371.2;**
    378.3
    UF   Bursaries
          Fellowships
          Scholarship funds
          Scholarships, fellowships, etc.
    SA   fields of study, ethnic groups,
          and classes of persons with
          the subdivision *Scholarships,*
          [to be added as needed]
    BT   **Education**
          Endowments
          Student aid
Scholarships, fellowships, etc.
    USE **Scholarships**
Scholastic achievement
    USE **Academic achievement**
Scholastic achievement tests
    USE **Achievement tests**
Scholastic Aptitude Test   **378.1**
    UF   SAT
    BT   **Colleges and universities—En-
            trance examinations**
          Examinations
School achievement tests
    USE **Achievement tests**

School administration and organization
USE **Schools—Administration**
School-age fathers
USE **Teenage fathers**
School-age mothers
USE **Teenage mothers**
School and community
USE **Community and school**
School and home
USE **Home and school**
School architecture
USE **School buildings**
School assembly programs   371.8
UF   Assembly programs, School
School entertainments
Schools—Exercises and recreations
Schools—Opening exercises
BT   **Student activities**
NT   **Commencements**
Recitations
RT   **Drama in education**
School athletics
USE **School sports**
School attendance (May subdiv. geog.)
371.2
UF   Absence from school
Absenteeism (Schools)
Attendance, School
Compulsory school attendance
BT   **Schools—Administration**
RT   **Compulsory education**
Dropouts
School boards (May subdiv. geog.)
353.8
UF   Boards of education
BT   **Schools—Administration**
School books
USE **Textbooks**
School buildings (May subdiv. geog.)
371.6; 727
UF   Buildings, School
School architecture
School houses
Schoolhouses
BT   **Buildings**
Schools
School buildings as recreation centers
USE **Community centers**

School busing
USE **Busing (School integration)**
School children—Transportation
School children (May subdiv. geog.)
155.42; 305.234
BT   **Children**
Students
School children—Food   371.7
UF   Food for school children
Meals for school children
School lunches
BT   **Children—Nutrition**
Diet
Food
School children—Medical examinations
USE **Children—Medical examinations**
School children—Transportation   371.8
UF   School busing
BT   **Transportation**
NT   **Busing (School integration)**
School choice (May subdiv. geog.)   **379.1**
Use for materials on choosing a school and on the right of parents to choose their children's school.
UF   Choice of school
Parents' choice of school
Schools—Selection
BT   **Education**
NT   **College choice**
School clubs
USE **Students—Societies**
School counseling   371.4
Use for materials on the assistance given to students by schools, colleges, or universities in understanding and coping with adjustment problems. Materials on the assistance given to students in the selection of a program of studies are entered under **Educational counseling.**
UF   Guidance counseling, School
BT   **Counseling**
RT   **Educational counseling**
School psychologists
School desegregation
USE **School integration**
School discipline   371.5
UF   Discipline of children
Punishment in schools
BT   **Schools—Administration**
Teaching
NT   **Classroom management**
Student government

621

School dropouts
USE **Dropouts**
School entertainments
USE **School assembly programs**
School excursions
USE **Field trips**
School fiction
USE **School stories**
School finance
USE **Education—Finance**
School furniture
USE **Schools—Equipment and supplies**
School grade retention
USE **Promotion (School)**
School houses
USE **School buildings**
School hygiene 371.7
BT **Children—Health and hygiene**
Health education
Hygiene
Public health
Sanitation
RT **School nurses**
School inspection
USE **School supervision**
Schools—Administration
School integration (May subdiv. geog.) **379.2**
UF Desegregated schools
Desegregation in education
Education—Integration
Integrated schools
Integration in education
Racial balance in schools
School desegregation
BT **Race relations**
NT **Busing (School integration)**
Magnet schools
RT **Segregation in education**
School journalism
USE **College and school journalism**
School libraries (May subdiv. geog.) **027.8**
BT **Instructional materials centers**
Libraries
NT **Elementary school libraries**
High school libraries
Libraries and students
RT **Libraries and schools**

School life
USE **Students**
School lunches
USE **School children—Food**
School management and organization
USE **Schools—Administration**
School media centers
USE **Instructional materials centers**
School music
USE **Music—Study and teaching**
School songbooks
Singing
School newspapers
USE **College and school journalism**
School nurses 371.7
BT **Nurses**
RT **Health education**
School hygiene
School organization
USE **Schools—Administration**
School playgrounds
USE **Playgrounds**
School plays
USE **Children's plays**
College and school drama
School prayer
USE **Prayer in the public schools**
School principals
USE **School superintendents and principals**
School promotion
USE **Promotion (School)**
School prose
USE **Children's writings**
School psychologists (May subdiv. geog.) **371.7**
BT **Psychologists**
RT **School counseling**
School readiness
USE **Readiness for school**
School reports 371.2
UF Educational reports
Reports, Teachers'
Teachers' reports
BT **Report writing**
RT **Grading and marking (Education)**
School shops 373.2
UF Industrial arts shops
BT **Technical education**

School songbooks   782.42
   UF   School music
   BT   **Songbooks**
          Songs
   NT   **Children's songs**
School sports (May subdiv. geog.)   371.8
   UF   Interscholastic sports
          School athletics
   BT   **Sports**
          Student activities
   RT   **College sports**
School stories   808.83; 813, etc.

   May be used for individual works, collections, or materials about school stories.

   UF   School fiction
          Schools—Fiction
   BT   **Fiction**
School superintendents and principals
      (May subdiv. geog.)   371.2
   UF   School principals
          Superintendents of schools
   BT   **Schools—Administration**
   RT   **School supervision**
School supervision   371.2

   Use for materials on the supervision of instruction. Materials on the management and organization of schools and on the administrative duties of educators are entered under **Schools—Administration.**

   UF   Inspection of schools
          Instructional supervision
          School inspection
          Supervision of schools
   BT   **Schools—Administration**
          Teaching
   RT   **School superintendents and principals**
School surveys
   USE   **Educational surveys**
School taxes
   USE   **Education—Finance**
School teaching
   USE   **Teaching**
School trips
   USE   **Field trips**
School verse
   USE   **Children's writings**
School violence (May subdiv. geog.)
      371.7
   UF   Student violence
          Violence in schools
   BT   **Juvenile delinquency**
          Violence

School yearbooks   371.8
   UF   Annuals
          College yearbooks
          High school yearbooks
          Student yearbooks
          Yearbooks
   BT   **Serial publications**
Schoolhouses
   USE   **School buildings**
Schools (May subdiv. geog.)   371
   SA   types of schools, e.g. **Church schools; Rural schools;** etc.; names of individual schools; and subjects with the subdivision *Study and teaching,* e.g. **Science—Study and teaching** [to be added as needed]
   NT   **Business schools**
          Charter schools
          Church schools
          Colleges and universities
          Correspondence schools and courses
          Elementary schools
          Evening and continuation schools
          Experimental schools
          High schools
          Junior high schools
          Kindergarten
          Libraries and schools
          Magnet schools
          Middle schools
          Museums and schools
          Nongraded schools
          Nursery schools
          Private schools
          Public schools
          Religious summer schools
          Rural schools
          School buildings
          Single-sex schools
          Summer schools
          Urban schools
   RT   **Education**
Schools—Accreditation (May subdiv. geog.)   379.1
   UF   Accreditation (Education) *[Former heading]*
          Educational accreditation

Schools—Accreditation—*Continued*

  SA types of educational institutions and names of individual institutions with the subdivision *Accreditation,* e.g. **Colleges and universities—Accreditation;** and subjects with the subdivision *Study and teaching,* for accreditation of programs of study in those subjects, e.g. **Mathematics—Study and teaching** [to be added as needed]

Schools—Administration (May subdiv. geog.) **371.2**

Use for materials on the management and organization of schools and on the administrative duties of educators. Materials on the supervision of instruction are entered under **School supervision.**

  UF Educational administration
      Inspection of schools
      School administration and organization
      School inspection
      School management and organization
      School organization
      Schools—Management and organization

  NT **Articulation (Education)**
      School attendance
      School boards
      School discipline
      School superintendents and principals
      School supervision
      Schools—Centralization
      Schools—Decentralization
      Student government

Schools and libraries
  USE **Libraries and schools**
Schools and museums
  USE **Museums and schools**
Schools as social centers
  USE **Community centers**
Schools—Centralization (May subdiv. geog.) **379.1**
  UF Centralization of schools
      Consolidation of schools
  BT **Schools—Administration**
Schools—Curricula
  USE **Education—Curricula**

Schools—Decentralization (May subdiv. geog.) **379.1**
  UF Decentralization of schools
  BT **Schools—Administration**
Schools—Equipment and supplies **371.6**
  UF School furniture
  BT **Furniture**
Schools—Exercises and recreations
  USE **School assembly programs**
Schools—Fiction
  USE **School stories**
Schools—Management and organization
  USE **Schools—Administration**
Schools, Military
  USE **Military education**
Schools, Nonformal
  USE **Experimental schools**
Schools—Opening exercises
  USE **School assembly programs**
Schools—Selection
  USE **School choice**
Schools—United States **371.0973**
  UF American schools
Science (May subdiv. geog.) **500**
  NT **Astronomy**
      Bible and science
      Biology
      Botany
      Chaos (Science)
      Chemistry
      Computer science
      Discoveries in science
      Earth sciences
      Forensic sciences
      Fossils
      Geology
      Life sciences
      Mathematics
      Natural history
      Petrology
      Physical sciences
      Physics
      Physiology
      Religion and science
      Science and civilization
      Science and the humanities
      Space sciences
      System theory
      Zoology

Science—*Continued*
RT   Scientific apparatus and in-
            struments
        Scientists
Science and civilization   306.4
    UF   Civilization and science
            Science and society
    BT   **Civilization**
            Progress
            Science
Science and religion
    USE   **Religion and science**
Science and society
    USE   **Science and civilization**
Science and space
    USE   **Space sciences**
Science and state
    USE   **Science—Government policy**
Science and the Bible
    USE   **Bible and science**
Science and the humanities   001.3
    UF   Humanities and science
    BT   **Humanities**
            Science
Science—Exhibitions   507.4
    UF   Science fairs
    BT   **Exhibitions**
    NT   **Science projects**
Science experiments
    USE   **Science—Experiments**
Science—Experiments   507
    UF   Experiments, Scientific
            Science experiments
            Scientific experiments
    SA   branches of science with the
            subdivision *Experiments,* e.g.
            Chemistry—Experiments [to
            be added as needed]
    RT   **Science projects**
Science fair projects
    USE   **Science projects**
Science fairs
    USE   **Science—Exhibitions**
Science fiction   808.83; 813, etc.
    May be used for individual works, collec-
    tions, or materials about fiction based on
    imagined developments in science and tech-
    nology.
    UF   Apocalyptic fantasies
            End-of-the-world fantasies
            Space flight (Fiction)

BT   Adventure fiction
        Fiction
NT   **Dystopias**
        Imaginary voyages
        Utopian fiction
RT   **Fantasy fiction**
        Interplanetary voyages
Science fiction comic books, strips, etc.
        741.5
    May be used for individual works, collec-
    tions, or materials about science fiction com-
    ics.
    BT   **Comic books, strips, etc.**
Science fiction films   791.43
    May be used for individual works, collec-
    tions, or materials about science fiction films.
    SA   types of science fiction films,
            e.g. **Star Wars films** [to be
            added as needed]
    BT   **Motion pictures**
    NT   **Star Wars films**
    RT   **Fantasy films**
Science fiction films—Catalogs
        016.79143
Science fiction plays   808.82; 812, etc.
    May be used for individual works, collec-
    tions, or materials about science fiction plays.
    BT   **Drama**
Science fiction poetry   808.81; 811, etc.
    May be used for individual works, collec-
    tions, or materials about science fiction poet-
    ry.
    BT   **Poetry**
Science fiction radio programs   791.44
    May be used for individual works, collec-
    tions, or materials about science fiction radio
    programs.
    BT   **Radio programs**
Science fiction television programs
        791.45
    May be used for individual works, collec-
    tions, or materials about science fiction televi-
    sion programs.
    BT   **Television programs**
    RT   **Fantasy television programs**
Science—Government policy (May subdiv.
        geog.)   353.7; 500
    UF   Science and state *[Former head-
            ing]*
            Science policy
Science journalism
    USE   **Scientific journalism**
Science—Methodology   501
    UF   Scientific method
    NT   **Logic**

Science policy
    USE   Science—Government policy
Science projects   507.8
    UF   Science fair projects
    BT   Science—Exhibitions
    RT   Science—Experiments
Science—Religious aspects
    USE   Religion and science
Science—Societies   506
    UF   Scientific societies
    BT   Societies
Science—Study and teaching   507
    UF   Scientific education
    NT   Nature study
Science—Study and teaching—Audiovisu-
    al aids   507.8
Science—Study and teaching—Evaluation
    507.6
Science—United States   509.73
Scientific apparatus and instruments
    502.8
    UF   Apparatus, Scientific
           Instruments, Scientific
           Scientific instruments
    SA   types of instruments, e.g. Aero-
           nautical instruments; and
           names of specific instruments
           [to be added as needed]
    NT   Aeronautical instruments
           Astronomical instruments
           Chemical apparatus
           Electric apparatus and appli-
           ances
           Electronic apparatus and ap-
           pliances
           Engineering instruments
           Meteorological instruments
           Optical instruments
    RT   Science
Scientific breakthroughs
    USE   Discoveries in science
Scientific creationism
    USE   Creationism
Scientific discoveries
    USE   Discoveries in science
Scientific education
    USE   Science—Study and teaching
Scientific errors
    USE   Errors

Scientific expeditions   508
    UF   Expeditions, Scientific
           Polar expeditions
    SA   names of regions explored with
           the subdivision *Exploration*
           for materials on scientific ex-
           peditions to regions that are
           unsettled or sparsely settled
           and largely unknown to the
           world at large, e.g. **Antarcti-
           ca—Exploration;** names of
           countries, states, etc., with the
           subdivision *Exploring expedi-
           tions* for materials on explora-
           tions sponsored by those gov-
           ernments; and names of expe-
           ditions [to be added as need-
           ed]
    BT   Voyages and travels
    NT   Antarctica—Exploration
           Arctic regions—Exploration
    RT   Exploration
Scientific experiments
    USE   Science—Experiments
Scientific instruments
    USE   Scientific apparatus and in-
           struments
Scientific journalism (May subdiv. geog.)
    070.4
    UF   Journalism, Scientific
           Science journalism
    BT   Journalism
Scientific management
    USE   Management
Scientific method
    USE   Science—Methodology
Scientific names of plants
    USE   Botany—Nomenclature
Scientific plant names
    USE   Botany—Nomenclature
Scientific recreations   793.8
    UF   Recreations, Scientific
    BT   Amusements
    NT   Mathematical recreations
Scientific societies
    USE   Science—Societies
Scientific writing
    USE   Technical writing

Scientists (May subdiv. geog.)   **509.2; 920**

    SA   types of scientists and names of individual scientists [to be added as needed]

    NT   **Astronomers**

           Biologists

           Chemists

           Geologists

           Mathematicians

           Naturalists

           Physicists

    RT   **Science**

Scottish clans

    USE   **Clans—Scotland**

Scottish personal names   **929.4**

    BT   **Personal names**

Scottish tartans

    USE   **Tartans**

Scouts and scouting   **369.4**

    BT   **Clubs**

           Community life

    NT   **Boy Scouts**

           Girl Scouts

Screen printing

    USE   **Silk screen printing**

Screening for drug abuse

    USE   **Drug testing**

Screenplays

    USE   **Motion picture plays**

           Television scripts

Scriptures, Holy

    USE   **Bible**

Scuba diving (May subdiv. geog.)   **797.2**

    Use for materials on free diving with the aid of a self-contained underwater breathing apparatus. Materials on free diving with mask, fins, and snorkel are entered under **Skin diving.**

    UF   Free diving

    BT   **Deep diving**

Sculling

    USE   **Rowing**

Sculptors (May subdiv. geog.)   **730.92; 920**

    BT   **Artists**

Sculptors—United States   **730.92; 920**

    UF   American sculptors [Former heading]

Sculpture   **730**

    UF   Statues

    SA   sculpture of particular countries, e.g. **Greek sculpture;** and specific types of sculpture [to be added as needed]

    BT   **Art**

           Decoration and ornament

    NT   **American sculpture**

           Brasses

           Bronzes

           Greek sculpture

           Kinetic sculpture

           Masks (Sculpture)

           Mobiles (Sculpture)

           Modeling

           Modernism in sculpture

           Monuments

           Plaster casts

           Soap sculpture

    RT   **Carving (Decorative arts)**

Sculpture—20th century   **735**

    UF   Modern sculpture—1900-1999 (20th century) [Former heading]

           Sculpture, Modern—20th century

Sculpture—21st century   **735**

Sculpture, Greek

    USE   **Greek sculpture**

Sculpture in motion

    USE   **Kinetic sculpture**

Sculpture, Modern

    USE   **Modernism in sculpture**

Sculpture, Modern—20th century

    USE   **Sculpture—20th century**

Sculpture—Technique   **731.4**

    RT   **Modeling**

SDI (Ballistic missile defense system)

    USE   **Strategic Defense Initiative**

Sea

    USE   **Ocean**

Sea animals

    USE   **Marine animals**

Sea bed

    USE   **Ocean bottom**

Sea farming

    USE   **Aquaculture**

Sea fisheries

    USE   **Commercial fishing**

Sea food

    USE   **Seafood**

Sea in art
    USE   **Marine painting**
Sea laboratories
    USE   **Undersea research stations**
Sea laws
    USE   **Maritime law**
Sea life
    USE   **Marine biology**
           Navies
           Sailors
           Seafaring life
Sea mosses
    USE   **Algae**
Sea poetry   808.81; 811, etc.; 811.008, etc.
    May be used for individual works, collections, or materials about poetry about the sea.
    BT   **Poetry**
    NT   **Sea songs**
Sea pollution
    USE   **Marine pollution**
Sea power   359
    UF   Dominion of the sea
          Military power
          Naval power
          Navy
    SA   names of countries with the subhead *Navy* or the subdivision *Naval history,* e.g. **United States. Navy; United States—Naval history;** etc. [to be added as needed]
    BT   **Naval art and science**
    NT   **Warships**
    RT   **Naval history**
          Navies
Sea resources
    USE   **Marine resources**
Sea routes
    USE   **Trade routes**
Sea shells
    USE   **Shells**
Sea-shore
    USE   **Seashore**
Sea songs   782.42
    UF   Chanties
          Sailors' song
    BT   **Sea poetry**
          Songs
Sea stories   808.83; 813, etc.
    May be used for individual works, collections, or materials about sea stories.

    UF   Sailors—Fiction
    BT   **Adventure and adventurers**
          Adventure fiction
          Fiction
Sea transportation
    USE   **Shipping**
Sea travel
    USE   **Ocean travel**
Sea water   551.46
    UF   Saline water
          Salt water
    BT   **Water**
Sea water aquariums
    USE   **Marine aquariums**
Sea water conversion   628.1
    UF   Conversion of saline water
          Desalination of water
          Desalting of water
          Saline water conversion
    BT   **Water purification**
Sea waves
    USE   **Ocean waves**
Seafaring life   910.4
    UF   Sailors' life
          Sea life
    SA   names of countries with the subhead *Navy,* e.g. **United States. Navy** [to be added as needed]
    BT   **Adventure and adventurers**
          Manners and customs
          Voyages and travels
    RT   **Sailors**
Seafood   641.3
    UF   Sea food
    SA   names of marine fish, shellfish, etc., used as food [to be added as needed]
    BT   **Food**
          Marine resources
    RT   **Fish as food**
Sealab project   551.46
    UF   Navy Sealab project
          Project Sealab
          United States. Navy—Sealab project
    BT   **Undersea research stations**
Seals (Animals) (May subdiv. geog.)   **599.79**
    BT   **Mammals**
          Marine mammals

Seals (Numismatics) (May subdiv. geog.)
737; 929.8
    UF   Emblems
          Signets
    BT   **Heraldry**
          History
          Inscriptions
          Numismatics
    RT   **National emblems**
Seamanship
    USE **Navigation**
Seamen
    USE **Sailors**
Search and rescue operations
    USE **Rescue work**
Searching the Internet
    USE **Internet searching**
Seascapes
    USE **Marine painting**
Seashore (May subdiv. geog.)   **551.45**
    UF   Sea-shore
    BT   **Landforms**
    NT   **Beaches**
          Sand dunes
    RT   **Coasts**
          Ocean
Seasons (May subdiv. geog.)   **508.2; 525**
    SA   names of the seasons [to be
          added as needed]
    BT   **Astronomy**
          Climate
          Meteorology
    NT   **Autumn**
Seaweeds
    USE **Algae**
Secession
    USE **State rights**
          United States—History—1861-
          1865, Civil War—Causes
Second Advent   **236**
    UF   Jesus Christ—Second Advent
          Second coming of Christ
    BT   **Eschatology**
          Jesus Christ
    RT   **Millennium**
Second coming of Christ
    USE **Second Advent**
Second economy
    USE **Underground economy**
Second hand trade
    USE **Secondhand trade**

Second job
    USE **Supplementary employment**
Second World War
    USE **World War, 1939-1945**
Secondary education (May subdiv. geog.)
373
    Use for materials on those levels of educa-
    tion higher than elementary and lower than
    college or university.
    UF   Education, Secondary
          High school education
          Secondary schools
    BT   **Education**
    NT   **Adult education**
          Evening and continuation
          schools
    RT   **High schools**
          Junior high schools
Secondary employment
    USE **Supplementary employment**
Secondary school libraries
    USE **High school libraries**
Secondary schools
    USE **High schools**
          Junior high schools
          Secondary education
Secondhand trade   **381**
    UF   Second hand trade
          Used merchandise
    SA   types of secondhand trade, e.g.
          Garage sales [to be added as
          needed]
    BT   **Selling**
    NT   **Garage sales**
Secret service (May subdiv. geog.)
363.28
    Use for materials on governmental service
    of a secret nature.
    SA   names of wars with the subdivi-
          sion *Secret service* [to be
          added as needed]
    BT   **Police**
    NT   **Espionage**
          World War, 1939-1945—Secret
          service
    RT   **Detectives**
          Intelligence service
          Spies
Secret service—United States   **363.28**
    UF   United States—Secret service

Secret societies (May subdiv. geog.)
 366; 371.8
 SA names of secret societies, e.g.
  Freemasons [to be added as
  needed]
 BT **Rites and ceremonies**
  Societies
 NT **Freemasons**
  Ku Klux Klan
 RT **Fraternities and sororities**
Secret writing
 USE **Cryptography**
Secretarial practice
 USE **Office practice**
Secretaries (May subdiv. geog.) **651.3**
 BT **Business education**
  Office management
Secrets, Trade
 USE **Trade secrets**
Sectionalism
 USE **Regionalism**
Sectionalism (United States)
 USE **Regionalism—United States**
Sects (May subdiv. geog.) **280; 291.9**
 Use for materials on independent religious
 groups whose teachings or practices fall with-
 in the normative bounds of the major world
 religions. Materials on the major world reli-
 gions are entered under **Religions.** Materials
 on groups or movements whose beliefs or
 practices differ significantly from the tradi-
 tional religions, often focused upon a charis-
 matic leader, are entered under **Cults.**
 UF Church denominations
  Denominations, Religious
  Religious denominations
 SA names of churches and sects
  within the major world reli-
  gions, e.g. **Presbyterian**
  Church; Hasidim; etc. [to be
  added as needed]
 BT **Church history**
  Religions
 NT **Christian sects**
 RT **Cults**
Secular humanism
 USE **Secularism**
Secularism (May subdiv. geog.) **171;**
 211
 Use for materials on any intellectual or
 philosophical movement or set of beliefs that
 promotes human values as separate and dis-
 tinct from religious doctrines.
 UF Humanism, Secular
  Secular humanism

 BT **Ethics**
  Utilitarianism
 NT **Atheism**
  Rationalism
 RT **Humanism**
Securities (May subdiv. geog.) **332.63**
 UF Capitalization (Finance)
  Dividends
 SA types of securities [to be added
  as needed]
 BT **Finance**
  Investments
  Stock exchanges
 NT **Bonds**
  Insider trading
  Mortgages
  Stocks
Securities exchange
 USE **Stock exchanges**
Securities fraud (May subdiv. geog.)
 345; 364.1
 UF Stock fraud
  Stock market fraud
 BT **Fraud**
Securities trading, Insider
 USE **Insider trading**
Security, Internal
 USE **Internal security**
Security, International
 USE **International security**
Security measures
 USE subjects with the subdivision *Se-*
  curity measures, e.g. **Nuclear**
  power plants—Security mea-
  sures [to be added as needed]
Sedition
 USE **Political crimes and offenses**
  Revolutions
Seeds **581.4**
 BT **Plant propagation**
  Plants
 NT **Nuts**
Seeds—Germination
 USE **Germination**
Seeing eye dogs
 USE **Guide dogs**
Segregation (May subdiv. geog.) **305.8**
 UF Desegregation
 SA segregation in particular areas,
  e.g. **Segregation in educa-**
  tion; and racial and ethnic

Segregation—*Continued*
        groups and classes of persons with the subdivision *Segregation,* e.g. **African Americans—Segregation** [to be added as needed]
  BT **Race relations**
  NT **African Americans—Segregation**
        Apartheid
        Blacks—Segregation
        Segregation in education
  RT **Discrimination**
        Minorities

Segregation in education (May subdiv. geog.) **379.2**
  UF Education—Integration
        Education—Segregation
        Integration in education
        Racial balance in schools
  BT **Segregation**
  RT **Discrimination in education**
        School integration

Segregation in housing
  USE **Discrimination in housing**

Segregation in public accommodations
  USE **Discrimination in public accommodations**

Seismic sea waves
  USE **Tsunamis**

Seismography
  USE **Earthquakes**

Seismology
  USE **Earthquakes**

Selection, Artificial
  USE **Breeding**

Selective service
  USE **Draft**

Self **126; 155.2**
  BT **Consciousness**
        Individuality
        Personality
  NT **Human body**
        Identity (Psychology)

Self-acceptance **155.2**
  UF Self-love (Psychology)
  BT **Psychology**
  RT **Self-confidence**
        Self-esteem
        Self-perception

Self-actualization
  USE **Self-realization**

Self-assurance
  USE **Self-confidence**
        Self-reliance

Self-awareness
  USE **Self-perception**

Self-care, Health
  USE **Health self-care**

Self-care, Medical
  USE **Health self-care**

Self-concept
  USE **Self-perception**

Self-confidence **155.2**
  UF Self-assurance
  BT **Emotions**
  RT **Assertiveness (Psychology)**
        Self-acceptance
        Self-consciousness
        Self-esteem
        Self-reliance

Self-consciousness **155.2**
  UF Embarrassment
  BT **Psychology**
  RT **Self-confidence**
        Self-esteem
        Self-perception

Self-control **153.8**
  UF Self-discipline
        Self-mastery
        Will power
        Willpower
  BT **Psychology**

Self-culture
  USE **Self-improvement**
        Self-instruction

Self-defense **613.6; 796.8**
  UF Fighting
  NT **Boxing**
        Judo
        Karate
        Self-defense for women
  RT **Martial arts**

Self-defense for women **613.6; 796.8**
  UF Fighting
        Women—Self-defense
        Women's self-defense
  BT **Self-defense**
  RT **Martial arts**

Self-defense in animals
  USE **Animal defenses**

Self-development
    USE   **Self-improvement**
           Self-instruction
Self-discipline
    USE   **Self-control**
Self-education
    USE   **Self-instruction**
Self-employed (May subdiv. geog.)
    331.12
    UF   Freelancers
    BT   **Businesspeople**
    NT   **Entrepreneurs**
           Home-based business
           Professions
Self-employed women (May subdiv. geog.)
    331.4
    UF   Women, Self-employed
    BT   **Women—Employment**
Self-esteem   **155.2**
    UF   Self-love (Psychology)
           Self-respect
    BT   **Psychology**
    RT   **Self-acceptance**
           Self-confidence
           Self-consciousness
           Self-perception
Self-evaluation in education
    USE   **Educational evaluation**
Self-examination, Medical
    USE   **Health self-care**
Self-expectations, Perfectionist
    USE   **Perfectionism (Personality**
              trait)
Self-fulfillment
    USE   **Self-realization**
Self-government
    USE   **Democracy**
           Representative government and
              representation
Self-government (in education)
    USE   **Student government**
Self health care
    USE   **Health self-care**
Self-help medical care
    USE   **Health self-care**
Self image
    USE   **Personal appearance**
Self-improvement   **158**
    UF   Personal development
           Personal growth
           Self-culture

Self-development
    BT   **Life skills**
    RT   **Self-instruction**
Self-instruction   **371.39**
    UF   Home education
           Home study courses
           Self-culture
           Self-development
           Self-education
           Teach yourself courses
    SA   subjects with the subdivision
           Programmed instruction, e.g.
           English language—Pro-
           grammed instruction [to be
           added as needed]
    BT   **Education**
           Study skills
    RT   **Correspondence schools and**
           courses
           Self-improvement
Self-love (Psychology)
    USE   **Self-acceptance**
           Self-esteem
Self-mastery
    USE   **Self-control**
Self-medication
    USE   **Health self-care**
Self-mutilation   **616.85**
    BT   **Abnormal psychology**
Self-perception   **155.2**
    UF   Self-awareness
           Self-concept
    BT   **Psychology**
    NT   **Body image**
    RT   **Self-acceptance**
           Self-consciousness
           Self-esteem
Self-protection in animals
    USE   **Animal defenses**
Self-realization   **155.2; 158**
    UF   Fulfillment, Self
           Self-actualization
           Self-fulfillment
    BT   **Psychology**
    RT   **Success**
Self-reliance   **179**
    UF   Self-assurance
    RT   **Self-confidence**
           Survival skills
Self-respect
    USE   **Self-esteem**

Selling   380.1; 658.8
   UF   Salesmanship
   BT   Business
        Retail trade
   NT   Auctions
        Direct selling
        Mail-order business
        Sales management
        Secondhand trade
   RT   Advertising
        Marketing
Selling of infants
   USE   Adoption—Corrupt practices
Semantics   121; 302.2; 401
   BT   Language and languages
        Linguistics
   NT   Semiotics
Semiconductors   621.3815
   BT   Electric conductors
        Electronics
   NT   Microelectronics
        Transistors
Semiotics   302.2; 401
   Use for materials on the relationship between signs and symbols and whatever it is they stand for.
   BT   Semantics
   NT   Visual literacy
   RT   Signs and symbols
Semitic peoples (May subdiv. geog.)
      305.892
   BT   Ethnology
Senate (U.S.)
   USE   United States. Congress. Senate
Senescence
   USE   Aging
Senior citizens
   USE   Elderly
Sense of direction
   USE   Direction sense
Senses and sensation   152.1; 612.8
   BT   Intellect
        Physiology
        Psychology
        Psychophysiology
        Theory of knowledge
   NT   Color sense
        Gestalt psychology
        Hearing
        Pain
        Perception
        Pleasure

        Smell
        Taste
        Touch
        Vision
Sensing, Remote
   USE   Remote sensing
Sensitivity training
   USE   Group relations training
Separate development (Race relations)
   USE   Apartheid
Separation anxiety in children   155.4
   BT   Anxiety
        Child psychology
Separation (Law)
   USE   Divorce
Separation of church and state
   USE   Church and state
Separation of powers (May subdiv. geog.)
      320.4; 342
   UF   Division of powers
        Powers, Separation of
   BT   Constitutional law
        Executive power
        Political science
Separation of powers—United States
      320.473
   UF   United States—Separation of
        powers
Separatism, Black
   USE   Black nationalism
Separatist movement in Québec (Province)
   USE   Québec (Province)—History—
        Autonomy and independence
        movements
Sepulchers
   USE   Tombs
Sepulchral brasses
   USE   Brasses
Sequences (Mathematics)   510
   UF   Mathematical sequences
        Numerical sequences
   BT   Algebra
        Mathematics
Serial publications (May subdiv. geog.)
      050
   Use for general materials on publications in any medium issued in successive parts bearing numerical or chronological designations and intended to be continued indefinitely.
   BT   Bibliography
        Publishers and publishing

Serial publications—*Continued*
  NT Almanacs
      Newspapers
      Periodicals
      School yearbooks
  RT International Standard Serial
      Numbers
Serigraphy
  USE Silk screen printing
Sermon on the mount   226.9
  UF Jesus Christ—Sermon on the
      mount
Sermons (May subdiv. geog.)   252;
  291.4
  Use for collections of sermons of several
  religions and for collections of Christian ser-
  mons not limited to a single topic, occasion,
  or Christian denomination. Materials on the
  art of writing and delivering sermons are en-
  tered under **Preaching.**

  SA sermons of particular countries,
      languages, or religions, e.g.
      **English sermons; Islamic
      sermons;** etc.; sermons
      preached at particular times of
      year or on particular occa-
      sions, e.g. **Lenten sermons;**
      and topics and Christian de-
      nominations with the subdivi-
      sion *Sermons,* e.g. **Christian
      life—Sermons; Presbyterian
      Church—Sermons;** etc. [to
      be added as needed]
  BT Christian literature
  NT Christian life—Sermons
      English sermons
      Islamic sermons
      Lenten sermons
      Presbyterian Church—Sermons
  RT Preaching
Serpents
  USE Snakes
Servants
  USE Household employees
Service books (Liturgy)
  USE Liturgies
Service, Customer
  USE Customer services
Service (in industry)
  USE Customer services

Service industries (May subdiv. geog.)
  338.4
  SA types of service industries [to be
      added as needed]
  BT Industries
  NT Food service
      Hotels and motels
      Lease and rental services
      Undertakers and undertaking
Service stations (May subdiv. geog.)
  629.28
  UF Filling stations
      Gas stations
  BT Automobile industry
      Petroleum industry
Servicemen
  USE Military personnel
Services, Customer
  USE Customer services
Services for
  USE classes of persons, ethnic
      groups, animals, and types of
      schools with the subdivision
      Services for, e.g. **Handi-
      capped—Services for** [to be
      added as needed]
Services for the handicapped
  USE Handicapped—Services for
Servicewomen
  USE Military personnel
Servitude
  USE Peonage
      Slavery
Servomechanisms   629.8
  UF Automatic control
  BT Automation
      Feedback control systems
Set theory   511.3
  UF Aggregates
      Classes (Mathematics)
      Ensembles (Mathematics)
      Mathematical sets
      Sets (Mathematics)
  BT Mathematics
  NT Arithmetic
      Boolean algebra
      Fractals
      Number theory
      Topology
  RT Symbolic logic

Sets, Fractal
  USE **Fractals**
Sets (Mathematics)
  USE **Set theory**
Sets of fractional dimension
  USE **Fractals**
Settlement of land
  USE **Land settlement**
Settlements, Social
  USE **Social settlements**
Seven Years' War, 1756-1763 940.2
  BT **Europe—History—1492-1789**
  NT **United States—History—1755-1763, French and Indian War**
Seventeenth century
  USE **World history—17th century**
Seville (Spain). World's Fair, 1992
  USE **Expo 92 (Seville, Spain)**
Sewage disposal (May subdiv. geog.)
      628.3
  BT **Public health**
     Refuse and refuse disposal
  RT **Water pollution**
Sewerage (May subdiv. geog.)   **628**
  UF Sewers
  BT **House drainage**
     Municipal engineering
     Plumbing
     Sanitary engineering
  RT **Drainage**
Sewers
  USE **Sewerage**
Sewing   646.2
  BT **Home economics**
  NT **Embroidery**
  RT **Dressmaking**
     Needlework
Sex
  USE **Sexual behavior**
Sex bias
  USE **Sexism**
Sex (Biology)   571.8; 612.6
  Use for materials on the physical traits that distinguish the male and female of a species and on the physiological aspects of sexuality. Materials on the social and behavioral aspects of sexuality are entered under **Sexual behavior.** Materials on the psychology of sexuality are entered under **Sex (Psychology).**
  UF Sex—Physiological aspects
      Sexuality

  BT **Biology**
  NT **Reproductive system**
      Sexual disorders
  RT **Reproduction**
      Sexual behavior
Sex change
  USE **Transsexualism**
Sex crimes (May subdiv. geog.)   **364.15**
  UF Sexual abuse
      Sexual crimes
      Sexual offenses
  SA types of sex crimes [to be added as needed]
  BT **Crime**
      Sexual behavior
  NT **Child sexual abuse**
      Incest
      Rape
Sex differences (Psychology)   155.3
  BT **Sex (Psychology)**
  NT **Androgyny**
      Sex role
Sex discrimination (May subdiv. geog.)
      305.3
  Use for materials on the restriction or denial of rights, privileges, or choice because of one's sex. Materials on prejudicial attitudes toward people because of their sex are entered under **Sexism.**
  BT **Discrimination**
      Sexism
  NT **Equal rights amendments**
      Women's rights
Sex disorders
  USE **Sexual disorders**
Sex education (May subdiv. geog.)
      372.3; 613.9071; 649
  UF Sex instruction
  BT **Family life education**
  RT **Sexual hygiene**
Sex in art
  USE **Erotic art**
Sex in mass media   302.23
  BT **Mass media**
Sex in popular culture   306.7
  BT **Popular culture**
Sex in the office
  USE **Sex in the workplace**
Sex in the workplace   306.7; 658
  UF Office romance
      Sex in the office
  BT **Sexual behavior**
  RT **Sexual harassment**

Sex instruction
USE **Sex education**
Sex organs
USE **Reproductive system**
Sex—Physiological aspects
USE **Sex (Biology)**
Sex—Psychological aspects
USE **Sex (Psychology)**
Sex (Psychology)   155.3
Use for materials on the psychology of sexuality. Materials on the social and behavioral aspects of sexuality are entered under **Sexual behavior.** Materials on the physiological traits that distinguish the male and female of a species and on the physiological aspects of sexuality are entered under **Sex (Biology).**
UF   Sex—Psychological aspects
Sexual behavior, Psychology of
Sexual psychology
Sexuality
BT   **Psychology**
NT   **Femininity**
Masculinity
Sex differences (Psychology)
RT   **Sexual behavior**
Sex role   305.3
Use for materials on the patterns of attitudes and behavior that are regarded as appropriate to one sex rather than the other.
UF   Female role
Gender identity
Male role
Sexual identity
BT   **Sex differences (Psychology)**
Sexual behavior
Social role
NT   **Androgyny**
Transsexualism
RT   **Sexism**
Sex therapy   616.6; 616.85
BT   **Psychotherapy**
RT   **Sexual disorders**
Sexism (May subdiv. geog.)   **305.3**
Use for materials on prejudicial attitudes toward people because of their sex. Materials on the restriction or denial of rights, privileges, or choice because of one's sex are entered under **Sex discrimination.**
UF   Sex bias
BT   **Attitude (Psychology)**
Prejudices
NT   **Sex discrimination**
RT   **Sex role**

Sexual abstinence   176; 306.73
Use for materials on abstinence from sexual activity. Materials on the virtue that moderates and regulates the sexual appetite in human beings are entered under **Chastity.** Materials on the renunciation of marriage for religious reasons are entered under **Celibacy.**
UF   Abstinence, Sexual
BT   **Asceticism**
Sexual behavior
RT   **Birth control**
Celibacy
Chastity
Sexual abuse
USE   **Child sexual abuse**
Sex crimes
Sexual harassment
Sexual assault
USE   **Rape**
Sexual behavior   306.7
Use for materials on the social and behavioral aspects of sexuality. Materials on the physiological traits that distinguish the male and female of a species and on the physiological aspects of sexuality are entered under **Sex (Biology).** Materials on the psychology of sexuality are entered under **Sex (Psychology).**
UF   Sex
Sexuality
SA   social groups and classes of persons with the subdivision *Sexual behavior,* e.g. **College students—Sexual behavior** [to be added as needed]
BT   **Human behavior**
NT   **College students—Sexual behavior**
Computer sex
Homosexuality
Sex crimes
Sex in the workplace
Sex role
Sexual abstinence
Sexual behavior in animals
Sexual deviation
Sexual harassment
RT   **Sex (Biology)**
Sex (Psychology)
Sexual disorders
Sexual ethics
Sexual behavior in animals   591.56
UF   Animal sexual behavior
Animals—Sexual behavior
Breeding behavior
Mating behavior

Sexual behavior in animals—*Continued*
    Reproductive behavior
  BT **Animal behavior**
       Sexual behavior
  NT **Animal courtship**
Sexual behavior, Psychology of
  USE **Sex (Psychology)**
Sexual crimes
  USE **Sex crimes**
Sexual deviation   306.7; 616.85
  UF Deviation, Sexual
       Perversion, Sexual
       Sexual perversion
  BT **Sexual behavior**
       Sexual disorders
Sexual disorders   616.6; 616.85
  UF Sex disorders
  BT **Sex (Biology)**
  NT **Sexual deviation**
  RT **Sex therapy**
       Sexual behavior
Sexual ethics (May subdiv. geog.)   **176**
  BT **Ethics**
  NT **Adultery**
       Chastity
       Free love
       Prostitution
       Sexual harassment
  RT **Sexual behavior**
Sexual harassment (May subdiv. geog.)
    331.13; 344
  UF Harassment, Sexual
       Sexual abuse
  BT **Sexual behavior**
       Sexual ethics
  RT **Sex in the workplace**
Sexual hygiene   613.9
  UF Hygiene, Sexual
       Social hygiene
  BT **Hygiene**
  NT **Birth control**
       Safe sex in AIDS prevention
       Sexually transmitted diseases—Prevention
  RT **Sex education**
       Sexually transmitted diseases
Sexual identity
  USE **Sex role**
Sexual offenses
  USE **Sex crimes**
Sexual perversion
  USE **Sexual deviation**

Sexual psychology
  USE **Sex (Psychology)**
Sexuality
  USE **Sex (Biology)**
       Sex (Psychology)
       Sexual behavior
Sexually abused children
  USE **Child sexual abuse**
Sexually transmitted diseases (May
    subdiv. geog.)   **616.95**
  UF VD
       Venereal diseases
  SA types of sexually transmitted dis-
       eases [to be added as needed]
  BT **Communicable diseases**
  NT **Syphilis**
  RT **Sexual hygiene**
Sexually transmitted diseases—Prevention
    616.95
  UF Safe sex
  BT **Sexual hygiene**
Shade gardens
  USE **Gardening in the shade**
Shades and shadows   741.2
  UF Light and shade
       Shadows
  BT **Drawing**
Shadow economy
  USE **Underground economy**
Shadow pantomimes and plays   791.5
  BT **Amateur theater**
       Pantomimes
       Puppets and puppet plays
       Shadow pictures
       Theater
Shadow pictures   793
  UF Hand shadows
       Shadowplay
  BT **Amusements**
  NT **Shadow pantomimes and plays**
Shadowplay
  USE **Shadow pictures**
Shadows
  USE **Shades and shadows**
Shady gardens
  USE **Gardening in the shade**
Shaft sinking
  USE **Drilling and boring (Earth and
       rocks)**
Shakers (May subdiv. geog.)   **289**
  BT **Christian sects**

Shakespeare, William, 1564-1616   822.3

When applicable, the subdivisions provided with this heading may be used for other voluminous authors, e.g. **Dante; Goethe;** etc. These headings are to be used for materials about Shakespeare and about his writings. The texts of his plays, etc., are not given subject headings.

Shakespeare, William, 1564-1616—Adaptations   822.3

May be used for individual works, collections, or materials about literary, cinematic, video, or television adaptations of Shakespeare's works.

UF   Shakespeare, William, 1564-1616—Paraphrases

Shakespeare, William, 1564-1616—Allusions   822.3

Shakespeare, William, 1564-1616—Anniversaries   822.3

Shakespeare, William, 1564-1616—Authorship   822.3

UF   Bacon-Shakespeare controversy

Shakespeare, William, 1564-1616—Bibliography   016.8223

Shakespeare, William, 1564-1616—Biography—Psychology

USE   **Shakespeare, William, 1564-1616—Psychology**

Shakespeare, William, 1564-1616—Characters   822.3

Shakespeare, William, 1564-1616—Comedies   822.3

Use for materials about the comedies, not for the texts of the plays.

Shakespeare, William, 1564-1616—Concordances   822.303

UF   Shakespeare, William, 1564-1616—Indexes

Shakespeare, William, 1564-1616—Criticism   822.3

Use for materials discussing the criticism of Shakespeare's works, including historical materials. Criticism of Shakespeare's works in general is entered under **Shakespeare, William, 1564-1616.** Criticism of the comedies is entered under **Shakespeare, William, 1564-1616—Comedies;** criticism of the sonnets under **Shakespeare, William, 1564-1616—Sonnets;** etc. Criticism of an individual play is entered under **Shakespeare, William, 1564-1616,** followed by the title of the play.

UF   Shakespeare, William, 1564-1616—Criticism, interpretation, etc.

Shakespeare, William, 1564-1616—Psychological studies

Shakespeare, William, 1564-1616—Criticism, interpretation, etc.

USE   **Shakespeare, William, 1564-1616—Criticism**

Shakespeare, William, 1564-1616—Dictionaries   822.303

BT   **Encyclopedias and dictionaries**

Shakespeare, William, 1564-1616—Discography   016.8223

Shakespeare, William, 1564-1616—Dramatic production   822.3

UF   Shakespeare, William, 1564-1616—Stage setting and scenery

Shakespeare, William, 1564-1616—Ethics   822.3

UF   Shakespeare, William, 1564-1616—Moral ideas

Shakespeare, William, 1564-1616—Religion and ethics

Shakespeare, William, 1564-1616—Filmography   016.8223

Shakespeare, William, 1564-1616—Histories   822.3

Use for materials about the histories, not for the texts of the plays.

Shakespeare, William, 1564-1616—Indexes

USE   **Shakespeare, William, 1564-1616—Concordances**

Shakespeare, William, 1564-1616—Influence   822.3

Use for materials on Shakespeare's influence on national literatures, literary movements, or specific persons.

Shakespeare, William, 1564-1616—Knowledge   822.3

Use for materials on Shakespeare's knowledge or treatment of specific subjects. May be subdivided by subject, e.g. **Shakespeare, William, 1564-1616—Knowledge—Animals;** etc.

Shakespeare, William, 1564-1616—Moral ideas

USE   **Shakespeare, William, 1564-1616—Ethics**

Shakespeare, William, 1564-1616—Paraphrases

USE   **Shakespeare, William, 1564-1616—Adaptations**

Shakespeare, William, 1564-1616—Parodies, imitations, etc.   822.3

UF   Shakespeare, William, 1564-1616—Parodies, travesties, etc.

Shakespeare, William, 1564-1616—Parodies, travesties, etc.
    USE **Shakespeare, William, 1564-1616—Parodies, imitations, etc.**
Shakespeare, William, 1564-1616—Poetic works 822.3
    Use for materials about the poetic works, not for the poetic texts themselves.
Shakespeare, William, 1564-1616—Portraits 822.3022
Shakespeare, William, 1564-1616—Psychological studies
    USE **Shakespeare, William, 1564-1616—Criticism**
          Shakespeare, William, 1564-1616—Psychology
Shakespeare, William, 1564-1616—Psychology 92; B
    UF Shakespeare, William, 1564-1616—Biography—Psychology
          Shakespeare, William, 1564-1616—Psychological studies
Shakespeare, William, 1564-1616—Quotations 822.3
Shakespeare, William, 1564-1616—Religion 822.3
    UF Shakespeare, William, 1564-1616—Religion and ethics
Shakespeare, William, 1564-1616—Religion and ethics
    USE **Shakespeare, William, 1564-1616—Ethics**
          Shakespeare, William, 1564-1616—Religion
Shakespeare, William, 1564-1616—Sonnets 822.3
    Use for materials about the sonnets, not for the texts of the sonnets.
Shakespeare, William, 1564-1616—Stage history 792; 822.3
    BT **Theater**
Shakespeare, William, 1564-1616—Stage setting and scenery
    USE **Shakespeare, William, 1564-1616—Dramatic production**
Shakespeare, William, 1564-1616—Style
    USE **Shakespeare, William, 1564-1616—Technique**

Shakespeare, William, 1564-1616—Technique 822.3
    UF Shakespeare, William, 1564-1616—Style
Shakespeare, William, 1564-1616—Tragedies 822.3
    Use for materials about the tragedies, not for the texts of the plays.
Shape 516
    UF Shapes
          Size and shape
    SA types of geometric shapes, e.g. **Square** [to be added as needed]
    BT **Concepts**
          Geometry
          Perception
    NT **Square**
Shapes
    USE **Shape**
Sharecropping (May subdiv. geog.) **333.33**
    BT **Farm tenancy**
Shared custody
    USE **Child custody**
Shared housing (May subdiv. geog.) **363.5; 643**
    Use for materials on two or more single, unrelated adults who live together.
    UF Home sharing
          House sharing
    BT **Housing**
    NT **Unmarried couples**
    RT **Roommates**
Shared parenting
    USE **Part-time parenting**
Shared reading books
    USE **Big books**
Shares of stock
    USE **Stocks**
Shareware (Computer software) 005.3
    Use for materials on computer software offered to consumers on a trial basis with the provision that they pay a voluntary fee if they want to use it.
    UF Software for sharing
    BT **Computer software**
Sharing of jobs
    USE **Job sharing**
Sheep 599.649; 636.3
    UF Lambs
    BT **Domestic animals**
          Mammals

Sheet metalwork   671.8
UF   Press working of metal
BT   **Metalwork**
NT   **Plate metalwork**
Sheffield plate   739.2
BT   **Plate**
Shellfish   594; 641.3
BT   **Aquatic animals**
NT   **Crabs**
Crustacea
Lobsters
Mollusks
Shells (May subdiv. geog.)   **591.47;**
594.147
Use for popular materials on seashells and
shell   collecting.   Systematic   and
comprehensive materials on shells are entered
under **Mollusks.**
UF   Sea shells
RT   **Mollusks**
Shells (Projectiles)
USE   **Projectiles**
Shelterbelts
USE   **Windbreaks**
Shelters, Air raid
USE   **Air raid shelters**
Sherlock Holmes (Fictitious character)
USE   **Holmes, Sherlock (Fictitious**
character)
Sherlock Holmes films   791.43
May be used for individual works, collec-
tions, or materials about Sherlock Holmes
films.
BT   **Motion pictures**
Mystery films
Shinto (May subdiv. geog.)   **299**
BT   **Religions**
RT   **Ancestor worship**
Ship building
USE   **Shipbuilding**
Ship models
USE   **Ships—Models**
Ship pilots (May subdiv. geog.)   **623.89**
UF   Pilots
Pilots and pilotage
BT   **Sailors**
RT   **Navigation**
Ship safety
USE   **Ships—Safety regulations**
Ship salvage
USE   **Marine salvage**

Shipbuilding (May subdiv. geog.)   **623.8**
UF   Ship building
Ships—Construction
BT   **Naval architecture**
NT   **Marine engines**
Steamboats
RT   **Boatbuilding**
Ships
Shipping (May subdiv. geog.)   **387.5**
UF   Marine transportation
Ocean—Economic aspects
Ocean transportation
Sea transportation
Water transportation
BT   **Transportation**
NT   **Harbors**
Inland navigation
Marine insurance
Maritime law
Territorial waters
RT   **Merchant marine**
Shipping—United States   387.00973
Ships (May subdiv. geog.)   **387.2; 623.8**
UF   Vessels (Ships)
SA   types of ships and vessels and
names of individual ships [to
be added as needed]
NT   **Clipper ships**
Hospital ships
Lightships
Merchant marine
Sailing
Steamboats
Submarines
Warships
Yachts and yachting
RT   **Boats and boating**
Shipbuilding
Ships—Construction
USE   **Shipbuilding**
Ships in art
USE   **Marine painting**
Ships—Models   623.8
UF   Model ships
Ship models
BT   **Models and modelmaking**
Ships—Safety regulations   341.7; 343
UF   Merchant marine—Safety regula-
tions
Ship safety

Ships—Safety regulations—*Continued*
BT Maritime law
Safety regulations
Shipwrecks 363.12; 910.4
UF Marine disasters
SA names of wrecked ships [to be
added as needed]
BT Accidents
Adventure and adventurers
Disasters
Navigation
Voyages and travels
RT Marine salvage
Survival after airplane acci-
dents, shipwrecks, etc.
Shoe industry (May subdiv. geog.)
338.4; 685
BT Clothing industry
Leather industry
RT Shoes
Shoes (May subdiv. geog.) 391.4; 646;
685
UF Boots
Footwear
BT Clothing and dress
RT Shoe industry
Shooting (May subdiv. geog.) 799.3
Use for materials on the use of firearms.
Materials on shooting game are entered under
Hunting.
NT Archery
Decoys (Hunting)
RT Firearms
Hunting
Shooting stars
USE Meteors
Shop management
USE Factory management
Shop practice
USE Machine shop practice
Shop windows
USE Show windows
Shoplifting 364.16
BT Theft
Shoppers' guides
USE Consumer education
Shopping
Shopping (May subdiv. geog.) 381; 640
Use for materials on consumer buying.
General materials on buying and materials on
buying by commercial enterprises are entered
under **Purchasing.**

UF Buyers' guides
Marketing (Home economics)
Shoppers' guides
SA types of products and services
with the subdivision *Purchas-
ing,* e.g. **Automobiles—Pur-
chasing** [to be added as need-
ed]
BT Home economics
Purchasing
NT Grocery shopping
Internet shopping
RT Consumer education
Shopping centers and malls (May subdiv.
geog.) 658.8
UF Malls, Shopping
Shopping malls
BT Commercial buildings
Retail trade
RT Stores
Shopping—Computer network resources
USE Internet shopping
Shopping—Internet resources
USE Internet shopping
Shopping malls
USE Shopping centers and malls
Shops
USE Stores
Short films 791.43
May be used for individual works, collec-
tions, or materials about short films.
BT Motion pictures
Short plays
USE One act plays
Short stories 808.83; 813, etc.
Use for collections of short stories by one
author or by several authors. Materials on the
short story as a literary form and on the tech-
nique of writing short stories are entered un-
der **Short story.**
UF Stories
BT Fiction
Short stories—Indexes 016.80883
Short story 808.3
Use for materials on the short story as a lit-
erary form and on the technique of writing
short stories. Collections of stories are entered
under **Short stories.**
BT Authorship
Fiction
Literature
RT Storytelling

Shorthand 653
 UF Stenography
 BT Business education
  Office practice
  Writing
 RT Abbreviations
Shortwave radio 621.3841
 UF High-frequency radio
  UHF radio
  Ultrahigh frequency radio
  Very high frequency radio
  VHF radio
 BT Radio
  Radio frequency modulation
 NT Amateur radio stations
  Citizens band radio
  Microwave communication sys-
   tems
  Microwaves
Shotguns 683.4
 UF Guns
 BT Firearms
Show business
 USE Performing arts
Show windows 659.1
 UF Shop windows
  Window dressing
 BT Advertising
  Decoration and ornament
  Windows
Showers (Parties) 793.2
 BT Parties
Shrines (May subdiv. geog.) 263; 291.3;
  726
 NT Tombs
 RT Pilgrims and pilgrimages
Shrubs (May subdiv. geog.) 582.1;
  635.9
 BT Plants
  Trees
 NT Evergreens
 RT Landscape gardening
  Ornamental plants
Shyness 155.2
 UF Bashfulness
 BT Emotions
Sibling rivalry 306.875
 BT Child psychology
  Siblings
Sibling sequence
 USE Birth order

Siblings 155.44; 306.875
 UF Brothers and sisters [Former
   heading]
  Sisters and brothers
 BT Family
 NT Brothers
  Sibling rivalry
  Sisters
  Twins
Sick 362.1
 UF Invalids
 BT Handicapped
 NT Church work with the sick
  Cooking for the sick
  First aid
  Mentally ill
  Terminally ill
 RT Diseases
  Home nursing
  Nursing
  Patients
Sick—Prayers 242; 291.4
 BT Prayers
Sickness
 USE Diseases
SIDS (Disease)
 USE Sudden infant death syndrome
Sieges
 USE Battles
Sight
 USE Vision
Sight saving books
 USE Large print books
Sign language 419
 UF Deaf—Sign language
 BT Language and languages
 NT Native American sign language
 RT Deaf—Means of communica-
   tion
  Signs and symbols
Sign painting 667
 BT Advertising
  Industrial painting
 NT Alphabets
 RT Lettering
  Signs and signboards
Signaling
 USE types of transportation and com-
   munication with the subdivi-
   sion Signaling, e.g.

Signaling—*Continued*
       Railraods—Signaling [to be added as needed]
Signals and signaling   388; 621.382
   UF   Coastal signals
         Fog signals
         Military signaling
         Naval signaling
   SA   types of transportation and communication with the subdivision *Signaling,* e.g.
       Railraods—Signaling [to be added as needed]
   BT   **Communication**
         Military art and science
         Naval art and science
         Navigation
         Signs and symbols
   NT   **Railroads—Signaling**
         Sonar
   RT   **Flags**
Signboards
   USE   **Signs and signboards**
Signets
   USE   **Seals (Numismatics)**
Signs (Advertising)
   USE   **Signs and signboards**
Signs and signboards   659.13
   UF   Billboards
         Road signs
         Signboards
         Signs (Advertising)
   BT   **Advertising**
   NT   **Electric signs**
   RT   **Posters**
         Sign painting
Signs and symbols (May subdiv. geog.)   302.2; 419
   UF   Emblems
         Symbols
   BT   **Communication**
   NT   **Ciphers**
         Cryptography
         Heraldry
         National emblems
         Signals and signaling
         State emblems
   RT   **Abbreviations**
         Semiotics
         Sign language
         Symbolism

Signs and symbols in literature
   USE   **Symbolism in literature**
Silage and silos   633.2
   UF   Silos
   BT   **Feeds**
         Forage plants
Silent films (May subdiv. geog.)   791.43
     May be used for individual works, collections, or materials about films made before the development of films with sound.
   UF   Silent motion pictures
   BT   **Motion pictures**
Silent motion pictures
   USE   **Silent films**
Silk (May subdiv. geog.)   677
   BT   **Fabrics**
         Fibers
   RT   **Silkworms**
Silk screen printing (May subdiv. geog.)   764
   UF   Screen printing
         Serigraphy
   BT   **Color printing**
         Stencil work
   RT   **Textile printing**
Silkworms   595.78; 638
   UF   Cocoons
   BT   **Beneficial insects**
         Insects
         Moths
   RT   **Silk**
Silos
   USE   **Silage and silos**
Silver (May subdiv. geog.)   332.4; 669
   BT   **Chemical elements**
         Precious metals
   NT   **Silverwork**
   RT   **Coinage**
         Money
Silver articles
   USE   **Silverwork**
Silver mines and mining (May subdiv. geog.)   622
   BT   **Mines and mineral resources**
   NT   **Prospecting**
Silver plate
   USE   **Plate**
         Silverware
Silver work
   USE   **Silverwork**
Silversmithing
   USE   **Silverwork**

Silverware (May subdiv. geog.)   642;
739.2
   UF   Flatware, Silver
        Silver plate
   BT   **Decorative arts**
        Silverwork
        Tableware
Silverwork (May subdiv. geog.)   739.2
   UF   Silver articles
        Silver work
        Silversmithing
   BT   **Art metalwork**
        Metalwork
        Silver
   NT   **Native American silverwork**
        Plate
        Silverware
Simple machines   621.8
   UF   Machines, Simple
   SA   types of simple machines, e.g.
        Wheels [to be added as need-
        ed]
   BT   **Machinery**
        Mechanical movements
        Mechanics
   NT   **Wheels**
Simulation, computer
   USE   **Computer simulation**
Simulation games in education   371.39
   UF   Educational gaming
        Educational simulation games
        Gaming, Educational
   BT   **Education**
        Educational games
        Game theory
Sin   241; 291.5
   BT   **Ethics**
        Good and evil
        Theology
Sinai Campaign, 1956   956.04
   UF   Anglo-French intervention in
        Egypt, 1956
        Arab-Israel War, 1956
        Israel-Arab War, 1956
   BT   **Egypt—History**
        Israel-Arab conflicts
Singers   782.0092; 920
   BT   **Musicians**

Singing   782; 783
   UF   School music
   BT   **Music**
   NT   **Songbooks**
        Voice culture
   RT   **Choirs (Music)**
        Vocal music
        Voice
Singing games   796.1
   BT   **Games**
Singing societies
   USE   **Choral societies**
Single child
   USE   **Only child**
Single men (May subdiv. geog.)   155.6;
305.38
   UF   Unmarried men
   BT   **Men**
        Single people
Single-parent families (May subdiv. geog.)
306.85
   Use for materials on households in which a
   parent living without a partner is rearing chil-
   dren. Materials on parents who were not mar-
   ried at the time of the birth of their children
   are entered under **Unmarried fathers** or **Un-**
   married mothers.
   UF   One parent family
        Single parent family *[Former*
        heading]
   BT   **Family**
   RT   **Single parents**
Single parent family
   USE   **Single-parent families**
Single parents (May subdiv. geog.)
306.85
   BT   **Parents**
        Unmarried couples
   NT   **Children of single parents**
        Unmarried fathers
        Unmarried mothers
   RT   **Single-parent families**
Single parents' children
   USE   **Children of single parents**
Single people (May subdiv. geog.)
155.6; 305.9
   UF   Unmarried people
   NT   **Single men**
        Single women
Single rail railroads
   USE   **Monorail railroads**
Single-sex education
   USE   **Single-sex schools**

Single-sex schools (May subdiv. geog.)
  370
  UF Single-sex education
  BT **Schools**
Single women (May subdiv. geog.)
  155.6; 305.48
  UF Unmarried women
  BT **Single people**
      Women
Sirius 523.8
  BT **Stars**
Sisterhoods
  USE **Monasticism and religious or-**
       ders for women
Sisters 306.875
  BT **Siblings**
      Women
Sisters and brothers
  USE **Siblings**
Sisters (Religious)
  USE **Nuns**
Sit-down strikes
  USE **Strikes**
Sit-ins for civil rights
  USE **Civil rights demonstrations**
Sitcoms
  USE **Comedy television programs**
Site oriented art
  USE **Earthworks (Art)**
Sitters (Babysitters)
  USE **Babysitters**
Situation comedies
  USE **Comedy television programs**
Six Day War, 1967
  USE **Israel-Arab War, 1967**
Sixteenth century
  USE **World history—16th century**
Size 530.8
  UF Large and small
      Size and shape
      Small and large
  BT **Concepts**
      Perception
Size and shape
  USE **Shape**
      Size
Skating
  USE **Ice skating**
      Roller skating
Skeletal remains
  USE **Anthropometry**

Skeleton 573.7; 611
  Use for materials limited to the morphology or mechanics of the skeleton, human or animal. Comprehensive and systematic materials on the anatomy of bones are entered under **Bones.**
  BT **Musculoskeletal system**
  RT **Bones**
Skepticism 149; 186; 211
  UF Scepticism
      Unbelief
  BT **Free thought**
      Philosophy
      Rationalism
  RT **Agnosticism**
      Belief and doubt
      Truth
Sketching
  USE **Drawing**
Skidoos
  USE **Snowmobiles**
Skiing (May subdiv. geog.) **796.93**
  UF Skis and skiing
      Snow skiing
  BT **Winter sports**
Skill
  USE **Ability**
Skilled labor (May subdiv. geog.) **331.7**
  BT **Labor**
Skills
  USE **Ability**
Skin 611; 612.7
  BT **Anatomy**
      Physiology
Skin—Care 616.5; 646.7
  UF Skin care
      Skin—Care and hygiene
Skin care
  USE **Skin—Care**
Skin—Care and hygiene
  USE **Skin—Care**
Skin—Diseases 616.5
  UF Dermatitis
  SA types of skin diseases [to be added as needed]
  BT **Diseases**
  NT **Acne**
Skin diving (May subdiv. geog.) **797.2**
  Use for materials on free diving with mask, fins, and snorkel. Materials on free diving with the aid of a self-contained underwater breathing apparatus are entered under **Scuba diving.**

Skin diving—*Continued*
UF Free diving
      Snorkeling
      Underwater swimming
BT **Deep diving**
Skinheads
USE **White supremacy movements**
Skins
USE **Hides and skins**
Skis and skiing
USE **Skiing**
Skits 791
BT **Amusements**
      Theater
Sky 520; 551.5
BT **Astronomy**
      Atmosphere
NT **Constellations**
Sky diving
USE **Skydiving**
Skydiving (May subdiv. geog.) 797.5
UF Sky diving
BT **Aeronautical sports**
Skyscrapers (May subdiv. geog.) 690;
    720
UF High rise buildings
BT **Buildings**
Skyscrapers—Earthquake effects 690;
    725
BT **Buildings—Earthquake effects**
      Earthquakes
Slander (Law)
USE **Libel and slander**
Slang
USE names of languages with the
      subdivision *Slang,* e.g. **En-**
      glish language—Slang [to be
      added as needed]
Slanted journalism
USE **Journalism—Objectivity**
Slapstick comedies
USE **Comedies**
      Comedy films
      Comedy television programs
Slave insurrections
USE **Slave revolts**
Slave revolts (May subdiv. geog.) 326;
    909
UF Slave insurrections
BT **Revolutions**
RT **Slavery**

Slave trade (May subdiv. geog.) 341;
    345; 380.1
BT **International law**
      Slavery
Slavery (May subdiv. geog.) 177; 306.3;
    326; 342
UF Abolition of slavery
      Antislavery
      Servitude
BT **Crimes against humanity**
NT **Slave trade**
      Slaves
RT **Abolitionists**
      Forced labor
      Peonage
      Slave revolts
      Slaves—Emancipation
Slavery—Emancipation
USE **Slaves—Emancipation**
Slavery—United States 306.3; 326.0973
RT **Southern States—History**
      Underground railroad
Slavery—United States—Fiction
    808.83; 813, etc.
    Use for collections of stories dealing with
    slavery in the United States.
Slaves (May subdiv. geog.) 305.5
BT **Slavery**
Slaves—Emancipation (May subdiv.
    geog.) 305.5
UF Abolition of slavery
      Antislavery
      Emancipation of slaves
      Slavery—Emancipation
BT **Freedom**
RT **Abolitionists**
      Slavery
Sledding 796.9
BT **Winter sports**
RT **Sleds**
Sledges
USE **Sleds**
Sleds 688.7
UF Sledges
      Sleighs and sledges
BT **Vehicles**
RT **Sledding**
Sleep 154.6; 612.8; 613.7
BT **Brain**
      Health
      Hygiene
      Mind and body

Sleep—*Continued*
        Psychophysiology
        Rest
        Subconsciousness
  NT **Bedtime**
  RT **Dreams**
        Insomnia
Sleeplessness
  USE **Insomnia**
Sleighs and sledges
  USE **Sleds**
Sleight of hand
  USE **Juggling**
        Magic tricks
Slide projectors
  USE **Projectors**
Slide rule **510.28**
  BT **Calculators**
        Logarithms
Slides (Photography) **778.2**
  UF Color slides
        Lantern slides
        Photographic slides
  BT **Photography**
  RT **Filmstrips**
Slovakia **943.73**
      May be subdivided like United States except for *History.*
  RT **Czechoslovakia**
Slow learning children **155.4; 371.92**
      Use for materials on children with less than average intelligence and slow social development who can nonetheless be educated and lead a normal life.
  BT **Exceptional children**
  NT **Learning disabilities**
  RT **Mentally handicapped children**
Slum clearance
  USE **Urban renewal**
Small and large
  USE **Size**
Small arms
  USE **Firearms**
Small business (May subdiv. geog.) **338.6; 658.02**
      Use for materials on small independent business enterprises.
  BT **Business**
  NT **Entrepreneurship**
        Home-based business
        Underground economy
Small cars
  USE **Compact cars**

Small loans
  USE **Personal loans**
Smell **152.1**
  BT **Senses and sensation**
  RT **Nose**
Smelting **669**
  BT **Furnaces**
  NT **Blast furnaces**
        Electrometallurgy
        Ore dressing
  RT **Metallurgy**
Smoke-ending programs
  USE **Smoking cessation programs**
Smoke prevention **363.738; 628.5**
  UF Prevention of smoke
  BT **Sanitation**
Smoke stacks
  USE **Chimneys**
Smokeless powder
  USE **Gunpowder**
Smoking (May subdiv. geog.) **178; 613.85**
  NT **Cigarettes**
        Cigars
        Tobacco habit
        Tobacco pipes
  RT **Tobacco**
Smoking cessation programs **613.85**
  UF How-to-stop-smoking programs
        Quit-smoking programs
        Smoke-ending programs
  BT **Tobacco habit**
Smuggling **364.1**
  UF Contraband trade
  BT **Crime**
        Tariff
Smuggling of drugs
  USE **Drug traffic**
Snakes (May subdiv. geog.) **597.96**
  UF Serpents
        Vipers
  SA types of snakes, e.g. **Rattlesnakes** [to be added as needed]
  BT **Reptiles**
  NT **Rattlesnakes**
        Snakes as pets
Snakes as pets **636.088**
  BT **Pets**
        Snakes

Snapshots
USE **Photographs**
Snorkeling
USE **Skin diving**
Snow (May subdiv. geog.)   **551.57**
BT **Precipitation (Meteorology)**
RT **Blizzards**
Storms
Snow skiing
USE **Skiing**
Snowmobiles   629.22; 796.94
UF Skidoos
BT **All terrain vehicles**
Soap   668
BT **Cleaning compounds**
RT **Detergents**
Soap box derbies   796.6
BT **Racing**
Soap carving
USE **Soap sculpture**
Soap operas   791.44; 791.45
May be used for individual works, collections, or materials about soap operas.
BT **Radio plays**
Television plays
RT **Radio serials**
Television serials
Soap sculpture   736
UF Soap carving
BT **Modeling**
Sculpture
Soaring flight
USE **Gliding and soaring**
Sobriquets
USE **Nicknames**
Soccer (May subdiv. geog.)   **796.334**
BT **Ball games**
Football
Sports
Soccer—Training   796.334
BT **Physical education**
Social action (May subdiv. geog.)   **361.2**
UF Social activism
SA subjects with the subdivision *Citizen participation*, e.g. **City planning—Citizen participation** [to be added as needed]
BT **Social policy**
NT **City planning—Citizen participation**
RT **Political participation**
Social problems

Social work
Social activism
USE **Social action**
Social adjustment   158; 303.3
UF Adjustment, Social
BT **Human behavior**
Interpersonal relations
Social psychology
NT **Socially handicapped**
Social alienation
USE **Alienation (Social psychology)**
Social anthropology
USE **Ethnology**
Social aspects
USE subjects with the subdivision *Social aspects,* e.g. **Genetic engineering—Social aspects** [to be added as needed]
Social behavior
USE **Human behavior**
Social case work   361.3
UF Case work, Social
Family social work
BT **Social work**
NT **Parole**
Probation
RT **Counseling**
Social change (May subdiv. geog.)   **303.4; 909**
UF Change, Social
Cultural change
Social evolution
BT **Anthropology**
Social sciences
Sociology
NT **Community development**
Modernization (Sociology)
Urbanization
Social classes (May subdiv. geog.)   **305.5; 323.3**
UF Class distinction
Rank
Social distinctions
BT **Caste**
Sociology
NT **Class consciousness**
Elite (Social sciences)
Intellectuals
Middle class
Rich
Upper class

Social classes—*Continued*
     Working class
Social conditions   306.09; 909
     Use for materials on the social aspects of
several of the following topics: labor, poverty,
education, health, housing, recreation, moral
conditions.
     UF   Social history
     SA   racial and ethnic groups, classes
          of persons, and names of
          countries, cities, etc., with the
          subdivision *Social conditions*
          [to be added as needed]
     BT   **Sociology**
     NT   **African Americans—Social**
          conditions
          Blacks—Social conditions
          Chicago (Ill.)—Social condi-
          tions
          Cost and standard of living
          Counter culture
          Economic conditions
          Jews—Social conditions
          Labor
          Men—Social conditions
          Moral conditions
          Native Americans—Social con-
          ditions
          Ohio—Social conditions
          Quality of life
          Social movements
          Social policy
          Social problems
          United States—Social condi-
          tions
          Urbanization
          Women—Social conditions
Social conflict (May subdiv. geog.)
     303.6
     UF   Class conflict
          Class struggle
          Conflict, Social
     BT   **Social psychology**
          Sociology
     NT   **Conflict of generations**
          Role conflict
Social conformity
     USE   **Conformity**
Social contract   320.01; 320.1
     BT   **Political science**
          Sociology

Social customs
     USE   **Manners and customs**
Social democracy
     USE   **Socialism**
Social distinctions
     USE   **Social classes**
Social drinking
     USE   **Drinking of alcoholic beverages**
Social ecology
     USE   **Human ecology**
Social equality
     USE   **Equality**
Social ethics (May subdiv. geog.)   **170**
     BT   **Ethics**
          Sociology
     NT   **Political ethics**
     RT   **Social problems**
Social evolution
     USE   **Social change**
Social geography
     USE   **Human geography**
Social group work   361.4; 362
     UF   Group social work
          Group work, Social
          Social work with groups
     BT   **Counseling**
          Social work
Social groups   302.3; 305
     UF   Group dynamics
          Groups, Social
     BT   **Sociology**
     NT   **Elite (Social sciences)**
          Leadership
          Neighborhood
          Social psychology
          Teams in the workplace
Social history
     USE   **Social conditions**
Social hygiene
     USE   **Public health**
          Sexual hygiene
Social insurance
     USE   **Social security**
Social isolation
     USE   **Loneliness**
Social learning
     USE   **Socialization**
Social life and customs
     USE   **Manners and customs**
          and names of ethnic groups,
          countries, cities, etc., with the

Social life and customs—*Continued*
          subdivision *Social life and
          customs,* e.g. **Native Americans—Social life and customs; Jews—Social life and customs; United States—Social life and customs;** etc. [to be added as needed]

Social medicine (May subdiv. geog.)
          306.4; 362.1

Use for materials on the study of social, genetic, and environmental influences on human disease and disability, as well as the promotion of health measures to protect both the individual and the community.

UF   Medical care—Social aspects
     Medical sociology
     Medicine—Social aspects
BT   **Medicine**
     Public health
     Public welfare
     Sociology
NT   **Hospices**
RT   **Medical ethics**

Social movements (May subdiv. geog.)
          303.48

SA   types of social movements, e.g.
        Environmental movement [to be added as needed]
BT   **Social conditions**
     Social psychology
NT   **Animal rights movement**
     Anti-apartheid movement
     Antinuclear movement
     Environmental movement
     Labor movement
     Militia movements
     New Age movement
     Peace movements
     Pro-choice movement
     Pro-life movement
     Protest movements
     Sanctuary movement
     Survivalism
     White supremacy movements
     Youth movement

Social planning
USE   **Social policy**

Social policy (May subdiv. geog.)   **361.6**

Use for materials on the ways a society regulates the relationships among individuals, groups, communities, and institutions, and on systematic procedures for achieving social

goals and managing available resources to attain social change.

UF   Government policy
     National planning
     Social planning
     State planning
SA   ethnic groups, classes of persons, and topics with the subdivision *Government policy,* e.g. **Homeless persons—Government policy;** and types of activities, facilities, industries, services, and undertakings with the subdivision *Planning,* e.g. **Transportation—Planning** [to be added as needed]
BT   **Planning**
     Social conditions
NT   **Arts—Government policy**
     Education—Government policy
     Homeless persons—Government policy
     Land reform
     Libraries—Government policy
     Multiculturalism
     Social action
     Welfare state
RT   **Economic policy**

Social policy—Chicago (Ill.)   361.6; 977.3

UF   Chicago (Ill.)—Social policy
     [Former heading]

Social policy—Ohio   361.6; 977.1

UF   Ohio—Social policy *[Former heading]*

Social policy—United States   361.6; 973

UF   United States—Social policy
     [Former heading]

Social problems (May subdiv. geog.)
          361.1

UF   Reform, Social
     Social reform
     Social welfare
BT   **Social conditions**
     Sociology
NT   **Alcoholism**
     Child labor
     Church and social problems
     Crime
     Discrimination
     Drug abuse
     Homelessness

Social problems—*Continued*
          Juvenile delinquency
          Poverty
          Prison reform
          Prostitution
          Public health
          Race discrimination
          Solvent abuse
          Suicide
          Unemployment
  RT   **Social action**
        Social ethics
Social problems and the church
  USE **Church and social problems**
Social problems in education
  USE **Educational sociology**
Social psychology (May subdiv. geog.)
      302
  UF   Mass psychology
  BT   **Human ecology**
        Psychology
        Social groups
        Sociology
  NT   **Alienation (Social psychology)**
        Class consciousness
        Discrimination
        Interpersonal relations
        Interviewing
        National characteristics
        Political psychology
        Popularity
        Public opinion
        Social adjustment
        Social conflict
        Social movements
        Social role
        Stereotype (Psychology)
        Violence
  RT   **Applied psychology**
        Crowds
        Ethnopsychology
Social reform
  USE **Social problems**
Social role   **302**
  UF   Role, Social
  BT   **Social psychology**
  NT   **Role conflict**
        Role playing
        Sex role
Social sciences (May subdiv. geog.)   **300**
  Use for general and comprehensive materials on the various branches of knowledge

dealing with human society, such as sociology, political science, economics, etc.
  UF   Social studies
  BT   **Civilization**
  NT   **Anthropology**
        Conservatism
        Cross-cultural studies
        Economics
        Gerontology
        History
        Human behavior
        Liberalism
        Political science
        Social change
        Social surveys
        Sociology
Social security (May subdiv. geog.)
      362; 368.4
  UF   Insurance, Social
        Social insurance
  BT   **Pensions**
  NT   **Workers' compensation**
Social service
  USE **Social work**
Social settlements (May subdiv. geog.)
      361.7; 362.5
  UF   Church settlements
        Neighborhood centers
        Settlements, Social
  SA   names of settlements, e.g. **Hull House (Chicago, Ill.)** [to be added as needed]
  BT   **Charities**
        Industrial welfare
        Social work
  NT   **Community centers**
        Hull House (Chicago, Ill.)
Social studies
  USE **Geography**
        History
        Social sciences
Social surveys (May subdiv. geog.)
      300.7
  Use for materials on the methods employed in conducting surveys of social and economic conditions.
  UF   Community surveys
  SA   names of regions, countries, cities, etc., with the subdivision *Social conditions* [to be added as needed]
  BT   **Social sciences**
        Surveys

Social surveys—United States 301
Social values (May subdiv. geog.) 303.3
  UF Group values
  BT **Values**
Social welfare
  USE **Charities**
      Public welfare
      Social problems
      Social work
Social work (May subdiv. geog.) 361.3
  Use for materials on the methods employed in welfare work, public or private. Materials on privately supported welfare activities are entered under **Charities.** Materials on tax-supported welfare activities are entered under **Public welfare.** General materials on the various policies, programs, services, and facilities to meet basic human needs, such as health, education, and welfare, are entered under **Human services.**
  UF Social service
      Social welfare
      Welfare work
  SA social work with particular groups of people, e.g. **Social work with the elderly;** and classes of persons and ethnic groups with the subdivision *Services for,* e.g. **Handicapped—Services for** [to be added as needed]
  BT **Human services**
  NT **Charities**
      Child welfare
      Community organization
      Community services
      Crisis centers
      Group homes
      Handicapped—Services for
      Hotlines (Telephone counseling)
      Industrial welfare
      Public welfare
      Social case work
      Social group work
      Social settlements
      Social work with the elderly
  RT **Social action**
Social work with groups
  USE **Social group work**
Social work with the elderly 362.6
  BT **Elderly**
      Social work

Socialism (May subdiv. geog.) 320.5; 335
  UF Collectivism
      Social democracy
  BT **Economics**
      Political science
  NT **Collective settlements**
      Dialectical materialism
      Government ownership
      Proletariat
      Utopias
  RT **Communism**
      Marxism
      National socialism
Socialism—United States 320.5; 335.00973
Socialization (May subdiv. geog.) 303.3
  Use for materials on the process by which individuals acquire group values and learn to function effectively in society.
  UF Children—Socialization
      Social learning
  BT **Acculturation**
      Child rearing
      Education
      Sociology
  NT **Americanization**
      Peer pressure
Socialization of industry
  USE **Government ownership**
Socialized medicine
  USE **National health insurance**
      State medicine
Socially handicapped (May subdiv. geog.) 362
  UF Culturally deprived
      Culturally handicapped
      Disadvantaged
      Underprivileged
  BT **Handicapped**
      Social adjustment
  NT **Socially handicapped children**
Socially handicapped children (May subdiv. geog.) 362.74
  UF Culturally deprived children
      Culturally handicapped children
      Disadvantaged children
      Underprivileged children
  BT **Handicapped children**
      Socially handicapped
  RT **At risk students**

Socials
   USE   **Church entertainments**
Societies (May subdiv. geog.)   **060**
   UF   Learned societies
   SA   types of societies, e.g. **Choral societies;** subjects, ethnic groups, classes of persons, corporate bodies, individual persons, and sacred works with the subdivision *Societies,* e.g. **Agriculture—Societies; Women—Societies;** etc.; and names of individual societies [to be added as needed]
   BT   **Associations**
   NT   **Agriculture—Societies**
         Boys' clubs
         Chemistry—Societies
         Choral societies
         Cooperative societies
         Education—Societies
         Elderly—Societies
         Girls' clubs
         History—Societies
         Labor unions
         Men—Societies
         Parent-teacher associations
         Science—Societies
         Secret societies
         Students—Societies
         Women—Societies
   RT   **Clubs**
Society and art
   USE   **Art and society**
Society and language
   USE   **Sociolinguistics**
Society and religion
   USE   **Religion and sociology**
Society of Friends (May subdiv. geog.)   **289.6**
   UF   Friends, Society of
         Quakers
   BT   **Christian sects**
Society, Primitive
   USE   **Primitive societies**
Society—Religious aspects
   USE   **Religion and sociology**
Sociobiology   **304.5; 577.8; 591.56**
   Use for materials on the biological basis of social behavior, especially as transmitted genetically.

   UF   Biology—Social aspects
   BT   **Comparative psychology**
         Sociology
Sociolinguistics (May subdiv. geog.)   **306.44**
   Use for materials on the study of the social aspects of language, particularly linguistic behavior, as determined by sociocultural factors.
   UF   Language and society
         Society and language
         Sociology of language
   BT   **Language and languages**
         Linguistics
         Sociology
Sociology (May subdiv. geog.)   **301**
   SA   sociology of particular religions, e.g. **Christian sociology;** and racial and ethnic groups, classes of persons, and names of countries, cities, etc., with the subdivision *Social conditions,* e.g. **United States—Social conditions** [to be added as needed[
   BT   **Social sciences**
   NT   **Christian sociology**
         Cities and towns
         Communication
         Educational sociology
         Equality
         Ethnic relations
         Ethnopsychology
         Family
         Human ecology
         Individualism
         Information society
         Labor
         Marxism
         Organizational sociology
         Population
         Race relations
         Religion and sociology
         Rural sociology
         Social change
         Social classes
         Social conditions
         Social conflict
         Social contract
         Social ethics
         Social groups
         Social medicine
         Social problems

Sociology—*Continued*
      Social psychology
      Socialization
      Sociobiology
      Sociolinguistics
      Urban sociology
  RT **Civilization**
      Culture
Sociology and art
  USE **Art and society**
Sociology and religion
  USE **Religion and sociology**
Sociology—Book reviews   301
Sociology, Christian
  USE **Christian sociology**
Sociology of language
  USE **Sociolinguistics**
Sociology of organizations
  USE **Organizational sociology**
Sociology of religion
  USE **Religion and sociology**
Sociology, Rural
  USE **Rural sociology**
Sociology, Urban
  USE **Urban sociology**
Sodium content of food
  USE **Food—Sodium content**
Softball   796.357
  BT **Ball games**
      Baseball
Software, Computer
  USE **Computer software**
Software for sharing
  USE **Shareware (Computer software)**
Software viruses
  USE **Computer viruses**
Soil conservation (May subdiv. geog.)
    631.4
  UF Conservation of the soil
  BT **Conservation of natural resources**
      Environmental protection
  RT **Erosion**
      Soil erosion
Soil engineering
  USE **Soil mechanics**
Soil erosion (May subdiv. geog.)   631.4
  UF Top soil loss
  BT **Erosion**
  RT **Soil conservation**

Soil fertility
  USE **Soils**
Soil mechanics   620.1
  UF Soil engineering
      Soils (Engineering)
  BT **Mechanics**
      Structural engineering
  RT **Foundations**
      Roads
      Soils
Soil microbiology   631.4
  UF Soils—Bacteriology
  BT **Microbiology**
      Sanitary engineering
  RT **Agricultural bacteriology**
Soilless agriculture
  USE **Hydroponics**
Soils (May subdiv. geog.)   631.4
  UF Soil fertility
  BT **Agriculture**
      Economic geology
  NT **Clay**
      Compost
      Fertilizers
  RT **Agricultural chemistry**
      Soil mechanics
Soils—Bacteriology
  USE **Soil microbiology**
Soils (Engineering)
  USE **Soil mechanics**
Soils, Lunar
  USE **Lunar soil**
Solace
  USE **Consolation**
Solar batteries   621.31
  UF Batteries, Solar
      Solar cells
      Sun powered batteries
  BT **Electric batteries**
      Photovoltaic power generation
      Solar radiation
Solar cells
  USE **Photovoltaic power generation**
      Solar batteries
Solar eclipses   523.7
  UF Eclipses, Solar
      Sun—Eclipses
  BT **Astronomy**

Solar energy (May subdiv. geog.)
        333.792; 621.47
    UF   Solar power
    BT   **Energy resources**
           Renewable energy resources
           Solar radiation
           Sun
    NT   **Photovoltaic power generation**
           Solar engines
           Solar heating
Solar engines   621.47
    BT   **Engines**
           Solar energy
Solar heating   621.47; 697
    SA   types of solar heating applica-
           tions, e.g. **Solar homes** [to be
           added as needed]
    BT   **Heating**
           Solar energy
    NT   **Solar homes**
Solar homes   697; 728
    BT   **Domestic architecture**
           Houses
           Solar heating
Solar physics
    USE **Sun**
Solar power
    USE **Solar energy**
Solar radiation   523.7; 621.47
    UF   Radiation, Solar
           Sun—Radiation
    BT   **Meteorology**
           Space environment
    NT   **Greenhouse effect**
           Solar batteries
           Solar energy
           Sunspots
Solar system   523.2
    SA   names of planets, e.g. **Saturn**
           (Planet) [to be added as
           needed]
    BT   **Astronomy**
           Stars
    NT   **Asteroids**
           Comets
           Earth
           Meteors
           Moon
           Planets
           Satellites
           Sun

Solder and soldering
    USE **Soldering**
Soldering   671.5
    UF   Solder and soldering
    BT   **Metals**
           Metalwork
    RT   **Welding**
Soldiers (May subdiv. geog.)   **355.0092;
920**
    UF   Army life
           Soldiers' life
    SA   names of countries with the sub-
           head *Army* and the subdivi-
           sion *Military life,* e.g. **United
           States. Army—Military life**
           [to be added as needed]
    BT   **Armies**
           Military personnel
    NT   **Mercenary soldiers**
           Missing in action
           **United States. Army—Military
           life**
           United States. Army—Officers
    RT   **Veterans**
Soldiers' handbooks
    USE **United States. Army—Hand-
           books, manuals, etc.**
Soldiers—Hygiene
    USE **Military personnel—Health
           and hygiene**
Soldiers' life
    USE **Soldiers**
           and names of countries with the
           subhead *Army* and the subdi-
           vision *Military life,* e.g. **Unit-
           ed States. Army—Military
           life** [to be added as needed]
Soldiers of fortune
    USE **Mercenary soldiers**
Soldiers' songs
    USE **War songs**
Soldiers—United States   355.0092; 920
    UF   GIs
           United States—Soldiers
Solicitors
    USE **Lawyers**
Solid Geometry   516.23
    UF   Geometry, Solid
    BT   **Geometry**
Solid waste disposal
    USE **Refuse and refuse disposal**

Solids 530.4; 531; 541
  BT **Physical chemistry**
      Physics
  NT **Crystals**
Solitaire (Game) 795.4
  UF Patience (Game)
  BT **Card games**
Solitude
  USE **Loneliness**
Solvent abuse (May subdiv. geog.)
        362.29
  UF Aerosol sniffing
      Glue sniffing
      Inhalant abuse
      Inhalation abuse of solvents
      Paint sniffing
      Substance abuse
  BT **Social problems**
  RT **Drug abuse**
Sonar 621.389
  UF Sound navigation
  BT **Signals and signaling**
Sonata 784.18
    Use for musical scores and for materials on
    the sonata as a musical form.
  UF Sonatas
  BT **Musical form**
Sonatas
  USE **Sonata**
Song books
  USE **Songbooks**
Song lyrics
  USE **Popular music—Texts**
Song writing
  USE **Composition (Music)**
      Popular music—Writing and
        publishing
Songbooks 782.42
    Use for general collections of songs that
    contain both words and music. Similar collec-
    tions limited to sacred songs are entered under
    Hymnals. Materials about songs are entered
    under **Songs.** Collections of songs on a single
    subject are entered under the subject with the
    subdivision *Songs.*
  UF Song books
  BT **Singing**
      Songs
  NT **Hymnals**
      School songbooks
Songs 782.42
    Use for materials about songs. General col-
    lections of songs that contain both words and

music are entered under **Songbooks.** Collections of songs that contain the words but not
the music are entered under **Poetry—Collections** for classical songs and under **Popular
music—Texts** for popular songs.
  SA types of songs, e.g. **Children's
      Songs;** songs of particular
      countries, e.g. **American
      songs;** subjects, classes of
      persons, and names of per-
      sons, corporate bodies, places,
      or wars, with the subdivision
      Songs, for collections or indi-
      vidual songs about the topic
      or associated with the entity
      named, e.g. **Cowhands—
      Songs; Surfing—Songs;
      United States Military Acad-
      emy—Songs; World War,
      1939-1945—Songs;** etc.; and
      names of individual songs [to
      be added as needed]
  BT **Poetry**
      Vocal music
  NT **African songs**
      American songs
      Ballads
      Carols
      Children's songs
      Cowhands—Songs
      Folk songs
      Hymns
      Lullabies
      National songs
      Popular music
      School songbooks
      Sea songs
      Songbooks
      Spirituals (Songs)
      State songs
      Students' songs
      Surfing—Songs
      United States. Army—Songs
      War songs
Songs, African
  USE **African songs**
Songs, African American
  USE **African American music**
Songs and music
  USE music of particular countries or
        ethnic groups, e.g. **American
        music; Native American mu-**

Songs and music—*Continued*

    sic; etc.; types of music, e.g.
Vocal music; and subjects,
classes of persons, and names
of individual persons, corporate bodies, places, or wars,
with the subdivision *Songs* for
collections of songs or materials about songs pertaining to
the topic or entity named, e.g.
**Cowhands—Songs; Surfing—
Songs; United States Military Academy—Songs** [to be
added as needed]

Songs for children
  USE **Children's songs**
Songwriters
  USE **Composers
       Lyricists**
Songwriting
  USE **Composition (Music)
       Popular music—Writing and
        publishing**
Sons 306.874
  BT **Family
      Men**
  NT **Father-son relationship
      Mother-son relationship**
Sons and fathers
  USE **Father-son relationship**
Sons and mothers
  USE **Mother-son relationship**
Soothsaying
  USE **Divination**
Soporifics
  USE **Narcotics**
Sorcery
  USE **Magic
      Occultism
      Witchcraft**
Sororities
  USE **Fraternities and sororities**
Sorrow
  USE **Bereavement
      Grief
      Joy and sorrow**
Soul 128; 233
  UF Spirit
  BT **Future life
      Human beings (Theology)
      Philosophy**

  NT **Immortality
      Psychology**
  RT **Reincarnation**
Sound 534; 620.2
  UF Acoustics
  BT **Physics
      Pneumatics
      Radiation**
  NT **Architectural acoustics
      Computer sound processing
      Hearing
      Noise
      Phonetics
      Sound effects
      Soundproofing
      Sounds
      Ultrasonics
      Vibration**
  RT **Music—Acoustics and physics**
Sound effects 534; 620.2
  BT **Sound**
Sound insulation
  USE **Soundproofing**
Sound navigation
  USE **Sonar**
Sound processing, Computer
  USE **Computer sound processing**
Sound recording
  USE **Sound—Recording and repro-
       ducing**
**Sound—Recording and reproducing
    621.389**

Use for materials on the equipment or the
process by which sound is recorded. Materials
on sound recordings that emphasize the content of the recording rather than the equipment, process, or format are entered under
Sound recordings. Materials about the format
are entered under the format, e.g. **Compact
discs.**

  UF Sound recording
  SA methods of recording, e.g. **Mag-
       netic recorders and record-
       ing** [to be added as needed]
  BT **Phonograph**
  NT **Compact disc players
      High-fidelity sound systems
      Phonograph
      Stereophonic sound systems**
  RT **Sound recordings**
Sound recordings (May subdiv. geog.)
    621.389; 780.26

Use for general materials and for materials
on sound recordings that emphasize the con-

Sound recordings—*Continued*
tent of the recording rather than the format. Materials about the format are entered under the format, e.g. **Compact discs.** Materials about the equipment or the process by which sound is recorded are entered under **Sound—Recording and reproducing.**

UF   Audio cassettes

        Audiotapes

        Cassette tapes, Audio

        Discography

        Phonograph records

        Recordings, Sound

        Records, Phonograph

        Tape recordings, Audio

SA   types of sound recordings, e.g. **Compact discs** [to be added as needed]

BT   **Audiovisual materials**

NT   **Audiobooks**

        Compact discs

RT   **Sound—Recording and reproducing**

Sound recordings—Copyright

USE   **Copyright—Sound recordings**

Sound waves   534; 620.2

BT   **Vibration**

        Waves

NT   **Ultrasonic waves**

Soundproofing   620.2; 693.8

UF   Insulation (Sound)

        Sound insulation

BT   **Architectural acoustics**

        Sound

Sounds   534; 620.2

BT   **Sound**

Soups   641.8

BT   **Cooking**

Sources

USE   historical subjects, periods of history, individual literary and sacred works, and names of wars with the subdivision *Sources,* e.g. **World War, 1939-1945—Sources;** and subjects, ethnic groups, classes of persons, coporate bodies, and names of countries, states, etc., with the subdivisions *History—Sources;* e.g. **United States—History—Sources** [to be added as needed]

South Africa   968

Use for materials on the Republic of South Africa.

UF   Republic of South Africa

        Union of South Africa

BT   **Africa**

        Southern Africa

South Africa—History   968

South Africa—Race relations   305.800968; 968

BT   **Race relations**

NT   **Anti-apartheid movement**

        Apartheid

South African Dutch

USE   **Afrikaners**

South Africans, Afrikaans-speaking

USE   **Afrikaners**

South America   980

BT   **America**

South American literature

USE   **Latin American literature**

South Atlantic States

USE   **Atlantic States**

South Korea

USE   **Korea (South)**

South Pacific region

USE   **Oceania**

South Pole   998

BT   **Polar regions**

RT   **Antarctica**

South Sea Islands

USE   **Oceania**

South Seas

USE   **Oceania**

South (U.S.)

USE   **Southern States**

Southeast Asia   959

Use for materials dealing collectively with the region of Asia that includes Burma, Thailand, Malaysia, Singapore, Indonesia, Vietnam, Cambodia, Laos, and the Philippines.

UF   Asia, Southeastern

BT   **Asia**

NT   **Indochina**

Southern Africa   968

Use for materials dealing collectively with the area south of the countries of Zaire and Tanzania. Southern Africa includes the political entities of Angola, Botswana, Comoros, Lesotho, Madagascar, Malawi, Mozambique, Namibia, South Africa, Swaziland, Zambia, and Zimbabwe. Materials on the Republic of South Africa are entered under **South Africa.**

Southern Africa—*Continued*
UF   Africa, Southern
BT   **Africa**
NT   **South Africa**
Southern cooking   641.5975
BT   **Cooking**
Southern lights
USE   **Auroras**
Southern literature
USE   **American literature—Southern States**
Southern States   975
UF   South (U.S.)
BT   **United States**
Southern States—African Americans
USE   **African Americans—Southern States**
Southern States—History   975
BT   **United States—History**
RT   **Slavery—United States**
Southwest, New
USE   **Southwestern States**
Southwest, Old
USE   **Old Southwest**
Southwest Pacific region
USE   **Oceania**
Southwestern States   979

Use for materials on that part of the United States that corresponds roughly with the old Spanish province of New Mexico, including the present Arizona, New Mexico, southern Colorado, Utah, Nevada, and California.

UF   Southwest, New
BT   **United States**
Sovereigns
USE   **Emperors**
        Kings and rulers
        Monarchy
        Queens
Soviet bloc
USE   **Communist countries**
Soviet communism
USE   **Communism—Soviet Union**
Soviet literature   890

Use for materials on several of the literatures of the Soviet Union. Materials on the individual literatures of the republics that made up the Soviet Union are entered with the appropriate adjective, e.g. **Russian literature;** etc.

UF   Literatures of the Soviet Union
        Soviet Union—Literatures
BT   **Literature**
RT   **Russian literature**

Soviet people
USE   **Soviets (People)**
Soviet Union   947.084

Use for materials on the Union of Soviet Socialist Republics between 1917 and 1991. Materials on Russia or the Russian empire before 1917 are entered under **Russia.** Materials on the independent republic of Russia since its establishment in December 1991 are entered under **Russia (Federation).** Materials on several or all of the countries that emerged from the dissolution of the Soviet Union in 1991 are entered under **Former Soviet republics.** Material specifically on the federation of former Soviet republics, which was established in December 1991 and does not include Georgia or the Baltic states, are entered under **Commonwealth of Independent States.** The Baltic states and the other republics of the former Soviet Union are: Armenia (Republic); Azerbaijan; Belarus; Estonia; Georgia (Republic); Kazakhstan; Kyrgyzstan; Latvia; Lithuania; Moldova; Tajikistan; Turkmenistan; Ukraine; and Uzbekistan; to be added as needed. The adjective **Soviet** is used to refer to the Soviet Union as a whole between 1917 and 1991, e.g. **Soviet literature.** Materials on the citizens of the Soviet Union between 1917 and 1991 are entered under **Soviets (People).** Materials on topics pertaining to individual republics, nationalities, or ethnic groups of the former Soviet Union are to be added as needed with the appropriate qualifier, e.g., **Russians; Russian language;** etc.

UF   Union of Soviet Socialist Republics
        USSR
NT   **Russians**
        Soviets (People)
RT   **Commonwealth of Independent States**
        Former Soviet republics
        Russia
        Russia (Federation)
Soviet Union—Communism
USE   **Communism—Soviet Union**
Soviet Union—History   947.084
UF   Soviet Union—History—1917-1991
Soviet Union—History—1917-1921, Revolution   947.084
UF   Russian revolution
BT   **Revolutions**
Soviet Union—History—1917-1925 947.084
Soviet Union—History—1917-1991
USE   **Soviet Union—History**
Soviet Union—History—1925-1953 947.084

Soviet Union—History—1939-1940, War
with Finland
  USE **Russo-Finnish War, 1939-1940**
Soviet Union—History—1953-1985
  947.085
Soviet Union—History—1953-1991
  947.085
Soviet Union—History—1985-1991
  947.085
Soviet Union—Literatures
  USE **Soviet literature**
Soviets (People) 920; 947.084
  Use for materials on the citizens of the So-
  viet Union between 1917 and 1991, not limit-
  ed to a single national or ethnic group. Mate-
  rials on the individual ethnic groups of the
  former Soviet Union are entered under the
  name for the ethnic group, e.g. **Russians;** etc.
  UF Soviet people
  BT **Soviet Union**
Soybean 633.3
  BT **Forage plants**
Space age
  USE **Astronautics and civilization**
Space and time 115
  UF Time and space
  BT **Fourth dimension**
      Metaphysics
      Space sciences
      Time
  NT **Cyberspace**
      Personal space
      Time travel
  RT **Relativity (Physics)**
Space-based weapons
  USE **Space weapons**
Space biology 571.0919; 612
  Use for materials on the biology of humans
  or other earth creatures while in outer space.
  Materials on the possibility of indigenous life
  in outer space are entered under **Life on oth-
  er planets.**
  UF Astrobiology
      Cosmobiology
  BT **Biology**
      Space sciences
  NT **Space medicine**
Space chemistry 523
  UF Astrochemistry
      Cosmochemistry
  BT **Chemistry**
Space colonies 629.44; 999
  Use for materials on communities estab-
  lished in space or on natural extraterrestrial

bodies. Materials on bases established on nat-
ural extraterrestrial bodies for specific func-
tions other than colonization are entered under
Extraterrestrial bases. Materials on manned
installations orbiting in space for specific
functions, such as servicing space ships, are
entered under **Space stations.**
  UF Colonies, Space
      Communities, Space
      Outer space—Colonies
  BT **Astronautics and civilization**
  RT **Extraterrestrial bases**
Space commercialization
  USE **Space industrialization**
Space communication
  USE **Astronautics—Communication
        systems**
       Interstellar communication
Space debris 629.4
  UF Debris in Space
      Junk in space
      Space pollution
  BT **Pollution**
      Space environment
Space environment 629.4
  UF Environment, Space
      Extraterrestrial environment
      Space weather
  BT **Astronomy**
      Outer space
  NT **Cosmic rays**
      Solar radiation
      Space debris
Space exploration (Astronautics)
  USE **Outer space—Exploration**
Space flight 629.4
  Use for materials on the physics and techni-
  cal details of flight beyond the earth's atmo-
  sphere. General materials and imaginary ac-
  counts of travel to other planets are entered
  under **Interplanetary voyages.**
  UF Humans in space
      Man in space
      Manned space flight
      People in space
      Rocket flight
      Space travel
  SA names of projects, e.g. **Gemini
        project;** and space flight to
      particular places, e.g. **Space
        flight to the moon** [to be
      added as needed]
  BT **Aeronautics—Flights**
      Astronautics

Space flight—*Continued*
  NT Astronauts
      Extravehicular activity (Space
        flight)
      Gemini project
      Orbital rendezvous (Space
        flight)
      Outer space—Exploration
      Space flight to the moon
  RT Astrodynamics
      Interplanetary voyages
      Navigation (Astronautics)
      Space medicine
      Space vehicles
Space flight (Fiction)
  USE Imaginary voyages
       Science fiction
Space flight—Law and legislation
  USE Space law
Space flight—Rescue work
  USE Space rescue operations
Space flight to the moon   629.45
  UF Flight to the moon
      Lunar expeditions
      Moon, Voyages to
      Voyages to the moon
  BT Astronautics
      Space flight
  NT Apollo project
      Moon—Exploration
Space heaters   644; 697
  BT Heating
  NT Fireplaces
      Stoves
Space industrial processing
  USE Space industrialization
Space industrialization (May subdiv.
      geog.)   629.44
  UF Commercial endeavors in space
      Industrial uses of space
      Manufacturing in space
      Space commercialization
      Space industrial processing
      Space manufacturing
      Space stations—Industrial appli-
        cations
  BT Industrialization
Space laboratories
  USE Space stations

Space law (May subdiv. geog.)   341.4
  UF Aerospace law
      Artificial satellites—Law and
        legislation
      Astronautics—Law and legisla-
        tion
      Space flight—Law and legisla-
        tion
      Space stations—Law and legisla-
        tion
  BT Astronautics and civilization
      International law
      Law
Space manufacturing
  USE Space industrialization
Space medicine   616.9
  UF Aerospace medicine
      Bioastronautics
  BT Medicine
      Space biology
      Space sciences
  NT Life support systems (Space
        environment)
      Weightlessness
  RT Aviation medicine
      Space flight
Space navigation
  USE Navigation (Astronautics)
Space nutrition
  USE Astronauts—Nutrition
Space optics   535
  BT Optics
      Space sciences
  NT Astronautical instruments
      Astronomical instruments
  RT Optical instruments
      Remote sensing
Space orbital rendezvous
  USE Orbital rendezvous (Space
        flight)
Space, Outer
  USE Outer space
Space, Personal
  USE Personal space
Space photography   778.3
  UF Photographs from space
      Photography in astronautics
  SA celestial bodies or objects in
        space with the subdivision
        Pictorial works [to be added
        as needed]

Space photography—*Continued*
  BT   **Photography**
       **Photography—Scientific appli-
       cations**
  NT   **Mars (Planet)—Pictorial works**
       Moon—Pictorial works
Space platforms
  USE   **Space stations**
Space pollution
  USE   **Space debris**
Space power
  USE   **Astronautics and civilization**
Space probes   629.43
  Use for materials on space exploration by
remote control from earth.
  SA   types of probes, e.g. **Lunar
       probes; Mars probes;** etc.;
       and names of space vehicles
       and space projects, e.g.
       Project Voyager [to be added
       as needed]
  BT   **Outer space—Exploration
       Space vehicles**
  NT   **Lunar probes
       Mars probes**
Space rescue operations   629.45
  UF   Rescue operations, Space
       Space flight—Rescue work
       Space vehicles—Rescue work
  BT   **Rescue work**
Space research
  USE   **Outer space—Exploration
       Space sciences**
Space rockets
  USE   **Space vehicles**
Space sciences (May subdiv. geog.)
       500.5
  Use for general materials and for scientific
results of space exploration and scientific ap-
plications of space flight.
  UF   Science and space
       Space research
  BT   **Science**
  NT   **Outer space
       Space and time
       Space biology
       Space medicine
       Space optics**
  RT   **Astronautics
       Astronomy**
**Space sciences—International cooperation
       500.5**
  BT   **International cooperation**

Space ships
  USE   **Space vehicles**
Space shuttles   629.44
  SA   names of individual space shut-
       tles [to be added as needed]
  BT   **Space vehicles**
  NT   **Challenger (Spacecraft)**
Space stations   629.44
  Use for materials on manned installations
orbiting in space for specific functions, such
as servicing space ships. Materials on bases
established on natural extraterrestrial bodies
for specific functions other than colonization
are entered under **Extraterrestrial bases.** Ma-
terials on communities established in space or
on natural extraterrestrial bodies are entered
under **Space colonies.**
  UF   Orbital laboratories
       Orbiting vehicles
       Space laboratories
       Space platforms
  BT   **Artificial satellites
       Astronautics
       Space vehicles**
  NT   **Orbital rendezvous (Space
       flight)**
Space stations—Industrial applications
  USE   **Space industrialization**
Space stations—Law and legislation
  USE   **Space law**
Space suits   629.47
  UF   Astronauts—Clothing
  BT   **Life support systems (Space
       environment)**
Space telecommunication
  USE   **Interstellar communication**
Space travel
  USE   **Interplanetary voyages
       Space flight**
Space vehicle accidents   363.12; 629.4
  UF   Astronautical accidents
       Astronautics—Accidents
       Space vehicles—Accidents
  BT   **Accidents**
Space vehicles   629.47
  UF   Space rockets
       Space ships
       Spacecraft
  BT   **Rocketry**
  NT   **Orbital rendezvous (Space
       flight)
       Rocket planes
       Space probes
       Space shuttles**

Space vehicles—*Continued*
      Space stations
  RT **Artificial satellites**
      Astronautics
      Space flight
Space vehicles—Accidents
  USE **Space vehicle accidents**
Space vehicles—Extravehicular activity
  USE **Extravehicular activity (Space flight)**
Space vehicles—Guidance systems
  629.47
Space vehicles—Instruments
  USE **Astronautical instruments**
Space vehicles—Piloting 629.45
  UF Piloting (Astronautics)
  BT **Astronauts**
      Navigation (Astronautics)
Space vehicles—Propulsion systems
  629.47
Space vehicles—Recovery 629.4
  UF Recovery of space vehicles
Space vehicles—Rescue work
  USE **Space rescue operations**
Space vehicles—Thermodynamics
  629.47
  BT **Thermodynamics**
Space vehicles—Tracking 629.4
  UF Tracking of satellites
Space walk
  USE **Extravehicular activity (Space flight)**
Space warfare 358
  Use for materials on interplanetary warfare, attacks on earth from outer space, and warfare among the nations of earth in outer space.
  UF Interplanetary warfare
      Interstellar warfare
      Space wars
  BT **Outer space**
      War
  NT **Space weapons**
      Strategic Defense Initiative
Space wars
  USE **Space warfare**
Space weapons 358
  UF Space-based weapons
      Star Wars weapons
      Weapons, Space
  BT **Military weapons**
      Space warfare
  RT **Strategic Defense Initiative**

Space weather
  USE **Space environment**
Spacecraft
  USE **Space vehicles**
Spain 946
  May be subdivided like United States except for *History*.
Spain—History 946
  NT **Spanish-American War, 1898**
      Spanish Armada, 1588
Spain—History—1898, War of 1898
  USE **Spanish-American War, 1898**
Spain—History—1936-1939, Civil War
  946.081
Spain—History—1939-1975 946.082
Spain—History—1975- 946.083
Spanish America
  USE **Latin America**
Spanish American literature
  USE **American literature (Spanish)**
      Latin American literature
Spanish-American War, 1898 973.8
  UF American-Spanish War, 1898
      Spain—History—1898, War of 1898
      United States—History—1898, War of 1898
  BT **Spain—History**
      United States—History—1865-1898
      United States—History—1898-1919
Spanish Armada, 1588 942.05; 946
  UF Armada, 1588
      Invincible Armada
  BT **Great Britain—History—1485-1603, Tudors**
      Spain—History
Spanish language 460
  May be subdivided like **English language**.
  BT **Language and languages**
      Romance languages
Spanish literature 860
  May use same subdivisions and names of literary forms as for **English literature**.
  BT **Literature**
      Romance literature
Sparring
  USE **Boxing**
Spas
  USE **Health resorts**
      Physical fitness centers

Speaking
    USE   **Debates and debating**
           Lectures and lecturing
           Preaching
           Public speaking
           Rhetoric
           Speech
           Voice
Speaking choirs
    USE   **Choral speaking**
Speaking in tongues
    USE   **Glossolalia**
Speaking with tongues
    USE   **Glossolalia**
Spear fishing   799.1
    BT   **Fishing**
Special collections in libraries
    USE   **Libraries—Special collections**
Special education (May subdiv. geog.)
    371.9
    SA   classes of exceptional children
           with the subdivision *Educa-*
           tion [to be added as needed]
    BT   **Education**
    NT   **Mentally handicapped chil-**
           dren—Education
    RT   **Mainstreaming in education**
Special libraries (May subdiv. geog.)
    026; 027.6
    Use for materials on libraries covering specialized subjects, containing special format materials, or serving a specialized clientele.
    SA   types of special libraries, e.g.
           Business libraries [to be added as needed]
    BT   **Libraries**
    NT   **Business libraries**
           Corporate libraries
           Government libraries
           Music libraries
Special Olympics   796.087
    BT   **Olympic games**
           Sports for the handicapped
Specialists exchange programs
    USE   **Exchange of persons programs**
Specie
    USE   **Coins**
Specifications
    USE   types of engineering, construction, industries, products, and merchandise with the subdivi-

sion *Specifications,* for works on the particular qualities prescribed for a product to meet specific requirements [to be added as needed]
Specimens, Preservation of
    USE   **Plants—Collection and preservation**
           Taxidermy
           Zoological specimens—Collection and preservation
           and types of natural specimens with the subdivision *Collection and preservation,* e.g.
           Birds—Collection and preservation [to be added as needed]
Spectacles
    USE   **Eyeglasses**
Specters
    USE   **Apparitions**
           Ghosts
Spectra
    USE   **Spectrum analysis**
Spectrochemical analysis
    USE   **Spectrum analysis**
Spectrochemistry
    USE   **Spectrum analysis**
Spectroscopy
    USE   **Spectrum analysis**
Spectrum analysis   535.8
    UF   Spectra
           Spectrochemical analysis
           Spectrochemistry
           Spectroscopy
    BT   **Astronomy**
           Astrophysics
           Chemistry
           Optics
           Radiation
    NT   **Mass spectrometry**
    RT   **Light**
Speculation (May subdiv. geog.)   **332.64**
    BT   **Finance**
    NT   **Real estate investment**
    RT   **Investments**
           Stock exchanges

Speech 302.2; 372.62; 410; 612.7
- UF Speaking
- BT **Language arts**
- NT **Speech disorders**
  Speech processing systems
  Speech therapy
  Voice culture
- RT **Language and languages**
  Phonetics
  Voice

Speech correction
- USE **Speech therapy**

Speech disorders 616.85
- UF Defective speech
  Speech pathology
  Stammering
  Stuttering
- BT **Speech**

Speech, Freedom of
- USE **Freedom of speech**

Speech pathology
- USE **Speech disorders**

Speech processing systems 006.5
- UF Computer speech processing sys-
  tems
  Electronic speech processing sys-
  tems
  Speech scramblers
- BT **Speech**
- NT **Automatic speech recognition**
  Speech synthesis
- RT **Computer sound processing**

Speech recognition, Automatic
- USE **Automatic speech recognition**

Speech scramblers
- USE **Speech processing systems**

Speech synthesis 006.5
- BT **Speech processing systems**

Speech therapy 616.85
- UF Speech correction
- BT **Speech**

Speeches 808.85; 815.008, etc.

Use for collections of speeches on several subjects and materials about speeches that have already been delivered. Materials on the art of delivering speeches are entered under **Public-speaking** or under **Lectures and lec-turing.** Collections of speeches on a single subject are entered under that subject.

- UF Addresses
  Orations
  Speeches, addresses, etc.
- SA speeches of particular countries,
  e.g. **American speeches** [to
  be added as needed]
- BT **Literature**
- NT **After dinner speeches**
  American speeches
  English speeches
  **Presidents—United States—In-
  augural addresses**
  Toasts
- RT **Lectures and lecturing**
  Public speaking

Speeches, addresses, etc.
- USE **Speeches**

Speeches, addresses, etc., American
- USE **American speeches**

Speeches, addresses, etc., English
- USE **English speeches**

Speed 531
- UF Velocity
- BT **Motion**

Speed (Drug)
- USE **Methamphetamine**

Speed reading 372.45
- UF Accelerated reading
  Faster reading
  Rapid reading
- BT **Reading**

Speed, Supersonic
- USE **Supersonic aerodynamics**

Speleology
- USE **Caves**

Spellers 418; 428.1, etc.
- BT **English language—Spelling**

Spelling
- USE names of languages with the
  subdivision *Spelling,* e.g. **English language—Spelling** [to
  be added as needed]

Spelling reform 418; 428.1, etc.
- UF English language—Spelling re-
  form
  Orthography
  Phonetic spelling
- BT **English language—Spelling**

Spells
- USE **Charms**
  Magic

Spherical trigonometry
- USE **Trigonometry**

Spices 641.3
  SA types of spices [to be added as needed]
  BT **Food**

Spiders (May subdiv. geog.) 595.4
  BT **Animals**

Spies (May subdiv. geog.) 327.12; 353.1; 355.3
  UF Intelligence agents
       Spying
  BT **Espionage**
       Subversive activities
  RT **Secret service**

Spinning 677; 746.1
  BT **Textile industry**
  RT **Yarn**

Spiral gearing
  USE **Gearing**

Spires 721
  UF Steeples
  BT **Architecture**
       Church architecture

Spirit
  USE **Soul**

Spiritism
  USE **Spiritualism**

Spirits
  USE **Angels**
       Apparitions
       Demonology
       Ghosts
       Spiritualism

Spiritual gifts 234
  Use for materials on extraordinary phenomena, such as glossolalia, visions, prophecies and interpretations, healings, discernment of spirits, etc. Materials dealing collectively with ordinary spiritual phenomena, such as faith, hope, love, patience, temperance, etc., are entered under **Virtue.**
  UF Charismata
       Gifts of grace
       Gifts of the Holy Spirit
       Gifts, Spiritual
  BT **Grace (Theology)**
  NT **Glossolalia**
       Spiritual healing
       Visions
  RT **Catholic charismatic movement**
       Holy Spirit
       Pentecostalism

Spiritual healing 234; 291.2; 615.8
  Use for materials on the use of faith, prayer, or other religious means to treat illness. Materials on psychic or psychological means to treat illness are entered under **Mental healing.**
  UF Divine healing
       Evangelistic healing
       Faith cure
       Faith healing
       Healing, Spiritual
  BT **Medicine—Religious aspects**
       Spiritual gifts
  RT **Christian Science**
       Mental healing
       Mind and body
       Miracles
       Subconsciousness
       Suggestive therapeutics

Spiritual life 248; 291.4
  Use for materials on spiritual practices and on the relationship that individuals may attain with the sacred. May be subdivided by religion or sect.
  BT **Religious life**
  NT **Conversion**
       Faith
       Hope
       Meditation
       Mysticism

Spiritualism (May subdiv. geog.) 133.9
  Use for materials on extraordinary spiritual phenomena, especially contact with the spirits of the dead.
  UF Spiritism
       Spirits
  BT **Occultism**
       Supernatural
  NT **Psychokinesis**
  RT **Apparitions**
       Parapsychology

Spirituals (Songs) 782.25
  BT **American songs**
       Folk songs—United States
       Hymns
       Songs
  RT **African American music**
       Gospel music

Splicing
  USE **Knots and splices**

Splicing of genes
  USE **Genetic engineering**

Split personality
  USE **Multiple personality**

Spoils system
USE **Political corruption**
Sponges (May subdiv. geog.)   **593.4**
BT **Aquatic animals**
Sporting equipment
USE **Sporting goods**
Sporting goods   796.028
UF   Sporting equipment
Sports—Equipment and supplies
RT **Sports**
Sports (May subdiv. geog.)   **796**
SA   types of sports and names of
sports competitions [to be
added as needed]
BT **Play**
Recreation
NT **Aeronautical sports**
Baseball
Basketball
Bullfights
Coaching (Athletics)
College sports
Cycling
Field hockey
Fishing
Football
Gymnastics
Olympic games
Orienteering
Professional sports
Racing
Rodeos
Rowing
School sports
Soccer
Sports cards
Sports records
Sports tournaments
Sportsmanship
Tennis
Track athletics
Water sports
Winter sports
RT **Amusements**
Athletes
Athletics
Games
Outdoor life
Physical education
Sporting goods
Sports facilities

Sports and drugs
USE **Athletes—Drug use**
Sports broadcasting
USE **Radio broadcasting of sports**
Television broadcasting of sports
Sports cards   769
UF   Cards, Sports
SA   types of cards for specific
sports, e.g. **Baseball cards** [to
be added as needed]
BT **Sports**
NT **Baseball cards**
Sports cars (May subdiv. geog.)
629.222
SA   names of specific sports cars [to
be added as needed]
BT **Automobiles**
Sports coaching
USE **Coaching (Athletics)**
Sports—Corrupt practices   796
UF   Cheating in sports
Corruption in sports
Sports scandals
BT **Criminal law**
Sports drama (Films)   791.43
May be used for individual works, collections, or materials about sports drama on film.
BT **Motion pictures**
Sports drama (Radio programs)   791.44
May be used for individual works, collections, or materials about sports drama on the radio.
BT **Radio programs**
Sports drama (Television programs)   791.45
May be used for individual works, collections, or materials about sports drama on television.
BT **Television programs**
Sports—Equipment and supplies
USE **Sporting goods**
Sports facilities (May subdiv. geog.)
796.06
SA   types of sports facilities [to be
added as needed]
NT **Playgrounds**
Stadiums
Swimming pools
RT **Recreation**
Sports
Sports—Fiction   808.83; 813, etc.
Use for collections of sports stories.

Sports—Fiction—*Continued*
   UF   Sports stories
   SA   types of sports with the subdivi-
         sion *Fiction,* e.g. **Baseball—**
         Fiction [to be added as need-
         ed]
Sports for the handicapped   796.01
   BT   **Handicapped**
   NT   **Special Olympics**
Sports in radio
   USE   **Radio broadcasting of sports**
Sports in television
   USE   **Television broadcasting of**
         sports
Sports—Lists   796
Sports—Medical aspects
   USE   **Sports medicine**
Sports medicine   613.7; 617.1
   UF   Athletic medicine
         Physical education—Medical as-
         pects
         Sports—Medical aspects
   BT   **Medical care**
         Medicine
Sports records (May subdiv. geog.)   **796**
   Use for materials on top performances or
   achievements.
   UF   Records, Sports
   BT   **Sports**
   RT   **Sports—Statistics**
         World records
Sports scandals
   USE   **Sports—Corrupt practices**
Sports—Statistics   796
   SA   types of sports with the subdivi-
         sion *Statistics* [to be added as
         needed]
   BT   **Statistics**
   RT   **Sports records**
Sports stories
   USE   **Sports—Fiction**
Sports tournaments (May subdiv. geog.)
         796
   UF   Tournaments
   SA   types of sports with the subdivi-
         sion *Tournaments,* e.g. **Ten-**
         nis—Tournaments [to be
         added as needed]
   BT   **Contests**
         Sports
   NT   **Tennis—Tournaments**

Sportsmanship   175
   BT   **Human behavior**
         Sports
Spot welding
   USE   **Electric welding**
Spouses
   USE   **Husbands**
         Wives
Spraying and dusting   632
   UF   Dusting and spraying
   BT   **Agricultural pests**
         Fruit—Diseases and pests
   NT   **Aeronautics in agriculture**
   RT   **Fungicides**
         Herbicides
         Insecticides
Spreadsheet software   005.3
   UF   Electronic spreadsheets *[Former*
         heading]
   BT   **Computer software**
Spun glass
   USE   **Glass fibers**
Spy films   791.43
   May be used for individual works, collec-
   tions, or materials about spy films.
   UF   Espionage films
         Suspense films
   BT   **Motion pictures**
   RT   **Mystery films**
Spy novels
   USE   **Spy stories**
Spy radio programs   791.44
   May be used for individual works, collec-
   tions, or materials about spy radio programs.
   UF   Suspense programs
   BT   **Radio programs**
Spy stories   808.83; 813, etc.
   May be used for individual works, collec-
   tions, or materials about spy stories.
   UF   Espionage stories
         Spy novels
   BT   **Adventure fiction**
   RT   **Mystery fiction**
         Romantic suspense novels
Spy television programs   791.45
   May be used for individual works, collec-
   tion, or materials about spy television pro-
   grams.
   UF   Espionage television programs
         Suspense programs
   BT   **Television programs**
   RT   **Mystery television programs**

Spying
USE **Espionage**
Spies
Square **516**
BT **Geometry**
Shape
Square dancing **793.3**
BT **Folk dancing**
Square root **513.2**
BT **Arithmetic**
Squirrels **599.36**
BT **Mammals**
NT **Chipmunks**
SST (Supersonic transport)
USE **Supersonic transport planes**
St. Bartholomew's Day, Massacre of, 1572
USE **Saint Bartholomew's Day,**
Massacre of, 1572
St. Francis, Order of
USE **Franciscans**
St. Valentine's Day
USE **Valentine's Day**
Stabilization in industry
USE **Business cycles**
Stadia
USE **Stadiums**
Stadiums (May subdiv. geog.) **796.06**
UF Ballparks
Stadia
BT **Sports facilities**
Staff
USE types of institutions, types of
public officials, and names of
individual public officials with
the subdivision *Staff*, e.g.
Presidents—United States—
Staff [to be added as needed]
Stage
USE **Acting**
Drama
Theater
Stage history
USE names of dramatists with the
subdivision *Stage history*, e.g.
Shakespeare, William, 1564-
1616—Stage history [to be
added as needed]
Stage lighting **792**
UF Television—Stage lighting
Theaters—Stage lighting
BT **Lighting**

Stage scenery
USE **Theaters—Stage setting and**
scenery
Stage setting
USE **Theaters—Stage setting and**
scenery
Stagecoaches
USE **Carriages and carts**
Stained glass
USE **Glass painting and staining**
Stalking (May subdiv. geog.) **364.1**
UF Antistalking laws
Stalking—Law and legislation
BT **Offenses against the person**
Stalking—Law and legislation
USE **Stalking**
Stamina, Physical
USE **Physical fitness**
Stammering
USE **Speech disorders**
Stamp collecting (May subdiv. geog.)
769.56
Use for materials on the collecting, buying,
and selling of postage stamps.
UF Philately
Postage stamp collecting
Postage stamps—Collectors and
collecting
Stamps—Collectors and collect-
ing
BT **Collectors and collecting**
RT **Postage stamps**
Stamps—Collectors and collecting
USE **Stamp collecting**
Stamps, Postage
USE **Postage stamps**
Standard book numbers
USE **Publishers' standard book**
numbers
Standard of living
USE **Cost and standard of living**
Standard of value
USE **Money**
Standard time
USE **Time**
Standards
USE subjects, types of school and in-
stitutions, and types of indus-
tries with the subdivision
Standards, e.g. **Environmen-**
tal protection—Standards;

Standards—*Continued*

    which may be further subdivided geographically [to be added as needed]

Standards of output

  USE **Production standards**

Star Wars (Ballistic missile defense system)

  USE **Strategic Defense Initiative**

Star Wars films **791.43**

    May be used for individual works, collections, or materials about Star Wars films.

  BT **Motion pictures**

      Science fiction films

Star Wars weapons

  USE **Space weapons**

Stars **523.8**

  SA names of constellations and of individual stars, e.g. **Sirius** [to be added as needed]

  NT **Black holes (Astronomy)**

      Galaxies

      Sirius

      Solar system

      Supernovas

  RT **Astronomy**

      Constellations

Stars—Atlases **523.8022**

  UF Astronomy—Atlases

      Atlases, Astronomical

  BT **Atlases**

Starting a business

  USE **New business enterprises**

Starvation **363.8**

  NT **Famines**

  RT **Fasting**

      Hunger

      Malnutrition

State aid to education

  USE **Government aid to education**

State aid to libraries

  USE **Government aid to libraries**

State and agriculture

  USE **Agriculture—Government policy**

State and environment

  USE **Environmental policy**

State and railroads

  USE **Railroads—Government policy**

State and the arts

  USE **Federal aid to the arts**

State birds **598**

  BT **Birds**

      State emblems

State constitutions

  USE **Constitutions**

      Constitutions—United States

State emblems (May subdiv. geog.) **929.9**

  UF Emblems, State

      State symbols

  SA types of state emblems and state symbols, e.g. **State birds; State flowers** [to be added as needed]

  BT **Signs and symbols**

  NT **State birds**

      State flowers

  RT **National emblems**

State encouragement of science, literature, and art

  USE **Cultural policy**

State encouragement of the arts

  USE **Arts—Government policy**

      Federal aid to the arts

State-federal relations

  USE **Federal-state relations**

State flowers **582.13**

  BT **Flowers**

      State emblems

State governments **352.13**

    Use for general materials on state government not limited to a single state.

  UF United States—State governments

  SA names of states with the subdivision *Politics and government,* e.g. **Ohio—Politics and government** [to be added as needed]

  BT **Political science**

  NT **Federal-state relations**

      Governors

      State-local relations

  RT **Federal government**

State, Heads of

  USE **Heads of state**

State libraries (May subdiv. geog.) **027.5**

    Use for materials on government libraries, maintained by state funds, that preserve state records and publications.

  BT **Government libraries**

State-local relations (May subdiv. geog.)
  342; 352.13
  UF City-state relations
      Local-state relations
  BT **Local government**
      Municipal government
      State governments
State-local tax relations
  USE **Intergovernmental tax relations**
State medicine (May subdiv. geog.)
  362.1; 368.4; 614
  Use for general materials on the relations of
  the state to medicine, public health, medical
  legislation, examinations of physicians by
  state boards, etc.
  UF Medicine, State
      National health service
      Socialized medicine
  BT **Medicine**
  NT **Medicaid**
      Medicare
      Public health
  RT **National health insurance**
State ministries
  USE **Executive departments**
State of the Union messages
  USE **Presidents—United States—**
      Messages
State ownership
  USE **Government ownership**
State ownership of railroads
  USE **Railroads—Government policy**
State planning
  USE **Economic policy**
      Regional planning
      Social policy
State police   363.2
  UF Police, State
  BT **Police**
State regulation of industry
  USE **Industrial policy**
State rights   321.02; 342
  UF Secession
      States' rights
  BT **Political science**
State songs   782.42
  BT **Songs**
State symbols
  USE **State emblems**

State, The   320.1
  UF Commonwealth, The
  NT **Church and state**
      Public interest
      Welfare state
  RT **Political science**
States, New
  USE **New states**
States' rights
  USE **State rights**
Statesmen (May subdiv. geog.)   **920**
  NT **Diplomats**
      Heads of state
      Politicians
Statics   531
  BT **Mechanics**
      Physics
  NT **Hydrostatics**
      Strains and stresses
  RT **Dynamics**
Statistical diagrams
  USE **Statistics—Graphic methods**
Statistical inference
  USE **Probabilities**
Statistics   001.4; 310
  Use for materials on the theory and meth-
  ods of statistics.
  SA subjects and names of countries,
      cities, etc., with the subdivi-
      sion *Statistics* [to be added as
      needed]
  BT **Economics**
  NT **Agriculture—Statistics**
      Average
      Census
      Chicago (Ill.)—Statistics
      Education—Statistics
      Libraries—Statistics
      Ohio—Statistics
      Probabilities
      Railroads—Statistics
      Sampling (Statistics)
      Sports—Statistics
      United States—Statistics
      Vital statistics
Statistics—Graphic methods   001.4
  UF Statistical diagrams
  BT **Graphic methods**
Statues
  USE **Monuments**
      Sculpture

Statutes
  USE   Law
Stealing
  USE   Theft
Steam   536; 621.1
  BT   Heat
       Power (Mechanics)
       Water
  RT   Steam engineering
Steam engineering (May subdiv. geog.)
       621.1
  BT   Engineering
  NT   Steam engines
       Steam navigation
       Steam power plants
  RT   Mechanical engineering
       Steam
Steam engines   621.1
  BT   Engines
       Steam engineering
  NT   Condensers (Steam)
       Marine engines
       Steam turbines
Steam heating   697
  BT   Heating
Steam locomotives (May subdiv. geog.)
       625.26
  BT   Locomotives
Steam navigation   387; 623.8
  BT   Navigation
       Steam engineering
       Transportation
  NT   Marine engineering
       Steam turbines
  RT   Steamboats
Steam power plants   621.1
  BT   Electric power plants
       Steam engineering
Steam turbines   621.1
  BT   Steam engincs
       Steam navigation
       Turbines
Steamboats (May subdiv. geog.)   387.2;
       623.8
  UF   Steamships
  BT   Boats and boating
       Naval architecture
       Ocean travel
       Shipbuilding
       Ships
  RT   Steam navigation

Steamships
  USE   Steamboats
Steel   669; 672
  BT   Iron
       Metalwork
  NT   Structural steel
Steel construction (May subdiv. geog.)
       693
  UF   Building, Iron and steel
       Iron and steel building
  BT   Building
       Structural engineering
  RT   Structural steel
Steel engraving
  USE   Engraving
Steel industry (May subdiv. geog.)
       338.4; 672
  UF   Steel industry and trade
  BT   Industries
  RT   Iron industry
Steel industry and trade
  USE   Steel industry
Steel industry—Labor productivity
       338.4
  BT   Labor productivity
Steel industry—Quality control   338.4;
       672
  BT   Quality control
Steel, Structural
  USE   Structural steel
Steeples
  USE   Spires
Steers
  USE   Beef cattle
Stencil work   686.2; 745.7
  BT   Decoration and ornament
       Painting
  NT   Silk screen printing
Stenography
  USE   Shorthand
Stepfamilies   306.85
  UF   Stepfamily [Former heading]
  BT   Family
Stepfamily
  USE   Stepfamilies
Stereo photography
  USE   Three dimensional photogra-
       phy
Stereo sound systems
  USE   Stereophonic sound systems

Stereophonic sound systems   621.389
    UF   Stereo sound systems
    BT   **High-fidelity sound systems**
          **Sound—Recording and repro-
          ducing**
Stereophotography
    USE **Three dimensional photogra-
          phy**
Stereopticon
    USE **Projectors**
Stereoscopic photography
    USE **Three dimensional photogra-
          phy**
Stereotype (Psychology) (May subdiv.
    geog.)   303.3
    UF   Mental stereotype
          Stereotyped behavior
    BT   **Attitude (Psychology)**
          Social psychology
          Thought and thinking
Stereotyped behavior
    USE **Stereotype (Psychology)**
Sterility in animals
    USE **Infertility**
Sterility in humans
    USE **Infertility**
Sterilization (Birth control) (May subdiv.
    geog.)   363.9; 613.9
    BT   **Birth control**
    NT   **Vasectomy**
Steroids   572; 612
    UF   Anabolic steroids
    BT   **Biochemistry**
          Drugs
    RT   **Athletes—Drug use**
          Hormones
Stewardesses, Airline
    USE **Flight attendants**
Stewards, Airline
    USE **Flight attendants**
Stills
    USE **Distillation**
Stimulants   613.8; 615
    SA   types of stimulants, e.g. **Am-
          phetamines;** and names of in-
          dividual stimulants [to be
          added as needed]
    BT   **Drugs**
          Psychotropic drugs
    NT   **Amphetamines**
          Hallucinogens

Stock car racing (May subdiv. geog.)
    796.72
    BT   **Automobile racing**
Stock control
    USE **Inventory control**
Stock exchange
    USE **Stock exchanges**
Stock exchange crashes
    USE **Financial crises**
Stock exchanges (May subdiv. geog.)
    332.64
    UF   Securities exchange
          Stock exchange *[Former head-
          ing]*
          Stock market
    BT   **Finance**
          Markets
    NT   **Bonds**
          Insider trading
          Securities
          Wall Street (New York, N.Y.)
    RT   **Investments**
          Speculation
          Stocks
Stock fraud
    USE **Securities fraud**
Stock judging
    USE **Livestock judging**
Stock market
    USE **Stock exchanges**
Stock market fraud
    USE **Securities fraud**
Stock market panics
    USE **Financial crises**
Stock raising
    USE **Livestock industry**
Stockings
    USE **Hosiery**
Stocks (May subdiv. geog.)   332.63
    UF   Dividends
          Shares of stock
    BT   **Commerce**
          Securities
    NT   **Corporations**
    RT   **Bonds**
          Investments
          Stock exchanges
Stocks—Insider trading
    USE **Insider trading**
Stockyards
    USE **Meat industry**

Stoics   188
> BT   **Ancient philosophy**
> **Ethics**

Stomach   612.3
> BT   **Anatomy**
> RT   **Digestion**

Stone   553.5; 693
> Use for materials on stone as a building material. General materials on naturally occurring solid minerals are entered under **Rocks.**
> SA   types of stone, e.g. **Marble** [to be added as needed]
> BT   **Building materials**
> **Economic geology**
> NT   **Granite**
> **Marble**
> **Masonry**
> **Stonecutting**
> RT   **Petrology**
> **Quarries and quarrying**
> **Rocks**

Stone Age (May subdiv. geog.)   **930.1**
> UF   Eolithic period
> Neolithic period
> Paleolithic period
> BT   **Civilization**
> RT   **Stone implements**

Stone-cutting
> USE   **Stonecutting**

Stone implements (May subdiv. geog.)   **930.1**
> UF   Flint implements
> Implements, utensils, etc.
> RT   **Stone Age**

Stone quarries
> USE   **Quarries and quarrying**

Stonecutting   693
> UF   Stone-cutting
> BT   **Masonry**
> **Stone**

Stoneware
> USE   **Pottery**

Storage
> USE   types of commodities, foods, materials, industrial products, etc., with the subdivision *Storage,* e.g. **Grain—Storage** [to be added as needed]

Storage batteries   621.31
> UF   Batteries, Electric
> BT   **Electric apparatus and appliances**

> RT   **Electric batteries**

Storage devices, Computer
> USE   **Computer storage devices**

Storage in the home   648
> UF   Home storage
> BT   **Home economics**

Store buildings
> USE   **Commercial buildings**

Stores (May subdiv. geog.)   **381**
> UF   Retail stores
> Shops
> SA   types of stores, e.g. **Drugstores** [to be added as needed]
> BT   **Commercial buildings**
> **Retail trade**
> NT   **Chain stores**
> **Department stores**
> **Discount stores**
> **Drugstores**
> **Supermarkets**
> RT   **Shopping centers and malls**

Stories
> USE   **Anecdotes**
> **Bible stories**
> **Fairy tales**
> **Fiction**
> **Legends**
> **Romances**
> **Short stories**
> **Stories in rhyme**
> **Stories without words**
> **Storytelling**
> and   national literatures and literary or musical forms with the subdivision *Stories, plots, etc.,* e.g. **Ballet—Stories, plots, etc.; Opera—Stories, plots, etc.;** etc. [to be added as needed]

Stories for children
> USE   **Children's stories**

Stories in rhyme   811, etc.
> Use as a form heading for narrative poems for very young children. Narrative poetry and materials about narrative poetry for older children and for adults are entered under **Narrative poetry.**
> UF   Stories
> BT   **Narrative poetry**
> **Rhyme**

Stories, plots, etc.   808
> Use for materials that analyze plots or discuss the technique of constructing plots. Col-

Stories, plots, etc.—*Continued*

lections of plots of a specific literary or musical form are entered under that form with the
subdivision *Stories, plots, etc.* General collections of literary plots are entered under **Stories, plots, etc.—Collections.**

  UF   Dramatic plots

          Fictional plots

          Plots (Drama, fiction, etc.) *[For-
          mer heading]*

          Scenarios

  SA   national literatures and literary
          or musical forms with the
          subdivision *Stories, plots, etc.,*
          e.g. **Ballet—Stories, plots,
          etc.; Opera—Stories, plots,
          etc.** [to be added as needed]

  BT **Literature**

Stories, plots, etc.—Collections   **802**

Use for collections of literary plots. Materials that analyze plots or discuss the technique
of constructing plots are entered under **Stories, plots, etc.**

  UF   Literature—Stories, plots, etc.
          [Former heading]

  SA   national literatures and specific
          genres of literature with the
          subdivision *Stories, plots, etc.*
          [to be added as needed]

Stories without words

Use as a form heading for stories for children told only through a sequence of pictures.

  UF   Nonword stories

          Picture books for children,
          Wordless

          Stories

          Wordless stories

  BT **Picture books for children**

Storms (May subdiv. geog.)   **551.55**

  SA   types of storms [to be added as
          needed]

  BT **Meteorology**

      Natural disasters

      Weather

  NT **Blizzards**

      Cyclones

      Dust storms

      Hurricanes

      Thunderstorms

      Tornadoes

      Typhoons

  RT **Rain**

      Snow

      Winds

Storytelling   **027.62; 372.67**

  UF   Stories

  BT **Children's literature**

  RT **Folklore**

      Short story

Storytelling—Collections   **808.85**

Use for collections of stories compiled primarily for oral presentation.

  UF   Collected works

          Collections of literature

Stoves   **697**

  BT **Heating**

      Space heaters

Strain (Psychology)

  USE **Stress (Psychology)**

Strains and stresses   **531; 620.1; 624.1**

  UF   Stresses

  BT **Mechanics**

      Statics

      **Structural analysis (Engineer-
      ing)**

  RT **Strength of materials**

Strangers and children

  USE **Children and strangers**

Strategic aspects

  USE areas of the world with the sub-
           division *Strategic aspects,* e.g.
           **Middle East—Strategic as-
           pects** [to be added as needed]

Strategic Defense Initiative   **358.1**

  UF   SDI (Ballistic missile defense
          system)

          Star Wars (Ballistic missile de-
          fense system)

  BT **Military policy—United States**

      Space warfare

      United States—Defenses

  RT **Space weapons**

Strategic materials

  USE **Materials**

Strategy   **355.4**

  UF   Military strategy

          Naval strategy

  SA   countries and areas of the world
          with the subdivision *Strategic
          aspects,* e.g. **Middle East—
          Strategic aspects** [to be add-
          ed as needed]

  BT **Military art and science**

      Naval art and science

  NT **Middle East—Strategic aspects**

      Tactics

Stratigraphic geology (May subdiv. geog.)
551.7

May be subdivided by geological period.

UF   Geology, Stratigraphic
      Historical geology
BT   **Geology**
NT   **Fossils**
Stratosphere   551.5
BT   **Upper atmosphere**
NT   **Ozone layer**
Stratospheric ozone
USE   **Ozone layer**
Straw votes
USE   **Public opinion polls**
Strawberries   634
BT   **Berries**
Stream animals (May subdiv. geog.)
578.76
UF   River animals
      Stream fauna
BT   **Animals**
      Rivers
Stream fauna
USE   **Stream animals**
Streamlining
USE   **Aerodynamics**
Street cars
USE   **Street railroads**
Street cleaning   363.72; 628.4
BT   **Cleaning**
      Municipal engineering
      Public health
      Roads
      Sanitary engineering
      Streets
RT   **Refuse and refuse disposal**
Street gangs
USE   **Gangs**
Street lighting
USE   **Streets—Lighting**
Street literature
USE   **Pamphlets**
Street people
USE   **Homeless persons**
Street railroads (May subdiv. geog.)
388.4; 625.6
UF   Interurban railroads
      Street cars
      Trams
      Trolley cars

BT   **Local transit**
      Railroads
RT   **Cable railroads**
      Electric railroads
Street traffic
USE   **City traffic**
      Traffic engineering
Streets (May subdiv. geog.)   **388.4;**
625.7
UF   Alleys
      Avenues
      Boulevards
      Thoroughfares
BT   **Cities and towns**
      Civil engineering
      Transportation
NT   **City traffic**
      Street cleaning
RT   **Pavements**
      Roads
Streets—Chicago (Ill.)   977.3
UF   Chicago (Ill.)—Streets
Streets—Lighting (May subdiv. geog.)
628.9
UF   Cities and towns—Lighting
      Street lighting
BT   **Lighting**
Streets—New York (N.Y.)   974.7
UF   New York (N.Y.)—Streets
RT   **Wall Street (New York, N.Y.)**
Strength of materials   620.1
UF   Resistance of materials
SA   types of materials with the sub-
      division *Testing,* e.g. **Con-**
      crete—Testing [to be added
      as needed]
BT   **Mechanics**
      Structural analysis (Engineer-
      ing)
NT   **Concrete—Testing**
RT   **Building materials**
      Strains and stresses
      Testing
Strength training
USE   **Weight lifting**
Stress (Physiology)   612; 616.8
UF   Physiological stress
      Tension (Physiology)
BT   **Adaptation (Biology)**
      Physiology
NT   **Job stress**

676

Stress (Psychology)   155.9; 616.89
  UF   Emotional stress
       Mental stress
       Psychological stress
       Strain (Psychology)
       Tension (Psychology)
  BT   **Mental health**
       Psychology
  NT   **Anxiety**
       Burn out (Psychology)
       Job stress
       Post-traumatic stress disorder
Stresses
  USE   **Strains and stresses**
Strikes (May subdiv. geog.)   331.892
       This heading may also be subdivided by in-
       dustry or occupation and then geographically,
       e.g. **Strikes—Automobile industry—United
       States.**
  UF   Lockouts
       Picketing
       Sit-down strikes
       Strikes and lockouts
       Work stoppages
  BT   **Industrial relations**
       Labor disputes
  NT   **Sabotage**
  RT   **Collective bargaining**
       Industrial arbitration
       Injunctions
       Labor unions
Strikes and lockouts
  USE   **Strikes**
Strikes—Automobile industry—United
       States   331.892
Strikes—United States   331.892
String orchestra music   784.7
  BT   **Orchestral music**
Stringed instruments   787
  UF   Bowed instruments
  SA   types of stringed instruments [to
       be added as needed]
  BT   **Musical instruments**
  NT   **Guitars**
       Violins
       Violoncellos
Strip films
  USE   **Filmstrips**
Stroke   616.8
  UF   Apoplexy
       Cerebrovascular disease
  BT   **Brain—Diseases**

Structural analysis (Engineering)   624
  UF   Architectural engineering
       Theory of structures
  BT   **Structural engineering**
  NT   **Strains and stresses**
       Strength of materials
Structural drafting
  USE   **Mechanical drawing**
Structural engineering (May subdiv.
       geog.)   624.1
  UF   Architectural engineering
  BT   **Civil engineering**
       Engineering
  NT   **Building**
       Foundations
       Hydraulic structures
       Soil mechanics
       Steel construction
       **Structural analysis (Engineer-
       ing)**
Structural failures   624.1
  UF   Collapse of structures
       Failures, Structural
  SA   types of structural failures, e.g.
       Building failures [to be add-
       ed as needed]
  BT   **Reliability (Engineering)**
  NT   **Building failures**
Structural materials
  USE   **Building materials**
Structural psychology
  USE   **Gestalt psychology**
Structural steel   691
  UF   Steel, Structural
  BT   **Building materials**
       Civil engineering
       Steel
  RT   **Steel construction**
Structural zoology
  USE   **Animals—Anatomy**
Structure in biology
  USE   **Morphology**
Structures
  USE   **Buildings**
Stucco   693
  BT   **Building materials**
       Decoration and ornament
       Plaster and plastering
Student achievement
  USE   **Academic achievement**

Student activities (May subdiv. geog.)
   371.8
   UF Extracurricular activities
   BT **Students**
   NT **After school programs**
       Cheerleading
       College and school drama
       College and school journalism
       College sports
       Field trips
       School assembly programs
       School sports
Student aid (May subdiv. geog.)   **371.2;**
   378.3
   UF Financial aid to students
       Student financial aid
   BT **College costs**
       Loans
   NT **Scholarships**
       Student loan funds
Student busing
   USE **Busing (School integration)**
Student clubs
   USE **Students—Societies**
Student councils
   USE **Student government**
Student dropouts
   USE **Dropouts**
Student evaluation of teachers   **371.14**
   UF Student rating of teachers
       Teachers, Student rating of
   BT **Teacher-student relationship**
Student financial aid
   USE **Student aid**
Student government   **371.5**
   UF Self-government (in education)
       Student councils
       Student self-government
   BT **School discipline**
       Schools—Administration
Student guidance
   USE **Educational counseling**
Student life
   USE **College students**
       Students
Student loan funds (May subdiv. geog.)
   371.2; 378.3
   UF Loan funds, Student
   BT **College costs**
       Student aid

Student movement
   USE **Youth movement**
Student promotion
   USE **Promotion (School)**
Student protests, demonstrations, etc.
   USE **Students—Political activity**
       Youth movement
Student rating of teachers
   USE **Student evaluation of teachers**
Student revolt
   USE **Students—Political activity**
       Youth movement
Student self-government
   USE **Student government**
Student societies
   USE **Students—Societies**
Student songs
   USE **Students' songs**
Student-teacher relationships
   USE **Teacher-student relationship**
Student teaching   **370.71**
   UF Practice teaching
       Teachers—Practice teaching
   BT **Teachers—Training**
       Teaching
Student to student counseling
   USE **Peer counseling**
Student violence
   USE **School violence**
Student yearbooks
   USE **School yearbooks**
Students (May subdiv. geog.)   **371.8**
   UF School life
       Student life *[Former heading]*
   SA types of students, e.g. **College**
       students [to be added as
       needed]
   NT **At risk students**
       College students
       Dropouts
       Foreign students
       High school students
       School children
       Student activities
Students and libraries
   USE **Libraries and students**
Students—Counseling
   USE **Educational counseling**
Students, Foreign
   USE **Foreign students**

Students—Grading and marking
    USE **Grading and marking (Education)**
Students' military training camps
    USE **Military training camps**
Students—Political activity   324; 371.8
    UF Politics and students
         Student protests, demonstrations, etc.
         Student revolt
    BT **Political participation**
         Youth movement
Students—Societies   371.8
    UF School clubs
         Student clubs
         Student societies
    BT **Societies**
    NT **Fraternities and sororities**
Students' songs   782.42
    UF College songs
         Student songs
    BT **Songs**
    NT **United States Military Academy—Songs**
Students—United States   371.80973
Students with problems
    USE **At risk students**
Study abroad
    USE **Foreign study**
Study and teaching
    USE **Education**
         and subjects with the subdivision *Study and teaching,* e.g.
         Science—Study and teaching [to be added as needed]
Study, Foreign
    USE **Foreign study**
Study guides
    USE named examinations with the subdivision *Study guides,* e.g. **Graduate Record Examination—Study guides;** and subjects, educational levels, and names of educational institutions with the subdivisions *Examinations—Study guides,* e.g. **English language—Examinations—Study guides** [to be added as needed]
Study guides for examinations
    USE **Examinations—Study guides**

Study methods
    USE **Study skills**
Study overseas
    USE **Foreign study**
Study skills   371.3028
    UF How to study
         Study methods
    SA subjects with the subdivision *Study and teaching,* e.g. **Art—Study and teaching** [to be added as needed]
    BT **Education**
         Life skills
         Teaching
    NT **Examinations—Study guides**
         Homework
         Independent study
         Self-instruction
Stunt flying   797.5
    UF Aerobatics
    BT **Airplanes—Piloting**
Stunt men
    USE **Stunt performers**
Stunt performers (May subdiv. geog.)   **791.4**
    UF Stunt men
    BT **Actors**
Stuttering
    USE **Speech disorders**
Style in dress
    USE **Clothing and dress**
         Costume
         Fashion
Style, Literary
    USE **Literary style**
Style manikins
    USE **Fashion models**
Style manuals
    USE **Printing—Style manuals**
Sub-Saharan Africa   960
    UF Africa, Sub-Saharan
         Black Africa
    BT **Africa**
Subconsciousness   127; 154.2
    BT **Parapsychology**
         Psychology
    NT **Hallucinations and illusions**
         Mental suggestion
         Sleep
    RT **Consciousness**
         Dreams

Subconsciousness—*Continued*
>> **Hypnotism**
>> **Mental healing**
>> **Mind and body**
>> **Psychoanalysis**
>> **Spiritual healing**

Subculture
> USE **Counter culture**

Subgravity state
> USE **Weightlessness**

Subject catalogs   016; 017
> UF   Catalogs, Subject
> BT   **Library catalogs**
> NT   **Subject headings**

Subject dictionaries
> USE   **Encyclopedias and dictionaries**

Subject headings   025.4
> UF   Thesauri
> BT   **Cataloging**
>> **Indexes**
>> **Subject catalogs**

Submarine boats
> USE   **Submarines**

Submarine cables   384.1; 384.6
> UF   Cables, Submarine
>> Ocean cables
> BT   **Telecommunication**
>> **Telegraph**

Submarine diving
> USE   **Deep diving**

Submarine engineering
> USE   **Ocean engineering**

Submarine exploration
> USE   **Underwater exploration**

Submarine geology (May subdiv. geog.)
551.46
> UF   Marine geology
>> Underwater geology
> BT   **Geology**
>> **Oceanography**
> NT   **Ocean bottom**
> RT   **Plate tectonics**

Submarine medicine   616.9
> UF   Underwater medicine
>> Underwater physiology
> BT   **Medicine**

Submarine oil well drilling
> USE   **Offshore oil well drilling**

Submarine photography
> USE   **Underwater photography**

Submarine research stations
> USE   **Undersea research stations**

Submarine vehicles
> USE   **Submersibles**

Submarine warfare   359.9
> UF   Naval warfare
>> Warfare, Submarine
> BT   **Naval art and science**
>> **War**
> NT   **Submarines**
>> **Torpedoes**
>> **World War, 1939-1945—Naval operations—Submarine**

Submarines (May subdiv. geog.)   **359.9;
623.8**

Use for materials on submarines only. Materials on other underwater craft are entered under **Submersibles.**
> UF   Submarine boats
> BT   **Ships**
>> **Submarine warfare**
>> **Submersibles**
>> **Warships**
> NT   **Nuclear submarines**

Submersibles   623.8
> UF   Submarine vehicles
>> Undersea vehicles
> SA   types of submersibles [to be added as needed]
> BT   **Vehicles**
> NT   **Bathyscaphe**
>> **Submarines**

Subscription television   384.55
> UF   Pay-per-view television
>> Pay television
>> Television, Subscription
> BT   **Television broadcasting**

Subsidies (May subdiv. geog.)   **338.9**

Use for materials on financial or other aid given, without equivalent recompense, by governments or governmental agencies to private enterprises.
> UF   Corporate welfare
>> Government subsidies
>> Grants
>> Subventions
> SA   types of subsidies, e.g. **Agricultural subsidies;** and federal aid to specific endeavors, e.g. **Federal aid to minority business enterprises** [to be added as needed]
> BT   **Domestic economic assistance**
>> **Economic policy**

Subsidies—*Continued*
NT **Agricultural subsidies**
     Federal aid to minority business enterprises
     Transfer payments
Subsistence economy (May subdiv. geog.) **330.9**
BT **Cost and standard of living**
NT **Barter**
RT **Poverty**
Substance abuse
USE **Drug abuse**
      Solvent abuse
Substantive due process
USE **Due process of law**
Substitute products   338
SA types of substitute products, e.g. **Sugar substitutes** [to be added as needed]
BT **Commercial products**
NT **Sugar substitutes**
RT **Synthetic products**
Subtraction   513.2
BT **Arithmetic**
Suburban areas
USE **Suburbs**
Suburban life (May subdiv. geog.) **307.74**
BT **Suburbs**
Suburbs (May subdiv. geog.)   **307.76**
UF Suburban areas
     Suburbs and environs
SA names of suburban areas, e.g. **Chicago Suburban Area (Ill.)** [to be added as needed]
BT **Cities and towns—Growth**
     City planning
     Metropolitan areas
NT **Suburban life**
Suburbs and environs
USE **Suburbs**
Subventions
USE **Subsidies**
Subversive activities (May subdiv. geog.) **322.4; 327.12**

Use for materials on any attempt to subvert, overthrow, or cause the destruction of any established or legally constituted government. Materials on the offense of acting to overthrow one's own government or to harm or kill its sovereign are entered under **Treason.**

UF Fifth column
BT **Insurgency**
NT **Espionage**
     Political crimes and offenses
     Sabotage
     Spies
     Terrorism
     Treason
RT **Internal security**
Subways (May subdiv. geog.)   **388.4; 625.4**
UF Underground railroads
BT **Local transit**
     Railroads
Success   158; 646.7
UF Fortune
     Personal development
BT **Business ethics**
     Wealth
NT **Academic achievement**
     Leadership
     Life skills
RT **Ability**
     Self-realization
Succession
USE presidents, prime ministers, and other rulers with the subdivision *Succession,* e.g. **Presidents—United States—Succession** [to be added as needed]
Sudden death in infants
USE **Sudden infant death syndrome**
Sudden infant death syndrome   618.92
UF Cot death
     Crib death
     Infant sudden death
     SIDS (Disease)
     Sudden death in infants
BT **Infants—Death**
Suffering   128; 152.1; 214
UF Affliction
RT **Joy and sorrow**
     Pain
Suffrage (May subdiv. geog.)   **324.6**
UF Franchise
     Voting
SA ethnic groups and classes of persons with the subdivision *Suffrage* [to be added as needed]

Suffrage—*Continued*
- BT **Citizenship**
  Constitutional law
  Democracy
  Elections
  Political science
- NT **African Americans—Suffrage**
  Blacks—Suffrage
  Naturalization
  Voter registration
  Women—Suffrage
- RT **Representative government and representation**

Suffragettes
- USE **Suffragists**

Suffragists (May subdiv. geog.)   324.6; 920
- UF Suffragettes
- BT **Reformers**
- RT **Feminism**
  Women—Suffrage

Sufism (May subdiv. geog.)   297.4
- BT **Mysticism—Islam**

Sugar   641.3; 664
- SA types of sugar [to be added as needed]
- BT **Food**
- NT **Maple sugar**
  Syrups

Sugar substitutes   641.3; 664
- UF Artificial sweeteners
  Nonnutritive sweeteners
- BT **Substitute products**

Suggestion, Mental
- USE **Mental suggestion**

Suggestive therapeutics   615.8
- UF Therapeutics, Suggestive
- BT **Therapeutics**
- RT **Hypnotism**
  Mental healing
  Mental suggestion
  Psychotherapy
  Spiritual healing

Suicidal behavior
- USE **Suicide—Psychological aspects**

Suicide (May subdiv. geog.)   179.7; 362.28
- UF Attempted suicide
  Suicide attempts

- SA classes of persons and ethnic groups with the subdivision *Suicide,* e.g. **Teenagers—Suicide** [to be added as needed]
- BT **Medical jurisprudence**
  Social problems
- NT **Teenagers—Suicide**
- RT **Homicide**
  Right to die

Suicide attempts
- USE **Suicide**

Suicide—Psychological aspects   616.85
- UF Suicidal behavior
- BT **Human behavior**

Suing (Law)
- USE **Litigation**

Suite (Music)   784.18
  Use for musical scores and for materials on the suite as a musical form.
- UF Partita
  Suites
- BT **Musical form**
  Orchestral music

Suites
- USE **Suite (Music)**

Suits (Law)
- USE **Litigation**

Suits of armor
- USE **Armor**

Sulfa drugs
- USE **Sulfonamides**

Sulfonamides   615
- UF Sulfa drugs
- BT **Drugs**

Sulfur
- USE **Sulphur**

Sulphur   546; 553.6; 661
- UF Sulfur
- BT **Chemical elements**

Summer camps
- USE **Camps**

Summer employment   331.1
- BT **Employment**
- RT **Teenagers—Employment**
  Youth—Employment

Summer resorts   790
- BT **Resorts**

Summer schools (May subdiv. geog.)   371.2
- UF Vacation schools
- BT **Public schools**
  Schools

Summer schools—*Continued*
  NT **Religious summer schools**
Sun 523.7
  UF Solar physics
  BT **Astronomy**
      Solar system
  NT **Solar energy**
      Sunspots
Sun-dials
  USE **Sundials**
Sun—Eclipses
  USE **Solar eclipses**
Sun (in religion, folklore, etc.)
  USE **Sun worship**
Sun powered batteries
  USE **Solar batteries**
Sun—Radiation
  USE **Solar radiation**
Sun-spots
  USE **Sunspots**
Sun worship (May subdiv. geog.) 291.2
  UF Sun (in religion, folklore, etc.)
  BT **Religion**
Sunday schools (May subdiv. geog.)
      268
  UF Bible classes
  BT **Church work**
      Religious education
  NT **Bible—Study and teaching**
Sundials 681.1
  UF Horology
      Sun-dials
  BT **Clocks and watches**
      Garden ornaments and furni-
      ture
      Time
Sunken cities
  USE **Extinct cities**
Sunken treasure
  USE **Buried treasure**
Sunspots 523.7
  UF Sun-spots
  BT **Meteorology**
      Solar radiation
      Sun
Super markets
  USE **Supermarkets**
Supercomputers 004.1
    Use for materials on extraordinarily power-
  ful computers.
  BT **Computers**

Superconducting materials
  USE **Superconductors**
Superconductive devices
  USE **Superconductors**
Superconductivity
  USE **Superconductors**
Superconductors 537.6; 621.3
  UF Superconducting materials
      Superconductive devices
      Superconductivity
  BT **Electric conductors**
      Electronics
Superhero comic books, strips, etc.
      741.5
    May be used for individual works, collec-
  tions, or materials about superhero comics.
  BT **Comic books, strips, etc.**
Superhero films 791.43
    May be used for individual works, collec-
  tions, or materials about superhero films.
  SA films with particular superheroes,
      e.g. **Superman films** [to be
      added as needed]
  BT **Adventure films**
  NT **Superman films**
Superhero radio programs 791.44
    May be used for individual works, collec-
  tions, or materials about superhero radio pro-
  grams.
  BT **Adventure radio programs**
Superhero television programs 791.45
    May be used for individual works, collec-
  tions, or materials about superhero television
  programs.
  BT **Adventure television programs**
Superhighways
  USE **Express highways**
Superintendents of schools
  USE **School superintendents and**
        principals
Superman films 791.43
    May be used for individual works, collec-
  tions, or materials about Superman films.
  BT **Superhero films**
Supermarket shopping
  USE **Grocery shopping**
Supermarkets (May subdiv. geog.)
      658.8
  UF Super markets
  BT **Grocery trade**
      Retail trade
      Stores

Supernatural   133; 291.2; 398.2
  BT **Religion**
  NT **Exorcism**
      Occultism
      Parapsychology
      Prophecies
      Revelation
      Spiritualism
  RT **Miracles**
Supernovae
  USE **Supernovas**
Supernovas   523.8
  UF Supernovae
  BT **Stars**
Supersonic aerodynamics   629.132
  UF Aerodynamics, Supersonic
      High speed aerodynamics
      Speed, Supersonic
  BT **Aerodynamics**
      High speed aeronautics
  NT **Aerothermodynamics**
Supersonic airliners
  USE **Supersonic transport planes**
Supersonic transport planes   629.133
  UF SST (Supersonic transport)
      Supersonic airliners
  BT **Jet planes**
Supersonic waves
  USE **Ultrasonic waves**
Supersonics
  USE **Ultrasonics**
Superstition (May subdiv. geog.)   001.9;
    398
  UF Folk beliefs
      Traditions
  BT **Folklore**
  NT **Charms**
  RT **Errors**
Supervision of employees
  USE **Personnel management**
Supervision of schools
  USE **School supervision**
Supervisors   331.7; 658.3
  UF Foremen
      Managers
  BT **Factory management**
      Personnel management
Supplementary employment   331.1
  UF Employment, Supplementary
      Moonlighting
      Second job

      Secondary employment
  BT **Labor**
      Part-time employment
Support of children
  USE **Child support**
Supreme Court—United States
  USE **United States. Supreme Court**
Surf
  USE **Ocean waves**
Surf riding
  USE **Surfing**
Surface of the earth
  USE **Earth—Surface**
Surfboarding
  USE **Surfing**
Surfing (May subdiv. geog.)   797.3
  UF Body surfing
      Surf riding
      Surfboarding
  BT **Water sports**
Surfing—Songs   782.42
  UF Surfing—Songs and music
  BT **Songs**
Surfing—Songs and music
  USE **Surfing—Songs**
Surgeons (May subdiv. geog.)   617.092;
    920
  BT **Physicians**
Surgery (May subdiv. geog.)   617
  UF Operations, Surgical
  SA classes of persons, names of dis-
      eases, and names of organs
      and regions of the body with
      the subdivision *Surgery* [to be
      added as needed]
  BT **Medicine**
  NT **Artificial organs**
      Cancer—Surgery
      Children—Surgery
      Cryosurgery
      Heart—Surgery
      Orthopedics
      Plastic surgery
      **Transplantation of organs, tis-
      sues, etc.**
      Vivisection
  RT **Anesthetics**
      Antiseptics
Surgery, Plastic
  USE **Plastic surgery**

Surgical transplantation
USE **Transplantation of organs, tissues, etc.**
Surnames
USE **Personal names**
Surplus government property (May subdiv. geog.) **352.5**
UF Excess government property
Government property, Surplus
BT **Property**
Surrealism (May subdiv. geog.) **709.04; 759.06; 809**
Use for the movement or style of surrealism in literature or in the visual arts.
BT **Arts**
Surrogate mothers **176; 306.874; 346.01**
BT **Mothers**
Surveying (May subdiv. geog.) **526.9**
UF Land surveying
Land surveys
SA names of countries, cities, etc., with the subdivision *Surveys,* for works containing the results of land surveys in those places, e.g. **United States—Surveys** [to be added as needed]
BT **Civil engineering**
Geography
Measurement
NT **Mine surveying**
Topographical drawing
RT **Geodesy**
Surveys **001.4**
UF Government surveys
SA types of surveys, e.g. **Market surveys;** and names of countries, cities, etc., with the subdivision *Surveys,* for works containing the results of land surveys in those places, e.g. **United States—Surveys** [to be added as needed]
BT **Research**
NT **Educational surveys**
Library surveys
Market surveys
Social surveys

Survival after airplane accidents, shipwrecks, etc. **613.6**
UF Castaways
RT **Aircraft accidents**
Rescue work
Shipwrecks
Wilderness survival
Survival of the fittest
USE **Natural selection**
Survival skills **613.6**
Use for materials on skills needed to survive in a hazardous environment, usually stressing self-reliance and economic self-sufficiency.
UF Emergency survival
Human survival skills
SA types of survival, e.g. **Wilderness survival** [to be added as needed]
BT **Civil defense**
Environmental influence on humans
Human ecology
Life skills
NT **Wilderness survival**
RT **Self-reliance**
Survivalism (May subdiv. geog.) **320.5; 613.6**
UF Survivalist movements
BT **Social movements**
Survivalist movements
USE **Survivalism**
Suspended sentence
USE **Probation**
Suspense films
USE **Adventure films**
Mystery films
Spy films
Suspense novels
USE **Adventure fiction**
Mystery fiction
Romantic suspense novels
Suspense programs
USE **Mystery radio programs**
Mystery television programs
Spy radio programs
Spy television programs
Sustainable development (May subdiv. geog.) **333.7; 338.9**
Use for materials on economic development that satisfies the needs of the present generation without depleting natural resources for

Sustainable development—*Continued*
the future or having adverse environmental effects. General materials on the environmental impact of economic development are entered under **Economic development—Environmental aspects.**

    UF   Economic sustainability
          Sustainable economic development
    BT   **Economic development**

Sustainable economic development
    USE **Sustainable development**

Swamp animals (May subdiv. geog.)
    578.768
    UF   Swamp fauna
    BT   **Animals**

Swamp fauna
    USE **Swamp animals**

Swamps (May subdiv. geog.)   **551.41**
    BT   **Wetlands**

Swashbucklers
    USE **Adventure fiction**
           Adventure films

Swedish language   **439.7**
    May be subdivided like **English language.**
    BT   **Language and languages**
           Scandinavian languages

Swedish literature   **839.7**
    May use same subdivisions and names of literary forms as for **English literature.**
    BT   **Literature**
           Scandinavian literature

Sweets
    USE **Candy**
           Confectionery

Swell
    USE **Ocean waves**

Swimming   **797.2**
    BT   **Water sports**
    NT   **Diving**
           Marathon swimming
           Synchronized swimming

Swimming pools   **690; 725; 797.2**
    UF   Pools
    BT   **Sports facilities**

Swindlers and swindling (May subdiv. geog.)   **364.16**
    UF   Con artists
           Con game
           Confidence game
    BT   **Crime**
           Criminals

    NT   **Counterfeits and counterfeiting**
           Credit card fraud
           Quacks and quackery
    RT   **Fraud**
           Impostors and imposture

Swine
    USE **Pigs**

Switchboard hotlines
    USE **Hotlines (Telephone counseling)**

Symbiosis   **577.8**
    UF   Mutualism (Biology)
    BT   **Biology**
           Ecology
    RT   **Parasites**
           Plant ecology

Symbolic logic   **511.3**
    UF   Logic, Symbolic and mathematical
           Mathematical logic
    BT   **Logic**
           Mathematics
    NT   **Boolean algebra**
    RT   **Set theory**

Symbolic numbers
    USE **Numerology**
           Symbolism of numbers

Symbolism (May subdiv. geog.)   **291.3; 302.2; 700**
    SA   symbolism of particular religions, e.g. **Christian symbolism;** and symbolism in particular subjects, e.g. **Symbolism in literature** [to be added as needed]
    BT   **Art**
           Mythology
    NT   **Christian symbolism**
           Heraldry
           Symbolism in literature
           Symbolism of numbers
    RT   **Signs and symbols**

Symbolism in literature   **809**
    UF   Signs and symbols in literature
    BT   **Literature**
           Symbolism
    RT   **Allegory**

Symbolism of numbers   **246; 291.3; 809**
    Use for general materials on the symbolism of numbers, as in philosophy, religion, or literature. Materials on the occult significance of numbers are entered under **Numerology.**

Symbolism of numbers—*Continued*
    UF   Number symbolism
          Sacred numbers
          Symbolic numbers
    BT   **Symbolism**
    NT   **Numerology**
    RT   **Cabala**
          Numbers

Symbols
    USE **Abbreviations**
          Signs and symbols

Symbols, Mathematical
    USE **Mathematical notation**

Sympathy
    USE **Bereavement**
          Consolation

Symphonic poems   784.2
    BT   **Orchestral music**

Symphonies
    USE **Symphony**

Symphony   784.18; 784.2
    Use for musical scores and for materials on the symphony as a musical form.
    UF   Symphonies
    BT   **Musical form**
          Orchestral music

Symptoms
    USE **Diagnosis**

Synagogues (May subdiv. geog.)   **296.6; 726**
    BT   **Buildings**
    RT   **Judaism**

Synchronized swimming   797.2
    UF   Water ballet
    BT   **Swimming**

Synods
    USE **Councils and synods**

Synonyms and antonyms
    USE names of languages with the subdivision *Synonyms and antonyms,* e.g. **English language—Synonyms and antonyms** [to be added as needed]

Synthesizer music
    USE **Electronic music**

Synthesizer (Musical instrument)
    USE **Synthesizers (Musical instruments)**

Synthesizers (Musical instruments)   786.7
    UF   Synthesizer (Musical instrument)
    BT   **Electronic musical instruments**

Synthetic chemistry
    USE **Organic compounds—Synthesis**

Synthetic detergents
    USE **Detergents**

Synthetic drugs of abuse
    USE **Designer drugs**

Synthetic fabrics   677
    SA   types of synthetic fabrics [to be added as needed]
    BT   **Fabrics**
          Synthetic products
    NT   **Nylon**
          Rayon

Synthetic foods
    USE **Artificial foods**

Synthetic fuels   662
    UF   Artificial fuels
          Nonfossil fuels
    BT   **Fuel**
          Synthetic products

Synthetic products   670
    SA   types of synthetic products and names of specific products [to be added as needed]
    BT   **Industrial chemistry**
    NT   **Artificial foods**
          Plastics
          Synthetic fabrics
          Synthetic fuels
          Synthetic rubber
    RT   **Organic compounds—Synthesis**
          Substitute products

Synthetic rubber   678
    UF   Rubber, Artificial
          Rubber, Synthetic
    BT   **Plastics**
          Synthetic products

Syphilis (May subdiv. geog.)   **616.95**
    BT   **Sexually transmitted diseases**

Syrups   641.3
    BT   **Sugar**

System analysis   003; 004.2; 658.4
    UF   Flow charts
          Flowcharting
          Linear system theory
          Network theory
          Systems analysis

System analysis—*Continued*
    BT   **Cybernetics**
           Mathematical models
           System theory
    NT   **Fuzzy systems**
           System design
           Systems engineering
System design   003; 004.2; 621.39
    UF   Systems design
    BT   **System analysis**
System engineering
    USE **Systems engineering**
System theory   003
    UF   Systems, Theory of
           Theory of systems
    BT   **Science**
    NT   **Chaos (Science)**
           Cybernetics
           Operations research
           System analysis
           Systems engineering
Systematic botany
    USE **Botany—Classification**
Systematic theology
    USE **Doctrinal theology**
Systems analysis
    USE **System analysis**
Systems, Database management
    USE **Database management**
Systems design
    USE **System design**
Systems engineering   620
    UF   System engineering
    BT   **Automation**
           Cybernetics
           Engineering
           Industrial design
           System analysis
           System theory
    NT   **Bionics**
           Reliability (Engineering)
    RT   **Operations research**
Systems, Fuzzy
    USE **Fuzzy systems**
Systems reliability
    USE **Reliability (Engineering)**
Systems, Theory of
    USE **System theory**
T groups
    USE **Group relations training**
Table decoration
    USE **Table setting and decoration**

Table etiquette   395.5
    BT   **Eating customs**
           Etiquette
    RT   **Dining**
Table setting and decoration   642
    UF   Table decoration
    BT   **Decoration and ornament**
    NT   **Flower arrangement**
           Tableware
Table talk
    USE **Conversation**
Table tennis   796.34
    UF   Ping-pong
    BT   **Ball games**
Tables   645; 749
    BT   **Furniture**
Tables (Systematic lists)
    USE subjects with the subdivision *Tables,* e.g. **Meteorology—Tables; Trigonometry—Tables** etc. [to be added as needed]
Tableware (May subdiv. geog.)   642
    UF   Dishes
    BT   **Table setting and decoration**
    NT   **Glassware**
           Porcelain
           Pottery
           Silverware
Tactics   355.4
    UF   Military tactics
    BT   **Military art and science**
           Strategy
    NT   **Biological warfare**
           Drill and minor tactics
           Guerrilla warfare
Tadpoles
    USE **Frogs**
Tailoring   646.4; 687
    UF   Garment making
    BT   **Clothing and dress**
           Clothing industry
    RT   **Dressmaking**
Taiwan   951.24
    Use for materials dealing with the island of Taiwan, regardless of time period, or with the post-1948 Republic of China. Materials dealing with mainland China, regardless of time period, or with the People's Republic of China and comprehensive materials on China including Taiwan are entered under **China.** May be subdivided like United States except for *History.*
    UF   China (Republic)
           Formosa

Taiwan—*Continued*
    Nationalist China
    Republic of China, 1949-
Takeovers, Corporate
  USE **Corporate mergers and acqui-
        sitions**
Talent
  USE **Ability
        Genius**
Talents
  USE **Ability**
Tales
  USE **Fables
        Fairy tales
        Folklore
        Legends**
Talismans
  USE **Charms**
Talk shows (May subdiv. geog.) **791.44;
    791.45**
  BT **Interviewing
       Radio programs
       Television programs**
Talking
  USE **Conversation**
Talking books
  USE **Audiobooks**
Tall tales **398.2; 808.83; 813, etc.**
    May be used for individual works, collec-
    tions, or materials about tall tales.
  BT **Folklore
       Legends
       Wit and humor**
Talmud **296.1**
  BT **Hebrew literature
       Jewish literature
       Judaism**
Tanks (Military science)
  USE **Military tanks**
Tanning **675**
  BT **Industrial chemistry**
  RT **Hides and skins
       Leather**
Taoism (May subdiv. geog.) **299**
  BT **Religions**
Tap dancing **792.7**
  BT **Dance**
Tap water
  USE **Drinking water**
Tape recorders
  USE **Magnetic recorders and re-
        cording**

Tape recordings, Audio
  USE **Sound recordings**
Tape recordings, Video
  USE **Videotapes**
Tapestry (May subdiv. geog.) **677;
    746.3**
  BT **Decoration and ornament
       Decorative arts
       Interior design
       Needlework**
Tardiness
  USE **Punctuality**
Tariff (May subdiv. geog.) **336.2; 382**
  UF Custom duties
       Customs (Tariff)
       Duties
       Revenue
  BT **Commercial policy
       Economic policy
       Public finance**
  NT **Smuggling**
  RT **Free trade
       Protectionism**
Tariff—United States **336.2; 382**
  UF United States—Tariff
Tarot **133.3; 795.4**
    Use for materials on the cards and the
  game.
  UF Tarot (Game)
  BT **Card games
       Fortune telling
       Playing cards**
Tarot (Game)
  USE **Tarot**
Tartans **391; 929.6**
  UF Highland costume
       Scottish tartans
  BT **Clans**
Taste **152.1**
  BT **Senses and sensation**
Taste (Aesthetics)
  USE **Aesthetics**
Tattooing (May subdiv. geog.) **391.6**
  UF Tattoos (Body markings)
  BT **Manners and customs
       Personal appearance**
Tattoos (Body markings)
  USE **Tattooing**
Taverns
  USE **Bars**

Tax assessment   336.2

Use for general materials on the valuation of property for determining tax liability. Materials on the assessment of property for tax purposes in a particular place are entered under **Taxation** followed by the appropriate geographical subdivision.

    UF   Appraisal
           Assessment
           Assessment, Tax
           Property tax—Assessment
           Real property tax—Assessment
    BT   **Taxation**
           Valuation

Tax avoidance
    USE **Tax planning**

Tax credits (May subdiv. geog.)   336.2
    BT   **Income tax**

Tax planning (May subdiv. geog.)
    343.04
    UF   Tax avoidance
           Tax saving
    BT   **Personal finance**
           Planning
           Taxation
    RT   **Estate planning**

Tax relations, Intergovernmental
    USE **Intergovernmental tax relations**

Tax saving
    USE **Tax planning**

Tax sharing
    USE **Intergovernmental tax relations**
           Revenue sharing

Taxation (May subdiv. geog.)   336.2
    UF   Direct taxation
           Duties
           Revenue
           Taxes
    SA   subjects with the subdivision *Taxation*, e.g. **Real estate investment—Taxation** [to be added as needed]
    BT   **Political science**
           Public finance
    NT   **Income tax**
           Inheritance and transfer tax
           Intergovernmental tax relations
           Internal revenue
           Real estate investment—Taxation
           Sales tax
           Tax assessment
           Tax planning

           Tithes

Taxation of legacies
    USE **Inheritance and transfer tax**

Taxation—United States   336.200973
    UF   United States—Taxation

Taxes
    USE **Taxation**

Taxidermy   590.75
    UF   Preservation of specimens
           Specimens, Preservation of
    SA   types of specimens with the subdivision *Collection and preservation*, e.g. **Birds—Collection and preservation** [to be added as needed]
    RT   **Zoological specimens—Collection and preservation**

Taxonomy (Botany)
    USE **Botany—Classification**

Tea   633.7; 641.8

Use for materials on the plant or on the beverage. Materials on the meal are entered under **Afternoon teas.**

    BT   **Beverages**
    RT   **Afternoon teas**
           Tea industry

Tea houses
    USE **Tearooms**

Tea industry (May subdiv. geog.)
    338.1; 338.4
    UF   Tea trade
    BT   **Beverage industry**
    NT   **Tearooms**
    RT   **Tea**

Tea rooms
    USE **Tearooms**

Tea shops
    USE **Tearooms**

Tea trade
    USE **Tea industry**

Teach yourself courses
    USE **Self-instruction**

Teacher exchange   370.116
    UF   Exchange of teachers
           Teacher exchange programs
    BT   **Exchange of persons programs**
           International education

Teacher exchange programs
    USE **Teacher exchange**

Teacher-parent conferences
    USE **Parent-teacher conferences**

Teacher-parent relationship
  USE **Parent-teacher relationship**
**Teacher-student relationship 371.1;
    378.1**
  UF Student-teacher relationships
      Teacher-student relationships
      [Former heading]
  BT **Child-adult relationship**
      Interpersonal relations
      Teaching
  NT **Student evaluation of teachers**
Teacher-student relationships
  USE **Teacher-student relationship**
Teacher training
  USE **Teachers—Training**
Teachers (May subdiv. geog.) **371.1;
    920**
  Use for materials on educators engaged in
classroom or other instruction. Materials on
people engaged professionally in the field of
education in general are entered under **Educa-
tors.**
  UF College teachers
      Faculty (Education)
      Professors
  BT **Educators**
  NT **Colleges and universities—Fac-
      ulty**
  RT **Teaching**
Teachers and parents
  USE **Parent-teacher relationship**
Teachers colleges (May subdiv. geog.)
    378.1
  Use for general and historical materials
about teachers colleges. Materials on their ed-
ucational functions are entered under **Teach-
ers—Training.**
  UF Normal schools
      Training colleges for teachers
  SA names of teachers colleges [to
      be added as needed]
  BT **Colleges and universities**
      Education—Study and teaching
  RT **Teachers—Training**
Teachers' institutes
  USE **Teachers' workshops**
Teachers—Pensions (May subdiv. geog.)
    331.25
  SA types of educational institutions
      and names of individual edu-
      cational insititutions with the
      subdivisions *Faculty—Pen-
      sions,* e.g. **Colleges and uni-**

versities—Faculty—Pensions
      [to be added as needed]
Teachers—Practice teaching
  USE **Student teaching**
Teachers' reports
  USE **School reports**
Teachers, Student rating of
  USE **Student evaluation of teachers**
Teachers—Training (May subdiv. geog.)
    370.71
  Use for materials on the history and meth-
ods of training teachers, including the educa-
tional functions of teachers colleges. Materials
on the study of education as a discipline are
entered under **Education—Study and teach-
ing.** Materials on the art of teaching and
methods of teaching are entered under **Teach-
ing.**
  UF Teacher training
      Teachers—Training of
  BT **Education—Study and teaching**
      Teaching
  NT **Student teaching**
      Teachers' workshops
  RT **Teachers colleges**
Teachers—Training of
  USE **Teachers—Training**
Teachers' workshops 371.1
  UF Teachers' institutes
      Workshops, Teachers'
  BT **Teachers—Training**
Teaching (May subdiv. geog.) **371.102**
  Use for materials on the art of teaching and
methods of teaching. Materials on the study of
education as a discipline are entered under
Education—Study and teaching. Materials
on the history and methods of training teach-
ers, including the educational functions of
teachers colleges, are entered under **Teach-
ers—Training.**
  UF Instruction
      Pedagogy
      School teaching
  SA subjects with the subdivision
      Study and teaching, e.g. **Sci-
      ence—Study and teaching**
      [to be added as needed]
  BT **Education**
  NT **Classroom management**
      Cooperative learning
      Educational psychology
      Examinations
      Lectures and lecturing
      **Montessori method of educa-
      tion**
      Project method in teaching

Teaching—*Continued*
    School discipline
    School supervision
    Student teaching
    Study skills
    Teacher-student relationship
    Teachers—Training
    Teaching teams
    Tutors and tutoring
  RT Teachers
Teaching—Aids and devices   371.33
  UF Educational media
      Instructional materials
      Teaching materials
  NT Audiovisual materials
      Bulletin boards
      Manipulatives
      Motion pictures in education
      Programmed instruction
      Radio in education
      Teaching machines
      Television in education
  RT Educational technology
Teaching—Data processing
  USE Computer-assisted instruction
Teaching—Experimental methods
  USE Education—Experimental
        methods
Teaching, Freedom of
  USE Academic freedom
Teaching machines   371.33
  BT Programmed instruction
      Teaching—Aids and devices
Teaching materials
  USE Teaching—Aids and devices
Teaching teams   371.14
  UF Team teaching
  BT Teaching
Teachings of Jesus Christ
  USE Jesus Christ—Teachings
Teahouses
  USE Tearooms
Team problem solving
  USE Group problem solving
Team teaching
  USE Teaching teams
Team work in the workplace
  USE Teams in the workplace
Teams in the workplace (May subdiv.
    geog.)   658.4
  UF Team work in the workplace
      Teamwork in the workplace

      Work groups
      Work teams
  BT Social groups
      Work environment
Teamwork in the workplace
  USE Teams in the workplace
Tearooms (May subdiv. geog.)   647.95
    Use for materials on public establishments devoted primarily to serving tea.
  UF Tea houses
      Tea rooms
      Tea shops
      Teahouses
      Teashops
  BT Restaurants
      Tea industry
Teas
  USE Afternoon teas
Teashops
  USE Tearooms
Technical assistance (May subdiv. geog.)
      338.91; 361.6
    Use for materials on foreign aid in the form of technical expertise. Materials on the transfer of innovations in technology from one country to another are entered under **Technology transfer.**
  UF Aid to developing areas
      Assistance to developing areas
      Foreign aid program
  SA technical assistance from particular countries, e.g. **American technical assistance** [to be added as needed]
  BT Foreign aid
      International economic relations
  NT American technical assistance
  RT Community development
      Technology transfer
Technical assistance, American
  USE American technical assistance
Technical chemistry
  USE Industrial chemistry
Technical education (May subdiv. geog.)
      370.11; 373.246; 374
  UF Industrial education
      Industrial schools
      Technical schools
      Trade schools
  SA technical subjects with the subdivision *Study and teaching,* e.g. **Engineering—Study and**

Technical education—*Continued*
    teaching [to be added as needed]
  BT **Education**
      Higher education
      Technology
  NT **Apprentices**
      Correspondence schools and courses
      Engineering—Study and teaching
      Evening and continuation schools
      Occupational retraining
      Occupational training
      School shops
  RT **Employees—Training**
      Industrial arts education
      Professional education
      Vocational education

Technical schools
  USE **Technical education**

Technical service
  USE **Customer services**

Technical services (Libraries)
  USE **Library technical processes**

Technical terms
  USE **Technology—Dictionaries**

Technical writing   **808**
  UF Scientific writing
  BT **Authorship**
      Technology—Language

Technique
  USE subjects and names of authors and artists with the subdivision *Technique,* e.g. **Fiction—Technique; Painting—Technique; Shakespeare, William, 1564-1616—Technique;** etc.
      [to be added as needed]

Technological literacy (May subdiv. geog.)   **302.2**
    Use for materials on a person's comprehension of technological innovation and the ability to use particular innovations appropriately.
  BT **Literacy**

Technological transfer
  USE **Technology transfer**

Technology (May subdiv. geog.)   **600**
  UF Applied science
      High tech
      High technology

  SA technology and other subjects, e.g. **Technology and civilization** [to be added as needed]
  NT **Distillation**
      Electronics
      Engineering
      Industrial chemistry
      Information technology
      Inventions
      Machinery
      Mills
      Technical education
      Technology and civilization
      Technology transfer
  RT **Industrial arts**

Technology and civilization   **303.4**
  UF Civilization and technology
  BT **Civilization**
      Technology
  NT **Computers and civilization**
  RT **Industrial revolution**

Technology—Dictionaries   **603**
  UF Technical terms
  BT **Encyclopedias and dictionaries**

Technology in the workplace
  USE **Machinery in the workplace**

Technology—Language   **601; 603**
  NT **Technical writing**

Technology transfer (May subdiv. geog.)   **338.9**
    Use for materials on the transfer of innovations in technology from one country to another. Materials on foreign aid in the form of technical expertise are entered under **Technical assistance.** May be subdivided by the region or country receiving the technology. Where applicable, make an additional entry under this heading subdivided by the region or country transferring the technology.
  UF Technological transfer
      Transfer of technology
  BT **Inventions**
      Technology
  RT **International cooperation**
      International relations
      Technical assistance

Teen age
  USE **Adolescence**

Teen suicide
  USE **Teenagers—Suicide**

Teenage consumers
  USE **Young consumers**

Teenage drinking
  USE **Teenagers—Alcohol use**

Teenage dropouts
  USE **Dropouts**
Teenage fathers (May subdiv. geog.)
  306.874; 362.7
    Use for materials focusing on fathers who
  are teenagers. Materials on fathers who at the
  time of a child's birth were not married to the
  child's mother are entered under **Unmarried
  fathers.** Materials focusing on fathers rearing
  children without a partner in the household
  are entered under **Single-parent families.**
  UF Adolescent fathers
      School-age fathers
  BT **Fathers**
      Teenage parents
Teenage gangs
  USE **Gangs**
Teenage literature
  USE **Young adult literature**
Teenage mothers (May subdiv. geog.)
  306.874; 362.7; 362.83
    Use for materials focusing on mothers who
  are teenagers. Materials on mothers who at
  the time of giving birth were not married to
  the child's father are entered under **Unmar-
  ried mothers.** Materials focusing on mothers
  rearing children without a partner in the
  household are entered under **Single-parent
  families.**
  UF Adolescent mothers
      School-age mothers
  BT **Mothers**
      Teenage parents
  RT **Teenage pregnancy**
Teenage parents (May subdiv. geog.)
  306.874; 362.7
  BT **Parents**
      Teenagers
  NT **Teenage fathers**
      Teenage mothers
Teenage pregnancy (May subdiv. geog.)
  362.7; 618.2
  UF Adolescent pregnancy
  BT **Pregnancy**
  RT **Teenage mothers**
Teenage prostitution
  USE **Juvenile prostitution**
Teenage suicide
  USE **Teenagers—Suicide**
Teenagers (May subdiv. geog.) **305.235**
    Use for materials about teen youth. Materi-
  als on the time of life extending from thirteen
  to twenty-five years, as well as on people in
  that general age range, are entered under
  Youth. Materials limited to people in the gen-
  eral age range of eighteen through twenty-five

years of age are entered under **Young men** or
Young women. Materials on the process or
state of growing up are entered under **Adoles-
cence.**
  UF Adolescents
      Teens
      Young adults
      Young people
      Young persons
  BT **Age**
      Youth
  NT **Runaway teenagers**
      Teenage parents
  RT **Boys**
      Girls
Teenagers—Alcohol use (May subdiv.
  geog.) **362.292; 613.81; 616.86**
  UF Alcohol and teenagers
      Drinking and teenagers
      Teenage drinking
      Teenagers and alcohol
  NT **Drinking age**
Teenagers and alcohol
  USE **Teenagers—Alcohol use**
Teenagers and drugs
  USE **Teenagers—Drug use**
Teenagers and narcotics
  USE **Teenagers—Drug use**
Teenagers—Attitudes **155.5; 305.235**
  BT **Attitude (Psychology)**
Teenagers—Books and reading **011.62;
  028.5**
    Use for materials on the reading interests of
  teenagers and for lists of books for teenagers.
  Collections or materials about literature pub-
  lished for teenagers are entered under **Young
  adult literature.**
  UF Books and reading for teenagers
      Books and reading for young
        adults
      Reading interests of teenagers
      Reading interests of young
        adults
      Young adults—Books and read-
        ing
  BT **Books and reading**
Teenagers—Development
  USE **Adolescence**
Teenagers—Drug use (May subdiv. geog.)
  362.29; 613.8; 616.86
  UF Drugs and teenagers
      Narcotics and teenagers
      Teenagers and drugs
      Teenagers and narcotics

Teenagers—Drug use—*Continued*
   BT   Youth—Drug use
   RT   Juvenile delinquency
Teenagers—Employment (May subdiv.
   geog.) 331.3
   BT   Age and employment
         Employment
         Youth—Employment
   RT   Summer employment
Teenagers—Literature
   USE Young adult literature
Teenagers—Psychiatry
   USE Adolescent psychiatry
Teenagers—Psychology
   USE Adolescent psychology
Teenagers—Religious life 248.4; 291.4
   BT   Religious life
         Youth—Religious life
Teenagers—Suicide 362.28; 616.85
   UF   Teen suicide
         Teenage suicide
   BT   Suicide
Teenagers—United States 305.2350973
   UF   American teenagers
   BT   Youth—United States
Teens
   USE Teenagers
Teepees
   USE Tepees
Teeth 611; 612.3; 617.6
   BT   Head
   RT   Dentistry
Teeth—Diseases 617.6
   BT   Diseases
Telecommunication (May subdiv. geog.)
   384; 621.382
   UF   Mass communication
   SA   subjects with the subdivision
         Communication systems, e.g.
         Astronautics—Communica-
         tion systems [to be added as
         needed]
   BT   Communication
   NT   Artificial satellites in telecom-
         munication
         Astronautics—Communication
         systems
         Broadcasting
         Computer networks
         Data transmission systems
         Electronic mail systems
         Fax transmission

         Intercommunication systems
         Interstellar communication
         Microwave communication sys-
         tems
         Radio
         Submarine cables
         Telecommuting
         Telegraph
         Telephone
         Television
Telecommuting (May subdiv. geog.)
   331.25
     Use for materials on employment at home
   with computers, word processors, etc., con-
   nected to a central work site, permitting em-
   ployees to substitute telecommunications for
   transportation.
   UF   Alternate work sites
         Work at home
         Working at home
   BT   Automation
         Telecommunication
Teleconferencing 384; 658.4
   UF   Conference calls
         (Teleconferencing)
         Telephone—Conference calls
   BT   Telephone
Telegraph 384.1; 621.383
   BT   Public utilities
         Telecommunication
   NT   Cipher and telegraph codes
         Submarine cables
Telegraph codes
   USE Cipher and telegraph codes
Telekinesis
   USE Psychokinesis
Telemarketing (May subdiv. geog.) 381;
   658.8
     Use for materials on the use of electronic
   media as a form of marketing that bypasses
   retail outlets in the advertising and selling of
   goods.
   UF   Electronic marketing
   BT   Direct selling
         Marketing
Telepathy 133.8
   UF   Mental telepathy
         Mind reading
   BT   Extrasensory perception
   RT   Clairvoyance
Telephone 384.6; 621.385
   BT   Public utilities
         Telecommunication

Telephone—*Continued*
   NT   Long distance telephone ser-
          vice
        Teleconferencing
        Video telephone
Telephone—Conference calls
   USE Teleconferencing
Telephone counseling
   USE Hotlines (Telephone counseling)
Telephone directories
   USE names of countries, cities, etc.,
          corporate bodies, classes of
          persons, ethnic groups, and
          types of organizations and in-
          dustries with the subdivision
          Telephone directories, e.g.
          Chicago (Ill.)—Telephone di-
          rectories [to be added as
          needed]
Telephone—Long distance
   USE Long distance telephone ser-
          vice
Telephotography   778.3
   BT   Photography
Telescope
   USE Telescopes
Telescopes   522; 681
   UF   Telescope
   BT   Astronomical instruments
        Optical instruments
Teletext systems   004.692; 384.3
      Use for materials on the one-way transmis-
      sion of computer-based data, such as weather
      forecasts or stock quotations, from a central
      source to a television set.
   BT   Data transmission systems
        Electronic publishing
        Information systems
        Television broadcasting
   RT   Videotex systems
Television (May subdiv. geog.)   302.23;
        384.55; 621.388
      Use for materials on the technology of tele-
      vision. Materials on what is seen on television
      are entered under **Television programs.**
   UF   TV
   SA   television and particular groups
          of people, e.g. **Television and
          children;** and television in
          various industries or fields of
          endeavor, e.g. **Television in
          education** [to be added as
          needed]

   BT   Telecommunication
   NT   African Americans on televi-
          sion
        Closed caption television
        Closed-circuit television
        Color television
        High definition television
        Home video systems
        Minorities on television
        Television and children
        Television and politics
        Television and youth
        Television broadcasting
        Television in education
        Video art
        Video telephone
        Violence on television
   RT   Videodiscs
        Videotapes
Television actors
   USE Actors
Television adaptations   791.45
      May be used for individual works, collec-
      tions, or materials about television adaptations
      of material from other media.
   UF   Adaptations
        Literature—Film and video adap-
          tations
        Motion pictures—Television ad-
          aptations
   SA   names of authors, titles of anon-
          ymous literary works, types of
          literature, and types of musi-
          cal compositions with the
          subdivision *Adaptations,* for
          individual works, collections,
          or criticism and interpretation
          of literary, cinematic, video,
          or television adaptations, e.g.,
          **Shakespeare, William, 1564-
          1616—Adaptations;
          Beowulf—Adaptations; Ar-
          thurian romances—Adapta-
          tions;** etc. [to be added as
          needed]
   BT   Television plays
        Television programs
        Television scripts
Television advertising (May subdiv. geog.)
        659.14
   UF   Commercials, Television
        Television commercials

Television advertising—*Continued*
  BT Advertising
      Television broadcasting
Television and children   305.23; 384.55;
      791.45
    Use for materials on the effect of television
    on children.
  UF Children and television
  BT Children
      Television
Television and infrared observation satellite
  USE TIROS satellites
Television and politics (May subdiv.
      geog.)   324
  UF Politics and television
      Television in politics
  BT Politics
      Television
  NT Equal time rule (Broadcasting)
      Fairness doctrine (Broadcast-
        ing)
Television and youth (May subdiv. geog.)
      305.235; 384.55; 791.45
  UF Youth and television
  BT Television
      Youth
Television authorship   808
  UF Television writing
  BT Authorship
  NT Television plays—Technique
Television broadcasting (May subdiv.
      geog.)   384.55
  UF Television industry
  SA television broadcasting of partic-
        ular kinds of programs, e.g.
        **Television broadcasting of
        sports** [to be added as need-
        ed]
  BT Broadcasting
      Mass media
      Television
  NT African Americans in television
        broadcasting
      Cable television
      Minorities in television broad-
        casting
      Public television
      Subscription television
      Teletext systems
      Television advertising
      Television broadcasting of
        news

Television broadcasting of
      sports
    Television—Production and di-
      rection
    Television programs
    Television scripts
    Television stations
    Videotex systems
Television broadcasting of news   070.1
  UF Television coverage of news
      Television journalism
      Television news
  BT Broadcast journalism
      Television broadcasting
Television broadcasting of sports   070.4
  UF Sports broadcasting
      Sports in television
      Television sports
  BT Broadcast journalism
      Television broadcasting
Television broadcasting—Vocational
      guidance   384.55
  BT Vocational guidance
Television cartoons
  USE Animated television programs
Television—Censorship (May subdiv.
      geog.)   384.55
  BT Censorship
Television, Closed-circuit
  USE Closed-circuit television
Television comedies
  USE Comedy television programs
Television comedy programs
  USE Comedy television programs
Television commercials
  USE Television advertising
Television coverage of news
  USE Television broadcasting of
        news
Television drama
  USE Television plays
Television—Equipment and supplies
      621.388
  NT Television—Receivers and re-
        ception
      Videodisc players
  RT Television supplies industry
      Video recording
Television equipment industry
  USE Television supplies industry

697

Television films
  USE **Television movies**
Television games
  USE **Video games**
Television in education (May subdiv.
    geog.) **371.33**
  UF Education and television
      Educational television
  BT **Audiovisual education**
      Teaching—Aids and devices
      Television
Television in politics
  USE **Television and politics**
Television industry
  USE **Television broadcasting**
      Television supplies industry
Television journalism
  USE **Broadcast journalism**
      Television broadcasting of
        news
Television movies   791.45
  May be used for individual works, collec-
  tions, or materials about television movies.
  UF Made-for-TV movies
      Television films
  BT **Motion pictures**
      Television programs
Television news
  USE **Television broadcasting of**
        news
Television novels
  USE **Radio and television novels**
Television personalities (May subdiv.
    geog.) **791.45**
  UF TV personalities
  BT **Celebrities**
Television plays   808.82; 812, etc.
  May be used for individual works, collec-
  tions, or materials about television plays.
  UF Scenarios
      Television drama
  BT **Drama**
      Television programs
  NT **Soap operas**
      Television adaptations
  RT **Television scripts**
Television plays—Technique   808.2
  UF Play writing
      Playwriting
  BT **Drama—Technique**
      Television authorship
  RT **Radio plays—Technique**

Television—Production and direction
    384.55; 791.45
  BT **Television broadcasting**
Television programs (May subdiv. geog.)
    791.45
  Use for materials on what is seen on televi-
  sion. Materials on the technology of television
  are entered under **Television.**
  UF Programs, Television
  SA types of television programs and
      names of specific programs
      [to be added as needed]
  BT **Television broadcasting**
  NT **Adventure television programs**
      Animated television programs
      Biographical television pro-
        grams
      Comedy television programs
      Fantasy television programs
      Horror television programs
      Legal drama (Television pro-
        grams)
      Medical drama (Television
        programs)
      Music videos
      Mystery television programs
      Science fiction television pro-
        grams
      Sports drama (Television pro-
        grams)
      Spy television programs
      Talk shows
      Television adaptations
      Television movies
      Television plays
      Television serials
      Variety shows (Television pro-
        grams)
      Violence on television
      War television programs
      Westerns (Television programs)
  RT **Television scripts**
Television—Receivers and reception
    621.388
  UF Television reception
      Television sets
  BT **Television—Equipment and**
        supplies
Television reception
  USE **Television—Receivers and re-**
        ception
Television—Repairing   621.388

698

Television scripts   791.45; 808.8; 818, etc.

May be used for individual works, collections, or materials about television scripts.
- UF   Screenplays
- BT   **Television broadcasting**
- NT   **Television adaptations**
- RT   **Television plays**
  Television programs

Television serials   791.45

May be used for individual works, collections, or materials about television serials.
- BT   **Television programs**
- RT   **Soap operas**

Television sets
- USE   **Television—Receivers and reception**

Television sports
- USE   **Television broadcasting of sports**

Television—Stage lighting
- USE   **Stage lighting**

Television stations   384.55
- BT   **Television broadcasting**

Television, Subscription
- USE   **Subscription television**

Television supplies industry (May subdiv. geog.)   338.4; 384.55
- UF   Television equipment industry
  Television industry
- RT   **Television—Equipment and supplies**

Television writing
- USE   **Television authorship**

Telstar project   621.382
- UF   Bell System Telstar satellite
  Project Telstar
- BT   **Artificial satellites in telecommunication**

Temperament   155.2
- BT   **Mind and body**
  Psychology
  Psychophysiology
- RT   **Character**

Temperance   178; 241; 613.81

Use for materials on the virtue of temperance or on the temperance movement.
- UF   Abstinence
  Drunkenness
  Intemperance
  Intoxication
  Total abstinence

- BT   **Virtue**
- RT   **Alcoholism**
  Drinking of alcoholic beverages
  Prohibition

Temperature   536
- NT   **Low temperatures**
- RT   **Cold**
  Heat
  Thermometers

Temperature, Animal and human
- USE   **Body temperature**

Temperature, Body
- USE   **Body temperature**

Temples (May subdiv. geog.)   291.3; 726
- BT   **Buildings**
  Church architecture
- NT   **Mosques**

Temporal power of the Pope
- USE   **Popes—Temporal power**

Temporary employment   331.25
- UF   Employment, Temporary
- BT   **Employment**

Ten commandments   222
- UF   Decalogue
- BT   **Bible. O.T.**

Tenant and landlord
- USE   **Landlord and tenant**

Tenant farming
- USE   **Farm tenancy**

Tenement houses (May subdiv. geog.)   647
- UF   Tenements (Apartment houses)
- BT   **Apartment houses**

Tenements (Apartment houses)
- USE   **Tenement houses**

Tennis (May subdiv. geog.)   796.342
- UF   Lawn tennis
- BT   **Sports**

Tennis—Tournaments (May subdiv. geog.)   796.342
- BT   **Sports tournaments**

Tenpins
- USE   **Bowling**

Tension (Physiology)
- USE   **Stress (Physiology)**

Tension (Psychology)
- USE   **Stress (Psychology)**

Tents   796.54
- BT   **Camping**

Tenure of land
- USE   **Land tenure**

Tenure of office
   USE **Civil service**
Tepees   **728; 970.004**
   UF   Teepees
         Wigwams
   BT **Native Americans—Dwellings**
Term limitations (Public office)
   USE **Term limits (Public office)**
Term limits (Public office) (May subdiv.
   geog.)   **328**
   UF   Term limitations (Public office)
   BT **Legislative bodies**
        Public officers
Term limits (Public office)—United
   States   **328.73**
   UF   United States—Term limits
        (Public office)
Term paper writing
   USE **Report writing**
Terminal care (May subdiv. geog.)
   362.1; 649.8
   UF   Care of the dying
   BT **Medical care**
   NT **Hospices**
        Life support systems (Medical
         environment)
        Terminally ill
   RT **Death**
        Living wills
Terminally ill (May subdiv. geog.)
   362.1; 649.8
   UF   Dying patients
         Fatally ill patients
   BT **Sick**
        Terminal care
   NT **Terminally ill children**
   RT **Death**
Terminally ill children (May subdiv.
   geog.)   **362.1; 649.8**
   UF   Dying children
         Fatally ill children
   BT **Terminally ill**
Terminals, Computer
   USE **Computer terminals**
Termination of pregnancy
   USE **Abortion**
Terminology
   USE **Terms and phrases**
        and subjects, classes of persons,
         sacred works, and religious
         sects with the subdivision

Terminology, for lists or discussions of words and expressions found in those works or
used in those fields, e.g. **Botany—Terminology;** names of
languages with the subdivision
Terms and phrases, e.g. **English language—Terms and
phrases;** scientific and technical disciplines and types of
substances, plants, and animals with the subdivision *Nomenclature,* for systematically
derived lists of names or designations that have been formally adopted or sanctioned,
and for discussions of the
principles involved in the creation and application of such
names, e.g. **Botany—Nomenclature;** and scientific and
technical disciplines and types
of animals, plants, and crops
with the subdivision *Nomenclature (Popular),* for lists or
materials about popular, non-
technical names or designations of substances, species,
etc., **Trees—Nomenclature
(Popular)** [to be added as
needed]
Terms and phrases   **030**
   UF   Commonplaces
        Terminology
   SA   names of languages with the
        subdivision *Terms and
        phrases,* e.g. **English lan-
        guage—Terms and phrases;**
        subjects, classes of persons,
        sacred works, and religious
        sects with the subdivision
        Terminology, for lists or dis-
        cussions of words and expres-
        sions found in those works or
        used in those fields, e.g. **Bot-
        any—Terminology;** scientific
        and technical disciplines and
        types of substances, plants,
        and animals with the subdivi-
        sion *Nomenclature,* for sys-
        tematically derived lists of

Terms and phrases—*Continued*

names or designations that have been formally adopted or sanctioned, and for discussions of the principles involved in the creation and application of such names, e.g. **Botany—Nomenclature;** and scientific and technical disciplines and types of animals, plants, and crops with the subdivision *Nomenclature (Popular),* for lists or materials about popular, non-technical names or designations of substances, species, etc., **Trees—Nomenclature (Popular)** [to be added as needed]

  BT **Names**

  RT **Allusions**

Terns 598.3

  BT **Birds**

       Water birds

Terra cotta 620.1; 691

  BT **Building materials**

       Decoration and ornament

       Pottery

Terrain sensing, Remote

  USE **Remote sensing**

Terrapins

  USE **Turtles**

Terrariums 635.9

  BT **Indoor gardening**

  RT **Miniature gardens**

Terrestrial physics

  USE **Geophysics**

Territorial expansion

  USE names of countries, regions, etc., with the subdivision *Territorial expansion,* e.g. **United States—Territorial expansion** [to be added as needed]

Territorial questions

  USE names of wars with the subdivision *Territorial questions,* e.g. **World War, 1939-1945—Territorial questions;** which may be further subdivided geographically [to be added as needed]

Territorial waters (May subdiv. geog.) **341.4**

  UF Economic zones (Maritime law)

       Three-mile limit

  BT **Shipping**

  RT **Continental shelf**

       Maritime law

Territorial waters—United States 341.4

  UF United States—Territorial waters

Territories and possessions

  USE names of countries with the subdivision *Territories and possessions,* or *Colonies,* e.g. **United States—Territories and possessions; Great Britain—Colonies;** etc. [to be added as needed]

Terror, Reign of

  USE **France—History—1789-1799, Revolution**

Terror tales

  USE **Ghost stories**

       Horror fiction

Terrorism (May subdiv. geog.) 303.6

  UF Political violence

  BT **Insurgency**

       Political crimes and offenses

       Subversive activities

  NT **Bombings**

       Hostages

       Sabotage

  RT **Anarchism and anarchists**

Terrorism—United States 303.6; 322.4

Terrorist bombings

  USE **Bombings**

Test pilots

  USE **Air pilots**

       Airplanes—Testing

Test preparation guides

  USE **Examinations—Study guides**

Test tube babies

  USE **Fertilization in vitro**

Test tube fertilization

  USE **Fertilization in vitro**

Testing 620

  UF Mechanical properties testing

  SA things tested with the subdivision *Testing,* e.g. **Ability—Testing; Airplanes—Testing; Concrete—Testing;** etc [to be added as needed]

Testing—*Continued*
   BT   **Reliability (Engineering)**
   NT   **Electric testing**
   RT   **Strength of materials**
Testing for drug abuse
   USE   **Drug testing**
Tests
   USE   **Educational tests and measurements**
         Examinations
Teutonic peoples (May subdiv. geog.)
      305.83
   UF   Nordic peoples
         Teutonic race
   SA   names of particular Teutonic peoples, e.g. **Goths** [to be added as needed]
   NT   **Anglo-Saxons**
         Goths
Teutonic race
   USE   **Teutonic peoples**
Textbooks   371.3
   Use for materials about textbooks. Textbooks themselves are entered under the subject only, e.g. **Arithmetic; Geography;** etc.
   UF   School books
   BT   **Books**
Textile chemistry   677
   UF   Chemistry, Textile
   BT   **Industrial chemistry**
         Textile industry
   NT   **Dyes and dyeing**
Textile design (May subdiv. geog.)   **746**
   UF   Fabric design
   BT   **Commercial art**
         Decoration and ornament
         Design
   NT   **Textile painting**
   RT   **Textile printing**
Textile fibers
   USE   **Fibers**
Textile industry (May subdiv. geog.)
      338.4; 677
   SA   types of articles manufactured, e.g **Rugs and carpets; Hosiery;** etc. [to be added as needed]
   BT   **Industries**
   NT   **Bleaching**
         Cotton manufacture
         Dyes and dyeing
         Hosiery
         Spinning
         Textile chemistry
         Textile printing
         Weaving
Textile painting   746.6
   BT   **Painting**
         Textile design
Textile printing   746.6
   UF   Block printing
   BT   **Printing**
         Textile industry
   RT   **Silk screen printing**
         Textile design
Textiles
   USE   **Fabrics**
Texts
   USE   types of lesser-known languages, dialects, early periods of languages, liturgies, and types of vocal music with the subdivision *Texts,* e.g. **Catholic Church—Liturgy—Texts; Popular music—Texts;** etc., for individual texts or collections of texts [to be added as needed]
Thanksgiving Day   394.2649
   BT   **Holidays**
         Religious holidays
Theater (May subdiv. geog.)   **792**
   Use for materials on drama as acted on the stage. Materials on drama as a literary form are entered under **Drama; American drama; English drama;** etc. Collections of plays are entered under **Drama—Collections; American drama—Collections;** etc. Materials on theater buildings are entered under **Theaters.**
   UF   Stage
   SA   names of wars with the subdivision *Theater and the war* e.g. **World War, 1939-1945—Theater and the war** [to be added as needed]
   BT   **Amusements**
         Performing arts
   NT   **Amateur theater**
         Arena theater
         Ballet
         Children's plays
         Experimental theater
         Little theater movement
         Masks (Plays)

Theater—*Continued*
        Morality plays
        Musicals
        Mysteries and miracle plays
        Pantomimes
        Passion plays
        Puppets and puppet plays
        Readers' theater
        Shadow pantomimes and plays
        Shakespeare, William, 1564-
          1616—Stage history
        Skits
        Vaudeville
        World War, 1939-1945—The-
          ater and the war
  RT Acting
      Drama
      Dramatic criticism
      Theaters
Theater and the war
  USE names of wars with the subdivi-
        sion *Theater and the war,* e.g.
        World War, 1939-1945—
        Theater and the war [to be
        added as needed]
Theater criticism
  USE **Dramatic criticism**
Theater-in-the-round
  USE **Arena theater**
Theater—Production and direction   792
  UF Direction (Theater)
      Play direction (Theater)
      Play production
      Theatrical direction
      Theatrical production
  RT **Theatrical producers and di-
      rectors**
Theater—United States   792.0973
Theaters (May subdiv. geog.)   725
    Use for materials on theater buildings, their
architecture, technical fixtures, decoration, etc.
Materials on drama as a literary form are en-
tered under **Drama.** Materials on drama as
acted on the stage are entered under **Theater.**
  UF Playhouses
  SA types of theaters [to be added as
      needed]
  BT **Buildings**
      **Centers for the performing
      arts**
  RT **Theater**

Theaters—Conservation and restoration
  (May subdiv. geog.)   725
  BT **Historic preservation**
Theaters—Stage lighting
  USE **Stage lighting**
Theaters—Stage setting and scenery
  792
  UF Scenery (Stage)
      Stage scenery
      Stage setting
      Theatrical scenery
  NT **Scene painting**
Theatrical costume
  USE **Costume**
Theatrical direction
  USE **Theater—Production and di-
      rection**
Theatrical directors
  USE **Theatrical producers and di-
      rectors**
Theatrical makeup   791.43; 791.45; 792
  UF Makeup, Theatrical
  BT **Cosmetics**
      Costume
Theatrical producers
  USE **Theatrical producers and di-
      rectors**
Theatrical producers and directors (May
  subdiv. geog.)   792; 920
  UF Theatrical directors
      Theatrical producers
  RT **Theater—Production and di-
      rection**
Theatrical production
  USE **Theater—Production and di-
      rection**
Theatrical scenery
  USE **Theaters—Stage setting and
      scenery**
Theft   364.16
  UF Larceny
      Stealing *[Former heading]*
  BT **Crime**
      Offenses against property
  NT **Art thefts**
      Shoplifting
  RT **Thieves**
Theism (May subdiv. geog.)   211
  BT **Philosophy**
      Religion
      Theology

Theism—*Continued*
  RT Atheism
      Deism
      God
Theme parks
  USE Amusement parks
Themes in art
  USE Art—Themes
Themes in literature
  USE Literature—Themes
Theological education
  USE Religious education
       Theology—Study and teaching
Theology (May subdiv. geog.) 230;
       291.2
  NT Apologetics
      Atheism
      Church
      Covenants
      Deism
      Doctrinal theology
      Eschatology
      Faith
      Feminist theology
      Good and evil
      Immortality
      Liberation theology
      Natural theology
      Pastoral theology
      Predestination
      Revelation
      Sin
      Theism
      Worship
  RT God
      Religion
Theology, Doctrinal
  USE Doctrinal theology
Theology of liberation
  USE Liberation theology
Theology—Study and teaching 230.07;
       291.2
  UF Education, Theological
      Religion—Study and teaching
      Theological education
  NT Catechisms
  RT Religious education
Theoretical chemistry
  USE Physical chemistry
Theory of games
  USE Game theory

Theory of graphs
  USE Graph theory
Theory of knowledge 001.01; 121
      Use for materials on the origin, nature,
    methods, and limits of human knowledge.
  UF Cognition
      Epistemology
      Knowledge, Theory of
      Understanding
  BT Consciousness
      Logic
      Metaphysics
      Philosophy
  NT Belief and doubt
      Certainty
      Empiricism
      Gestalt psychology
      Ideology
      Intuition
      Perception
      Pragmatism
      Rationalism
      Senses and sensation
  RT Apperception
      Intellect
      Reality
      Truth
Theory of numbers
  USE Number theory
Theory of structures
  USE Structural analysis (Engineer-
          ing)
Theory of systems
  USE System theory
Theosophy (May subdiv. geog.) 299
  BT Mysticism
      Religions
  NT Reincarnation
      Yoga
Therapeutic systems
  USE Alternative medicine
Therapeutic use
  USE subjects with the subdivision
          Therapeutic use, e.g. Cold—
          Therapeutic use; Herbs—
          Therapeutic use etc. [to be
          added as needed]
Therapeutics 615.5
  UF Diseases—Treatment
      Therapy
      Treatment
      Treatment of diseases

Therapeutics—*Continued*
   SA   types of therapies, e.g. **Hydro-therapy;** diseases with the subdivision *Treatment,* e.g. **AIDS (Disease)—Treatment;** subjects with the subdivision *Therapeutic use,* e.g. **Cold—Therapeutic use; Herbs—Therapeutic use;** etc.; diseases with the subdivision *Diet therapy,* e.g. **Cancer—Diet therapy;** and types of drugs and names of specific drugs [to be added as needed]
   BT   **Medicine**
         Pathology
   NT   **AIDS (Disease)—Treatment**
         Antiseptics
         Cold—Therapeutic use
         Diet in disease
         Diet therapy
         Drug therapy
         Drugs
         Electrotherapeutics
         Gene therapy
         Herbs—Therapeutic use
         Hydrotherapy
         Materia medica
         Medicine
         Naturopathy
         Nursing
         Nutrition
         Occupational therapy
         Pet therapy
         Phototherapy
         Physical therapy
         Psychotherapy
         Radiotherapy
         Suggestive therapeutics
   RT   **Pharmaceutical chemistry**
Therapeutics, Suggestive
   USE **Suggestive therapeutics**
Therapy
   USE **Therapeutics**
Therapy, Gene
   USE **Gene therapy**
Therapy, Psychological
   USE **Psychotherapy**
Thermal insulation
   USE **Insulation (Heat)**

Thermal waters
   USE **Geothermal resources**
         Geysers
Thermoaerodynamics
   USE **Aerothermodynamics**
Thermodynamics 536
   SA   subjects with the subdivision *Thermodynamics,* e.g. **Space vehicles—Thermodynamics** [to be added as needed]
   BT   **Dynamics**
         Physical chemistry
         Physics
   NT   **Aerothermodynamics**
         Heat engines
         Heat pumps
         Space vehicles—Thermodynamics
   RT   **Heat**
         Heat engines
         Quantum theory
Thermometers 536
   UF   Thermometry
   BT   **Heat**
         Meteorological instruments
   RT   **Temperature**
Thermometry
   USE **Thermometers**
Thesauri
   USE **Subject headings** and names of languages with the subdivision *Synonyms and antonyms,* e.g. **English language—Synonyms and antonyms** [to be added as needed]
Theses
   USE **Dissertations**
Thieves (May subdiv. geog.) **364.3**
   UF   Bandits
         Brigands
         Burglars
         Highwaymen
         Outlaws
         Robbers
   BT   **Criminals**
   RT   **Theft**
Think tanks
   USE **Group problem solving**
Thinking
   USE **Thought and thinking**

Third parties (United States politics)
    324.273
    BT   **Political parties**
          United States—Politics and
            government
Third World
    USE **Developing countries**
Third World War
    USE **World War III**
Thirteenth century
    USE **World history—13th century**
Thirty Years' War, 1618-1648   **909.08;**
    940.2
    BT   **Europe—History—1492-1789**
          Germany—History—1517-1740
Thoroughfares
    USE **Roads**
          Streets
Thought and thinking   **153.4**
    UF   Thinking
    BT   **Educational psychology**
          Psychology
    NT   **Attention**
          Critical thinking
          Ideology
          Memory
          Perception
          Reasoning
          Stereotype (Psychology)
    RT   **Intellect**
          Logic
Thought control
    USE **Brainwashing**
Threatened species
    USE **Endangered species**
Three dimensional photography   **778.4**
    UF   3-D photography
          Photography, Stereoscopic
          Stereo photography
          Stereophotography
          Stereoscopic photography
    BT   **Photography**
    RT   **Holography**
Three-mile limit
    USE **Territorial waters**
Three Stooges films   **791.43**
    May be used for individual works, collections, or materials about Three Stooges films.
    BT   **Comedy films**
          Motion pictures
Three (The number)   **513**
    BT   **Numbers**

Thrift
    USE **Saving and investment**
Thrillers
    USE **Adventure fiction**
          Adventure films
Throat   **611; 612; 617.5**
    BT   **Anatomy**
    NT   **Voice**
Thunderstorms (May subdiv. geog.)
    551.55
    BT   **Meteorology**
          Storms
    NT   **Lightning**
Tiananmen Square Incident, Beijing
    (China), 1989   **951.05**
    UF   Beijing Massacre, 1989
          China—History—1989, Tiananmen Square Incident *[Former heading]*
Ticks   **595.4**
    BT   **Animals**
Tidal waves
    USE **Tsunamis**
Tides (May subdiv. geog.)   **551.47**
    BT   **Ocean**
Tie dyeing   **746.6**
    BT   **Dyes and dyeing**
Tiles (May subdiv. geog.)   **666; 693;**
    738.6
    UF   Ceramic tiles
    BT   **Building materials**
          Ceramics
Timber
    USE **Forests and forestry**
          Lumber and lumbering
          Trees
          Wood
Timber—Harvesting
    USE **Logging**
Time   **529**
    UF   Horology
          Standard time
    NT   **Calendars**
          Chronology
          Clocks and watches
          Day
          Night
          Punctuality
          Space and time
          Sundials
          Time management

Time—*Continued*
RT Cycles
 Nautical astronomy
Time and space
 USE **Space and time**
Time management 640; 650.1
 UF Allocation of time
 Personal time management
 BT **Management**
 Time
Time production standards
 USE **Production standards**
Time saving cooking
 USE **Quick and easy cooking**
Time sharing (Real estate)
 USE **Timesharing (Real estate)**
Time study 658.5
 BT **Factory management**
 Industrial efficiency
 Job analysis
 Personnel management
 Production standards
 RT **Motion study**
Time travel 115
 BT **Fourth dimension**
 Space and time
Timesharing (Real estate) (May subdiv.
 geog.) **333.3; 333.5; 643**
 UF Condominium timesharing
 Real estate timesharing
 Time sharing (Real estate)
 Vacation home timesharing
 BT **Condominiums**
 Housing
Tin 669
 BT **Chemical elements**
 Metals
Tinsmithing
 USE **Tinwork**
Tinwork (May subdiv. geog.) **673**
 UF Tinsmithing
 BT **Metalwork**
Tiny objects
 USE **Miniature objects**
Tires 678
 UF Rubber tires
 BT **Wheels**
Tiros (Meteorological satellite)
 USE **TIROS satellites**
TIROS satellites 551.5
 UF Television and infrared observa-
 tion satellite

Tiros (Meteorological satellite)
 [Former heading]
 BT **Meteorological satellites**
Tissue donation
 USE **Donation of organs, tissues,**
 etc.
Tissues—Transplantation
 USE **Transplantation of organs, tis-**
 sues, etc.
Tithes (May subdiv. geog.) **248; 254**
 BT **Church finance**
 Ecclesiastical law
 Taxation
Toadstools
 USE **Mushrooms**
Toasts 808.5; 808.85
 UF Healths, Drinking of
 BT **Epigrams**
 Speeches
 RT **After dinner speeches**
Tobacco (May subdiv. geog.) **633.7**
 BT **Plants**
 NT **Cigarettes**
 Cigars
 RT **Smoking**
Tobacco habit (May subdiv. geog.) **178;**
 613.85; 616.86
 UF Addiction to nicotine
 Addiction to tobacco
 Nicotine habit
 BT **Habit**
 Smoking
 NT **Smoking cessation programs**
Tobacco pipes 688
 UF Pipes, Tobacco
 BT **Smoking**
Toilet preparations
 USE **Toiletries**
Toilet training 649
 BT **Child rearing**
Toiletries 646.7
 UF Toilet preparations
 BT **Personal grooming**
 RT **Cosmetics**
Tolerance
 USE **Toleration**
Toleration (May subdiv. geog.) **179;**
 323
 UF Bigotry
 Intolerance
 Tolerance

Toleration—*Continued*
  BT Interpersonal relations
  NT Academic freedom
       Freedom of conscience
       Freedom of religion
  RT Discrimination
Toll roads
  USE Express highways
Tombs (May subdiv. geog.) 726
  UF Graves
       Mausoleums
       Rock tombs
       Sepulchers
       Vaults (Sepulchral)
  SA classes of persons, and names of
       families, royal houses,
       dynasties, etc., with the subdi-
       vision *Tombs,* e.g. **Presi-
       dents—United States—
       Tombs** [to be added as need-
       ed]
  BT Archeology
       Architecture
       Burial
       Monuments
       Shrines
  NT Brasses
       Catacombs
       Epitaphs
       Mounds and mound builders
  RT Cemeteries
Tomography 616.07; 621.36
  UF CAT scan
       Computerized tomography
  BT X-rays
Tongue twisters 398.8
  BT Children's poetry
       Folklore
       Nonsense verses
Tools (May subdiv. geog.) 621.9
  UF Implements, utensils, etc.
  SA types of tools [to be added as
       needed]
  NT Agricultural machinery
       Carpentry tools
       Machine tools
       Machinery
       Power tools
       Saws
       Weapons
Top soil loss
  USE Soil erosion

Topographical drawing 526.022
  BT Drawing
       Surveying
  RT Map drawing
Topology 514
  UF Position analysis
  BT Geometry
       Set theory
  NT Fractals
       Graph theory
  RT Linear algebra
Tories, American
  USE American Loyalists
Tornadoes (May subdiv. geog.) 551.55
  UF Twisters (Tornadoes)
  BT Meteorology
       Storms
       Winds
Torpedoes 623.4
  BT Explosives
       Naval art and science
       Submarine warfare
Tort liability of professions
  USE Malpractice
Tortoises
  USE Turtles
Torture (May subdiv. geog.) 365
  BT Criminal procedure
       Cruelty
       Punishment
Total abstinence
  USE Temperance
Totalitarianism (May subdiv. geog.)
       321.9
  UF Authoritarianism
  BT Political science
  NT Communism
       Dictators
       Fascism
Totem poles (May subdiv. gcog.) 299;
       730.89
  BT Totems and totemism
Totems and totemism (May subdiv.
       geog.) 299
  BT Ethnology
       Mythology
  NT Totem poles
Touch 152.1; 612
  UF Feeling
  BT Senses and sensation
  NT Hugging

Touring, Bicycle
USE **Bicycle touring**
Tourism
USE **Tourist trade**
Travel
Tourist accommodations
USE **Hotels and motels**
Youth hostels
Tourist industry
USE **Tourist trade**
Tourist trade (May subdiv. geog.) 338.4
UF Tourism
Tourist industry
Tourists
Travel industry
BT **Commerce**
RT **Travel**
Tourists
USE **Tourist trade**
Travelers
Tournaments
USE **Medieval tournaments**
Sports tournaments
and types of sports and games
with the subdivision *Tourna-*
ments, e.g. **Tennis—Tourna-**
ments [to be added as need-
ed]
Town life
USE **City and town life**
Town meeting
USE **Local government**
Town officers
USE **Municipal officials and em-**
ployees
Town planning
USE **City planning**
Towns
USE **Cities and towns**
Towns, abandoned
USE **Ghost towns**
Township government
USE **Local government**
Toxic dumps
USE **Hazardous waste sites**
Toxic plants
USE **Poisonous plants**
Toxic substances
USE **Hazardous substances**
Poisons and poisoning

Toxic wastes
USE **Hazardous wastes**
Toxicology 571.9; 615.9
Use for materials on the science that treats
of poisons and their antidotes. Materials on
poisonous substance and their use are entered
under **Poisons and poisoning.**
UF Chemicals—Toxicology
SA types of poisons or poisoning,
e.g. **Lead poisoning;** and
types of poisonous substances
with the subdivision *Toxicolo-*
gy, for materials on the influ-
ence of particular substances
on humans and animals, e.g.
Insecticides—Toxicology [to
be added as needed]
BT **Medicine**
Pharmacology
RT **Poisons and poisoning**
Toy and movable books
UF Movable books
Pop-up books
BT **Picture books for children**
NT **Glow-in-the-dark books**
Toys (May subdiv. geog.) 688.7; 790.1
SA types of toys [to be added as
needed]
BT **Amusements**
NT **Dollhouses**
Dolls
Electric toys
Electronic toys
RT **Miniature objects**
Track and field
USE **Track athletics**
Track athletics (May subdiv. geog.)
796.42
UF Field athletics
Track and field
SA types of track sports [to be add-
ed as needed]
BT **Athletics**
Sports
NT **Running**
Tracking and trailing (May subdiv.
geog.) 799.2
UF Trailing
BT **Hunting**
NT **Animal tracks**
RT **Animal behavior**

Tracking of satellites
USE **Artificial satellites—Tracking**
     Space vehicles—Tracking
Tracks of animals
USE **Animal tracks**
Traction engines
USE **Tractors**
Tractors 629.225; 631.3
UF Traction engines
BT **Agricultural machinery**
Trade
USE **Business**
     Commerce
Trade agreements (Labor)
USE **Industrial arbitration**
     Labor contract
Trade and professional associations (May
    subdiv. geog.) **380.1; 650**
UF Professional associations
     Trade associations
BT **Associations**
Trade associations
USE **Trade and professional associa-
     tions**
Trade, Balance of
USE **Balance of trade**
Trade barriers
USE **Commercial policy**
Trade, Boards of
USE **Chambers of commerce**
Trade catalogs
USE **Commercial catalogs**
Trade deficits
USE **Balance of trade**
Trade expositions
USE **Trade shows**
Trade fairs
USE **Trade shows**
Trade, International
USE **International trade**
Trade marks
USE **Trademarks**
Trade, Restraint of
USE **Restraint of trade**
Trade routes (May subdiv. geog.) **387**
UF Ocean routes
     Routes of trade
     Sea routes
BT **Commerce**
     Commercial geography
     Transportation

Trade schools
USE **Technical education**
Trade secrets 346.04; 658.4
UF Business secrets
     Commercial secrets
     Industrial secrets
     Secrets, Trade
BT **Right of privacy**
     Unfair competition
Trade shows (May subdiv. geog.) **659.1**
UF Industrial exhibitions
     Trade expositions
     Trade fairs
BT **Exhibitions**
     Fairs
Trade surpluses
USE **Balance of trade**
Trade-unions
USE **Labor unions**
Trade waste
USE **Industrial waste**
     Waste products
Trademarks (May subdiv. geog.)
    346.04; 929.9
UF Company symbols
     Corporate symbols
     Trade marks
SA types of industries and products
     with the subdivision *Trade-
     marks,* for materials on the
     words, letters, or symbols
     used by the manufacturers or
     dealers of those goods to dis-
     tinguish them from the goods
     of others, e.g. **Glassware—
     Trademarks** [to be added as
     needed]
BT **Commerce**
     Manufactures
NT **Glassware—Trademarks**
RT **Brand name products**
     Patents
Trades
USE **Industrial arts**
     Occupations
Traditional medicine (May subdiv. geog.)
    615.8
UF Folk medicine
     Folklore, Medical
     Medical folklore

Traditional medicine—*Continued*
SA   traditional medicine of particular ethnic groups, e.g. **Native American medicine** [to be added as needed]
BT   **Medicine**
     Popular medicine
Traditions
USE   **Folklore**
     Legends
     Manners and customs
     Rites and ceremonies
     Superstition
Traffic accidents (May subdiv. geog.) **363.12**
UF   Automobile accidents
     Automobiles—Accidents
     Car accidents
     Car wrecks
     Highway accidents
BT   **Accidents**
Traffic, City
USE   **City traffic**
Traffic control
USE   **Traffic engineering**
     Traffic regulations
Traffic engineering (May subdiv. geog.) **388.4**
    Usc for materials on the planning of the flow of traffic and related topics, largely as they concern street transportation in cities and metropolitan areas.
UF   Street traffic
     Traffic control
BT   **Engineering**
     Highway engineering
     Transportation
NT   **Car pools**
     City traffic
     Express highways
     Local transit
RT   **Traffic regulations**
Traffic regulations (May subdiv. geog.) **388.4**
UF   Traffic control
BT   **Safety regulations**
RT   **Automobiles—Law and legislation**
     Traffic engineering
Trafficking in drugs
USE   **Drug traffic**

Trafficking in narcotics
USE   **Drug traffic**
Tragedies   **808.82; 812, etc.**
    May be used for individual works or for collections. Materials about tragedy as a literary form are entered under **Tragedy.**
BT   **Drama**
Tragedy   **792.1; 809.2**
    Use for materials on tragedy as a literary form. Individual works and collections of tragedies are entered under **Tragedies.**
BT   **Drama**
Trailer camps
USE   **Trailer parks**
Trailer parks (May subdiv. geog.)   **647; 796.54**
UF   Mobile home parks
     Trailer camps
BT   **Campgrounds**
     Mobile home living
Trailers
USE   **Mobile homes**
     Travel trailers and campers
Trailing
USE   **Tracking and trailing**
Train wrecks
USE   **Railroad accidents**
Training
USE   types of sports activites, plants and crops, animals, and classes of persons with the subdivision *Training,* e.g. **Soccer—Training; Horses—Training; Teachers—Training;** etc. [to be added as needed]
Training camps, Military
USE   **Military training camps**
Training colleges for teachers
USE   **Teachers colleges**
Training, Occupational
USE   **Occupational training**
Training of animals
USE   **Animals—Training**
Training of children
USE   **Child rearing**
Training of employees
USE   **Employees—Training**
Training, Vocational
USE   **Occupational training**
Trains
USE   **Railroads**

Traitors (May subdiv. geog.) **364.1**
  NT **Collaborationists**
  RT **Treason**
Tramps (May subdiv. geog.) **305.5**
    Use for materials on homeless persons who travel about from place to place and work in occasional jobs.
  UF Hoboes
       Vagabonds
       Vagrants
  BT **Homeless persons**
       Poor
  RT **Begging**
       Unemployed
Trams
  USE **Street railroads**
Transactional analysis **158**
  BT **Psychotherapy**
Transatlantic flights
  USE **Aeronautics—Flights**
Transcendental meditation **158**
  BT **Meditation**
Transcendentalism **141**
  BT **Philosophy**
  RT **Idealism**
Transcontinental journeys (American continent)
  USE **Overland journeys to the Pacific**
Transcultural studies
  USE **Cross-cultural studies**
Transfer of technology
  USE **Technology transfer**
Transfer payments (May subdiv. geog.) **339.5**
  UF Government transfer payments
  BT **Domestic economic assistance**
       Economic policy
       Subsidies
Transfer tax
  USE **Inheritance and transfer tax**
Transformation (Genetics)
  USE **Genetic transformation**
Transformers, Electric
  USE **Electric transformers**
Transgenics
  USE **Genetic engineering**
Transistor amplifiers **621.3815**
  UF Amplifiers, Transistor
       Audio amplifiers, Transistor
       Transistor audio amplifiers

  BT **Amplifiers (Electronics)**
       Transistors
Transistor audio amplifiers
  USE **Transistor amplifiers**
Transistors **621.3815**
  BT **Electronics**
       Semiconductors
  NT **Transistor amplifiers**
Transit systems
  USE **Local transit**
Translating and interpreting (May subdiv. geog.) **418**
  UF Interpreting and translating
  BT **Language and languages**
Transmission of data
  USE **Data transmission systems**
Transmission of power
  USE **Electric lines**
       Electric power distribution
       Power transmission
Transmissions, Automobile
  USE **Automobiles—Transmission devices**
Transmutation (Chemistry) **539.7**
    Use for materials on the transmutation of metals in nuclear physics. Materials on medieval attempts to change base metals into gold are entered under **Alchemy.**
  UF Transmutation of metals
  BT **Atoms**
       Nuclear physics
       Radioactivity
  NT **Cyclotrons**
  RT **Alchemy**
Transmutation of metals
  USE **Alchemy**
       Transmutation (Chemistry)
Transplantation
  USE **Transplantation of organs, tissues, etc.**
       and organs of the body with the subdivision *Transplantation*, e.g. **Heart—Transplantation** [to be added as needed]
Transplantation of organs, tissues, etc. **617.9**
  UF Medical transplantation
       Organ transplants
       Organs—Transplantation
       Surgical transplantation
       Tissues—Transplantation

Transplantation of organs, tissues, etc.—
Continued

>Transplantation
SA organs of the body with the
>>subdivision *Transplantation,*
>>e.g. **Heart—Transplantation**
>>[to be added as needed]
BT **Surgery**
NT **Heart—Transplantation**
RT **Donation of organs, tissues,
>>etc.**
>>**Preservation of organs, tissues,
>>etc.**

**Transplantation of organs, tissues, etc.—
Ethical aspects 174**

UF Transplantation of organs, tis-
>>sues, etc.—Moral and reli-
>>gious aspects
BT **Bioethics**

Transplantation of organs, tissues, etc.—
Moral and religious aspects

USE **Transplantation of organs, tis-
>>sues, etc.—Ethical aspects**
>>**Transplantation of organs, tis-
>>sues, etc.—Religious aspects**

**Transplantation of organs, tissues, etc.—
Religious aspects 241; 291.1**

UF Transplantation of organs, tis-
>>sues, etc.—Moral and reli-
>>gious aspects

Transportation (May subdiv. geog.) **388**

SA subjects, classes of person, and
>>names of wars with the sub-
>>division *Transportation,* e.g.
>>**Hazardous substances—
>>Transportation; School chil-
>>dren—Transportation;
>>World War, 1939-1945—
>>Transportation;** etc. [to be
>>added as needed]
BT **Locomotion**
NT **Bridges
>>Canals
>>Car pools
>>Commercial aeronautics
>>Express service
>>Freight
>>Harbors
>>Hazardous substances—Trans-
>>portation
>>Highway transportation
>>Inland navigation**

>**Local transit
>Merchant marine
>Military transportation
>Ocean travel
>Pipelines
>Postal service
>Railroads
>Roads
>School children—Transporta-
>tion
>Shipping
>Steam navigation
>Streets
>Trade routes
>Traffic engineering
>Trucking
>Vehicles
>Waterways
>World War, 1939-1945—Trans-
>portation**
RT **Commerce**

Transportation, Highway
USE **Highway transportation**

Transportation, Military
USE **Military transportation**

Transportation of criminals
USE **Penal colonies**

Transportation—Planning (May subdiv.
geog.) **338**
BT **Planning**

Transsexualism 305.3; 616.85
UF Change of sex
>>Sex change
>>Transsexuality *[Former heading]*
BT **Sex role**

Transsexuality
USE **Transsexualism**

Trapping (May subdiv. geog.) **639**
NT **Fur trade**
RT **Game and game birds
>>Hunting**

Traumatic stress syndrome
USE **Post-traumatic stress disorder**

Travel 910

>Use for materials on the art and enjoyment
of travel and advice for travelers. Descriptions
of actual voyages are entered under **Voyages
and travels** or under the name of a place with
the subdivision *Description.* An account of an
extinct city or town by a traveler in ancient
times is entered under the name of the extinct
city or town, without further subdivision, e.g.
Delphi (Extinct city).

Travel—*Continued*
- UF   Group travel
  - Journeys
  - Tourism
- SA   names of cities (except extinct cities), countries, states, etc., with the subdivision *Description,* e.g. **United States—Description;** and ethnic groups, classes of persons, and names of individuals with the subdivision *Travel,* e.g. **Handicapped—Travel** [to be added as needed]
- BT   **Manners and customs**
- NT   **Automobile travel**
  - **Bicycle touring**
  - **Handicapped—Travel**
  - **Ocean travel**
  - **Travel in literature**
  - **Voyages around the world**
- RT   **Tourist trade**
  - **Voyages and travels**

Travel books
- USE   **Voyages and travels**
  - **Voyages around the world**

Travel guides
- USE   **Automobile travel—Guidebooks** and names of cities (except ancient cities), countries, states, etc., with the subdivision *Guidebooks,* e.g. **Chicago (Ill.)—Guidebooks; United States—Guidebooks;** etc. [to be added as needed]

Travel in literature   **809**

Use for materials about the theme of travel in literature. Materials about non-fiction travel writing, collections of travel writings, and accounts of voyages and travels not limited to a single place are entered under **Voyages and travels.** Accounts of voyages and travels limited to a single place are entered under the name of the place with the subdivision *Description.*
- UF   Voyages and travels in literature
- BT   **Literature—Themes**
  - **Travel**
- RT   **Voyages and travels**

Travel industry
- USE   **Tourist trade**

Travel trailers and campers   **629.226; 796.7**

Use for materials on structures mounted upon a truck or towed by a truck or automobile for the purpose of temporary dwelling or cargo hauling. Materials on stationary transportable structures designed for year-round living are entered under **Mobile homes.**
- UF   Automobiles—Trailers
  - Campers and trailers
  - House trailers
  - Pickup campers
  - Trailers
- BT   **Camping**
  - **Recreational vehicles**
- NT   **Vans**
- RT   **Mobile homes**

Travelers (May subdiv. geog.)   **910.92; 920**
- UF   Tourists
  - Voyagers
- SA   travelers from particular countries, e.g. **American travelers;** and ethnic groups, classes of person, and names of individuals with the subdivision *Travel,* e.g. **Presidents—United States—Travel** [to be added as needed]
- BT   **Voyages and travels**
- NT   **American travelers**
- RT   **Explorers**

Traveling sales personnel
- USE   **Sales personnel**

Travels
- USE   **Voyages and travels**

Travesties
- USE   **Parodies**

Tray gardens
- USE   **Miniature gardens**

Treason (May subdiv. geog.)   **364.1**

Use for materials on the offense of acting to overthrow one's own government or to harm or kill its sovereign. Materials on any attempt to subvert, overthrow, or cause the destruction of any established or legally constituted government are entered under **Subversive activities.**
- UF   High treason
- BT   **Crime**
  - **Political crimes and offenses**
  - **Subversive activities**
- RT   **Traitors**

Treasure trove
- USE   **Buried treasure**

Treaties   341; 341.3
   SA   names of countries with the sub-
        division *Foreign relations—*
        Treaties, and names of wars
        with the subdivision *Treaties*
        [to be added as needed]
   BT   **Diplomacy**
        International law
        International relations
   NT   **International arbitration**
        **United States—Foreign rela-
        tions—Treaties**
        **World War, 1939-1945—Trea-
        ties**
Treatment
   USE   **Therapeutics**
         and types of diseases with the
         subdivision *Treatment,* e.g.
         AIDS (Disease)—Treatment
         [to be added as needed]
Treatment of diseases
   USE   **Therapeutics**
Tree planting (May subdiv. geog.)
        635.9
   UF   Planting
   BT   **Forests and forestry**
   NT   **Windbreaks**
   RT   **Christmas tree growing**
        Reforestation
        Trees
Trees (May subdiv. geog.)   **582.16; 635.9**
   Names of nuts and tree fruits may be used
   for either the nut or fruit or the tree.
   UF   Arboriculture
        Timber
   SA   types of trees, e.g. **Oak** [to be
        added as needed], in the sin-
        gular form
   BT   **Plants**
   NT   **Christmas trees**
        Dwarf trees
        Evergreens
        Fruit culture
        Lumber and lumbering
        Oak
        Pruning
        Shrubs
        Wood
   RT   **Forests and forestry**
        Landscape gardening
        Tree planting

Trees—Nomenclature (Popular)   **582.16**
   BT   **Popular plant names**
Trees—United States   **582.160973**
Trent Affair, 1861   **973.7**
   BT   **United States—History—1861-
        1865, Civil War**
Trial by jury
   USE   **Jury**
Trial by publicity
   USE   **Freedom of the press and fair
         trial**
Trial marriage
   USE   **Unmarried couples**
Trials (May subdiv. geog.)   **345; 347**
   May be qualified by topic, e.g. **Trials
   (Homicide).**
   BT   **Criminal law**
   NT   **Courts martial and courts of
        inquiry**
        Trials (Homicide)
        War crime trials
        Witnesses
   RT   **Crime**
Trials—Fiction
   USE   **Legal stories**
Trials (Homicide) (May subdiv. geog.)
        345
   UF   Homicide trials
        Murder trials
        Trials (Murder)
   BT   **Homicide**
        Trials
Trials (Murder)
   USE   **Trials (Homicide)**
Tricks   **793.5**
   SA   types of tricks [to be added as
        needed]
   BT   **Amusements**
   NT   **Card tricks**
        Juggling
        Magic tricks
Tricycles   **629.227; 796.6**
   UF   Trikes
   BT   **Vehicles**
   RT   **Cycling**
Trigonometry   **516.24**
   UF   Plane trigonometry
        Spherical trigonometry
   BT   **Geometry**
        Mathematics

Trigonometry—Tables   516.24
  BT Mathematics—Tables
  NT Logarithms
Trikes
  USE Tricycles
Trinity   231
  BT Christianity—Doctrines
        God—Christianity
  NT Holy Spirit
  RT Jesus Christ—Divinity
Tripoline War, 1801-1805
  USE United States—History—1801-
        1805, Tripolitan War
Tripolitan War, 1801-1805
  USE United States—History—1801-
        1805, Tripolitan War
Trivia
  USE Curiosities and wonders
        Questions and answers
Trolley cars
  USE Street railroads
Tropical diseases
  USE Tropical medicine
Tropical fish   597.17
  BT Fishes
Tropical hygiene
  USE Tropical medicine
Tropical jungles
  USE Jungles
Tropical medicine (May subdiv. geog.)
    614
  UF Diseases, Tropical
        Tropical diseases
        Tropical hygiene
  SA types of tropical diseases, e.g.
        Yellow fever [to be added as
        needed]
  BT Medicine
  NT Yellow fever
Tropical rain forests
  USE Rain forests
Tropics   910.913
  SA subjects with the subdivision
        Tropics, or *Tropical condi-*
        tions [to be added as needed]
  BT Earth
  NT Agriculture—Tropics
Troubadours   849.1; 920
  BT French poetry
        Minstrels
        Poets

Trout fishing (May subdiv. geog.)   799.1
  BT Fishing
Truck crops
  USE Truck farming
Truck farming (May subdiv. geog.)   635
  UF Garden farming
        Market gardening
        Truck crops
        Truck gardening
  BT Agriculture
        Gardening
        Horticulture
  RT Vegetable gardening
Truck freight
  USE Trucking
Truck gardening
  USE Truck farming
Trucking (May subdiv. geog.)   388.3
  UF Truck freight
  BT Freight
        Transportation
Trucks (May subdiv. geog.)   629.224
  UF Motor trucks
  SA types of trucks and names of
        specific makes and models [to
        be added as needed]
  BT Automobiles
        Highway transportation
  RT Materials handling
Trucks—Weight   629.224
Trust companies (May subdiv. geog.)
    332.2
  BT Business
        Corporations
  RT Banks and banking
        Trusts and trustees
Trust funds
  USE Trusts and trustees
Trustees
  USE Trusts and trustees
Trusts and trustees (May subdiv. geog.)
    346.05
  UF Boards of trustees
        Fiduciaries
        Trust funds
        Trustees
  SA types of trustees, e.g. **Library**
        trustees [to be added as
        needed]

Trusts and trustees—*Continued*
BT   Contracts
NT   Library trustees
RT   Estate planning
      Executors and administrators
      Inheritance and succession
      Trust companies
Trusts, Industrial
USE   Industrial trusts
Truth   121
BT   Belief and doubt
      Philosophy
NT   Reality
      Truthfulness and falsehood
RT   Certainty
      Pragmatism
      Skepticism
      Theory of knowledge
Truth in advertising
USE   Deceptive advertising
Truthfulness and falsehood   177
UF   Credibility
      Falsehood
      Lying
      Untruth
BT   Human behavior
      Truth
NT   Lie detectors and detection
RT   Honesty
Tsunamis (May subdiv. geog.)   551.47
UF   Earthquake sea waves
      Seismic sea waves
      Tidal waves
BT   Natural disasters
      Ocean waves
Tuberculosis (May subdiv. geog.)   362.1; 616.9
BT   Lungs—Diseases
Tuberculosis—Mortality (May subdiv. geog.)   362.1
Tuberculosis—Vaccination (May subdiv. geog.)   614.4
BT   Vaccination
Tugboats   623.8
BT   Boats and boating
Tuition
USE   College costs
      Colleges and universities—Finance
      Education—Finance
Tumbling   796.47
BT   Acrobats and acrobatics

Tumors   616.99
NT   Cancer
Tuning   784.192
SA   types of instruments with the subdivision *Tuning* [to be added as needed]
NT   Pianos—Tuning
RT   Musical instruments
Tunnels (May subdiv. geog.)   388; 624.1
BT   Civil engineering
NT   Excavation
RT   Drilling and boring (Earth and rocks)
Turbines   621.406
BT   Engines
      Hydraulic machinery
NT   Gas turbines
      Steam turbines
Turkeys   598.6; 636.5
BT   Birds
      Poultry
Turncoats
USE   Defectors
Turning   621.9
UF   Lathe work
      Wood turning
BT   Carpentry
RT   Lathes
      Woodwork
Turnpikes (Modern)
USE   Express highways
Turtles (May subdiv. geog.)   597.92
UF   Terrapins
      Tortoises
BT   Reptiles
Tutoring
USE   Tutors and tutoring
Tutors
USE   Tutors and tutoring
Tutors and tutoring (May subdiv. geog.)   371.39

Use for general materials on one-on-one instruction. Materials on the adaptation of instruction to meet individual needs within a group are entered under **Individualized instruction.**

UF   Tutoring
      Tutors
BT   Teaching
NT   Independent study
      Individualized instruction
TV
USE   Television

TV personalities
  USE **Television personalities**
Twelfth century
  USE **World history—12th century**
Twelve-step programs   362.29
    UF   Programs, Twelve-step
         Twelve steps (Self-help)
    SA   names of specific twelve-step
         programs [to be added as
         needed]
    BT   **Behavior modification**
    RT   **Alcoholism**
         Compulsive behavior
         Drug abuse
Twelve steps (Self-help)
  USE **Twelve-step programs**
Twentieth century
  USE **World history—20th century**
Twenty-first century
  USE **World history—21st century**
Twins   155.44; 306.875
    BT   **Multiple birth**
         Siblings
Twisters (Tornadoes)
  USE **Tornadoes**
Two-career couples
  USE **Dual-career families**
Two-career families
  USE **Dual-career families**
Two-career family
  USE **Dual-career families**
Two-income families
  USE **Dual-career families**
Two-year colleges
  USE **Junior colleges**
Type and type-founding (May subdiv.
    geog.) **686.2**
    UF   Type and type founding *[Former
         heading]*
    BT   **Founding**
         Printing
    NT   **Linotype**
    RT   **Initials**
         Printing—Specimens
         Typesetting
         Typography
Type and type founding
  USE **Type and type-founding**
Type design
  USE **Typography**

Type-setting
  USE **Typesetting**
Type specimens
  USE **Printing—Specimens**
Typefaces
  USE **Typography**
Typesetting   686.2
    UF   Composition (Printing)
         Type-setting
    BT   **Printing**
    NT   **Linotype**
    RT   **Type and type-founding**
Typewriters   652.3; 681
    BT   **Office equipment and supplies**
Typewriting   652.3
    BT   **Business education**
         Office practice
         Writing
    RT   **Keyboarding (Electronics)**
Typhoid fever   616.9
    UF   Enteric fever
    BT   **Diseases**
         Fever
Typhoons (May subdiv. geog.)   **551.55**
      Use for cyclonic storms originating in the
    region of the China Seas and the Philippines.
    BT   **Cyclones**
         Storms
         Winds
    RT   **Hurricanes**
Typography   686.2
    UF   Type design
         Typefaces
    BT   **Graphic arts**
         Printing
    NT   **Advertising layout and typog-
         raphy**
    RT   **Type and type-founding**
UFOs
  USE **Unidentified flying objects**
UHF radio
  USE **Shortwave radio**
Ultrahigh frequency radio
  USE **Shortwave radio**
Ultrasonic waves   534.5
    UF   Supersonic waves
         Waves, Ultrasonic
    BT   **Sound waves**
         Ultrasonics
**Ultrasonic waves—Industrial applications
    620.2**

718

Ultrasonics   534.5
   UF   Inaudible sound
          Supersonics
   BT   **Sound**
   NT   **Ultrasonic waves**
Ultraviolet rays   535.01; 621.36
   UF   Rays, Ultra-violet
   BT   **Electromagnetic waves**
          Radiation
   RT   **Phototherapy**
          Radiotherapy
Umbrellas and parasols   391.4; 685
   UF   Parasols
   BT   **Clothing and dress**
UN
   USE   **United Nations**
Unbelief
   USE   **Skepticism**
Unborn child
   USE   **Fetus**
Unconventional warfare
   USE   **Guerrilla warfare**
Undenominational churches
   USE   **Community churches**
Underdeveloped areas
   USE   **Developing countries**
Undergraduates
   USE   **College students**
Underground architecture (May subdiv.
     geog.)   **624.1; 690; 720**
   UF   Underground design
   BT   **Architecture**
   NT   **Basements**
          Earth sheltered houses
Underground design
   USE   **Underground architecture**
Underground economy (May subdiv.
     geog.)   **381**
     Use for materials on goods and services that are produced and sold legally but not reported or taxed. Materials on illegal trade aimed at avoiding government regulations, such as fixed prices or rationing, are entered under **Black market.**
   UF   Economy, Underground
          Hidden economy
          Informal sector (Economics)
          Parallel economy
          Second economy
          Shadow economy
          Untaxed income
   BT   **Economics**
          Small business

   NT   **Barter**
          Illegal aliens
   RT   **Black market**
Underground films
   USE   **Experimental films**
Underground houses
   USE   **Earth sheltered houses**
Underground literature
   USE   **Alternative press**
Underground movements
   USE   names of wars with the subdivision *Underground movements,* e.g. **World War, 1939-1945—Underground movements** [to be added as needed]
Underground press
   USE   **Alternative press**
Underground railroad (May subdiv.
     geog.)   **326**
   RT   **Slavery—United States**
Underground railroads
   USE   **Subways**
Underprivileged
   USE   **Socially handicapped**
Underprivileged children
   USE   **Socially handicapped children**
Underprivileged students
   USE   **At risk students**
Undersea engineering
   USE   **Ocean engineering**
Undersea exploration
   USE   **Underwater exploration**
Undersea research stations   551.46
   UF   Manned undersea research stations
          Sea laboratories
          Submarine research stations
          Underwater research stations
   SA   names of special research projects and stations, e.g. **Sealab project** [to be added as needed]
   BT   **Oceanography—Research**
          Underwater exploration
   NT   **Sealab project**
Undersea vehicles
   USE   **Submersibles**
Understanding
   USE   **Intellect**
          Theory of knowledge

Undertakers and undertaking (May
  subdiv. geog.)   **363.7; 393**
  UF   Funeral directors
        Morticians
  BT   **Service industries**
Underwater diving
  USE   **Deep diving**
Underwater drilling (Petroleum)
  USE   **Offshore oil well drilling**
Underwater exploration (May subdiv.
  geog.)   **551.46; 627**
  UF   Submarine exploration
        Undersea exploration
  BT   **Exploration**
        Oceanography
  NT   **Buried treasure**
        Deep diving
        Undersea research stations
Underwater geology
  USE   **Submarine geology**
Underwater medicine
  USE   **Submarine medicine**
Underwater photography   **778.7**
  UF   Deep-sea Photography
        Submarine photography
  BT   **Photography**
Underwater physiology
  USE   **Submarine medicine**
Underwater research stations
  USE   **Undersea research stations**
Underwater swimming
  USE   **Skin diving**
Undocumented aliens
  USE   **Illegal aliens**
Unemployed (May subdiv. geog.)   **331.13**
  UF   Jobless people
        Out-of-work people
  BT   **Labor supply**
        Poor
        Unemployment
  NT   **Food relief**
        Occupational retraining
  RT   **Domestic economic assistance**
        Tramps
Unemployment (May subdiv. geog.)
  331.13
  UF   Joblessness
  BT   **Employment**
        Labor supply
        Social problems

  NT   **Employment agencies**
        Unemployed
Unemployment insurance (May subdiv.
  geog.)   **368.4**
  UF   Insurance, Unemployment
        Labor—Insurance
        Payroll taxes
  BT   **Insurance**
Unfair competition   **338.6**
  UF   Competition, Unfair
        Fair trade
        Unfair trade practices
  BT   **Commercial law**
  NT   **Trade secrets**
  RT   **Restraint of trade**
Unfair trade practices
  USE   **Unfair competition**
Ungraded schools
  USE   **Nongraded schools**
Unidentified flying objects   **001.9**
  UF   Flying saucers
        Saucers, Flying
        UFOs
  BT   **Aeronautics**
        Astronautics
Uniforms (May subdiv. geog.)   **391**
  SA   classes of persons and names of
        individual corporate bodies
        and military services with the
        subdivision *Uniforms*, e.g.
        **United States. Army—Uni-
        forms** [to be added as need-
        ed]
  BT   **Clothing and dress**
        Costume
  NT   **Military uniforms**
Uniforms, Military
  USE   **Military uniforms**
Uniforms, Naval
  USE   **Military uniforms**
Union churches
  USE   **Community churches**
Union of South Africa
  USE   **South Africa**
Union of Soviet Socialist Republics
  USE   **Soviet Union**
Union shop
  USE   **Open and closed shop**
Unions, Labor
  USE   **Labor unions**

Unison speaking
USE **Choral speaking**
Unitarianism 289.1
 BT **Christian sects**
   Congregationalism
United Brethren
 USE **Moravians**
United Nations 341.23
 UF UN
 BT **International arbitration**
   International cooperation
   International organization
United Nations—Armed forces 341.23
 UF Peace keeping forces
 BT **Armed forces**
United Nations—Employees
 USE **United Nations—Officials and**
    employees
United Nations—Finance 341.23
 BT **Finance**
United Nations—Information services
  341.23
 BT **Information services**
United Nations—Officials and employees
  341.23
 UF United Nations—Employees
United States 973
 The subdivisions under **United States**, with
 the exception of the period divisions of his-
 tory, may be used under the name of any
 country or region. The subdivisions under
 Ohio may be used under names of states, and
 those under **Chicago (Ill.)** under cities. Corporate name headings for corporate entities within the United States government, such as gov-
 ernment agencies and departments, which are
 used either as authors or as subjects, have a
 period rather than a dash between the parts,
 e.g. **United States. Army;** and may be added
 as needed.
 UF US
   USA
 SA regions of the United States and
   groups of states, e.g. **New**
   England; Southern States;
   etc. [to be added as needed]
 NT **Atlantic States**
   Gulf States (U.S.)
   Middle West
   Mississippi River Valley
   New England
   Old Northwest
   Old Southwest
   Oregon Trail
   Pacific Northwest

   Southern States
   Southwestern States
   West (U.S.)
 RT **Americans**
United States—Annexations
 USE **United States—Territorial ex-**
    pansion
United States—Antiquities 973
 BT **Antiquities**
United States—Appropriations and ex-
  penditures 352.4
 UF Federal spending policy
   Government spending policy
 BT **Budget—United States**
United States—Archives
 USE **Archives—United States**
United States—Armed forces 355.00973
 SA official names and branches of
   the armed forces, e.g. **United**
   States. Army; United States.
   Navy; etc. [to be added as
   needed]
 BT **Armed forces**
 NT **United States. Army**
   United States. Navy
United States—Armed forces—Gays
 USE **Gays and lesbians in the mili-**
    tary
United States—Armed forces—Military
  life 355.10973
 BT **Military personnel**
United States—Armed Forces—Recruit-
  ing, enlistment, etc. 355.2
 BT **Recruiting and enlistment**
United States. Army 355
 Subdivisions used under this heading may
 be used under armies of other countries as ap-
 propriate.
 BT **Armies**
   Military history
   United States—Armed forces
 NT **United States Military Acade-**
   my
United States. Army—Appointments and
  retirements 355.1
 UF United States. Army—Retire-
   ments
United States. Army—Biography 920
 BT **Biography**
United States. Army—Chaplains 355.3;
  920
 BT **Chaplains**

United States. Army—Crimes and misde-
    meanors
    USE **Military offenses—United
        States**
**United States. Army—Demobilization
    355.2**
United States. Army—Desertions
    USE **Military desertion—United
        States**
United States. Army—Enlistment
    USE **United States. Army—Recruit-
        ing, enlistment, etc.**
**United States. Army—Examinations
    355.1**
    UF Army tests
    BT **Examinations**
**United States. Army—Handbooks, manu-
    als, etc. 355**
    UF Soldiers' handbooks
        United States. Army—Officers'
            handbooks
        United States. Army—Soldiers'
            handbooks
United States. Army—Insignia 355.1
    BT **Insignia**
**United States. Army—Medals, badges,
    decorations, etc. 355.1**
    BT **Insignia
        Medals**
**United States. Army—Military life
    355.1**
    BT **Military personnel
        Soldiers**
United States. Army—Music
    USE **United States. Army—Songs**
United States. Army—Officers 355.3
    BT **Military personnel
        Soldiers**
United States. Army—Officers' handbooks
    USE **United States. Army—Hand-
        books, manuals, etc.**
United States. Army—Ordnance 355.8
    UF United States. Army—Ordnance
        and ordnance stores
    BT **Ordnance**
United States. Army—Ordnance and ord-
    nance stores
    USE **United States. Army—Ord-
        nance**

**United States. Army—Parachute troops
    356**
    UF United States—Parachute troops
    BT **Parachute troops**
**United States. Army—Recruiting, enlist-
    ment, etc. 355.2**
    UF United States. Army—Enlistment
    BT **Recruiting and enlistment**
United States. Army—Retirements
    USE **United States. Army—Appoint-
        ments and retirements**
United States. Army—Soldiers' handbooks
    USE **United States. Army—Hand-
        books, manuals, etc.**
United States. Army—Songs 782.42
    UF United States. Army—Music
        United States. Army—Songs and
            music
    BT **Songs**
United States. Army—Songs and music
    USE **United States. Army—Songs**
United States. Army—Uniforms 355.1
United States—Atlases
    USE **United States—Maps**
**United States—Bibliography 015.73;
    016.973**
United States—Bicentennial celebrations
    USE **American Revolution Bicenten-
        nial, 1776-1976**
United States—Bill of rights
    USE **United States. Constitution.
        1st-10th amendments**
United States—Bio-bibliography 012
United States—Biography 920.073
    BT **Biography**
**United States—Biography—Dictionaries
    920.073**
**United States—Biography—Portraits
    920.073**
    UF United States—History—Portraits
United States—Boundaries 973
    BT **Boundaries**
United States—Budget
    USE **Budget—United States**
United States—Campaign funds
    USE **Campaign funds—United
        States**
United States—Census 317.3; 352.7
    BT **Census**

United States—Centennial celebrations,
etc. 973
   NT   **American Revolution Bicenten-
nial, 1776-1976**
United States—Church and state
   USE   **Church and state—United
States**
United States—Church history   277.3
   UF   Church history—United States
       United States—Religious history
   BT   **Church history**
   RT   **United States—Religion**
United States—Cities and towns
   USE   **Cities and towns—United
States**
United States—Civil defense
   USE   **Civil defense—United States**
United States—Civil service
   USE   **Civil service—United States**
United States—Civilization   973
   BT   **Civilization**
   NT   **Americana**
United States—Civilization—1960-1970
973.92
United States—Civilization—1970-
973.92
United States—Civilization—Foreign in-
fluences   973
United States—Climate   551.6973
   BT   **Climate**
United States—Commerce   380.1;
382.0973
   BT   **Commerce**
United States—Commerce—Japan   382
United States—Commercial policy
   USE   **Commercial policy—United
States**
United States. Congress   328.73
   UF   Congress (U.S.)
   BT   **Legislative bodies**
   NT   **United States. Congress. House
United States. Congress. Senate**
United States. Congress. House   328.73
   UF   House of Representatives (U.S.)
       Representatives, House of (U.S.)
   BT   **United States. Congress**
United States. Congress. Senate   328.73
   UF   Senate (U.S.)
   BT   **United States. Congress**
United States. Constitution   342.73
   Use for the text of the United States Consti-
tution and for materials about that document.

UF   American constitution
       Constitution (U.S.)
United States. Constitution. 1st-10th
amendments   342.73
   Use for the text of the United States Bill of
rights and for materials about that document.
   UF   American Bill of rights
       Bill of rights (U.S.)
       United States—Bill of rights
United States—Constitutional history
   USE   **Constitutional history—United
States**
United States—Constitutional law
   USE   **Constitutional law—United
States**
United States—Constitutions
   USE   **Constitutions—United States**
United States—Courts
   USE   **Courts—United States**
United States—Cultural policy
   USE   **Cultural policy—United States**
United States—Declaration of indepen-
dence   973.3
   UF   Declaration of independence
(U.S.)
United States—Defenses   355.4
   BT   **Military readiness**
   NT   **Strategic Defense Initiative**
United States—Description   917.3
   UF   United States—Description and
travel
       United States—Travel
   BT   **Geography**
United States—Description and travel
   USE   **United States—Description**
United States—Description—Guidebooks
   USE   **United States—Guidebooks**
United States—Description—Views
   USE   **United States—Pictorial works**
United States—Diplomatic and consular
service
   USE   **American diplomatic and con-
sular service**
United States—Directories   917.30025
   Use for lists of names and addresses. Lists
of names without addresses are entered under
United States—Registers.
   BT   **Directories**
   RT   **United States—Registers**
United States—Economic conditions
330.973
   May be subdivided by period using the sub-
divisions under **United States—History,** e.g.

United States—Economic conditions—
Continued
    United States—Economic conditions—1600-
    1775, Colonial period.
    UF   National resources
    BT   **Economic conditions**
United States—Economic policy
    USE   **Economic policy—United States**
United States—Elections
    USE   **Elections—United States**
United States—Emigration and immigration
    USE   **United States—Immigration**
            and emigration
United States—Employees
    USE   **United States—Officials and**
            employees
United States—Environmental policy
    USE   **Environmental policy—United**
            States
United States—Ethnic relations   305.8
United States—Ethnology
    USE   **Ethnology—United States**
United States—Executive departments
    USE   **Executive departments—United**
            States
United States—Executive departments—Re-
organization
    USE   **Administrative agencies—Reor-**
            ganization—United States
United States—Executive power
    USE   **Executive power—United**
            States
United States—Exploration   973
    UF   Exploration—United States
    BT   **America—Exploration**
          Exploration
    NT   **West (U.S.)—Exploration**
United States—Exploring expeditions
    910.973; 973
    Use for materials on exploring expeditions
    sponsored by the United States. Materials on
    early exploration of a particular place are en-
    tered under the name of the place with the
    subdivision *Exploration.*
    UF   American exploring expeditions
    SA   names of expeditions, e.g. **Lewis**
            and Clark Expedition (1804-
            1806) [to be added as need-
            ed]
    BT   **Explorers**
    NT   **Lewis and Clark Expedition**
            (1804-1806)

United States—Fiscal policy
    USE   **Fiscal policy—United States**
United States—Flags
    USE   **Flags—United States**
United States—Foreign economic rela-
    tions   337.73
    UF   Foreign economic relations—
            United States
    BT   **International economic rela-**
            tions
United States—Foreign opinion (May
    subdiv. geog.)   **303.3; 973**
    Use for materials on foreign public opinion
    about the United States. May be further subdi-
    vided by the country holding the opinion, e.g.
    United States—Foreign opinion—France.
    UF   Anti-Americanism
          Antiamericanism
          United States—Foreign public
          opinion
    BT   **Public opinion**
United States—Foreign opinion—France
    303.3; 973
    Use for materials on French public opinion
    about the United States.
United States—Foreign policy
    USE   **United States—Foreign rela-**
            tions
United States—Foreign population
    USE   **Aliens—United States**
            Immigrants—United States
United States—Foreign public opinion
    USE   **United States—Foreign opinion**
United States—Foreign relations (May
    subdiv. geog.)   **327.73**
    When further subdividing geographically,
    provide an additional subject entry with the
    two places in reversed positions, i.e. **United**
    States—Foreign relations—Iran and also
    Iran—Foreign relations—United States.
    UF   United States—Foreign policy
    BT   **Diplomacy**
          International relations
          World politics
    NT   **Monroe Doctrine**
    RT   **Neutrality—United States**
United States—Foreign relations—Iran
    327.73055
    NT   **Iran hostage crisis, 1979-1981**
United States—Foreign relations—Trea-
    ties   327.73; 341.3
    UF   United States—Treaties
    BT   **Treaties**

United States—Gazetteers   917.3003
   BT   **Gazetteers**
United States—Geographic names
   USE   **Geographic names—United
       States**
United States—Geography   917.3
   BT   **Geography**
United States—Government
   USE   **United States—Politics and
       government**
United States—Government buildings
   USE   **Public buildings—United States**
United States—Government employees
   USE   **United States—Officials and
       employees**
United States—Government publications
   USE   **Government publications—
       United States**
United States—Governmental investigations
   USE   **Governmental investigations—
       United States**
United States—Guidebooks   917.304
   UF   United States—Description—
       Guidebooks
United States—Historic buildings
   USE   **Historic buildings—United
       States**
United States—Historical geography
   911
   BT   **Historical geography**
United States—Historical geography—
   Maps   911
   BT   **United States—Maps**
United States—Historiography   973.07
   UF   United States—History—Histori-
       ography
   BT   **Historiography**
United States—History   973
   UF   American history
   NT   **Americana
       Constitutional history—United
       States
       Southern States—History
       West (U.S.)—History**
United States—History—1600-1775, Colo-
   nial period   973.2
    Use for materials on American history from
    the earliest permanent English settlements on
    the Atlantic coast up to the American Revolu-
    tion. Materials on the period of discovery are
    entered under **United States—Exploration.**
   UF   American colonies
       Colonial history (U.S.)

   NT   **Bacon's Rebellion, 1676
       King Philip's War, 1675-1676
       Pilgrims (New England colo-
       nists)
       Pontiac's Conspiracy, 1763-
       1765
       United States—History—1689-
       1697, King William's War
       United States—History—1755-
       1763, French and Indian
       War**
United States—History—1675-1676, King
   Philip's War
   USE   **King Philip's War, 1675-1676**
United States—History—1689-1697, King
   William's War   973.2
   UF   King William's War, 1689-1697
   BT   **Native Americans—Wars
       United States—History—1600-
       1775, Colonial period**
United States—History—1755-1763,
   French and Indian War   973.2
   UF   French and Indian War
   BT   **Native Americans—Wars
       Seven Years' War, 1756-1763
       United States—History—1600-
       1775, Colonial period**
United States—History—1775-1783, Rev-
   olution   973.3
    May be subdivided like **United States—
    History—1861-1865, Civil War.**
   UF   American Revolution
       Revolution, American
       War of the American Revolution
   BT   **Revolutions**
   NT   **American Loyalists
       Canadian Invasion, 1775-1776
       Fourth of July**
United States—History—1775-1783, Revo-
   lution—Centennial celebrations, etc.
   USE   **American Revolution Bicenten-
       nial, 1776-1976**
United States—History—1783-1809
   973.3; 973.4
   UF   Confederation of American colo-
       nies
   NT   **Lewis and Clark Expedition
       (1804-1806)
       Louisiana Purchase**
United States—History—1783-1865
   973.3-973.7
   NT   **War of 1812**

United States—History—19th century
973.5

United States—History—1801-1805, Tripolitan War   973.4

   UF Tripoline War, 1801-1805
       Tripolitan War, 1801-1805

United States—History—1812-1815, War of 1812

   USE **War of 1812**

United States—History—1815-1861
973.5; 973.6

   NT **Black Hawk War, 1832**
       Mexican War, 1846-1848

United States—History—1845-1848, War with Mexico

   USE **Mexican War, 1846-1848**

United States—History—1861-1865, Civil War   973.7

   UF American Civil War
       Civil War—United States

   NT **Confederate States of America**
       Trent Affair, 1861

United States—History—1861-1865, Civil War—Biography   920; 973.7092

   BT **Biography**

United States—History—1861-1865, Civil War—Campaigns   973.7

   SA names of battles, e.g. **Gettysburg (Pa.), Battle of, 1863**
       [to be added as needed]

   NT **Gettysburg (Pa.), Battle of, 1863**

United States—History—1861-1865, Civil War—Causes   973.7

   UF Secession

United States—History—1861-1865, Civil War—Centennial celebrations, etc. 973.7

United States—History—1861-1865, Civil War—Drama   808.82; 812, etc.

Use for collections of plays dealing with the Civil War.

   BT **Historical drama**

United States—History—1861-1865, Civil War—Fiction   808.83; 813, etc.

Use for collections of stories dealing with the Civil War.

United States—History—1861-1865, Civil War—Health aspects   973.7

United States—History—1861-1865, Civil War—Historiography   973.7

   BT **Historiography**

United States—History—1861-1865, Civil War—Medical care   973.7

   BT **Medical care**

United States—History—1861-1865, Civil War—Naval operations   973.7

United States—History—1861-1865, Civil War—Personal narratives   973.7

Use for collective or individual eyewitness reports or autobiographical accounts of the war in general. Accounts limited to a specific topic are entered under that topic.

   BT **Autobiographies**
       Biography

United States—History—1861-1865, Civil War—Pictorial works   973.7022

United States—History—1861-1865, Civil War—Prisoners and prisons 973.7

   BT **Prisoners of war**
       Prisons

United States—History—1861-1865, Civil War—Reconstruction

   USE **Reconstruction (1865-1876)**

United States—History—1861-1865, Civil War—Sources   973.7

United States—History—1865-1898 973.8

   NT **Reconstruction (1865-1876)**
       Spanish-American War, 1898

United States—History—1898-1919 973.9; 973.91

   NT **Spanish-American War, 1898**

United States—History—1898, War of 1898

   USE **Spanish-American War, 1898**

United States—History—20th century 973.9

United States—History—1914-1918, World War

   USE **World War, 1914-1918—United States**

United States—History—1919-1933 973.91

United States—History—1933-1945 973.917

United States—History—1939-1945, World War

   USE **World War, 1939-1945—United States**

United States—History—1945-   973.92

United States—History—1945-1953 973.918

United States—History—1953-1961
973.921

United States—History—1961-1974
973.922-973.924

NT Vietnam War, 1961-1975
Watergate Affair, 1972-1974

United States—History—1974-1989
973.925-973.927

NT Iran-Contra Affair, 1985-1990

United States—History—1989- 973.928

NT Iran-Contra Affair, 1985-1990
Persian Gulf War, 1991

United States—History—21st century
973.9

United States—History—Bibliography
016.973

United States—History—Chronology
973

United States—History—Dictionaries
973.03

BT History—Dictionaries

United States—History—Drama
808.82; 812, etc.

Use for collections of plays dealing with
American history.

BT Historical drama

United States—History—Examinations
973.076

UF United States—History—Examinations, questions, etc.

BT United States—History—Study
and teaching

United States—History—Examinations,
questions, etc.

USE United States—History—Examinations

United States—History—Fiction
808.83; 813, etc.

Use for collections of stories dealing with
American history.

United States—History—Historiography

USE United States—Historiography

United States—History—Library resources 973.07

United States—History—Outlines, syllabi,
etc. 973.02

BT United States—History—Study
and teaching

United States—History—Periodicals
973.05

United States—History—Poetry 808.81;
811, etc.; 811.008, etc.

Use for collections of poetry dealing with
American history.

BT Historical poetry

United States—History—Portraits

USE United States—Biography—
Portraits

United States—History—Societies
973.06

BT History—Societies

United States—History—Sources 973

United States—History—Study and
teaching 973.07

NT United States—History—Examinations

United States—History—Outlines, syllabi, etc.

United States—Immigration and emigration 325; 325.73

UF United States—Emigration and
immigration

SA names of immigrant groups, e.g.
Mexican Americans; Mexi-
cans—United States [to be
added as needed]

BT Americanization
Immigration and emigration

RT Aliens—United States
Immigrants—United States

United States—Industrial policy

USE Industrial policy—United
States

United States—Industries

USE Industries—United States

United States—Insular possessions

USE United States—Territories and
possessions

United States—Intellectual life 973

BT Intellectual life

United States—Intelligence service

USE Intelligence service—United
States

United States—Internal security

USE Internal security—United
States

United States—Land settlement

USE Land settlement—United States

United States—Land surveys

USE United States—Surveys

United States—Languages   306.44
   Use for materials on the several languages spoken in the United States.
United States—Law
   USE   **Law—United States**
United States. Library of Congress
   USE   **Library of Congress**
United States—Local history   973
   BT   **Local history**
United States—Mail
   USE   **Postal service—United States**
United States—Manufactures
   USE   **Manufactures—United States**
United States—Maps   912.73
   UF   United States—Atlases
   BT   **Atlases**
        Maps
   NT   **United States—Historical geography—Maps**
United States Military Academy   355.0071
   UF   USMA
        West Point (Military academy)
   BT   **Colleges and universities**
        United States. Army
United States Military Academy—Registers   355.0071
United States Military Academy—Songs   782.42
   UF   United States Military Academy—Songs and music
   BT   **Students' songs**
United States Military Academy—Songs and music
   USE   **United States Military Academy—Songs**
United States—Military history   355.00973; 973
   BT   **Military history**
United States—Military offenses
   USE   **Military offenses—United States**
United States—Military personnel
   USE   **Military personnel—United States**
United States—Military policy
   USE   **Military policy—United States**
United States—Militia   355.3
   BT   **Armed forces**
   NT   **United States. National Guard**
United States—Monetary policy
   USE   **Monetary policy—United States**

United States—Moral conditions   973
   BT   **Moral conditions**
United States—Municipal government
   USE   **Municipal government—United States**
United States—National characteristics
   USE   **American national characteristics**
United States. National Guard   355.3
   UF   National Guard (U.S.)
   BT   **United States—Militia**
United States—National parks and reserves
   USE   **National parks and reserves—United States**
United States—National security
   USE   **National security—United States**
United States—National songs
   USE   **National songs—United States**
United States—Naval history   359.00973
   BT   **Naval history**
United States. Navy   359
   Subdivisions used under **United States. Army** may be used under this heading and under navies of other countries as appropriate.
   BT   **Navies**
        United States—Armed forces
United States. Navy—Biography   920
   BT   **Biography**
United States. Navy—Enlistment
   USE   **United States. Navy—Recruiting, enlistment, etc.**
United States. Navy—Handbooks, manuals, etc.   359
   UF   Sailors' handbooks
        United States. Navy—Officers' handbooks
        United States. Navy—Sailors' handbooks
United States. Navy—Insignia   359.1
   BT   **Insignia**
United States. Navy—Medals, badges, decorations, etc.   359.1
   BT   **Insignia**
        Medals
United States. Navy—Officers   359.3
   BT   **Military personnel**
United States. Navy—Officers' handbooks
   USE   **United States. Navy—Handbooks, manuals, etc.**

United States. Navy—Recruiting, enlistment, etc.   359.2
  UF   United States. Navy—Enlistment
  BT   **Recruiting and enlistment**
United States. Navy—Sailors' handbooks
  USE   **United States. Navy—Handbooks, manuals, etc.**
United States. Navy—Sealab project
  USE   **Sealab project**
United States—Neutrality
  USE   **Neutrality—United States**
United States—Occupations
  USE   **Occupations—United States**
United States—Officials and employees 351.73
  UF   United States—Employees
        United States—Government employees
  RT   **Civil service—United States**
United States—Parachute troops
  USE   **United States. Army—Parachute troops**
United States—Peoples
  USE   **Ethnology—United States**
United States—Pictorial works 917.30022
  UF   United States—Description—Views
United States—Police
  USE   **Police—United States**
United States—Politicians
  USE   **Politicians—United States**
United States—Politics
  USE   **United States—Politics and government**
United States—Politics and government 973

> May be subdivided by period using the subdivisions under **United States—History,** e.g. **United States—Politics and government—1600-1775, Colonial period.**

  UF   American government
        American politics
        United States—Government
        United States—Politics
  BT   **Political science**
        Politics
        Public administration
  NT   **Third parties (United States politics)**
United States—Popular culture
  USE   **Popular culture—United States**

United States—Population   304.60973
  BT   **Population**
United States—Postal service
  USE   **Postal service—United States**
United States—Presidents
  USE   **Presidents—United States**
United States—Prisons
  USE   **Prisons—United States**
United States—Public buildings
  USE   **Public buildings—United States**
United States—Public debts
  USE   **Public debts—United States**
United States—Public health
  USE   **Public health—United States**
United States—Public lands
  USE   **Public lands—United States**
United States—Public schools
  USE   **Public schools—United States**
United States—Public works
  USE   **Public works—United States**
United States—Race relations 305.800973
  BT   **Race relations**
United States—Registers   917.30025

> Use for lists of names without addresses. Lists of names that include addresses are entered under **United States—Directories.**

  RT   **United States—Directories**
United States—Religion   200.973; 277.3
  BT   **Religion**
  RT   **United States—Church history**
United States—Religious history
  USE   **United States—Church history**
United States—Rural conditions 307.720973
  BT   **Rural sociology**
United States—Secret service
  USE   **Secret service—United States**
United States—Separation of powers
  USE   **Separation of powers—United States**
United States—Social conditions   973
  BT   **Social conditions**
United States—Social life and customs 973
  BT   **Manners and customs**
United States—Social policy
  USE   **Social policy—United States**
United States—Soldiers
  USE   **Soldiers—United States**
United States—State governments
  USE   **State governments**

United States—Statistics   317.3
   BT   **Statistics**
United States. Supreme Court   347.73
   UF   Supreme Court—United States
   BT   **Courts**
United States. Supreme Court—Biography   920
   BT   **Biography**
United States—Surveys   972
     Use for materials containing the results of land surveys of the United States.
   UF   United States—Land surveys
United States—Tariff
   USE   **Tariff—United States**
United States—Taxation
   USE   **Taxation—United States**
United States—Term limits (Public office)
   USE   **Term limits (Public office)—United States**
United States—Territorial expansion   973
   UF   Expansion (United States politics)
       Manifest destiny (United States)
       United States—Annexations
       Westward movement
United States—Territorial waters
   USE   **Territorial waters—United States**
United States—Territories and possessions   325; 973
   UF   United States—Insular possessions
United States—Travel
   USE   **United States—Description**
United States—Treaties
   USE   **United States—Foreign relations—Treaties**
United States—Vice-presidents
   USE   **Vice-presidents—United States**
United States—World War, 1914-1918
   USE   **World War, 1914-1918—United States**
United States—World War, 1939-1945
   USE   **World War, 1939-1945—United States**
United States—World War, 1939-1945—Casualties
   USE   **World War, 1939-1945—Casualties—United States**

United States—World War, 1939-1945—Casualties—Statistics
   USE   **World War, 1939-1945—Casualties—United States—Statistics**
United Steelworkers of America   331.88
   BT   **Labor unions**
Universal bibliographic control
   USE   **Bibliographic control**
Universal history
   USE   **World history**
Universal language   401
   UF   International language
       Language, International
       Language, Universal
       World language
   BT   **Language and languages**
       Linguistics
   NT   **Esperanto**
Universal military training
   USE   **Draft**
Universe   113; 523.1
     Use for materials limited to the physical description of the universe. General and theoretical materials on the science or philosophy of the universe are entered under **Cosmology.**
   UF   Cosmogony
       Cosmography
   NT   **Astronomy**
       Cosmology
       Life on other planets
   RT   **Creation**
Universities
   USE   **Colleges and universities**
Universities and colleges
   USE   **Colleges and universities**
University degrees
   USE   **Academic degrees**
University extension (May subdiv. geog.)   378.1
   BT   **Colleges and universities**
       Distance education
       Higher education
   NT   **Adult education**
       Correspondence schools and courses
University graduates
   USE   **College graduates**
University libraries
   USE   **Academic libraries**
University students
   USE   **College students**

Unmarried couples (May subdiv. geog.)
    306.7
    UF   Cohabitation
           Common law marriage
           Living together
           Trial marriage
           Unmarried people
    BT   **Lifestyles**
           Shared housing
    NT   **Single parents**

Unmarried fathers (May subdiv. geog.)
    306.85; 362.82
    Use for materials on fathers who at the time of childbirth were not married to the child's mother. Materials on fathers rearing children without a partner in the household are entered under **Single-parent families.** Materials on fathers who are teenagers are entered under **Teenage fathers.**
    UF   Parents, Unmarried
           Unmarried parents
           Unwed fathers
    BT   **Fathers**
           Single parents
    RT   **Illegitimacy**

Unmarried men
    USE   **Single men**

Unmarried mothers (May subdiv. geog.)
    306.85; 362.83
    Use for materials on mothers who at the time of giving birth were not married to the child's father. Materials on mothers rearing children without a partner in the household are entered under **Single-parent families.** Materials on mothers who are teenagers are entered under **Teenage mothers.**
    UF   Parents, Unmarried
           Unmarried parents
           Unwed mothers
    BT   **Mothers**
           Single parents
    RT   **Illegitimacy**

Unmarried parents
    USE   **Unmarried fathers**
            Unmarried mothers

Unmarried people
    USE   **Single people**
            Unmarried couples

Unmarried women
    USE   **Single women**

Unsafe products
    USE   **Product safety**

Unskilled labor (May subdiv. geog.)
    331.7
    UF   Unskilled workers
    BT   **Labor**

Unskilled workers
    USE   **Unskilled labor**

Untaxed income
    USE   **Underground economy**

Untruth
    USE   **Truthfulness and falsehood**

Unwed fathers
    USE   **Unmarried fathers**

Unwed mothers
    USE   **Unmarried mothers**

Upholstery   **684.1; 747**
    BT   **Interior design**
    NT   **Draperies**
    RT   **Furniture**

Upper atmosphere   **551.5**
    UF   Atmosphere, Upper
    BT   **Atmosphere**
    NT   **Stratosphere**

Upper class (May subdiv. geog.)   **305.5**
    UF   Fashionable society
           High society
           Upper classes
    BT   **Social classes**
    NT   **Aristocracy**
           Nobility

Upper classes
    USE   **Upper class**

Uranium   **669**
    BT   **Chemical elements**
    RT   **Radioactivity**

Urban areas
    USE   **Cities and towns**
            Metropolitan areas

Urban development
    USE   **Cities and towns—Growth**
            City planning
            Urbanization

Urban education
    USE   **Urban schools**

Urban-federal relations
    USE   **Federal-city relations**

Urban homesteading (May subdiv. geog.)
    363.5
    BT   **Houses—Buying and selling**
           Housing
           Urban renewal

Urban housing
USE **Housing**
Urban life
USE **City and town life**
Urban planning
USE **City planning**
Urban renewal (May subdiv. geog.)
307.3

Use for materials on the economic, sociological, and political aspects of urban redevelopment. Materials on the architectural and engineering aspects are entered under **City planning.**

UF Slum clearance
BT **Metropolitan areas**
Urban sociology
NT **Community development**
Urban homesteading
RT **City planning**
Community organization
Urban renewal—Chicago (Ill.) 307.3
UF Chicago (Ill.)—Urban renewal
Urban renewal—United States 307.3
Urban-rural migration
USE **Internal migration**
Urban schools (May subdiv. geog.) **371**
UF City schools
Inner city schools
Urban education
BT **Schools**
Urban sociology (May subdiv. geog.)
307.76
UF Sociology, Urban
BT **Sociology**
NT **City and town life**
Urban renewal
Urbanization
RT **Cities and towns**
Urban traffic
USE **City traffic**
Urban transportation
USE **Local transit**
Urbanization (May subdiv. geog.)
307.76

Use for materials on the process by which
town and communities acquire urban characteristics.

UF Cities and towns, Movement to
Urban development
BT **Cities and towns**
Rural sociology
Social change
Social conditions

Urban sociology
RT **Cities and towns—Growth**
US
USE **United States**
USA
USE **United States**
Usage
USE names of languages and groups
of languages with the subdivi-
sion *Usage,* e.g. **English lan-
guage—Usage** [to be added
as needed]
Used merchandise
USE **Secondhand trade**
Useful insects
USE **Beneficial insects**
Usenet newsgroups
USE **Electronic discussion groups**
USMA
USE **United States Military Acade-
my**
USSR
USE **Soviet Union**
Utensils, Kitchen
USE **Kitchen utensils**
Utilitarianism 144
BT **Ethics**
NT **Secularism**
RT **Pragmatism**
Utilities (Computer programs) 005.4

Use for materials on software used to perform standard computer system operations
such as sorting data, searching for viruses,
copying data from one file to another, etc.

UF Computer utility programs
Computers—Utility programs
Utility programs (Computer pro-
grams)
BT **Computer software**
Utilities, Public
USE **Public utilities**
Utility programs (Computer programs)
USE **Utilities (Computer programs)**
Utilization of waste
USE **Salvage**
Utopian fiction 813, etc.

May be used for individual works, collections, or materials about imaginative accounts
of ideal societies. Theoretical materials about
ideal societies and accounts of practical attempts to create such societies are entered under **Utopias.**

UF Ideal states
Utopian literature

Utopian fiction—*Continued*
- BT **Fantasy fiction**
  Science fiction
- RT **Dystopias**
  Utopias

Utopian literature
- USE **Utopian fiction**
  Utopias

Utopias   321; 335

Use for theoretical materials on ideal societies and for accounts of practical attempts to create such societies. Imaginative accounts of ideal societies are entered under **Utopian fiction.**
- UF Ideal states
  Utopian literature
- BT **Political science**
  Socialism
- RT **Collective settlements**
  Paradise
  Utopian fiction

Vacation church schools
- USE **Religious summer schools**

Vacation home timesharing
- USE **Timesharing (Real estate)**

Vacation schools
- USE **Summer schools**

Vacation schools, Religious
- USE **Religious summer schools**

Vacations (May subdiv. geog.)   **331.25; 658.3**
- BT **Recreation**
- RT **Holidays**

Vaccination (May subdiv. geog.)   **614.4**

Use for materials on active immunization with a vaccine. Materials on any process, active or passive, that leads to increased immunity are entered under **Immunization.**
- UF Inoculation
- SA types of animals and types of diseases with the subdivision *Vaccination*, e.g. **Cattle—Vaccination; Tuberculosis—Vaccination** [to be added as needed]
- BT **Immunization**
  Preventive medicine
  Public health
- NT **Cattle—Vaccination**
  Poliomyelitis vaccine
  Tuberculosis—Vaccination

Vacuum tubes   537.5; 621.3815
- UF Electron tubes
- BT **Electronic apparatus and appliances**
- NT **Cathode ray tubes**
- RT **X-rays**

Vagabonds
- USE **Tramps**

Vagrants
- USE **Tramps**

Valentine's Day   394.2618
- UF Saint Valentine's Day
  St. Valentine's Day
- BT **Holidays**

Valuation   338.5

Use for general materials on the appraisal of property. Materials on valuation of particular types of property are entered under the type of property, e.g. **Real estate.** Materials on valuation for taxing purposes are entered under **Tax assessment.**
- UF Appraisal
  Capitalization (Finance)
- NT **Tax assessment**

Values   121; 170; 303.3

Use for materials on moral and aesthetic values.
- UF Axiology
  Human values
  Worth
- BT **Aesthetics**
  Ethics
  Psychology
- NT Social values

Vampire films   791.43

May be used for individual works, collections, or materials about vampire films.
- UF Vampires in motion pictures
- BT **Horror films**
  Motion pictures

Vampires (May subdiv. geog.)   **398.21**
- BT **Folklore**

Vampires in motion pictures
- USE **Vampire films**

Van life   796.7
- UF Vanning
  Vans—Social aspects
- BT **Mobile home living**
  Vans

Van pools
- USE **Car pools**

Vandalism 364.16
    UF   Destruction of property
    BT   **Offenses against property**
    NT   **Graffiti**
Vanishing species
    USE **Endangered species**
Vanning
    USE **Van life**
Vans 728.7
    BT   **Travel trailers and campers**
    NT   **Van life**
Vans—Social aspects
    USE **Van life**
Variation (Biology) 576.5
    UF   Mutation (Biology)
    BT   **Biology**
           Genetics
           Heredity
    NT   **Adaptation (Biology)**
           Mendel's law
           Natural selection
    RT   **Evolution**
Variety shows (Radio programs)
       791.44
    May be used for individual works, collections, or materials about variety shows on the radio.
    BT   **Radio programs**
Variety shows (Television programs)
       791.45
    May be used for individual works, collections, or materials about variety shows on television.
    BT   **Television programs**
Varnish and varnishing 667; 698
    BT   **Finishes and finishing**
Varsity sports
    USE **College sports**
Vascular system
    USE **Cardiovascular system**
Vasectomy 613.9
    BT   **Sterilization (Birth control)**
Vases (May subdiv. geog.) 731; 738
    RT   **Glassware**
           Pottery
Vassals
    USE **Feudalism**
Vatican City 945.6
    Use for geographical and descriptive materials on the independent papal state in Rome. Materials on the central administration of the Roman Catholic Church are entered under **Catholic Church.**

Vatican City—Foreign relations
    USE **Catholic Church—Foreign relations**
Vatican Council (2nd : 1962-1965) 262
    BT   **Councils and synods**
Vaudeville (May subdiv. geog.) 792.7
    BT   **Amusements**
           Theater
Vaults (Sepulchral)
    USE **Tombs**
VCRs
    USE **Video recording**
VD
    USE **Sexually transmitted diseases**
Vedas 294.5
    BT   **Hinduism**
           Sacred books
Vegetable gardening (May subdiv. geog.)
       635
    UF   Kitchen gardens
    BT   **Gardening**
           Horticulture
    RT   **Truck farming**
           Vegetables
Vegetable kingdom
    USE **Botany**
           Plants
Vegetable oils
    USE **Essences and essential oils**
           Oils and fats
Vegetables (May subdiv. geog.) 635;
       641.3
    SA   types of vegetables [to be added as needed]
    BT   **Food**
           Plants
    NT   **Celery**
           Cooking—Vegetables
           Potatoes
           Root crops
    RT   **Vegetable gardening**
Vegetables—Canning
    USE **Vegetables—Preservation**
Vegetables—Preservation 641.4
    UF   Vegetables—Canning
    BT   **Canning and preserving**
Vegetarian cookery
    USE **Vegetarian cooking**

Vegetarian cooking (May subdiv. geog.)
    641.5
  UF   Vegetarian cookery
  BT   **Cooking**
  RT   **Cooking—Vegetables**
Vegetarianism (May subdiv. geog.)
    613.2
  BT   **Diet**
Vehicles   **388; 629.2**
  SA   types of vehicles and names of
       specific makes and models of
       vehicles [to be added as
       needed]
  BT   **Transportation**
  NT   **Air-cushion vehicles**
       All terrain vehicles
       Automobiles
       Bicycles
       Carriages and carts
       Military vehicles
       Recreational vehicles
       Sleds
       Submersibles
       Tricycles
Vehicles, Military
  USE **Military vehicles**
Velocity
  USE **Speed**
Veneers and veneering   **674; 698**
  BT   **Cabinetwork**
       Furniture
Venereal diseases
  USE **Sexually transmitted diseases**
Ventilation   **697.9**
  SA   types of buildings with the sub-
       division *Heating and ventila-*
       tion, e.g. **Houses—Heating**
       and ventilation [to be added
       as needed[
  BT   **Air**
       Home economics
       Household sanitation
       Hygiene
       Sanitation
  RT   **Air conditioning**
       Heating
Ventriloquism   **793.8**
  BT   **Amusements**
       Voice
Verbal abuse
  USE **Invective**

Verbal learning   **153.1; 370.15**
    Use for materials on the process of learning
  and understanding written or spoken language,
  ranging from learning to associate two non-
  sense syllables to solving problems presented
  in verbal terms.
  UF   Learning, Verbal
  BT   **Language and languages**
       Psychology of learning
  NT   **Reading comprehension**
Vermin
  USE **Household pests**
       Pests
Vers libre
  USE **Free verse**
Verse epistles
  USE **Epistolary poetry**
Versification   **808.1**
  UF   English language—Versification
       Meter
       Prosody
  BT   **Authorship**
       Poetics
       Rhythm
  NT   **Rhyme**
Vertebrates (May subdiv. geog.)   **596**
  BT   **Animals**
Very high frequency radio
  USE **Shortwave radio**
Vessels (Ships)
  USE **Ships**
Vesta (Roman deity)   **292.2**
  BT   **Gods and goddesses**
Veterans (May subdiv. geog.)   **305.9;**
    920
  UF   War veterans
  BT   **Military art and science**
  RT   **Military hospitals**
       Military pensions
       Military personnel
       Soldiers
Veterans Day   **394.264**
  UF   Armistice Day
  BT   **Holidays**
Veterans—Education (May subdiv. geog.)
    362.86
  UF   Education of veterans
  BT   **Education**
Veterans—Employment   **331.5**
  BT   **Employment**
Veterans—Hospitals
  USE **Military hospitals**

Veterans—Legal status, laws, etc.   343
   BT   Military law
Veterans—United States   305.9;
   353.5390973; 920
Veterinary medicine (May subdiv. geog.)
   636.089
   SA   types of animals with the subdivi-
       sion *Diseases,* e.g. **Horses—**
       Diseases; or with the subdivi-
       sion *Wounds and injuries,* e.g.
       Horses—Wounds and inju-
       ries [to be added as needed]
   BT   Medicine
   RT   Animals—Diseases
VHF radio
   USE   Shortwave radio
Viaducts
   USE   Bridges
Vibration   531; 620.3
   BT   Mechanics
       Sound
   NT   Sound waves
       Waves
Vicarious atonement
   USE   Atonement—Christianity
Vice   170
   UF   Vices
   SA   types of vices [to be added as
       needed]
   BT   Conduct of life
       Ethics
       Human behavior
   RT   Crime
Vice-presidents (May subdiv. geog.)
   352.23; 920
   BT   Presidents
Vice-presidents—United States   352.23;
   920
   UF   United States—Vice-presidents
Vices
   USE   Vice
Victimless crimes
   USE   Crimes without victims
Victims of atomic bombings
   USE   Atomic bomb victims
Victims of crime
   USE   Victims of crimes
Victims of crimes (May subdiv. geog.)
   362.88
   UF   Crime victims
       Victims of crime

   BT   Crime
   NT   Abused women
       Adult child abuse victims
Victorian literature
   USE   English literature—19th
       century
Victoriana   745.1; 747.2
   BT   Antiques
       Collectibles
Video art (May subdiv. geog.)˙   700;
   791.45
   Use for materials on works of art created
   with the use of television and video recording
   technology.
   UF   Electronic art
   BT   Art
       Television
       Video recording
Video cameras, Home
   USE   Camcorders
Video cassette recorders and recording
   USE   Video recording
Video cassettes
   USE   Videotapes
Video disc players
   USE   Videodisc players
Video discs
   USE   Videodiscs
Video display terminals
   USE   Computer monitors
Video games   688.7; 794.8
   UF   Electronic games
       Television games
   SA   types of video games and names
       of individual games [to be
       added as needed]
   BT   Electronic toys
       Games
Video recording   384.55; 621.388;
   778.59
   Use for materials on either the equipment
   or the process by which video or video and
   audio materials are recorded.
   UF   VCRs
       Video cassette recorders and re-
       cording
       Videorecorders
       Videotape recorders and record-
       ing
   NT   Camcorders
       Video art
       Videodiscs
       Videotapes

Video recording—*Continued*
 RT Home video systems
  Television—Equipment and
   supplies
Video recordings
 USE **Videodiscs**
  Videotapes
Video recordings, Closed caption
 USE **Closed caption video record-
   ings**
Video recordings for the hearing impaired
 USE **Closed caption video record-
   ings**
Video tapes
 USE **Videotapes**
Video telephone 384.6; 621.386
 UF Picture telephone
  Videophone
 BT **Data transmission systems**
  Telephone
  Television
Videocassettes
 USE **Videotapes**
Videodisc players 384.55; 621.388
 UF Video disc players
 BT **Television—Equipment and
   supplies**
Videodiscs 384.55; 621.388
 UF Video discs
  Video recordings
 BT **Audiovisual materials**
  Optical storage devices
  Video recording
 NT **Closed caption video record-
   ings**
  Music videos
 RT **Television**
Videophone
 USE **Video telephone**
Videorecorders
 USE **Video recording**
Videos, Music
 USE **Music videos**
Videotape recorders and recording
 USE **Video recording**
Videotapes 384.55; 778.59
 UF Tape recordings, Video
  Video cassettes
  Video recordings
  Video tapes
  Videocassettes

 BT **Audiovisual materials**
  Home video systems
  Video recording
 NT **Closed caption video record-
   ings**
  Music videos
 RT **Television**
Videotex systems 004.69; 384.3
 Use for materials on the transmission of
 computer-based data from a central source to
 a television set or personal computer allowing
 for two-way interactions, such as with home
 shopping or home banking.
 UF Interactive videotex
  Viewdata systems
 BT **Data transmission systems**
  Information systems
  Television broadcasting
 RT **Teletext systems**
Vietnam War, 1961-1975 959.704
 May use appropriate subdivisions under
 World War, 1939-1945.
 UF Vietnamese Conflict, 1961-1975
  Vietnamese War, 1961-1975
 BT **United States—History—1961-
   1974**
Vietnamese Conflict, 1961-1975
 USE **Vietnam War, 1961-1975**
Vietnamese refugees (May subdiv. geog.)
  325
 BT **Refugees**
Vietnamese War, 1961-1975
 USE **Vietnam War, 1961-1975**
Viewdata systems
 USE **Videotex systems**
Views 910.22
 Use for collections of pictures of many
 places.
 UF Scenery
 SA countries, states, cities, etc., and
  named entities, such as indi-
  vidual parks, structures, etc.,
  with the subdivision *Pictorial
  works,* e.g. **Chicago (Ill.)—
  Pictorial works; United
  States—Pictorial works; Yo-
  semite National Park
  (Calif.)—Pictorial works;** etc.
  [to be added as needed]
 BT **Pictures**

Vigilance committees (May subdiv. geog.)
    364.1; 364.4
  UF Vigilantes
  BT **Crime**
        Criminal law
  RT **Lynching**

Vigilantes
  USE **Vigilance committees**

Vikings (May subdiv. geog.) **948**
    Use for materials on early Scandinavian people. Materials on the people since the tenth century are entered under **Scandinavians.**
  UF Norsemen
        Northmen
  BT **Scandinavians**
  RT **Normans**

Villages (May subdiv. geog.) **307.76**
  BT **Cities and towns**

Vines
  USE **Climbing plants**

Vineyards (May subdiv. geog.) **634.8**
  UF Viticulture
  BT **Farms**
  RT **Grapes**
        Wine and wine making

Vintage automobiles
  USE **Antique and classic cars**

Vintage cars
  USE **Antique and classic cars**

Vintage motorcycles
  USE **Antique and vintage motorcycles**

Violence (May subdiv. geog.) **303.6**
  SA types of violence [to be added as needed]
  BT **Aggressiveness (Psychology)**
        Social psychology
  NT **Domestic violence**
        Hate crimes
        School violence

Violence in mass media **302.23**
  BT **Mass media**

Violence in popular culture **306.4**
  BT **Popular culture**

Violence in schools
  USE **School violence**

Violence in television
  USE **Violence on television**

Violence on television **302.23; 791.45**
  UF Violence in television *[Former heading]*

  BT **Television**
        Television programs

Violin
  USE **Violins**

Violin music **787.2**
  BT **Music**

Violin players
  USE **Violinists**

Violinists (May subdiv. geog.) **787.2092; 920**
  UF Violin players
  BT **Instrumentalists**

Violins **787.2**
  UF Fiddle
        Violin
  BT **Stringed instruments**

Violoncellists (May subdiv. geog.)
    787.4092
  UF Cellists
        Cello players
        Violoncello players
  BT **Instrumentalists**

Violoncello
  USE **Violoncellos**

Violoncello players
  USE **Violoncellists**

Violoncellos **787.4**
  UF Cello
        Violoncello
  BT **Stringed instruments**

Vipers
  USE **Snakes**

Virgin Mary
  USE **Mary, Blessed Virgin, Saint**

Virtual reality **006**
  UF Artificial reality
  BT **Computer simulation**
  RT **Computer graphics**

Virtue **170**
  UF Virtues
  SA types of virtues [to be added as needed]
  BT **Conduct of life**
        Ethics
        Human behavior
  NT **Charity**
        Chastity
        Courage
        Courtesy
        Faith
        Forgiveness

Virtue—*Continued*
>> Hope
>> Justice
>> Loyalty
>> Obedience
>> Patience
>> Punctuality
>> Temperance

Virtues
> USE **Virtue**

Viruses 579.2
> UF Microbes
> BT **Microorganisms**
> NT **Chickenpox**

Viruses, Computer
> USE **Computer viruses**

Visceral learning
> USE **Biofeedback training**

Viscosity 532; 620.1
> BT **Hydrodynamics**
>> **Mechanics**

Vision 152.14; 573.8; 612.8; 617.7
> UF Sight
> BT **Optics**
>> **Senses and sensation**
> NT **Color sense**
>> **Optical illusions**
>> **Vision disorders**
> RT **Eye**

Vision disorders 362.4; 617.7
> UF Defective vision
>> Impaired vision
>> Visual handicaps
>> Visual impairments
> BT **Vision**
> NT **Blind**
>> **Color blindness**

Visions 133.8; 248.2; 291.4
> BT **Parapsychology**
>> **Religion**
>> **Spiritual gifts**
> NT **Dreams**
>> **Hallucinations and illusions**
> RT **Apparitions**

Visitation rights (Domestic relations)
> (May subdiv. geog.) **306.8**
> BT **Domestic relations**
> RT **Child custody**

Visitors' exchange programs
> USE **Exchange of persons programs**

Visual handicaps
> USE **Vision disorders**

Visual impairments
> USE **Vision disorders**

Visual instruction
> USE **Audiovisual education**

Visual literacy 153; 707
> Use for materials on the ability to interpret and evaluate visual objects and symbols, such as television, motion pictures, art works, etc.
> UF Literacy, Visual
> BT **Arts**
>> **Literacy**
>> **Semiotics**

Vital records
> USE **Registers of births, etc.**

Vital statistics 304.6; 310
> UF Burial statistics
>> Death rate
>> Marriage statistics
>> Mortuary statistics
>> Records of births, etc.
> SA names of countries, cities, etc., and names of ethnic groups with the subdivision *Vital statistics,* for compilations of birth, marriage, and death statistics; and names of wars with the subdivision *Casualties—Statistics,* e.g. **World War, 1939-1945—Casualties—Statistics; World War, 1939-1945—Casualties—United States—Statistics;** etc. [to be added as needed]
> BT **Statistics**
> NT **Birth rate**
>> **Census**
>> **Life expectancy**
>> **Mortality**
>> **Population**
> RT **Registers of births, etc.**

Vitamins 572; 613.2; 615
> BT **Food**
>> **Nutrition**

Viticulture
> USE **Grapes**
>> **Vineyards**
>> **Wine and wine making**

Vivisection 179
> BT **Animal experimentation**
>> **Surgery**

Vocabulary   418; 428, etc.

    UF   English language—Vocabulary

              Languages—Vocabulary

              Words

    BT   **Language and languages**

    NT   **New words**

Vocal culture

    USE **Voice culture**

Vocal ensembles

    USE **Ensembles (Music)**

Vocal music (May subdiv. geog.)   782

    BT   **Music**

    NT   **Cantatas**

            Carols

            Choral music

            Folk songs

            Hymns

            Opera

            Operetta

            Oratorio

            Songs

    RT   **Singing**

Vocation, Choice of

    USE **Vocational guidance**

Vocational education (May subdiv. geog.)
        370.11; 373.246; 374

Use for materials on teaching a skill during the educational process. Materials on teaching people a skill after formal education are entered under **Occupational training.** Materials discussing on-the-job training are entered under **Employees—Training.** Materials on retraining are entered under **Occupational retraining.**

    UF   Career education

    SA   types of industries, professions,

              etc., with the subdivision

              Study and teaching, e.g. **Agri-**

              culture—Study and teaching

              [to be added as needed]

    BT   **Education**

    NT   **Agriculture—Study and teach-**

              ing

            Employees—Training

            Industrial arts education

            Occupational retraining

            Occupational training

            Vocational guidance

    RT   **Professional education**

            Technical education

Vocational guidance (May subdiv. geog.)
        331.7; 371.4

Use for materials on the activities and programs designed to help people plan, choose, and succeed in their careers. Materials on the assistance given to students by schools, colleges, or universities in the selection of a program of studies suited to their abilities, interests, future plans, and general circumstances are entered under **Educational counseling.**

    UF   Career counseling

              Career development

              Career guidance

              Careers

              Choice of profession, occupation,

                vocation, etc.

              Employment guidance

              Guidance, Vocational

              Job placement guidance

              Occupational guidance

              Vocation, Choice of

    SA   vocational guidance for particu-

              lar classes of persons, e.g.

              Vocational guidance for the

              handicapped; and fields of

              knowledge, corporate bodies,

              military services, professions,

              and industries and trades with

              the subdivision *Vocational*

              guidance [to be added as

              needed]

    BT   **Counseling**

            Vocational education

    NT   **Career changes**

            Job hunting

            Law—Vocational guidance

            Television broadcasting—Voca-

            tional guidance

            Vocational guidance for the

            handicapped

    RT   **Educational counseling**

            Employment

            Occupations

            Professions

Vocational guidance for the handicapped
    (May subdiv. geog.)   371.4

    BT   **Handicapped**

            Vocational guidance

Vocational training

    USE **Occupational training**

Vocations

    USE **Occupations**

          Professions

Vodun

    USE **Voodooism**

Voice   783
      UF   Speaking
      BT   **Language and languages**
            Throat
      NT   **Automatic speech recognition**
            Ventriloquism
      RT   **Phonetics**
            Public speaking
            Singing
            Speech
Voice culture   808.5
      UF   Vocal culture
            Voice training
      BT   **Public speaking**
            Singing
            Speech
Voice training
      USE   **Voice culture**
Volatile oils
      USE   **Essences and essential oils**
Volcanoes (May subdiv. geog.)   551.21
      SA   names of volcanoes [to be added
            as needed]
      BT   **Geology**
            Mountains
            Physical geography
Volleyball   796.325
      BT   **Ball games**
Volume (Cubic content)   389; 530.8
      UF   Cubic measurement
      BT   **Geometry**
            Measurement
            Weights and measures
Volume feeding
      USE   **Food service**
Voluntarism
      USE   **Volunteer work**
Voluntary associations
      USE   **Associations**
Voluntary military service (May subdiv.
      geog.)   355.2
      UF   Military service, Voluntary
            Volunteer military service
      BT   **Armed forces**
            Recruiting and enlistment
Voluntary organizations
      USE   **Associations**
Volunteer military service
      USE   **Voluntary military service**

Volunteer work (May subdiv. geog.)
      361.3
      UF   Voluntarism
            Volunteering
            Volunteerism
            Volunteers
      SA   types of volunteer work and
            names of volunteer programs,
            e.g. **Meals on wheels pro-**
            grams [to be added as need-
            ed]
      BT   **Public welfare**
      NT   **Caregivers**
            Foster grandparents
      RT   **Charities**
            National service
Volunteering
      USE   **Volunteer work**
Volunteerism
      USE   **Volunteer work**
Volunteers
      USE   **Volunteer work**
Volunteers in church work
      USE   **Lay ministry**
Voodoo
      USE   **Voodooism**
Voodooism (May subdiv. geog.)   299
      UF   Vodun
            Voodoo
            Voudou
            Voudouism
      BT   **Religions**
Voter registration (May subdiv. geog.)
      324.6
      UF   Registration of voters
      BT   **Elections**
            Suffrage
Voting
      USE   **Elections**
            Suffrage
Voudou
      USE   **Voodooism**
Voudouism
      USE   **Voodooism**
Voyager project
      USE   **Project Voyager**
Voyagers
      USE   **Explorers**
            Travelers
Voyages and travels   910.4
      Use for materials about non-fiction travel
      writing, for collections of travel writings, and

Voyages and travels—*Continued*
for accounts of voyages and travels not limited to a single place. Materials about the
theme of travel in literature are entered under
Travel in literature. Materials on the art and
enjoyment of travel and advice for travelers
are entered under **Travel.**

UF Journeys
    Travel books
    Travels
SA names of cities (except extinct
    cities), states, countries, conti-
    nents, etc., with the subdivi-
    sion *Description;* e.g. **United
    States—Description;** names
    of extinct cities or towns,
    without further subdivision,
    for accounts of those places
    by travelers in ancient times,
    e.g. **Delphi (Extinct city);**
    names of individual ships;
    names of regions, e.g. **Arctic
    regions;** ethnic groups, classes
    of persons, and names of in-
    dividuals with the subidivision
    Travel, e.g. **Handicapped—
    Travel;** names of countries
    sponsoring exploring expedi-
    tions with the subdivision *Ex-
    ploring expeditions;* e.g. **Unit-
    ed States—Exploring expedi-
    tions;** and names of places
    that were unsettled or sparsely
    settled and largely unknown
    to the world at large at the
    time of exploration, with the
    subdivision *Exploration,* e.g.
    America—Exploration [to be
    added as needed]
BT **Geography**
NT **Aeronautics—Flights**
    Northeast Passage
    Ocean travel
    **Overland journeys to the Pa-
    cific**
    Papal visits
    Pilgrims and pilgrimages
    Scientific expeditions
    Seafaring life
    Shipwrecks
    Travelers
    Voyages around the world
    Whaling

    Yachts and yachting
RT **Adventure and adventurers**
    Exploration
    Explorers
    Travel
    Travel in literature
Voyages and travels in literature
USE **Travel in literature**
Voyages around the world   910.4
UF Circumnavigation
    Travel books
BT **Travel**
    Voyages and travels
Voyages to the moon
USE **Imaginary voyages**
     Space flight to the moon
Wage-price controls
USE **Wage-price policy**
Wage-price policy (May subdiv. geog.)
     331.2
UF Government policy
    Price controls
    Price-wage policy
    Wage-price controls
BT **Inflation (Finance)**
    Prices
    Salaries, wages, etc.
Wages
USE **Salaries, wages, etc.**
Wagons
USE **Carriages and carts**
Waiters and waitresses (May subdiv.
     geog.) **642**
UF Waitresses
BT **Food service**
Waitresses
USE **Waiters and waitresses**
Wakefulness
USE **Insomnia**
Walking (May subdiv. geog.) **796.51**
BT **Locomotion**
RT **Hiking**
Walking in space
USE **Extravehicular activity (Space
     flight)**
Wall decoration
USE **Mural painting and decoration**
Wall painting
USE **Mural painting and decoration**
Wall Street (New York, N.Y.)   332.6
     Use for materials on the activities of Wall
     Street as a financial district. Historical and de-

Wall Street (New York, N.Y.)—*Continued*
scriptive materials on Wall Street as a street
are entered under **Streets—New York (N.Y.)**.

- BT **Stock exchanges**
- RT **Streets—New York (N.Y.)**

Wallpaper 676; 747

- BT **Interior design**
- RT **Paperhanging**

Walls 690; 721

- BT **Buildings**
  Civil engineering

Walt Disney World (Fla.) 791.06

- UF Disney World (Fla.)
- BT **Amusement parks**

War 172; 303.6; 355.02

- UF Fighting
  Wars
- SA names of wars, battles, etc., e.g.
  United States—History—1861-1865, Civil War; Gettysburg (Pa.), Battle of, 1863; and war and other subjects, e.g. **War and civilization** [to be added as needed]
- NT **Arms control**
  Battles
  Chemical warfare
  Children and war
  Guerrilla warfare
  Intervention (International law)
  Military aeronautics
  Military occupation
  Military personnel
  Nuclear warfare
  Prisoners of war
  Psychological warfare
  Space warfare
  Submarine warfare
  War and civilization
  War and emergency powers
  War crimes
  War—Religious aspects
  World War III
- RT **Armed forces**
  International law
  Military art and science
  Military law
  Naval art and science
  Peace

War and children

- USE **Children and war**

War and civilization 172; 303.4

- UF Civilization and war
- BT **Civilization**
  War

War and emergency powers (May subdiv. geog.) **342**

- UF Emergency powers
  War powers
- BT **Constitutional law**
  Executive power
  Legislative bodies
  War

War and industry

- USE **War—Economic aspects**

War and religion

- USE **War—Religious aspects**

War, Articles of

- USE **Military law**

War crime trials (May subdiv. geog.) **341.6**

- BT **Trials**

War crimes (May subdiv. geog.) **341.6; 364.1**

- UF Military atrocities
- SA names of wars with the subdivision *Atrocities,* e.g. **World War, 1939-1945—Atrocities;** and names of specific atrocities [to be added as needed]
- BT **Crimes against humanity**
  International law
  War

War—Economic aspects (May subdiv. geog.) **303.6**

Use for materials discussing the economic causes of war and the effect of war on industry and trade.

- UF Economics of war
  Industry and war
  War and industry
- SA names of wars with the subdivision *Economic aspects* [to be added as needed]
- NT **Industrial mobilization**
  World War, 1939-1945—Economic aspects
- RT **International competition**

War films 791.43

May be used for individual works, collections, or materials about war films in general, not limited to a particular war.

- UF Anti-war films
  Apocalyptic fantasies

War films—*Continued*

    End-of-the-world fantasies

  SA   names of wars with the subdivision *Motion pictures and the war;* e.g. **World War, 1939-1945—Motion pictures and the war** [to be added as needed]

  BT   **Historical drama**

        Motion pictures

  NT   **World War, 1939-1945—Motion pictures and the war**

War of 1812   **940.2; 973.5**

  UF   United States—History—1812-1815, War of 1812 *[Former heading]*

  BT   **Great Britain—History—1714-1837**

        United States—History—1783-1865

War of nerves

  USE **Psychological warfare**

War of the American Revolution

  USE **United States—History—1775-1783, Revolution**

War pensions

  USE **Military pensions**

War poetry   **808.81; 811, etc.; 811.008, etc.**

    May be used for individual works or collections of war poetry, or for materials about war poetry in general, not confined to a particular war.

  UF   Anti-war poetry

  SA   names of wars with the subdivision *Poetry* [to be added as needed]

  BT   **Poetry**

  NT   **World War, 1939-1945—Poetry**

  RT   **War songs**

War powers

  USE **War and emergency powers**

War protest movements

  USE **Peace movements**

War radio programs   **791.44**

    May be used for individual works, collections, or materials about war radio programs.

  BT   **Radio programs**

War—Religious aspects   **261.8; 291.1**

    May be subdivided by religion or sect.

  UF   Religion and war

        War and religion

  SA   names of wars with the subdivision *Religious aspects,* e.g. **World War, 1939-1945—Religious aspects** [to be added as needed]

  BT   **Religion**

        War

  NT   **Conscientious objectors**

        Pacifism

War ships

  USE **Warships**

War songs   **782.42**

  UF   Battle songs

        Soldiers' songs

  BT   **National songs**

        Songs

  NT   **World War, 1939-1945—Songs**

  RT   **War poetry**

War stories   **808.83; 813, etc.**

    May be used for individual works, collections, or materials about war stories.

  UF   Anti-war stories

        Apocalyptic fantasies

        End-of-the-world fantasies

  SA   names of wars and battles with the subdivision *Fiction,* e.g. **World War, 1939-1945—Fiction** [to be added as needed]

  BT   **Fiction**

        Historical fiction

War television programs   **791.45**

    May be used for individual works, collections, or materials about war television programs.

  BT   **Television programs**

War use

  USE subjects with the subdivision *War use,* e.g. **Dogs—War use** [to be added as needed]

War use of animals

  USE **Animals—War use**

War use of dogs

  USE **Dogs—War use**

War veterans

  USE **Veterans**

War work

  USE names of wars with the subdivision *War work,* e.g. **World War, 1939-1945—War work** [to be added as needed]

Warfare, Submarine

  USE **Submarine warfare**

Warm air heating
USE **Hot air heating**
Wars
USE **Military history**
Naval history
War
and ethnic groups with the subdivision *Wars,* e.g. **Native Americans—Wars** [to be added as needed]
Wars of the Roses, 1455-1485
USE **Great Britain—History—1455-1485, Wars of the Roses**
Warships (May subdiv. geog.) **359.8; 623.8**
UF Battle ships
Battleships
War ships
SA names of countries with the subhead *Navy,* e.g. **United States. Navy;** and names of individual warships [to be added as needed]
BT **Naval architecture**
Naval art and science
Sea power
Ships
NT **Aircraft carriers**
Submarines
RT **Navies**
Washing
USE **Laundry**
Wasps 595.79
BT **Insects**
Waste as fuel
USE **Waste products as fuel**
Waste disposal
USE **Refuse and refuse disposal**
and types of waste disposal, e.g. **Radioactive waste disposal; Sewage disposal;** etc.; and types of industries, plants, and facilities with the subdivision *Waste disposal,* e.g. **Chemical industry—Waste disposal** [to be added as needed]
Waste (Economics) 339.4
BT **Economics**

Waste products 628.4
UF By-products
Junk
Trade waste
BT **Industrial chemistry**
Manufactures
NT **Industrial waste**
RT **Recycling**
Refuse and refuse disposal
Waste products as fuel 333.793; 662
UF Energy conversion from waste
Organic waste as fuel
Waste as fuel
BT **Salvage**
RT **Biomass energy**
Waste reclamation
USE **Salvage**
Wastes, Hazardous
USE **Hazardous wastes**
Wastes, Medical
USE **Medical wastes**
Watches
USE **Clocks and watches**
Water 551.4; 553.7
UF Hydrology
BT **Earth sciences**
Hydraulics
NT **Drinking water**
Floods
Frost
Geysers
Hydrotherapy
Ice
Lakes
Ocean
Ponds
Precipitation (Meteorology)
Rivers
Sea water
Steam
RT **Hydraulic engineering**
Water rights
Water—Analysis 546; 628.1
BT **Analytical chemistry**
RT **Water pollution**
Water animals
USE **Aquatic animals**
Water ballet
USE **Synchronized swimming**

Water birds (May subdiv. geog.)
598.176
UF   Aquatic birds
Water fowl
Wild fowl
SA   types of water birds [to be added as needed]
BT   **Birds**
NT   **Geese**
Terns
Water conduits
USE   **Aqueducts**
Water conservation (May subdiv. geog.)
333.91
UF   Conservation of water
BT   **Conservation of natural resources**
RT   **Water supply**
Water cure
USE   **Hydrotherapy**
Water farming
USE   **Hydroponics**
Water flow
USE   **Hydraulics**
Water fluoridation   628.1
UF   Fluoridation of water
Water—Fluoridation
BT   **Water supply**
Water—Fluoridation
USE   **Water fluoridation**
Water fowl
USE   **Water birds**
Water—Oil pollution
USE   **Oil pollution of water**
Water plants
USE   **Freshwater plants**
Marine plants
Water pollution (May subdiv. geog.)
363.739; 628.1
UF   Detergent pollution of rivers, lakes, etc.
Pollution of water
River pollution
SA   types of pollution, e.g. **Oil pollution of water** [to be added as needed]
BT   **Environmental health**
Pollution
Public health
NT   **Acid rain**
Marine pollution

Oil pollution of water
RT   **Industrial waste**
Sewage disposal
Water—Analysis
Water power   333.9; 621.2
UF   Hydroelectric power
Water-power
BT   **Energy resources**
Hydraulics
Power (Mechanics)
Renewable energy resources
Rivers
Water resources development
NT   **Hydraulic engineering**
Hydraulic machinery
Hydroelectric power plants
Water-power
USE   **Water power**
Water—Purification
USE   **Water purification**
Water purification   628.1
UF   Purification of water
Water—Purification
BT   **Sanitation**
Water supply
NT   **Sea water conversion**
Water resources development (May subdiv. geog.)   **333.91**
BT   **Energy development**
Natural resources
NT   **Irrigation**
Water power
RT   **Water supply**
Water rights (May subdiv. geog.)
333.91; 346.04
BT   **Law**
RT   **Water**
Water safety   363.14; 797.028
UF   Aquatic sports—Safety measures
Drowning prevention
Water sports—Safety measures
BT   **Accidents—Prevention**
Water skiing   797.3
BT   **Water sports**
Water sports (May subdiv. geog.)   **797**
UF   Aquatic sports
SA   types of water sports [to be added as needed]
BT   **Sports**
NT   **Boats and boating**
Canoes and canoeing

Water sports—*Continued*

　　　　Deep diving
　　　　Diving
　　　　Rowing
　　　　Sailing
　　　　Surfing
　　　　Swimming
　　　　Water skiing
　　　　Yachts and yachting
Water sports—Safety measures
　　USE　**Water safety**
Water supply (May subdiv. geog.)
　　　　363.6; 628.1
　　UF　Waterworks
　　BT　**Natural resources**
　　　　Public utilities
　　NT　**Aqueducts**
　　　　Dams
　　　　Drinking water
　　　　Forest influences
　　　　Irrigation
　　　　Water fluoridation
　　　　Water purification
　　RT　**Water conservation**
　　　　Water resources development
　　　　Wells
Water supply engineering (May subdiv.
　　geog.)　**628.1**
　　BT　**Civil engineering**
　　　　Engineering
　　NT　**Drilling and boring (Earth and
　　　　rocks)**
　　RT　**Hydraulic engineering**
Water transportation
　　USE　**Shipping**
Watercolor painting (May subdiv. geog.)
　　　　751.42
　　UF　Watercolors
　　BT　**Painting**
Watercolors
　　USE　**Watercolor painting**
Watergate Affair, 1972-1974　973.924
　　BT　**United States—History—1961-
　　　　1974**
Watering places
　　USE　**Health resorts**
Waterways (May subdiv. geog.)　**386**
　　　　Use for materials on rivers, lakes, and ca-
　　　nals used for transportation.
　　BT　**Transportation**
　　NT　**Canals**
　　　　Lakes

　　　　Rivers
　　RT　**Inland navigation**
Waterworks
　　USE　**Water supply**
Wave mechanics　530.12; 531
　　BT　**Mechanics**
　　　　Quantum theory
　　　　Waves
Waves　531
　　BT　**Hydrodynamics**
　　　　Vibration
　　NT　**Electric waves**
　　　　Ocean waves
　　　　Radiation
　　　　Sound waves
　　　　Wave mechanics
Waves, Electromagnetic
　　USE　**Electromagnetic waves**
Waves, Ultrasonic
　　USE　**Ultrasonic waves**
Wealth (May subdiv. geog.)　**330.1**
　　UF　Distribution of wealth
　　　　Fortunes
　　　　Riches
　　BT　**Economics**
　　　　Finance
　　NT　**Cost and standard of living**
　　　　Economic conditions
　　　　Income
　　　　Inheritance and succession
　　　　Profit
　　　　Saving and investment
　　　　Success
　　RT　**Capital**
　　　　Money
　　　　Property
Wealthy people
　　USE　**Rich**
Weaponry
　　USE　**Weapons**
Weapons (May subdiv. geog.)　**355.8;
　　　　623.4**
　　UF　Arms and armor
　　　　Weaponry
　　BT　**Tools**
　　NT　**Bow and arrow**
　　　　Firearms
　　　　Military weapons
　　RT　**Armor**
　　　　Military art and science

Weapons, Atomic
USE **Nuclear weapons**
Weapons industry
USE **Defense industry**
Firearms industry
Weapons, Nuclear
USE **Nuclear weapons**
Weapons, Space
USE **Space weapons**
Weariness
USE **Fatigue**
Weather 551.6

Use for materials on the state of the atmosphere at a given time and place with respect to heat or cold, wetness or dryness, calm or storm. Scientific materials on the atmosphere, especially weather factors, are entered under **Meteorology.** Materials on climate as it relates to humans and to plant and animal life, including the effects of changes of climate, are entered under **Climate.**

SA names of countries, cities, etc.,
with the subdivision *Climate,*
e.g. **United States—Climate**
[to be added as needed]
NT **Humidity**
Precipitation (Meteorology)
Storms
Weather control
Weather forecasting
Winds
RT **Climate**
Meteorology
Weather control 551.68
UF Artificial weather control
Cloud seeding
Rain making
Weather modification
BT **Meteorology**
Weather
Weather—Folklore 398.26
UF Weather lore
BT **Folklore**
Meteorology
Weather forecasting
Weather forecasting (May subdiv. geog.)
551.63
UF Precipitation forecasting
BT **Forecasting**
Meteorology
Weather
NT **Weather—Folklore**
Weather lore
USE **Weather—Folklore**

Weather modification
USE **Weather control**
Weather satellites
USE **Meteorological satellites**
Weather stations
USE **Meteorological observatories**
Weaving (May subdiv. geog.) **677;**
746.1; 746.41
UF Hand weaving
SA types of woven articles, e.g.
Rugs and carpets [to be added as needed]
BT **Handicraft**
Textile industry
NT **Basket making**
Beadwork
Lace and lace making
Looms
RT **Fabrics**
Web pages
USE **Web sites**
Web publishing
USE **Electronic publishing**
Web servers 004.67
UF World Wide Web servers *[Former heading]*
BT **World Wide Web**
Web sites 005.7
UF Web pages
Websites
World Wide Web pages
World Wide Web sites
SA names of individual web sites;
and topics, geographic names,
categories of persons, ethnic
groups, etc., with the subdivision *Internet resources* [to be added as needed]
BT **Internet resources**
Web sites—Design 005.7
BT **Design**
Websites
USE **Web sites**
Weddings (May subdiv. geog.) **392.5;**
395.2
BT **Marriage**
NT **Marriage customs and rites**
Weed killers
USE **Herbicides**

Weeds (May subdiv. geog.)　**632**
　　BT　**Agricultural pests**
　　　　Economic botany
　　　　Gardening
　　　　Plants
Week　**529**
　　BT　**Calendars**
　　　　Chronology
　　RT　**Days**
Weight　**530.8**
　　UF　Weight (Physics)
　　SA　types of objects and substances
　　　　with the subdivision *Weight*,
　　　　e.g. **Trucks—Weight** [to be
　　　　added as needed]
　　BT　**Physics**
　　NT　**Body weight**
　　RT　**Weights and measures**
Weight control
　　USE　**Weight loss**
Weight lifting　**796.41; 613.7**
　　UF　Strength training
　　　　Weight training
　　　　Weightlifting
　　BT　**Athletics**
　　　　Exercise
　　RT　**Bodybuilding**
Weight loss　**613.2**
　　UF　Dieting
　　　　Diets, Reducing
　　　　Reducing
　　　　Weight control
　　BT　**Body weight**
　　RT　**Diet**
　　　　Exercise
Weight (Physics)
　　USE　**Weight**
Weight training
　　USE　**Weight lifting**
Weightlessness　**531**
　　UF　Free fall
　　　　Gravity free state
　　　　Subgravity state
　　　　Zero gravity
　　BT　**Environmental influence on
　　　　humans**
　　　　Space medicine
Weightlifting
　　USE　**Weight lifting**

Weights and measures (May subdiv.
　　geog.)　**389; 530.8**
　　UF　Measures
　　　　Metrology
　　SA　types of objects and substances
　　　　with the subdivision *Weight*,
　　　　e.g. **Trucks—Weight** [to be
　　　　added as needed]
　　BT　**Physics**
　　NT　**Electric measurements**
　　　　Measuring instruments
　　　　Volume (Cubic content)
　　RT　**Measurement**
　　　　Metric system
　　　　Weight
Welding　**671.5**
　　UF　Oxyacetylene welding
　　BT　**Blacksmithing**
　　　　Forging
　　　　Ironwork
　　　　Metalwork
　　NT　**Electric welding**
　　RT　**Soldering**
Welding, Electric
　　USE　**Electric welding**
Welfare agencies
　　USE　**Charities**
Welfare, Public
　　USE　**Public welfare**
Welfare reform
　　USE　**Public welfare**
Welfare state (May subdiv. geog.)
　　　　330.12; 361.6
　　BT　**Economic policy**
　　　　Public welfare
　　　　Social policy
　　　　State, The
Welfare work
　　USE　**Charities**
　　　　Social work
Welfare work in industry
　　USE　**Industrial welfare**
Well boring
　　USE　**Drilling and boring (Earth and
　　　　rocks)**
Well drilling, Oil
　　USE　**Oil well drilling**
Wells (May subdiv. geog.)　**551.49; 628.1**
　　BT　**Hydraulic engineering**
　　RT　**Drilling and boring (Earth and
　　　　rocks)**

Wells—*Continued*
  Water supply
West Africa 966
  Use for materials dealing collectively with the southern half of the western bulge of the African continent, bounded on the north by the Sahara and on the south and west by the Atlantic Ocean. The term usually includes Benin, Burkina Faso, Cameroon, Gambia, Ghana, Guinea, Guinea-Bissau, Ivory Coast, Liberia, Nigeria, Senegal, Sierra Leone, and Togo, and sometimes Mali, Mauritania, and Niger as well.
  UF Africa, West
  BT **Africa**
  NT **French-speaking West Africa**
West Germany
  USE **Germany (West)**
West Indian literature (French) 840
  Use for collections and for materials on West Indian literature written originally in French.
  BT **Literature**
West Point (Military academy)
  USE **United States Military Academy**
West (U.S.) 978
  Use for the region west of the Mississippi River.
  UF Western States
  SA names of individual states in this region [to be added as needed]
  BT **United States**
  NT **Pacific Northwest**
    Pacific States
West (U.S.)—Exploration 978
  BT **United States—Exploration**
  RT **Overland journeys to the Pacific**
West (U.S.)—History 978
  UF Westward movement
  BT **United States—History**
Western civilization 306.09; 909
  Use for materials on the culture and society stemming from the Greco-Roman traditions of the occident rather than those of Islam, India, or the Far East.
  UF Civilization, Western
    Occidental civilization
  BT **Civilization**
    East and West
Western comic books, strips, etc. 741.5
  May be used for individual works, collections, or materials about Western comics.
  BT **Comic books, strips, etc.**

Western Europe
  USE **Europe**
Western films 791.43
  May be used for individual works, collections, or materials about Western films.
  UF Westerns
  SA types of Western films, e.g.
    Lone Ranger films [to be added as needed]
  BT **Adventure films**
    Historical drama
    Motion pictures
  NT **Lone Ranger films**
Western States
  USE **West (U.S.)**
Western stories 808.83; 813, etc.
  May be used for individual works, collections, or materials about post-19th-century fiction set in the 19th-century American West.
  UF Westerns
  BT **Adventure fiction**
    Fiction
    Historical fiction
Westerns
  USE **Western films**
    Western stories
    Westerns (Radio programs)
    Westerns (Television programs)
Westerns (Radio programs) 791.44
  May be used for individual works, collections, or materials about Westerns on the radio.
  UF Westerns
  BT **Radio programs**
Westerns (Television programs) 791.45
  May be used for individual works, collections, or materials about Western on television.
  UF Westerns
  BT **Television programs**
Westminster Abbey 726.5
  BT **Abbeys**
    Church buildings
Westward movement
  USE **Land settlement—United States**
    United States—Territorial expansion
    West (U.S.)—History
Wetlands (May subdiv. geog.) **551.41**
  SA types of wetlands, e.g. **Marshes** [to be added as needed]
  BT **Landforms**
  NT **Bogs**
    Marshes

Wetlands—*Continued*
    Swamps
Whales (May subdiv. geog.) **599.5**
    BT **Mammals**
         Marine mammals
Whaling (May subdiv. geog.) **639.2**
    BT **Commercial fishing**
         Hunting
         Voyages and travels
Wheat (May subdiv. geog.) **633.1**
    BT **Grain**
Wheels **621.8; 629.2**
    UF Car wheels
    BT **Simple machines**
    NT **Gearing**
         Tires
Which-way stories
    USE **Plot-your-own stories**
Whistle blowing (May subdiv. geog.)
    174; 342; 353.4
    Use for materials on the practice of calling public attention to corruption, mismanagement, or waste in government, business, the military, etc.
    UF Blowing the whistle
         Whistleblowing
    BT **Political corruption**
         Public interest
Whistleblowing
    USE **Whistle blowing**
White collar crimes (May subdiv. geog.)
    364.16
    UF Occupational crimes
    BT **Crime**
    NT **Fraud**
White supremacist movements
    USE **White supremacy movements**
White supremacy movements (May subdiv. geog.) **320.5**
    UF Skinheads
         White supremacist movements
    BT **Race relations**
         Racism
         Social movements
Whittling
    USE **Wood carving**
Whodunits
    USE **Mystery and detective plays**
         Mystery fiction
         Mystery films
         Mystery radio programs
         Mystery television programs

Whole language **372.62**
    Use for materials on the integration of listening, speaking, writing, and reading skills in meaningful situations in which children participate actively.
    UF Integrated language arts (Holistic)
         Language arts (Holistic)
         Language experience approach in education
    BT **Education—Experimental methods**
         Language arts
Wholistic medicine
    USE **Holistic medicine**
Wica
    USE **Wicca**
Wicca **133.4**
    UF Wica
    BT **Folklore**
         Paganism
    RT **Goddess religion**
         Witchcraft
Wickedness
    USE **Good and evil**
Widowers (May subdiv. geog.) **305.38; 306.88**
    BT **Men**
Widows (May subdiv. geog.) **305.48; 306.88**
    BT **Women**
Wife abuse (May subdiv. geog.) **362.82**
    UF Abuse of wives
         Abused wives
         Battering of wives
         Wife battering
         Wife beating
    BT **Domestic violence**
    RT **Abused women**
Wife battering
    USE **Wife abuse**
Wife beating
    USE **Wife abuse**
Wigs **391.5**
    BT **Clothing and dress**
         Costume
         Hair
Wigwams
    USE **Tepees**
Wild animal dwellings
    USE **Animals—Habitations**

Wild animals
USE **Animals**
Wildlife
Wild cats (May subdiv. geog.) **599.75;**
636.8
Use for materials on non-domesticated species of cats or domestic cats living in a wild state. Materials on domestic cats are entered under **Cats.**
UF Felidae
Feral cats
Wildcats
SA types of wild cats [to be added as needed]
BT **Mammals**
RT **Cats**
Wild children (May subdiv. geog.)
155.45
Use for materials on children who have been raised by animals or have lived their formative years in the wild without contact with human society.
UF Feral children
Wolf children
BT **Exceptional children**
Wild flowers (May subdiv. geog.)
582.13
UF Wildflowers
BT **Flowers**
Wild flowers—Conservation
USE **Plant conservation**
Wild fowl
USE **Game and game birds**
Water birds
Wildcats
USE **Wild cats**
Wilderness areas (May subdiv. geog.)
333.78
UF Scenery
BT **Forest reserves**
RT **Conservation of natural resources**
National parks and reserves
Wilderness survival (May subdiv. geog.)
613.6; 796.5
UF Bush survival
Outdoor survival
BT **Camping**
Outdoor life
Survival skills
RT **Survival after airplane accidents, shipwrecks, etc.**

Wildflowers
USE **Wild flowers**
Wildlife (May subdiv. geog.) **333.95;**
639
Use for materials on wild animals in their natural environment, especially mammals, birds, and fishes that are hunted for sport or food.
UF Feral animals
Wild animals
SA types of wildlife, e.g. **Desert animals** [to be added as needed]
BT **Animals**
NT **Game and game birds**
RT **Wildlife conservation**
Wildlife and pesticides
USE **Pesticides and wildlife**
Wildlife conservation (May subdiv. geog.)
639.9
UF Conservation of wildlife
Preservation of wildlife
Protection of wildlife
BT **Conservation of natural resources**
Economic zoology
Endangered species
Environmental protection
Nature conservation
NT **Birdbanding**
Birds—Protection
Game protection
Game reserves
Pesticides and wildlife
Wildlife refuges
RT **Rare animals**
Wildlife
Wildlife refuges (May subdiv. geog.)
639.9
UF Wildlife sanctuaries
SA names of specific refuges [to be added as needed]
BT **Wildlife conservation**
Wildlife sanctuaries
USE **Wildlife refuges**
Will
USE **Brainwashing**
Free will and determinism
Will power
USE **Self-control**
Willpower
USE **Self-control**

Wills   346.05
   UF   Bequests
          Legacies
   BT   Genealogy
          Registers of births, etc.
   NT   Living wills
   RT   Executors and administrators
          Inheritance and succession
Wind
   USE   Winds
Wind instruments   788
   SA   types of wind instruments [to be
          added as needed]
   BT   Musical instruments
   NT   Brass instruments
          Flutes
          Woodwind instruments
Wind power (May subdiv. geog.)   333.9;
   621.4
   BT   Energy resources
          Power (Mechanics)
          Renewable energy resources
   RT   Windmills
Windbreaks   634.9
   UF   Shelterbelts
   BT   Tree planting
Windmills (May subdiv. geog.)   621.4
   RT   Wind power
Window dressing
   USE   Show windows
Window gardening   635.9
   UF   Windowbox gardening
          Windowsill gardening
   BT   Gardening
          Indoor gardening
   NT   House plants
   RT   Container gardening
          Flower gardening
Windowbox gardening
   USE   Window gardening
Windows   721
   BT   Architecture—Details
          Buildings
   NT   Show windows
Windows, Stained glass
   USE   Glass painting and staining
Windowsill gardening
   USE   Window gardening
Winds   551.51
   UF   Gales
          Wind

   BT   Meteorology
          Navigation
          Physical geography
          Weather
   NT   Cyclones
          Hurricanes
          Tornadoes
          Typhoons
   RT   Storms
Windsurfing (May subdiv. geog.)   797.3
   UF   Board sailing
          Sailboarding
   BT   Sailing
Wine and wine making (May subdiv.
   geog.)   641.2; 663
   UF   Viticulture
   BT   Alcoholic beverages
   RT   Grapes
          Vineyards
Winter resorts (May subdiv. geog.)
   796.9
   BT   Resorts
Winter sports (May subdiv. geog.)
   796.9
   UF   Ice sports
   SA   types of winter sports [to be
          added as needed]
   BT   Sports
   NT   Hockey
          Ice skating
          Skiing
          Sledding
Wire services
   USE   News agencies
Wireless
   USE   Radio
Wiretapping   363.25
   BT   Criminal investigation
          Right of privacy
   RT   Eavesdropping
Wiring, Electric
   USE   Electric wiring
Wishes   153.8
   BT   Motivation (Psychology)
Wit and humor   808.87; 817, etc.
     May be used for individual works, collec-
   tions, or materials about wit and humor.
   UF   Facetiae
          Humor
   SA   wit and humor of particular
          countries, e.g. American wit
          and humor; and subjects

Wit and humor—*Continued*

    with the subdivision *Humor*,
    e.g. **Music—Humor** [to be
    added as needed]

  BT   **Literature**

  NT   **American wit and humor**
        Black humor (Literature)
        Chapbooks
        Comedies
        Comedy
        Comic books, strips, etc.
        English wit and humor
        Epigrams
        Humorists
        Humorous fiction
        Humorous poetry
        Jokes
        Mock-heroic literature
        Music—Humor
        Nonsense verses
        Parody
        Practical jokes
        Puns
        Satire
        Tall tales
        World War, 1939-1945—Humor

  RT   **Anecdotes**

Witchcraft (May subdiv. geog.)   **133.4**

  UF   Black art (Magic)
        Black magic (Witchcraft)
        Sorcery

  BT   **Folklore**
        Occultism

  NT   **Witches**

  RT   **Magic**
        Wicca

Witches (May subdiv. geog.)   **133.4**

  UF   Covens

  BT   **Witchcraft**

Witnesses (May subdiv. geog.)   **345; 347**

  UF   Cross-examination

  BT   **Litigation**
        Trials

Wives (May subdiv. geog.)   **306.872**

  UF   Married women
        Spouses

  BT   **Family**
        Marriage
        Married people
        Women

Wives of presidents—United States
  USE   **Presidents' spouses—United States**

Wives, Runaway
  USE   **Runaway adults**

Wolf children
  USE   **Wild children**

Woman
  USE   **Women**

Woman-man relationship
  USE   **Man-woman relationship**

Women (May subdiv. geog.)   **305.4**

  UF   Woman

  SA   women of particular racial or
        ethnic groups, e.g. **Mexican
        American women;** women in
        various occupations and pro-
        fessions, e.g. **Women artists;
        Policewomen; Women in the
        motion picture industry;**
        etc.; and names of wars and
        military services with the sub-
        division *Women,* e.g. **World
        War, 1939-1945—Women** [to
        be added as needed]

  NT   **Abused women**
        African American women
        Black women
        Businesswomen
        Daughters
        Lesbians
        Mexican American women
        Mothers
        Native American women
        Nuns
        Policewomen
        Single women
        Sisters
        Widows
        Wives
        Women air pilots
        Women artists
        Women authors
        Women clergy
        Women in the motion picture industry
        Women judges
        Women physicians
        World War, 1939-1945—Women
        Young women

Women—*Continued*
    RT   **Femininity**
Women actors
    USE **Actresses**
Women air pilots (May subdiv. geog.)
    629.13092; 920
    BT   **Air pilots**
          Women
Women artists (May subdiv. geog.)
    709.2; 920
    Use for materials on the attainments of several women in the area of art.
    BT   **Artists**
          Women
Women authors   809; 920
    Use for collections and for materials on the attainments of several women authors not limited to a single national literature or literary form.
    SA   literary forms and national literatures with the subdivision *Women authors,* e.g. **American literature—Women authors** [to be added as needed]
    BT   **Authors**
          Women
Women—Biography   920
    BT   **Biography**
Women—Biography—Dictionaries
    920.72
Women, Black
    USE **Black women**
Women—Civil rights
    USE **Women's rights**
Women clergy (May subdiv. geog.)
    200.92; 270.092
    BT   **Clergy**
          Women
    RT   **Ordination of women**
Women—Clothing
    USE **Women's clothing**
Women—Clubs
    USE **Women—Societies**
Women—Diseases   616.0082; 618.1
    UF   Diseases of women
          Gynecology
    BT   **Diseases**
    NT   **Breast cancer**
    RT   **Women—Health and hygiene**
Women—Dress
    USE **Women's clothing**

Women—Education (May subdiv. geog.)
    371.822
    UF   Education of women
    BT   **Education**
    RT   **Coeducation**
Women—Emancipation
    USE **Women's rights**
Women—Employment (May subdiv. geog.) **331.4**
    UF   Girls—Employment
          Working women
    SA   women in various occupations and professions, e.g. **Women artists; Policewomen; Women in the motion picture industry;** etc. [to be added as needed]
    BT   **Employment**
    NT   **Equal pay for equal work**
          Self-employed women
Women—Enfranchisement
    USE **Women—Suffrage**
Women—Equal rights
    USE **Women's rights**
Women—Health and hygiene   613
    UF   Gynecology
          Women—Hygiene
    BT   **Health**
          Hygiene
    NT   **Women—Mental health**
    RT   **Women—Diseases**
Women—History   305.409
    Use for comprehensive materials on the history of women, their socio-economic, political, and legal position, their participation in historical events, and their contributions to society. Materials dealing specifically with women's social condition and status, including historical discussions of the same, are entered under **Women—Social conditions.**
    BT   **Feminism**
          History
Women—Hygiene
    USE **Women—Health and hygiene**
Women—Identity   305.4
    UF   Female identity
          Feminine identity
    BT   **Identity (Psychology)**
Women in art   704.9
    Use for materials on women depicted in works of art. Materials on the attainments of several women in the area of art are entered under **Women artists.**
    BT   **Art—Themes**

Women in business

USE **Businesswomen**

Women in literature   809

Use for materials on the theme of women in works of literature. Collections and materials on several women authors not limited to a single national literature or literary form are entered under **Women authors.**

BT   **Literature—Themes**

Women in motion pictures   791.43

Use for materials discussing the portrayal of women in motion pictures. Materials discussing all aspects of women's involvement in motion pictures are entered under **Women in the motion picture industry.**

BT   **Motion pictures**

Women in the Bible   220.8

UF   Bible—Women

BT   **Bible—Biography**

Women in the motion picture industry 791.43

Use for materials discussing all aspects of women's involvement in motion pictures. Materials discussing the portrayal of women in motion pictures are entered under **Women in motion pictures.**

BT   **Motion picture industry**

Women

Women judges (May subdiv. geog.) **347; 920**

BT   **Judges**

Women

Women-men relationship

USE   **Man-woman relationship**

Women—Mental health   362.2

BT   **Mental health**

Women—Health and hygiene

RT   **Women—Psychology**

Women—Ordination

USE   **Ordination of women**

Women physicians (May subdiv. geog.) **610.69; 920**

BT   **Physicians**

Women

Women police officers

USE   **Policewomen**

Women—Political activity (May subdiv. geog.)   **324**

BT   **Political participation**

NT   **Women politicians**

Women politicians (May subdiv. geog.) **324.2092; 920**

BT   **Politicians**

Women—Political activity

Women—Psychology   155.3

UF   Feminine psychology

BT   **Psychology**

RT   **Women—Mental health**

Women—Relations with men

USE   **Man-woman relationship**

Women—Religious life   248.4; 291.4

BT   **Religious life**

RT   **Goddess religion**

Women—Self-defense

USE   **Self-defense for women**

Women, Self-employed

USE   **Self-employed women**

Women—Social conditions (May subdiv. geog.)   **305.42**

Use for materials dealing specifically with women's social condition and status, including historical discussions of the same. Comprehensive materials on the history of women are entered under **Women—History.**

BT   **Social conditions**

NT   **Prostitution**

Women's movement

Women—Societies (May subdiv. geog.) **367**

UF   Women—Clubs

Women's clubs

Women's organizations

BT   **Clubs**

Societies

Women—Suffrage (May subdiv. geog.) **324.6**

UF   Women—Enfranchisement

Women's suffrage

BT   **Suffrage**

Women's rights

RT   **Suffragists**

Women—United States   305.40973

Women's clothing (May subdiv. geog.) **646**

UF   Women—Clothing

Women—Dress

BT   **Clothing and dress**

Women's clubs

USE   **Women—Societies**

Women's liberation movement

USE   **Women's movement**

Women's movement (May subdiv. geog.) **305.42; 323.3**

Use for materials on activities aimed at obtaining equal rights and opportunities for women. Materials on the theory of the political and social equality of the sexes and wom-

Women's movement—*Continued*
en's perspectives on various subjects are entered under **Feminism.**

  UF Women's liberation movement

  BT **Women—Social conditions**

        Women's rights

  RT **Feminism**

Women's organizations

  USE **Women—Societies**

Women's rights (May subdiv. geog.)
    323.3; 342

  UF Emancipation of women

        Rights of women

        Women—Civil rights

        Women—Emancipation

        Women—Equal rights

  BT **Civil rights**

        Sex discrimination

  NT **Women—Suffrage**

        Women's movement

  RT **Feminism**

        Pro-choice movement

        Pro-life movement

Women's self-defense

  USE **Self-defense for women**

Women's suffrage

  USE **Women—Suffrage**

Wonders

  USE **Curiosities and wonders**

Wood (May subdiv. geog.)   **620.1; 674**

  UF Timber

        Woods

  SA types of wood, e.g. **Oak** [to be added as needed]

  BT **Building materials**

        Forest products

        Fuel

        Trees

  NT **Lumber and lumbering**

        Oak

        Plywood

        Woodwork

  RT **Forests and forestry**

Wood block printing

  USE **Wood engraving**

        Woodcuts

Wood carving   **731.4; 736**

  UF Carving, Wood

        Whittling

  BT **Carving (Decorative arts)**

        Decoration and ornament

        Woodwork

Wood engraving   **761**

  UF Block printing

        Wood block printing

  BT **Engraving**

Wood finishing   **698**

  BT **Finishes and finishing**

  NT **Furniture finishing**

Wood—Preservation   **674**

  UF Preservation of wood

Wood turning

  USE **Turning**

Woodcuts   **761**

  UF Block printing

        Wood block printing

  BT **Prints**

Woods

  USE **Forests and forestry**

        Lumber and lumbering

        Wood

Woodwind instruments   **877.2**

  BT **Wind instruments**

Woodwork (May subdiv. geog.)   **684**

  BT **Architecture—Details**

        Decorative arts

        Wood

  NT **Furniture making**

        Wood carving

  RT **Cabinetwork**

        Carpentry

        Turning

Woodworking machinery   **621.9; 684**

  SA types of woodworking machines [to be added as needed]

  BT **Machinery**

  NT **Lathes**

Wool (May subdiv. geog.)   **677**

  BT **Animal products**

        Fabrics

        Fibers

Word books

  USE **Picture dictionaries**

Word building

  USE **Word skills**

Word games   **793.734**

  SA types of word games, e.g. **Crossword puzzles** [to be added as needed]

  BT **Games**

        Literary recreations

  NT **Crossword puzzles**

Word histories
  USE **Language and languages—Ety-**
       mology
Word processing   652.5
  BT   **Office management**
       Office practice
  RT   **Desktop publishing**
       Word processing software
Word processing software   005.3
  BT   **Computer software**
  RT   **Word processing**
Word processor keyboarding
  USE **Keyboarding (Electronics)**
Word skills   372.4; 418
    Use for educational materials on conso-
    nants, blends, vowels, prefixes and suffixes,
    digraphs, syllables, root words, rhyming, and
    alphabet, etc.
  UF   Word building
       Words
  BT   **Reading**
  RT   **English language—Spelling**
Wordless stories
  USE **Stories without words**
Words
  USE **Vocabulary**
       Word skills
Words, New
  USE **New words**
Work   158.7; 306.3
    Use for materials on the physical or mental
    exertion of individuals to produce or accom-
    plish something. Materials on the collective
    human activities involved in the production
    and distribution of goods and services in an
    economy, as well as materials on the group of
    workers who render these services for wages,
    are entered under **Labor.**
  NT   **Job satisfaction**
       Work and family
       Work environment
       Work ethic
  RT   **Labor**
       Occupations
Work addiction
  USE **Workaholism**
Work and family (May subdiv. geog.)
       306.3; 306.87; 646.7
    Use for materials on the conflict or balance
    in people's lives between the demands of
    work and family.
  UF   Family and work
  BT   **Family**
       Work
  RT   **Dual-career families**

Work at home
  USE **Home-based business**
       Telecommuting
Work environment (May subdiv. geog.)
       331.25; 620.8
  UF   Places of work
       Work places
       Working environment
       Workplace environment
       Worksite environment
  BT   **Environment**
       Work
  NT   **Machinery in the workplace**
       Teams in the workplace
Work ethic (May subdiv. geog.)   **174**
  UF   Protestant work ethic
  BT   **Ethics**
       Work
Work groups
  USE **Teams in the workplace**
Work performance standards
  USE **Performance standards**
Work places
  USE **Work environment**
Work satisfaction
  USE **Job satisfaction**
Work standards
  USE **Production standards**
Work stoppages
  USE **Strikes**
Work stress
  USE **Job stress**
Work teams
  USE **Teams in the workplace**
Workaholic syndrome
  USE **Workaholism**
Workaholism   155.2; 616.85
  UF   Addiction to work
       Compulsive working
       Work addiction
       Workaholic syndrome
  BT   **Compulsive behavior**
Workers
  USE **Employees**
       Labor
       Working class
Workers' compensation (May subdiv.
       geog.)   **368.4**
  UF   Compensation
       Employers' liability

Workers' compensation—*Continued*
      Insurance, Workers' compensation
      Workmen's compensation
  BT **Accident insurance**
      Health insurance
      Social security
Workers' participation in management
  USE **Participative management**
Working animals 636.088
  SA animals in specific working situations [to be added as needed]
  BT **Animals**
      Domestic animals
      Economic zoology
  NT **Animals in police work**
      Animals—War use
      Guide dogs
Working at home
  USE **Home-based business**
      Telecommuting
Working children
  USE **Child labor**
Working class (May subdiv. geog.)
     305.5
    Use for materials on the social class composed of persons who work for wages, usually in manual labor.
  UF Blue collar workers
      Factory workers
      Industrial workers
      Labor and laboring classes
      Laborers
      Laboring class
      Laboring classes
      Manual workers
      Workers
      Working classes
  BT **Social classes**
  NT **Proletariat**
  RT **Labor**
Working classes
  USE **Working class**
Working couples
  USE **Dual-career families**
Working day
  USE **Hours of labor**
Working environment
  USE **Work environment**
Working hours
  USE **Hours of labor**

Working parents' children
  USE **Children of working parents**
Working robots
  USE **Industrial robots**
Working women
  USE **Women—Employment**
Workmen's compensation
  USE **Workers' compensation**
Workplace environment
  USE **Work environment**
Workshop councils
  USE **Participative management**
Workshops, Teachers'
  USE **Teachers' workshops**
Worksite environment
  USE **Work environment**
World
  USE **Earth**
World economics
  USE **Commercial geography**
      Commercial policy
      Economic conditions
      International competition
World government
  USE **International organization**
World history 909
  UF Universal history
  BT **History**
  NT **Ancient history**
      Geography
      Middle Ages
      Modern history
World history—12th century 909
  UF Twelfth century
  SA names of regions, countries, cities, etc., with the subdivision *History—12th century* [to be added as needed]
  BT **Middle Ages**
World history—13th century 909
  UF Thirteenth century *[Former heading]*
  SA names of regions, countries, cities, etc., with the subdivision *History—13th century* [to be added as needed]
  BT **Middle Ages**
World history—14th century 909
  UF Fourteenth century *[Former heading]*

World history—14th century—*Continued*

    SA   names of regions, countries, cities, etc., with the subdivision *History—14th century* [to be added as needed]

    BT   **Middle Ages**

World history—15th century   909

    UF   Fifteenth century *[Former heading]*

    SA   names of regions, countries, cities, etc., with the subdivision *History—15th century* [to be added as needed]

    BT   **Middle Ages**

World history—16th century   909

    UF   History, Modern—16th century

        Sixteenth century *[Former heading]*

    SA   names of regions, countries, cities, etc., with the subdivision *History—16th century* [to be added as needed]

World history—17th century   909

    UF   History, Modern—17th century

        Seventeenth century *[Former heading]*

    SA   names of regions, countries, cities, etc., with the subdivision *History—17th century* [to be added as needed]

World history—18th century   909.7

    UF   Eighteenth century *[Former heading]*

        History, Modern—18th century

    SA   names of regions, countries, cities, etc., with the subdivision *History—18th century* [to be added as needed]

World history—19th century   909.81

    UF   History, Modern—19th century

        Modern history—1800-1899 (19th century) *[Former heading]*

        Nineteenth century *[Former heading]*

    SA   names of regions, countries, cities, etc., with the subdivision *History—19th century* [to be added as needed]

World history—20th century   909.82

    UF   History, Modern—20th century

        Modern history—1900-1999 (20th century) *[Former heading]*

        Twentieth century *[Former heading]*

    SA   names of regions, countries, cities, etc., with the subdivision *History—20th century* [to be added as needed]

    NT   **World War, 1914-1918**

        World War, 1939-1945

World history—1945-   909.82

    UF   History, Modern—1945-

        Modern history—1945- *[Former heading]*

World history—21st century   909.83

    UF   History, Modern—21st century

        Twenty-first century *[Former heading]*

    SA   names of regions, countries, cities, etc., with the subdivision *History—21st century* [to be added as needed]

World language

    USE **Universal language**

World order

    USE **International relations**

World organization

    USE **International organization**

World politics   909

    Use for historical accounts of international political affairs. Materials on the theory of international relations are entered under **International relations.**

    UF   International politics

    SA   names of countries with the subdivisions *Foreign relations* and *Politics and government* [to be added as needed]

    BT   **Political science**

    NT   **United States—Foreign relations**

        World War, 1914-1918

        World War, 1939-1945

        World War III

    RT   **Geopolitics**

        International organization

        International relations

World politics—1945-   909.82

World politics—1945-1965   909.82

World politics—1945-1991   909.82
 NT   Cold war
World politics—1965-   909.82
World politics—1991-   909.82
World records   030
 UF   Human records
        Records of achievement
        Records, World
        World's records
 BT   **Curiosities and wonders**
 RT   **Sports records**
World War I
 USE   **World War, 1914-1918**
World War II
 USE   **World War, 1939-1945**
World War, 1914-1918 (May subdiv.
        geog.)   **940.3; 940.4**
    May be subdivided like **World War, 1939-
1945.**
 UF   First World War
        World War I
 BT   **Europe—History—1871-1918**
        World history—20th century
        World politics
**World War, 1914-1918—Chemical war-
        fare   940.4**
 UF   World War, 1914-1918—Gas
        warfare
 BT   **Chemical warfare**
**World War, 1914-1918—Economic as-
        pects   940.3**
 RT   **Reconstruction (1914-1939)**
World War, 1914-1918—Gas warfare
 USE   **World War, 1914-1918—Chem-
        ical warfare**
World War, 1914-1918—Peace   940.3
 BT   **Peace**
 NT   **League of Nations**
World War, 1914-1918—Reconstruction
 USE   **Reconstruction (1914-1939)**
**World War, 1914-1918—Territorial ques-
        tions** (May subdiv. geog.)   **940.3**
 BT   **Boundaries**
**World War, 1914-1918—United States
        940.3; 940.4; 973.91**
 UF   United States—History—1914-
        1918, World War
        United States—World War,
        1914-1918

World War, 1939-1945 (May subdiv.
        geog.)   **940.53; 940.54**
    Subdivisions used under this heading may
be used under other wars.
 UF   Second World War
        World War II
 SA   names of battles, campaigns,
        sieges, etc., e.g. **Ardennes,
        Battle of the, 1944-1945;
        Pearl Harbor (Oahu, Ha-
        waii), Attack on, 1941;** etc.
        [to be added as needed]
 BT   **Europe—History—1918-1945**
        World history—20th century
        World politics
**World War, 1939-1945—Aerial opera-
        tions   940.54**
 UF   World War, 1939-1945—Battles,
        sieges, etc.
 BT   **Military aeronautics**
**World War, 1939-1945—African Ameri-
        cans   940.53; 940.54**
 BT   **African Americans**
**World War, 1939-1945—Amphibious op-
        erations   940.54**
 BT   **World War, 1939-1945—Naval
        operations**
World War, 1939-1945—Antiwar move-
        ments
 USE   **World War, 1939-1945—Pro-
        test movements**
**World War, 1939-1945—Armistices
        940.53**
World War, 1939-1945—Arms
 USE   **World War, 1939-1945—
        Equipment and supplies**
**World War, 1939-1945—Art and the
        war   940.53**
 UF   World War, 1939-1945—Iconog-
        raphy
        World War, 1939-1945, in art
 BT   **Art**
**World War, 1939-1945—Atrocities
        940.54**
 SA   names of specific atrocities and
        crimes [to be added as need-
        ed]
 BT   **Atrocities**
 NT   **Handicapped—Nazi persecution**
**World War, 1939-1945—Battlefields
        940.54**

World War, 1939-1945—Battles, sieges,
etc.
  USE **World War, 1939-1945—Aerial
operations
World War, 1939-1945—Cam-
paigns
World War, 1939-1945—Naval
operations**
**World War, 1939-1945—Biography
920**
  BT **Biography**
**World War, 1939-1945—Blockades
940.54**
World War, 1939-1945—Campaigns
(May subdiv. geog.) **940.54**
  UF World War, 1939-1945—Battles,
sieges, etc.
  SA names of battles, campaigns,
sieges, etc., **Ardennes, Battle
of the, 1944-1945** [to be add-
ed as needed]
  NT **Ardennes, Battle of the, 1944-
1945
Normandy (France), Attack on,
1944
Pearl Harbor (Oahu, Hawaii),
Attack on, 1941**
**World War, 1939-1945—Cartoons and
caricatures 940.53**
  BT **Cartoons and caricatures**
World War, 1939-1945—Casualties (May
subdiv. geog.) **940.54**
**World War, 1939-1945—Casualties—Sta-
tistics 940.54**
**World War, 1939-1945—Casualties—
United States 940.54**
  UF United States—World War,
1939-1945—Casualties
**World War, 1939-1945—Casualties—
United States—Statistics 940.54**
  UF United States—World War,
1939-1945—Casualties—Statis-
tics
World War, 1939-1945—Causes 940.53
  NT **National socialism**
**World War, 1939-1945—Censorship
940.54**
  BT **Censorship**
World War, 1939-1945—Charities
  USE **World War, 1939-1945—Civil-
ian relief**

**World War, 1939-1945—War
work**
**World War, 1939-1945—Chemical war-
fare 940.54**
  BT **Chemical warfare**
**World War, 1939-1945—Children
940.53**
  BT **Children and war**
World War, 1939-1945—Civilian evacua-
tion
  USE **World War, 1939-1945—Evac-
uation of civilians**
**World War, 1939-1945—Civilian relief
940.54**
  UF World War, 1939-1945—Chari-
ties
  BT **Charities
Food relief
Foreign aid
Reconstruction (1939-1951)
World War, 1939-1945—War
work**
  RT **World War, 1939-1945—Refu-
gees**
**World War, 1939-1945—Collaborationists
940.53**
  UF Fifth column
Quislings
  BT **Collaborationists**
**World War, 1939-1945—Conferences
940.53**
  UF World War, 1939-1945—Con-
gresses *[Former heading]*
  BT **Conferences**
World War, 1939-1945—Congresses
  USE **World War, 1939-1945—Con-
ferences**
**World War, 1939-1945—Conscientious
objectors 940.53**
  BT **Conscientious objectors**
World War, 1939-1945—Correspondents
  USE **World War, 1939-1945—Jour-
nalists**
**World War, 1939-1945—Desertions
940.54**
  BT **Military desertion**
**World War, 1939-1945—Destruction and
pillage 940.54**

World War, 1939-1945—Diplomatic history   940.53
   NT   World War, 1939-1945—Governments in exile

World War, 1939-1945—Displaced persons
   USE   World War, 1939-1945—Refugees

World War, 1939-1945—Draft resisters   940.54
   BT   Draft resisters

World War, 1939-1945—Economic aspects   940.53

Use for materials on the economic causes of the war and the effect of the war on commerce and industry.

   BT   War—Economic aspects
   NT   World War, 1939-1945—Finance

        World War, 1939-1945—Manpower

        World War, 1939-1945—Reparations
   RT   Reconstruction (1939-1951)

World War, 1939-1945—Education and the war   940.53
   BT   Education

World War, 1939-1945—Engineering and construction   940.54
   BT   Military engineering

World War, 1939-1945—Equipment and supplies   940.54
   UF   World War, 1939-1945—Arms

        World War, 1939-1945—Military supplies

        World War, 1939-1945—Military weapons

        World War, 1939-1945—Ordnance

        World War, 1939-1945—Supplies

        World War, 1939-1945—Weapons
   BT   Military weapons

World War, 1939-1945—Ethical aspects   940.53
   UF   World War, 1939-1945—Moral and religious aspects
   BT   Ethics

World War, 1939-1945—Evacuation of civilians   940.54
   UF   Civilian evacuation

        World War, 1939-1945—Civilian evacuation
   BT   Civil defense

        World War, 1939-1945—Refugees

World War, 1939-1945—Fiction   808.83; 813, etc.

Use for collections of stories dealing with the Second World War. Materials about the depiction of the war in literature are entered under **World War, 1939-1945—Literature and the war.**

World War, 1939-1945—Finance   940.53

Use for materials on the cost and financing of the war, including war debts, and the effect of the war on financial systems, including inflation.

   BT   World War, 1939-1945—Economic aspects

World War, 1939-1945—Food supply   940.53
   BT   Food relief

World War, 1939-1945—Forced repatriation   940.53
   RT   World War, 1939-1945—Refugees

World War, 1939-1945—Governments in exile   940.53
   BT   World War, 1939-1945—Diplomatic history

World War, 1939-1945—Guerrillas
   USE   World War, 1939-1945—Underground movements

World War, 1939-1945—Health aspects   940.54

World War, 1939-1945—Hospitals
   USE   World War, 1939-1945—Medical care

World War, 1939-1945—Human resources
   USE   World War, 1939-1945—Manpower

World War, 1939-1945—Humor   940.53
   BT   Wit and humor

World War, 1939-1945—Iconography
   USE   World War, 1939-1945—Art and the war

World War, 1939-1945, in art
   USE   World War, 1939-1945—Art and the war

World War, 1939-1945, in literature
    USE **World War, 1939-1945—Literature and the war**
World War, 1939-1945, in motion pictures
    USE **World War, 1939-1945—Motion pictures and the war**
World War, 1939-1945—Influence 940.53
World War, 1939-1945—Jews   940.53
    BT **Jews**
    RT **Holocaust, 1933-1945**
World War, 1939-1945—Jews—Rescue 940.54
    UF Rescue of Jews, 1939-1945
    BT **Jews—Persecutions**
    NT **Righteous Gentiles in the Holocaust**
World War, 1939-1945—Journalists 940.54
    UF World War, 1939-1945—Correspondents
         World War, 1939-1945—War correspondents
    BT **Journalists**
World War, 1939-1945—Literature and the war   809; 810, etc.; 940.53
    Use for materials on the depiction of the war in literature. Collections of stories dealing with the Second World War are entered under **World War, 1939-1945—Fiction.**
    UF World War, 1939-1945, in literature
    BT **Literature**
World War, 1939-1945—Manpower 940.54
    UF World War, 1939-1945—Human resources
    BT **World War, 1939-1945—Economic aspects**
World War, 1939-1945—Maps   940.53
    BT **Maps**
World War, 1939-1945—Medical care 940.54
    UF World War, 1939-1945—Hospitals
    BT **Medical care**
World War, 1939-1945—Military supplies
    USE **World War, 1939-1945—Equipment and supplies**
World War, 1939-1945—Military weapons
    USE **World War, 1939-1945—Equipment and supplies**

World War, 1939-1945—Missing in action   940.54
    BT **Missing in action**
         World War, 1939-1945—Prisoners and prisons
World War, 1939-1945—Monuments 725
    BT **Monuments**
World War, 1939-1945—Moral and religious aspects
    USE **World War, 1939-1945—Ethical aspects**
         World War, 1939-1945—Religious aspects
World War, 1939-1945—Motion pictures and the war   791.43; 940.53
    Use for materials about films dealing with the Second World War or about the use of motion pictures in the war effort.
    UF World War, 1939-1945, in motion pictures
    BT **Motion pictures**
         War films
World War, 1939-1945—Museums 940.53
    BT **Museums**
World War, 1939-1945—Naval operations   940.54
    UF World War, 1939-1945—Battles, sieges, etc.
    NT **World War, 1939-1945—Amphibious operations**
World War, 1939-1945—Naval operations—Submarine   940.54
    UF World War, 1939-1945—Submarine operations
    BT **Submarine warfare**
World War, 1939-1945—Occupied territories   940.54
    SA names of occupied countries with the appropriate subdivision under *History,* e.g., **Netherlands—History—1940-1945, German occupation; Japan—History—1945-1952, Allied occupation;** etc. [to be added as needed]
    BT **Military occupation**
         World War, 1939-1945—Territorial questions

World War, 1939-1945—Ordnance
   USE **World War, 1939-1945—**
       Equipment and supplies
World War, 1939-1945—Peace   940.53
World War, 1939-1945—Personal narra-
   tives   940.53; 940.54

   Use for collective or individual eyewitness
   reports or autobiographical accounts of the
   war in general. Accounts limited to a specific
   topic are entered under that topic.

   BT **Autobiographies**
       Biography
World War, 1939-1945—Pictorial works
   940.53022
World War, 1939-1945—Poetry   808.81;
   811, etc.; 811.008, etc.

   Use for collections of poetry dealing with
   the Second World War.

   BT **Historical poetry**
       War poetry
World War, 1939-1945—Prisoners and
   prisons   940.54
   BT **Concentration camps**
       Prisoners of war
       Prisons
   NT **World War, 1939-1945—Miss-**
       ing in action
World War, 1939-1945—Propaganda
   940.54
   BT **Propaganda**
World War, 1939-1945—Protest move-
   ments   940.53
   UF World War, 1939-1945—Antiwar
       movements
       World War, 1939-1945—Pro-
       tests, demonstrations, etc.
   BT **Protest movements**
World War, 1939-1945—Protests, demon-
   strations, etc.
   USE **World War, 1939-1945—Pro-**
       test movements
World War, 1939-1945—Psychological
   aspects   940.53
   BT **Psychological warfare**
World War, 1939-1945—Public opinion
   940.53
   BT **Public opinion**
World War, 1939-1945—Railroads
   USE **World War, 1939-1945—Trans-**
       portation
World War, 1939-1945—Reconstruction
   USE **Reconstruction (1939-1951)**

World War, 1939-1945—Refugees
   940.53
   UF World War, 1939-1945—Dis-
       placed persons
   BT **Political refugees**
   NT **World War, 1939-1945—Evac-**
       uation of civilians
   RT **World War, 1939-1945—Civil-**
       ian relief
       World War, 1939-1945—
       Forced repatriation
World War, 1939-1945—Regimental his-
   tories   940.54
World War, 1939-1945—Religious as-
   pects   940.53
   UF World War, 1939-1945—Moral
       and religious aspects
World War, 1939-1945—Reparations
   940.53
   BT **Reconstruction (1939-1951)**
       World War, 1939-1945—Eco-
       nomic aspects
World War, 1939-1945—Resistance move-
   ments
   USE **World War, 1939-1945—Un-**
       derground movements
World War, 1939-1945—Secret service
   940.54
   BT **Secret service**
World War, 1939-1945—Social aspects
   940.53
World War, 1939-1945—Social work
   USE **World War, 1939-1945—War**
       work
World War, 1939-1945—Songs   782.42
   UF World War, 1939-1945—Songs
       and music
   BT **Military music**
       War songs
World War, 1939-1945—Songs and music
   USE **World War, 1939-1945—Songs**
World War, 1939-1945—Sources
   940.53
World War, 1939-1945—Submarine opera-
   tions
   USE **World War, 1939-1945—Naval**
       operations—Submarine
World War, 1939-1945—Supplies
   USE **World War, 1939-1945—**
       Equipment and supplies

World War, 1939-1945—Territorial questions (May subdiv. geog.) 940.53
BT Boundaries
NT World War, 1939-1945—Occupied territories
World War, 1939-1945—Theater and the war 792; 940.53
BT Theater
World War, 1939-1945—Transportation 940.54
UF World War, 1939-1945—Railroads
BT Transportation
World War, 1939-1945—Treaties 940.53
BT Treaties
World War, 1939-1945—Underground movements 940.54
UF Anti-fascist movements
Anti-Nazi movement
World War, 1939-1945—Guerrillas
World War, 1939-1945—Resistance movements
World War, 1939-1945—United States 940.53; 940.54; 973.917
UF United States—History—1939-1945, World War
United States—World War, 1939-1945
World War, 1939-1945—War correspondents
USE World War, 1939-1945—Journalists
World War, 1939-1945—War work 940.53
UF World War, 1939-1945—Charities
World War, 1939-1945—Social work
NT World War, 1939-1945—Civilian relief
World War, 1939-1945—Weapons
USE World War, 1939-1945—Equipment and supplies
World War, 1939-1945—Women 940.53; 940.54
BT Women

World War III 355
UF Third World War
BT War
World politics
World Wide Web 004.67
UF World Wide Web (Information retrieval system)
BT Internet
NT Web servers
World Wide Web (Information retrieval system)
USE World Wide Web
World Wide Web pages
USE Web sites
World Wide Web servers
USE Web servers
World Wide Web sites
USE Web sites
World's Fair (1992 : Seville, Spain)
USE Expo 92 (Seville, Spain)
World's fairs
USE Exhibitions
Fairs
World's records
USE World records
Worms 592
BT Animals
Worry 152.4
BT Emotions
RT Anxiety
Worship 248.3; 264; 291.3
UF Devotion
BT Religion
Theology
NT Church year
Devotional exercises
Prayer
Public worship
Sacrifice
Worship of the dead
USE Ancestor worship
Worth
USE Values
Wounded, First aid to
USE First aid
Wounds and injuries 617.1
UF Injuries
SA classes of persons, animals, organs of the body, and plants and crops with the subdivision *Wounds and injuries*, e.g.

Wounds and injuries—*Continued*
>>> Horses—Wounds and injuries; Foot—Wounds and injuries; etc. [to be added as needed]
- BT **Accidents**
- NT **Fractures**

Wrapping of gifts
- USE **Gift wrapping**

Wrecks
- USE **Accidents**

Wrestling (May subdiv. geog.)   796.812
- BT **Athletics**
- NT **Judo**

Writers
- USE **Authors**

Writing   411
>>> Use for materials on the process or result of recording language in the form of conventionalized visible marks or signs on a surface. Materials limited to writing with a pen or pencil and practical or prescriptive guides to penmanship or the art of writing are entered under **Handwriting**. Materials on handwriting as an expression of the writer's character are entered under **Graphology**. Materials on the alphabet or writing of a particular language are entered under the name of the language with the subdivisions *Alphabet* and *Writing*.
- BT **Communication**
  Language and languages
  Language arts
- NT **Abbreviations**
  Alphabet
  Autographs
  Calligraphy
  Cryptography
  Graphology
  Handwriting
  Hieroglyphics
  Picture writing
  Shorthand
  Typewriting
  Writing of numerals
- RT **Ciphers**

Writing (Authorship)
- USE **Authorship**
  Creative writing

Writing of numerals   513
- UF Numeral formation
  Numeral writing
  Numerals, Writing of
- BT **Handwriting**
  Numerals
  Writing

Writing—Patterning
- USE **Language arts—Patterning**

Writing—Study and teaching
- USE **Handwriting**

Writings of gay men
- USE **Gay men's writings**

Writings of lesbians
- USE **Lesbians' writings**

Wrought iron work
- USE **Ironwork**

X-15 (Rocket aircraft)   629.133
- BT **Rocket planes**

X-rays   539.7
- UF Radiography
  Roentgen rays
  X rays
- BT **Electromagnetic waves**
  Radiation
- NT **Gamma rays**
  Tomography
- RT **Radiotherapy**
  Vacuum tubes

X rays
- USE **X-rays**

Xerographic art
- USE **Copy art**

Xerography
- USE **Photocopying**

YA literature
- USE **Young adult literature**

Yacht basins
- USE **Marinas**

Yachting
- USE **Yachts and yachting**

Yachts and yachting (May subdiv. geog.)   797.1
- UF Yachting
- BT **Boatbuilding**
  Boats and boating
  Ocean travel
  Ships
  Voyages and travels
  Water sports
- NT **Marinas**
- RT **Sailing**

Yard sales
- USE **Garage sales**

Yarn   677
- NT **Cotton**
  Flax
- RT **Spinning**

Yearbooks
USE **Periodicals**
School yearbooks
and subjects with the subdivision *Periodicals,* e.g. **Engineering—Periodicals** [to be added as needed]
Yeast 641.3
BT **Fungi**
Yellow fever 616.9
BT **Tropical medicine**
Yeti 001.9
UF Abominable snowman
BT **Monsters**
Mythical animals
Yiddish language 439
May be subdivided like **English language.**
UF Jewish language
Jews—Language
BT **Language and languages**
Yiddish literature 839
May use same subdivisions and names of literary forms as for **English literature.**
BT **Jewish literature**
Yoga 181; 613.7
BT **Hindu philosophy**
Hinduism
Theosophy
NT **Hatha yoga**
Yoga exercises
USE **Hatha yoga**
Yoga, Hatha
USE **Hatha yoga**
Yom Kippur 296.4
UF Atonement, Day of
Day of Atonement
BT **Jewish holidays**
Yom Kippur War, 1973
USE **Israel-Arab War, 1973**
Yoruba (African people) 305.896
BT **Africans**
Native peoples
Yosemite National Park (Calif.) 719; 979.4
BT **National parks and reserves—United States**
Yosemite National Park (Calif.)—Pictorial works 979.4
Young adult literature 808.8; 809; 810.8, etc.
Use for collections or materials about literature published for teenage readers. Materials

on the reading interests of teenagers and lists of books for teenagers are entered under **Teenagers—Books and reading.**
UF Books for teenagers
Teenage literature
Teenagers—Literature
YA literature
Young adults' literature
BT **Literature**
Young adults
USE **Teenagers**
Youth
Young adults—Books and reading
USE **Teenagers—Books and reading**
Young adults' libraries (May subdiv. geog.) 027.62
UF Library services to teenagers
Library services to young adults
Young adults' library services
[Former heading]
BT **Libraries**
Young adults' library services
USE **Young adults' libraries**
Young adults' literature
USE **Young adult literature**
Young consumers 640.73; 658.8
UF Children as consumers
Teenage consumers
Youth market
BT **Consumers**
Young men (May subdiv. geog.) 305.31
Use for materials on men in the general age range of eighteen through twenty-five years. Materials on the time of life between thirteen and twenty-five, as well as on people in that greater age range are entered under **Youth.**
BT **Men**
Youth
RT **Boys**
Young people
USE **Teenagers**
Youth
Young persons
USE **Teenagers**
Youth
Young women (May subdiv. geog.) 305.4
Use for materials on women in the general age range of eighteen through twenty-five years. Materials on the time of life between thirteen and twenty-five, as well as on people in that greater age range are entered under **Youth.**
BT **Women**
Youth

Young women—*Continued*
  RT **Girls**
Youngest child
  USE **Birth order**
Youth (May subdiv. geog.)   **305.235**
    Use for materials on the time of life be-tween thirteen and twenty-five years, as well as on people in this general age range. Materi-als limited to teen youth are entered under **Teenagers.** Materials limited to people in the general age range of eighteen through twenty-five years of age are entered under **Young men** or **Young women.** Materials on the pro-cess or state of growing up are entered under **Adolescence.**
  UF Young adults
       Young people
       Young persons
  SA youth of particular racial or eth-nic groups [to be added as needed]
  BT **Age**
  NT **African American youth**
       Church work with youth
       Dropouts
       Teenagers
       Television and youth
       Young men
       Young women
Youth—Alcohol use (May subdiv. geog.)
     613.81; 616.86
  UF Alcohol and youth
       Drinking and youth
  NT **Drinking age**
Youth and drugs
  USE **Youth—Drug use**
Youth and narcotics
  USE **Youth—Drug use**
Youth and television
  USE **Television and youth**
Youth—Drug use (May subdiv. geog.)
     613.8; 616.86
  UF Drugs and youth
       Narcotics and youth
       Youth and drugs
       Youth and narcotics
  NT **Teenagers—Drug use**
  RT **Juvenile delinquency**
Youth—Employment (May subdiv. geog.)
     331.3
  BT **Age and employment**
       Employment
  NT **Teenagers—Employment**
  RT **Summer employment**

Youth hostels (May subdiv. geog.)
     647.94
  UF Tourist accommodations
  BT **Community centers**
       Hotels and motels
Youth market
  USE **Young consumers**
Youth movement (May subdiv. geog.)
     322.4
  UF Student movement
       Student protests, demonstrations, etc.
       Student revolt
  BT **Social movements**
  NT **Students—Political activity**
Youth—Religious life   **248.4; 291.4**
  BT **Religious life**
  NT **Teenagers—Religious life**
Youth—United States   **305.230973**
  UF American youth
  NT **Teenagers—United States**
Zen Buddhism (May subdiv. geog.)
     294.3
  BT **Buddhism**
Zeppelins
  USE **Airships**
Zero gravity
  USE **Weightlessness**
Zeus (Greek deity)   **292.2**
  BT **Gods and goddesses**
Zinc   **669**
  BT **Chemical elements**
       Metals
Zionism (May subdiv. geog.)   **320.5**
  UF Zionist movement
  RT **Jews—Restoration**
Zionist movement
  USE **Zionism**
Zip code (May subdiv. geog.)   **383**
  UF Postal delivery code
  BT **Postal service**
Zodiac   **133.5; 523**
  BT **Astrology**
       Astronomy
Zoning (May subdiv. geog.)   **346.04; 354.3**
  UF City planning—Zone system
       Districting (in city planning)
  BT **City planning**
Zoological gardens
  USE **Zoos**

**Zoological specimens—Collection and
preservation   590.75**
   UF   Collections of natural specimens
        Preservation of zoological speci-
        mens
        Specimens, Preservation of
   SA   types of specimens with the sub-
        division *Collection and pres-
        ervation,* e.g. **Birds—Collec-
        tion and preservation** [to be
        added as needed]
   BT   **Collectors and collecting**
   NT   **Birds—Collection and preser-
        vation**
   RT   **Taxidermy**
Zoology   590
   Use for materials on the science of animals.
   Nonscientific materials on animals are entered
   under **Animals.**
   UF   Animal kingdom
        Animal physiology
        Fauna
   SA   names of divisions, classes, etc.,
        of the animal kingdom, e.g.
        **Invertebrates; Vertebrates;
        Birds; Mammals;** etc.; and
        names of animals [to be add-
        ed as needed]

   BT   **Biology**
        Science
   NT   **Animal behavior**
        Animals—Anatomy
        Comparative anatomy
        Comparative psychology
        Economic zoology
        Embryology
   RT   **Animals**
        Natural history
        Zoos
Zoology—Anatomy
   USE   **Animals—Anatomy**
Zoology, Economic
   USE   **Economic zoology**
Zoology of the Bible
   USE   **Bible—Natural history**
Zoology—United States
   USE   **Animals—United States**
Zoos (May subdiv. geog.)   **590.73**
   UF   Zoological gardens
   SA   names of individual zoos [to be
        added as needed]
   BT   **Parks**
   NT   **Petting zoos**
   RT   **Animals**
        Zoology